THE

# ENCYCLOPÆDIA

OF

# GEOGRAPHY:

COMPRISING A

COMPLETE DESCRIPTION OF THE EARTH,

PHYSICAL, STATISTICAL, CIVIL, AND POLITICAL;

EXHIBITING ITS RELATION TO THE HEAVENLY BODIES,

ITS PHYSICAL STRUCTURE,

THE NATURAL HISTORY OF EACH COUNTRY,

AND THE INDUSTRY, COMMERCE, POLITICAL INSTITUTIONS,

AND CIVIL AND SOCIAL STATE

OF

ALL NATIONS.

---

BY HUGH MURRAY, F.R.S.E.

ASSISTED IN

ASTRONOMY, &c. BY PROF. WALLACE, | BOTANY, &c. BY PROFESSOR HOOKER
GEOLOGY, &c. BY PROF. JAMESON, | ZOOLOGY, &c. BY W. SWAINSON, ESQ

---

ILLUSTRATED BY EIGHTY-TWO MAPS,

AND ABOUT ELEVEN HUNDRED OTHER ENGRAVINGS ON WOOD

REPRESENTING THE MOST REMARKABLE OBJECTS OF NATURE AND ART
IN EVERY REGION OF THE GLOBE,

TOGETHER WITH A

NEW MAP OF THE UNITED STATES.

---

REVISED, WITH ADDITIONS,

BY THOMAS G. BRADFORD.

---

IN THREE VOLUMES.

VOL. I.

---

PHILADELPHIA:

BLANCHARD AND LEA.

1855.

STEREOTYPED BY J. FAGAN.....PHILADELPHIA.
PRINTED BY C. SHERMAN AND CO.

# PREFACE TO THE ENGLISH EDITION.

The value and importance of the study of Geography are so obvious, and indeed so universally acknowledged, as to require little illustration. Nothing can be more interesting to man, or more gratify his thirst for knowledge, than a survey of the earth which he inhabits, peopled as it is by beings of the same nature with himself. To visit and observe foreign climes and regions is an object of general desire, and forms one of the most effectual means of enlarging and enlightening the human mind. This wish, however, unless in the case of a few individuals, can be gratified only to a very limited extent, and in none can embrace more than a small portion of the vast variety of interesting objects which the earth comprises. This necessary defect of personal observation may, however, be in a great measure supplied, by collecting the reports and narratives of those intelligent individuals who have explored and described its various regions, and forming out of these a general description of the world and its inhabitants.

Works of this class have always possessed a peculiar attraction. Even in ancient times, when the extent of the known world, and the information with respect to the inhabitants and productions of its remoter regions, were comparatively limited, the geographical descriptions of Herodotus, Strabo, Pomponius Mela, and Pliny, rank among the most valuable productions of the classic ages. But in modern times, and particularly in the present age, Geography has acquired a much more prominent place among the departments of human knowledge. The discovery of America in the fifteenth century awakened a spirit of enterprise, and a desire to explore unknown regions, that have continued to gain new strength. During the last half century more especially, the most civilised nations of Europe have been contending with each other for the glory of discovery; and there is now scarcely a shore however remote, or the interior of a continent however barbarous or difficult of access, which has not been surveyed and described. Materials have thus been provided for a much more complete, interesting, and authentic description of the earth, than could have been drawn up at any former period.

The extensive discoveries thus recently made have thrown a wonderful light on the structure and productions of the earth, and afforded large contributions to all the departments of natural history They have also displayed man in every varied condition, from the highest refinement of civilised society, to the rudest and most abject condition of savage life. These representations are not only interesting in themselves, but throw light on the history of past ages. Communities are still found exactly similar to some of those described in the earliest records of antiquity. The tent of the Arab sheik differs little from that which Abraham pitched on the plains of Mamre; many of the Tartar tribes are a people exactly similar to those who roamed in early ages over the plains of Scythia; and the splendid courts of Babylon and Persepolis have their representatives in the existing world. We may thus, in fact, trace back man to an earlier and ruder stage than any represented in the ancient records; for these convey only faint and fabulous notions of what mankind had been at a very early period. But the wilds of America, and the shores of the Pacific, exhibit the state of savage simplicity, which doubtless existed in Europe before the light of authentic history had begun to dawn. Hence it is that Geography, in its present extended range, not only shows man as he actually exists, but delineates, as it were, the progressive history of the species.

Besides the gratification thus afforded to a liberal curiosity, the knowledge of even the remotest regions has, through recent events, become an object of the utmost practical importance. In many of these, colonies have been founded, political relations formed, and a commercial intercourse with them opened, by the civilised nations of Europe, and particularly by Britain. Regions the most distant to which a ship can sail form integral portions of her dominion, and have their ports crowded with her vessels. There are thousands in this country who have a more intimate connection with Calcutta or Sydney, than with towns in their immediate vicinity. The manufacturer labours to supply the markets of countries, the very existence of which, fifty years ago, was unknown; the circumnavigation of the globe is now an ordinary trading voyage. The knowledge of Geography has thus become a necessary qualification for the pursuits of commerce and industry, and for much of the ordinary and current business of life. A great proportion of the youth of Britain are trained for employments in countries which lie far beyond the limits of Europe.

The same causes have, moreover, given to the knowledge of distant countries a peculiar hold on the domestic and social affections. There are few amongst us who have not a near relation, perhaps a brother or a child, residing in another hemisphere. Oceans now separate us from those to whom we are united by the tenderest ties; the objects of our affection have their abode on the banks of the Ganges, or the shores of the Pacific; and many, whose hearts are knit in the closest friendship, are divided from each other by half the earth. In this situation, a description of the place in which our friend or relative dwells, the objects which meet his eye, the society in which he mingles, must afford peculiar gratification, and soothe the mind under this painful separation.

Deeply impressed with a sense of the great extent and difficult execution of a complete geographical work, the Editor, during nearly ten years in which he has been engaged upon it, has used the utmost exertion to procure from every quarter information and aid. He has studiously collected the most recent, authentic, and accurate accounts of the extent, natural features, population, productions, industry, political constitution, literature, religion, and social state of the various regions of the globe, with the leading details as to their districts and cities. The sciences connected with the natural history of the earth have, however, attained to such an extent and importance, that a thorough knowledge of them can only be possessed by individuals who have specially devoted themselves to one particular branch. The Editor, therefore, considered it essential to procure the co-operation of writers who had risen to acknowledged eminence in the departments of Geology and Mineralogy, Zoology and Botany. He considered that he had fully succeeded, when Professor Jameson undertook to delineate the geological structure of the globe, and the distribution of minerals over its surface; Mr. Swainson to explain the distribution of animals, and the most remarkable of those found in each particular region; and Dr. Hooker to perform the same task in regard to the vegetable kingdom. Professor Wallace has illustrated the relations of the earth as a planet, the trigonometrical surveys, the construction of maps, and other subjects connected with mathematical science. These tasks have been executed in a manner which, it is hoped, will fully support the high reputation of their respective authors. In preparing the sections relating to commerce, the editor derived much assistance from Mr. M'Culloch's Dictionary of Commerce, and he is also indebted to that gentleman for many valuable communications. Various parts relating to remote countries have been revised by gentlemen recently returned from them.

The Maps, which are so numerous as to form a complete Atlas, have been executed from drawings by Hall; and having been carefully revised by the Editor, they will, it is hoped, be found to be accurate, and to include all the most recent discoveries. Notwithstanding the smallness of the scale, they are illustrated by the letter-press in a manner which enables them to comprise equal information with others of much larger dimensions.

The other Wood Engravings are mostly original, or have been carefully selected from the most faithful representations of the objects described; and they are executed in the best style by the eminent artists whose names appear on the title-page. They exhibit the most remarkable plants and animals, the chief cities, public buildings, natural curiosities, and picturesque scenery, with the characteristic figures and costumes of the natives, in the countries described. It is not believed that any work of this kind is similarly embellished, at least to nearly the same extent. These representations are by no means introduced for the sake of mere ornament; they will be found of the greatest utility, conveying an infinitely better idea of the objects than could be derived from the most laboured description.

Notwithstanding all these efforts, it is impossible to lay this volume before the Public without the painful reflection, that, in a subject involving such an infinite number and variety of details, many of which are often very difficult to procure, not a few imperfections and even errors must inevitably occur. M. Balbi, whose exertions to collect the most recent geographical information are well known, and to whose labours the present volume is much indebted, candidly observes:—"One of the greatest obstacles to be surmounted in the composition of an elementary treatise of Geography is the want of contemporary documents. Geography is almost necessarily a compound of things which are, with things which have ceased to be. How can one be informed of all the changes that take place in the course of a few years, even in the capitals of Europe, still more in those of Asia, Africa, and America? To compose a Geography which should exhibit a complete picture of the globe at a particular period, it would be necessary to have authentic documents, all of the same date and that a recent one; which never has been, and never can be."

## ADVERTISEMENT

TO THE

# AMERICAN EDITION.

---

THE object and plan of the ENCYCLOPÆDIA OF GEOGRAPHY have been very fully set forth in the Preface to the English Edition, and the names of the editor and his collaborators are sufficient vouchers for its value. It is due, however, to the American reader, to inform him in what respects these volumes differ from the original. The whole of the English work is here given, with the single exception, that the description of Great Britain, which occupied more than one-third of the Book devoted to Europe, and considerably more than the space given to the whole of America, has been somewhat abridged; but, it is believed, without the omission of any thing of importance. The text has been carefully revised and corrected throughout, and in most cases more recent statistical details have been substituted for those of the original. The additions to the first volumes are not considerable in amount, but are generally such as have been required by changes in our knowledge or in the condition of things. The Book relating to America has been enlarged as far as the limits of the work would allow, principally by the addition of local details; the condition of the new American states is too unsettled to render it worth while to fill much space with accounts of their political relations, which might be entirely changed before these pages met the eye of the reader. The Chapter which treats of the United States has been written anew, the original being extremely imperfect and incorrect, as all European treatises on the subject are.—Our growth is so rapid, the increase of our population, wealth, commerce, manufactures, and other industrial resources, so amazing, the creation of new towns, cities, nay, states, is continually making such a change in the face of things, public works are conceived, planned, and executed on so great a scale and with such promptitude, that it is not at all surprising that a distant writer should be entirely baffled in his attempts to describe the country as it is. The Zoological section has alone been retained, but it has been much enlarged, chiefly from a later work of Mr. Swainson's; and some general remarks upon the shells of the United States have been added. For the account of the Geology of our country, the reader is indebted to Prof. Rogers, of the University of Pennsylvania. The Botanical section has also been prepared by a gentleman of high reputation in the scientific world. The Editor is painfully sensible of the imperfection of the other parts of this Chapter, but he trusts that the difficulties of the subject will obtain for him the indulgence of the reader.

Philadelphia, *October 1st*, 1836.

# CONTENTS OF VOL. I.

## BOOK II.

GEOLOGICAL PRINCIPLES.



## BOOK III.

GENERAL PRINCIPLES OF GEOGRAPHY UNDER ITS RELATION TO ORGANISED AND LIVING BEINGS.



# PART III.

GEOGRAPHY CONSIDERED IN RELATION TO THE VARIOUS REGIONS OF THE GLOBE.

## BOOK I.—EUROPE.

# ENCYCLOPÆDIA OF GEOGRAPHY.

## INTRODUCTION.

Geography consists in the description and delineation of the Earth. It considers that planet in respect to its form, its connexion with other bodies in the universe, the various parts into which it is divided, their relations to each other, and the objects with which each is respectively filled. Geography indeed could not attempt a scientific analysis of all these objects, without seeking to comprehend within itself a complete circle of science. It views only their obvious and visible characters, and chiefly those features which are peculiar to each respective country and region on the face of the globe.

The great importance of this branch of knowledge must be sufficiently obvious. It embraces a vast variety of those objects which are most interesting in themselves, and with which it most concerns man to be conversant. It enables the navigator, the merchant, the military commander, to carry on their respective operations. Geography is moreover essential to the clear understanding of every branch of the history both of man and nature. The transactions of bordering states are unintelligible without a knowledge of their relative extent and position, and of the theatre on which the great events of their history are acted. Every form, both of animal and vegetable nature, is modified in the most striking manner by the climate or the country in which it is placed. Still more intimate is its relation with geology and other sciences, which investigate the materials composing the substance and crust of the earth. None of these branches of knowledge can be distinctly understood, or viewed under its proper relation and arrangement, without a previous knowledge of geography.

This important and extensive subject seems to divide itself naturally into three parts.

The *First* Part treats of the "History of Geography;" the origin and progress of the Science; and the steps by which man, who seemed fixed by nature in a local and limited position, has made himself acquainted with the immense circuit of the globe. This Part is divided into—I. Ancient Geography;—II. Geography of the Middle Ages;—III. Modern Geography.

The *Second* Part comprises the *Principles* of the Science. These are—I. *Mathematical:* those which relate to the form of the earth, its movements, its place in the Solar System, the great circles by which it is divided, the operations by which it is surveyed, and the modes in which its spherical outline can be represented on the plane surface of a map. II. *Physical:* those which treat of the substances which cover the earth's surface, the elements which compose and surround it; rock, earth, water, air, as they appear under the various forms of mountain, plain, river, sea, and present all the changing phenomena of the atmosphere. III. Geography may be considered in its relation to other objects and sciences. 1. To Zoology, or the distribution of animals over the globe. 2. To Botany, or the diffusion of vegetable productions. 3. To the human race, and the various branches into which it has been formed, considered in relation to numbers, wealth, political union, social, intellectual, and moral condition.

The *Third* Part considers Geography in detail, as it applies to the various quarters and countries into which the world is divided, the outline and extent of each, its natural features, the revolutions through which it has passed, its political constitution, the industry and wealth, the civil and social condition of its inhabitants. The description of each country will conclude with a local and topographical survey of its districts, cities, and towns.

This Part will divide itself into five general heads:—I. Europe. II. Asia. III. Africa. IV. Australia. V. America.

An Index will be added, which, being extremely copious, and containing references to all the places mentioned in the work, will answer in a great degree the purposes of a Geographical Gazetteer.

# PART I.

## HISTORY OF GEOGRAPHY.

The History of Geography may be divided into three books:—I. Ancient Geography. II. Geography of the middle ages. III. Modern Geography.

---

# BOOK I.

## ANCIENT GEOGRAPHY.

The Geography of the Ancients may be considered under the heads of, I. Hebrew and Phœnician Geography; the principal features of which may be found in the Jewish Scriptures. II. Greek Geography, in its early state, before the expedition of Alexander. III. The first Alexandrian school formed by Eratosthenes. IV. The Roman school, formed chiefly by Mela and Pliny. V. The second Alexandrian school, formed by Ptolemy.

---

### CHAPTER I.

#### HEBREW AND PHŒNICIAN GEOGRAPHY.

The Sacred Records, in addition to their higher claims on the attention of mankind, possess the important secondary advantage, that they enable us to trace human existence, and the forms of society, back to a much earlier period than the information derived from any other source. They were long anterior in this respect to the classic story of Greece and Rome; the faintest light even of whose fabulous history cannot be traced back to the period when Abraham was driving his flocks over the seats of future empire on the Euphrates. Among Abraham's contemporaries we discern the germ of the great monarchies which first changed the face of human affairs. Nimrod, the founder of Babylon, almost like an Iroquois chief, is mainly celebrated for his activity and success in the chase. Modern discovery has indeed made us acquainted with tribes existing in a still ruder form; but there is no narrative in which we can trace so distinctly the gradual, yet somewhat rapid, transition made in these favoured regions, from the hunting and pastoral, to the commercial and agricultural states of society.

#### Sect. I.—*The Patriarchal Ages.*

In the early patriarchal records we discover first the rich Mesopotamian plain, not yet covered with cities and harvests, but standing as an open common, over which the sons of Terah drove unmolested their flocks and herds. In these favourable circumstances, and surrounded by simple and rural plenty, the flocks and the shepherds multiplied in an extraordinary manner. The heads of the families became petty princes, and were as such at once respected and feared. As they went on increasing, the land became "not able to bear them;" and the most intimate friends were able to prevent dissension among their adherents only by an entire though painful separation; nay, even by striking into routes so opposite, as to prevent the possibility of a future union. This, however, was rather a palliation than a cure for the evil; for, in whatever quarter each directed his course, he came into contact with other families. The difficulty was still augmented, when all the more fertile tracts began to be cultivated by a fixed population, subject to regular government. The first regions which came under these circumstances appear to have been Lower Egypt and Gerar, on the coast of Philistia, along the Mediterranean. In the latter we find Isaac attempting to settle and cultivate the ground; but the king, though evidently afraid to offend so potent a tribe, insisted, in a determined though courteous manner, upon their quitting his territory. The family were therefore obliged finally to establish themselves in the vicinity of Hebron, collecting the somewhat scanty herbage which grew amid the rugged mountains to the west of the Dead Sea. It was, therefore, an auspicious change when they were transported into the Land of Goshen, a rich pastoral district of Egypt. The circumstances attending the captivity of Joseph enable us already to observe the activity of that interior caravan-trade, which afterwards on so great a scale, traversed

Arabia. Two caravans, destined for the supply of Egypt, appear meeting each other in opposite directions; and that cruel trade, of which men were the object, is already carried on in the same remorseless manner, and by the same unjust means, by which it has ever since been conducted.

Sect. II.—*The Kingdom of Israel.*

The Israelites, after being established in Egypt for more than two centuries, were led back into the promised land, so long the seat of their ancestors. Every thing there, since the patriarchal age, had assumed quite a different aspect: it presented walled cities, and high cultivation, accompanied with that gross superstition and dissolute voluptuousness which are the too common attendants of early wealth. The guilty inhabitants of Canaan with their country were delivered into the hands of the Israelites; and the territory being divided among the ten tribes, gave occasion to a very careful topographical survey; but nothing yet occurred to attract the views of the nation beyond these limits, or towards the world in general. Still less could this take place during the subsequent period, when they were forsaken of heaven, and reduced to servitude under the neighbouring nations. It was *under the favoured reign of David* that Israel finally triumphed over all her enemies. That great prince left to Solomon, either as subject or tributary, a territory extending from the Euphrates to the Mediterranean and the borders of Egypt, forming the most powerful state then in western Asia. *Solomon*, by the terror of his father's name, and of the powerful army transmitted to him, was enabled to preserve the whole of this kingdom, during a long reign, in peaceful submission. This accomplished prince devoted himself to the arts of peace, to the extension of commerce, to the culture of science, and to the improvement and embellishment of his dominions in every direction. By the alliance with Hiram, he was enabled to accomplish voyages more remote than had, perhaps, been ever undertaken under any former sovereign. His alliance, and even his society, were courted by distant princes; and the observation of the Jews began to extend over a considerable portion of the globe.

The separation of the kingdoms after the death of Solomon, was a fatal blow to the greatness of the house of Israel. Their divided power could no longer maintain numerous tributaries in submission, nor was it adequate to distant and extensive enterprises. All the states beyond the Jordan shook off the yoke; the attempts to navigate the Red Sea were abandoned; and all distant regions in a great measure lost sight of. Their view, however, was enlarged by unexpected and unwelcome events from another quarter.

The successive invasions of Assyria and Babylon, which terminated in the downfall of both the kingdoms, forced upon the Israelites a knowledge of the existence of these proud and powerful empires. At the same time, the colossal grandeur of Egypt, the only power capable of contending with them, was brought into prominent notice. Ample materials were thus afforded for those lofty and awful images, those pictures of the shaking of the world and the downfall of nations, which abound in the writings of the prophets during the regal times. Another and nearer object attracted wonder, and afforded the means of knowledge respecting regions still more distant. This was Tyre, the earliest seat of commerce, in whose markets were found collected the tin of Britain, the gold of Africa, the cotton of India, and, perhaps, the silks of China. This forms so grand a feature, and the descriptions of it tend so much to illustrate early geography, that it must claim some separate notice.

Sect. III.—*Commerce of Tyre.*

Tyre, which under Solomon was already great and flourishing, continued to increase till, with the exception of one of its own colonies, it became the most splendid emporium of the ancient world. It appears, indeed, truly wonderful that, at this early period of arts and history, when Rome yet consisted only of a few straw-thatched cottages, merchants in Tyre should vie with the pomp of kings. So magnificent was the scene, that the prophet, in announcing the divine intention to destroy Tyre, considers it as implying a purpose "to stain the pride of all glory, and to bring into contempt all the honourable of the earth." (*Isai.* xxiii. 9.) Perhaps, however, commerce in its earlier efforts has a particular tendency to concentrate itself in one point, where alone it finds protection, information, and regular channels; while in the advance of society its streams begin to be more widely diffused.

In the interesting picture of Tyrian commerce drawn by Ezekiel, the foundation of the intercourse with Damascus and other contiguous districts, is stated to be "the multitude of the wares of her making;" that is, it consisted in the exchange of her manufactured produce for the raw produce of these rich agricultural districts. There is little specification of the Tyrian manufactures, but the returns were all made in natural products, of the first quality which the soils of Judea and of Syria afforded; from Judea, the finest wheat, honey, oils, and balsam; from Syria, white wool, and the wine of Helbon. No situation could be more fortunate than that of Tyre for the formation of a navy, with the magnificent forests of Lebanon, Senir, and Bashan, rising immediately behind. The timbers, it appears, were constructed of fir; the cedar supplied masts; while the oak was used for those long and powerful oars, which were then the chief instruments of navigation. The vessels appear to have been fitted up with a luxury unknown to modern times. The benches were of the finest cypress wood, inlaid with ivory; the fine linen of Egypt, adorned even with embroidery, was spread out in sails. Tyre, like Carthage, appears to have adopted the policy of employing mercenary troops, which she drew even from the mountainous districts of Persia and the upper Euphrates. The immediate guard of the city, however, was intrusted to its neighbours of Arvad and Gammadin, who, standing round the walls in brilliant armour, are said to have "made its beauty perfect."

With regard to the distant commerce of Tyre, the quarters to which it was carried on must become the subject of some discussion, in the course of which we shall introduce the interesting particulars given by the prophet.

### Sect. IV.—*The World according to the Hebrews.*

No system of Geography can be traced in the sacred writers, who, occupied with higher objects, do not even allude to any such as existing among the Hebrews. The ideas of that people with regard to the structure and boundaries of the earth may, however, be *inferred* from the genealogical chapters (*Gen.* x., repeated 1 *Chron.* i.), which contain, in fact, a view of the known divisions of the earth, agreeing in some striking particulars with the records of profane history; also from the accounts of the commerce of Tyre, and from various detached notices in the historians and prophets.

The Hebrews obviously never attempted to form any scientific theory respecting the structure of the earth. The natural impression, which represents it as a flat surface, with the heaven as a firmament or curtain spread over it, is found universally prevalent. Beneath was conceived to be a deep pit, the abode of darkness and the shadow of death. In one place we find the grand image of the earth being hung upon nothing; but, elsewhere, the *pillars* of the earth are repeatedly mentioned; and sometimes the pillars of heaven. In short, it is evident, that every writer caught the idea impressed on his senses and imagination by the view of these grand objects, without endeavouring to arrange them into any regular system. Although, however, the Jews never indulged in speculative geography, yet there are copious examples of minute and careful topography for practical purposes. Our object, however, is not to mark the divisions of Judea, but to trace the ideas of the Jews respecting the extent and boundaries of the known world. We shall at the same time be able to collect all that is now to be known of the Phœnician Geography; for it is evident that Ezekiel visited Tyre, as Herodotus did Babylon, with the eye of an intelligent observer; and he would doubtless hold intercourse with the best informed men in that great school of commerce and navigation. The objects always alluded to, as placed at the farthest limits of their knowledge, are Tarshish; Ophir; The Isles; Sheba and Dedan; The River; Gog, Magog, and the north. (*Fig.* 1.)

#### Subsect. 1.—*Tarshish.*

Tarshish is the name which, in the annals of Jewish and Phœnician navigation, occurs most frequently, and ranks next to Tyre; yet nothing has been found more difficult than to fix that name to any precise place. The peculiar difficulty is this; that there are two voyages from Tarshish: one up the Mediterranean, bringing iron, silver, lead, and tin, the produce of Spain and Britain (*Ezek.* xxvii. 12.); the other up the Red Sea, bringing gold, ivory, and apes, the produce of tropical Africa (1 *Kings*, x. 22.). How these two voyages can be from the same place, appears at first sight to baffle research.

Various places have been suggested, among which I should not think it necessary to mention Tarsus, in Cilicia, were it not supported by such names as Volney and Malte Brun. Except the resemblance of name, it has not a single feature which can be reconciled to the Tarshish of Scripture. Besides, the name *Tarsus* is evidently of Greek origin (*See Steph. Byzant. in v. Strabo*, l. 14. *Bochart's, Phaleg., and Wetstein's Nov. Test.* vol. ii. p. 511. and 608.), whereas Tarshish is manifestly of oriental derivation, and is doubtless of Phœnician origin. Indeed, Malte Brun admits it to be tenable only on the clumsy and improbable supposition of there being two places of the name of Tarshish. Tartessus or Cadiz is certainly more plausible, and agrees with the Mediterranean voyage; but the distance is too great, and notice might have been expected to be taken of not a few intermediate objects, particularly of the Straits of Gibraltar. It is altogether foreign to the voyage by the Red Sea. This last objection appears also to hold against Carthage, which, in every other respect, seems preferable to Tartessus, and of which more will be said in the sequel.

To solve the problem of the two voyages, the only attempt, so far as I know, has been in the ingenious hypothesis of Gosselin: Tarshish, according to him, signifies the great or open sea, as distinguished even from the largest of its inclosed gulfs. The name may then be applied equally to the Atlantic and the Indian Ocean; and the voyage to and

*Fig.* 1.—GEOGRAPHICAL SYSTEM OF THE HEBREWS.

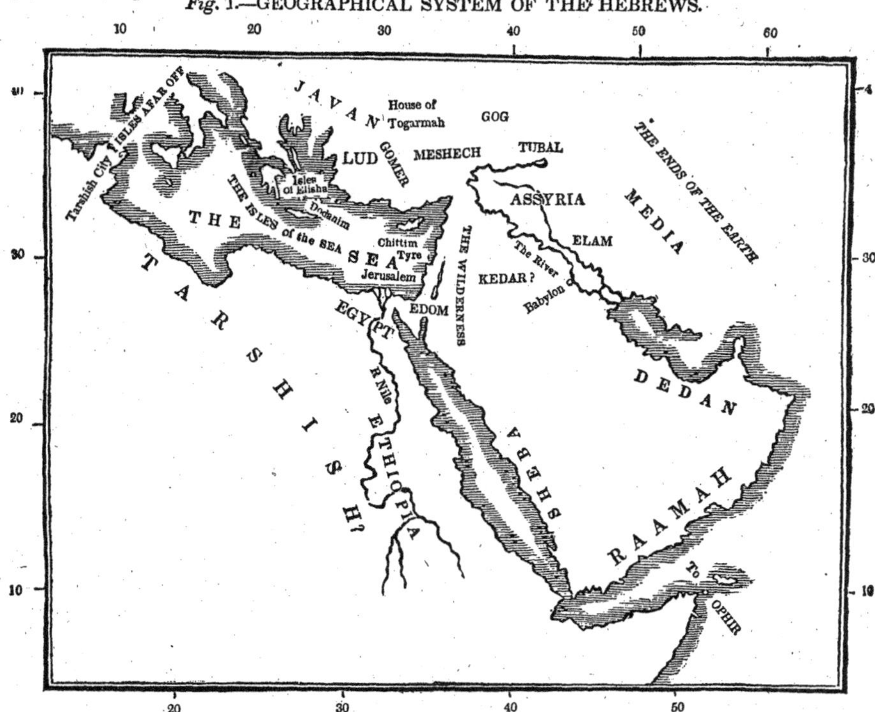


from Tarshish may equally be by the Red Sea or the Mediterranean. But though this hypothesis be supported by the signification of an old Hebrew term, and though it solve the great problem, I think any one, who attentively traces the various occasions on which Tarshish is mentioned in Scripture, will be satisfied that it has a sense quite different from the loose and vague one here ascribed to it. Let us only read the following verse:—"But Jonah rose up to flee into Tarshish from the presence of the Lord, and went down to Joppa, and he found a ship going to Tarshish; so he paid the fare thereof, and went down into it, to go with them into Tarshish from the presence of the Lord." Do not these words unavoidably suggest a precise port, to which there was a regular packet, with a fixed rate of fare?—not a mere vague setting out into the wide and open sea. If the following expressions can be reconciled to M. Gosselin's hypothesis, it is only by very strained interpretations:—"The kings of Tarshish;—the merchants of Tarshish;—pass ye over to Tarshish;—Tarshish was thy merchant:—with silver, &c. they traded in the fairs;—silver in plates is brought from Tarshish, and gold from Ophir;—the daughter of Tarshish," &c. In the genealogical chapters, Tarshish is introduced as one of the sons of Javan. But the other three sons, and every other name mentioned in these chapters, are the fathers of a country and nation; and it would be quite singular if Tarshish alone should have had only *the sea* for his offspring. What a strange idea to call the sea one of the sons of Javan! Indeed, this is so glaringly improbable, that M. Gosselin has recourse to the hypothesis of interpolation—a supposition very unlikely in regard to books held so sacred, and in respect to these chapters among a people so fond of genealogy, and altogether a most unsound principle, as applied to the sacred volume. Finally, I think it very evident, from the general tenour of Hebrew writers, that they had no distinct notion of the Mediterranean as an inclosed sea, and of an ocean beyond it. The expression, "the sea," used in that vague and wide sense, will, I apprehend, be always found to signify the Mediterranean, the Red Sea being designated by that particular term. Thus, there appears to be no motive for adopting M. Gosselin's hypothesis, except the want of any other by which the problem of the two voyages can possibly be solved. But if another can be stated, which shall solve that problem, and at the same time make Tarshish the very place it might be expected to be, this great question may, perhaps, be considered as settled in a more satisfactory manner than heretofore.

That Tarshish must be, fundamentally, Carthage, cannot, I think, admit of a moment's doubt. The strongest argument is, that if it be not, then that grand emporium of Mediterranean trade, the colony of Tyre, the place of all others with which Tyre held always the closest intercourse, must never have been named by the prophets, who give such copious and detailed accounts of Tyrian commerce. When Ezekiel was enumerating every place, even the most obscure, with which Tyre held intercourse, can it be supposed that this, the chief of all others, would have been totally omitted? But if Tarshish be Carthage, then that celebrated city holds exactly the prominent place which, according to every circumstance, it ought to have held in relation to Tyre. This general negative argument does appear to me quite irresistible. The details are equally conformable. Carthage in her glory monopolized, almost entirely, the commerce of Spain and Britain. She even took the most violent measures to prevent any maritime power from penetrating to the west of Sicily. There appears no trace of the Tyrians ever proceeding further. They found, apparently, in Carthage, a complete assortment of the commodities of all the countries to the west, and on the ocean—silver, iron, lead, and tin, which were thus naturally viewed by the Jews, and perhaps by the Tyrians themselves, as Carthaginian commodities. With regard to the name, considering that both Tarshish and Carthage are corruptions of the original Phœnician term, they have that rude resemblance which might be expected. The connexion is rendered stronger by Carchedon, the Greek name of Carthage, which forms a sort of middle term between them.

The voyage from Tarshish by the Red Sea, however, which forms the grand difficulty, remains yet unaccounted for; and it can only, I think, be solved in the following manner: I conceive the name of this great African metropolis must have been generally extended to the whole of the continent of Africa. All the names of the continents, we may observe, were originally derived from one of their remarkable and frequented districts. The name of Asia was extended by the Greeks from a tract of that name immediately opposite to their shore, including Troas, Ionia, and some other of the more eastern districts of Asia Minor. With the Romans, Africa derived its name from the very district now in question, called always Africa Propria, being the finest on that coast, and including Carthage. It appears, then, quite natural that a place so very prominent, with which Tyre held such close and constant intercourse, apparently the only place much frequented by her on the coast of Africa, should be associated in her conception with the whole continent in which it was situated. On any other supposition, the Jews and Phœnicians must have had no name for Africa, which is not very probable. It is observable that Tarshish evidently does not comprehend either Egypt or Upper Ethiopia, which countries, in fact, were never by the ancients considered as decidedly African, that continent, according to their conception, having the Nile for its eastern boundary. If we admit Tarshish to be Africa, the whole difficulty respecting the two voyages at once disappears. As the voyage to the northern coast was by the Mediterranean, so that to the eastern coast was of course by the Red Sea. It is in favour of this solution that Jerome, in fact, calls the voyage to Tarshish "an African voyage." The Jews, unacquainted with intermediate countries, had probably a very inadequate conception of the distance between these coasts; at all events, they justly considered them as parts of the same vast expanse of continent.

### SUBSECT. 2.—*Ophir.*

The name of Ophir, combined, as it always is, with the most precious of metals, and the most coveted of all commodities, ranks among the distant countries known to the Jews, almost superior in splendour to Tarshish, though not equal in greatness and commercial importance. The voyages of Solomon to Ophir for gold, form the greatest naval enterprise in which the kingdom of Judea was ever engaged. Yet this name has been attended with little less difficulty, and produced scarcely less controversy, than that of Tarshish.

The belief that Ophir was in Arabia has certainly not a little to urge in its favour. In the genealogical chapters it is always combined with Sheba, or Sabea, which was undoubtedly situated at the south-west angle of Arabia. It was from Sheba that gold (doubtless, the gold of Ophir,) was regularly brought to Judea and Phœnicia. Even Bochart, who thinks himself obliged to seek in India a more distant Ophir, clumsily compounds the matter by making another Ophir in Arabia. He is followed by M. Malte Brun. M. Gosselin, with his usual zeal to restrict ancient knowledge, insists, that there never was any Ophir except the Arabian, and places it in the modern interior district of Dofar. There appear to me, I confess, vast improbabilities in this Arabian Ophir. As an interior district, it must have been nearer, or certainly as near, to Judea as Sheba; and it appears strange, that no direct land communication should ever have been opened with it. Let us consider the mighty operations of Solomon; his utmost efforts combined with those of Hiram; the materials of shipbuilding conveyed by land over a vast desert; the most skilful workmen transported to Ezion Geber; a fleet composed of large vessels, called ships of Tarshish, at last formed, and undertaking a series of voyages, in each of which three years were employed. What a waste of labour and expenditure to obtain a commodity which could have been conveyed across Arabia in two months on the backs of camels! Yet the repetition of the voyage shows that the article was, in fact, procured on better terms than by the usual channel. In the voyage from Ophir, also, we find new articles never mentioned in relation to Sheba or Arabia, but characteristic of equatorial Africa—ivory, apes, and peacocks. With regard to the close combination in which Sheba and Ophir are always found, it will appear natural enough, when we consider that, unless during the short expedition of Solomon, Sheba appears to have been the channel by which the gold of Ophir was transmitted to Judea and Phœnicia. This circumstance might readily lead the inhabitants of those countries to consider the two as closely connected, though Ophir might be beyond Sheba, and even be separated from it by seas and territories of considerable extent.

The hypothesis which places Ophir in India, though supported by great names, appears quite untenable. The trade of Ophir bears not the least resemblance to an Indian trade. It does not include the fine manufactures and rich spices which India has always furnished; and its staple is gold, which never, at any time, was an article of export from that quarter of Asia. India has, on the contrary, always demanded a large balance of specie, and has formed a gulf in which the gold of the west has been absorbed. If we reject India, we shall not certainly, with some *savans*, travel as far as Peru in quest of our object, notwithstanding the slight resemblance of name, and the attempt to eke it out by the expression "gold of Parvaim," which has some appearance of being synonymous.

The eastern coast of Africa is the quarter to which all the indications appear very clearly to point. In the voyage to Tarshish by the Red Sea, its name and that of Ophir are always combined; nay, the voyage, which in the Book of Kings is called the voyage to Tarshish, in the Chronicles is called the voyage to Ophir; so that it is evident the two are one and the same voyage; and, if Tarshish was Africa, Ophir must clearly be *in* Africa. There is, however, on this coast no abundant supply of gold till we reach as far south as Sofala; thus implying an extent of navigation which is certainly somewhat startling. M. Gosselin particularly urges, that in the time of Alexander there was no longer any knowledge of eastern Africa; and that even the Romans never appear to have penetrated beyond Cape Delgado. On the other hand, it is to be considered that the alliance of Hiram and Solomon united advantages which never existed again in an equal degree. The wealth, naval skill, and ample materials which those great princes could command were scarcely equalled, even by the Ptolemies. After the death of Solomon, the kingdom, split into two, and weakened by continued dissention, abandoned entirely these distant commercial enterprises. A solitary attempt to renew the trade was made by Jehoshaphat, but the vessels prepared for that purpose were wrecked in the very mouth of the port of Ezion Geber; after which the undertaking was entirely given up. In the calamities, which afterwards befel Israel and Judah, and the revolutions which subverted the whole political system of western Asia, it is not wonderful that every trace of this distant intercourse should have been obliterated; and that the successors of Alexander should have had to enter on a new field of discovery. In support of the supposition of Sofala, there may also be noticed a certain resemblance of name; and the duration of the voyage, stated at three years, would afford very ample time to reach the Zambese, even under all the imperfections of ancient navigation.

### Subsect. 3.—*The Isles.*

The Isles, a term which occurs much in Scripture, might be supposed to describe generally those portions of the globe which come under this description; yet a careful comparison of the different passages in which the word occurs will probably show, that it is used in a much more precise and determinate sense, and is applied to a wide and connected range of territory. The whole of the southern coasts of Europe, consisting either of real islands or of peninsular tracts, appears by the Jews and Phœnicians to have been viewed as a long range of islands. Besides, the terms *νησος* and *insula* were, in periods of remote antiquity, applied loosely to peninsulas as well as islands proper. Among many examples which might be adduced, *one* will suffice—Peloponnesus. The isles, relative to Tyre, appear to have ranked only second to Tarshish as a source of wealth, and in respect of close and intimate intercourse. Tyre is called expressly, "a merchant of many isles:" and the consternation which shook the isles at the sound of her fall; the dismay of their kings, who are said to have then cast off their robes, and sat on the ground,—all point out the extent and importance of this commerce. *Tarshish, Elisha, Chittim,* and *Dodanim* are named in the genealogical chapter as the *four* who divided among them the isles of the Gentiles; but, though Tarshish is so often named in combination with "the isles" among the most distant maritime territories, there is never any indication as if it were itself an island. The combination is probably produced by the extensive possessions and commerce of the Carthaginians in the western islands and coasts of Europe. These, including the southern point of Italy, were, as already observed, probably considered as insular, and were distinguished by the appellations of the "isles afar off," and "the distant isles of the sea." The "isle" in particular, which Isaiah mentions in such close connexion with Tarshish, and which the merchants of Sidon, "by passing over the sea, had replenished," can scarcely be any other than Sicily, an island almost Carthaginian, and containing so many flourishing cities. With regard to the isles of Elisha, they are evidently Hellas, the Greek name of Greece. The only distinctive characteristic, indeed, that of furnishing Tyre with the blue and purple dye, does not recall to us any of the features under which we have been accustomed to recognize that celebrated region. But Greece was not yet the seat of arts and arms; and, had she been so, the Tyrian merchants might still have viewed her only as she served their purpose. Bochart has collected ample testimonies to show that the murex, the shell which yielded those celebrated dyes, was found in peculiar abundance on the coast of Laconia. Chittim appears very evidently Cyprus, and its early capital of Citium. The alarm being given thence of the approach of the king of Babylon, and its being considered as the natural place of refuge for the inhabitants of Tyre, where yet they would not be fully secure, mark a proximity which belongs to no other island. The name, indeed, is in one instance given to Greece, and in another to Italy; but this seems merely to be, that, as the nearest known island, its name is sometimes thus vaguely extended to the whole of that territory considered by the Jews as insular. The attempts of Bochart to find the name of Chittim in Italy have been wholly abortive; for we cannot consider as worthy of notice the observation that it and *Latium*, in the respective Greek and Latin languages, both signify "to hide." In regard to Dodanim, convertible into Rodanim(ד and ר being perpetually interchanged and confounded), though it is mentioned only once, we seem justified in fixing on Rhodes, already flourishing and commercial, though not yet become the rival of kings. Bochart seems to go much too far, when he seeks for it on the Rhone or the Ebro.

### SUBSECT. 4.—*Sheba and Dedan.*

Of the internal trade of western Asia during the early ages, the most extensive and important was that carried on across Arabia. It consisted, not so much in the productions of the region, itself, as in those of India and Africa, which found their way by this channel to Judea and Phœnicia.

Sheba, among the Arabian states, holds the most prominent place, being undoubtedly the same with the Sabæa or Arabia Felix of the classic writers. Its imports were the precious commodities of gold and incense: the latter anciently in most extensive demand for the purpose of sacrifice. These articles appear to have been brought to Judea, not by any maritime channel, but in crowded caravans. The "companies of Sheba" are mentioned even in Job. Isaiah speaks of the "multitude of camels;" and of "all they from Sheba." Yet the incense, it is now certain, must have come chiefly from the opposite African coast of Berbera; and the gold, we have some reason to think, must have been derived from a still more remote part of that continent.

The commerce of Dedan rivalled that of Sheba, being carried on from the opposite or eastern coast. The mention of "many isles" in combination with Dedan, seems to fix it to that point at the entrance of the Persian Gulf, which is, in fact, bordered by numerous islands. One of these, Ormuz, became afterwards the seat of a kingdom, which, from a situation and commerce similar to that of Dedan, derived a splendour which made it the pride of the East. The imports from Dedan—"ivory and precious cloths"—point out the source of this prosperity. These were the commodities of India, brought to the mouth of the Persian Gulf, and thence transported across the desert to the western regions. The caravan trade of Dedan appears to have been most extensive; insomuch that the prophet, in denouncing the judgment upon Arabia, mentions the "travelling companies of Dedanim" as its most conspicuous feature. In the prophets, Edom and Dedan are almost universally named together, and the same judgments represented as affecting both. Hence they are usually considered as parts of the same country, and the ordinary maps include Dedan as a district of Edom. Even Bochart, whose learning showed him that there must be a more distant Dedan, adopts the hackneyed scheme of supposing that there were two Dedans. There is no occasion for so unskilful a theory to explain the intimate connexion between these two states. When caravans came across Arabia from the Persian Gulf, it was at Edom or Idumea that they first touched on the civilized world. A depôt was thus naturally formed there of the commodities in which they traded. This traffic raised Idumea and its capital, Petra, to a high pitch of wealth and importance. So close a connexion necessarily caused Dedan to be deeply affected by any calamity which desolated Edom, and rendered her no longer the channel through which this commerce could flow. But these disasters are by no means represented as touching her so closely or so deeply; and while Edom is represented as utterly spoiled, and converted into a waste and reproach, the inhabitants of Dedan are merely warned to "turn back and dwell deep;" (Jer. xlix. 8.) and the expression, "they of Dedan shall fall by the sword," is more correctly interpreted in the margin, "they shall fall by the sword *unto* Dedan." These circumstances appear to mark, along with an intimate connexion, a complete distance and separation between these two great Arabian states.

Raamah is mentioned among other nations of Arabia, along with Sheba, as producing the same articles, but as a much less remarkable country. It appears to be the modern Hadramuth, neither situated so commodiously as Sheba for the African, nor as Dedan for the

Indian, trade. Some of the best-watered districts probably of the Nedsjed, appear to have composed the kingdom of *Kedar*, enriched by the breeding of numerous sheep and goats, with which it supplied even Tyre, and rose to such prosperity, as to make it be considered a mighty catastrophe "when all the glory of Kedar should fail."

### Subsect. 5.—*Countries on the Euphrates.*

The river (for such is the import of the term) presents itself as a grand feature of the landscape after passing across the wide Syrian desert, towards the eastern extremity of the known world. This name, in preference even over the Nile and the Jordan, was always applied to the Euphrates, which, holding so immense a course through kingdoms the most celebrated in history, was considered as one of the grand boundaries of the earth. The great empires and capitals of Assyria and Babylon gave to it a lustre, which was scarcely divided by the *Tigris*, whose name was little known to the Jews before the captivity. Along this line of territory Ezekiel enumerates a number of cities, Haran, Canneh, Eden, Ashur, &c., from which great caravans proceeded to Tyre with cloths and other articles of the most valuable description. In such early accounts, however, the country from which commodities last came is seldom distinguished from their original seat. I therefore entirely agree with Dr. Vincent, that they must have been brought by a long overland voyage across Asia; that these chests of rich apparel, so carefully bound with cords, came, probably, by interior caravans from Hindostan, and, perhaps, already from the frontier of China.

Of the countries beyond the Euphrates, only some broken fragments of knowledge appear to have reached Judea before the captivity. Elam is particularly noticed; the residence of a warlike people, occupying the long mountainous tract east of the Tigris. Media and Persia are also named on a few occasions, but so as to prove that they were only contemplated in dim and obscure distance. At a vague and indefinite distance beyond, the *ends of the earth* were imagined to exist. The early Greeks and, after them, the Arabians, viewed the habitable earth as an island, surrounded on every side by water. Ptolemy, on the contrary, places at every extremity of his map a vague expanse of unknown land. The Hebrews combined in some measure these two views of the subject. To the west, the remotest object for them was the sea, studded with numerous and distant isles; but to the east, where land was seen indefinitely extending, they formed the idea of an inland termination, without being able to attach to it any precise limits. Such a boundary was apparently supposed to exist in various directions, since "all the ends of the earth" is an expression frequently occurring. It was to the east, however, that this idea peculiarly attached itself; and "from the river to the ends of the earth," is the farthest point to which the figurative kingdom of the Messiah is made to extend.

### Subsect. 6.—*Gog, Magog, and the North.*

The north quarter is the only part of the circuit of the geographical knowledge of the Jews which remains to be surveyed. It presented features of peculiarly rude and formidable aspect. Ezekiel, in anticipating an approaching inroad, draws the most gloomy feature of the hordes which it poured forth: Gog, with all his bands, coming like a storm or a cloud to cover the land; Gomer with all his bands; the house of Togarmah, from the north quarter: "a great company and a mighty army," directing their course against those nations which "were at rest, dwelt safely, and had gotten cattle and goods;" and with the eager purpose "to take a prey, to carry away their silver and gold, to take a great spoil." This picture, these hostile and tumultuous crowds, "all riding upon horses," with their wide-roaming and predatory habits, has always suggested the idea of Scythian invasion; and the Arabian geographers have placed the castle of Gog and Magog at the remotest extremity of Tartary. On looking narrowly into the matter, however, we shall find it difficult to suppose this inroad to have proceeded from any part of those unbounded plains. The fact is, we have no occasion to look so far; for the high table-lands in the interior and north of Asia Minor, Phrygia, Galatia, Cappadocia, and Paphlagonia, have always presented the same rude pastoral aspect, and have bred tribes of migratory shepherds and warriors, very similar to those of Scythia itself. These tracts, in fact, continue still to pour forth vast bodies of irregular cavalry, which form the main strength of the Turkish armies. This view of the subject appears completely fixed by the account of the commercial intercourse maintained by these nations with Tyre. The prophet mentions Meshech and Tubal, elsewhere completely identified with Gog, who is called their "chief prince." There never has been the least doubt as to the position of these countries in Upper Armenia, and on the southern border of Caucasus. There the classical writers mention in the Moschi and the Tibareni, which are, perhaps, the same names. The imports into Tyre are stated to be "vessels of brass, and persons of men." This somewhat curious combination is, however, altogether characteristic of the region in question, which was, in ancient time, highly distinguished for the copiousness and excellence of its copper and iron, which last is not wholly excluded by the term used in the original. The skill with which it was worked into steel by the Chalybes, a people of this region, caused their name to be generally given to this product.

Even in the present state of neglect, the neighbourhood of Trebisond supplies with excellent copper all the Lesser Asia. The other article, also, is but too descriptive. The expression, "persons of men," marks the trade in slaves, with which it has always been the fate of Caucasian countries to supply the East. Horses and mules are reported as brought by the "house of Togarmah." Horses have always been a boast of Tartary; and an alliance has been imagined between this name and that of the Turcomans, who still furnish the finest horses. But there was a race called Trogmi, in the upland tracts of Paphlagonia, a region celebrated for its horses, and also for its mules, in which last respect it has a decided advantage over Tartary, to which this last breed is a stranger. Thus we seem justified in finding Gog, with all his rude and terrible appendages, in the northern extremity indeed of the civilized and classical world of Asia, but still far distant from those boundless wastes which composed the ancient Scythia and the modern Tartary.

Javan, which is described as furnishing the same objects of trade with Meshech and Tubal, but not as having any concern in the desolating invasion of Gog, is, in fact, the same word with Ion, or Ionia, an extensive appellation, which comprehended all the western part of the Lesser Asia. The Jews and Phœnicians, overlooking the long range of narrow straits which separated it from Europe, not yet recognised as a separate continent, appear to have extended the name to Thrace, and the interior of continental Greece. Alexander the Great is in one place called king of Javan. That a similar extension was recognised in the early ages of Greece itself, appears by the celebrated ancient inscription at the Isthmus of Corinth. "This is Peloponnesus, not *Ionia*." The Javan slaves were probably drawn from Thrace, whose barbarous regions amply supplied the ancient markets with this cruel species of commodity.

---

## CHAPTER II.

### ANCIENT VOYAGES OF DISCOVERY.

The early voyages of discovery formed the most important materials for those delineations of the globe which were made by the geographical schools of Greece and Rome in their more advanced and perfected state. Before proceeding, therefore, to consider the systems of these schools, it may be proper to take a survey of the exploratory voyages performed by ancient navigators. These do not appear very considerable in the eyes of a modern mariner. There is not one of them, perhaps, which the captain of a tolerably appointed merchant-vessel would not, in the course of his ordinary business, be ready to undertake But in steering along an unexplored coast, in vessels which could scarcely rank above boats without the use of the compass, or any correct means of astronomical observation, even these limited voyages were fraught with peril and adventure. The record of them is however, involved in much mystery and controversy. They were not reported to the world in those regular narratives with which the modern press teems. The ancient narratives are always meagre, and in many cases we have only fragments of hearsay testimony, collected by careless or prejudiced writers. A learned investigation, therefore, is usually necessary, to discover along what coast the navigator sailed, to what point of it he reached and sometimes whether he ever sailed along any coast. In several cases the most skilful disputants are still divided on questions, which, sunk in the deep abyss of time, must probably remain for ever undecided. Faint and dubious, however, as are these records, they will lead us over some of the most interesting problems of antiquity, and will enable us to trace, in some degree, the infant steps of maritime enterprise.

### SECT. I.—*Circumnavigation of Africa under Necho.*

To perform the circuit of the coast of Africa was the favourite object of ancient maritime enterprise, as it continued to be of that of modern times, till the era of its final happy accomplishment. The manner in which its coasts, beyond the Mediterranean and the Red Sea, begin to converge, suggested the idea of a peninsula, the circumnavigation of which might be effected, even by the limited resources of ancient navigation. The wide sphere, both of knowledge and trade, which such a discovery would open to the enterprising maritime nations round the Mediterranean, was sufficiently obvious. The first attempt of this description originated in a quarter which had usually been accustomed to keep aloof from every species of naval enterprise.

Egypt had long held itelf as a country strictly agricultural; but *Necho*, who, next to Sesostris, raised its military glory to the greatest height, appears, like other conquerors, to have been animated by an active spirit, which exerted itself in every direction. Not possessing fit instruments among his own subjects, he engaged some Phœnician navigators to descend the Red Sea, and endeavour to find their way back to the Mediterranean, by the Pillars of Hercules. The narrative is so very short, that we may easily give it in the words of Herodotus: "The Phœnicians, setting sail from the Red Sea, made their way into the southern sea; when autumn approached, they drew their vessels to land, sowed a crop, and waited till it was grown, when they reaped it, and again put to sea. Having spent two years in this manner, in the third year they reached the Pillars of Hercules, and returned to Egypt, reporting what does not find belief with me, but may, perhaps, with some other person; for they said that in passing Africa they had the sun on their right hand (i. e. the north). In this manner Libya was first known."

The authenticity of this narrative has been in a remarkable degree the object of learned curiosity, and has produced a mass of controversy, greater, perhaps, than its short and vague nature is well able to admit. The arguments appear to have been exhausted on the believing side by Rennell, on the sceptical by Gosselin and Vincent. Formidable as the achievement was, it does not seem to involve any absolute impossibility, since the whole voyage might be performed without losing sight of the shore, or launching into the open sea, through which the ancients had no means of guiding their course; and their smaller vessels, keeping close to the shore, might even possess some advantage over our larger ones, obliged to stand out to sea, and encounter the stormy waves of the Atlantic. Herodotus seems inclined to credit the information, unless, on the ground of one general statement, which, being the very thing that should have happened, and disbelieved only through his ignorance, strongly fortifies our inclination to credit the story.

## Sect. II.—*The Voyage of Sataspes.*

The Persian monarchs, after their sway was established over the eastern coasts of the Mediterranean, found the exploration of Africa in some degree their peculiar province. This nation, however, laboured under an aversion and dread of the sea, greater, perhaps, than that of the other orientals. The only effort of theirs on record was one which arose in a singular and rather casual manner.

Sataspes, a Persian nobleman, having committed a heinous offence, was condemned by Xerxes to a cruel death. His friends, however, persuaded the monarch, that by commuting this sentence into that of a voyage round Africa, he would inflict sufferings scarcely less severe, and might render a national benefit. They prevailed, and Sataspes, having procured in Egypt a vessel and crew, passed the Straits of Gibraltar, and bent his course southwards. He is represented as having beat about for several months, at the end of which he probably reached the coasts of the Sahara. The view of those frightful and desolate shores, and of the tempestuous ocean which dashed against them, might well intimidate a navigator bred in the luxurious indolence of the Persian court. Sataspes was struck with a panic, and measured back his course to the straits. Yet, hoping that time and the degree in which he had accomplished his mission might efface the impression, both of former offence and of present failure, he again presented himself before Xerxes. In giving an account of his voyage, he merely related, that wherever he landed he had seen little men wearing a Phœnician dress, who immediately fled into the mountains; but his people had done them no injury, beyond carrying off the cattle of which they stood in need. The failure of the ultimate object of the expedition he imputed to the occurrence of an insurmountable obstacle, the nature of which has not been satisfactorily explained. Xerxes, however, accustomed to expect that all nature should be subservient to his will, would listen to no excuse, and ordered the original sentence to be immediately executed.

## Sect. III.—*Voyage of Hanno.*

The Carthaginians, as the greatest maritime and commercial people of antiquity, might have been expected to make earlier and further progress in the discovery of Africa than any other nation. In general, however, a veil of deep mystery shrouded all the proceedings of that powerful and aspiring people. It is even asserted that they considered as exclusively theirs the whole Mediterranean west of a line drawn across to Sicily, and that they captured all the vessels, and put to death the crews, that were found navigating within these forbidden precincts. The Romans, on the other side, animated by inextinguishable enmity, are said to have industriously destroyed all the records of the literature and history of their fallen rivals. The only fragment that escaped is the Periplus of Hanno, which, notwithstanding the scepticism of Dodwell, its editor, the learned world are now generally agreed in considering as ancient and authentic. This celebrated document is so short, that we may find space here for a complete translation of it.

"It pleased the Carthaginians that Hanno should sail beyond the Pillars of Hercules, and should found cities of the Liby-Phœnicians. He set sail, therefore, with a fleet of sixty vessels, each of which was impelled by fifty oars. They carried with them men and women to the number of thirty thousand, with provisions and supplies of various kinds. We sailed two days beyond the straits, and founded a city overlooking an ample plain, and which we called Thymiaterium. Thence we proceeded westward to Soloe, a promontory of Libya, thickly shaded with trees, where we founded a temple to Neptune; then turning eastward for half a day's sail, we came into a lake not far from the sea, overgrown with numerous and high reeds, and on whose banks elephants and a number of wild animals were feeding. Having passed this lake in the course of a day's sail, we founded cities on the sea coast, Caricum-Teichos, Gytte, Acra, Melissa, and Arambys. Then setting sail, we made our way to the great river Lixus, which flows from Libya. On its banks the Lixitæ, a pastoral race, fed their flocks; with whom we formed ties of friendship, and spent a short interval. The country above them was inhabited by inhospitable Ethiopians, filled with wild beasts, and traversed by very high mountains, whence the Lixus is said to descend; and it was added, that these mountains were inhabited by men dwelling in caves, of a strange appearance, who outran even horses in the chase. Having received interpreters from the Lixitæ, we proceeded along a desert coast till the middle of the second day; when we sailed one day to the eastward, and in the recess of a little bay found a small island, five stadia in circuit. We left inhabitants there, and named it Cerne. This island, on taking an account of our course, we conjectured to be opposite to Carthage; for the navigation from Carthage to the Pillars, and from the Pillars to Cerne, corresponded. Then we came to a lake through which flows a great river called Chretes. That lake contained three islands greater than Cerne; by these, in the course of a day's navigation, we reached the interior shore of the lake, where very great mountains impended over it, inhabited by a rough people dressed in skins of wild beasts, who by throwing stones repelled us, and prevented us from landing. We then sailed into another river, large and broad, full of crocodiles and river horses. We then returned to Cerne. From Cerne, renewing our course to the south, we passed for twelve days along a shore, the whole of which was in the possession of the Ethiopians, who showed a trembling dread of our aspect, and spoke a language unknown to our Lixite interpreters. On the last day, we came to high mountains covered with trees, the wood of which was odoriferous and variously tinted. Passing round these mountains by a navigation of two days, we came to an immense opening of the sea, bordered by plains in which we saw fires of different magnitude glittering at intervals from every spot. Having watered there, we proceeded five days along the shore, till we came to an immense bay, which the interpreters called the Western Horn. In it was a large island, and in that island a salt water lake, in which again there was another island. Entering this lake, we saw in the day nothing but forest; but in the night there were many fires burning; and we heard various sounds of musical instruments, and the cries of numberless human beings. Being terrified by these objects, and the prophets also exhorting us to quit the island, we made off, and reached next the fiery region of Thymiamata, whence torrents of flame poured down into the sea. Here the heat of the earth was such, that the foot could not tread upon it. We therefore took our speedy departure from this place, and after four days' further sail, saw the earth in the night full of flames. There appeared also in the midst of them one lofty fire greater than the rest, which seemed to reach to the very stars; this, when seen by daylight, proved to be a very lofty mountain, called the chariot of the gods. Thence by a navigation of three days, having passed these fiery torrents, we came upon another bay, called the Southern Horn. In its inmost recess was an island similar to that formerly described, which contained in like manner a lake with another island, inhabited by a rude description of people. The females were much more numerous than the males, and had rough skins: our interpreters called them ***Gorillæ***. We pursued but could take none of the males; they all escaped to the top of precipices, which they mounted with ease, and threw down stones; we took three of the females, but they made such violent struggles, biting and tearing their captors, that we killed them, and stripped off the skins, which we carried to Carthage: being out of provisions, we could go no further."

Such is the entire narrative of this most celebrated of the ancient voyages; but it would be impossible to comprise within the same limits even a sketch of the commentaries to which it has given rise among the learned.

Three leading hypotheses have been formed; one, that of Bougainville, who conceives Hanno to have reached the Gulf of Benin; another, of Major Rennell, who carries his course only to Sherbro Sound, a little beyond Sierra Leone; while M. Gosselin insists upon terminating it about the river of Nun. (*Fig.* 2.) When we reflect that the first of these courses is upwards of three thousand miles, and the last under seven hundred, an idea may be formed of the extremely vague nature of these data, where all the names are changed, and no one point fixed with such certainty that the others can rest upon it.

Bougainville contends that his assigned limits do not exceed what may reasonably be supposed to have been passed over by the most skilful navigator of antiquity; in fact, the period of thirty-eight days is precisely the time employed by the squadron sent in 1641 to found the Portuguese fort of Elmina. All the grand features of man and nature described by Hanno are to be found in tropical Africa only; Ethiopians or Negroes, Gorillæ, who are evidently apes or orang-outangs; rivers so large as to contain crocodiles and hippopotami. The great conflagrations of the grass, and the music and dancing prolonged through the night, are phenomena which have been observed only in the negro territories.

Major Rennell's system retains all the arguments by which that of Bougainville is sup

*Fig.* 2.—MAP ILLUSTRATING THE VOYAGE OF HANNO.

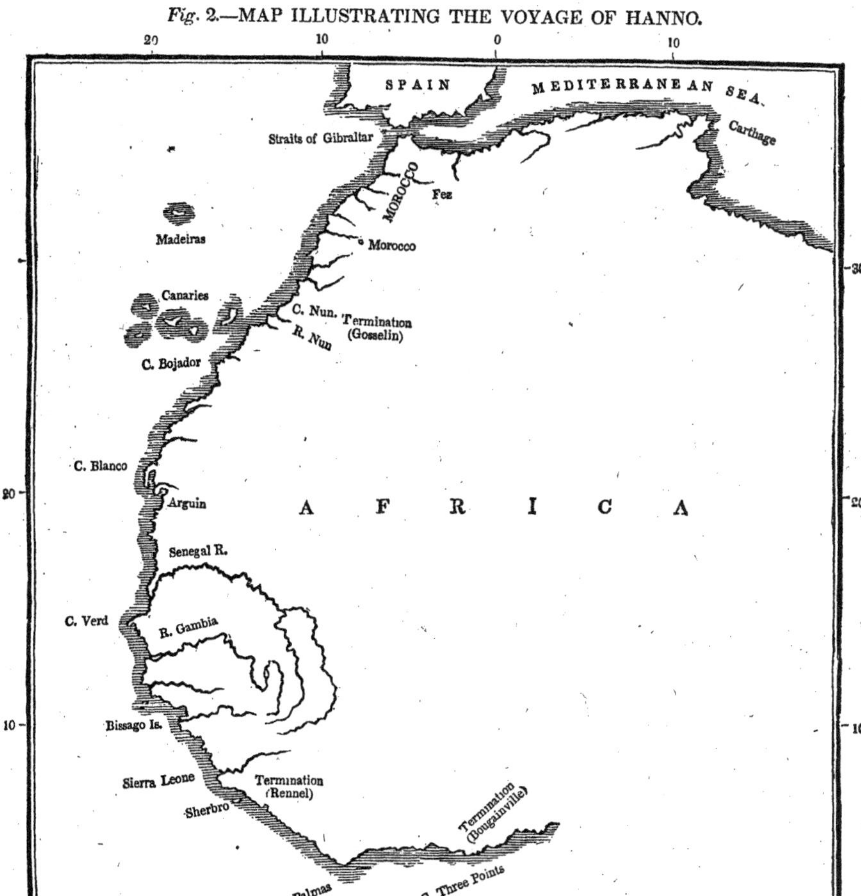


ported, at the same time that it avoids the extravagant supposition of ancient vessels having made a course of seventy geographical miles in the day. The Gulfs of Bissago and Sherbro present those numerous islands described by Hanno, and not found on any other part of the coast; and even their form seems to correspond to the appellation of Horn, applied by him to these great gulfs. If, then, Hanno's career reached central Africa, there can be little doubt that Major Rennell's hypothesis, or something near it, exhibits his real progress.

M. Gosselin restricts the voyage within much narrower limits. It was impossible, he urges, that the course could be otherwise than slow in a voyage of discovery upon an unknown sea, where the mariner could sail only by daylight, with constant precautions, and minutely examining every part of the coast. The motions of Hanno were clogged also by the large and incumbered fleet of which he was the escort. Destitute of the compass, and without the power of standing out to sea, he could never, it is alleged, have doubled Cape Bojador, which so long baffled the efforts of the Portuguese. With regard to the features supposed to be exclusively characteristic of tropical Africa, M. Gosselin conceives that Morocco, yet in no degree civilized or subdued, but in the full possession of rude native tribes, would bear a much more similar aspect than now to the interior portions of the continent. The ape tribe and the wild river amphibia might probably fill a region unoccupied by man, though now, it is supposed, expelled by culture and a more crowded population. The term Ethiopians has been applied, not to negroes only, but to all nations of a dark colour. He conceives, therefore, that Hanno's course could never pass much beyond the frontier of Morocco, and could have reached only a very little further than the estuary of the river of Nun.

To decide a point on which such learned men so widely disagree, is what we do not feel very forward to undertake; and really the difficulties appear very great in any view of the subject. The detail of the positions would, on the whole, lead us to prefer the most limited space. Of these positions the island of Cerne forms the key; and the identifying of it with Arguin is essential to the support of the two remote hypotheses. But though it is evident that the whole of the sailing period to Cerne is not given, the time being omitted during which the five cities were founded, yet the general tenour seems hardly consistent with so great a way being made along such a difficult and unknown shore. The defect is in some degree supplied by an ancient nautical guide of some authority, called the Periplus of Scylax, in which the sail from the straits to Cerne is given at twelve days, a period which Major Rennell admits to be wholly insufficient for reaching Arguin. Ptolemy, indeed, carries Cerne to almost a tropical latitude; but as he keeps it still north of the Canaries, his graduation here is manifestly erroneous, and his authority, on the whole, is in favour of retaining Cerne within the limits of Morocco. The details of Hanno do not appear to be always very satisfactory; but perhaps they might prove more so, did we possess a more accurate survey of this coast than has yet been taken. On the whole, then, the great question is, whether M. Gosselin's solutions can account for the aspect of nature and life being so different from that of Morocco, and so like that of a negro coast: perhaps here, too, some light might be obtained from a careful observation of the ruder borders of the former empire.

### SECT. IV.—*Voyages of Eudoxus.*

The ambition of performing the circuit of Africa, the grand maritime problem of antiquity, was not solely confined to princes and states. Even private adventurers, animated by the ambition of achieving so great an enterprise, and hoping, perhaps, to combine with it opportunities of lucrative commerce, are found in the list of the explorers of Africa. Eudoxus was the most memorable of these adventurers, whose story, however, has come down to us through a very clouded medium. In ancient, still more than in modern times, there existed men whose habit it was to treat with doubt and derision all narratives of discovery that extended beyond the ordinary limits. At the head of this sceptical band stands Strabo, one of the greatest geographers whose works survive, and who forms the chief medium by which these narratives have reached our time; a most unfortunate circumstance to the fame of these early discoverers. However, in many instances, nature herself has stood forth as their vindicator; and our more extended knowledge has enabled us to detect the fallacy of the arguments by which Strabo has endeavoured to refute them. This is not particularly the case with regard to Eudoxus; but really, in Strabo's notices respecting the adventurous life of the bold navigator, we cannot see any thing which tends to controvert the general belief of antiquity, that he had made repeated and spirited attempts to explore the unknown coasts of the African continent.

According to the narratives of Strabo, Eudoxus was a native of Cyzicus, sent on a mission to Alexandria, then the great seat of maritime enterprise and geographical knowledge. His ardent mind was strongly imbued with the spirit which reigned there; and he offered himself to Ptolemy Evergetes, the reigning king, as a zealous instrument to be employed in any expedition having these objects in view. There was, at first, some talk of ascending the Nile, and endeavouring to reach its unknown sources; but their views received a new direction from the arrival of a person who was, or professed to be, a native of India, escaped alone from the wreck of his vessel near the foot of the Arabian Gulf. Ptolemy immediately fitted out a naval armament, with which Eudoxus proceeded on this destination. He appears to have made a prosperous voyage, and to have returned with a cargo of aromatics and precious stones, which last had either been washed down by the rivers, or dug out in a concrete state. It is scarcely probable, however, that Eudoxus ever reached the real shores of India, or went beyond the southern shore of Arabia, and, at farthest, the Persian Gulf. Of this wealth, Evergetes appears to have plundered him; which Strabo insinuates was in resentment of some dishonest conduct on his own part. We cannot, in these days, attempt to judge between the two parties. However, Evergetes dying, his widow Cleopatra took Eudoxus again into favour, and sent him on a fresh voyage. He was now driven by unfavourable winds to the coast of Ethiopia, where he was well received by the inhabitants, and carried on some advantageous trade. His return to Alexandria was again unfortunate. Cleopatra was dead; and her son, who succeeded, treated him as ill as Evergetes had done. Eudoxus brought with him, however, one trophy from the extremity of his voyage—the prow of a vessel, said to have come from the westward as a portion of a wreck, and on which was sculptured the figure of a horse. This prow being exhibited by Eudoxus on the harbour, some mariners from Cadiz declared it to be the very form peculiar to a species of large vessel which went from that port for purposes partly of trade, and partly of fishing, to the coast of Mauritania. Eudoxus listened with enthusiastic credulity, and determined now to renounce the deceitful patronage of courts, and to fit out a new expedition from the commercial city of Cadiz. He proceeded thither by way of Massilia and other maritime stations, where he loudly proclaimed his hopes, and invited all who were animated with any spirit of enterprise to accompany him. He accordingly succeeded in equipping an expedition on a considerable, and even magnificent scale. He had one ship and two large boats, on board of which he carried, not only goods and provisions, but artisans, medical men, and even players on musical instruments. A crew so gay, and filled, probably, with extravagant hopes, were ill fitted to encounter the hardships of African discovery. They took fright at the swell of the open sea, through which Eudoxus was anxious to conduct them, and insisted, according to the usual timid system, on being brought near to the shore. This led to the disaster which Eudoxus had foreseen: the ships were stranded, and the cargo with difficulty saved. The most valuable articles were then put on board one vessel of a lighter construction, and he prosecuted the voyage till he came to a race of people who appeared to him to speak the same language with those whom he had met on the opposite shore of the continent. Conceiving himself to have thus ascertained the object of his voyage, he returned, and endeavoured to procure the barbaric aid of Bocchus, king of Mauritania; but, suspecting that monarch of a treacherous design against him, he again betook himself to Spain. Here he succeeded in equipping a fresh expedition, consisting of one large vessel fitted for the open sea, and another of smaller dimensions for exploring the coast. Here, unfortunately, the narrative breaks off, referring to the Spaniards and Gaditanians, as likely to know more; but as nothing more is stated on any authority, we fear that this last expedition must have had an unfortunate issue. Such is the narrative given by Strabo, upon information which seems to have been originally obtained from Eudoxus himself; and we see nothing in it unworthy of belief, or which might not very well be accomplished by a man of bold and enthusiastic character, possessed of science and talent, and devoted with such ardent zeal to the cause of discovery. Eudoxus cannot be made responsible for the fables which antiquity has put into his mouth. He is represented by some as having actually made the circuit of Africa; by others as having come to one nation that was dumb, and another whose mouth was entirely closed, and which received food through an orifice in the nose. But none of these fables are found in the report of Eudoxus himself, as coming through the medium of Strabo his enemy.

### Sect. V.—*Voyage of Pytheas.*

The voyage of Pytheas, the Massilian navigator, is of peculiar interest, as it is the only one described in any detail, having Europe, and particularly the British Isles, for its object. It comes to us, however, still more deeply tinged by the same dim and discoloured medium through which that of Eudoxus has passed. It is known almost solely by the hostile quotations of the sceptical Strabo, adduced for the purpose of proving Pytheas to be "a liar of the first magnitude." Yet, the nature of the grounds on which this conclusion is made to rest, is such as to place in the clearest light Strabo's own ignorance, and the superior information of Pytheas. This last will become more conspicuous, if we suppose, as seems probable, that the errors of the geographer were transmitted to him from Massilia itself; in which case, Pytheas being found possessed of knowledge of which his countrymen were destitute, there appears no mode in which he could have obtained it, except the actual performance of the voyages.

The following are statements on which Strabo rests his refutation of Pytheas. That navigator stated, that the *Calbium Promontorium*, the extremity of Bretagne, pointed to the west, while Strabo affirms it to be perfectly notorious that its direction was to the *north.* This last strange idea was connected with what we shall find to be the general error of this school, which allowed to France a southern coast only, and not a western one. Again, Pytheas represented Britain as having one of its sides much longer than five hundred miles, whereas, his adversary maintains this to be the dimensions of its longest side, which, according to him, is that opposite to and seen from the shores of Gaul. Finally, Pytheas asserts that his *Ultima Thule* was farther north than Ireland; whereas, all well-informed persons, knowing Ireland to be four hundred miles north from Britain, and scarcely habitable on account of the cold, considered it as forming on that side the extreme boundary of the inhabited earth. Thus far it is necessary only to name the charges against Pytheas, to make him shine conspicuous above his enemies.

There are other statements, it must be confessed, which appear at first sight a little startling. Pytheas describes the longest side of Britain not only as more than five hundred miles in length, but as exceeding two thousand. It is to be observed, however, that while Strabo described Britain as a triangle, having its longest side opposite to Gaul, Pytheas conceived it to have only *two* sides, one of which, consequently, reached from the Land's End, or the Lizard Point, to the extremity of Scotland. If we consider this vast extent of coast, with so many winding shores and deep bays, all the sinuosities of which an ancient navigator was obliged to follow, the estimate will appear not very extravagant. Again Pytheas described the coast of Kent as several days' sail from that of Gaul. But the term by which Strabo designates Gaul, is Κηλτικη (Celtica); and it appears from Cæsar, that Celtica formed only one of the three parts into which Gaul was divided, and was bounded on the east by the Seine. Pytheas probably used the term in this restricted and more proper sense; when the distance assigned became strictly correct. He moreover described the coast of Spain as inhabited by Gallic nations; it would even seem, that he considered the Calbium Promontorium as Spanish. Here he was clearly in the wrong; but the error will probably be found to have rested not in his observations and facts, but in mixing them with an erroneous theory prevalent at Massilia, according to which, France had not a western coast, nor one facing the Atlantic; such a coast belonged to Spain only. Under this impression, Pytheas, so long as he sailed along the western coast of Gaul, and till he came to that opposite to Britain, would naturally imagine that he was sailing along the coast of Spain.

Strabo at last traces Pytheas to Thule, and "her utmost isles," when he does, certainly, present a narrative assuming somewhat of a fabulous aspect. The most daring navigator, as he approached the dreary boundaries of earth and ocean, and saw only the high billows of the North Sea dashing against a rocky and misty shore, might become liable to some sinister impressions. Pytheas, it seems, said, that beyond Thule there commenced what was neither earth, sea, nor air, but a confused blending of all the three, similar to the substance called *pulmo marinus* (a species of medusa common on our shores). He added, that this substance was the basis of the universe, and that in it, air, earth, and sky hung as it were suspended. If we place ourselves in the situation of Pytheas, seeing before him the northern sea, overhung by thick and gloomy mists, shrouded in twilight, and darkened by tempest, we may suppose him very easily persuaded, that what he beheld was a confused blending of all the elements, not very dissimilar even to that thick viscid animal substance to which it was compared. Nor can we feel much wonder, if, after this long and difficult navigation through so many perils, he should lend somewhat of a ready ear to a *report* which represented him to have reached that farthest boundary of nature, beyond which it was no longer possible for mortal sail to penetrate. Another report of Pytheas was, that at Thule the phenomenon took place which belongs only to the polar circle,—a summer of one long day, and a winter of one long night. Antiquity is somewhat full of rumours of this phenomenon, which science had pointed out as likely to take place at a certain latitude; and there was a general disposition in those who had made any progress northwards to anticipate the term. Considering the loose way in which rumour then spread, it may easily be supposed, that the partisans of this idea might support it by an exaggerated representation of the real statements of Pytheas. One of these (Geminius) merely reports him as saying that the nights appeared to him to last only for two or three hours, a statement which at midsummer would be quite correct. Indeed, we have been assured by persons who have resided in the Shetland islands, that at that season there was scarcely any sensible term of darkness. A foreigner, then, visiting the islands, might very readily imagine he had arrived at that point on the globe where the summer was one uninterrupted day.

The theories, which would make Thule any other place than Shetland, seem not to require much discussion, though there are not wanting learned partisans in favour of each. Iceland would imply too great an extent of open sea for an ancient navigator; and the period of five days' sail from the continent would be very inadequate. Some Scandinavian writers have claimed Thule as belonging to their own region; Rudbeck for Sweden; Saxo Grammaticus, and Schœnning for the Norwegian Tellemach; Malte Brun for Jutland. These theories seem sufficiently refuted by the single consideration, that Pytheas invariably considered Thule as British, and expressly calls it the "farthest of the Britains." But Jutland or the Baltic he could have only reached by a long navigation along the coasts of Germany, which could never have been performed without the clear perception of having left far behind him every thing belonging to Britain.

### SECT. VI.—*The Voyage of Nearchus.*

Alexander the Great was animated beyond, perhaps, any other ancient monarch or sage, with an ardent zeal for discovery His expedition became almost as much one of exploration as of conquest. Its course was in general by land, and through the interior of the continent; but his mind was not less deeply fixed upon commerce and maritime discovery. On reaching, therefore, the banks of the Indus, and being obliged by the mutiny of his troops to fix there the termination of his career, he was seized with a desire to explore the lower course of that river, and afterwards the southern coasts of Asia; a long range completely unknown to the Greeks. The prospects of this voyage, however, were such as to appal the most enterprising of his naval officers. The perils of tempest and shipwreck on this wide and unknown ocean, with those of being driven upon a barbarous and desert coast, appeared almost to preclude the hope of reaching by this long circuit the destined station of the army on the banks of the Euphrates. The inferior officers variously excused themselves from so heavy a task; and the enterprise appeared ready to fail for lack of instruments, when Nearchus, the admiral of the fleet, came forward and proffered his own services. Alexander unwillingly committed this task to an officer so high in rank, and his intimate friend; but the earnestness of Nearchus, and the backwardness of all the others, left him at length no alternative.

The voyage down the Indus was brilliant. Alexander conveyed his army in a crowded fleet of two thousand vessels. The sound of the numberless oars, echoed by the surrounding woods, as they floated down this majestic stream, excited the admiring gaze of the natives. Alexander even accompanied his admiral down the Delta of the Indus, and took a view of the ocean, after which he returned, to lead his army by a most perilous and difficult route through Gedrosia and Karamania to Babylon.

Nearchus now began his arduous naval route (*Fig.* 3.), after the usual antique preparation

*Fig.* 3.—MAP OF THE VOYAGE OF NEARCHUS.

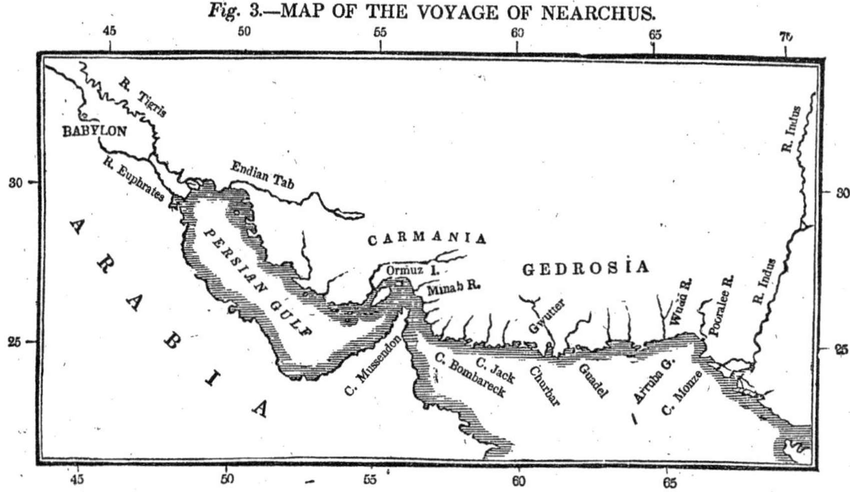


of sacrifices and games. At the mouth of the river appeared a most formidable obstacle, a rock barring the passage, and against which the waves broke with fury. This was surmounted by cutting a canal across the softest part of the rock, through which the vessels were able to pass at full tide. He then passed the sandy island of Krokali (Corachie,) and Mount Eirus (Cape Monze,) when, being now in the open ocean, a series of gales began, so heavy and continued, as obliged him to seek the shelter of an excellent harbour formed by an island called Bibacta. The crews here landed, threw up an entrenchment to defend themselves against the natives, and remained for twenty-three days, subsisting chiefly on shell-fish. The wind having abated, they set sail, and came to a coast where water, of which they appear to have needed almost daily supplies, was only to be got by going several miles up into the country. They then passed between a range of rocks, so close to each other, that the oars struck against them on each side. After sailing a considerable space, partly in a narrow channel between a wooded island and the shore, they came to the river Arabius (the modern Pooralee). It gave name to a numerous people, inhabiting all the territory between this river and the Indus. On the other side was the coast of the Oritæ. In proceeding, however, Nearchus met with a dreadful tempest, in which three of his vessels perished, though the crews were saved by swimming, and he with difficulty brought his shattered vessels to the coast. Here he found Leonatus, whom Alexander had detached to open a communication with him, which he obtained only by very hard fighting. Nearchus here spent some time in refitting his shattered vessels, and exchanged those of his crew who had proved themselves less efficient, for fresh men out of the Greek army. Having laid in corn for ten days, they sailed with a prosperous wind, and reached the rapid stream of Tomerus (the modern Wudd). Here the natives, six hundred strong, were drawn up to oppose their landing; a barbarous race, armed with lances six cubits long, pointed not with iron, but with wood hardened in the fire. Nearchus caused a band of his light troops to swim on shore, and to make no movement till they were drawn up in a triple line, then suddenly to raise a general shout, and pour in clouds of darts and missiles. This sudden attack, their shouts, and the glitter of their armour, produced instant and total rout on the part of the natives. They are described as presenting an aspect almost incredibly savage, being covered in a great measure with hair, and having long nails like the claws of wild beasts. Their dress consisted in the skins of animals and of large fishes.

The expedition now steering out to sea, and taking a southerly course, observed phenomena belonging to the midsummer of the tropic, the novelty of which struck them with surprise. When the sun was in the meridian no shadow was projected, and when there came to be a little shadow, it declined to the southward. Stars, which were wont to be seen high in the heavens, were now little above the horizon. At Bagaziri (Cape Arrubah) they left the coast of the Oritæ, and entered that of the Ichthyophagi, or fish-eaters, a food which is said to have so remarkably abounded, that even the flesh of the cattle savoured of fish, from their making it, like sea-birds, their daily food. The people were hospitable, but could give only fishes and goats. It was not till the Greeks had sailed a considerable distance that at Barna they found some palms, gardens, and verdure. After passing Cophantæ (Guadel,) where they obtained a supply of fine water, and Cyzia (Gwutter) on a desert and rocky shore, they came to a small town on a hill a little inland (probably Churbar,) where it appeared probable that a supply of grain might be obtained. To possess himself of this, Nearchus had recourse to measures that harmonized much more with the character of a buccaneering freebooter, than with that of an officer of the first prince in the world. The people met him in the most kindly manner, and presented to him roasted fish and other victuals. Meeting their friendly advances, he expressed a wish to visit their city, and being cordially admitted, his first step was to take military occupation of it, and command the natives to lay open to him all their stores of grain. The poor citizens at first flew to arms, but having no means of effectual resistance, were obliged to yield. It proved, however, that they had little except dried fish reduced to powder, and Nearchus could get only a very small stock of grain. In sailing now along an almost desert coast, the stock of provisions became excessively scanty; and they obtained only a poor supply by landing and cutting off the leaves of wild palm-trees. The pressure became so extreme, and was so impatiently borne by the crews, that Nearchus did not think it safe to land at night, lest they should all take flight into the interior. In one place he found a paltry village, all the inhabitants of which fled; but the Greeks found seven camels, which they killed and eagerly devoured. The same distress continued to press upon them so long as they sailed along the coast of the "fish-eaters." Notwithstanding this name, few of them were fishers, or had even boats. They procured this food by immense nets, sometimes a quarter of a mile long, formed out of the fibrous bark of the palm tree. These they placed at high tide across the mouth of little bays, so that when the waters receded, the nets retained all the fish which had been carried up with the tide. The houses of the rich were built with the bones of whales cast ashore, those of the poor with the back-bones of smaller fishes. Nearchus descried a number of whales, whose presence was at first made sensible only by the quantity of water thrown up into the air, and tossed as in a whirlpool, a spectacle which struck the sailors with terror, and made the oars drop from their hands. The commander, however, on being informed of the cause, made his crews raise the loudest possible sound by shouts, trumpets, and dashing of oars, which at once kept up their own spirits, and was supposed to induce these monsters of the deep to replunge into their abysses.

The coast of Caramania was next reached by Nearchus, after passing the fabulous abode of a Persian Circe, who, according to report, was accustomed to seduce the navigator by voluptuous pleasures, and then convert him into a fish. Nearchus now found his distresses nearly at an end, as the soil was tolerably productive in grain and fruits, and there was plenty of good water. After passing Capes Jask and Bombareek, they came in view of a huge promontory, stretching far into the sea, called Cape Maceta (Mussendoon), and forming the entrance of the Persian Gulf. The great body of the sailors, and even Onesicrotus, an officer high in command, weary of this long navigation, earnestly proposed to land, and march on foot to Babylon. Nearchus justly and strongly insisted that this was in no degree to fulfil the intention of Alexander, whose injunction it was, to survey every coast, every harbour, and every bay, between India and the Euphrates; and that besides they incurred great hazard of being involved in those arid and burning deserts, of which Arabia in a great measure consists. This wise opinion prevailed, and in ascending the Persian Gulf they found, for the most part, a fertile and beautiful coast. In the delightful country at the mouth of the river Anamis (the modern Minab) they landed, and began to refresh themselves after so many hardships. Nay, a party having proceeded to some distance into the interior, met, with tears of surprise and joy, a man in a Greek dress, and speaking the Greek language. This proved to be a soldier who had straggled from the army of Alexander, which he reported to be at a distance of only five days' journey. On receiving this intelligence, Nearchus caused the ships to be drawn on shore, a rampart to be formed round them, and the crews to take rest and refreshment, while he and Archias set out alone for the camp. On their arrival they presented an aspect so haggard, pale, and squalid, that the persons they met did not know them, but on being told their name, hastened to carry the first tidings to Alexander. They added (a hasty conclusion formed from appearances,) that the fleet and the army had perished. Alexander received Nearchus with a kindness mingled with sorrow, and after the first salutations, began to ask particulars of the catastrophe of his favourite armament; but when Nearchus replied, "O king! thy ships and men are safe," the conqueror burst into a flood of tears, and swore by Jupiter Ammon, that he derived more pleasure from this event than from the entire conquest of Asia.

The rest of the navigation of Nearchus, when he had with some difficulty regained the fleet, was easy, care being taken that he should find on the coast every kind of supply. They passed the barren and desert rock of Organa, afterwards so celebrated under the name of Ormuz, the large and fertile Oaracta (the modern Kishme). Soon after they quitted the coast of Caramania and entered that of Persia proper (the modern Fars,) which they followed till its termination at the river Arosis (the modern Endian Tab,) which appeared to them the largest they had seen since they had left the Indus. They were now in Susiana, and soon reached the mouth of the Tigris where the voyage terminated.

The circumnavigation of Arabia, and the opening of a communication between the Red Sea and the Persian Gulf, formed to Alexander an object of almost equal ambition. He accordingly appears to have sent expeditions down both seas, in the hope of accomplishing this object. Those, however, who went from Persia were never able to double that formidable promontory (the Mussendoon) which Nearchus had passed at the entrance of the gulf; while those who went from Egypt, after making a certain progress, were always obliged to return for want of water. The narrator chose to conclude with inferring, that such an achievement must be beyond human skill or power, otherwise the daring curiosity of Alexander would certainly have accomplished it. He reinforces this argument by observing, that as caravans which crossed Arabia were able to travel only during the night and in the day were unable to bear the intense heat of the sun, it was unreasonable to suppose that a region still farther to the south should be at all habitable.

### Sect. VII.—*Periplus of the Erythrean Sea.*

The complete establishment of the dominion of Rome produced a long period of comparative peace. The encouragement of industry and commerce never formed part of the policy of that powerful empire; but the demand for luxuries of every description in its overgrown capital, where the wealth of the world was collected, and to procure which the remotest extremities of the earth and sea were ransacked, powerfully stimulated mercantile enterprise. Alexandria continued still the great nautical school, by whose mariners the obstacles which in the time of Alexander had been deemed insurmountable were completely overcome. Regular voyages were established across to India, and for a considerable extent along the eastern coast of Africa. The course of this commercial voyage is related by Arrian, not the historian of Alexander, but a merchant of Alexandria; and though not so much a voyage of discovery as a coasting guide, it is founded, probably, upon personal observation, and will enable us to complete the survey of the great naval routes of the ancient world.

The voyage down the west coast of the Red Sea began with Berenice, founded by the Ptolemies, and the site of which, after being long sought for in vain, seems to have been nearly fixed by Belzoni. The coast on the African side was wild, and occupied only by a few rude huts of barbarous Nubians. The small port called Ptolemais Theron was the only place where refreshments could be obtained. At length, the navigator came to Aduli, a great emporium, whose site Mr. Salt seems to have ascertained in the vicinity of Arkeeko. Here was a profusion of excellent ivory, collected and sent down from Axum, the metropolis, about eight days' journey in the interior. In return for this single staple of Ethiopia was exchanged that variety of showy colours, suited to a rude taste; pottery and glass vessels, the manufacture of Diospolis; brass for vessels and ornaments, iron for pointing lances, arms, and cutting instruments. Some fine cloths, and ornaments of gold and silver, were brought as presents or tribute to the king. Farther down, apparently in the Gulf of Zeyla, was the kingdom of Zoskales, a prince who is described in glowing terms as adorned with every virtue, and eminently skilled in Grecian literature; but these seeds of civilization, if they ever existed, did not ripen in so ungenial a climate. The coast now turns eastward to the Indian Ocean.

A view of the passage down the opposite or eastern coast of the Red Sea must now be taken. Navigators do not seem to have ventured across the breadth of that sea from Berenice, but went by Myos Hormus, along the mouth of the Gulf of Suez, touching at *Leuke Kome*, the fair village, which formed the port of the great commercial capital of Petra. The coast downwards was most unfavourable to navigation, "full of danger, without harbours, beset with rocks, everywhere full of horror;" and such the whole of the Red Sea is described to be by modern navigators. If a vessel was driven too near the shore, it was immediately plundered by the barbarous inhabitants, and all who survived carried into slavery. At length they came to the Burnt Island, which seems to be Gebel Tor, on the coast of Yemen, where they found a fine country and a friendly people. The emporium of this coast was Moosa, near the modern Mocha, said to be inhabited by a race skilled in maritime affairs. The imports were of the same description as at Aduli, but of finer quality, including a considerable quantity of dye-stuffs. The exports were myrrh, gum, alabaster (no mention yet of coffee). They then proceeded downwards, and passed the straits now called Bab el Mandel.

The southern coast of Arabia formed the next object of navigation. Ocelis (the modern Ghella) was a good harbour, though with little trade; but Arabia Felix, which seems to have been near the site of Aden, had been a most flourishing port, forming a depot in which the merchants of Alexandria found all the commodities of India. It had lately, however, been destroyed by the Romans. In coasting along Arabia, they found Kane (the modern Macculla); the Gulf of Sachalites, in which is found the modern Sahar; and Syagros, described as the largest promontory in the world, usually supposed to be Ras el Had, but which Vincent appears clearly to fix in the much more westerly position of Cape Fartash. This region is described as yielding a considerable quantity of incense, but as extremely moist and unhealthy. They now passed Mosca (Morebat), Asichone (Hasec), the islands of Zenobius (Curia Muria), and came to Ras el Had, where the coast turns northward to the Persian Gulf. The writer observes, and truly, that the entrance of the Gulf is bordered by very lofty and rugged mountains; he mentions the celebrated pearl fishery on its western shore, and Apologos, otherwise called Oboleh, then the emporium of the Euphrates. He does not dwell, however, on these details, and passes also, with very slight notice, the southern coast of Persia, which the observations of Nearchus had shown to be destitute of any materials for commerce.

The coast of India (*fig.* 4.) now commences, and forms the most important era in the voyage. He reaches the mouth of the great river *Sinthus*, by which name he designates the Indus. It is represented as entering the sea by seven mouths, only one of which is navigable, and on which is situated a place called Emporium Barbaricum, subject to the interior metropolis of Minnagara, which last is described as a Scythian city. The idea of Scythia attached to this part of India could only be suggested by the rude pastoral manners of the people, and, combined with the circumstance of its being included in the Parthian empire, points out Minnagara as belonging to what is now called the kingdom of Caubul, to which, in fact, the Delta of the Indus is still subject. The merchants were obliged to go up to Minnagara, and to negotiate with the prince himself. After passing the Indus, navigators found successively the gulfs of Eirin (Cutch) and of Barygaza (Baroach). The narrator here remarks the dangers of every kind with which these gulfs are beset, shallows, concealed rocks, narrow and difficult entrances, but above all, the extraordinary occasional violence of the tide; in consequence of which, unexperienced navigators often saw their vessels either sunk or driven on shore. Frequently, when they were sailing in perfectly smooth water, a sound was heard as of an advancing army; and soon the tide rushed on with such force, that no anchor could secure the vessels. Barygaza was a very great emporium, at which were found the same commodities as at Emporium Barbaricum, with much finer cloths, and a quantity of long pepper. Ozene (Ougein) was a great interior capital, the prince of which it was necessary to propitiate, by sending up handsome presents of the very best wine, rich unguents, cloth, and beautiful female slaves.

*Fig.* 4.—PERIPLUS—COAST OF INDIA.

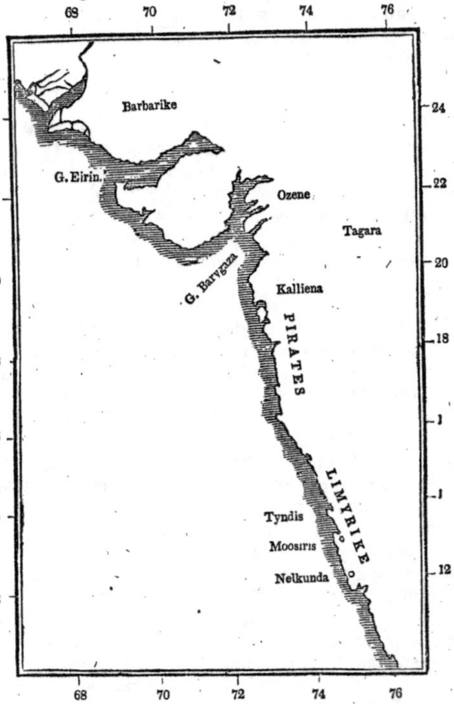

The region of Dachinabades (the Decan, i. e. the South, for Arrian remarks, Δαχανος καλειται ὁ νοτος τη αὐτων γλωσση) extended to the south of Barygaza, and is described as combining "many regions, deserts, huge mountains, wild beasts of every kind, and finally, many great and populous nations." It had two large interior capitals, Plithana and Tagara; the one twenty days' journey south from Barygaza, the other ten days farther. The grandeur of both has sunk under the changes to which eastern cities are subject; but the site of the former seems recognised in Piltanah on the Godavery, that of the latter in Deoghir, now Dowlatabad, in whose vicinity are the magnificent sculptured temples of Ellora. A number of ports are now described, which cannot be very precisely determined; but Kalliena, mentioned as the seat, though with some interruptions, of a very great commerce, is pretty clearly recognised at or near the modern Bombay. Afterwards we may know the Concan by the mention of pirates. At length the Greeks reached Limyrike, a fine port, and the seat of a great trade. The three chief emporia were Tyndis (Barcelore), Moosiris (Mangalore), and Nelkunda (Nelisuram). This last, which has sunk into a place of very secondary importance, was then the chief southern, as Barygaza was the chief northern, emporium of western India. The larger Greek vessels had even, by availing themselves of the monsoon, been enabled, with a daring course very foreign to the usual habits of ancient navigation, to steer directly across from the mouth of the Red Sea to Nelkunda. The grand staple then, as now, was pepper; to which were added pearls, and precious stones of various descriptions, among which were diamonds and hyacinths, cotton cloths, tortoise-shell, and betel-leaf, from the interior. Among the imports, according to the usual course of Indian trade, stood foremost "much money," a little cloth, and a little wine; but a considerable quantity of metals and toys, brass, lead, tin, glass, coral, stibium for painting the eyes, orpiment, and cinnabar. There is much appearance that Nelkunda was the farthest point to which the Greek navigators actually penetrated, and that they found there a supply of the commodities produced in the more eastern regions.

All beyond Nelkunda is faint and tinctured with fable. We recognise, however, Comar (Cape Comorin), Taprobane (Ceylon), and its great pearl-fishery. The Coromandel coast is nearly a blank, till we arrive at Masalin, which, with the great abundance of its cotton cloths, speaks clearly Masulipatan. In proceeding northwards, navigators came to a strange and barbarous people, with visages sometimes of enormous length, at others resembling those of horses, and some eating human flesh: an exaggerated picture of the fierce predatory races who occupy the mountain and jungle tracts of Orissa. Arrian describes accurately, however, the direction to the east which the coast of the ocean takes, before it receives the mighty flood of the Ganges. At its mouth there was then, it seems, a great emporium bearing the name, which no city now does, of the river itself. The staple was "superlatively fine cotton cloths, called Gangetic," and which still exist in the superb fabrics of Dacca and Moorshedabad.

In the regions beyond Ganges the author of the Periplus gropes almost in total darkness. Mention is made of an island, the farthest part of the world to the east, and which is richly stored with the most precious productions of the countries that lie on the shore of the Red Sea. This cannot seemingly be any other than Sumatra, though erroneously placed near the Ganges. The only ulterior position is Thinæ, a great interior city, situated opposite to Pontus and the Caspian Sea, and near to where the Palus Mœotis flows into the ocean. This strange site we shall afterwards find reason to consider as a combination of some actual rumours with the theory formed by the first Alexandrian school respecting the form and dimensions of the continent of Asia. There seems some reason, however, to conclude with Dr. Vincent, that this Thinæ, whence caravans came by way of Bactria to Barygaza, must have obscurely indicated the capital of China. Nor can we be easily persuaded that in the *malabathrum*, though most usually applied to betel-leaf, some confused idea of *tea* is not involved. Its being so strictly characteristic of China, and being brought by persons of a broad forehead, short body, and flat nose, features decidedly Mongol and Chinese, seem all in favour of this supposition, and inconsistent with that which would make it merely betel-leaf, a product of Indostan; though there is doubtless a great and manifest confusion between the two substances.

*Fig.* 5.—Periplus—African Coast.

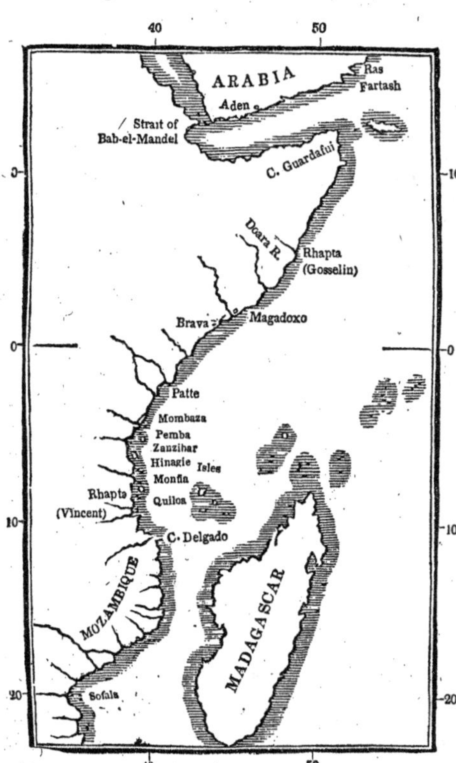


We must now look back to the Straits of Bab-el-Mandel, and follow our author along the African coast. (*Fig.* 5.) From those straits vessels proceeded eastward along the shore opposite to Arabia, the modern Berbera. Its ports, Avalites, Mosyllum, Mundos, Daphnon, and others, cannot be easily identified on a coast, with respect to which we have scarcely any modern data. The imports were nearly the same as at Adulis; the exports were myrrh, frankincense, a species of cinnamon called casia, some other aromatics, slaves, and a little ivory. At length they doubled the promontory of Aromata (Guardafui), when they came to a coast stretching to the southward and facing the Indian Ocean. Here was a port, the seat of a considerable trade, but by no means secure; however, when the north wind began to blow with dangerous violence, the vessels found shelter in the neighbouring promontory and port of Tabai. Proceeding onwards, they found Opone, Apokapa the less and greater, Nicon, Serapion, seven successive rivers, with anchorages at the mouth of each. Soon after, at the distance of about three hundred stadia from the continent, there occurred a low wooded island, bearing the very expanded name of

Eitenediom-menouthesias, which other writers wisely contract into Menuthias. It contained no wild animals, but abounded in fish, particularly tortoises, which the inhabitants were very diligent in catching. Two days' voyage farther brought them to Rhapta, a promontory and port, and the seat of a great trade. Beyond this point, the ocean was not yet explored; but it turned to the west and south, and was supposed to continue in that direction till it joined the Atlantic. The exports from this coast were ivory in great abundance, but not equal in quality to that of Aduli; tortoise-shell, superior to every other except that of India; and a number of valuable slaves, chiefly destined for the Egyptian market. The territory was governed by a number of petty kings, all owning the supremacy of Mopharites, who was himself tributary to Moosa, by the vessels of which great commercial state the trade of this coast was almost entirely carried on.

The extent of coast thus described by the author of the Periplus has been the subject of considerable controversy. Dr. Vincent fixes Rhapta, its farthest point, at Quiloa, thus allowing a navigation of upwards of fifteen hundred miles; while the rigid scepticism of M. Gosselin, placing it at Brava near the mouth of the Doara, allows a good deal less than half that distance. Dr. Vincent here, however, appears to carry the question triumphantly, by means of his seven mouths of rivers, of which M. Gosselin admits that no trace can be found within his limits. They are clearly presented by the estuaries of the Quillimanci, on which are the important harbours of Patte, Melinda, and Mombaza. But we cannot, with Dr. Vincent, pass by Pemba and Zanzibar, to find in the little island of Monfia the Menuthias of Arrian. Zanzibar, from its size and its proximity to the coast, appears a feature which it was impossible to overlook, and its position is in much better bearing with the seven estuaries previously passed. The next cape must then be Rhapta, and this will be that opposite to which is situated the small group of the Hinagie Islands. Beyond it for a considerable distance the coast runs in the direction of south-west, which does not at all admit the placing Rhapta beyond Quiloa, nor, indeed, on any other part of the coast till after we pass Mosambique.

---

## CHAPTER III.

### GREEK GEOGRAPHY BEFORE ALEXANDER.

GREECE is regarded by all civilized nations as their instructress in the sciences, many of the most brilliant of which she carried to the utmost perfection. In that of geography, however, little progress was made until the formation of the Greek kingdom in Egypt under the Ptolemies. Neither extensive commerce nor distant conquest characterised the Grecian states, otherwise so illustrious for all the arts of peace and war. It was not till the conquering career of Alexander, that the survey of the Greeks was extended over the wide circuit of the ancient world. Engaged before that era in the glorious defensive war against Persia, and the contests with each other for pre-eminence, they confined their views very much within the limits of Greece and its neighbouring coasts and islands.

The first traces of Greek geography are found among its poets, whose brilliant fancy has spread its lustre over all the regions with which Greece ever held intercourse. Homer took the lead, and his high authority gave to the geography of the Greeks a poetical cast, which they transmitted to the nations whom they taught, and of which the traces are not entirely obliterated.

### SECT. I.—*Geography of Homer.*

It is in Homer that we find the first trace of the widely-prevalent idea, that the earth is a flat circle, begirt on every side by the ocean. This was indeed a natural idea in a region so entirely insular and peninsular, nowhere presenting, like Judea, a vast tract stretching so far as to give the idea of immeasurable distance. The circular shape was suggested by that of the visible horizon; and until science demonstrated the globular form of our planet, the very natural opinion prevailed that the earth was a flat circle, with the vault of heaven above, darkness, and the abode of departed souls beneath.

Homer, like Hesiod and the ancient poets generally, delights in topographical detail, and scarcely allows a city or natural object to pass without applying to it some characteristic epithet. It was only, however, within a very limited range that he could give these distinct and animated notices. The Greek islands, beautiful and fertile spots, which seem to have been the first cradle of European civilization, were the central point from which his knowledge emanated. He knew well, and had probably visited, on one side Peloponnesus, Attica, and the regions immediately adjoining; on the other, the western coast of Asia Minor, and the banks of the beautiful rivers by which it is watered. Perhaps scarcely any other tract on the globe presents within the same compass such a variety of grand and beautiful objects to rouse the imagination. Beyond this circuit the world of Homer was soon involved in mysterious obscurity. Some grand and distant features, discernible through the gloom, were exaggerated and distorted by ignorance and superstition. Thebes, the mighty capital of

Egypt, when that kingdom was in its greatest glory, is celebrated for its hundred gates, and the hosts of warriors which they sent forth to battle. Beyond lay the Ethiopians, deemed the remotest of men, dwelling on the farthest verge of the earth, and to whose distant confines Jupiter repaired to hold an annual festival. In the western part of the same continent the stupendous ridges of Atlas had excited in Grecian fancy the image of a gigantic deified being, to whom was intrusted the support of the heavens. Even farther to the west, the exploits and wanderings of the great Grecian demigod had conveyed a tradition of the strait leading into the ocean, and of the rocks on each side, celebrated under the denomination of the Pillars of Hercules. On the east, Colchos was distinguished by its early wealth and commerce; it was considered a city on the ocean, with which, therefore, the Black Sea must have been confounded; and being supposed to contain the palace of the Sun, where during the night he gave rest to his coursers, and whence in the morning he drove his chariot to its diurnal career, Colchos must have been regarded by Homer as placed on the most eastern verge of the earth. On the north, Rhodope, under the name of the Riphæan Mountains, was considered a chain of indefinite extent, closing in the northern limits of the world. The poet, however, had heard a vague report of the Scythians, under the description of a people subsisting on mares' milk. The vessels which conveyed the Grecian army to Troy were evidently little better than large boats; and all distant voyages, or those in which land was lost sight of, were considered as fraught with the extremest peril. A navigation to Africa or to Sicily took place only through tempest, terminating usually in shipwreck; and a return from these shores was esteemed almost miraculous. In regard to Sicily, indeed, Homer has largely communicated his ideas, having made it the theatre of the woes and wanderings of the hero of the Odyssey. Making every allowance for poetical license, we see evident traces of the terrified and excited state of mind in the navigators who returned from these shores. Monsters of strange form and magnitude, who watched for the destruction of the mariner, and even fed upon his quivering limbs; delusive syrens, who lured but to destroy; imprisonment under the transformed shape of wild beasts; these, probably, are only a highly-coloured repetition of the terrific rumours brought by the few whose bark had been wafted to those as yet savage coasts.

## Sect. II.—*Poetical Geography.*

An ideal and poetical character was communicated to the science of geography itself by the fables with which Homer thus tinged his narrative. This tendency indeed did not rest solely upon Homeric influence, but proceeded from certain secret workings of the human heart. There exist in man ideas and wishes for which, in the sphere of his actual existence, he can find no corresponding objects; these he creates for himself in that dim boundary which separates the known from the unknown world. There involuntarily arises in his breast a longing after a more exalted state of existence than the world before him presents—bright scenes, which he seeks but never finds in the circuit of realities. In a newly-discovered region, however, which possesses any share of beauty, imagination soon heightens the colours of nature, till they appear to fulfil its fond anticipations. Such were those brilliant spots celebrated by the poets under the title of the Gardens of the Hesperides—the Fortunate Islands—the Isles of the Blest—for which, when knowledge had dispelled the first illusion, and brought them down to the ordinary level, a place was still found in some more distant extremity of the globe. Northern Africa, as it stretched westward, was peculiarly adapted, by its striking and brilliant contrasts, to excite these illusions. The first site of the Hesperian gardens was at the frontier of Cyrene, where they are described by Scylax as forming a luxuriant grove, in which the lotus and the palm were mingled with the finest trees of Europe. Other and more western sites were successively found, both for them and the Fortunate Islands, which last were finally fixed, probably on very imperfect observation, at the Canaries. These islands have not altogether lost the appellation; and they are painted by Horace in glowing colours as a refuge still left for mortals from that troubled and imperfect existence which they experience in every other quarter of the globe. Independent, however, of this bright and romantic enjoyment, there are other objects of fond desire to the human heart. In this agitated world it sighs after peace—a scene of profound repose, exempt from the tumults of passion and the corrosion of care. Such a scene, indeed, would never fulfil the hopes thus formed; yet these hopes spring from a natural illusion, to flatter which Grecian poetry conjured up a fabled race, the Hyperboreans, seated in the recesses of the North, and sheltered by vast mountains from the rage of the elements. They were represented as exempted from all ills, physical and moral, the change of seasons, sickness, and even from death. The original seat assigned to them was behind the Riphæan Mountains, which seem to have been originally Rhodope, the northern boundary of the Homeric world. The Greeks having soon acquired knowledge sufficient to ascertain that no such people was there to be found, sought them next on the banks of the Danube; but every thing there was remote from that tranquil aspect under which the poets had painted the Hyperborean world. Some traditions carry them westward; but their seat was finally fixed in that northern extremity of Asiatic Russia which the ancients never explored. They even carried with them the Riphæan Mountains, which became thus an ideal chain, delineated in modern maps as extending along the extreme frontier of Europe. Impressions of gloomy darkness, and even of the termination of existence, are, in other moods of the human mind, associated with images of distance and obscurity. These influences gave birth to the Cimmerians, a people who dwelt in perpetual darkness, and were never illumined by the cheerful rays of the sun. Their favourite seat was on the straits at the mouth of the peninsula of Taurida, the farthest point, probably, of which rumour had spoken in the poetical ages, and which was called the Cimmerian Bosphorus. It was probably from similitude of name that they were afterwards confounded with the people called Cimbri. The learned, however, have found traces of Cimmerians in the extremities both of the east and the west; and the idea of the earth as terminated by a boundary of darkness, being founded on natural impressions, has very generally prevailed. Park mentions it as the reigning belief among the Mandingos at this day; and the world, in the system of the Arabian geographers, was enclosed by a sea of darkness.

Other fabulous creations, springing from those of Homer, continued long to hold a place in geography. The one-eyed Cyclops appears under the name of Arimaspian on the frontier of India, and in the remotest extremity of Africa. The Pigmies multiplied still more extensively; they had seats on the Strymon, the Hebrus, in India, and the north of Europe. According to Strabo they were spread over the whole southern border of the earth; and this representation even induced Banier to suspect that, on that side, they have been confounded with the monkeys.

## Sect. III.—*School of Miletus.*

The astronomical schools of Miletus and Samos appear, so far at least as there is any precise record, to have made the first attempts to form geography into a system, and to apply to it the lights derived from astronomy. These and other cities of Asia Minor rank high among the early seats of commerce, and they established colonies in various quarters of the Mediterranean and the Euxine. While they continued independent they were very wealthy and prosperous, and the sciences were cultivated with ardour and success. To a commercial people practical mathematics, and especially those branches subservient to geography and navigation, must have peculiarly recommended themselves. Thales, Anaximander, Anaximenes, and Pythagoras, are celebrated by their countrymen as the inventors of all the processes by which the phenomena of the globe are calculated. The gnomon or sundial, for ascertaining the progress of the sun from tropic to tropic, and finally the latitude of particular places, the division of the year into 365 days, and into four seasons, are represented as having originated in this school. It appears doubtful, however, whether these discoveries were due to their own exertions or borrowed from the Egyptians and Chaldeans, whose fame, amid the dim traditions of antiquity, stands pre-eminent for astronomical observation.

The first rude mode of forming a division of the earth was into *climates*, determined by the species of animals and plants produced in each. Thus the negro, the rhinoceros, the elephant, were considered as characteristic of the torrid zone. This very loose method gave place to another, formed by observing at each place the length of the longest and shortest days. This could only be done with accuracy by a gnomon or dial, erected on a horizontal plane, and showing, by the length or shortness of its shadow, the elevation of the sun above the horizon. There is much reason to think that this simple instrument was employed by the Egyptians, especially in the operation, which they undoubtedly performed, of adding five days and a quarter to 360, the number originally supposed to form a complete year. It has even been imagined by some, that the pyramids, those enormous structures by which this people excited the astonishment of the world, were only huge sundials; and though it might doubtless be extravagant to conclude this to have been their sole object, yet it really appears that, being placed in the direct position of the cardinal points, they are perfectly fitted for being thus employed. But, though it is clear that Thales and his disciples had largely drawn from these early sources, they probably made considerable additions to the information thence derived. Two books, one on the tropic, and the other on the equinoxes, are reported to have been written by Thales himself. The degree of knowledge thus attained enabled him to discover the error of the vulgar in supposing the earth to be a plane surface; but he could not reach the precise idea of its globular form. Anaximander viewed it as a cylinder; some compared its form to that of a boat; others to that of a lofty mountain. The details of the Pythagorean cosmography have not reached us; but the fact that they placed the sun in the centre of the system, with the earth moving round it, indicates at that infant era attainments which were lost during many ages, and only recovered at a far more advanced stage of modern science.

The map must, as soon as geography was cultivated, have occurred as the best and most perspicuous form of embodying its results. Anaximander is the first who is reported to have constructed a map of the world, embracing that limited sphere of objects which were then comprehended under that term. But the most celebrated production of this nature was that employed by Aristagoras, the prince of Miletus, to induce Cleomenes, the Spartan king to undertake the conquest of Persia. He entered, it is said, the presence of that monarch, holding in his hand a tablet of brass, on which were inscribed "the whole circuit of the earth, the sea, and all the rivers." Under this pompous description, however, was probably included little more than a route from the Ionian sea to Susa, which was specially pointed to as that by which the Spartan prince might lead his victorious troops to the Persian capital. Even of this line, respecting which he was so deeply interested, the short detail of Herodotus shows him to possess by no means complete information. Beyond Cilicia his descriptions are very indistinct. He has omitted Media altogether, and has given to Armenia quite an undue extension.

The continental Greeks, during the era of their greatest power, did not cultivate systematic geography, nor indeed any sciences dependent upon mathematical principles, with much activity; indeed, they did not even keep them up to the state in which they had been received from the Ionian cities. One solitary observation of latitude is recorded as having been made at Athens, by Meton and Eudemon, 432 years A. C. The different states, in the course of their extensive wars, must have acquired a great portion of that topographical knowledge which is indispensable for military operations. Engrossed by these internal objects, their attention was little directed to the general system of the world. One individual alone, by extensive travels and diligent enquiries, procured an ample accession to the science of history and of historical geography.

## Sect. IV.—*Geography of Herodotus.*

The system of geography included in the great historical work of Herodotus is as complete as could be formed from the materials within his reach. It comprises a general summary of all that he could learn respecting the human race, and the regions which they inhabited. His information was obtained not solely or chiefly from books, but mostly by travelling, the only mode in which at that era geographical knowledge could be effectually collected. He assures us that he had visited Persia, Assyria, Egypt, Thrace, Scythia, and all the distant regions which he describes. He viewed them, however, only as tracts of territory, the abode of men, and did not attempt to combine them into any system of the earth; nor did he possess, or, at least, apply any of the mathematical or astronomical principles of the Milesian school. He even derides some of its conclusions; as that of the earth being round and encompassed by the ocean. His strange statement, that the sun in India was vertical in the morning instead of at midday, is evidently a misunderstood report of what he had been informed respecting the difference of time in the different parts of the earth's circumference. His knowledge, however, such as it is, consisting of plain facts, untinctured with theory, is both solid and extensive.

The division of the earth into three quarters, or continents, was by this time completely formed. Sea, or at least water, seems to have been the principle of separation, though not required to be altogether complete. Setting out from Europe, for the origin of which appellation we have nothing but the fable of Europa, the Greeks seem to have named the other continents from the districts immediately beyond the intervening sea. Homer already mentions the name of Asia as applied to a large and fine tract on the coast of Ionia. Thence it spread through the spacious peninsula of which it forms part, and which Europeans continue to call Asia Minor; but soon passing these limits, it was vaguely extended through the boundless regions of the East, till it finally embraced entirely the largest of the three continents. On the other side, directly to the south, the Greeks first landed on the coast of Libya; and the name of Libya was by them applied to the entire continent. With the Romans, on the contrary, whose position and political relations attached them entirely to the district of Africa proper, in which Carthage is situated, the name of Africa soon prevailed over every other.

These grand divisions of the ancient world were already known to Herodotus; but he has astonished European readers in an extraordinary degree by the assertion, that Europe is longer and of greater extent than Asia and Africa united. The severe judgment of M. Gosselin pronounces such an assertion, made in the midst of the nations which carried on the most extensive navigation, to be a proof that they had not formed the least idea of the distance which their vessels sailed along the Mediterranean. Before pronouncing so severe a sentence, we must consider attentively what, in the conception of Herodotus, was Europe, and what was Asia. He mentions two boundaries: one formed by the Black Sea and the Don, which, though it does not form a very appropriate boundary of a continent, continues still to prevail, being connected with the Northern Ocean by the mountain chain of the Urals. But in the other, which is that preferred by Herodotus, the Black Sea is continued by the Caspian; the boundary line being carried along the north of that sea, and thence indefinitely eastward. Taking Europe in this sense, we find it in the west co-extended with the opposite coast of Africa, which the ancients necessarily considered as marking the length of that continent, while, in the east, however far Asia might be prolonged, Europe was stil regarded as co-extensive. With regard to the boundaries of Africa, too, there was an extreme want of precision. Our limit of the Isthmus of Suez is certainly the most accurate;

but the ancients, who could not readily admit the notion of a continent bounded by any thing but water attached themselves more to the Nile, and did not well know whether to consider Egypt as Asiatic or African.

### Subsect. 1.—*The Europe of Herodotus.*

Scythia was the extremity of Europe, beyond Greece, with which Herodotus appears to have been most familiar, and which, in fact, he knew better than almost any other ancient writer. This name, which became ultimately Asiatic, was restricted by him to the tracts that now form the southern provinces of the Russian empire. These regions were then, and in a great measure still are, possessed by the same description of rude Nomadic and pastoral people, who have always occupied the central plains of Asia. The attention of the historian was specially called to them by the rash and daring expedition of Darius into a region secured by its natural barriers, and the wandering and untamed character of its people, against every form of regular subjection. Darius, crossing the Hellespont, marched along the southern shore of the Euxine, reached the banks of the Volga, and after the fruitless labour of erecting there several fortresses, returned by a more inland route, in which Major Rennell even supposes him to have passed the site of Little Novogorod. The knowledge acquired by this expedition, however, did not enable Herodotus to avoid great errors in the delineation of European Scythia. He imbibed a most exaggerated idea of the dimensions of the Palus Mœotis, which he calls the "mother of the Euxine." This appears to have arisen chiefly from the false *orienting* of the side which faces Russia, and which is made to stretch almost due north, instead of west, while the sea itself is represented as forming the eastern boundary of that great space of four hundred miles square, within which Herodotus comprises Scythia. The southern boundary was formed by the Euxine, and the other two by the land, so that he does not connect it in any shape with the Northern Ocean.

The details of this extensive region are given by Herodotus with considerable accuracy. Of its rivers, after the Danube, which he ranks second to the Nile, he mentions the Tyres or Dniester, the Hypanis, or Bog (and even describes the close approach of these rivers to each other in the upper part of their course), the great channel of the Borysthenes, or Dnieper, and the Tanais or Don. Between the last he mentions several streams, the Panticapes, Hypacyris, and Gerrhus, which not being recognized by modern geography, Major Rennell supposes to be creeks or branches of the greater rivers.

Milesian colonies had, by the active enterprise of that commercial people, been already formed even on these rude shores. One, called the port of the Borysthenes, is described as the centre of the trade of Scythia. On the banks of this great river dwelt a people, bearing the rare character of the *ploughing* Scythians, who renouncing the almost universal habits of their race, raised crops of grain in this fertile district, which still furnishes to the ports of Taganrog and Odessa those supplies, which render them the granary of the Mediterranean. The Milesians had also a colony established at the mouth of the Danube.

The northern interior countries of Europe, which lay beyond the limits of the Scythia explored by the expedition of Darius, were covered for Herodotus with a veil of dim obscurity. On the Scythian frontier, along the heads of the Dniester and Borysthenes, he represents several nations; the Melanchleni, "men clothed in black;" the Androphagi, "men eaters;" the Neuri, "once a year converted into foxes." These Greek names, and partly fabulous attributes, show the very imperfect nature of the notices collected on the subject. The regions beyond the Danube are expressly stated to be occupied by nations to him unknown. Two precious commodities, the amber from the coast of Prussia, and the tin of the Cassiterides, under which last name a vague idea of the British Islands seems to be included, communicated the knowledge, that there was a great ocean in the north, but without the means of ascertaining its extent and limits. On the east, however, as already observed, he had attached to Europe a vast extent of territory which has been entirely severed from it in subsequent systems. The expanse of northern and even middle Asia, which the ancients afterwards called Scythia, and which forms the modern Tartary, inhabited by races exactly similar to the Scythians already described, appeared to Herodotus decidedly European. It was bounded by the Phasis, the Caspian, the Aral (not distinctly recognized), and the Jaxartes. The Massagetæ, celebrated for their contest with Cyrus, gave name with Herodotus to all the wandering tribes in this eastern part of Europe; but they were afterwards merged into the prevailing appellation of Scythians.

### Subsect. 2. *Asia of Herodotus.*

Asia, according to the conception of it formed by Herodotus, will appear, from what has been said, to include only a small portion of the vast continent to which we assign that name. On the north it had the same seas and rivers just enumerated as the boundaries of eastern Europe; to the east it terminated with India; while even to the south, a large portion of the desert tracts of Arabia were not yet believed to exist. When this great historian wrote, all the various kingdoms and petty states, into which, in the infancy of the world, Asia had been partitioned, were absorbed into one vast empire. The Persians claimed Asia as their own, and had distributed it into twenty-four satrapies, which have been illustrated in a very learned manner by Major Rennell. They included, with the exception of the northern part, which he considered as European, all of Asia that was known to the Greeks. In collecting therefore from Major Rennell's investigation the following table of those satrapies, we exhibit not only the outline of that great empire, but, with the somewhat dubious exception of a small part of Greece, the whole of the civilized world. The tribute paid in talents of silver will exhibit their relative wealth and importance.

TABLE OF THE DIVISION OF ASIA INTO SATRAPIES.

| | Talents. |
|---|---|
| 1. Ionia, Magnesia, Caria, Æolia, Lycia, Pamphylia (the west and south coast of Asia Minor)........ | 400 |
| 2. Mysia, Lydia, &c. (the western interior)........ | 500 |
| 3. Phrygia, Paphlagonia, Cappadocia, &c. (the north coast and the great interior table-land of Asia Minor) | 360 |
| 4. Cilicia (including part of Syria, and reaching to the Euphrates)........ | 500 |
| 5. Phœnicia, Palestine, and Cyprus (which furnished also a third part of the naval force of the empire) | 360 |
| 6. Egypt, including Cyrene and Barca (half of the tribute paid in grain)........ | 1400 |
| 9. Babylon and Assyria, including Syria, and furnishing also 500 eunuchs........ | 1000 |
| 8. Susiana, or Southern Persia........ | 300 |
| 10. Media, (Northern Persia)........ | 450 |
| 11. The Caspians, Pæsicæ, Pantimathi, and Daritæ (the Caspian provinces of Persia)........ | 200 |
| 18. The Matieni, Saspires, &c. (Aderbijan and the Armenian provinces)........ | 200 |
| 13. Armenia........ | 400 |
| 19. The Mosynœci, Tibareni, Moschi, &c. (the Western Caucasus, Georgia, Mingrelia, as far as Trebisond)........ | 300 |
| 14. The Sagartians, Sarameans, &c. (Seistan, Caramania, Lar, and other territories along the Indian Ocean, and the eastern part of the Persian Gulf)........ | 600 |
| 16. The Parthians, Choasmians, Sogdians, and Arians (Khorasan, Herat, Candahar)........ | 300 |
| 7. The Gandarii, the Dadicæ, &c. (Margiana, the country on the Murghab, between Khorasan and the Oxus........ | 170 |
| 12. Bactria (Balk)........ | 360 |
| 15. The Sacæ and Caspicæ (Kashgar, Pamer, and other tracts of mountainous country about the head of the Oxus)........ | 250 |
| 17. The Paricanii and Ethiopians of Asia (Mekran, including, perhaps, Caubul, and the Delta of the Indus)........ | 400 |
| 18. India, the largest of all, being 360 talents in gold, which amounts in silver to........ | 4680 |

Some tracts of this vast empire, not formed into regular satrapies, were privileged to furnish only presents, or gifts, under an appearance of voluntary homage. Among these were ranked the Persians proper, inhabiting the modern Fars, who obtained this distinction as the conquering people by whom the empire was originally founded. The Southern Arabians, and the Ethiopians above Egypt, derived the same immunity from the difficult access to those rude regions in which they dwelt. The Southern Arabians are said to have propitiated the favour of the great king by the present of a thousand talents of incense. The Colchians, and the occupants of the neighbouring heights of Caucasus, were also numbered among the "givers of gifts;" while the inhabitants of the northern parts of that great range, secure in their mountain fastnesses, are said to have cared very little about the mighty ruler of Persia.

These delineations of Asia display, upon the whole, a surprising accuracy and extent of knowledge; yet several remarkable errors occur with regard to points of which the investigation does not appear very difficult. Thus the breadth of Asia Minor was reduced almost a half; that between Babylon and the capital of Egypt was underrated at least a fourth; and the country between the Black Sea and the Caspian was placed in the same meridian with the Persian Gulf, while it is really four degrees to the westward. These errors are the more remarkable, as the distances, instead of being in *excess*, according to almost every other ancient example, fall short of the truth. The early travellers exaggerated every space over which they actually passed; but it sometimes happened that two points were approached from different quarters, and then united to each other by a hypothetical line, which, as men usually undervalue what they know nothing of, was made generally too small. It would not appear that any regular route had been formed across the high and rugged table-land in the interior of Asia Minor from Cilicia to Trebisond. These two points, being approached respectively along the southern and northern coasts of the peninsula, might be supposed nearer to each other than they really were. Egypt was approached through Syria and Palestine, and Babylon by descending the Euphrates; but the direct line between them lying across the Arabian desert, was scarcely known or frequented, and therefore became an ideal line in the view of Herodotus. The line from Armenia to the Persian Gulf was of course measured along the Euphrates, the general course of which was south; and as the ancients oriented all their lines to a cardinal point, they overlooked the gradual but constant bend which that river takes to the eastward.

The ideas of Herodotus concerning the extent of Asia, even including all that portion of it which he assigned to Europe, could not fail to be defective. He knew nothing of India beyond the Ganges, Thibet, China, Eastern Tartary, or Siberia, more than half the superficial extent of the continent. Even his notions concerning India were most imperfect. He describes it as bounded on the east by sand, stretching into an unknown and measureless desert. From this statement it clearly appears that his India comprehended merely the western part watered by the Indus and its five tributaries; he knew nothing of its widest and richest regions, the Gangetic provinces, Delhi, Bengal, and the Deccan; large portions were also cut off from the southern coasts of Asia, which were supposed to be washed by an ocean called the Red or Erythrean Sea, without any distinction of the Persian Gulf, and very little of that which we now call the Red Sea.

### SUBSECT. 3.—*Africa of Herodotus.*

In his inquiries respecting Africa, Herodotus appears to have been equally diligent as concerning the other regions of the globe; but as he never proceeded beyond Egypt, and as the formidable barriers which nature opposes to him who attempts to penetrate the interior had been very imperfectly overcome, much in what he collected is obscured with mystery or perplexed with conjecture.

Egypt is described with great accuracy, and under some features which no longer exist; for the Tanitic and Pelusiac branches of the Nile, of which little more than the channels can now be traced, were then in full flow. It appears, however, that considerable confusion prevailed respecting the quarter of the world to which Egypt was to be adjudged. As water formed the basis of the division into continents, the sandy isthmus of Suez, believed to be broader than it really was, appeared very ill-fitted to form such a limit. The Nile, therefore, in the opinion of all the Greeks, was the boundary of the continents: all to the east was Arabia; all to the west Libya; but a difficulty here arose in fixing the lot of Egypt itself. The Greeks, it appears, considered nothing as Egypt beyond the Delta; but this opinion is ridiculed by Herodotus, who observes, that in that case there must formerly have been no Egypt at all, since this its lower branch was evidently produced by the gradual alluvial depositions of the Nile. He contends reasonably, that all the banks of the Nile as far up as Elephanta, which was inhabited by Egyptians, was clearly Egypt. He accuses the Greeks of referring the Delta, or their Egypt, neither to Asia nor Libya. If we rightly understand his own idea, it is that the middle or Sebennytic branch was the proper point of division between those continents.

In tracing the Nile above Egypt, Herodotus states a line of two months' journey partly along the banks, partly in boats which were dragged by ropes along the current through the rocky channel. At the end of this journey they came to Meroe, the capital of Ethiopia above Egypt, an ancient and celebrated kingdom, whose monuments were viewed with almost religious veneration, and whose monarchs had repeatedly conquered Egypt and founded dynasties. Two months' journey farther was the country of the Egyptian exiles, a numerous body, who, having revolted from Psammeticus, sought the protection of the king of Ethiopia, and were cantoned by him in this remote district, which may be Sennaar, or rather, perhaps, the branch of the Bahr-el-Abiad opposite to it; for Herodotus shows his knowledge of this last stream by observing that it comes from the west.

The long tract of desert to the west of Egypt is also described by Herodotus in some detail, though apparently only from hearsay. The most conspicuous objects here are the oases, particularly that which contains the ancient and venerated temple of Jupiter Ammon, and which has been identified with the modern Siwah. To the west he gives the names of a succession of wandering and pastoral tribes, such as still roam over these arid and sandy regions, deriving from the soil only the produce of the date-tree. Many of them stand charged with morals peculiarly shameless and dissolute, the females indulging openly in the most irregular conduct, and making even a boast of the number of their paramours. Probably there may be scandal mixed in these very evil reports of the African ladies. An exception to this rude pastoral character existed on the coast of Cyrenaica, where the Greeks established flourishing colonies, which could be approached, however, only by the dangerous route of the Syrtis or quicksand, proverbial in ancient times as the scene of disastrous shipwreck.

The Nasamones, the most westerly as well as the most numerous of the wandering tribes, in general drove their herds along the sea-coast, but in summer repaired to the Oasis of Ægila (Augila) to collect the dates produced in that district. A tribe among this people were called the Psylli, or devourers of serpents; and in fact appear to have had a peculiar power of charming those noxious reptiles with which their deserts abound. Within their borders, on the side of Cyrene, where verdure first began to adorn the waste, Herodotus has fixed the fabled site of the Hesperian gardens.

The Garamantes, to the south-west of Augila, and the Nasamones, are represented by our historian as inhabitants of a region infested by wild beasts, and of a timid character flying the view and intercourse of other men, destitute of arms, and unacquainted with war. These characters do not apply to the people of modern Fezzan, which, however, is undoubtedly the tract pointed out. To the north-west were the Gindanes (the modern Gadamis), among whom the license of public morals had risen to a greater height than among all the wandering tribes of Libya. Still proceeding north-west, the traveller came to the lake Tritonis, celebrated in ancient fable as the birth-place of Minerva, who, according to one legend, was sprung from Neptune and the nymph of the lake. This lake forms the western limit of the long range of nomadic tribes. Beyond it, Herodotus gives us the Maxyes, who cultivated the ground. He had now reached that fine range of territory belonging to Carthage, stretching along the coast, watered and enriched by streams from the Atlas. It is very remarkable, however, that he should pass by entirely that mighty and celebrated state, which was not only the most powerful in Africa, but was also the centre of industry and commerce with respect to the ancient world. Major Rennell has suspected that this arose from a national feeling of enmity on account of their alliance with the Persians; but when we consider that no such feeling has prevented the fullest account from being given of the Persians themselves, it can scarcely be supposed that the being merely friends to the Persians would exclude so great a people from his notice. It seems really very difficult to conjecture his motive, unless, according to the suggestion of a learned friend, we suppose that Herodotus, writing almost entirely to illustrate what was obscure, or communicate knowledge on points respecting which the world were in ignorance, might think it superfluous to describe what must have been well known to the bulk of his readers, for the same reason that he has given no regular description of Greece. In reference to the transactions of this people with other nations, he takes repeated occasion to mention them, so that the omission could not arise from absolute ignorance.

Atlas and the desert border behind it next engage the attention of our historian; a tract reaching as far as the straits, which he calls the *high forehead* of Africa. He describes Atlas as a long and lofty range, whose highest pinnacles are wrapped in perpetual clouds and he ascribes to the natives the origin of the belief adopted by the Greeks, which made it the pillar of heaven. Even in this extreme boundary of the continent, he mentions some peculiarities that really exist:—the enormous size and formidable character of the serpent tribe; oxen with large and crooked horns; houses of salt which would melt away if a single shower were to interrupt the continued drought. When he begins, however, to speak of people with horses' heads, and others without heads at all, it is time to take our leave; though some learned writers suppose this to be a mere exaggerated description of some animals of the desert. We must still follow him, however, to the western coast beyond the straits, where the Carthaginians, he was informed, carried on trade with the natives in a peculiar manner. The parties did not see each other, but after a signal made by smoke, one laid down his proffer, went away, and left room for the other to do the same; when the first came, and either accepted or rejected the bargain, till the terms were adjusted. There have been reports in various quarters of this mode of traffic, but all, we suspect, exaggerated representations of the timid manner in which civilized traders make their approaches to those savage people who possessed any valuable commodities. The product sought upon this shore was gold: and, as it does not exist in any latitude north of the Senegal, Major Rennell concludes that the trade of Carthage extended to that distant river. A sceptic might surmise that the gold was brought across the desert to the coast of Barbary; yet, considering the formidable character of this desert, it seems doubtful if at so early a period a commercial route across it could have been opened.

The interior of Africa could not fail deeply to attract the curiosity of Herodotus. The part already noticed as described by him forms only a belt along its northern coast, and includes none of the vast inland tracts. On this subject, however, he has only one tale to tell. Several Nasamonian youths of distinction, seized with that desire to penetrate the continent which has prevailed throughout all ages, departed on an expedition to the southward. They traversed three successive belts; first, the cultivated, or at least verdant and inhabited tract along the sea-shore; then, another occupied only by wild beasts; and, lastly, a region arid and desolate. Here, while plucking fruits, they were surprised by some men of small stature, who carried them by the way of very great lakes, to a city inhabited by black inhabitants, and situated on a large river flowing from west to east. This river Herodotus, naturally enough, judges to be the Nile. Major Rennell conceives it to be probably the river of Tombuctoo, which Europeans call the Niger; but we think, since the late discoveries, there can scarcely be any hesitation in fixing it as the Yeou, the river which rolls through Bornou, while the Tchad may be identified with the great lakes along which the expedition was conducted.

---

## CHAPTER IV.

### FIRST ALEXANDRIAN SCHOOL.—ERATOSTHENES AND STRABO.

### Sect. I.—*The Expedition of Alexander.*

The geography of the Greeks became little more than a topographical delineation of military routes, after the intestine wars in which they were involved caused them to lose sight of the more distant regions of the earth. Besides, as they never cultivated mathematical science with any care or to any extent, they had not the power of arranging even these limited materials into a systematic form.

The expedition of Alexander gave a much greater degree of expansion to the human mind. That monarch transferred the seat of war into the Persian empire, and carried his victorious arms into the remotest regions of the East. Whatever might be the faults and follies with which his career was stained, it cannot be denied that an enlightened curiosity animated all his proceedings. Wherever he went, he was accompanied by skilful surveyors, Diognetus and Bæton, who measured the length and direction of every route over which the army passed. Alexander himself carefully inspected these itineraries, employed all practicable means for obtaining the best materials, and his letters are even quoted by Pliny as authorities for many geographical statements. These itineraries are said to have been afterwards published by Bæton, under the title of "the Marches of Alexander." From the defective state of the science, however, which that prince could not remedy, all these materials were necessarily imperfect. They could include nothing beyond mechanical measurement, nor is there any record, throughout this long career, of a single attempt to fix the position of any spot by celestial observation. Imperfect as they were, however, these documents did not the less form a completely new era in geographical science. After the death of Alexander, they passed through the hands of Seleucus into those of Ptolemy Philadelphus, who spared no efforts to render Alexandria the greatest seat of learning and science in the ancient world; and among the sciences there cultivated, geography and astronomy held the most distinguished place.

The progress of Alexander led him at first through Syria, Egypt and Persia, but did not bring the Greeks to the knowledge of any countries, of whose existence and limits they were not already fully apprised. But after he began the pursuit of Bessus, who had carried off Darius into Bactriana, his march became a sort of exploratory route. In his vain pursuit of the Scythian armies he reached the banks of the Jaxartes, though he did not fully trace the course either of that river or of the Oxus. On his way thence to India, he had to penetrate the narrow passes overhung by the snowy ramparts of the Hindoo Coosh, and, with much difficulty and many hardships to his troops, learned to appreciate the magnitude of that great inland barrier of Asia. In India, Alexander could not penetrate beyond the region watered by the five rivers. Yet he did not consider it as the boundary of the earth; he learned the existence and beauty of the fine regions on the Ganges, whither he in vain attempted to persuade his fatigued and refractory troops to follow him. He consoled himself by conveying his army in pomp down the Indus, to view the entrance of that great stream into the ocean, and with instructions, as we have already seen, to trace the shores of Asia round the Persian Gulf. He himself, upon very bad information, undertook to lead back his army through Gedrosia and Caramania, the greater part of which he found, as modern travellers have done, to be a desert of the most dreary and formidable character, in which his army was with difficulty saved from total destruction.

### Sect. II.—*Expedition of Seleucus.*

Seleucus, on the partition of the empire of Alexander, succeeded to the dominion of Syria and the East. Neither that prince nor his successors were either learned or patrons of learning; but as the owner of extensive dominions, and aiming at farther conquest, he cherished the natural wish to be acquainted with what he possessed or hoped to obtain. He employed his admiral, Patrocles, to make a survey of the Caspian Sea, which had not entered into the line of Alexander's route; but the information gained by this voyage must, as we shall see, have been far from complete. It would also seem as if he had employed the same admiral in an attempt to circumnavigate Asia; but the assertion which obtained credit in that age, that he had sailed round from India to the Caspian, sufficiently attests the failure of the enterprise. Seleucus, also, finding, probably, that the inroad of Alexander into India had been of very transient result, undertook a military expedition, the details of which are little known, and which enabled him to establish no permanent footing in the country; but he collected some further materials for the geographer, and the record of his marches appears to have been of important service to Pliny. He sent also an embassy under Megasthenes to Palibothra, capital of the great Indian kingdom situated on the Ganges, from which the ancients derived a more accurate knowledge of these eastern parts of the world than they had previously possessed.

### Sect. III.—*Eratosthenes.*

Eratosthenes at length succeeded in reducing geography to a system *under the patronage of the Ptolemies*, which gave him access to all the materials collected by Alexander, his generals, and successors, and to the immense mass of documents assembled in the Alexandrian library. The astronomical observations made in this school were now sufficient to prove the globular form of the earth. Eratosthenes, proceeding upon this principle, made it his study to adjust to it all the known features of the globe. He did not, however, attend to the grand original divisions of the equator, the pole, or even the tropics. The line which formed the basis of his geography, and generally of that of the Alexandrian school, was a parallel drawn across the Mediterranean, and thence prolonged through Asia. It was formed in a very rough manner, upon no actual observation, and comprising all leading positions which came nearly though not strictly within its sphere. It was called generally, the parallel of Rhodes. The most westerly point was the Sacred Cape of Iberia (Cape St. Vincent), after which followed the "Strait of the Pillars" (of Hercules). The next point was the Strait of Sicily, erroneously considered to be under the same meridian with Rome and Carthage. Then came Rhodes, the centre of the line. Issus, celebrated as the site of the victory of Alexander, was with little difficulty brought within the limit. Next followed the somewhat doubtful position of the Caspian gates, and the line was extended along the chain of Mount Taurus, supposed to divide Asia into two parts, till it terminated at the remote city of Thinæ, situated on the eastern ocean. This entire length of the habitable world, as it was called, amounted to about 70,000 stadia, or, according to his estimate, one hundred degrees, not quite a third of the circuit of the globe.

In determining a meridian to exhibit his breadth of the habitable world, Eratosthenes laboured under still greater difficulties. On the extreme south was "the limit of the habitable earth;" for, according to this school, a certain tract around the equator was, from the excess of heat, unfit for human habitation. The uninhabitable zone was supposed to extend 8,300 stadia, or about twelve degrees to the north of the equator. Under the next parallel were included the "Isle of the Exiles," in or near Sennaar; the cinnamon-bearing region, which appears to be Berbera, and Taproban, or Ceylon. Next comes Meroe, the capital of Ethiopia, which was supposed, though with great error, to correspond as to latitude with the southern extremity of India: thence descending the Nile the geographer marks the celebrated position of Syene, which was concluded to be immediately under the tropic, since there was a well, in the depth of which at noon-day, at the precise time of the vernal equinox, the disk of the sun was seen reflected entire. The observation was very nearly correct. Next came Alexandria, of which, as the centre of all these observations, the position as to latitude was very closely approximated. Then followed Rhodes in the centre of the great parallel already described as exhibiting the length of the habitable globe. Continuing northward, though not upon the same line, were found the Hellespont, Byzantium, the mouth of the Borysthenes, and passing over the vast obscurely-known tracts of Germany, Gaul, and Britain, the farthest Thule, which, on the report of Pytheas, Eratosthenes regarded as the extreme northern boundary of the earth. As the same authority placed Thule under the Arctic circle, or at sixty-six degrees of latitude, the interval between that position and the limit of the habitable earth on the side of the equator amounted to about fifty-four degrees, or according to his estimate 38,000 stadia, which formed thus the supposed breadth from north to south of the habitable earth.

### Sect. IV.—*Hipparchus.*

Hipparchus, carrying still farther the system adopted by Eratosthenes, subjected the whole science of geography to astronomical principles. His labours in numbering the stars, and arranging them according to their place in the heavens, were such as appeared marvellous to the ancients, and are esteemed by Pliny as achievements that would have been arduous even for a god. In this career, however, he had been preceded by Timocharis and Aristillus, who, more than a century before, had made some observations which paved the way for the present extended discoveries. Hipparchus appears to have first conceived the idea of transferring the observed latitudes and longitudes of the stars to their corresponding places on the earth's surface, thus fixing the latter with a precision which no itinerary measurements could ever attain. He made a considerable number of observations of latitude, in addition to the very few previously existing, and he pointed out the mode in which the longitudes might be ascertained by observing the eclipses of the sun and moon. It does not appear to what extent he carried the difficult operations requisite for this investigation; but he is said to have calculated the eclipses for six hundred years, including the moments of their appearance at different places; a performance which seems to indicate a knowledge of their astronomical position. Thus Hipparchus distinctly perceived all the principles upon which an accurate system of geography might be founded, and made some progress in their application; but these important principles, like others which were beyond the comprehension of the age in which they were made, remained for a long time dormant or misapplied, and were not brought into full practical application until a much more advanced period in the progress of science.

### Sect. V.—*The world according to Eratosthenes and Strabo.*

The application to the different parts of the earth's surface of the principles according to which the globe was to be delineated, formed a task still more arduous than that of the first establishment of those principles. The longitudes and latitudes of the ancients are both erroneous; more especially the longitudes, to which astronomical observation was never very extensively applied; hence it is not wonderful that the errors should be great;

but the regular and rapid manner in which they accumulate appears very surprising. They begin from the Sacred Cape of Iberia (Cape St. Vincent), which the ancients made their first meridian, and continue regularly increasing as we proceed eastward. To the Pillars of Hercules were assigned more than two degrees beyond the truth; to Alexandria, nearly seven; to Issus, ten; to the Caspian gates, fourteen; to Pattalena, or the Delta of the Indus, twenty-three; to the mouth of the Ganges, nearly twenty-seven. We have already had occasion to observe, and the remark is found in the best ancient geographers, that merchants and travellers of that age gave an exaggerated report of all the distances over which they passed. The windings of the route, the hardships and obstacles encountered by them, the desire to magnify their own achievements, all concurred in inducing them to view and present this particular through an amplified medium. All the itineraries continued along the line upon which Eratosthenes measured his length of the habitable globe being thus unduly extended, the degrees calculated out of them were of course equally in excess; and this excess became always the greater in proportion to the length to which the line was protracted beyond its commencement at the Sacred Cape. The latitude of the principal places in and round the Mediterranean is in general not far from the truth, probably because it was determined by such rude observations as were within the compass of Greek science at that early period.

In tracing the outline of the known world, and especially of the continents, geographers still proceeded amid obscurity and doubt. This school had laid down the fundamental principle of a great circumambient ocean, embracing the entire circuit of the three continents. This idea, inherited from Homer, was doubtless supported by facts to a considerable extent; but its application to the world in general, and especially to the northern shores of Europe and Asia, was manifestly hypothetical. Eratosthenes, in comparing the magnitude of his known world, even under its exaggerated dimensions, with the general circumference of the earth, became sensible that only a third part of this last was filled up. He indulges in conjecture as to the contents of this vast unknown region, which, he observes, might either be supposed to consist of one great ocean, the whole of which he denominates the Atlantic, or of lands and islands which might be discovered in sailing to the westward. With a degree of caution, however, not very common in that age, he declines to give any decisive opinion on this question.—The system of Eratosthenes may now be considered in regard to Europe, Asia, and Africa.

### SUBSECT. 1.—*Europe.* (*Fig.* 6.)

The imperfection of ancient geography is often conspicuous with respect to countries which were very near and familiar. In regard to the very centre of the Mediterranean, Eratosthenes committed a capital error. Following the propensity to include all the leading positions under some one line to which they approximate, he placed in the same meridian Rome, the Sicilian strait (that of Messina), and Carthage. The mistake with regard to the first and last of these points did not much exceed a degree; but the middle point is nearly four degrees east from Rome, and five from Carthage. Such an error could not fail to produce others. M. Gosselin shows that it has led to a signal mistake respecting the position of Sicily, as the geographer, in order to retain its relative position towards Carthage, necessarily represented its greatest length as from north to south, instead of from east to west. The promontory of Lilybæum, facing Carthage, became the southern instead of the western extremity of Sicily; while Cape Pachynum, instead of the southern, became the eastern. Sicily being thus projected so unreasonably towards the south, Carthage also was made to recede too far in the same direction; and the coast leading thither from the straits of Gibraltar was supposed to bend to the south instead of the north. The same erroneous process, placing Sicily too far west, enlarged beyond measure the eastern basin of the Mediterranean comprehended between it and Asia Minor. This deformity became still more serious from another application, to Alexandria and Rhodes, of the system of placing leading points under the same meridian. As the former error had made Sicily too far west, this made Rhodes too far east, and rendered the sea between these islands too large by at least a half.

Strabo, ever alive to the faults of his predecessors, detected the mistake of Eratosthenes with respect to the relative positions of Rome and Carthage. He has been far, however, from rectifying all the wrong positions established by his predecessor. He has

---

*References to the Map of Europe according to Eratosthenes.*

| | | | | |
|---|---|---|---|---|
| 1. Gades | 11. Roma | 20. Rhegium | 29. Pola | d Liger |
| 2. Calpe | 12. Ostia | 21. Scylacium | 30. Epidaurus | e Garumna |
| 3. Carthago Nova | 13. Circeii | 22. Thurii | 31. Epidamnus | f Durius |
| 4. Narbo | 14. Puteoli | 23. Tarentum | 32. Apollonia | g Tagus |
| 5. Massilia | 15. Neapolis | 24. Brundusium | | h Anas |
| 6. Antipolis | 16. Posidonia | 25. Sipus | *Rivers* | i Boetis |
| 7. Genua | 17. Velia | 26. Teanum | a Albis | j Iberus |
| 8. Luna | 18. Laus | 27. Ancona | b Rhenus | k Rhodanus |
| 9. Populonium | 19. Hipponium | 28. Ariminum | c Sequana | l Varus |
| 10. Cossa | | | | |

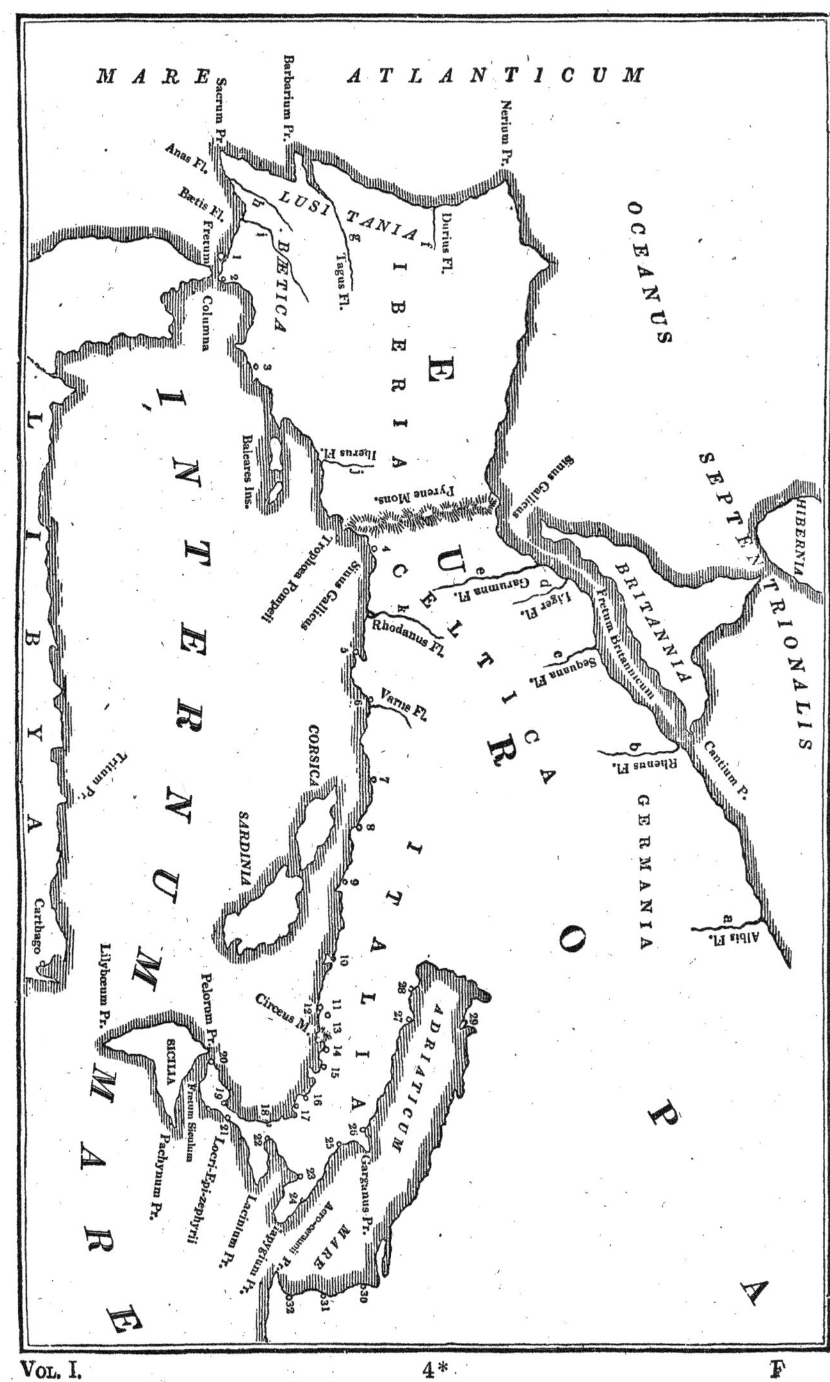
MARE ATLANTICUM
Sacrum Pr.
Barbarium Pr.
Nerium Pr.
OCEANUS SEPTENTRIONALIS
Anas Fl.
Bætis Fl.
Fretum
Columna
LUSITANIA
BÆTICA
IBERIA
Tagus Fl.
Durius Fl.
EUROPA
Baleares Ins.
Iberus Fl.
Pyrene Mons.
Sinus Gallicus
Tropæa Pompeii
Sinus Gallicus
CELTICA
Garumna Fl.
Liger Fl.
Rhodanus Fl.
Sequana Fl.
Varus Fl.
Rhenus Fl.
BRITANNIA
Fretum Britannicum
HIBERNIA
Cantium P.
GERMANIA
Albis Fl.
CORSICA
SARDINIA
ITALIA
ADRIATICUM
MARE
LIBYA
INTERNUM MARE
Carthago
Lilybæum Pr.
SICILIA
Pelorum Pr.
Circeus M.
Fretum Siculum
Pachynum Pr.
Locri-Epi-zephyrii
Lacinium Pr.
Iapygium Pr.
Acro-ceraunii Pr.
Garganus Pr.

left untouched the false orienting of Sicily, and all the errors dependent upon it. Both he and Eratosthenes describe Italy as extending from north to south, which, allowing for the early tendency to orient all lines towards a cardinal point, may be taken as a pretty fair representation. M. Gosselin has undertaken to show that such a direction would be inconsistent with the other data given by these geographers, in conformity to which Italy must stretch from east to west. Considering, however, the imperfect state of geographical delineation at that period, it seems going too far to follow each error into all its consequences, or to suppose that all the views given can be brought into complete harmony.

The outline of the central and northern countries of Europe drawn by these geographers is excessively vague. Strabo indeed makes some approach to accuracy in comparing the Spanish peninsula to a "hide spread out," or to a parallelogram. Various countries were by the ancients denominated from a fancied resemblance to some object in nature, nor are examples wanting in modern times. But the eastern side of this figure is formed by the Pyrenees, which are thus made to extend from north to south, to form the western boundary of Gaul, and to be parallel to the Rhine. Hence arises the greatest of all these errors; for Gaul is allowed to have on the ocean only one coast, which is that looking to the north, and every where opposite to Britain. Strabo treats with derision the report of Pytheas, that the *Calbium promontorium*, the extreme point of Brittany, looked to the west, and he represents vessels as sailing to Britain as readily from the mouth of the Loire and Garonne as from that of the Rhine and the Seine. Great as these errors are, we shall easily trace their origin in considering the sources whence the Greeks derived their information respecting these extremities of Europe. Whatever may have been the case with regard to the Carthaginians, it is evident that neither Greeks nor Romans ever navigated its exterior seas. Pytheas alone performed that daring voyage; but having no witnesses to bring in support of his relation, it was denounced as fabulous, in common with others made by early discoverers. The regular channel of communication was Marseilles. The merchandise of Britain being brought across the British channel to the mouths of the Rhine and the Seine, was conveyed up those rivers, and by land carriage to that great emporium of Gaul. Hence the geography of Gaul and Britain, in that age, was ruled entirely by Massilian ideas. From the causes stated, the Massilians had no communication with Britain unless by the northern coast of Gaul, and by routes directed from south to north through that country. Reasoning only from what they knew, they might soon arrive at the conclusion, that Gaul had only a northern coast, and might apply to it the whole of the erroneous system now described. The result of this system was, that the Cassiterides, Islands of Tin, in which term the Scilly islands were evidently blended with Cornwall, were made to approach to Spain, and came to be considered as much Spanish as British. So prevalent was this idea, that even afterwards, when the conquests of Rome had made known the wide separation between the two countries, the Cassiterides are found in some maps still attached to Spain, and at a little distance from Cape Ortegal.

Britain, under this system, was represented as a triangle, of which the base, or longest side, was that along the channel and opposite to Gaul. As the coast, after passing the two extremities of this line, begins on one side to bend inward towards the Bristol Channel, and on the other to the Thames, navigators then probably considered it as continuing in these directions till it came to a point, far short of its real termination. Ierne, or Hibernia, (Ireland) appears in dim obscurity. It is said to be situated four hundred miles north from the centre of Britain, under a climate so excessively cold that there could not possibly be any inhabited country nearer to the pole. If the four hundred miles be measured from the centre of the southern coast, and allowance be made for false orienting, it will not be found so very wide of the truth. The rest of the description was probably made out by confused ideas of Scotland, and particularly the bleak mountainous tracts in the north. Eratosthenes, indeed, has derived from Pytheas a knowledge of the far northern limit of Thule, and of its appendant islands, stretching towards the Arctic sea; but, as the proud scepticism of Strabo rejected this statement, he was thrown back upon the more imperfect information afforded by the merchants of Marseilles.

The eastern shores of northern Europe occasioned still more embarrassment to the Greeks. They had, in general, the idea of this continent having the sea for its boundary; but this seems mainly to rest upon the general vague belief of a circumambient ocean, and an understanding that Germany had on the north a maritime boundary, indicated by the amber brought from the shores of the Baltic. Here, too, Pytheas, either by personal investigation or by careful inquiry, had collected some particulars which if Strabo had not disdained, he would not have been left in such total darkness. After proceeding far along the German coast, that navigator, it is said, came to a great gulf (evidently the Baltic). He found Basilia, a very large island, the same which Pliny calls Baltia; being, in fact, the peninsula of Scandinavia, which, until it was circumnavigated, must have been regarded by navigators as an island. Then, it is said, he came to the Tanais, which appears, no doubt, a very startling assertion; but we must remember that, in this school, the circumambient ocean was supposed to have a coast only a little north of the Euxine and the Caspian, and to communicate with these seas or gulfs (as they were supposed to be) by narrow straits, one of which was the Tanais, and the mouth of one of the great Baltic rivers might very easily be imagined to form the termination of this strait.

Subsect. 2.—*Asia*. (*Fig.* 7. *page* 44.)

The limits assigned to Asia, already too small, were contracted by the geographers of the Alexandrian school, notwithstanding the additional sources of information which they possessed respecting that continent. This error arose partly from their theory of a surrounding ocean, and partly from their neglect of the important information obtained by Herodotus respecting the countries along the heads of the Euxine and Caspian. The expedition of Alexander, indeed, and the embassy of Megasthenes, made them acquainted with the Ganges, rolling eastward through the fine plain of Upper Hindostan. Seeing it pursue this direction to the utmost limit of the then known world, they were led to conclude that its course continued eastward, and that it fell into the eastern ocean, which formed, on that side, the boundary of the continent. Connecting this with the Caspian, the only northern Asiatic sea known to them, they drew a line from one to the other, by which they excluded nearly two-thirds the extent of Asia; the Birman empire, China, the greater part of Tartary, and the whole of Siberia. On the shore of the eastern ocean was placed Thinæ, evidently known only by vague rumour, and which they fixed at the extremity of the line measuring the length of the habitable globe. What may be the import of this mysterious name, and whether it be the capital of Siam or of China, is a discussion which will be better reserved until we come to the more precise notices of Ptolemy. One other grand feature was known to this school; the cape of the Coliaci or Cape Comorin; but conceiving the coast of Coromandel to follow the line of the Ganges, and, consequently, to verge towards the west, they made it several degrees more easterly than even Thinæ.

Asia within and Asia beyond Taurus were made the grand divisions of that continent. That great mountain chain arising in Asia Minor was supposed to be prolonged by those of the Elburz, of Khorasan, and of Hindoo Coosh, which, in fact, there is much reason to believe, may form a chain nowhere wholly interrupted. Within Taurus were all the fertile, populous, and splendid kingdoms and countries of Asia; Syria, Assyria, Babylon, Persia, Susiana, Ionia, Cilicia; beyond, were the ruder tracts of Scythia, Bactria, Sogdiana; and more westerly, the Caucasian territory, and the part of Asia Minor situated along the shore of the Black Sea.

Subsect. 3.—*Africa*.

In regard to Africa, the knowledge of these geographers, though accurate in some respects, was extremely limited. They believed its boundary to be the sea; but this correct judgment proceeded rather from a casual coincidence with their theory of an encircling ocean, than from any actual knowledge; since Strabo rejected even the possibility of circumnavigation. This scepticism was founded upon the hypothesis of an uninhabitable torrid zone, which formed an essential part of the reigning system at this period. It is a belief manifestly African, founded on the observation of those vast and burning deserts, which extend indefinitely beyond the narrow inhabited stripe bordering on the Mediterranean. The Nile, then, being still considered as the eastern boundary, Africa became a sort of right-angled triangle, of which the two smaller sides were formed by that river and the Mediterranean, while the hypotenuse, or largest side, was the unexplored shore. It was upon the Nile that Eratosthenes measured the habitable world of Africa; yet he does not trace that river so high as Herodotus, his details reaching only between three and four hundred miles above Meroe. In these details, however, he is very accurate: on the eastern side, he represents it as receiving two great rivers, the Astapus and the Astaboras, the former of which flows from lakes in the south, and, when swelled by the summer rains, forms almost the main body of the Nile. He describes also the bend which the river makes in its passage through Nubia. The source, being imagined to exist in regions rendered inaccessible by extreme heat, could not be considered as within the reach of discovery. The idea, however, still prevailed, that it came from the west, and Strabo even mentions a report, that its source was in the remote region of Mauritania, south of the Atlas. This is the only statement made by geographers of this school, which can be considered as indicating any idea of the existence of the Niger.

---

## CHAPTER V.

### ROMAN GEOGRAPHY.

The Roman geographers attained no proficiency in the mathematical branch of the science. M. Gosselin does not even hesitate to assert, that they remained always strangers to its very first elements. They made no attempt, therefore, to combine their materials into one harmonious system, or to fix their positions with that strict accuracy, which astronomi-

THE WORLD ACCORDING TO ERATOSTHENES. FIG. 7

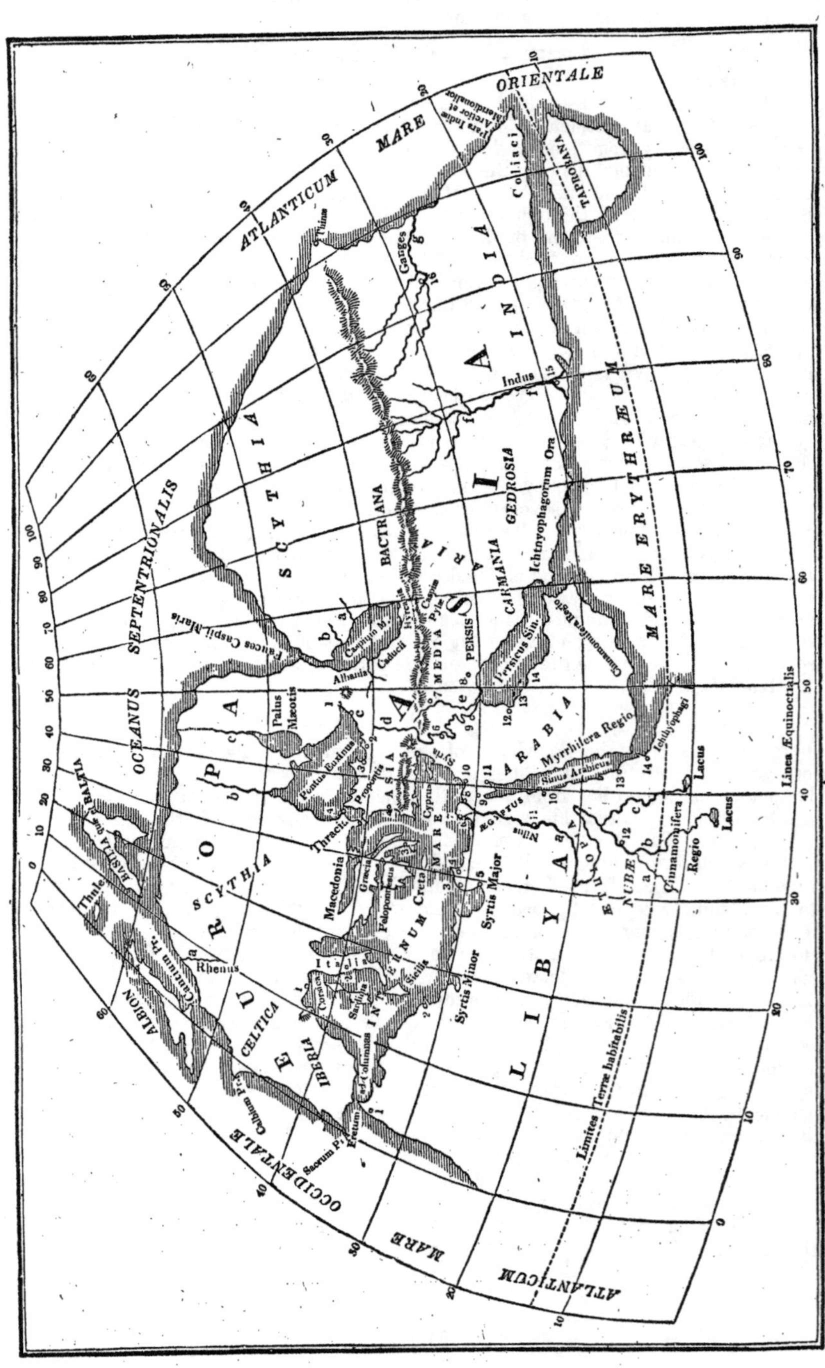

cal observation alone can reach. Yet no nation employed greater diligence in the operations of practical survey. This was, indeed, absolutely requisite, with a view to that incessant warfare in which they were engaged; they could not conquer the world without previously surveying it. Their geographical researches were, however, held strictly subservient to this ambitious design.

Itineraries were thus the only form in which the results of Roman investigation were presented. Vegetius informs us that when war was to be carried into any country, the first care was to procure a complete set of routes, and place them in the hands of the general. These itineraries, it is observed, ought, if possible, to contain, not merely the intervals, in paces and Roman miles, between one place and another, but the quality of the roads, the surrounding objects, mountains and rivers, delineated with the utmost possible precision. They were not only to be noted, but painted, that the commanders might not know merely, but see before their eyes, the route by which they were to proceed. The Romans became thus the surveyors as well as the conquerors of the world; and every new war in which they engaged, every new conquest which their arms achieved, produced a fresh accumulation of materials for the use of the geographer. Even after a country was subdued, the necessity of accurate survey did not cease. The empire was long held in a state of mere military occupation; camps formed at proper distances were connected by those excellent and durable roads, many of which remain to this day. An accurate acquaintance with the position and intervals of these camps, and the nature of the intervening territory, was essential to the maintenance of their dominion over the vast extent of their conquered countries. No sooner, therefore, had Julius Cæsar seated himself on the undisputed throne of the empire, than he caused a *senatûs consultum* to be passed for a general measurement of the Roman world. This task, it is said, was intrusted to "the most prudent men, adorned with every endowment of philosophy." The east was assigned to Zenodoxus, the west to Theodotus, and the south to Polycletus. In the course of twenty-five years, as we are informed by Æthicus, the whole was completed. Julius Cæsar, however, did not long survive the commencement of this great work, which the civil wars probably suspended. It was apparently resumed and completed under the reign of Augustus and the ministry of his son-in-law Agrippa, to whom it appears, from Pliny, to have been afterwards ascribed. The exact principles upon which this grand measurement was conducted have nowhere been stated. The reform of the calendar, effected by Cæsar, seems to point out that some elements of astronomy existed among those with whom he consulted.

Rome, in the most flourishing era of its literature, produced *two eminent geographers*, Mela and Pliny.

## Sect. I.—*Mela*.

The personal history of this eminent geographer is a subject respecting which scarcely any particulars have transpired. From the allusions, however, in his own writings, to the conquest of Britain by Claudius as a recent event, made in those flattering terms which only a contemporary would have employed, it would appear that his work was written under the reign of that inglorious prince, and is, consequently, anterior to that of Pliny.

Mela, in forming his system, does not appear to have possessed those extensive measurements and itineraries, which were probably deposited in the imperial archives. Faithful, however, to the object of his treatise, "de situ orbis," he discovers very considerable anxiety to determine the position of the globe, and trace with accuracy its general outlines. He adopts the general principles of the school of Eratosthenes, incorporating into it the new features which had been afforded by Roman conquest. He does not appear, however, to have comprehended their idea of the globular form of the earth, nor is he very perspicuous in any thing that he says upon that subject. He begins—"All that, whatever it is, to which we give the name of the world and heaven, is one thing, and in one circuit embraces itself and all things;" vague and pompous expressions, to which no determinate idea can be attached. We find him, however, adopting in its fullest extent the belief of a circumambient ocean; and when he speaks of "the high earth in this middle part of it," and describes the sea as going under and washing round it, we are led to believe, that he viewed the earth as a sort of cone, or as a high mountain raised by its elevation above the abyss of waters. Having made a vague division of the world into east, west, and north, he distributed it into five zones, two temperate, one torrid, and two frigid. Only the first two were habitable;

*References to the Map of the World according to Eratosthenes.*

EUROPA.
1. Massilia
2. Roma
3. Athenæ
4. Byzantium

*Rivers.*
a Rhenus
b Borysthenes
c Tanais

ASIA.
1. Dioscurias
2. Amisus
3. Sinope
4. Ephesus
5. Issus
6. Thapsacus
7. Ninus
8. Susa
9. Babylon
10. Rhinocolura
11. Ælana
12. Gerra
13. Tirus Insula
14. Aradus Insula
15. Patala
16. Palibothra

*Rivers.*
a Oxus
b Jaxartes
c Phasis
d Euphrates
e Tigris
f Indus
g Ganges

AFRICA.
1. Lixus
2. Carthago
3. Ptolemais
4. Cyrene
5. Berenice
6. Alexandria
7. Canopus
8. Pelusium
9. Arsinoe
10. Berenice
11. Syene
12. Meroe
13. Ptolemais
14. Aduli

*Rivers*
a Nilus
b Astapus
c Astaboras.

*Fig.* 8.—SYSTEM OF MELA.

and that on the south was inaccessible to man, on account of the torrid regions intervening. According to this system, however, there was on that side another earth, inhabited by people, whom he calls *Antichthones*, from their opposite position with respect to that part which we inhabit. The form and boundaries of the known and habitable earth are thus delineated:—The Mediterranean, with its branches of the Straits, the Euxine, and the Palus Mœotis; its great tributaries, the Nile and the Tanais;—these combine, in his conception, to form the grand line by which the universe is divided. The Mediterranean itself separates Europe from Africa; and these continents are bounded on the east, the former by the Tanais, the latter by the Nile; all beyond or to the east of these limits was Asia. (*Fig.* 8.)

In drawing the outline of Asia, Mela adheres very strictly to his Alexandrian models. He describes it as bounded by an ocean on every side except the western, where it confines with Africa and Europe. It presents, he says, a huge and perpetual front to the eastern ocean, its shores being occupied by the three farthest known nations, the Indians on the south, the Seres in the middle, and the Scythians on the north; but the territory of the Indians and Scythians is rendered in a great measure uninhabitable by the extremes of heat and cold. The limited extent of his accurate information, however, is apparent from the representation he gives of this ocean, as flowing directly north from the point of Colis (Cape Comorin), the Ganges flowing into it, and the Scythians occupying its shores as far as "the Caspian *Bay*." He even inclines to credit the report of an Indian vessel having been driven round by stress of weather to the coast of Germany. Thus he gave to Asia the same truncated form which it had received from the authors whom he followed; but he certainly rendered the dimensions of its eastern shore more ample, when he made it to consist, not of India only, but also of Serica and part of Scythia. With regard to the southern shores of Asia, they were known with sufficient accuracy, ever since the expedition of Alexander, and the voyage of Nearchus. He calls the Indian ocean the Red Sea, and recognises the Red Sea of modern geographers only under the name of the Arabian gulf; but this is plainly a mere nominal difference.

Europe, as described by Mela, extends from the Tanais to Cadiz, and, with the exception of its eastern river-limit, is bounded every where by seas and oceans. Its leading feature is the Mediterranean, joined to the Euxine and the Palus Mœotis, which are considered only as prolongations of that sea; while the Ægean, the Ionian, and the Adriatic seas, form its three great gulfs. The western part he divides into the Tuscan and the Libyan seas. His delineation of the exterior coasts marks a great advance of knowledge. He assigns to Spain a northern, and to France a western coast of great extent, and adds that the Pyrenees, after separating France from Spain, enter the latter country and penetrate to its extremity, when they face the Atlantic. Here the whole chain of the Cantabrian mountains is considered, by no very strained meaning, as Pyrenean. In treating of these outer shores of Europe, and the "huge and infinite sea" on which they border, Mela relates, with exaggerating wonder, the phenomena, unknown to a Mediterranean people, of the tides, "that mighty movement by which the sea alternately advances and returns into itself, overflowing the lands, driving back mighty rivers, and sweeping away the strongest land animals." His speculations on the cause are singular; either the world is a great animal whose breathings excite in its breast these alternate movements; or it contains deep caves, into which the waters are alternately absorbed and ejected. He does, however, mention the theory which supposes them influenced by the moon, and remarks their correspondence with the movements of that body. In treating of the Cassiterides, or Islands of Tin, which include, as already observed, the Scilly Islands and Cornwall, he shows considerable perplexity, only observing that they are "in Celticis," indicating their close alliance with France. In regard to Britain itself, however, he confidently undertakes to give the world better information, in consequence of the victories of "the greatest of princes" over nations hitherto unsubdued and unknown; and he certainly makes a great progress beyond the imperfect notions of Strabo. He describes Britain as presenting two extensive oblique coasts, one looking towards France, the other towards Germany; the two forming a great angle nearly opposite to the mouth of the Rhine. The coasts then began to bend inwards, and form a triangle varied with numerous points and angles, and somewhat similar in form to Sicily. The country is described as flat, large, and fruitful, but contrary to what now obtains, more favourable to the support of flocks than of men. The natives were uncultivated, warlike, and ignorant of wealth; they were accustomed to paint their bodies, and to ride in chariots. Above Britain was Juverna (Ireland), nearly equal in size, and of an oblong form, its soil scarcely fit for the production of grain, but its pastures so luxuriant, that if the cattle were allowed to feed for more than a short period of the day, they died of repletion. The relative dimensions assigned to Britain and Ireland would seem to show that the former was known only in its southern part, yet the writer discovers himself not unacquainted with the Scottish islands. He mentions thirty Orcades, in which number the Shetland Islands are probably included.

In proceeding to the east and north, Germany is described by Mela as a region of great extent, intersected by many rivers, and covered in a great measure with woods and marshes. The inhabitants were tall and remarkable for courage and strength, continually exercised in war and hard labour, eating raw flesh, and clothed partly in the bark of trees. Passing the Vistula, we enter into Sarmatia, extending to the Danube, rather a vague limit, but the term is evidently meant to comprehend the greater part of modern Poland. The people are some stages in barbarism beyond even the Germans, having no cities or even settled abodes, and carrying their fierceness to such a pitch, that hunting and bending the bow were considered the best accomplishments of their females, no one of whom, the writer even asserts, could enter the matrimonial state till she had killed her man. On this shore he represents the Codanus Sinus, a great bay filled with large and small islands; nowhere presenting an expanse resembling a sea, but dispersed and scattered in narrow channels like rivers; a description very applicable to the entrance of the Baltic and the Danish islands. In common with all the ancients, however, Mela appears to have been ignorant of any thing like a continent on the other side of this great bay.

The outline of Africa, drawn by this geographer, sufficiently shows his limited range of information. This continent he views as a triangle, the greatest length of which, measured in his system from the Nile to the Atlantic, is considerably less than the length of Europe. Of this triangle, the Nile forms the base; and from thence the southern coast, or that of the Ethiopic ocean, continually approximates to the northern, till, beyond the Pillars of Hercules, it tapers almost to a point. The origin and course of the Nile are to Mela a subject of much speculation. One account, esteemed by him as tolerably credible (*aliquâ credibile*) identifies it with a great Ethiopian river, called in the language of the natives Nuchul; which, while all other rivers tend towards the ocean, alone flows eastward to the central region, and no one knows where it terminates; a striking coincidence with the actual observation of the moderns, respecting that celebrated stream denominated the Niger. Elsewhere, however, Mela propounds an hypothesis of a much more extraordinary character He says, that if there be another earth (on the south of the equator), and *Antichthones* opposite to us, "it might not be departing too far from the truth" to suppose that the Nile arose in that earth, and reached our side of the globe by a channel beneath the ocean. Thus it would naturally swell during the summer solstice, which, on the side of the world from which it came, was the season of winter. Bertius and Vincent, however, have perhaps dealt too hardly with the author, in embodying this wild conception into a map, and giving it to the world as the system of Mela, who mentions it merely as a conjecture. The lower part of the course of the Nile he describes with less accuracy than Strabo, the two channels of the Astapus and Astaboras being made branches of the Nile itself, first separating and then re-uniting. His ignorance respecting even the shores of the Red Sea is proved by their being filled with poetical wonders; the pigmies waging their ancient war with the cranes; the phœnix, after a life of four hundred years, dying, and reviving from its ashes. Proceeding to the interior and remoter shores of Ethiopia, he finds always new wonders, sphynxes, birds with horns, flying horses. He refers to the voyages of Hanno and of Eudoxus, to whom he ascribes a variety of fables, by which the reputation of that navigator has been much and perhaps unjustly tarnished; lastly, he comes to the Fortunate Islands, of which the soil produces all things spontaneously, and the fountains are possessed of miraculous virtues. In short, every thing that Mela says of Africa beyond the mere Mediterranean coast betrays a remarkable ignorance of the mysteries of that continent.

### Sect. II.—*Pliny.*

Pliny, the most learned of the Roman writers, devotes two books of his extensive work on natural history to a system of geography. He appears to have possessed a greater store of authentic materials than any former writer. From his intimate connexion with the imperial family, and with many of the most eminent commanders, all the military measurements, as well as the general survey of the Roman empire, were placed at his disposal. He has introduced, therefore, a multitude of itinerary details, which are generally very accurate and valuable. But he employs no astronomical elements, and appears to have taken no pains to construct a regular system. All the general ideas which we can trace in his delineation appear to be founded on the same basis with those of Mela.

Pliny begins with Europe, which he considers as by far the most beautiful and fruitful of the three quarters of the globe; and he applauds the opinion of those who consider it not merely as a third, but as a half of the whole globe, separated from the other half by the Tanais and the Mediterranean. This capital error, however, will not appear so surprising, when we consider that the regions here compared with Europe were Asia terminated by the Ganges and the Jaxartes, and Africa extending only a few hundred miles inland from the Mediterranean. Europe had been computed by Agrippa at 3440 miles in length, by Polybius at only 2440; which last dimension is nearly correct. Pliny discovers a clear conception of the form of Spain, drawing the Pyrenees not from south to north, but from south-east to north-west, and observing that Spain, "where it begins from them, is narrower than France, and even than itself." The position of Britain in the map of Europe is very fairly given; though, to enumerate Spain, with France and Germany, among the countries to which it is opposite, partakes too much of antiquated theories. He states the belief of Agrippa that Britain was eight hundred miles in length, and three hundred in breadth; Ireland the same in breadth, but shorter by two hundred miles; which is a tolerable estimate, the last particular excepted. His disposal of the islands around Britain is not a little confused. He mentions the Orkneys, seven Æmodæ, and thirty Ebudæ, but without showing any precise idea of how they stand. Not only the Isle of Man, but that of Wight also, is placed between England and Ireland. He commits also a remarkable error when he mentions Cassiterim or Cattiterim, where tin is produced, as an island at the distance of six days' sail from Britain. To the remotest point, Thule, he assigns the attributes of a region beneath the Arctic circle, having only one day and one night in the year; and only a day's sail from the Cronium or Concrete Sea. Here, also, he mentions reports of other islands, Scandia, Bergos (Bergen), Nerigon, which have intercourse with Thule. These features evidently belong to the coast of Norway.

In describing the north of Europe, Pliny begins from the northern shores of the Euxine, and Palus Mœotis. The latter receives the Tanais, flowing from the Riphæan Mountains, and forming the boundary of Europe. Beyond that celebrated and demi-fabulous range, he still finds the Hyperboreans, a people screened from every noxious blast, leading a happy life exempt from old age, sickness, discord, and grief; till at length, satiated with felicity, they throw themselves from a rock into the sea. These fables are, however, qualified with the saving clause, "if we are to believe them," which shows that the faith of Pliny was not implicit. The shores of the ocean, he confesses, are "marked by uncertainty." On the authority, however, of Xenophon Lampsacenus and of Pytheas, he reports Basilia or Baltia as an island of immense magnitude, three days' journey from the Scythian coast. Proceeding westward, he comes to the Cimbric Chersonese, and opposite to it another island. Scandinavia, of unexplored magnitude, but which was by many described as forming quite another world. Thus Baltia and Scandinavia, approached from different points, are considered as two distinct insular territories, the vast extent of which, however, appears to be better apprehended by Pliny than by any other ancient writer.

Asia, in Pliny, is delineated according to the general ideas of Strabo and Mela. The Caspian or Hyrcanian Sea is a gulf opening into the northern or Scythian ocean, which is in communication with that called Seric or Oriental. Pliny seems to have fuller information of the grandeur and wealth of India than any of his predecessors. Its inhabitants and its cities were innumerable, and it was reported on good authority to form a third of the whole world. It enjoyed gentle breezes, two summers, two harvests, one before, another after the periodical winds. Blessed with these advantages, this happy people were never known to emigrate beyond their own territories. He describes the marches of Alexander, from the measurements of Diognetus and Bæton, and where these fail, he continues them by those of Seleucus, and by the embassy of Megasthenes, as far as the mouth of the Ganges. These itineraries seem very good. In treating of Taprobane, he observes, that it had been believed by some to be an opposite continent or earth, but that the inquiries of Alexander had clearly proved it to be an island. His report, however, that the country of the Seres was seen from it, implies a most inadequate and erroneous conception of the eastern coasts of Asia.

The Africa of Pliny does not differ in its general outline from that of Mela. His access, however, to the archives of the empire, and his acquaintance with some of the Roman generals, enabled him to give new details as to some of its most interior tracts. The region of Atlas had been first penetrated in the reign of Claudius, by Ædemon, an adherent of the extinct family of the Ptolemies, who sought refuge there. Suetonius Paulinus, with whom Pliny had conversed, found it of immense height, covered with snow even in summer; on one side rising from the sands, rough, horrid, and bare; on the other, covered with thick groves of unknown species of trees, and sparkling with fountains. An account is given of a voyage along the western coast, which Polybius had made by order of Scipio. Only the names of the places and the distances are given. The former coincide in a great measure with those of Hanno; and if Polybius was right in this coincidence, his report tends much to confirm M. Gosselin's view of the limited extent of Hanno's discoveries. In the time of Vespasian, another expedition, under Cornelius Balbus, penetrated into and conquered Garama (Germa), and Cydamus (Gadamis). The Romans here beheld with surprise houses built of salt, and on digging to a small depth, water sprung out of the sand. A number of names of conquered places are here given, which it is difficult to recognize; for it seems too hasty to identify Boin with Bornou.

A theory of the course of the Niger was formed by Pliny from these materials with considerable pains, but very imperfect success. Its source, according to king Juba, existed in Mauritania, and it is even said to have been found by Suetonius Paulinus after a few days' march to the south of the Atlas. The Niger springs here from a lake; but soon, indignant at flowing through sandy and squalid tracts, it passes under ground for several days, and emerges into another lake of Mauritania. After a circuit, however, of some extent, it again disappears, and having pursued a subterranean course of twenty days, re-appears, dividing Africa from Ethiopia. At last, in its passage through Ethiopia itself, it assumes the character of the Nile, first in two channels, Astusapes and Astaboras, enclosing the island of Meroe, and afterwards uniting to form the entire and proper Nile. This wild and absurd detail evidently includes the course of several rivers belonging to different and widely remote regions of Africa. It may even be doubted, if any part belongs to what by moderns has been considered the Niger. It seems very probable, however, that the middle part, which divides Africa from Ethiopia, has been suggested by the river of Bornou, or the Yeou, as it has been called by our recent discoverers.

### Sect. III.—*Itineraries.—Peutingerian Table.*

Of the itineraries composed by the masters of the world, and employed by them as an instrument in its conquest, some fragments yet remain. The most memorable is that which bears the name of Antoninus. It has been ascribed by some to Severus, by others to Theodosius, and in fact contains many particulars which could not have been written prior to the era of the last sovereigns; but it seems probable that there were successive editions, with such amendments and alterations as time suggested. It is a mere skeleton road-book, with nothing but the names of places and their distance from each other. The same may be said of the Jerusalem Itinerary, exhibiting in great detail the route from Bordeaux to that holy city.

The Peutingerian Table (the Italian portion of which is exhibited in *Fig.* 9. p. 50.) is a more remarkable monument, and may be considered, probably, as a specimen of the "painted roads" of the ancients. It forms a map of the world, constructed, however, on the most novel and peculiar principles. Its dimensions being twenty feet in length and one in breadth, an idea may be formed of the correctness with which the proportion of the different parts is exhibited. The high road which traversed the Roman empire in the general direction of east and west is made the first meridian, and to this every other part is subjected. The ob-

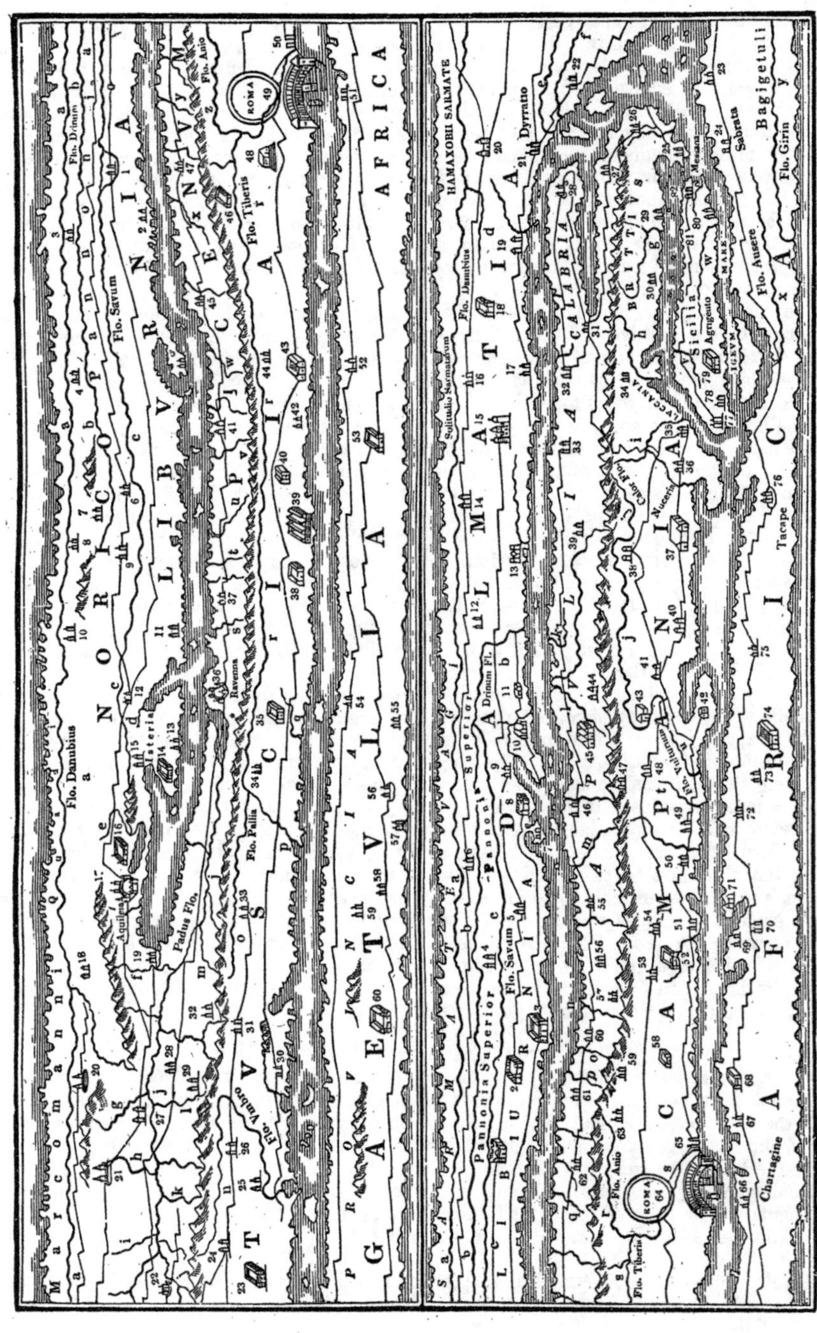
Flo. Danubius
Flo. Savum
Aquileia
Padus Flo.
Ravenna
Flo. Pallia
Flo. Tiberis
ROMA
AFRICA
HAMAXOBII SARMATE
Solitudo Sarmatarum
Pannonia Superior
Dyrratio
CALABRIA
BRITTIVS
Nuceria
Flo. Anio
Sicilia
Agrigento
Messana
Tacape
Chartagine
Sabrata
Bagigetuli
Flo. Ausere
Flo. Girin

jects along this line are minutely and faithfully exhibited; of those lying to the north and south of it only some general notion can be conveyed: these are all represented, of course, most enormously extended in length and reduced in breadth.

---

## CHAPTER VI.

### SECOND ALEXANDRIAN SCHOOL.

ALEXANDRIA by her contributions to geography supplied to a great extent the deficiencies of the Romans, who, amid the success with which they cultivated history and literature, never attained to any eminence in this science. That capital, even in its subject state, retained still the impulse received from the Ptolemies, and continued to be the second in magnitude, and the foremost in learning, of all in the empire. In the second century there was established, here and at Tyre, a geographical school, possessing more ample materials and resources than any that had hitherto existed. To the conquests and itineraries of Alexander were now added those of Rome, which, extending in a different direction, embraced many countries to the north and to the west, Gaul, Britain, Germany, Spain, and Mauritania, respecting which the Greeks had possessed only confused and imperfect notions. Thus a greater portion of the globe than at any former period was now united under one government, which, by a standing army and a regular system of laws, preserved the whole in peace and order. The terror of the Roman arms enabled travellers to penetrate with safety even beyond the limits of the empire. Lastly, the unbounded luxury of the great capitals, and above all of imperial Rome, enriched with the spoils of the globe, fired the enterprise of the merchant, who found his way into those remotest markets of the eastern world, the rich commodities of which had hitherto been either brought by caravans or found at intermediate stations.

These enlarged materials were connected together by a much more accurate and scientific arrangement than had been adopted under the school of Eratosthenes. The method suggested by Hipparchus of subjecting the whole of geography to astronomical principles, and of fixing the position of every spot upon the globe according to its longitude and latitude, was now attempted to be carried into full effect. The attempt, however, was made but in a very rude manner, and upon a very narrow basis of observation. Not only, therefore, did it present a very imperfect edition of the new system, but involved errors which caused it in some respects to retrograde even from the rude state to which it had been brought by the former school of Alexandria.

### SECT. I.—*Marinus of Tyre.*

No Tyrian system of geography has come down to us, notwithstanding the commercial greatness of its people at an early period. From the Hebrew writers we have accounts perhaps of nearly the whole of the distant countries with which the Tyrians held intercourse;

---

*References to the Peutingerian Table (page 50).*

NORTH PART.

1. Siscia
2. Sardona
3. Aquinco
4. Brigantio
5. Jadera
6. Ragadone
7. Sabarie
8. Carnunto
9. Celeia
10. Vindobona
11. Tarsatica
12. Emona
13. Pola
14. Silvo
15. Parentio
16. Fonte-tumaia
17. Aquileia
18. Ovilia
19. Altino
20. Regino
21. Tridente
22. Placentia
23. Aquæ Populanie
24. Florentia Tuscorum
25. Sena Julia
26. Bituriba
27. Verona
28. Mantua
29. Mutina
30, Cosa
31. Adretio
32. Bononia
33. Clusio
34. Volsinis
35. Aquas Passaris
36. Ravenna
37. Arimino
38. Granisca
39. Contum cellis
40. Aquas tuari
41. Ancone
42. Castro-novo
43. Aquas Apollinaris
44. Soleto
45. Polentia
46. Reate
47. Castello Firmani
48. Ad Sem. Petrum
49. Roma
50. Hostis
51. Chartagine
52. Utica Colonia
53. Aquis
54. Ipponte diarito
55. Capsa Colonia
56. Ad Medera
57. Theleote Col.
58. Theneste
59. Sicca-veria
60. Ad Aquas Cæsaris

*Rivers.*

a Danubius
b Drinum
c Savum
d Arsia
e Frigido
f Licenna
g Afesia
h Cleusis
i Umatia
j Padus
k Paala
l Aninio
m Isex
n Umbro
o Pallia
p Armenita
q Marta
r Tiberis
s Rubicum
t Nelurum
u Matana
v Miso
w Flosis
x Tuma
y Nerninum
z Anio

SOUTH PART.

1. Ad Pretorum
2. Servitio
3. Ad Pretorum
4. Mursa Major
5. Indenea
6. Tittoburgo
7. Ragurio
8. Siclis, run.
9. Salona
10. Epetio
11. Inarona
12. Sirmium
13. Narona
14. Tauruno
15. Ad Matricem
16. Singiduna
17. Epitauro
18. Stanedi
19. Lissun
20. Viminatio
21. Dyrratio
22. Aulona
23. Osa Col.
24. Sabrata
25. Regio
26. Caulon
27. Lacenium
28. Castra Minervæ
29. Vibona Valentia
30. Temsa
31. Tarento
32. Brindisi
33. Gnatie
34. Nerulos
35. Salerno
36. Nuceria
37. Oplontis
38. Benevento
39. Venusie
40. Neapoli
41. Capua
42. Cumas
43. Syllas
44. Aeras
45. Pretonium Laucrianum
46. Siponto
47. Esernie
48. Teano Scedicino
49. Sinuessa
50. Menturnis
51. Fundis
52. Terracina
53. Ferentinum
54. Febraterie
55. Istonum
56. Corsinio
57. Marrubio
58. Tres Tabernas
59. Carsulis
60. Ostia eterni
61. Pinna
62. Castro nova
63. Preneste
64. Roma
65. Hostis
66. Chartagine
67. Maxula
68. Ad Aquas
69. Misua Clipeis
70. Gurra
71. Ad Horrea
72. Lepteminus
73. Thiforo Col.
74. Ad Aquas
75. Taparura
76. Tacape
77. Drepanis
78. Lilybeo
79. Aquas Labodes
80. Siracusis
81. Aethna Mons
82. Messana

*Rivers.*

a Danubius
b Drinum
c Savum
d Margum
e Genesis
f Hapsum
g Tanno
h Crater
i Silarum
j Color
k Aveldium
l Aufidenus
m Larinum
n Clocoris
o Sannum
p Cumara
q Nernum
r Arno
s Tiberis
t Safo
u Vulturnus
v Himera
w Niranus
x Ausere
y Gerin

but if those writers are supposed to have borrowed from them their ideas respecting the general structure and boundaries of the earth, geography among the early Phœnicians will not appear to have passed its infancy. As Tyre, however, even under the Roman empire, remained still the seat of an extensive commerce, some of her intelligent citizens availed themselves of the lights afforded by the learning of Alexandria, and applied them to the illustration of those subjects on which the greatness and prosperity of their city depended. If the merchants of Tyre had nothing left of that proud rule, and those monopolizing profits, which enabled them to rival the pomp of princes, their commercial relations probably extended over a wider surface of the globe than ever. They seem to have been engaged in that vast caravan route which was opened from Byzantium across the whole interior of Asia, conducting the merchants by a journey of ten or eleven months to the Chinese frontier, whence they brought silk, the staple product of that great country. Collecting these enlarged materials, Marinus, a native of Tyre, sought to apply to them the astronomical principles of Hipparchus, and thus to arrange geography into a new and more accurate form.

The works of Marinus have perished, and are known to us only by the references and extracts of Ptolemy; but these are sufficient to show that his system partook largely of the imperfection of a first effort. Aware that the degree of longitude diminished as it receded from the equator, he yet did not attempt to express this difference by representing the meridians with curved lines approaching each other, although this had been already shown by Hipparchus to be the proper course. He made them parallel to each other, not at the equatorial distance, but at that which belonged to them at the meridian of Rhodes. Thus in the part of the globe which came into his immediate observation he avoided any material error; but the meridians, adjusted only to this latitude, became too near each other as they were carried southward, and too distant as they went northward. He fell into a still more pernicious error in adopting the geodesic measurement of Posidonius, according to which the circumference of the earth was made to consist of only 180,000 stadia, and consequently the degree to contain only 500 stadia. This short degree, being calculated out of the exaggerated itineraries upon which the maps of those days were constructed, enormously amplified all the dimensions of the globe. Marinus appears also to have admitted with excessive credulity the extravagant reports of the merchants who had penetrated across the vast mountain and desert tracts in the east of Asia. The rugged and difficult character of the region, the circuitous route which they were frequently obliged to follow, and the obstacles often encountered from the rude inhabitants, caused this journey to occupy a much longer time than those performed through districts better known; and time, as already observed, was the element out of which the ancients were chiefly accustomed to calculate space. Ptolemy also accuses the merchants of vain-glorious propensities, which led them to magnify beyond truth the extent and vastness of the regions which they traversed. Hence the great line upon which Marinus measured the length of the habitable globe, instead of one hundred and twenty-nine degrees given to it in the measurement of Eratosthenes, is swelled out to two hundred and twenty-five degrees, not much less than two-thirds of the globe; whereas the actual length, placing Thinæ even at the eastern extremity of China, is not much more than one third. The exaggeration is enormous chiefly with respect to the country beyond India, which is made to comprise one hundred degrees. This being probably a new route opened through the Himaleh, and across the vast deserts of Eastern Tartary, had been affected by all the sources of amplification in a remarkable degree.

## Sect. II.—*Ptolemy.*

Ptolemy, the last and greatest of the geographers of antiquity, and equally illustrious as an astronomer, instituted a complete reform of the science, and undertook to purify it from all the false elements with which it had been alloyed. The principles, in fact, which he adopted were strictly correct; for though, as an astronomer, his theory of the universe was substantially false, yet, in admitting the globular form of the earth and the revolution of the heavenly bodies, he admitted all the elements which were requisite for the less lofty sphere of earthly delineation. He adopted the system of Hipparchus in its utmost extent, subjecting every spot on the known globe to astronomical data, and constructing his tables, never according to itinerary distance, but according to the supposed latitude and longitude of each place. He saw and corrected the error of Marinus in making the degrees of longitude equal under every latitude. Thus, though Ptolemy did not actually introduce any new principle into geography, he was the first who combined together all the sound views of his predecessors, and formed out of them a just and harmonious delineation. Yet he was far from reaching his aim of forming a perfect system. He still retained the erroneous measurement of the degree formed by Posidonius, and of which Marinus had made so unfortunate a use. Hence, while he felt the extravagance of the distances assigned by his predecessor, in consequence of the adoption of the degree of 500 stadia, he extricated himself but partially from the same error. All his longitudes, extended along the length of the known world, present a similar accumulation of errors, only somewhat diminished in amount. These errors, beginning from Cape St. Vincent, constantly increase till, in India, they amount to upwards of forty degrees. M. Gosselin has even accused him of an error which, as he justly observes, would mark a strange departure from every principle, and a neglect of what ought to be the first care of a geographer. This consists in giving to his degrees of latitude a different dimension from that of the degrees of longitude, and retaining, with regard to the former, Eratosthenes's standard of 700 stadia. I suspect, however, that M. Gosselin has been somewhat precipitate in advancing so serious a charge against the first geographer of antiquity. The ground on which he proceeds seems to be, that while Ptolemy has changed materially all the longitudes of Eratosthenes, the latitudes along the great line continue unaltered and generally correct. The real cause of this, however, appears to be, that the latitudes of Rhodes and several other leading points of this great line were determined by observations which, though not perfect, at least approached to the truth, while the longitudes were calculated merely out of the itineraries. This central line, therefore, bisecting the breadth of the known world, was fixed upon sound data, and the errors could accumulate only to the north and south of it. In fact, we shall find that they did accumulate as rapidly as in the longitudes, when the sphere of observation was passed, which was bounded by Syene on the south, Marseilles and Byzantium on the north. The mouth of the Seine is placed one degree too far north; that of the Rhine, nearly two degrees; that of the Elbe, more than two degrees; York is three degrees; and the farther accumulation is only prevented by that singular conformation which we shall find given by Ptolemy to the northern part of Britain. To the south, again, Axum is placed three degrees too far south; Cape Aromata (Guardafui), nearly six degrees; and from that point the errors continually become greater. Thus it appears, that as soon as Ptolemy quits the sphere of observation, his latitudes are calculated exactly as his longitudes, out of itineraries, and exhibit the same accumulation of errors.

The manuscripts of Ptolemy are clearly shown by M. Gosselin to have reached us in a very imperfect state. In collating with care the different editions, that learned writer has found a greater number of variations than in those of almost any other ancient writer. These variations were of course very likely to occur in copying cyphers where there was no connexion of sense to check the copyist. The manuscripts and the maps appear to have been copied by different hands, holding no communication with each other; and accordingly these two parts of the same work do not, in many instances, correspond. Lastly, the work of Ptolemy appears, for several centuries, to have been carried about as a guide by mariners and travellers, who, wherever they found any feature which did not agree with their observations, altered the writing or the map accordingly. This process appears in the numerous variations of the Latin copies with regard to the western part of the Mediterranean, and of the Greek with regard to the eastern. The alterations thus made would often, and indeed, most generally, be improvements; but the great discrepancies which they introduced into the different copies, must have greatly bewildered the public.

In delineating the geographical system of Ptolemy, we can only consider the general outline, which is pretty much the same in all the editions. Ptolemy begins with rejecting the theory of his predecessors, from Homer to Strabo downwards, who represent the whole earth as enclosed by a circumambient ocean. Mercantile caravans, especially in the east of Asia, had now proceeded considerably beyond the line of coast which, according to the last school, had marked the eastern bounding ocean. They had passed that line without reaching the distant corresponding one by which the Pacific and Arctic seas were actually drawn around this vast continent. The eastern Atlantic, and the Northern Oceans were, therefore, effaced from the delineation of Asia, and an indefinite expanse of *terra incognita* (unknown land) was substituted as the boundary of the world. This proceeding must certainly be considered as more precise and philosophical than the gratuitous theoretical one for which it was substituted. Men, however, seldom know exactly where to stop: Ptolemy, having once formed the idea of a bounding terra incognita, extended it round nearly the entire circuit of the known world. All the reports of the circumnavigation of Africa were rejected; that continent was represented as stretching indefinitely south, and it was even carried round to join the east of Asia, and form the Erythrean or Indian sea into a vast basin. Thus the whole system and structure of these two continents underwent, in the hands of Ptolemy, a complete transmutation.

### Subsect. 1. *Europe.* (*Fig.* 10.)

In regard to all the remoter boundaries of Europe, Ptolemy displays an advancement in knowledge, truly wonderful, considering the short period which had elapsed since the days of Strabo. The facts which we have stated under the head of Roman geography show the vast additional mass of information derived from the conquests of Cæsar, and from the imperial surveys. This having been incorporated into the writings of Mela and Pliny, a century before the age of Ptolemy, would easily, through these and other channels, reach his knowledge. It is not surprising that the crude delineation of the exterior coasts of Europe under the Strabonic system should have been materially amended; that Spain

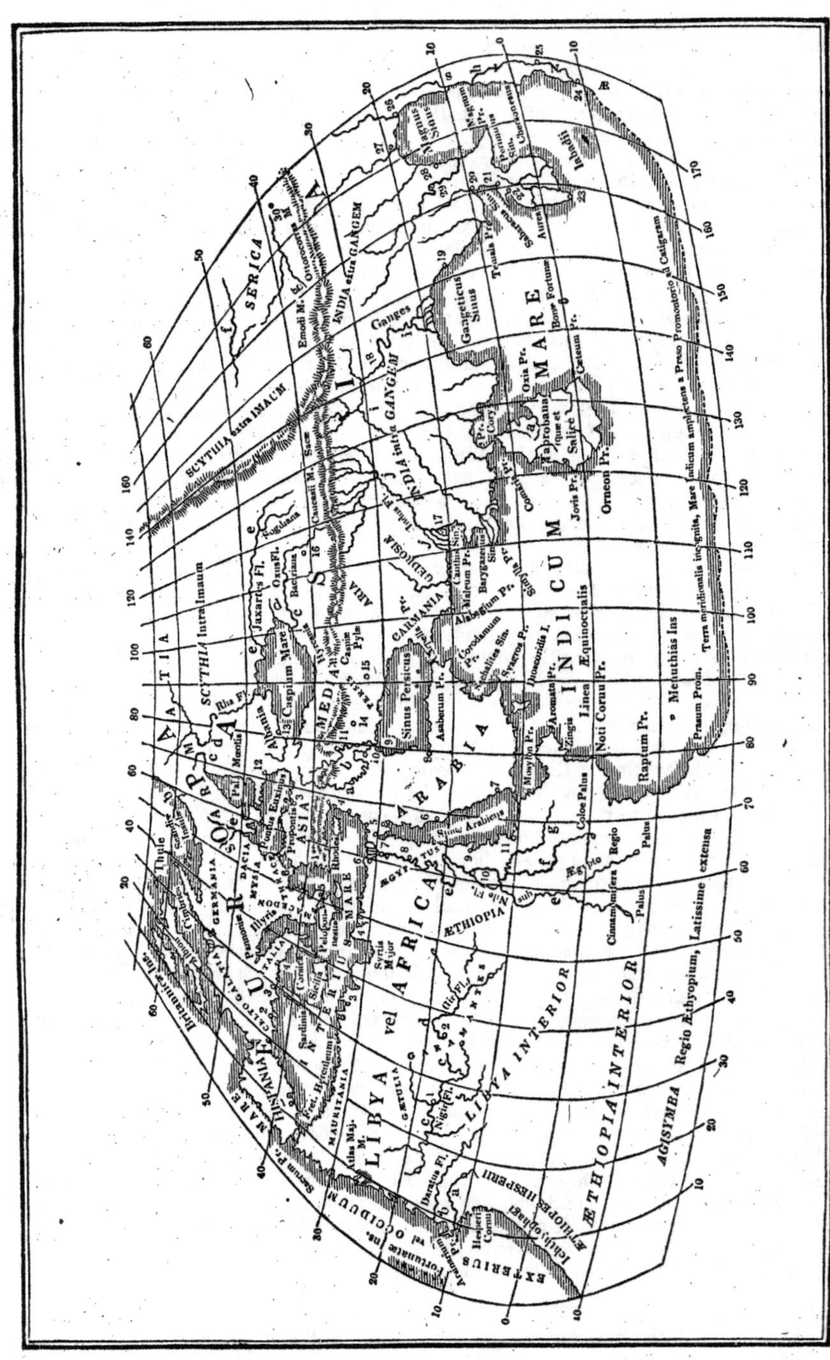
SERICA
SCYTHIA extra IMAUM
SCYTHIA Intra Imaum
INDIA extra GANGEM
INDIA intra GANGEM
Gangeticus Sinus
MARE INDICUM
Taprobana
Caspium Mare
Sinus Persicus
ARABIA
AFRICA
LIBYA
ÆTHIOPIA
LIBYA INTERIOR
ÆTHIOPIA INTERIOR
Linea Æquinoctialis
Regio Æthyopium, Latissime extensa
Terra meridionalis incognita
Menuthias Ins
Rapum Pr.
Noti Cornu Pr.
Pontus Euxinus
Propontis
ASIA
EUROPA
SARMATIA
GERMANIA
HISPANIA
Thule
MARE OCCIDUUS vel EXTERIUS
Fortunatæ Ins.
Ganges
Cattigara
Ægypto
Cinnamonifera Regio
Palus
Aurea
Jaxartes Fl.
Oxus Fl.
Sicilia
Sardinia
Creta
Rhodes
Syrtis Major
Nile Fl.
ÆTHIOPES HESPERII
AGISYMBA

should have now a southern, and Gaul a western coast; and that the Bay of Biscay should appear clearly under the appellations of the Cantabrian Ocean and the Aquitanian Sea. In regard to Britain, also, or, at least, England, a great reform had been effected. Its coast, after passing the promontory of Kent, bends inward toward the estuary of the Thames, called here Idumanus. Still more decided, on the opposite side, is the "*Sabrina estuarium*" (the estuary of the Severn), a very appropriate appellation for the Bristol Channel. The projection of Wales, and its entire outline, appears then drawn in a very unexceptionable manner. With regard to Ireland, Ptolemy has not been able wholly to shake off the erroneous impressions of the first Alexandrian school, according to which that country lay to the north of Britain. He makes it west, indeed, but at the same time greatly too far north, its southern coast being on a line with that of Lancashire, or, at least, with the north-western point of Wales. The consequence is, that the island of Mona (Man) is placed off the south-eastern point of Ireland, not far from Wexford. Having pointed out this great error, we must add, that the whole form and circuit of Ireland is given with a correctness which appears very surprising, when contrasted with so great a mistake as to its relative position. Again, the eastern coast of England proceeds correctly till it reaches the vicinity of York, when an aberration takes place of the most extraordinary nature. The rest of the English coast, with the whole of that of Scotland, instead of ranging from north to south, runs from west to east. The eastern coast becomes thus the southern, the western becomes the northern; and the coast of Germany appears opposite and parallel throughout its whole extent. The most northerly extremity of Britain is thus fixed at a point which Mr. Pinkerton supposed to be the Mull of Galloway, but which seems more probably to be some point near Port Patrick, which might be supposed the most westerly, for the west is here the north. It is part of this arrangement, that the Æbudæ (Hebrides) are placed in the Deucaledonian Ocean, which washes the western coast of Scotland, made here the northern; and the Orkneys are in the same ocean; for, instead of following the line of the main land, they are placed, as, indeed, they ought to be, north, becoming thus at right angles to that line.

To account for this strangely distorted form of northern Britain, M. Gosselin has formed a very ingenious theory. The southern extremity of the island being in lat. 52° N., and Thule, the remotest extremity, in 63°, Ptolemy could not, within these limits, find space for that vast expanse of coast, which the itineraries represented to him as belonging to Britain. To make out this space he had no alternative but to give to the northern part the form it actually bears in his maps, and under which the latitude is augmented only by the breadth of Scotland, a much smaller dimension than the length. The question, however, is, by what circumstance Ptolemy was checked in his latitude of Thule, and why he should not have driven it out to the north as far as his itineraries seemed to require. We at one time thought it possible that this grand boundary point might have been fixed by some rude observation which was not applied to the intermediate points. But it appears very improbable, that any expedition which should have made an observation of latitude at Shetland, should not have done the same in the southern and much more accessible parts of Britain. I rather incline to adopt the following solution. We have seen, that, in the ideas of the Roman navigators, Thule was in a great measure separated from Britain, and attached to the east of Germany, or rather to Scandinavia; whether its existence was made known to them by Scandinavian navigators, or whether a part of the coast of Norway was actually fixed upon by them instead of Shetland for this most northern limit of the earth. This idea, which attached Thule to Scandinavia, appears to have been combined in Ptolemy's mind with that of Pytheas, who made it the remotest extremity of Britain. Such a combination could be accomplished only by stretching Scotland across the German ocean in that strange direction.

The details of Scotland, if we pass over this radical error, are given in a manner much more tolerable than could have been expected in a country unsubdued by the Romans, and with their imperfect navigation. Thule, in Ptolemy, is not a cluster of islands, like those of Shetland, but one large island, upwards of a hundred miles in length: this circumstance more and more strengthens the suspicion that Norway, to a considerable extent, entered into the idea attached to that celebrated name.

---

*References to the Map of the World according to Ptolemy.*

EUROPA.
1. Carthago Nova
2. Massilia
3. Genua
4. Roma
5. Athenæ
6. Byzantium

*Rivers*
a Rhenus
b Chesinus
c Tanais
d Rha
e Borysthenes

ASIA.
1. Ephesus
2. Sinope
3. Amisus
4. Issus
5. Elana
6. Zaaram
7. Musa
8. Gerra
9. Teredon
10. Babylon
11. Ninus
12. Dioscurias
13. Gagara
14. Susa
15. Persepolis
16. Bactra
17. Patala
18. Palibothra
19. Baracura
20. Besynga
21. Barabæ
22. Tacola
23. Sabana
24. Catigara
25. Thinæ
26. Aspithra
27. Tomara
28. Sinda
29. Daiona
30. Sera

*Rivers.*
a Euphrates
b Tigris
c Oxus
d Polytimetus
e Jaxartes
f Œchardes
g Bautisus
h Senus
i Ganges
j Indus

*Taprobana Insula.*
a Ganges

LIBYA VEL AFRICA.
1. Nigira
2. Gira
3. Carthago
4. Phycus
5. Cyrene
6. Alexandria
7. Heroopolis
8. Syene
9. Ptolemais
10. Meroe
11. Adulis

*Rivers*
a Stachir
b Daratus
c Nigir
d Gir
e Nilus
f Astapus
g Astaboras

Under the heads of great Germany and of Sarmatia, Ptolemy has given all the knowledge he had acquired of the north and east of Europe, which was not inconsiderable. The line of the German coast is very well formed, and the Amasius or Ems, the Visurgis or Weser, the Albis or Elbe, the Vedra or Oder, and the Visula or Vistula, appear in regular succession, and almost under their modern names. Jutland appears as the Cimbric Chersonese, and the southern coast of the Baltic is carried on very correctly; but, in regard to Scandinavia, he fails entirely. Evidently ignorant that the Baltic is an enclosed gulf, he calls it "the Sarmatic Ocean," and places in it four islands. Three of these, close to the Cimbric Chersonese, are clearly recognised in the islands of Denmark; but the other, of greater extent, farther to the east and opposite to the mouth of the Vistula, is probably part of Sweden, and perhaps Gothland. It is clear, that navigators had not then rounded Jutland, and passed through the Skagerrack or Cattegat, otherwise they must have noticed these straits, and the great extent of continent opposite the Cimbric Chersonese. The Aloecian islands, however, situated off the northern extremity of Jutland, must have been suggested by some part of the Norwegian coast, as there are no islands in that quarter. The more northern part of the Norwegian coast was probably, as already observed, identified with Thule.

The coast of Sarmatia is described by Ptolemy on passing the Vistula, and he traces with accuracy the great bend which it takes northward to the gulf of Riga. Four rivers are given, which cannot be recognised by their names, but which M. Gosselin conceives to be the Pregel, the Niemen, the Windau, and the Dwina. Beyond this he places "the end of the sea of the known land," and immediately commences that boundary of *terra incognita* which he carries around the whole of Asia.

In regard to the south of European Russia, Ptolemy recovers much of the knowledge which had been wholly or partially lost under Strabo. He appears indeed to have gone back in a great measure to Herodotus, whom he imitates in giving most unreasonable extension to the Palus Mæotis. There is little room for complaint as to the Tanais, the Borysthenes, and the other great rivers which fall into the Euxine. In this remote and wild extremity of Europe, however, he has found a place for certain poetical and historical fictions, which experience had banished from better known quarters, but which could not find a place here with any propriety;—the grove of Diana, the race-course of Achilles, the altars of Cæsar and of Alexander; neither of whom ever carried their arms into this part of the ancient Scythia.

In tracing the Mediterranean, Ptolemy improves considerably upon the labours of his predecessors. Sicily, in particular, is much better constructed, and the straits of Messina are placed nearly in their true latitude. He still, however, merits deep reproach for the utterly barbarous form which he has given to Italy, that ruling country, which must of all others have appeared to him the most interesting, and for which he must have possessed the most ample materials. Yet Italy, with the exception of a slight bend at its extremity, is oriented almost entirely east and west, having the Adriatic for its northern, and the Tyrrhenian for its southern boundary. I cannot find any account of an error so strange, except by supposing that Ptolemy must have been led into it by one of those itinerary maps which, like the Peutingerian, made every thing subservient to the direction of the Roman high road, and drew it in a straight line from one extremity to the other. It is easy to suppose that he might not comprehend the very odd principle upon which this map was constructed, and might conceive that being made with regard to Italy, a country so near, and so completely within reach, it might be implicitly relied on. This suspicion is strengthened when we find, after passing Dyrrachium, the port of embarkation for Greece, this being the direction of the great road of the empire, that the coast of Italy suddenly resumes its just form, and the peninsula of Campania makes even too abrupt a bend to the south.

### Subsect. 2.—*Asia.*

In regard of Asia also, important discoveries had been made since the time of Eratosthenes. Immense territories, included by that geographer within the domain of the ocean, were known to Ptolemy as occupied by the wandering hordes of Scythia, or by the peaceful and industrious nation of the Seres or Chinese. This advantage might be partly due to the military itineraries, especially that of Trajan in his victorious expedition into Parthia. The grand source, however, evidently was that bold spirit of commercial enterprise, to which an impulse was given by the vast consumption of Rome, when the wealth of the world centred in that mighty and voluptuous capital. The East was the region mainly resorted to for the supply of the boundless wants which arose in that artificial and luxurious state of society. The merchants soon learned to trace routes, both by land and sea, much longer and more adventurous than had been achieved by their predecessors at any former period. Under the narrative entitled "the Periplus of the Erythrean Sea," we have followed the maritime career by which the merchants of Alexandria were led to the coast of Malabar. Whether, in the time of Ptolemy, the Greek navigators had actually proceeded farther, it may be difficult to say with certainty. He has certainly, however obtained a considerable accession of knowledge with regard to this eastern extremity of the known world. He goes far beyond the mouth of the Ganges, at which we have observed the termination of all precise knowledge in the author of the Periplus. After delineating a coast, with a succession of ports which it is difficult to identify, he comes to a grand feature, which he calls "the Golden Chersonese," formed by three great estuaries discharging their waters into the sea. These phenomena are actually presented by the mouths of the Irrawaddy at the southern extremity of Pegu. This is followed by an extensive feature, the *Magnus Sinus*, or Great Bay, penetrating far inland, and receiving some considerable rivers. The gulf of Malacca is not nearly so large or so deep as this *Magnus Sinus*; but its mouth being very broad, and its shores very winding, it is not very improbable that, in the eyes of ancient and unskilful navigators, it might assume this exaggerated form and dimension. Beyond the *Magnus Sinus* the coast, in continuity with its eastern shore, stretches due south to the farthest known extremity of the world. On this coast the leading features are Thinæ, a great interior metropolis, and Cattigara, its sea-port at the mouth of the river Cotiaris. This coast, it should seem, can only be that of Malacca and the Isthmus of Kraw, which runs exactly in the direction here assigned by Ptolemy. Gosselin identifies Thinæ with Tenasserin; but there seems more reason for acceding to Dr. Vincent's opinion that it is Siam. This exposition, which is supported by Vossius, Gosselin, and Vincent, appears to me undoubtedly preferable to the more general one supported by the authority of d'Anville, which makes the coast of the Sinæ extend along the gulf of Siam and the sea of China. Such a line would involve Ptolemy in the strange and incredible blunder of making a coast face the east which really faces the west. Sumatra, indeed, is so land-locked that it might easily enough have been taken for a part of the continent, and have been called the Golden Chersonese. But it seems inconceivable how the straits of Malacca and of Sunda, so important and so critical to navigators, and by one or the other of which they must have entered the sea of China, could have been overlooked. On this supposition, indeed, the coasts are swelled very far beyond their due dimensions; but we have often remarked how enormously this is apt to be the case, in regard to routes, and above all coasts which are traversed for the first time, and by inexperienced navigators. Ptolemy, as we have seen, after retrenching the eastern itineraries of Marinus one half, left them still greatly too large; and he does not mention any similar retrenchment in regard to the coasts. If, on the other hand, those of Ptolemy extend to the Chinese sea and to China, then, contrary to every ancient example, he must have immensely underrated the extent of these imperfectly discovered tracts; an error which would be contrary to all precedent:—this, however, does not imply that there may not, within this line of positive knowledge, have been a confused blending of features that lay in reality beyond.

The increased knowledge of Ptolemy respecting the eastern part of the Asiatic continent was chiefly derived, as we have already remarked, from the great caravan which proceeded from Byzantium, having the country of Serica for its ultimate destination. This caravan, having traversed Asia Minor, crossed the Euphrates at Hierapolis, and journeyed through Media, by way of Ecbatana (Hamadan), to Hecatompylos (Daumghaun), the capital of Parthia. It then advanced north to Hyrcania (Horkan or Jorjan), thence south, to take in the fine province of Aria (Herat). It now again turned north, to include the capital of Margiana (Meru Rood), thence due east to Bactria (Balk), which then formed, as at present, the main centre of the commerce of interior Asia. The caravan now quitted the easy and level tract through which its route had hitherto led, and began to ascend that vast and rugged mountain world which fills the eastern interior of Asia. After accomplishing the steep ascent of the *Montes Comedorum*, which seems to be the chain of the Beloor, it reached a station called the "Stone Tower," which there is nothing to identify, except that the direction towards it is north-east, and it may be either Ladauk or Yarcund, the great modern emporium of this part of the East. From the Stone Tower to the frontier of Serica, Marinus, on the authority of the merchants, reported a journey of seven months, which Ptolemy considers as monstrous and incredible, though he admits that the road is exposed to the greatest hardships and difficulties. The question, what is the country described by Ptolemy and his contemporaries as Serica, is the most curious in the ancient geography of Asia. The earliest modern opinion identified Serica with northern China, while the country of the Sinæ composed the southern part. D'Anville, however, who transported the Sinæ into the coast of Cambodia, carried westward also the Seres into the country of the Igours, or Eygurs, including in their territory only the small projecting portion of the Chinese province of Shensee. Mr. Pinkerton places it still farther west, in Little Bucharia. M. Gosselin, followed generally by the present French school, contends that Serinagur, in the north of Hindostan, is the real Sera metropolis of Ptolemy. I can see no reason for altering the grounds on which I concluded formerly, and endeavoured to prove, Serica to be simply China. (See *Edinburg Phil. Trans* vol. viii. On the ancient Geography of Central and Eastern Asia.) All the natives of India whom Ptolemy saw assured him that the Seres lay beyond the Sinæ, and China is beyond Siam. The Sinæ (Siam) had to the north Scythia beyond Imaus, which country had Serica on the east. Serica is described as traversed by two great rivers, flowing eastward, as the Hoang-ho and Yang-tse-kiang actually do. Serica, according to Ptolemy's graduation, was fourteen hundred miles from north to south, and eleven hundred from east to west, a very close approach to the dimensions of modern China. Serica, then, in form, extent, geographical features, and relations to the neighbouring countries, exactly corresponds to the modern China. Not less conformable is the report given of the national character. The Seres are represented as frugal, quiet, sedate, and tranquil beyond all other nations; as of all others the most unwarlike, and the most averse to the use of arms; as shunning, with the most studious care, the society and intercourse of strangers, and scarcely ever allowing them to enter their territory; as carrying on trade at a fixed frontier station only, and under the strictest precautions; as selling their own commodities without receiving the commodities of other nations in return. Silk was the staple of Serica, and it is of China. With regard to M. Gosselin's Indian theory, it must now, we suppose, be on all hands given up, since Thibet and Northern India, instead of being connected by the valley of the Ganges, have been found separated by the unbroken continuity of the loftiest ridge of the Himmaleh, which can be penetrated only by a few most perilous and tremendous passes.

Respecting Hindostan, and its limitary regions, the details given by Ptolemy include a great mass of sound information. In some important particulars, indeed, his map is decidedly superior to those possessed by the moderns, previous to the late important accessions to their knowledge. He describes the Ganges rising, as it really does, on the southern side of the Himmaleh, and in the outer limits of Hindostan, while, prior to the mission sent by Col. Colebrooke, in 1808, its origin, and a considerable part of its early course, were supposed to be in Little Thibet. The mission to Caubul first found that all the great western rivers emptied themselves by one channel into the Indus, as they had been represented by Ptolemy, while modern maps had exhibited them entering by two great separate channels. The same mission discovered two very considerable rivers, western tributaries of the Indus, the Kaumeh and the Suaut, of which no trace had yet appeared in modern delineation; but, on turning to Ptolemy, we find them accurately traced under the names of the Coe and the Suaste. Thus we find him delineating with success geographical features in the most secret recesses of Asia, which remained unknown till lately to the best-informed of modern geographers.

The site of Palibothra is one main point in which, after much discussion, geographers have in vain endeavoured to form an unanimous opinion. It was found by Megasthenes the proud capital of the Gangetic kingdom, and the greatest city of all India. Yet modern geographers have not been able to agree within several hundred miles upon this marked and celebrated position. Arrian states that it is situated at the junction of the Ganges with the Erranaboas, the third river of India as to magnitude, being surpassed only by the Ganges and the Indus. This scale of magnitude suggests the Jumna, and at the confluence of the Jumna with the Ganges actually stands Allahabad, a city of great magnitude and high antiquity, which is even revered by the Hindoos as the "king of holy cities." Upon this general idea D'Anville and, after him, Robertson, have considered Allahabad as occupying the site of Palibothra. On examination, however, this is found in contradiction to the most positive statements of Pliny and Ptolemy. Pliny, in express words, states Palibothra to be 425 miles *distant from* the junction of these two rivers. Ptolemy makes the distance somewhat greater still. In considering Allahabad, then, as Palibothra, we abandon altogether the authority of these two great geographers, a step in which we should be very little justified, either by a reference to their general character, or by our knowledge of their remarkable accuracy with regard to the other features of central and northern India. Their account of Palibothra, too, is given upon the authority of Greek ambassadors, who actually visited that capital. The river next in magnitude is the Gogra or Sarayu. But the junction of this river with the Ganges is not nearly so far from that of the Jumna as the above statements would require. Besides, Ptolemy actually gives us the Sarabus (Sarayu), with its junction in the due relative position to that of the Jumna, but Palibothra much farther down. Major Rennel has made choice of Patna, and considers the junction of the Soane, at present thirty miles above that city, as having taken place formerly by a different and nearer channel. This theory stands on much higher ground than the other; yet it by no means closely corresponds with the ancient data. Pliny mentions both the Sonus and the Erranaboas as quite distinct tributaries of the Ganges, and he places the city considerably farther down than Patna is. Ptolemy, also, in giving the junction of the Soa and the Ganges, places Palibothra more than two hundred miles below. Major Rennell's theory, then, brings us considerably short of the point at which this great capital ought to be situated.

Another point which appeared to me to unite the name and position of Palibothra has been mentioned (*Discoveries in Asia*, v. i. p. 491.), and, without being inclined very confidently to dogmatize, it still appears to me to combine better the different requisites than any other yet named. The name of *Boglipoor* may be considered identical with Paliboor; for, in transferring Indian terms into our characters, P and B, O and A, are always used promiscuously; and the termination attached by the Romans is evidently according to their system of harmonizing foreign sounds with their own. A name is of little consequence when it is not accompanied with a corresponding position; but here this appears to coincide nearly, though not indeed quite exactly, with Pliny. He makes Palibothra 430 miles from the junction of the Ganges and Jumna, and 600 from Gange, a capital situated at the mouth of the former. Boglipoor, however, instead of being only two-fifths of the distance between these two points, is about exactly midway. The space lower down the river, being less known, might more readily have been exaggerated, and Gange being on the most easterly branch of the Ganges, might occupy nearly the position of Islamabad. The place assigned by Ptolemy is exactly midway, and therefore coincides strictly with the position of Boglipoor. Near it the Ganges receives the Coosy, or river of Nepaul, certainly not the third in India as to magnitude; but the ambassadors might not have very precise means of ascertaining the relative dimensions of the Indian rivers. There is, therefore, a great weight of evidence, as to name and position, in favour of the theory here proposed. I must confess, however, that I find no description of any monuments, such as might be expected to mark the ancient site of so splendid a capital. Indian structures, however, are not usually composed of materials sufficiently solid to resist the ravages of sixteen centuries. If the local data could at all have allowed us to fix upon the thrice ancient and holy Benares, its character would have given it at once a pre-eminence; but this is impossible. Rajemahl, suggested, is not very distant from Boglipoor; but besides losing the coincidence of name, it agrees less than the other position with the statements both of Ptolemy and Pliny.

### Subsect. 3.—*Africa.*

In the delineation of Africa, Ptolemy, himself an African, had obvious advantages. Accordingly his delineations of several of the most interior features have, as in the case of southern India, proved to be more accurate than those given by modern geographers down to a very recent period. The course of the Nile, up to its highest probable source in the central range of the mountains of the Moon, has been justified by recent inquiry, in opposition to the Portuguese missionaries, who drew it from the mountains and lakes of Abyssinia. This original fountain-head has not yet been traced by the daring foot of the modern traveller; but the description given to Brown, of its descent from the great mountain chain south of Darfoor, corresponds very exactly with Ptolemy, making allowance only for his erroneous graduation. With equal fidelity, he delineates the Astaboras, or Atbara, the Astapus, or river of Abyssinia, successively falling into it from the east. He has, indeed, made Meroe an island, enclosed by branches of the Nile; but modern discovery has shown it to be so very nearly insular, in consequence of the great bend taken to the south, that the error cannot be considered excessive.

In regard to central Africa, Ptolemy had not equal advantages, on account of the distance, because no track had yet been formed across the vast ocean of desert which intervened. It appears to me a matter of some difficulty to ascertain the precise extent of his knowledge as to this region. M. Gosselin has not hesitated to assert, that he knew nothing of Africa south of the desert, and that all the features which he has assigned to interior Libya, and the course of the Niger, belong in fact to Fezzan and that region behind the Atlas which we call the B'led-el-Jereede, or Land of Dates. This opinion certainly receives much countenance when we find the Garamantes and the Garamantica vallis placed on the same line with the Niger, the lake of Nigritia, and the other leading central features. I still, however, think it probable that Ptolemy might, by way of the Upper Nile, have obtained intelligence respecting a portion at least of these vast regions, the approach to which by way of Dongola and Sennaar was not obstructed by any very insurmountable barriers. Besides the agreement of several names, as Gana, Tagana, Panagra, the general picture of this region as one of lakes, rivers, and mountains, agrees much better with the interior than with the arid tract between Atlas and the desert. My suspicion therefore is, that Ptolemy, unacquainted with any route across the great desert, was not aware of the wide interval between the features to the north and those to the south of it, and linked them together in his description as contiguous and connected. As his knowledge of central Africa was thus obtained only in a westerly course from the Nile, it was not likely to extend beyond the eastern part of the vast breadth between the Nile and the ocean. The Mons Mandrus, his most western feature, with a great river flowing from it into the lake of Nigritia, may perhaps be recognized in the mighty range of the mountains of Mandara and the river Shary flowing from them into the lake or sea of the Tchad. About this quarter I should conceive the knowledge which reached Ptolemy by inland channels probably terminated; and the Atlantic coast, known to exist by the voyages of Hanno, Scylax, and Polybius, was united to these objects by a merely hypothetical construction. In regard to the course of the Niger, it is difficult to say very precisely what were Ptolemy's views, and we only perceive that he made it an inland river, neither flowing into the Atlantic, nor by the Nile into the Mediterranean.

Respecting this great central region of Africa, however, Ptolemy had obtained some notices from which he might have estimated its magnitude. Two Roman expeditions had been reported to him, one made by Septimius Flaccus from Garama, and the other by Julius

Maternus from the coast of Cyrene. The former in three, and the latter in four months, had penetrated into the country of the Ethiopians. Ptolemy expresses himself very sceptical as to the possible length of this march; nevertheless he lays down the country of Agisymba as that farthest region of interior Ethiopia into which these commanders had penetrated. Agisymba we suspect to be Agadez; at least as the march comprehends no rivers or lakes, it cannot well have reached the line of the Niger. Nevertheless Ptolemy places it considerably to the south of Nigritia; which is doubtless in favour of the limited extent which M. Gosselin allows to his information. But we may observe that, supposing Ptolemy to have formed, in the manner above supposed, his idea of the plain of the Niger as little removed to the south of Fezzan, he must, in protracting marches of three or four months, necessarily have carried the line much farther to the south.

In regard to the western coasts of Africa, Ptolemy's delineation is not very luminous, but appears on the whole to favour M. Gosselin's views respecting the extent of Hanno's voyage and of the knowledge of the ancients. He does indeed present two rivers, the Daradus and the Stachir, flowing on a line with the plain of Nigritia. But I have no idea that Ptolemy could have any precise information reaching across the entire breadth of the continent, and conceive, as already hinted, that the coast and interior were here hypothetically united. As Ptolemy placed the plain of the Niger much too far north, he might make these rivers on a line with it, without identifying them with the Senegal and Gambia. His position of the Fortunate Islands (Canaries) opposite to their mouths, and south of Cerne, is not at all in favour of the opinion which carries these last features deep into central Africa.

On the eastern coast of Africa, Ptolemy adds to the line described by the author of the Periplus a coast extending from the promontory of Rhaptum to that of Prasum. At this point the coast, hitherto running south-west, changes to south-east. No details are given of this coast, which is described as rough and difficult to navigate. We can neither, with M. Gosselin, limit Prasum to Brava, nor with Vincent carry it so far as Mosambique. There is no part of the coast to which the direction assigned to it belongs, except from Quiloa to Cape Delgado; and if Rhaptum be at or near Quiloa, the latter, allowing for some exaggeration of distance on a coast so little known, will be the promontory Prasum. Five degrees east and three degrees south of this promontory is the island of Menuthias. The Menouthesias of the Periplus appeared pretty plainly to be one of the smaller islands near the African coast, and probably Zanzibar; but none of these could be the Menuthias of Ptolemy, which is manifestly Madagascar.

# BOOK II.

## GEOGRAPHY OF THE MIDDLE AGES.

UNDER the "geography of the middle ages" may be comprehended that of the Arabian or Saracen nations, during the period when science was successfully cultivated among them; and the geographical ideas prevalent in Europe, during that long darkness which preceded the revival of learning, and the commencement of maritime discovery.

## CHAPTER I.

### ARABIAN GEOGRAPHY.

THE Arabs were for some time the most learned of nations. As the mantle of science dropped from the sages of Greece and Rome, it fell upon this wild and strange race, sprung from the bosom of bigotry and barbarism. The fanatic hordes, who, under the guidance of their false prophet, rushed from the heart of Arabia, at first owned no law but the Koran and the sword. When they had conquered half the world, however, and founded splendid capitals on the banks of the Euphrates and the Guadalquivir, there arose a race of humane and polished princes, who studiously sought to relumine the almost extinguished lamp of science. Almamoun above all, in the ninth century, may rank among the most distinguished of its patrons who have ever filled a throne.

Geography among the Arabian states, appears to have been studied with greater ardour than at any other place or country, except at Alexandria. It employed the pens of several of their most eminent writers; Masudi and Ebn Haukal in the ninth and tenth centuries; Abulfeda and Edrisi in the twelfth and thirteenth; to whom may be added the respectable names of Ibn-al-Vardi, Bakoui, and Scheabeddin. Although none of their works have become at all familiar to the European reader, yet learned men have translated portions, which not only convey a general idea of their system, but have enabled geographers to delineate some districts of the globe which otherwise would have long remained unknown.

### Sect. I.—*General System.* *Fig.* 11.

The mathematical sciences, and above all astronomy, were among the most favourite pursuits of the court of Bagdad; and the ample resources which they afforded were applied with considerable care to the improvement of geography. In 833, the caliph Almamoun endeavoured, by observations of latitude made at Kufa, and at a point in the desert of Palmyra, to measure the circumference of the globe. In all the countries subject to the Mahomedan arms, numerous observations are recorded which, though not always rigorously correct, appear at least to have been real, and not merely calculated out of itineraries, like those of the Alexandrian geographers. The tables of Abulfeda, of Ulug Beg, and of Nazir Eddin, edited by Grævius, and republished by Hudson, afford materials that are still useful for the construction of the maps of interior Asia.

*Fig.* 11.—MAP OF THE WORLD TAKEN FROM AN ARABIAN MANUSCRIPT OF AL EDRISI, IN THE BODLEIAN LIBRARY.

1. Mountains of the Moon and Sources of the Nile
2. Berbara (kingdom of Adel)
3. Al-Zung (Zanguebar)
4. Sefala (Sofala)
5. Al-Wak Wak
6. Serendeeb (Ceylon)
7. Al-Comor (Madagascar)
8. A-Dasi
9. Al-Yeman (Arabia Felix)
10. Tehama
11. Al-Hejaz (Arabia Deserta)
12. Al-Shujar (Seger)
13. Al-Imama (Yamama)
14. Al-Habesh (Ethiopia, Abyssinia)
15. Al Nuba (Nubia)
16. Al Tajdeen
17. Al-Bejah
18. Al-Saneed (Upper Egypt, Said)
19. Al-ouhat-what (Oasis)
20. Gowas
21. Kanun
22. Belad Al-lemlum
23. Belad Mufrada
24. Belad Nemaneh
25. Al-Mulita u Sinhajeh
26. Curan (Karooan, Kurene)
27. Negroland
28. Al-Sous Nera
29. Al-Mughrub Al Amkeen (Mogreb the West)
30. Afreekeea (Africa)
31. Belad el Gerid (Date Country)
32. Seharee, Bereneek (or Desert of Berenike)
33. Missur (Egypt)
34. Al-Sham (Syria)
35. Al-Irak (Persian empire)
36. Fars (Persia Proper)
37. Kirman (Carmania)
38. Alfazeh
39. Mughan
40. Al-Sunda (Scindi)
41. Al-Hind (India)
42. Al-Seen (China)
43. Khorasān
44. Al-Beharus
45. Azerbijan (Media)
46. Khuwarizm
47. Al-Shash
48. Khirkeez
49. Al-Sefur
50. Al-Tibut (Tibet)
51. Al-Nufuz Izz
52. Kurjeea (Georgia)
53. Keymak
54. Kulhœa
55. Izzea
56. Azkush
57. Turkesh
58. Iturab
59. Bulghar (Bulgaria)
60. Al-Mutenah
61. Yajooj (Gog)
62. Majooj (Magog)
63. Asiatic (Russia)
64. Bejeerut
65. Al-Alman
66. Al-Khuzzus Khozr (Caspian Sea)
67. Turkea (Turkey)
68. Albeian (Albania)
69. Makedunoeah (Macedonia)
70. Baltic Sea
71. Jenubea (probably Sweden)
72. Germania (Germany)
73. Denmark
74. Afranseeah (France)
75. Felowiah (Norway)
76. Burtea or Burtenea (Britain)
77. Corsica, Sardinia, &c
78. Italy
79. Ashkerineah (part of Spain, Q. Andalusia)

Many countries, hitherto unknown and barbarous, were explored, and in some degree civilized, by the Moslem arms. Those on the Oxus and the Jaxartes, the Asiatic Scythia of the ancients, and occupied then only by Nomadic hordes, were covered by them with great and flourishing cities. Among these, Samarcand became afterwards the capital of an empire that extended over half of Asia. At the opposite extremity, Mauritania, which had been regarded by the Romans as almost beyond the limits of social existence, became a flourishing kingdom, and possessed in Fez an eminent school of learning. Even beyond the limits of the Mahomedan world, missions were sent to explore the remotest limits of the east and west. One interesting result of these has been communicated in the relation of two Mahomedan travellers, Wahad and Abuzaid, who in the ninth century penetrated into China; and gave a description of that country; which, though only recently known to us by the translation of Renaudot, must have been the earliest ever communicated to the nations of the west. From Lisbon, also, the brothers Almagrurim sailed, endeavouring to anticipate the discoveries of Columbus, by exploring unknown countries beyond "the sea of darkness." For ten or eleven days they steered westward; but seeing a storm approaching, the light faint, and the sea tempestuous, they dreaded having come to the dark boundaries of the earth. They turned therefore south, sailed twelve days in that direction, and came to an island, which they called Ganam, or the island of birds; but the flesh of these birds was too bitter to be eaten. They sailed on twelve days farther, and came to another island, the king of which assured them that their pursuit was vain: that his father had sent an expedition for the same purpose; but that, after a month's sail, the light had wholly failed, and they had been obliged to return. The adventurers, therefore, made their way back to the coast of Africa, which they reached in three days. The bearings stated seem to point out Madeira and the Canaries as the two islands visited in this expedition.

In regard to the general outline of the earth, the Arabs seem to have closely adhered to ancient theories. They revived the early impression of an ocean, which, like a zone, encompassed the whole earth. This, according to a natural feeling, was characterized as the "Sea of Darkness," an appellation most usually given to the Atlantic; but the northern sea of Europe and Asia, inspiring still more mysterious and gloomy ideas, is called the "Sea of pitchy Darkness." Edrisi has even imagined the land as floating in the sea, and only part appearing above, like an egg in a basin of water. At the same time he divides it into seven seas, fancifully appropriated to the seven climates into which the earth was divided. According to these climates, he describes the earth beginning at the western and proceeding to the eastern extremity; an ill-judged arrangement, which, by a mechanical section, separates portions of territory the most intimately connected. The knowledge of the Arabs was subjected to another and a voluntary limitation. They studiously desisted from all inquiry respecting those blinded nations, whose minds had never been illumined by the light of the Koran. Ibn Haukal even makes it a subject of glory, that he had found nothing worthy of remark among nations who could not be viewed without horror by men who had any innate principles of virtue, wisdom, or religion. These views of the subject greatly restricted their means of knowledge in respect to Europe, and rendered it of little value, unless with regard to those two continents, which their arms had rendered to a great extent Mahomedan.

### SECT. II.—*Asia.*

The Asia of the Arabs comprised a wider range than had belonged to that continent under any former system. China is distinctly marked, partly under the appellation of Seen, and partly under that of Cathay; the former term appearing to comprehend India beyond the Ganges. Lamery, productive in camphor, gold, ivory, and dye-woods, appears by these products to be Sumatra, and mention is even made of Al Djavah. The countries on the Oxus and Jaxartes having become the seat of an extended Moslem empire, of which Samarcand was the capital, Tartary, both eastern and western, was, for the first time, delineated with tolerable accuracy; many of the leading positions, in this hitherto inaccessible part of the continent, were even fixed by astronomical observation; and some positive though faint and indistinct notice appears to have been received respecting the people situated along the shores of the Northern Ocean. Unfortunately the main objects of curiosity and inquiry were Gog and Magog. The authentic application of these names has been observed under the Hebrew system as belonging to a devastating race from the shores of the Euxine and Caspian. Oriental fancy had transformed them into two enormous giants, who had erected an impregnable castle on the borders of Scythia. The efforts made by the court of Bagdad in pursuit of this chimera were very extraordinary. The first expedition was undertaken with the hope of finding it somewhere on the shores of the Caspian; but as their conquests soon embraced the whole of that region, without the slightest trace of this tremendous castle, the more southern country of Bokhara was the next object of search. When that also had been surveyed in vain, the court was involved in much perplexity, and scarcely knew to what ulterior region their view was to be directed. At length one of the caliphs dispatched a mission, with strict injunctions on no account to return without having discovered the castle of Gog. The envoys, according to Edrisi's report, proceeded first along the shores of the

Caspian, then through a vast extent of desert, probably the country of the Kirghises, when they arrived at a stupendous range of mountains, which must have been the Altai. Here they did actually find or pretend to find something which they concluded to be the castle of Gog and Magog. Perhaps they reached some of those ancient monuments which have been found along this range, and gladly embraced this pretext to rid themselves of so troublesome a commission. The picture they drew of it was certainly very highly coloured, according to Oriental taste. The walls were of iron cemented with brass, and a gate fifty cubits high was secured by bolts and bars of enormous magnitude. The minds of the Arabs were thus set at rest, and in all the future delineations of Asia this mighty castle was seen towering at its farthest extremity.

### Sect. III.—*Africa.*

In regard to Africa, the wide-extended settlements of the Arabs afforded them new sources of information. The Mediterranean coast, indeed, as far as Numidia, had been fully explored by the ancients, and had even formed a more intimate part of their political system than it has done of that of the moderns. By the Arabs, however, who had established here a succession of kingdoms, it was described in greater detail than ever; and as the most western of these kingdoms was the flourishing one of Morocco, this region, comprising the nearly unknown tracts of ancient Mauritania, formed an almost entirely new acquisition to knowledge. But their grandest achievement consisted in forming a road across the Great Desert, and in colonising a considerable part of the central regions of Africa. They here founded a series of powerful kingdoms: Ghana, the modern Kano; Tocrur, which we conceive to be Sackatoo; Kuku and Kauga, which recent travellers have found in and near the modern region called Bornou. They described those countries as situated on the Nile of the Negroes, which, contrary to ancient opinions, they represented as rising indeed from the same fountain with the Nile; but as flowing westward across all Africa, and falling into the Atlantic ocean or sea of darkness. At its mouth they placed the island of Ulil, whence salt was conveyed to all the Negro territories, which were entirely destitute of that necessary of life. This view of the subject, though erroneous, was naturally suggested by the course of the rivers within the region with which they were alone intimately acquainted; but we reserve this discussion for a separate chapter, when we propose to give a succinct view of the successive theories respecting this great African river. We shall at present only observe, that, as Tocrur is described to be only eighteen days' journey from the ocean, it is plain that the knowledge of the Arabs did not extend to Tombuctoo; that they knew nothing of the Senegal or Gambia, or the countries upon these rivers; and that the ocean into which they represented the Nile of the Negroes as falling was either a hypothetical feature altogether, or was at least hypothetically connected with all that they knew of the eastern tracts of interior Africa.

---

## CHAPTER II.

### EUROPEAN GEOGRAPHY DURING THE DARK AGES.

Even the imperfect knowledge possessed by the ancient geographers became involved in the general progress of that intellectual darkness, which ensued on the decline of the Roman empire. Europe, overwhelmed with a deluge of barbarism, no longer cultivated art or science; and the rude states into which it was divided had only a vague idea of each other's situation. The advance of this darkness may be observed in an anonymous work, published at Ravenna in the eighth century. The writer presents only confused fragments of the information contained in Ptolemy and Pliny. The coast of India, indeed, the mercantile route to which appears to have been kept open, is still delineated with some degree of correctness. But the whole interior of Asia, from China to Bactriana, is included under the name of "Seric India:" the Caspian re-appears as a gulf of the Northern Ocean; in short, all these distant regions are viewed, in the manner natural to ignorance, as a dim and indefinite expanse, the features of which were all confusedly blended with each other.

The monasteries during the dark ages afforded an asylum for all that remained of ancient knowledge; in them the manuscripts of many of the classic writers were still preserved, though little consulted. The reading aloud of histories, and descriptions of neighbouring, and even of distant countries, formed a mode of beguiling the tedious hours; but these being recorded under the title of "Wonders of the World," and crowded with the most extravagant fables, served rather for the amusement of the fire-side, than for any real instruction.

The missions undertaken for the conversion of the northern pagans were the principal channel by which any geographical knowledge was conveyed. The missionaries did not, at this time, attempt to pass the limits of Europe; but directed their efforts towards the conversion of the Slavonic tribes, who occupied Poland, Prussia and Livonia. Other appears even to have penetrated through the interior of Russia to the White Sea; he undertook also an extensive voyage along the coasts of Norway. The Anglo-Saxon Wilfrid, named by the pope the apostle of the Germans, appears to have been the person who transmitted the most full details relative to the Slavonic tribes. St. Otto, bishop of Bamberg, and Anscaire, a monk of Corbie, penetrated to the kingdoms of Sweden and Denmark; but the details of their mission have not been preserved. Although, however, the monks thus did something to illustrate the geography of Europe, there is sufficient evidence that they laboured, in many instances, under the grossest ignorance; some of them knew not even the capital of their own country, or the cities nearest to their own.

The great monarchs made some efforts to rescue the age from this state of profound ignorance. The two illustrious monarchs, Charlemagne and Alfred, distinguished themselves by their endeavours to promote geography: the former constructed a silver table of large dimensions, on which was delineated the whole world so far as known to him; unfortunately the materials were too costly, and the silver world was soon melted down to supply the necessities of one of its kingdoms. Alfred produced a more valuable monument in a description of the north of Europe, from the best materials which could be then collected, and which forms still the best record of the geographical knowledge of that age. Under the direction of William the Conqueror was drawn up that important document called Doomsday Book, in which the population, the culture, and the taxes paid by each district, are exhibited in the greatest detail. A similar survey of Denmark was made in the thirteenth century, by its sovereign Waldemar II.; and of the Mark of Brandenburg, in the fourteenth century, by the emperor Charles IV.

The Danes and Norwegians, the Northmen as they were called, while under their mighty sea-kings they spread desolation over the maritime districts of Europe, necessarily acquired a very extensive knowledge of its seas and coasts. Such knowledge, though nowhere formed into any regular system, may be traced in the sagas, or metrical histories in which they celebrate the gallant exploits of their countrymen. They were, of course, familiar with all the countries bordering on the Baltic. They knew by conquest Orkney, Shetland, the Hebrides, and the western coast of Ireland. Their fleets reached even the shores of Italy and Sicily. Towards the north, they established colonies in Iceland and Greenland. But the most important discovery of the Northmen was, undoubtedly, America, if their claim to the merit of that discovery shall be admitted to be made good. In the beginning of the eleventh century, Thorwald and Leif, two natives of Iceland, having sailed far to the south-west, came to a country which appeared to them, doubtless by comparison, to be mild and agreeable; the natives were of dwarfish stature, and maintained with them sometimes a hostile, but oftener a friendly intercourse. Finding that the rivers abounded with fish, and that the finest furs could be procured, they and their countrymen repeated their visits; and in 1211, Bishop Eric is said to have repaired thither with the view of converting the natives. The name given to the region is Vinland, from the *vines* growing in it; a feature which certainly occurs to us as very foreign to this part of the world; but, in fact, wild vines are found growing in all the most northerly districts of America. It is highly probable that the continent was not reached by the Icelandic adventurers, and that Vinland was merely a southerly district of Greenland.

---

## CHAPTER III.

### GEOGRAPHICAL KNOWLEDGE DERIVED FROM THE CRUSADES.

The crusades formed a series of events which roused the European mind from its local and limited range, and directed its ken into the regions of another continent. The high-wrought enthusiasm which impelled Europe to pour itself, as it were, in one mass on the eastern world, however blind might have been the zeal which inspired it, was, on the whole, highly beneficial: it drove back the tide of Saracen and Turkish conquest, which might have swallowed up the whole West, and involved it in the same gloom of barbarism and superstition that pervaded the East. Above all, the crusades had a powerful influence in dispelling the mental darkness in which the western regions were involved, and in preparing that light of science and intelligence which was so soon to dawn upon them. The attention of Europe was thus directed to these interesting and memorable regions, known hitherto only by the meagre report of some occasional pilgrims. Not only the Holy Land, with the kingdoms of Jerusalem and Edessa, founded by the victorious crusaders, but the extensive domains belonging to the Saracen and Turkish empires, became objects of inquiry; search was now made in the writings of the ancient geographers, and perhaps some lights were derived even from the Arabian writers. Sanudo compiled a map of the world, annexed to Bongar's "Gesta Dei per Francos," (*fig.* 12.) in which the ideas formed out of the crusading expeditions are fully exemplified: Jerusalem is placed in the centre of the world, as the point to which every other object is to be referred; the earth is made a circle surrounded by the ocean, the shores of which are represented as everywhere nearly equidistant from that spiritual capital, the site of which is, indeed, remarkable for its relation to the three continents, Asia, Europe, and Africa. Persia stands in its proper place; but India, under the modifications of Greater and Lesser, is confusedly repeated at different points, while the river Indus is mentioned in the text as the eastern boundary of Asia. To the north, the

*Fig.* 12.—SANUDO'S MAP OF THE WORLD.

castle of Gog and Magog, an Arabian feature, crowns a vast range of mountains, within which it is said that the Tartars had been imprisoned by Alexander the Great. The Caspian appears, with the bordering countries of Georgia, Hyrcania, and Albania; but these features stand nearly at the northern boundary of the habitable earth. Africa has a sea to the south, stated, however, to be inaccessible, on account of the intensity of the heat. The European countries stand in their due place, not even excepting Russia and Scandinavia; though some oversights are observable in the manner in which the two are connected together.

---

## CHAPTER IV.

### TARTAR GEOGRAPHY.

The revolutions of the north of Asia next attracted the eyes of Europeans to the distant quarters of the world. The roaming tenants of those boundless wilds, known under the ancient name of Scythia, and the modern one of Tartary, have at various periods conquered and desolated the civilized world of Asia. The offspring of Tartar chiefs sat for many centuries on the thrones of Pekin, of Delhi, of Ispahan, and of Constantinople: but, of the Tartar rulers, none ever raised so terrible a name, or established so wide an empire, a Gengis or Zingis; originally an individual chief of the Monguls, he attained the general swa over that warlike race, and led them as conquerors from empire to empire. His first and most signal exploit was the conquest of China; having thence crossed the whole breadth of Asia, he died on the shores of the Caspian. His successors pressed on westward, overran Russia, and penetrated through Poland into Hungary and Silesia; their approach, their rapid movements, and the exaggerated reports of their ravages, struck the nations of Europe with inexpressible terror; this was greatly heightened by the prevailing ignorance of geography, which was such that none knew when they might arrive, or where they might be encountered. The

Danes were thus deterred one season even from going to the herring-fishery, on the coast of Scotland. The Tartars defeated and killed the Duke of Silesia; but a general muster of the German chivalry being made to oppose them, they retreated into the interior of Poland, and even further to the east, leaving only a numerous vanguard; but it was suspected that they were only mustering their strength, again to invade Europe, in more dreadful and destructive array.

Embassy, at this crisis, was deemed the expedient most likely to appease the fury of these dreaded invaders. According to the ideas of the age, the pope appeared the most respectable character, in whose name a mission could be undertaken, and monks the most fitting ambassadors. The choice was injudicious: these envoys, ignorant of the political relations of countries, of the usages of society, and the mode of treating with mankind, obtained no respect in the eyes of the fierce conquerors of Asia. They returned without fulfilling any object of their mission; and if Europe was not again exposed to this barbarous inundation, it owed its safety only to the division of the immense empire of Kaptchak, and the dissensions among its princes. These ambassadors, however, traversed a large portion of the continent, before unknown to Europeans. One mission, indeed, under Ascelin, which met the Monguls on the frontier of Persia, does not communicate any geographical information; but the journey of Carpini, and after him of Rubruquis, (*fig.* 13.) led them through the north of

*Fig.* 13.—MAP OF THE JOURNEY OF RUBRUQUIS.

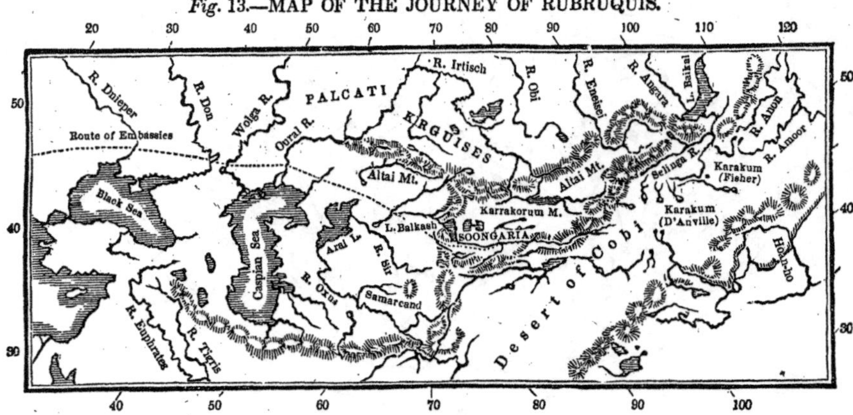


Russia, along the shores of the Black Sea, and the Caspian, and thence into the very heart of the immense plains of interior Asia, where they found the great Tartar capital of Karakorum, the chief seat of the posterity of Zingis. Here the masters of the world, while embassies and presents were waiting them from all the courts of southern Asia, were living in the rudest Scythian fashion, feeding scantily on horse-flesh and mares' milk, roving about in tents, destitute of arts, and occupied only with war and plunder. The Tartars, however, treated with a proud disdain all other nations, over whom they held themselves as commissioned by heaven to rule, while they paid the most abject submission to their own Khan, revering him as the appointed representative of the deity on earth.

Karakorum was found scarcely entitled to the name of city, being little larger than one of the suburbs of Paris, and its most sumptuous edifices scarcely suitable to a European country town. The situation of this capital of so great an empire has been a subject of some controversy. D'Anville places it at a point to the north of China, near the eastern limit of the great desert of Shamo or Cobi, while Fischer fixes it on the Orchon, one of the rivers which unite in forming the Selingha. I have elsewhere endeavoured to show (Discoveries in Asia, I.) that both these positions must be about a thousand miles to the eastward of the real site. It is true that upwards of four months was occupied in passing from the western frontier of Russia to this capital; and the missionaries complain of the grievous rapidity with which they were conveyed. They estimate the daily rate as equal to the distance from Paris to Orleans, or about seventy miles; and this time and route would doubtless be sufficient to carry them to the most eastern extremity of the continent. But whenever they give us the time actually employed in travelling between known points, a rate is found which does not even approach to the above. Two months are spent by Carpini in travelling from the Dnieper to the Volga, and by Rubruquis from the Danube to the Don, "riding post as the Tartars do;" yet neither of these spaces exceeds in direct distance six hundred miles. Then from the Volga to the Ural, which may be two hundred and fifty miles, we have twelve days; while the journey from the Ural to the inland sea of Balkash, or Palcati, occupied above forty-three days. Thus down to that point it required four months to travel not quite eighteen hundred miles. From the Balkash to Karakorum, the journey was performed in three weeks.

Is it possible to suppose that they could in that time have travelled fifteen hundred miles, the space which would be necessary to enable them to reach the Karakorum either of D'Anville or of Fischer? They could not have passed the great table plain of Soongaria, compared by the Oriental histories to a great sea of verdure, and consequently of all others the best fitted to form the central encampment of this great pastoral and military empire. All the geographical indications given by Rubruquis agree with this position; and disagree wholly with the other two. He says all the rivers observed by him flowed to the westward, which is true as far as Soongaria, but directly contrary to what takes place in the other positions, both of which are even placed upon rivers that flow to the eastward. China is said to lie to the south-east, as it does from Soongaria; but from the two other positions it would be directly south. The Kirghises are said to lie to the north, and the Baschkirs to the west; but these, according to the ordinary site, would have been at a distance quite immense, and could have had no relations with Karakorum. The hypothesis which places that city in Mongolia is founded upon the latter having been the original seat of Zingis; but Rubruquis expressly states, that this arrangement had now ceased, and that Tartaria was "the chief and royal city." Such a change was, indeed, almost necessary to an empire which was to embrace at once the East and the West; to hold China in one hand, and Russia in the other.

---

## CHAPTER V.

### VENETIAN GEOGRAPHY.

The republics of Italy, and above all that of Venice, were the states in which the spirit of commerce and inquiry, after being long dormant, revived with the most brilliant lustre. The commerce which they carried on was one which connected them with the most distant regions: they traded in the jewels, the spices, and the fine cloths of India, a country situated at a distance really vast, and which then appeared almost immeasurable. It was not by Venetians, however, or by any Europeans, that the vast intervening space was traversed. They found the Indian commodities in the ports of the Mediterranean or the Black Sea, to which they were brought by the Arabs up the Red Sea, or by the interior caravans across central Asia. It was impossible, however, that they could see these precious and profitable commodities continuing to enter their ports, without feeling some curiosity as to the splendid and beautiful regions whence they came; and, in that age of enterprise, it was likely that some would be impelled to brave even the obstacles presented by this vast unknown space, occupied by people of a hostile and bigoted faith. The Abbé Zurla has collected notices of a considerable number who, actuated by this spirit of discovery, penetrated to a considerable depth into the interior of Asia. But the fame of all these is eclipsed by one, whose travels extended far beyond the rest, and who has always ranked among the greatest of discoverers of any age.

Marco Polo was a noble Venetian, whose family, like many others of the same rank, was engaged in extensive commerce. His uncles, Maffeo and Nicolo, had visited Tartary, and afterwards China, though without leaving any narrative of their observations. The pope, however, being apprized of their discoveries, sent out an ecclesiastical mission, accompanied by the young Marco Polo, then only nineteen. They spent twenty-four years in traversing the most remote regions of Asia. The result of their religious mission is not stated; but they returned laden with precious jewels, with which they dazzled the eyes of their countrymen, by whom they were not at first recognised. Marco being afterwards made prisoner by the Genoese, was persuaded to amuse the hours of confinement by dictating a narrative of his travels, which was read with avidity, and soon translated into all the European languages. He has suffered like many other eminent travellers, under those injurious suspicions which arise in the minds of persons unwilling to believe any event or object which goes beyond the sphere of their ordinary experience. His name even furnished the nickname given to a personage introduced into the comedies of the age, to recite every species of extravagant fable. But modern information has verified in all its most essential points the narrative of Marco Polo, leaving only a slight tincture of that credulity which was characteristic of the age, and is confined to what was told him by others of countries which he did not himself visit. He appears to have first proceeded along the northern shore of Asia Minor, then the seat of a flourishing Turkish dynasty. He passed through Armenia, along the lofty ridges of Ararat, and descending the Euphrates through Curdistan came to Bagdad, no longer the capital of the caliphate, but still a flourishing and civilized city under its Tartar conquerors. He visited the great commercial capital of Ormuz, and thence proceeded eastward through the southern part of Persia by Kerman and Kubbees, across the great salt desert. At length he reached Balkh, which, though still a considerable emporium of central Asia, presented only in its ruined temples and spacious squares the vestiges of its ancient grandeur. Then passing along the borders of Cashmire and the mountain tract of Balashan (Badakshan), celebrated for its mines of rubies, he ascended to the elevated plain of Pamere, forming the summit of that cross branch of the Himmaleh called the Beloor. On this, which appeared to him the highest ground in the world, he felt that difficulty in respiration, and in producing combustion, which is peculiar to the most elevated mountain sites. He afterwards reached the large Tartar cities of Yarkund and Cashgar, and entered on that great eastern table-land which, before and since, has formed the *Terra Incognita* of Asia. He then entered Northern China, which he calls Cathay, and visited its capital Cambalu, his description of which strikingly coincides with that of the modern Pekin. He afterwards visited Mangi or Southern China, and found in its capital, Quinsai, a scene eclipsing all that he had beheld either in Europe or in the East. It is described as a most immense, and, from its splendour and the beauty of its situation, almost a magic city. In fact Hangtchoofoo, which corresponds with Quinsai, though it has long ceased to be the capital of China, is still a very large city, very charmingly situated. From China, Marco Polo passed through the Indian Archipelago, hearing only of Great Java, but visiting Sumatra, which he calls Little Java. He touched at the coasts both of Malabar and Coromandel, and learned many particulars respecting India and its people, which have since been confirmed by modern observation. He returned by the Red Sea to Europe.

A map of the world on a large scale, (*fig.* 14.) by Fra Mauro, which is preserved at Venice, and of which a highly finished copy exists in the British Museum, exhibits a view of the geographical ideas formed by the Venetians, founded upon the information derived from their Asiatic travellers, and prior to the discovery of America.

*Fig.* 14.—MAP OF THE WORLD BY FRA MAURO.

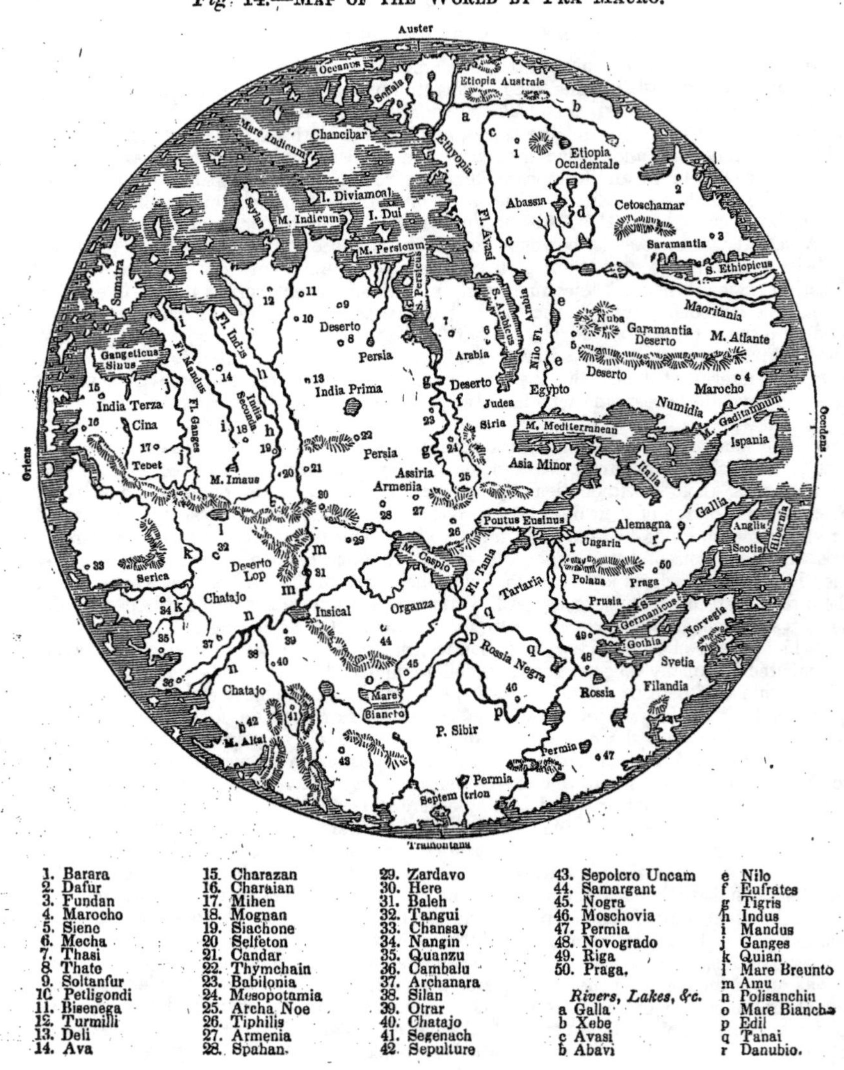


| | | | | |
|---|---|---|---|---|
| 1. Barara | 15. Charazan | 29. Zardavo | 43. Sepolcro Uncam | e Nilo |
| 2. Dafur | 16. Charaian | 30. Here | 44. Samargant | f Eufrates |
| 3. Fundan | 17. Mihen | 31. Baleh | 45. Nogra | g Tigris |
| 4. Marocho | 18. Mognan | 32. Tangui | 46. Moschovia | h Indus |
| 5. Siene | 19. Siachone | 33. Chansay | 47. Permia | i Mandus |
| 6. Mecha | 20 Selfeton | 34. Nangin | 48. Novogrado | j Ganges |
| 7. Thasi | 21. Candar | 35. Quanzu | 49. Riga | k Quian |
| 8. Thato | 22. Thymchain | 36. Cambalu | 50. Praga. | l Mare Breunto |
| 9. Soltanfur | 23. Babilonia | 37. Archanara | | m Amu |
| 10. Petligondi | 24. Mesopotamia | 38. Silan | *Rivers, Lakes, &c.* | n Polisanchin |
| 11. Bisenega | 25. Archa Noe | 39. Otrar | a Galla | o Mare Biancho |
| 12. Turmilli | 26. Tiphilis | 40. Chatajo | b Xebe | p Edil |
| 13. Deli | 27. Armenia | 41. Segenach | c Avasi | q Tanai |
| 14. Ava | 28. Spahan. | 42. Sepulture | b Abavi | r Danubio. |

# BOOK III.

## MODERN GEOGRAPHY.

Geography was now to assume a new aspect, and worlds before unknown were to be comprehended within her domain. Although the Italian states produced, almost exclusively, eminent astronomers, skilful pilots, and hardy navigators, their attention was nearly engrossed by land conveyance, and the navigation of the interior seas of Europe: they did not originate, or even attempt to follow out, any trains of oceanic discovery. The rulers of the exterior coasts of Europe, and especially of the Iberian peninsula, carried off all the prizes in this new and brilliant career. Between 1492 and 1498, the American continent, and the passage to India by the Cape, were discovered by Gama and Columbus: the face of the world was changed; and all the daring and enterprising spirits of the age embarked in this career of discovery, conquest, and commerce.

---

## CHAPTER I.

### DISCOVERY OF AMERICA AND THE EAST INDIES.

The progress of discovery over the globe, when the first steps had been taken, was astonishingly rapid; no cost, no peril, deterred even private adventurers from equipping fleets, crossing the oceans, and facing the rage of savage nations in the remotest extremities of the earth. Columbus had not yet seen the American continent, and the mouth of the Orinoco, when Cabot, of Venetian descent, but sailing under English auspices, discovered Newfoundland, and coasted along the present territory of the United States, probably as far as Virginia. In the next two or three years, the Cortereals, a daring family of Portuguese navigators, began the long and vain search of a passage round the north of America: they sailed along the coast of Labrador, and entered the spacious inlet of Hudson's Bay, which they seem to have mistaken for the sea between Africa and America; but two of them unhappily perished. In 1501, Cabral, destined for India, struck unexpectedly on the coast of Brazil, which he claimed for Portugal. Amerigo Vespucci had sailed along a great part of Terra Firma, and Guiana, and he now made two extensive voyages along the coast of Brazil; services which obtained for him the high honour of giving his name to the whole continent. Grijalva and Ojeda went round a great part of the circuit of the coasts of the gulf of Mexico. In 1513, Nunez Balboa, crossing the narrow isthmus of Panama, beheld the boundless expanse of the Pacific Ocean. These discoveries afforded the impulse which prompted Cortez and Pizarro to engage in their adventurous and sanguinary career; in which, with a handful of daring followers, they subverted the extensive and populous empires of Mexico and Peru. Expeditions were soon pushed forward on one side to Chili, and on the other to California, and the regions to the north. Nearly a full view was thus obtained, both of the great interior breadth of America, and of that amazing range of coast which it presents to the southern ocean.

In the Eastern world, the domain which the papal grant had assigned to Portugal, discovery was alike rapid. Twenty years had not elapsed from the landing of Vasco da Gama, when Albuquerque, Almeida, Castro, Sequeira, Perez, and many others, as navigators or as conquerors, had explored all the coasts of Hindostan, those of Eastern Africa, of Arabia, of Persia; had penetrated to Malacca and the Spice Islands; learned the existence of Siam and Pegu; and even attempted to enter the ports of China. But the characteristic jealousy of that power was soon awakened: the Portuguese embassy was not admitted into the presence of the emperor; and a mandate was issued, that none of the men with long beards and large eyes should enter the havens of the celestial empire. After all these discoveries, the grand achievement yet remained, of connecting together the ranges of eastern and western discovery; and of laying open to the wondering eyes of mankind that structure of the globe, which, though demonstrated by the astronomer, seemed to the generality of mankind contrary to the testimony of their senses.

Magellan, in 1520, undertook, by circumnavigating the earth, to solve this mighty problem: he passed through the straits which bear his name, and crossed the entire breadth of the Pacific. He himself was unhappily killed at the Philippine Islands, but his companions sailed on, and presented themselves to the astonished eyes of the Portuguese at the Moluccas. They arrived in Europe, after a voyage of three years; and it could no longer be doubted by the most sceptical that the earth was a spherical body.

## CHAPTER II.

### EARLY SYSTEM OF MODERN GEOGRAPHY.

The systematic arrangement of the immense regions thus discovered, their adjustment to each other, and to the mass of knowledge previously possessed, was a task as yet beyond the resources of modern geography. It was to Venice that the results of discovery were still referred to be arranged and systematised; but the Venetian geographers, however skilful, laboured under many difficulties. The navigators seldom furnished them with any celestial observations, or even accurate surveys; for which, indeed, science had as yet provided no suitable instruments: they gave only rude delineations, on which the geographer was obliged to trace his uncertain way; most of the countries formerly known were touched at new points, and recognised under new names; and the continents, being made to contain both the old and the new features, were swelled to a preposterous magnitude. The east of Asia was obliged to contain at once the Serica of Ptolemy, the Mangi and Cathay of Marco Polo, and the China of the Portuguese, all as separate empires. The relative site of the two continents of Asia and America, the presentation of the west coast of the one to the east coast of the other, was of course the problem which they had the fewest means of solving. In a series of Venetian maps, preserved in the king's library, the two continents are described throughout their whole extent as either united or separated only by the narrow Strait of Anian: the former delineation is retained even in a map by Bertelli, dated 1571; and in one by Cimertinus (1566), Cathay is placed upon the Gulf of Mexico. The expedition of Magellan, it might be supposed, would already have opened their eyes to the extent of that vast ocean which here intervened: but Magellan scarcely penetrated into the northern Pacific; and his ill-understood course was probably supposed to reach direct from Cape Horn to the Moluccas, which did not interfere with the hypothesis of the two continents meeting each other in a different latitude. The breadth of America, like all unknown spaces, was vastly exaggerated in the early maps; while eastern Asia, by the process above pointed out, was tripled in all dimensions, and thus made to cover an ample portion of the Pacific.

Sebastian Munster, in 1572, produced a delineation of the world, which is cleared of some of the grossest mistakes, and which very tolerably delineates the general outline of the earth. He commits, however, a very discreditable mistake, in taking Ptolemy for his guide in regard to Scotland, and consequently representing that country as extending from west to east; a blunder the more singular, as his forms of Scandinavia and Ireland are liable to little exception. Singular flights of fancy are found in the works of these early geographers. Munster undertakes to describe, not only the surface of the earth, but also its interior: this is stated to be occupied by hell, a huge cavern two or three thousand German miles in length and breadth, and "capable of holding many millions of damned souls." Its existence was proved by the spirits which, in the depth of mineral caverns, as he had been assured by Cornelius Agrippa, often killed instantly a great number of men. The inflammatory gases, which are still frequently producing such disasters, afford certainly no unplausible ground for that strange conclusion.

Ortelius, in the commencement of the sixteenth century, exhibits a remarkable improvement in geography. In his maps, all the parts of the globe begin to assume their real form and dimensions; America and Asia are widely separated, the expanse of the South Sea interposing between them. The south pole is invested with a *Terra Australis Incognita;* which, as it relates to New Holland, is said to rest on the authority of Marco Polo and Barthema, and in regard to the West, on that of Magellan. *Terra del Fuego* is made a portion of this Austral continent: while in lat. 41° S., and long. 10° west of Ferro, is *Promontorium Terræ Australis.* There is a *Terra Septentrionalis Incognita*, nearly as extensive, and seeming to include Nova Zembla. Greenland, however, exists distinct from it. In the interior of Asia, the Caspian, under the appellation of Mer de Bachu, presents the same form and dimensions as in Ptolemy, and receives all the rivers falling really into the Aral, the existence of which seems not to be suspected by this geographer.

Mercator advanced considerably farther, particularly by showing the imperfections of Ptolemy, and the injudicious manner in which the delineations given by him had been mixed with those furnished by modern authority. Mercator retains the Austral continent, including in it *Terra del Fuego.* The lakes of Canada appear for the first time in his maps, as a sea of fresh water, the termination of which is unknown. In Africa, Abyssinia, enormously amplified, is made the principal and almost sole feature; it extends southward to the vicinity of the Cape, comprehending Mosambique, and bordering on Caffraria: the Nile rises only about ten degrees north of the Cape, and consequently traverses all Africa from south to north. With respect to the extreme northern regions, this very learned man has indulged in some extraordinary flights of imagination. The ocean resumes, as in Homer, the character of a river, and is seen rushing by four mouths into the Polar Gulf, to be absorbed, it is said, into the bowels of the earth. On one of the river branches are placed pigmies, scarcely four feet high; a notion suggested, perhaps, by the diminutive stature of the Laplanders and Samoyedes: on another is placed a sort of northern paradise, while the Pole itself, a black and immense rock, towers to a prodigious height.

From the time of Mercator modern geography made rapid and continued progress, till it attained the state approaching towards perfection, in which it now exists: this will appear, when we consider it as astronomical, critical, or statistical; and when we view it in its relation to the different quarters of the globe.

---

## CHAPTER III.

### MODERN ASTRONOMICAL GEOGRAPHY

The astronomical geography of the Greeks rested on a basis exceedingly narrow. It was only at Alexandria, Syene, Rhodes, and a few other leading points, that observations of latitude appear to have been made with a tolerable approach to accuracy; all the others seem to have been only extended from rude itineraries. With regard to the longitudes, although the mode of calculating them by means of eclipses appears to have been understood, only one or two actual observations of this nature are recorded; nor does it seem to have exerted any important influence on geography in general. The Arabs made much greater progress in this department; but, through the separation produced by religious antipathy, their works were scarcely at all known in Europe at the period of the revival of letters. At that time, the pompous display of latitudes and longitudes made by Ptolemy, venerable as it had become from its antiquity, commanded universal assent.

Modern observations have gradually shown the magnitude of Ptolemy's errors. The first great shock to his authority was given by the latitude of Constantinople, which Amurath III. caused to be taken in 1574, when it proved to be two degrees lower than ancient authorities had assigned: the idea of such a difference, however, was treated with derision by some European geographers, till it was confirmed, in 1638, by Greaves, who had been sent to the East by Archbishop Laud. Even then, many, rather than renounce the authority of Ptolemy, believed that a change had taken place in the position of the earth; but this notion became no longer tenable to any extent when Alexandria and other points were found very nearly to coincide with ancient observation. But the great alarm as to the unsoundness of ancient graduation was given in 1635, when M. de Peiresc caused an eclipse of the moon to be observed at Marseilles and at Aleppo; and the difference of longitude, instead of 45° as it had been represented, was found to be only about 30°: such an enormous error, in a dimension which ought of all others to have been most exactly ascertained, shook altogether the blind confidence hitherto reposed in the longitudes of Ptolemy. It was at last perceived, that an entire reform of his graduations must be effected, before geography could rest on any secure basis. Numerous observations upon eclipses now began to be made; but it was then discovered, that this only known mode of ascertaining the longitude was attended with many imperfections. In the observation of fifty-six eclipses, collected by Ricciolus, there were no two, observed in the same two places by the same men, which exhibited the same quantity of longitude: even the same eclipse gave different results, when observed at its four critical periods. As it was found impossible to guard against errors amounting even to three or four degrees, an opinion became prevalent, in the middle of the seventeenth century, that unless for very great distances, even itinerary measures would give the result with greater accuracy; yet Galileo, in 1610, had already pointed out a source of more accurate knowledge: he had in that year discovered three of the satellites of Jupiter, and in his Nuncius Sidereus, pointed out the use to which they might be applied. As his hints did not meet with the attention they merited, he communicated them more fully, in 1631, to Philip II. of Spain; but that bigoted prince was unable to estimate their importance. Galileo met with a more favourable reception from the Dutch, who sent Hortensius and Bleau to Florence, to communicate with him on the subject. They found that great man involved in the storm of persecution which the ignorant bigotry of the Romish church had raised against him: he was thrown into prison; and, after having asked pardon on his knees, for asserting that the earth moved round the sun, obtained only a mitigation of his confinement. This discovery was therefore of little use till 1668, when Cassini published his tables of the revolutions and elipses of these satellites; and three years afterwards, he and Picard made joint observations at Paris, and in the observatories of Tycho Brahe at Copenhagen, by which the longitude of these two important points, which had been the subject of long controversy, was finally fixed.

The French government now took the most active measures for extending geographical observation. Two academicians, Picard and De la Hire, were employed to construct a new map of France upon astronomical principles. In this operation they almost everywhere reduced the previous dimensions, which had been founded upon itinerary measures, and were liable to their usual excess: they took off a whole degree from the western coast between Britany and Gascony, and half a degree from the coasts of Languedoc and Provence; so that on their return, Louis XIV. facetiously reproached them with having robbed him of a part of his kingdom. Other academicians were employed to determine the longitude of Goree on the coast of Africa, and of Guadaloupe and Martinico in the West Indies; and M. Chazelles was sent up the Levant on a similar mission. Expeditions on a much grander scale were dispatched, under Maupertuis to the Arctic circle, and Condamine to the equator The primary object of these was to determine the figure of the earth by the application of the pendulum; but the opportunity was taken of making various observations of longitude and latitude, in regions which had been formerly delineated only by processes of the most vague description.

In the operation of determining the position of places on the globe, important improvements have been made since the above eras. Although there can be no more accurate mode of determining the longitude, than by the eclipses of Jupiter's satellites, these are of too unfrequent occurrence to answer the practical purposes required. Observations of the transits of Mercury and Venus over the sun, of the occultations of the fixed stars, and of what are called lunar distances; processes, the nature of which will be fully explained in the following book, have been employed with success. Nay, to such perfection have chronometers been brought, that, by showing the difference of time between known and unknown points, they serve many of the ordinary purposes of navigation. The voyages undertaken by Capt. Cook, under the auspices of George III., afforded the means not only of exploring many islands and regions of the Pacific and Polar seas, but of throwing much light upon the general structure of the earth. The expeditions of Capt. Parry, and the nautical surveys executed under the direction of the British government by Flinders, King, Owen, and other officers, have gone far to fix the outlines of the great continents. The trigonometrical surveys of France and England, executed within the last thirty years, have almost completed the delineation of those countries. Still this branch of geography remains very imperfect.

---

## CHAPTER IV.

### MODERN CRITICAL GEOGRAPHY.

THE application of a sound criticism to geographical materials cannot be discerned in the rude and infant stages of the science. There is no branch in which the inquirer is so likely to be misled by false and fabulous rumours. The persons from whom he must draw his information,—the navigator, the merchant, the traveller,—make observations often only in a rough and superficial manner, and are swayed in their reports by fancy or vanity. The results of their own observation, or the authentic relations of well-informed persons, are confounded with the most vague rumours which float among the vulgar. Hence almost all the early systems have a portion of truth, mingled with many ideal and fabulous creations. The human mind unwillingly owns its ignorance even to itself. The geographer was reluctant to stop short at the point where his authentic information ceased. Having to delineate a kingdom or a continent, he filled up the really unknown parts from vague rumour, or a fanciful prolongation of those that were known. Whatever object had once found a place was copied mechanically without any inquiry, until modern maps and descriptions became crowded with objects, for the position of which no reason could be assigned.

Strabo, among the ancient geographers, was alone endowed with a critical spirit: but not having a sufficiently ample stock of materials, he exercised his judgment with a blind severity, which appears to have done injustice to several individuals whose exertions in the infant cause of discovery were highly meritorious. This extreme of scepticism, opposite to that of credulity, has indeed thrown unjustly into shade the merits of some of the most eminent discoverers, both ancient and modern. It is only by the collation of numerous authorities, accumulated by time and extended intercourse, that the just medium can be observed, and an equitable sentence pronounced on the reports of each party.

D'Anville, in the eighteenth century, possessed of ample materials, endued with indefatigable patience and sound judgment, undertook to revise the whole system, upon which the world and its regions had been hitherto delineated. The maps of the age were still covered with many obsolete and many fanciful particulars; and large portions of the world, concerning which absolutely nothing was known, were filled with imaginary cities and countries. D'Anville subjected every geographical feature to the strictest revision, and expunged without mercy those which rested on no positive and actual authority. The world, under his hands, assumed a new, and in some respects, a less flattering aspect. Maps, which had before been amply and regularly covered, now exhibited vast and unseemly blanks, which amid the boasted learning of this age, implied a mortifying confession of ignorance. It was impossible, however, to deny, that this was the sound system upon which to proceed Geography rested at last upon sure bases, and proceeded in a regular course of improvement.

Major Rennell, with a skill and sagacity not inferior to that of D'Anville, arranged and illustrated the mass of important materials collected respecting India and Africa; and, though additional contributions of vast importance have in some degree superseded his actual delineation, his example has introduced a still greater precision into the mode of treating the subject.

The comparison of ancient and modern geography, and the tracing of the infant steps of early discovery, constitute an interesting field of inquiry, which has been much cultivated during the present age. Vossius, Bochart, and other learned scholars of the seventeenth century, had exercised much diligence in these researches; but they were not always guided by the soundest judgment, nor were they sufficiently acquainted with the objects actually existing, to be able to recognise them under the early descriptions. Rennell, Vincent, and Mannert, seemed to have carried this research nearly as far as it can go, though without being able to dispel that impenetrable darkness in which some questions are still involved. Gosselin has applied to the science an extent of investigation, and a critical acumen, which, perhaps, none of his predecessors have equalled; but animated by too *Strabonic* a spirit, and seeking to subvert all the bases on which ancient geography had before rested, he has in many instances rather given lustre to bold and ingenious paradoxes, than made solid additions to the science.

---

## CHAPTER V.

### MODERN DESCRIPTIVE AND STATISTICAL GEOGRAPHY.

The mere outline of the globe, its continents and countries, the leading features of mountains, rivers, and cities, their distance and position with respect to each other, constitute all that in the very strictest sense can be called geography. But the mind cannot pass these in review, without feeling its interest excited, in even a superior degree, by other objects, for which these only serve as the basis. The productions of the earth, whether natural or artificial; the treasures hid in its bosom; the animals which roam or are bred on its surface; above all, the men by whom each region is peopled,—their manners, laws, industry, commerce, the revolutions through which they have passed,—these possess the strongest claim on our attention, and are of an importance superior to that of the mere geometrical outline.

The ancients did not occupy themselves with much more than the simple and fundamental bases of the science. The delineation of these formed alone an arduous task, which the geographer was required to accomplish before he could attend to the accessary and ornamental parts. Eratosthenes does not appear to have extended his research beyond those branches which were connected with astronomy. The work of Ptolemy forms a mere naked tabular list of positions, rarely enlivened by any historical or descriptive notices. Pliny does not go much farther. Strabo alone has enriched his work with numerous anecdotes and descriptions which, though not given on any complete or systematic principle, constitute a great portion of its value.

Early modern writers confined themselves, like the ancient geographers, to mere outlines. All the first treatises were formed on the model of Ptolemy; D'Anville, the head of the French school, applied himself solely to the boundaries and positions of countries, which he fixed with a precision before unknown, but without directing much attention to their physical and social relations.

Statistics, the science which treats of kingdoms and states in their relations of population, wealth, productions, commerce, and public force, is, as a separate branch of knowledge, only of recent origin. From the first it had a natural alliance with geography. Busching may be considered as the father of statistical geography: his vast research, strict fidelity, and access to the best sources, enabled him, in his description of Europe, to assemble a mass of information unequalled by any of his predecessors. He has arranged it, however, nearly in the same mechanical manner in which they had drawn the mathematical outlines of the globe. His writings, instead of conveying to the mind striking general views, are loaded with minute and burdensome details, which can be useful only as matter of reference, and would therefore have most properly appeared in the form of a dictionary. His successors have been numerous, and their labours are of similar character and value. Bruns, with regard to Africa, and Ebeling to Asia, continued the series. The great geographical work recently completed by Hassel, Cannabich, Gaspari, and Gutsmuth, in twenty-five octavo volumes, each equal to three or four of ordinary size, comprises, probably, the largest mass of statistical information ever assembled into one work.

The English compilations of Bowen, Guthrie, Salmon, and others of the same school were, perhaps, the first works which embraced nearly all the objects that can give interest to a system of geography; and though indifferently executed, and devoid of any charms of style, they acquired a very extensive popularity. Mr. Pinkerton has executed a work on the same plan, in a superior manner, adding notices of the different branches of natural history, and of the different languages of nations. M. Malte-Brun, by his acquaintance with the eastern and northern literature of Europe, and by an animated and interesting style, has produced a work in some respects superior. M. Balbi has distinguished himself by the industry with which he has collected geographical facts.

We shall now take a view of modern discovery in the remoter quarters of the globe.

## CHAPTER VI.

### MODERN GEOGRAPHY OF ASIA.

ASIA was the first continent which attracted the attention of Europeans, and the journeys of all the early travellers. The enterprise of the Venetians penetrated into some of the wide and perilous tracts of its interior, which the boldest of more modern travellers have in vain essayed to reach. Since the passage of the Cape, the career of discovery has been chiefly maritime. We have seen how rapidly the Portuguese fleets explored all the southern coasts and islands. The eastern shores beyond Japan, as they presented nothing tempting to commercial avidity, were left to be examined by expeditions having science and curiosity for their object. This task was effected by Cook, Perouse, Broughton, and Krusenstern. Jesso, which had figured as a large continental tract, stretching between Asia and America, was reduced by them to its insular form and dimensions, and its separation from Saghalien established; the range of the Kurile islands was also traced; but some questions respecting this very remote and irregular coast remain yet to be solved. Along its northern boundary, beset by the almost perpetual ices of the polar sea, the progress of navigation was slow and laborious. The English and Dutch, the chief maritime states, made extraordinary efforts and braved fearful disasters, in the hopeless attempt to effect by this route a nearer passage to India; but though they penetrated beyond Nova Zembla, they never could pass the formidable promontory of Severovostochnoi, the most northern point of the Asiatic continent. The Russians now claimed for themselves the task of advancing farther. They had most rapidly discovered, and conquered the whole south and centre of Siberia, and reached the eastern ocean at Ochotzk; but the frozen bounds of the north for some time defied their investigation. Proceeding in little barks, however, they worked their way from promontory to promontory. Behring and Tchirikoff, early in the last century, sailed through the Northern Pacific, discovered the American coast, and the straits, bearing the name of the former, which divide Asia from America. Deschnew and Shalaurof, by rounding the Asiatic side of this Cape, and discovering the coast stretching away to the westward, were supposed to have established the fact of the entire separation of the two continents. There still remained a portion of coast on the side of Asia, which, it was alleged, might, by an immense circuit, have connected the two together; but the late voyage of Baron Wrangle seems to have removed every ground on which such conjecture could rest, and to have established beyond doubt or dispute, the existence of Asia and America as continents altogether distinct.

Respecting the interior of Asia, the British obtained much additional information from India, after they became undisputed masters of that region. This information was in many respects only a revival of ancient knowledge. The mountain boundary of India was traced, and found to rise to a height before unsuspected. The sources and early courses of the Ganges and the Indus, were found in quarters quite different from those which modern geography had long assigned to them. The mountain territories of Cabul and Candahar, the vast sandy plains of Mekran, were illustrated by the missions of Elphinstone and Pottinger; while Turner and Moorcroft penetrated into the high interior table-land of Thibet. Recent and authentic information has also been furnished by Burnes respecting Bochara and Samarcand, those celebrated capitals of the early masters of Asia: but there remains still a great central Terra Incognita, respecting which our information rests chiefly upon the desultory and somewhat clouded reports of Marco Polo, and the meagre narrative of Goez; though some important and more precise information has recently been afforded by the researches of Humboldt and Klaproth.

---

## CHAPTER VII.

### MODERN GEOGRAPHY OF AFRICA.

AFRICA, more than any other quarter of the globe, has defied the research, and humbled the pride, of modern inquiry. After accurate surveys had been made of the remotest oceans and shores, this continent, placed almost in view of Europe, still baffled every attempt to penetrate the mighty secrets which it held in its bosom. This vast and unbroken region enclosed by huge expanses of desert, and occupied by barbarous and predatory tribes, for a long period proved fatal to every daring mortal who attempted to penetrate into its depths. The Portuguese, however, at an early period, made very extraordinary exertions, impelled by the odd chimera of Prester John, a Christian prince, whom they expected to find in the interior. With this view they explored Abyssinia, of which they vastly exaggerated the dimensions, making it extend even to the Cape, in the vicinity of which, according to their idea, the Nile took its origin. In their progress also along the western coast, they sent repeated embassies into the interior, to discover, if possible, the abode of Prester John; and though that favourite object always eluded their search, they appear to have reached on one occasion as far as Timbuctoo, and learned at Benin some particulars respecting the great interior kingdom of Ogane or Ghana.

The great interior river called by Ptolemy the Niger, was the object which from the first excited the chief interest in respect to the African interior. All the early European navigators, on coming to the two broad estuaries of the Senegal and Gambia, concluded that one or both formed the termination of the long course which the Niger had been described as taking across the entire breadth of Africa. For several centuries the European nations, intent only on the trade in slaves, merely touched at different points of the coast, to which those unhappy victims were brought down by large caravans. In the beginning of the seventeenth century, however, the French and English having respectively settled on the Senegal and Gambia, were tempted, by the report and view of the gold brought from the interior, to push up these rivers and endeavour to reach Timbuctoo. They had not ascended far, when they became sensible that the extraordinary magnitude and distant origin ascribed to both was altogether chimerical. They were traced so near to their sources as to be little more than rivulets; yet still the explorers were far from Timbuctoo, and from the great central plain, through which the main course of the Niger was understood to flow. At the same time, notices were transmitted to the French geographers Delisle and D'Anville, which led them to infer that there was in that region another and greater river, which flowed eastward towards the interior, and of which they were unable to learn the termination. Yet this delineation of these great geographers had been in a great measure lost sight of, even among their own countrymen.

The information obtained by the African Association at first tended to confirm this impression. The persons who had crossed the Niger at the most eastern part of the central African plain, described it to Mr. Lucas as flowing westward: but these conflicting statements were silenced by the first expedition of Mr. Park, who at Sego beheld it a broad and majestic stream, flowing through the plain of Bambarra from west to east, and directing its course into the depths of interior Africa. From that time, the termination of the Niger became the grand problem which the science and the enterprise of the age were exerted to solve. A boundless field was open to conjecture. By one theory, the Niger was lost in some great inland seas or lakes of the interior; by another, it bent to the south and west, and reached the Atlantic either in the Gulf of Benin, or by the estuary of the Congo; lastly, it rolled to the eastward, till, under the name of the Abiad, or White River, it became the principal head of the Nile of Egypt. At last, by the persevering exertions of the British government, an expedition fairly succeeded in penetrating into the hitherto unknown interior of Africa, and in throwing a wonderful addition of light upon its structure. This mission, however, broke up the grand question. They discovered, flowing through the great African plain, not one river in one direction, but several in different directions; all of which, it appears, have been considered at different times, and under different circumstances, as the Niger. These rivers are four:—1. The Senegal, considered by the Arabians and modern Europeans as the embouchure by which the Niger entered the ocean. 2. The Joliba, which ever since it was visited, and its course ascertained, by Park, has been fixed in the mind of Europeans as the only Niger; though probably not known to any of the ancient geographers who used that term. 3. The Quarrama, or river of Zirmie, first discovered by the late mission, flowing from east to west, and falling into the Joliba or Quolla. This is evidently the Arabian Nile of the negroes, on or near which are situated all their great cities—Ghana, now known under the name of Cano; Berissa, under that of Bershee; Tocrur, as I apprehend, under that of Sackatoo. 4. The Yeou, flowing eastward into the great lake of Bornou, and which appears to have been the western Nile of Herodotus, visited by the Nasamonian adventurers from Tripoli. The mission also ascertained the site of the kingdom of Bornou, which had been very erroneously placed; they discovered the fertile kingdom of Loggun, perhaps the Cauga of Edrisi, and the great mountain region of Mandara, which appears to be the *Mons Mandrus* of Ptolemy. The subsequent expedition of Clapperton from the Gulf of Benin showed the connexion between the Atlantic coast and the interior, and completed the diagonal section made across the greatest breadth of the African continent. It showed also the continuity of large and populous kingdoms extending in this direction: Eyeo, the Gago of Leo and the early geographers; Zegzeg, with its large capital Zaria; Nyffe, the most industrious of the African states; Boussa, Koolfu, and other flourishing cities. The Niger of Park was here seen holding a southerly direction towards the Gulf of Benin; but it was reserved for Lander finally to solve the grand problem by tracing the Niger down to its termination in the Gulf of Benin. This discovery, with that of its numerous tributaries, opens to commerce the prospect of being able to penetrate into the most interior and finest regions of the African continent.

Among partial but important contributions to the knowledge of Africa, may be mentioned the observations of Bruce and Salt in Abyssinia; those of Brown in Darfur; of Waddington and Caillaud in the upper part of the Nile; and, lastly, of Lichtenstein, Campbell, and Burchell, upon the countries which lie in the interior northward from the Cape of Good Hope. Yet a vast field still remains for future discovery. In particular, all the southern interior, from the equator nearly to the Cape, has scarcely been the subject even of rumour. The sources of the Nile, after the search of so many ages, are yet unexplored: as well as that wide range of territory which intervenes between it and the series of rivers which we have just noticed as assuming the name of Niger. The continuity and structure also of that vast chain of mountains, which, according to recent travellers, appears to cross Africa at its greatest breadth, and gives rise to so many mighty streams, have yet by no means been completely traced.

---

## CHAPTER VIII.

### MODERN GEOGRAPHY OF AMERICA.

THE discovery of America, as formerly observed, was made in the first instance with extraordinary rapidity. The thirst for gold and the spirit of adventure urged nation after nation to explore its coasts, and penetrate its interior. Within twenty years was formed a full and tolerably precise outline of the whole eastern coast, from the mouth of Hudson's Bay to the Straits of Magellan. The conquest of Cortez, of Pizarro, and of their immediate successors, soon conveyed a pretty accurate idea of the western coast of South America, of Mexico, and even of the peninsula of California. But the northern regions, stretching into the ices of the Pole, presented barriers of a formidable description, which long baffled the utmost efforts of navigators. America on this side resisted for a longer time the attempts to complete its delineation than any other continent.

To explore the north-western coast seems to have been an undertaking properly belonging to Spain, the possessor of all the vast and opulent regions which extend along the Pacific. Recent notices have shown that they did not neglect that inquiry, for Cortez and several of the other viceroys sent expeditions along this coast, to which they gave the name of New-Mexico. The Spaniards, however, as usual, shrouded in deep mystery even these limited discoveries, and were long able to prevent the other nations of Europe from visiting this coast, the most remote and inaccessible of any in the circuit of the globe. Europeans, therefore, were not aware of the vast breadth to which this continent expanded towards the north. They rather supposed that, like South America, it narrowed to a point or cape, upon passing which the navigator would enter upon the expanse of the Pacific, and might bear down upon Japan, China, and the East Indies. The commercial nations therefore, made vigorous and almost ceaseless efforts to turn this point, and effect, as they imagined, a nearer and more direct route into the eastern seas.

The English took the lead in this important career. Under the reign of Queen Elizabeth, Frobisher and Davis made each three successive voyages. One discovered the entrance into Hudson's Bay, the other found the entrance into the great sea which bears the name of Baffin's Bay; but, partly arrested by the well known obstructions to which these seas are liable, partly diverted by a chimerical search after gold, they could not penetrate beyond the numerous islands and inlets by which these entrances are beset. Hudson, in 1610, steered a bolder course, and entered the vast bay, which has received its appellation from that great navigator, who there unfortunately terminated his adventurous career. The treachery of a ferocious and mutinous crew exposed him on these frozen and desolate shores, where he miserably perished. Sir Thomas Button followed in 1612, and finding himself in the middle of this capacious basin, imagined himself already in the Pacific, and stood full sail to the westward. To his utter dismay he came to the long continuous line of shore which forms the western boundary of Hudson's Bay. He expressed his disappointment by giving to the coast the name of "Hope checked." Bylot and Baffin, who followed three years after, were stopped by the ice at Southampton Island. Baffin, however, made afterwards a more important voyage, in which he completely rounded the shores of that great sea which bears his name, and which, appearing to him to be inclosed on all sides by land, has been denominated Baffin's Bay. The error involved in this appellation deterred subsequent navigators from any further attempt; for Baffin, in passing the great opening of Lancaster sound, had concluded it to be merely a gulf. From that period the English navigators, though they ceased not to view this object with ardour, hoped to fulfil it only by the channel of Hudson's Bay. In 1631, two vessels were sent thither under Fox and James. The latter, entangled in some of the southern bays, returned after dreadful sufferings from the cold of the winter; but the former, quaintly calling himself North-west Fox, explored a part of that great opening called Sir Thomas Roe's Welcome, which appeared now to afford almost the only hope of a passage; but he stopped short at a point which he termed "Fox's farthest." Under Charles II. a company was formed for the purpose of settlement and commerce in Hudson's Bay, and engaged to make the most strenuous exertions to discover western passage; but it is believed that the only exertions really made by the Company ended to prevent any such discovery. Middleton, an officer in their service, was sent out in 1741, sailed up the Welcome, and believed himself to have discovered that the head of that channel was completely closed. He was strongly charged with having received a high bribe from the Hudson's Bay Company to stifle the discovery, and Moor and Smith were sent out in the following year with the most sanguine hopes; but when they returned with out having effected any thing, the public expectations were greatly abated. It became the general impression that America, on this side, formed a mass of unbroken land, and that the long sought passage had no existence.

New views of the extent and form of the northern extremities of America were opened by the discoveries of Cook, corroborated by those of some other English navigators in the Northern Pacific. It appeared that America there stretched away to the north-west, till it reached a breadth equal to one-fourth part of the circumference of the globe. Cook penetrated, indeed, through the strait which bounds the continent and separates it from Asia; but the coast appeared there extending indefinitely north; and it became a general impression that America formed a huge unbroken mass of land approaching the Pole, and perhaps reaching that ultimate point of the globe. This belief received a sudden shock from Hearne's voyage down the Copper Mine River, and his discovery of the sea into which it fell, in a latitude not higher than that of the north of Hudson's Bay. Soon after, Sir Alexander Mackenzie traced also to the sea another river twenty degrees farther west. There was now a strong presumption that a sea bounded the whole of America to the north, and that there really was such a passage as had been so long sought, and might be found, were it not too closely barred by ice and tempest. The British administration, animated with an active and laudable zeal in the cause of discovery, determined that no possible effort should be omitted by which this important and long agitated question might be brought to a final decision.

A series of exploratory voyages was now begun. Capt. Ross, in 1818, made the circuit of Baffin's Bay, and returned with the belief that no opening existed: Lieut. Parry, second in command, formed a different judgment, and having satisfied the Admiralty as to his grounds of belief, was sent out with the command of a new expedition. In this memorable voyage, Capt. Parry penetrated through Lancaster Sound, which he found to widen gradually, until it opened into the expanse of the Polar Sea. He did not touch on any part of the American coast, but found parallel to it a chain of large islands; and his progress through these was arrested, not by land, but by straits and channels encumbered with ice. In consideration of these obstacles, his next attempt was made through Hudson's Bay, by the yet imperfectly explored channel of the Welcome. Struggling through various obstacles, he reached at length a point considerably beyond that where Middleton had stopped, and found a strait opening from Hudson's Bay into the Polar Sea. This strait was, however, so narrow, and so completely blocked with ice, that there appeared no room to hope that it would ever afford an open passage. Capt. Parry was therefore again sent out in his first direction; but he made no material addition to his former discoveries. Meantime a land journey, under Capt. Franklin, following in the footsteps of Hearne, reached the sea, and discovered a considerable extent of the hitherto unknown northern coast of the American continent. A tolerably clear glimpse was thus obtained of its extent and boundaries; and the zealous efforts of government were employed to verify the whole by actual survey. A second expedition under Capt. Franklin extended this survey over three-fourths of this boundary coast, and reached beyond the 149th degree of longitude. Meantime an expedition, under Captain Beechy, sent to meet Captain Franklin from the westward, passed the Icy Cape of Cook, and arrived at nearly 156° W. longitude; between which point and Captain Franklin's farthest limit there intervened only 7°, or 150 miles.

The belief was hence entertained, that the whole coast extended in a line not varying much from the 70th degree of latitude; but the important expedition which Captain Ross has just achieved through so many difficulties, proves the existence of a large peninsula, extending as far north as 74° N. latitude. It remains still probable that a naval passage may exist farther north, in the line of Captain Parry's first voyage. But the encumbering ice is so thick, and so wedged into various straits and channels, that probably no vessel will ever be able even once to work its way through; and certainly a ship could never set out with any assurance of thus finding its way from the Atlantic into the Pacific. Britain has, however, reaped an ample share of glory in contributing so essentially to delineate the boundaries and dimensions of this great and important continent.

---

## CHAPTER IX.

### MODERN GEOGRAPHY OF THE AUSTRAL SEAS AND ISLANDS.

More than half the surface of the globe, including long groups of islands and vast expanses of ocean, remained unexplored, even after regular naval routes had been formed round the Cape of Good Hope, and Cape Horn; yet there soon arose the belief of an Austral continent, as extensive and as abounding in wealth as that which had been discovered by Columbus. An ideal balance was fancied, which it was supposed must exist between the lands of the northern and those of the southern hemispheres; and the more disproportionate the extent of sea which existed in the known parts of the latter, the greater it was supposed must be the mass of southern continent which was to establish this ideal, imaginary balance. In all the early maps, a huge continental mass encircles the Antarctic pole, and presents to the great ocean a continuous circuit of shore reaching round the globe: the above analogies were doubtless aided by discoveries made on great insular tracts of the South Sea, so partial that they might be mistaken for promontories, or portions of a great mass of Antarctic land.

The Portuguese, so long the most skilful and intrepid navigators of the ocean, appear to have been the first who threw any light upon this fifth and most remote portion of the earth; in less than twenty years after their passage of the Cape they had reached the most extreme islands of the Oriental Archipelago, including Java and the Moluccas, and appear even to have observed some parts of the coast of New Guinea. There are no records of their having proceeded farther; but maps have been found in the British Museum, and other collections, which exhibit an extensive land to the south of Java, under the title of Java Major, on which occur a number of names, some of them Portuguese: one of these maps, partly translated into French, has the "*Côte des Herbages*," a name somewhat curiously coinciding with Botany Bay. None of these discoveries, however, have been embodied in any known narration.

The Spaniards also, during their early and adventurous career, made strenuous efforts to explore the southern seas: Magellan, as already observed, by his first circumnavigation of the globe, effected a grand step in geographical discovery. Alvaro Mendana, in 1568, sailed from Lima, and, after crossing the breadth of the Pacific, discovered a group of large maritime lands, to which, from a chimerical reference to Ophir, he gave the name of "Islands of Solomon:" they appear to be part of that great group which forms the outer range of Australasia. Mendana set out on a second voyage, and reached the same quarter, but, by some fatality, could not again find the islands formerly discovered. Quiros made a still more important expedition; he passed through the Polynesian group; and Sagittaria, one of the islands discovered by him, appears clearly identified with Otaheite; he terminated his voyage, like Mendana, among the exterior islands of Australasia; and with him expired the spirit of Spanish enterprise.

The Dutch, when they had expelled the Portuguese from Java and the Spice Islands, and had established in them the centre of their Indian dominion, were placed in such close proximity with New Holland, that it was scarcely possible for a great maritime nation to avoid extending their search to that region. Van Diemen, the Dutch governor of India about the middle of the seventeenth century, greatly promoted this object, and sent successive vessels to explore the coast of New Holland. Hertog, Carpenter, Nuytz, and Ulaming made very extensive observations on the northern and western shores, but found them so dreary and unpromising, that no settlement of any description was ever attempted. Abel Tasman, however, went beyond his predecessors; he reached the southern extremity of this great mass of land, to which he gave the name of Van Diemen, without discovering it to be an island: he then sailed across, surveyed the western coast of New Zealand, and returned home by the Friendly Islands. This important range of discovery was not followed up; it refuted, however, the delineation by which New Holland had been made part of the imagined Austral continent. In the newly arranged charts, that continent still remained, but with its position shifted farther to the south, and New Zealand probably contributing to form part of its fancied outline.

The English nation, by the voyages of several navigators, and particularly of Cook, secured the glory of fully exploring the depths of the great Pacific. The previous voyages of Byron, Wallis, and Carteret had already made known some of the interesting groups of islands with which its vast surface is studded. Cook fully traced the great chains of the Society Islands, and of the Friendly Islands; he discovered and surveyed the eastern coasts of New Holland and Van Diemen's Land. He settled the form and relations of New Zealand, New Caledonia, and the other great Australasian lands and islands. This side he passed thrice the Antarctic circle, and ranging along the yet unvisited borders of the southern pole, solved, by refuting, the famous modern hypothesis of an Austral continent. He navigated also through the northern Pacific, observed carefully the group of the Sandwich Islands, and established, in the manner before pointed out, the relation between the continents of Asia and America. Many eminent navigators, among the French, La Perouse, Marchand, D'Entrecasteaux; among the Russians, Kotzebue and Krusenstern; among the English, Vancouver and Beechey, followed; and, though the grand prizes of discovery had been carried off, found still some gleanings in so vast a field. The circumnavigation of the globe has ended in becoming a mere trading voyage, which conveys neither name nor glory to him by whom it is achieved. Captain Weddell, however, has lately, in New South Shetland, found a tract of land situated nearer to the Antarctic pole than any previously supposed to exist.

New Holland, much the most extensive of the lands belonging to the southern hemisphere, and rendered doubly interesting by its recent relations with Europe, has formed the theatre of late southern discoveries. Bass, in an open boat, found the strait which bears his name, separating New Holland from Van Diemen's land, and making the latter a separate island. Baudin and Flinders, contemporaneously employed by the French and English nations, made a continuous survey of the vast circuit of its coasts, which had been before touched only at partial points. At a later period, Freycinet made some additional observations; and King found still a great extent of north and north-western coast to survey for the first time. More recently, the discovery of Swan River and its shores promises to redeem the reproach of sterility which had been attached to the whole western coast of this continent: the interior on the eastern side also, though guarded by steep and lofty barriers, has been penetrated to a considerable depth, and found to contain extensive plains traversed by large rivers. Still the explored tracts form only a small proportion of the vast surface of this southern continent.

# PART II.

## PRINCIPLES OF GEOGRAPHY.

AMONG the various branches of human knowledge there is so intimate a connexion, that no science can be truly said to be independent of all others. Some, indeed, may be regarded as primary, because, to a certain extent, they have had an independent existence, and because other sciences have sprung from them. Such, for example, are arithmetic and geometry, the prolific parents of all the branches of modern mathematics. Other sciences, again, are connected by collateral relationship, in respect of their affording mutual aid: and in this manner all the branches of human knowledge depend one on another, each repaying the advantages which it has received.

The subject of this treatise, GEOGRAPHY, which in common with other sciences owes its origin to the wants of man, joined with his inherent desire of knowledge, has arrived at its present state of improvement by the aid of several sciences, and of a very great number of the arts which are the fruit of human ingenuity. It is more particularly indebted to the mathematical sciences, either directly, as furnishing rules and methods by which the magnitude of the earth, its figure, and the position of the different parts of its surface, may be determined; or indirectly, inasmuch as it has been improved by astronomy, navigation, and other sciences which owe their perfection to the mathematics. To the arts its obligations are innumerable: for every step of progress which has been made in the construction and management of ships, in the fabrication of mathematical, optical, and nautical instruments, and in the collateral arts on which these depend, has contributed to the advancement of geographical knowledge.

The doctrines of geography strongly support, and have a close affinity with, those of astronomy. It is only by the application of this latter science that we have been able to discover the true figure of the earth, and its magnitude: and some of the most important divisions of the earth's surface are marked out by astronomical phenomena. On the other hand, an exact knowledge of the figure and magnitude of the earth is of the highest importance in the explication of the more recondite doctrines of astronomy. Hence, while the doctrines of astronomy involve the principles of geography, it holds equally true that the principles of geography can only be understood by a due application of some of the more simple theories of astronomy.

The science of geology has, if possible, a still more intimate connexion with the description of the earth. While astronomy delineates the form and movements of that planet, and its relation to other bodies in the universe, geology describes the materials which compose its surface, and the order in which they are arranged, with the composition and phenomena of the surrounding atmosphere. The various inequalities into which it is formed, the distinction of land and sea, with their origin and effects, come all within the sphere of this important science.

The organized and living beings which cover the surface of our planet, form a most interesting feature in its delineation. For the support and nourishment of these, the whole of its vast structure was originally destined. In taking a survey of this interesting range of objects, we may begin with plants; then ascend to animals; and, lastly, to man, who holds the chief rank in the constitution of this lower world.

Three divisions, comprehending each a separate book, will, on the grounds now stated, comprehend the Principles of Geography: these are—I. Astronomical Principles. II. Geological principles. III. Geography considered in relation to the organized living and rational natures which cover the surface of the earth.

# BOOK I.

## ASTRONOMICAL PRINCIPLES.

### CHAPTER I.

#### GENERAL VIEW OF THE PHENOMENA OF THE HEAVENS, APPARENT MOTIONS, FIXED STARS, PLANETS, &c.

THE succession of day and night brings under our observation the sun, the moon, and an innumerable multitude of luminous bodies, which appear like points on the concave surface of the heavens. Of these the sun and the moon are the most remarkable. The sun at all times presents to us a circular disc: the disc of the moon is also at certain periods circular, but she undergoes a succession of changes in the appearances of her luminous part, which are denominated *phases*. With regard to the distances of the sun and moon from this earth, we are certain that they are very remote; for we observe that their apparent magnitude is not sensibly affected by any change in our local position. We may with probability suppose the stars to be bodies of the same nature with the sun and moon, appearing smaller only because they are at a greater distance.

The apparent motion of the heavens from east to west about a fixed point in the northern quarter of the sky, as seen in this country, is a phenomenon quite familiar to every one. If we change our position on the earth by going always south, this fixed point appears to descend, and at last it sinks below the horizon: but we now perceive that there is another fixed point in the southern region of the heavens, exactly opposite to the former, about which the diurnal motion is also in like manner performed. These two points are the NORTH and SOUTH, or the ARCTIC and ANTARCTIC POLES of the heavens.

From what we see on the earth's surface, we learn by experience that *the real and apparent motions of bodies may be very different*. An observer in a vessel carried along by the current of a river, will feel disposed to believe himself at rest; and then, if he were to judge from appearances, he would suppose that trees and fixed objects on the banks were in motion, because of the apparent change in their relative positions. Hence we may infer, that we cannot judge immediately respecting the absolute motions of the heavenly bodies from their apparent motions. It has only been by a series of nice observations, and the application of the doctrines of mathematics, that the former have with absolute certainty been deduced from the latter.

The general phenomena of the apparent motions have, however, been discovered by the ordinary observation of mankind from the remotest ages. To a spectator in any place of the earth, the whole system of the celestial bodies appears as if placed on the surface of a concave sphere, the centre of which is the place where he stands; and this sphere appears to revolve daily on an ideal line which passes through the poles of the heavens, and is called the AXIS of the world. Although the supposition that the celestial bodies are all situated in the surface of a sphere, of which the eye is the centre, be perfectly consistent with the appearance of the heavens, it is easy to understand that this may be a consequence of their immense distances. To an observer standing on an extensive plain, objects very remote around him, though at unequal distances, would appear in the circumference of a circle having his eye in the centre.

Besides the diurnal motion of the heavenly bodies, which is common to them all, we discover that some of them have *peculiar motions by which they change their apparent places in respect of one another*. Thus we see the MOON in the course of about a month describe a circle quite round the heavens from west to east. The SUN also appears to change his position daily, and to go round the heavens from west to east in a year. It is in consequence of this peculiar motion of the sun, that we find different stars at different seasons of the year set immediately after him, or rise immediately before him; and that the appearance of the heavens through the course of the year is continually changing.

From the remotest antiquity *five* stars had been observed to change their position; and in modern times five others have been discovered. These "wandering stars" have been appropriately denominated PLANETS; and, generally speaking, they can be seen at all times, except when their feeble light is rendered insensible by the effulgence of the sun. The planets have received particular names, and are distinguished by particular characters; these are Mercury ☿, Venus ♀, Mars ♂, Vesta ⚶, Juno ⚵, Ceres ⚳, Pallas ⚴, Jupiter ♃, Saturn ♄, Uranus ♅.

There are other luminous bodies having a proper motion, which are seen for a short time and afterwards disappear. Their existence, however, is permanent. They are distinguished from the planets by their being visible only for a short period, and also by a train of light proceeding from them on one side, forming a *tail;* these bodies are called COMETS. Their number is not known, but it appears to be very considerable.

Besides the sun, moon, planets, and comets, there are other luminous bodies visible every clear night; these retain always the same position in respect of each other, and for this reason are denominated **FIXED STARS.** Their apparent motion about the axis of the celestial sphere is perfectly uniform, and a complete revolution is performed in about 23 hours 56 minutes.

By the permanence of the relative situations of the fixed stars on the concavity of the celestial sphere, we are enabled to determine the apparent motions of the other heavenly bodies. Of these the motions of the sun and moon are the most conspicuous and simple. The motions of the planets appear more complicated, and are considerably different from one another. This dissimilarity might well lead to a conjecture, that the real motions of the heavenly bodies are very different from the apparent motions, and that these last are modified by the real motion of the earth. This conjecture we shall afterwards find fully verified.

All the heavenly bodies which this general survey has brought under our notice, with their motions and mutual relations, form the subject of **ASTRONOMY**, which of all the natural sciences presents the most extensive series of discoveries. By observing for ages, and determining with exactness, the positions of the sun, moon, and stars; by tracing and measuring with precision their various motions; and by employing all the resources of mathematical science in investigating the constant laws to which these motions are subject, the human mind has succeeded in passing from the first cursory view of the heavens, to that comprehensive survey by which, in the present state of astronomical science, we contemplate the past and future states of the system of the universe.

---

## CHAPTER II.

### THE HEAVENS AS SEEN THROUGH THE TELESCOPE.

FROM the discovery of the telescope, and its application to the purposes of astronomy, a new era may be dated in that science. The number of stars visible to the naked eye is about three thousand, which appear scattered over the concave surface of the heavens. Even in the clearest night, and in the absence of the moon, seldom more than two thousand are seen at once. They are not distributed indiscriminately over the heavens, but are disposed in groups, which from the remotest antiquity have received distinct names, and these have been employed to facilitate the description of the heavens, and the reference to any particular star. The ancients imagined the figures of various personages of their mythology, and of animals, &c. to be traced on the concave surface: these figures they called *constellations*, and considered a group of stars to belong to each. To some of the brighter stars, and to those more remarkable for their position, proper names have been given.

The distinction founded on the different degrees of brightness of the fixed stars, is the most obvious which occurs to the spectator while his vision is unassisted by the telescope, and has accordingly been employed for the purpose of classifying them. The stars visible to the naked eye have been, on this principle, arranged under six *magnitudes*. The brightest are reckoned to be of the first magnitude, the next in brightness of the second, and so on to the sixth magnitude. The arrangement of the stars has been still farther facilitated by combining the principle of this last-mentioned arrangement with the method of constellations. In maps of the heavens and on celestial globes the constellations are delineated, and the stars in each constellation are marked with the letters of the Greek alphabet according to their degrees of brightness.

The use of the telescope has greatly increased *the number of visible stars;* and has at the same time discovered to us many particulars before unknown respecting those that are visible to the naked eye. Many of the stars which to unaided vision appear single, are found, when observed through a telescope of high magnifying powers, to consist of two, sometimes of three or more stars extremely near to one another. Seven hundred of these multiple stars were observed by Sir William Herschel, and the number has been increased by the joint labours of his son and Sir James South, also by the German astronomer Struve. In some of them the small stars are different in brightness and in the colour of their light. Thus $\alpha$ Herculis is double; the larger of the stars is red, the smaller blue: $\varepsilon$ Lyræ is composed of four stars; three white, and one red: $\gamma$ Andromedæ consists of two stars very unequal, the largest a reddish white, the smallest a sky-blue inclining to green. Some single stars evidently differ in their colour: Aldebaran is red, Sirius of a brilliant white.

Nebulæ are small luminous spots of a cloudy appearance and irregular shape, seen in many places of the heavens. The most remarkable appearance of this kind is the Galaxy, or Milky Way, which encompasses the whole heavens, and is visible to the naked eye. The Sword of Orion contains a beautiful nebula. Two occur in the head of the Great Bear, one of an oval shape the other round like a comet without a tail. Viewed through a telescope of great magnifying power, these luminous spots are resolved into a multitude of small stars, distinctly separate, but apparently very near one another, whose light being blended together produces the luminous appearance. In a portion of the Galaxy, about fifteen degrees in length, and two in breadth, Dr. Herschel found no fewer than fifty thousand stars large enough to be distinctly counted. The number of nebulæ is very considerable. Herschel discovered two thousand; before his time only one hundred and three were known.

Continued observation has shown that *the fixed stars are not altogether exempt from change.* Several stars mentioned by the ancient astronomers are no longer visible, while some are now seen by the naked eye which are not in the ancient catalogues. Some stars have suddenly appeared, and after having been seen for a short time have ceased to be visible. In 1572 a new star appeared in Cassiopeia's Chair; and in 1604 another appeared in Serpentarius. These stars did not change their places: but having gradually increased in brilliancy, until they exceeded Venus or Jupiter in brightness, and were even seen in the day-time, they diminished in the same gradual manner, and in a few months entirely disappeared. Some stars are observed to have periodical changes of brightness. Of this description is Algol, or β Persei: when brightest it is of the second, and when least bright of the fourth magnitude. It goes through all its changes of lustre in four days, twenty-one hours. Other stars like β in the Whale, have gradually increased in brilliancy; or, like δ in the Great Bear, have continually diminished in brightness.

The fixed stars, when viewed through the telescope, appear like luminous points on the concave surface of the heavens; but the planets are found to exhibit the appearance of discs of greater or less diameter. Mercury and Venus accompany the sun, appearing at one time on the east, and at another time on the west of that luminary, and never receding from him beyond a certain distance. The other planets recede from the sun to all possible angular distances. Connected with this circumstance is a distinction which it is useful to make of *inferior* planets and *superior* planets; the former appellation being applied to Mercury and Venus, and the latter to the remaining planets.

Mercury and Venus, as they oscillate about the sun, exhibit all the phases of the moon. From having the appearance of a crescent, they gradually assume that of the half-moon. The illuminated part of the disc increasing, they become gibbous, and at last present a complete circular disc, like the full moon. From this state of illumination they again pass through the same appearances in an inverted order, until they disappear altogether. Sometimes these planets are seen like black spots in the sun; these appearances are called *transits* of the planets over the sun's disc. They are rare, but when observed, particularly the transit of Venus, they give the best means of determining the magnitude of the solar system. In all the phases of Mercury and Venus the convexity of the illuminated portion of the disc is turned towards the sun.

The discs of the other planets are always nearly circular. Mars, however, in certain positions with regard to the sun, assumes a gibbous appearance; but he never becomes cornicular like Venus. He has no satellite. As viewed from the earth, he is known by his red and fiery appearance. Dr. Herschel observed that the polar regions of Mars, after having been turned from the sun, appeared brighter than the rest of the planetary disc; just as if these regions had in the absence of the sun's heat been covered with snow.

Certain spots appear on the discs of the sun and the four planets Venus, Mars, Jupiter, and Saturn, when they are viewed through the telescope, and are distinguished from other parts of the discs by the colour or intensity of their light. Similar spots are seen on the moon with the naked eye. Jupiter has also his disc marked with several parallel belts or stripes, which stretch across it. They are subject to considerable variation with regard to number, breadth, and distance from each other. Mercury is too much immersed in the solar rays; Vesta, Ceres, Juno, and Pallas, are too small; and Uranus is too distant to allow points of unequal brilliancy to be observed on their surface. The spots upon the sun are very variable in their number, position, and magnitude. Often they are numerous, and of great extent. Each of them, in general, consists of a dark space, or *umbra*, surrounded by a *penumbra*, or fainter shade, beyond which is a border of light more brilliant than the rest of the sun's disc. Sometimes, though seldom, the sun has been without spots for several years; this was the case from 1676 to 1684. The dark nucleus of the spot is seen to form and disappear amidst the greater brilliancy that surrounds it. After the nucleus ceases to be seen, the umbra continues visible for some time: the place where it at length disappears becomes like the other parts of the solar surface, unless it be succeeded, which is sometimes the case by a luminous spot. Umbræ of great extent have, with few exceptions, a nucleus in their centre; but small umbræ are often seen without it.

The solar spots are never stationary, but are seen to move slowly over the sun's disc from east to west. Their paths across the disc, when accurately traced, are found to be rectilineal in the beginning of June, and in the beginning of December; but in the intermediate seasons they are found to be elliptic. Between June and December the convexity of the path is towards the upper part of the disc, and between December and June it is towards the lower part.

The planet Jupiter, when viewed through the telescope, appears to be attended by fou small stars, ranged nearly in a straight line, which are seen sometimes on the same side, and at other times on opposite sides of the planet. These small stars occasionally pass between us and Jupiter, and then they are found to project shadows which are seen to traverse his disc. On the other hand, they are often immersed in the shadow of Jupiter, and exhibit the phenomenon called an *eclipse*. The planets Saturn and Uranus are also similarly attended, the former by seven, and the latter by six, little stars. These accompanying stars are called satellites, and also *secondary planets*, in contradistinction to the others, which are called *primary*.

Saturn is distinguished from all the other planets, in being surrounded by a circular ring concentric with itself. When first examined by the telescope, this planet was almost always seen between two small luminous bodies of an irregular form, which seemed to be attached to it, and which, as they suggested the idea of handles, were denominated *ansæ*. Sometimes the ansæ disappeared, and then Saturn appeared round like the other planets. By tracing with care these singular appearances, and combining them with the positions of Saturn relatively to the sun and the earth, Huygens at last discovered that they are produced by a ring which encompasses the body of the planet, and which is everywhere separated from it. Being seen obliquely, the ring appears of an oval or elliptic form. Before the time of Herschel the ring of Saturn was supposed to be single; but this distinguished astronomer discovered that it is double: so that two rings concentric, and in the same plane, constitute what was formerly supposed to be a single ring. The ring, which is very thin, is inclined to the plane of the ecliptic. It revolves from west to east in $10^h\ 39'\ 54''$. Its breadth is nearly equal to its distance from Saturn; that is, about one third of the diameter of the planet. The interval between the rings is very little; yet Dr. Herschel saw a star through it. The inner ring is somewhat broader than the outer.

---

## CHAPTER III.

### APPROXIMATION TO THE FIGURE AND MAGNITUDE OF THE EARTH.

The true figure and exact magnitude of the earth are elements of the highest importance in geography. Their determination, however, has required the aid of astronomy in its most improved state; yet it is necessary, to the explanation of the general doctrines of astronomy, that we should, in the outset, know nearly its figure and magnitude: we shall afterwards explain by what means the first conceptions have been corrected, and its true figure and magnitude found. Having now pointed out, generally, the phenomena of the heavens—taking into view the more remarkable discoveries made by aid of the telescope—we are next to consider *the causes and mutual dependence of these phenomena*. The first step towards obtaining an explication of the motions of the heavenly bodies, is to form some notion of the figure and magnitude of the earth which we inhabit, and from which all the celestial phenomena are observed. To a person placed in an elevated situation in an open country, where the view is unconfined on all sides, the earth appears an extended plane, with the concave sphere of the heavens resting upon it,—the horizon being the common boundary. This appearance is, however, altogether illusory.

The earth is a round body, and is isolated in space. This is sufficiently established by the following facts:—

1. To an observer who travels from north to south the nocturnal heavens appear continually to change their aspect. The stars, indeed, retain the same relative position in respect of each other, and the points on which the heavens appear to revolve remain unchanged; but the angle, which the axis of their motion forms with the horizon, continually decreases; so that stars which, at the place from which he set out, appeared to reach their greatest elevation to the south of the point directly over his head, now that he has changed his position, appear, when highest, on the north of that point. This clearly indicates that his path on the earth's surface has not been a straight line, but a curve of which the convexity is turned towards the sky.

2. The convexity of the earth is quite apparent to a spectator in a ship receding from the shore. At first low objects disappear; then those more elevated; and at last the highest points of the land sink in the horizon, on account of the direct visual ray being broken by the interposed curved surface of the ocean. In like manner, when two ships approach each other, the navigators in each see at first the upper part of the rigging of the other vessel the hull being still invisible: as the distance becomes less the body of each vessel comes gradually into view. The reverse happens if the distance between the vessels is increasing. From these appearances it is evident, that a straight line joining any two points of the earth's surfaces passes within the body of the earth.

3. That the horizon of the sea, which, to the eye, terminates its surface, is only an apparent limit in reference to the position of the observer, is evident from the fact, that if we advance towards it we find it recede; and, at the same time, we still imagine ourselves placed in the centre of an extended plane, bounded by the line in which the heavens and

earth appear to meet. This is what the navigator uniformly experiences; while, to an observer on the shore, his vessel appears to sink below the horizon; and by continuing to sail in the same direction, he will at last arrive at the same port from which he set out,—having thus circumnavigated the earth. This enterprise has, it is well known, in numerous instances, been accomplished by navigators, who have left the shores of Europe and returned home, some by sailing always towards the west, and others by holding an easterly course. This great experiment demonstrates that the sea and land have a curved surface which returns into itself, so that no part of it is touched by the heavens.

There are other phenomena which prove that the earth, if not an exact sphere, is at least nearly of that figure. The various appearances of the moon, in the course of her revolution round the earth, show that she is an opaque body, and is visible only by the reflected light of the sun. The earth being also an opaque body, must project a shadow in a direction opposite to the sun. It will afterwards be shown that the moon, when full, must sometimes pass through this shadow. In this case, when the moon begins to penetrate, or is about to leave, the shadow, the greater part of the disc is still illuminated by the sun; and it is found that this luminous part is always of the form of a crescent, having its concave side bounded by an arch of a circle. The section of the earth's shadow, shown by its projection on the moon, is, therefore, as to sense, circular,—a proof that the earth is a sphere, or nearly of a spherical figure; whence we may conclude that there is a point within the earth which is its centre.

That the earth is a round body, is thus completely proved by experience and observation; yet, when this doctrine is presented to the mind for the first time, there is some difficulty in believing that the earth is balanced, as it were, on its centre, without any visible support; while all things at rest on its surface require to be supported. We must, however, consider that the bodies which we see fall towards the centre of the earth are mere atoms in comparison to the earth itself; and that, although their tendency to its centre is another fact established by experience, yet it does not thence follow that the earth itself should move towards one point of space rather than towards another. A little reflection will show that there is no inconsistency in supposing the earth, an immense mass, to be at rest, and all things to be retained on its surface by some force analogous to that by which a piece of iron is drawn towards a magnet. This is really the fact; and a consequence of it is, that on opposite sides of the earth its inhabitants stand in opposite directions, with their feet towards each other, for which reason they are called *Antipodes;* and every country has its own Antipodes.

The knowledge of the true figure and magnitude of the earth is of the greatest importance in geography, and on this account we shall treat of them in a particular manner. In the mean time, as a near approximation to the truth, the earth may be considered as differing but little from a sphere, 7916 miles in diameter, and consequently nearly 24,870 miles in circumference. In geometry, the circumference of every circle is supposed to be divided into 360 equal parts, called degrees; and each of these into 60 equal parts, called minutes, and so on. A degree, therefore, of any circle on the earth's surface, whose centre is the same with that of the earth, will be rather more than 69 miles; and a minute of a degree will be about $1\frac{3}{20}$ mile.

---

## CHAPTER IV.

### DOCTRINE OF THE SPHERE.

THE motions of the celestial bodies being in appearance all performed on a sphere, of which the eye of the spectator is the centre; with a view to describe the nature of these motions, it has been found expedient to suppose certain circles to be traced on this sphere, to which, also, the positions of the heavenly bodies in space are referred.

The distance of the fixed stars is immensely great in respect of the earth's semi-diameter; for it is found that, when viewed from any two points of the earth's surface, they have the very same relative position, and the same apparent distances, at a given instant of time. Hence it follows, that the appearance of the heavens, and the angular distances of the fixed stars, will be, as to sense, the same, whether they be viewed from the centre of the earth, or from a point on its surface. We may, therefore, conceive the axis of the diurnal revolution to pass through the centre of the earth, which will be also the centre of the celestial sphere.

#### DEFINITIONS.

A great circle of the sphere is that whose plane passes through its centre; and all others are called small circles.

A circle of the celestial sphere, whose plane passes through the earth's centre, and is perpendicular to the axis, is called the EQUATOR. The line in which this plane meets the earth's surface is called the EQUATOR of the earth, or the EQUINOCTIAL.

To illustrate this by a diagram, let c be the centre of the sphere (*fig.* 15.), which we suppose to coincide with the centre of the earth, and let P c p be the axis; then the circle, whose diameter is E Q, which passes through c, and is perpendicular to P p, is the *Equator.* The circles which the stars describe by the diurnal revolution, are all parallel to the Equator. Such is the circle whose diameter is A B.

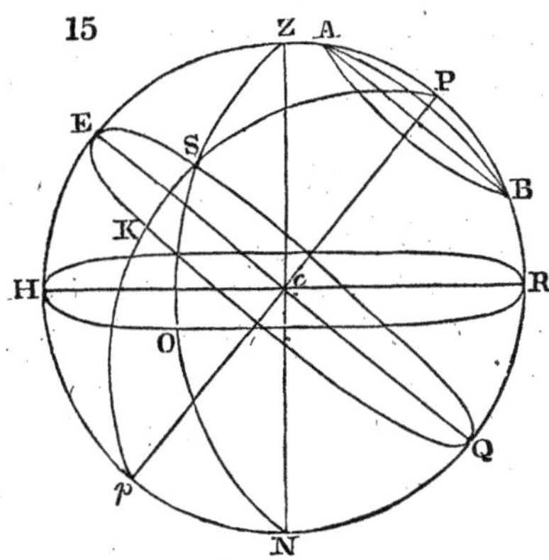


A circle, whose plane passes through the poles, is called the Meridian, and the section of the earth's surface made by this plane is called the Meridian of all the places through which it passes. Thus P E p Q is a meridian circle in the heavens. The number of these circles is indefinite.

By the geometrical properties of a sphere, the plane of any meridian cuts the planes of the equator and all circles parallel to it at right angles.

We know by observation, that any body at rest, and let fall from a point above the earth, will, by its weight or gravity, descend in a straight line. This line is the *direction of gravity:* it is also indicated by the direction of a cord to which a plummet is suspended, and is everywhere perpendicular to the surface of water at rest. If, now, a line in the direction of gravity at any point on the earth's surface be produced indefinitely upward and downward, this line, called a vertical, will mark, on the celestial sphere, two points called the Zenith and Nadir. The former is the point in the heavens immediately over head. A plane conceived to pass through any plane on the earth's surface at right angles to the line joining its zenith and nadir, will, when extended to the heavens, meet the sphere in a circle, which is the Horizon of that place. A plane that passes through the earth's centre, and is parallel to the plane just now defined, will meet the sphere in a circle, which is also called the Horizon, but, to distinguish the one from the other, the former is called the Sensible, and the latter the Rational Horizon. On account, however, of the smallness of the earth's semidiameter, when compared with the immense distances of the fixed stars, the two horizons are, as to sense, the same.

The zenith is at Z (*fig.* 15.), and nadir at N. The circle H O R is the horizon.

If the earth were a perfect sphere, the direction of gravity being everywhere perpendicular to its surface, all bodies would tend towards its centre. But if there be *any deviation from the exact spherical figure*, (and this is really the case,) then the direction of gravity will not, in general, pass through the centre; though, if the deviation be small, it will nearly pass through that point.

The plane of the horizon of any place touches the earth's surface, and divides the whole expanse of the heavens into two Hemispheres; one of which, *viz.* that above the horizon, is Visible, and the other Invisible. To an eye placed close to the earth's surface, or to the surface of the sea, the two hemispheres will appear exactly equal. A spectator, however, on the top of a mountain, can see more than half of the heavens; because, if a line drawn from his eye to touch the earth's surface were carried round, it would generate the surface of a cone. The portion of the heavens within this cone would be invisible; but he would see all the space without the cone, which would manifestly be the larger portion. His apparent horizon would still be a circle; but it would be below the plane passing through his eye perpendicular to the vertical. The depression of the horizon of a spectator so situated below this plane is called the Dip.

Circles whose planes pass through the zenith and nadir of any place are called Vertical Circles. Such, for example, as the circle Z O N. These, by the properties of a sphere, are all perpendicular to the horizon. The meridian is, of course, a vertical circle; and the vertical circle whose plane is perpendicular to the meridian is called the Prime Vertical.

The meridian cuts the horizon in the North and South points, and the prime vertical cuts it in the East and West. These four are the Cardinal Points. They divide the horizon into four equal parts.

Let a vertical circle be supposed to pass continually through a star, or any point of the heavens, the arc of that circle between the star and the horizon is called the Altitude of the star; and the arc of the horizon between the vertical circle and the meridian is called its Azimuth, which may be measured either from the north or south. Thus, in *fig.* 15., suppose a star at S, then its altitude is the arc S O, and its azimuth the arc H O.

Vertical circles are called Circles of Azimuth.

The altitude of a star will evidently be greatest when it is on the meridian, and it will have equal altitudes when it is at equal distances from the meridian; that is, when its eastern and western azimuths are equal.

Suppose a meridian to pass through a star, then the arc intercepted between the star and the equator is called the DECLINATION of the star. Thus P S *p* being a meridian that passes through the star S, and meets the equator in K, the arc S K is the declination of the star.

If the meridian circle pass through the zenith of any place, the arc intercepted between the zenith and the equator is called the LATITUDE of that place. Thus Z being the zenith of any place, and E K Q the equator, the latitude of the place is the arc Z E.

Assuming the meridian circle that passes through the zenith of any particular place as the FIRST MERIDIAN, the arc of the equator intercepted between the first meridian and the meridian circle passing through the zenith of any other place, is called the LONGITUDE of that place. It is usual, in this country, to reckon the longitude of places from the meridian circle that passes through the zenith of the Observatory at Greenwich.

Because the arcs Z R, the distance of the zenith from the horizon, and P E, the distance of the pole from the equator, are each one-fourth of the circumference of a circle or a quadrant, they are equal, and consequently, leaving out the common arc P Z, the arcs Z E and P R are equal. Hence it appears that P R, the distance of the pole from the horizon of any place, called the *elevation* or *altitude* of the pole, is equal to the latitude of that place.

---

## CHAPTER V.

### ROTATION OF THE SUN, MOON, AND PLANETS ON THEIR AXES. THEIR FIGURE.

FROM the phenomena of the spots which, by aid of the telescope, are visible on his disc, we are led to conclude that the sun *revolves from west to east* on an axis, in about twenty-five days and a half. Though these spots are subject to many variations, they are sufficiently permanent to enable us to discover that they have regular motions across the disc, exactly the same as must belong to corresponding points on the surface of the sun, supposing him actually to have a motion of rotation from west to east on an axis nearly perpendicular to the plane of the PATH or ORBIT, which, in virtue of his apparent motion, he describes round the heavens in the course of a year. When a spot is first discovered on the eastern edge of the disc, it appears like a fine line: as it approaches the centre of the disc its breadth increases; as it advances towards the western edge the breadth again diminishes, until the spot at length entirely disappears. The same spot is sometimes again observed, after fourteen days, on the east side of the disc; but more frequently the spot is dissolved, and is no more seen. By careful observation of the time occupied by a spot in crossing the disc, taking also into account the proper motion of the sun from west to east during that period, the time of the sun's rotation on his axis is found to be about twenty-five and a half days.

That the moon, and the planets Mercury, Venus, Mars, Jupiter, and Saturn, have each a motion of rotation from west to east, on an axis inclined to the plane of the sun's orbit, is inferred in like manner from the spots that are seen to traverse their discs. The moon presents always nearly the same side to the earth; and must, therefore, revolve on her axis in the same time in which she is carried round the heavens by her apparent motion, namely, in $27^{d}\ 7^{m}\ 43^{s}$. Mercury revolves in $24^{h}\ 5^{m}$; Venus in $23^{h}\ 30^{m}$; Mars in $24^{h}\ 39^{m}$; Jupiter in $9^{h}\ 56^{m}$; Saturn in $10^{h}\ 29^{m}$. In the remaining planets no appearances have been discovered which enable us to ascertain whether or not they revolve on axes; though, from analogy, it is highly probable that they do.

With regard to the figure of the sun and of those planets which are known to revolve on axes, we may conclude that they are nearly spherical; because no other but a spherical body can, when revolving on an axis in the manner of the planets (with the exception of the moon), present in every position the appearance of a circular disc. The spherical figure of the moon, and, indeed, of the other planets which exhibit phases, may be inferred from the fact, that the concavity of the crescent which they from time to time display is bounded by an elliptic line. The planet Uranus always presents a disc that is nearly circular, and it has not been ascertained that he revolves on an axis; but it is very improbable, when we consider how very irregular his motions among the fixed stars appear when seen from the earth, that he should keep the same side always turned towards us. His apparent motion is sometimes direct, that is from west to east, sometimes retrograde, or in the contrary direction; so that to present constantly the appearance of a circular disc, the planet would require, were it not spherical, to have motions in opposite directions about the same axis. The same reasoning will apply to the remaining planets. We may conclude, therefore, that the sun, moon, and planets, are bodies nearly spherical.

## CHAPTER VI.

### DISTANCES AND MAGNITUDES OF THE HEAVENLY BODIES.

Distances of the fixed stars. From whatever point of the earth's surface we observe the fixed stars, they always appear to preserve the very same relative positions. We may hence conclude that these bodies are situated at immeasurable distances from the earth; and that though to us who inhabit it the dimensions of the earth appear very great, they are insensible when compared with these immense distances. The earth is in reality but as a point in space. But though the fixed stars are vastly too remote to admit of their distances being determined, we have reason to believe that they are placed at very different degrees of remoteness. They shine with very various degrees of brilliancy; multitudes are not visible without the aid of the telescope, and it may reasonably be supposed that many more have not yet been discovered by the most powerful instruments which have been directed to the heavens.

The distances of the fixed stars being unknown, we can only form conjectures from hypothesis and analogy respecting their true magnitudes. When viewed through the best telescopes, they have no apparent diameter, but appear like points in the heavens.

Mode of determining the distance of the sun, moon, and planets. In reference to the sphere of *the fixed stars*, then, the earth is to be regarded as a point. To a spectator, at the sun, moon, and planets, however, it would present a disc subtending an angle of greater or less magnitude, and, even when smallest, admitting of measurement. This angle can be determined by an observer on the earth's surface; and as we know the true magnitude of the earth, it affords us the means of estimating the distances of these bodies. Let O *o* (*fig.* 16) be the places of two observers under the same meridian, but very distant from each other. Let P be a planet in the meridian of these places, and let some fixed star which comes to the meridian at the same time with the planet, be seen by the observers at O and *o*, in the directions O S, *o s*. Join O P, *o* P, and produce O P, to meet *o s* in A. Then, because O S, *o s*, are parallel (the distance of the star S being regarded as infinite), the angles O A *o*, A O S are equal; and, because O P *o* is the exterior angle of the triangle *o* A P, it is equal to the sum of the two interior and opposite angles A *o* P, *o* A P. Wherefore the angle O P *o* is equal to the sum of the angles A *o* P, P O S; that is, the angle subtended at the planet by the chord of the terrestrial arc intercepted between the points of observation, is equal to the sum of the apparent distances of the planet from the star, provided the planet is seen (as we have here supposed) on opposite sides of the star by the two observers. If the star is seen on the same side by both, the angle at the planet will then be equal to the difference of the apparent distances.

If the observers are so situated that P O, P *o* (*fig.* 17) are tangents to the circle O E *o* at the points O and *o*, the angle O P *o* will be the angle subtended by the disc of the earth at the planet.

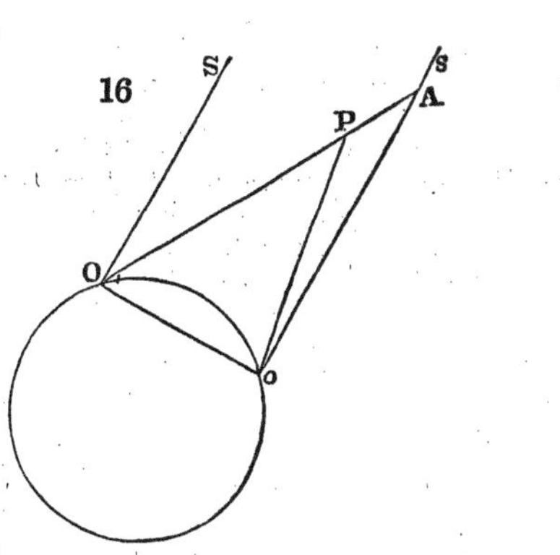


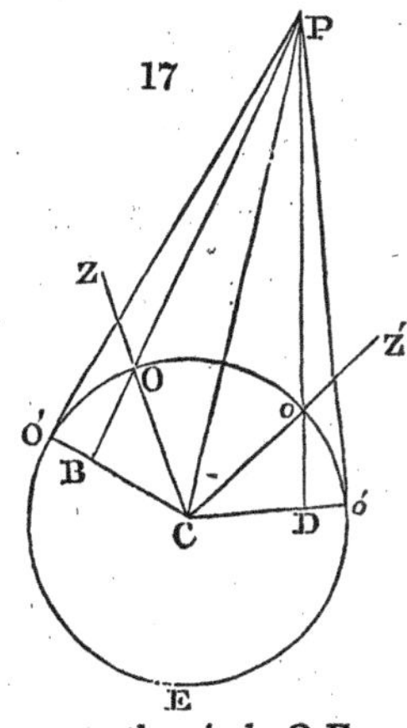


But if P O, P *o* are not tangents, draw P O′ and P *ó* tangents to the circle O E *o*, and from C the centre draw C O′, C *ó* to the points of contact: draw also the vertical lines C Z and C Z′ through O and *o* the places of the observers, and produce P O, P *o* to meet C O′, C *ó* in B and D. Now, for the sun and planets the angle O P *o* is very small, and even for the moon it is not very considerable. The distance P C may therefore be regarded, in every case, as much greater than C O′, or C *ó*. Hence the lines C O′, C B, C D may without sensible error be considered as proportional to the angles C P O′, C P B, C P D; so that we have $\angle$ C P O′: $\angle$ C P O = C O′: C B and $\angle$ C P O: $\angle$ C P *o* = C O′: C D; wherefore $\angle$ C P O′: $\angle$ C P O + $\angle$ C P *o* or $\angle$ O P *o* = C O′: C B + C D But the angles at B and D are very nearly right angles, and therefore, to radius C O′, we have C B = Sin. C O B = Sin. P O Z; and C D = Sin. C *o* D = Sin. P *o* Z′: Hence we obtain ∠ C P O′: ∠ O P *o* = (C O: C B + C D =) Rad.: Sin. P O Z + Sin. P *o* Z′: And 2 ∠ C P O′ or ∠ O′ P *ó* = 2 ∠ O P *o* × $\frac{\text{Rad.}}{\text{Sin. P O Z + Sin. P } o \text{ Z}'}$

If the planet be on the same side of the zenith to both observers, then the difference, instead of the sum of the sines of the zenith distances, must be taken for the denominator. Expressing the above formula in words, we give the following simple rule:—*Divide the arc, (expressed in parts of the radius,) which measures the observed angle at the planet, by the sum of the sines of the zenith distances of the planet, if it is between the zeniths of the two observers; or by the difference of these sines if the planet is on the same side of the zenith to both observers; and twice the result will be the arc, expressed in parts of the radius, that measures the angle subtended at the planet by the disc of the earth.*

Since small angles, that require for their measurement only the use of the micrometer can be determined with much more accuracy than large angles requiring the whole telescope to be moved, it is best to employ, in finding the angle O P *o* a star which is near the planet; a small error in taking the zenith distances of the planet will produce no sensible error in the result.

Another method of determining this angle, is by observations on the transit of Venus over the disc of the sun; a phenomenon in which the planet is seen like a dark spot on the disc; but the method now explained is sufficient for our present purpose.

The following are *the angles subtended by the earth's disc at the sun, moon, and planets,* when the earth is nearest to each:

| | | Seconds. | | | Seconds. |
|---|---|---|---|---|---|
| Angle at the | Sun | = 17 | Angle at | Uranus | = 1 |
| | Mercury | = 28 | | Vesta | |
| | Venus | = 62 | | Juno | = 9 |
| | Mars | = 42 | | Ceres | |
| | Jupiter | = 4 | | Pallas | |
| | Saturn | = 2 | | Moon | = 2° 2′ |

To determine, now, the distance of the sun or moon, or of a planet:—In the right angled triangle P O C we have given the angle P equal to half the angle subtended by the earth's disc at the body whose distance is to be found; also O C the earth's semi-diameter: therefore the distance P C may be determined by the proportion Sin. P : Rad. = C O : P C. Since the angle P is small, its sine must be nearly equal to the arc which measures it. Observing therefore that the arc to which the radius is equal, expressed in seconds, is 206265″ we have ∠ P (in seconds) : 206265 = C O : P C. Hence

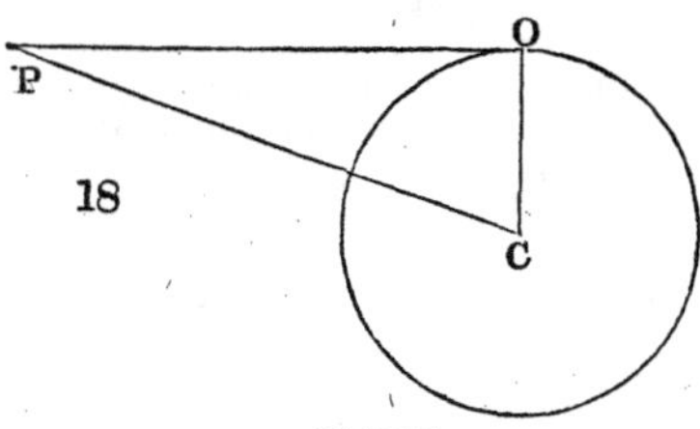


P C = 2 C O × $\frac{206265}{2\text{ P}}$. Whence we derive the following rule:—*Divide the constant number* 206265 *by the number of seconds in the angle subtended by the earth's disc as seen from the body whose distance is to be determined; multiply the result by the diameter of the earth, and the product is the distance required.* In the case of the sun; assuming the diameter of the earth as unity, we have the distance equal to $\frac{206265}{17}$ or 12133 diameters of the earth. In like manner, taking 4″, 2″, 1″ for the angles subtended by the earth's disc at Jupiter, Saturn, and Uranus, the distances of these planets from the earth, when least, will be 51566, 103132, 206265 diameters of the earth respectively. The mean distance of the moon is about sixty semi-diameters of the earth.

The apparent diameter of any one of the heavenly bodies, is the number of seconds in the measure of the angle under which its circular disc is seen by a spectator upon the earth. When measured by a micrometer, the apparent diameters of the sun, moon, and planets are found to be, when greatest, as follows:

| | | Seconds. | | | Seconds. |
|---|---|---|---|---|---|
| Diameter of the | Sun | = 1923 | Diameter of | Jupiter | = 46 |
| | Mercury | = 12 | | Saturn | = 18 |
| | Venus | = 61 | | Uranus | = 4 |
| | Mars | = 18 | | Moon | = 2020 |

The four remaining planets, according to the most careful observations, appear to subtend only a small part of a second.

Now, for deducing the real diameters from the apparent, we have this rule:—*As the apparent diameter of the earth, (or the seconds in the angle which its disc subtends,) as seen from the planet, is to the apparent diameter of the planet as seen from the earth, so is the true diameter of the earth to the true diameter of the planet.*

Calling the diameter of the earth unity, or 8000 miles in round numbers, we obtain,

| | | | Diameters of the Earth. | | Miles. |
|---|---|---|---|---|---|
| Diameter of the | Sun | = | 111.454 | = | 882,000 nearly. |
| | Mercury | = | 0.398 | = | 3,140 — |
| | Venus | = | 0.9 | = | 7,200 — |
| | Mars | = | 0.517 | = | 4,100 — |
| | Jupiter | = | 10.860 | = | 87,000 — |
| | Saturn | = | 9.982 | = | 76,068 — |
| | Uranus | = | 4.332 | = | 34,500 — |
| | Moon | = | 0.273 | = | 2,160 — |

As the sun, moon, and planets are spherical bodies, *their magnitudes* compared with the magnitude of the earth, may be found upon the principle that similar solids are to one another as the cubes of their similar dimensions; so that *as the cube of the diameter of the earth is to the cube of the diameter of the sun, moon, or a planet, so is the magnitude of the former to the magnitude of the latter.*

Assuming the magnitude of the earth as unity:

| | | | |
|---|---|---|---|
| The magnitude of the | Sun | = | 1384472.000 |
| | Mercury | = | .063 |
| | Venus | = | .927 |
| | Mars | = | .139 |
| | Jupiter | = | 1280.900 |
| | Saturn | = | 995.000 |
| | Uranus | = | 80.490 |
| | Moon | = | .020 |

Having now ascertained the distances and magnitudes of the heavenly bodies, we proceed to inquire whether the diurnal motion which we observe in them be a real or only an apparent motion; and whether the earth is the centre to which the proper motion of any of them is to be referred.

---

## CHAPTER VII.

### ROTATION OF THE EARTH.

The diurnal motion of the heavenly bodies suggests the existence of some cause, under the influence of which they either perform or appear to perform a revolution from east to west round the axis of the celestial sphere in the space of a day and a night. Now, there are two suppositions, on either of which the diurnal motion may be explained. We may suppose the heavens to be carried round the earth, while the latter remains immoveable in the centre; or we may suppose the heavens to be at rest, and the earth to revolve on an axis in an opposite direction; that is, from west to east. To which of these hypotheses the preference is due, will be evident if we consider that the heavenly bodies are independent one of another, and are placed at very different distances from the earth; that variations in the apparent diameters of the planets indicate great changes in their distances, while the comets traverse the heavens in all directions; so that it is difficult to conceive that one and the same cause should impress on all these bodies a common motion of rotation.

Since the earth is a globe of about 8000 miles diameter, it is small when compared with the immense mass of the sun. Were the centres of the sun and earth brought into coincidence, the former body would fill the orbit of the moon and extend as far again beyond it. Besides, the sun is distant from us about twelve thousand diameters of the earth; so that to revolve round the heavens in the interval of twenty-four hours, he must move at the immense velocity of about twenty-five millions of miles in an hour. It is therefore more reasonable to suppose the earth to have a motion of rotation on an axis, than to suppose the sun, a body so distant and of such immense magnitude, to move with the vast rapidity that would be requisite to carry him round the heavens in so short an interval. With regard to the fixed stars, we may reason in the same manner with still greater force: for the velocity necessary to carry the sun round in twenty-four hours is really insensible when compared with the rapidity with which the fixed stars must move to accomplish a like revolution. In order to account for the diurnal motion of the heavens on the hypothesis that the earth is at rest, it must be supposed that the sun, moon, and stars have their velocities so adapted to their respective distances, that all of them complete their revolutions round the earth in exactly the same number of seconds. Such an adaptation among innumerable independent bodies, placed at such a variety of distances, it is impossible to admit.

There are other phenomena of the heavens which serve still farther to confirm the conclusion, that the diurnal motion of the heavenly bodies is not a real motion. Every difficulty, however disappears, if we suppose the earth to have a motion of rotation on an axis from west to east. Carried round with a velocity common to all the objects which surround us on the earth's surface, we are in a situation similar to that of a spectator placed in a vessel in motion. At the first careless glance he imagines himself at rest, while the shore, and all the objects which he sees, unconnected with the vessel, appear to be in motion. By reflecting, however, on the extent of the shore, on the magnitude of the mountains, and other objects on land, when compared with the vessel from which he observes them, he frees his mind from this momentary illusion, and becomes convinced that the motion of these objects is only apparent, and that it is produced by the real motion of the vessel. The multitude of stars scattered over the heavens are, with respect to us, what the shore and the objects upon it are with regard to the spectator placed in the vessel: and by the same considerations, by which his first impressions are so corrected that he becomes assured of the reality of his motion, we are led to the conclusion that the rotation of the earth on an axis produces the apparent diurnal motion of the heavens.

An argument for the rotation of the earth may also be drawn from analogy. Several of the planets are known to have a motion on an axis similar to that which we have supposed to belong to the earth. Jupiter, for example, which is many times greater than the earth, revolves on his axis from west to east in less than half a day; and to an observer on his surface, the heavens would appear to revolve round that planet in the same manner as we see them revolve round the earth, but in about half the time. This motion of the heavens in reference to a spectator on the planet Jupiter would, however, be only apparent; and hence we may reasonably conclude, that the case is the same in reference to a spectator on the earth.

Lastly, if the earth is actually in motion, there will be generated a *centrifugal force*, or a tendency to throw off objects from its surface, which must diminish the force of gravity, particularly at the equator, where the motion is most rapid. Now, by observations made with the pendulum, this diminution of the force of gravity has been found to exist. The same cause affects also the figure of the earth, which has been found to be flattened somewhat at the points of rotation, and elevated at the equatorial regions. The same is observed to be the figure of Jupiter,—a circumstance which greatly strengthens the argument drawn from analogy. The evidence which has now been adduced leaves no doubt respecting the earth's motion of rotation; and thus we are enabled to ascertain the true place which the globe that we inhabit holds in the universe.

The points in which the axis of rotation meets the surface are called the POLES of the earth; and it is evident that the axis, if produced, must pass through the poles of the heavens.

---

## CHAPTER VIII.

### APPARENT ANNUAL MOTION OF THE SUN. VICISSITUDE OF SEASONS.

WHILE the sun participates in the diurnal motion of the heavens, he also appears to move eastward among the fixed stars. This motion it will be of importance now to trace out, and to explain the change of seasons to which it gives rise. If we observe each day of the year the meridian altitude of the sun, and note the time which elapses between his passage over the meridian and the passage of any particular star, we shall have the apparent motion of the sun in the direction of the meridian, and of the circles parallel to the equator in which he appears daily to be carried by the diurnal motion of the heavens. The result of the composition of these two motions will give the true motion for each day. In this manner it has been found that the sun moves in a path or orbit which cuts the equator in two opposite points, and makes with it an angle equal to 23° 28′ nearly.

The name of ecliptic is given to the circle which the plane of this orbit marks out on the sphere of the heavens. It passes through twelve constellations, which are called the TWELVE SIGNS. This has given rise to the division of the ecliptic into twelve equal parts, called SIGNS, each containing, of course, 30°. The twelve signs are contained in a zone of the starry heavens, called the ZODIAC. The names of these constellations, with the characters by which they are usually denoted, are as follow:—Aries ♈, Taurus ♉, Gemini ♊, Cancer ♋, Leo ♌, Virgo ♍, Libra ♎, Scorpio ♏, Sagittarius ♐, Capricornus ♑, Aquarius ♒, Pisces ♓.

The vicissitude of seasons arises from the combination of the apparent motion of the sun in the ecliptic with his apparent diurnal motion. When the sun is in either of the points in which the ecliptic intersects the equator, he describes the equator on that day in virtue of his diurnal motion; and as by the properties of the sphere this circle is divided into two equal parts by the horizon, at whatever point of the earth's surface the spectator is situated, the day is then equal to the night over all the globe.

The points of intersection of equator and ecliptic are called the EQUINOCTIAL POINTS. The first point of the sign *Aries* is supposed to coincide with the point of the vernal equinox; and from that point the signs of the ecliptic are reckoned: the first point of the sign *Libra* will therefore coincide with the point of the autumnal equinox. As the sun, when he leaves the point of the vernal equinox advances in the ecliptic, his meridian altitude above our horizon daily increases, and a larger portion of the parallel which he daily describes becomes visible. Hence arises a gradual increase in the length of the day in all countries to the north of the equator; until the sun having reached his greatest altitude, the day acquires its greatest length, and begins to shorten. As the variations of the altitude on each side of the points at which it is greatest are insensible, the sun, if we attend only to his altitude, appears stationary, and the day continues, for some time, very nearly of the same length. The point of the ecliptic at which the *maximum* takes place is therefore denominated the point of the Summer Solstice. The sun, having reached this point, now returns towards the equator, which he crosses at the point of the autumnal equinox. His meridian altitude gradually diminishes until it reaches the *minimum* at the point of the Winter Solstice. The day, which has been gradually shortening from the summer solstice, is then the shortest in the year, and for some time does not sensibly lengthen. The sun, however, again gradually approaches the equator, and reaches it at the vernal equinox.

Such is the constant progress of the sun in the heavens, and such the succession of the seasons of the year. The Spring is the time comprised between the vernal or spring equinox, which falls about the 21st of March, and the summer solstice, which happens about the 21st of June: the interval between the solstice and the autumnal equinox, which falls about the 23d of September is the Summer: the time between the autumnal equinox and the winter solstice, which occurs about the 22d of December, is the Autumn: and, lastly, the Winter is the time that elapses between the winter solstice and the spring equinox.

The two circles parallel to the equator, which the sun describes on the longest and shortest days, are called, one the summer or northern Tropic, and the other the winter or southern Tropic. They are also respectively denominated the tropic of Cancer and the tropic of Capricorn, in reference to the points in which they touch the ecliptic.

The presence of the sun above the horizon being the cause of heat, and the temperature increasing as the altitude increases, it might be inferred that the temperature should be the same in summer as in spring, and in winter as in autumn; because the altitudes of the sun in these seasons exactly correspond. But it is to be observed that the temperature is not an instantaneous effect of the sun's presence; but is the result of the continued action of his rays. On this account it is not greatest on the day when the altitude is greatest, but some time between the summer solstice and autumnal equinox. In like manner, the greatest cold of winter does not occur on the shortest day, but some time between the winter solstice and the spring equinox.

With regard both to temperature and the length of the day, great differences arise from the different elevations of the pole above the horizon, as we proceed from the equator towards either of the poles. The horizon of an observer at the equator passes through the poles, and by the geometrical properties of the sphere it divides the equator and all the circles, parallel to it into two equal parts. It also cuts them at right angles; and hence the position of the celestial sphere, in reference to the horizon of an observer at the equator, is called the Right position of the sphere. In whatever point of the ecliptic the sun is situated, his diurnal course is therefore at right angles to the horizon, and one half of it is in the visible hemisphere, and the other half in the invisible; hence, at the equator, the day is at all seasons equal to the night.

When the sun is in either of the equinoctial points, he passes through the zenith at mid-day. When he is in either of the solstitial points his meridian altitude is the least, and is equal to the complement of the inclination of the ecliptic to the equator. In these two positions of the sun the shadows of objects fall, at mid-day, in opposite directions,—a phenomenon which at no season occurs in our climate, where the solar shadows are at mid-day always directed towards the north: there are, then, properly speaking, two summers and two winters in the year at the equator. The same thing takes place in all the countries where the elevation of the pole above the horizon is less than the obliquity of the ecliptic. In every country beyond this region there is only one summer and one winter in the year, with the intervening seasons of spring and autumn: the sun is never in the zenith: the length of the longest day increases, and that of the shortest day diminishes, as we advance towards either of the poles; and when we have reached such a position, that the zenith is distant from the pole by an arc of the meridian equal to the obliquity of the ecliptic, the sun does not set at the summer solstice, nor rise at the winter solstice.

The polar circles. About each of the poles of the celestial sphere, suppose a circle to be described distant from it by an arc equal to the obliquity of the ecliptic; these two circles are called the Polar Circles. In the region of the earth situated around either of its poles, at every point whose zenith lines within the polar circle, the time of the sun's presence above the horizon and of his absence below it, at certain seasons, exceeds twenty-four hours: it increases as we approach the pole, and may amount to days or even to months. Thus, when the sun's declination north, increasing, becomes equal to the distance of the zenith of any place in the northern polar region from the north pole of the heavens, he ceases to set at that place, and continues above the horizon until he has reached the same declination in returning towards the equator. From that time the sun rises and sets in the course of twenty-four hours, until the sun's declination south becomes equal to the distance of the zenith from the pole, and then he ceases to rise and continues below the horizon till he has again acquired the same declination in returning northward.

At the pole, the equator coincides with the horizon, and all the circles parallel to the equator are also parallel to the horizon. This is called the PARALLEL position of the sphere. To an observer, placed at the pole, the heavenly bodies would appear to move round, either in the horizon or parallel to it. Hence the sun is constantly above the horizon when he is on the same side of the equator with the pole, and constantly below it when on the other side; so that at either of the poles of the earth there is only one day and one night in the year.

At any point on the earth's surface, between the equator and either of the poles, the equator and the circles parallel to it, are oblique to the horizon. This is called the OBLIQUE position of the sphere; and by the geometrical properties of the sphere, the horizon, in this position, divides all the circles parallel to the equator into two unequal parts; hence arises the inequality of the days and nights at all places between the equator and either pole. In this country, for example, in summer, when the sun is on the north side of the equator, the larger portion of his diurnal course lies in the visible hemisphere, and the less in the invisible, so that the day is longer than the night. The reverse is the case in the winter when the sun is on the south side of the equator.

If two places are situated on opposite sides of the equator, the spring and summer of the one will, it is evident, correspond to the autumn and winter of the other.

With regard to the temperature, it is higher in the equatorial regions than in any other part of the earth, because there the action of the sun's rays is most direct. To every point of the earth's surface, whose zenith lies between the tropics, the sun is vertical twice in the year; so that his rays, acting perpendicularly, produce their greatest effect. In the polar regions the temperature is lowest, in consequence of the obliquity with which the sun's rays fall on the earth's surface, and the great length of the winter night. In the countries situated between the equatorial region and the two polar regions, there prevails a medium temperature, increasing as the zenith approaches the nearer of the two tropics, and diminishing as it approaches the nearer of the polar circles.

A division of the earth's surface into five zones has been suggested by this difference of temperature from the equator towards either pole.

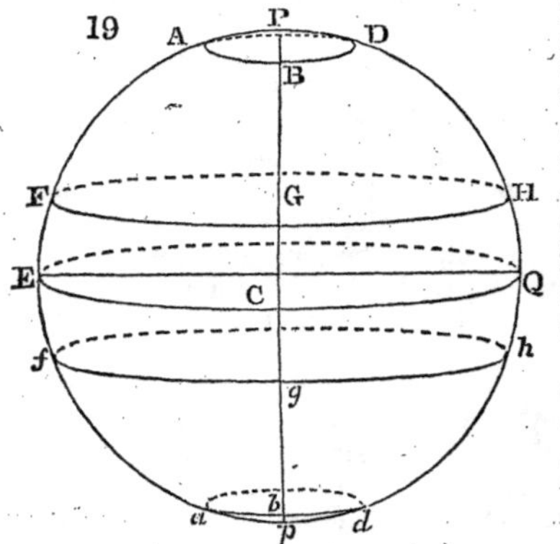


In the adjoining figure let P *p* represent the earth's axis, P E *p* Q, a meridian, and E Q the equatorial diameter. Let E C Q be the representation of a circle on the earth's surface equally distant from the poles, which will therefore be the *equator:* and F G H, *f g h* circles on the earth's surface parallel to the equator, and at the distance of about 23½ degrees; on each side of it, and A B D, *a b d* circles round the poles P, *p*, and at the same distance of 23½ degrees.

At the times of the year when the sun is in the tropic of Cancer, he will, in his apparent revolution, be vertical to all places on the circle F G H; and when he is in the tropic of Capricorn, he will be vertical to the circle *f g h*. The space on the earth's surface between these circles is the *Torrid Zone.*

When the sun is in the southern tropic he will not be seen anywhere in the space bounded by the circle A B D This is, therefore, the northern *Frigid Zone:* and when he is in the northern tropic there is a like tract, bounded by the circle *a b d*, round the south pole, where he will then be invisible. This is the southern *Frigid Zone.* The two tracts between the torrid zone and the frigid zones are the temperate zones.

Another division of the earth into zones was used by the ancient geographers, founded on the different lengths of the longest day, as we proceed from the equator towards either of the poles. These zones were denominated CLIMATES, and were each of such a breadth, that the longest day at the boundary nearer the pole exceeded the longest day at the boundary nearer the equator by some certain space of time, as half an hour or an hour. Within the polar circle, the climates were supposed of such a breadth as to make the longest day at the opposite sides differ by a month.

The points in which the equator and ecliptic intersect each other are not immoveable, but appear, with respect to the fixed stars, to recede towards the west at the rate of $50\frac{1}{10}'$ nearly, annually, or about 1° in 72 years. This motion is called the PRECESSION of the Equinoxes. When the constellations of the zodiac were first delineated by the ancient astronomers, the middle of the sign *Aries* was at the point of the vernal equinox, from which it is now distant more than 58° towards the east. In consequence of the precession of the equinoxes, the time in which the sun moves from the vernal equinox to the vernal equinox again, is less than the time in which he moves from any star to the same star again;—the point of the vernal equinox moving westward, so as to meet the sun, and thus anticipate the time of his crossing the equator in the preceding year.

The intervals of time which separate the equinoxes or the solstices are unequal. Almost eight days more elapse from the spring to the autumnal equinox, than from the latter to the former. We may therefore conclude, that the motion of the sun is not uniform. From precise and multiplied observations, it has been ascertained that his motion is most rapid at a point of the ecliptic situated near the winter solsticial point, and slowest at the opposite point towards the summer solstice. At the former point the sun describes daily 1° 1′ 10″, at the latter only 57′ 11½″. The distance of the sun from the earth is also variable. This is proved by variations observed in his apparent diameter, which increases and diminishes at the same time with his angular velocity, but not in the same ratio. The angular velocities at any two instants of time are, to one another, as the squares of the apparent diameters.

If $v$ and $v'$ be the angular velocities of the sun, or his daily advances in the ecliptic at any two seasons of the year, and $d$ and $d'$ his apparent diameters at the same time, then $v : v' = d^2 : d'^2$.

To diminish the apparent motion of the sun, it would be sufficient to suppose that body removed to a greater distance from the earth, without altering his true angular velocity. But if the diminution of his motion depended entirely on this cause, the apparent velocity would diminish in the same ratio with the apparent diameter. Since it diminishes, however, as the square of the diameter, there must necessarily be an actual diminution of the velocity of the sun while he recedes to a greater distance from the earth.

His distance being reciprocally as his apparent diameter, if D and D′ be his distances at the two seasons when his diameters are $d$ and $d'$, we have $v : v' = D'^2 : D^2$; and $vD^2 = v'D'^2$. Hence it appears, that from the combined effect of the two causes influencing the sun's apparent motions,—namely, the diminution of his velocity and the increase of his distance,—his daily angular motion diminishes as the square of his distance increases; so that the product of the square of the distance by the velocity is a constant quantity.

Let us imagine a straight line to join the centres of the sun and of the earth. This line is usually called the Radius Vector. It is not difficult to prove that the small sector, or the area which the Radius Vector traces in a day, in consequence of the sun's motion, is proportional to the product of the square of this radius by the sun's daily motion, that is, to $v D^2$. This area is therefore constant; and the whole area, described by the Radius Vector, setting out from a fixed radius, increases as the number of days reckoned from the epoch when the sun was at the fixed radius.

Since $vD^2 = v'D'^2$, we have $D' = D\sqrt{\frac{v}{v'}}$. Assuming, therefore, any line whatever for D, and finding, by observation, the sun's angular velocity for every day of the year, the value of D′ for each day may be found.

Thus we shall be able to trace a curve line representing the orbit of the sun. This curve is found to be not exactly circular, but a little elongated in the direction of the straight line passing through the centre of the earth, and joining the points in the orbit at which the sun is at its greatest and least distances. The resemblance of this curve to an *ellipse* having given rise to a comparison between them, their identity has been discovered. Hence we conclude, that *the apparent solar orbit is an ellipse having the centre of the earth in one of its foci.*

The solar ellipse is not much different from a circle; for its eccentricity, which, from the geometrical properties of the ellipse, is equal to half the difference of the sun's greatest and least distances from the earth, is a quantity which bears but a very small proportion to the distance of the sun. It appears, from observation, that there is a small diminution of the eccentricity,—so small, indeed, as scarcely to be perceptible in a century.

The position of the greater axis of the solar ellipse is not constantly the same. Its extremities have an annual motion eastward, in reference to the fixed stars, of about 12″ in the direction of the sun's motion.

The obliquity of the sun's orbit, or of the ecliptic to the equator, is also subject to change, and appears to have been continually diminishing from the remotest date of astronomical observation. Its present rate of diminution may be stated at nearly 48″ in a century.

The apparent elliptic motion of the sun does not represent, with perfect exactness, the results of modern observation. The great precision now attained in the art of observing has made known to us small inequalities, the laws of which it would have been almost impossible to determine by mere observation. These laws can be investigated only after the physical cause has been discovered upon which the phenomena depend.

## CHAPTER IX.

### DIVISION AND MEASURE OF TIME.

THE notion of time is suggested by the succession of phenomena in the universe. When two events exactly correspond in all their circumstances, they are conceived to occupy equal portions of time. The descent of a heavy body to the earth, for example, from a given height, if repeated under precisely similar circumstances, will in every case be performed in the same interval of time. Suppose then that a number of heavy bodies fall to the ground one after another from the same height,—the descent of the second and of each succeeding body commencing at the instant in which the body that preceded it had reached the ground; the whole time occupied by the fall of these bodies will be divided into equal portions, one of which may be assumed as the measuring unit of time. The vibrations of a pendulum, performed under precisely the same circumstances, are employed for estimating the smaller portions of time: the larger portions are determined by the motions of the sun; from which arise the vicissitude of day and night, and the change of seasons.

The DAY, in civil life, is the time that elapses between the rising and setting of the sun; and the NIGHT the time between his setting and rising. The ASTRONOMICAL or SOLAR DAY, on the other hand, comprehends the whole period of the sun's diurnal revolution, and is reckoned from the time of his passing any particular meridian, to the time of his returning to the same meridian. The pendulum usually employed is of such a length as to divide the mean astronomical day into $24 \times 60 \times 60 = 86400$ equal parts called *seconds;* 60 of these parts make a *minute;* 60 minutes make an *hour;* and 24 hours complete the day.

As the apparent motion of the sun carries him eastward among the fixed stars, the time that elapses between his passing the meridian, and his returning to it again, is longer than the time that intervenes between two successive passages (called transits) of any particular star. This latter period is the exact time of the earth's revolution on its axis, and is called a SIDEREAL day: it is about $23^h\ 56^m\ 4^s$ in length.

The motion of the earth on its axis being perfectly uniform, *the length of the sidereal day* is always the same. This is not, however, the case with respect to the astronomical or solar day, which is affected by the unequable motion of the sun, and by the obliquity of the ecliptic. At the summer solstice, towards which the sun's motion in the ecliptic is slowest, the solar day is more nearly equal to the sidereal day than at the winter solstice, when the sun's motion is quickest.

With regard to the effect of the obliquity of the ecliptic in reference to the length of the solar day, it is to be observed, that, by the geometrical properties of the sphere, equal portions of any circle, whose plane is perpendicular to the axis of revolution, pass over the meridian in equal times; but if the plane of a circle is oblique to the axis, the arcs that pass over the meridian in equal times are not equal. Hence, if the sun moved uniformly in the equator, the solar day would be always of the same length: but as he moves in the ecliptic, whose plane is oblique to the axis, even if he did proceed with a uniform motion, the equal arcs which he daily described would pass over the meridian in unequal times; so that the solar day would be longer or shorter according to the sun's place in the ecliptic.

The motion of the shadow on a sun-dial marks out time as measured by the sun's motion in the ecliptic: but if the sun moved uniformly in the equator at such a rate as to complete the annual circuit of the heavens, in the same time as he does by his actual motion in the ecliptic, time measured by his motion would then correspond with that of a well-regulated clock.

The difference between the time shown by the sun-dial, and that shown by the clock, is called the EQUATION OF TIME. The part of this equation which depends on the obliquity of the ecliptic, vanishes at the equinoxes and at the solstices; because at these seasons the sun comes to the meridian at the same moment as he would do if he moved in the equator.

From the vernal equinox till the summer solstice, and from the autumnal equinox till the winter solstice, the time as shown by the sun-dial is in advance of that indicated by the clock; because then the sun's distance from the first point of *Aries*, and first point of *Libra*, passes sooner over the meridian than the equal arc upon the equator, which the sun would have described had he moved in that circle.

Again, the hour shown by the sun-dial is behind that shown by the clock, from the summer and winter solstices, till the autumnal and vernal equinoxes; because at these two seasons the distance of the sun from the first point of *Aries*, and from the first point of *Libra*, requires longer time to pass over the meridian, than the equal arc upon the equator.

The part of the equation of time which arises from the unequable motion of the sun, will vanish when he is at his greatest and least distances from the earth; because he is in these two points of his orbit at the same instants of time as he would be if he moved uniformly with his mean velocity; that is, with a rate of motion by which he would describe equally the ecliptic in the same time in which he describes it by his unequable motion.

The dial, during the time when the sun is moving from the point of his greatest, to the point of his least distance from the earth, is faster than the clock; because the sun is then at no instant so far advanced in his orbit, as he would have been if he had been moving uniformly with his mean velocity. The reverse is the case while the sun is moving from the point of his least to that of his greatest distance. Time measured by the dial is called APPARENT time; that shown by a well-regulated clock is called TRUE time. The effect of the obliquity of the ecliptic, and that of the sun's unequable motion, in rendering the dial faster or slower than the clock, sometimes combine with and at other times counteract each other. The amount of each is given in the two following tables for every fifth day of the year; and by taking the sum or difference, according as the obliquity of the ecliptic and the sun's unequable motion produce similar or opposite effects, a table may be formed of the equation of time.

*Table showing the Part of the Equation of Time that arises from the Obliquity of the Ecliptic.*

| Dial Faster. | | | | Dial Slower. | | | | Dial Faster. | | | | Dial Slower. | | | |
|---|---|---|---|---|---|---|---|---|---|---|---|---|---|---|---|
| | | M. | S. | | | M. | S. | | | M. | S. | | | M. | S. |
| March | 21 | 0 | 0 | June | 21 | 0 | 0 | September | 23 | 0 | 0 | December | 21 | 0 | 0 |
| | 25 | 1 | 39 | | 26 | 1 | 48 | | 28 | 1 | 39 | | 26 | 1 | 48 |
| | 30 | 3 | 15 | July | 1 | 3 | 32 | October | 3 | 3 | 15 | | 31 | 3 | 32 |
| April | 4 | 4 | 46 | | 7 | 5 | 8 | | 8 | 4 | 46 | January | 5 | 5 | 8 |
| | 9 | 6 | 9 | | 12 | 6 | 35 | | 13 | 6 | 9 | | 10 | 6 | 35 |
| | 14 | 7 | 22 | | 17 | 7 | 48 | | 18 | 7 | 22 | | 15 | 7 | 48 |
| | 19 | 8 | 23 | | 22 | 8 | 45 | | 23 | 8 | 23 | | 20 | 8 | 45 |
| | 24 | 9 | 9 | | 28 | 9 | 26 | | 28 | 9 | 9 | | 25 | 9 | 26 |
| | 30 | 9 | 40 | August | 2 | 9 | 49 | November | 2 | 9 | 40 | | 29 | 9 | 49 |
| May | 5 | 9 | 53 | | 7 | 9 | 53 | | 7 | 9 | 53 | February | 3 | 9 | 53 |
| | 10 | 9 | 49 | | 12 | 9 | 40 | | 12 | 9 | 49 | | 8 | 9 | 40 |
| | 15 | 9 | 26 | | 17 | 9 | 9 | | 17 | 9 | 26 | | 13 | 9 | 9 |
| | 20 | 8 | 45 | | 22 | 8 | 23 | | 22 | 8 | 45 | | 18 | 8 | 23 |
| | 26 | 7 | 48 | | 28 | 7 | 22 | | 27 | 7 | 48 | | 23 | 7 | 22 |
| | 31 | 6 | 35 | September | 2 | 6 | 9 | December | 2 | 6 | 35 | | 28 | 6 | 9 |
| June | 5 | 5 | 8 | | 7 | 4 | 46 | | 7 | 5 | 8 | March | 5 | 4 | 46 |
| | 10 | 3 | 32 | | 12 | 3 | 15 | | 12 | 3 | 32 | | 10 | 3 | 15 |
| | 16 | 1 | 48 | | 17 | 1 | 39 | | 17 | 1 | 48 | | 15 | 1 | 39 |
| | | | | | | | | | | | | | 20 | 0 | 0 |

*Table showing the Part of the Equation of Time that arises from the Inequality of the Sun's Motion.*

| Dial Faster than Clock. | | | | | | | | Dial Slower than Clock. | | | | | | | |
|---|---|---|---|---|---|---|---|---|---|---|---|---|---|---|---|
| | | M. | S. | | | M. | S. | | | M. | S. | | | M. | S. |
| July | 1 | 0 | 0 | October | 3 | 7 | 43 | December | 31 | 0 | 0 | March | 30 | 7 | 43 |
| | 7 | 0 | 40 | | 8 | 7 | 42 | January | 5 | 0 | 41 | April | 4 | 7 | 40 |
| | 12 | 1 | 19 | | 13 | 7 | 37 | | 10 | 1 | 22 | | 9 | 7 | 34 |
| | 17 | 1 | 57 | | 18 | 7 | 29 | | 15 | 2 | 2 | | 14 | 7 | 24 |
| | 22 | 2 | 35 | | 23 | 7 | 18 | | 20 | 2 | 41 | | 19 | 7 | 12 |
| | 28 | 3 | 12 | | 28 | 7 | 3 | | 25 | 3 | 19 | | 24 | 6 | 56 |
| August | 2 | 3 | 47 | November | 2 | 6 | 45 | | 29 | 3 | 56 | | 30 | 6 | 36 |
| | 7 | 4 | 21 | | 7 | 6 | 24 | February | 3 | 4 | 30 | May | 5 | 6 | 14 |
| | 12 | 4 | 52 | | 12 | 5 | 39 | | 8 | 5 | 2 | | 10 | 5 | 50 |
| | 17 | 5 | 22 | | 17 | 5 | 32 | | 13 | 5 | 32 | | 15 | 5 | 22 |
| | 22 | 5 | 50 | | 22 | 5 | 2 | | 18 | 5 | 39 | | 20 | 4 | 52 |
| | 28 | 6 | 14 | | 27 | 4 | 30 | | 23 | 6 | 24 | | 26 | 4 | 21 |
| September | 2 | 6 | 36 | December | 2 | 3 | 56 | | 28 | 6 | 45 | | 31 | 3 | 47 |
| | 7 | 6 | 56 | | 7 | 3 | 19 | March | 5 | 7 | 3 | June | 5 | 3 | 12 |
| | 12 | 7 | 12 | | 12 | 2 | 41 | | 10 | 7 | 18 | | 10 | 2 | 35 |
| | 17 | 7 | 24 | | 17 | 2 | 2 | | 15 | 7 | 29 | | 16 | 1 | 57 |
| | 23 | 7 | 34 | | 21 | 1 | 22 | | 20 | 7 | 37 | | 21 | 1 | 19 |
| | 28 | 7 | 40 | | 26 | 0 | 41 | | 25 | 7 | 42 | | 26 | 0 | 40 |

The difference between the apparent and the true time, is very observable about the season when the day is lengthening or shortening with most rapidity. It is a common remark, that when the day is shortening, the change is more observable in the evening than in the morning; but that the reverse is the case when the day is lengthening. This arises from the clock being before or after the sun. Thus, in the end of October, the dial is upwards of sixteen minutes faster than the clock; so that the time of sun-rise, and the time of sun-set, will each, as indicated by the clock, appear earlier by 16 minutes, than as indicated by the motion of the solar shadow. Hence the instant of noon, as shown by the clock, appears not to divide equally the time during which the sun is above the horizon: the time from sun-rise till noon, appears longer than from noon till sun-set. Again, about the middle of February, the dial is about 15 minutes slower than the clock; so that the time of sun-rise and the time of sun-set will each, as indicated by the clock, be later by 15 minutes than as indicated by the dial; and the time from sun-rise till noon, as shown by the clock, will appear shorter than the time from noon till sun-set.

As the return of the sun to the meridian marks out the day, so his return to the same equinox marks out *another portion of time* of much importance to be determined with accuracy; namely, *the* YEAR. This period comprehends the seasons which divide it into four parts. Within this period also, the moon goes twelve times through all her phases, which occupy the space of nearly twenty-nine and a half days: hence the year has been divided into twelve months, three of which are allotted to each season. By accurate observation it is found, that the time which elapses between the instant at which the sun passes the vernal equinox, and the period of his return to it, is $365^d\ 5^h\ 48^m\ 48^s$. This period is called the TROPICAL year. It is found to be shorter than the interval between two successive returns of the sun to the same star by $20^m\ 29^s$. This last-mentioned period is called the SIDEREAL year, and consists of $365^d\ 6^h\ 9^m\ 11^s$.

In order to make such a distribution of time as is accommodated to the purposes of life, it is necessary so to adjust the reckoning of the solar revolution to the length of the mean solar day, that the beginning of the year may coincide with the beginning of the day, and the seasons may always recur in the same months. If the solar revolution consisted of an exact number of days, there would be no difficulty; but as it includes a fraction of a day, it is evident that one year cannot be made equal to one revolution, without incurring the inconvenience of making the year commence at a different point of time from the beginning of the day. But though one year cannot be made equal to one revolution, a certain number of years may be made equal to a like number of revolutions.

Julius Cæsar introduced the first near approximation to accuracy on this subject, in the 45th year before the commencement of the Christian era. The Romans had before that time estimated the year according to the course of the moon, in imitation of the Greeks; dividing it into twelve months, which consisted in all of 354 days; but as an odd number was thought the more fortunate, one day was added which made the year consist of 355 days. To make the lunar year correspond with the course of the sun, on which depends the vicissitude of seasons, an intercalary month was inserted every other year, between the 23d and 24th day of February. The intercalation of this month was left to the discretion of the priests, who, from interested motives, inserted often more or fewer than the proper number of days, so as to make the year longer or shorter, according as it suited their own purposes. This caused the months to be transposed from their stated seasons, the winter months being carried back into autumn, and the autumnal months into summer. When Julius Cæsar became master of the state, he resolved to put an end to this disorder, by abolishing the use of intercalations which had been the source of it; and for that purpose, by the assistance of Sosigenes, a celebrated astronomer of Alexandria, he adjusted the year to the course of the sun, and assigned to the respective months the number of days which they still contain. That matters might proceed with regularity from the beginning of the ensuing January, he made the current year, which was called the last year of *confusion*, consist of fifteen months, or 445 days.

The JULIAN *year* is founded upon the supposition that the solar revolution is exactly $365^d\ 6^h$. For three successive years the six hours are omitted; but in the fourth year an additional day is inserted in the month of February, which makes the four years correspond with four solar revolutions. This fourth year, consisting of 366 days, is called BISSEXTILE or LEAP year. But as the true length of the solar revolution is not $365^d\ 6^h$, but only $365^d\ 5^h\ 48^m\ 48^s$, the Julian year is too long by $11^m\ 12^s$; so that before a new year begins, the sun has passed the point of the ecliptic where the preceding year began. The error thence arising is, however, so small, that it was long before it was observed. The Julian Calendar was introduced into the church at the time of the Council of Nice, in the year 325 of the Christian era; and the vernal equinox was at that time fixed to the 21st of March. In the year 1582, however, it was found that the vernal equinox fell, not on the 21st of March, but on the 11th of that month; so that the Julian year had fallen about ten days behind the sun. If this erroneous reckoning had been continued, the seasons would have entirely changed their places. *It was therefore resolved to reform the calendar*, which was done by *Pope Gregory* XIII., and the first step was to correct the loss of the ten days, by counting the day after the 4th of October, not the 5th, but the 15th day of the month. The error in the Julian year reckoning, being about eleven minutes yearly, amounts to nearly three days in four centuries. Hence to prevent its accumulation in future, it was agreed to suppress three intercalary days in the course of four hundred years, by considering the last of three successive centuries common, instead of leap years. The years in which the inter calary days are omitted are 1700, 1800, 1900: and, in general, the last year of every century not divisible by four, is reckoned a common year, which in the Julian account is bissextile. The degree of accuracy thus attained is very considerable; for taking the annual error at $11\frac{1}{5}$ minutes, in four centuries, it will amount to 4480 minutes, or to $3^d\ 2^h\ 40^m$. Of this error, the fractional part, $2^h\ 40^m$, is all that remains uncorrected; and this error will require the lapse of 3600 years before it amounts to a day.

*Other modes of intercalation.* If the tropical year were $365^d\ 5^h\ 49^m\ 12^s$, the Gregorian intercalation would be perfectly exact. Accurate observation proves, however, that the year is shorter by about 24 seconds. If scientific principles had been strictly followed, they would have pointed out other modes of intercalation still more accurate, though perhaps not more convenient, than that which has been adopted. The determination of the methods of intercalation best suited to make the computations in the calendar correspond as nearly as possible with the real motions of the sun, requires all the integer numbers to be found, which most nearly express the ratio of $5^h\ 48^m\ 48^s$ to a day. These numbers are easily determined by the method of *continued fractions.* In the Gregorian calendar, 97 days are intercalated in the course of 400 years; but it would be much more exact to intercalate 109 days in the course of 450 years. If the tropical year were precisely $365^d\ 5^h\ 48^m\ 48^s$, this intercalation would, indeed, be quite accurate: for $5^h\ 48^m\ 48^s$, multiplied by 450, give exactly 109 days.

The reformation of the calendar, or the change from the Old Style to the New Style, did not take place *in England*, till the year 1752, at which time it was established by an act of parliament. The alteration was ordered to be made on the 2d of September; and as the error of the Julian reckoning now amounted to 11 days, the 3d was to be counted the 14th of September.

*Correspondence between the days of the week and month.* As the common year consists of 52 weeks and one day, it is evident that the beginning and end of each common year will fall on the same day of the week. In a series of years, therefore, if no leap years occurred, the first day of each month would, year after year, be one day farther advanced in the week, till, in the course of seven years, the same days of the month would return to the same days of the week. But since leap year contains 52 weeks and 2 days, and occurs every fourth year, it follows that the days of the week cannot correspond to the same days of the month, till after the lapse of four times seven or twenty-eight years. This period is called the Cycle of the Sun. When this period is completed, the sun's place in the ecliptic returns to the same signs and degrees on the same months and days, so as not to differ a degree in a century; and the leap years, as well as the common years, begin the same course over again with respect to the days of the week on which the days of the month fall. The year of our Saviour's birth, according to the vulgar era, was the ninth year of the solar cycle: hence, to find the current year of that cycle, we must add nine to the given year of the Christian era, and divide the sum by twenty-eight; the quotient will be the number of cycles which have been completed since the birth of Christ, and the remainder will be the current year of the present cycle. Thus, for the year 1829, the cycle of the sun is found to be 18. The first seven letters of the alphabet have been employed to mark the several days of the week. As one of those seven letters must necessarily stand against Sunday, it is printed in the calendar in a capital form, and called the Dominical Letter: the other six letters are inserted in a different character, to denote the other six days of the week. When January begins on Sunday, A is the Dominical letter for that year: but because the next year begins on Monday, the Sunday will of course fall on the seventh day, to which is annexed the seventh letter G, which will therefore be the Dominical letter for all that year: and as the third year will begin on Tuesday, Sunday will fall on the sixth day, so that F will be the Dominical letter for that year, and so on. Hence it is evident that the Dominical letters will succeed each other in a retrograde order, viz. G, F, E, D, C, B, A. As the days of the week correspond to the same days of the month only once in twenty-eight years, it follows that it is only after the lapse of the same period, that the series of Dominical letters can proceed in the same order in reference to the days of the month. Every leap year has two Dominical letters; one answering from the beginning of January till the end of February; the other being the letter immediately preceding, answering for the remainder of the year. The Dominical letter may be found for any year of any century by the following rule: *divide the centuries by 4, and take twice what remains from 6: then add together this last remainder, the odd years above the even centuries, and the fourth part of these odd years, neglecting the remainder if any: divide the sum by 7, and the excess of 7 above the remainder is the number answering to the letter required.* Thus, for the year 1830, the Dominical letter is C. For the centuries 18 divided by 4 leave 2; and twice this remainder taken from 6 also leaves 2; by adding to which the odd number of years 30, and their fourth part 7, we obtain 39: this sum divided by 7 leaves the remainder 4, which taken from 7 leaves 3, answering to C, the third letter of the alphabet.

---

## CHAPTER X.

### PROPER MOTION OF THE MOON. HER PHASES. ECLIPSES OF THE SUN AND MOON.

The moon, next to the sun, is the most interesting to us of all the heavenly bodies. Her phases, or that series of changes in her figure and illumination which she undergoes in the course of about a month, are one of the most striking of the celestial phenomena; and present a division of time so remarkable that it has been the first in use among all nations.

The moon has an apparent motion among the fixed stars similar to that of the sun, but much more rapid: it carries her eastward at the rate of nearly 13° 10½′, at an average, in 24 hours. When this motion is accurately traced out, it is found, that the moon describes round the earth, in 27ᵈ 7ʰ 43ᵐ, a path or orbit inclined to the ecliptic at an angle of nearly 5° 9′. The line in which the plane of the orbit cuts the plane of the ecliptic is called the LINE OF THE NODES. The point in which the moon crosses the ecliptic when *ascending* to the north, is called the ASCENDING node; and the opposite point, in which she crosses it when *descending* to the south, is called the DESCENDING node.

The figure of the lunar orbit is determined in the same manner as that of the solar, by observing the changes in the apparent diameter of the moon, and comparing these with the variations in her angular velocity. It is thus found, that the moon's orbit, like that of the sun, is in appearance an ellipse, having the centre of the earth in one of the foci, and that the radius vector, or the line joining the centres of the earth and moon, describes areas proportional to the times. Neither the line of the nodes nor the greater axis of the lunar orbit is fixed. The former has a slow retrograde motion, by which it makes an entire revolution in something more than 18⅔ years; the latter has a progressive motion, by which it completes a revolution in something less than 9 years. The elliptic orbit is liable, indeed, to so many changes, that the full investigation of the lunar motion has been found one of the most difficult problems in astronomy. At the same time it is one of the most useful, as connected with the finding of the longitude of places on the surface of the earth. Accordingly, the efforts of astronomers have been assiduously directed to the perfecting of the lunar theory; and by employing the resources of modern science, and combining these with continued and accurate observation, their labours have been crowned with wonderful success.

The phases of the moon depend on her position with regard to the sun. Let E be the earth, M the moon revolving in her orbit round the earth, E S the direction of the sun, and let us suppose all the solar rays which illuminate the moon to proceed in straight lines parallel to S E. The moon is an opaque body like the earth, and is visible only in consequence of reflecting the light of the sun. When she comes to the meridian, therefore, about the same time with the sun, that is, when she is at M, she must be invisible, on account of the unenlightened side being turned towards us. It is then said to be NEW moon: and, in reference to her position with regard to the sun, the moon is said to be in CONJUNCTION. Again, when the moon comes to the meridian about midnight, that is, when she is at *m*, she is said to be in OPPOSITION, and in that position she presents an entire circular disc; because the whole of the enlightened side is then turned towards the earth. It is then said to be FULL moon. At any point of her orbit, between the points of conjunction and opposition, the moon turns more or less of her enlightened side towards the earth, according to her angular distance from the sun, and presents exactly the same appearances as an opaque spherical body, of which one side is illuminated, would exhibit, if viewed from a distance, and in the same positions in which the moon is seen from the earth. After the conjunction, as soon as she has emerged sufficiently from the solar rays, she is seen in the western sky, after sunset, in the form of a CRESCENT, as at M′, having the convex side turned towards the sun, and the concave bounded by an elliptic line. On every succeeding night the luminous part increases, while the elliptic boundary continually approaches to a straight line. On the seventh night from the time of new moon, the moon reaches the position M″, where her distance from the sun is 90°: she is then said to be in her first QUADRATURE, and exhibits the appearance of HALF moon; that is, the disc is a semicircle. The enlightened part still continuing to increase on the same side, the rectilineal boundary of the semicircular disc passes again into an elliptic line, and the moon becomes GIBBOUS, as at M‴: on all sides the disc is convex, though it does not become entirely full orbed until she reaches the point of opposition, at *m*, about the end of seven days from the time of half moon. From the instant of opposition the moon begins to return to the sun on the western side; and in her progress towards the conjunction she goes through the same series of changes in an inverted order, becoming first gibbous, as at *m*′; then half moon at the time when she reaches the position *m*″, her second quadrature; then a crescent, as at *m*‴, which, continually diminishing, at last disappears altogether. Thus, on the supposition that the moon is an opaque body and nearly spherical, and that she revolves in an orbit round the earth, the phenomena of her phases are easily explained.

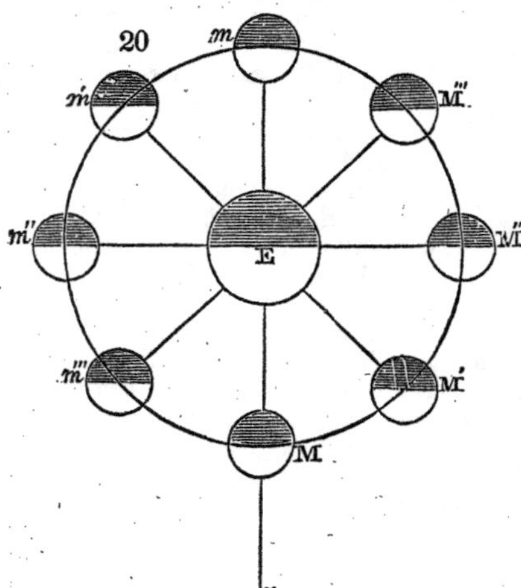

Strictly speaking, the moon is not exactly 90 degrees distant from the sun when she presents the appearance of half moon. This phasis occurs at the moment when the moon is in such a position that two straight lines drawn from her centre,—the one to the centre of the earth, the other to the centre of the sun,—form a right angle. By observing, therefore, the moon's distance from the sun, at the instant when the boundary between the enlightened and dark part exactly bisects the lunar disc, we should have in the right-angled triangle S M F the angle at F; and hence, since the side F M is also known, S F, the distance of the sun may be determined. This was the first method employed for finding the sun's distance from the earth; but, from the nicety of the observations required, it cannot be expected to lead to any very satisfactory result.

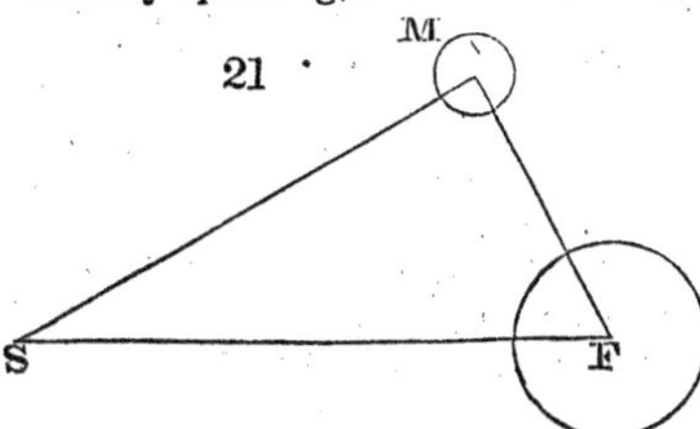


To a spectator on the moon the earth must evidently exhibit a series of changes similar to the lunar phases as seen from the earth. At the time of conjunction the moon is on the illuminated side of the earth, so that the earth must then appear, as seen from the moon, an entire circular disc. Again, at the time of opposition, the moon is on the dark side of the earth; so that the earth must then be invisible. When the moon is seen as a crescent, the earth will appear gibbous; and when the moon appears gibbous, the earth will be seen as a crescent.

The fact of the earth appearing to a spectator on the moon an entire luminous disc, at the time of the moon's conjunction with the sun, furnishes an explanation of a phenomenon with which every one is familiar. In clear weather, when the moon is three or four days old, her whole body is visible. The horns of the enlightened crescent appear to project beyond the old moon as if they were part of a sphere of considerably larger diameter than the unenlightened part. Now, the part of the moon not directly illuminated by the sun is seen by the light reflected from the earth. The appearance of a lucid bow, connecting the horns of the crescent, is produced by the circumstance of the eastern edge of the moon's disc being more luminous than the adjacent regions towards the centre. With regard to the enlightened crescent appearing a portion of a larger sphere, this is an optical deception, and furnishes a remarkable proof that of two objects of equal magnitude, but of different degrees of brightness, the brighter appears larger.

A lunation or lunar month is formed by the time that elapses between one new moon and another. It consists of $29^d\ 12^h\ 44^m\ 3^s$ nearly; and therefore exceeds the period of her mean sidereal revolution, which is $27^d\ 7^h\ 43^m\ 11\frac{1}{2}^s$. This excess arises from the proper motion of the sun in the ecliptic; for it is evident that the period in which the moon goes through all her phases must be equal to the time required to describe 360°, with an angular velocity equal to the difference between angular velocities of moon and sun.

*Cycle of the moon.* In 19 Julian solar years there are 235 lunations, and about one hour and a half more Hence, after 19 years, the conjunctions, oppositions, and other aspects of the moon recur on the same days of the month, and only about an hour and a half sooner. This period is accordingly called the Cycle of the Moon, and has been found of so much use in adjusting the lunar to the solar year, in order to know the time of new and full moon, and to determine the time of Easter, and other moveable feasts, that the numbers of it have been called Golden Numbers. The year of our Saviour's birth, according to the vulgar era, was the first year of the lunar cycle: hence, to find the golden number, or the current year of that cycle, we must add one to the year of Christ for which the golden number is required, and divide the sum by 19: the quotient will be the number of cycles which have elapsed since the birth of Christ, and the remainder will be the golden nnmber or current year of the cycle.

The epact is the difference between the solar and lunar periods at the end of each year, or the moon's age on the first of January. Since the Julian solar year is $365^d\ 6^h$, and the lunar year, or twelve lunations, $354^d\ 8^h\ 48^m\ 36^s$, if we suppose new moon to have happened on the first of January, so that the epact for that year is 0, it follows that the epact for the next succeeding year will be $10^d\ 21^h\ 11^m\ 24^s$, or nearly 11 days. For the third year, the epact will be nearly 22 days. For the fourth year it will be 33 days, or (rejecting 30 days for a complete lunation), 3 days, and so on.

The annexed table contains the *golden numbers* with the corresponding *epacts* adapted to the Gregorian calendar, till the year 1900. The epact for each month of the year is, in like manner, the moon's age on the first day of the month, supposing new moon to have happened on the first of January.

| Golden Numbers. | Epacts. | Golden Numbers. | Epacts. | Golden Numbers. | Epacts. |
|---|---|---|---|---|---|
| I. | 0 | VIII. | 17 | XV. | 4 |
| II. | 11 | IX. | 28 | XVI. | 15 |
| III. | 22 | X. | 9 | XVII. | 26 |
| IV. | 3 | XI. | 20 | XVIII. | 7 |
| V. | 14 | XII. | 1 | XIX. | 18 |
| VI. | 25 | XIII. | 12 | I. | 0 |
| VII. | 6 | XIV. | 23 | | |

The epacts for the months of the common and leap year are as follows:—

| | Jan. | Feb. | Mar. | Apr. | May. | June. | July. | Aug. | Sep. | Oct. | Nov. | Dec. |
|---|---|---|---|---|---|---|---|---|---|---|---|---|
| Common year | 0, | 1, | 0, | 2, | 2, | 3, | 4, | 5, | 7, | 7, | 9, | 9. |
| Leap year | 0, | 1, | 1, | 3, | 3, | 4, | 5, | 6, | 8, | 8, | 10, | 10. |

It is evident that the moon's age will be found by adding together the epact of the year, the epact of the month, and the day of the month, rejecting thirty if the sum amount to that number. Thus, if it is required to find the moon's age on the 11th November 1829; by adding 1 to 1829 and dividing by 19, we obtain a remainder 6, which is the golden number for the year 1829. Now, against VI. in the table, we find 25 for the epact of the year, and 9 is the epact for November: hence $25 + 9 + 11 - 30 = 15$, which is the moon's age; so that the moon is full on that day.

The lunar cycle of 19 years, though remarkably simple, is however far from being accurate. Nineteen years contain about an hour and a half more than 235 lunations; so that at the termination of that period the moon has advanced about an hour and a half in the next lunation. This error amounts to a day in the course of 16 cycles, or about 300 years. But, to compensate this excess, the epacts may be advanced one day every 300 years, and in this manner the lunar and solar periods will be made to agree. In consequence of her apparent motion eastward, the moon is about 48 minutes later after every diurnal revolution of coming to the meridian. As 48 minutes is equal to $\frac{4}{5}$ of an hour, an approximation is made to the time of her southing, by multiplying her age by 4, and dividing by 5. This gives the time, nearly, before or after noon, according as the moon is past the opposition or conjunction.

The time of her rising and setting is affected by the same cause. In one part of the orbit, however, this is in a great measure counteracted by the smallness of the angle which the orbit makes with the horizon. For facilitating the illustration of this phenomenon, let us suppose the moon to move in the ecliptic, from which she never deviates much more than 5°. By turning round the celestial globe, it will be seen that the ecliptic makes with the horizon very different angles, as the points of their intersection vary. If the first point of *Aries* be brought to coincide with the east point of the horizon, the angle which the ecliptic makes with the horizon is equal to the difference of the obliquity of the ecliptic and the complement of the latitude: but if the first point of *Libra* be brought into coincidence with the east point, the angle between the ecliptic and the horizon is equal to the sum of the obliquity and the complement of the latitude. When the moon is in *Pisces* or *Aries*, her motion in her orbit will therefore produce a considerable change, each succeeding night, on the distance between the east and the point of rising, but the time of rising will not be much affected. The reverse will be the case when the moon is in *Virgo* or *Libra*. Hence it is obvious that in every lunation, at a certain time, the moon must rise nearly at the same hour for several days together. This phenomenon, however, for the most part, passes unobserved; but in the harvest season it attracts attention, as being then much more conspicuous than at any other time of the year. In the autumnal months the moon is *full* in the signs *Pisces* and *Aries*, (the sun being at that season in the opposite signs *Virgo* and *Libra*,) and on that account rises an entire orb (or nearly so) for about a week, almost at the time of sunset, thus affording a supply of light very beneficial to the husbandman, in gathering in the fruits of the earth. This lunation has accordingly been distinguished by the name of the HARVEST MOON.

The inclination of the moon's orbit to the ecliptic, makes the *harvest moon* rise, more or less, nearly at the same time that she would if she moved in the ecliptic, according to the position of the line of the nodes. If we suppose the ascending node to be in *Aries*, the moon's orbit makes with the horizon an angle upwards of 5° less than the angle which the ecliptic makes with it, and consequently the harvest moon will rise more nearly at the same time than if the moon had been in the ecliptic. In a little less than $9\frac{1}{3}$ years, however, the line of the nodes will have made half a revolution, and the descending node will be in *Aries*. The moon's orbit will then make with the horizon an angle more than 5° greater than that which the ecliptic makes with it; and, consequently, the harvest moon will not rise so nearly at the same time as if the moon had been in the ecliptic.

The quantity of moonlight which we enjoy in winter is much greater than in summer. As the moon is always on the same side of the heavens with the sun, at the time of new moon, and on the opposite side at the time of full moon; it is evident that at midsummer the moon, when seen as a crescent, will rise at a point of the horizon to the north of east, and set at a point to the north of west, and will be seen high in the heavens when she passes the meridian. As she approaches full moon, however, she will rise farther and farther to the south of east, will appear low in the heavens when on the meridian, and will set farther and farther to the south of west. The reverse takes place at mid-winter: the moon is low when seen as a crescent, and rises higher and higher in the heavens as she approaches full moon. She also rises to the south of east when a crescent, and sets to the south of west; but, when full, rises and sets to the north of these points. Thus the great quantity of moonlight during the long nights of winter arises from the moon being full in the northern signs of the ecliptic, and is analogous to that of sunshine in the long days of summer. As we approach the pole, the quantity of moonlight in winter becomes still more remarkable; and at the pole itself, at mid-winter, the moon does not set for fifteen days together, namely, from the first to the last quarter.

The lunar disc is diversified with a great variety of spots, which are quite permanent, but differ very considerably from each other in degrees of brightness. These inequalities of illumination are visible to the naked eye. Since the discovery of the telescope they have engaged the particular attention of several astronomers, by whom their relative positions have been carefully ascertained, and laid down in maps of the lunar surface. From an attentive examination of the lights and shades seen on the moon's disc, it has been inferred that her surface is very irregular, being diversified by lofty mountains, precipitous rocks, and deep caverns. The existence of these irregularities of surface is strikingly evident from the serrated appearance of the line which separates the enlightened from the dark part of the moon, and by a variety of bright detached spots, almost always visible on the dark part and near the line of separation between light and darkness. These bright spots are the tops of mountains illuminated by the sun, while his rays have not yet reached the bottom of the intervening valleys. The dark spots of the moon are smooth, and apparently level, while the luminous parts are elevated regions, which either rise into high mountains or sink into deep and immense cavities. The general smoothness of the dark spots naturally led to the conclusion that they were collections of water; but more careful observation has made it appear that the line which separates the enlightened from the dark part of the moon is not smooth and regular, even when it passes over a dark spot; so that there is no reason to suppose that there is any large collection of water in the moon: and this conclusion is strengthened by the constant serenity of her appearance, which seems undisturbed by any of those atmospherical phenomena which arise on our globe from the existence of water. The mountainous scenery of the moon, and more especially the immense caverns with which her surface is broken, bear little analogy to what we see on the surface of the earth. The resemblance may, however, be conceived to be considerably increased if all the waters of the earth were removed, and the beds of the ocean, seas, and lakes were left dry with all the inequalities of their surfaces exposed to view. The earth would then be diversified, not only with the rocks and mountains now seen upon its surface, but likewise with deep caverns of immense extent, and having detached mountains and rocks rising from the bottom, similar to the cavities discovered in the moon. From certain light spots which have sometimes been seen on the dark part of the moon, at such a distance from the enlightened portion that they could not arise from the light of the sun, astronomers have inferred the existence of volcanoes in the moon. Dr. Herschel, in particular, two or three different times, observed such spots.

The height of a lunar mountain may be measured by the following method. Let D A E be a section of the moon made by a plane passing through O, the eye of an observer on the earth, M the summit of a mountain situated in the dark part of the lunar disc, and S the sun. It is evident that this plane will be perpendicular to the line which joins the horns of the moon. Let D A be the arch of the circle D A F, which passes over the visible portion of the enlightened hemisphere. Whenever the point M becomes visible to a spectator at O, it must be illuminated by a ray of the sun S A M, which will be a tangent to the circle D A F at the point A, and therefore at right angles to the diameter A F. Produce O M to meet the diameter D E in $m$, and draw A $r$ and A $n$ parallel to D E and M $m$; also produce E D to meet S M in C. Because D A E is a section of that hemisphere of the moon which is turned towards the earth, the visual ray O M $m$ is perpendicular to D E: hence the angles $m$ M C, M C $m$ are together equal to two right angles. But because C A is perpendicular to A B, the angles A B C and A C B (or M C $m$) are also together equal to two right angles: whence it is evident that the angle $m$ M C is equal to A B C; and that the triangles A M $r$, A B $n$ are similar. We have, therefore, A $n$ : A B = A $r$ : A M. Hence $\mathrm{A\,M} = \dfrac{\mathrm{A}\,r \times \mathrm{A\,B}}{\mathrm{A}\,n}$.

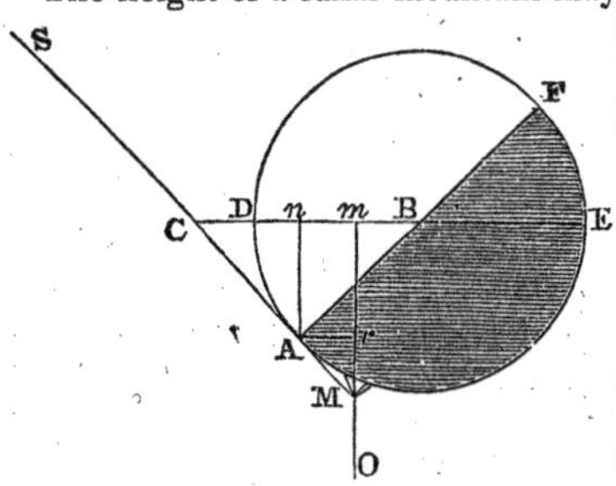

Now, A $r$ is the projection of A M on the lunar disc, and will be found by measuring, with the micrometer, in a direction perpendicular to a line joining the horns of the moon, the distance of the illuminated summit M from the enlightened disc at A; also $\dfrac{\mathrm{A}\,n}{\mathrm{A\,B}}$ = Sin. ∠ A B C, radius being unity, the angle A B C is equal to S M $m$ the moon's distance or elongation from the sun: wherefore we obtain $\mathrm{A\,M} = \dfrac{\mathrm{A}\,r}{\text{Sin. elongation}}$, a given quantity.

Next, let A G H be a section of the moon made by a plane passing along the tangent A M, and through the centre K: draw M K G; then, by a well-known property of the circle, $AM^2 = GM \times MH = MH \times (GH + HM)$, or, H M being much smaller than G H, we have $AM^2 = MH \times GH$, and $MH = \frac{AM^2}{GH}$ nearly. Now, A M and G H are both given; therefore H M, the height of the mountain above the general surface, may be determined.

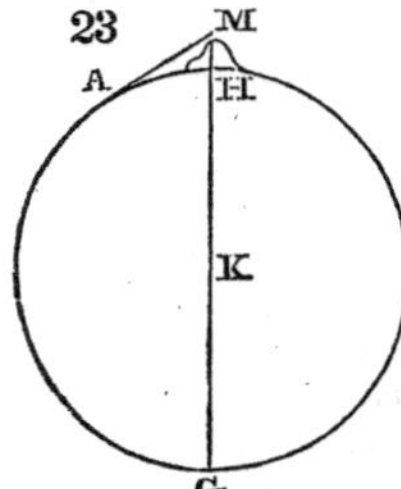


Suppose, for example, that when the apparent diameter of the moon is 31′ 15″, and her elongation from the sun 93° 57½′, the distance between the enlightened part of her disc, and the summit of a mountain situated in the dark part of it is found to be 41½″; and let it be required thence to determine the height of the mountain.

The diameter of the moon is about 2180 miles; hence 31′ 15″ or 1875″ : 41½″ = 2180 : 48·25, which is the number of miles in 41½″ on the lunar disc; so that we have $Ar = 48{\cdot}25$ miles.

Again, the Nat. Sin. of the elongation 93° 57½ = ·9976; therefore $AM = \frac{Ar}{\text{Sin. elongation}} = \frac{48{\cdot}25}{{\cdot}9976} = 48{\cdot}36$ miles.

Lastly. The height $= \frac{AM^2}{GH} = \frac{(48{\cdot}36)^2}{2180} = 1{\cdot}07$ mile.

Thus the height of the lunar mountain in question is found to be about a mile. The principle now explained is correct in theory; but with regard to the results obtained from the practical application of it, a greater difference of opinion exists than might have been expected. These results are, however, highly curious and interesting.

*Moon's motion round the earth.* The moon's surface, when viewed through a telescope, is so strongly characterised by the spots visible upon it, as to leave no doubt of its being always the same. From this the inference is obvious, since we are certain from the moon's motion round the earth, that she must revolve on an axis nearly perpendicular to the plane of her orbit in the same time that she revolves about the earth, namely in 27¼ days nearly. Her rotation on her axis is equable; but this is not the case with her motion in her orbit, which is periodically variable: and hence there are parts of the eastern and western edges of the moon which are seen occasionally. This appearance is called the LIBRATION OF THE MOON IN LONGITUDE. It is entirely optical, and argues no inequality in the moon's motion on her axis.

The moon's axis of rotation is not altogether perpendicular to the plane of her orbit, but inclined to it at an angle of 88° 29′ 49″. In consequence of this position of her axis her poles are alternately visible, and a small portion of the polar regions; this phenomenon is called the LIBRATION OF THE MOON IN LATITUDE.

The diurnal libration of the moon is another optical appearance arising from the moon being viewed from the surface instead of the centre of the earth. At rising, a part of the western edge is seen, which is invisible at setting; and, at setting, a part of the eastern edge is seen, which is invisible at rising.

The explication of the lunar phases leads to that of ECLIPSES—those occasional obscurations of the sun and moon which have, in ages of ignorance, been objects of superstitious terror to mankind, and at all times objects of curiosity to the philosopher. At the time of new moon, the moon is upon the same side of the heavens with the sun, but, for the most part, passes either above or below the solar disc without obscuring any part of it. This arises from her orbit being inclined to the ecliptic: for it is evident that if the planes of the orbit and ecliptic coincided, the centres of the sun, moon, and earth would, at every new moon, be in the same straight line; so that the moon would be seen to pass over the sun's disc, and the sun would appear to be totally or partially eclipsed, according to the position of an inhabitant upon the earth's surface. Again, at the time of full moon, the moon is on the opposite side of the heavens from the sun; and therefore she is on the same side of the heavens with the shadow, which the earth, as an opaque body, projects into space. In most cases, however, the moon passes above or below this conical shadow; so that she is not deprived of the sun's rays. But if the plane of the orbit coincided with that of the ecliptic, the centres of the sun, moon, and earth would evidently be in the same straight line at every full moon as well as at every new moon: the moon would therefore fall into the earth's shadow, and would be eclipsed to all the inhabitants on that side of the earth which is turned towards the moon at the time.

Though the inclination of the lunar orbit to the ecliptic prevents the occurrence at every new and full moon of these phenomena, there are certain distances from the nodes of the moon's orbit, called ECLIPTIC LIMITS, within which, if the moon is situated at the time of new or full moon, there will be a solar or lunar eclipse.

To illustrate the general phenomena of lunar eclipses. Let A B, D E be sections of the sun and earth, by a plane perpendicular to the plane of the ecliptic. Draw A V, B V touching

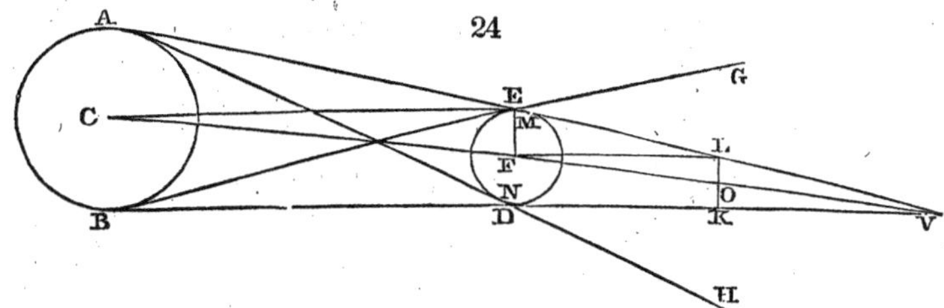


the circles A B, D E on the corresponding sides in E and D, and meeting each other in V: also draw B G, A H, touching these circles on the opposite sides in M and N. Then, if we suppose the figure A B H G to revolve about the line C F, which joins the centres of the circles, as an axis, the cone generated by the line E V represents the shadow which the earth projects into space; and from every point of that conical shadow the light of the sun is entirely excluded. The spaces between E V, M G, and between D V, N H, will receive the light of a part of the sun: and hence the space round the shadow, which is generated by the motion of the lines G M, E V, is called the PENUMBRA.

Join C E. It is evident that the angle E V F is equal to the difference of the angles A E C, E C F. But A E C is the angle under which the sun's semidiameter is seen from the earth; and E C F is the angle under which the earth's semidiameter is seen from the sun. Both of these angles being known, their difference E V F is a given angle. Now, in the right angled triangle E V F we have given the angle at V, and the side E F, which is the earth's semidiameter: hence F V, the height of the earth's shadow, may be determined. The height of the shadow varies from 213 to 220 semidiameters of the earth.

Again, let F O be the distance of the moon from the earth: draw K O L perpendicular to F V, and join F L. The angle L F O, under which the semidiameter of the section of the earth's shadow is seen from the earth, is equal to the difference of the angles, F L E, F V L. But F L E is the angle under which the semidiameter of the earth is seen from the moon, and F V L is, as has been shown, equal to the difference between the angle under which the sun's semidiameter is seen from the earth, and the angle under which the earth's semidiameter is seen from the sun: hence, to find the angle under which the section of the earth's shadow through which the moon passes in a lunar eclipse is seen from the earth, we must add together the two angles under which the semidiameter of the earth appears when seen from the sun and moon, and from the sum subtract the sun's apparent semidiameter, the remainder is the angle required. The angle L F O, when greatest, is about 46′: but the inclination of the lunar orbit to the ecliptic is upward of 5°, and to this distance the moon may recede from the ecliptic. It is evident, therefore, that an eclipse of the moon can take place only when she is near her nodes.

Let the circle A H B be the section of the earth's shadow at the moon; A B a portion of the ecliptic, and D F a portion of the moon's orbit near the ascending node. Draw C G from the centre of the shadow, (which must be the point of the ecliptic directly opposite the sun,) perpendicular to A B, and let it meet D F in G; then G is the point of opposition at which the moon will be 180 degrees of the ecliptic distant from the sun. Now, in moving from D to G, the moon must enter the earth's shadow, and will therefore be eclipsed. The beginning of the eclipse will be the moment that she enters on the shadow at K: the middle of the eclipse will be the moment when her centre reaches the point E, the extremity of the perpendicular drawn from C to D F; and the end of the eclipse will be the moment when she leaves the shadow at the point L. The portion of the moon's disc that is obscured will depend on the distance between E and C, which will vanish when the point of the opposition coincides with the node. It is evident that had the eclipse happened on the other side of the node, the opposite edge of the moon would have been immersed in the shadow.

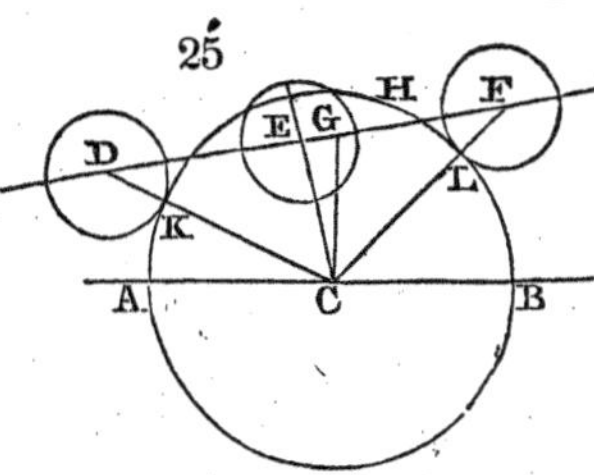


In eclipses there are various degrees of immersion. When this is entire, it is said to be *total;* when only a part of the moon is immersed, the eclipse is said to be *partial;* and when the centre of the moon passes through the centre of the shadow, the eclipse is said to be *central* and *total.* The breadth of the shadow at the moon is about three times her diameter, so that in the case of a total central eclipse, the moon may be entirely obscured for nearly two hours.

The time when eclipses shall happen may be computed from the laws which regulate the motions of the sun and moon. This computation requires astronomical tables, and is performed with considerable labour. But it may be observed that in 223 lunations, or 18 years 10 days (or 11 days according as four or five leap years occur in the interim), 7 hours 43 minutes, the moon returns to the same position nearly with regard to the sun, and the lunar nodes, and therefore the eclipses, will return nearly in the same order and circumstances. This is thought to be the period called the Chaldean *Saros*, being used by the Chaldeans in predicting eclipses.

When it is known that a lunar eclipse is to happen, it is easy to compute its general circumstances. The distance of the moon from the ecliptic at opposition, the time of opposition, the angles under which the earth's semidiameter is seen at the sun and moon, also the apparent diameters of these two luminaries, are known from the tables. In the right angled triangle C E G we have given C G, and the angle G C E, which is equal to the inclination of the moon's orbit to the ecliptic, nearly; hence we find C E and E G. From C E and C F, the sum of the semidiameters of the section of the earth's shadow and the moon, we find E F, which is equal to E D; thence D G, G F become known. We can compute from the tables the angular motion of the moon in her orbit relatively to the sun, the latter body being supposed at rest. Her motion relatively to the opposite point C is evidently the same: hence we can determine the time of describing D G and G F; that is, the time that elapses between the beginning of the eclipse and the opposition, and between the opposition and the end of the eclipse. But the time of the opposition is known, therefore the times of the beginning and end of the eclipse will also be known.

For estimating the quantity of an eclipse, the diameter of the solar or lunar disc is conceived to be divided into twelve equal parts called DIGITS; and according to the number of those parts which are obscured, so many digits are said to be eclipsed.

Let it be supposed that the edge of the moon's disc just touches the edge of the section of the earth's shadow at P, and that at the same time the diameters of the moon and shadow are each at the *maximum*, and we shall find the ecliptic limit for lunar eclipses. Produce E D and B A to meet in N: then N C is the limit of the distance of the node from the opposition at which an eclipse can happen. Since the line in which the centre of the moon moves (which for a short distance may be considered as a straight line) must be supposed parallel to the tangent to the circle A P B at the point P, the angle at E is a right angle. The angle N, is the inclination of the lunar orbit to the ecliptic: also C E is equal to the sum of the semidiameters of the moon and shadow. Hence from the spherical triangle C E N, C N may be determined; and is found to be about $11\frac{1}{2}°$. Unless when the node and the point of opposition, which are both liable to continual change of position, come within this distance, there cannot possibly be a lunar eclipse.

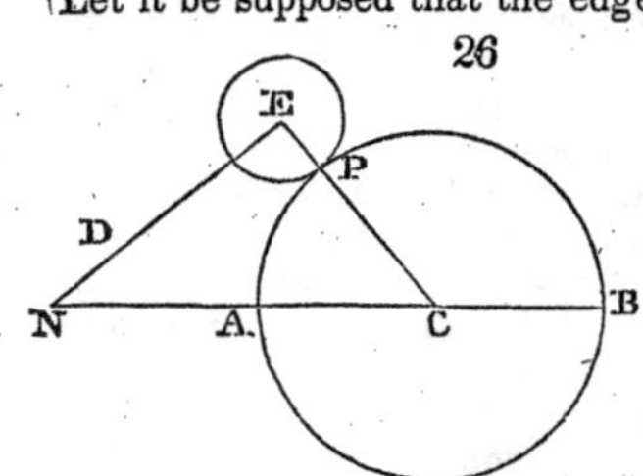


Calculation of longitude. The penumbra makes it very difficult to observe, with precision, the beginning or end of a lunar eclipse; so that though these periods may be employed for determining the longitude of places on the earth, no great degree of accuracy is to be expected. The best method is to note the time of the arrival of the boundary of the shadow at the different spots on the lunar surface, which may be considered as so many different observations.

The moon seldom disappears entirely in lunar eclipses, but is seen of a dusky red colour: even the spots on the lunar surface may be distinguished through the shade. This effect is to be attributed to a portion of the sun's light, which enters the conical shadow in consequence of being refracted by the atmosphere of the earth. The nature and effects of atmospherical refraction will afterwards be explained.

Eclipses of the sun. With regard to the general phenomena of solar eclipses, we may begin with remarking, that when the sun's light is intercepted by the moon, so that at any place on the earth's surface he becomes partly or wholly invisible, properly speaking, it is an eclipse of *that portion of the earth* on which the moon's shadow or penumbra falls.

The semi-angle at the vertex of the moon's shadow is determined in a similar manner to that on which the semi-angle at the vertex of the earth's shadow was found. It is equal to the difference of the angles under which the semi-diameters of the sun and moon would be seen, if each of these bodies were viewed from the other at the time of their conjunction; and will therefore not be very far from being equal to the apparent semi-diameter of the sun as seen from the earth. Computing, then, the length of the conical shadow of the moon, we shall find it vary from about $60\frac{1}{2}$ to $55\frac{1}{2}$ semi-diameters of the earth. The length of the shadow at the time of the conjunction may therefore at one time exceed, and at another time fall short of the moon's distance from the earth, which varies from 64 to 56 semi-diameters. In the former case, if the conjunction happen when the moon is within a certain distance of the node, the lunar shadow will reach the earth, and a section of it will traverse a portion of the earth's surface, producing, wherever it falls, a total eclipse of the sun.

Wherever the penumbra falls, the sun will appear partially eclipsed; more or fewer digits being eclipsed according as the place is less or more removed from the shadow, Beyond the penumbra the sun is not eclipsed at all. The section of the lunar shadow is so near the vertex, that, even when greatest, the portion of the earth's surface which it covers is not very extensive, being only about 180 miles in diameter: the penumbra, however extends over a considerable part of that hemisphere of the earth which is turned towards the sun. A total eclipse in any place cannot exceed 7′ 58″. If the vertex of the lunar shadow just reaches the surface, the total eclipse then produced will be instantaneous.

When the vertex of the lunar shadow falls short of the earth's surface, at no place will there be a total eclipse: but at places near the axis of the cone, there will be seen *an* ANNULAR *eclipse;* that is, the central parts of the sun's disc will be obscured, but a bright ring will be left visible round the dark body of the moon. Thus let A B, C D be sections of the sun and moon and V the vertex of the lunar

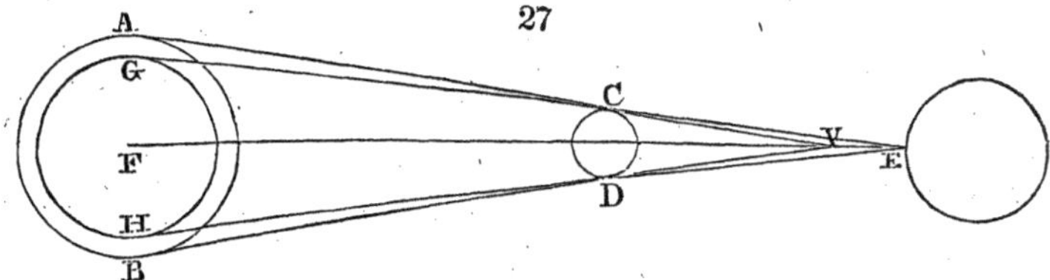


shadow which is supposed not to reach the earth. Produce F V the axis of the shadow to meet the surface of the earth in E. From E draw E C G, E D H tangents to the moon, and intersecting the sun's disc in G and H. The circle of which the line joining G H is the diameter, marks out the portion of the sun that is hid by the body of the moon from an observer at E, and the *annulus*, of which the breadth is A G, will be visible.

The general circumstances of a solar eclipse may be represented by projection; and a map may be constructed to show the progress of the shadow over the surface of the earth. The most simple projection is that which supposes the observer to be placed in the sun, and to see the path which any place on the earth's surface describes in consequence of the diurnal motion projected into an ellipse on the plane of the earth's disc, while the path of the moon's shadow is projected into a straight line on the same disc. The geometrical construction thus obtained is sufficiently accurate for the prediction of eclipses.

The circumstances of a solar eclipse may, however, be computed with considerable accuracy. Thus, find for the given place, from the tables, the time of the conjunction of the sun and moon. The position of the heavenly bodies in reference to the ecliptic is determined by latitude and longitude, in the same manner as the position of a place on the surface of the earth in reference to the equator. Find, then, for the time of the conjunction, the latitude and longitude of the moon, and apply to them the small change produced by the spectator being placed on the surface instead of the centre of the earth; a change which depends on the angle which the earth's semidiameter subtends at the sun and moon at the time: this will give us the apparent latitude and longitude of the moon as seen on the concave surface of the heavens. Compute from these and the longitude of the sun, that is, his distance from the first point of *Aries*, the apparent distance of the centres of the sun and moon at the instant of conjunction; whence we may nearly conclude the time of the beginning and ending of the eclipse, by taking into account the apparent horary motion of the moon in latitude and longitude at the time of conjunction, computed from the tables. About the conjectured time of the beginning of the eclipse, compute two or three apparent latitudes and longitudes of the moon, and thence, combined with the longitude of the sun, the apparent distances of the centres. From these results the time may be computed by proportion when the apparent distance of the centres is equal to the sum of the apparent semi-diameters, that is, the time of the beginning of the eclipse.

The magnitude also of the eclipse at any time may be thus determined: let S E (*fig.* 28.) be the computed apparent difference of longitude of the centres S, M, of the sun and moon, and M E the computed apparent latitude of the moon. In the right-angled triangle M E S, we have therefore given the two sides to find the hypothenuse M S, which, being known, we obtain $m\ n$ the eclipsed part of the sun: for $m\ n = \text{S}\ m + \text{M}\ n - \text{M S}$.

The ecliptic limits of the sun may be determined in the following manner: let S and M (29—*fig.* 1.) be the sun and moon, seen from E the centre of the earth at the moment of conjunction; that is, when their centres are in the same circle S B perpendicular to the ecliptic. Let the angle $a$ E $b$, formed by tangents drawn from E to the adjacent edges of the solar and lunar discs, be equal to the *greatest* difference between the true place B and apparent

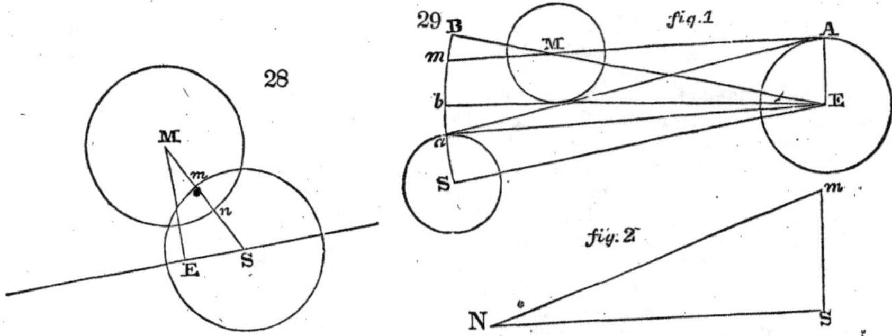


place *m* of the moon, which can arise from her being viewed from the surface instead of the centre of the earth. It is not difficult to see that this difference will be greatest when the moon is in the horizon, and that its effect will be to depress her altitude. The distance of the sun is so great, that we may at present consider his true and apparent place as coincident. Suppose now an observer on the earth's surface at A, whose horizon is at right angles to S B, to have the moon in his horizon at the moment of conjunction; it is evident that to him the two discs would appear to be in contact: but to an observer on any other point of the earth's surface, the discs would appear asunder. In the moment of conjunction, therefore, the penumbra must have just touched the earth at the point A; and when the centres of the sun and moon approach nearest to each other before or after the conjunction, it will spread over a very small portion of the earth's surface near A, so as to produce *barely* an eclipse. Hence the distance of the sun from the node at the time of conjunction will be the solar ecliptic limit, nearly. In the right-angled spherical triangle S *m* N (*fig.* 2.) let N S be a portion of the ecliptic, and N *m* a portion of the moon's orbit, N being the node, and let the perpendicular S *m* be equal to S *m* in *fig.* 1. The arc N S is the ecliptic limit required: and to find it, we have given the angle at N equal to the inclination of the moon's orbit to the ecliptic, and S *m* equal to the sum of the apparent diameters of the sun and moon together with the angle *b* E *a*, which is equal to B M *m* or A M E, the angle subtended by the semidiameter of the earth's disc as seen from the moon. The angle N and the perpendicular S *m* being known, the base N S is easily determined. The three quantities to the sum of which S *m* is equal, are variable in their values. Taking for S *m* the sum of the semidiameters of the solar and lunar disc, and of the disc of the earth as seen from the moon when they are greatest, we find S N equal to 17° 12′ nearly. But if S *m* be made equal to the sum of the semidiameters when they are least, S N is found to be nearly equal to 15° 19′. Within the former of these limits an eclipse of the sun *may* happen, within the latter it *must* happen.

If the moon's apparent diameter be greater than or equal to that of the sun, the eclipse will be total wherever the lunar shadow falls. But if the sun's apparent diameter be greater than that of the moon, the eclipse will be annular within the lunar shadow.

*Number of eclipses.* The ecliptic limits of the sun taken on each side of the node, give an arc of the ecliptic exceeding 30°, so that the sun will be more than a month in passing through these limits. Hence there must be two eclipses of the sun every year. Since the ecliptic limits of the moon, however, taken on each side give an arc only of about 23°, and since through this portion of the ecliptic the sun passes in less than a month, there may be no eclipse of the moon in the course of a year.

When a total and central eclipse of the moon happens, there may be an eclipse of the sun at the preceding and following conjunctions, because between new and full moons the sun describes only about 15 degrees of the ecliptic, so that each conjunction may happen within the solar ecliptic limits. The same may take place at the opposite node: there may therefore be six eclipses in the course of a year. The retrogradation of the node at the rate of 20° yearly renders it possible, when the first eclipse of the year happens early in January, that another eclipse of the sun may occur in the end of the year. On the whole, there may be seven eclipses in the course of one year; five of the sun, and two of the moon: and there never can be fewer than two, but though more solar eclipses happen than lunar, there are fewer of the former visible than of the latter; because a lunar eclipse is visible at every place on the earth which is turned towards the moon during its continuance; but in a solar eclipse the sun continues visible at all places over which the penumbra does not pass. The greatest possible duration of the annular appearance of a solar eclipse is $12^m\ 24^s$, and the greatest possible time during which the sun can be wholly obscured is $7^m\ 58^s$.

As the beginning and end of a solar eclipse can be observed with considerable accuracy, they are useful for determining the longitude, though the method which they furnish is complex and laborious.

*Effects of atmospherical refraction and parallax.* In the preceding explanation of solar eclipses we have had occasion to refer to the effects of ATMOSPHERICAL REFRACTION; also to the difference between the apparent places of the sun and moon, called their PARALLAX, produced from their being viewed from the surface instead of the centre of the earth. Before leaving this subject, we shall state a little more fully the effects arising from these causes.

*Atmospherical refraction.* The earth is surrounded on all sides by an aeriform elastic fluid, which is called the ATMOSPHERE. This fluid possesses weight, and is compressible; and hence the parts near the surface of the earth are more dense than those above them, on account of the greater superincumbent pressure which they sustain. The same thing holds true of every *stratum* when compared, in reference to density, with that immediately below it; so that from the surface upwards the density gradually diminishes, at a few miles' elevation becomes very small, and at some point may be considered as altogether evanescent. Now, it is a well known principle, that if a ray of light, after passing through one medium (air, for instance), enters another (say water) of a different density, in a direction *not* perpendicular to its surface, it is bent out of its course *towards* the perpendicular to the surface on which the ray is incident, if the second medium is the denser of the two; but *from* that perpendicular if the second medium is the rarer. In passing through the atmosphere, therefore, a ray of light will be continually deflected from the rectilineal into a curvilineal path; because at every point of its course it is entering a medium of a greater density. The ray is said to be *refracted;* and as the tangent draws from the eye to the curve which it describes is the direction in which celestial objects appear, it follows, that refraction renders the apparent altitude of all the heavenly bodies greater than the true. Hence they often appear above the horizon when they are actually below it.

The deviation of the refracted ray from its original course increases with the angle of incidence, and vanishes when the direction of the ray is perpendicular to the surface of the second medium. Hence atmospherical refraction is greatest when the object is in the horizon, where it may be about 34′: at 45° altitude, it is about 57½″: in the zenith it vanishes.

Whatever alters the density of the atmosphere must affect also its refractive power. In all accurate observations, therefore, the state of the barometer and thermometer must be taken into account. At the same zenith distances, the quantity of refraction varies nearly as the height of the barometer, supposing the temperature to remain the same. The effect of a variation in the temperature is to diminish the quantity of refraction about $\frac{1}{480}$th part for every increase of one degree in the height of the thermometer.

In passing through the atmosphere *light is reflected* as well as refracted. The reflective power of the atmosphere produces the splendour of day by diffusing light in every direction. Combined with its refractive power, it causes that faint light called TWILIGHT, which is perceived before sunrise and after sunset;—beginning in the morning in our latitude, and ending in the evening, when the sun's depression below the horizon is about 18°. Various other phenomena are to be attributed to the same cause: the red and orange colour of the morning and evening clouds; the ruddy appearance of all the heavenly bodies when near the horizon; the blue colour of the sky; and the bright azure of the distant mountains, are all the effects of the refractive powers of the atmosphere.

Refraction is also the cause of *the oval appearance of the sun and moon when near the horizon.* The diameter of the disc that is parallel to the horizon remains unaffected in its apparent length, because both extremities are equally refracted; but the diameter perpendicular to the horizon is shortened by about $\frac{1}{6}$th of its length, because the lower edge of the disc, being nearer the horizon, is refracted nearly five minutes more than the upper.

The great apparent magnitude of the sun and moon when in the horizon is another remarkable phenomenon which we may here notice. This illusion, which is altogether optical, is usually accounted for on this principle, that we form an erroneous judgment respecting the distances of these bodies when they are in the horizon, compared with their distances when they have attained a considerable elevation. When we see the moon, for example, in the heavens at a considerable altitude, we intuitively suppose her nearer than when she is in the horizon; because, in the latter case, we see a multitude of objects,—many of them at great distances, and the moon beyond them all; but, in the former case, we have no intervening objects by which to form an estimate of her distance. The angle under which she is seen being nearly the same, we infer a greater magnitude when we imagine the distance greatest, that is, when the moon is in the horizon. Such is the error into which we, in this instance, fall, in the rapid judgments of the mind respecting magnitude and distance connected with vision. The more deliberate conclusion on this subject drawn by reason is, that the moon must indeed be at a greater distance from an observer on the earth, when she is in his horizon, than when she is in or near his zenith; but that, however the eye may be deceived, her apparent diameter must, when exactly measured, be found less. This is accordingly the case; for, when accurately measured with the micrometer, the moon's apparent diameter, when she is in the horizon, is actually found to be less than when she has attained a considerable altitude.

*Parallax.* We have formerly shown that, in comparison with the distances of the fixed stars, the earth is but as a point in the universe; so that their positions in the heavens appear the same when viewed from the earth's surface, as they would if they were viewed from its centre. This, however, is not the case with regard to the sun, moon, and planets. At each of these bodies the earth presents a disc of an appreciable magnitude: and, on the other hand, their positions among the fixed stars, when viewed from different points of the surface of the earth, vary, and are different from what they would be were they seen from the centre of the earth.

Let A B E (*fig.* 30.) be the earth, C its centre, and M, M'', M' (a heavenly body, for example) the moon in the sensible horizon, the zenith, and any intermediate position. The true places of the moon in these positions, as seen from the centre C, and referred to the starry heavens, will be $m$, $m''$, $m'$; and their apparent places, as seen from B, will be $n$, $m''$, $n'$. It is evident, that in the zenith the true and apparent places coincide, so that there is no parallax. In the horizon the parallax is greatest: it is measured by the arc $m\ n$, and is equal to the angle B M C, under which the semidiameter of the earth's disc appears when viewed from the moon. At the intermediate position M' the parallax is measured by the arc $m'\ n'$: it is less than in the horizon, and decreases as the body ascends until it vanishes when the body reaches the zenith. From the horizon to the zenith, parallax diminishes the apparent altitude of a body; but as the altitude increases, this diminution becomes less and less. Its effect, therefore, is contrary to that of refraction, which always increases the apparent altitude of a body.

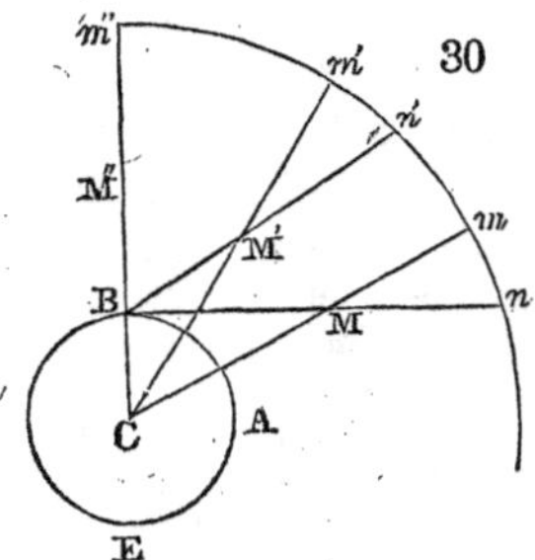


---

## CHAPTER XI.

### MOTION OF THE PLANETS ROUND THE SUN.

THE phenomena of the motions of the other planets differ from those of the moon, which, as we have shown, are all easily accounted for, on the supposition that the moon revolves round the earth in an elliptic orbit, subject to various changes; which are confined, however, within certain limits. The attempts which the ancient astronomers made to explain the celestial phenomena, by supposing the earth to be the centre of the universe, introduced a system, the PTOLEMAIC, which was received for about 1500 years, as affording the true explanation of the planetary motions; but which the progress of scientific discovery has proved to be absurd. Ptolemy, an astronomer of Egypt, who flourished about 140 years after the Christian era, supposed the planets to revolve about the earth in the following order; viz. the Moon, Mercury, Venus, the Sun, Mars, Jupiter, Saturn. Beyond the region of the planets he placed the sphere of the fixed stars. While he thus accounted for the proper motions of the planets from west to east, he conceived the whole to be carried round the earth by a diurnal motion, in the opposite direction, in twenty-four hours. The irregularities of the planetary motions,—these being sometimes direct, at other times retrograde; sometimes swift, and at other times slow,—were imagined by him to arise from each planet moving in a small circle, called an EPICYCLE, whose centre was carried round a larger circle, called the DEFERENT, having the earth placed a little to the one side of its centre. The motions in these circles he imagined to be produced by the revolution of transparent globes; each planet being supposed to be attached to a globe, which carried it round in its epicycle; and this globe again supposed to be contained in the shell of another globe of sufficient thickness to receive it within its solid substance, and to allow it to revolve on its own centre, at the same time that it was carried in the deferent round the earth.

Setting aside the obvious objections to this theory, arising from the extravagance of the suppositions, as well as the awkwardness and complication of the machinery which it employs, an insuperable difficulty remains; viz. that the whole system is entirely hypothetical, and offers no proof of the existence of the agents to which it attributes such mighty effects. It is not surprising, therefore, that instead of being confirmed by subsequent discoveries, it fell to the ground as soon as the true method of investigating the laws of nature was understood and adopted.

Of the planets, two, Mercury and Venus, always accompany the sun, never receding from him beyond certain limits: the rest are seen at all possible angular distances from the sun. Let us, then, fix upon Venus as the most conspicuous of the two which accompany the sun, and upon Mars as one of the most conspicuous among those which recede to all angular distances from him; and by tracing out the apparent motions of these planets, let us endeavour to ascertain the centre about which they revolve.

When the planet Venus is near the sun, she is invisible; but when she has emerged sufficiently from his rays, she is seen in the twilight of the morning or evening, according as she is to the west or east of the sun. In the former case she is the **MORNING STAR**; in the latter, the **EVENING STAR**. When she begins to be seen in the evening, she is found to be receding from the sun towards the east, and thus disengaging herself more and more from his rays. Having reached her greatest angular distance, or elongation, which is from 45° to 48°, she begins again to approach him, and continues to do so till her angular distance is about 28°. During all this time her motion is *direct*, that is, in the order of the signs; but now she becomes *stationary*, and in a short time she is seen moving in a direction contrary to the order of the signs, and has thus acquired a *retrograde* motion; but still she continues to approach the sun, until in a short time she is lost in his light. After being invisible for about six weeks, she is again seen; but now in the morning to the west of the sun, emerging from the solar rays. Her motion is still retrograde; but when she has reached about 28° distance from the sun, she again becomes stationary; and in a short time resumes a direct motion, receding from him night after night, until her angular distance exceeds 45°. She then returns to the sun; is for a time lost in his rays; and at length is seen in the evening to the east of the sun, to repeat the same round of phenomena. While Venus thus appears to have an oscillatory motion to the east and west of the sun, she is found, when viewed through a telescope, to present phases exactly similar to those of the moon, the illuminated portion being always turned towards the sun. We may hence infer that Venus is an opaque body, and shines in consequence of reflecting the solar light. At the same time her apparent diameter also varies, its variations having an evident relation to the position of the planet with regard to the sun. The diameter appears least when the planet is about to be immersed in the rays of the sun in the morning, or immediately after her emerging from them in the evening. On the other hand, it appears greatest when she is about to be lost in the solar rays in the evening, or when she emerges from them in the morning. Such is a general view of the apparent motion of Venus; and by attending to the phenomena which she exhibits, we are led to the conclusion that she revolves round the sun. When in the morning she begins to disengage herself from the solar rays, she is seen to rise before the sun in the form of a crescent; and it is then that her diameter appears greatest. At that time, therefore, she must be nearer to us than the sun is, and not far from being in conjunction with him. Her crescent increases, and her diameter diminishes, as she recedes from the sun: when she has reached her greatest elongation and returns again towards him, she continues to discover to us more and more of her enlightened hemisphere, her diameter all the time diminishing, until she is lost, in the morning, in the sun's rays. At the instant of her disappearing, Venus is seen as a full disc; and at the same time her diameter is least. Hence we may with certainty infer, that she is then at a greater distance from us than the sun, and again nearly in conjunction with him. After having remained for some time invisible, she reappears in the evening to the east of the sun; and in receding from and returning towards him exhibits, in an inverted order, the same phenomena, in reference to the changes in her disc and apparent diameter, which she had presented when seen in the morning, on the west of the sun: her enlightened hemisphere turns more and more from us, and her apparent diameter continually increases, until she again disappears, or is seen as a black spot traversing the disc of the sun.

From these phenomena only one inference can be drawn; viz. that Venus revolves in an orbit, near the centre of which the sun is placed. This conclusion, which rests on the firm basis of observation, leads to a natural and simple explanation of all the peculiarities of her motion.

The planet Mars, the next to be considered, appears to be carried round the earth by a motion which is subject to great inequalities. When he begins to be seen in the morning emerging from the solar rays, his motion is direct, and at its greatest rapidity; but it gradually diminishes until the planet's angular distance from the sun is about 137°. At that time it changes into a retrograde motion, whose rapidity increases till the moment that the planet comes into opposition with the sun, or is on the meridian at midnight. It is then at its greatest rate, and presently begins to decrease, continuing to do so till the planet becomes stationary when at the angular distance of about 137° from the sun. The motion now returns to its direct state, after having been retrograde for about seventy-three days; and in that period the planet describes an arc of retrogradation of about 16°. Mars continues to approach the sun, until he becomes immersed in his rays in the evening. These phenomena are repeated at every opposition of the planet, with considerable differences, however, in reference to the duration and extent of the retrogradations. At different points of his course round the heavens, the apparent diameter of Mars is very different: it varies from about 13.3″ to 29.1″. It is greatest when the planet is in opposition to the sun.

The phenomena now described can be satisfactorily explained in no other way but by supposing Mars to revolve round the sun. As he recedes from the sun to all possible angular distances, the earth must be situated within his orbit; but the increase of his apparent diameter as he approaches his opposition, and its decrease when he approaches the sun, show that the earth is not the centre of his motion. Before he reaches the point of opposition, his motion from being direct, becomes retrograde; after the opposition it resumes its direct state, when the planet is at the same distance from the sun, at which he was situated when the motion became retrograde; and it is at the moment of conjunction that this last motion is most rapid. Now, all these circumstances evidently indicate that the apparent motion of Mars is the result of two combined motions, which alternately conspire with and oppose each other, and of which one depends on the apparent motion of the sun. As we have found that Venus revolves round the sun, and accompanies him in his apparent annual motion round the earth, we are led by analogy to extend the same law to Mars, and to conclude that he also revolves in an orbit round the sun.

The disc of Mars changes its figure, and becomes sensibly oval, according to his position relatively to the sun: hence we may conclude that Mars is an opaque body, and derives his light from the sun.

The same reasoning being applicable in the case of the other planets, we may extend to all of them the conclusion which we have now established in reference to Venus and Mars,—namely, that they are opaque bodies, and revolve about the sun in orbits nearly circular; while that luminary of the system either describes or appears to describe an orbit about the earth in the course of a year. This general law, which affords a simple and complete explication of the planetary motions, receives additional confirmation from the phenomena of the satellites of Jupiter and the ring of Saturn; for these phenomena prove directly that Jupiter and Saturn revolve about the sun in nearly circular orbits.

---

## CHAPTER XII.

### MOTION OF THE EARTH ROUND THE SUN.

THE conclusion to which we have now been led,—that all the planets describe orbits that have the sun near to their centre,—naturally suggests the question, *whether the earth itself is not subject to the same law*, and therefore to be ranked among the planets which revolve round the sun. With regard to the celestial motions, every appearance would remain the same to us, whether the earth described an orbit round the sun, or the sun with his accompanying planets revolved round the earth. To which of these hypotheses the preference is due will appear from the following considerations:—

The immense masses of the sun and of several of the planets, combined with their great distances from the earth, render it much more simple to suppose that the earth describes an orbit round the sun, than that the whole planetary system revolves round the earth. What an inconceivable rapidity of motion is it necessary to assign to Saturn, almost ten times more distant from us than the sun, or to Uranus, at about double the distance of Saturn, in order that these planets may complete a revolution round the earth in a year, at the same time that they revolve about the sun! It is a law which is found to pervade the planetary system, that the less body revolves about the greater body which is in its neighbourhood; and by supposing the earth, in conformity with this law, to revolve about the sun, which in magnitude greatly exceeds all the planets taken together, we avoid all the complication and rapidity of motion which follow from the supposition of the earth being at rest.

The analogy which subsists between the earth and the planets confirms the hypothesis of the earth being carried round the sun by a motion of translation: Jupiter, for example, is known to have a revolution on his own axis, and to be attended by four satellites. In these particulars the earth resembles that planet, having also a revolution on its own axis, and being attended by one satellite, the moon. An observer placed on Jupiter would be led from appearances to imagine that the planetary system revolved round him, in like manner as an inhabitant of the earth supposes himself placed at the centre of the celestial motions: and the greater magnitude of Jupiter would give to such a conclusion, when drawn by an observer placed on that planet, a greater resemblance to the truth than it would have when drawn by an inhabitant of the earth. With such a close analogy in these respects before our eyes, may we not naturally conclude that it extends still farther; and that as Jupiter revolves in an orbit round the sun, the earth must also have a similar motion?

Let us imagine ourselves to be placed on the surface of the sun, and from that position to observe the earth and the planets. All these bodies would appear to move from west to east; the planets would be found free from all that complication in their motion to which they appear subject when viewed from the earth; and the motion of the earth itself would in every circumstance correspond with that of the planets. The more distant a planet is from the sun, the longer is the time which it requires to perform its revolution round him; but throughout the planetary system this remarkable law prevails, connecting the periodic times with the distances,—the squares of the former are proportional to the cubes of the latter. If we compute, by this principle, what should be the time of revolution of a planet situated at the distance of the earth from the sun, we find the result correspond exactly with the sidereal year; thus, the earth's distance from the sun being assumed as unity, the distance of

Mars is known to be 1·523693: his periodic time is 686·9796 days. Hence we have $(1·52693)^3 : 1^3 :: (686·9796)^2 : (365·256)^2$. The periodic time of a planet, at the same distance from the sun as the earth is, should therefore be 365·256 days, which is the length of the sidereal year. This result leaves no doubt that the motion which the earth would be seen to have, if it were viewed from the sun, arises from the same causes, and is regulated by the same laws as the motions of the planets: hence we may conclude that it is no less real.

The motion of the earth in an orbit round the sun, which the preceding considerations render so highly probable, is directly *proved* by the phenomena of *the aberration of light* It was long supposed that light was propagated from the sun and other luminous bodies instantaneously; but modern observations have proved that this hypothesis is erroneous, and that light, like all other projectiles, occupies a certain time in passing from one point of space to another. The fact that light has a progressive motion was first discovered by Roemer, a celebrated Danish astronomer, from observations made on the eclipses which the satellites of Jupiter undergo when they fall into his shadow. He found that these eclipses happened sometimes sooner and sometimes later than the time deduced from the tables of their motions; the observation being before or after the computed time, according as the earth was nearer to or farther from Jupiter than the mean distance. Repeated observations have proved, that when the earth is between the sun and Jupiter, his satellites are seen eclipsed about 8¼ minutes sooner than they should be according to the tables; but that when the earth is on the opposite side of the sun from Jupiter, the eclipses of his satellites happen about 8¼ minutes later than the time shown by the tables. The only conclusion that can be drawn from these facts is, that light occupies about 16½ minutes in traversing a space equal to the diameter of the earth's orbit, which is upwards of 190 millions of miles; it must therefore move at the enormous rate of nearly 210,000 miles in a second.

Now, if the earth is really in motion, it must be moving at the rate of about 20 miles in a second, in order to accomplish its revolution round the sun in the course of a year. This rate of motion, although small when compared with the velocity of light, bears to it a sensible proportion; so that an evident consequence of the earth's motion will be, that the apparent places of the heavenly bodies will not be the same as they would be if the earth were at rest.

Suppose A B to be a portion of the earth's orbit, S a fixed star, and S A the direction of light proceeding from the star to the earth at A. It is evident that if the earth were at rest at A, a telescope presented in the direction A S would receive the light of the star, which, proceeding along the axis of the telescope, would reach the eye at A, and show the star in its true position. But if the earth be supposed to move from A towards B with a velocity that bears a sensible proportion to the velocity of light, the ray S A, which enters the telescope at C, cannot reach the eye, but must, in consequence of the motion, be lost against the interior of the tube. In order that the light from the star may reach the eye when carried forward by the earth's motion, the telescope must have such an inclination to A B, that S F being supposed a ray parallel to S A, and meeting the axis of the telescope in D, A F may have to F D the same ratio as the earth's velocity in its orbit has to the velocity of light; that is, of 1 to 10,000 nearly. In this position of the telescope, the light entering at D will pass along the axis as it moves from A to F, and will reach the eye at F; but the star will be seen in the direction, not of F S, but of F E: so that its apparent place differs from its true by a quantity measured by the angle S F E or A D F. The angle D F E is the aberration which will evidently be towards that part of the heavens to which the earth is moving. Let the axis F E be supposed to be produced to the starry heavens: it will trace out on the convex surface a circle, if the star S is in the pole of the ecliptic; but an ellipse in every other position of the star. The true place of the star is the centre of the circle or ellipse.

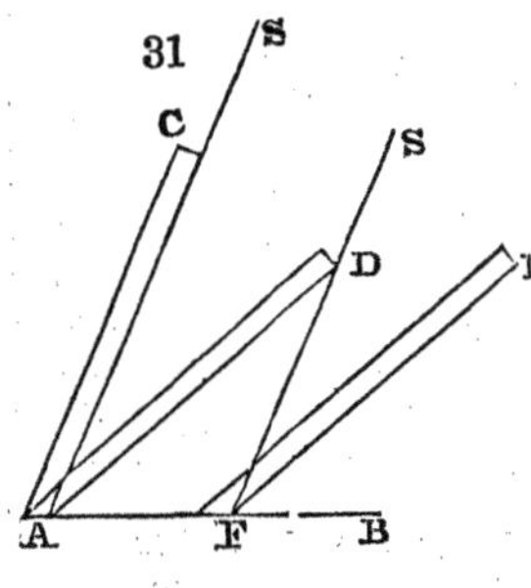


If the star be in the pole of the ecliptic, the angle D A F may be considered as a right angle; for the line joining the star and the earth will always be perpendicular to the direction of the earth's motion. In this case, therefore, the angle A D F will be the greatest possible; for the ratio of sin. A D F to sin. D A F is constant, being the same with the ratio of A F to F D, or of 1 to 10,000 nearly: so that sin. A D F is greatest, and therefore A D F is greatest when sin. D A F is the greatest possible; that is, when D A F is a right angle. In the case of any other star the greater axis of the ellipse which it appears to describe round its true place as a centre will be equal to the diameter of the circle which a star in the pole of the ecliptic would appear to describe about the pole as a centre: for the ellipse will be the orthographic projection of a circle equal to that described about the pole, the greater axis being the diameter, which is perpendicular to a circle of the sphere passing through the star and the pole of the ecliptic, and at right angles to the ecliptic. When the star is in the ecliptic, it will appear to describe an arch equal to the greater axis of the ellipse described by a star not in the ecliptic, or to the diameter of the circle of aberration that would be described by a star in the pole of the ecliptic.

When angle D A F is a right angle, we have D F : F A : : rad : sin. ∠ A D F; that is, 10,000 : 1 : : 1 : ·0001 = sine of greatest aberration, which will therefore be 20″ nearly. The aberration of a planet will depend on its own motion as well as on that of the earth. If the motion of the planet were equal and parallel to that of the earth, no aberration would take place. The aberration of a planet may be found by first considering the effect of the motion of the earth on the apparent place, and then the aberration arising from the planet's own motion.

Such are the effects which, if the earth have actually a motion of translation that carries it in an orbit round the sun, must arise from that motion combined with the progressive motion of light. To obtain, therefore, decisive proof of the earth's annual motion, it is only necessary to ascertain by accurate observation the existence of these phenomena.

The true system of the world, which supposes the sun to be at rest in the centre, and the earth and planets to revolve round him, while the moon revolves about the earth, and the diurnal motion of the heavens arises from the motion of the earth on its axis, was taught by several of the ancient philosophers, and particularly by Pythagoras. It was also held by Archimedes; but after him it was neglected, and even forgotten for many ages, until at length, in the beginning of the sixteenth century, it was revived and improved by Copernicus, from whom it took the name of the COPERNICAN System. Notwithstanding the beauty and simplicity which distinguished this theory, it was at first coldly received or utterly rejected. Tycho Brahe, an illustrious Dane, was among its adversaries. He regarded the doctrine of the earth's motion as untenable, without abandoning the testimony of Scripture: hence he was led to imagine another system, which bears his name; in which the sun, with all the planets and comets revolving round him, is supposed to perform a revolution about the earth in a solar year, while at the same time all the heavenly bodies are supposed to be carried round the earth from east to west in twenty-four hours.

The only apparent difficulty connected with the Copernican system arises from the fact, that the earth's axis is always pointed to the same star, and that the stars preserve always the same relative positions; though by the annual motion of the earth, a spectator on its surface views them at any two instants of time separated by the period of about six months, from two points nearly 200,000,000 miles asunder. During the seventeenth century the supporters of the Copernican system laboured to remove this objection, by detecting a change in the position of the fixed stars.

The minute and accurate observations instituted for this purpose led, in the end, to the important discovery made by the celebrated Dr. Bradley, that the very effects which we have shown, must result from the annual motion of the earth combined with the progressive motion of light. He found that each star describes, round its true place as a centre, a small ellipse of which the greater axis is about 40″; and that this ellipse approaches to a circle or to a straight line, which are its limits, according as the star is situated towards the pole of the ecliptic, or towards the ecliptic itself. No parallax is observable in the fixed stars arising from the earth's annual motion; and hence it must be inferred that their distance is so great, that even the diameter of the earth's orbit is to be regarded as a point in the universe.

From an attentive consideration of the celestial motions, *we are therefore led to reject as erroneous the notions which appearances at first suggest respecting the system of the world.* Instead of the globe which we inhabit being at rest in the centre of the universe, it is a planet in motion about its own axis and about the sun. In regarding it under this aspect, we find all the celestial phenomena explained in the most simple manner, the laws of the motions of the heavenly bodies appear uniform, and every analogy subsisting among them is preserved unbroken. Like Jupiter, Saturn, and Uranus, the earth is accompanied by a satellite; it revolves on its own axis as Venus, Mars, Jupiter, Saturn, and perhaps all the planets; like them it receives light from the sun; and to complete the analogy, it revolves about the sun in the same direction, and according to the same laws. By following out the results arising from the earth's motion being combined with the real motions of the planets and of light, we find all the phenomena of the heavens flow, as necessary consequences, from one great principle. Thus the motion of the earth acquires all the certainty of which a physical truth is susceptible.

The vicissitudes of seasons arise, as we have already explained, from the obliquity of the ecliptic to the equator. The ecliptic, which we have hitherto considered as the path of the sun round the earth, we have now proved to be the orbit of the earth round the sun. The axis of the earth's diurnal motion is inclined to the plane of its orbit at an angle of about 66° 32′, and remains, as the earth revolves round the sun, nearly parallel to itself. Hence the circle which the sun appears to trace in the heavens in the course of a year forms with the equator an angle of about 23° 28′. This produces the differences in the distribution of the solar light and heat which we observe throughout the seasons of the year.

The parallelism of the earth is not absolute; for the axis is found to have a slow motion of revolution from east to west round a line passing through the centre of the earth, and perpendicular to the ecliptic; its revolution being completed in the period of 25,745 years. In consequence of this motion the poles in the sphere of the starry heavens describe each a circle round the pole of the ecliptic, at the distance of 23° 28′ nearly; and the two points in which the terrestrial equator, when produced to the starry heavens, cuts the ecliptic, shift to the westward, at the rate of about 50⅓ seconds yearly, which causes the precession of the equinoxes. A small inequality has been observed in the precession of the equinoxes, and in the mean obliquity of the ecliptic, which arises from a slight motion in the earth's axis, whereby its inclination to the ecliptic is not always exactly the same, but varies backwards and forwards some seconds. This is called the nutation of the earth's axis, and was discovered by Dr. Bradley while employed in verifying his theory of aberration. The period of the changes of this inequality is nearly nine years.

---

## CHAPTER XIII.

### ORBITS OF THE PLANETS.

To an observer placed on the sun, all the planets would appear to trace on the concave surface circular paths, cutting each other at various angles, but all comprehended within a certain zone of the heavens of some degrees in breadth. The angle which the plane of the orbit of a planet makes with the ecliptic is called the INCLINATION of that orbit; and the line of their intersection is called the LINE OF THE NODES. If a planet be observed twice in the same node, the node being supposed to have in the mean time remained stationary, the position of the line of the nodes can be determined, and also the distance of the planets from the sun at the times of observation.

Let a superior planet be observed in its node N from the earth at E, (*Fig*. 32), and after the planet has made an entire revolution let the earth be at E′. Then, from the time and the theory of the earth's motion, E E′ is given, and the angles S E E′, S E′ E. But the angles S E N, S E′ N are known by observation; therefore, in the triangle E E′ N, the angles E E′ N, E′ E N, and the base E E′ are given; and hence the sides N E and E′ N may be found. Wherefore from either of the triangles S E N, S E′ N the distance S N is determined; also the angle E S N, which ascertains the position of the node as seen from the sun.

From observations of this kind, made at times considerably distant from each other, it found that the nodes of each planet have a slow retrograde motion.

Again, the distance of a planet from the sun, and its place as seen from the sun, may be determined from observations made at the time of its opposition to the sun.

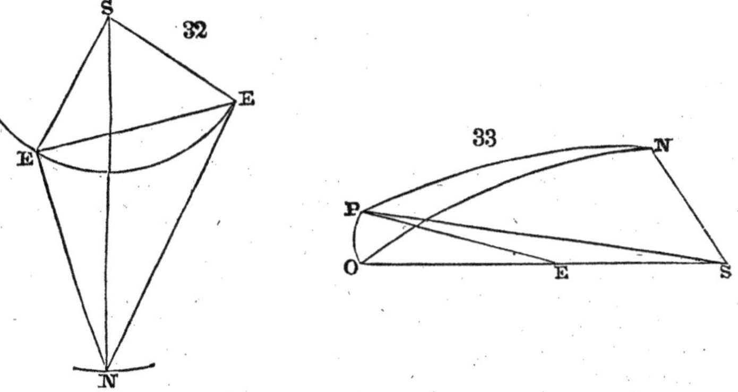


(*Fig*. 33). Let E be the earth, S the sun, P the planet, O its place reduced to the ecliptic, S N the line of the nodes passing through the sun. Since the planet is in its opposition, the points S, E, O are in the same straight line. The angle E S N is known by the last problem, which determines the position of the line of the nodes; therefore the arch O N in the heavens, which measures it, is also given. The angle P N O is equal to the inclination of the planet's orbit to the ecliptic, and is therefore given; also the angle P O N is a right angle. Hence in the spherical triangle P N O, the perpendicular P O and the hypotenuse P N may be found. Now the arc P O is the measure of the angle P S O, and P N is the measure of P S N; therefore these two angles are given. In the rectilineal triangle P S E, the exterior angle P E O can be determined by observation; the angle P S E or P S O is given, and the base E S is known by the theory of the earth's motion; whence P S, the distance of the planet from the sun, may be computed.

*Orbit of a planet.* Since the angle P S N is also known, the line P S is given in position as well as in magnitude. If many oppositions of a planet are thus observed, and if the radii obtained be laid down, the line connecting their extreme points will represent the orbit of the planet. In this manner it is found that the orbits of all the planets are ellipses, having the sun in their common focus; and that the angular motions of a planet round the sun are inversely as the squares of its distance from the sun: so that the sectors described by the radius vector are proportional to the times. This exactly corresponds with what was proved respecting the apparent motion of the sun in the ecliptic, and therefore the motion of the earth is regulated by the same law.

The planets which move immediately round the sun are called PRIMARY, their satellites are called SECONDARY PLANETS. Thus, the moon is a secondary planet to the earth. In considering the lunar motion, we found that the moon describes round the earth an elliptic orbit, and that the radius vector describes equal areas in equal times. The same holds of the satellites of Jupiter, Saturn, and Uranus; so that the same principle runs through the motions of all the bodies of the planetary system.

When the mean distances of the planets are compared, and also their periodical times, it is found that the squares of the periodic times are as the cubes of the distances.

The great general facts which have now been pointed out respecting the orbits of the planets, and their motions in these orbits, were first discovered by Kepler, after he had employed immense labour and ingenuity in the research, and are usually called KEPLER'S LAWS. It may be proper to bring them under one point of view:—

I. The primary planets all revolve in elliptic orbits round the sun, which occupies one of the foci of the ellipse; the plane of the orbit passing through the centre of the sun.

II. The radius vector describes equal areas in equal times.

III. The squares of the times of revolution in the planetary bodies are as the cubes of their distances from the sun.

---

## CHAPTER XIV.

### COMETS.

THE fixed stars and the planets are always visible when not obscured by the superior light of the sun; but the class of bodies called COMETS are seen only when they are in that part of their several paths which lies nearest to the sun: at all other times they move through regions of space far beyond the reach of our vision, even when assisted by the most powerful telescopes. The motions of the comets are, like those of the planets, performed in elliptic orbits according to Kepler's laws; but, unlike the planetary orbits, the ellipses which the comets describe are extremely elongated: so that the small portion of their orbits through which we have an opportunity of tracing them coincides very nearly with a parabola, the curve of which is the limit of the ellipse when its greater axis is indefinitely increased. The inclination of the orbits of the comets is very various; some move in planes almost coincident with the ecliptic, and others in planes nearly perpendicular to it. They move also in very different directions; the motion of some being *direct*, and of others *retrograde.*

The comets differ widely from the planets in their appearance, as well as in the figure and position of their orbits. When a comet is first seen, it is usually surrounded by a faintly luminous vapour, which becomes more bright as the comet approaches the sun, and at length shoots out into a long luminous and transparent train, very much resembling a *streamer*, and extending in a direction opposite to the sun. The dense part of the comet, which both to the naked eye, and when viewed through a telescope, resembles much the planetary bodies, is called the *nucleus;* the faintly luminous vapour by which it is surrounded is called the *coma;* and the long luminous train proceeding from the comet in an opposite direction from the sun is called the *tail.* Between the nucleus and the coma lies a part fainter than the former, but brighter than the latter, and in which the nucleus appears involved: this is called the *head* of the comet.

The length of the tail is very various. Sometimes it extends only a few degrees; in other cases it has been found to reach over more than a fourth part of the heavens. If a comet does not come very near the sun, the coma does not shoot into a tail, but retains the appearance of a nebulosity round the comet during the whole period of its being visible. The tail sometimes consists of two or more diverging streams of light, and is always so transparent that the smallest stars are seen through it without any sensible diminution of their brilliancy.

*Nature of comets.* In ages of ignorance, comets have always, from their extraordinary appearance, been sources of superstitious terror to mankind. This fear has been dissipated by the light of science, which has shown that the appearances of comets are regulated by the same laws as other celestial phenomena. We are still, however, almost entirely ignorant of the nature of these bodies, though a great many hypotheses have been formed concerning them. They were considered by some of the ancients, and particularly by Aristotle, as accidental fires or meteors generated in the atmosphere of the earth; but this opinion is obviously groundless. If they were connected with the earth or its atmosphere, they would partake of the diurnal motion on the axis, and could not therefore appear to have a diurnal revolution in the heavens along with the other celestial bodies. Besides, their having no diurnal parallax proves that they are at a great distance from the earth; while the fact of their apparent motion being affected by the annual motion of the earth shows that they are situated in the planetary regions. Observation has demonstrated that, like the planets, they are permanent bodies, and, in all probability, derive their light from the sun.

From the small portion of the orbit of any comet which we have an opportunity of observing, we cannot ascertain with sufficient accuracy the elements necessary for determining the period of its return; but supposing that their orbits are not disturbed by any cause in those distant regions of space through which the greater portion of the paths of comets lie, it is evident that by accurately observing all the comets that come within view, and carefully recording the results, in the course of ages the return of many comets may be detected and their periodic times ascertained. Hence the greater axis of the orbit of each may be determined by Kepler's third law; and the comet's least distance from the sun being found by observation, the less axis will also become known. In this manner the periodic time of some comets has been found, and their return predicted.

The first and most remarkable instance is that of Dr. Halley, who, by comparing his observations on the comet of 1682, with those of Kepler on the comet of 1607, and those of Apian on the comet of 1531, found reason to conclude, from the agreement of the circumstances of each, that what had been considered three distinct comets were only re-appearances of the same comet after a period of about 76 years. In all the three cases the distance of the comet from the sun when nearest to him was almost the same; the position of the comet in the heavens at the time of its nearest approach to the sun likewise corresponded; as did also the inclination of the orbit, the place of the nodes, and the variableness of the motion, as being direct or retrograde.

These coincidences rendered the identity of the comet almost absolutely certain. Hence Halley predicted its return in the end of 1758 or the beginning of 1759. It appeared about the end of December 1758, and made its nearest approach to the sun on the 13th of March 1759, differing not many days from the time expected. Again it made its appearance, as predicted, at the completion of its period, toward the end of August, 1835.

Though there can be no doubt of the identity of the comet of 1531, 1607, 1682, 1759, and 1835, the appearances were considerably different. In 1531 the comet was of a bright gold colour; in 1607, it was dark and livid; it was bright again in 1682; and obscure in 1759.

The mean distance of this comet from the sun is about eighteen times that of the earth; but in consequence of the great eccentricity of its orbit, its distance, when at the farther extremity of its greater axis, is nearly double that of Uranus, the most distant of the planets. When nearest to the sun, its distance from him is about $\frac{6}{10}$th parts of the earth's mean distance.

A very remarkable comet was seen in the end of 1680 and beginning of 1681. Its tail extended 70°, and was very brilliant. This comet, of all those which have been observed, approaches nearest to the sun. Descending with immense velocity in a path almost perpendicular to his surface, it proceeded until its distance from his centre was only about 540,000 miles. Sir Isaac Newton computed that, in consequence of so near an approach to the sun, it must have received a heat 2000 times greater than that of iron almost going into fusion; and that if it was equal in magnitude to our earth, and cooled in the same manner as terrestrial bodies, its heat would not be expended in less than 50,000 years.

Three observations on comets are recorded in history, agreeing in remarkable circumstances with the comet of 1680:—one in the 44th year before Christ; another in the consulate of Lampadius and Orestes, about the year of Christ 531; and the third in the reign of Henry I. of England, in the year 1106. These dates are nearly at equal distances of time, namely, 575 years; which is also the period between 1106 and 1681. Hence Dr. Halley conjectured that these might be successive appearances of one and the same comet, revolving about the sun in the period of about 575 years. If this conjecture is well founded, this comet may be expected again, after finishing the same period, about the year 2255.

A comet remarkable for its beauty appeared in 1811. The tail of this comet was composed of two diverging streams of faint light, slightly coloured, which made an angle of from 15° to 20°, and sometimes much more, and were bent outwards. The space between was comparatively obscure. When at its greatest length, the tail subtended an angle of at least 16°; and was then computed to extend about 23,000,000 miles in length.

Besides Dr. Halley's comet there are two others whose returns have been observed, and the elements of their orbits determined, with such certainty, as to enable astronomers to predict their re-appearance. One of these was recognised for the first time in 1819 as a periodic comet. Encke, a German astronomer, has determined the time of its revolution about the sun to be three years and three months nearly. The other was last seen in 1832. Its periodic time was determined by Biela, a Bohemian astronomer, to be six years and three quarters. Altogether, then, there are only three comets whose periods are certainly known.

*Danger from comets.* As the comets traverse the planetary regions in all directions, it is natural to inquire whether there is not a possibility that some one of them may approach so near to the earth as greatly to disturb its motion, or by an actual contact to produce the most disastrous effects. Upon this subject there is no reasonable ground for fear. If it is not absolutely impossible that a comet may come in contact with the earth, the probabilities against such an event happening are as millions to one. Among bodies so small in comparison with the immense space in which they move; and moving with all velocities, and in orbits that are inclined in all directions, and are of all dimensions, how small must be the probability that any two shall come in contact! Small, however, as this probability is for any one age, if we take into account a long series of ages, the probability may be greatly increased.

If we suppose the earth actually to receive such a shock, it is easy to imagine the calamitous consequences which must follow. The axis and motion of rotation being changed, the waters of the ocean would leave their ancient position, and would be precipitated towards the new equator. A great part of the human race, and of the lower animals, would be drowned by this universal deluge, or destroyed by the violent shock impressed on the terrestrial globe. Whole species of animals might be annihilated. All the monuments of human industry and invention would be overthrown. In such a catastrophe we find, too, a cause adequate to account for the ocean having overflowed lofty mountains, on which it has left incontestable evidence of its presence; and to explain how the animals and plants of the south may have existed in the climates of the north, where we find the remains and impressions of them. Lastly, such an event accounts for the recentness of the modern world, the monuments of which go back scarcely 3000 years. The human race, reduced to a small number of individuals, and to the most miserable condition, would for a long time be mainly occupied in providing for their preservation, amidst the wreck which surrounded them, and would lose all remembrance of arts and sciences; and when, by the progress of civilization, they at length became sensible of the want of these, they would find it necessary to recommence, as if man had been newly placed upon the earth.

It seems impossible to contemplate the picture of calamity here drawn, without being forcibly struck with this singular coincidence;—that if we suppose the period of the comet of 1680 (which in that year made a considerably near approach to the earth's orbit) to be 575½ years; and count back, from the year 1680, seven revolutions, or a period of 4028 years, we reach the year 2349 before Christ,—the year of the deluge, as fixed by chronologers.

If we take into consideration the great velocity with which the comets move in approaching to and receding from the sun, it is evident that *the mere approximation of a comet to the terrestrial orbit, would be productive of little or no effect.* Accordingly, though a comet is said to have eclipsed the moon, in which case it must have been very near the earth, no sensible effect was produced.

---

## CHAPTER XV.

### LAW OF UNIVERSAL GRAVITATION.

HAVING now taken a brief view of the planetary motions, and pointed out generally their laws, we may next inquire whether from these any *general principle* can be deduced to which the motions regulated by them may be referred as to their cause.

The motions of the heavenly bodies have been variously accounted for. We have already adverted to the rude mechanism of deferent and epicyclic spheres, by which some of the ancient philosophers attempted to explain the celestial motions. This doctrine originated with Eudoxus and Callipus. But a more sensible attempt was made by Cleanthes, another philosopher of Greece, who, from observing that bodies are easily carried round by whirlpools or vortices of water, imagined that the celestial spaces are filled with an ethereal fluid, which is in continual motion round the earth, and that it carried the sun and planets round with it. Though this hypothesis affords no real explanation of the phenomena, it was revived in modern times, and maintained by two of the most eminent mathematicians and philosophers in Europe, namely, by Des Cartes and Leibnitz, and for a long time met with general acquiescence. But a much nearer approximation to right conceptions on this subject was made by many philosophers, both of ancient and modern times, who supposed that the planets were deflected from uniform rectilineal motions, by forces similar to what we observe in the motions of magnetical and electrical bodies, or in the motion of common heavy bodies; where one body seems to influence the motion of another at a distance from it, without any intervening impulsion. Fermat was the first who suggested that the weight of a body is the sum of the tendencies of each particle of matter in the body to every particle of the earth. Kepler made another approximation to the truth when he said, that if there were two bodies placed out of the reach of all external forces, and at perfect liberty to move, they would approach each other with velocities inversely proportional to their quantities of matter· when he asserted that the earth and the moon mutually attract each other, and are prevented from meeting by their revolution round their common centre of attraction; and when he attributed the tides to the attractive influence of the moon in heaping up the waters immediately under her.

But Dr. Hooke made the most precise surmise to this purpose. At a meeting of the Royal Society, May 3, 1668, he expressed himself in the following manner:—"I will explain a system of the world very different from any yet received, and it is founded on the three following propositions:

"1. That all the heavenly bodies have not only a gravitation of their parts to their own proper centres, but that they also mutually attract each other within their spheres of action.

"2. That all bodies having a simple motion will continue to move in a straight line unless continually deflected from it, by some extraneous force causing them to describe a circle, an ellipse, or some other curve.

"3. That this attraction is so much the greater as the bodies are nearer. As to the proportion in which these forces diminish by an increase of distance, I own I have not yet discovered it, although I have made some experiments to that purpose. I leave this to others who have time and knowledge sufficient for the task."

The truly philosophical views stated in these propositions relatively to the celestial motions were illustrated by a very pretty experiment, which Hooke had some time before exhibited to the Society. A ball, suspended by a long thread from the ceiling, was made to swing round another ball laid on a table immediately below the point of suspension. When the impulse given to the pendulum was very nicely adjusted to its deviation from the perpendicular, it described a perfect circle round the ball on the table; but when the impulse was very great or very little, it described an ellipse having the other ball in its centre. The force, under the influence of which this circular or elliptic motion was produced, Hooke showed to be a deflecting force, proportional to the distance from the other ball. But he added, that although this illustrated the planetary motions in some degree, yet it was not suitable to their case; for the planets describe ellipses, having the sun not in their centre but in their focus, so that they are not retained in their orbits by a force proportional to the distance from the sun.

Thus we see that certain points of resemblance between the motions of the planets and the motions of magnets and heavy bodies, had attracted the attention of many philosophers; but these observers failed to deduce from the principles which they so dimly perceived any satisfactory conclusion.

At length the powerful genius of Sir Isaac Newton was directed to the subject, and by his penetrating sagacity the law of universal gravitation was brought fully into view, and successfully applied to explain the celestial phenomena. He had retired from Cambridge to the country on account of the plague, and while walking in his garden he was led to meditate on the planetary motions, and on the nature of that central force which retains the planets in their orbits. The thought happily occurred to him that the same force, or some modification of the same force, which causes a heavy body to descend to the earth, might extend to the moon, and might retain that body in its orbit by deflecting it from the rectilineal path. However plausible this conjecture might appear, the mind of Newton was too deeply imbued with the true spirit of philosophy to adopt it as the groundwork of a theory, unless it could be shown by calculation to be coincident with fact. But before it could be brought to this test, it was necessary that he should form some conditional hypothesis respecting the modification of the force as the distance increased, and also that he should know nearly the magnitude of the earth. The hypothesis which he assumed with regard to the modification of the force according to the increase of the distance was correct; namely, that the force decreases as the square of the distance increases. But he made a false estimation of the bulk of the earth; so that his calculations showed that his conjecture did not agree with the phenomenon: he accordingly abandoned it. A few years afterwards he was induced, however, to renew his calculations, having in the interval obtained more correct *data*, in consequence of the measurement of a degree in France by Picard. The attempt now succeeded; and it is said that, as his calculations drew to a close, he became so agitated that he was obliged to request a friend to finish them. His former conjecture was found to agree with the phenomena with the utmost precision; and in exploring the grand scene which was now laid open before him, he was led to an explanation of the system of the world, consisting simply in an accurate narration of facts, and such an arrangement of them as showed their mutual dependence, and, at the same time, their reference to one great fact of which they were all necessary consequences.

We are now to explain briefly the theory of gravitation; but our account of it must of course be very limited.

There is no phenomenon in nature more familiar to us than motion; and although it be greatly diversified according to the causes by which it is produced, yet all motions are subject to the three following laws:—

1st LAW. Every body continues in a state of rest, or of uniform rectilinear motion, unless affected by some mechanical force.

2d LAW. Every change of motion is proportional to the force impressed, and is made in the direction of that force.

3d LAW. Every action is accompanied by an equal and contrary re-action.

It is a consequence of the first two laws, that if a body or particle of matter be subjected at the same time to the action of two moving forces, each of which would separately cause it to describe the side of a parallelogram uniformly in a given time, the body will describe the diagonal uniformly in the same time. By these very simple laws, the result of experience, and by the principles of geometry, Newton established the sublime doctrines of the planetary motions.

It will not be expected that we should enter at any considerable length into the recondite doctrines of physical astronomy. This subject requires for its full discussion ample space, and all the resources of the higher mathematics: the mere elements of geometry, however, are sufficient to indicate generally some of the fundamental principles. Let us suppose that S (*fig.* 34.) is a fixed point, and that a body moves in the direction A B with an uniform velocity, at such a rate, that if not disturbed by any external cause, it would move from B to *b* in a second of time. Let us also suppose that when the body arrives at B, it receives an impulse in the direction B S, and of such intensity, that, if acting alone, it would cause the body to move uniformly from B to H in a second. Complete the parallelogram H B *b* C, and draw the diagonal B C: the impulse at B, combined with the tendency to continue its motion in the line B *b*, will cause the body to move along the diagonal B C; so that at the end of a second it will actually be at the point C; and if no external cause acted on the body, by the first law, it would continue to move uniformly ever after in the direction B C *c*; so that in the next second it would describe a line C *c*, equal to B C. But now suppose that the body, when at C, receives a second impulse in the direction C S, by which it would be carried uniformly from C to I in a second: then, completing the parallelogram D I C *c*, the actual path of the body will be the diagonal C D, which will be uniformly described in a second; and if undisturbed, the motion would be continued uniformly in the straight line C D *d*, the distance D *d* described in the next second being equal to C D. A third impulse at D, in the direction D S, such as would carry the body uniformly from D to K in a second of time, would, when combined with the tendency to move in the direction D *d*, produce a motion along D E, the diagonal of the parallelogram E K D *d*, and a fourth impulse in the direction E S, would, when combined with the motion in the direction E *e*, produce a motion along the diagonal E F, and so on. In this way, by successive instantaneous impulses, a body may be made to describe the path A B C D E F, &c., which will be all in one plane.

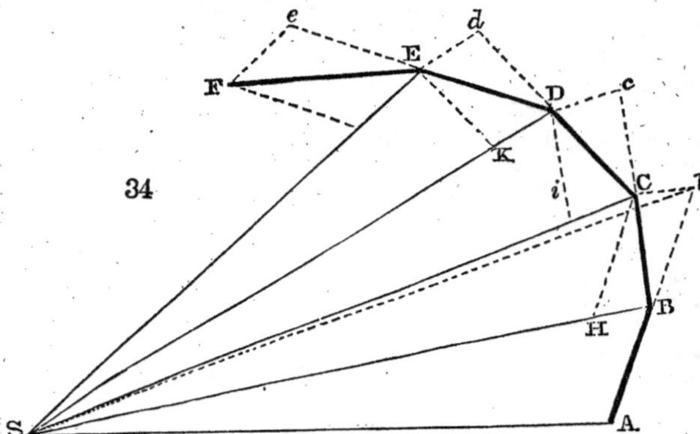


Since the lines A B, B *b* are equal, the triangles A S B, B S *b* are equal; but because C *b* is parallel to S B, the triangle B S *b* is equal to the triangle B S C; therefore the triangle B S C is equal to A S B. In like manner, it may be proved that C S D is equal to B S C, and D S E to C S D, and so on: thus it appears that the triangles A S B, B S C, C S D, D S E, &c. are all equal. If we suppose a straight line to be drawn from the moving body to the fixed point S, and to be continually carried along with it, it is evident that this line will pass over or generate the equal areas A S B, B S C, C S D, D S E, &c. in equal intervals of time: it is also evident that the shorter the interval between the impulses communicated to the moving body, the greater will be the number of sides of the figure formed by the diagonals of the parallelograms, and the nearer will the line composed of these diagonals approach to a curve. If we suppose, therefore, that the body is urged towards F by a force acting, not at intervals, but incessantly, the body will move in that curve to which, as its limit, the line, composed of the diagonals continually approaches, while the line drawn from the moving body A S, or *radius vector*, will continue to describe areas proportional to the times.

The force which urges the body towards S, is called a CENTRIPETAL FORCE. If the action of that force were to cease, the body would proceed in a straight line,—a tangent to its curvilinear path. The tendency of the body to proceed in the direction of the tangent, is called its CENTRIFUGAL FORCE.

From the important conclusion to which we have now been led, we may infer, conversely that if a body revolve in a curvilinear path about a point, and if the radius vector drawn from that point describe round it areas proportional to the times, the body is deflected from the rectilineal path by a force directed to that point. Now, this is exactly the case of the planets, both primary and secondary. The former describe curvilinear orbits round the sun and, according to the second of Kepler's laws, the radius vector describes areas proportional to the times. Hence we may infer, that each is retained in its orbit by a centripetal force directed towards the sun; and that this force is counteracted by a centrifugal force generated by the planet's motion in its orbit. In like manner, each secondary planet revolves about its primary, the areas described by the radius vector following the same law; so that the secondary must be acted upon by a centripetal force directed towards the primary planet.

The next thing to be determined is the law of the centripetal force when a body moves in an elliptic orbit, the force being directed towards one of the foci. First, let us suppose a body to revolve in the circumference of a circle A D C (*fig.* 35.), about any point S, as the centre of its motion, and let us inquire into the law of the centripetal force in that case.

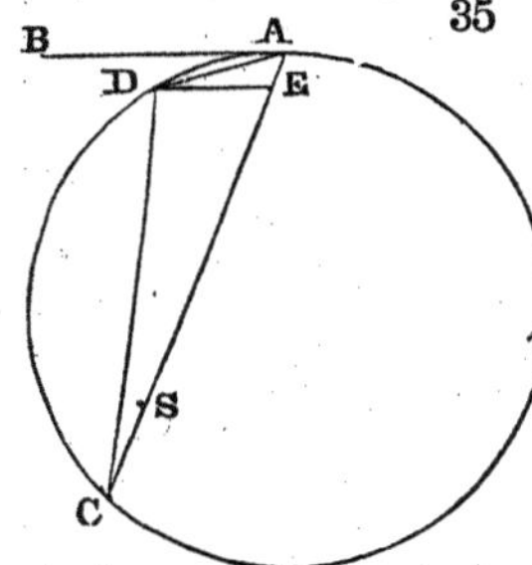


Draw the chord A S C, and let A D be so small an arc, that it may be considered coincident with its chord. Draw D E parallel to the tangent A B, and join C D. Then A D will measure the velocity of the body in its orbit at the point A, and A E the space over which the centripetal force directed towards S, if acting alone, would cause the body to move in the time in which it moves from A to D. Put $v$ to denote the velocity, and $f$ the centripetal force. Since the triangles A D C, A E D, are equiangular and similar, we have A C : A D = A D : A E; that is,

$$AC : v = v : f : \text{therefore } f = \frac{v^2}{AC}$$

Next, let A P B (*fig.* 36.) be the elliptic orbit of a planet, S the focus in which the sun is placed, A the point at which the planet is at its greatest distance from the sun, and P any other point in its orbit. Join P S; draw the tangent P D, and draw S D perpendicular to P D. Let $v$ and $v'$ denote the velocities of the planet at A and P respectively; and $c$ and $c'$ the chords of the equicurve circles at A and P which pass through the point S, and let $f$ be the deflecting force at A, and $f'$ the deflecting force at P. Then from what we have proved respecting a body moving in the circumference of a circle round any point F as the centre of its motion, we have $f : f' = \frac{v^2}{c} : \frac{v'^2}{c'} = v^2c' : v'^2c$. But since the small arcs which represent the velocities at A and P must be supposed to be described in equal times, the corresponding areas described by the radius vector will also be equal. Hence it is not difficult to see that $v \times AS = v' \times SD$, and $v : v' = SD : SA$. We obtain, therefore, $f : f' = SD^2 \times c' : SA^2 \times c$. Draw P E perpendicular to the tangent P D, meeting the axis in E, and draw E G perpendicular to P E, and E H perpendicular to P G. From the properties of the ellipse, P H is equal to half the principal parameter, and consequently to half of $c$, the chord of the circle, of equal curvature at A, which passes through S. Also P G is half of $c'$, the chord of the equicurve circle at P, which passes through S. Therefore,

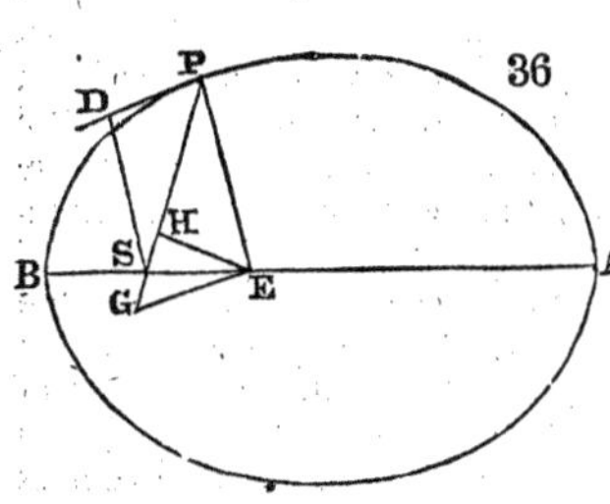


$$f : f' = 2\,SD^2 \times PG : 2\,SA^2 \times PH.$$
$$= SD^2 \times PG : SA^2 \times PH.$$

Now, from the similar triangles G P E, E P H, we have G P : P E = P E : P H; hence G P : P H = $GP^2 : PE^2$. But the triangles G P E, P S D being also similar, $GP^2 : PE^2 = PS^2 : SD^2$; therefore, G P : P H = $PS^2 : SD^2$; and $PS^2 \times PH = SD^2 \times GP$: and since it was shown that $f : f' = SD^2 \times PG : SA^2 \times PH$, wherefore $f : f' = PS^2 \times PH : SA^2 \times PH$; or leaving the common factor P H out of the two consequents we have

$$f : f' = PS^2 : SA^2.$$

Thus we have arrived at this important conclusion; that *the force by which the planets evolve round the sun in elliptical orbits, the sun being in one of the foci, and the radius vector describing areas proportional to the times, is always inversely as the squares of the distances.*

There remains yet another point to be determined respecting *the forces which retain the different planets in their orbits;* namely, whether there is *any analogy between them.* From Kepler's third law, we know that the squares of the periodical times of any two of the planets are proportional to the cubes of their mean distances from the sun. This law is independent of the eccentricities of the orbits; and the same relation would subsist between the mean distances and the periodic times, though the eccentricities were to become infinitely small; or, what is the same thing, the orbits were to become circles. Let us then suppose the planets to move with uniform velocities in circular orbits, having the sun in the centre. This supposition differs very little from the truth. Put $v$, $v'$ to denote the velocities of two of the planets, $r$, $r'$ the radii of their orbits, $t$, $t'$ their periodic times, and $f$, $f'$ the forces by which they are retained in their orbits. From what we have already shown respecting a body moving in a circle round any point as the centre of its motion, we have $f=\frac{v^2}{2r}$ and $f'=\frac{v'^2}{2r'}$, therefore $f:f'=\frac{v^2}{r}:\frac{v'^2}{r'}$. But since the circumferences of circles are to one another as their radii, and the velocity or the space passed over by the planet in the unit of time is equal to the circumference of its orbit, divided by the periodic time expressed in that unit, it is evident that $v:v'=\frac{r}{t}:\frac{r'}{t'}$: hence $\frac{v^2}{r}:\frac{v'^2}{r'}=\frac{r}{t^2}:\frac{r'}{t'^2}$; or, since $t^2:t'^2=r^3:r'^3$, $\frac{v^2}{r}:\frac{v'^2}{r'}=\frac{r}{r^3}:\frac{r'}{r'^3}=\frac{1}{r^2}:\frac{1}{r'^2}=r'^2:r^2$. Wherefore we obtain $f:f'=r'^2:r^2$.

This result shows that the forces which, acting on two planets, would cause them to describe circular orbits, agreeing with Kepler's third law, are inversely as the squares of the distances. Hence we may infer the sameness of the force which retains the planets in their respective orbits; since it varies from orbit to orbit, according to the very same law which regulates its intensity at different distances in the same orbit. This conclusion is fully established by the fact, that the force which acts upon the comets during their descent to the sun, varies exactly according to the law which we have now assigned as the law of the planetary force. The comet of 1759, which was predicted by Dr. Halley, came from regions far beyond the most distant of the known planets, and approached nearer to the sun than Venus; and when it arrived at the same distance from the sun as any of the planets, its deflection from the rectilineal course by the action of the centripetal force, was the very same as that of the planet. We may, therefore, conclude, that it is one and the same force which deflects all the planets as well as the comets.

From what has now been shown, it is evident that if all the planets were placed at the same distance from the sun, they would all be deflected equally by the centripetal force independently of the quantity of matter in each. Hence it follows that, at equal distances, the centripetal force must act equally on every particle of matter of which the planets are composed; so that if one planet contain exactly double the quantity of matter that another planet contains, and if both are placed at exactly the same distance from the sun, the former will receive a double impulse. We may infer, therefore, that another law of the force which retains the planets in their orbits is, that, *at equal distances, it is proportional to the mass on which it acts;* and that *if two bodies act on the same particle of matter, the forces which they exert are proportional to their masses.* The force may be supposed to be produced either by a cause residing in the body which is placed in the centre of motion, or by a cause residing in the revolving body. In the former point of view, it is called a force of ATTRACTION; in the latter, a force of GRAVITATION. The truth is, however, that the cause of this force is absolutely unknown. We see only the effects produced, and from these we investigate the laws which connect them with each other, and the general principles on which they depend.

Thus, from the facts discovered by Kepler respecting the planetary motion, we have shown that each planet has a tendency towards the sun, in consequence of which from a state of rest it would move towards him, acquiring at every instant an increase of velocity according to a fixed and determinate *rule* or law which applies alike to all the planets. This tendency, if not counteracted, would bring the matter of the sun and planets into one mass. This, however, is prevented from taking place, in consequence of an impulse having been originally communicated to each planet, giving it a constant tendency to move in a straight line with an uniform velocity. The effects arising from these two tendencies are so adjusted, as to produce elliptic orbits. But the law which regulates the effects arising from the tendency of the planets towards the sun remaining the same, such a velocity might have been communicated to each planet, by the original impulse which gave it its tendency to move uniformly in a straight line, as would have produced parabolic or hyperbolic orbits. In a circular orbit, if the centre of motion coincide with the centre of the orbit, the velocity of a planet is uniform, and of such rapidity as at every point to produce a tendency to move in a tangent to the orbit, exactly sufficient to counterbalance the tendency to move towards the centre of the orbit. If the orbit be elliptical, and one of the foci the centre of motion, the motion of the planet is variable, and its tendency to move uniformly in a tangent to the orbit sometimes exceeds, and at other times falls short of, that which would be necessary to cause it to revolve in a circle at the same distance from the centre of motion.

Let A D B E be the elliptic orbit of a planet revolving about the sun, which is supposed to be placed in the focus S. Suppose the planet to set out from A in the direction A P, A being the point of its greatest distance from the sun. At A the direction of the planet's motion is at right angles to the radius vector, and if the velocity were such as to produce a tendency to move in the direction of the tangent A G, exactly equivalent to the tendency of the planet to move towards the sun, the planet would revolve in a circle of which S is the centre, and S A the radius. But the velocity being supposed less, the path of the planet will fall within the circle, and the angle S P H contained between the radius vector and the tangent P H, which shows the direction of the planet's motion, changes from a right angle to an acute angle. The tendency of the planet towards the sun is now exerted partly in accelerating its velocity in its orbit, and partly incurvating its path. While the planet describes the quadrant A P D, its velocity is always less than that which would produce a circular motion; until it is at the point D, and then the velocity is precisely what would be sufficient for a circular motion about S, if its direction were perpendicular to the radius vector: the direction, however, being oblique, the planet is brought still nearer to S. The tendency towards the sun is, in a great measure, still exerted in accelerating the motion, and as soon as the planet passes D, its velocity becomes greater than what might produce a circular motion about S. The angle S D K is, therefore, the least angle which the radius vector makes with the direction of the planet's motion, and from the moment when the planet passes the point D, that angle begins to increase; and the effect of this is to cause the tendency of the planet towards the sun to be principally exerted in incurvating the orbit. Its influence in accelerating the planet's motion, though it still exists, is gradually diminished, until the planet arrives at the point B, where it ceases altogether, in consequence of the radius vector being at right angles to the tangent B L.

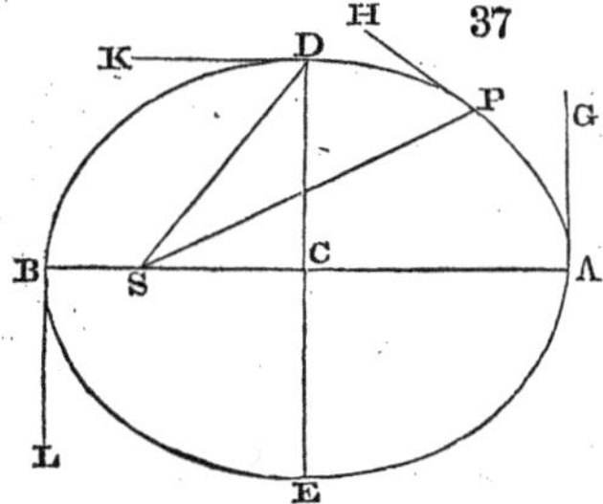


As the velocity of the planet at B is greater than what is sufficient to produce a motion in a circle of which the radius is S B, the path of the planet falls wholly without that circle; and consequently, it is now receding from the sun. The angle which the radius vector makes with the direction of its motion becoming obtuse, the tendency of the planet towards the sun is now partly employed in retarding its motion, so that its velocity is diminished. The angle contained between the radius vector and the direction of the planet's motion increases while the planet is moving from B to E, and decreases from E to A, when it becomes a right angle, as it had formerly decreased from A to D, and increased from D to B. The velocity of the planet in its orbit must, therefore, decrease from B to A, as it had formerly increased from A to B; at the point E it will be equal to what it was at D, and from E to A, the influence of the planet's tendency towards the sun to diminish its velocity will become less and less, until when the planet has arrived at A, it will cease altogether. The velocity is then the same as at first, and the motion goes on in this way for ever.

Whatever has now been deduced from Kepler's Laws respecting the orbits of the primary planets, and the law of the force by which they are described, will apply equally to the orbits of the secondary planets: for in each of these little systems, there is the same analogy between the periodic times and the distances, which takes place in the general system; the figure of the orbits is also elliptic, and the areas described by the radius vector is proportional to the times. We may legitimately conclude, therefore, that *the satellites revolving about any planet, are retained in their orbits by a force inversely proportional to the squares of their distances from their primary planet;* so that all the celestial motions are produced by forces regulated by this general law.

The force that keeps the Moon in her orbit is, then, the attraction of the earth, or her gravitation towards the earth. But we find that the earth attracts all the bodies near its surface by a force which is proportional to the mass of the body attracted. Whatever be the weight of a body, it falls to the earth from the same height in the same time, and with the same velocity. Thus, if the resistance of the atmosphere be removed, it is found by experiment that the lightest feather falls to the earth, from a given height, in the very same time, and with the very same velocity, as a stone, however great its weight. Let us inquire whether the force which retains the moon in its orbit may not be identified with this attractive force which causes the descent of heavy bodies to the surface of the earth.

We may without great error suppose the lunar orbit to be circular, and its semidiameter to be equal to sixty semidiameters of the earth. Let it be represented by the circle C M A, the earth being supposed to be placed at the centre E; and let M C be the small portion

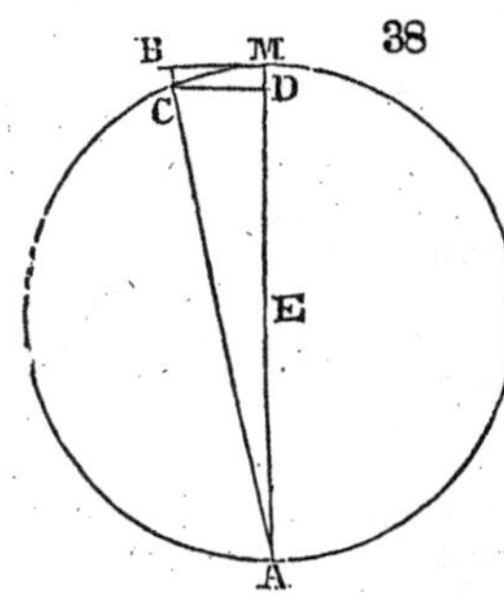


of the orbit which the moon describes in a second of time. Draw M B a tangent to the orbit at M: draw also C D parallel to M B, and C B parallel to M A, the diameter of the orbit. The arch M C may be regarded as coincident with its chord; therefore, joining A C, it is evident that in the right angled triangle A C M we have A M : M C=M C : M D. Hence, since A M and M C are known, M D or B C, the deflection of the moon from the tangent in a second, by the attraction of the earth, may be found.

The moon describes her orbit round the earth in about $27^d$ $7^h$ $43^m$ or 2,360,580 seconds; the circumference of her orbit is about 60 times the circumference of the earth, that is, if we reckon $69\frac{1}{2}$ English miles to a degree, 7,926,336,000 feet; therefore the length of the arc M C, which the moon describes in a second, will be found nearly equal to 3358 feet. Again, A M, the diameter of the moon's orbit, is about 2,523,031,140 feet. Hence we obtain M D equal to 00447 feet nearly. This small fractional part of a foot is the space which a body, placed at the distance of the moon, and falling from a state of rest by the action of the force which retains the moon in her orbit, would pass over in the first second of time. Observing, now, that this force increases as the squares of the distances decrease, we may determine the space which a body at the surface of the earth (or at the distance of one semidiameter from the earth's centre), and falling from a state of rest, would pass over in the first second of time, if urged by the same force. For, since the moon's distance from the earth is equal to about sixty times the semidiameter of the earth, we have $1^2 : 60^2 = 00447$: the space required, which is found to be 16·09 feet. Now, this is exactly the space which a body, falling from rest by its own weight, is found by experiment to pass over in the first second of time. Hence we may infer, that *the moon is retained in its orbit by the very same force which produces pressure in a body supported, or causes a body when unsupported to fall to the ground.*

Though the attraction of the earth on bodies near its surface is only a particular case of a general principle, which produces all the planetary motions, the effects are, to appearance, considerably modified. At all the heights to which we are able to ascend above the general surface of the earth, or to which we can project a body, the force of gravity acts, as to sense, uniformly: it also acts in the direction of straight lines, perpendicular to the horizon, and therefore parallel to one another, for the greatest range that can be given to a projectile. Hence the phenomena, which depend on the force diminishing in intensity, as the square of the distance increases, and on its emanating in the direction of straight lines drawn to the centre of the attracting sphere, become imperceptible. In consequence of the comparatively small velocity with which human power can project a body, its path always meets the earth, and its motion terminates. But if the whole matter of the earth were collected into a point at the centre, a body projected from a point 4000 miles distant from the centre, and with such a velocity as human power can communicate, would be acted upon by the same forces, with a body similarly projected from the surface of the earth. But on the supposition now made, the body would meet with no obstacle, but would approach within a certain distance of the centre, and would then recede from it until it reached another limit, when it would again approach, and go on in this manner, approaching and receding alternately, for ever. The path of the body would be an ellipse, resembling in figure the orbit of a comet. The extreme portions of the path would, as to sense, be portions of a parabola. Hence it is usually laid down as a law regulating the motion of projectiles, that *if a heavy body be projected in a straight line, not perpendicular to the horizon, it will describe a parabola situated in the vertical plane passing through that straight line, and having its axis perpendicular to the horizon.* This physical truth was first discovered by Galileo.

The force of gravity near the surface of the earth being uniform in its action, it is found that the motion which it produces corresponds in all its circumstances with that which mathematical reasoning shows should result from the action of a constant force. *The spaces through which the body falls are proportional to the squares of the times, and the velocity is proportional to the time during which the body has been falling.*

From the third law of Kepler, it is not difficult to see that *the periodic time of a planet* in its orbit is determined entirely by the mean distance, that is, half the transverse axis; and is not at all affected by the increase or decrease of the conjugate axis. By supposing, then, the conjugate axis to be continually diminished, we are led to this conclusion, that the time in which a body would descend to the sun, if allowed to fall from a state of rest at any distance from him, is equal to half the time of revolution in an ellipse the semitransverse axis of which is half of that distance. Let T be the time of revolution of a planet at any distance, and $t$ the time of revolution at half that distance; then, by the third law of Kepler, $T^2 : t^2 : 2^3 : 1^3$; hence we have $t = \frac{T}{\sqrt{8}}$, and $\frac{1}{2}t = \frac{T}{\sqrt{32}}$. But $\frac{1}{2}t$ is the time in which a body would fall from the distance corresponding to T. Hence *the time in which a planet would fall to the sun by the action of the centripetal force is equal to the periodic time divided by* $\sqrt{32}$; or (what amounts to the same thing) to the periodic time multiplied by 0·176776, the reciprocal of the square root of 32. By this general rule, the times in which the different planets would reach the sun, if the action of *their* centrifugal force entirely ceased at the moment when they are at their mean distances, are as follow:

| | Days. | Hrs. | | Days. | Hrs. |
|---|---|---|---|---|---|
| Mercury in | 15 | 13 | Juno | 354 | 19 |
| Venus | 39 | 17 | Vesta | 205 | 0 |
| The Earth | 64 | 13 | Jupiter | 765 | 19 |
| Mars | 121 | 10 | Saturn | 1901 | 0 |
| Ceres | 297 | 6 | Georgium Sidus | 5425 | 0 |
| Pallas | 301 | 4 | The Moon would fall to the Earth in | 4 | 20 |

The principle in the Newtonian philosophy, that the effects produced by the attraction of a body depend very much upon the quantity of matter which it contains, furnishes the means of resolving a problem which at first sight may appear of such difficulty as to transcend the powers of the human mind; namely, to determine the quantity of matter in the sun and planets. Let $f$ and $f'$ denote the forces by which two bodies revolve in circular orbits round two central bodies, of which the masses are denoted by $m$ and $m'$. Let $r$ and $r'$ be the radii of the orbits, and $t$ and $t'$ the periodic times. From what we have already proved with regard to a force that retains a body in a circular orbit, we have

$f : f' = \frac{r}{t^2} : \frac{r'}{t'^2}$ But we have also $f : f' = \frac{m}{r^2} : \frac{m'}{r'^2}$; therefore, $\frac{m}{r^2} : \frac{m'}{r'^2} = \frac{r}{t^2} : \frac{r'}{t'^2}$; and consequently, $m : m' = \frac{r^3}{t^2} : \frac{r'^3}{t'^2}$

Thus it appears that *the masses of matter in the bodies which compose the solar system are directly as the cubes of the mean distances of any bodies which revolve round them, and inversely as the squares of the times in which the revolutions are performed.* By means of this principle, the masses of the sun and of the planets which have satellites may be compared with one another. With regard to the planets which have no satellites, the quantity of matter contained in them can only be guessed from the effects they produce on the motions of the other planets. The quantity of matter in the moon can, however, be determined with greater certainty, by comparing together the influence of the sun and moon in producing the tides and the precession of the equinoxes. Hence we learn, that the matter in the moon is about $\frac{1}{70}$ of the matter in the earth.

The following table exhibits the masses of the planets, that of the sun being considered as unity:

TABLE.

| | | | |
|---|---|---|---|
| Mercury | $\frac{1}{2025810}$ | Jupiter | $\frac{1}{1070.5}$ |
| Venus | $\frac{1}{405871}$ | Saturn | $\frac{1}{3512}$ |
| The Earth | $\frac{1}{354936}$ | Uranus | $\frac{1}{17918}$ |
| Mars | $\frac{1}{2546320}$ | | |

If we add together the numbers given in this table, it will be found that the whole matter in all the planets is not one-six-hundredth part of the matter in the sun.

Knowing the masses of the planets and their diameters, we can determine the force of gravity at their surfaces; for, supposing them to be spherical bodies, and to have no rotation on their axes, the forces with which a body placed on their surfaces gravitates to them will be *proportional to their masses, divided by the squares of their diameters.*

From the masses of Jupiter and the earth, La Place calculates that if we suppose them to have no rotation, a body which at the earth's equator weighs one pound would, if carried to the equator of Jupiter, weigh 2.509 pounds, supposing the weights to be measured by the pressures exerted in the two situations. If the centrifugal force produced by the rotation of the planets be taken into account, however, this weight must be diminished by about one-ninth part. The same body would weigh about 27.65 pounds at the surface of the sun. Hence it follows that a heavy body would there descend about 425 feet in the first second of time.

We have hitherto attended chiefly to the action of the central body upon that which revolves round it; but, in reality, the action is mutual. The planets attract the sun in the same manner as the sun attracts the planets; and the same action and re-action have place among the primary planets and their satellites. Indeed, the gravitation of all the great bodies of the system towards one another, appears only to be a consequence of a similar action between every particle of matter and every other particle of matter. This great fact, to which all the celestial phenomena are ultimately to be referred—*that the particles of matter mutually attract each other by a force varying inversely as the squares of the distances*—is commonly called the principle of UNIVERSAL GRAVITATION.

The mutual attraction of the bodies composing the planetary system gives rise to a train of consequences which it has required the utmost efforts of human ingenuity to unfold. We have already remarked that the planetary motions are liable to a variety of irregularities with which accurate observation has made us acquainted. Now, here we see the cause to which all these irregularities are to be referred. If the sun were fixed immovable in the centre, and only one planet revolving round him, then the path of that planet would be an ellipse, from which there would not be the least deviation; and that focus which is the centre of motion would coincide with the centre of the sun, supposing that body to be spherical and composed of matter of uniform density. But since the planet attracts the sun as well as the sun attracts the planet, with a force directly proportional to the mass and inversely proportional to the square of the distance, it follows that the sun must also move in an elliptic orbit round that point of which the condition is in no way disturbed by the mutual action of the revolving bodies, namely, their CENTRE OF GRAVITY. It is with this point that the focus of the orbit of the planet, and that of the solar orbit, would coincide, and about which the radius vector of each would describe areas proportional to the times. In reference to this point also, the squares of the periodic times would be proportional to the cubes of the distances.

If we suppose two or more planets to revolve about the sun, it is evident that the motions of all would be disturbed by their mutual gravitation. The immense magnitude of the sun compared with that of any of the planets, or of all the planets taken together, might, however, give to his attraction such a preponderance as would preserve all the planetary orbits nearly elliptical; while his own orbit would become a more complicated curve, but such as to furnish a centrifugal force in respect of each planet, just able to counterbalance the gravitation towards it. The centre of gravity of the whole system would be a point to which all their motions are to be referred. Now this is actually the case of the planetary system. Accurate observation proves that the sun is not at rest in the centre, though his motion is very small. His centre is never distant from the centre of gravity of the system so much as his own diameter; and hence the orbit which he describes must be very inconsiderable, when compared with the orbits of the planets. With regard to those planets which are accompanied by satellites, it is not the centre of the primary which traces the elliptic orbit round the sun, but the common centre of gravity of the primary planet and secondary planets which revolve round it.

The perturbations which the mutual attraction of the planets produce in each other's motions are divided into two classes. The one class affect the figure and position of the elliptic orbits, and increase with extreme slowness: these are called SECULAR INEQUALITIES. The other class depend on the mutual situation of the different planets, and acquire the same amount whenever the same relative positions occur: these are called PERIODIC INEQUALITIES. Both these classes of inequalities have been demonstrated to be periodical; that is, they increase only to a certain extent, and then decrease. Amidst all the changes which arise from the mutual actions of the heavenly bodies, there are two things which remain perpetually the same; namely, the greater axis of the orbit which the planet describes, and its periodic time. Thus the permanency of the planetary system is secured.

To subject to calculation the perturbations of the system, requires the solution of the following problem: three bodies of given magnitudes, as the sun, the earth, and the moon, being projected into space with given velocities, and in given directions, and attracting each other according to a given law, namely, inversely as the squares of their distances from each other, and directly as their masses; it is required to determine the nature of the curve, that one of them, as the moon, describes about one of the other two, as the earth. This is the celebrated PROBLEM OF THE THREE BODIES, stated in all its generality, but under this aspect its solution is beyond the reach of the most refined methods of analysis which the mathematical sciences in their present state furnish. In its application to the purposes of physical astronomy, there are certain conditions which render the problem less difficult: viz. 1. That the sun greatly exceeds in magnitude the other two bodies, and is nearly at rest. 2. Its distance from the earth and moon is so great, that it may be considered the same for both. This condition fails, however, in reference to the action of the primary planets on one another, a circumstance which augments the difficulty of investigating the perturbations arising from their mutual gravitation. 3. The planetary orbits are nearly elliptical, and the aberrations from the ellipses in reference to each, are all that is required. Even with these limitations the problem is sufficiently difficult, and has engaged the attention, and exercised the skill of the most celebrated mathematicians of modern times.

The general view which we have now given of the planetary disturbances is all that our present object requires. We shall only, therefore, farther advert to the explanation which he theory of gravitation affords of the figure of the earth, and of the tides.

---

## CHAPTER XVI.

### FIGURE AND CONSTITUTION OF THE EARTH DEDUCED FROM THE THEORY OF GRAVITATION

In the beginning (Chap. III.) we proved that the earth must be nearly spherical, in order to account for the general phenomena which we constantly observe. As soon, however, as the general *law of gravitation* was discovered, it was a necessary consequence that the earth could not be a perfect sphere, but must rather be an oblate spheroid flattened at the poles, and swelled out at the equator, and this inference is independent of all actual measurement, but may be confirmed by observation, and in fact has been so, as will be afterwards fully proved. This deviation from the spherical figure is to be attributed to the influence of the centrifugal force, arising from the earth's diurnal rotation, in diminishing the force of gravity from the pole towards the equator, where the centrifugal force, in reference to the surface, is the greatest possible. This tendency which every particle of matter in the earth has to fly off in the direction of a tangent to the circle in which the particle is carried by the earth's motion of rotation would be increased if that motion were to be accelerated: and may be conceived to be increased to such power as not only to overcome the force of gravity, but also the force by which the particles adhere to one another, and so to cause the earth to separate into fragments. Suppose a small satellite to revolve round the earth close to its surface at the equator; its periodic time may be deduced from that of the moon, on the principle that the squares of their periodic times would be to one another as the cubes of their distances. For we have (since the moon's distance is about sixty times the semi-diameter of the earth, and the time of her periodic revolution 39343 minutes),

$$60^3 : 1^3 = 39343^2 : \text{sq. of the periodic time of the satellite.}$$

Hence we obtain the periodic time nearly equal to $84\frac{1}{2}$ minutes. If the earth revolved about its axis in $84\frac{1}{2}$ minutes while such a satellite described a circular orbit close to its surface, the satellite would therefore appear to be at rest on the surface, but would not in the least degree press upon it, because the force of gravity would be exactly counterbalanced by the centrifugal force produced by the motion of the satellite in its orbit. Now, all the objects on the surface at the equator would be in the very same circumstances with the satellite; for they actually describe circles in consequence of the earth's motion, and if the earth revolved in $84\frac{1}{2}$ minutes, their centrifugal force would become exactly equal to the force of gravity; so that they would no longer have weight. If the earth's motion of rotation became still more rapid, they would fly off from the surface.

At the equator a body describes a circle of which the circumference is about 132,105,600 feet in $23^h\ 56^m$ nearly: it must therefore describe an arc of about 1528 feet in a second of time. From what we have shown already respecting central forces, it is evident that, by dividing the square of this arc by the diameter of the earth, we shall find the deflection from the tangent in a second, which will be the measure of the centrifugal force. This deflection amounts to about $\frac{67}{100}$ of an inch, or $\frac{1}{288}$ of $16\frac{1}{12}$ feet, the space through which a body would fall in a second by the force of apparent gravity. The centrifugal force at the equator is therefore the $\frac{1}{288}$ part of the sensible weight of a body, or $\frac{1}{289}$ part of its real weight. Suppose, then, a body, when weighed at the equator by a spring-steel yard, to be found capable of drawing out the spring to the division 288: if that body were weighed at the pole, where the centrifugal force vanishes, it would draw out the spring to the division 289.

It admits of being demonstrated that, proceeding from the equator where the centrifugal force is *the greatest* toward either pole, where it vanishes, *the increase of gravity in different latitudes is as the square of the sine of the latitude.*

Such being the nature of the forces that act upon every particle of matter of which the earth is composed, *the determination of its figure from physical principles* involves the solution of the two following problems:—

1. What is the law according to which a particle will gravitate towards a solid of a given form and constitution, the particle being supposed situated either within or without the solid?

2. What figure will a mass of matter, either wholly or partly fluid, assume in consequence of the joint effect of the attraction of its particles (that attraction varying inversely as the squares of their distances), and a centrifugal force arising from the rotation of the mass about an axis? Both these problems involve a great degree of difficulty; and the second is even more intricate than the first, in consequence of the reciprocal relations subsisting between the figure of the attracting body and the law of gravitation at its surface, which renders a knowledge of the one necessary to the determination of the other. Assuming that an homogeneous fluid of the same mean density with the earth has the figure of an oblate spheroid, and revolves on its axis in $23^h\ 56^m\ 4^s$ of solar time, it would be *in equilibrio*, if the axis of revolution were to the equatorial diameter in the proportion of 229 to 230. This is the figure which Newton ascribed to the earth; and though th assumption which he made of such a figure was certainly gratuitous, the result of his investigation is almost the same as later writers have obtained by a more rigorous as well as direct mode of reasoning than that which he employed. Again, it has been demonstrated by La Place, that a fluid and homogeneous mass, of the mean density of the earth, cannot remain in equilibrium and possess at the same time an elliptic figure, if the time of its rotation be less than $2^h\ 25^m\ 17^s$. If the time of revolution exceed this, there may always be two elliptic spheroids, and not more, in which the equilibrium may be maintained. In the

case of the mass revolving in $23^h\ 56^m\ 4^s$, the one spheroid is that which has already been mentioned; the other is one in which the polar diameter is to the equatorial in the ratio of 1 to 681. The extreme flatness of this spheroid must render the force of gravity at the equator almost nothing; the fluid, therefore, would be so easily dissipated that this equilibrium can scarcely be regarded as stable.

Another conclusion on this subject, deduced by Clairault, is, that if the fluid mass supposed to revolve on its axis, instead of being homogeneous, be composed of strata which increase in density towards the centre, in order to remain in equilibrium, it must still possess the figure of an elliptic spheroid, but the oblateness will be diminished.

The oblateness of the earth at its poles is a phenomenon which the measurements that have been made of arcs of the meridian have placed beyond all doubt; but there is still an uncertainty as to the exact quantity of the compression. The results obtained, however, render it highly probable that it is less than $\frac{1}{230}$, which Newton, proceeding on the supposition of a uniform density, assigned for the compression. Hence we may conclude, that if the earth is a spheroid of equilibrium, it is denser in the interior than at its surface. This inference has been verified by very accurate experiments made by the late Dr. Maskelyne on the sides of the mountain Schehallien, in Perthshire. The object was to determine the derangement of the plummet by the vicinity of this lofty and solid mountain; and the results, obtained from observation made at two stations on the south and north sides of it, showed that the plummet deviated from the direction of gravity towards the mountain more than 7″. The quantity of this change of direction gives the ratio of the attraction of the mountain to that of the whole earth, or to the force of gravity, equal to the ratio of 1 to 17804. But the bulk and figure of the mountain being also obtained by a trigonometrical survey, its mean density was found to be to the mean density of the earth nearly as 5 to 9. Thus it appears that the mean density of the earth is not much less than double the density of the rocks which compose the mountain Schehallien; and these, again, seem considerably more dense than the mean of those which form the exterior crust of the earth.

It may appear an objection to this mode of reasoning concerning the figure of the earth, that it is not evident how a centrifugal force should produce the same effect on a solid body, like the earth, that it does upon a fluid mass. But the fact that the earth has made an approximation to the spheroid of *equilibrium*, is an indication that either the entire mass was originally fluid, from whatever cause; or the repeated waste and reconsolidation of the parts near the surface has gradually produced the spheroidal figure. In either of these modes the power of cohesion, which in the solid body resists the effects of the centrifugal force, may have been overcome. However irregular a body, whose surface is composed of land and water, may be in its primitive form; by the process of constant waste, the more prominent parts are gradually worn down, and the matter which composed them is deposited in the lower parts which are occupied by the water: here it acquires a horizontal stratification; and having, by certain mineral operations, under the transforming hand of nature, been consolidated into stone, the water being removed, it may again form a part of the solid crust of the earth. In this manner the primitive irregular form will gradually disappear, and the surface in the course of ages acquire a position at right angles to the direction of gravity; so that, by the action of the centrifugal force, there will be a constant approximation made to the spheroid of equilibrium. The irregular distribution of the heterogeneous materials which compose this terraqueous globe may, perhaps, prevent the coincidence from ever being complete.

It admits of being demonstrated, that if the earth were a perfect sphere, and composed of matter of uniform density at equal distances from its centre, the action of the solar and lunar attraction upon it would be the same as if the whole terraqueous mass were condensed into a point at the centre. Hence the position of its axis would not, in that case, be in the least degree affected by its gravitation towards the sun and moon, but would remain parallel to itself while the earth performed its annual revolution. In consequence of the spheroidal figure, however, the earth may be considered as composed of a sphere of which the radius is half the polar axis, and of a quantity of redundant matter, which is distributed over it in such a manner as to swell out the equatorial regions. The action of the solar and lunar attraction on this redundant matter produces the precession of the equinoxes and the nutation of the earth's axis. The complete explanation of these phenomena affords one of the happiest illustrations of the Newtonian doctrine of attraction; but requires at the same time the aid of some of the most abstruse theories both in pure mathematics and mechanics.

---

## CHAPTER XVII.

### THE TIDES.

THE alternate rise and fall of the surface of the sea, or it flux and reflux, known by the name of the TIDES, is a phenomenon which has attracted the attention of mankind from the earliest periods. Herodotus and Diodorus Siculus take notice of the daily flux and reflux of the waters of the Red Sea or Arabian Gulf, the latter historian describing it as a great and rapid tide; but neither of these writers forms any conjecture respecting its cause. Observation must soon have shown, that this periodical ebbing and flowing of the waters of the ocean had an intimate connexion with the position of the sun and moon in the heavens; and, accordingly, we find that Pliny not only describes the phenomena of tides, but expressly attributes them to the action of these luminaries.

It was not, however, until Newton applied the principle of universal gravitation to explain these phenomena that the theory of the tides was fully understood. The weight of a body on the surface of the earth arises from the tendency which the particles composing it have to the centre (or to a point near the centre), in obedience to the law of gravity. But as every object on the earth's surface gravitates towards the sun and moon, as well as towards the earth, it follows that the solar and lunar attraction must affect the weight of terrestrial objects. Upon solid bodies, between the particles of which adhesive force is powerful, no discernible effects are produced by this attraction. But the case is altogether different with regard to the waters of the ocean, the component particles of which yield to the slightest impulse; so that any alteration in their weight that does not equally affect the whole must be followed immediately by a motion of the parts of the fluid mass, which will continue until, by a new arrangement of the particles, the equilibrium is restored.

To see what must be the general effect, arising from the action of the sun, if the whole surface of the globe were covered with water; let A C B O (*fig.* 39.) be the watery sphere, S the

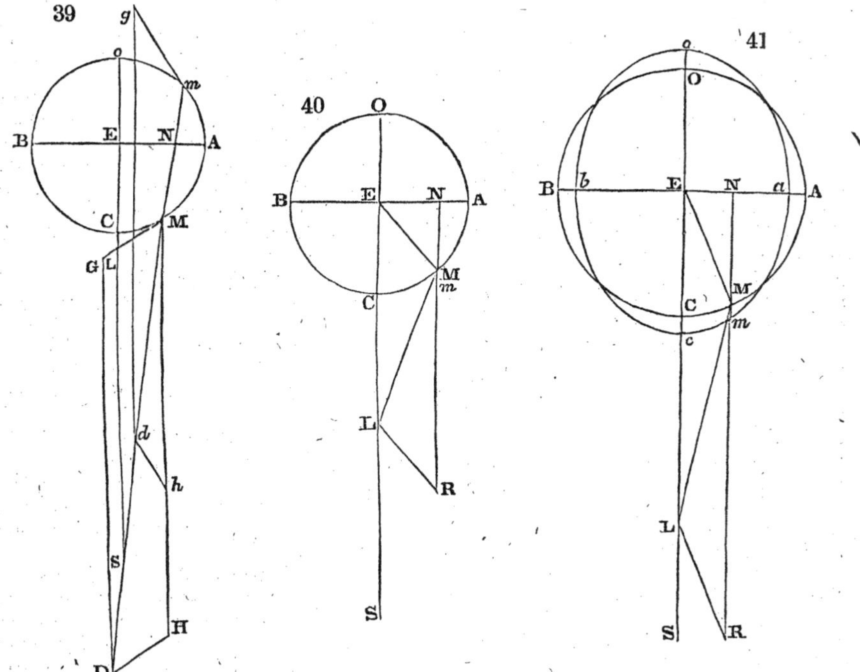


sun, and E the centre of the earth. Let the gravitation of the central particle E to the sun be represented by the line E S, and the gravitation of any other particle M by the line M S D. Let the force M D be resolved into two forces, M H equal and parallel to E S, and M G. The force M H does not in the least degree affect the gravitation of the particle M towards the centre E; and M G is, therefore, the only disturbing force. If S M be produced to meet the circle A C B O in the point *m*, the action of the sun on a particle situated at *m* is less than its action on the central particle E; so that if *m d* represent the gravitation of the particle *m* towards the sun, the point *d* will fall on the opposite side of S from the point D; and the force *m d* being resolved into two forces, *m h* equal and parallel to E S, and the disturbing force *m g*, it is evident that the tendency of the force *m g* is to diminish the gravity of the particle *m*, in like manner as the force M G diminishes the gravity of the particle M. When the point M coincides with A, the angle E S M is the angle under which the semidiameter of the earth is seen from the sun; therefore E S M can never exceed $8\frac{1}{2}''$: whence, in determining the direction and quantity of the disturbing force from the geometrical relations of the lines, we may consider the lines D G, S L, and D M as coincident, and M L may be taken for the disturbing force. Again, the difference between

S M and S E is greatest when the point M coincides with C or O. But if we consider that C E, the difference between S E and S M when greatest, is only about $\frac{1}{24000}$ part of S E, it is evident that we commit but a very small error in supposing S M, S N, and S E in every position equal. Now, since S E and D M represent the gravitation of the particles E and M towards the sun respectively, we have $SE : DM = SM^2 : SE^2$; therefore, since S E and S N may be considered equal, $DM = \frac{SN^3}{SM^2}$. But $SN = SM + MN$, therefore $SN^3 = SM^3 + 3SM^2 \times MN + 3SM \times MN^2 + MN^3$. The quantity M N is so small, compared with S M, that the two last terms of this expression for $SN^3$ may be neglected: we have, therefore, $SN^3 = SM^3 + 3SM^2 \times MN$, and $\frac{SN^3}{SM^2} = SM + 3MN$: wherefore, also, $DM = SM + 3MN$; and taking S M from each, we find $SD = 3MN$. Now, since G D may be considered equal to $LS + SD$, and E S is by construction equal to G D, it is evident that $ES = LS + SD$, or taking L S from each, $EL = SD$. Hence $EL = 3MN$, and the disturbing force for any point M is determined both in direction and magnitude.

Suppose now that A C B O (*fig.* 40.) is the terraqueous globe, E S a line directed to the sun, and A E B a section by that circle which separates the enlightened from the dark hemisphere. Let M be any particle on or within the mass. Through the point M draw a straight line M N perpendicular to the plane A E B, and in E S take E L, equal to 3 M N: join L M; then L M represents the direction and intensity of the disturbing force which the sun exerts on the particle M. Let the force L M be resolved into two forces, one, M E, directed towards the centre of the earth, and the other, M R, tending from the plane A E B towards the sun. Suppose the same construction to be made for every point of the sphere, the whole being supposed covered with water, it is evident that the forces represented by M E will balance one another, and therefore need not be considered. But the force represented by M R will diminish the gravity of every particle M, reckoned in the direction of a line perpendicular to the plane of that great circle of the earth which separates the illuminated from the dark hemisphere. The force thus diminishing the gravity will be proportional to three times the distance of the particle from the same plane; for R M is equal to L E or 3 M N. Every particle in any column M N being thus acted on by a force which evidently tends to destroy the equilibrium of the fluid mass, the water in that column cannot remain at rest. Its equilibrium may be restored, however, by the addition of a small portion M *m*, which, by restoring the weight of the column, enables it to resist the pressure of the adjacent columns. A similar addition may be made to each column, perpendicular to the plane A E B: and the result will be that, from being spherical, the figure of the globe will be changed into that of an oblong elliptical spheroid, having its axis directed towards the sun, and its poles in those points of the surface which have the sun in the zenith and nadir.

Let the figure into which the watery sphere would be transformed by the solar action be represented by the ellipse *a c b o* (*fig.* 41.): the points *o* and *c* are the poles of the spheroid; and at these points the waters are highest above the sphere A C B O of equal capacity, while all round the circumference B E A the waters are below their natural level. By calculation it is found that the difference between E *c* and E *a* is about twenty-four and a half inches; so that the deviation from the spherical figure is not great.

The figure which the watery spheroid assumes must be in a slight degree influenced by the spheroidal figure of the earth; but the deviation from the spherical figure is so small, that its effect in changing the spheroidal figure of the waters on the surface of the earth must be quite inconsiderable. If the earth were at rest, the watery spheroid would acquire that form which would produce an equilibrium among all its particles. This, however, can never happen under the actual circumstances of the case, because some time must elapse before an accelerating force can produce a finite change in the disposition of the waters; but, by the motion of the earth on its axis, the disturbing force is every instant applied to a different part of the surface, so that the position of equilibrium can never actually be attained. Such, then, is the general effect which the solar action would produce if the whole globe were fluid, or a spherical nucleus covered with a fluid of equal density. To explain the phenomena of the tides, however, it is indispensably necessary to take into account the action of the moon.

It is with the moon that the tides are principally connected; and the sun's influence is known only by its increasing or diminishing the effects of her more powerful action. This greater influence of the moon in producing the tides arises from her vicinity to the earth, when compared with the sun, her distance being only about $\frac{1}{400}$ part of his. It must be carefully kept in view, that it is not the mere action of the sun and moon that produces the tides in the ocean, but the *inequalities* in the action of each: and the gravitation of the waters of the ocean to the moon is much more unequal than their gravitation to the sun. Whatever has been proved with regard to the influence of the sun in producing tides in the ocean is equally applicable to the moon. The waters will be accumulated immediately under her, and on the opposite side of the globe, producing a spheroid of the same kind with that which we have shown must be produced by the unequal action of the sun, but more elongated; and this spheroid, directed toward the moon, will follow her in her apparent daily revolution about the earth. In consequence of this simultaneous gravitation towards both luminaries, the ocean must assume a figure different from both of these spheroids; which will become blended and undistinguishable. The resulting figure resembles each of the spheroids in being elongated, and its most elevated parts are found to follow the more powerful of the disturbing bodies, namely, the moon, in her apparent diurnal revolution about the earth. We may, without sensible error, suppose that the change produced in any part of the ocean by the combined action of the sun and moon, is the sum or the difference of the changes which they would have produced if acting separately.

We have already remarked that the rapid motion of the waters, in consequence of the diurnal motion, prevents them from ever assuming the figure which would be requisite for the equilibrium of the forces acting on them; so that they oscillate continually, alternately approaching to that figure and receding from it. The motion thus communicated to them is one not of transference, but of undulation, one part rising and another sinking, unless when from want of depth of water the balance between the adjacent columns is destroyed. We may, therefore, regard the two elevations produced in the ocean by the inequalities in the solar and lunar actions as two vast waves which follow the moon in her apparent diurnal motion. The line joining the tops of these two waves is not directed to the moon, as would be the case if the earth and moon were at rest, but is directed to a point about 30° to the eastward of the moon. This arises from the *inertia* of the water, which causes it, when once put in motion, to continue to rise for a time after the impulse communicated has ceased. If we consider the tides relatively to the whole surface of the globe, there is a meridian, therefore, about 30° eastward of the moon where it is always HIGH WATER, both in the hemisphere where the moon is, and the opposite hemisphere. On the west side of the meridian the tide is *flowing*, and on the east side of it the tide is *ebbing*. On the meridian which is at right angles to the former, it is everywhere LOW WATER. If we suppose, then, the sun and moon to be in the equator, and an observer to be situated on the surface of the water under the equator; when the moon has risen 30° above his horizon, the state of the tide to that observer will be low water. As the moon advances towards his zenith, the tide will flow; and when she has reached a point about 30° to the westward of his zenith, the summit of the wave will reach him, and then the state of the tide will be high water. As the moon approaches the western horizon, the observer will see the water gradually subside as it had formerly risen; and when she has descended 30° below the horizon, it is again low water. As the moon continues her course below the horizon, the waters again gradually rise by the approach of the other wave until its summit arrives at the observer, and again produces high water; when the moon has passed the opposite meridian, and reached a point 30° beyond it, the tide again begins to ebb as the wave rolls on, and the same phenomena are repeated in the same order. Thus, in the space of time in which the moon performs her diurnal revolution, which may be called a lunar day, and consists of nearly $24^h\ 50^m$, there occur two tides of flood and two of ebb. The time between one high water to the next is about $12^h\ 25^m$, and the instant of low water is nearly but not exactly the middle of this interval, the tide in general taking about nine or ten minutes more in ebbing than in flowing.

*Spring and neap tides.* As the magnitude of the two waves which produce the rise and fall of the tide depends on the action of the sun as well as on that of the moon, it is evident that the height to which the water rises and falls must be affected by the relative position of the two luminaries. At new moon and full moon the actions of the sun and moon are combined, but at the quadratures they counteract each other. In the former case, the two spheroids produced by the solar and lunar actions have their axes coincident or nearly so; in the latter, their axes are at right angles to each other. Hence, at new and full moon the flood tide will rise higher, and the ebb tide will sink lower, than usual. The reverse of this will happen when the moon is in either of her quadratures: the flood tide will not rise so high as usual, nor will the ebb tide sink so low. This is exactly coincident with experience; and we here perceive the cause of what are called SPRING TIDES and NEAP TIDES. About the time of full moon and change the tides rise higher than when the moon presents any other phasis. The highest tide does not happen, however, the first after the opposition or conjunction, though the disturbing forces are then united, but some time after; and the cause of this is the same which prevents the time of high water of any one tide coinciding with the time of the moon being on that meridian under which the tide happens; namely, the *inertia* of the water, or that tendency which all matter has to retain its state whether of rest or motion. At Brest, where an accurate register was kept of the phenomena of the tides about the beginning of the last century, it was found that the highest tide happened about a day and a half after the new and full moon. If the time of high water coincide with the very time of conjunction or opposition, the third high water after that is the highest of all. This is called 1e SPRING TIDE. From this period the tides gradually decrease, until the third high water after the moon's quadrature, which is the lowest of all, and is called the **NEAP TIDE.** But having reached their utmost depression, the tides again increase until the occurrence of the next spring tide; and so on continually. The higher the tide of flood rises, the lower the ebb tide generally sinks on that day. The total magnitude of the tide is estimated by the difference between high and low water. At Brest the medium spring tide is about 19 feet, and the medium neap tide about 9 feet.

*Effect in different hemispheres.* Let us next suppose the sun and moon to be situated in one of the tropics; the two waves raised in the ocean by their actions on opposite sides of the globe will now roll along under the tropics. If an observer be placed on the surface of the water, and under the same tropic in which the sun and moon are situated, he will still see two tides of flood and two of ebb; but they will not correspond in all their circumstances, as they did on the former supposition. The depth of the high water produced by the wave situated in the same hemisphere with the moon, will evidently be greater than that of the high water produced by the wave which rolls along under the other tropic in the opposite hemisphere from the moon; for the observer will see the very summit of the one wave, and only the sloping side of the other. To an observer situated under the tropic on the opposite side of the equator from the sun and moon, the case would be reversed; and if he were so far removed from the equator as to be situated under the polar circle, no part of the wave accumulated in the same hemisphere with the moon would reach him; so that he would see only one tide of flood and one tide of ebb daily produced by the motion of the other wave.

This also is consistent with what we know respecting the tides from observation. All the phenomena are found to be modified by the latitude of the place of observation; and some phenomena are found to occur in high latitudes, which are not at all seen when the place of observation is under the equator. In particular when the moon and the observer are on the same side of the equator, that tide in which the moon is above the horizon is greater than the other tide of the same day which happens when the moon is below the horizon. The contrary takes place when the moon and the observer are on opposite sides of the equator: in this latter case, if the polar distance of the observer be equal to the moon's declination, he will see but one tide in the day, continuing to flow for twelve hours and to ebb for twelve hours. We have supposed for simplicity the sun and moon to be in the equator, or in one of the tropics; but it is evident that this can seldom be the case. The two luminaries are capable of an infinite variety of positions in reference to each other, as well as in reference to any particular point of the earth's surface. The phenomena with regard to particular places must, therefore, be endlessly diversified; but by tracing the general features, the principles become apparent upon which all the phenomena depend.

The influence of the sun and moon in producing tides in the ocean will evidently be augmented when these bodies are nearer to the earth, and diminished when their distances are increased. From this cause it arises, that when the moon is in that part of her orbit where she approaches nearest to the earth, the spring tide which happens at that time is the highest, and the next spring tide is the smallest; because the moon is then nearly at her greatest distance from the earth. This makes a difference of $2\frac{3}{4}$ feet from the mean height of the spring tide at Brest; and consequently of double that quantity, or $5\frac{1}{2}$ feet, between the greatest spring tide and the least. The neap tide which happens between these two very unequal spring tides is regular, because the moon is then nearly at her mean distance. The reverse of this takes place when the moon is at her mean distance at the time of the change: the spring tide is regular, but the two neap tides differ considerably in height. The increased distance of the sun is the reason why the spring tides in our summer are not so great as in our winter. At the mean intensities of the disturbing forces, the sun tends to raise the waters about $24\frac{1}{2}$ inches, and the moon about 58. Hence the spring tide should be about $58+24\frac{1}{2}=82\frac{1}{2}$ inches, and the neap tide about $58-24\frac{1}{2}=33\frac{1}{2}$ inches.

*Variations caused by continents, islands, &c.* We have hitherto supposed the two waves which produce the phenomena of the tides to meet with no interruption in their progress round the world. This is, however, far from being the case; they are interrupted by continents and islands, and may be propelled or retarded by the action of the wind; their velocity and direction may also be changed by irregularities in the bed of the ocean: so that, to explain all the phenomena at any particular place, the effect of local circumstances, which is often great, must be taken into the account. The great Pacific Ocean is, perhaps, the only part of the terraqueous globe in which all the forces have room to operate. But the wave which they form must, in rolling westward, encounter the coasts of Asia and New Holland, with the interjacent islands; and amidst these obstacles it must force its way to the Indian Ocean. Its figure will thus be changed, and the phenomena of the tides, which it produces, powerfully modified. On its eastern side the Pacific is bounded by a vast stretch of coast, extending without interruption from Cape Horn to Behring's Straits. This barrier prevents all supply from the eastward for making up the watery spheroid, and must be equally effectual in arresting the progress of the waters accumulated to the eastward of the American continent. So far as we have information respecting the tides in the Pacific

Ocean, they appear to be very unlike the European tides, until we reach about 40° or 50° west from the coast of America. In the neighbourhood of that coast, scarcely any tide occurs when the moon is below the horizon. Even in the middle of the Pacific Ocean the tides are very small, but at the same time very regular.

As a great extent of surface is necessary in order that the sea should be sensibly affected by the inequalities in the actions of the sun and moon, the *tides* which are experienced in narrow seas, and on shores far removed from the main body of the ocean, are not produced in those seas, but are waves propagated from the great diurnal undulation, and moving with much less velocity. The tides which visit the coasts of England, must, in a great measure, be supplied from the accumulation of water in the Indian and Ethiopic Ocean, from the eastward, and by what is brought or kept back from the South Sea. The undulations will be diffused as proceeding from a collection coming round the Cape of Good Hope, and round Cape Horn. Consistently with this supposition, it is found that high water, which occurs at the Cape of Good Hope at new and full moon about three o'clock, is later and later as we proceed northward along the coast of Africa; later and later still as we follow it along the western coasts of Spain and France, until we reach the mouth of the English Channel. The wave now divides itself into three branches; one part passing up St. George's Channel, another proceeding northward along the western coast of Ireland, and the third passing up the English Channel, between the British and French coasts. The two branches that proceed along the east and west sides of Ireland unite and form one ridge or wave, which continues its progress along the western coasts and islands of Scotland, and then diffuses itself eastward towards Norway and Denmark, and circling round the eastern coasts of Britain, comes southward through the German Ocean, until it reaches Dover, where it meets the branch which passes up the English Channel. It is to be remarked, however, that this tide which comes up the channel is not the same with that which meets it from the north, but is a whole tide earlier if not two, as appears from the fact of the spring tide at Rye being a tide earlier than the spring tide at the Nore: it even seems two tides earlier, for it appears the one as often as the other. By tracing the hour of high water from the Lizard up St. George's Channel, and along the west coasts of Scotland, it appears that the two tides which pass along the east and west sides of Ireland and unite into one wave to the north of it, travel round Britain in about twenty-eight hours, in which time the primitive tide has gone round the whole circumference of the earth, and nearly 45 degrees more. By attending also to the successive hours of high water along the western coasts of Africa and Europe, it appears that the wave, which divides into three branches at the mouth of the English Channel, takes up nearly two days, or between four and five tides, in travelling thither from the Cape of Good Hope. A similar progress of the same high water from the southward is observed along the eastern shores of South America; but beyond Brazil and Surinam the Atlantic Ocean is sufficiently extensive to contribute greatly to the formation of the regular spheroid; so that the effect of this high water from the southward, being blended with the tide raised in the Atlantic itself, becomes insensible. In an ocean of such a breadth from east to west as the Atlantic, the water can rise on the one shore only by descending on the other. In the middle, therefore, it will retain nearly the mean height between its elevations on the two opposite coasts: this appears to be the reason why the tides are small in islands that are very far distant from the shores.

The reflection of the tide from shore to shore is a great cause of irregularity in the tides. The coasts may be so situated that the time in which the undulation that constitutes the tide would of itself vibrate backward and forward from shore to shore, may be so exactly accommodated to the recurring action of the moon that the succeeding impulses, being always added to the natural undulation, may raise it to a height altogether disproportioned to what the action of the moon can produce in the open sea, where the undulation diffuses itself to a vast distance.

The inequalities which undoubtedly obtain in the bottom of the ocean affect the tides, by changing the direction of the waters; also their velocity either absolutely or in respect of particular places. They may also influence the height by causing the tide to rush with increasing velocity towards a particular point, where the waters must at length be suddenly checked, and therefore be accumulated in an extraordinary degree: this appears to be the cause of the astonishingly high tides which occur in the Bay of Fundy. The high water of the Atlantic Ocean at St. Helena does not exceed four or five feet; but, setting in obliquely on the coast of North America, it seems to range along that coast in a channel or bed, gradually narrowing till it is stopped in the Bay of Fundy, where the accumulation of the waters becomes tremendous. The tide approaches with a prodigious noise in one vast wave, that is seen many miles off, and the waters rise to the height of more than seventy feet in the gulf of Cumberland basin; the rapidity of the waters is so great as to overtake animals feeding on the shores.

In consequence of the length of time required for a tide to propagate itself up a great river, one or two succeeding tides may reach the mouth of the river before the first tide has arrived at the highest point to which it ranges up the stream. The second tide will also have propagated itself so far up the river, by the time that the third tide reaches the mouth; and thus there may be three co-existent high waters in the river. The two intervening low waters in the ocean will also produce two corresponding low waters in the river: these changes in the depth of the stream are produced by the high waters which arrive at its mouth checking its velocity, and the low waters accelerating it. To cause high water at any particular point, it is by no means necessary that the water should be raised to that level all the way from that point to the mouth of the river. Before such an accumulation could take place, in many instances, places farther down the stream would be inundated. At many places that are far from the sea, the stream at the moment of high water is down the river, and sometimes it is considerable. At Quebec, the current in the St. Lawrence runs at the rate of not less than three miles per hour: this is a clear proof that the water is not heaped up, for there can be no stream without a declivity. The phenomenon termed the **bore** of a river, which occurs chiefly in large rivers that have a wide outlet, and where the greatest tides are experienced, arises from the waters accumulated in the gulf or outlet by one tide not being, in such circumstances, discharged before the approach of the ensuing tide. These accumulated waters encounter, therefore, the waters of the ocean flowing in an opposite direction; so that the re-action of the conflicting waves produces an elevation of the water far above the natural level. The surge formed in this manner rolls up the river with irresistible force, overwhelming every thing which it encounters; until, exhausted by the resistance which it has to overcome, it at length sinks into a feeble undulation. The violence and elevation with which the bore rushes along in some rivers is almost incredible: at the mouth of the Severn the flood comes up in one head about ten feet in height; but in the great rivers of America, and particularly in the Amazon, it becomes a rolling mountain of water, which is said to attain the height of 180 feet.

In confined seas of small extent, such as the Caspian, the Euxine, the Baltic, and the great lakes of North America, the tides must necessarily be almost insensible; the disturbing forces in such situations have not room to act to any extent: the greatest height to which the waters of the Caspian can rise above their level on the shore, in consequence of a spheroidal shape being given to them by the lunar action, does not exceed seven inches; an accumulation which a slight breeze of wind is sufficient to counteract. Even in cases where a confined sea is connected with the ocean by a narrow channel, no sensible tide can happen; for the tide in the ocean cannot diffuse itself through the contracted inlet during the period that elapses between two consecutive tides.

The Mediterranean is a confined sea of considerable extent; and the tides there might be very sensible if the effects of the solar and lunar actions were not diminished by its distance from the equator. As the moon approaches the meridian of the eastern part of the Mediterranean, there is a considerable elevation of the waters on the Syrian coast, and a considerable depression at Gibraltar. In the middle of the length the water is at the mean height; in the Atlantic Ocean, an open and extensive surface of water, the regular spheroidal form is nearly attained, and the water stands considerably higher on the outside of the straits than on the inside; it is nearly low water within, while it is about one third or one half flood without. Notwithstanding this accumulation, the communication is too narrow to allow the tide of the ocean to diffuse itself in a regular manner into the basin of the Mediterranean. As the moon moves westward, toward Gibraltar, the water will begin to rise, but slowly, within the straits, while without it is flowing very rapidly. The accumulation within increases with the progress of the moon westward, until it reaches high water; but by this time the tide has been ebbing for some hours without the straits. It will now be low water on the coast of Syria; and during all this time the water at the middle between the eastern and western extremities will not have sensibly altered its depth.

The singular currents which prevail in the Straits of Gibraltar appear in a great measure explained by these peculiarities with regard to the tides in the Mediterranean Sea and Atlantic Ocean. Changes of tide, always different and frequently quite opposite, are observed on the east and west sides of the narrow neck which connects the rock with Spain; and the general tenor of those changes has a very great analogy with what has now been described.

It is a fact which strikes the attention, upon the most cursory observation of the phenomena of the tides, that they fall later every day. This variation in the interval of the tides is called the **priming** or **lagging** of the tides, according as we refer them to lunar or solar time. If we suppose the sun and moon to be in the equator, and the watery spheroid to attain *instantaneously* the form suited to its equilibrium, then the line joining the summits of the two waves produced in the ocean by their combined actions will always be directed to a point situated between their centres; except in the case of the sun and moon being in conjunction or opposition, when it will be directed towards their centres. The following table calculated on the above supposition, and for the mean distances of the sun and moon from the earth, exhibits the minutes of solar time that the moment of high water precedes or follows the moon's southing, corresponding to every tenth degree of the moon's elongation (eastward) from the sun or from the point opposite to the sun. It shows also the hour and minute of the day, nearly, when it is high water; and the height of the tide, supposing the height of a spring tide to be 1000:—

| Moon's Elongation at southing. | Time of High Water. | | Height of Tide. | Time of High Water. | | Moon's Elongation at southing. |
|---|---|---|---|---|---|---|
| | Before Moon's southing. | Afternoon or Midnight. | | Afternoon or Midnight. | After Moon's southing. | |
| Deg. | Min. | Ho. Min. | | Ho. Min. | Min. | Deg. |
| 0 | 0 | 0 0 | 1000 | 12 0 | 0 | 180 |
| 10 | 11½ | 0 28½ | 987 | 11 31 | 11½ | 170 |
| 20 | 22 | 0 58 | 949 | 11 2 | 22 | 160 |
| 30 | 31½ | 1 28½ | 887 | 10 31 | 31½ | 150 |
| 40 | 40 | 2 0 | 806 | 10 0 | 40 | 140 |
| 50 | 45 | 2 35 | 715 | 9 25 | 45 | 130 |
| 60 | 46½ | 3 13½ | 610 | 8 46½ | 46½ | 120 |
| 70 | 40½ | 3 59½ | 518 | 8 0½ | 40½ | 110 |
| 80 | 25 | 4 55 | 453 | 7 5 | 25 | 100 |
| 90 | 0 | 6 0 | 429 | 6 0 | 0 | 90 |

If we note the exact time of high water of spring tide for any harbour, and the exact position of the sun and moon at that time, we can easily make a table of the monthly series for that port, by noticing the difference of that time from the table, and making the same difference for every succeeding phasis of the tide.

---

## CHAPTER XVIII.

### GENERAL VIEW OF THE SOLAR SYSTEM.

Ten stars, among the countless number with which, in a clear night, the heavens appear so resplendent, have been proved, by the observations and reasonings of which we have now given a brief outline, to be *planets* revolving about the sun, and deriving their light from him. The earth which we inhabit has been proved to have a similar motion, and to belong to the same class of bodies. Several of these primary planets are accompanied by satellites; and the whole are preserved in their respective orbits by a centripetal combined with a centrifugal force. Thus there subsist among these bodies relations which are regarded as uniting them in one system, having the sun in the centre; and which is therefore called the SOLAR SYSTEM.

In regard to the other planets, as we have employed the obvious analogy subsisting between them and our earth, in proving its annual and diurnal motion; so, on the other hand, from the same grounds, it seems reasonable to conclude that, like the earth, they are designed and fitted by Infinite Wisdom for the accommodation of inhabitants, and that in all probability millions of beings are placed upon them. Though our observations in relation to the subserviency of the arrangements of nature to the enjoyment of sentient beings is confined to this narrow scene; yet, seeing this small portion of the universe crowded with examples of utility, why should we imagine that Divine Goodness has not throughout the system in like manner diffused its bounty? As our knowledge of the celestial phenomena is extended, the probability becomes proportionably stronger that the other planets are stored with inhabitants who share in the blessings of rational and sentient existence. Their rotation, their *atmospheres*, of which the telescope has enabled us to detect the existence, and the changes which we see going on in these atmospheres, so much resemble what we experience on the earth, that no man who clearly conceives them can divest his mind of the thought that this is not the only part of the system where the Creator has displayed his bounty by giving existence to sentient beings. There is nothing that forbids us to suppose that in each of the other planets there is the same inexhaustible store of subordinate contrivances that we see here for living creatures in every situation, possessing appropriate forms, desires, and abilities. Before abandoning such an opinion, there may surely be expected, from those who require us to do so, some good reason for its rejection.

In regard to the fixed stars, as the sun, if viewed from a sufficient distance, would be diminished into a luminous point, while the planets that revolve round him would become invisible; so, on the other hand, it is highly probable that each fixed star is itself a sun, and the centre of a particular system, being surrounded with a certain number of planets and comets, which, at different distances and in different periods, perform their revolutions around it.

There appears strong reason to suppose that *the sun, with his accompanying planets, has a motion among the fixed stars*, round a centre. From a comparison of ancient and modern observations, it appears that while the stars in one quarter of the heavens are receding from each other, those in the opposite region are gradually approaching. Dr. Herschel has found that these motions of the stars are nearly in the direction that would result from a motion of the sun towards the constellation of Hercules. It is the opinion of Lalande that there is a kind of equilibrium among all the systems of the universe, and that they have a periodic circulation about their common centre of gravity.

## TABULAR VIEW OF THE SOLAR SYSTEM.

### I. SECONDARY PLANETS.

#### 1. THE MOON.

| Revolutions. | D. | H. | M. | S. |
|---|---|---|---|---|
| Synodical | 29 | 12 | 44 | 2.9 |
| Anomalistic | 27 | 13 | 18 | 37.4 |
| Sidereal | 27 | 7 | 43 | 11.5 |
| Tropical | 27 | 7 | 43 | 4.7 |
| Nodical | 27 | 5 | 5 | 36.0 |

Inclination of Orbit to plane of Ecliptic.... 5° 8′ 47″.9
Greater semi-axis of Orbit = 1.000000
Eccentricity = .054844

Semidiameter of Terrestrial Equator = 1.
Moon's mean distance = 59.96435.
in miles = 237000.
Moon's mean diameter = 2160 miles.
Her volume = $\frac{1}{49}$ of volume of the Earth.
Her mass = $\frac{1}{79.89}$ of mass of the Earth.
Her density = $\frac{1}{1.623}$ = .615 of density of the Earth.
Her light is $\frac{1}{300000}$th of the light of the Sun.

#### 2. SATELLITES OF JUPITER.

| Satellites. | Sidereal Revolution. D. H. M. | Mean distance in semidiameters of Jupiter's Equator. |
|---|---|---|
| 1 | 1 18 28 | 6.049 |
| 2 | 3 13 14 | 9.623 |
| 3 | 7 8 43 | 15.350 |
| 4 | 16 16 32 | 26.998 |

#### 3. SATELLITES OF SATURN.

| Satellites. | Sidereal Revolution. D. H. M. | Mean distance in semidiameters of Saturn's Equator. |
|---|---|---|
| 1 | 0 22 38 | 3.351 |
| 2 | 1 8 53 | 4.300 |
| 3 | 1 21 18 | 5.284 |
| 4 | 2 17 45 | 6.819 |
| 5 | 4 12 45 | 9.524 |
| 6 | 15 22 41 | 22.081 |
| 7 | 79 7 55 | 64.359 |

#### 4. SATELLITES OF URANUS.

| Satellites. | Sidereal Revolution. D. H. M. | Mean distance in semidiameters of Uranus's Equator. |
|---|---|---|
| 1 | 5 21 25 | 13.120 |
| 2 | 8 16 58 | 17.022 |
| 3 | 10 23 4 | 19.845 |
| 4 | 13 10 56 | 22.752 |
| 5 | 38 1 48 | 45.507 |
| 6 | 107 16 40 | 91.008 |

### II. PRIMARY PLANETS AND SUN.

| Planets. | Sidereal Period. D. | Mean Distance. | Eccentricity. | Mean Longitude. Jan 1, 1801. ° ′ ″ | Long. Perhelion. Jan. 1, 1801. ° ′ ″ | Inclin. of Orbit. Jan. 1, 1801. ° ′ ″ | Long. Nodes. Jan. 1, 1801. ° ′ ″ | Mean Daily Motion in Orbit. ° ′ ″ |
|---|---|---|---|---|---|---|---|---|
| Mercury | 87.9692580 | 0.3870981 | .20551494 | 166 0 48.6 | 74 21 46.9 | 7 0 9.1 | 45 57 30.9 | 4 5 32.6 |
| Venus | 224.7007869 | 0.7233316 | .00686074 | 11 33 3.0 | 128 43 53.1 | 3 23 28.5 | 74 54 12.9 | 1 36 7.8 |
| Earth | 365.2563612 | 1.0000000 | .01678357 | 100 39 10.2 | 99 30 5.0 | - - - | - - - | 0 59 8.3 |
| Mars | 686.9796458 | 1.5236923 | .09330700 | 64 22 55.5 | 332 23 56.6 | 1 51 6.2 | 48 0 3.5 | 0 31 26.7 |
| Vesta | 1325.7431 | 2.3678700 | .08913000 | 278 30 0.4 (1820) | 249 23 44.4 (1820) | 7 8 9.0 (1820) | 103 13 18.2 (1820) | 0 16 17.9 |
| Juno | 1592.6608 | 2.6690090 | .25781800 | 200 16 19.1 (1820) | 53 33 46.0 (1820) | 13 4 9.7 (1820) | 171 7 40.4 (1820) | 0 13 32.9 |
| Ceres | 1681.3931 | 2.7672450 | .07843900 | 123 16 11.9 (1820) | 147 7 31.5 (1820) | 10 37 26.2 (1820) | 80 41 24.0 (1820) | 0 12 50.9 |
| Pallas | 1686.5388 | 2.7728860 | .24164800 | 108 24 57.9 (1820) | 121 7 4.3 (1820) | 34 34 55.0 (1820) | 172 39 26.8 (1820) | 0 12 48.4 |
| Jupiter | 4332.5848212 | 5.2027760 | .04816210 | 112 15 23.0 | 13 8 34.6 | 1 18 51.3 | 98 26 18.9 | 0 4 59.3 |
| Saturn | 10759.2198174 | 9.5387861 | .05615050 | 135 20 6.5 | 89 9 29.8 | 2 29 35.7 | 111 56 37.4 | 0 2 0.6 |
| Uranus | 30686.8208296 | 19.1823900 | .04667938 | 177 48 23.0 | 167 31 16.1 | 0 46 28.4 | 72 59 35.3 | 0 0 42.4 |

| Planets and Sun. | True Diameter. | Volume. | Mass. | Density. | Gravity. | Sidereal Rotation. h. m. s. | Inclination of Axis to Axis of Ecliptic. ° ′ ″ | Light and Heat. |
|---|---|---|---|---|---|---|---|---|
| Mercury | 0.398 | 0.398 | $\frac{1}{2025810}$ | - - | 1.03 | 24 5 28 | not known | 6.680 |
| Venus | 0.975 | 0.927 | $\frac{1}{405871}$ | - - | 0.98 | 23 21 7 | not exactly known | 1.911 |
| Earth | 1.000 | 1.000 | $\frac{1}{354936}$ | 3.9326 | 1.00 | 24 0 0 | 23 27 56.5 | 1.000 |
| Mars | 0.517 | 0.139 | $\frac{1}{2546320}$ | - - | .33 | 24 39 21 | 30 19 10.8 | 0.431 |
| Jupiter | 10.860 | 1280.900 | $\frac{1}{1070.5}$ | .9924 | 2.72 | 9 55 50 | 3 5 30.0 | 0.037 |
| Saturn | 9.982 | 995.000 | $\frac{1}{3512}$ | .5500 | 1.01 | 10 29 17 | 31 19 0 | 0.011 |
| Uranus | 4.332 | 80.490 | $\frac{1}{17918}$ | 1.1000 | - - | unknown | not known | 0.003 |
| Sun | 111.454 | 1384472.000 | 1 | 1.0000 | 27.90 | 25 12 0 | 7 30 0 | |
| Moon | .0275 | .000 | $\frac{1}{26620200}$ | 2.4185 | 0.16 | 27 7 43 | 1 30 10.8 | 1.000 |

## CHAPTER XIX.

### FIGURE AND MAGNITUDE OF THE EARTH.

We have sufficiently established the important proposition that the earth is a round body; and have inferred from the figure of its shadow, as seen on the moon's disc in lunar eclipses, that it must be a sphere, or at least that it approaches to that figure. The hypothesis of its being exactly spherical is sufficient to explain, in a satisfactory manner, the general appearance of the heavens, as seen from different points of its surface; and before the true doctrine of motion and the law of gravitation, which connects the most remote bodies in the universe, were discovered, a sphere was considered to be an exact representation of its shape, and the ingenuity of mathematicians was exerted to discover its magnitude.

The determination of the magnitude of the earth might appear, to one altogether ignorant of mathematical science, as a problem of insuperable difficulty, and, indeed, as too sublime to be resolved by a human being. If, however, we suppose the earth an exact sphere, the theory of the solution is by no means difficult; it is within the bounds of elementary geometry, and has been known from the earliest ages: but the case is very different with the practice. In the actual resolution, instruments of the greatest nicety are required; and to produce these, the ingenuity of man has been tasked to the utmost during the last two hundred years; besides, the application of them demands, in addition to the principles of geometry, some of the most refined theories in physics: so that, on the whole, few problems present a more ample field for the exertion of the mind of man, or have more extensively called forth the assistance of arts and sciences.

It is now about two thousand years since Eratosthenes attempted to resolve this important problem. He knew that on the day of the summer solstice the sun illuminated the bottom of a well at Syené. At the same instant he observed at Alexandria that the sun was 7° 12′ from the zenith: and it was supposed that Syené was due south from that place, and therefore that both were under the same meridian. Let C (*fig.* 42.) be the earth's centre, A Alexandria, Z its zenith in the heavens, B Syené, and S the sun at the instant when it illuminated the bottom of the well, and consequently was in the zenith of that place. The angular measure of the celestial arc Z S, or the corresponding terrestrial arc A B, is the angle Z C S at the earth's centre. Eratosthenes observed the angle Z A S, which by the elements of geometry, is less than the former by the angle A S C. However, this difference is so small, that it may be altogether neglected in the present case; and thus the angle A C B will be nearly 7° 12′, that is, one fiftieth part of 360°; and consequently the arc A B of the terrestrial meridian one fiftieth of the earth's circumference. The distance between Alexandria and Syené had been determined to be 5000 stadia. Hence it immediately followed that the earth's circumference was 250,000 stadia. As it could not be supposed that this result was very accurate, Eratosthenes reckoned the circumference to be 252,000 stadia, which give in round numbers 700 stadia to the length of a degree.

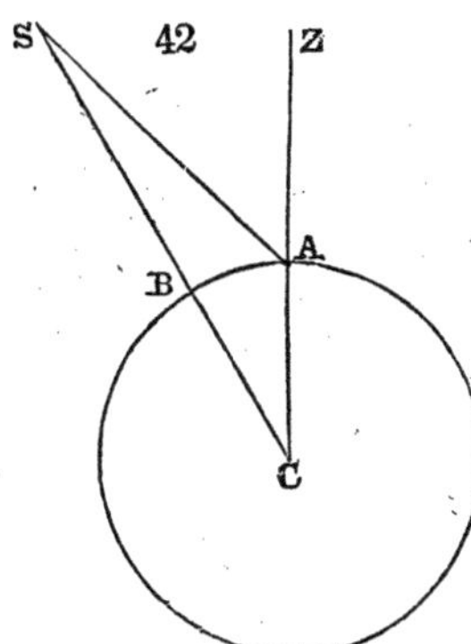


The geometrical principle here employed was quite correct, and indeed was the same which is used at this time; but the data were very inaccurate and uncertain, for Syené, instead of being exactly south from Alexandria, lies considerably to the east; and it may well be supposed that the assigned distance between Alexandria and Syené was not an accurate measurement, but merely a rude approximation. It is impossible, however, now to determine how near Eratosthenes came to the truth, for want of a knowledge of the exact length of the stadium by which the distance was reckoned.

The principles by which Eratosthenes was directed in his measurement of the earth appear to have been afterwards employed by Posidonius. This astronomer had remarked, that at Rhodes the star Canopus was just visible in the horizon, but never rose above it; while at Alexandria it attained an altitude of 7½°, or $\frac{1}{48}$th part of the circumference of a great circle. The direct distance between these two places, which were supposed to be on the same meridian, was accounted to be 5000 stadia; and therefore, according to this observation, the circumference should have been 240,000: but here the uncertainty of a distance reckoned by a sea-voyage, not to speak of other causes of error, renders the conclusion of no value.

About the year 800 of the Christian era, the caliph Almaman directed that his astronomers should measure a degree of the meridian in the plains of Mesopotamia. The method which they employed was susceptible of greater accuracy than that of the Greeks. They divided themselves into two parties: after observing the altitude of the pole, one went directly north and the other south, measuring as they proceeded, and taking from time to time the altitude of the pole, until each party had changed its latitude by a degree. Thus the measure of two degrees was obtained; but, at the present time, our ignorance of the exact length of the unit of measure renders all their labour useless to us, even if (what is very unlikely) its accuracy might have been relied on. It appears, however, that their estimation of the earth's magnitude was less accurate than that of the astronomer of Alexandria.

The method of Eratosthenes was practised in modern times, first by Fernel, a Flemish physician. He travelled from Paris towards Amiens, which places are nearly under the same meridian, until he had passed over a degree of latitude; and, by a contrivance attached to the wheel of his carriage, he ascertained the number of revolutions it made in that distance. In this way he found the length of the degree to be 57,070 French toises.

The same degree was afterwards measured by La Caille, and found to be 57,074 toises. The near agreement of Fernel's result with this last, obtained by a more accurate and scientific process, is very remarkable.

The Dutch astronomer Snellius was the first who attempted to resolve this most interesting and difficult problem in practical geometry with those scientific aids which its importance required. In the year 1617 he published his *Eratosthenes Batavus*, in which he has detailed the whole process. The extreme points of his meridional arc are terminated in the parallels of Alcmaer, in lat. 52° 40½′, and Bergen-op-Zoom, lat. 51° 29′, the arc between them being 1° 11½′. He formed a series of triangles between these places along the earth's surface, and determined (as well as the imperfect instruments of the time enabled him to determine) their angles; and by several base lines, actually measured, he found their sides. He reduced the positions of his stations to the meridian; and he concluded that a degree of the meridian was 28,500 perches, which were equivalent to 55,100 toises of that period; which, however, were rather longer than the toise as it is now estimated. The error of Snellius appears to have been about 2000 toises on the length of a degree, of which 1900 may have arisen from the error in measuring the celestial arc, and the rest from the imperfection of his geodetical measurements. Snellius measured his original base over again, and corrected his conclusion: he died, however, before he could publish the result. Cassini made certain corrections in his calculations, by which the length of the degree came out 56,675 toises; and Muschenbroek, by an examination of Snellius's papers, found that the degree ought to have been reckoned 57,033 toises.

Richard Norwood made a remarkable approximation to the true length of a degree in 1635, by apparently inadequate means. He measured the distance between London and York, observing the bearings as he proceeded, and reducing all to the direction of the meridian and the horizontal plane. He determined the difference of latitude to be 2° 28′; and from the whole distance he determined the degree to be 367,176 feet English, or 57,800 toises.

As far as pure mathematical theory was concerned, the method of Snellius was excellent; the chief imperfection was in his instruments: but an immense improvement was made by Picard, in the application of the telescope and the micrometer to the measurement of angles; and, with the assistance of instruments constructed on the new principle, this astronomer, by the direction of the French Academy, began the measurement of an arc of the meridian, taking for its extremities the parallels of Sourdon near Amiens, and Malvoisine. His general manner of conducting the process was the same as that of Snellius. He connected the extreme parallels by a series of triangles, the sides of which were determined from a base of 5663 toises, measured twice with great care at one extremity of the series. There was a base of verification of 3902 toises measured at the other extremity. The horizontal angles were measured by a quadrant of thirty-eight inches' radius; and the celestial arc, which was about 1° 12′, by a sector ten feet in radius. He concluded the length of a degree to be 57,060 toises.

This was the first measurement in which confidence could be placed. It is true there were several elements wanting in the determination of the celestial arc, owing to the imperfect state of astronomical science at that time; but, by a fortunate compensation, the errors thence arising corrected each other. This measurement of Picard was of service to Newton, in verifying his happy thought of the law of universal gravitation.

The measurement begun by Picard was continued northward to Dunkirk by La Hire, and in the opposite direction, as far as Perpignan, by the second Cassini, who published the whole in 1718, in a work on the magnitude and figure of the earth.

The labour of the French astronomers determined the magnitude of the earth with a degree of accuracy sufficient for the general purposes of geography; but science was now proceeding with rapid strides, and a new question was agitated,—Is the earth an exact sphere, as had been hitherto supposed? or, if it be not a sphere, what is its true figure?

Huygens and Newton had established the doctrine of the centrifugal force of bodies revolving in circles; and from this it was justly inferred that the earth, in consequence of its rotation on an axis, must necessarily deviate from a spherical figure, and assume that of an oblate spheroid; that is, a solid generated by the revolution of an ellipse on its lesser axis, the extremities of which in this case were the poles.

This opinion received support from some astronomical observations made by Richer, who was sent by the Academy of Sciences, in 1672, to Cayenne. He there found that his clock, which had been regulated to mean time at Paris, went slower by a sensible quantity. This interesting observation showed that the weight of the pendulum was less at the equator than it had been at Paris; and hence the increase of the force of gravity in proceeding from the equator towards the pole, as shown theoretically by Newton, was completely established; and consequently also the oblateness of the earth at the poles, and its elevation at the equator which are the consequence of this diminution.

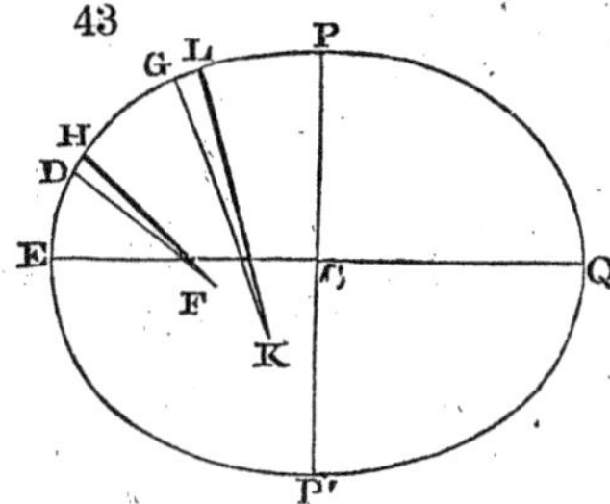


If the earth were a perfect sphere, then all the degree of the terrestrial meridian from the equator to the pole would be equal in length. But this will by no means be the case if the earth be a spheroid. For, supposing the earth to be an oblate spheroid (*fig.* 43.), of which the lesser axis is P P′, that diameter of the earth which passes through P P′ the poles. Let E Q be any equatorial diameter, and E P Q P′ a section of the earth, through the axis P P′, which will therefore be a terrestrial meridian. Because the direction of gravity is always in a line perpendicular to the earth's surface; at the poles and equator, the direction of gravity will pass through the centre. It will be otherwise, however, at any point, D, between the equator and poles; for, by the nature of the ellipse, a line, D F, drawn perpendicular to the curve at D will pass on one side of the centre. Now let us suppose that D F, H F, are two straight lines perpendicular to the earth's surface at D and H, which meet in F, and contain an angle D F H, of one degree; also let G K, L K, be other two lines perpendicular to the earth's surface at points nearer the pole; and suppose these also to contain an angle G K L, of one degree. The elliptic arc D H, because of its smallness, may be considered as an arc of a circle of which D F or H F is the radius; and similarly the elliptic arc G L may be considered as an arc of a circle whose radius is G K or L K. The curvature of the ellipse is greatest at E, the extremity of the greater axis, and gradually decreases to P, the extremity of the lesser axis, where it is least. Hence the arc D H will be more incurvated than G F; and since the angles at F and K are equal, each being one degree, the almost equal lines G K, L K, will be greater than the almost equal lines D H, H F; and the arc G L must therefore be greater than the arc D H. Thus, if the earth is an oblate spheroid, a degree of the terrestrial meridian will, by actual measurement, be found to be least at the equator; and the degrees will gradually increase as we proceed towards either pole.

It is manifest that the case would be just the reverse if the earth were an oblong spheroid, generated by the rotation of an ellipse on its greater axis E Q. Hence the important question, What is the figure of the terrestrial meridian? may be resolved by measuring arcs of the meridian in different latitudes.

None of the measurements before that begun by Picard were made with such accuracy as to enable mathematicians to resolve the question. But it was then supposed that this had been performed with such care as to afford the necessary data. Such, however, appears not to have been the case. The degrees actually measured were found to be unequal; but, instead of increasing in going from south to north, the reverse was supposed to be the fact; and had this been really true, the polar axis would have been greater than the equatorial,—a conclusion quite in opposition to that derivable from the doctrine of centrifugal force.

To determine this most important question, the Academy of Sciences resolved that degrees of the meridian should be measured in various latitudes which might differ as much as possible; and it was determined that one party should be sent to the neighbourhood of the equator, and another to the polar circle. Two scientific expeditions were accordingly undertaken. Maupertuis, Clairaut, Comus, Lemonnier, and Outhier, went to Lapland, where the Swedish astronomer Celsius joined them; and there they measured an arc of fifty-seven minutes of a degree, from which they concluded that a degree under the polar circle, viz. in lat. 66° 20′, was 57,419 toises, that is, about 349 toises greater than that of Paris. This degree has been since remeasured with great care by Svanberg and other Swedish mathematicians, who found it to be 57,196 toises. This is 223 toises less than the determination of the French academicans; but it is certainly more correct.

The other party, composed of Godin, Bouguer, and La Condamine, performed a similar but more extensive operation in Peru. After ten years' labour, they, with the assistance of two Spanish officers, Don Jorge Juan and Antonio de Ulloa, accomplished the measurement of an arc of about 3° 7′. From this they concluded that the length of a degree was 56,758 toises, which was shorter than the French degree by 302 toises. These measurements set the question completely at rest. There could no longer be any doubt that the polar diameter of the earth was shorter than the equatorial.

The measurement of different degrees has been since performed many times in different countries; as again in France, and also at the Cape of Good Hope, by La Caille; in Italy, by Maire, Boscovich, and Beccaria; in Pennsylvania, by Mason and Dixon; in Hungary, by Liesganig; in India, by Lambton.

There have been, in addition to these, two admeasurements of arcs of the meridian which deserve particular notice, on account of their extent, the excellence of the instruments employed, and the skill with which the operations have been conducted. We are indebted to the spirit of reform and improvement which sprung out of the French revolution for one of these, and to the liberal and enlightened views of the English government for the other.

The great diversity in the units of a measure is an evil which has been long felt and complained of in every commercial country. The French Constitutional Assembly took up this most important subject in the year 1790; and, at the suggestion of Talleyrand, it was decreed, that the king should request his Britannic majesty to engage the parliament of England to concur with the National Assembly in fixing a natural unit of weights and measures; that, under the auspices of the two nations, commissioners of the Academy of Sciences, and an equal number of members of the Royal Society of London, should determine the length of the pendulum in the latitude of 45°, or other preferable latitude, and from this deduce an invariable standard for all weights and measures.

The Academy named a commission, composed of Borda, Lagrange, Laplace, Monge, and Condorcet, who gave a report, which is printed in the Memoirs of the Academy for 1788. Three different fundamental units were suggested in their report. The first is the pendulum which beats seconds in a given parallel. That of 45° was thought preferable to any other, because there the pendulum is a mean among all those which beat seconds in the different latitudes between the equator and the pole. They observed, however, that the pendulum contains a heterogeneous element, namely, time; and an arbitrary element, viz. the division of the day into 86,400 seconds. They, therefore, considered it to be less proper as a standard unit of lineal measure, than another which they regarded as unexceptionable. This is the length of a quadrant of the meridian, a linear magnitude of the same kind as the thing to be determined, and therefore more natural than the pendulum, which involved the consideration of time. There is yet another linear unit, namely, the circumference of the earth's equator. But this is not better known than the elliptic meridian; nor does it admit of being determined with so much precision. On the whole, therefore, it was recommended that the quadrant of the meridian should be taken as the primary unit, and that its ten-millionth part (a lineal space about $39\frac{10}{27}$ English inches) should be the ordinary unit for the measurements which occur in the affairs of life. This was named a *mètre*.

Although in the beginning it had been proposed to invite the English philosophers to assist in establishing a standard unit, yet, as the object to be attained could be accomplished perfectly by the French mathematicians, without any foreign aid, it was recommended to commence immediately the measurement of the arc of the meridian between Dunkirk and Barcelona, an extent of nearly $9\frac{1}{2}$ degrees. The operations necessary for this labour were, 1. To determine the difference of latitude between Dunkirk and Barcelona; and, in general, to make such astronomical observations on the whole line as might be thought useful. 2. To measure again the bases which had served for the measurement of the degree made at Paris, and the construction of the map of France. 3. To verify by new observations the series of triangles which had formerly been employed for the measurement of the meridian, and to prolong them to Barcelona. 4. To make, at the 45th degree, such observations as might determine the number of vibrations which a pendulum equal in length to one ten-millionth part of the meridian would make in a day, in a *vacuum* at the level of the sea, and at the temperature of melting ice, in order that, this number being once known, the *mètre* might be determined at any time by the length of the pendulum. In this way the advantages of the two methods of forming a standard would be united. 5. To verify by new experiments the specific gravity of pure water in a *vacuum*, and at the temperature of water just beginning to freeze. 6. And lastly, To reduce all the old measures of every kind employed in commerce to the new standards.

To accomplish these objects, it was recommended that six distinct commissioners should be appointed. This was done by a decree of the National Assembly, dated 26th March, 1791; only it was thought to be better to commit the astronomical and geodetical observations to a single commission. Immediately directions were given for the construction of the necessary instruments. Lenoir, a celebrated French artist, was employed to make repeating circles, long rules of platina for the measurement of the bases, and a shorter rule; also, balls of platina and gold for the pendulum observations.

About the middle of the year 1792, Cassini and Borda began a series of experiments on the pendulum; and, in the following year, Lavoisier was engaged in experiments on the expansion of metals. And about the same time Mechain began his operations for the determination of the portion of the meridian between Rodez and Barcelona, an extent of 170,000 toises. Delambre had undertaken the portion of the arc between Dunkirk and Rodez, 38,000 toises in extent. This, however, had been twice measured before; and for this reason the labour was expected to be less than was requisite for the other portion, which was entirely new. Besides the privations and hardships, the ordinary accompaniments of a service which requires those who perform it to live in elevated situations, with little shelter, with few of the comforts to which they have been accustomed, and exposed to the vicissitudes of heat and cold, and the influence of the nocturnal dews, they had to encounter the perils arising from a disorganized state of society. Mechain was stopped in the neighbourhood of Paris; but when he pursued his labours at a distance from the capital, he met with no farther interruption; while Delambre, in the north of France, was often exposed to the most imminent danger. In the heat of the French revolution, the people were jealous of what they did not understand; and the astronomers were at once exposed to the machinations of their enemies at Paris, and to the brutality of the ignorant peasants in the provinces.

In the course of their operations they measured two bases, on the accurate determination of which the utility of all their labours was to depend. One base, of 6075.9 toises, was measured by Delambre at Melun; and the other, of 6006.2478 toises, at Perpignan. The distance between them was 360,330 toises, about 436 English miles. They were connected by a chain of triangles, the sides and angles of which were all known; so that the length of one base being known, that of the other might be found by computation. It is a remarkable fact, that when the base of Perpignan was inferred by calculation from that of Melun, the result was found to be only ten or eleven inches less than that obtained by actual measurement. This striking agreement affords a strong presumptive proof of the accuracy with which the operations had been conducted.

The determination of the latitudes of the two extremities of the arc was also a matter of the utmost importance. The pains which the astronomers took to arrive at true results are almost incredible. Delambre made 800 observations to ascertain the true latitude of the Dunkirk extremity; and a corresponding degree of attention was bestowed on different intermediate points.

This most important undertaking was at last, after seven years' labour, brought to a conclusion in the year 1799. Although the result was, in its first application, to be directed to the establishment of a standard unit of lineal measure for the French nation, yet the advantages which may be deduced from it extended much farther, and were available to every nation enlightened by science. For this reason, the states living in peace with France had been invited to send eminent mathematicians and astronomers to assist in a rigorous examination of every step of the operation. The astronomical and geodetical observations, in particular, were subjected to the examination of Tralles, the deputy of the Helvetian republic; Van Swinden, the Batavian deputy; and the two French philosophers Laplace and Legendre. They entered into all the details of the measurement of the bases; and they examined the three angles of every triangle, and determined their values. The calculations were then separately performed by four different persons—Tralles, Van Swinden, Legendre, and Delambre; and this last astronomer calculated the length of the meridian by four different and independent methods; and a report was made to the National Institute at Paris, in June 1799, in the name of the Class of Physical and Mathematical Sciences, on the Measure of the Meridian of France, and its Results.

The general fact, that the degrees of the meridian increase as we recede from the equator towards the pole, was again fully confirmed; so that the oblateness of the earth in the direction of the polar axis is a truth now placed beyond all controversy. Notwithstanding, however, the almost incredible care with which the operations were conducted, the exact quantity of this compression was still left in some uncertainty. The limits between which the true measure of the oblateness is contained are, however, narrower; and it is likely that the problem, What is the exact proportion of the polar to the equatorial axis? does not, from its nature, admit of a nearer approximation to the truth than has been already obtained.

If we could suppose the measurements of lines and angles to be perfectly correct, it would follow, that although on the whole, taking considerable intervals, the length of arcs of the meridian corresponding to equal celestial arcs go on increasing from south to north, yet the law of the increase is irregular, and not that which ought to result from an exact elliptic meridian. The result of the measurement will be seen in the following table:—

| | Latitudes. | Intervals. | Intervals in Toises. | Length of a Degree. | Mean Latitude. | Arc of one Second. |
|---|---|---|---|---|---|---|
| | ° ′ ″ | ° ′ ″ | | Toises. | ° ′ ″ | Toises |
| Dunkirk | 51 2 9.20 | | | | | |
| | | 2 11 19.83 | 124944.8 | 57082.63 | 49 56 29.30 | 15.856283 |
| Pantheon | 48 50 49.37 | | | | | |
| | | 2 40 6.83 | 152293.1 | 57069.31 | 47 30 45.91 | 15.852586 |
| Evaux | 46 10 42.54 | | | | | |
| | | 2 57 48.24 | 168846.7 | 56977.80 | 44 41 48.37 | 15.827167 |
| Carcassone | 43 12 54.30 | | | | | |
| | | 1 51 9.34 | 105499.0 | 56946.68 | 42 17 19.60 | 15.818508 |
| Montjouy | 41 21 44.96 | | | | | |

From this table we see that the length of a degree in the four mean latitudes goes on increasing. Also, from the column of mean latitudes, and that of the length of a degree, it appears that a diminution of 2° 25′ 43″.39 in the first mean latitude corresponds to a diminution of 13.13 toises in the terrestrial meridian: this gives 5.5 toises to a degree. Again, that a farther diminution of 2° 48′ 57″.54 produces a diminution of 91.51 toises, which is at the rate of 32.4 toises to a degree. Lastly, that a third diminution of 2° 24′ 28″.77 gives a diminution of 31.17 toises, which is at the rate of about 12.9 toises to a degree. These changes of 5.5, 32.4, and 31.17 toises in the length of a degree in going southward evidently do not follow a regular law, such as should result from a continuous increase of curvature. We may, therefore, reasonably suppose that all the observations have not been equally perfect, or that, in addition to unavoidable errors in the estimation of lines and angles, some disturbing cause must have operated: probably, an inequality of density, in the density of the strata over which the measurement was performed, may have had great influence in producing the irregularity.

The small discrepancies in the results of the observations must produce corresponding uncertainty in the determination of the great objects to be attained. On the whole, however, it was concluded that the length of the terrestrial meridian between the pole and the equator was 5,130,740 toises; and hence the mètre, or ten-millionth part of the meridian, was .513074 of a toise, which is 443.295986 lines.

Another most important result, deducible from these observations, was the *ratio* of the *polar axis* of the earth to the *equatorial axis*. This must partake of the uncertainty of the data by which it is to be determined. We may, however, assume, without sensible error, that the equatorial axis is to the polar as 334 to 333. The difference, therefore, of the semi-axes, compared with the equatorial radius, will be one part in 334. The fraction $\frac{1}{334}$—that is, the difference of the semi-axes divided by the equatorial radius,—is called the *compression* of the earth at the poles.

The astronomer Mechain had contemplated the extension of the measurement of the meridian beyond the limit at first proposed; but he did not live to carry his views into execution. However, the undertaking was resumed, after a cessation of three years, by Biot and Arago, French astronomers, with whom were associated MM. Chaix and Rodriguez, Spaniards, all eminently distinguished for their talent and devotedness to the object to be accomplished. By their exertions, a train of triangles was carried southward from the point where Mechain and Delambre had stopped, to Formentera, a small island near Ivica, in the Mediterranean. This is the southern limit of a most interesting labour: but, if ever European civilization extends into Africa, the measurement may be extended to Cape de Gata, and thence across the Mediterranean to the coast of Africa, and continued to the city of Algiers, which is nearly in the meridian of Paris; so that in time the southern extremity may be actually carried to the summit of Mount Atlas.

The other measurement of a considerable portion of the earth, to which we have alluded, was begun under the auspices and at the expense of the British government as long ago as the year 1784. At that time a memoir, drawn up by Cassini de Thury, was presented to the minister (Mr. Fox) by the French ambassador. It stated the advantages which would accrue to geography and astronomy by determining the difference of longitude between the observatories of Greenwich and Paris, by means of a series of triangles from the former to Dunkirk, to which place the meridian of Paris had previously been extended. The proposal was communicated to the Royal Society; and having been approved of, the execution was committed to general Roy. The first step was to measure a base, from the length of which the sides of all the triangles might be inferred; and a line rather more than five miles in length was traced out on Hounslow Heath, and measured with the most scrupulous care. It may at first sight appear a very simple matter to measure a straight line on the ground; but if the utmost exactness is required, the operation must be performed with instruments constructed with the greatest ingenuity, and the application of much physical knowledge. Generally all solid bodies expand by heat, and contract by cold; and, moreover, some change their dimensions by moisture and dryness. To counteract or to estimate precisely these changes, so as to allow for them in the final result, is a matter of great difficulty, and only to be accomplished by infinite care and perseverance.

The measurement of the base was first undertaken with deal rods, twenty feet in length. These, however, were found to be much affected by the changes in the atmosphere from moisture to dryness: they were therefore laid aside; and instead of them glass rods, of the same length in frames, were employed. This substance was chosen, from a belief that it was less affected by changes of temperature than the metals. The measurement, which had been begun about the middle of June, was completed in the end of October; and it was found that the base measured exactly 27404.08 feet, or 5.19 miles.

The work in the field was not carried farther at that time: it was, however, resumed in 1787. A theodolite of greater dimensions than had ever been employed in geodetical operations was constructed by the celebrated artist Ramsden. The series of observations was begun at the base in the beginning of August, by General Roy, assisted by Isaac Dalby, an excellent mathematician, and most veracious astronomical observer. After continuing to a certain length, it was judged to be expedient to break off, and proceed with the instruments to Dover. A series of observations was there made, in conjunction with the French academicians Cassini, Mechain, and Legendre, by which the triangulation between Paris and Dunkirk might be connected with that between Dover and Greenwich. As a check on the operations, a base of verification was also measured on Romney Marsh; and in this, instead of the glass rods, a steel chain, constructed for the purpose by Ramsden, was employed; it having been found by experience that there was no sensible difference in point of accuracy between this and the glass rods, while the chain manifestly was more convenient. Afterwards, when the two bases were connected by calculating the sides of the triangles, it was found that the measured base differed from its computed value by only twenty-eight inches, although Romney Marsh is more than sixty miles from Hounslow Heath. The junction of the observatories of Greenwich and Paris, by a series of triangles, was completed in 1788, and an account of the operations communicated to the Royal Society; but the death of General Roy again suspended the survey until the year 1791.

At this time, by the exertions of the Duke of Richmond, Master-general of the Ordnance, the survey was resumed with great vigour. A new theodolite, and various other instruments, in addition to those formerly employed, were liberally supplied, and placed under the direction of Captain (afterwards Colonel) Mudge of the Royal Artillery, and Mr. Dalby. Beginning their labours by a re-measurement of the base on Hounslow Heath with steel chains, they found the difference between this and the former, in which glass rods were employed, to be no more than two inches and three quarters. They also measured another base of verification, 36574.4 feet in length, on Salisbury Plain. When this was connected by a chain of triangles with the base on Hounslow Heath, and its length computed, the result did not differ more than an inch from the actual measurement; a convincing proof of the accuracy with which all the operations had been conducted.

Although an accurate survey of the island was the main object for which all this labour was undertaken, yet, as its complete accomplishment requires a knowledge of the figure and dimensions of the earth, no opportunity of solving this grand problem is to be neglected. The two stations of Beachy Head in Sussex, and Dunnose in the Isle of Wight, are visible from each other, and more than sixty-four miles asunder, nearly in a direction from east to west: their exact distance was found by the geodetical operations to be 339397 feet. The azimuth, or bearing of the line between them with respect to the meridian, also the latitude of Beachy Head, were determined by astronomical observations. From these data the length of a degree perpendicular to the meridian was computed; and this, compared with the length of a meridional degree in the same latitude, gave the proportion of the polar to the equatorial axis.

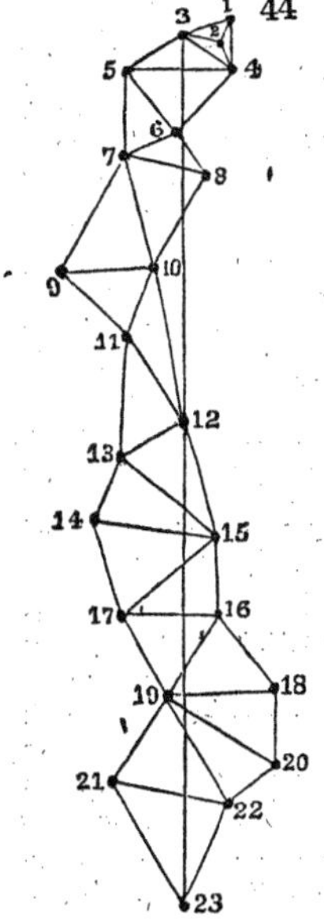


The result thus obtained, however, differed considerably from that obtained by meridional degrees. It has been found impossible to explain the want of agreement in a satisfactory way; and, for this reason, it has been thought better to rest the solution of the problem entirely on the measurement of degrees of the meridian in different latitudes, which, on the whole, give results more consistent with one another.

Without noticing in detail all the steps by which the survey has advanced, we shall next advert to the measurement of an arc of the meridian between Dunnose, in the Isle of Wight, and Clifton, near Doncaster; the former in lat. 50° 37′ 5″, and the latter in 53° 27′ 30″ To accomplish this, the ingenuity of the artist Ramsden was again exercised in the construction of an instrument, a zenith sector, for finding the latitude of the different points of the arc: this was almost the last work of a man to whose genius astronomy and geography are highly indebted; and it was superior to any thing of the kind ever before constructed.

To give the reader a distinct notion of this most important operation, we here present a sketch (*fig.* 44.) of the series of triangles, twenty-two in number, which connect the extreme points together with the angles contained by the straight lines which join the different stations, and the length of their sides. The numbers marked on the diagram indicate the names of the *stations*, by referring to the following table. The northern extremity of the base, Beacon Hill, or Clifton, is marked No. 3.; and the southern extremity, Dunnose, is 23. The names of the intermediate points may be seen in the table.

| No. of Triangles. | Names of Stations. | Angles corrected for Calculation. | Distance. | Feet. |
|---|---|---|---|---|
| | | ° ′ ″ | | |
| | Butser Hill (22) | 76 12 21.5 | From Dunnose to | |
| 1. | Dean Hill (21) | 48 4 31.75 | Butser Hill | 140580.4 |
| | Dunnose (23) | 55 43 6.75 | to Dean Hill | 183496.2 |
| | Dean Hill (21) | 62 22 47 | Dean Hill from | |
| 2 | Butser Hill (22) | 48 28 40 | Butser Hill | 156122.1 |
| | Highclere (19) | 69 8 33 | Highclere | 125084.9 |
| | Butser Hill (22) | 81 31 44.5 | Butser Hill from | |
| 3. | Hind Head (20) | 66 15 54.25 | Hind Head | 78905.7 |
| | Highclere (19) | 29 12 21.25 | Highclere | 148031.0 |
| | Highclere (19) | 34 46 15 | Highclere from | |
| 4. | Hind Head (20) | 83 20 14 | Bagshot Heath | 142952.6 |
| | Bagshot Heath (18) | 61 53 31 | Hind Head | 160972.2 |
| | Bagshot Heath (18) | 55 32 25.25 | Nnffield from | |
| 5. | Highclere (19) | 46 10 17.75 | Bagshot Heath | 105321.2 |
| | Nuffield (16) | 78 17 17 | Highclere | 120374. |
| | White Horse Hill (17) | 63 7 53.5 | White Horse Hill from | |
| 6. | Highclere (19) | 63 18 17 | Nuffield | 120557.7 |
| | Nuffield (16) | 53 33 49.5 | Highclere | 108563.1 |
| | White Horse Hill (17) | 38 48 12.5 | Brill from | |
| 7. | Nuffield (16) | 86 4 15 | White Horse Hill | 146603.2 |
| | Brill (15) | 55 7 32.5 | Nuffield | 92805.5 |
| | Brill (15) | 50 14 45 | Stow from | |
| 8. | White Horse Hill (17) | 64 45 42.5 | White Horse Hill | 124365.6 |
| | Stow on the Weld (14) | 64 59 32.5 | Brill | 146326.3 |
| | Brill (15) | 32 34 42.25 | Epwell from | |
| 9. | Stow on the Weld (14) | 60 56 5.5 | Stow | 78938.2 |
| | Epwell (13) | 86 29 12.25 | Brill | 128140 |
| | Brill (15) | 34 23 57.5 | Arbury Hill from | |
| 10. | Epwell (13) | 85 0 17.5 | Epwell | 83098.4 |
| | Arbury Hill (12) | 60 35 45 | Brill | 146530 |
| | Arbury Hill (12) | 89 57 5.5 | Corley from | |
| 11. | Epwell (13) | 54 45 18.25 | Arbury Hill | 117463 |
| | Corley (11) | 35 17 36.25 | Epwell | 143827.8 |

The distance of Butser Hill (22.) from Dunnose, 140580.4 feet, had been previously found, by a series of triangles connecting these stations with the bases measured on Hounslow Heath and Salisbury Plain; but, for greater security against error, a new base of 26342.7 feet was measured on Misterton Carr, in the northern part of Lincolnshire. From this the sides of the triangles proceeding from the north to the south were computed, as exhibited in the remainder of the table.

| No. of Triangles. | Names of Stations. | Angles corrected for Calculation. | Distance. | Feet. |
|---|---|---|---|---|
| | | ° ′ ″ | | |
| | Beacon Hill (3) | 20 47 20 | Beacon Hill from | |
| 12. | North end of Base (1) | 60 17 13 | North end of Base | 64461.7 |
| | South end of Base (2) | 98 55 27 | South end of Base | 73321.9 |
| | Beacon Hill (3) | 34 44 42 | Gringley from | |
| 13. | North end of Base (1) | 74 46 56 | North end of Base | 44338.2 |
| | Gringley (4) | 70 28 22 | Beacon Hill | 75068.0 |
| | Beacon Hill (3) | 13 57 23 | | |
| 14. | Gringley (4) | 51 11 5 | Gringley from | |
| | South end of Base (2) | 114 51 52 | Beacon Hill | 75068.2 |
| | Heathersedge (5) | 18 40 38 | Heathersedge from | |
| 15. | Beacon Hill (3) | 138 9 16 | Beacon Hill | 92227.2 |
| | Gringley (4) | 23 10 6 | Gringley | 156384.8 |
| | Sutton Ashfield (6) | 78 47 1 | Sutton Ashfield from | |
| 16. | Heathersedge (5) | 54 52 35 | Gringley | 130399.7 |
| | Gringley (4) | 46 20 24 | Heathersedge | 115339.9 |
| | Orpit (7) | 80 28 57 | Orpit from | |
| 17. | Heathersedge (5) | 39 8 38 | Heathersedge | 101660 3 |
| | Sutton Ashfield (6) | 60 22 25 | Sutton Ashfield | 73826.6 |
| | Hollan Hill (8) | 44 43 31 | Hollan Hill from | |
| 18. | Sutton Ashfield (6) | 113 49 7 | Sutton Ashfield | 38375.2 |
| | Orpit (7) | 21 27 22 | Orpit | 95975.3 |
| | Bardon Hill (10) | 42 58 59 | Bardon Hill from | |
| 19. | Hollan Hill (8) | 74 52 37 | Hollan Hill | 124454.7 |
| | Orpit (7) | 62 8 24 | Orpit | 135895.3 |
| | Castle Ring (9) | 55 32 43 | Castle Ring from | |
| 20. | Bardon Hill (10) | 68 24 3 | Orpit | 153235.2 |
| | Orpit (7) | 56 3 14 | Bardon Hill | 136717.8 |
| | Corley (11) | 72 32 46 | Corley from | |
| 21. | Castle Ring (9) | 47 54 42 | Bardon Hill | 106357.3 |
| | Bardon Hill (10) | 59 32 32 | Castle Ring | 123539.7 |
| | Arbury Hill (12) | 34 14 33 | Arbury Hill from | |
| 22. | Corley (11) | 107 20 14 | Bardon Hill | 180426.0 |
| | Bardon Hill (10) | 38 25 13 | Corley | 117457.1 |

From the last triangle the distance between Corley and Arbury Hill comes out 117457.1 feet. This result has been found from the base on Misterton Carr: but the same distance, deduced from the bases on Hounslow Heath and Salisbury Plain, either of which is more than 150 miles distant from Misterton Carr, was found to be 117,463 feet, only six feet different. Here we have a remarkable proof of the extreme accuracy with which the operations have been conducted; so that, from whatever cause any uncertainty in the conclusion sought may proceed, it can hardly be found either in the want of perfection in the instruments, or of care in those who used them.

By observations on the pole star, the exact bearing of Butser Hill from Dunnose (that is, the azimuth or angle which the line joining them makes with the meridian,) was found: and by like observations the bearing of the station at Gringley from Clifton was determined. By these data, and by the known lengths of the sides of the triangles, the portions of the meridian intercepted by perpendiculars on it from the stations was obtained. Their sum gave 1,036,337 feet for the meridional distance on the surface of the earth, between Dunnose and Clifton. Moreover, by the zenith sector, the arc of the celestial meridian between them was found to be 2° 50′ 23″.38, or 2.8398 of difference of latitude. The length of the measured arc of the meridian, viz. 1,036,337 feet, divided by this number, gives 364,933 feet, or 6082 fathoms for the length of a degree in the parallel midway between Dunnose and Clifton, which is 50° 2′ 20″.

In the same way that the length of a degree, at the middle point between Clifton and Dunnose, was determined, the length of degrees at other intermediate points was found. The latitude of the station at Arbury Hill was carefully observed with the sector. The latitude of Greenwich was well known; and that of Blenheim, an observatory belonging to the Duke of Marlborough, had been determined from five years' observations. The two observatories were assumed as stations, in addition to those in the meridional chain of triangles, and their position in respect of the others was found.

By comparing the celestial with the terrestrial arcs, the length of degrees in various parallels was determined, as in the following table:—

| | Latitude of Middle Point. | Fathoms. |
|---|---|---|
| Arbury Hill and Clifton | 52° 50′ 29″.8 | 60,766 |
| Blenheim and Clifton | 52 38 56.1 | 60,769 |
| Greenwich and Clifton | 52 28 5.7 | 60,794 |
| Dunnose and Clifton | 52 2 19.8 | 60,820 |
| Arbury Hill and Greenwich | 51 51 4.1 | 60,849 |
| Dunnose and Arbury Hill | 51 35 18.2 | 60,864 |
| Blenheim and Dunnose | 51 13 18.2 | 60,890 |
| Dunnose and Greenwich | 51 2 54.2 | 60,884 |

This table presents a singular deviation from the common rule; for, instead of the degrees increasing as we proceed from north to south, they appear to decrease, as if the earth were an oblong instead of an oblate spheroid. The oblateness of the earth at the poles is, however, a fact so well established by more extensive measurements, that we must suppose either that some error has been committed in the observations,—a thing, however, not probable; or else, what is more probable, that by inequality in the density of the strata, producing a local attraction, the plumb-line of the sector has suffered a deflection at some of the stations.

Notwithstanding the discrepancy of the results of the measurements in this particular arc, the length of a degree at the middle station (viz. lat. 52° 2′ 20″) agrees very well with the measurements of the meridian in France and other places. Indeed, the measurements of the small arcs of the meridian in other countries have presented similar anomalies, although in general not so remarkable. It is, therefore, only by comparison of the measures of extensive arcs at considerable intervals that we can arrive at certain conclusions. The British survey has now been extended from the southern parts of the island to Unst, the northernmost of the Shetland Islands. At present the engineer officers who carried it on are employed in the survey of Ireland; but we may expect that at no remote period they will resume the British survey, and supply the observations still wanting. When this is done, and the complete triangulation is published, it will then appear how far local attraction may have disturbed the plummet in passing over the variety of rocks throughout the island.

Although the compression of the earth be small, yet an exact knowledge of its quantity is of great importance, because of the deductions which are to be made from it. It has been explained, that the direction of a plumb-line is always perpendicular to the earth' surface; therefore, and because of the continual change of curvature of the meridian in going from north to south, the direction of gravity can only pass through the earth's centre at the poles and equator. Thus it appears that there is a necessary connexion between the form of the earth and terrestrial gravity; so that the small variations in the latter, which are owing to the deviations from the exact spherical figure, being known, that deviation itself may be determined.

If the earth were spherical and homogenous, the attraction of its mass upon different points of its surface, or the force which solicits every particle of matter at its surface towards the centre, would be everywhere the same. But the elliptic form produces a small deviation from this equality, which increases in going from the equator towards the poles, as the square of the sine of the latitude; and this would be true even if the earth were at rest: but, by its revolution about its shorter axis, there is produced a centrifugal force, which acts in a direction perpendicular to that axis, and therefore diminishes the force of gravity most of all at the equator, because there the two forces act in contrary directions. At the pole its direction is perpendicular to the direction of gravity, and produces no effect.

By the united operation of these two causes, in going from the equator towards the poles, is produced a variation in the degree of quickness of descent of a heavy body, which increases as the square of the sine of the latitude.

The oscillations of a pendulum afford a simple means of verifying this fact. The increase of weight in a heavy body,—that is, the force of gravity in proceeding from the equator to the poles,—will be indicated by a diminution of the time in which an invariable pendulum performs a vibration. Accordingly the pendulum has been employed to determine the figure of the earth; and the results obtained have been found to accord perfectly with the geodetical measurements which we have described.

The British and French governments have both instituted observations on the pendulum. The latter, on the recommendation of the Academy of Sciences, directed that the intensity of the force of gravity should be determined at different points of the arc of the meridian between Dunkirk and Formentera; and committed the labour to MM. Biot, Arago, Mathieu, Bouvard, and Chaix: subsequently, Biot extended his observations to the northern extremity of the British islands. These operations were begun in the year 1807. At a somewhat later period the British government, with the assistance of the Royal Society, employed Captain Kater, an eminent observer and experimenter, in the same labour; and also sent Captain Sabine, a British artillery officer, with invariable pendulums, to the equator on the one hand, and the highest accessible latitudes of the northern hemisphere on the other. It was expected that, by thus multiplying the places of observation, the combination of results would destroy the irregular influences of local density, and give the true variations of the force of gravity, which are owing to the earth's ellipticity. From a mean of all the observations made by the British and French experimenters, it was found that the compression or ellipticity of the earth was about $\frac{1}{288 \cdot 7}$ or $\frac{1}{288 \cdot 86}$ Laplace had previously concluded, from the combined measurements of terrestrial degrees and pendulum experiments, and the lunar inequalities dependent on the figure of the earth, that the same important element was $\frac{1}{306 \cdot 75}$. There is a difference between the two conclusions; but, on the whole, all the results which have been obtained are comprehended within limits which may be deemed moderate, considering the difficulty of the inquiry.

The following tables exhibit numerical values of the magnitudes of the degrees of latitude and longitude, and their proportion to each other.

The first is from a valuable collection of astronomical tables and formulæ by F. Baily, Esq., President of the Astronomical Society of London. It shows the length of a degree of latitude and longitude on the earth's surface, assuming the compression to be $\frac{1}{300}$, together with the length of the pendulum beating seconds there, supposing the compression to be $\frac{1}{307}$, the measures at the equator being considered as unity; also the increase in the number of vibrations of an invariable pendulum beating seconds at the equator on proceeding towards the pole. This merely shows the relative values of the quantities therein stated.

The second and third tables are from Mendoza's Tables for Navigation and Nautical Astronomy. And the fourth is from the very valuable Introduction to Practical Astronomy by Dr. Pearson, where it is stated to be computed from a Formula given by Lieut.-Col. Lambton in the Asiatic Researches, vol. xii.

The tables are constructed from different values of the earth's compression at the poles. The uncertainty of this important element, in all questions of geography and astronomy, is an inconvenience which cannot yet be got rid of.

In Tables II. and III., the dimensions of the degrees of latitude and longitude are given in minutes of the equator. To change these into feet or fathoms, we must know the number of them in a degree of the equator.

According to Puissant and Svanberg, the equatorial degree, or 60 geographical miles, is 60,847 fathoms.

Cagnoli has assumed = 60,893 fathoms.

Lieut.-Col. Lambton reckoned it to be 60,857 fathoms.

General Mudge concluded it to be 60,845 fathoms.

Mr. Baily, as an accompaniment to his table (Table I.), assumes the equatorial diameter of the earth to be 7924 miles, and the polar = 7916 miles. A degree of longitude at the equator will, on this supposition, be 69.15 miles, = 60,852 fathoms, = 365,110 feet: so one second of time, or fifteen seconds of a degree of longitude, will be 1521 feet.

Table IV. gives the measure of each degree of latitude and longitude in fathoms.

TABLE I.

| | Compression $= \frac{1}{300}$. | | Compression $= \frac{1}{307}$. | |
|---|---|---|---|---|
| Lat. | Degree of Longitude. | Degree of Latitude. | Length of the Pendulum. | Increase of Vibrations. |
| ° | | | | ″ |
| 0 | 1.00000 | 1.000000 | 1.00000 | 0.0 |
| 5 | 0.99622 | 1.000076 | 1.00004 | 1.77 |
| 10 | .98490 | 1.000301 | 1.00016 | 7.02 |
| 15 | .96614 | 1.000669 | 1.00036 | 15.60 |
| 20 | .94006 | 1.001168 | 1.00063 | 27.24 |
| 25 | .90685 | 1.001783 | 1.00096 | 41.59 |
| 30 | .86675 | 1.002496 | 1.00135 | 58.21 |
| 35 | .82005 | 1.003284 | 1.00177 | 76.60 |
| 40 | .76710 | 1.004125 | 1.00223 | 96.21 |
| 45 | .70828 | 1.004992 | 1.00269 | 116.42 |
| 50 | .64404 | 1.005858 | 1.00316 | 136.64 |
| 55 | .57485 | 1.006699 | 1.00362 | 156.25 |
| 60 | .50126 | 1.007487 | 1.00404 | 174.63 |
| 65 | .42377 | 1.008200 | 1.00443 | 191.26 |
| 70 | .34302 | 1.008815 | 1.00476 | 205.61 |
| 75 | .25960 | 1.009315 | 1.00503 | 217.25 |
| 80 | .17421 | 1.009682 | 1.00523 | 225.82 |
| 85 | .08764 | 1.009907 | 1.00535 | 231.08 |
| 90 | .00000 | 1.009983 | 1.00539 | 232.85 |

TABLE II.

The Measure of a Degree of Longitude, on each Parallel of Latitude in Minutes of the Equator, on the Sphere and Spheroid. Compression $= \frac{1}{321}$.

| Par. of Lat. | Degree on the Sphere. | Degree on the Spheroid. | Par. of Lat. | Degree on the Sphere. | Degree on the Spheroid. | Par. of Lat. | Degree on the Sphere. | Degree on the Spheroid. |
|---|---|---|---|---|---|---|---|---|
| ° | ′ | ′ | ° | ′ | ′ | ° | ′ | ′ |
| 0 | 60.000 | 60.000 | 30 | 51.962 | 52.002 | 60 | 30.000 | 30.070 |
| 1 | 59.991 | 59.991 | 31 | 51.430 | 51.473 | 61 | 29.089 | 29.158 |
| 2 | 59.963 | 59.964 | 32 | 50.883 | 50.927 | 62 | 28.168 | 28.237 |
| 3 | 59.918 | 59.918 | 33 | 50.320 | 50.367 | 63 | 27.239 | 27.307 |
| 4 | 59.854 | 59.855 | 34 | 49.742 | 49.791 | 64 | 26.302 | 26.369 |
| 5 | 59.772 | 59.773 | 35 | 49.149 | 49.199 | 65 | 25.357 | 25.422 |
| 6 | 59.671 | 59.673 | 36 | 48.541 | 48.593 | 66 | 24.404 | 24.468 |
| 7 | 59.553 | 59.556 | 37 | 47.918 | 47.972 | 67 | 23.444 | 23.506 |
| 8 | 59.416 | 59.420 | 38 | 47.281 | 47.336 | 68 | 22.476 | 22.537 |
| 9 | 59.261 | 59.266 | 39 | 46.629 | 46.686 | 69 | 21.502 | 21.562 |
| 10 | 59.088 | 59.094 | 40 | 45.963 | 46.022 | 70 | 20.521 | 20.578 |
| 11 | 58.898 | 59.904 | 41 | 45.283 | 45.343 | 71 | 19.534 | 19.589 |
| 12 | 58.689 | 58.697 | 42 | 44.589 | 44.651 | 72 | 18.541 | 18.593 |
| 13 | 58.462 | 58.471 | 43 | 43.881 | 43.945 | 73 | 17.542 | 17.592 |
| 14 | 58.218 | 58.228 | 44 | 43.160 | 43.225 | 74 | 16.538 | 16.586 |
| 15 | 57.956 | 57.963 | 45 | 42.426 | 42.493 | 75 | 15.529 | 15.574 |
| 16 | 57.676 | 57.689 | 46 | 41.680 | 41.747 | 76 | 14.515 | 14.558 |
| 17 | 57.378 | 57.394 | 47 | 40.920 | 40.988 | 77 | 13.497 | 13.537 |
| 18 | 57.063 | 57.080 | 48 | 40.148 | 40.217 | 78 | 12.475 | 12.512 |
| 19 | 56.731 | 56.750 | 49 | 39.364 | 39.434 | 79 | 11.449 | 11.483 |
| 20 | 56.382 | 56.402 | 50 | 38.567 | 38.638 | 80 | 10.419 | 10.450 |
| 21 | 56.015 | 56.037 | 51 | 37.759 | 37.831 | 81 | 9.386 | 9.414 |
| 22 | 55.631 | 55.665 | 52 | 36.940 | 37.011 | 82 | 8.350 | 8.376 |
| 23 | 55.230 | 55.257 | 53 | 36.109 | 36.181 | 83 | 7.312 | 7.335 |
| 24 | 54.813 | 54.841 | 54 | 35.267 | 35.339 | 84 | 6.272 | 6.292 |
| 25 | 54.378 | 54.409 | 55 | 34.415 | 34.487 | 85 | 5.229 | 5.246 |
| 26 | 53.928 | 53.960 | 56 | 33.552 | 33.624 | 86 | 4.185 | 4.193 |
| 27 | 53.460 | 53.495 | 57 | 32.678 | 32.750 | 87 | 3.140 | 3.149 |
| 28 | 52.997 | 53.013 | 58 | 31.795 | 31.866 | 88 | 2.094 | 2.100 |
| 29 | 52.477 | 52.002 | 59 | 30.902 | 30.973 | 89 | 1.047 | 1.050 |
| 30 | 51.962 | 52.002 | 60 | 30.000 | 30.070 | 90 | 0.000 | 0.000 |

### TABLE III.

The Measures of different Arcs of the Meridian in the Spheroid from the Equator to the Pole; and also the respective Degrees of Latitude in Minutes of the Equator. Compression $= \frac{1}{321}$.

| ° | ′ | ′ | ° | ′ | ′ | ° | ′ | ′ |
|---|---|---|---|---|---|---|---|---|
| 0 | 0.000 | 59.628 | 30 | 1790.302 | 59.772 | 60 | 3587.515 | 60.051 |
| 1 | 59.628 | 59.629 | 31 | 1850.074 | 59.781 | 61 | 3647.566 | 60.059 |
| 2 | 119.257 | 59.630 | 32 | 1909.855 | 59.789 | 62 | 3707.625 | 60.067 |
| 3 | 178.887 | 59.631 | 33 | 1969.644 | 59.798 | 63 | 3767.692 | 60.075 |
| 4 | 238.518 | 59.632 | 34 | 2029.442 | 59.807 | 64 | 3827.767 | 60.082 |
| 5 | 298.150 | 59.634 | 35 | 2089.249 | 59.816 | 65 | 3887.849 | 60.090 |
| 6 | 357.784 | 59.636 | 36 | 2149.065 | 59.826 | 66 | 3947.939 | 60.097 |
| 7 | 417.420 | 59.638 | 37 | 2208.891 | 59.835 | 67 | 4008.036 | 60.104 |
| 8 | 477.058 | 59.641 | 38 | 2263.726 | 59.844 | 68 | 4068.140 | 60.111 |
| 9 | 536.699 | 59.644 | 39 | 2328.570 | 59.854 | 69 | 4128.251 | 60.117 |
| 10 | 596.343 | 59.647 | 40 | 2388.424 | 59.863 | 70 | 4188.368 | 60.124 |
| 11 | 655.990 | 59.651 | 41 | 2448.287 | 59.873 | 71 | 4248.492 | 60.130 |
| 12 | 715.641 | 59.655 | 42 | 2508.160 | 59.883 | 72 | 4308.622 | 60.135 |
| 13 | 775.296 | 59.659 | 43 | 2568.043 | 59.893 | 73 | 4368.757 | 60.141 |
| 14 | 834.955 | 59.663 | 44 | 2627.936 | 59.902 | 74 | 4428.898 | 60.146 |
| 15 | 894,618 | 59.668 | 45 | 2687.838 | 59.912 | 75 | 4489.044 | 60.151 |
| 16 | 954.286 | 59.673 | 46 | 2747.750 | 59.922 | 76 | 4549.195 | 60.155 |
| 17 | 1013.959 | 59.679 | 47 | 2807.672 | 59.931 | 77 | 4609.350 | 60.160 |
| 18 | 1073.638 | 59.685 | 48 | 2867.603 | 59.941 | 78 | 4669.510 | 60.164 |
| 19 | 1133.323 | 59.691 | 49 | 2927.544 | 59.951 | 79 | 4729.674 | 60.167 |
| 20 | 1193.014 | 59.697 | 50 | 2987.495 | 59.960 | 80 | 4789.841 | 60.171 |
| 21 | 1252.711 | 59.703 | 51 | 3047.455 | 59.970 | 81 | 4850.012 | 60.174 |
| 22 | 1312.414 | 59.710 | 52 | 3107.425 | 59.979 | 82 | 4910.186 | 60.176 |
| 23 | 1372.124 | 59.717 | 53 | 3167.404 | 59.989 | 83 | 4970.362 | 60.179 |
| 24 | 1431.841 | 59.724 | 54 | 3227.393 | 59.998 | 84 | 5030.541 | 60.181 |
| 25 | 1491.565 | 59.732 | 55 | 3287.391 | 60.007 | 85 | 5090.722 | 60.182 |
| 26 | 1551.297 | 59.739 | 56 | 3347.398 | 60.016 | 86 | 5150.904 | 60.184 |
| 27 | 1611.036 | 59.747 | 57 | 3407.414 | 60.025 | 87 | 5211.088 | 60.185 |
| 28 | 1670.783 | 59.755 | 58 | 3467.439 | 60.034 | 88 | 5271.273 | 60.185 |
| 29 | 1730.538 | 59.764 | 59 | 3527.473 | 60.042 | 89 | 5331.458 | 60.186 |
| 30 | 1790.302 | | 60 | 3587.515 | | 90 | 5391.644 | |

### TABLE IV.

The Measure of each Degree of Latitude and of a Degree of Longitude in each Parallel of Latitude from the Equator to either Pole. Compression $\frac{1}{304}$.

| Par. of Lat. | Degree of Latitude in Fathoms. | Degree of Longitude in Fathoms. | Par. of Lat. | Degree of Latitude in Fathoms. | Degree of Longitude in Fathoms. | Par. of Lat. | Degree of Latitude in Fathoms. | Degree of Longitude in Fathoms. |
|---|---|---|---|---|---|---|---|---|
| ° | | | ° | | | ° | | |
| 0 | 60458.6 | 60857.1 | 30 | 60607.4 | 52746.9 | 60 | 60906.6 | 30503.5 |
| 1 | 60458.8 | 60847.8 | 31 | 60616.5 | 52210.0 | 61 | 60915.7 | 29578.2 |
| 2 | 60459.8 | 60820.2 | 32 | 60625.8 | 51657.2 | 62 | 60924.5 | 28643.8 |
| 3 | 60460.3 | 60774.2 | 33 | 60635.2 | 51088.6 | 63 | 60933.1 | 27700.6 |
| 4 | 60461.5 | 60709.8 | 34 | 60644.8 | 56504.5 | 64 | 60941.4 | 26748.8 |
| 5 | 60463.2 | 60627.0 | 35 | 60654.5 | 49904.9 | 65 | 60949.6 | 25788.7 |
| 6 | 60465.1 | 60525.8 | 36 | 60664.4 | 49290.2 | 66 | 60957.5 | 24820.7 |
| 7 | 60467.5 | 60406.4 | 37 | 60674.3 | 48660.3 | 67 | 60965.3 | 23845.0 |
| 8 | 60470.1 | 60268.6 | 38 | 60684.4 | 48015.6 | 68 | 60972.7 | 22861.9 |
| 9 | 60473.2 | 60112.6 | 39 | 60694.6 | 47355.2 | 69 | 60979.8 | 21871.7 |
| 10 | 60476.5 | 59938.4 | 40 | 60704.8 | 46682.4 | 70 | 60986.7 | 20874.8 |
| 11 | 60480.3 | 59746.1 | 41 | 60715.1 | 45994.2 | 71 | 60993.4 | 19871.4 |
| 12 | 60484.3 | 59535.6 | 42 | 60725.4 | 45292.0 | 72 | 60999.7 | 18861.8 |
| 13 | 60488.7 | 59307.1 | 43 | 60735.8 | 44576.0 | 73 | 61005.7 | 17846.4 |
| 14 | 60493.4 | 59060.6 | 44 | 60746.3 | 43846.2 | 74 | 61011.5 | 16825.4 |
| 15 | 60498 4 | 58796.3 | 45 | 60756.7 | 43103.0 | 75 | 61016.8 | 15799.3 |
| 16 | 60503.8 | 58514.1 | 46 | 60767.2 | 42346.6 | 76 | 61022.0 | 14768.2 |
| 17 | 60509.4 | 58214.2 | 47 | 60777.6 | 41577.3 | 77 | 61026.7 | 13732.6 |
| 18 | 60515.4 | 57896.6 | 48 | 60788.0 | 40795.1 | 78 | 61031.2 | 12692.7 |
| 19 | 60521.6 | 57561.4 | 49 | 60798.4 | 40000.5 | 79 | 61035.3 | 11648.9 |
| 20 | 60528.2 | 57208.8 | 50 | 60808.7 | 39193.5 | 80 | 61039.1 | 10601.4 |
| 21 | 60535.0 | 56838.9 | 51 | 60819.0 | 38374.5 | 81 | 61042.5 | 9550.7 |
| 22 | 60542.0 | 56451.6 | 52 | 60829.2 | 37543.7 | 82 | 61045.6 | 8497.0 |
| 23 | 60549.4 | 56047.2 | 53 | 60839.3 | 36701.4 | 83 | 61048.3 | 7440.6 |
| 24 | 60557.0 | 55625.8 | 54 | 60849.3 | 35847.8 | 84 | 61050.7 | 6382.0 |
| 25 | 60564.8 | 55187.5 | 55 | 60859.3 | 34983.1 | 85 | 61052.7 | 5321.4 |
| 26 | 60572.9 | 54732.4 | 56 | 60869.0 | 34107.6 | 86 | 61054.3 | 4259.1 |
| 27 | 60581.2 | 54260.6 | 57 | 60878.7 | 33221.5 | 87 | 61055.6 | 3195.5 |
| 28 | 60589.7 | 53772.4 | 58 | 60888.2 | 32325.5 | 88 | 61056.5 | 2130.9 |
| 29 | 60598.4 | 53267.8 | 59 | 60897.5 | 31419.4 | 89 | 61057.1 | 1065.6 |
| 30 | 60607.4 | 52746.9 | 60 | 60906.6 | 30503.5 | 90 | 61057.2 | 0000.0 |

## CHAPTER XX.

### DETERMINATION OF LATITUDE AND LONGITUDE.

There are three important problems in geography which require for their solution the doctrines of astronomy. The first requires to find the direction of the meridian at any point of the earth's surface; the second, to find the latitude of any place; and the third, to find the longitude.

Problem I.—*To determine the Meridian, or to draw a Meridian Line.*

This problem, like many others in practical astronomy, admits of a comparatively easy solution, if no great degree of accuracy is required; but to obtain a very accurate result, much care, and instruments of the most perfect construction, are indispensable.

The general principle of the solution is the fact, that the celestial bodies which do not sensibly change their declination in the course of a day, have the same apparent altitude at equal intervals of time before and after passing the meridian: also, that their altitude is greatest or least when in the plane of the meridian; that is, when they are due south or due north.

About the time of the summer and winter solstice, the sun changes his declination very little in the course of a day: and hence it happens that the shadow of an upright rod or *gnomon* is almost exactly of the same length when the sun is at equal distances from the meridian. To determine the position of the meridian, then, let a number of concentric circles be described on a horizontal plane, and let a wire or rod be placed directly over their common centre, and perpendicular to the plane; and, the sun shining on the plane, let the two points in which the extremity of the shadow of the wire crosses each circle be exactly noted. Then, through any point of the plane which is at equal distances, from each pair of intersections draw a straight line through the centre of the circle; and this will be in the plane of the meridian, or will be a *meridian line.* It is easy to see that one circle, and one pair of intersections of the path of the extremity of the shadow and the circle, would be sufficient: but several circles will fulfil the object with greater accuracy and more certainty; because a mean position of the meridian line may be found among all the results; and besides, one of a pair, or both, may be lost by clouds intercepting the light of the sun.

The imperfection of this method of finding the meridian arises from the indistinctness of the termination of the shadow of the upright wire, and from the change of the sun's declination between the observations. There is, however, another as simple and exact as can be expected, without the assistance of a telescope. It is known that the pole star and the star Alioth, or ε of the Great Bear, pass the meridian within about nine minutes of each other. If, therefore, we suspend two plummets by threads to the ends of a rod which turns horizontally on a pivot, and by moving the rod, keep the two plumb-lines exactly between the eye and Alioth when near the meridian, then, at the moment when the pole star is also seen along the two plumb-lines, the two stars and the plumb-lines will be all nearly in the plane of the meridian. To keep the plumb-lines steady in the vertical plane, the plummets may hang in vessels filled with water.

If we could determine the position of a star when its altitude is greatest or least, we would then have a point of the heavens in the plane of the meridian: but that position cannot be found with certainty, because the change of altitude is imperceptible to a sensible distance on each side of the meridian.

The exact determination of the meridian requires the aid of the telescope, a well-regulated clock, and an instrument for determining the altitude of the sun or a star: Hadley's sextant, or a reflecting circle, are the proper instruments for this purpose. By the sextant we can determine two instants of time when the star has the same altitude; the clock will give the interval of time between them: and half this interval will be the time between each observation and the passage of the star over the meridian. If we next day note the time by the clock when the star again attains that altitude, and add to that time the above-mentioned half interval, we shall have the time by the clock when the star will be on the meridian. If at that instant a telescope, moveable in a vertical plane, be directed to the star, so that in passing the meridian the star may be in the axis of the telescope, the position of the plane of the meridian will be obtained: and if the telescope be fixed to a horizontal axis which is perpendicular to that plane, it will have a vertical motion in the plane of the meridian, and will be what is called a *transit instrument.* By this instrument the exact instant when any celestial phenomenon is on the meridian is known. It is, therefore, one of the most essential instruments in an observatory.

In a variable climate, it may happen that the observations necessary to determine the meridian may be interrupted by cloudy weather. This, however, is an inconvenience to which all astronomical observations are liable. It must also be observed, that a single set of observations will not give so perfect a result as a considerable number of sets, from which a mean may be deduced.

If the celestial object change its position otherwise than by the diurnal motions of the earth, as happens when it is the sun, still the problem may be resolved, as has been explained, by making allowance for the change of position, by applying the principles of spherical trigonometry to the laws of the motion.

### PROBLEM II.—*To determine the Latitude.*

In treating of the doctrine of the sphere, it has been already shown that the distance of the pole of the world (that is, the point of the heavens about which all the stars turn) from the horizon of any place is equal to its latitude. Now, in the course of twenty-four hours, every star passes the meridian twice, at equal distances from the pole, and on opposite sides of it. When the star passes the meridian below the pole,—that is, between the pole and the horizon,—its altitude is the *least* possible; and when it crosses the meridian above the pole, or between the pole and the south part of the horizon, its distance from the north point of the horizon will be the *greatest* possible. If, therefore, with a suitable instrument, (a quadrant for instance,) we take the star's altitude when it is least, and also when it is greatest, and correct these for refraction, it is manifest that half their sum will be the latitude of the place where the observations were made.

We have supposed the star to pass the meridian between the pole and the zenith, and then its greatest altitude will be its distance from the north point of the horizon: but it may pass to the south of the zenith, and then its altitude, reckoned from the south, must be subtracted from 180° to get its distance from the north point of the horizon; and half the sum of the two distances, as before, will be the latitude.

Any one star that never sets, the pole star for instance, will serve to determine the latitude: but it will be proper, if circumstances allow, to observe various stars, and the mean of all the observations may be expected to be more correct than a single pair.

If, instead of the greatest and least altitudes of a star, its greatest and least distances from the zenith be found, then half their sum will be the *complement* of the latitude; that is, the difference between the latitude and ninety degrees.

For example, by observations made on the pole star at the Dublin Observatory, it was found that

| | | | |
|---|---|---|---|
| Its greatest zenith distance, corrected for refraction, was - - - | 38° | 19′ | 43″.11 |
| Least - - - - - - - - - - - - - - - - - - - - - - | 34 | 53 | 49.55 |
| The sum - - - - - - - - - - - - - - - - - - - - | 73 | 13 | 32.66 |
| Half the sum, or co-latitude of the observatory - - - - - - - | 36 | 36 | 46.33 |
| The latitude - - - - - - - - - - - - - - - - - - - | 53 | 23 | 13.67 |

When the latitude of one place is known, the latitude of another place may be found by observing with a quadrant, or other suitable instrument, the zenith distances of any star at both places. The difference of these zenith distances, when corrected for refraction, will be the difference of latitude of the two places.

Thus, for example, to determine the difference between the latitudes of Greenwich Observatory and Dunnose in the Isle of Wight, it was found that

| | | | |
|---|---|---|---|
| At Dunnose the Z. D. of β Draconis was - - - - - - - - - - | 1° | 50′ | 5″.24 |
| And at Greenwich - - - - - - - - - - - - - - - - - | 0 | 58 | 33.13 |
| Difference of latitude - - - - - - - - - - - - - - - - - | 0 | 51 | 32.11 |
| The latitude of Greenwich was known to be - - - - - - - - | 51 | 28 | 30.05 |
| The latitude of Dunnose is - - - - - - - - - - - - - - - | 50 | 37 | 8.39 |

The navigator has daily occasion to determine his latitude at sea. For this purpose, he finds the sun's zenith distance, or its altitude at noon, by Hadley's sextant. The Nautical Almanac gives him the sun's declination, or distance from the equator at the time he makes his observation: the sum or difference of these is his latitude, according as the ship and the sun are on the same or opposite sides of the equator.

Ex. On July 24, 1783, at a place in longitude 54° ($3^h$ $36^m$) west of Greenwich, the altitude of the sun's lower limb, when cleared from refraction and parallax, was observed by a sextant to be 59° 15′ 30″. By the Nautical Almanac, the sun's semidiameter was 15′ 48″, and his declination at the time of noon in that longitude 19° 51′ N. The calculation for the latitude will stand thus:—

| | | | |
|---|---|---|---|
| Altitude of the sun's lower limb - - - - - - - - - - - - - | 59° | 15′ | 30″ |
| Add sun's semidiameter - - - - - - - - - - - - - - - - | | 15 | 48 |
| Subtract altitude of sun's centre - - - - - - - - - - - - - - | 59 | 31 | 18 |
| From - - - - - - - - - - - - - - - - - - - - - - | 90 | 0 | 0 |
| To sun's zenith distance - - - - - - - - - - - - - - - - | 30 | 28 | 42 |
| Add sun's declination - - - - - - - - - - - - - - - - - | 19 | 51 | 0 |
| The latitude of the place is - - - - - - - - - - - - - - - | 50 | 19 | 42 |

The navigator cannot always obtain an observation of the sun or a star when on the meridian. He may, however, be able to observe two latitudes out of the meridian, and the interval of time between them. With these data, and the aid of spherical trigonometry and the Nautical Almanac, he may find his latitude by rules given by writers on navigation and astronomy. It is, in general, by one or other of these methods that the recorded latitudes of all places have been obtained, and arranged in a table for the use of the geographer and navigator.

### Problem III.—*To determine the Longitude.*

The interval of time between two successive passages of the sun over the meridian of any place is twenty-four hours. If, therefore, we suppose a number of meridians to be drawn at equal intervals,—that is, to form successively with each other equal angles at the poles,—then, in the course of twenty-four hours, each of these meridians (supposing their planes produced) will pass through the sun. Therefore twenty-four hours of mean solar time will correspond to 360 degrees of longitude; for the whole scale of longitude must be contained between the eastern and western sides of the meridian at the same place. At places situated on the meridian opposite that on which the sun was at $0^h$, or, in civil reckoning, at 12 at noon, the time would be $12^h$, or 12 at night; and $12^h$ would correspond to 180 degrees of longitude. At places situated on the meridian at right angles to the former, the time would be $6^h$ or $18^h$, or, in civil reckoning, six in the morning or six in the evening; and, accordingly, six hours and eighteen hours of mean solar time will correspond to 90° or 270° of longitude; and so on for intermediate meridians.

The selection of a meridian, from which the longitude is to be reckoned, is entirely arbitrary. The English take the meridian passing through Greenwich Observatory for the *first meridian*, and reckon its longitude to be 0° or $0^h$. The first meridian of the French is that which passes through the observatory of Paris. An interval of $9^m\ 21^s$ elapses between the passages of the sun over the meridians of Paris and Greenwich: the longitude of Paris Observatory is, therefore, by English geographers, accounted to be $9^m\ 21^s$ east in time; or in degrees, 2° 20′ 15″.

Since it is noon at all places on the meridian of Greenwich from pole to pole at the same instant, it will be an hour past noon, or $1^h$, at all places on the meridian 15° to the east of that of Greenwich; and two hours past noon, or $2^h$, at all places on the meridian 30° east from that of Greenwich; and so on. On the other hand, it will want an hour to noon, or will be $11^h$, at all places on the meridian 15° west from that of Greenwich; and it will be two hours before noon, or $10^h$, at places on the meridian 30° west from that of Greenwich; and so on, reckoning an hour, or sixty minutes of time, to correspond to fifteen degrees, and four minutes of time to one degree.

Since it appears that all places on the same meridian have noon, or any assumed hour, at the same instant, and that the instant of noon is different at places on different meridians,—being earlier or later on meridians having west longitude, according as they are nearer to or farther from the first meridian, and the reverse on meridians having east longitude; and moreover, that the difference between the time of noon on two meridians is proportional to the difference of their longitude, and therefore a *measure* of that difference; it follows that if, knowing the hour of the day at any place, we can at the same instant by any means know the hour at a place on any other meridian, then we can determine the difference of longitude between the meridians: for it will be the difference between the times of the day, as estimated on the two meridians, reckoned in hours, minutes, &c.; and this may be converted into degrees, minutes, and seconds, by reckoning fifteen degrees to an hour, and proportionally for minutes and seconds of time.

The practical methods of determining the longitude are the following:—

#### 1. *By a Chronometer or Time-keeper.*

Let us suppose that a traveller departs from any place, (St. Paul's, London, for example,) and carries with him a watch regulated to mean solar time, and which indicates $12^h$ at the instant of *mean noon* at London: then, supposing the watch to go with perfect regularity, if he go to Edinburgh, and compare the estimated solar time there with that shown by his watch, he will find that they differ by twelves minutes twenty-one seconds; so that when it is $12^h$ at Edinburgh Observatory, it will be $12^h\ 12^m\ 21^s$ by his watch. He may therefore conclude, that the difference of longitude between London and Edinburgh is $12^m\ 21^s$ west; and since St. Paul's is twenty-three seconds of time west from Greenwich, the longitude of Edinburgh Observatory is $12^m\ 44^s$ west, which corresponds to 3° 11′. If, leaving London, he had gone to Paris, he would there have found the estimated time to be $9^m\ 44^s$ earlier than that shown by his watch: hence the difference between the meridians of London and Paris is $9^m\ 44^s$, and the longitude of Paris (from Greenwich) $9^m\ 21^s$ east.

In the same way the navigator at sea may determine his longitude by a good chronometer. He can determine the hour of the day by the sun's altitude, and the principles of spherical trigonometry. Or he may take equal altitudes, noting the times; the middle point of time between them will be the instant of noon, as shown by the watch: he must, however, make a correction for the change of the sun's declination, and the distance run by the ship in the interval. Supposing now the chronometer to have been set to the true time at the port from whence he sailed, and to have gone uniformly with a small known daily acceleration or retardation, called its *rate;* this correction being applied, he will have the time at the port corresponding to his observed time of noon, and their difference will be the longitude of the ship eastward or westward from the meridian whence she sailed.

The longitude of any point on the earth, either at sea or on land, may be determined by a good chronometer; in the latter case, however, the jolting it must suffer by carriage will disturb its motion, and render the result sought uncertain. At sea, the mode of transport is not so liable to sudden jerks; and, therefore, the chronometer may be expected to go with more regularity. If several be employed, considerable accuracy may be obtained. The Board of Admiralty sent ten or twelve chronometers from Greenwich to Falmouth, and thence in a vessel to Madeira, and in this way determined the longitude of Funchal from a mean of their results.

The facility of this mode of determining the longitude makes perfection in the construction of chronometers an object of high importance in a maritime nation like Britain. It was, therefore, for many years encouraged by acts of parliament offering high rewards for prescribed degrees of excellence. These, however, are now repealed; but the government has not lost sight of this important subject.

### 2. *The Longitude by Eclipses of Jupiter's Satellites.*

If a celestial phenomenon can be seen at the same absolute instant of time in two different places of the earth, this appearance gives the means of determining the difference of their longitudes; for if the phenomenon be seen at both places, and the times, according to their reckoning, be noted, it is manifest that their difference will be the difference of longitude, in time, of the two places.

Now the eclipses of Jupiter's moons are phenomena of this kind. They may be seen, almost at the same instant, everywhere in the hemisphere in which Jupiter is visible: and such is the perfection of astronomy, that the times at which they will happen can be predicted with considerable accuracy. These are computed according to Greenwich time, and published, along with various other matters, in the Nautical Almanac, several years before they happen, for the benefit of travellers. This method of finding the longitude can, however, only be applied on land; for at sea the rolling of the ship makes it next to impossible to direct a telescope so steadily to Jupiter as to view the eclipse of a satellite.

*Example.*—Suppose an immersion of the first satellite should be observed at the Cape of Good Hope, April 16, 1805, at $13^h\ 25^m\ 35^s$ mean time; the predicted time given by the Ephemeris being $12^h\ 12^m\ 2^s$ at Greenwich. Here the difference is $1^h\ 13^m\ 33^s$; whence the longitude of the Cape should be 18° 23′ 15″ east of Greenwich.

In this example, the observed time at the Cape is compared with the computed time of the eclipse at Greenwich. If, instead of this, the observed time at Greenwich had been used, greater accuracy might have been expected.

This method is easy, and therefore much practised; but it is liable to uncertainty: for two observers in the same room, but using different telescopes, will sometimes differ in noting the time of an eclipse of the first satellite by as much as fifteen or twenty seconds. Delambre thinks that the time of an eclipse of the fourth satellite may be doubtful to the amount of four minutes.

### 3. *Longitude by an Eclipse of the Moon.*

An eclipse of the moon has exactly the same appearance, at the same instant, wherever seen; but it is impossible to be quite sure, by observation, of the exact time of their beginning or end, because of the penumbra which bounds the earth's shadow. The results to be obtained from them are therefore uncertain, to perhaps two minutes of time; and therefore only to be regarded as approximations to the truth.

*Example.* An eclipse of the moon was observed Aug. 28. 1729, by the astronomer Cassini at Paris, and by Mr. Stephenson at Barbadoes.

| | | | | | | |
|---|---|---|---|---|---|---|
| At Paris, Imm. ☽ - | $12^h$ | $19^m$ | $13^s$ | Emer. ☽ - | $13^h$ | $59^m$ |
| At Barbadoes, Imm. ☽ | 8 | 11 | 0 | Emer. ☽ - | 9 | 51 |
| | 4 | 8 | 13 | | 4 | 8 |

By the mean of the two, the difference of longitude is $4^h\ 8^m\ 6^s{\cdot}5$; that is, Barbadoes is 62° 1′ 30″ west of Paris.

### 4. *Longitude by Lunar Distances, or by Occultations of Stars by the Moon.*

The moon is, of all the celestial bodies, the most convenient for determining the longitude, because of the greater quickness of her apparent motion among the stars. She makes the complete circuit of the heavens in $27^{d}$ $7^{h}$ $43^{m}$ $4^{s}.7$ (this is her mean sidereal revolution): therefore she changes her place among the stars more than half a degree, or her own apparent diameter, in an hour; so that in two minutes of time she passes over one minute of a degree. This, or even its half, is quite a measurable quantity by a good sextant.

By the theory of the moon's motion, her place among the stars is known at any time that is, knowing the time of the day at Greenwich, the place of the moon is known; and, on the other hand, knowing the place of the moon, the time at Greenwich is known. The Nautical Almanac gives the distance of the moon's centre from the sun, and some of the brighter stars, as it would be seen from the earth's centre, for every third hour of the day, Greenwich time. If, therefore, the Almanac show that the moon, considered as seen from the earth's centre, will be 10° from a certain fixed star at six o'clock in the evening at Greenwich; and we make an observation at a distant place, and find that the moon's distance from the same star, reduced by computation to what it would be if seen at the earth's centre, is 10°, we immediately conclude that at that instant it is six o'clock at Greenwich. Thus the moon, with the brighter fixed stars near her path, serve the purpose of a chronometer.

To determine the longitude in this way, one observer measures the moon's distance from the sun or a bright star (one of those in the Ephemeris); another observer at the same time finds the altitudes of the moon and star; and a third should observe the exact time by a chronometer or good watch at which the observations were made. These observations, corrected for refraction, give *data* for finding what would be the apparent place of the moon in the heavens, if it could be seen from the centre of the earth at that time. The Nautical Almanac enables the observer to find the hour at Greenwich, when the position of the moon in the heavens was such as he observed it, and the interval between the Greenwich time and his own gives him his longitude.

This method of finding the longitude is commonly practised in the service of the East India Company, and in the navy. By it the longitude may be generally known to within twenty miles, and very often much nearer. This, although less accurate than the latitude, is yet an invaluable acquisition to the navigator. A striking proof how much it may be depended on has been given by a distinguished navigator (Capt. Basil Hall, R. N.). After a voyage of 8000 miles, occupying eighty-nine days, he arrived off Rio de Janeiro, having passed through the Pacific Ocean, rounded Cape Horn, and crossed the South Atlantic, without making any land. When within a week's sail of Rio, he set about determining, by lunar observations, the ship's course and place at a determinate moment; and having found this, within from five to ten miles, he trusted to the ordinary and more compendious way of finding his position, such as is used in short trips, for the remainder of his voyage. When he arrived within fifteen or twenty miles of the coast (according to his estimation), he hove to at four in the morning, waiting for day-break. He then proceeded, although the weather was hazy; but about eight it become so foggy that he did not like to stand in farther. The fog suddenly cleared off, and then he had the satisfaction to see the Great Sugar-loaf Rock, which stands on one side of the harbour, so nearly right a-head, that he had not to alter his course above a point in order to hit the entrance of Rio.

Occultations of stars by the moon serve exactly the same purpose as a distance of the moon from a star: these, however, are not so generally observed at sea as on land. They give the distance of the moon from the star with almost perfect accuracy, and therefore are an excellent method of determining the longitude. When an occultation has been observed, we can, by the lunar tables or the Nautical Almanac, which is a species of lunar and solar tables, compute the distance between the centre of the moon and star as it would appear at the earth's centre at the moment the occultation was observed, provided we know the longitude of the place where the observation was made: but this longitude is the very thing we want; therefore we cannot proceed by a direct process. However, we may know the longitude nearly by some other means; an eclipse of one of Jupiter's satellites, for example. With this, as if it were the true longitude, we may calculate the apparent distance between the star and centre of the moon reduced to the earth's centre at the time the occultation was seer If the longitude had been correctly assumed, this would have been exactly the moon's semidiameter; but it will differ more or less, according to the magnitude of the error we have made in the assumed longitude. There will, however, be such a determinate connexion between the error of the longitude and the difference between the moon's semidiameter and computed distance of the star and moon's centre, that the one will be deducible from the other by calculation. In this way, then, the error may be estimated, and a nearer approximation to the longitude obtained; and a repetition of the process will give a still more correct result.

### 5. *Longitude by the Transit of the Moon over the Meridian.*

Let T be the time by the clock when the moon is observed on the meridian of any place, $t$ the time of transit of a known fixed star, $24 + x$ the interval between two successive transits of the same star: then $24 + x : T - t :: 360° :$ difference of right ascension of the moon and star at the instant the moon was on the meridian; to which adding the known right ascension of the star, the right ascension (A) of the moon when on the meridian is determined. Now the moon's right ascension when on the meridian of Greenwich is given in the Nautical Almanac for every day of the year, from whence the daily increment of her right ascension may be determined: let, therefore, $a$ be the moon's right ascension when on the meridian of Greenwich, E the increment of right ascension in the time between two successive transits over the same meridian; then, considering the change of right ascension as uniform,

$$E : a - A :: 360° : \text{the required longitude.}$$

### 6. *Longitude by Signals.*

The most accurate way of determining small differences of longitude is by signals made on the earth's surface. A rocket fired from an elevated spot on a clear night may be seen distinctly with a telescope at the distance of twenty or thirty miles: therefore, by observing the times at which the same explosion is seen at two places, the difference of longitude of the places may be found.

The same method will apply to places at any distance, if they be connected by a chain of stations sufficiently near to each other to admit of a rocket to be seen from every two adjoining stations. The difference of longitude between Greenwich and Paris was determined in 1825 in this way. Rockets were exploded at Wrotham, and seen simultaneously at Greenwich and Fairlight Down: also at La Canche on the French coast, which were seen at Fairlight and Ligniers; and at Mont Javoult, which were observed at Ligniers and Paris.

In the same way the difference of longitude between Geneva and Milan has been determined by signals made by illumination on the tops of intermediate mountains.

The intensely brilliant light which Lieutenant Drummond, of the Royal Engineers, has proposed for light-houses, and which is produced by placing a ball of lime, about the size of a pea, in a flame supported by oxygen gas, may be employed in determining differences of longitude. We believe that, in favourable weather, this light exhibited on the top of Ben Lomond may be seen at the same time at Edinburgh and in Ireland: indeed, we know that it has actually been seen in the north of Ireland. Here, then, we have the means of determining with great exactness the difference between the longitude of Dublin and Edinburgh.

### 7. *Longitude by Triangulation.*

The trigonometrical survey of Britain has determined the longitude of all the principal points on the coast, as well as the mountains and cities in the interior, particularly in England. At present the survey is suspended in Britain, but is going on in Ireland. When this is completed, the British survey will doubtless be resumed, and the geography of the northern part of the island made as perfect in its minute details as the southern, which, from its proximity to the continent, is more necessary to be known in preparing plans of national defence.

---

## CHAPTER XXI.

### REPRESENTATION OF THE EARTH.

THE most natural and correct representation which can be given of the geographical divisions of the earth's surface is that which is made on a sphere or globe. In this way the different countries may be truly delineated, so as to exhibit perfectly to the eye their relative position, their magnitude, and boundaries; and by such a representation of the earth, all the problems in geography may be resolved with elegance and facility.

But although the surface of a solid having the exact figure of the earth, or differing but little from it, affords in theory the most complete and the only perfect representation of any considerable tract of country, yet there is a limit in practice to this precious advantage. A globe of a moderate size serves very well to give a distinct notion of the figure, the magnitude, the position, and general features of the great continents and islands: but the largest globe that can conveniently be constructed is insufficient for minute details; and then we must have recourse to the more simple, although less perfect, representations of MAPS.

It is impossible to represent on a plane a large extent of the earth's surface, so that the distances of places in the plane map shall have to each other precisely the same proportion as their distances on the globe. To obviate this difficulty, geographers have had recourse to different methods of representing portions of the globe on a plane.

By one method the countries are represented by the rules of perspective, as they would appear to an eye that should view them on the surface of a sphere from a given point. The different positions which may be assumed for the point from which the sphere is viewed give rise to different *projections*, which all answer very well when the surface to be represented is of small extent, and the point of view, or *projecting point*, is nearly over its centre. However, when the surface is of great extent, a whole hemisphere for instance, those places which lie near the border of the projection are in them all much distorted.

According to another method, the spherical surface to be represented is supposed to be cone whose vertex is somewhere in the polar axis produced, and its curved surface eithe touches the sphere at the middle parallel of the map, or falls within the sphere at the middle parallel, and without it at the extreme parallels. The surface of the cone is then supposed to be extended into a plane. This way of constructing maps is called the method of *development.*

There are other mathematical hypotheses according to which maps are delineated, and one in particular by which marine charts are constructed. In this, the parallels of latitude and circles of longitude are all represented by straight lines (that is, a line making always the same angle with the meridian), and the course of a ship sailing always on the same rhomb is also a straight line. A representation of the earth in this way is commonly called *Mercator's chart*, although the invention is due to an English mathematician, Edward Wright. Charts of this construction are of great importance in navigation.

## I. CONSTRUCTION OF MAPS BY PROJECTION.

There are two projections of the sphere by which portions of its surface may be truly delineated by the rules of perspective: the ORTHOGRAPHIC and the STEREOGRAPHIC. In each, the plane on which the projection is made is called the *plane of projection.*

### 1. ORTHOGRAPHIC PROJECTION.

To project any point in space orthographically on a plane, a perpendicular is to be drawn from the point on the plane and the bottom of the perpendicular; that is, the point in which it meets the plane is the orthographic projection of the point.

The orthographic projection of a line of any kind on a plane is found by supposing perpendiculars to be drawn from every point in the line, and that line on the plane which passes through the bottom of all the perpendiculars in the orthographic projection of the proposed line.

It is easy to see that the orthographic projection of a straight line must be a straight line, because the perpendiculars drawn from every point in it to the plane of projection will all lie in a plane, and the common section of two planes is a straight line. It is also apparent that the projection of a rectilineal figure will be a rectilineal figure.

If a circle be parallel to the plane of projection, its orthographic projection or representation will be a circle: for the perpendiculars supposed to be drawn from every point in the circle to the plane of projection will all be on the curve surface of a cylinder, and they may be considered as constituting that surface. The circle and its projection will be the top and bottom of the cylinder; and since they are parallel, they will be alike and equal.

If the plane in which a circle lies be perpendicular to the plane of projection, its projection will manifestly be a straight line, which will be equal in length to the diameter; and the projection of any arc reckoned from the extremities of the diameter will be projected into its versed sine; also the complement of the arc, or what it wants of ninety degrees, will be projected into its sine.

But if a circle be in a plane which is neither parallel nor perpendicular to the plane of projection, then its projection will neither be a circle nor a straight line; it will be an oval figure. The bounding line will be an *ellipse*, a curve formed by cutting a cylinder by a plane oblique to its axis; and it is also one of the *conic sections.*

An exact notion may be formed of the orthographic projection of any line or figure by holding it in the light of the sun, and observing its shadow formed on a plane which is perpendicular to the direction of the solar rays. The rays which pass close to the figure are the perpendiculars to the plane, and the shadow is the projection of the figure.

The plans and sections by which artificers execute different constructions are no other than orthographic projections of the things to be constructed; with these all workmen are familiar.

The orthographic projection of any object,—the *terrestrial globe*, for example,—with all its circles, and the continents and islands on its surface, is *nearly* the representation or picture which an artist would delineate on a plane surface, if he meant to represent the globe at a great distance from the eye; and it is *exactly* the appearance which the globe would have, supposing an eye could view it at an infinite distance.

From the nature of this projection, it appears that the orthographic representation of half the surface of the globe will show nearly the true figure and proportions of countries about the middle; that is, directly opposite to the supposed position of the eye: but, towards the extremities of the map, the graphic representations of places will imperfectly exhibit their true figure and position. For this reason it is seldom employed in geography, although its use is frequent in astronomy.

(A.) *To project the Sphere orthographically on the Plane of the Equator.*

About any point, C, as a centre (*fig.* 45), with any radius, C A, describe a circle B A 90 to represent the equator. Draw two diameters, A C 180, B C 90, perpendicular to each other: these will be the projections of meridians distant 90° from each other, and C will be the projection of the pole.

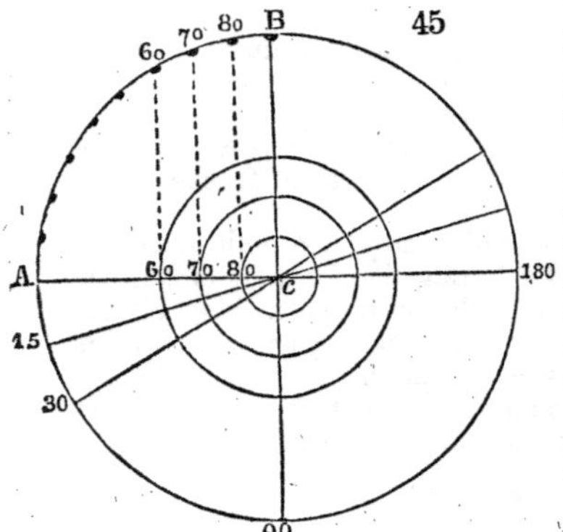


Divide each quadrant into six equal parts, and let A 15, 15 30 be two of these; draw diameters through 15 and 30, and these will be the projections of meridians 15° and 30° from A C 180; and, in this way, meridians dividing the equator into twenty-four equal parts may be represented. Of these, any one, C A, may be assumed as the first meridian.

To project the parallels of latitude: divide A B, one of the quadrants, into nine equal parts; let 80, 70, 60 be the three of these points of division adjoining to B: draw perpendiculars from these, and all the other points on the radius A C meeting it in 80, 70, 60, &c. About C as a centre at the distances C 80, C 70, C 60, &c. describe circles, and these will be the projections of parallels of latitude at the distance of ten degrees.

The polar circles and tropics may be found by laying off an arc of 23½° from A towards B, and from B towards A, and drawing perpendiculars from the points thus determined on C A, circles described about C, through the bottoms of the perpendiculars, will be the projections of the polar circle and tropic. In this way, the projection may be completed.

It is easy to see that the regions within the polar circle may be represented by this projection so as to give a tolerable notion of their position and magnitude, judging by the eye; but that the appearance of the equatorial regions will be altogether distorted.

(B.) *To project the Sphere orthographically on the Plane of the Meridian.*

Describe any circle, N E S Q (*fig.* 46.), to represent the meridian, and draw two diameters, E C Q, N C S, perpendicular to each other; the former may be taken as the projection of the equator, and then the latter will represent a meridian 90° from the meridian N E S.

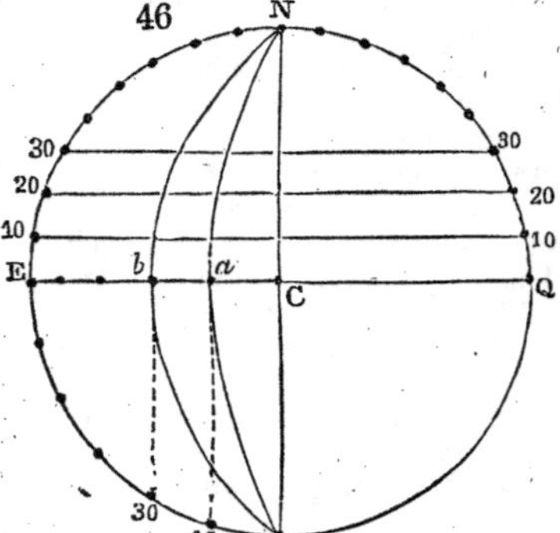


To represent other meridians: divide a quadrant S E into six equal parts, as at 15, 30, &c.; from these points of division draw perpendiculars 15 *a*, 30 *b*, &c. on E Q. Describe ellipses N *a* S, N *b* S, having a common transverse axis N S, and the lines C *a*, C *b*, &c. for their semiconjugate axes; and these will be the projections of meridians which pass through every fifteenth degree of the equator. Or, by dividing E S into nine equal parts, they may be made to pass through every tenth degree.

For the parallels of latitude: divide the quadrants E N, N Q each into nine equal parts at 10, 20, 30, &c.; join the corresponding numbers by straight lines, and these will be the projections of parallels of latitude at distances of 10°, 20°, 30°, &c. from the equator. The tropics and polar circles are to be drawn in the same way; the former at 23½° on each side of the equator, and the latter 23½° from the poles.

In this projection, the polar regions, and all places near the meridian N E S Q, are very much distorted in appearance to the eye: it is only towards the centre that there is any considerable resemblance of a projected portion of the earth's surface to its appearance on a globe.

## 2. STEREOGRAPHIC PROJECTION.

In the stereographic projection, the eye is supposed to be situated at a point in the surface of the sphere, and the plane on which the projection is to be made is the plane of that great circle, which is everywhere 90° distant from the position of the eye: hence it must be evident that the eye can see only the inside or concave surface; however, we may suppose the sphere to be transparent, and its various circles, and the islands, continents, &c. delineated on its surface to be seen through it. If we now conceive a line to be drawn from the eye to any point on the concave surface, the point in which that line cuts the plane of projection will be the *projection* of the point on the spherical surface.

To illustrate what has been said, let E A C B (*fig.* 47.) be a great circle of the sphere, *p q r s* a plane passing through its centre, and perpendicular to the plane of the great circle; let C E be a diameter of the sphere perpendicular to the plane; then assuming *p q r s* as the plane of projection, E, one end of that diameter, may be taken as the place of the eye or projecting point. If, now, straight lines E A, E B, E C, E D, &c. be drawn to A, B, C, D, any points on the surface of the sphere, the points *a*, *b*, *c*, *d*, &c. in which these lines meet the plane *p r*, will be the projections of the corresponding points on the surface of the sphere. Let A D B be any circle of the sphere: conceive a straight line to be drawn from E, the place of the eye, to D, any point in the circumference. If D, the end of this line, be now carried round the circle, supposing it always to pass through the fixed point E, the line will generate the surface of a cone whose base is the circle, and vertex the place of the eye; and the curve line *a d b*, which is the common section of the plane *p r*, and the surface of the cone will be the *projection* of the *circle*.

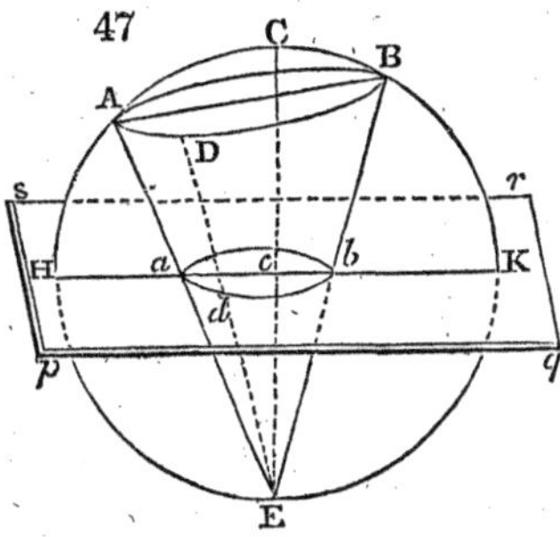


It will now be sufficiently obvious,

1. *That every circle which passes through the eye will be projected into or represented by a straight line on the plane of projection.*

2. *That every circle whose plane is parallel to the plane of the circle will be projected into a circle.*

These two properties hold true wherever the eye be situated. The assumption, however, that it is in the surface of the sphere gives rise to geometrical properties which are peculiar to this projection, and which by their simplicity and elegance give it great value.

One geometrical property is this: whatever be the position of the circle A D B (or base of the cone) on the surface of the sphere, the portion of the cone between the projecting point E and the plane of projection *p r* is always similar to the whole cone. If the plane of the base be parallel to the plane of projection, the truth of this proposition is obvious; but writers on geometry prove, that when it is oblique, still the cones whose bases are A D B and *a d b*, and common vertex E, are similar; only they have contrary positions. From the similarity of the whole cone to the part cut off, it follows that,

3. *In the stereographical projection of the sphere, the representation of any circle that does not pass through the eye will always be a circle.*

There is another proposition demonstrated by writers on spherical geometry which is of great importance in this projection; viz. if two straight lines be drawn from any point on the surface of the sphere to touch it in that point, their representation on the plane of projection will contain an angle exactly equal to the angle contained by the lines themselves. Since straight lines touching the surface of a sphere at any point may be regarded as tangents to any circles of the sphere passing through that point, we have this other remarkable property:—

4. *The angle made on the surface of the sphere by two circles which cut each other, and the angle made by circles which are their representations, are in all cases equal.*

This projection is extremely convenient in practice, because a circle may be easily described when three points in its circumference are given, or when two points and its radius are known; also, the property of lines making angles at their intersection on the surface of the sphere equal to those formed by their projections, is of great value in the representation of the surface of the sphere of a plane. Moreover, the contraction of the map towards the extremities of an hemisphere is not so great as in the orthographical projection; on all these accounts, the stereographical projection deserves a preference.

Supposing E to be the projecting point, or place of the eye, and *p r* the plane of projection, let C be the point of the sphere opposite to E, and therefore 90° everywhere from the circle, which is the common section of the sphere and plane of projection; it is evident that any arc, A C, of a great circle passing through C and E will be projected into a straight line *a c*. now this line is manifestly the tangent of the angle A E C to the radius E *c*, and the measure of this angle is half the arc A C.

5. Hence it follows, that if a great circle pass through the projecting point, *any arc of that circle, reckoned from the opposite point of the sphere, is projected into a straight line passing through the centre, and equal to the tangent of that arc.*

(A) *To project the Sphere stereographically on the Plane of the Equator.*

Describe a circle, A B D (*fig.* 48.), to represent the equator, and draw any diameter A C D and a radius C B perpendicular to A D. Supposing now that the parallels of latitude to every tenth degree are to be represented in the map, divide A B, a quadrant of the circle, into nine equal parts, as at the points 10, 20, 30, &c. and draw straight lines from the points of division to D, the extremity of the diameter A C D, meeting the radius B C in the points 10, 20, 30, &c. Then, about the centre C describe circles to pass through the points 10, 20, 30, &c., and these will represent the parallels of 10, 20, 30, &c. degrees of latitude. In this way, all the parallels of latitude may be found, as also the tropic and polar circle, by laying off arcs of 23½° and 66½° from B towards A.

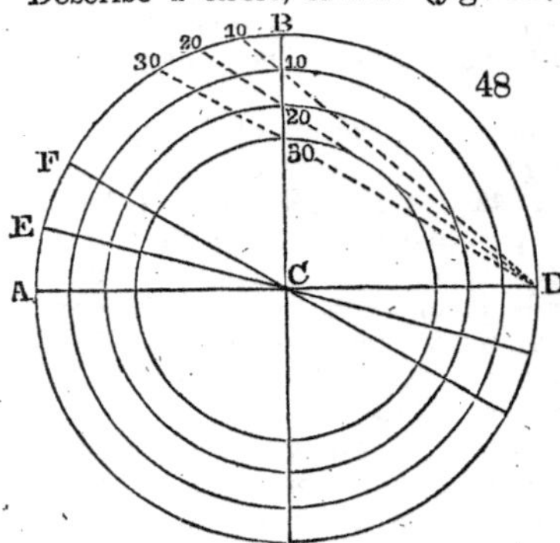


Next divide the circumference of the circle into into 24 equal parts, and draw radii from the centre to the points of division. These will represent the meridians which differ in longitude by one hour.

(B) *To project the Sphere stereographically on the Plane of a Meridian.*

Describe any circle N Q S E (*fig.* 49.), to represent the meridian on which the projection is to be made; which should be so chosen as to include nearly one of the continents,—the eastern, for instance: this will be accomplished if N E S be the meridian 20° west from London. Draw the diameter N C S, which will represent the meridian that passes through the projecting point, and therefore is perpendicular to the plane of projection. Then N will represent the north, and S the south pole; draw another diameter, E C Q, which will represent the equator.

Since, by the nature of the projection, all the meridians will be represented by circles which pass through the poles N, S, it will be sufficient if we determine the points in which they cut the equator: we shall suppose the meridians to pass through every tenth degree of longitude: the points where they cut the equator will be found by dividing one of the quadrantal arcs, N Q, into nine equal parts, as at 10, 20, 30, &c., and drawing straight lines from S to the points of division, meeting C Q in 1, 2, 3, &c. Then, a circle described through the points N 1 S will represent the meridian which cuts the equator 10° from Q, and a circle through N 2 S will be the meridian that cuts the equator 20° from Q. The remaining meridians N 3 S, &c. will be determined exactly in the same way; and it appears from the construction, that the centres of the circles will be in the diameter E Q and its prolongation, and their distances from the centre will be the tangents of 10°, 20°, &c.; viz. the inclination of the circles to the plane of the primitive; also, that their radii will be the secants of the same inclinations.

To describe the parallels of latitude, divide the four quadrants each into nine equal parts, as at 80, 70, 60, &c., and draw straight lines from E, one end of the diameter E Q, to the points of division, meeting N S in 8, 7, 6, &c. Then circles described through 80, 8, 80; 70, 7, 70, &c., will represent the parallels of 80°, 70°, &c. The centres of all the circles will be in the line N S, and distant from it by the secants of the distances of the parallels from the pole: also, the radii will be the tangents of the same distances. The polar circles and tropics being described by the same rules at the distances 23½° and 66½° from the poles, the projection will be completed.

(C.) *To project the Sphere stereographically on the Plane of the Horizon for a given Latitude.*

In this projection, the eye is supposed to be in the nadir of the place for which the projection is made.

On C (*fig.* 50.) and C (*fig.* 51.) as centres with any radius, describe circles W N E S, W′N′E′S′, of which *fig.* 50. is to be the primitive or horizon; the other, *fig.* 51., is to serve for determining the position of the circles to be described on *fig.* 50. Draw the diameters N S, W E, N′S′, W′E′ in both circles perpendicular to one another; then N S in *fig.* 50. will be the projection of the meridian, and W E the projection of the circle passing through the east and west points of the horizon and the zenith,—that is, the prime vertical; N will be the north point of the horizon, S the south, and E and W the east and west points.

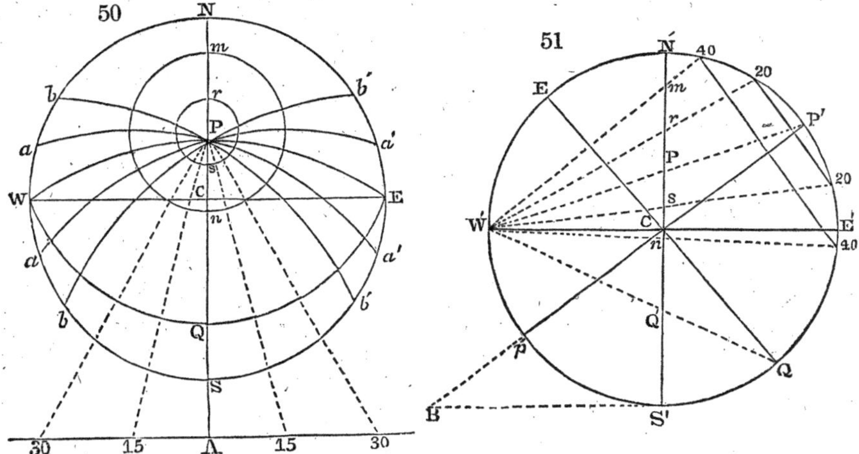


Make the arc N′P′, or the angle N′ C P′, *fig.* 51., equal to the latitude of the place; join W′P′ cutting C N′ in P; make C P in *fig.* 50. equal to C P in *fig.* 51., and P, *fig.* 50., will be the projection of the north pole. Draw the diameter E Q, *fig.* 51., perpendicular to P′ C *p′*; join W′Q′ meeting C S′ in Q′. Take C Q, *fig.* 50., equal to C Q′, *fig.* 51.; describe a circle through the points W, Q, E, and the arc W Q E will represent the equator. Next, to project the parallels of latitude,—for example, those which are 40° and 20° from the pole,—from P′, *fig.* 51., take P′ 40 and P′ 40, each arcs of 40° on opposite sides of P′; also, P′ 20, P′ 20, arcs of 20°. Join W′ 40, W′ 40, meeting C N′ in *m* and *n*; also W′ 20, W′ 20, meeting C N′ in *r* and *s*. In N C S, *fig.* 50., take C *m*, C *n*, C *r*, C *s*, equal to C *m*, C *n*, C *r*, C *s*, *fig.* 51.; describe circles on *m n*, *r s* as diameters, and these will be projections of parallels of latitude at the distances of 40° and 20° from the pole. In this way may all the parallels, also the tropics and polar circle, be projected.

*To project the meridian:* in *fig.* 51. draw S′ B perpendicular to N′ S′, meeting P′ *p* produced in B; take C A, *fig.* 50., equal to S′ B, *fig.* 51., and through A draw a perpendicular to C A. Let us suppose that the meridians are to make with each other angles of 15°: at P, in the line P A, draw P 15 and P 15 on each side of P A, making angles with it of 15°; and, in like manner, P 30, P 30, making angles of 30°, and so on to angles of 75°. On A, as a centre, describe a circle to pass through P; this will pass through W and E, and will be the projection of the six o'clock hour circle in the heavens, or that meridian on the globe that is perpendicular to the meridian of the place for which the projection is made. On the points 15, 15 describe arcs *a* P *a′*, *a* P *a′* to pass through P, and meet the projection of the horizon in *a*, *a′*; *a*, *a′*; and in like manner on 30, 30 as centres describe the arcs *b* P *b′*, *b* P *b′*, &c. all passing through P: these will be the projections of meridians on the terrestrial sphere, or of hour circles on the celestial sphere. In this way, the projection may be completed.

### 3. GLOBULAR PROJECTION.

In the orthographic projection, equal portions of the earth's spherical surface are represented by unequal plane surfaces; and the deviation from equality in the surface to be represented, and its plane representation, increases from the centre to the circumference of the projection.

The same is true of the stereographic projection, but with this difference, that the distortion in the representation of the figure of any portion of the spherical surfaces proceeds in a contrary direction: in the former case, the degrees of longitude and latitude are gradually contracted from the centre to the circumference; but in the latter, they are enlarged.

In the stereographic projection, the projecting point, or point of view, is the pole of the circle on which the projection is made; and in the orthographic, it may be supposed in the axis, and at a very great, or rather indefinitely great, distance. It is this change of position of the point of view that produces the change in the direction in which the degrees of latitude or longitude are contracted. Hence it may be supposed, that, by taking a point of view at some finite distance greater than the radius of the sphere, a perspective representation will be obtained, in which the degrees in the representation will be nearly equal, and the deviation from equality in the representation of equal portions of the spherical surface in some measure corrected.

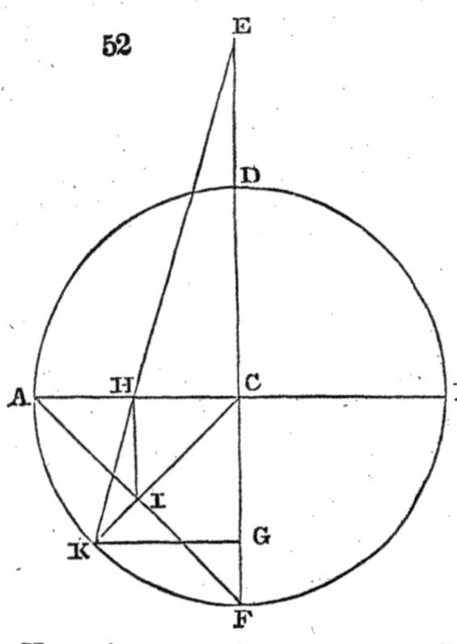


Let A D B (*fig.* 52.) be a section of the sphere by a plane passing through E, the point of view, and C the centre; draw the diameter F D to pass through E, and draw A C B perpendicular to D F. Since the whole quadrant A F is to be projected into the radius A C, if it be possible to make the representations of equal portions of it nearly equal, its halves A K and K F may be assumed as represented by A H and H C, halves of the radius: therefore, a line drawn from K to E must bisect the radius in H. This determines D E, *the distance of the projecting point, to be equal to* K G, *a perpendicular from the middle of the quadrant.*

To prove this geometrical proposition, draw A F and K C intersecting in I, and join H I. Then A I=I F and A I : I F : : A H : H C; therefore H I is parallel to C F,: hence, K I : I C : : K H : H E : : G C : C E. Now, K I=F G and I C=G C; therefore F G : G C : : G C : C E: hence F G·C E=G $C^2$=K $G^2$=F G·G D; therefore C E=G D, and, taking away the line C D common to both, D E is equal to C G or to K G.

Hence it appears that the distance D E is the sine of 45°; and therefore nearly 71 of such parts as the radius C A contains 100. This projection was first suggested by M. Delahire, and is now commonly called the Globular projection. If we suppose the quadrant A F divided into ten equal parts, then the projections of the arcs of 9°, reckoning from F to A, will be as in this table, in which the radius C A is supposed to be 10.

| Arc. | Representation. | Arc. | Representation. |
|---|---|---|---|
| 0°... 9° | .991 | 45°... 54° | 1.017 |
| 9 ... 18 | .994 | 54 ... 63 | 1.020 |
| 18 ... 27 | .999 | 63 ... 72 | 1.015 |
| 27 ... 36 | 1.004 | 72 ... 81 | .997 |
| 36 ... 45 | 1.013 | 81 ... 90 | .950 |

From this table it appears, that the approximation to equality in the projection of equal arcs of a circle perpendicular to the plane of projection is considerable.

According to the principles of perspective, in this projection the circles of the sphere will be represented by ellipses; and they have been so delineated in two hemispheres, projected, drawn, and beautifully engraved by Mr. Joseph Lowry, of London. He has placed London at the centre of the northern hemisphere, and instead of .707, Delahire's distance of the projecting point, he has made it .68 of the radius.

In general, however, the projection is made on a meridian, and the circles of the sphere are represented by circles, and without any regard to the distance of a point of view. Also, the degrees of longitude on the equator, and of latitude on a meridian, are made all equal. With these simplifications, the meridians and parallels on a hemisphere of the earth's surface may be represented by the following construction:—

Let us suppose the parallels of latitude to be traced through every tenth degree, and that the meridians are to be an hour from each other.

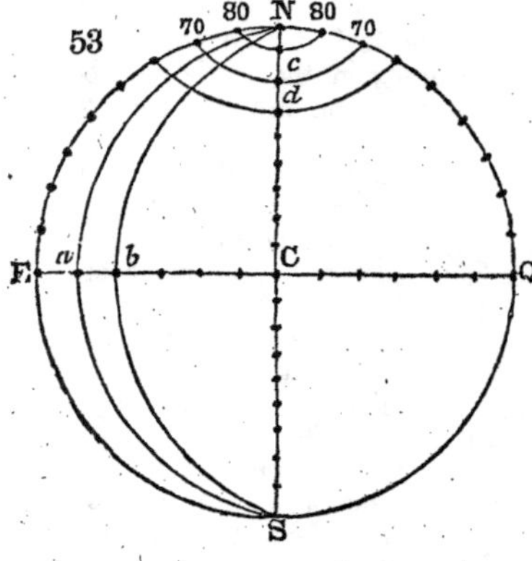


Describe a circle, E N Q S (*fig.* 53.), for the representation of the meridian. Draw the diameters E Q, N S perpendicular to each other; one, E Q, to represent the equator, and the other, N S, the meridian, which is 90° from that on which the projection is made; N being the north, and S the south pole.

Divide the quadrants E N, Q N, and the radius C N, each into nine equal parts; let N 80, 80 70, &c. be the equal divisions of the quadrants, and N *c*, *c d*, &c. the equal divisions of the radius: describe a circle through the three points 80, *c*, 80, and it will be the representation of the parallel of 80° of latitude; in like manner a circle described through the points 70, *d*, 70 will represent the parallel of 70°; the remaining parallels, the tropics and polar circles, on both sides of E Q, the equator, are to be found in the same manner.

Next for the meridians: divide the radii C E, C Q each into six equal parts at the points *a*, *b*, &c.: describe circles through the points N *a* S, N *b* S, &c. and these will be the representations of the meridians, any one of which, in laying down the positions of places by their latitude and longitude, may be assumed as the first meridian.

## II. CONSTRUCTION OF MAPS BY DEVELOPEMENT.

The three methods of projection which have been explained are usually employed in the representation of a hemisphere, but are seldom used in delineating the geographical features of a single country. For these, the method of *developement* is commonly employed.

A perfect geographical representation of a country should represent all its parts in just proportion, and should exhibit its true figure. This is exactly done on the sphere; but it can only be nearly accomplished on a plane surface.

The purposes of civil government require maps that give the true figure and dimensions of territory. Military affairs require such as give correct distances; and navigation demands the exact bearing of one place from another. Ordinary maps fulfil approximately the two first purposes. The last is completely satisfied by a map of a peculiar construction, called Mercator's chart; but this is not immediately applicable to the other purposes.

It is a known property of a cone that its curve surface can be expanded into a plane: hence any figure delineated on it can always be exhibited exactly in all its dimensions on a plane surface. Now, a part of the surface of a sphere contained between two parallels of latitude, not very remote, will not differ much from the surface of a frustum of a cone that touches the sphere in the parallel midway between them; and this will also be true if it pass along the chord, or if it pass partly within and partly without the sphere, cutting it between the middle and extreme parallels: in each case the length of the slant side of the frustum must be supposed equal to the length of the meridian between the extreme parallels. On this principle, different constructions have been given for representing the surface of a sphere on a plane.

### 1. *Conical Developement.*

Let P A Q (*fig.* 54.) be a section of the meridian, P Q the axis, C the centre, E C the radius of the equator, B D any arc of the meridian, and A the middle point between B and D: draw the tangent A O, meeting the axis in O. Suppose now the plane figure O A E to revolve about the axis P Q; the semicircle P A Q will generate a sphere, and the tangent O A will generate the surface of a cone which touches the sphere in A. The points B, A, D will generate the parallels of latitude B *b*, A H *a*, D *d*, of which the middle parallel A H *a* will be a section of the cone perpendicular to its axis.

Take H any point in the parallel A H *a*; draw F H to its centre, and join H O. Conceive now the cone to be expanded into a plane, and that the surface O A H becomes, by developement, O′ A′ H′. The expansion of A H, the arc of the parallel of latitude on the sphere, whose radius is F H, the cosine of the latitude, will now become A′ H′, an arc of a circle whose radius is A′ O′ = A O, the cotangent of the latitude of the parallel.

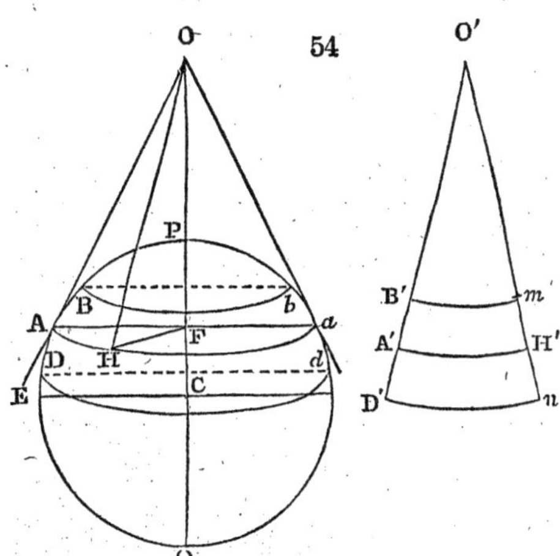


In O′ A′ take A′ B′ and A′ D′, each equal to A B or A D, and with the radii O′ B′, O′ D′ describe arcs B′ *m*, D′ *n*. The plane figure B′ *m n* D′ may now be taken as nearly equal to the spherical surface bounded by meridians passing through A and H, and the portions of the parallels B *b*, A *a* intercepted between them: and any tract of country delineated on the sphere may be nearly shown by a delineation on the plane; the approximation being the more accurate as the breadth of the spherical zone is less.

Let the middle latitude E A and the angle A F H, or breadth in longitude of the spherical surface, be supposed given, to determine the radius O′ A′ and the angle O′ A′ H′ Because the middle latitude is known, its cotangent O H is given in parts of the radius by the trigonometrical tables, or it may be expressed in minutes of latitude, by considering that half the circumference (to radius = 1) is 3.1416; therefore, the radius in minutes will be expressed.

$$\frac{60 \times 180}{3\ 1416} = 3437.7'.$$

Hence O′ A′, the radius of the middle parallel in the developement, will be expressed in minutes of latitude by

$$3437.7' \times \text{cot. middle lat.}$$

Next, to find the angle A′ O′ H′. The arc A H on the sphere and the arc A′ H′ on the plane being equal; by the principles of geometry, the angle A F H will be to the angle A′ O′ H′ as A′ O′ to A F: now, A′ O′ = A O is the cotangent of the middle latitude, and A F is its cosine, and the cotangent is to the cosine as radius to the sine; therefore, putting L to denote the degrees of longitude between two meridians on the sphere, the angle A′ O′ H′, contained by the straight lines which represent them in the developement, will be in degrees

$$L \times \text{Sine middle lat.}$$

The angle O′, and the lines O′ A′, A′ B′, A′ D′, in the developement, are now known; it remains only to divide B′ D′, the representation of the arc of the meridian, and B′ *m*, D′ *n*, the parallels of latitude, into equal parts to form scales of latitude and longitude: then, circles described about O′ as a centre, through the proper divisions of B′ D′, will form the parallels of latitude; and straight lines drawn joining corresponding degrees on the extreme parallels B′ *m*, D′ *n*, will represent the meridians on the map; which is now ready for the delineation of the geographical features of the tract it is to represent. This is the way in which the common maps are constructed.

*Example.* Let it be required to construct a map to comprehend the British islands, which extend from 50° to about 61° of north latitude, and from 2° east to 11° west, about 13° of longitude. The middle latitude is 55° 30′, of which the cotangent in the tables is .68728 and sine = .82413. From these *data*, O′ A′, the radius of the middle parallel, is 3437.7 × .68728 = 2362′.7: the length of the arc B D is 11° = 660′; therefore, A′ B′ = A′ D′, its half, is 330, and hence

$$O\,B = 2362.7 \times 330 = 2692'.7$$
$$O\,A = 2362.7 - 330 = 2032'.7.$$

The number of degrees of longitude (L) in this case is 13°; therefore, angle A′ O′ H′ = 13° × .82413 = 10° 42.

Knowing now the radii O′ B′, O′ D′, and the angle O′, we can find the arcs B′ *m*, D′ *n*; or we can find their chords.

Thus we have,

$$\text{chord of arc } B'\,m = 2\,O\,B\,\text{Sin.}\,\tfrac{1}{2}\,O' = 375'.6.$$
$$\text{chord of arc } D'\,n = 2\,O\,D\,\text{Sin.}\,\tfrac{1}{2}\,O' = 502'.1.$$

We have now obtained the chords of 13° of longitude on the extreme parallels, and the meridians which form their extremities in minutes of a degree of the meridian; also the radii of the parallels of latitude: with these, the intelligent student of geography will find no difficulty in constructing a map of Britain.

### 2. *Murdoch's Conical Developement.*

There have been various modifications of the conical developement: of these, one was given by the Rev. Patrick Murdoch, in the Lond. Phil. Trans. 1758. Let M denote the arc of the meridian which is to be represented in a map: he proposed to make O′ A′, the radius of the middle parallel, equal to

$$\frac{\text{chord of arc M}}{\text{arc M}} \times \text{Cot. mid. lat.}$$

the cotangent being supposed expressed by the radius of the sphere. The remainder of the construction is the same as the ordinary conical projection.

By Murdoch's method, the surface of the developement is exactly equal to the spherical surface which it represents, and the cone passes through points of the meridian between the middle latitudes and the extremities of the projected arc, its side being parallel to the tangent at the middle latitude.

### 3. *De Lisle's Conical Developement.*

The astronomer De Lisle employed the conical projection in constructing a general chart of the Russian empire, which extended from 40° to 70° of north latitude. He, however, supposed the cone to enter the sphere so as to cut it in two parallels midway between the mean and extreme parallels: these, in the developement, had the same dimensions as the corresponding circles of the sphere, and its whole extent differed but little from that of the tract it was meant to represent; because the excess at the two extremities of the chart was compensated, at least in part, by the opposite error in the middle.

### 4. *Euler's Method.*

Euler was also occupied with this projection: but he substituted for the determination of parallels which should be common with the sphere, that of the point of concourse of straight lines which represent the meridians, and of the angle which they make when they contain one degree of longitude. His calculations rest on the following conditions:—1. That the errors are equal at the northern and southern extremities of the map. 2. That they are also equal to the greatest of those towards its middle. Hence he concluded that the point of concourse of the meridians should be situated beyond the pole by a quantity equal to 5° of latitude, and that the angle of two consecutive meridians should be 48° 44′.

### 5. *Flamsteed's Projection.*

The English astronomer Flamsteed, in constructing his celestial atlas, developed all the parallels of latitude on the sphere into straight lines, and also one of the meridians; *viz.* tha which passes through the middle of the chart: then the parallels, which are all perpendicular to that meridian, are exactly of the same length as on the globe, and consequently the degrees of longitude on the parallels will be shown in their just proportion, that is, as the cosines of the latitude. If, now, the parallels on the map be divided into equal parts, just as the parallels on the globe are, by the meridians, curve lines traced through corresponding points of division will represent the meridians.

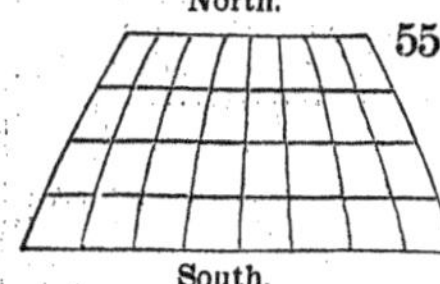


The adjoining figure (*fig.* 55.) exhibits a sketch of a map of this construction.

According to Flamsteed's method, any distance on the map in the direction of the parallels is everywhere equal to the corresponding distance on the globe; but the configuration of places near the extremities is considerably distorted by the obliquity of the meridians to the parallels, so that the spherical quadrilaterals, the sides of which cross at right angles, are in the map represented by mixtilineal trapeziums, of which the angles are very unequal. Flamsteed employed this projection in representing the positions of the stars; but it is also employed in geography, particularly in delineating countries which extend on both sides of the equator: Africa, for instance.

### 6. *Modification of Flamsteed's Projection.*

There is a modification of Flamsteed's projection (*fig.* 56.), which has been extensively employed, and which deserves particular attention, because it corrects, in part, the defect of the obliquity of the meridians. This substitutes arcs of concentric circles for the straight lines, which he proposed to represent the parallels of latitude. The common centre of the circles is in a straight line drawn through the middle of the map as an axis, and which represents a meridian; and its position in the axis ought to be such, that the obliquity of the angles made at the intersection of the curves which represent the meridians, and the circles which represent the parallels, should be as little as possible.

The position of the centre is so assumed, that the radius of the middle parallel of latitude is equal to its cotangent; and in this the modified projection of Flamsteed agrees with the ordinary conical projection.

To exemplify this construction, let it be proposed to describe the parallels and meridians for a map of Europe, which shall extend from 35° north latitude to 70°.

Let us, as before, assume a minute of a degree of latitude for the unit of the scale from which the measures of the lines are to be taken. Therefore, as before, the radius of the sphere, of which a portion of the spherical surface is to be represented, will be 3437.7 minutes.

Let O A C B (*fig.* 56.) be assumed as the axis or middle meridian of the map; and let A D, B E be the halves of the part of the extreme parallels of latitude to be represented, and C the point in which the middle parallel (52° 30′) cuts the axis; also, let O be the centre of the circles, arcs of which are to represent the parallels.

By the nature of the projection, O C must be taken equal to the cotangent of 52° 30′; this, to radius = 1, is .76733, and to a radius expressed by minutes, we have

$$O\,C = .76733 \times 3437.7 = 2637'.8.$$

Having found O C, the radius of the middle parallel, the radius of any other parallel may be found by adding or subtracting its distance in minutes of the meridian from the middle parallel. Thus we find the radii of parallels differing by 5°, as in the annexed table:—

| Parallel. | Radius. | Parallel. | Radius. |
|---|---|---|---|
| 35° | 3687.8 | 55 | 2487.8 |
| 40 | 3387.8 | 60 | 2187.8 |
| 45 | 3087.8 | 65 | 1887.8 |
| 50 | 2787.8 | 70 | 1587.8 |

Next, we must find the points in which some one meridian cuts all the parallels. We shall suppose it to be 30° of longitude from O C, the axis of the map.

From the nature of the developement, the arc of longitude on any parallel in the map is equal to the arc of the parallel on the sphere which it represents. This has to an arc of the same number of degrees of the meridian the proportion of the cosine of the latitude of the parallel to the radius. Therefore, an arc of 30° = 1800′ on a parallel whose latitude is L will be in minutes,

$$1800 \times \text{cosine L}.$$

By this formula, the lengths of the arcs may be easily computed by a table of logarithmic sines; but, for a practical construction, it will be more convenient to have the chords of the arcs. Now, in arcs not exceeding 30°, the arc diminished by a fraction whose numerator is the cube of the arc, and denominator 24 times the square of the radius, is very near equal to the chord; that is, $a$ being put for any arc, and $r$ its radius,

$$\text{chord } a = a - \frac{a^3}{24r^2} \text{ nearly.}$$

From this formula, the chords may easily be deduced from the arcs.

As an example, let the arc of 30° of longitude, and its chord on the parallel 35°, be required. For facility of calculation, we shall use logarithms.

| Calculation of Arc. | Logarithms. | Calculation of Log. of $24r^2$. | Logarithms. |
|---|---|---|---|
| 30°=1800′ | 3.25527 | Radius of arc 687.8 | 3.56677 |
| Cosine 35° | 9.91336 | | 2 |
| Arc $a$=1474′.5 | 3.16863 | Log. of square of radius | 7.13354 |
| | 3 | 24 | 1.38021 |
| From log. of cube of arc | 9.50589 | Logarithm $24r^2$ | 8.51375 |
| Subtract Log. $24r^2$ | 8.51375 | | |
| Differ. of arc and chord 9′.8 | 099214 | | |

| Par. of Lat. | Arcs. | Chord of Arc. |
|---|---|---|
| 35 | 1474.5 | 1464.7 |
| 40 | 1378.9 | 1369.4 |
| 45 | 1272.8 | 1263.8 |
| 50 | 1157.0 | 1148.7 |
| 55 | 1032.4 | 1025.0 |
| 60 | 900.0 | 893.6 |
| 65 | 760.7 | 755.5 |
| 70 | 615.6 | 611.8 |

Thus, by an easy logarithmic calculation, we have found the arc to be 1474′.5, and its excess above the chord to be 9′.8. Therefore, the chord is 1464′.7 of the meridian. By a like process, we have found the arcs of 30° of longitude, and their chords on the parallels to every fifth degree, as in this table.

Having now found the chord of 30° of longitude on the parallel of 35° to be 1464′.7 of the meridian, we must, with compasses, place that distance taken from a scale of minutes from B to E, and to $e$; and the points E, $e$ will be in the representations of meridians 30° of longitude from the axis on each side. In the same way, the intersections of these meridians with the other parallels are found. Curve lines E D, $e$ $d$ must now be traced through all the intersections, and these will be the meridians on the map.

The intersections of the intermediate meridians with the parallels may be found by dividing each parallel into thirty equal parts, from the axis both ways; and as many meridian lines may be exhibited as may be thought necessary. In the figure here given, they are traced to every tenth degree.

If the map is to extend further than 30° on each side of its middle meridian, the divisions of the parallels may be repeated on each, and meridians drawn.

This construction of a map is memorable, because it was adopted by the general *depôt* of war of France, about the year 1803, as the groundwork of a system of geographical charts which should exhibit the French original territory, as well as the additions which had been made, and were expected to be made, by conquest or negotiation.

### *Developement of the Curve Surface of a Cylinder.*

The mariner, in navigating a ship between remote points on the globe, directs his course by the *compass;* steering as nearly as possible always in the same direction, supposing there are no obstacles to prevent him. If the place from which he sets out, and that of his destination, be due north and south from each other, the ship's path will evidently be a great circle, *viz.* the meridian passing through them. If, again, they have the same latitude, he must sail on a parallel of latitude; that is, his course must be due east or west. But if the places differ both in latitude and longitude, then it becomes a question, what is the nature of the line on the globe along which a ship must sail, with her head always in the same direction, as indicated by the compass, so as to pass from one to the other?

The line in question, which is called a *rhumb line* or *loxodromic line*, has manifestly this property,—*it cuts all the meridians on the globe at the same angle.* By this property, a ship sailing along it will move always in the same direction, as shown by a compass: but it will not be a great circle; for the equator is the only great circle that cuts all the meridians at the same angle; and hence it appears that the line on the globe by which a ship passes from one place to another is never the shortest possible, except when they are on the same meridian, or on the equator.

Supposing a navigator had a perfect delineation of the earth on a sphere, it is by no means evident how he should find the course he ought to steer to reach a remote port. By due consideration, however, he would see that the path must be a spiral. It would also be represented by a spiral curve on a map, formed by the developement of a cone; but navigators required charts before the theory of such curves was understood; therefore at that period his art must have been imperfect.

The wants of the navigator, accordingly, gave rise to the construction of a chart, in which the meridians and parallels were straight lines; and in this the developement of the curve surface of a cylinder was employed. Let us conceive that a zone of the earth's surface, of no great extent in latitude, is inscribed in or circumscribed about a right cylinder, whose axis coincides with that of the globe: the planes of the meridians will cut the curve surface of the cylinder in straight lines, parallel to the axis; and the planes of the parallels will cut it in sections perpendicular to the axis, which will be circles equal to the base of the cylinder. But in supposing the surface of the cylinder developed into a plane, these circles will become straight lines, perpendicular to the meridians. This developement has received the name of the *plane chart:* its invention is attributed to Henry, son of John, king of Portugal. This kind of chart has nothing but its simplicity to recommend it; for the degrees of longitude have, indeed, their just proportion to the degrees of latitude in the parallel common to the cylinder and sphere, but in no other parallel.

In the developement of a cylinder circumscribing the whole sphere, the area of any zone in the sphere is exactly equal to that of its representation in the chart; and indeed the same equality may be observed in all cases, by a proper assumption of a parallel of latitude as the base of the cylinder. The developement, however, has this great fault,—the degrees of longitude always err in excess towards the north and in defect towards the south of the mean parallel, which is assumed as the base of the cylinder.

There is a construction, described in books of navigation under the name of a *plane chart*, the principle of which is somewhat different from that just described. In the seaman's plane chart the meridians are parallel straight lines, and so also are the parallels of latitude; and both are so laid down that a degree of latitude and a degree of longitude are equal in all latitudes. It may easily be conceived how incompetent such a representation must be to the purposes of navigation or geography.

### *Mercator's Chart.*

The utter inadequacy of the old plane charts to the wants of geography and navigation induced ingenious men to consider whether a chart might not be so constructed as to represent the meridians and parallels by straight lines, and at the same time readily show the true bearings of places from one another. The first that gave a true solution—at least an approximate one—of this important problem was Gerard Mercator, who was born at Ruremond, in Upper Guelderland, in the year 1512, and published a chart in 1556, wherein the rhumbs, which on the globe are spirals, were represented by straight lines, as in the plane chart; and so also were the meridians and parallels. It is not known by what principle Mercator constructed his chart; it has been supposed that he observed on a globe furnished with rhumbs what meridians the rhumbs passed in each degree of latitude: it is certain he did not know the true principles of the construction; for these were first found by Edward Wright, of Caius College, in Cambridge, who communicated his discovery to his friend Thomas Blundeville, with a short table, showing the correct distances of the parallels of latitude from the equator, which was published in 1594 by Blundeville, among his *Exercises.* The truth of the divisions of Mercator's chart was then tried by the numbers given by Wright, and they were found to be inaccurate; hence it appears that Mercator did not understand the principles of the map bearing his name, and that this important invention is due to Wright, who explained it himself, in his treatise entitled *The Correction of certain Errors in Navigation*, published 1599, but written many years before.

Although Wright's numbers were sufficiently correct for all nautical purposes, and might be carried to any degree of accuracy, yet, in the progress of mathematical science, an improvement was made in his theory. Napier's invention of logarithms had proved an inestimable advantage to navigation and geography, by shortening calculations: this, however, was not the only advantage that the navigator derived from the invention; for, about the year 1645, Henry Bond showed that the division of the meridian in Wright's chart was altogether analogous to the logarithmic tangents of half the complements of the latitudes, and might be expressed by them. He seems to have found this by chance: such accidental discoveries are, however, never made but by men of genius. He could not demonstrate his important theorem. At last James Gregory proved its truth in his *Exercitationes Geometricæ*, published in 1668. The construction of the chart was now made perfect.

The invention of Mercator's chart, one of the most important in the 16th century, affords a notable instance of the slowness with which men adopt improvements in science. Although designed for the use of sailors, it was at first by no means generally used by them. William Burrough, a celebrated navigator, who had entered on his profession at the age of fifteen, and risen by his merit to the rank of controller of Queen Elizabeth's navy, objected to its usefulness. He said—"By Mercator's augmenting his degrees of latitude towards the poles, the same is more fit for such to behold as study in cosmography, by reading authors upon the

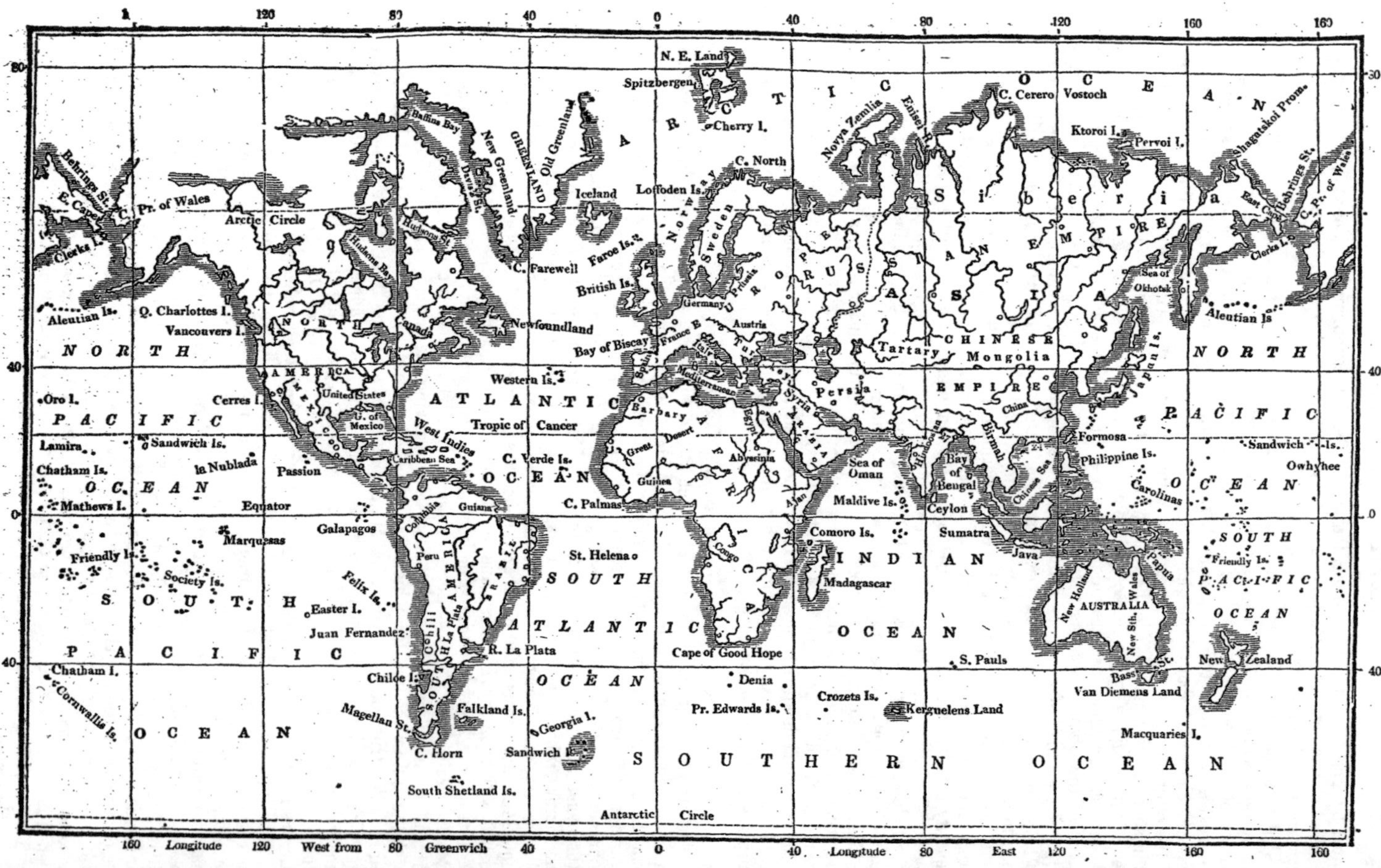
ARCTIC OCEAN
NORTH PACIFIC OCEAN
SOUTH PACIFIC OCEAN
ATLANTIC OCEAN
SOUTH ATLANTIC OCEAN
INDIAN OCEAN
SOUTHERN OCEAN
N. E. Land
Spitzbergen
Cherry I.
C. North
Loffoden Is.
Iceland
Faroe Is.
British Is.
Bay of Biscay
Old Greenland
GREENLAND
New Greenland
Davis St.
Baffins Bay
Hudsons Bay
C. Farewell
Newfoundland
Western Is.
Tropic of Cancer
C. Verde Is.
C. Palmas
St. Helena
R. La Plata
Falkland Is.
Georgia I.
Sandwich Is.
South Shetland Is.
C. Horn
Magellan St.
Chiloe I.
Juan Fernandez
Easter I.
Felix Is.
Galapagos
Passion
Equator
Marquesas
Society Is.
Friendly Is.
Chatham I.
Cornwallis Is.
Mathews I.
Chatham Is.
Lamira
Oro I.
Aleutian Is.
Behrings St.
E. Cape
Clerks I.
Pr. of Wales
Q. Charlottes I.
Vancouvers I.
Cerres I.
la Nublada
Sandwich Is.
Arctic Circle
Antarctic Circle
West Indies
Caribbean Sea
G. of Mexico
United States
NORTH AMERICA
MEXICO
SOUTH AMERICA
Cape of Good Hope
Pr. Edwards Is.
Denia
Crozets Is.
Kerguelens Land
S. Pauls
Madagascar
Comoro Is.
Maldive Is.
Ceylon
Sumatra
Java
Bay of Bengal
Sea of Oman
Persia
Syria
ARABIA
Egypt
Abyssinia
AFRICA
Congo
Guinea
Great Desert
Barbary
Mediterranean
Turkey
Austria
Germany
France
Spain
Italy
Sweden
Norway
Prussia
EUROPE
RUSSIA
ASIA
Siberia
RUSSIAN EMPIRE
Tartary
Mongolia
CHINESE EMPIRE
China
Chinese Sea
Birmah
Formosa
Philippine Is.
Japan Is.
Carolinas
Papua
New Holland
AUSTRALIA
New Sth. Wales
Bass St.
Van Diemens Land
Macquaries I.
New Zealand
Friendly Is.
Owhyhee
Sandwich Is.
Aleutian Is.
East Cape
Clerks I.
Behrings St.
Shelagskoi Prom.
C. Pr. of Wales
Sea of Okhotsk
Pervoi I.
Ktoroi I.
Vostoch
C. Cerero
Eniesei R.
Novya Zemlia
160 Longitude 120 West from 80 Greenwich 40
0
40 Longitude 80 East 120
160
160

land, than to be used in navigation at the sea." It is curious to observe that logarithms, the other grand auxiliary of navigation, met with a like reception from the German mathematicians that were somewhat advanced in years.

Mercator's chart may be produced by developement, as follows:—Conceive that a sphere with the meridians and parallels and countries delineated on it, is inclosed in a hollow cylinder, and that the axis of the sphere coincides with that of the cylinder. Imagine now that the sphere is expanded in its dimensions, just as a soap-bubble is produced by blowing air into it, or as a bladder would swell in all directions by inflation, the parts always stretching uniformly; the meridians will lengthen in the same proportion as the parallels, till every point of the expanding spherical surface comes into contact with the concave surface of the cylinder: the meridians will at last become straight lines, and the parallels, circles on that surface; the former in the direction of its length, and the latter parallel to its base, which is the equator. Suppose now the surface of the cylinder to be cut open along one of the meridians, and spread into a plane; the surface thus produced will be Mercator's chart.

Mercator's chart is constructed, then, on the following geometrical principles:—1. The meridians are parallel straight lines at equal distances, for equal differences of longitude; and the parallels of latitude are also straight lines, perpendicular to the meridians. 2. Supposing a meridian on the globe be divided into minutes of a degree; one of these, at any parallel of latitude, will be to a minute of longitude taken on that parallel in the proportion of the radius of the equator to the radius of the parallel, which is the cosine of the latitude; that is, as the secant of the latitude to radius. Now the same holds true in the chart; that is, a minute of the meridian, at any parallel, has to a minute of longitude in that parallel the proportion of the secant of the latitude of the parallel to radius.

By the first of these properties a minute of longitude in the map is represented by a line of the same length in every parallel; therefore, by the second the minutes of the meridian will be represented by lines which go on increasing from the equator towards the poles. From this it follows that, if a minute on the equator be taken as the unit of a scale, and that unit be considered as the radius of a circle, then the representation of a minute of the meridian, at any latitude, will be expressed by the number in the trigonometrical tables which is the secant of that latitude. Thus it appears that, while the degrees of longitude on the equator form a scale of which the divisions are all equal in the map, the degrees of latitude marked on a meridian form a scale of which the divisions go on increasing from the equator towards both poles, each being the sum of the secants of all the minutes in the degree.

The numbers which result from the addition of the secants of 1 minute, 2 minutes, and so on to the last minute of any arc of the meridian, reckoned from the equator, are given in books on navigation. They form the table of *meridional parts*, and serve for laying down the position of any place in the chart. The addition of the secants is, however, only an approximation to the true length of the enlarged meridian in the chart; but it is sufficiently near the truth for nautical or geographical purposes. In strictness, also, it must be considered that the earth is not a sphere, but a spheroid, and on that account allowance ought to be made for its compression at the poles. The following short table shows the length of the enlarged meridian, both on the sphere and the spheroid, to every fifth degree of latitude. The compression is assumed to be $\frac{320}{321}$.

| Lat. | Meridional Parts. | | Lat. | Meridional Parts. | |
|---|---|---|---|---|---|
| | Sphere. | Spheroid. | | Sphere. | Spheroid. |
| 0° | 0.00 | 0.00 | 50° | 3474.47 | 3457.39 |
| 5 | 300.38 | 298.37 | 55 | 3967.97 | 3950.57 |
| 10 | 603.07 | 599.01 | 60 | 4527.37 | 4509.41 |
| 15 | 910.46 | 905.28 | 65 | 5178.81 | 5159.93 |
| 20 | 1225.14 | 1217.69 | 70 | 5965.92 | 5945.51 |
| 25 | 1549.99 | 1541.17 | 75 | 6970.34 | 6951.07 |
| 30 | 1888.38 | 1877.99 | 80 | 8375.29 | 8352.24 |
| 35 | 2244.29 | 2232.09 | 85 | 10764.62 | 10741.75 |
| 40 | 2622.69 | 2608.35 | 90 | Infinite. | Infinite. |
| 45 | 3029.94 | 3014.41 | | | |

To construct Mercator's chart (*fig.* 57.), draw two straight lines W E, N S at right angles to each other, intersecting in C; of these W E is to represent the equator, and N S a meridian, in the middle of the chart: from any convenient scale lay off equal parts along the equator, from C both ways, to represent degrees of longitude, and each of which should, if there be room, contain 60 subdivisions for minutes.

Assuming the equator as a scale of minutes, lay off from C, north and south on the middle meridian, the number of minutes in the enlarged meridian, corresponding to each degree of latitude as shown by a table of meridional parts, of which that just given is an abridgement.

Draw straight lines through every fifth or every tenth degree of the equator and divided meridian, and perpendicular to them. The perpendiculars to the equator will be *meridians*, and the lines parallel to it *parallels of latitude*.

FIG. 57.

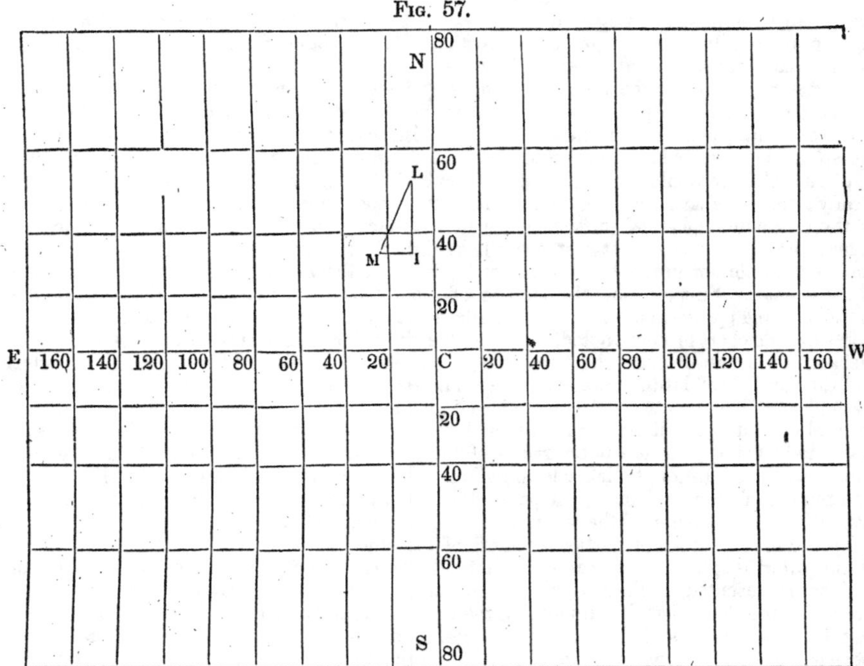


To put any place in its proper position on the chart, assume some one meridian for the first, and lay off from its intersection with the equator, and along it in the proper direction, the longitude of the place in minutes; draw a line through the point thus found perpendicular to the equator: this will be the meridian of the place.

On this meridian lay off the latitude, as shown by the table of meridional parts; and the point thus determined will be the true position of the place in the chart.

To find the bearing of one point from another, or *course* in which a ship ought to sail in passing from one to the other, draw a straight line joining the two points, and the angle which that line makes with the meridians is the *course* or bearing.

Thus, if L be the Lizard Point on the chart, and M the east end of the Island of Madeira, draw L I parallel to the meridian N S, and the angle I L M will be the course on which a ship ought to steer from the Lizard to reach Madeira.

The course may be found by a trigonometrical calculation, by considering that the *meridional difference of latitude* of the two places (as given by the table of meridional parts), and the difference of longitude in minutes, are the sides of a right-angled triangle, of which the line joining the places is the hypotenuse, and the course one of the acute angles, viz. that made by the meridian and line joining the places.

Again, the distance of the places, measured on the rhumb line passing through them, may also be found by trigonometry. It is the hypotenuse of a right-angled triangle, of which the *proper difference* of latitude (not the meridional difference) is one side, and the course the adjacent angle.

These properties of the chart apply alike to the bearings and distances of all places on the globe measured on rhumb lines. The bearing and distances of London, Edinburgh, and Dublin, for instance, from each, may be found in this way from a table of meridional parts and their known latitudes and longitudes.

It is evident that Mercator's chart does not serve well to show the figure of the countries on the globe, nor their relative magnitudes. These are purposes, however, which it is not intended to serve; but it does serve perfectly the purposes for which it was first constructed, and which, before its invention, were a *desideratum* in geography.

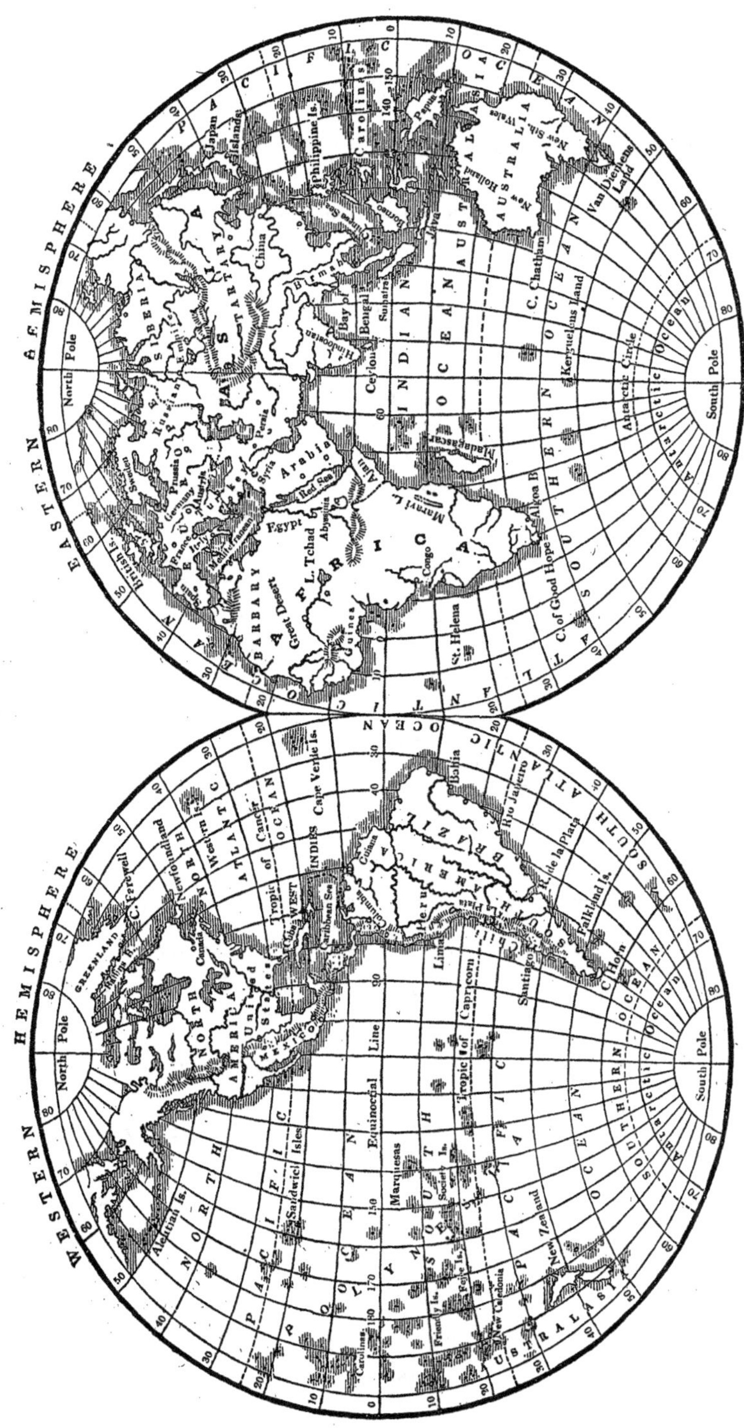
EASTERN HEMISPHERE
North Pole
South Pole
SIBERIA
Russian Empire
Sweden
Prussia
Germany
Austria
France
Italy
Spain
British Is.
Mediterranean
Turkey
Persia
Arabia
Syria
Red Sea
Egypt
Abyssinia
BARBARY
Great Desert
L. Tchad
Guinea
Congo
AFRICA
St. Helena
C. of Good Hope
Algoa B.
Madagascar
INDIAN OCEAN
Ceylon
Bay of Bengal
Hindoostan
Sumatra
Java
Borneo
China
Philippine Is.
Japan Islands
Papua
New Holland
AUSTRALIA
New South Wales
Van Diemens Land
Kerguelens Land
Antarctic Circle
SOUTHERN OCEAN
WESTERN HEMISPHERE
GREENLAND
C. Farewell
Newfoundland
Canada
NORTH AMERICA
United States
MEXICO
Cuba
WEST INDIES
Caribbean Sea
Tropic of Cancer
Cape Verde Is.
NORTH ATLANTIC OCEAN
Columbia
Guiana
BRAZIL
Bahia
Rio Janeiro
Peru
Lima
Chili
Santiago
R. de la Plata
Falkland Is.
C. Horn
Tropic of Capricorn
Equinoctial Line
SOUTH ATLANTIC
Aleutian Is.
Sandwich Isles
Marquesas
Society Is.
Friendly Is.
New Caledonia
New Zealand
Carolinas
NORTH PACIFIC OCEAN
SOUTHERN OCEAN

# BOOK II

# GEOLOGICAL PRINCIPLES.

Geology is that branch of natural history which treats of the atmosphere, the waters of the globe, and of the mountain-rocks of which the earth is composed. No department of natural history abounds more in important facts and interesting conclusions; and therefore we shall lay before our readers a short view, 1st, Of the natural history of the atmosphere, or *meteorology;* 2dly, Of the natural history of the waters of the globe, or *hydrology;* and, 3dly, Of the solid materials of which the earth is composed, or *geognosy.*

---

## CHAPTER I.

### METEOROLOGY.

This beautiful department of science makes us acquainted with all the properties and relations of the *atmosphere* which surrounds our planet. Although in general but little studied by geologists, a knowledge of it is, nevertheless, most useful in a geological point of view, of which the details we shall now lay before our readers will afford ample proof.

#### Sect. I.—*Pressure, Height, Form, and Temperature of the Atmosphere.*

The air in which we breathe, with the clouds and vapours floating in it, surrounds the earth on all sides to an unknown height, and forms a moveable envelope denominated the *atmosphere.* The human species, and other land animals, being thus entirely immersed in this fluid, may with some propriety be said to inhabit an ocean as really as the fishes which live in the great deep. But the latter have the advantage in being able to mount up, remain, or descend at pleasure in their element: whereas, without some additional aid, we must content ourselves with the more humble allotment of remaining on the bottom of our ocean. The winged tribes, doubtless, have the power of ascending to great heights; still they can never reach the summit. There is nothing more essential to the existence or health of man himself, or of the various inferior animals and vegetables which live on our globe, than the air or atmosphere; nor has any agent a greater share in the innumerable changes which are daily taking place in the inanimate materials composing our planet. It is not wonderful, then, that the composition and properties of the atmosphere should have so often excited inquiry. To give an account of these, and of their relations to other bodies, particularly to the various substances which are diffused in the atmosphere, and really or apparently deposited from it, constitutes the science of meteorology. Whilst engaging in this task, so far as our limits permit, it will be fully as instructive, and scarcely more tedious, occasionally to introduce a very brief sketch of the mode in which some of the leading facts were first discovered; but there is reason to think that a few of the more obvious properties of air have been known, as it were instinctively, from the remotest antiquity.

That air is a body or substance possessing the essential properties of matter, appears from the resistance which it offers to the occupation of its place by other bodies. Thus, if an apparently empty glass jar be first inverted, and then immersed in a vessel of water, that liquid will only enter a very little way into the jar, the rest being occupied by the air. This familiar experiment shows that air is a body, by its resisting the entry of the water. At the same time it shows the air to be an elastic or compressible substance, otherwise it should have completely excluded the water. That it is a fluid is evident from the ease with which bodies move in it, from its pressing equally in every direction, and passing with great facility through extremely minute openings.

The ancients must have been aware of these properties, or at least of some of their practical applications, otherwise they could not have constructed their powerful air-guns, nor availed themselves of the principle of the diving-bell: for, in those early ages, the adventurers who dived in search of pearls, &c. were accustomed to hold large pots or kettles inverted on their heads. The air which these open vessels contained both excluded the water, and for a short time supported respiration; thus forming diving-bells in a portable shape. The ancients likewise, in some of their mechanical contrivances, availed themselves of that property of air by which it expands with heat and contracts with cold. It was on this principle that, in more modern times, Sanctorio constructed the air thermometer.

Weight and pressure are properties of the air as of all other bodies: it presses on the earth's surface, and on every other body with which it comes into contact. This was conjectured even by the ancients. But the effects which are now known to result from the weight and elasticity of the air were for a long time ascribed to a principle called nature's horror of a vacuum. So late as the beginning of the seventeenth century, it was generally believed, that the ascent of water in pumps was owing to this principle, and that by means of suction fluids might be raised to any height whatever. But Galileo, though still inclining to the old opinion, remarked that water did not rise in a common pump unless the sucker or bucket reached within 34 feet of its surface in the well. Hence he was forced to conjecture, that not the power of suction, but the pressure of the atmosphere on the surface of the well, was the cause of the water's ascent; that a column of water 34 feet high was a counterpoise to one of air on an equal base, but reaching to the top of the atmosphere; and that, for this reason, water could not follow the sucker any farther.

Torricelli, a disciple of Galileo, profited by this hint. It occurred to him that the same force which supported water to the height of 34 feet would sustain a column of any other fluid which weighed as much on an equal base; and therefore mercury, being 13.6 times as heavy as water, should only be suspended to the height of 29 or 30 inches. Accordingly, he took a glass tube from three to four feet long, and closed at one end; this he filled with mercury; then, stopping its mouth with his finger, he inverted the tube, and on re-opening its mouth in a vessel of quicksilver the result verified his expectation. The mercury, obeying the laws of hydrostatics, descended in the tube till the vertical column was about 30 inches above the level of the cistern, leaving the remaining space at the top empty or nearly a vacuum. Hence he inferred that it was only the weight or pressure of the atmosphere on the mercury in the cistern, which balanced the column in the tube. This is usually called the Toricellian experiment, and is the foundation of the barometer.

The mean pressure is everywhere the same at the level of the sea, and equal to about $14\frac{1}{2}$ lbs. on the square inch. It becomes less as the place is elevated above the sea, and greater if below its level. The pressure of the atmosphere, as measured by the mercurial column, varies somewhat at every place on the earth's surface. Generally speaking, its variations are greatest in the temperate zones, decreasing towards the equator and poles. The annual range rarely exceeds half an inch in the torrid zone. It is about two inches at London, and the same at St. Petersburg, but rather less at Melville Island. It nowhere exceeds $3\frac{1}{2}$ inches. The annual range is more considerable at the level of the sea than on mountains; and under the same latitude it is less, as the height of the place above the sea is greater. The barometer has a tendency to rise from 4 P. M. to 10 P. M.; to fall from 10 P. M. to 4 A. M.; to rise from 4 A. M. to 10 A. M.; and again to fall from 10 A. M. to 4 P. M. Different authors, however, differ a little both as to the hours and the amount of the diurnal variation, which appears to be greater as the latitude is lower. The barometer is likewise elevated a little at the quarters of the moon, and depressed at the new and full. The range of this instrument is greater in winter than in summer.

The barometer ranges higher in proportion as the weather is more serene and settled; calm weather, with a tendency to rain, depresses it; high winds have a similar effect. In extra-tropical climates, a fall in the barometer, with a change or rise of wind, is usually followed by rain.

The law which regulates the elasticity of the air formed the next important step, after the discovery of the pressure. Boyle in England, and Mariotte in France, discovered, much about the same time, that the temperature being the same, the pressure or elastic force of air is directly as its density, or inversely as the space it occupies. This law, though received as correct at the time of its discovery, continued to be suspected till within these few years. But Dulong and Petit have recently examined it through a wide range of temperature; Professor Oersted has tried it under a great variety of pressures; and within the limits of their experiments it was found to hold good.

The variable capacity for heat forms another property of air of no less importance, but which seems to have been little known or attended to till towards the end of the last century. When air undergoes a change of volume, it at the same time changes its capacity for heat; becoming hotter by compression, and colder by rarefaction. The want of acquaintance with this circumstance led Newton, and many others after him, into the mistake of concluding, that the particles of elastic fluids repel each other with forces inversely as their central distances; which cannot be the case if the capacity be affected, no matter in what manner or degree, by a change of density. But very extensive experiments, made by some of the most eminent scientific men in France, and repeated in England, are favourable to the idea that the particles of air observe the same law as magnetism and electricity, repelling each other with forces inversely as the *squares* of their distances.

There is a gradation of density in the air. Being, as already stated, a compressible body, it is obvious that the lower parts of the atmosphere, by sustaining the greater weight or pressure of the air above them, must be so much the more condensed; and therefore, as we ascend in the atmosphere, the density will continually diminish. Accordingly, it may be shown from the principles already laid down, that were the temperature and the force of gravity uniform at all heights above the earth's surface, the densities of the strata would decrease in geometrical progression for altitudes taken in arithmetical progression, so as nearly to halve the density for every 3.5 miles of ascent. But, independently of a trifling change in the force of gravity, this is not exactly the law of nature; for it is found that the temperature generally decreases as we go upward, and that not according to any fixed law

Hence the relation between the density and altitude is not of a steady character, and can only be obtained in any particular case from observing the pressure, temperature, and hygrometric state of the air. This is a research to which many eminent men have turned their attention; and their successive labours have led to the formation of convenient rules, by which the heights of mountains can be obtained to a considerable degree of accuracy, and with great facility, by means of the barometer, &c.

The height and form of the atmosphere are objects of interest. With an uniform temperature, the law of Boyle would involve the notion that its height is infinite; but this is an idea which has scarcely any supporters, and is generally believed to be incompatible with the laws of motion. Dr. Wollaston, whose opinion is entitled to great deference, maintains that the atmosphere must terminate at the height where the repulsive force between its particles equals their tendency to gravitate towards the earth. The law of gravity may be admitted as known, but the same can hardly be affirmed of the law which regulates the repulsive force, so long as the temperature at great heights is unknown; and this circumstance leaves the boundary undetermined. A doubt of a more serious nature, however, attaches to this speculation, on the ground that we are totally ignorant with what materials the air may be mixed at great elevations. The atmosphere is generally supposed to be higher at the equator than at the poles; but we have neither data for computing the heights, nor the proportion in which they differ: so that the oblate spheroidal figure which some give to the atmosphere can be considered as little else than an ingenious conjecture.

The temperature of the atmosphere has great influence on most meteorological phenomena; but it is exceedingly variable, and can as yet be determined only by actual observation on the spot. Nothing would tend to throw greater light on many of the unresolved questions in meteorology, than a ready mode of computing with certainty the temperature which obtains at any instant in a point of the atmosphere remote from the contact of the earth's surface, and at any point on the surface remote from the observer: but these are likely to continue desiderata. The very little that is known of the temperature of air remote from the earth's surface has been derived from a few aëronautic excursions, particularly the ascent of M. Gay-Lussac to the height of 7630 yards.

The heat of the air in one shape or another is no doubt greatly derived from the sun, either immediately, by intercepting the solar rays, or indirectly, from its contact with the earth's surface, which is more or less heated according as it is turned more or less towards the sun: but whether heat, in return, be projected from the earth or its atmosphere towards other regions of space, is a disputed question. Professor Leslie maintains that heat, which is not accompanied with or rather is not in the state of light, cannot pass through a vacuum, and, of course, that it cannot pass the boundary of the atmosphere. If so, it would follow that the atmosphere does not continually draw off heat from the earth, but may oftener be the warmer of the two. Many philosophers, however, are of a different opinion, among whom was the ingenious Dr. Wells, with most of those who embraced his theory of dew. These allege, that heat is constantly projected from the earth and atmosphere towards the boundless regions of space. Observation shows, that much heat passes upward from the earth's surface, especially when the air is clear. In this way, the stratum of air in contact with the surface is cooled more than that which is somewhat higher. It is probable that there exists a natural tendency in the atmosphere, as in most other bodies, towards an uniform temperature throughout its whole height; and since currents in its upper regions usually come from a warmer quarter, and the lower currents from a colder, there is upon the whole, independently of aëronautic observations, some ground for supposing that the decrease of temperature on ascending in the atmosphere should be slower than the law of capacity as increased by dilatation requires.

The following list of temperatures, chiefly observed at stations employed in the barometrical measurements of heights, is taken from M. Ramond's work on that subject. Only a few of these measurements embrace the whole heights of the mountains on which they were made, and the first case is of a different class. We have reduced the temperatures to Fahrenheit's scale:—

| Places. | Height. | Temp. at bot. | Temp. at top. | Places. | Height. | Temp. at bot. | Temp. at top. |
|---|---|---|---|---|---|---|---|
| | Yards. | ° | ° | | Yards | ° | ° |
| Gay-Lussac's ascent | 7630 | 87.4 | 14.9 | Pic d'Eyre, Tarbes | 2347 | 79.3 | 51.8 |
| Chimborazo | 6427 | 77.5 | 29.1 | Pic du Montaign | 2244 | 58.1 | 37.6 |
| Mont Blanc | 4762 | 82.9 | 26.8 | Pic du Midi, Bareges | 1808 | 80.1 | 61.5 |
| Ditto | — | 81.7 | 29.1 | Ditto | — | 71.4 | 46.4 |
| Pic de Teneriffe | 4077 | 76.8 | 47.1 | Ditto | — | 70.3 | 46.8 |
| Mont Blanc, Chamouny | 4070 | 73.4 | 26.8 | Ditto | — | 65.3 | 42.8 |
| Etna | 3540 | 73.6 | 39.9 | Ditto | — | 50.6 | 36.5 |
| Mont Perdu, Tarbes | 3408 | 78.1 | 44.4 | Ditto | — | 64.0 | 44.6 |
| Col du Geant | 3346 | 76.8 | 40.1 | Ditto | — | 66.0 | 42.4 |
| Maladette | 3174 | 69 4 | 38.1 | Ditto | — | 65.1 | 41.4 |
| Pic du Midi, Tarbes | 2858 | 81.5 | 52.9 | Puy de Dome, Clermont | 1163 | 70.3 | 57.9 |
| Ditto | — | 67.3 | 47.5 | Ditto | — | 64.0 | 51.4 |
| Ditto | — | 72.5 | 46.6 | Ditto | — | 65.5 | 53.1 |
| Ditto | — | 74.3 | 50.7 | Ditto | — | 76.6 | 59.4 |
| Ditto | — | 65.8 | 46.6 | Ditto | — | 91.2 | 74.1 |
| Ditto | — | 66.4 | 39.2 | Bedat du Bagneres, Tarbes | 611 | 51.6 | 46.4 |
| Ditto | — | 58.6 | 39.7 | Pont du Berges, Clermont | 537 | 32.5 | 26.8 |
| Col du Geant, Chamouny | 2606 | 70.9 | 40.1 | La Barrague, Clermont | 415 | 74.5 | 71.2 |
| Mont Perdu, Bareges | 2354 | 77.0 | 44.4 | | | | |

This table shows, in a very striking manner, with how little certainty the decrease of temperature can be estimated from the increase of height; and how unsteady the rate of decrease is often at the same place. M. Ramond, however, has collected some cases which are still more discordant.

The preceding table contains the temperatures of the air at different heights for one or a few particular instants; but we shall now add *a table from Baron Humboldt of the mean temperatures of elevated situations*, as deduced from several years observations. The degrees are those of Fahrenheit's scale.

| Height in English feet. | Equatorial zone from lat. 0° to 10°. | | Temperate zone from lat. 45° to 47° | |
|---|---|---|---|---|
| | Mean Temp. | Difference. | Mean Temp. | Difference. |
| | ° | ° | ° | ° |
| 0 | 81.5 | | 53.6 | |
| 3195 | 71.2 | 10.3 | 41.0 | 12.6 |
| 6393 | 65.1 | 6.1 | 31.6 | 9.4 |
| 9587 | 57.7 | 7.4 | 23.4 | 8.2 |
| 12792 | 44.6 | 13.1 | | |
| 15965 | 34.7 | 9.9 | | |

From this table it appears, that, in the mean state of the atmosphere, the temperature does not decrease uniformly for a uniform ascent. At the equator, the thermometer falls 10° in the first 1000 yards of ascent, or about 1° for 310 feet. In the next 1000 yards, it is only 1° for 524 feet; but in the third and fourth stages there is a remarkable acceleration, which having attained its maximum rate, is diminished again in the fifth stage to somewhat less than it was in the first, or to 1° in 320 feet. The mean rate in the variation of temperature, throughout the whole height of 15965 feet, at the limit of perpetual snow, is 1° for every 341 feet. The smaller rate of decrease in the second and third stages is ascribed by Humboldt to the large dense clouds which are suspended in this region, and which, he alleges, have the triple effect of absorbing the sun's rays, forming rain, and intercepting the radiation of heat from the earth. In the temperate zone, the decrease is at the rate of 1° for 253 feet, during the first 1000 yards of ascent. But throughout the whole height of 9587 feet, to the limit of perpetual snow, where the mean temperature is 23.4°, the decrease is 1° for 317 feet, or almost 1° for 100 yards. As already remarked, observations made in the free regions of the atmosphere have not yet been so numerous as to warrant any certain conclusion regarding the temperature; but, so far as such observations go, they do not differ very widely from the mean of those observed on the sides and summits of mountains. But generally in the temperate zone, a difference of 1000 yards in height will produce a difference of 12° of temperature; and so on in proportion for smaller heights. In higher regions, the difference between the heats of day and night, summer and winter, seem to be less than at the level of the sea; though from this there are some exceptions. Extensive table-lands are usually warmer than insulated peaks of the same height. Humboldt calculates that, in the temperate zone, an ascent of 110 yards diminishes the temperature as much as an additional degree of latitude.

*Temperature of air in mines.* Having thus noticed the lower temperatures which obtain in more elevated situations, we shall now give some account of the increased temperature which generally prevails in air occupying deep caverns and mines. There can be no doubt as to such facts, but the source of the heat is still a subject of controversy. There are some mines intensely cold; and as these were first observed, the explanation offered was, that the colder portions of air had, by their greater weight, descended into the mines: but this solution entirely vanished when it was known that mines are generally hot. The heat of the workmen, their fires and lights, have been stated as sources of heat; as likewise the chemical action of air and water on the minerals. Some again allege that a high temperature obtains in the interior of our globe, and consequently that the heat will always be greater as we penetrate farther. However, it is found that on boring into the solid strata in the bottom of warm mines, and letting down a thermometer, the temperature, so far from increasing, comes short of that in the mine. This sufficiently proves that, whatever be the sources of heat, some of them at least must operate in or be situated about the mine itself. That a high temperature obtains in the interior, is in many instances evident from the streams of hot water and vapour which issue from fissures in the strata: but in many warm mines nothing of this is observable. Professor Leslie, Dr. Forbes, and afterwards Mr. Matthew Miller, have suggested the heat evolved by a current of air, while it undergoes an increase of pressure in descending into the mine. The first two of these philosophers did not deem this an adequate source of heat; and Mr. Miller seems to entertain similar doubts. But from what is now known of the great heat evolved by the compression of air, there can be little room to question that this furnishes a considerable supply, wherever there is a sufficient current of air. Thus, if air at the temperature of 62° F. have its density suddenly increased by the 170th part, the temperature will be raised 1°; supposing no heat to be lost on the sides of the shaft. This would give 1° for a descent of 170 feet, which is still short of the rate at which the temperature is observed to increase in British mines; but when added to the heat caused by the presence of the workmen and horses, their lights, blasting of rocks, fires, &c. together with some increase of temperature belonging to the deeper strata, there does not seem any mystery in the heat of some, although probably not of all, mines. Those mines, again, in which there is almost no circulation of air, and which present a wide mouth to a clear sky, may have their temperature reduced by radiating heat upwards, in the same way that plants are starved with cold by being too much sheltered from the wind while they are exposed to a clear sky.

An immense collection of facts and observations relating to this subject may be seen in the *Transactions of the Geological Society of Cornwall*, and in the first number of the *Edin. Phil. Journal*. From the latter we extract the following summary of Mr. Bald's observations, made in the deepest coal-mines in Great Britain:—

*Whitehaven Colliery, County of Cumberland.*

Air at the surface ....................55° F
A spring at surface ....................49
Water at depth of 480 feet ....................60
Air at same depth ....................63
Air at depth of 600 feet ....................66

*Workington Colliery, Cumberland.*

Air at the surface ....................56
A spring at surface ....................48
Water at depth of 180 feet ....................50
Water 504 feet beneath the surface of the Irish Sea ....................60

*Teem Colliery, County of Durham.*

Water at surface ....................49
Water at depth of 444 feet ....................61° F
Air at same depth ....................68

*Percy Main Colliery, Northumberland.*

Air at the surface ....................42
Water at surface ....................49
Air at depth of 900 feet below the level of the sea, and immediately under the bed of the river Tyne ....................70
Water at same depth ....................68
Here Leslie's hygrometer indicated dryness ....83

*Jarrow Colliery, County of Durham.*

Air at the surface ....................49½
Water at surface ....................49
Air at depth of 882 feet ....................70
Water at same depth ....................68

The engine pit of Jarrow is the deepest perpendicular shaft in Britain, being 900 feet to the foot of the pumps, where the temperature of the air was 64°.

*Killingworth Colliery, Northumberland.*

Air at surface ....................48° F
Water at surface ....................49
Air at bottom of shaft 790 feet deep ....................51
Air at depth of 900 feet, and a mile and half from bottom of down-cast pit ....................70
Water at most distant forehead and 1200 feet below surface ....................74° F
Air at same depth ....................77
At this depth, distilled water boiled at ....................213
When at surface it boiled at ....................210·5

The temperature of springs and caverns, in many places, coincides with the mean annual temperature of the air: but Humboldt alleges that, in latitudes above 45°, the mean heat of springs and caves exceeds that of the atmosphere. As connected with this subject, Mr. Ferguson, of Raith, had four large thermometers sunk in his garden, to the respective depths of 1, 2, 4, and 8 feet, in lat. 56° 10′, and 50 feet above the sea. The stems and scales rose above ground, and indicated the following monthly mean temperatures:

| | 1816. | | | | 1817. | | | |
|---|---|---|---|---|---|---|---|---|
| | 1 Foot. | 2 Feet. | 4 Feet. | 8 Feet. | 1 Foot. | 2 Feet. | 4 Feet. | 8 Feet. |
| January | 33.0° | 36.3° | 40.7° | 43.0° | 35.6° | 38.7° | 40.5° | 45.1° |
| February | 33.7 | 36.0 | 39.0 | 42.0 | 37.0 | 40.0 | 41.6 | 42.7 |
| March | 35.0 | 36.7 | 39.6 | 42.3 | 39.4 | 40.2 | 41.7 | 42.5 |
| April | 39.7 | 38.4 | 41.4 | 43.8 | 45.0 | 42.4 | 42.6 | 42.6 |
| May | 40.0 | 43.3 | 43.4 | 44.0 | 46.8 | 44.7 | 44.6 | 44.2 |
| June | 51.6 | 50.0 | 47.1 | 45.8 | 51.1 | 49.4 | 47.6 | 47.8 |
| July | 54.0 | 52.5 | 50.4 | 47.7 | 55.2 | 55.0 | 51.4 | 49.6 |
| August | 50.0 | 52.5 | 50.6 | 49.4 | 53.4 | 53.9 | 52.0 | 50.0 |
| September | 51.6 | 51.3 | 51.8 | 50.0 | 53.0 | 52.7 | 52.0 | 50.7 |
| October | 47.0 | 49.3 | 49.7 | 49.6 | 45.7 | 49.4 | 49.4 | 49.8 |
| November | 40.8 | 43.8 | 46.3 | 45.6 | 41.0 | 44.7 | 47.0 | 47.6 |
| December | 35.7 | 40.0 | 43.0 | 46.0 | 35.9 | 40.8 | 44.9 | 46.4 |
| Mean of the Year | 43.8 | 44.1 | 45.1 | 46.8 | 44.9 | 45.9 | 46.2 | 46.6 |

Had the thermometers been sunk considerably deeper, they might have been expected to have indicated 47° 7′, which is the constant temperature of a neighbouring spring issuing from a trap rock.

The local temperature or climate of a country depends very much upon its distance from the equator, and its height above the level of the sea: but the nature of the surface, the proportion of humidity, the distance of the sea, of lakes, of mountains, of arid or frozen plains, and perhaps, also, the internal heat of the earth, have each their share in the fertility or salubrity of a country. The decrease of heat as we recede from the equator follows different laws in the two hemispheres, being greater in the southern than in the northern, and is also affected by the longitude. On the west of Europe, the cold increases less with the latitude than in any other quarter. Under meridians which are 90° either east or west of London, the increase of cold, as we go northward, is more rapid than in England. According to Humboldt, continents and large islands are warmer on their western sides than on the eastern. The annexed table shows the mean temperatures of western Europe and North America continued to the equator.

| Lat. | Old World. | New World. | Diff. |
|---|---|---|---|
| 0° | 81.5° | 81.5° | 0° |
| 20 | 77.9 | 77.9 | 0 |
| 30 | 70.7 | 67.1 | 3.6 |
| 40 | 63.5 | 54.5 | 9.0 |
| 50 | 50.9 | 38.3 | 12.6 |
| 60 | 41.0 | 25.0 | 16.0 |
| 70 | 33.0 | 0.0 | 33.0 |

Isothermal lines have been considered as measuring the heat and cold of the earth. The climate of Eastern Asia comes nearer to that of Eastern America than of Western Europe. Thus the latitudes of Naples, Peking, and Philadelphia are respectively 41°, 40°, and 40°, whilst their mean temperatures are 63.3°, 54.8°, and 53.4°. Such differences are rendered more sensible when we connect the places having the same mean temperature by lines which Humboldt denominates isothermal lines. Thus, the isothermal line of 59° F. traverses the latitude of 43° in Europe, but descends to lat. 36° in America; the isothermal line of 41° F. passes from lat. 60° in Europe to lat. 48° in America: but since the western coast of North America is warmer than the eastern, the isothermal lines, being traced round the northern hemisphere, would have concave summits at the east side of both worlds, and convex at the west.

The difference between the mean temperature of summer and winter is nothing at the equator, and increases continually with the latitude. But the extreme difference of the seasons is comparatively small in Western Europe, and great where the mean annual temperature is low, as on the east coasts of Asia and America. If we draw a line in a north-east direction from Bordeaux to Warsaw, and continue it to the Wolga, in lat. 55°, then all places under this line, at the same elevation, will have nearly the same summer temperature of 69° or 70° F. The lines of equal winter temperature decline in an opposite direction. Thus a straight line drawn from Edinburgh to Milan, almost at right angles to the former line, would pass over places which, if equally elevated, would have nearly the same winter temperature of 37° or 38° F.

The extremes of temperature are experienced chiefly in large inland tracts, and little felt in small islands remote from continents. In the United States intense cold is felt when the wind blows from the frozen regions round Hudson's Bay. From snow-clad mountains, gusts of cold wind, called *snow winds*, rush down and cool the adjacent plains. The heat accumulates to an astonishing degree when the wind passes over extensive deserts of burning sand, which are said, in some instances in Africa, to be heated to the boiling point. This fine sand, or rather dust, sometimes rises in the air and obscures it like a fog, communicating to it an intolerable heat. In arctic countries the temperature is very much regulated by the freezing of the water and the melting of the ice; by the freezing of the water great quantities of heat are given out which moderate the severity of the winter's cold, and thus save from destruction the arctic land animals, and plants; while in summer, the intensity of the heat, produced by the long continuance of the sun above the horizon, is moderated by the abstraction of a considerable portion of that heat by the water during the melting of the ice. Had the arctic regions been entirely of land, neither plants nor animals could have existed in them: for during summer, owing to the sun remaining above the horizon for months, an elevation of atmospheric temperature would have been produced fatal to animals and plants; and in winter, the long darkness and intense cold would have proved equally fatal to animated beings. The cold of the icy regions of the north has been alleged to reach, by currents of air, southern latitudes, and thus to lower their temperature.

Baron Humboldt has added more to our knowledge of the distribution of temperature over the globe than any other who had laboured in the same boundless field of research. The table on the following page contains his general summary, to which is added Melville Island. The temperatures have been reduced to Fahrenheit's scale, and the longitudes are reckoned from Greenwich. An asterisk is prefixed to those places whose temperatures have been most accurately determined, and in general by means of 8000 observations.

In treating on the mean annual temperature which obtains at different places, it is customary to give a table which makes the temperature depend entirely on the *latitude*. But observation shows, that the temperature is usually higher at the same latitude in the old world than in the new, and in north latitude than in south; and, as was already mentioned, it differs in the same continent under different meridians. So that more than one table would be required for each quarter of the globe; or else one very extensive table, involving the longitude as well as latitude, which is the case with Humboldt's table, so far as it goes.

As the earth and its atmosphere are continually receiving heat from the sun, it is plain that their mean annual temperature must be continually on the increase, if no heat be thrown off by them into surrounding space. Professor Leslie accordingly alleges, that the increase of temperature is at the rate of about 1° in 80 years. This would help to explain some of the changes of climate which seem to have been gradually taking place during successive ages in many places, and particularly in the west of Europe. But the late celebrated Marquis de la Place has endeavoured to show, from astronomical observations, that the mean temperature of the earth has undergone no sensible change during the last two thousand years. His arguments, however, are not free from objection.

### SECT. II.—*Effect of Climate on Plants and Animals.*

The geographical distribution of plants and animals appears to be chiefly regulated by the temperature of the atmosphere. Each has generally a particular climate in which it thrives best, and beyond certain limits it ceases to exist. Since an increase of height has an effect

| Isothermal Bands. | Names of Places. | Position. | | | Mean Temperature of the Year. | Mean Temperature of | | | | Mean Temperature of | |
|---|---|---|---|---|---|---|---|---|---|---|---|
| | | Lat. | Long. | Hght. | | Winter. | Spring. | Summer. | Autumn. | Warmest Month. | Coldest Month. |
| | | ° ′ | ° ′ | Feet | ° | ° | ° | ° | ° | ° | ° |
| Band from 32° to 41°. | Melville Island .... | 74 47 | 110 48 W. | 0 | — 2.00 | —31.33 | — 6.60 | 33.78 | — 3.84 | 39.08 | —35.52 |
| | Nain ........... | 57 8 | 61 20 W. | 0 | +26.42 | — 0.60 | 23.90 | 48.38 | 33.44 | 51.80 | —11.20 |
| | *Enontekies ...... | 68 30 | 20 47 E. | 1356 | 26.96 | 0.68 | 24.98 | 54.86 | 27.32 | 59.54 | — 0.58 |
| | Hospice de St. Gothard.......... | 46 30 | 8 23 E. | 6390 | 30.38 | 18.32 | 26.42 | 44.96 | 31.82 | 46.22 | +15.08 |
| | North Cape ....... | 71 0 | 25 50 E. | 0 | 32.00 | 23.72 | 29.66 | 43.34 | 32.08 | 46.58 | 22.10 |
| | *Ulea ........... | 65 3 | 25 26 E. | 0 | 35.08 | 11.84 | 27.14 | 57.74 | 35.96 | 61.52 | 7.70 |
| | *Umea ........... | 63 50 | 20 16 E. | 0 | 33.26 | 12.92 | 33.80 | 54.86 | 33.44 | 62.60 | 11.48 |
| | *St. Petersburg ..... | 59 56 | 30 19 E. | 0 | 38.84 | 17.06 | 38.12 | 62.06 | 38.66 | 65.66 | 8.60 |
| | Drontheim ........ | 63 24 | 10 22 E. | 0 | 39.92 | 23.72 | 35.24 | 61.24 | 40.10 | 64.94 | 19.58 |
| | Moscow ......... | 55 45 | 37 32 E. | 970 | 40.10 | 10.78 | 44.06 | 67.10 | 38.30 | 70.52 | 6.08 |
| | Abo ............. | 60 27 | 22 18 E | 0 | 40.28 | 20.84 | 38.30 | 61.88 | 40.64 | —— | —— |
| Band from 41° to 50° | *Upsal............ | 59 51 | 17 38 E. | 0 | 42.08 | 24.98 | 39.38 | 60.26 | 42.80 | 62.42 | 22.46 |
| | *Stockholm ........ | 59 20 | 18 3 E. | 0 | 42.26 | 25.52 | 28.30 | 61.88 | 43.16 | 64.04 | 22.82 |
| | Quebec........... | 46 47 | 71 0 W. | 0 | 41.74 | 14.18 | 38.84 | 68.00 | 46.04 | 73.40 | 13.81 |
| | Christiania ........ | 59 55 | 10 48 E. | 0 | 42.80 | 28.78 | 39.02 | 62.60 | 41.18 | 66.74 | 28.41 |
| | *Convent of Peissenberg.......... | 47 47 | 10 34 E. | 3066 | 42.98 | 28.58 | 42.08 | 58.46 | 42.98 | 59.36 | 30.20 |
| | *Copenhagen ....... | 55 41 | 12 35 E. | 0 | 45.68 | 30.74 | 41.18 | 62.60 | 48.38 | 65.66 | 27.14 |
| | *Kendal .......... | 54 17 | 2 46 W. | 0 | 46.22 | 30.86 | 45.14 | 56.84 | 46.22 | 58.10 | 34.88 |
| | Falkland Islands ... | 51 25 | 59 59 W. | 0 | 46.94 | 39.56 | 46.58 | 53.06 | 48.46 | 55.76 | 37.40 |
| | *Prague ......... | 50 5 | 14 24 E. | 0 | 49.46 | 31.46 | 47.66 | 68.90 | 50.18 | —— | —— |
| | Gottingen ........ | 51 32 | 9 53 E. | 456 | 46.94 | 30.38 | 44.24 | 64.76 | 48.74 | 66.38 | 29.66 |
| | *Zurich .......... | 47 22 | 8 32 E. | 1350 | 47.84 | 29.66 | 48.20 | 64.04 | 48.92 | 65.66 | 26.78 |
| | *Edinburgh ........ | 55 57 | 3 10 W. | 150 | 47.84 | 38.66 | 46.40 | 58.28 | 48.56 | 59.36 | 38.30 |
| | Warsaw .......... | 52 14 | 21 2 E. | 0 | 48.56 | 28.76 | 47.48 | 69.08 | 49.46 | 70.34 | 27.14 |
| | *Coire ........... | 46 50 | 9 30 E. | 1876 | 48.92 | 32.36 | 50.00 | 63.32 | 50.36 | 64.58 | 29.48 |
| | Dublin .......... | 53 21 | 6 19 W. | 0 | 49.10 | 39.20 | 47.30 | 59.54 | 50.00 | 61.16 | 35.42 |
| | Berne .......... | 46 5 | 7 26 E. | 1650 | 49.28 | 32.00 | 48.92 | 66.56 | 49.82 | 67.28 | 30.56 |
| | *Geneva ......... | 46 12 | 6 8 E. | 1080 | 49.28 | 34.70 | 47.66 | 64.94 | 50.00 | 66.56 | 34.16 |
| | *Manheim ......... | 49 29 | 8 28 E. | 432 | 50.18 | 38.80 | 49.64 | 67.10 | 49.82 | 68.72 | 33.44 |
| | Vienna .......... | 48 12 | 16 22 E. | 420 | 50.54 | 32.72 | 51.26 | 69.26 | 50.54 | 70.52 | 26.60 |
| Band from 50° to 59°. | *Clermont.......... | 45 46 | 3 5 E. | 1260 | 50.00 | 34.52 | 50.54 | 64.40 | 51.26 | 66.20 | 28.04 |
| | *Buda ........... | 47 29 | 19 1 E. | 494 | 51.08 | 33.98 | 51.08 | 70.52 | 52.34 | 71.60 | 27.78 |
| | Cambridge, Mass... | 42 22 | 71 7 W. | 0 | 50.36 | 33.98 | 47.66 | 70.70 | 49.82 | 72.86 | 29.84 |
| | *Paris .......... | 48 50 | 2 20 E. | 222 | 51.08 | 38.66 | 49.28 | 64.58 | 51.44 | 65.30 | 36.14 |
| | *London .......... | 51 30 | 0 5 W. | 0 | 50.36 | 39.56 | 48.56 | 63.14 | 50.18 | 64.40 | 37.76 |
| | Dunkirk .......... | 51 2 | 2 22 E. | 0 | 50.54 | 38.48 | 48.56 | 64.04 | 50.90 | 64.76 | 37.76 |
| | Amsterdam ....... | 52 22 | 4 50 E. | 0 | 51.62 | 36.86 | 51.62 | 65.84 | 51.62 | 66.92 | 35.42 |
| | Brussels ......... | 50 50 | 4 22 E. | 0 | 51.80 | 36.68 | 53.24 | 66.20 | 51.08 | 67.28 | 35.60 |
| | *Franeker.......... | 52 36 | 6 22 E. | 0 | 51.80 | 36.68 | 51.08 | 67.28 | 54.32 | 69.08 | 32.90 |
| | Philadelphia ...... | 39 56 | 75 10 W. | 0 | 53.42 | 32.18 | 51.44 | 73.94 | 56.48 | 77.00 | 32.72 |
| | New York ....... | 40 40 | 73 58 W. | 0 | 53.78 | 29.84 | 51.26 | 79.16 | 54.50 | 80.70 | 25.34 |
| | *Cincinnati......... | 39 6 | 84 27 W. | 510 | 53.78 | 32.90 | 54.14 | 72.86 | 54.86 | 74.30 | 30.20 |
| | St. Malo ......... | 48 39 | 2 1 W. | 0 | 54.14 | 42.26 | 52.16 | 66.02 | 55.76 | 66.92 | 41.74 |
| | Nantes .......... | 47 13 | 1 32 W. | 0 | 54.68 | 40.46 | 54.50 | 68.54 | 55.58 | 70.52 | 39.02 |
| | Peking........... | 39 54 | 116 27 E. | 0 | 54.86 | 26.42 | 56.30 | 82.58 | 54.32 | 84.38 | 24.62 |
| | *Milan ........... | 45 28 | 9 11 E. | 390 | 55.76 | 36.32 | 56.12 | 73.04 | 56.84 | 74.66 | 36.14 |
| | Bordeaux ........ | 44 50 | 0 34 W. | 0 | 56.48 | 42.08 | 56.48 | 70.88 | 56.30 | 73.04 | 41.00 |
| Band from 59° to 68°. | Marseilles......... | 43 17 | 5 22 E. | 0 | 59.00 | 45.50 | 57.56 | 72.50 | 60.08 | 74.66 | 44.42 |
| | Montpellier ....... | 43 36 | 3 52 E. | 0 | 59.36 | 44.06 | 56.66 | 75.74 | 60.98 | 78.08 | 42.08 |
| | *Rome............ | 41 53 | 12 27 E. | 0 | 60.44 | 45.86 | 57.74 | 75.20 | 62.78 | 77.00 | 42.26 |
| | Toulon .......... | 43 7 | 5 50 E. | 0 | 62.06 | 48.38 | 60.80 | 75.02 | 64.40 | 77.00 | 46.40 |
| | Nangasaki ........ | 32 45 | 129 55 E. | 0 | 60.80 | 39.38 | 57.56 | 82.94 | 64.22 | 86.90 | 37.40 |
| | *Natchez .......... | 31 34 | 91 24 W. | 180 | 64.76 | 48.56 | 65.48 | 79.16 | 66.02 | 79.70 | 46.94 |
| 68° to 72°. | *Funchal .......... | 32 37 | 16 56 W. | 0 | 68.54 | 64.40 | 65.84 | 72.50 | 72.32 | 75.56 | 64.04 |
| | Algiers .......... | 36 48 | 3 1 E. | 0 | 69.98 | 61.52 | 65.66 | 80.24 | 72.50 | 82.76 | 60.08 |
| Band above 72°. | *Cairo ............ | 30 2 | 30 18 E. | 0 | 72.32 | 58.46 | 73.58 | 85.10 | 71.42 | 85.82 | 56.12 |
| | *Vera Cruz ........ | 19 11 | 96 1 W. | 0 | 77.72 | 71.96 | 77.90 | 81.50 | 78.62 | 81.86 | 71.06 |
| | *Havana........... | 23 10 | 82 13 W. | 0 | 78.08 | 71.24 | 78.98 | 83.30 | 78.98 | 83.84 | 69.98 |
| | *Cumana .......... | 10 27 | 65 15 W. | 0 | 81.86 | 80.24 | 83.66 | 82.04 | 80.24 | 84.38 | 79.16 |

on climate in some respects similar to an increase of latitude, it has been commonly supposed that there are properly no plants peculiar to high latitudes, because such may be raised on the mountains under the equator, which embrace every variety of climate between their summit and base, at least in so far as temperature is concerned. In point of atmospheric pressure, however, the two situations differ essentially; and some naturalists allege, that pressure is of vital importance to the growth of plants. Professor Dobereiner is of opinion that the diminutive size of plants, in elevated situations, depends more on the diminution of pressure than of temperature. To ascertain this, he put equal quantities of barley and moist earth into two equal receivers: the air in the one had a pressure of 14 inches of mercury, and the other 56; germination commenced in both at the same time, and the leaves had the same green tint. At the end of fifteen days, the shoots in the rarefied air were 6 inches long, and in the other from 9 to 10. The first were expanded and soft and wet on the surface, especially towards their extremities; the others were firm, rolled round the stem, and nearly dry. In some respects, this accords with what Humboldt observed of the trees on the Andes, that water transpires from them even in the driest weather. But such experiments are inconclusive, unless there were some contrivance employed to renew the confined air frequently. Independently of pressure, the barley in the condensed air had the use of four times the quantity of air in the other vessel.

Plants are most numerous, and exhibit the greatest variety of species, and the most luxuriant growth, within the tropics, beyond which they gradually diminish. In the arctic regions, and in the north of Russia, the vegetable kingdom has dwindled to almost nothing. The lines which limit the growth of certain plants depend on the average summer temperature, for plants which require a long and moderate heat; on the temperature of the warmest month, for those which require a short but great heat; and on the temperature of the coldest month, for those which cannot bear cold. The transparency of the air is also of importance to many plants; but our limits will not admit of enlarging, and therefore we shall confine ourselves to a short account of the climates of cultivated plants. The plantain, which is a primary article of food in tropical America, requires a temperature from 82° to 73° F., which occurs between lat. 0° and 27°: but, in the equinoctial zone (lat. 0° to 10°), its fruit does not ripen at a greater altitude than 3300 feet. The sugar-cane has nearly the same range, but is cultivated, though with less advantage, in the old world to lat. 36° 5′, where the mean temperature is about 67°. The severity of the North American winter prevents the cultivation of the sugar-cane beyond lat. 31°; but it succeeds at an altitude of 5700 feet on the table-land of Mexico. The favourite climate of the cotton plant lies between lat. 0° and 34°; but it succeeds with a mean summer heat of 75° or 73° F., if that of winter do not descend below 36° or 38°. In America, it is cultivated at lat. 37°; in Europe, at lat. 40°; and in Astracan, at lat. 46°. The date palm thrives best between lat. 29° and 35°; but, when sheltered from the north wind, it is cultivated on the shores of Italy to lat. 44°. The citron has nearly the same range, but is cultivated at Nice, at altitudes of 400 feet. This tree, with the sweet orange, grows in Louisiana to lat. 30°, but beyond that it is injured by the cold. The olive ranges in Europe between lat. 36° and 44° 5′; it succeeds wherever, with a mean annual temperature from 66° to 58° F., that of summer is not below 71°, nor that of the coldest month below 42°, which excludes all North America beyond lat. 34°. The favourite climate of the vine in the old world is between lat. 36° and 48°; but it thrives wherever the mean temperature is from 62° to 47.5°, provided that of winter is not below 33°, nor summer under 66° or 68°. Such is the case on the shores of Europe to lat. 47°, and in the interior to lat. 50°, but only to lat. 40° in North America. The *cerealia* or common grain, as wheat, rye, barley, and oats, thrive where the mean annual temperature descends to 28° F., provided that of summer rise to 52° or 53°. In Lapland, barley ripens wherever the mean temperature of summer rises to 47° or 48°. The rapid growth of barley and oats adapts them to the short summers of the north: they are found as high as lat. 69½° in Lapland, along with the potato. In some parts of eastern Russia, no grain is found beyond lat. 60°. Wheat, which is a precarious crop, and little cultivated beyond lat. 58° in western Europe, yields good returns in this part of the temperate zone, when the mean heat, while the grain is on the ground, is 55°; but if no more than 46°, none of the *cerealia* come to maturity. These species of grain are cultivated at a height of 3500 feet on the Alps, in lat. 46°. Barley and oats succeed at double that height on Caucasus, and at almost a triple height on the Andes, along with wheat and rye. In the west of Europe, maize has the same range as the vine, but reaches farther north on the east. In its native American soil, it forms the chief article of food, from the river Plata to the lakes of Canada. Requiring a short but warm season of four months, it is well suited to the climate of the New World up to the latitude of 45°. The oak ceases at lat. 63° in Norway, at 60° or 61° in Finland, and at 57° in the government of Perm. The pinus silvestris, or Scots fir, grows to a height of 60 feet in Lapland, at lat. 70°, and 850 feet above the level of the sea: there the birch is found at double that elevation. In eastern Russia, the larch, pine, birch, and mountain-ash, disappear about lat. 68°; and, at Hudson's Bay, all trees cease about lat. 60°.

SECT. III.—*Composition of the Atmosphere.—Aqueous Meteors.*

Regarding the composition of the atmosphere, abundantly vague and fanciful notions prevailed for many ages. The ancients considered air as one of the four simple elements, of which they supposed all other bodies to be compounded. These were earth, air, fire, and water. How far the opinion was correct, which made fire an element, is a question on which nothing is yet known; but the researches of modern chemistry have shown that the other three are all compound bodies. The chief, and perhaps the only essential, component substances in the atmosphere, are the two gases called oxygen and azote; its other ingredients, occurring only in small and variable quantities, are rather to be considered as foreign bodies. The analysis of air is a difficult problem. Many chemists have found it to consist of 21 parts by volume of oxygen to 79 of azote; and this proportion is sensibly the same whether the air be from the polar or tropical regions, from the level of the sea or a mountain top, from the most healthy or insalubrious countries. But Dr. Prout, guided by the laws of definite proportions, alleges, that if the two gases of which air principally consists be really combined, they ought to be 20 oxygen to 80 azote; and it must be allowed that similar conjectures of the same eminent chemist have been verified regarding the composition of other bodies, which had apparently deviated farther from the atomic system.

The investigation of the component parts of the atmosphere did not keep pace with that of its mechanical properties. Boyle, however, and his cotemporaries, put it beyond doubt that it contained an elastic fluid and water in the state of vapour. They also conjectured that it contained various other substances, which rose from the earth in the form of vapours, and often altered its properties, rendering it noxious or fatal. Since the discovery of carbonic acid by Dr. Black, it has been ascertained that this elastic fluid always constitutes a part, though a very minute one, of the atmosphere.

With respect to moisture, or the state in which water exists in air, two opinions have been formed: 1. Water may be dissolved in air, in the same manner as salt is held in solution by water; 2. It may be mixed with air in the state of steam or vapour, after having been converted into vapour. The first of these was hinted at by Dr. Hooke, and afterwards proposed by Dr. Halley. It has been adopted by many others in succession, among whom is Professor Leslie; and it cannot be denied that many of the phenomena agree with that theory. The second opinion seems to have originated with Mr. Deluc; but it is to Mr. Dalton and M. Gay Lussac that we are indebted for subjecting this theory to the test of experiment.

Evaporation from the waters on the surface of the earth is undoubtedly the source whence the moisture which exists in air is derived. Accordingly we find that water exposed to the air suffers a gradual diminution of bulk, till it entirely disappears. It is then said, in common language, to have dried up, or to have *evaporated*. Under an exhausted receiver, water diminishes even more rapidly than in the open air. Were this owing to solution, the very reverse ought to follow; because, in place of vapour being caused by the presence of air, it goes on more rapidly in its absence. By comparing a set of experiments made at Geneva, with a similar set on the Col-du-Géant, 10,950 feet higher, Saussure found that, supposing the temperature and dryness of the air the same at both places, the evaporation at the upper would be to that at the lower nearly as 7 to 3; so that a diminution of about one third in the density of the air more than doubled the rate of evaporation. It is well known, that cold is always generated during spontaneous evaporation; that is to say, that water, as it disappears, carries off a quantity of heat. Dr. Black has rendered it probable, that the quantity of heat which disappears during spontaneous evaporation is as great as that which is required to form water into steam. A wet body is always cooled by exposure to dry air, owing to the evaporation from its surface. Hence, in warm countries, liquors are cooled by wrapping wet cloths round the bottles and exposing them to the air. M. Saussure observed, that the evaporation from the surface of melting snow caused it to freeze again, when the temperature of the air was 4° or 5° above the freezing point. The simplest mode of illustrating the cooling influence of evaporation, is to cover the ball of a thermometer with wet cloth and expose it to the air, when it will be found to indicate a greater or less degree of cold. This, it is true, does not take place if the air be very damp, because there is then no evaporation. Wind tends to promote evaporation, both by communicating its heat to the colder evaporating surface, and also by sweeping away the vapour as it is formed. On the contrary, there is scarcely any evaporation in perfectly still air, unless some substance be present which absorbs the vapour as it forms.

On this principle, Professor Leslie contrived an elegant mode of producing ice in any climate. A cup with water is placed within the receiver of an air-pump, along with some substance which absorbs the vapour. The rate of evaporation is then increased in an astonishing degree, by exhausting the air from the receiver; and the portion of the water which is converted into vapour abstracts so much heat from the remainder, that the latter is speedily converted into ice.

Dew is a remarkable product of atmospheric moisture. The quantity of aqueous vapour which can exist in a given space, as a cubic foot, is pretty generally believed to be the same, whether there be air present in the space, or nothing but the vapour alone. The quantity is always (*cæt. par.*) the same at the same temperature, but it is greater as the temperature is higher; and therefore, supposing the space to be saturated with vapour at a particular temperature, a portion of this will return into drops of water whenever the temperature falls. It is on this principle that a cold body, such as a bottle of liquor, being carried into a warm moist apartment, becomes bedewed on the outside, till, perhaps, the water trickles down its sides: the contact of the cold surface chills the air, which in return deposits a portion of its moisture. Now this is similar to the mode in which moisture is insensibly deposited from the atmosphere on bodies at the earth's surface, and which is known by the name of *dew*. All bodies, placed in still air and exposed to the aspect of a clear sky, are found to become colder than they would be if some screen or awning were interposed between them and the sky. In such circumstances, bodies often become much colder than the surrounding air, which, if sufficiently moist, deposits on them a portion of its moisture or dew. When the temperature is low, the dew is frozen, and forms *hoar frost*.

The radiation of heat also deserves notice. About the commencement of the present century, Professor Leslie discovered that bodies possess very different powers of radiating heat; and that this depends on the nature and condition of their surfaces. Metals possess this quality in a degree inferior to vitreous bodies, and it is diminished in all of them by polishing the surface. Most fibrous and filamentous vegetable substances are good radiators, as are likewise bodies in general which are bad conductors or bad reflectors of heat. Now the degrees of cooling, which different bodies undergo when exposed together to the aspect of the sky, is observed to follow the same order as that of their radiating powers; and, of course, the order in which they begin to acquire dew, as also the quantity acquired, is regulated by a similar law, as will be seen from what follows.

For the investigation of the causes of dew we are chiefly indebted to the late ingenious Dr. Wells. The ancients maintained, that dew appears only on calm and clear nights. Dr. Wells found that, in opposite circumstances, very little is ever deposited, and that little only when the clouds are very high. Dew never occurs in nights both cloudy and windy; and if in the course of the night, the weather, from being serene, should become dark and stormy, dew which had been deposited will disappear. In calm weather, more dew will appear if the sky be partially covered with clouds, than if it were quite clear. It often happens, that even before sunset, dew begins to adhere to grass in spots which are sheltered from both sun and wind; for, in clear weather, such spots suffer much from the chilling aspect of the sky, and may often continue to acquire dew during the whole night, and for some time after sunrise. The quantity of dew depends on the moistness of the air, being greater after rain than after long-continued dry weather. It is more abundant, in Europe, with southerly and westerly winds, than with those which blow from the opposite points. The reason of this seems to be the direction of the sea rendering the wind moist; for, in Egypt, dew rarely occurs unless the wind come from the sea. But with a southerly wind, which has passed along the floods of the Nile, dew is usually observed in the Delta five or six days before the inundation. After a long period of drought, Dr. Wells exposed to the clear sky, 28 minutes before sunset in a calm evening, known weights of wool and swan-down, upon a smooth, unpainted, dry fir table about 3 feet in height, and which had been placed an hour before in the sunshine in a large grass field. At 12 minutes after sunset the wool was 14° colder than the air, but had gained no weight. The swan-down was 13° colder than the air, but had got no additional weight; nor was it any heavier at the end of 20 minutes longer, but it had then become 14½° colder than the air; whilst the grass was 15° colder than the air 4 feet above ground.—From these, and many similar experiments, Dr. Wells concluded that bodies become colder than the neighbouring air *before* they are dewed.—He bent a sheet of pasteboard into the form of a penthouse, making the angle of flexure 90°, and leaving both ends open. This was placed one evening, with its ridge uppermost, upon a grass-plat, and, as nearly as could be guessed, in the direction of the wind. On the middle of the spot of grass sheltered by the roof, was placed 10 grains of wool, and an equal quantity on a spot of the grass fully exposed to the sky. In the morning, the first 10 grains were only 2 grains heavier, whilst the other had gained 16. The wool does not here acquire moisture from the grass by capillary attraction, for the same effect happens if it be placed in a saucer; nor is it by hygrometric attraction, for in a cloudy night, wool placed on an elevated board scarcely gained any weight.

The quantity of dew varies according to circumstances. When wool is placed upon a bad conductor of heat, as a deal board, a few feet from the ground, it will become colder and acquire more dew than if laid on the grass. At the windward end of the board, it is less bedewed than at the sheltered end; because, in the former case, the wind keeps up the temperature nearer to that of the atmosphere. Rough and porous surfaces, as shavings of wood, straw, &c., take more dew than smooth and solid bodies. Raw silk and fine cotton collect more than even wool. Glass, being a good radiator of heat, is much more quickly coated with dew than bright metals, which, indeed, receive it more readily than many other bodies. This circumstance has given rise to the strange idea that metals absorb dew, though they be the most compact bodies known. If we coat a piece of glass partially with bright tin-foil, or silver leaf, the uncovered portion of the glass quickly becomes cold by radiation, on exposure to a clear nocturnal sky, and acquires moisture; which, beginning on those parts most remote from the metal, gradually approaches it. Thus, also, if we coat a part of the outside of a window-pane with tin-foil in a clear night, then moisture will be deposited inside, on every part but that opposite to the metal; but if the metal be inside, then the outside of the coated part of the pane will be sooner and more copiously bedewed. In the first case, the tin-foil prevents the glass under it from dissipating its heat, and therefore it can receive no dew; in the second case, the tin-foil prevents the part of the glass which it coats from receiving the calorific influence of the apartment, and hence it is sooner cooled on the outside than the rest of the pane. When the night, after having been clear, becomes cloudy, though there be no change with respect to calmness, a rise in the temperature of the glass always ensues. In clear nights the temperature always falls, but, unless the air be sufficiently moist, dew does not necessarily follow; from which it is evident, that the cold cannot be the effect of dew. For a more particular account of these interesting phenomena, we must refer the reader to Dr. Wells's elegant *Essay on Dew.*

*Clouds.* The various forms of clouds were first successfully attempted to be arranged under a few general modifications by Mr. Luke Howard, and published in the 16th and 17th vols. of the *Philosoph. Magazine.* The modifications of clouds is a term used to express the structure or manner of aggregation, in which the influence of certain constant laws is sufficiently evident amidst the endless subordinate diversities resulting from occasional causes. Hence the principal modifications are as distinguishable from each other, as a tree from a hill, or the latter from a lake; although clouds, in the same modification, compared with each other, have often only the common resemblance which exists among trees, hills, and lakes, taken generally.

There are three simple and distinct modifications, which are thus named and defined by Mr. Howard:—

(1.) *Cirrus.* A cloud resembling a lock of hair or a feather. Parallel, flexous, or diverging fibres, unlimited in their extent or direction.

(2.) *Cumulus.* A cloud which increases from above in dense convex or conical heaps.

(3.) *Stratus.* An extended continuous level sheet of cloud, increasing from beneath.

There are two modifications which appear to be of an *intermediate* nature: these are—

(4.) *Cirro-cumulus.* A connected system of small roundish clouds, in close order or contact.

(5.) *Cirro-stratus.* A horizontal or slightly inclined *sheet,* attenuated at its circumference, concave downward, or undulated. Groups or patches have these characters.

There are two modifications which exhibit a compound structure, viz.:—

(6.) *Cumulo-stratus.* A cloud in which the structure of the *cumulus* is mixed with that of the *cirro-stratus* or *cirro-cumulus.* The *cumulus* flattened at top, and overhanging its base.

(7.) *Nimbus.* A dense cloud spreading out into a crown of *cirrus,* and passing beneath into a shower.

Regarding the mode in which clouds are suspended in the air, philosophers are not agreed. About the commencement of the last century, it was supposed that the aqueous particles of clouds were in the form of hollow shells, specifically lighter than the air in which they float. But as no evidence or probability could be adduced in favour of this theory, it has given place to other speculations; and, at present, many consider the suspension of clouds as an electrical phenomenon. On attentively observing the forms of clouds, it will be found that they have a tendency to assume one or other of the seven distinct modifications above mentioned; the peculiar characters of which may be discovered in all the endless configurations exhibited by clouds under different circumstances. It may be observed farther, that the most indefinite and shapeless masses of clouds, if attentively watched, will sooner or later show a tendency to assume the form of some of these modifications; a circumstance which shows not only their distinct nature, but also proves that there are some general causes, as yet undiscovered, why aqueous vapour, suspended in the air, should assume certain definable and constant modifications.

A more minute description of the formation and changes of the clouds, and of the prognostics of the weather to be deduced from their peculiar appearances, shall now be attempted.

The cirrus or curl-cloud* may be distinguished from every other by the lightness of its nature, its fibrous structure, and the great and perpetually changing variety of figures which it presents to the eye. It is generally the most elevated of clouds, occupying the higher regions of the atmosphere. As this cloud, under different circumstances, presents consider-

* This, and the other additional terms which follow, have been proposed as English names by Dr. Thomas Forster.

able varieties of appearances, it will be proper to consider these separately, with reference to the particular kind of weather in which they prevail. After a continuance of clear fine weather, a whitish line of cloud may often be observed at a great height, like a white thread stretched across the sky, the ends seeming lost in each horizon: this is often the first indication of a change to wet weather. To this line of cirrus, others are added laterally, and sometimes, as it were, propagated from the sides of the line in an oblique or transverse direction; the whole having the appearance of net-work. At other times the lines become gradually denser; descend lower in the atmosphere; and, uniting with others below, produce rain without exhibiting the above-mentioned transverse reticulations. The above-described varieties of cloud, though composed of straight lines, are ranged under the general head of *cirrus*, from their resemblance to this cloud when it appears under curved and contorted forms. The *comoid cirrus*, popularly known under the name of the *grey mare's tail*, is the proper cirrus. It somewhat resembles a distended lock of white hair, or a bunch of combed wool, and from this it got the name *comoid*. It usually occurs in variable weather, and is reckoned a precursor of wind and rain. In changeable weather it varies considerably in a few hours; but when the fibres have a constant direction to the same point of the compass for any considerable time, a gale of wind generally springs up from that quarter. During warm changeable weather, when there are light breezes of wind, long and obliquely descending bands of cirrus are often observed in the air, and sometimes seem to connect distant clouds. Frequently, by means of the interposition of these cirri between a cumulus and some other cloud, as, for instance, cirro-stratus, the cumulo-stratus, and ultimately the nimbus or rain-cloud, is formed. The cirrus, when attentively examined, is found to be in constant motion, not merely changing its form, but often exhibiting an internal commotion in the substance of the cloud, especially in the larger end of it. Every particle seems alive and in motion, while the whole mass scarcely changes its place. This motion, on a minute examination, often appears to consist of the fibres which compose the cirrus, gently waving to and from each other; frequently, however, it seems like minute specks all in commotion. This takes place more frequently in those large and lofty *cirri*, with rounded heads and long pointed tails, so common in dry winds during summer and autumn.

The formation of the cumulus is best viewed in fine settled weather, about sunrise or a little after. Small specks of cloud are seen here and there in the atmosphere. These seem to be the result of small gatherings of the stratus or evening mist, which rising in the morning grows into small masses of cloud, whilst the rest of the sky becomes clearer. About sunrise these clouds increase; two or more of them unite, till a large cloud be formed, which, assuming a cumulated and irregularly hemispherical shape, has received the name of *cumulus* or *stacken-cloud*. This is properly the cloud of day, as it usually subsides in the evening by retracing the steps of its formation in the morning. It separates into small fragments and evaporates, giving place to the stratus or fall-cloud, which is therefore styled the cloud of night.

Some varieties in the forms of the cumulus deserve particular notice, as they are supposed to be connected with electrical phenomena. The hemispherical form is more perfect in fine than in changeable weather. When such well-formed cumuli prevail during many successive days, the weather is settled, and the electrometer pretty steady in its indications. They are whitish coloured, and when opposed to the sun reflect a silvery light. Cumuli which occur during intervals between showers are more fleecy, and variable in form and colour. Sometimes they are blackish, and may at any time increase till they obscure the sky, or assume the form of the twain-cloud or cumulo-stratus.

The stratus or fall-cloud comprehends fogs, and all those creeping mists which, towards evening, fill the valleys, and disappear in the morning. The cumuli which have prevailed during a hot summer's day decrease towards evening, and by degrees there is formed a white mist near the ground, increasing in density till midnight or even till morning, and generally disappearing after sunrise. In autumn, this cloud sometimes lasts longer in the morning. In winter it becomes still more dense, and sometimes continues a whole day or many successive days. A remarkable instance of this occurred in January, 1814, when a dense fog prevailed for about a fortnight, extending over a great part of the south and west of England. It was particularly felt at London, where the stagnation and subsidence of the smoke more than doubled the dismal visitation. The stratus is often positively electrified, and its component parts do not wet leaves or other substances connected with the earth. On this, however, it may be remarked that dry bodies, which continue warmer than the fog, must remain dry on the ordinary principles of evaporation. The stratus may be distinguished from some varieties of cirro-stratus which resemble it, by the circumstance that the latter wets every object it alights on.

The cirro-cumulus or sonder-cloud is subject to some variations in the size and figure of the orbicular masses of which it is composed, and in their distances from each other. About the time of thunder storms, the component parts are denser in their structure, rounder in their form, and closer together than usual. This has been frequently noticed by poets as a prognostic of thunder and tempestuous weather. In rainy changeable weather, this cloud has a light fleecy texture, and is very irregular in the form of its component parts; so that it then approaches to the form of the cirro-stratus. Sometimes, indeed, it consists of *nebeculæ*, so small and light coloured as to be scarcely discernible. In fine summer weather, the cirro-cumulus is neither so dense as the stormy variety, nor so light as the one last described; its parts vary in size, and in their proximity. During fine dry weather with light breezes, small detachments of cirro-cumulus rapidly form and subside, which do not lie in one plane; but their arrangement is commonly horizontal. The cirro-cumulus sometimes commences in the clear sky. At other times the cirrus, the cirro-stratus, or some other cloud, changes into cirro-cumulus, and *vice versâ*. In summer, this cloud forebodes heat: in winter, the breaking up of frost, and mild wet weather.

The cirro-stratus is remarkable for its shallowness, compared with its horizontal extent; so that when any other cloud assumes this form, it seldom fails to end in a cirro-stratus. This cloud is constantly changing its form, and gradually subsiding; hence it has been called the *wane-cloud*. There are many varieties in its figure; sometimes it is disposed in waving bars or streaks, varying almost infinitely in size and shape. A flat horizontal cloud, consisting of such streaks, frequently occurs during changeable summer weather; its bars are generally confused in the middle, but more distinct towards the edges. A variety of this sort constitutes what is called the mackerel-back sky. It is often very high in the atmosphere, as is proved from its still appearing high when viewed from the top of a lofty mountain. The cumulus, on the contrary, may be seen on a level with, or even lower than, the observer. The cirro-stratus often appears in the form of a long plain streak, tapering towards the extremities. Sometimes such a figure seems to alight on the cumulo-stratus; and, in these cases, the density of the latter increases in proportion as the former alternately appears and evaporates again on its summits. The usual result is the formation of the nimbus, and a fall of rain. Another principal variety of the cirro-stratus consists of small rows of little clouds, curved in a peculiar manner: it is called the *cymoid* cirro-stratus, and is a sure indication of approaching storms. The last variety of this cloud which we shall now notice, is that large and shallow veil of cloud which covers a large portion of the sky, particularly towards night, and through which the sun and moon are indistinctly seen. Those peculiar refractions of the light of these luminaries, called halos and mock suns, usually appear in this cloud. These are the most certain signs, yet known, of approaching rain or snow.

The cumulo-stratus or twain-cloud is a stage towards the production of rain, and is frequently formed in the following manner:—The cumulus which usually passes along in the wind, seems retarded in its progress, grows denser, spreads out laterally till it overhangs the base in dark and irregular protuberances. This change often takes place in all the cumuli which are near to each other; their bases unite, whilst the superstructure remains asunder, rising up like so many mountain summits, or masses of rocks. The cumulo-strati, in which hail showers and thunder storms occur, look extremely black and menacing before the rain commences. Sometimes the cumulo-stratus evaporates, or changes again to cumulus, but it oftener ends in the nimbus and rain.

The nimbus remains to be described; a cloud which always precedes the fall of rain, snow, or hail. Any of the others above described may increase so much as to obscure the sky, without ending in rain, before which the peculiar characteristic of the rain-cloud may always be distinguished. The best way of obtaining a clear idea of the formation of the nimbus or rain-cloud is to observe a distant shower in profile, from its first formation to its fall in rain. The cumulus seems first arrested in its progress: then a cirrus or cirro-stratus may appear to alight on the top of it. The change to cumulo-stratus then goes on rapidly; and this cloud, increasing in density, assumes that black and threatening aspect which is a known indication of rain. This blackness is soon changed for a more gray obscurity; and this is the criterion of the actual formation of rain drops, which now begin to fall, while a *cirriform* crown of fibres extends from the upper parts of the clouds, and small cumuli enter into the under part. After the shower has spent itself the different modifications appear again in their several stations: the cirrus, the cirro-stratus, or perhaps the cirro-cumulus, appear in the upper regions of the air; while the remaining part of the broken nimbus assumes the form of flocky cumuli, and sails along in the lower current of wind. The reappearance of large cumulo-strati indicates a return of the rain. In showery weather, the alternate formation and destruction of rain-clouds goes on rapidly, and is attended by the other modifications in succession, as above described. From its connexion with local showers, the nimbus is distinguished almost exclusively by bearing in its broad field of sable the honours of the rainbow.

***Rain.*** Theories of rain have been founded on the above observations. Since, as already mentioned, a greater quantity of moisture can exist in a given space as the temperature is higher, it is plain that there is a certain temperature at which air containing some moisture, will just be saturated, and which is called the point of deposition, or the *dewing* point; for, if cooled in the least below this, the air will deposit moisture. When the cooling in the body of air below the dew point is very slight, the effect is merely to disturb the transparency, or produce a *fog*. In the case of dew, formerly considered, the transparency is not affected; because it is not the *mass* of air that is cooled below the point of deposition, but only a minute portion of it which comes into contact with surfaces cooled by radiation. When the cooling in a body of air below the dewing point is considerable, the water is deposited more copiously, and collecting into drops, descends to the earth in the form of *rain;* or, if the temperature be sufficiently low, the drops are partially frozen, and form *sleet;* if fully frozen, *snow;* and if such drops be large and compact, they receive the appellation of *hail*.

Dr. James Hutton of Edinburgh made the first attempt to account for the phenomena of rain, &c. on known principles. Without deciding whether moisture be simply mixed or chemically combined in the air, he conjectured from the phenomena, as is now established by experiment, that the quantity of aqueous vapour which can exist in air varies in a higher ratio than the temperature. Hence he inferred that whenever two volumes of air saturated with moisture are mixed at different temperatures, a precipitation of moisture must ensue, in consequence of the *mean* temperature not being able to support the *mean* quantity of vapour. But if the air, before mixture, was not fully saturated with moisture, then a smaller quantity, or none at all, may be deposited. This theory has been adopted by various meteorologists, particularly Professor Leslie and Mr. Dalton: but Mr. Luke Howard has justly remarked, that it involves the assumption that the mixture should have the *mean* temperature,—a point which was then, and is even yet, not quite settled; although so far as experiment goes, it is fully more favourable to the theory than the *mean* would be.

Mr. Howard accordingly rejects Dr. Hutton's theory, and alleges that rain is almost in every instance the result of the electrical action of clouds upon each other. This idea, he thinks, is confirmed by observations made in various ways upon the electrical state of the clouds and rain; and he supposes that a thunder storm is only a more sudden and sensible display of those energies which are incessantly operating for more general purposes.

There are two circumstances deserving of notice *in the formation of the nimbus or rain-cloud*, the spreading of the superior masses of cloud in all directions, until they become, like the stratus, one uniform sheet; and the rapid motion and visible decrease of the cumulus, when brought under the latter. The cirri, also, which so frequently stretch from the superior sheet upwards, like so many bristles, are supposed by some to be temporary conductors for the electricity evolved by the union of minute particles of vapour into the larger drops which form the rain. In an experiment of Cavallo's with a kite sent up 360 feet in an interval between two showers, and kept up during rain, it seems that the superior clouds were positively electrified before the rain; but on the arrival of a large cumulus, a strong negative electricity took place, which lasted while the cumulus was passing over the kite. We are not, however, warranted to conclude that the cumulus which brings on rain is always negative; as the same effect might ensue from a positive cumulus uniting with a negative stratus: yet the general negative state of the lower atmosphere during rain, and the positive indications commonly given by the true stratus, render this the more probable opinion. It is not, however, absolutely necessary to determine the several states of the clouds which appear during rain; since there is sufficient evidence in favour of the conclusion, that clouds formed in different parts of the atmosphere operate on each other when brought near enough, so as to occasion their partial or entire destruction,—an effect which can be attributed only to their possessing beforehand, or acquiring at the moment, the opposite electricities. Such is Mr. Howard's view of the subject; but until electricity itself, and, in particular, the electricity of the atmosphere, be better understood, it is doubtful if the phenomena of rain be brought any nearer home by being ascribed to electricity. In the present state of science, Dr. Hutton's theory has rather the advantage of depending on principles which are better known, though there is some uncertainty regarding their fitness for the purpose.

Rain is very unequally distributed to the different regions of the globe; but nature has so arranged it, that it is most copious in those latitudes where evaporation is most rapid. There are, however, exceptions to this rule; for, on several tracts on the earth's surface, it hardly ever rains. These are usually far inland, and are generally extensive plains utterly sterile and uninhabitable. The want of rain is in some places partially supplied by the copious deposition of dew. On the contrary, there are some spots where it always rains, and which are mostly on the sea. As the whole atmosphere, when fully charged with humidity, is calculated to hold no more water than would form a sheet 5 inches in depth, while the mean annual deposit is about 35 or 40 inches, it is plain that the supply must be frequently renewed. Rain is more abundant toward the equator than the poles, at the sea-coast than towards the interior, and on elevated situations than on plains.

From the most authentic sources, Mr. Dalton has constructed the following table, showing the mean monthly and annual quantities of rain which have fallen at several places, being the average for many years:—

| | Manchester. 33 Years. | Liverpool. 18 Years. | Chatsworth. 16 Years. | Lancaster. 20 Years. | Kendal. 25 Years. | Dumfries. 16 Years. | Glasgow. 17 Years. | London. 40 Years. | Paris. 15 Years. | Viviers. 40 Years. |
|---|---|---|---|---|---|---|---|---|---|---|
| | Inch. | Inch. | Inch. | Inch. | Inch. | Inch. | Inch. | Inch. | Fr. Inch. | Fr. Inch. |
| January | 2.310 | 2.177 | 2.196 | 3.461 | 5.299 | 3.095 | 1.595 | 1.464 | 1.228 | 2.477 |
| February | 2.568 | 1.847 | 1.652 | 2.995 | 5.126 | 2.837 | 1.741 | 1.250 | 1.232 | 1.700 |
| March | 2.098 | 1.523 | 1.322 | 1.753 | 3.151 | 2.164 | 1.184 | 1.172 | 1.190 | 1.927 |
| April | 2.010 | 2.104 | 2.078 | 2.180 | 2.986 | 2.017 | 0.979 | 1.279 | 1.185 | 2.686 |
| May | 2.895 | 2.573 | 2.118 | 2.460 | 3.480 | 2.568 | 1.641 | 1.636 | 1.767 | 2.931 |
| June | 2.502 | 2.816 | 2.286 | 2.512 | 2.722 | 2.974 | 1.343 | 1.738 | 1.697 | 2.562 |
| July | 3.697 | 3.663 | 3.006 | 4.140 | 4.959 | 3.256 | 2.303 | 2.448 | 1.800 | 1.882 |
| August | 3.665 | 3.311 | 2.435 | 4.581 | 5.039 | 3.199 | 2.746 | 1.807 | 1.900 | 2.347 |
| September | 3.281 | 3.654 | 2.289 | 3.751 | 4.874 | 4.350 | 1.617 | 1.842 | 1.550 | 4.140 |
| October | 3.922 | 3.724 | 3.079 | 4.151 | 5.439 | 4.143 | 2.297 | 2.092 | 1.780 | 4.741 |
| November | 3.360 | 3.441 | 2.634 | 3.775 | 4.785 | 3.174 | 1.904 | 2.222 | 1.720 | 4.187 |
| December | 3.832 | 3.288 | 2.569 | 3.955 | 6.084 | 3.142 | 1.981 | 1.736 | 1.600 | 2.397 |
| | 36.140 | 34.118 | 27.664 | 39.714 | 53.944 | 36.919 | 21.331 | 20.686 | 18.649 | 33.977 |

The depth of rain, according to Humboldt, at the latitudes of 0°, 19°, 45°, and 60°, is, respectively, 96, 80, 29, and 17 inches. In the torrid zone, a small thick rain falls almost every day on that side of the equator where the sun is; but it generally intermits during the night. In many places, there are two wet and two dry seasons in the year; and in some regions, from the effect of the mountains and peculiar winds, places under the same parallel have their wet and dry seasons at opposite periods. Though the annual depth of rain be greatest toward the equator, the number of rainy days increases with the latitude.

Aqueous meteors, so essential to vegetation, have their salutary effects modified by the *chemical qualities* of the moisture in the atmosphere. The salt rain and dew of the vicinity of the Caspian Sea, owing to the vapours which are exhaled from the soil, probably contribute to those saline efflorescences which are said to be gradually overspreading the once fertile soil of Persia. The salt fogs in the west of Jutland are very injurious to the foliage of trees, without being hurtful to the grass. Rain has also been known to be impregnated with sulphur, and with various substances approaching to that of animal and vegetable matters. Some of these communicate to the rain a peculiar colour, as that of blood, &c. On the other hand, fogs occur in which little or no moisture is present: such are called *dry fogs;* and are supposed to be the vapours and ashes ejected by volcanoes, and diffused in the atmosphere by the winds. Their occurring about the time of great eruptions strengthens this conjecture.

*Glaciers.* Ice and snow absorb a large portion of heat during liquefaction, which they give out again on freezing; for, in the ordinary process of nature, water does not cool below 32° F. till the whole be frozen; nor does its temperature rise above that point, while in contact with ice or snow,—that is, till the whole be melted. This property has an important effect on the temperature of snowy districts. It retards and often prevents the occurrence of extreme cold, and it opposes a sudden rise of temperature above the freezing point. The cold in the atmosphere, as was formerly stated, continually increases with the elevation; and, at a certain height, depending on the climate or latitude, perpetual frost prevails. Where the earth's surface attains this height, it is, with the exception of some steep or vertical cliffs, continually covered with snow. The snow acquires new additions from time to time; for, though it may melt slowly from the heat of the ground on which it rests, yet it suffers little decay externally, except what the air carries off by evaporation. The warmth of the solar rays may soften it a little, but this only tends to its farther consolidation. Masses of this sort are called *glaciers.* By accumulating in the manner just mentioned, they often become top-heavy, or acquire such an enormous weight as to break their hold, or crush their lower parts, which are besides liable to be undermined by the warmth of the mountain on which they rest. Hence it not unfrequently happens, that huge masses of ice or conglomerated snow slide or roll down the sides of mountains, transporting, perhaps, large stones or fragments of rocks to which they had adhered, or which had been separated from their beds by the agency of the weather. Detached glaciers often descend into districts having a mean temperature considerably above the melting point of snow. But so great is the heat consumed in liquefying such huge masses, that years may elapse before they entirely disappear; and during that interval others descend; and so on continually. So that the limit of perpetual snow may be found in a climate where little snow falls from the clouds. When glaciers descend into the sea, and particularly when detached and floating, they are termed *icebergs.*

The snow-line, or lower limit in mountains covered with perpetual snow, descends in winter and rises again in summer. Under the equator, this change is scarcely perceptible but it increases with the latitude, and in high latitudes the snow-line has a great range. The direction of the prevailing winds, with many circumstances too numerous to be detailed, has each its effect. The snow-line is lower on the sides of mountains turned from the sun, than on acclivities which receive his rays more perpendicular to their surfaces. Hence it happens, that one side of a mountain may be covered with perpetual snow, whilst at the same height on the opposite side it is in a state of cultivation. The snow-line, therefore, depends so much on localities, that no general rule can be given for computing its altitude. Though often employed for estimating the heights of mountains, it is a most fallacious criterion.

Humboldt gives the following heights of perpetual snow in different parts of the world:— Andes of Quito (lat. 1° to 1° 30′), 2460 toises. Volcano of Puracé (lat. 2° 18′), 2420 toises. Tolima (lat. 4° 46′), 2380 toises. Nevados of Mexico (lat. 19°), 2350 toises. Himáláya (lat. 31°), northern side, 1950 toises; southern side, 2605 toises. Summit of Sierra Nevada, Grenada (lat. 37° 10′), 1780 toises. Caucasus (lat. 42° to 43°), 1650 toises. Pyrenees (lat. 42° 5′ to 43°), 1400 toises. Swiss Alps (lat. 46°), 1370 toises. Carpathian mountains (49° 10′), 1330 toises. Norway (lat. 61° to 67°), 850 to 600 toises; and (lat. 70° to 71° 30′) 550 to 366 toises.

*Colour of the Atmosphere.* That the air has a blue colour, has been conjectured because a distant landscape appears of that cast, which, however, is greatly diminished by a good telescope. Newton ascribed this phenomenon to the greater refrangibility of the blue rays; and some consider it the effect of vapour. The appearance of the sky, when viewed from a high mountain, is of a deep blue, approaching to black. But this must be in some way illusory; because the upper atmosphere is highly transparent, as the heavenly bodies shine with increased splendour.

### Sect. IV.—*Luminous Meteors.*

The refraction and reflection of light by air produce a remarkable phenomenon. While the rays of light move in a medium of uniform density and composition, they are straight; but when they pass obliquely into a medium of a different density, they are bent or *refracted* toward the denser medium. The rays of light, therefore, whilst coming through the atmosphere from the heavenly bodies, are always entering into a denser and denser stratum of air, and are consequently bent down towards the earth. The different rays suffer different degrees of refraction, according to their colour. That of red is the least, then orange, yellow, green, light blue, indigo, and violet. All solid bodies have the property of reflecting light; and it is probable that all bodies whatever reflect light in a greater or less degree. The clouds and air possess this property. The rays which are the most refrangible, are also the most easily reflected. When the sky shines with a fine azure hue, it is by means of the more reflexible rays, which are first reflected from the earth, and afterwards returned by the atmosphere. The refraction and reflection of light enable it to diffuse itself over the atmosphere, illuminating our hemisphere for a considerable time after the sun has gone down and before he has arisen, producing the morning and evening *twilight.*

The rainbow is a circular image of the sun, variously coloured, and produced thus:— The solar rays, by entering the drops of falling rain, are refracted to their farther surfaces, and thence, by one or more reflections, transmitted to the eye. But on escaping from the drop, they undergo a second refraction, by which the rays are separated into their different colours; and in this state are exhibited to an eye properly placed to receive them. The rainbow is never seen but when rain is falling, and the sun and bow are always on opposite sides of the observer.

The halo is a broad circle of a variable diameter, sometimes white, but more commonly exhibiting a faint representation of the colours of the rainbow. It appears in a thin cloud, or in a haze, around the sun and moon's disc.

The corona is a circular space, full of mild whitish light, around the moon's disc. It sometimes passes into a yellowish or brownish colour towards the edges. This and the *halo* are popularly known by the name of *burrs;* and the latter is accounted a prognostic of rain, especially when its diameter is large.

Parhelia or *mock-suns* are images which appear sometimes above and sometimes below the disc of the true sun. They are supposed to be seated in the points of intersection of different halos, and to derive their brightness from the union of several reflections. Parhelia are sometimes surrounded by a whitish border, sometimes by the colours of the rainbow. They are rarely quite circular, and some have luminous trains, as has likewise the sun himself, when near the horizon, in the vicinity of Hudson's Bay. It is there, and in similar cold foggy situations, that parhelia are usually seen.

Mock-moons or paraselenæ are of less frequent occurrence than parhelia, but they are generally ascribed to a similar cause.

Luminous shadows or glories are remarkable phenomena, in which a spectator sees his shadow projected on a cloud with a luminous ring, sometimes coloured like the rainbow, encircling his head. The spectator, in such cases, must either be on an elevation, or the cloud must be very low. The shadow is usually of an enormous size.

*Looming* is the term used by sailors to express a curious optical deception, by which objects come into view, though materially altered as to their real situation or position. The French call it *mirage*, and the Italians *fata morgana*. It often happens at sea, that a distant ship appears as if painted in the sky, perhaps in an inverted position, and not supported by the water. Sunken rocks and sands appear as if raised above the surface. The Swedes long searched in vain for an illusory island of this sort, which they saw from a distance, as if placed between the isles of Aland and the coast of Upland. The shipping and buildings on the shore of Naples have, from Messina, sometimes appeared floating inverted in the air. In 1798, the French coast appeared distinctly raised above the sea, for an hour, as viewed from the opposite shore of Sussex. To the French, whilst marching in the Egyptian deserts, the sandy plain covered in the distance by a dense vapour presented the illusive image of a vast lake, towards which they hastened, but could never reach it.

The aurora borealis, or northern light, is a remarkable luminous phenomenon which occurs during night, and most commonly in clear or frosty weather. It is unknown in low latitudes, and becomes more frequent as we recede from the equator. But it is doubtful if its maximum either as to frequency or brilliancy be at the pole; for in the late north polar expeditions it was seen to the south of the observer, whereas at greater distances from the pole it appears to the north or a little to the west of north of the spectator. It is usually of a reddish colour, inclining to yellow, and sends out frequent coruscations of pale light, which seem to arise from the horizon in pyramidal undulating forms, and shoots with great velocity towards the zenith. Some maintain that a whizzing noise accompanies this phenomenon, but this is not very well ascertained. The light appears sometimes remarkably red, as was the case in many parts of Europe, Dec. 5, 1737. The aurora borealis frequently appears in the form of a luminous arch, chiefly in the spring, and in the autumn of a dry season. The arch is partly bright and partly dark, but generally transparent. This kind of meteor is almost constant during the long winter nights, in high latitudes. The "merry dancers," as it is called in Shetland, afford the inhabitants great relief amid the gloom of their long dreary nights. They commonly appear at twilight near the horizon, of a dun yellow, and sometimes continue so for several hours, without motion; afterwards they break into streams of a stronger light, passing into columns and innumerable different shapes. During this, the colour varies from all the tints of yellow to the most obscure russet, exhibiting the most beautiful appearance. In the northern parts of Sweden and Lapland, the aurora borealis is singularly beautiful, and affords to travellers a very fine light during the whole night. In Hudson's Bay it diffuses a variegated splendour sometimes equal to that of the full moon. Similar lights were observed by Dr. Forster towards the south pole, but they were much feebler than in the northern hemisphere. The cause of such phenomena is unknown. Some ascribe them to electricity and magnetism.

The electricity of the atmosphere is very imperfectly understood. In storms, the clouds usually exhibit the vitreous or positive electricity. In summer, when the earth is dry, and the day warm and serene, the electricity of the air increases from sunrise to noon; in which state it continues for an hour or two, and again diminishes, till the dew appear. It revives towards midnight, and again decreases till it become insensible.

The phenomena of thunder are so well known, as to require no description; but no satisfactory explanation has yet been discovered, except that it is intimately connected with electricity, which being itself in a great measure among the *incognita*, leaves us still in the dark. Thunder is more frequent as we approach the equator, and decreases as the latitude increases, being totally unknown in the arctic regions. It is a very rare phenomenon in intensely cold weather, and seldom occurs during night in the temperate zones. It is usually attended by heavy showers of hail or sleet, and less frequently by rain. The distance of thunder may be estimated, by allowing 1100 feet for each second which elapses between seeing the flash of lightning and hearing the report. It is seldom heard at a greater distance than two miles, and only does mischief when very near.

St. Elmo's fire is a faint light which seems to adhere to the points of bodies carried swiftly through the air. It appears on the tops of ship masts, and at the points of spears and other warlike instruments when in motion. It is generally believed to be an accumulation of electric matter. A single flame of this sort was called by the ancients *Helena*. When seen in pairs, they were called *Castor* and *Pollux*.

Fire-balls are those luminous bodies which appear usually at a great height above the earth, and were on that account long known by the term *meteor*, which is now applied to many other aërial phenomena. They present a very imposing appearance, and are seen of an immense size, sometimes red, but oftener of a vivid dazzling white. They traverse the atmosphere with amazing velocity. This, and their great height, have been inferred from their being seen from various distant places almost at the same instant. Sometimes they burst in pieces, or discharge torrents of flames, with a detonation making both the air and earth to tremble. Some of these balls descend like lightning, break through the roofs of buildings, destroy animals, and shatter vessels at sea; in short, they are often attended with all the disastrous effects of thunder and lightning, with which they are occasionally accompanied. Some consider these balls to be great masses of electric matter, passing from one place to another. Others suppose them to be the same with the aërolites.

Aërolites, or meteoric stones, have frequently descended from the atmosphere from the remotest antiquity. Both the above opinions may be in so far correct; because the fire-balls exhibit very different appearances. Philosophers are very much divided regarding the origin of meteoric stones. Some imagine them to be ejected from volcanoes on the earth's surface; others from volcanoes on the moon. A third class maintain, that they are generated by the combination and condensation of their component parts, previously diffused in the atmosphere in the gaseous form. Others allege, that they are detached stones moving through the boundless regions of space, and which casually come into contact with our planet. All these are little else than conjecture, although their formation in the atmosphere is the most plausible. A numerous list of the most authentic falls of such bodies is given in *Phil. Mag.* vol. lxvii.

Falling stars are very ordinary phenomena everywhere, but still they belong to a class which is not well understood. Near the place of their apparent descent, a fœtid gelatinous substance has frequently been found, of a whitish yellow colour.*

The zodiacal light is a luminous appearance, seen after sunset, or before sunrise, somewhat similar to the milky way, but of a fainter light, in the figure of an inverted cone or pyramid, with its base towards the sun. Its axis is variously inclined to the horizon, and makes an angle of nearly 7° with the plane of the ecliptic. The earliest distinct account of it was given by Cassini in 1683; but this affords no ground for supposing that it had not existed or been seen prior to that date: it is always observable, when the sky is clear, in the torrid zone; but is more rarely to be found as we recede from the equator. The season most favourable for observing it is about the beginning of March: it is much brighter in some years than others, and was particularly brilliant at Paris, 16th February, 1769. The zodiacal light lies in the plane of the sun's equator, and is therefore supposed by some to be connected with his rotation.

## Sect. V.—*Winds.*

Winds are currents of air occasioned by the disturbance of the equilibrium of the atmosphere by the unequal distribution of heat. The general tendency, in such circumstances, is for the heavier columns to displace the lighter; and for the air at the earth's surface to move from the poles toward the equator: in consequence of the rotation of the earth on its axis, another motion is combined with the currents just described. The air, which is constantly moving from points where the earth's motion on its axis is slower to those where it is quicker, cannot have precisely the same motion eastward with the part of the surface over which it is passing, and therefore must, relatively to that surface, acquire a motion somewhat westerly. The two currents, therefore, from the opposite hemispheres, will, on meeting, about the equator, destroy that part of each other's motion which is in the direction of the meridian, leaving nothing but their united motion towards the west. Such is the cause of the *trade-wind*, as proposed and rejected by Dr. Halley: it was shortly after revived by Hadley, and is pretty generally received. The trade-wind (with certain exceptions) blows constantly from the east, between the latitudes of 30° N. and 30° S.; it declines somewhat from due east, towards the parallel to which the sun is vertical at different seasons of the year. The only supply for the air constantly abstracted from the higher latitudes must be made by a counter current, in the upper regions of the atmosphere, carrying back the air from the equator to the poles. In a zone of variable breadth, within the region of trade-winds, calms and rains prevail, caused probably by the mingling and ascending of the opposite currents. High lands change or interrupt the course of the trade-winds: thus, under the lee of the African shore, calms and variable winds prevail near the Cape Verd islands, while an eddy, or counter current of air from the south-west, is generated under the coast of Guinea. The lofty barrier of the Andes shelters the sea on the Peruvian shores from the trade-winds, which are not felt till a ship has sailed eighty leagues westward; but the intervening space is occupied by a wind from the south. In the Indian ocean, the trade-wind is curiously modified by the surrounding land: the southern trade-wind blows regularly from the east and south-east, from 10° to 23° south latitude; but between 10° south and the equator north-west winds prevail from October to April, and south-east the rest of the year; while north of the equator, the wind is south-west in summer, and north-east in winter: these are called *monsoons*, but are not fully understood.

As to the parts of the globe that lie beyond the region of trade-winds, calms prevail pretty generally over a narrow space; beyond which, the region of variable winds extends probably to the poles. Mr. Forster observes, that beyond the tropics the west winds are most common. He also supposes that east winds have an ascendency within the antartic circle. According to Robins, a westerly wind almost constantly prevails about latitude 60° S. in the Pacific

* Professor Brandes, of Breslau, has published a curious Treatise on Falling Stars, to which we may direct the attention of our readers.

Ocean. In Hudson's Bay, westerly winds prevail during three fourths of the year, as also in Kamtschatka. At Melville island, the north and north-west winds prevail: on account of these winds, the Atlantic may be crossed eastward in about half the time of returning westward.

Sea and land breezes arise from the same general principle which chiefly occasions the trade-winds: during the day, when the sun renders the surface of the land warmer than that of the sea, the warmer rarefied air of the land ascends, being buoyed up and displaced by the heavier air rushing from the sea, and thus forming the *sea breeze;* but the reverse often happens during the night, when the surface of the land becomes colder than the sea, and occasions a wind from the land, or a *land breeze.* Winds of this sort are more frequent about islands and small peninsulas than in other situations; but they are not confined to any particular latitude.

A variety of local winds have also been observed. The *etesian*, which is a northerly or north-easterly wind, prevails very much in summer all over Europe. Pliny describes it as blowing regularly in Italy for forty days after the summer solstice. It is supposed to be a part of the great lower current moving towards the equator. Another northern wind, which often continues about a month in February and March, is called the *ornithian* wind, because some birds of passage then make their appearance in the south of Europe. A *squall*, or sudden gust of wind, is common in many places; and when its impetuosity is sufficient to bear along trees, buildings, &c., it is called a *hurricane;* such winds have frequently a whirling motion, and are accompanied with torrents of rain or hail, and even thunder; these are sometimes called *tornadoes:* they are principally confined to the torrid zone. The *sirocco* is a hot southern wind, known on the shores of the Mediterranean; when it reaches Naples and Sicily, it is very moist and relaxing to the human frame. Some warm climates are occasionally visited by excessive hot pestilential winds, generally from the south, and known under a great variety of names in different quarters. Such are the *kamsin* of Egypt, the *simoom* or *samiel* of Arabia and the Desert. The deleterious effects, which frequently cut off whole hordes or caravans, are sometimes ascribed to the predominance of one of the component gases of the air, or to a mixture of nitrous gas, &c.; but this is not well ascertained. The very arid state of the air, bearing along vast quantities of burning sand and dust, must of itself be very prejudicial to animal life. The *harmattan* is a warm, dry, east wind, which occurs in Guinea, and is also of an unwholesome description.

The velocity of the wind varies from nothing up to 100 miles in an hour; but the maximum is variously stated by different authors. According to Smeaton, a gentle breeze moves between 4 and 5 miles per hour, and has a force of about 2 ounces on a foot; a brisk pleasant gale moves from 10 to 15 miles, with a force of 12 ounces; a high wind, 30 to 35 miles, with a force of 5 or 6 pounds; a hurricane, bearing along trees, houses, &c. has a velocity of 100 miles, and a force of 49 pounds on the square foot.

The force of the wind is nearly as the square of the velocity multiplied by the density of the air. Some interesting experiments are described by Colonel Beaufoy, *Annals Phil.* vol. viii. p. 94.

The atmosphere is the vehicle of sound, and we shall close this brief sketch by noticing this property. Till lately, the velocity of sound used to be greatly over-rated. From the experiments of Dr. Moll, in the plains of Utrecht, in 1823, it appears, that the mean velocity of sound is nearly 1100 feet per second; but it varies a little with the temperature and humidity of the air. See *Phil. Trans.* for 1824.

---

## CHAPTER II.

### HYDROLOGY.

THIS branch of natural history makes us acquainted with the various properties and relations of the waters of the globe. Any definition of water is unnecessary; but mankind must have remarked, at a very early period, that the waters distributed over the globe differ considerably in their fitness for drinking, for preparing food, and for other domestic purposes. These differences are occasioned by the foreign bodies which this liquid holds in a state of solution or suspension; for water is capable of dissolving a greater number of substances than any other fluid. Hence it is scarcely ever found native in a state of absolute purity: in some cases, the quantity of foreign matter is so minute, as to have little influence on the taste or other properties; but in other instances they are so abundant, as to render it unfit for common use, or even noxious; while at other times it is medicinal, &c., according to the nature of the substances with which it is impregnated. Native water, free from colour, is almost never poisonous, especially if it be at the same time tasteless; but if blue from copper, green from iron, or brown from vegetable impregnation, it is unfit for the use of man. Water performs the most important functions in the vegetable and animal kingdoms, and enters largely into their compositions, as a constituent part.

The substance of water presents itself under three different forms of aggregation. It under sufficient pressure, it is liquid at all temperatures above 32°, so far as is known. It is densest at the temperature of 40°. When cooled down to 32°, it ordinarily assumes the solid form of ice; but if great care be taken to avoid agitation, it may be cooled almost to zero, without freezing. Congelation commences in the form of prismatic crystals, crossing each other at angles of 60° or 120°, and the temperature, however low before, instantly rises to 32°. During this process, the mass expands with a prodigious force, the volume suddenly increasing about a ninth part. Glass bottles filled with water, and properly stopped, are burst during its congelation, and the same has happened to a strong bomb-shell. Water passes into vapour at all temperatures, and under any pressure; when the elasticity of the vapour equals or exceeds the incumbent pressure, the process proceeds with violence, and is called boiling. Under the ordinary pressure of the atmosphere, this takes place at about 212° of Fahrenheit's scale; but the boiling temperature varies with the pressure: hence, water boils at a lower temperature on a mountain top, and at a higher in a deep pit.

The relations of water to heat are very remarkable. With the exception of hydrogen gas, it absorbs more heat in warming, and parts with more in cooling, than other bodies do. Hence, large bodies of water have a powerful influence in checking or retarding sudden alterations of temperature in the surrounding air. Ice, in melting, absorbs as much heat as would raise its temperature 140°, and gives out the like quantity again in freezing,—a property that enables it to resist or retard sudden alterations of temperature in cold climates, in a more remarkable degree than the other; which, however, exerts its influence in the torrid and temperate as well as in the frigid zone. Lastly, water, in assuming the elastic form, absorbs heat sufficient to raise its temperature 1000°, and parts with as much during re-condensing into water; so that water possesses an almost boundless influence in tempering climate.

Water, as to its composition, was long ranked among the simple elements; but the researches of modern chemistry have ascertained that it is a compound of 88.9 of oxygen, and 11.1 of hydrogen; or its composition by volume and weight may be thus stated: one volume of oxygen combined with two of hydrogen, or eight parts by weight of oxygen, with one of hydrogen. It is composed and decomposed, during many of the operations of nature, and its chemical agency is almost universal. It is an ingredient in most bodies which appear under the crystalline form.

## Sect. I.—*The Ocean.*

The ocean is the origin and fountain of all the other waters which occur, in whatever form, on the face of the globe. According to some naturalists, it forms the remains of the menstruum or chaotic fluid, in which all solid bodies were originally held in a state of solution, and from which they have been precipitated or crystallized, in short, brought to their present state, during the countless ages which these processes are supposed to have occupied, anterior to the creation of man: be this as it may, we are certain, that it is from the vapours exhaled by the ocean that the atmosphere is furnished with sufficient moisture to support and refresh the organized beings which inhabit the earth. All nature languishes when the atmosphere withholds its rain and dews; plants fade and droop; animals feel their strength failing; even man himself, breathing nothing but dust, can with difficulty procure shelter from the sultry heat by which his frame is parched and overpowered. The ocean is the grand thoroughfare of commerce, forming a medium of communication between the most distant and otherwise inaccessible portions of the earth. It consists of one continuous fluid, spread round the land, and probably extending from pole to pole. All the gulfs, all the inland seas, form only portions detached, but not entirely separated, from that universal sea, denominated the ocean. Geographers roundly estimate the ocean and its branches to occupy three fourths of the entire surface of the globe. But to ascertain the exact proportion between the land and water will afford them ample employment for ages to come, though every day adds to the stock of information already acquired.

The ocean is variously subdivided by different authors: it may be conveniently divided into five great basins.

The Pacific, so named from its comparative tranquillity, and often called also the Great South Sea, separates Asia from America. It is the largest of the basins, and somewhat exceeds the entire surface of dry land. Its greatest extent, from east to west, is about 3700 leagues, and breadth 2700. It is bounded on the east by the western and north-west shores of America, and on the west by the eastern coasts of Asia: on the western side, and between the tropics, its surface is studded with innumerable groups of islands, all remarkably small; and consisting generally of coral reefs, rising up like a wall from unknown depths, and emerging but a very little above the sea. These islands are the works of innumerable minute insects, whose incessant labours are thus gradually forming new lands in the bosom of the ocean. On the western side, it communicates with the inland seas of Japan and Okotsk, the Yellow and Chinese seas; and on the eastern side, it has the inlets of California and Queen Charlotte's Sound. The small isles of the Pacific, scattered over the torrid zone, have their temperature so moderated by the ocean as to enjoy the most delightful climate in the world.

The second basin, or Atlantic Ocean, is usually divided into the North Atlantic, and the South Atlantic, or Ethiopic Ocean. The Atlantic is bounded on the east by Europe and Africa; and on the west, by America: that part of it between Europe and North America is frequently called the Western Ocean. The Atlantic basin extends from 70° N. to 35° and 50° S. latitude; but it is only about half the size of the Pacific Ocean. The length is about 2800 leagues, but the breadth, which is very unequal, varies from 600 to 1800. The South Atlantic contains few islands of any size, and no inlets of consequence; but the North Atlantic abounds in large islands, and in deep and numerous inland seas, which penetrate far on each side into both the old and new worlds, and have fitted it for the most extensive commerce on the globe. On its eastern shores it receives few large rivers except the Niger; but on the west it receives the Plata, Orinoco, Amazons, and Mississippi,—the largest rivers on the face of the earth.

The third basin is the Indian Ocean, which washes the shores of the south-east coasts of Africa and the south of Asia. It is bounded on the east by the Indian islands, New Holland, and New Zealand: its length and breadth are each about 1500 leagues: it contains many islands, the two large bays of Bengal and Oman, with the deep inlets of the Persian Gulf and Red Sea. The half-yearly winds called monsoons prevail in its northern parts.

The fourth basin is the Arctic Ocean, an immense circular basin, surrounding the North Pole, and communicating with the Pacific and Atlantic by two channels; the one separating America from Europe, the other America from Asia. Few points of the coasts of Europe and Asia, which occupy a full half of the circumscribing circle, extend much beyond the 70th parallel; and it is doubtful if the other boundaries, consisting of the northern coasts of America and Old Greenland, reach nearer the Pole; so that the mean diameter of this basin may be taken at 800 leagues. Its interior or central parts are little known: several islands are scattered over its southern extremities, the largest of which is Old Greenland, whose northern limit is unknown; the others are Spitzbergen, Nova Zembla, the Isles of New Siberia, those lately discovered by Captain Parry, and several towards Baffin's Bay. The White Sea, on the north coast of Europe, is the only deep gulf connected with this basin, which is of any importance to navigation.

The fifth basin is the Antarctic, which is still less known than the preceding: it joins the Pacific in the latitude of 50° S., and the Indian Ocean in that of 40°. Floating ice occurs in every part of it; but it is very abundant within the parallel of 60°. It was long supposed, that a large continent of land and fixed ice occupied the greater part within the antarctic circle. In 1819, Captain Smith discovered land lying between the longitudes of 55° and 65° W., and beginning at the latitude of 62°. Mr. Weddell has since examined this quarter nearer the Pole, which he believes to be free from fixed ice.

Of the inland seas, the Mediterranean is the largest and most important: it is deserving of notice on various accounts, and in particular as having been the scene of by far the greater number of the nautical adventures of antiquity. It is the "Great Sea" of the Sacred Writings, though we find it there spoken of under other names. Its greatest length, from east to west, is about 2350 miles; and the breadth, which is sometimes small, is at the greatest 650. It is bounded on the south by Africa, on the east by Asia, and on the north by Europe. It communicates on the west with the Atlantic by the Straits of Gibraltar, and with the Black Sea by the Dardanelles Strait on the east. It has many islands, gulfs, and bays, with a very deep inlet on the north called the Adriatic Sea, or Gulf of Venice. The Black Sea is connected with the Sea of Azof; but these containing only brackish water, and being so far inland, have more of the character of lakes than branches of the ocean. Proceeding still farther eastward, we come to the Caspian Sea, which is abundantly salt, and of great dimensions; but being wholly unconnected with the ocean, will be afterwards spoken of under the character of a lake.

The Baltic is pretty much allied to the Black Sea, in having only brackish waters, which are sometimes wholly frozen over for several months in winter, and the ice so strong, that armies have been marched across. The Baltic communicates with the German Sea by the strait called the Cattegat: its greatest length is 1200 miles. The North Sea, or German Ocean, is bounded by Britain and the Orkneys on the west, and the continent of Europe on the east; and reaches from the Straits of Dover to the Shetland Islands, where it joins the Northern Ocean. On the west of the Atlantic are the Gulfs of Mexico and St. Lawrence, and Hudson's and Baffin's Bays; but we must now proceed to treat of the different properties and relations of the ocean, so far as our limits will permit.

The usual colour which sea water exhibits is a bluish green, of various shades. Some maintain, that this is its true and proper colour; others, that it is an optical illusion, occasioned by the greater refrangibility of the blue rays of light,—opinions which may both be true to a certain extent. The ocean seems often to assume various other colours; some of them no doubt real, but as often illusory. Among the more general sources of deception, may be reckoned the aspect of the sky: thus, an apparently dark-coloured sea is a common prognostic of an approaching storm; not that the water then is really blacker than usual, but because the dark colour of the clouds indistinctly seen in, or reflected from the waves, is mistaken for the colour of the sea itself. Whatever other colour the sky happens to wear has a greater or less influence on the appearance of the ocean: thus red clouds seem to tinge it red, &c. On some occasions, the edges of the waves, by refracting the solar beams like a prism, exhibit all the different colours of the rainbow, which is still more nearly imitated by the refraction of the rays in the spray. Not unfrequently, an indistinct image of the neighbouring coast reflected from the ruffled surface is mistaken for the colour of the water.

The variety of colours in the sea may probably arise from animal and vegetable matters diffused through the waters in a putrescent state, and communicating various tints. The yellow and bright green shades seem to be owing to living marine vegetables, which grow at the bottom, stretch their fibres through the water, or spread over the surface; and it is supposed that the colour of innumerable minute animals is often confounded with that of the sea. Near the shore, and especially towards the mouths of rivers, the diffusion of mud and other earthy matters cannot fail to affect the colour of the sea: where it is shallow or very transparent, the colour of the bottom is frequently mistaken for that of the water.

The colour of the Greenland Sea, according to Mr. Scoresby, varies from ultramarine blue to olive-green, and from the most pure transparency to great opacity. These appearances, he thinks, are not transitory, but permanent; not depending on the state of the weather, but on the quality of the water. Hudson, in 1607, noticed these changes, and observed that the sea was blue where there was ice, and green where it was open. This, however, was only accidental. Phipps does not mention the green water; it forms, perhaps, one-fourth of the Greenland Sea, between the latitudes of 74° and 80°; often it constitutes long bands or currents, lying north and south, or N. E. and S. W. Mr. Scoresby sometimes passed through stripes of pale green, olive-green, and transparent blue, in the course of ten minutes. The food of the whale occurs chiefly in the green water, and there the fishers look for them. Whales are more easily taken in the opaque green water than in the transparent blue, because they do not readily see their enemies through the former. On examining the differently-coloured sea waters, Mr. Scoresby found various substances and animalcules, especially in the olive-green water. The number of medusæ was immense: they were about one-fourth of an inch asunder. Hence a cubic foot would contain 110,592. From these, and many similar observations, Mr. Scoresby concludes, that the Arctic Sea owes its colour to animalcules, and that they occasion the opacity of the olive-green water. The blue water contains few animalcules, and is uncommonly transparent. The surface of the Mediterranean sometimes appears of a purple tint. In the Gulf of Guinea, the sea is sometimes white; and around the Maldive islands, black.

The transparency of the sea may in many places be very great, without such property being readily noticed. Thus, where the water is sufficiently deep to be dark at the bottom, it may seem quite opaque, unless some fish or other object happen to come within view. Agitation of the surface will likewise tend to conceal the transparency. In general, the sea is more transparent as we recede from the shore, and in cold climates than in hot; owing perhaps, to the smaller quantity of organic matter diffused in the waters of high latitudes. From this, however, there are exceptions; as in the opacity of the Arctic Sea just noticed, and in the case of the Caribbean Sea, which is often remarkably transparent. Admiral Milne observed the bottom at a depth of 150 feet in the Caribbean Sea. Authors are not agreed to what depth the solar rays penetrate; and indeed we have every reason to suppose that this must depend upon and be as various as the transparency. Some limit the penetration to a depth of 100 yards; while others more than double that quantity. The light should surely penetrate to at least double the depth to which an observer can see from the surface.

The temperature of the sea has probably a tendency to follow the mean temperature of the climate; but many powerful causes must interfere and modify it. Thus, between the tropics, the mean temperature of the surface of the ocean is about 80°, and generally ranges between 77° and 84°. Beyond the tropics, it begins to decrease, but without observing any strict connexion with the latitude; because, on account of the great specific heat of water, powerful currents cannot fail partially to preserve, for some time, the temperature of the place from which they come. Hence, currents from the torrid zone, on passing into higher latitudes, raise the temperature of the sea above what usually belongs to such parallels; the reverse holds of cold icy currents from the arctic regions. The temperature of the ocean is much more steady than that of the superincumbent air, and has likewise a smaller annual range: unless where very shallow, it has scarcely any diurnal range.

The temperature of the sea on descending below the surface generally decreases, but not according to any uniform or known law. Thus, at a depth of five fathoms, it is sometimes 1° colder, while in other instances it requires 100 fathoms for 1°. Sometimes the cold attains its maximum at a depth of 100 fathoms, and sometimes it requires 400 or 500 fathoms. According to an experiment related by Capt. Sabine, the temperature of the Caribbean Sea was 45.5° at a depth of 1000 fathoms, while its surface was 83°. But the enormous pressure at the bottom probably compressed the ball of the thermometer, and kept the apparent temperature 45.5° above the truth. In the Arctic Sea, however, the temperature increases with the depth. Mr. Scoresby, who first ascertained this, found an increase of 6.6° and 8° at the respective depths of 120 and 730 fathoms; Capt. Parry, 6° at 240 fathoms; Capt. Sabine, 7.5° at 680 fathoms; Lieut. Beechy, 10° at 700 fathoms; and Mr. Fisher, 9.5° at a depth of 188 fathoms. Thus, the rate of increase of temperature in the Arctic Sea has as inconstant a connexion with the depth as the decrease in the temperate and torrid zones. Sea water freezes about 28°; after which, the ice has been observed to cool down to — 55°; but we cannot thence infer, that a lower temperature does not occur in the polar regions.

The phosphorescence of the sea is a common but very remarkable phenomenon, concerning the cause of which authors are not agreed. But most probably, as Newton conjectured, it proceeds from a variety of causes. Since his time, it has engaged the attention of many eminent philosophers. The appearance of these lights is by no means uniform. Sometimes a vessel, in traversing the ocean, seems to mark out a track of fire; while each stroke of an oar emits a light, sometimes brilliant and dazzling, at other times tranquil and pearly. These lights are grouped in endless variety. Perhaps, at one time, innumerable shining points float on the surface, and then unite into one extensive sheet of light. At another time, the spectator fancies he sees large sparkling figures, like animals in pursuit of each other, incessantly vanishing and re-appearing. Such lights have been ascribed to luminous animals, and to the phosphorescence of semiputrescent matter diffused in the ocean. It is well known, that various fishes and other marine animals emit light, which does not in every instance appear to be voluntary, or to depend on the vital principle, as, in some of them, it continues, and perhaps increases, after death: but motion seems to be either a principal cause, or at least an exciting one; for this light more rarely occurs, and is much fainter, in still water, whilst it becomes more and more brilliant as the motion increases. It is also more abundant immediately before and during storms. In vol. v. p. 303. of the *Edin. Phil. Jour.*, Dr. Francis Buchanan has given a very interesting account of an extraordinary shining of the sea, which he observed, 31st July, 1785, in longitude 61° 25′ E., latitude 6° 32′ N. "About a quarter past seven P. M.," says he, "the sea was observed to be remarkably white. The sky was everywhere clear, except around the horizon, where, for about 15°, it was covered with a dark haze, as is usual in such latitudes. The whiteness gradually increased till past eight. The sea was then as high-coloured as milk, not unlike the milky way, the luminous appearance very much resembling the brighter stars in that constellation. It continued in this state till past midnight, and only disappeared as daylight advanced. The whiteness prevented us from being able to see either the break or the swell of the sea, although both were considerable, as we knew from the motion of the ship and the noise. There was much light upon deck, as we could discern all the ropes much more distinctly than usual. We drew several buckets of water, in which, even when at rest, there appeared a great number of luminous bodies. The bulk of them did not appear to be more than one quarter of an inch in length, and nearly as much in breadth. Some, however, were one inch and a half long, and of the same breadth as the others. These were seen to move in the same manner as a worm does in water. When taken up on the finger, they retained their shining faculty even when dry. When brought near a candle, their light disappeared; but, by minute attention, an extremely fine white filament could be observed and lifted upon the point of a pin. It was of a uniform shining colour and form, and about the thickness of a spider's thread. In a gallon of water there might be about 400 of these animals emitting light. The water itself, when in the bucket, had a natural appearance. The atmosphere was seemingly free from fog. The stars were bright, and there was no moonlight. The night before, the same appearance was observed at ten P. M.; it lasted only 20 minutes; but as I was below, I did not hear of it till it was over."—"The animalcules which occasion the unusual luminousness of the sea emit light only when strongly agitated, and hence appear close by the sides of the ship, or when any larger fish passes swiftly, or when a bucket of water is drawn and suddenly poured out."—"In the year 1805, on returning from St. Helena to England, a little north from the equinoctial line, and near the coast of Africa, I had an opportunity of seeing a still more splendid appearance of the luminous animalcules. Soon after dark in the evening, it being nearly calm, we saw numerous lights at a distance, like the lamps of a great city. The lights gradually approached the frigate, and on reaching us appeared to arise from a great many large fishes (albicores) sporting in the water, and agitating the animalcules, so as to excite their luminous powers."

The depth of the sea is a question on which our information is very imperfect, and there is little likelihood that much accurate information will ever be obtained on the subject, so far as regards the wide ocean. According to the speculations of the late celebrated Marquis Laplace, the depth of the ocean is comparatively small, and nearly uniform. If, however, it be recollected that the bottom of the sea is still a part of the earth's surface, and by much the greater part too, one would be apt to ask, why that larger part of the surface should be more level than what appears as dry land? The soundings which have been made in the ocean are quite inadequate to decide the question. They, however, often indicate great inequalities in the depth; but how far hollows may have been filled with *débris*, or asperities worn down, it is not easy to say; though it is more likely that the summits of mountains exposed to the alternate or combined actions of air and moisture suffer a more rapid abrasion than those which are wholly under water. In general, the slope of the adjacent shore is continued downward for a good way under water; that is, the sea is usually shallow where the shore is flat, while its depth increases rapidly by the side of a cliff or steep mountain. It is therefore probable, that some islands, though very small, may be the tops of sub-marine mountains as large, perhaps, as the highest which occur on the earth's surface. In many instances, no bottom has been found; but this might proceed either from the shortness of the line, or from its being borne aside by rapid currents. We have already mentioned a sounding of 6000 feet in the Caribbean sea; but Lord Mulgrave's line of 4680 feet did not reach the bottom of the Northern Ocean. In the entrance of the German or North Sea, at the Straits of Dover, the central depth is 29 fathoms. This extensive basin contains various shallows and sand-banks; yet, generally speaking, the depth increases in going northward, and near to Bergen in Norway it amounts to 190 fathoms. A very interesting account of the bed of the German Sea is given by Mr. Stevenson, *Edin. Phil. Jour.* iii. 42.; and in the third volume of the *Memoirs of the Wernerian Society*.

The level of the open sea is believed, generally speaking, to be everywhere the same; or to form a portion of the surface of an oblate spheroid, to which the surface of the land approaches with less accuracy. Some gulfs and inland seas appear to deviate in some measure from the general rule. This is more particularly the case where the communication of such seas with the ocean is narrow; and there are a few other exceptions.* When the general motion of the ocean or of the trade-winds is directed into the mouth of an inland sea, it has a tendency to raise its level above that of the ocean. On this account it is that the Arabian Gulf or Red Sea is higher than the ocean, and still higher than the Mediterranean, which, from the opposite action of the wind and the great evaporation, is supposed to be a little below the general level.† Some gulfs and inland seas, as the Baltic and Black Sea, rise in spring, from the copious influx of river water, and are lowered in summer by evaporation and the efflux at their mouths. Of late years, there has been considerable discussion regarding the subsidence of the Baltic below the level it had formerly maintained. Whilst some support this opinion, and venture to explain the cause of the subsidence, others deny the fact altogether. The trade-winds and general westward motion of the ocean force the water into the Gulf of Mexico, so as to maintain a higher level there than on the western coast of the Isthmus of Darien.‡ The consequence of this accumulation of water is, that it generates a current moving northwards; and which, after various windings through the Atlantic, at length reaches the western shores of Europe, as will be more particularly noticed hereafter. Some naturalists allege, that the *débris*, or alluvial matters daily abraded by the action of the weather on the surface of the land, and swept into the ocean by the rain and rivers, must, at length, raise the level of the ocean till it cover the whole globe, and restore the reign of ancient chaos. Unless there be some compensating process, which either makes up for the exhausted materials, or gradually elevates the entire continents above the water, it is not very easy to guess at an alternative. A compensating power is situated deep in the crust of the earth.

The taste of sea water is disagreeable and bitter, at least when taken from the surface or near the shore; but when drawn from great depths, its taste is only saline. It would therefore seem that the bitterness is owing to the greater abundance of animal and vegetable matter near the surface. Man, in a civilized state, cannot make use of sea water as drink; yet it is said that the inhabitants of Easter Island, in the Pacific Ocean, make it their usual beverage. Some of the lower animals occasionally travel far to drink sea water. Sheep are very fond of licking the dry salt; and so are horses and cattle. With them it is a cure for various complaints. Several attempts have been made to render sea water potable, or to free it from salt. Distillation is the most effectual; but the expense of fuel is a serious objection to this method at sea, and, after all, it does not divest it of all its bitterness. Thus, in the midst of water, mariners are frequently in danger of dying of thirst, when they run short of fresh water. Sea ice, when melted, affords nearly fresh water; but being devoid of air, its taste is not very agreeable, though it would be highly prized in time of need. A temporary, and in some degree an imaginary, relief may be obtained, by holding salt water in the mouth.

The saline contents of the waters of the wide ocean do not, so far as experience has gone, vary much in different latitudes and under different meridians, although we ought to find the sea fresher in the spaces occupied by the internal limits of the trade-wind, and also in those tracts of the ocean where calms and a high temperature prevail, as on the west coast

---

* Strabo says the level of the Gulf of Corinth is higher than that of the Gulf of Cenchreæ.

† *Vide* Maclaren on the level of the Red Sea, in the Edinburgh Philosophical Journal.

‡ The mean height of the Pacific above the Atlantic is said to be 3.52 feet.

of Africa. The mean is about 3.5 per cent. in the weight of the water; but the saltness is more or less affected by currents and storms. It is diminished at the surface during heavy rains, and by the discharge of rivers; but increased by evaporation, which carries off the water fresh, and leaves the salt behind: hence there is often little consistency in detached observations. From a great variety of experiments, Dr. Marcet concludes: 1. That the Southern Ocean contains more salt than the Northern, in the ratio of 1.0291 to 1.02757. 2. That the mean specific gravity of sea water near the equator is 1.02777, intermediate between those of the northern and southern hemispheres. 3. That there is no notable difference in sea water under different meridians. 4. That there is no satisfactory evidence that the sea at great depths is more salt than at the surface. 5. That the sea, in general, contains more salt where it is deepest and most remote from land; and that its saltness is always diminished in the vicinity of large masses of ice. 6. That small inland seas, though communicating with the ocean, are much less salt than the open ocean. 7. That the Mediterranean contains rather larger proportions of salt than the ocean. This last is explained from the fact, that a pretty strong current from the Atlantic always flows inward at the mouth of the Mediterranean, to supply, as was supposed, the water which escaped by evaporation, and left its salt behind. So great, however, is the influx, that this inland sea ought to have become perfect brine, or perhaps to have deposited beds of salt, if there were *no efflux;* and accordingly it is maintained that there is an outward current at the bottom, very deep, which carries off this excess of salt, and prevents its deposition in the vast hollows in the bottom. The water drawn up from this lower current is salter, in a small degree, than at the surface.

The following are the mean specific gravities of the waters of different seas, according to Dr. Marcet's experiments:—

| | | | |
|---|---|---|---|
| Arctic Ocean | 1.02664 | Black Sea | 1.01418 |
| Northern Hemisphere | 1.02829 | White Sea | 1.01901 |
| Southern Hemisphere | 1.02882 | Baltic | 1.01523 |
| Yellow Sea | 1.02291 | Lake Ourmia, in Persia | 1.16507 |
| Mediterranean | 1.02930 | Dead Sea | 1.11100 |
| Sea of Marmora | 1.01915 | | |

The saltness of inland seas is subject to many varieties. In the entrance to the Black Sea, the water is much salter at the bottom than the surface. To account for this, it is said that an under current enters from the Mediterranean. It is well known that there is an outward current at the surface, which brings with it the less salt water of the Black Sea. The saltness of inland seas is often affected by the direction and strength of the wind, either forcing in, or retarding the entrance of, water from the ocean. Accordingly, from the experiments of Wilcke, it appears that the saltness of the Baltic is increased by a west wind, and still more so by a north-west wind; but it undergoes a diminution when the wind is from the east. Thus, the specific gravities are, for a

| | | | |
|---|---|---|---|
| Wind at W. | 1.0067 | Storm at W. | 1.0118 |
| Ditto at N. W. | 1.0098 | Wind at E. | 1.0039 |

Hence, the proportion of salt in the Baltic depends in no small degree on the different winds; a proof that the salt is not only derived from the neighbouring ocean, but that storms have a much greater effect on it than has been commonly supposed.

The constituent parts of sea water have been an object of examination to many chemists, and various sets of experiments made to determine them. The late Dr. Murray of Edinburgh was of opinion that there were various sources of fallacy in analysing sea water; and that different modes of operating on the same water gave very different results. Two reasons are assigned for this; viz. that some of the different salts mutually decompose each other in the process, and that a part is lost altogether by evaporation, especially if the temperature be high. According to this eminent chemist, 10,000 parts of water from the Frith of Forth, which is not sensibly different from that of the ocean, contain 220 parts of common salt, 33 of sulphate of soda, 42 of muriate of magnesia, and 8 of muriate of lime. On analysing sea water from N. latitude 25° 30′, W. longitude 32° 30′, Dr. Marcet made the numbers respectively 266, 47, 52, and 12. According to Bladh, the saltness is greater about the tropics than at the equator. Dr. Trail maintains the contrary; and also that the saltness increases with the depth.

Ice is formed on the sea, though its saltness enables it to resist the process of congelation at the ordinary freezing point of fresh water. This quality does not withstand the rigour of the Arctic regions, where the temperature of the air has been observed so low as 55° F. Sea water freezes about 28°, but the temperature varies a little with the saltness.—It is a curious circumstance, that sea water parts with its salt in freezing. Hence compact transparent sea ice affords fresh water on being melted. When, however, the ice is of a loose or cellular texture, its pores sometimes contain liquid brine; and therefore, on being melted, it affords brackish water. It is supposed to be the affinity between the water and salt which retards the congelation of sea water; because the greater the saltness, the lower is the freezing temperature. Detached masses of ice are occasionally met with, floating in the ocean at so low a parallel of latitude as 40° in both hemispheres; having been conveyed thither by currents from the polar regions.* At the parallel of 50° they are more abundant; and there it is common, in winter, to see the shallow edges of the sea covered with ice. At 60° N. latitude, the gulfs and inland seas are frequently frozen over their whole surface. As we proceed toward the poles, the ice becomes more and more abundant, and of larger dimensions, till at length we come to *fields* of ice, and *icebergs* or mountains of ice. The process of congelation commences at the surface of the sea, with the formation of slender prismatic crystals resembling wet snow: this the seamen call *sludge*. The surface is at first rough; but, by the union of the crystals and the accumulation of the *sludge*, the surface becomes smooth and forms a continued sheet, which is next broken, by the agitation of the water, into fragments of about three inches diameter; these again coalesce into a continued sheet of a stronger texture, which is in its turn broken as before, but into larger fragments called *pancake ice*. Where the water is free from all agitation, the congelation goes on more regularly, and some allege more rapidly. During 24 hours of keen frost, the ice frequently attains a thickness of from two to three inches, and is soon fit for walking on: it is then called *bay ice*. When the thickness is about a foot, it is called *light ice;* and when three feet thick, *heavy ice*. The term *field* is given to a sheet of ice so extensive that its farther end cannot be seen from a mast-head. Very large loosened pieces, whose boundaries may be seen readily, are called *floes*. Fragments of thick ice floating together are called *brash ice*. Floating ice of any sort, sufficiently loose to allow a vessel to pass through, is called *open* or *drift ice*. Indeed, there is no end to the terms which seamen apply to different sorts of ice. The sudden disruption of extensive fields is sometimes produced by that powerful tendency to undulation of the surface, communicated by the motions of the adjoining liquid surface of the ocean during a continued storm, which is denominated a *ground swell*. The ice, when thin, merely yields; but, if thick and little flexible, it is broken with tremendous noise. A very interesting account of such a phenomenon is given by a party of missionaries who passed along the coast of Labrador in sledges drawn by dogs. They narrowly escaped destruction; but were near enough to witness all its grandeur. "The missionaries met a sledge with Esquimaux turning in from the sea, who threw out some hints that it might be as well for them to return. After some time, their own Esquimaux hinted that there was a ground swell under the ice. It was then scarcely perceptible, except on lying down and applying the ear close to the ice, when a hollow disagreeable grating noise was heard ascending from the abyss. As the motion of the sea under the ice had grown more perceptible, they became alarmed, and began to think it prudent to keep close to the shore. The ice also had fissures in many places, some of which formed chasms of one or two feet; but as these are not uncommon even in its best state, and the dogs easily leap over them, they are frightful only to strangers. As the wind rose to a storm, the swell had now increased so much that its effects on the ice were extraordinary, and really alarming. The sledges, instead of gliding smoothly along as on an even surface, sometimes ran with violence after the dogs, and sometimes seemed with difficulty to ascend a rising hill. Noises, too, were now distinctly heard in many directions, like the report of cannon, from the bursting of the ice at a distance. Alarmed by these frightful phenomena, our travellers drove with all haste towards the shore; and as they approached it, the prospect before them was tremendous. The ice, having burst loose from the rocks, was tossed to and fro, and broken in a thousand pieces against the precipices with a dreadful noise; which, added to the raging of the sea, the roaring of the wind, and the driving of the snow, so completely overpowered them as almost to deprive them of the use both of their eyes and ears. To make the land was now the only resource that remained; but it was with the utmost difficulty that the frightened dogs could be driven forward; and as the whole body of the ice frequently sunk below the summits of the rocks, and then rose above them, the only time for landing was the moment it gained the level of the coast,—a circumstance which rendered the attempt extremely nice and hazardous. Both sledges, however, succeeded in gaining the shore, and were drawn up on the beach, though not without great difficulty. Scarcely had they reached it, when that part of the ice from which they had just escaped burst asunder, and the water, rushing up from beneath, instantly precipitated it into the ocean. In a moment, as if by signal, the whole mass of ice for several miles along the coast, and extending as far as the eye could reach, began to break and to be overwhelmed with the waves. The spectacle was awfully grand. The immense fields of ice rising out of the ocean, clashing against one another, and then plunging into the deep with a violence which no language can describe and a noise like the discharge of a thousand cannon, was a sight which must have struck the most unreflecting mind with solemn awe. The brethren were overwhelmed with amazement at their miraculous escape; and even the pagan Esquimaux expressed gratitude to God for their deliverance."†

The term *iceberg* is applied to huge masses of ice resembling mountains, whether resting on the land or floating on the sea. The latter part appear to be sometimes formed in the

* Horsburgh mentions icebergs having been met with in South lat. 35° 54¼′, and West long. 17° 59′.—*Phil. Mag.*

† Brown's History of the Propagation of Christianity, vol. ii. p. 57

sea itself, by the accumulation of ice and snow; at other times to be fragments of land icebergs or glaciers, which have been piling up on the shore till quite overgrown, and ultimately broken and launched into the ocean by their own weight. Masses of this sort abound in Baffin's Bay, where they are sometimes two miles long, and half or one third as broad. They are bristled with various spires, rising, perhaps, 100 feet above the surface, and descending half as much below it. When compact ice floats in water, the part under the surface is about nine times as great as that above it; and hence the icebergs may sometimes descend to a great depth, though they should be far from consisting of very compact ice. Icebergs of an even surface, rising 90 feet above the sea, and having an area of five or six square miles, are very common. Those of East Greenland are of inferior size, and they are still smaller around Spitzbergen, where some of enormous dimensions occur on shore. The reason which Mr. Scoresby assigns for this is, that, owing to the shallowness of the water into which the huge masses are precipitated, they are all shattered against the bottom into a thousand pieces before they are fairly launched into deep water. "On an excursion to one of the Seven Icebergs, in July 1818," says Mr. Scoresby, "I was particularly fortunate in witnessing one of the grandest effects which these polar glaciers ever present. A strong north-westerly swell, having for some hours been beating on the shore, had loosened a number of fragments attached to the iceberg, and various heaps of broken ice denoted recent shoots of the seaward edge. As we rowed towards it, with a view of proceeding close to its base, I observed a few little pieces fall from the top; and while my eye was fixed upon the place, an immense column, probably 50 feet square and 150 feet high, began to leave the parent ice at the top; and leaning majestically forward, with an accelerated velocity fell with an awful crash into the sea. The water into which it plunged was converted into an appearance of vapour or smoke, like that from a furious cannonading. The noise was equal to that of thunder, which it nearly resembled. The column which fell was nearly square, and in magnitude resembled a church. It broke into a thousand pieces. This circumstance was a happy caution; for we might have inadvertently gone to the very base of the icy cliff, from which masses of considerable magnitude were continually falling." A huge mass of this sort which fell on a Russian ship, broke the fore and main masts, sprung the bowsprit, and flung the ship over with such violence that a piece of ordnance was thrown overboard from under the half-deck, and the captain and some of the crew were projected in the same manner. The captain, however, escaped unhurt; but the mate and two others were killed, and many were wounded.

Icebergs variously affect navigation. They are often highly useful by protecting navigators from gales, as well as from the concussions of drift ice, which moves more quickly when acted on by the wind than the massy iceberg. To the latter, ships are sometimes moored, but not without danger; for these floating masses are sometimes so nicely balanced as to be easily overturned, should they happen to catch the bottom of the sea. The concussion produced in this way sometimes detaches large fragments; and sometimes the iceberg rolls forward, to the imminent danger of the vessel, though perhaps 100 yards distant,—so great are the waves and whirls caused by such an occurrence. Many dangers and discouragements attend the navigation of the polar seas: but the recent attempts to discover a north-west passage through the Arctic Sea have rendered the ice a subject of considerable interest. These attempts have not yet been crowned with success: but different navigators have brought such different accounts of the state of the ice, that it is probably very changeable and very difficult to examine. It is not quite agreed that any navigator has been within 6° of the North Pole; although some accounts pretend to a still nearer approach. Captain Parry, in his last voyage, reached to 82° 45′ N. lat. The failure of Captain Cook's attempt to penetrate to the South Pole gave rise to an idea, which has been pretty generally entertained since his time, that the South Pole is surrounded with fixed ice to the distance of 18° or 19°; and a more recent Russian expedition gave still worse hopes, as they could not get beyond the latitude of 70° S. Mr. Weddell, however, has since reached 255 miles nearer the pole, and met with no such obstruction: this enterprising navigator contends strenuously that the South Pole must be free from ice, and might be reached by sea. Some of his arguments are rather plausible; but the question is involved in so many uncertainties, that nothing less than actual trial can decide it.

The expansion and contraction of ice has important effects. Though water undergoes a great expansion in the act of freezing, yet ice obeys the ordinary law of solids,—that of expanding by heat and contracting by cold. The effect, therefore, of intense cold is to contract ice, which, if of large dimensions, or fixed all around, has no alternative but to rend where it is contracting most. This is often attended with a tremendous report. On the contrary, a rise of temperature may not only bring the parts to meet again, but often makes them lap over, or burst up with great violence.*

The motion of the waters of the ocean is almost perpetual; and it is believed, that without

* The most satisfactory account of the polar ice is that of Scoresby, first published in the Memoirs of the Wernerian Natural History Society

this provision in the economy of nature the sea, in place of tempering and purifying the air, would both become putrid and exhale noxious vapours.

*Waves.* The motions which first present themselves to our notice are the partial and alternate rising and falling of the surface, known by the name of undulations or *waves.* This sort of motion is caused by the wind, which, by dislodging or depressing a certain portion of the waters, has destroyed the equilibrium or level, which they naturally endeavour to recover. Waves may be compared to the reciprocation of water in a syphon or bent tube. It was in this way that Newton deduced the velocity of waves, and the time required to an undulation. If water ascend and descend alternately in the legs of a bent tube, and a pendulum be constructed whose length between the point of suspension and centre of oscillation is equal to half the length of the water in the tube, then this fluid will ascend and descend during each oscillation of the pendulum. Hence the velocity of the waves is as the square roots of their breadths; the breadth being the distance between the tops of the ridges. In the same way, it may be shown that the apparent progressive motions of waves through spaces equal to their breadths are performed in the times in which pendulums oscillate whose lengths are equal to these breadths. Hence waves, whose breadth is 39⅛ inches, will seem to pass over that space in one second. Waves are scarcely ever without progressive motion; but the real progress of the surface of the water is generally small, compared to the apparent motion of the waves; as is easily proved from any floating body which does not rise above the surface so as to be hurried forward by the wind. Waves are distinguished into natural and accidental. The natural are proportional to the strength of the wind producing them:—the accidental are occasioned by repercussion of the wind from hills and bold coasts, and by the dashing of the waves on rocks and shoals. Divers, it is said, find the waters perfectly still at the depth of thirty yards, during the greatest tempest. But this can only be known of some sheltered spots; for when do divers descend in an open sea during a tempest? Waves are always seen rolling towards the shore; but an obstacle opposed to them becomes the centre of a new series which spreads in circles. One set of waves, however, may not interfere with the motion of another, and they may mutually cross without interruption. Sometimes the ordinary oscillations are combined with a distant swell, called the *bore,* which rises impetuous after certain intervals. Breakers, or waves which break against some obstacle, when formed over a great extent of shore, are distinguished by the name of *surf.* The surf is greatest in those parts of the ocean where the wind blows always nearly in the same direction.

*Currents.* There are two permanent and general sorts of currents in the ocean, which are supposed to originate in two great movements,—that of the tropical waters westward round the globe, and that of the polar waters towards the equator. But it is plain that the latter, or polar currents, imply the existence of a *third* set, moving in the opposite direction; otherwise the waters at the poles would soon be exhausted, together with the ice from which they are partly derived. It is well known that the rain, fog, or snow, which falls in the polar regions, could never supply any perceptible current towards the equator. The movement of the tropical waters westward is ascribed to the agency of the trade winds, which, blowing constantly from the east, must impress their motion on the sea to a certain extent. But the resulting current is necessarily modified by the position of the great continents. This grand westerly motion prevails generally between 30° S. and 30° N. latitude. According to Humboldt, its mean velocity is from nine to ten miles a-day. In the Atlantic it separates into two branches, one of which forms the well-known Gulf Stream. This branch flows northward, through the middle of the Atlantic, till it reaches the Cape Verd Islands: it then turns west, passes through the Caribbean Sea, and the strait between Cuba and Yucatan, winds round the Mexican Gulf, and rushes out by the Bahama Channel; then spreading out to a greater breadth, it sweeps along the shores of the United States to Newfoundland. At this point it is deflected south-eastward by a southerly current from Baffin's Bay, and passing the Azores and Canary Isles, returns in a great measure into itself, and repeats its circumgyration. The waters of the North Atlantic, between the latitudes of 11° and 43°, thus form a continued whirlpool, completing a circuit of 3800 leagues in about 34 months. Its velocity is greater as the depth and breadth are less. Its breadth is 51 leagues in the Bahama Channel, and velocity from three to five miles an hour. In its retrograde course from longitude 50° to the Azores the breadth is 160 leagues, and velocity from seven to eight miles a-day. An insulated expanse of almost motionless water, 140 leagues in breadth, occupies the interior of the circuit. This grand current sends off one branch near Newfoundland, which proceeds north-eastward, and sometimes deposits tropical fruits on the shores of the British isles and Norway. In 1776, Dr. Franklin traced this current, by means of its high temperature, quite across the Atlantic; and, since his time, it has been more closely traced, especially by Captain Sabine. A second branch, escaping at the Azores, enters the Straits of Gibraltar, and forms the upper and middle current which prevails in that strait. Another branch of the great tropical current sets along the coast of Brazil, and at length passes through the Straits of Magellan. In the Pacific Ocean the waters have a general westward motion from the coast of Peru, which must be partly supplied by the last-mentioned current after doubling Cape Horn. The current from the coast of Peru is less perceptible, till it enters the Indian Ocean; when, strengthened by the northerly currents there, it flows along the eastern coast of Africa, and doubles the Cape of Good Hope, in a rapid stream, 130 miles broad, and from 7° to 8° warmer than the contiguous sea. A current from the South Pole sets along the west side of New Holland into the Bay of Bengal: it is supposed that other portions of the general polar current deflect the great westerly current northward, after it has passed the southern promontories of Africa and America. In the Northern Ocean, in the space comprised between Greenland and the coasts of Britain and Norway, and between Labrador and Spitzbergen, a great body of waters, acted on by three or four lateral currents, is supposed to perform a perpetual circuit. These waters receive their impulse eastward from a branch of the Gulf Stream, which passes from Newfoundland along the north-west coasts of Scotland and Norway. At the North Cape in Lapland, a great westerly current from Nova Zembla turns the waters north-westward along both sides of Spitzbergen. Beyond this island, being met by a current from the pole, they turn south-westward, and pass along the coast of Greenland to Davis's Straits, where they are deflected southward by a fourth current from Baffin's Bay; and having returned to Newfoundland, recommence their revolution. Thus two great whirlpools, connected with one another, touch at the Bank of Newfoundland, which seems to be a bar cast up by their conflicting waters; and revolving in opposite directions, occupy four-fifths of the North Atlantic. The small current which sets from the Bay of Biscay across the mouth of the English Channel, and through St. George's Channel, is most probably a branch of the Gulf Stream which had come off at the Azores. Were other parts of the ocean as minutely examined as the North Atlantic, it is to be expected that other great vortices would be discovered.

Local or temporary currents are produced by winds, the discharge of rivers, the melting of ice, &c. In general, currents which do not descend to a great depth are liable to change with the winds, particularly when they blow for a long time with equal force, as the monsoons do. These winds give by turns entirely opposite directions to the currents which prevail from the Maldivia Islands to Arabia and Zanguebar. When the supply of fresh water in an inland sea falls short of what is carried off by evaporation, its level will have a tendency to fall below that of the ocean; and hence the water will flow into it from the ocean. But, as formerly noticed, a continual influx of salt water, to be concentrated by evaporation, must have a tendency to render such inland sea salter than the ocean; and the salter water being the heavier, naturally endeavours to keep under the lighter, which enters from the ocean. In this way, it forms an outward current in the bottom of the entrance. Such is said to be the case with the Mediterranean, as was first hinted by Dr. Hudson in 1724. The reverse of all this takes place where the supply of fresh water in an inland sea exceeds the evaporation, as is the case with the Baltic, the Black Sea, and the Sea of Azof. In these the outward fresher current is uppermost, while the heavier salter current enters below. Since the mean quantity of salt brought in must equal what is carried out, if no permanent change take place in the saltness of the inland sea, it follows that the salter current is the smaller of the two. However, the weather sometimes produces temporary exceptions to this general rule. The current which flows into the Mediterranean by the Straits of Gibraltar sets along the shores of Africa and Egypt to Syria, where it turns north-westward; and, joined by the current from the Dardanelles, it makes the circuit of the Adriatic, then of the coasts of Tuscany, France and Spain, and ultimately returns to the Straits. In the Cattegat, a northern current proceeds from the Baltic along the coasts of Sweden; and another, a southern current, enters into the Baltic along the coasts of Jutland. In the German Sea, a north current sets from the Straits of Dover along the continental shore, while a south current comes from the Orkneys along the British coast.

Whirlpools or eddies are produced by the meeting of currents which come in different directions. These, by encountering in a narrow passage, turn, as it were, about a centre, which is sometimes spiral, till they unite or one of them escapes. The most celebrated whirlpools are the Euripus near the coast of Negropont, the Charybdis in the Straits of Sicily, and the Malstroem on the northern coast of Norway. Such eddies sometimes augment their force by means of two contrary high tides, or by the action of the winds. In certain states of the tide, some of them cease altogether; but they do not fail to make up for this afterwards. Their danger to navigation is well known; but is, perhaps, inferior to the dread which they inspire. They draw vessels along, and dash them against the rocks, or engulf them in the eddies. The wrecks, perhaps, do not appear till some time afterwards; or, indeed, they may never be seen at all. This has given rise to the notion that these vortices have no bottom. The phenomena and dread of whirlpools have afforded excellent matter for marvellous fables, both to the ancient poets and more modern writers.

The tides form a remarkable phenomenon, consisting in the alternate rise and fall of the surface of the sea twice in the course of a lunar day, or at a mean rate every $12^h\ 25^m\ 14^s$. The instant of low water is nearly, but not exactly, in the middle of the interval between two high waters. The tide generally takes nine or ten minutes longer in ebbing than flowing. At the new and full moon the tides attain the greatest height, and the interval between two high waters is least, viz. 12h 19m 28s. At the quarters of the moon the tides are the least, and the intervals the greatest, viz. 12h 30m 7s. The time of high water is mostly regulated by the moon; and in general, in the open sea, is from two to three hours after that planet passes the meridian, either above or under the horizon. On the shores of large continents, and where there are shallows and obstructions, great irregularities take place in this respect; and when these exceed six hours, it may seem as if the high water preceded the moon's passage over the meridian. Though the tides seem to be regulated chiefly by the moon, they appear also in a certain degree to be under the influence of the sun. Thus, at the syzigies, when the sun and moon come to the meridian together, the tides, every thing else considered, are the highest. At the quarters, when the sun and moon are 90° distant, the tides are least. The former are called the *spring*, the latter the *neap* tides. The highest of the spring tides is not that immediately after the new or full moon; but is in general the third, and in some cases the fourth. The lowest of the neap tides occurs much about the same time after the quarters. The total magnitude of the tide is estimated by the difference between the heights of high and low water. The higher the flood tide rises, the lower the ebb tide generally sinks on the same day. At Brest, the medium spring tide is about 19 feet, and the mean neap tide about 9. On other parts of the coast of France opposite to England, the waters, being confined, rise to a great height, and do so on both sides of the Channel. At St. Malo it is from 45 to 50 feet. Nearly as high tides occur at Annapolis Royal, in Nova Scotia. It is the obstruction which the land presents to the motions of the waters which occasions tides of any consequence at all: were the globe entirely covered with water, the tides would be very insignificant. Thus, in the Pacific Ocean, the spring tide amounts only to 5 feet, and the neap to from 2 to 2.5 feet. On the other hand, a free communication with the ocean is indispensable, to produce a high tide. Thus, in inland seas, the tides are very trifling, because the luminaries act nearly equally over the whole surface at the same time.

The height of the tide increases as the sun or moon is nearer the earth, but in a higher ratio. The rise of the tides is likewise greater when the sun or moon is in the equator, and less as they decline from it. When the observer and the moon are on the same side of the equator, the tide which happens when the moon is above the horizon is greater than when she is below it. The reverse occurs when the observer and the moon are on opposite sides of the equator. If the tides be considered relatively to the whole globe and to the open sea, it appears that there is a meridian about 30° eastward of the moon, where it is always high water, both in the hemisphere where the moon is and in the opposite. On the west side of this circle the tide is flowing; on the east it is ebbing; and on the meridian, which is at right angles to the same, it is everywhere low water. These meridian circles move westward, keeping nearly at the same distance from the moon: only approaching nearer to her when new or full, and withdrawing at the quarters. In high latitudes the tides are very inconsiderable. It is probable that at the poles there are no diurnal tides; but there is some ground for thinking that the water will rise higher at the pole to which the luminaries are at any time nearest, than at the opposite.

The great wave which follows the moon as above described, and constitutes the tide, is to be considered as an undulation or reciprocation of the waters of the ocean; in which there is, except when it passes over shallows or approaches the shore, very little progressive motion. In all this we are as yet overlooking the operation of local causes, winds, currents, &c., by which these general laws are modified, overruled, or even reversed. Most people find little difficulty in conceiving how the waters should rise on the side of the globe which is next the moon; but there can scarcely be a harder task than bringing many to see *why the waters should at the same time rise on the side which is turned from the moon.* We must, however, confine ourselves to a very brief and palpable explanation. The force by which the moon draws any particle of our globe towards her is greater when it is nearer to her, and less when more remote. The force, therefore, with which the moon attracts the particles on the side nearest her is greater than the average force which she exerts on the whole globe. These particles, therefore, rise or endeavour to come near the moon. On the other hand, the force by which the moon draws the particles which are farthest from her being less than the average force, these particles endeavour to recede from the moon, and in so doing they also recede from the earth's centre; that is, they rise higher than the general level. The action of the sun is similar to that of the moon; but his being almost four hundred times as distant, greatly diminishes his effect. At the new and full moon the luminaries act together, and produce *spring* tides. The highest of all are a little after the autumnal, and before the vernal, equinox; and the least spring tides occur a little after the solstices. At the quarters of the moon her action is opposed by that of the sun, and therefore *neap* tides are the result.

The time of high water deserves consideration. The preceding is sufficient to show that the phenomena of the tides are effects that might be expected from the principle of attraction or gravitation; but since the waters necessarily occupy some time in moving from one place to another, this is the reason why the high water occurs, not when the moon is on the meridian but from two to three hours afterwards. For the same reason, when the sun is before or west of the moon, he hastens the rise of the tide; and when behind her, he retards it. Considerable extent of surface is necessary, in order that the sea should be sensibly affected by the action of the sun and moon; for it is only by the inequality of such action on different parts of the mass of waters that their level is disturbed. In narrow seas, and on shores far from the main body of the water, the tides are not caused by the direct action of the sun and moon, but are waves propagated from the great diurnal undulation. Of this the tides on the coast of Britain, and in the German sea, are remarkable examples. The high water transmitted from the tide in the Atlantic reaches Ushant between three and four hours after the moon has passed the meridian, and its ridge stretches north-west, so as to fall a little south of the coast of Ireland. This wave soon after divides itself into three branches; one passing up the British Channel, another ranging along the west side of Ireland and Scotland, and the third entering the Irish Channel. The first of these flows at the rate of about 50 miles an hour, so as to pass through the Straits of Dover, and to reach the Nore about midnight at the time of spring tide. The second being in a more open sea, moves more rapidly, reaching the north of Ireland by six P. M.; about nine it has got to the Orkneys, and forms a wave or ridge stretching due north; at twelve the summit of the same wave extends from the coast of Buchan eastward to the Naze of Norway; and in twelve hours more it passes southward through the German Sea and reaches the Nore, where it meets the morning tide that left the mouth of the Channel only eight hours before. Thus, these two tides travel round Britain in 28 hours; in which time the primitive tide has gone quite round the globe, and nearly 45 degrees more. Various curious anomalies are observed in the tides of particular places: such as their ceasing altogether for a day or two, at a certain age of the moon; while at other times they become considerable, though perhaps occurring only once a day It is said that on some coasts there is never more than one tide in the course of a lunar day, which is probably owing to some oversight: but it may be shown from theory, that if the observer's distance from the pole be equal to the moon's declination, he will see but one tide in the day. Small tides occur six times a day on the shore of the Isle of Negropont.*

The agency of the tides is probably very extensive in many of the operations of nature, and in particular in those which regard geology. The late Professor Robison suggested how experiments might be made to determine the mean density of the globe, from the temporary change which is undoubtedly caused on the direction of gravity by the great body of water brought to Annapolis Royal, and then withdrawn by the stream tides.

### SECT. II.—*Springs.*

Springs are composed of the waters issuing from crevices in the earth. Of such there are great varieties. Some of the principal distinctions, independently of the qualities of their waters, are,—*temporary* springs, which only flow during a certain season of the year; *perennial*, which always run; *intermitting*, which alternately run and cease, either wholly or in part, at short intervals; *periodical*, which flow and ebb regularly at particular periods; *spouting*, which issue with considerable force, forming, perhaps, a jet of water. The magnitude of springs passes through every gradation, from being scarcely perceptible, to considerable rivulets. They have, likewise, a wide range of temperature; but necessarily limited between the freezing and boiling points. It is most usual for springs which are large, and which appear to issue from a considerable depth, to have nearly the mean temperature of the place; and in some instances the temperature is remarkably steady,—not the slightest variation being perceptible in the course of the year. Hence apparently, or relatively to the air, they are colder in summer and hotter in winter. It is, no doubt, this contrast which has given rise to the popular notion, that good springs are really colder in summer and hotter in winter. Nothing is more common than to see a well smoking during intense frost, which shows nothing of the kind during warm weather; but it does not require a really high temperature to exhibit such an appearance, but only a temperature not so low as that of the air. The most that any spring keeps within the range of both seasons, is to remain always at one temperature. The greater number of the smaller springs, however, become a little warmer in summer and colder in winter; particularly those which come along for a considerable way at a small depth under ground. By so doing, they participate in the temperature of the surface, which varies with the season: but all springs preserve a greater warmth than the mean temperature of winter; and, excepting the thermal or hot springs, they do not reach the mean heat of summer.

Hot springs are those which preserve a heat above the mean temperature of the place. Such as are merely tepid are common in most countries, especially in mines. Those having a considerably higher temperature are less frequently met with, and mostly in volcanic districts; but some of them reach the boiling point, or are actually boiling and spouting forth

* *Vide* Stevenson's great work on the Bell-Rock Light-house, for observations on Tides in the British seas

with great violence, which indicates their having had a still higher temperature before getting vent. The most remarkable are the hot springs of Iceland, some of which are considered among the greatest wonders of the world. They are believed to be more abundant in Iceland than in any other country. But the interest which the number and variety of these hot springs excites in a person who never saw any thing similar, is quickly lost in the feelings which are roused on beholding the magnificent and tremendous explosions of the Geysers, as they are called. Besides the principal fountains, there is a great number of boiling springs, cavities full of hot water, and several from which steam issues. There are also some places full of boiling mud of gray and red colours. The silicious depositions of the waters of the Great Geyser have formed for it a basin 56 feet in diameter in one direction, and 46 in the other; a projection from one side causing it to deviate from the perfect circle. In the centre of this basin is a cylindrical pit or shaft 10 feet in diameter. Through this the hot water rises gradually, filling it and the basin, after which it runs over in small quantities. At intervals of some hours, when the basin is full, explosions are heard from below, like the report of distant cannon, and at the same time a tremulous motion of the ground is felt all around the basin: immediately the water rises in a mass from the pit, and sinking again, causes the water in the basin to be agitated and to overflow: another and a stronger propulsion follows, and clouds of vapour ascend. At length, strong explosions take place, and, large quantities of steam escaping, the water is thrown to a height of from 30 to 90 feet, and even to 200 or 300 feet. The steam, coming into contact with the cold air of that climate, is condensed into thick clouds, which are tossed and rolled with great rapidity; the whole forming a very singular and magnificent exhibition. After continuing for some time, the explosions cease, when the basin and pit are found empty. Bursts of steam sometimes take place, when the water is rising, without any warning by subterraneous noise. These phenomena seem to be occasioned by steam finding its way from below into cavities, where part of it is condensed into water, which water is at length forced out by the action of the steam under high pressure. The New Geyser is somewhat smaller than the other. There are many hot springs of less note in Iceland; but perhaps the most curious of the whole is the Tunguhver. Among a great number of boiling springs are two cavities, within a yard of each other, from which the water spouts alternately: while from one the water is thrown about ten feet high in a narrow jet, the other cavity is full of water boiling violently. This jet continues about four minutes, and then subsides; when the water from the other immediately rises, in a thicker column, to the height of three or four feet. This continues about three minutes; when it sinks and the other rises, and so on alternately.

The natural jets of water, called spouting springs, only differ from the rest in comir down some close canal from a fountain on a higher level. Being thus closely confined, they burst forth in consequence of the pressure, in the same manner as the artificial spouting fountains do.*

Intermitting fountains have sometimes been viewed by the multitude as of a miraculous nature. One at Como, in Italy, rises and falls every hour: another at Colmars, in Provence, rises eight times as often. At Fronzanches, in Languedoc, one has a period of 24 hours 15 minutes. England affords many examples of such springs; particularly those on the sea coast, whose waters rise and fall with the pressure of the tides. The town of Tideswell, in Derbyshire, is named from a noted fountain of this sort which once flowed there, but has now ceased to observe its tides. The principles on which intermitting springs depend are attempted to be explained in every popular treatise on hydrostatics and hydraulics.†

Various have been the opinions of philosophers concerning the origin of springs. Some suppose that sea water is conveyed through subterraneous ducts or canals to the places where the springs flow out of the earth: but in this way fresh-water springs could not be produced; because sea water cannot be freed from its salt by filtration. It is, besides, difficult to conceive how the water should filter *upwards*. In order to overcome these objections, recourse has been had to subterranean heat, by which the water is conceived to rise upwards in vapour through certain fissures and cavities of the mountains where it is collected, and issues forth, as we see, in springs. Others vary the hypothesis a little, by saying that the sea water is raised through the mountains by capillary action; but here we ought still to have salt springs; and it has been further objected that a current cannot be produced by capillary action.

The most probable theory is that proposed by Dr. Halley, who maintained that springs are nothing more than a part of the water which falls on higher ground filtrating through, and afterwards issuing forth at a lower level. This, it is true, does not at first sight appea to account for the permanent flow of springs during dry weather. To complete the theory it is supposed that the water at first collects in large subterranean cavities, from which it afterwards filtrates slowly, and passes towards the springs. The disposition of the rocks in

* Vide Ed. New Phil. Journal, vol. ix. for observations on spouting springs and Artesian wells.

† Vide Ed. New Phil. Journal, vol. viii. for an account of intermitting springs.

strata contributes much to the collecting of the waters under the surface, and conveying them without waste, as if in close pipes, till they are united in fountains, lakes, rivers, &c. Dr. Halley showed that the evaporation from the sea alone is a sufficient supply for all the waters that the rivers carry into it. His calculation was founded on a very complex view of the subject, and liable to several objections. Buffon took a more simple view of the matter, by selecting one of those lakes that send out no stream to the ocean, and showing that the probable evaporation from the surface of the lake is equal to all the water carried into it.

The theory of hot springs is deserving of consideration. It has been ascertained that the greater number of warm and hot springs occur in volcanic countries—where volcanoes formerly burnt or are still in a state of activity; and of those that do not occur in volcanic districts, some are associated with trap and granite rocks, to which most geologists assign an igneous origin. Hence it is inferred that they owe their temperature to the same cause or causes as gave rise to volcanic and ignigenous rocks. That the heat of such springs is often connected with volcanic action cannot admit of doubt; for, from the Geyser of Iceland, the transition is almost uninterrupted to the hot springs in the dormant volcano of the island of Ischia, and from thence to those connected with the process which formerly took place in the now extinct volcanoes of Hungary and Auvergne. The hot and warm springs of Bath and Bristol, however, occur in a limestone country where no igneous rocks are visible; but these may be under the limestone. This opinion is further countenanced by the fact that many of the hot springs met with in primitive, and also in secondary, formations, occur in spots where the strata appear to have been disturbed by igneous agency. Of this there is a striking example at the hot springs of Carlsbad in Bohemia; the hot springs of Clifton issue from a limestone which appears, at an early period, to have been disturbed by igneous action: the hot springs of Pfeffers, in the Grisons, gush from a ravine from 400 to 654 feet in depth, and so perpendicular that the provisions required for the inmates of the bath are lowered from ropes attached to the summit of the cliff, and so narrow that the rocks in some places touch overhead, and nowhere, perhaps, are more than 30 feet apart. The most obvious explanation of such a phenomenon is to be found in some convulsion of nature, such as that caused by an earthquake, or the sudden elevation of a large tract of country. The other hot springs in Switzerland appear in circumstances for the most part similar. Those of Weissenburg, in the canton of Berne, rise out of a gorge of the same kind as that of Pfeffers: those of Louechi appear at the foot of the mural precipice of the Gemmi: whilst the spring of Baden, in the canton of Argovia, from which the only remaining one, that of Schinzath, is not far removed, lies near the point where, in consequence of the two mountains of Staffelegg and Lagern having been severed asunder by some great convulsion, the waters of the Rhine and of the other rivers,—which appear to have once constituted a single lake extending from Coire in the Grisons to this mountain ridge, including the lakes of Zurich and of Wallenstadt, with the intermediate country,—in one continuous sheet of water, flowed off by the channel now taken by one of the rivers, the Limmat alone. Thus the Rhine, says Dr. Daubeny, may be supposed to owe its original direction to the event which produced one hot spring, and its present course to that which occasioned another.

Some springs apparently emit inflammable matter; for when a light is applied, it seems to take fire like ardent spirits. But it is not so much the water that is inflammable, as some gas which it exhales, or bituminous matter floating on its surface.

*Springs in the sea.* Powerful springs are occasionally met with boiling up in the bottom of the sea, so as, in some instances, to rise above the surface. From some of them navigators can draw up fresh water fit for taking on board as store. The natives, in certain places, know where to dive under the surface of the sea for fresh water; which, perhaps, may be the only source whence they could obtain it.

*Mineral waters, and the quantity of matter they deposit.* Springs in their course through strata convey along with them portions of the strata, not only from higher to lower situations, but also from below upwards. They contain salts, earths, acids, metals, and inflammable matters, of very varied nature: the variety depending sometimes on the nature of the strata through which they pass; at other times, as in those that rise upwards in volcanic districts, on igneous agency. Hoffman remarks, that when warm and hot springs, and those richly impregnated with mineral matters, occur in countries at a distance from active and extinct volcanoes, we observe the strata from which they issue to be much deranged, thus intimating that formerly earthquakes and other igneous agencies were at work in the districts where these springs now flow. The quantity of mineral water brought from the interior of the earth by springs is very great; whether that matter is abstracted from the strata traversed by the springs, or is brought by them from a great depth, as in volcanic countries. Even some calcareous springs in Britain deposit annually vast quantities of calcareous tuffa and calcareous sinter. In the neighbourhood of Edinburgh there are great calcareous deposits from calcareous springs that flow through limestone rocks; and appearances of the same description abound around all the calcareous springs in England. Near to Clermont, in France, some calcareous springs, rising through rocks of *granite and gneiss,* have formed a mound or hill 240 feet high. Many of the great edifices in Rome are built of calcareous deposits from calcareous springs. The hot springs of Carlsbad annually deposit much calcareous tuffa and sinter. Other springs, as the hot springs in Iceland and in the Azores, deposit annually great quantities of silica. Salt springs also bring from the interior of the earth, and spread over their vicinity, much salt, which salt may be derived from the saline clays and salt beds through which they pass; in other instances the salt may come from a great depth as an igneous production.

*Chemical nature of spring waters.* The water of springs, when very pure, is named *soft;* if impregnated with calcareous salts, *hard;* and if impregnated with various mineral matters, *mineral.* It was long believed that hard water was unfit for brewing and distillation; and hence soft water was often procured for these operations, at great expense; but it is now found that water which owes its hardness to lime is the most proper of all for the fermentation of worts. A time will, however, be necessary to remove the popular prejudice in favour of soft water. We have, in the Table on the following page, given a view of the composition of the most celebrated mineral springs.

According to some chemists, the salts found by chemical analysis in springs are considered as existing in the waters; the late Dr. Murray considers the compound existing before concentration of the water as, in all cases, the most soluble salts that can be formed out of the ingredients present. But, in reality, so far from our having determined in any given case the nature of the existing combinations between the ingredients, we are ignorant even of any method by which such knowledge is attainable. If, says Berzelius, the physician inquires of the chemist, what the proportion these salts bear to each other in any given case may be, the latter must reply, that this is a question as to which we are at present entirely in the dark; as the proportion depends not only on the quantity of acids and bases present, which admits being ascertained, but also on the relative force of affinity subsisting between the one and the other, for determining which we have as yet no data whatever.

## Sect. III.—*Lakes.*

A lake is a body of water which does not communicate with the ocean. Independently of the qualities of their waters, lakes are distinguished into several sorts:—1. Those which receive streams of water, and have an outlet, are the class of lakes best known. It is rare for a lake to give rise to more than one river, which often bears the name of the principal stream which flows into the lake, though the two rivers may differ materially in every respect. 2. Those which receive streams of water, and often great rivers, without having any visible outlet. This class is less numerous than the former, and is confined to warm climates; but the largest of all lakes, the Caspian Sea, belongs to it. 3. Those which receive no running water, but have an outlet,—circumstances which imply that such lakes are fed with springs from beneath, or with small imperceptible streams from the adjacent land. 4. Those which receive no running water, and have no visible outlet. Lakes of this class, exclusive of marshes, are for the most part small, and merit little attention. Without regarding the foregoing distinctions, some writers subdivide lakes into two kinds, according to the general character of the surface in which their basins are situated: viz. those which are formed in deep hollows between the ridges or at the foot of mountains, and fed by springs or torrents; and those which are formed in low and level countries for want of a general declivity, or dammed up by a mere accumulation of alluvial matter.

Subterranean lakes form a class of lakes differing remarkably from all the preceding, and are bodies of water contained in cavities quite covered over by earthy strata. It is only when such cavities are laid open by earthquakes, by the falling asunder of mountains, by the action of the weather or of rivers, by the operations of mining, or when the roof falls in, that their situation becomes known. But they are probably very numerous, though perhaps often of small size. It is not easy to account for the permanent and uniform flow of many springs on any other supposition. Some of them appear to give rise to rivers, while others are known to receive very considerable streams which lose themselves in the interior. Such are the numerous cavities of the Julian Alps. It is to similar reservoirs that we must attribute the periodical disappearance of certain lakes situated above ground. There are some caverns in Norway which afford a passage to rapid currents of water, as appears from the sound heard through their roofs. It is natural to suppose that many streams, finding no readier outlet, flow into subterranean cavities, are absorbed by the earth, or discharge themselves under ground into the sea. In this way may be explained the origin of those springs of fresh water that are to be seen spouting up even in the midst of the waves of the ocean. The waters thrown up by volcanoes, the sudden and terrible inundation of mines, the number of rivers which disappear, the mountains which are suddenly engulfed in the bosom of new lakes,—all these facts leave no doubt of the existence of extensive subterranean cavities containing large bodies of water. The digging of wells has supplied a fact still more interesting to physical geography. It appears that there are lakes, or rather sheets of water, which extend under ground to considerable distances. In digging wells near Aire, in the province of Artois, they always come to a clayey bed; which being pierced, the water gushes

## TABLE OF THE COMPOSITION OF THE MOST CELEBRATED MINERAL SPRINGS, &c.

| Names of the Springs, &c. | | Chemists. | Grains of Water. | Cubic inches of Gases. | | | | Carbonates of | | | | Sulphates of | | | | Muriates of | | | | Silica. | Alumina. | Resins. | Temp. |
|---|---|---|---|---|---|---|---|---|---|---|---|---|---|---|---|---|---|---|---|---|---|---|---|
| | | | | Oxygen. | Carbonic Acid. | Sulph. Hydrogen. | Azote. | Soda. | Lime. | Magnesia. | Iron. | Soda. | Lime. | Magnesia. | Iron. | Soda. | Lime. | Magnesia. | Potash. | | | | |
| | | | | | | | | Grains. | Grains. | Grains. | Grains. | Grains. | Grains. | Grains. | Grains. | Grains. | Grains. | Grains. | Grains. | Grains. | Grains. | Grains. | |
| Acidulous. | Seltzer | Bergmann | 8949 | 43.5 | 13.1 | | | 5.2 | 78.3 | 6.3 | | | | | | 13.7 | | | | | | | Cold. |
| | Pyrmont | Ditto | 8950 | | 19.6 | | | | 4.3 | 9.8 | 0.7 | | 8.4 | 5.4 | | 1.7 | | | | | | | Cold. |
| | Spa | Ditto | 8933 | | 9.8 | | | 1.9 | 1.9 | 4.4 | 0.7 | | | | | 0.2 | | | | | | | Cold. |
| | Carlsbad | Klaproth | 25320 | | 50.0 | | | 38.5 | 12.5 | | 0.1 | 66.8 | | | | 32.5 | | | | 2.3 | | | 165° |
| | Kilburn | Schmesser | 138240 | | 84.0 | 36.0 | | | 2.4 | 1.3 | 0.3 | 18.2 | 13.0 | 91.0 | | 6.0 | 0.6 | 2.8 | | | | 6.0 | Cold. |
| Sulphureous. | Harrowgate | Garnet | 103643 | | 8.0 | 19.0 | 7.0 | | 18.5 | 5.5 | | | | 0.5 | | 615.5 | 3.0 | 9.1 | | | | | Cold. |
| | Moffat | Ditto | 103643 | | 1.0 | 10.0 | 4.0 | | | | | | | | | 3.6 | | | | | | | Cold. |
| | Aix-la-Chapelle | Babington | 8940 | | | 13.1 | | | 15.3 | 5.9 | | | | | | 6.2 | | | | | | | 143° |
| | Enghien | Fourcroy | 92160 | | 18.5 | 7.0 | | | 21.4 | 1.3 | | | 33.3 | 5.8 | | 2.4 | | 8.0 | | | | | Cold. |
| Saline. | Sedlitz | | 58309 | | 8.0 | | | | 6.7 | 21.0 | | | 41.1 | 1444 | | | | 36.5 | | | | | Cold. |
| | Cheltenham | Fothergill | 103643 | | 30.3 | 3.0 | 12.0 | | | 12.5 | 5.0 | 48.0 | 40.0 | | | 5.0 | | 12.5 | | | | | Cold. |
| | Plombieres | Vauquelin | 14600 | | | | | 36.0 | 0.4 | | | 1.0 | | | | 2.0 | | | | | | | Cold. |
| | Dunblane | Murray | 7291 | | | | | | 0.5 | | 0.2 | 3.7 | | | | 21.0 | 20.8 | | | | | | Cold. |
| | Pitcaithley | Ditto | 7291 | | 1.0 | | | | 0.5 | | | 0.9 | | | | 12.7 | 20.2 | | | | | | Cold. |
| Chalybeate. | Tunbridge | Babington | 103643 | 1.4 | 10.6 | | 4.0 | | | | 1.0 | | 1.3 | | | 0.5 | | 2.3 | | | | | Cold. |
| | Brighton | Marcet | 58309 | | 18.0 | | | | | | | | 32.7 | | 11.2 | 12.2 | | 6.0 | | 1.1 | | | Cold. |
| | Toplitz | John | 22540 | | | | | 13.5 | 16.5 | | 32.5 | | | | | 61.3 | 28.5 | | | | 15.1 | | Cold. |
| Calcareous, nearly pure. | Bath | Phillips | 15360 | | 2.4 | | | | 1.6 | | .004 | 3.0 | 18.0 | | | 6.6 | | | | 0.4 | | | 114° |
| | Buxton | Pearson | 58309 | | | | 2.0 | | 10.5 | | | | 2.5 | | | 1.5 | | | | | | | 82 |
| | Bristol | Carrick | 58309 | | 30.3 | | | | 13.5 | | | 11.2 | 11.7 | | | 4.0 | | 7.3 | | | | | 74 |
| | Matlock | | 58309 | | | | | | | | | | trace | | | | | | | | | | 66 |
| | Malvern | Philip | 58309 | | | | | 5.3 | 1.6 | 0.9 | 0.6 | 2.9 | | | | 1.6 | | | | | | | Cold |
| Dead Sea, sp. gr. 1.211 | | Marcet | 100 | | | | | | | | | | .054 | | | 10.7 | 3.8 | 10.1 | | | | | |
| Ditto 1.245 | | Klaproth | 100 | | | | | | | | | | | | | 7.8 | 10.6 | 24.2 | | | | | |
| Ditto 1.283 | | Gay-Lussac | 100 | | | | | | | | | | | | | 7.0 | 4.0 | 15.3 | | | | | |
| Frith of Forth | | Murray | 7291 | | | | | | | | | 25.6 | | | | 159.3 | 5.7 | 35.5 | trace | | | | |

forth in large bubbles, and forms permanent springs. In the country of Modena, we find everywhere, at the depth of twenty yards, a bed of clay five feet thick; which being pierced, the water spouts up with considerable force—indicating that it is connected with a reservoir which stands at a higher level. There is a district in the interior of Algiers, where the inhabitants, after digging to a depth of about 200 fathoms, invariably come to water, which flows up in such abundance that they call it the subterranean sea.

Lakes which receive much water, but have no outlet, were believed necessarily to communicate with the ocean by some subterraneous channel. The great distance of some of them from the ocean seemed to stand in the way of such an explanation; and doubts might still have remained, were it not for the discovery of the remarkable fact, that some of the principal lakes of this description have their surfaces far depressed below the level of the ocean. Thus the surface of the Caspian Sea, which is the largest known lake, and without an outlet, was found by Engelhardt and Parrot to be 334 feet beneath the level of the Black Sea. A similar depression has been ascertained of the level of the famous Dead Sea, in Judea, which is also a lake without an outlet. Its surface is below that of the Mediterranean in its neighbourhood, and consequently still farther below the higher level of the Red Sea. The true explanation as to the consumption of the waters of such lakes seems to be, that it is carried off by evaporation. The climates in which the two last-mentioned are situated accord well with this supposition. The level of these lakes, however, varies with the weather, and with the abundance or scarcity of the waters discharged into them by rivers at particular seasons of the year. The variation in the height of the Caspian Sea is from four to eight feet; but the level, at a particular point of its shore, must be affected by the direction of the wind, and probably by a very trifling tide. When the banks of lakes are very porous, they cannot fail, during very dry weather, to absorb a large portion of the water, and to throw it off by evaporation.

The depth of great lakes has been seldom ascertained with much exactness. The general depth of the Caspian Sea is from 60 to 70 fathoms; but this increases towards the south end to such a degree, that no bottom can be found with a line of 380 fathoms. In lakes, as in the ocean, the slope of the bank is continued downward for a considerable way below the water; that is, deep lakes are to be found in mountainous districts, and shallow marshy ones in flatter countries. The depth of Loch Ness, in the Highlands of Scotland, is in some places 130 fathoms, which is four times the mean depth of the German Sea; and its bottom is actually 30 fathoms below the deepest part of that sea, between the latitudes of Dover and Inverness.* The Lake of Geneva attains the still greater depth of 161 fathoms. Many other lakes are known to be exceedingly deep, without the amount being ascertained. Several have passed for ages as bottomless; but this opinion now obtains little credit. It is more probable, that most lakes are daily getting more shallow, from being filled up with mud or débris.

The temperature of the surface of lakes depends on the climate and season; but at the bottom of deep lakes it undergoes little or no change throughout the year, and approaches to that which corresponds to the maximum density of water, which different writers estimate variously, from 39° F. to 42.5°; but 40° is most commonly received. In Loch Catrine and Loch Lomond, the temperature, at all depths below 40 fathoms, is 41°; but the mean for the climate is 47°. The deep lakes of Thun and Zug, in Switzerland, have a temperature of 42° at the depth of 15 brasses. Thun was 41.5° at the depth of 105 brasses, while the surface was 60°; and Zug, 41° at 38 brasses, with surface 58°. The bottom of the Lake of Geneva has a temperature of 42°: that of the Lago Sabatino at Rome is 44.5°, at a depth of 80 fathoms. Tepid springs may, in some cases, keep up the temperature, when they occur at the bottom of lakes. From what we mentioned of the Caribbean Sea, it does not appear that the climate has much influence; and yet most powerful springs of fresh water are known to boil up in its shallower parts. Such springs probably approach to the mean temperature of the climate; or, perhaps, those who contend for an increase of heat with the depth of the solid strata would claim for them a higher temperature. Deep lakes almost never freeze, except in a very cold climate; because the whole body of water must cool below 40° before congelation could commence. Accordingly, neither Loch Ness nor its effluent river of the same name are ever frozen over.

The qualities of the waters of lakes are various, according to the nature of the substances with which they may be mixed or contaminated. The principal distinctions, in this respect, are *fresh*, *saline*, and *alkaline*. Lakes which receive much fresh water, and have a copious efflux, are almost always fresh; but those which lose much of their water by evaporation may be slightly saline, especially if the neighbouring soil abound in salt. When lakes have no outlet, they are invariably saline. To account for this, two reasons have been given, which are quite compatible with each other. The one is, that salt lakes having no outlet are concentrated portions of the waters of the deluge, retained by the hollows of the earth's surface; and that all other lakes were originally such, and saline; but those have had their

* Vide Stevenson, Wernerian Memoirs, and Edinburgh Phil. Journal.

salt washed out and carried to the ocean, which are traversed by rivers or other fresh water The other opinion is, that the salt in lakes has come from springs, or been washed from the soil of the adjacent country by means of the rain and rivers: for such lakes are most abundant where the soil contains saline matter; and where lakes only lose water by evaporation, the vapour goes off fresh and leaves the salt behind. The Dead Sea is the saltest of all known lakes, and appears to have been so for upwards of 4000 years; for in the book of Genesis it is called, by way of distinction, the "Salt Sea," even at a time when the adjacent plain was as noted for fertility as it is now for barrenness. The waters of this lake are in a state of saturation, containing about eight times as much salt as those of the ocean. The salt must be accumulating in beds at its bottom; for the river Jordan, which is brackish, necessarily carries in more. Masses of bitumen frequently float on the surface, and seem to rise from the bottom of the lake. The same thing occurs in other Asiatic lakes, some of which are impregnated with borax. In the island of Trinidad, there is a lake which produces an enormous quantity of bitumen fit for naval purposes.

Some lakes are both saline and alkaline, as is the case with a series of lakes in Lower Egypt. These are called the Natron Lakes, from their abounding in soda, which is there called *trona* and *natron*, the *nitre* of the Sacred Writings.

Lakes appear to have been much more numerous at a former period than at present, and to have occupied a large proportion of the surface of the land. Traces of their existence occur everywhere. Many of them have been filled up with débris, and become level plains traversed by a river; some have been drained by the gradual deepening of their outlets; or both causes have often operated together. Others have got vent through cracks caused by earthquakes, or by the subsiding of a part of the basin. The kingdom of Hungary is supposed to have been originally the basin of a lake; and some go so far as to allege the same of the Mediterranean Sea. Geological phenomena also show that new lakes arise, and old ones disappear, during those great risings and sinkings of the land which have taken place during former periods, and even now are not without example.

There are several modes in which new lakes may be formed. In hot tropical climates, many large lakes are formed during the rainy season, and entirely disappear on a change of weather; but such hardly deserve the name, being rather land-floods, though they would be permanent lakes in a colder country. We have already mentioned the formation of a visible or open lake from the falling in of the roof of a subterranean one. When a mountain falls asunder, it often happens that it stops up a neighbouring river and valley, and forms a lake. But the water of a river obstructed in this manner will always overflow, and can scarcely fail to regain its former level, either by wearing away a cut for itself above, or by undermining the ruins beneath. Shallow marshy lakes are frequently formed by the surplus waters of rivers detained on flat ground by an accumulation of mud. Ice and snow sometimes accumulate in narrow passes between mountains, so as to obstruct and make the water stagnant, and form a temporary lake, increasing perhaps for years, till at length the pressure of the water is augmented to such a degree as to burst the icy barrier. The consequences are sometimes dreadful. So great a discharge of water and ice, precipitated from the mountains, tears up not only alluvial substances, but frequently portions of rocks, which are scattered over the plain below. Thus villages and fertile fields are almost instantly converted into deep hollows and heaps of rubbish. These cavities perhaps continue filled with water, forming small lakes.

There are certain lakes which disappear and re-appear periodically, without regard to the rainy season. Such are supposed to be filled and emptied in a manner similar to the cavities of intermitting springs, or to communicate with some subterranean lake which undergoes such periodical changes. That any lakes, remote from the sea, should communicate with it under ground, so as to rise and fall with the tide, is very improbable. In Portugal there is a small lake near Beja, which emits a loud noise on the approach of a storm. Other lakes appear agitated by the disengagement of gas. Near Boleslaw, in Bohemia, a lake of unfathomable depth sometimes emits blasts of wind which raise up pieces of ice. Some of the Scottish lakes, and the Wetter in Sweden, experience violent agitations even during serene weather. A coincidence of dates has given ground for believing that these agitations are connected with earthquakes in distant countries.

### SECT. IV.—*Rivers.*

The origin and progress of rivers have been compared by Pliny to the life of man. "Its beginnings are insignificant, and its infancy is frivolous; it plays among the flowers of a meadow, it waters a garden, or turns a little mill. Gathering strength, in its youth it becomes wild and impetuous. Impatient of the restraints which it still meets with in the hollows among the mountains, it is restless and fretful; quick in its turning, and unsteady in its course. Now it is a roaring cataract, tearing up and overturning whatever opposes its progress, and it shoots headlong down from a rock; then it becomes a sullen and gloomy pool, buried in the bottom of a glen. Recovering breath by repose, it again dashes along, till tired of uproar and mischief, it quits all that it has swept along, and leaves the opening of the valley strewed with the rejected waste. Now quitting its retirement, it comes abroad into the world, journeying with more prudence and discretion, through cultivated fields, yielding to circumstances, and winding round what would trouble it to overwhelm or remove. It passes through the populous cities, and all the busy haunts of man, tendering its services on every side, and becomes the support and ornament of the country. Increased by numerous alliances, and advanced in its course, it becomes grave and stately in its motions, loves peace and quiet, and in majestic silence rolls on its mighty waters till it is laid to rest in the vast abyss." The sun and the host of heaven have, in all ages and nations, been objects of sincere worship, Next to them, the rivers seem to have attracted the grateful acknowledgements of the inhabitants of the neighbouring countries. They have everywhere been considered a sort of tutelar deities, and each little district, every retired valley, had its river god, who was preferred to the others. The expostulation of Naaman the Syrian, who was offended with the prophet for enjoining him to wash in the river Jordan, was the natural effusion of this attachment. "What (said he), are not Abana and Pharpar, rivers of Damascus, more excellent than all the waters of Judea? Might I not wash in them and be clean? so he went away wroth." In those countries particularly where the labours of the husbandman and shepherd depended on what took place in a far distant country by the falling of periodical rains, or the melting of the collected snows, the Nile, the Ganges, the Indus, were the sensible agents of nature in procuring to the inhabitants of their fertile banks all their abundance, and they became objects of grateful adoration. Their sources were sought for even by conquering princes, and when found were worshipped with the most affectionate devotion. These rivers preserve to this day the fond adoration of the inhabitants of the countries through which they pass, and their waters are still held sacred.

The term *river* is applied to any large current of water which is not in the ocean or its branches, and which may discharge itself into the ocean, into lakes, marshes, or into other rivers; for the waters of some rivers never reach the ocean; as is the case with the Wolga, the Jordan, and others, which discharge themselves into salt lakes, having usually the name of *seas*. When the atmosphere supplies a country with more water than it has an opportunity of carrying off again by evaporation, the surplus either penetrates through the surface or collects into small streams, which, afterwards uniting and receiving the water of springs, gradually form larger and larger currents, which, if allowed to proceed increasing, at length become rivers. Some rivers proceed from lakes or marshes, but none come immediately from the sea. They invariably occupy the lowest parts of the districts from which their waters are derived, and these districts are called their *basins*. The basins are usually bounded by high lands, and sometimes by mountains. They form natural divisions in physical geography. Those of the Rhone, Garonne, Loire, Seine, and part of the basin of the Rhine, comprehend the greatest part of France. In some cases, the boundaries of basins are not well defined; as where the surface becomes flat or marshy. This is the case between the basins of the Amazon and Orinoco, which are connected by a natural and navigable communication. In Europe, the sources of the Dwina, of the Niemen, and of the Borysthenes, are nearly united in a marshy plain. It is evident that the deep ravines through which rivers flow could not in many instances be the work of the rivers themselves; because the margins of such ravines are often higher than other places of the district, through which the rivers ought to have flowed before such valleys were cut, as some fancy, out of solid rock. A more rational explanation is, that a crack or rent,—the effect of some earthquake or subsidence,—had taken place; and that the water, getting through such rent, had gradually widened it by the attrition of its sand and gravel: the still more corroding action of the weather would materially assist in widening the upper part of the ravine. Many rivers appear to have been at first a series of lakes and cataracts alternately, through which the water was conveyed from higher to lower ground. The bottoms of these lakes are gradually filled up with débris, the outlets are by degrees deepened, or the basins rent through as above described. The lakes at length become dry plains, traversed by the river; the cataracts, clefts or deep ravines; and the river acquires, upon the whole, a pretty uniform descent. There are traces of these changes everywhere: the parallel roads of Lochaber, as they are called, seem to be nothing else than the horizontal shelves with which lakes are usually surrounded. From these it appears that the valleys of Glen Gluoy, Glen Roy, and Glen Spean, have formerly been the basins of lakes, which are now cut through and emptied. Three distinct basins are observed in the course of the Rhine: first, that of the Lake of Constance; the second reaches from Basle to Bingen; and the third from this to the sea. They are separated from each other by rocky straits. In many cases, the subsidence of the water, at successive stages, can be traced from one level to another, by means of the different horizontal shelves still visible on the sides of the valleys. Sir Thomas Lauder remarked this, in the above named glens in the Highlands of Scotland. In the valley of the Rhine, Professor Playfair distinguished four or five such terraces, at the successive heights of twenty, thirty, or forty feet above one another. The same thing occurs on the banks in the great chain of North American lakes which are not yet empty.

The larger rivers are, their fall or declivity is generally so much the smaller. The reason of this is, that large rivers necessarily occupy the lowest parts of the country; and also, that there are no materials of which beds of rivers are ordinarily formed, that could have resisted the action of a great river, having a rapid fall, during the lapse of ages. In the last 200 leagues of the Amazons, the fall is only 10.5 feet; and in the 3000 miles above that, the mean fall is only five inches per mile. The Seine, between Valvins and Sevres, has a fall of about 9.5 inches per mile. The Loire, between Briaire and Orleans, has only one foot in 13,596. Between the Himalaya chain and the sea, the Ganges has only four inches per mile. The entire fall of the Wolga is 957 French feet, or five inches per mile. Notwithstanding the rapidity of the Rhine, it has only a fall of four feet per mile between Schaffhausen and Strasburg; and of two feet between that and Schenckenschantz. Sometimes a river falling into another with great rapidity, and at an acute angle, will at the time of flood force the latter to flow back for a short way. Such is sometimes the effect of the Arve on the Rhone, which is forced back into the Lake of Geneva.

The *bore* is a phenomenon which occurs on some great rivers, which enter the sea with considerably velocity, and experience a sudden check or obstruction from the flow of the tide: the consequence is, that an enormous wave, known by the term *bore*, and various other names, is generated and sent backward or up the river with great velocity, to the no small danger of the navigation. The principle on which this phenomenon depends is nearly allied to that of the hydraulic ram: at the spring tides, it appears of a correspondingly greater magnitude. In the Amazons, the height of this wave is estimated at 180 feet.

Rivers are subject to inundation. In the Sacred Writings, some allusions are made to the overflowings of the Nile; but those of the Jordan are distinctly mentioned, as covering all the banks during harvest, and expelling the lions which lurked in the thickets, so as to drive them infuriated through the country. Modern travellers, however, assert that this river does not now overflow; and they allege as a reason, that its channel is become deep enough to hold the floods. It is as likely that the banks have been raised by the deposition of mud and the growth of vegetables: perhaps the fall of snow and rain upon Mount Lebanon, from which the floods came, is not so abundant since its forests of cedars were cut down; for some travellers are of opinion that this river must, from the accounts of the ancients, have been formerly of much greater magnitude, at all seasons of the year, than it now appears to be.

The excessive rains which fall in tropical regions, during a certain season of the year, occasion the inundation or overflowing of the rivers which originate in the torrid zone. The following is nearly the general rule for the rainy season; viz., that periodical rains everywhere prevail from the equator to the parallel of latitude over which the sun is vertical. Humboldt mentions as another pretty correct and still more general rule, applying likewise to the frigid zone, that the season of floods falls within four months of midsummer. The floods of rivers originating in high latitudes proceed principally from the melting of the ice and snow on the mountains, by means of the summer's heat. Such floods are violent, but of short duration, and occur in the four months preceding the summer solstice. Some of these rivers have two, or perhaps three, successive floods, corresponding to the seasons of thaw in the low ground, on the sides of mountains, and on their summits.

The ancients were quite aware that some rivers derived their floods from the sources we have just mentioned; but the overflowings of the Nile, in a country remote from both rain and snow, excited their surprise. The mystery was, however, dispelled, when once it was known that the Nile principally draws its waters from the tropical regions, where the excessive periodical rains cause other rivers to overflow. The Nile begins to swell in June, and continues to do so till the middle of August, when it has reached its maximum height of from 24 to 28 feet. With the exception of a few elevated spots, and some of the higher accumulations of alluvial matter, on the margin of the river, the whole of the Delta and the long valley of Egypt is then covered with water. The rising of the Ganges, which is partly owing to the melting of snow and partly to the rainy season, commences in April, and, like the Nile, attains its maximum of about 31 or 32 feet in the middle of August. Tropical rivers which move parallel to the equator spread their waters pretty uniformly over the low ground: such is the case with the Orinoco and the Senegal. In rivers which descend from great elevations, or move at right angles to the equator, the action of the tropical rains is extremely unequal; for the surplus water only overflows the low and flat districts. This is exactly what happens with the Nile: but it is sufficient here to mention the general principles; as the inundations of particular rivers will be described along with their respective countries.

Waterfalls, or cascades and cataracts, are often formed by rivers in descending from primitive mountains into secondary countries. Compact durable rocks are requisite for producing a permanent effect of this kind: such are the cataracts of the Nile, of the Ganges, and various other rivers. Some cataracts, like those of Tunguska, in Siberia, have gradually lost their elevation by the wearing away of the rocks, and have now only a rapid descent. According to Humboldt, the height of the great cataract of the Rio de Bogota, in South America, long estimated at 1500 feet, is about 800 feet; that of Staubbach is about

900 feet. The small river Ache, in Bavaria, which rises in the cavern of the glacier of Mount Tauren, runs through the valley of Achenthal, and, after reaching the Gulf of Tauren, throws itself over an elevation of 2000 feet. It has five great falls; the last of which forms a most magnificent arch of waters, which is resolved into spray before it reaches the ground. The noise of the waters is so terrible, that it is heard at the distance of more than a league; and the current of air produced by the descent of the water is so violent, that it drives back those who attempt to advance towards the gulf: it is necessary, therefore, to approach it by walking backwards. The fall of Garispa in India is 1000 feet. One of the most considerable known falls takes place on the river Niagara, which connects Lakes Erie and Ontario. The river here, just before the fall, is divided by Goat Island into two parts: the one, 600 feet broad, falls to the depth of 150 feet; while the other, 35 yards broad, falls 164 feet in perpendicular height. In Scotland the most considerable falls are those on the river Clyde, near Lanark, where the river is precipitated down three successive precipices of red sandstone. In the upper fall, that of *Bonniton*, the whole river throws itself over a precipice 30 feet high: lower down, at *Corra Linn*, it is precipitated from a height of 84 feet. The lowest fall, that of *Stonebyres*, consists of three stages, being broken by two projecting rocks; its fall is 80 feet. In the course of the river Foyers, on the side of Loch Ness, there are two falls; the upper fall is 40 feet high, the lower 90 feet. In the mineralogical report of Lapland, presented to the Swedish government, the discovery of a great waterfall in the river Lulea is particularly mentioned. It is said to be one eighth of a mile broad, and to fall 400 feet; if the mile be German, as is most likely (equal to four and a half English miles), the breadth exceeds half an English mile.

---

## CHAPTER III.

### GEOGNOSY.

This branch of natural history makes us acquainted with the structure, materials, relative position, and mode of formation, of the great mineral masses of which the crust of the earth is composed.

In conveying to our readers a short view of this important subject, we shall adopt the following arrangement:—

I. Describe the physiognomy of the earth's surface.
II. Give an account of the action of water and air on that surface.
III. Give an account of the action of volcanoes and earthquakes on the earth's surface.
IV. Describe the different structures observable in the solid mass of the globe.
V. Define and describe the different classes and species of rocks of which the crust of the earth is composed.

#### Sect. I.—*Physiognomy of the Earth's surface.*

*Dry land.* The dry land, or the land above the level of the sea, is arranged into masses of various magnitudes and forms. It is not equally distributed; for a much larger portion of it occurs to the north than to the south of the equator; and the difference in this respect is so great, that the southern half of the globe is principally water, while the northern is chiefly land. About the middle of the last century, it was asserted that a great continent must exist towards the south pole, in order to counterbalance the mass of land in the northern hemisphere; but by the voyages of Cook and Bellinghausen, and particularly the late enterprise of Weddel, it has been shown that in high southern latitudes, in place of a continent, there are but a few groups of islands. The absence of a continent near the south pole does not itself prove that there is less land there than in the north, since it is possible that the land in general may be only rather more depressed in the south, and consequently the ocean is spread more extensively over the surface of the earth in that quarter. The dry land is arranged into two grand divisions named *worlds*, viz. the *Old World* and the *New World*. The Old World, in the eastern hemisphere, extends from S. W. to N. E., and comprehends the three continents of Europe, Asia, and Africa. The *New World*, in the western hemisphere, extends from N. to S., and is composed of two continents, viz. North and South America.

The general direction of the land in the two worlds is different. In America, it is from N. to S.: in the Old World, it is S. W. to N. E: and, if we omit Africa, it is almost parallel with the equator. The longest straight line that can be drawn on the Old World commences on the western coast of Africa, from about Cape Verd, and extends to Behring' Strait, on the north-east coast of Asia: it is about 11,000 miles in length. A similar line traced along the New World from the Strait of Terra del Fuego to the northern shore of North America measures nearly 9000 miles.

The Old and New Worlds have the following features in common: northern and southern halves, connecting isthmuses, a peninsula on the one side, and a group of islands on the other. This arrangement will appear evident from the following details.

The old world may be considered as composed of two great halves: the one, the western, includes Europe and Africa; the other, the eastern, Asia and New Holland. In the western half, the two continents, viz. Europe and Africa, are connected together by the isthmus of Suez, and have on the one hand the islands of the Mediterranean, and on the other the peninsula of Arabia. In the eastern half, the two continents of Asia and New Holland are, to a certain extent, connected together by the islands of Java, Sumatra, &c.; and in front of this *broken isthmus* is Papua and other islands, and on the other side the peninsula of India. The New World is composed of two halves, a northern and a southern: these are connected together by the isthmus of Darien; and on the front are situated the West India islands, and behind the peninsula of California.

Another general feature in the general distribution of the dry land, is the tapering of all the great peninsulas to the south. This, for example, is the case with the continent of Africa, with Arabia, India, South America, Scandinavia, Spain, Italy, Greece, Corea, Alashka, Kamtchatka, California, Florida, and Greenland.

Besides the Old and New Worlds, as above described, there occur, dispersed through the ocean, numerous smaller masses of land, forming islands of various magnitudes and forms. Those islands situated near to the continents are considered as belonging to them. Thus the British isles belong to Europe, those of Japan to Asia, the West India islands to America, and Madagascar to Africa. But besides these there are other islands and groups of islands, situated at a distance from continents, and which cannot be referred to any of the preceding divisions, but to the oceans in which they occur; as, for example, the Sandwich Islands, in the North Pacific Ocean.

### SUBSECT. 1.—*Inequalities of the Surface of the Dry Land.*

The surface of the land exhibits great variety in aspect, forming mountains, hills, valleys, and plains. The most general of these features are what geographers term *high land* and *low land*. *High lands* are lofty, uneven, and widely extended masses of land: thus, the mountainous tract of country extending from the Naze of Norway to the North Cape is a high land. *Low lands* are widely extended low and flat countries: thus, the northern part of France, the Netherlands, Holland, part of Germany, and Silesia; Poland, and European Russia form what may be called the great European low land. We shall first explain the structure of high land, and next that of low land.

(1.) *Structure of high land.* In a high land, the central parts are generally the most rugged and lofty, while the exterior districts, those which border on the low land, are lower, and less rugged. The central part is named *alpine*, the lower and the exterior part *hilly*. The alpine part of a high land is composed of a central and lofty chain of mountains, named the *central*, or *high mountain chain*, towards which there tend a greater or lesser number of *lateral* or principal; and from these again *subordinate* chains. The high mountain chain forms the *water-shed* (*divortia aquarum*) of the district; and the hollows that traverse the upper part of this chain are named *passes* (*cols.*) On passing from one side to another of the alpine land, we do not always travel through a pass or *col*, but sometimes across a comparatively flat tract, many leagues in extent; such are named *table-lands*. In crossing from Norway to Sweden, we pass in some parts across a table-land; also in travelling from Vera Cruz by Mexico to Acapulco. The inclined planes on which the lateral, or principal and subordinate, chains are distributed are named the *acclivities* of the high land. The hollows that separate these chains from each other are named *valleys:* those valleys bounded by principal chains are named *principal valleys*, and sometimes *transverse valleys;* while the valleys between subordinate chains are named *subordinate valleys*. The hilly or lower part of the high land is composed of comparatively low and less rugged chains, called *chains of hills*, which are irregularly grouped, being entirely without a central or high mountain chain. The valleys in this hilly land are shorter, less steep, and not so rugged as in the more central or alpine part of the high land.

(2.) *Structure of low land.* Low land is formed principally of extensive plains, little elevated above the level of the sea, in which we occasionally observe gentle risings and undulations of the surface, that often extend to a considerable distance, and sometimes form the limits between neighbouring rivers. Now and then conical and table-shaped hills rise up singly and suddenly in a low country, as is the case with volcanic and igneous hills. The plains of the low land are characterised by the presence of particular hollows or concavities, which are named *river-courses* or *river-valleys;* because in these rivers flow. In such hollows we distinguish the *bed* of the river, and the *holm* or *haugh land;* further we observe the *high* and *low* banks of the river, and the *ravines* or small valleys, that traverse the high bank and terminate in the low bank. There is still another kind of hollow met with in the low land; it is that in which lakes, generally shallow, are contained.

*Coasts.* The margin of the dry land, where it meets the waters of the ocean, has received the general name of *coast.* It varies in its aspect. Sometimes it is low and shelving, and then the neighbouring sea is shallow to a considerable distance; at other times it is steep, lofty, and rugged, and then the sea is deep. In many parts of Great Britain, and on the continent, as in Holland, the coast is low and sandy, and the sand is occasionally blown into hills.

*Caves.* These are cavities of greater or less extent, which are either *open* to day, as in the case of the magnificent caves in the Isle of Isla, those in Arran, those near Wemyss on the coast of Fifeshire, &c., when they are named *external* or *open caves;* or they are more or less concealed in the interior of the rocks in which they are contained, as Maclean's Cave in the Isle of Egg, and many caves in the limestone of Derbyshire: such are named *internal caves.*

SUBSECT. 2.—*Inequalities of the Surface of the Submarine Land.*

The bottom of the sea, like the surface of the dry land, varies in form. In some seas there occur flats and plains ranging to a considerable extent, and near to the surface of the water, forming what are called *shoals;* in other cases, plains, of great extent, occur deeply seated, or much below the surface of the sea, which are denominated *deep submarine plains.* These submarine plains, like the plains on the dry land, sometimes contain hollows of considerable extent, and of great depth; the deep hollows under the sea off the coast of Scotland, known under the name of *Montrose pits*, are of this description. The sea bottom is sometimes *hilly;* these hills vary in form and magnitude, and are either deeply seated, or rise above the surface of the water, forming rocks or islands. In tropical seas, the bottom, when not very deep, becomes encrusted with coral; which coral sometimes rises to the surface, and then forms *coral shoals, coral reefs*, or *coral isles.* If the bottom is very deep, but sends up from below hills whose summits are not far below the level of the ocean, these in tropical seas also become covered with coral.

SECT. II.—*Effects of Water and the Atmosphere on the Surface of the Land.*

Water is a very active agent in altering and variously modifying the surface of the earth, and its energy is increased when it carries along with it mechanical matter, as sand, gravel, &c., and particularly when aided by the gnawing influence of the atmosphere. Through these agents the whole surface of the dry land is kept more or less in a state of motion, by their breaking up the strata, and removing with greater or less rapidity, the broken rocky matters from point to point, and often into lakes and the sea.

Water acts mechanically and chemically: it acts *mechanically* when it removes part of the soil or broken rocky matter over which it passes, or corrodes the channel in which it flows, or the reservoirs in which it is contained; it also acts mechanically, when, on being imbibed by rocks, it increases their weight, and thus favours their rending, slipping, and overturning; and, lastly, it acts mechanically, when, by its freezing in fissures, it breaks up mountain masses and rocks. It acts *chemically*, when it dissolves particular mineral substances, as rock-salt, out of the rocks through which it percolates.

SUBSECT. 1.—*Mechanical destroying Effects of Water.*

(1.) *Rivulets and Rivers.* Running waters, in their course from the higher to the lower parts of a country, carry along with them the débris already prepared by the action of the weather on exposed rocks, and also more or less considerable portions of the strata of the basin in which they flow. The quantity of abraded matter depends in a great degree on the quantity of sand or gravel the river carries along with it; it being a fact, that running water, when pure, acts but feebly on compact strata, and displays its scooping or excavating power only when carrying along with it sand, gravel, and such other matters, which communicate to it a mechanical destroying action. As the velocity of the river diminishes, its carrying power diminishes; and frequently, long before it has reached the marsh, lake, or the sea into which it disembogues itself, it carries only slime and sleech, leaving the gravels and larger solid masses in higher parts of its course. The transporting power of water is much greater than many are aware of: it is strikingly shown by the enormous quantities of rubbish, and great blocks of stone, which are swept along by rivulets when in the state of flood or swollen. This transporting power is materially assisted by the diminished specific gravity of the rocks when immersed in the water, by which their weight is often diminished one-third, and even one-half. The transporting of heavy stones by water in situations where ice occurs is assisted by the ice which adheres to them, and which diminishes the specific gravity of the mass.

(2.) *Lakes.* Around the margins of many lakes we observe a beach, formed of the fragments of the neighbouring strata, broken off in part by the waters of the lake. The bursting of lakes also occasions great changes in the neighbouring country, which changes are of a mechanical destroying nature.

(3.) *Ocean.* The waters of the ocean exercise a powerful destroying effect on coasts. If the coasts are bold and rugged, they are violently assaulted by the waves of the ocean; the crags and cliffs split and tumble down, in frightful and irregular succession. The perforated rock, the Doreholm, on the west coast of Shetland; the perforated rocks described by Captain Cook near New Zealand; the stalks, holms, and skerries on the coasts of Shetland,

Scotland, and Norway, are effects of the destroying power of the waves of the ocean, conjoined with the gnawing action of the weather. On those rocky coasts where the strata are of unequal hardness, the softer portions, and also part of the surrounding harder mass, are removed by the action of the waves; and thus *sea-caves* are formed.

The waters of the ocean often also cause dreadful ravages in low countries exposed to their fury. Holland furnishes many striking examples of its devastating power. In the year 1225 the waters of the ocean, agitated by a violent tempest, inundated the country; the Rhine. swollen at the time by extraordinary floods, and retained at a great height, partly by the waters of the ocean, and partly by the wind blowing in a contrary direction to its course, spread over the neighbouring country: but, the tempest having suddenly subsided, the highly elevated waters retired, with such velocity and force as to carry with them a considerable portion of the soil, and left in its place the sea now named the *Zuyder Sea*. In the year 1421, a great inundation submerged the southern part of the province of Holland, drowned 60,000 persons, and on retiring formed the *Bies-Boos*.

The action of the sea on the submarine land is also worthy of notice. Stevenson speaks of agitations of the sea reaching to a depth of upwards of 200 feet; stating that, at a considerable depth the power of the ocean is so considerable as to break rocks in pieces, and throw them upon the coasts in masses, of various sizes and forms. Thus he says, "numerous proofs of the sea being disturbed to a considerable depth have also occurred since the erection of the Bell-Rock Light-house, situated upon a sunken rock in the sea, twelve miles off Arbroath, in Forfarshire. Some *drift-stones* of large dimensions, measuring upwards of thirty cubic feet, or more than two tons weight, have, during storms, been often thrown upon the rock from the deep water. These large boulder-stones are so familiar to the light-house keepers at this station, as to be by them termed travellers.* On the coast of the *main land* of Shetland, particularly on the west coast, we have observed many striking displays of the power of the waves in moving enormous masses of rocks.

The currents that traverse the ocean, like rivers on the dry land, probably scoop out beds for themselves, and carry away, and often to distant places, great quantities of abraded matter. The gulf stream, and other branches of the great equinoctial current, may act powerfully in this way; and the same may be the case with the currents in other seas, and those that enter mediterranean seas and wind round them, as the Baltic and Mediterranean.

(4.) *Action of water by its own weight.* Water by its own weight contributes very much to the degradation of the surface of the globe. Sometimes great masses of rock, particularly those of a soft and porous nature, imbibe much water, by which their weight is increased, and thus occasions breaking and rending, and slipping of masses often of enormous magnitude. Clay beds sometimes become soft from the percolation of rain or snow water from the superincumbent strata. When this takes place the superincumbent beds lose their support, and if the clay and superimposed rocks are inclined at a considerable angle, the rocks in vast masses separate, and slide down into the lower part of the country. The fall of the Rossberg, in Switzerland, in September 1802, may be mentioned as an example of this phenomenon. This mountain (Rossberg) is 5193 feet high, and lies opposite to the Rigiberg, which rises 6182 feet above the level of the sea. The Rossberg is composed of molasse, with beds of clay, and all inclined at an angle of 45° to 50°. It is said that the clay in some of the beds was much softened by the percolating water, and the thick superincumbent beds of molasse, in this way losing their support, were separated from the inclined and soft surface underneath, and slid into the valley below. This avalanche of debris and mud overwhelmed several villages, and destroyed from 800 to 900 persons. In the year 1714, the west side of the Diablerets, in the Valais, separated, and in its course downwards covered the neighbouring country with its ruins for two miles in length and breadth; the immense blocks of stones and heaps of rubbish interrupted the course of the rivers, and lakes were thus formed. In the year 1618, the once considerable town of Pleurs, in the Grisons, with the neighbouring village of Schelano, were overwhelmed by a vast mass of rock, which had imbibed much water, and separated from the south side of the mountain of Corto.

(5.) *Effects of the freezing of water.* In those regions of the earth where the freezing and thawing of water takes place, the expansive and destroying action of ice is often displayed on a grand scale. In the history of northern countries we meet with many accounts of the noises and rendings of rocks, occasioned hy the expansion of water during its freezing in the fissures of rocks. Terrible disasters take place in alpine countries by the bursting and fall of great masses of rock, split by the freezing of the water in rents.

(6.) *Destroying effects of ice and snow.* Water in the form of ice causes considerable changes on the surface of the earth. Thus, when floated along in great masses by rivers, it breaks up their banks, and thus affords them an opportunity of devastating the lower country; and the masses are often so great, that enormous heaps of the strata are thereby torn off and carried to a distance. When sea ice is drifted against the cliffs and precipices on the coast, the breaking and destruction it occasions sometimes almost pass belief. For the breaking

* Vide Wernerian Soc. Memoirs vol. iii.

up and moving of large masses of rock, one of the most powerful engines employed by nature are the glaciers. These masses of congealed water and snow, in their course downward, push before them enormous quantities of broken rocky matter, which form great mounds, named moraine.

### Subsect. 2.—*Chemical destroying Effects of Water.*

Atmospheric water enters into the fissures of rocks in a pure state, but issues forth again more or less impregnated with mineral matters of various kinds abraded from the strata through which they pass. The most abundant substance brought out in this way from the interior of the crust of the earth is lime, which is deposited from these calcareous waters in the form of tuffa. Many of the excavations in limestone are partly owing to this destroying effect of water. Spring waters, in passing through beds of gypsum and rock salt, dissolve a portion of them, and in this way sometimes occasion considerable changes in the interior and even the surface of the earth, by the superincumbent strata yielding over the hollows formed by the removal of the salt and gypsum.

### Subsect. 3.—*Mechanical forming Effects of Water.*

(1.) *Forming effects of springs.* Springs bring from the interior of the earth muddy matter of various descriptions; and in the course of time, if the springs are spouting-springs, hillocks and hills of considerable magnitude are thus formed.

(2.) *Lakes.* When lakes are filled up, or are emptied, we find the space formerly occupied by them covered, to a greater or less depth, with the alluvial matter brought into them by the rivers that flow into them. When lakes burst their barriers, at different times, they leave on their sides a series of natural terraces or platforms, of which we have a splendid example in Glen Roy. In Glen Roy these terraces are known under the name of *Parallel Roads of Glen Roy;* because some have fancied they were not natural arrangements, but works of art,—roads formed by the ancient inhabitants.

(3.) *Rivers.* When rivers are in a state of flood they often overflow their banks, and cover the neighbouring country with their waters. Thus the Ganges, near its mouth, in the rainy season overflows the country to the breadth of one hundred miles, and to the depth of nearly twelve feet, and the Indus, during its period of inundation, extends thirty or forty miles from its banks. This flood water carries with it muddy and other matters, and deposits them upon the land. Gerard says that the annual floods of the Nile had raised the surface of Upper Egypt about six feet four inches, English measure, since the commencement of the Christian era, or four inches in a century. In other countries extensive deposits, extending along the sides of rivers, are formed by the overflowing of their waters. Where rivers enter lakes and the sea, they form triangular pieces of land named *dèltas*, from their resemblance in form to the triangular-shaped Greek letter Δ. These deltas are more strongly marked in lakes than in nearly inclosed seas, as the Mediterranean; and in these seas than in the ocean, where the depositions are much interrupted by currents. The most famous in history of these deltas is that of the Nile. This delta has been considerably enlarged since the time of Herodotus, but not to the extent stated by many writers. At no great distance from the shore of the delta the depth of the Mediterranean is about seventy-two feet, and farther out the sea suddenly deepens to 2000 feet,—a depth very probably beyond reach of the delta, and which may be conjectured to be the original depth of this part of the Mediterranean sea. The deltas of the other rivers that flow into the Mediterranean, as the Rhone and the Po, exhibit phenomena similar to those observed in the delta of Egypt; and by their considerable extent, and annual growth, furnish ample proofs of the forming power of rivers, and of the resemblance of alluvial matters to strata of an older date. The great sea-deltas, or those formed where rivers flow into the ocean, are sometimes on a great scale, as is the case with the Ganges, of which a most interesting account has been given by Rennel and some other writers. A full description of this magnificent delta, as also of the vast deposites at the mouths of the Mississippi, Orinoco, and other great rivers, will be given in the body of this work. At present, however, we may remark, that the quantity of matter carried into the sea by all the rivers on the globe is very great, and fully as considerable as that stated by some authors, who have been held as exaggerating the amount of this earthy matter carried from the dry land to the shores of the ocean. The alluvial matter brought down by rivers not only forms great tracts of land at their mouths, but also, through the agency of currents, assisted by the waves of the ocean, gives rise to extensive tracts of low and flat land, which extend along the coasts.

*Downs.* When the sea-coast is low, and the bottom consists of sand, the waves push this sand towards the shore, where, at every reflux of the tide, it becomes partially dried, and the winds, which often blow from the sea, drift up some portions of it upon the beach. By this forming action of the ocean, sandy flats and *downs*, or ranges of sand-hills, are formed along the coast. When this sand is moved about by the wind, it forms what is called the *sand-flood.* Westward from the mouth of the river Findhorn, in Morayshire, a district consisting of upwards of ten square miles of land, which, owing to its fertility, was once named the Granary of Moray, has been depopulated, and rendered utterly unproductive by the sand-flood. This barren waste may be characterised as hilly; the accumulations of sand composing these hills frequently varying in their height, and likewise in their situations. The sand hills of Barry, at the mouth of the Tay, composed of blown sand, are from 200 to 300 feet high. Belhelvie links, in Aberdeenshire, and the extensive sandy tracts in the Shetland and Western Islands, are of the same description. These blowing sands sometimes block up the mouths of rivers and rivulets: thus, many years ago, the mouth of the river Findhorn in Moray having become blocked up with blowing sand, it cut out for itself its present channel, which conducts it by a more direct course to the sea. In consequence of this, the old town of Findhorn had changed its situation from the east to the west side of the river, and its site has since been covered by the sea. The lake at Strathbeg, which covers a square mile of country, on the coast of Aberdeenshire, about ten miles north from Peterhead, was formed about 170 years ago, by the choking up by blowing sand of a small stream that fell into the sea. These barriers sometimes give way, when the tract is again, for a time, covered by the sea; a new barrier again rises, and the sea is excluded a second time. These operations, on a great scale, would afford alternation of productions of the land and of the sea. The sands of the African deserts may be sea sands, or land sands, or both together. Dr. Oudney, Major Denham, and Captain Clapperton have added to our knowledge of the blowing sands of the African deserts. The coloured engraving of the sand-hills of the African desert in Denham, Oudney, and Clapperton's Narrative, is a striking and interesting representation of the form of the moving sand-hills of Africa.

*Sand banks.* The bed of the German Ocean supports many accumulations of sand, called sand-banks. One of these extends from the Frith of Forth, in a north-easterly direction, to a distance of 110 miles, while another, the Dogger Bank, extends, north and south, for upwards of 350 miles. The average height of these submarine sand-banks is estimated at about seventy-eight feet: the whole surface of the various shoals in this sea laid down in charts, according to Stevenson, is equal to about one-fifth of the whole area of the German Ocean, or about one-third of the whole extent of England and Scotland. These banks are composed of quartz sand, varying in the size of the grain, from coarse to fine, which is abundantly mixed with broken shells and fragments of corals. These banks are conjectured to owe their origin to the action of currents and the tides.

### SUBSECT. 4.—*Chemical forming Effects of Water.*

(1.) *Springs.* Many spring waters, after dissolving, by means of the superabundant carbonic acid with which they are impregnated, calcareous matter abraded from limestone rocks, or rocks containing lime, allow the carbonate of lime to crystallize, in consequence of the escape of the acid, and in this way form depositions of calc-sinter, or calcareous alabaster, on the roofs, sides, and floors of caves; or fill up fissures in rocks, and form veins; or when flowing over the surface of rocks, form, if the surface is horizontal, horizontal beds—if inclined, inclined beds—of calcareous sinter and calcareous tuffa. These beds sometimes extend very far, and with a thickness of 200 or 300 feet. The water of such springs, when collected into hollows so as to form lakes, often deposits vast quantities of calcareous sinters and tuffas; and hence such lakes, when emptied, present extensive calcareous deposits. The travertine employed at Rome for building is a lake or spring calcareous deposit of sinter and tuffa; and the town of Guancavelica in South America is built of a compact calcareous tuffa from the calcareous springs in the neighbourhood. In the mountain limestone districts in England, also in the lias districts both in England and Scotland, the roofs, walls, and floors of caves are often elegantly ornamented by numerous varieties of calcareous sinter. In Persia, as mentioned by Sir John Malcolm, there are great deposits of a very fine calc sinter, which is extensively employed for ornamental purposes; and in the marshes of the great plain of the vast circular valley of Hungary, according to Beudant, there is a constant deposition of horizontal strata of calcareous tuffa and sinter, which are so hard as to be used for building, all the houses of Czlea being constructed of these minerals. The pea-stone, a beautiful calcareous carbonate, is formed in very considerable abundance from the waters of calcareous hot springs, as those at Carlsbad in Bohemia. As these calcareous springs often flow into rivers, and these rivers terminate in the sea, it is evident that in this way a vast quantity of carbonate of lime must reach the ocean where it will be deposited in the various forms of sinter, tuffa, and limestone. The Geysers, or hot springs of Iceland, and those of St. Michael's in the Azores, deposit on the dry land vast quantities of siliceous sinter. This siliceous mineral, which is sometimes like opal, although generally pure, is not always so, being occasionally intermixed with other earths, and thus giving rise to particular mineral substances. Such springs also pour their waters into the ocean, and even rise from the bottom of the sea sometimes a considerable way upwards, or even jet above the surface level of the sea, all the time throwing out much water impregnated with silica, which is deposited on the submarine land in various forms and states, depending on a variety of circumstances, which our limits prevent our noticing.

(2.) *Lakes.* Having already noticed the calcareous depositions from the waters of some lakes, we may now mention some other deposits that appear to owe their origin to lakes. The bog iron-ore, or hydro-phosphate of iron, is often found in such situations as to show that it has been deposited from the waters of lakes; and in some countries it is collected from the sides and bottoms of lakes once in a certain number of years; thus showing that it is still forming in such situations. In salt lakes considerable depositions of salt take place; and when such collections of water dry up, or are drained off, the sides and bottoms of the hollows are found incrusted with salt, which is sometimes disposed in beds alternately with beds of clay.

(3.) *Marine incrustations.* Collections of perfect and broken sea-shells and of corals are sometimes found agglutinated by calcareous, clayey, or ferruginous matters, forming banks or beds of considerable extent. Beds of this kind, particularly those formed of shells, are met with in many parts of the coasts of this island. In other countries, as in the West Indies, a solid conglomerate of shells and corals lines a considerable extent of coast on several of the islands. The human skeleton from the island of Guadaloupe, in the British Museum, is imbedded in a rock of this description.

### Subsect. 5.—*Effects of the Atmosphere, &c.*

*Effects of the atmosphere.* The air and moisture of the atmosphere effect great changes on the rocks at the surface of the earth. They either simply disintegrate the rock, or not only break it down, but also occasion a change in its chemical constitution. Sandstone, and other rocks of the same general description, often yield very readily to the weather; their basis or ground is washed away, and the quartz, mica, and other particles remain in the form of sand and gravel. When trap veins intersect strata, it frequently happens that the softer parts of the rock are destroyed, while the harder trap appears rising several feet or yards above the neighbouring surface, and crossing the country like walls; hence, in Scotland, they are named *dykes.* The variously shaped *summits* of mountains and hills owe much of their form to the destroying influence of the weather. Some caves, as certain open caves in sandstones and limestones, are also formed by the destroying powers of the atmosphere. The various changes in the form of rocks, by which they assume columnar, globular, tabular, and indeterminate angular forms, and fall into *scales, crusts, layers, gravels,* and *sands,* are, to a certain extent, effects of the destroying powers of the atmosphere. Valleys owe much of their form and extent to the destroying influence of the atmosphere. Their sides and summits, everywhere exposed to its action, become covered with débris; and in this way valleys experience greater changes than are produced on their bottom by the passage of the river, and on its sides by the rushing of the torrent. The chemical destroying effects are to be traced to the carbonic acid of the atmosphere, and to the vast quantities of the same matter which rise from the interior of the earth: this acid dissolves lime, abstracts alkaline matters from granite and other similar rocks, and by combining with iron, converts that universally distributed substance into a soluble carbonate. The oxygen of the atmosphere also, by its action on the iron and other constituents of rocks, assists in breaking them down.

*Effects of electricity on rocks.* Electricity, as a chemical agent, may be considered not only as directly producing an infinity of changes, but also as influencing almost all that take place. There are not two substances on the surface of the globe that are not in different electrical relations to each other; and chemical attraction itself seems to be a peculiar form of the exhibition of electric attraction: and whenever the atmosphere, or water, or any part of the surface of the earth, gains accumulated electricity of a different kind from the contiguous surfaces, the tendency of this electricity is to produce new arrangements of the parts of those surfaces. Thus, a positively electrified cloud, acting even at a great distance on a moistened stone, tends to attract its oxygenous, or acidiform, or acid ingredients; and a negatively electrified cloud has the same effect upon its earthy, alkaline, or metallic matter; and the silent and slow operation of electricity is much more important in the economy of nature than its grand and impressive operation in lightning and thunder.

## Sect. III.—*On Volcanoes, and the Changes they produce on the Land and the Bottom of the Sea.*

The agents which the globe conceals in its interior, and whose existence is manifested at its surface, are made known to us by the phenomena of *volcanoes* and *earthquakes.* We shall first describe these phenomena, and afterwards add some observations on their causes.

### Subsect. 1.—*Distribution of Volcanoes.*

Volcanoes, as is well known, are openings in the crust of the earth, whence there issue from time to time jets of burning substances and currents of melted matters which bear the name of *lavas.* These openings are generally on the summit of isolated mountains; they have the form of a funnel, and take the name of *craters.*

*Position of volcanoes.* Volcanoes occur in all quarters of the globe, and are often distributed in a linear direction.

*Distribution.*—Europe contains but few burning volcanoes. On the coast of Sicily, we see Ætna rising like a colossus to a height of 10,870 English feet. On the opposite coast of Italy we have Vesuvius, which does not attain more than the third of this elevation, viz. 3932 feet. Between them, in the Lipari islands, we find the small volcano of Stromboli, and the volcanoes of Vulcano and Vulcanello, which still smoke. The islands of the Archipelago, at Milo and Santorino, contain mountains which, during an early historic period, produced terrible igneous phenomena. Iceland in the north, in the midst of snow and ice, presents to our view many volcanoes, of which the most prominent, Hecla, rises to a height of 5500 feet. Farther to the north, in the desolate and dreary Jan Mayen's Island, extending between north latitude 70° 49′ and 71° 8′, is the volcano of Esk Mount, which rises to a height of 1500 feet above the sea-beach in Jameson's Bay. The continent of *Asia*, as far as is known at present, exhibits but few volcanoes. We can scarcely reckon three or four on its western shores, or on the edges of the Caspian: there are none in its northern part: some but vaguely known exist in Central Asia: in the east, the peninsula of Kamtschatka contains five or six; but in the islands which surround this continent their number is great. The islands on the coast of *Africa*, such as Bourbon, Madagascar, the Cape de Verd Islands, the Canaries, and the Azores, also contain several volcanoes. In *America*, if we except those of the West India islands, we observe the greater part of them on the ridge of that great Cordillera, which, like an immense wall or lofty terrace, borders the western part of that continent. They are remarkable not only on account of their position, but also for their colossal form, the nature of the masses of which they are composed, and the materials they throw out. Torrents of fire rarely issue from them, but streams of water and mud are of frequent occurrence: the total number of American volcanoes is about eighty-six; they are placed as it were in groups. The kingdom of Guatemala presents about twenty; in Mexico there are six, in the number of which is the Jorullo, so well known from the account of Humboldt. But it is in Peru that the greatest occur: there are seven in that country, of which we shall mention Pichincha, nearly 15,931 feet high; Cotopaxi, wich rises to the height of 18,867 feet; and Antisana, which attains a height of 19,136 feet. On a rough estimate, we state the number of burning volcanoes including solfataras at 303; of these 194 are in islands, and the other 109 are on the continents: the most distant from the sea are those of America and Asia; in Peru there are volcanoes thirty leagues from the sea; and that of Popocatepetl near Mexico, which, however, is now only a smoking volcano, is fifty-six leagues; and they occur in the very centre of Asia. The circumstance of the most active volcanoes being situated in the vicinity of the sea, is a fact worthy of being recollected; it becomes still more so when we observe, that there are submarine volcanoes burning in the midst of the waters. The islands, and the phenomena which they have been observed to produce, at Santorino, on the coast of Iceland, in the Azores, &c., leave no doubt respecting their existence.

Independently of volcanoes in a state of activity, the interior of our continents contains a great number of *extinct volcanoes*, but which still present their original form, or incontestable remains of that form: perhaps no country contains more numerous and splendid displays of them than France; there are more than a hundred in Auvergne, Vivarais, and Cevennes. They are conical mountains, composed of lavas, scoriæ, and volcanic ashes heaped upon each other; many of them present a crater, which has retained its form in a greater or less degree; and sometimes there are seen as it were issuing from their bases lavas which extend to a distance of several thousand yards, and which have perfectly preserved the form of *currents:* the matter of which they are composed resembles that of lava trap. We may further remark, that volcanoes are never or scarcely ever isolated; they are collected into groups. This is the case with the American volcanoes; those of Asia, and the different Archipelagoes are similarly situated: in Europe, the Greek islands and southern Italy present distinct groups. Sometimes volcanoes are arranged one after the other in the same line, as is the case in South America, and in the extinct volcanoes in the neighbourhood of the Puy de Dôme.

### SUBSECT. 2.—*Phenomena and Theory of Volcanoes.*

Volcanoes do not incessantly emit flames, nor do lavas constantly flow from them; they remain for ages in a state of inactivity. Vesuvius was extinct from time immemorial, when, awakening from its slumber, it suddenly rekindled, in the reign of Titus, and buried the cities of Pompeii, Herculaneum, and Stabiæ under its ashes. It became quiet again at the end of the fifteenth century; and in 1630, when it resumed its action, its summit was inhabited, and covered with wood. The inhabitants of Catania regarded as fables the accounts of history respecting eruptions of Ætna, till the period when their city was ravaged, and in part destroyed, by the fires of that volcano.

Subterranean noises, and the appearance or increase of smoke, which issues from the crater, are generally the first symptoms of volcanic action. Presently the noise becomes louder, the earth trembles, it experiences shocks, and every thing proclaims that it is in labour. The smoke increases, thickens, and becomes charged with ashes. When the air is tranquil, the smoke is seen rising, under the form of an immense column, to a very great height. There, finding itself in a rarer atmosphere, it ceases to rise; its upper part dilating, forms as it were an expanded summit, placed upon a lengthened shaft. The cloud, with the supporting column, in favourable circumstances, has the figure of an immense umbrella, or of the Italian pine, to which Pliny the Elder compared that of the eruption of Vesuvius in A. D. 79, and which was accurately represented in October, 1822. At other times the smoke disperses in the air: it there forms thick and vast clouds which obscure the day, and cover the surrounding country with darkness. These columns and clouds are often traversed by enormous jets of red-hot sand, resembling flames, and rising to extraordinary heights. Sometimes they are traversed by flashes of lightning, and on all sides loud explosions are heard. Then there are projected red-hot stones and masses in fusion. They issue from the volcano with a noise which is frequently very loud. They rise into the air, spreading out in their progress, and fall around the mouth of the volcano under the form of showers of ashes, scoriæ, or stones. The shocks and quakings of the ground continue and increase in violence. In the midst of these convulsions, and on these accessions, the melted matter which filled the subterranean furnaces, already carried into the mountain, is raised up by elastic fluids; it ascends to the crater, fills it up, and passing over the least elevated part of this enormous cavity, spreads out upon the flanks of the volcano. It then descends, sometimes very quickly; sometimes, and more frequently, as a majestic river, quietly rolled along its peaceful waters. Very frequently, when the lava rises, the walls which contain it being unable to resist its immense pressure or its heat, give way and burst asunder. It rushes forth like an impetuous torrent through this new aperture: rivers and torrents of fire make their way to the foot of the mountain; they spread out upon the neighbouring ground, carrying along or burying all that they find in their way, breaking down or overthrowing every obstacle that opposes their passage. In the midst of torrents of fire, enormous currents of water and mud sometimes issue from volcanoes, and deluges falling from the atmosphere increase the ravages, lay waste fields which lavas had spared, and carry desolation into places which had already thought themselves happy in having escaped the scourges of the eruption. Mephitic gases and noxious exhalations sometimes arise, particularly in low situations; they destroy animals and blast vegetation, and thus complete the scene of misery and desolation.

After the emission of the lavas the earth seems freed of the evil which agitated it, the earthquakes cease, the explosions and ejections diminish for some time, and the volcano enjoys a moment of rest: but presently a new accession takes place, reproducing in a still more terrible manner the same phenomena; and this state of things continues during a variable period of time. At length the crisis ceases, and the volcano finally resumes its original tranquillity.

Having premised this general account of volcanic action, we shall next treat of the substances ejected or projected into the atmosphere by volcanoes, and the lavas which they pour out.

### a. *Ejected Matters.*

These are, 1. Smoke. 2. Ashes. 3. Sands. 4. Scoriæ. 5. Volcanic bombs. 6. *Unaltered Masses?*

(1.) *Smoke.* The enormous columns of smoke which are seen issuing from the crater, sometimes with extraordinary rapidity, are chiefly composed of aqueous vapour. This vapour is generally charged with gaseous substances, and particularly with hydrogen gas, sometimes also with carbonic acid. Sulphurous acid and muriatic acid are also given out. The smoke is gray or white; sometimes also brownish black, or fuliginous, and then the smell is not unlike that of asphaltum, or mineral pitch. It often contains a great quantity of volcanic ashes.

(2.) *Ashes.* These ashes, which appear to be nothing else than the substances of the lava reduced to a state of minute mechanical division, are formed of flocculent and extremely minute particles of a gray colour, and forming a paste with water. They are always mixed with a greater or less quantity of sand, which gives them the blackish colour which they sometimes exhibit. The torrents of gas and vapour which issue from the craters carry these ashes along with them, bearing them into the atmosphere, where they form vast clouds, sometimes so dense as to cover the surrounding country with darkness. During the eruption of Hecla in 1766, clouds of this kind produced such a degree of darkness that at Glaumba, which is more than fifty leagues distant from the mountain, people could only find their way by groping. During the eruption of Vesuvius in 1794, at Caserta, four leagues distant, people could only walk by the light of torches. On the 1st of May, 1812, a cloud of volcanic ashes and sand, coming from a volcano in the island of St. Vincent, covered th whole of Barbadoes, spreading over it so intense a darkness, that at mid-day, in the open air one could not perceive the trees or other objects near him, or even a white handkerchief placed at the distance of six inches from the eye. The distance to which these volcanic ashes are carried by the winds is truly astonishing. Barbadoes is more than twenty leagues from St. Vincent's, and Hecla is fifty leagues from Glaumba. Procopius relates, that in 472 the ashes of Vesuvius were carried as far as Constantinople; that is to say, to a distance of

250 leagues. These showers of ashes produce, in the countries where they fall, earthy beds, often of great thickness, which, on being heaped up and penetrated by water, form some kind of volcanic tuffa.

(3.) *Volcanic sands.* These are small particles of lavas which have been ejected into the air in the form of drops, and there harden. They are nothing but very small sized scoriæ, or fragments of ordinary scoriæ. They are, moreover, mingled with numerous small crystals of augite and felspar, or with fragments of these crystals. The quantity of these sands which volcanoes eject is immense. They form the greater part of the ejections, and of the mass of many volcanic mountains, of Ætna for example, according to M. Dolomieu. The finest mingle with the ashes, and form part of the clouds already mentioned. Others, accumulating in too great quantity to be sustained upon the acclivities of the mountain, slide down and spread out at its base. In the eruption of Vesuvius of 1822, a current of sand of this description, still red-hot, was taken at a distance for a torrent of lava.

(4.) *Scoriæ.* The gases which come from the depths of the volcano, passing through the mass of melted lava with great force and velocity, carry off some parts of that viscid matter, and bear them along with them into the atmosphere. They are there further divided, in consequence of the resistance which the air opposes to them; and, in cooling, they assume the intumesced and slaggy appearance which the scoriæ of forges so frequently have.

(5.) *Volcanic bombs.* When the matter of lavas is projected in a soft state, as is most commonly the case, it sometimes on cooling in the air assumes the form of drops, tears, or elongated spheroids, to which the name of *volcanic bombs* is given. They abound in the extinct volcanoes of Auvergne.

(6.) *Unaltered ejected masses.* Volcanoes sometimes eject stones, many of which bear no marks of common fusion. These, by some, are considered as fragments of rocks, which form the walls of internal cavities, and which may have been torn off and projected by some current of elastic fluids; others, again, maintain that they are fragments of rocks, which have been formed by igneous solution and crystallization. Fragments of these dubious masses are found in great numbers on the Monte Somma. There they are of granular limestone, containing mica, and many other minerals besides.

*Projectile power of volcanoes.* Did our space allow of it, it would be interesting to inquire what is the intensity of that force which throws such quantities of matter to so great a height. We can only remark, that the greatest velocity in the case of Ætna and Vesuvius was found to be equal to that of a cannon-ball at the moment when it issues from a cannon, the velocity being from four to five hundred yards per second. The gigantic Cotopaxi projected a piece of rock about an hundred cubic yards in magnitude to the distance of three leagues.

### b. *Lavas.*

*Eruptions of lavas.* When we have an opportunity of seeing the liquid lava in the crater, it resembles the melted matter in our furnaces, and appears as it were boiling with greater or less violence. Jets of the melted matter are thrown up from the liquid surface, through the agency of elastic fluids. It is by these elastic fluids that the lava is raised upwards in the crater. When the mountain is high, as Teneriffe or Ætna, these fluids are not sufficiently powerful to raise the lava to the summit, or rather the sides of the mountain are not sufficiently strong to resist the weight and force of the long and heavy column of lava; it therefore presses or melts the walls which surround it, and thus forms an opening, through which it issues with great rapidity. When, on the contrary, the mountains are comparatively low, as Vesuvius for example, the lava reaches the mouth of the crater and flows over its lips, and from thence downwards along the acclivities of the mountain. On reaching the bottom they divide into several branches, according to the nature and slope of the ground over which they flow. The currents or streams of lava vary much in regard to the velocity with which they move. This velocity depends upon the slope of the ground upon which it flows, as well as upon the quantity and viscidity of the lava. At Vesuvius, M. de la Torre saw currents passing over a space of about 800 yards in an hour. Sir William Hamilton observed one which traversed 1800 yards in the same time. The eruption of 1776 presented another, which moved more than 2000 yards in 14 minutes. Buchk observed, during the eruption of 1805, a torrent flow from the summit to the sea-shore, a distance, in a straight line, of about 7000 yards. Those we have mentioned, however, are extraordinary velocities; for in general lavas move slowly. Those of Ætna, flowing upon an inclined plane, are considered quick when they traverse a space of 400 yards in an hour. In flat grounds they sometimes occupy whole days in advancing a few yards.

The slowness with which lavas cool is not less remarkable than that with which they move. If their surface is quickly cooled and consolidated, the case is different with the interior; the heat concentrates there, and is retained for whole years. Currents are mentioned which were flowing ten years after emerging from the crater, and lavas were seen smoking in Ætna twenty years after an eruption.

The heat of liquid lava is nearly that of liquid trap, as greenstone or basalt. The particular temperatures are given by Dr. Kennedy, Sir James Hall, and Professor Jameson.

The magnitude of lava currents varies much. The largest current which has ever issued from Vesuvius was about 14,000 yards long; that of the eruption of 1805 was 8000; that of 1794 was in length 4200 yards, in breadth from 100 to 400 yards, and in depth from eight to ten yards; that which issued from Ætna in 1787 was four times larger; and Dolomieu relates that that volcano furnished one more than ten leagues in length. But the largest current known is that which in Iceland, in 1783, covered an cxtent of twenty leagues in length by four in breadth.

These currents, by being superinduced on each other, and having interposed between them other products of eruptions, as sand, ashes, and scoriæ, form a series of inclined beds that give rise to the cone of the mountain. In short, the cone is composed of a series of concentric layers or coats of lava, scoriæ, &c.; the outgoings of which are sometimes well seen in natural sections in the mountain.

### c. *Different Kinds of Eruptions.*

*Watery and muddy eruptions.* In the accounts of volcanic eruptions, mention is often made of torrents of water and mud vomited forth by volcanoes. Many of these watery and muddy eruptions are external actions, as is the case with those mentioned as having taken place in Vesuvius, Ætna, and Hecla; others are internal, as those of Quito.

(1.) *External aqueous and muddy eruptions.* These are owing to great rains, which frequently take place by the condensation of the great volumes of aqueous vapour that rise from the craters during volcanic action. This rain, on mixing with the ashes and sands, forms currents, more or less charged with earthy matters, which descend on the sides of the mountain, spread themselves at its base, and sometimes to a distance in the low country. The melting of bodies of snow by the lavas also occasions great floods of water and mud. Of this a striking instance is related as having taken place on Mount Ætna in 1755, where, by the sudden melting of a great body of snow by a stream of liquid lava, a terrible inundation was produced, which devastated the sides of the mountain for eight miles in length, and afterwards covered the lower parts of Ætna, together with the plains near the sea, with great deposits of sand, ashes, scoriæ, and fragments of lava. Similar floods of ashes and sand are mentioned by authors as taking place in Iceland and in America, where the summits reach above the snow line.

(2.) *Internal aqueous and muddy eruptions.* These waters also frequently make their way into the mountain by infiltration. They there collect in particular reservoirs; and at the period of explosion, or when the mountain happens to split in consequence of some shock, they issue forth, and cover the neighbouring countries. During the earthquake which overturned Lima in 1746, four volcanoes opened at Lucanos and in the mountains of Concepcion, and occasioned a frightful inundation. The mountains of Quito sometimes present the same phenomena: but it is there accompanied with extraordinary circumstances. The enormous cones of Cotopaxi, Pichincha, Tunguragua, &c., are but in some measure the summits of the volcanoes to which they belong, and whose acclivities are probably encased in the great mass of the Andes. No true lavas, within the memory of man, have been vomited forth by these volcanoes; yet Humboldt saw consolidated lava currents on Sanguay, and even on Antisana. It might be said, says Humboldt, that the volcanic agents, which seldom have force sufficient to raise the column of lava to the summit of Ætna and of the Peak of Teneriffe, would still less be able to raise it in volcanoes of nearly double the height. In Ætna and Teneriffe, the lava may force an opening at the lower part of the mountains, and thus burst out; but this could not happen in volcanoes whose sides are strengthened, to a height of nearly 3000 yards, by the whole breadth of the Cordilleras. These volcanoes confine themselves to the emission of ashes, scoriæ, and pumice. They also vomit immense quantities of water and mud, but much more frequently by openings which take place on the sides of the cone than by the craters. These muddy waters form, as it were, great lakes in the different cavities which these enormous mountains contain. They issue from these cavities, as we have said, when a communication is opened with the exterior. Thus, in 1698, the volcano of Carguarazo, which is in the neighbourhood of Chimborazo, and perhaps forms a part of it, broke down, and covered with mud eighteen square leagues of country. Similar muddy waters are still contained in parts of the same country, which are of volcanic origin, but which no longer present any indication of fire; and they are equally vomited forth during great commotions of the ground. In Peru and Quito it is not by fire and currents of burning matters that the volcanoes commit their ravages, but by the water and enormous streams of mud. This substance is mud which is at first of a soft consistence, soon hardens, and bears the name of *moya*. It presents two curious phenomena. Sometimes, as in the moya which inundated the country of Pilielo, and which destroyed the village of that name during the earthquake of 1797, it contains a combustible matter, which renders it blackish and soiling, and which exists in so large a quantity in it that the inhabitants make use of this moya as a kind of fuel. Frequently the same muddy waters, issuing from subterranean caverns, carry with them a great quantity of small fishes. These fishes are a species of *pimelodes* (P. cyclopum). Most of them are not more than four inches long. Their number is sometimes so great that diseases are occasioned in the country by their putrefaction. They are the same as those which live in the brooks of the country. What, then, has introduced them into these subterranean lakes? It would appear that there are some communications between the upper and lower level of these lakes and the surface of the ground; but what could have raised them from the level of this surface to the summit of the volcanoes, for they sometimes issue from the crater? It is very difficult to give any explanation of this. From all that has been said above, it does not appear that the mud which issues from these volcanoes comes from the subterranean caverns where the volcanic fires have their focus, and prepare the matter of lava.

*Air and mud volcanoes.* In some countries we observe issuing from the ground jets impelled by gases and charged with earth, which, on being deposited in the form of mud, in the neighbourhood of and chiefly around the apertures which have vomited them, form cones, which represent on a very small scale volcanic cones, and which are therefore named *air volcanoes.* One of the most remarkable of these is that of Macalouba in Sicily. It consists of a hill of dried mud about 160 feet high. Its upper part, which is 2600 feet in circumference, presents a multitude of small cones of which the largest are not above a yard in diameter. They have a small crater full of soft clay, which is every instant traversed by large bubbles of gas, which burst with an exploding noise, and scatter the clay around. Some of these explosions have been seen throwing jets of mud to the height of 160 feet. In the neighbourhood of Modena there are many of these small mud volcanoes, where they are called *salses* on account of the saltness of the water they scatter about. The gas which occasions the phenomena is hydrogen gas charged with petroleum and carbonic acid. Similar mud volcanoes occur in the Crimea, Java, Trinidad, and America.

### d. *Periods of Activity of Volcanoes, and the Theory of their Formation.*

*Periods of activity of volcanoes.* The periods of activity of volcanoes are but transitory and of short duration. They are followed by years, and even ages, of rest. Humboldt is of opinion that the frequency of eruptions seems to be in the inverse ratio of the size of the volcano. The smallest of them, Stromboli, is continually throwing up volcanic matter; the eruptions of Vesuvius are less frequent, there having been but eighteen recorded since 1701; those of Ætna are much rarer; those of the Peak of Teneriffe still more so; and the colossal summits of Cotopaxi and Tunguragua scarcely exhibit one in the course of a hundred years. To periods of activity there sometimes succeed periods of repose. The crater is filled up and becomes covered with forests. These burning furnaces, whence torrents of fire have issued, become the reservoirs of subterranean lakes, whose waters are peopled with fishes, and in elevated situations the sides and summits of the mountains become covered with snow and ice. But most commonly the state of rest is not complete; the crater remains open, and there is exhaled from it a greater or less quantity of vapours, which attack the masses that lie in their way. Sometimes they produce different saline and metallic incrustations Volcanic districts in which, however, no eruption has taken place since the commencement of our history, and in which the volcanic cones are nearly effaced, still betray by their vapours and exhalations the fire which formerly ravaged them, and which is not yet extinct. Such are the *Phlegrean Fields*, on the coast of Puzzoli, in the kingdom of Naples.

*Cause of volcanoes.* This is an obscure subject. A conjecture, hazarded many years ago, may be stated. There being no decided proof of a central heat, in the commonly received sense, it may be assumed that the matter of lavas is seated deep in the crust of the earth, in spaces of greater or less extent, from whence it is sent up from time to time among the previously existing strata, by the agency of elastic fluids.

## SECT. IV.—*Earthquakes.*

*On earthquakes, and the changes they produce on the earth's surface.* Werner distinguishes two kinds of earthquakes. Some, he says, appear to be connected with a particular volcano, and to have their focus in the same region as it. They are only felt to the distance of a few leagues around, and their paroxysms are almost always connected with those of the volcano. Others, which appear to have their focus at a much greater depth, and whose effects are much greater, are propagated to immense distances with incredible celerity, and are felt almost at the same time at points thousands of miles distant from each other. Some of the latter however approach the former, and are still connected with volcanic phenomena. Thus, during the earthquake which overturned Lima in 1746, and which was one of the most terrible that has been recorded, four volcanoes opened in one night, and the agitation of the earth ceased.

*Universality of earthquakes.* If in the more violent we include the slighter agitations of the earth's surface in particular places, earthquakes may be said to be universal or general, and we may affirm that no considerable country is entirely exempted from them. Sandy deserts and fertile regions, primitive, secondary, and tertiary hills, extensive plains, and even marshy districts but little elevated above the level of the sea, afford no protection against these destructive phenomena, which are equally prevalent in cold, in temperate, and in tropical climates. They are, however, generally considered more frequent near to coasts; thus, Syria, the coasts and islands of Asia, America, the European coasts of the Mediterranean, and Iceland, are most subject to them; while the plains of Africa, Asia, and the North of Europe are least exposed. Viewing the whole earth, and including every slighter agitation, earthquakes appear to be exceedingly numerous, and it may be maintained that not a week passes in which the earth's surface in some place or other is not more or less agitated. The great number of concussions observed in civilized countries, and the fact that some districts are constantly agitated by them, entitle us to draw the conclusion. Their return in the places most subject to them, and in the places where they are less frequent, is not regulated by any precise period of time. Their appearance is not connected with any particular season of the year or state of the atmosphere, and they take place by day as well as by night.

*Phenomena of Earthquakes.* The phenomena peculiar to earthquakes are in themselves sufficiently simple. They consist in tremblings and oscillations of the earth's surface, called shocks; extending over greater or smaller tracts of country, and frequently following a particular direction. The shocks appear at first chiefly as perpendicular heavings; then as horizontal undulations or oscillations; lastly, in some instances, there is a violent agitation: the motion is more or less rotatory. If to these we add the rending, slipping, rising and sinking of the ground, the violent agitations of the sea, lakes, rivers, and springs; consisting, in springs, in their drying up or bursting forth with great violence; in lakes, rivers, and the ocean, in their falling and rising, and rushing backwards and forwards, owing to the sinking and rising of the land, we obtain an enumeration of the principal phenomena. As the subject is very interesting, we shall view it somewhat in detail, and under the following heads: — 1. Shocks. 2. Extent of earthquakes. 3. Duration of shocks. 4. Magnitude of rents formed, and the phenomena connected with them. 5. Elevation and subsidence of the land. 6. Agitations in the sea. 7. Notice of particular earthquakes.

(1.) *Shocks.* The slighter shocks of an earthquake, consisting of perpendicular heavings and horizontal undulations, commonly produce rents in houses, moving light objects in them, as articles of furniture. Persons unacquainted with the phenomenon, or who do not perceive it from the subterraneous noise resembling thunder which accompanies it, feel unsteady while in their beds, but particularly when sitting, and believe themselves seized with a sudden giddiness. The shocks proceed gradually to be more violent, and then they are very easily perceived even by the inexperienced. Then the most substantial buildings are shattered to pieces, and the inhabitants buried beneath their ruins: while buildings of a lighter construction are only rent, and very slender reed huts are least of all exposed to destruction. In some cases the fracturing, or as it were trituration, surpasses description. Hence, for the plainest reasons, it is most dangerous to remain in houses or inhabited places; but even the fields and mountains themselves afford no perfect security, inasmuch as the fields frequently in some places open into fissures, and are rent asunder; while mountains are not only rent, but slide down into the valleys, dam up rivers, form lakes, and cause inundations. Although the desolation produced by these convulsions exceeds all description, this is much more the case with the rotatory motions; a species of motion, however, the existence of which has been denied by some geologists. In proof of it, however, it may be mentioned, that during the earthquake of Catania, whose general direction was from S. E. to N. W., many statues were turned round, and a large mass of rock was turned 25° from South to East. But the rotatory motion was more strikingly exemplified in the earthquake at Valparaiso, on the 19th November, 1822, by which many houses were turned round, and three palm-trees were found twisted round one another like willows. These rotatory motions of masses of rock are particularly interesting when viewed in connexion with the phenomena of faults or shifts among strata in non-volcanic districts. It is only the slighter earthquakes that pass by with a single shock; in most of them more shocks follow at short intervals, and for the most part the number is proportioned to the violence of the concussion. The first shock is sometimes the most powerful, but the second is as often, if not oftener, equally violent. Further, the concussions are also repeated after longer intervals, as the earthquakes in Syria, that sometimes continue for a number of months, with longer or shorter intermissions; but the first catastrophe is generally the most violent and destructive.

(2.) *Extent of earthquakes.* It is the agitation of the sea that points out the great extent of the tracts of land convulsed by earthquakes. In this respect, the earthquake at Lisbon, in 1755, was the most remarkable and most violent that ever visited Europe. In consequence of it, by the concussion on the bottom, or momentary rising or upheaving of the submarine land, the sea overflowed the coasts of Sweden, England, and Spain, and of the islands of Antigua, Barbadoes, and Martinique in America. In Barbadoes the tide, which rises only 28 inches, rose 20 feet in the bay of Carlisle, and the water appeared as black as ink, owing probably to bituminous matter thrown up from the bed of the ocean. On the 1st of November, when the concussion was most violent, the water at Guadaloupe retreated twice, and on its return rose in the channel of the island to a height of from 10 to 12 feet

Similar appearances were witnessed at Martinique. A wave of the sea, 60 feet high, overflowed a part of the city of Cadiz; and the lakes of Switzerland, such as Geneva, were observed to be in commotion six hours after the first shock. It is also remarkable that agitations were noticed in lake Ontario, in October, 1755. During the earthquake at Lima, 1586, a wave of the sea rose 84 feet high in the harbour of Callao. During the earthquakes in Calabria in 1783, the sea not only overflowed the coast and drowned many people, but was in general so much agitated that the guns on shipboard sprung from the deck to a height of several inches.

(3.) *Slipping of Mountains.* Besides the common operations of earthquakes already mentioned, others occur that do not immediately succeed the concussions, and therefore happen less frequently. To these belong the sliding down of parts of mountains, as at Dobratch in 1345, and the falling together of two mountains in Jamaica in 1692, by which the bed of a river was dammed up. In the latter place, a part of a mountain slid down and covered many plantations; the city of Port Royal sunk to the depth of eight fathoms; and a plain of 1000 acres fell in, with all the buildings upon it.

(4.) *Duration of shocks.* Single shocks frequently succeed one another very rapidly, and often after greater or smaller intervals of time; they are occasionally single, frequently very numerous; and in volcanic districts, shocks sometimes happen after a lapse of months or years, are then followed by longer or shorter intervals, and even periods of 10 or 100 years. In regard to this, it is remarkable that since the earthquake which in 1204 shook Antioch, Damascus, and Tripoli, Syria was spared till the latter half of the seventeenth century, although no region of the earth suffers more from these destructive phenomena than that country. It is, in short, difficult to define the duration of a single shock. It is undoubtedly brief in general; and in slighter shocks, witnessed by tranquil spectators and consequently observed with greater attention, it is not longer than a few seconds. In the greater convulsions, for instance at Lima, Caraccas, Calabria, Catania, Zante, Antioch, &c. the time is reckoned from fifty seconds to one minute and five seconds, or indefinitely from a few minutes to a few seconds. When we consider how exceedingly distracted the attention is when the shock is first perceived, that the duration cannot be measured by means of a watch, but by supposition, and that by such a mode of computation we are in the habit of reckoning time much longer than it really is, we may with great probability conclude that the duration of a single shock does not go beyond a few seconds, and we may affirm that, at the most, it rarely exceeds half a minute.

(5.) *Magnitude of rents formed by earthquakes.* These vary from a few feet to many fathoms in extent. They have either a direction which is nearly straight or more or less winding, or they run in all directions from a centre. During the terrible Calabrian earthquakes of 1783, rents were formed of great dimensions; in the territory of San Fili there was formed a rent half a mile long, two feet and a half broad, and twenty-five feet deep; in the district of Plaisano, a rent, of nearly a mile in length, one hundred and five feet broad, and thirty feet deep opened; and in the same district two gulfs arose, one at Cerzulli, three quarters of a mile long, one hundred and fifty feet broad, and about one hundred feet deep; and another, nearly a quarter of a mile long, about thirty feet broad, and two hundred and twenty-five feet deep. Ulloa relates that in the earthquake of 1746, in Peru, a rent took place, which was two miles and a half long, and four or five feet wide. These rents sometimes close again; thus, in the year 1692, in the island of Jamaica, during an earthquake, the ground heaved like a boiling sea, and was traversed by numerous rents, two or three hundred of which were often seen at a time opening and closing rapidly again.

(6.) *Elevation and subsidence of land during earthquakes.* It is evident that, if the land is fractured and then traversed with vast rents by earthquakes, that portion of the land will in some places sink and in others rise, and this not once but several times in the same place. In the year 1772, during an eruption of one of the loftiest mountains in Java, the ground began to sink, and a great part of the volcano, and part of the neighbouring country, estimated to be fifteen miles long and six miles broad, was swallowed up. During the earthquake at Lisbon in 1755, a new quay entirely disappeared; thousands of the inhabitants had taken shelter on it, to be out of the reach of the tottering and falling buildings, when suddenly the quay sunk down with its thousands of human beings, and not one of their dead bodies ever floated to the surface. In the year 1692, during an earthquake in Jamaica, a tract of land about a thousand acres in extent sank down in less than a minute, and the sea immediately took its place. On the north side of the island several large tracts with their whole population were swallowed up, and a lake appeared in their place covering above a thousand acres. Numerous examples of the upraising of the land by earthquakes might be given; we shall enumerate a few of them. On the 19th of November, 1822, a most dreadful earthquake visited the coast of Chili; the shock was felt at the same time throughout a space of one thousand two hundred miles from north to south. When the country around Valparaiso was examined on the morning after the shock, it was found that the entire line of coast, for the distance of more than a hundred miles, was raised above its former level. The area over which this upraising took place was estimated at one hundred thousand square miles: the rise upon the coast was from two to four feet; at the distance of a mile inland, it was estimated from five to seven feet. On the 18th of March in the year 1790, at St. Maria di Niscomi, some miles from Terranuovo, near the south coast of Sicily, a loud subterranean noise was heard under the town just mentioned, and the day after earthquakes were felt; then the ground gradually sunk down for a circumference of three Italian miles, during seven shocks, and in one place to a depth of thirty feet; as the subsidence was unequal, rents were formed, some of which were so wide that they could not be leaped over: this gradual sinking continued to the end of the month. About the middle of this period an opening took place in the subsiding land, about three feet in diameter; through these continued to flow, for three hours, a stream of mud, which covered a space sixty feet long and thirty feet broad; the mud was saltish and composed of chalky marl and a viscid clay, with fragments of crystalline limestone; it smelt of sulphur and petroleum. On the 16th June, 1819, at Cutch in Bombay, a violent earthquake took place, during which, independent of other changes, the eastern and almost abandoned channel of the Indus was much altered: this estuary was, before the earthquake, fordable at Luckput, being only a foot deep when the tide was at ebb, at flood tide never more than six feet; but it was deepened at the fort of Luckput, after the earthquake, to more than eighteen feet at low water, showing that a considerable depression had taken place. The channel of the river Runn was so much sunk that, instead of being dry as before, during that period of the year, it was no longer fordable except at one place; and it is remarked by Captain Macmurdoch,—and the observation is of high geological import, as connected with the formation of valleys, of river districts, &c.—"should the water continue throughout the year, we may perhaps see an inland navigation along the northern shore of Cutch; which, from stone anchors, &c. still to be seen, and the tradition of the country, I believe to have existed at some former period." Sindree, a small mud fort and village belonging to the Cutch government, situated where the Runn joins the Indus, was overflowed at the time of the shock. The people escaped with difficulty, and the tops of the houses and walls are now alone seen above water. In the year 1790, in the Caraccas, during an earthquake, a portion of granite soil sunk, and left a lake 800 yards in diameter, and from eighty to an hundred feet deep; it was a part of the forest of Aripao which sunk, and the trees remained green for several months under water.

(7.) *Agitations of the sea.* We have already noticed, in a general way, the agitations observed in the sea during earthquakes; we shall now add some particulars illustrative of these motions. During the Lisbon earthquake of 1755, the sea rose along the coast of Spain; and at Cadiz it advanced in the form of vast waves sixty feet high. At Lisbon about sixty thousand persons perished. The sea first retired, and laid the bar dry; it then rushed in, rising upwards of fifty feet above its ordinary level. At Kinsale, in Ireland, the sea rushed into the harbour, and invaded the land. At Tangier, in Africa, it rose and fell eighteen times on the coast. At Funchal, in Madeira, it rose fifteen feet above high-water mark; although the tide, which ebbs and flows there seven feet, was then half ebb. Even ships at sea, a considerable distance from land, felt, in the midst of these convulsive motions, as if hurried across a ridge of rocks. This took place, to a distance of 100 or 270 nautical miles from the coast, during the earthquake at Lisbon in 1816. During the Lisbon earthquake of 1755, the shock was felt at sea, on the deck of a ship to the west of Lisbon, and produced nearly the same feeling as on land. At San Lucar, the captain of the Nancy frigate felt his ship so violently agitated that he thought he had struck on the ground; but, on heaving the lead, found he was in deep water. Captain Clark, from Derina, in N. lat. 36° 24′, between nine and ten in the morning, had his ship shaken as if she had struck upon a rock, so that the seams of the deck opened. Dr. Shaw relates, that in 1724, being on board the Gazello, an Algerine ship of 50 guns, they felt such violent shocks, one after another, as if the weight of twenty or thirty tons had been let fall from a good height on the ballast. Schouten, speaking of an earthquake which happened in the Moluccas, says, that the mountains were shaken, and ships that were at anchor in thirty or forty fathoms' water were jerked as if they had run ashore, or come foul of rocks. Le Genil says, "that ships at sea and at anchor suffer, during earthquakes, such violent agitations that they seem to be falling asunder; their guns break loose, and their masts spring."

(8.) *Notices of particular Earthquakes.* A full account of all the principal earthquakes that are known would much exceed our limits; we shall, therefore, select only a few of the more interesting.

No part of Europe is more visited by earthquakes than Italy and the neighbouring islands. The first earthquake particularly worthy of notice was that which, in the year 63, destroyed Herculaneum and Pompeii. Since that period they have frequently visited Italy and Sicily, but much seldomer from A. D. 63 to the twelfth century, than from that period till modern times, that is, till the eighteenth and nineteenth centuries. Of these we shall describe one of the most recent in Calabria, and another of still later date in Sicily.

*Earthquake of* 1783. The earthquake that so much affected Calabria, and destroyed the city of Messina, raged at unequal periods from the 5th of February till the 28th of March,

1783. According to Sorcia, its principal seat was the small town of Oppido in the neighbourhood of Atramonte, a snow-covered peak of the Apennines. From this point, says Sir William Hamilton, around to a distance of twenty-five miles, comprehends the surface of country which suffered most, and where all the towns and villages were destroyed. If we describe the circle with a radius of seventy-two miles, it will include the whole country which was in any way affected by the earthquake. The first shock, on the 5th February, in two minutes threw down the greatest part of the houses in all the cities, towns, and villages from the western acclivities of the Apennines, in Calabria Ultra, to Messina in Sicily, and convulsed the whole surface of the country. Another shock, which took place on the 25th of March, was nearly equally violent. The granite chain which extends through Calabria from north to south was but slightly agitated, the principal shocks being propagated with a wave-like motion through the tertiary sands, sand-stones, and clays, from west to east. It was remarked that the violence of the shock was greatest at the line of junction of the granite and tertiary rocks, occasioned probably by the interruption of the undulatory movement of the softer strata by the harder granite. The granite range also prevented the passage of the shocks to the countries on the opposite side of the mountain-range. About 200 towns and villages were destroyed, more than one hundred hills slid down, fell together, dammed up rivers, and formed lakes: numerous rents, often of vast magnitude, were formed; many subsidences and also upraisings of the ground took place; and the general features of the country were so much changed that they could scarcely be recognised. Thus, in a very short space of time, the whole country was as much changed as if it had been exposed to common influences for many thousand years. The total number of human beings that perished was estimated at 100,000, and it was difficult to find even distant relations to succeed to the property of some families.

*Earthquake of Lisbon in* 1755. In no part of southern Europe has so tremendous an earthquake occurred as that which began on the 1st of November, 1755. On the morning of that day, at thirty-five minutes after nine, without the least warning, except a noise like thunder heard under ground, a most dreadful earthquake shook, by short but quick vibrations, the foundations of Lisbon, so that many of the principal edifices fell to the ground in an instant: then, with a scarcely perceptible pause, the nature of the motion changed, now resembling that of a wagon driven violently over rough stones, which laid in ruins almost every house, church, convent, and public building, with an incredible destruction of the people. It continued in all about six minutes. At the moment of its beginning, some persons on the Tagus, near a mile from the city, heard their boat make a noise as if it had run aground, though then in deep water, and saw at the same time houses falling on both sides of the river. Four or five minutes after, the boat made the like noise, caused by another shock, which brought down more houses. The bed of the Tagus was in many places *raised to its surface.* Ships were driven from their anchors, and jostled together with great violence; and the masters did not know if they were afloat or aground. The large quay called *Caes de Prada,* was overturned, crowded with people, and sunk to an unfathomable depth in the water, not so much as one body afterwards appearing. *The bar was seen dry from shore to shore;* then suddenly the sea, like a mountain, came rolling in, and about Belem castle the water rose fifty feet almost in an instant; and had it not been for the great bay opposite the city, which received and spread the great flux, the lower part must have been under water. As it was, it came up to the houses, and drove the inhabitants to the hills. About noon, there was another shock, *when the walls of several houses which were yet standing were seen to open from top to bottom more than a quarter of a yard, but closed again so exactly as to leave scarce any mark of injury.* It is remarked, that on the 1st of November, 1756, being the anniversary of the fatal tragedy of this unhappy city, another shock gave the inhabitants so terrible an alarm that they were preparing for their flight into the country, but were prevented by several regiments of horse placed all around by the king's orders. Many of the largest mountains in Portugal during the great earthquake were shaken as it were to their foundation, and many of them opened at their summits, split, and rent, and huge masses of them were cast down into the subjacent valleys. The same dreadful visitation was experienced at Oporto. We are told that at about forty minutes past nine in the morning, the sky being serene, was heard a dreadful hollow noise like thunder or the rattling of coaches over rugged stones at a distance; and almost at the same instant was felt a severe shock of an earthquake, which lasted six or seven minutes, during which every thing shook and rattled. It rent several churches. *In the streets the earth was seen to heave under the people's feet, as if in labour,* The river was also amazingly affected; for in the space of a minute or two, it rose and fell five or six feet, and continued to do so for four hours. The river Douro was observed to burst open in some parts, and discharge vast quantities of air; and the agitation was so great in the sea, beyond the bar, that it was imagined the air got vent there also.

On the fatal day of the great earthquake of Lisbon, at Ayamonte, near where the Guadiana falls into the bay of Cadiz, a little before ten o'clock, immediately on a rushing noise being heard, a terrible earthquake was felt which during fourteen or fifteen minutes damaged almost all the buildings. In little more than half an hour after, the sea and river, with all their canals, overflowed their bounds with great violence, laying under water all the coasts of the islands adjacent to the city and its neighbourhood, flowing into the streets. The water rose three times, after it had as many times subsided. One of the swells was at the time of ebb. The water came on in vast black mountains, white with foam at the top, and demolished more than half of the town at the bar called De Canala. The earth was observed to open in several places, and from the apertures flowed vast quantities of water.

At Cadiz, in the same morning, some minutes after nine, the whole town was shaken with a violent earthquake, which lasted about five minutes. The water in the cisterns under ground rolled backwards and forwards. At ten minutes after eleven, a wave was seen coming from sea, eight miles off, at least sixty feet higher than usual. It dashed against the west part of the city; at last it came upon the walls, beat in the breast-work, and carried pieces of eight or ten tons weight forty or fifty yards from the wall. When the wave was gone, some parts that are deep at low water were left quite dry, for the water returned there with the same violence as it came. On the same eventful morning Gibraltar was agitated by an earthquake. It lasted about two minutes. *The guns on the battery were seen to rise, others to sink, the earth having an undulating motion.* Most people were seized with giddiness and sickness, and some fell down, others were stupefied, though many that were walking or riding felt no motion, but were sick. The sea rose six feet every fifteen minutes, and fell so low that boats and all the small craft near the shore were left aground, as were numbers of fish. Ships in the bay seemed as if they had struck on rocks. The flux and reflux lasted till six next morning, having decreased gradually from two in the afternoon.

This earthquake excited much attention, from the incredibly great extent at which slighter contemporary shocks were experienced. They extended from Greenland and Iceland to Norway, Sweden, Germany, Britain, Switzerland, France, Spain, Morocco, Salee, Fez, Teutan, and even to the West Indies and the lake Ontario in North America.

However dreadful many of the earthquakes of Europe were, they bear no comparison with those which have desolated many parts of Asia. Passing over those which were observed in the islands, on the eastern continent, and in the environs of the Caspian Sea, our attention is particularly drawn towards Syria, on account of the ravages it has frequently experienced.

Gibbon, in the forty-third chapter of his Decline and Fall of the Roman Empire, gives the following account of the earthquake that took place at Antioch in A. D. 526, May 30. "The near approach of a comet may injure or destroy the globe which we inhabit; but the changes on its surface have been hitherto produced by the action of volcanoes and earthquakes. The nature of the soil may indicate the countries most exposed to these formidable concussions, since they are caused by subterraneous fires, and such fires are kindled by the union and fermentation of iron and sulphur. But their times and effects appear to lie beyond the reach of human curiosity, and the philosopher will discreetly abstain from the prediction of earthquakes, till he has counted the drops of water that silently filtrate on the inflammable mineral, and measured the caverns which increase by resistance the explosion of the imprisoned air. Without assigning the cause, history will distinguish the periods in which these calamitous events have been rare or frequent, and will observe, that this fever of the earth raged with uncommon violence during the reign of Justinian. Each year is marked by the repetition of earthquakes, of such duration, that Constantinople has been shaken above forty days; of such extent, that the shock has been communicated to the whole surface of the globe, or at least of the Roman empire. An impulsive or vibratory motion was felt: enormous chasms were opened, huge and heavy bodies were discharged into the air, the sea alternately advanced and retreated beyond its ordinary bounds, and a mountain was torn from Libanus, and cast into the waves, where it protected, as a mole, the new harbour of Botrys, in Phœnicia. The stroke that agitates an ant-hill, may crush the insect myriads in the dust; yet truth must extort a confession, that man has industriously laboured for his own destruction. The institution of great cities, which include a nation within the limits of a wall, almost realizes the wish of Caligula, that the Roman people had but one neck. *Two hundred and fifty thousand persons* are said to have perished in the earthquake of Antioch, whose domestic multitudes were swelled by the conflux of strangers to the festival of the Ascension. The loss of Berytus was of smaller account, but of much greater value. That city, on the coast of Phœnicia, was illustrated by the study of the civil law, which opened the surest road to wealth and dignity: the schools of Berytus were filled with the rising spirits of the age, and many a youth was lost in the earthquake who might have lived to be the scourge or the guardian of his country. In these disasters, the architect becomes the enemy of mankind. The hut of a savage, or the tent of an Arab, may be thrown down without injury to the inhabitants; and the Peruvians had reason to deride the folly of their Spanish conquerors, who with so much cost and labour erected their own sepulchres. The rich marbles of a patrician are dashed on his own head; a whole people is buried under the ruins of public and private edifices, and the conflagration is kindled and propagated by the innumerable fires which are necessary for the subsistence and manufactures of a great city. Instead of the mutual sympathy which might comfort and assist the distressed, they dreadfully experience the vices and passions which are released from the fear of punishment: the tottering houses are pillaged by intrepid avarice; revenge embraces the moment, and selects the victim; and the earth often swallows the assassin or the ravisher in the consummation of their crimes. Superstition involves the present danger with invisible terrors; and if the image of death may sometimes be subservient to the virtue or repentance of individuals, an affrighted people is more forcibly moved to expect the end of the world, or to deprecate with servile homage the wrath of an avenging Deity." In 1169 single shocks continued for four months; and in 1202 another earthquake destroyed many cities, filled up the valleys of Lebanon, and shattered the basaltic districts of Hauran, so that, according to the expression then current, *it was no longer possible to say, Here stood this or that city.* A dreadful earthquake took place in 1759; the shocks continued for six months. At the first shock the cities of Antioch, Balbec, Acre, Tripoli, &c. were laid in ruins, and 30,000 persons killed. The more recent earthquake, of 1822, lasted still longer, and committed dreadful ravages. On the 13th of August, in one horrible night, Aleppo, Antioch, Biha, Gesser, indeed every single village and cottage within the pashalic of Aleppo, was, within ten or twelve seconds, completely destroyed, and converted into a heap of rubbish: no less than 20,000 people lost their lives, and many more were mutilated; a very great number, considering the low population of these places.

Africa is very little known, and we are therefore ignorant of any earthquakes in its interior, where they may occur as frequently as in other places. The southern extremity of this continent is rarely visited by slight shocks, but they are more numerous in the north, where, in March, 1825, they did considerable damage to Algiers and Blida. On the contrary, *America*, particularly in the southern parts, is inferior to no part of the world for the magnitude, number, and duration of its earthquakes. We shall now mention a few of the greatest recorded by naturalists. To these belong the earthquake of 1746, which, within five minutes, destroyed the greater part of Lima; Callao was inundated; and of 4000 persons, 200 only escaped. The destruction of New Andalusia, on the 21st of October, 1766, was equally terrible. The shocks extended over Cumana, Caraccas, Maracaibo, the shores of the Casanar, the Meta, the Orinoco, and Ventures; and the granite districts in the mission of Encaranada were also shaken by their violence. An earthquake, in 1797, destroyed a great part of Peru. It proceeded from the volcano Tunguragua, continued with slight shocks during the whole of February and March, and returned on the 15th of April, with increased violence. Many places were filled up by the summits of mountains tumbling down; muddy water flowed from the volcano; and, spreading over the country, became afterwards an indurated crust of clay. The entire number of persons who perished on this occasion was 16,000. No earthquake could well be more destructive to any place than that which destroyed the Caraccas in 1812, and of which Humboldt has given an excellent description. The Caraccas was thought secure on account of its primitive mountains, although in 1641, 1703, and 1778, violent earthquakes were experienced, and a slighter shock in 1802. Humboldt, from actual inspection, had no doubt but this country, from being in a volcanic region, must be liable to such disasters. In December, 1811, various shocks were felt; on the 12th of March, 1812, the city of Caraccas was destroyed. The sky was clear, and in Venezuela, there had not been a drop of rain for five months: there was no forewarning prognostic, for the first shock at seven minutes past four in the afternoon came on unexpectedly, and set the bells a ringing. This was immediately succeeded by a second shock, which caused a waving and rolling motion in the earth, then a subterraneous rumbling noise was heard, and there was a third shock, in which the motion was perpendicular, and sometimes rolling horizontally, with a violence which nothing could withstand. The people, in place of flying directly to the open fields, flocked in crowds to the churches, where arrangements had been made for a procession; and the multitudes assembled there were buried beneath the ruins. Two churches 150 feet high, and supported by columns of from twelve to fifteen feet in diameter, fell in a mass of rubbish, and were for the most part ground into dust. The Caserne el Quartel vanished almost entirely, and a regiment of soldiers stationed there, and about to join the procession, disappeared at the same time along with it; a few individuals only escaped; nine-tenths of the city were completely destroyed, and most of the houses that remained were rendered uninhabitable; the number of people killed was reckoned at nearly 10,000, without including those who perished afterwards from bruises and want of sustenance. The clouds of dust having fallen, were succeeded by a serene night, which formed a frightful contrast with the destruction on the earth, and with the dead bodies lying scattered among the ruins. The duration of each particular shock was reckoned by some 50 seconds, by others 1 minute 12 seconds. These shocks extended over the provinces of Venezuela, Varinas, Maracaibo, and into the mountains in the interior. La Guayra, Mayquatia, La Vega, St. Felipe and Merida, were almost entirely destroyed. In La Guayra and St. Felipe the number of persons killed was about 5000. On the 5th of April another violent earthquake took place, during which enormous fragments were detached from the mountains. It was said that the mountain Silla lost from 350 to 360 feet of its height by sinking.

*Cause of Earthquakes.*—The original hypothesis, which attributed volcanic eruptions and earthquakes to the operation of central fire, was at first attacked chiefly by Stukely, who, from the phenomena of two earthquakes observed at London on the 8th February, and 8th of March, 1749, endeavoured to prove that they were caused by a highly overcharged state of the electric fluid. Andrew Bena affirms, that they are sudden explosions, caused by gas in the interior of the earth, which he believes would be found there inclosed in reservoirs of sulphur and bitumen. Beccaria, as is known, endeavoured to attribute to electricity every thing that had any probable affinity for it; hence he believed that an accumulation of it in the crust of the earth produced concussions with the clouds, and then exhibited the appearance of earthquakes. Humboldt found it to be a prevailing opinion in America that earthquakes are electrical phenomena; but observes, that this must be excused by reason of the partiality entertained for Franklin. The invention of the Voltaic pile, and the observation of its singular operations, induced many philosophers, at least those naturalists who were perfectly intimate with the nature of this remarkable apparatus, to consider the whole earth as a column or pile of this description, or that it contains an apparatus of this description in its interior. These fancies, however, lead to nothing satisfactory. Where then can we seek for the cause or causes of earthquakes? The subject is entirely hypothetical, as we have no means of reaching the seat of these remarkable phenomena. The theory of the earthquake is the same as that of the volcano. The agitations may be produced by the motions of the liquid and gaseous matter at a *great depth in the crust of the earth endeavouring to escape.*

Sect. V.—*Account of the different Structures observable in the Crust of the Earth.*

Before the time of Werner, little had been accomplis' ed in regard to the determination of the structures that occur in the crust of the earth. Some maintained that everywhere irregularity prevailed, and that it was in vain to look for order or regularity in the coarse rocky masses of which mountains, hills, and plains are composed. Werner, however, on general grounds, assumed that if determinate structures and arrangements occurred in the vegetable and animal kingdoms, the same must be the case in the mineral kingdom, not only in simple minerals, but also in the great and more generally distributed masses of which the crust of the earth is principally composed. His investigations fully confirmed the truth of this opinion, for minerals he found as well characterised as plants and animals and the following details will show that there exists among *mountain rocks*, or those grea masses of which the crust of the earth is composed, a beautiful series of structure, from that of *hand-specimens* to the general arrangements of the great rock formations. We shall consider these structures in the following order, beginning with the smallest and terminating with the greatest.

Subsect. —*Different Structures.*

1. Structure of mountain rocks in hand-specimens.
2. Structure of strata and beds.
3. Structure of formations.
4. Arrangements of formations in regard to each other.
5. Structure of veins.

(1.) *Structure of mountain rocks.* The kinds of structure occurring in mountain rocks are the following:—1. Compact. 2. Slaty. 3. Granular. 4. Porphyritic. 5. Amygdaloidal. 6. Conglomerated. In the *compact structure*, the mass is uniform, without slaty or any other arrangement, and when broken exhibits various fractures as earthy, splintery, conchoidal, even, &c. Common compact quartz is an example of this kind of structure. In the *slaty structure* the rocks split readily into thin layers or slates, as in common roofing slate. Rocks having the *granular structure* are composed of granular concretions or imperfect crystals, as in primitive limestone or statuary marble. In the *porphyritic structure* there is a basis or ground with imbedded crystals, generally of felspar or quartz, or both, as in porphyry: in the *amygdaloidal structure* there is also a basis or ground; but here the base does not contain imbedded crystals, but amygdaloidal cavities, which are either nearly empty, half filled, or completely filled with minerals. The rock named amygdaloid exhibits this kind of structure. Lastly, the *conglomerated structure* is that which we observe in the rock named conglomerate, which is composed of fragments imbedded in a basis or ground.

(2.) *Structure of strata and beds.* When a mountain or hill is composed of tabular masses of the same kind of rock, as of sandstone, that extend throughout the hill, it is said to be stratified, and the individual tabular masses are named *strata*, as in *fig.* 58. If among these strata there occur tabular masses of a different rock, the masses are named *beds*: *a. fig*

58. represents a bed of limestone in the cliff of stratified sandstone. These strata and beds

58

vary in *position*; sometimes they are flat or *horizontal*, or they are more or less inclined until they become *vertical*, or are set on their edges. They also vary in the point of the compass towards which they are *inclined*, or *dip*; but it is worthy of remark that the dip is always at right angles to the range or direction of the strata; and that if the dip is given, we know the direction: but a knowledge of the direction will not give us the dip. Their *direction* also varies. The position of strata is determined by a well-known instrument, the clinometer, which is a compass with an attached quadrant. When we examine the structure of individual strata and beds, several varieties may be discovered: thus, in some beds, the rock is arranged in *columns*, as in basalt; in others, the arrangement is in *tables*, as in porphyry; or in *balls*, as in granite and greenstone.

(3.) *Structure of formations.* The idea of formations was first clearly brought out by Werner. To his views on this most important subject we can trace the new character of geology, and the great progress made in geognosy within these last thirty years. But this is not the place for discussing the subject. All those rocks which appear to have been formed at the same time, and in the same or similar circumstances, and which agree in position, structure, mass, petrifactions, imbedded minerals, &c. are said to belong to the same formation. These formations are divided into *simple* and *compound*. *Simple formations* are those principally composed of one rock; *compound formations*, of more than one species of rock: granite is an example of a simple formation; the first secondary sandstone, or the great coal formation, of a compound formation, because it contains several rocks; viz. sandstone, slate, limestone, coal, and ironstone.

(4.) *Arrangement of formations in regard to each other.* When two formations occur together, and the one rests upon the other, the subjacent formation is named the *fundamental rock*, and that which covers or lies upon the other, the *superincumbent*. The line where the two rocks or formations meet is called the *line of separation* or *line of junction*. In *fig*. 59. *a* is the fundamental rock, and *b* the superimposed rook, and *c c* the line of junction.

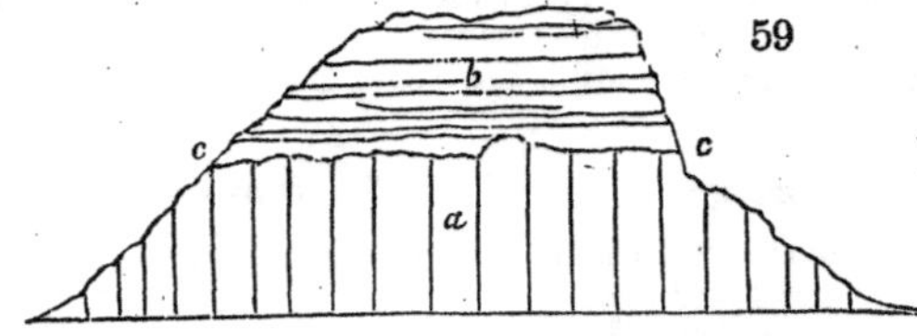

59

When the strata of the superimposed formation is parallel with the strata of the fundamental or subjacent rock, the stratification is said to be *conformable*, as *fig*. 60 where a formation *a*

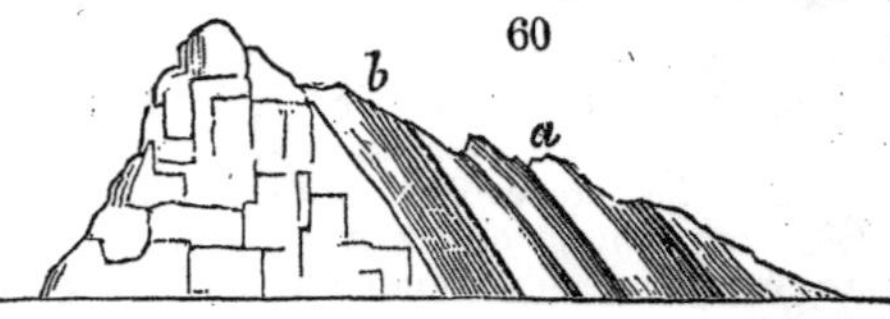

60

we shall say of limestone, rests on *b*, of sandstone. If the strata of the superimposed formation are disposed as at *c*, *fig*. 61., they are said to be *unconformable*. Lastly, if the

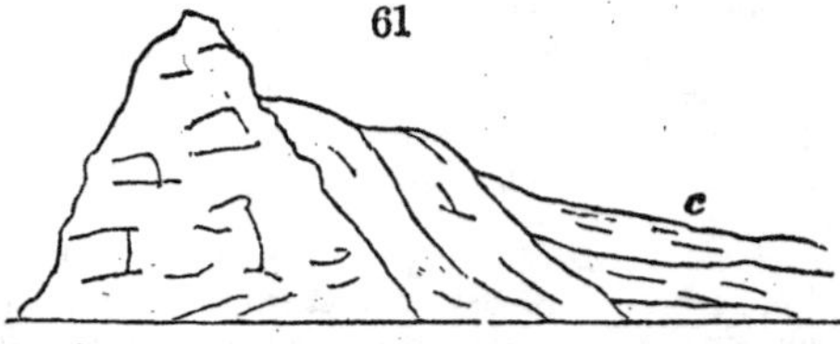

61

strata lie over the ends of the strata of the fundamental rock, as at *b*, in *fig*. 59., they are said to be *unconformable* and *overlying*. If the strata rest on the fundamental rock. as represented

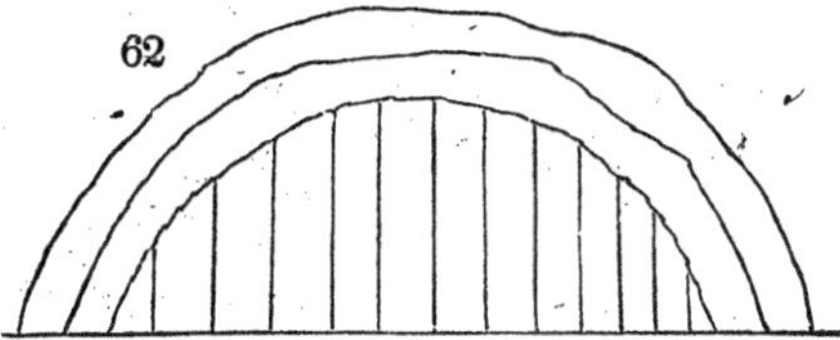


in *fig*. 62., they are said to be *saddle-shaped;* if as represented in *fig*. 63., they are said to

be *mantle-shaped;* if disposed in a bason-shaped hollow, as in *fig*. 64., they are said to be

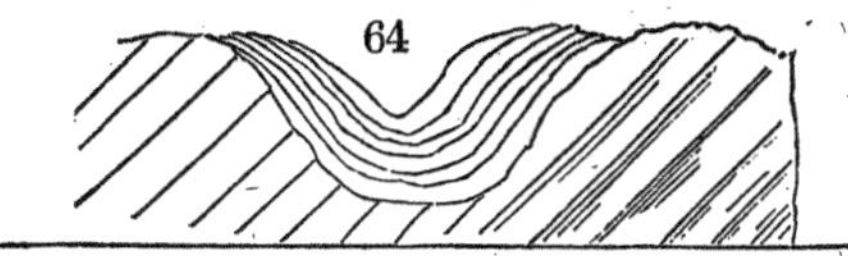


*bason-shaped;* if in a lengthened or trough-like hollow, as in *fig*. 65., thev are said to be

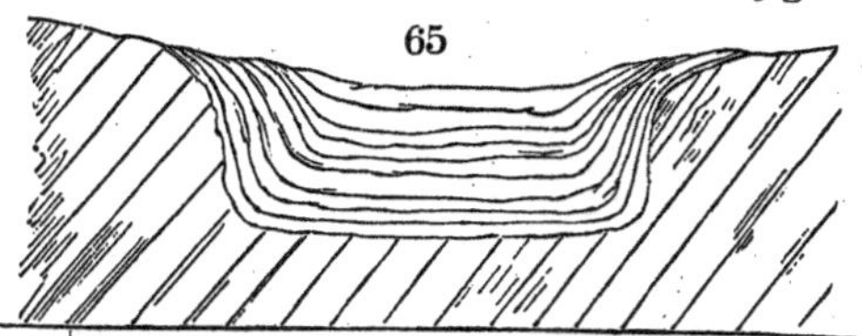


*trough-shaped.* In a mountain or natural section of Neptunian or aquatic rocks, as limestone, sandstone, slate, &c., the undermost or lowest-lying strata are considered to be the oldest: therefore, on ascending a mountain, as that in *fig*. 66., from *a* to *b*, we pass from the newer

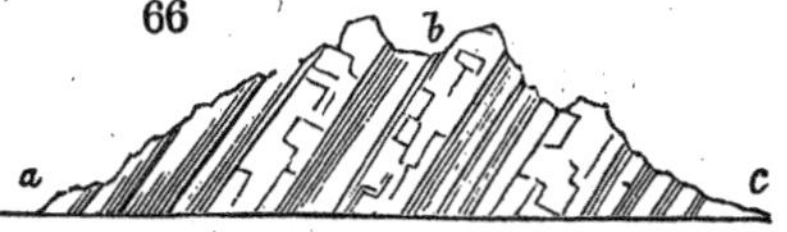


to the older rocks; but if from *c* to *b*, from the older to the newer. Formations were formerly more continuous than at present, portions only remaining of extensive deposits. The remaining portions occupying different situations have received particular names, according to the situations in which they occur. When in patches on the summits of hills, as represented at *a a a* in *fig*. 67., they are called *mountain-caps*. When in hollows, as at *b b*, they are named *upfillings*.

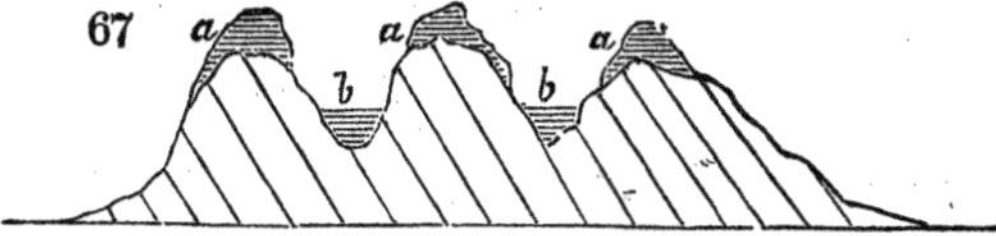


(5.) *Structure of Veins.* These are tabular masses that intersect the strata and beds of the mountain or tract in which they occur. The tabular masses of trap or whinstone veins that cut across the strata of Great Britain are there popularly known under the name of *whin dykes*. Veins, like strata, vary in position, being sometimes vertical, at other times not much inclined to the horizon; their direction, inclination, and dip are determined in the same manner as in strata. These intersecting masses vary in *breadth* from an inch or less to many fathoms; in *length*, from a few inches to several miles; and in *depth*, from a few inches to an unknown and vast depth. Veins appear to have been originally open rents or fissures traversing the strata, which have been filled by an after-process with the mineral matters they now contain. This being the case, we naturally expect to find the strata on the walls of veins exhibiting the same phenomena as occur in the walls of rents. When rents cut across strata, they sometimes, as in *fig.* 68., at *a*, *b*, produce no derangement;

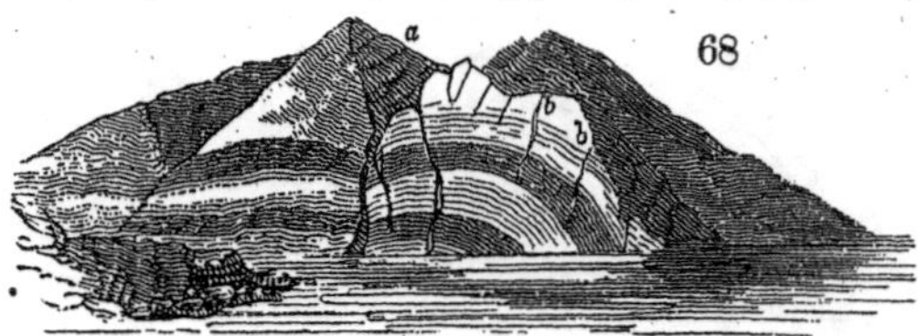

68

while, in other cases, the strata on the opposite sides of the rent do not correspond, owing to the strata on one side sinking down, as represented in *fig.* 69.: this derangement is called a *shift*, *slip*, or *fault*.

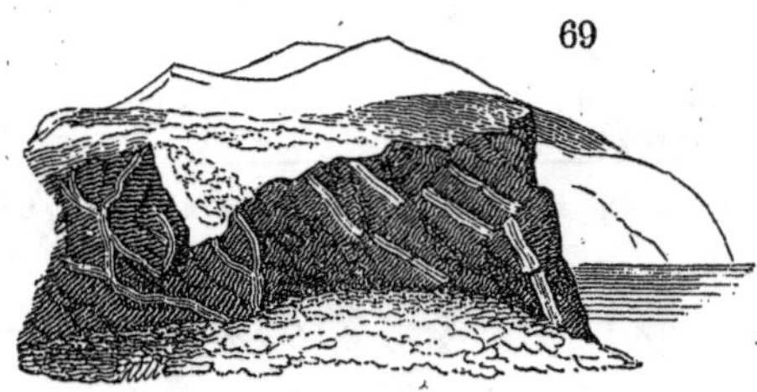
69

Such, then, are the different structures observable in the great masses of which the crust of the earth is composed. We next proceed to give—

## SECT. VI.—*An Account of the different Classes and Species of Rocks of which the Crust of the Earth is composed.*

It was at one time a general opinion that the formations of which the crust of the earth is composed were destitute of all regularity in distribution and in individual characters. Lehman, a German miner, was early convinced of a certain degree of order in their arrangement; and in his well-known work, first stated their division into *Primitive* and *Secondary*; under the first including those destitute of fossil organic remains, while under the other he arranged all those containing petrifactions or fossil organic remains. The first, he said, were generally in highly inclined strata, the other in horizontal strata. Werner first distinctly characterised these two classes of rocks, and added to them other two classes, viz. the *Transition* and *Local*, or what are now called the *Tertiary*. The whole rocks, from the oldest to the newest, were arranged by Werner under the following names and in the following order:—1. Primitive. 2. Transition. 3. Secondary. 4. Local, the Tertiary of the present geology. 5. Alluvial. 6. Volcanic. This arrangement, more or less modified, still remains, being adopted by the principal geologists in Europe and America.

*Primitive rocks.* The rocks of this class lie under those of the succeeding classes. Countries in which they predominate are in general more rugged and lofty than those composed of rocks of the other classes; further, their cliffs are more extensive, their valleys narrower and deeper, and more uneven, than those in secondary countries. The strata of primitive mountains are very frequently highly inclined; a circumstance which contributes in an especial manner to the increase of the ruggedness and inequalities of the surface of primitive regions. The primitive strata in many countries maintain a wonderful uniformity of direction. Thus, in Scotland the general direction of the strata of primitive mountains is from N. E. to S. W.; and the same is nearly the case in the vast alpine regions of Norway, and in many of the lofty and widely extended primitive lands of other parts of Europe. The rocks of which primitive mountains and plains are composed are throughout of a crystalline nature, and present such characters as intimate their formation from a state of solution These characters are the intermixture of the concretions of which they are composed at their line of junction, their mutual penetration of each other, their considerable lustre, pure colours, and translucency. Thus, in granite the concretions of felspar, quartz, and mica are joined together without any basis or ground; and at their line of juncture are either closely attached together, or are intermixed; and frequently branches of the one concretion shoot into the other, thus occasioning a mutual interlacement, as is observed in bodies that have been formed simultaneously and from a state of solution. These characters show that the concretions of granite (and the same applies to the concretions of limestone, gneiss, mica slate, and other rocks of the primitive class,) are of a crystalline nature, and have been formed at the same time. The strata are so arranged as to show that they are crystalline formations. Primitive rocks contain no organic remains, hence are inferred to have been formed before animals and vegetables were called into existence. Primitive rocks abound very much in metalliferous minerals, and hitherto no metal has been met with which does not occur, either exclusively or occasionally, in this class of rocks. Tin, wolfram, lead, copper, iron, cobalt, zinc, manganese, arsenic, and mercury, occur either disseminated, in beds and veins, or imbedded in various rocks of this class, and many primitive districts are characterised by the metalliferous deposits they contain.

The most beautiful of all productions of the mineral kingdom, the gems, occur in great variety in primitive rocks. Nothing can be more beautiful than the *drussy cavities* met with in primitive mountains, whose walls are lined with pure and variously tinted and crystallized topaz, beryl, rock crystal, fluor spar, and calcareous spar; the gneiss, granite, and mica slate, with their *imbedded* crystals and grains of sapphire, chrysolite, and garnet; and the *veins* in granite, clay slate, and other primitive rocks, with their emeralds, axinites, and spinel rubies, afford to the mineralogist highly interesting combinations.

*Species of primitive rocks.*—The following are the species of rocks that form the primitive parts of the crust of the earth:—1. Granite. 2. Syenite. 3. Protogine. 4. Trap. 5. Serpentine. 6. Porphyry. 7. Gneiss. 8. Mica slate. 9. Clay slate. 10. Quartz rock. 11. Limestone.

Of these rocks one set, consisting of certain granites, with trap, gneiss, mica slate, clay slate, quartz rock, and limestone, are said to be of *Neptunian* origin, that is, have been deposited from a liquid, probably water; the other set, including certain granites, with syenite, porphyry, protogine, serpentine and diallage rock, are named *Plutonic* or *igneous*, it being probable that they have been formed from a state of igneous solution. We shall describe first the Neptunian, and next the Plutonian primitive rocks.

### Subsect. 1.—*Neptunian Primitive Rocks.*

(1.) *Granite* is a granular compound of felspar, quartz, and mica. It occurs in beds and in imbedded masses, and also in included veins in gneiss, mica slate, and clay slate. From its intimate connexion with these rocks, it is inferred to be a Neptunian deposit.

(2.) *Trap.* Under this name we include all those granular primitive rocks in which hornblende is the sole or predominant constituent part. These rocks sometimes appear arranged like the steps of a stair; hence the name trap, from the Swedish word *trappa*, a stair.

(3.) *Gneiss* is a granular slaty compound of felspar, mica, and quartz.

(4.) *Mica slate* is a slaty compound of mica and quartz. *Talc slate* and *micaceous talc rocks* may be arranged under this head.

(5.) *Clay slate* is a slaty rock, frequently entirely composed of minute scales of mica.

(6.) *Quartz rock.* This rock is almost entirely composed of quartz, either in granular concretions or in the compact form; and grains of felspar and scales of mica not unfrequently occur in it. When the felspar increases in quantity, the compound at length passes into granite. When the scales of mica increase and the felspar disappears, mica slate is formed.

(7.) *Limestone.* This rock has generally a white or gray colour, is composed of shining granular concretions, and is more or less translucent. It frequently contains scales of mica and grains of quartz, seldom or never grains and crystals of felspar.

### Subsect. 2.—*Plutonian or Ignigenous Primitive Rocks.*

(1.) *Granite.* The structure and composition of this granite is in general the same as that of the Neptunian kind already noticed. It differs from it in occurring in vast and often widely extended masses, which form the central parts of mountain groups, and appear to have come from below after the deposition of the Neptunian rocks that rest upon them. The highly inclined position of the primitive strata is considered to have been occasioned by this granite, with its syenites and porphyries.

(2.) *Syenite* is a compound of felspar, hornblende, and quartz: in short, it is a granite in which the mica is replaced by hornblende. Some of the primitive traps belong to this head.

(3.) *Porphyry* is a rock with a felspar basis, including grains and crystals of felspar and quartz, and sometimes scales of mica. This porphyry is a mere modification of granite.

(4.) *Protogine* is a granular compound of felspar, quartz, and chlorite. It differs from granite in the mica being replaced by chlorite.

(5.) *Serpentine* is a simple green-coloured rock, with a compact fracture, feeble translucency on the edges, which yields readily to the knife, and feels greasy.

(6.) *Diallage rock* is a compound of felspar and diallage. It belongs probably to the primitive trap series.

## Sect. VII.—*Transition Rocks.*

The rocks of this class, in the regular succession, rest immediately upon those of the primitive class. Most of the rocks are distinctly stratified, and the strata are frequently vertical, and, like those of the primitive class, exhibit the same general direction throughout great tracts of country. Some of the deposits are of a chemical, others of a mechanical nature; limestone is an example of a chemical, greywacke of a mechanical deposit. They are distinguished from primitive rocks by the presence of fossil organic remains, and the positive characters are drawn from the occurrence of certain fossil crustaceous animals, shells, and corals. The extensive deposits of limestone, particularly of the variegated kinds so highly prized for ornamental purposes, which they contain; the fine granites and porphyries which they afford; and the ores of lead and copper distributed among them, are proofs of their importance in the arts. In this class there are also Neptunian and Plutonian rocks. The *Neptunian* are the following, viz. 1. Greywacke. 2. Transition clay slate. 3. Gneiss and mica slate. 4. Quartz rock. 5. Red sandstone. 6. Limestone. 7. Glance coal. The *Plutonian* are, 1. Granite. 2. Syenite. 3. Porphyry. 4. Trap. 5. Serpentine.

### Subsect. 1.—*Neptunian Transition Rocks.*

(1.) *Greywacke* is a conglomerated rock, having a basis of clay slate, in which fragments of various primitive rocks, as clay slate, quartz rock, &c. occur imbedded. When the imbedded fragments become very small, and the quantity of the basis increases, the rock acquires a slaty fracture, and is named *greywacke slate.*

(2.) *Transition clay slate.* This is the rock known under the name *roofing slate.* It sometimes contains trilobites.

(3.) *Gneiss and mica slate.* These have the same general aspect as the varieties met with in primitive regions.

(4.) *Quartz rock.* This rock very much resembles the kinds met with in primitive mountains.

(5.) *Limestone.* It frequently occurs with less lustre and translucency than primitive limestones, and often exhibits in the same bed various tints and shades of beautiful colours. It is frequently traversed by veins of calcareous spar. Some varieties are conglomerated, forming the *brecciated marble* of artists; and others contain fossil shells and corals, and also the characteristic *trilobite.*

(6.) *Glance coal,* or *Anthracite.* Beds of this coal, known by its metallic lustre, and burning without flame or smoke, are met with in transition districts.

### Subsect. 2.—*Plutonian Transition Rocks.*

(1.) *Granite.* This rock does not differ materially from that of the primitive period. It is principally distinguished by its being intermingled with greywacke and other transition rocks.

(2.) *Syenite.* This rock, which has the same mineralogical characters with the primitive varieties, very generally contains crystals of sphene.

(3.) *Porphyry.* This porphyry has sometimes a basis of felspar, sometimes of clay stone, and as usual contains imbedded grains and crystals of felspar. It occurs either alone, or associated with syenite and trap, forming mountains, and even ranges of mountains.

(4.) *Trap.* In this as in the primitive trap, the sole or predominating mineral is horn blende. It passes into syenite.

(5.) *Serpentine.* This rock does not differ materially from the primitive rock of the same name: geognostically it is distinguished from it by its alternating with, and sometimes traversing in the form of veins, greywacke and other characteristic transition rocks.

## Sect. VIII.—*Secondary Rocks.*

This very interesting class of rocks rests, in the regular succession, immediately upon those of the transition class. Much of the mineral matter of which they are composed appears to have been deposited from a state of mechanical suspension, a circumstance which may be considered as distinguishing them, in some measure, from the transition class, where chemical deposits prevail over those of a mechanical nature. They abound in fossil organic remains, and it is here that for the first time we meet with remains of vertebrated animals, as *lacertæ* and other species of the same general description. *Coal,* which occurs but in small quantity in transition deposits, is profusely distributed among secondary formations. Of ores, by far the most abundant, and at the same time most important in an economical view, are those of *iron* and *lead:* of these the iron (it is the common clay ironstone, the aluminous carbonate of iron,) is the most abundant and most widely distributed. In this, as in the preceding class, there are Neptunian and Plutonian rocks. The Neptunian rocks are the following:—1. Sandstone. 2. Slate. 3. Limestone. 4. Gypsum. 5. Coal. The Plutonian are, 1. Granite. 2. Porphyry. 3. Trap.

### Subsect. 1.—*Neptunian Secondary Rocks.*

In the primitive and transition classes geologists have not hitherto observed any very determinate arrangement among the Neptunian deposits; whereas in the present class a determinate order has been discovered throughout the whole series. In our sketch we shall follow the order of succession, beginning with the oldest, and finishing our account with a description of the newest formation. The whole Neptunian series is divided into formations of sandstone and formations of limestone; the other members of the series, as the slate, gypsum, coal, and ironstone, occurring subordinate to these.

*First secondary formation;* or the *old red sandstone.* This formation is a sandstone of a red colour, and, being the oldest of the sandstones, is named the *old red sandstone.* It is composed of particles of quartz, with occasional scales of mica and fragments of felspar, held together by an iron-shot basis or ground. Sometimes it is associated with a *conglomerate* made up of fragments of transition and primitive rocks.

*Second secondary formation*, or *mountain limestone*, or *metalliferous limestone*, or *carboniferous limestone* of geologists. This deposit rests, generally conformably, sometimes also unconformably, on the old red sandstone. It is distinctly stratified, and the strata are frequently more or less inclined. Its colours are generally gray; the fracture is compact. Sometimes it has a granular foliated structure, particularly where it occurs in contact with trap rocks. Some varieties, viz. those named *lucullite*, have a black colour. It contains fossil organic remains of animals of various descriptions. Of these the most characteristic are genera of the *trilobite* tribe.

*Third secondary formation;* or the *second secondary sandstone*, or the *great coal formation.* This very important deposit is a compound formation, therefore consists of different rocks. Of these rocks the predominating one is sandstone. The rocks of the formation are the following:—1. Sandstone. 2. Slate. 3. Clay. 4. Limestone. 5. Coal. 6. Ironstone. 1. *Sandstone.* The general colours are white and gray; sometimes also it is reddish, and then it much resembles the old red sandstone. Some varieties are entirely composed of particles of quartz, held together by a very inconsiderable basis or ground; others contain, besides quartz, also felspar and mica; these are by some geologists named *arkose.* It frequently contains coaly matter, and casts and impressions of plants.—2. *Slate.* Of the slate there are two kinds, named slate clay and bituminous shale, both of which are mere modifications of clay with the slaty structure. These also contain fossil organic remains.—3. *Clay.* This is compact clay without the slaty structure, and from its use in the arts is named fire clay.—4. *Limestone.* This limestone very much resembles the mountain limestone which lies below the coal; but hitherto no trilobites have been found in it. It alternates in beds with the other rocks of this formation. Some geologists refer it to the mountain limestone, and consequently that limestone to the coal formation; an opinion which may be correct.—5. *Coal.* The coal in this formation occurs in beds that alternate with the slates, sandstone, and limestones. The coal is bituminous or black coal.—6. *Ironstone.* This ironstone is the common gray clay ironstone of mineralogists. It is an aluminous carbonate of iron, and is the species of ironstone which affords most of the iron manufactured in Great Britain. It occurs in beds or imbedded, and most frequently in the slate of this formation.

*Fourth secondary formation;* the *second secondary limestone;* the *magnesian and alpine limestone* of authors. This formation, in the regular succession, rests immediately upon the coal formation. It contains several varieties of limestone. One of these, which frequently occupies the lowest part of the deposit, has a brownish black colour, a thick slaty fracture, and emits an animal bituminous smell, and is named *bituminous marl slate.* Another variety has a yellowish gray, or even at times an ochre yellow colour, with a compact or small granular foliated structure, with a low degree of lustre, and is named *magnesian limestone.* Another variety has a brownish or yellowish colour, is sometimes compact, sometimes granular or cavernous, impregnated with sparry iron, forms the upper part of the deposit, and is called *calcaire ferrifère.* When this variety becomes charged with bitumen and cavernous, it is named by German miners *rauchwacke.* It abounds in the fossil shell named *Productus aculeatus.* This formation does not abound in fossil organic remains. No true ferns, but fossil *fuci* and *zosteræ*, occur in it. Remains of the *monitor*, and it is said also of the *crocodile*, have been met with in it. Fishes of the genus chætodon and of other tribes, and numerous remains of shells and corals, occur more or less frequently in different varieties of the limestone. The *trilobite* tribe, so abundant in the transition period, and also in the first secondary limestone, occur here along with *orthoceratites.* It is the species named *trilobites bituminous.* *Entrochi* and *pentacrini* of great size also occur in it. The shells are not distributed throughout the whole mass of the beds, but rather occur in particular parts. The following are the shells:—

*Orthoceratites*, very rare.
*Ammonites gibbosus.*
*Terebratula paradoxa.*
*Terebratula elongata.*
*Spirifer alatus.*
*Encrinus racemosus.*
*Productus rugosus.*
*Mytilus rostratus.*
*Terebratula ovata, lacunosa, trigonella.*

*Fifth secondary formation;* the *third secondary sandstone*, or *variegated sandstone*, or *new red sandstone.* In this formation, besides the sandstone, there are, when the deposit is complete, also beds of marl, with gypsum and rock-salt. The *inferior part* of this formation is a red coloured sandstone conglomerate, which rarely contains subordinate beds of dolomite, but no fossil organic remains. Above this reposes what may be called the *middle part* of the deposit, which is the variegated sandstone, so named because it sometimes exhibits different colours, principally red, with yellow and gray blotches. It is composed of fine grains of quartz, with a little mica, and sometimes felspar, held together by a base of ferruginous clay. It contains but few organic remains, principally of vegetables. The *upper part* of the deposit is generally composed of beds of a clayey marl, always more or less slaty, and generally alternating in the lower part with beds of the sandstone. Its colours are red, gray, and yellow; sometimes it is variegated in the same manner as the sandstone with which it alternates. It contains subordinate beds of *gypsum*, and *rock-salt*, and sometimes also beds of *dolomite*. It contains littoral shells and bones of *saurian* animals.

*Sixth secondary formation;* the *shell limestone*, or *muschel kalkstein*. This interesting deposit, in the regular succession, rests immediately on the variegated or new red sandstone formation. This limestone is of a gray, yellow, or reddish tint of colour.—It is compact, but the fracture surfaces exhibit numerous shining facets from animal fossil remains. Beds of marl, which are sometimes oolitic, alternate with it. It often abounds in well preserved fossil shells; hence the name shell limestone. It sometimes contains *gypsum* and *rock-salt*. It contains besides numerous species of fossil shells, often very well preserved, bones of great saurian animals, and impressions of fuci and ferns. Corals and echinites are rare, but entrochites are sometimes so abundant that in some parts of Germany it is named trochital limestone (trochiten kalk). The encrinites liliiformis, very common in this formation, is considered to be characteristic of it. Of the fossil shells, the *Ammonites nodosus* and *Avicula socialis* are considered as characteristic of the shell limestone.

*Seventh secondary formation;* the *third secondary sandstone, red ground, marnes irisées, Keuper*. This deposit is principally composed of sandstone, marls, and dolomites with *salt* and *gypsum*. It has been divided into the following four groups:—1. Keuper salt and gypsum. 2. Inferior keuper, 3. Variegated marls. 4. Upper or superior keuper.—The *salt* and *gypsum*, with their marls and beds of saline clay, the most important members of this formation in an economical point of view, occupy the lowest part of the series. Several extensive salt-mines occupy this situation.—The *inferior keuper*, that which rests on the gypsum and salt, is a sandstone which is red in the upper strata, but gradually passes into gray in the lower. This sandstone sometimes alternates with marls, slate clay, and dolomites, and contains beds of gypsum and coal. The slate clay contains bivalve shells, a species of *Ophiura*, and several species of *Equisetum*, *Filices*, and also some *Cycadaceæ*.—The *variegated marls* (marnes irisées), resting upon the inferior keuper, exhibit alternate stripes of white, green, violet, red, gray, and blue; they are generally compact or slaty, and soft. They contain few or no organic remains, very little gypsum, and no rock-salt.—The *upper keuper* is sandstone of a gray, yellow, or variegated colour. It is composed principally of grains of quartz, generally but loosely held together, so that the mass can frequently be pressed into grains between the fingers. Contains some traces of coal, and a few fossil shells and impressions of plants.

*Eighth secondary formation*, or *fourth secondary limestone*, contains the *lias and oolite limestones* and *Jura limestone* of authors. This, which is one of the most extensive and important of the secondary formations, may be divided into the following members; proceeding, as usual, from below upwards:—1. Lias. 2. Oolite. 3. Oxford clay. 4. Coral rag. 5. Kimmeridge clay. 6. Portland oolite.

(1.) *Lias*. Lias is a provincial name applied to limestone shales, and marl stones, and some sandstones that occur along with them. The marls are sometimes very bituminous, and contain beds of lignite or brown coal, and also fossil shells, and occasionally beds of gypsum. The fossil vegetables of the lias are lignites, fossil wood, sometimes siliceous impressions of ferns, cycadaceæ, and fuci. The animal remains are numerous and interesting. It is in this deposit that bones and skeletons of extinct tribes of saurian animals are met with; such as the genera *geosaurus*, *ichthyosaurus*, and *plesiosaurus*. Different species of *fishes* and of *crabs* also occur. The lias contains an immense quantity of fossil shells, of which the predominating one is the *Gryphæa arcuata;* hence the marl stones or limestones of the lias have been named gryphite limestones. Besides, the following may also be mentioned as characteristic fossils, viz. *Ammonites Buclandii*, *Plagiostoma gigantea*, *Belemnites paxillosus*, and *Belemnites digitalis*.

(2.) *Oolite*. The oolite is divided into inferior oolite and great oolite. *Inferior oolite*. This is a limestone composed of round granular concretions, resembling the roe of fishes; hence the name oolite, or roestone, given to it. It is associated with compact limestones and marls, and sometimes it abounds in fossil organic remains. It contains, as at Brora in Sutherland, beds of coal. The fossil vegetables, which are numerous and often well preserved, are of the fern and cycas tribes. It also contains bones and skeletons of great extent, saurian animals, also tortoises and crabs. Species of the tribe echinus, which makes its first appearance in the eighth secondary formation, are not uncommon; the crinoid family has also representatives here, so also have several genera of the coral tribe. The characteristic fossil shells of the inferior oolite are the *Belemnites aalensis* and *Bel. sulcatus*.—*Great oolite*. This is a thick deposit, composed chiefly of an oolitic limestone. It contains beds of dolomite, and sometimes rests upon beds of *fullers' earth*. Resting upon this oolite is the *Bradford clay;* next the *forest marble*, to which belongs the *lithographic limestones* of Bavaria. This forest marble, which includes also the *Stonesfield slate*, contains remains of *flying reptiles, terrestrial mammifera? saurian animals, insects, marine shells,* and *vegetables.* The upper member of this great oolite series is named *cornbrash,* which is a bluish and whitish compact limestone with marl.

(3.) *Oxford clay* and *Kelloway rock.* The Oxford clay is a bluish argillaceous marl, which becomes brown on exposure to the air. It contains subordinate beds of calcareous marl, and also the calcareous clayey nodules, named *septaria.* Underneath is the Kelloway rock, a particular kind of calcareous rock. The marls sometimes contain bones of the ichthyosaurus. The fossil shells are pretty numerous, but our limited space will not allow an enumeration of them.

(4.) *Coral rag* is a loosely aggregated calcareous rock, abounding in different species of madrepores; the rock is sometimes marly, and of a gray colour. Below the coral rag is a bed of ferruginous siliceous sand, containing a calcareous grit or sandstone, and siliceo-calcareous concretions. It is in this part that the fossil organic remains are most abundant and most perfectly preserved. Fossil *Cycadaceæ* occur; also, as in the *calcareous grit,* bones of saurian animals. Nearly all the *madrepores* belong to the genera *Astrea, Caryophyllea,* and *Meandrina. Echinites* of the genera *Cidaris* and *Clypeus* are met with. The fossil shells have not been thoroughly examined.

(5.) *Kimmeridge clay.* The lower beds of the preceding deposit alternate with a blue or yellowish gray marl, which is more or less slaty, and contains beds of a very bituminous slate, and even true lignite or brown coal, sometimes forming beds of considerable thickness. An ichthyosaurus different from that in the lias is found here; also remains of the plesiosaurus, and bones of whales, it is said, have been found in the Kimmeridge clay; also fine impressions of fishes. *Serpula,* also species of *cidaris* and *asterias,* occur in this formation. Many species of different genera of marine shells are enumerated as occurring in it, particularly *ammonites, belemnites,* &c. It would appear that the prevailing fossil shells in the whole oolite formation are *ammonites* and *belemnites.* The belemnites do not occur lower down in the series than the lias.

(6.) *Portland oolite.* This is a limestone which is frequently loosely aggregated, sometimes oolitic, forming the last deposit of secondary limestone with this structure, none of the superior or newer secondary limestones possessing it. It contains petrified monocotyledonous and dicotyledonous plants. Remains of large saurian animals, and also of fishes, are met with in it. *Ammonites, trigonia,* and *gryphites,* are abundant. The most characteristic shells are the *Ammonites triplicatus* and the *Pecten lamellosus.* A *cidaris* and *madrepore* have also been discovered in it.

*Ninth secondary formation. Wealden clay* and *Purbeck stone.* This remarkable formation abounds in fresh-water shells and land plants; but, in England at least, contains no marine species; hence it is an example of a fresh-water deposit between two marine deposits, viz. the oolite and chalk. It is probable, however, that future observations will prove that even in England it contains marine shells. There are two members of this formation, viz. the Weald clay, and Purbeck stone.

(1.) *Weald Clay.* This is a bluish or grayish coloured clay, containing subordinate beds of argillaceous limestone. The limestone abounds in shells belonging to the fresh-water genus *paludinæ;* also a great quantity of the crustaceous tribe named *cypris. Brown iron ore,* beds of *lignite,* and beds of sandstone much resembling some of the varieties of the coal formation, also occur in it. It contains impressions of ferns, but of different species from those in the coal formation.

(2.) *Purbeck stone* is a clayey limestone, which alternates with marls. It abounds in *paludinæ,* also contains beautiful impressions of fresh-water fishes, and of tortoises and crocodiles.

*Tenth secondary formation,* or *chalk formation.* This formation is well characterised, by its organic remains and flints. Five beds occur in this formation; viz. 1. *Lower green sand;* 2. *Gault clay;* 3. *Upper green sand;* 4. *Tuffaceous chalk;* 5. *Chalk.*

(1.) *Lower green sand.* This sand does not differ from the upper; but the fossil organic remains are less abundant. The shells are ammonites, terebratulites, trigonia, &c. In Great Britain the *trigonia alæformis* is considered as characteristic of this lower green sand.

(2.) *Gault.* The green sand is divided into two by a very thick bed of bluish gray clay, known in many of the districts where it occurs under the name of gault. It contains *ammonites* and other shells, particularly the *Inoceramus sulcatus.*

(3.) *Upper green sand.* The lower part of the tuffaceous chalk, containing a prodigious quantity of fossils and of iron pyrites, becomes more and more charged with green points, and we reach a mass composed of a green sand more or less marly, and often a green coloured calcareous sandstone. Fragments of silicified wood, and also parts of shells penetrated with silica; teeth of fishes, but parts of no other vertebrated animals, occur in it. The fossil shells are very numerous: species of the genera *cidaris* and *spatangus* are met with, and also corals of various kinds.

(4.) *Tuffaceous chalk,* which is generally composed of a cretaceous matter, clay and sand.

It is softer than chalk, and towards the lower part of the mass the clay predominates, and slaty clay marl is found. When the sand predominates, a loosely aggregate grayish sandstone is formed. No flints occur in this tuffaceous chalk, their place being taken by chert. Fossil vegetables, even lignite, are found in it. Fossils are most abundant in the lower part of this deposit. The chief are *belemnites*, *ammonites*, *nautilites*, *hamites*, *baculites*, *turrilites*, *echinites*, with *madrepores* and *encrinites*.

(5.) The *uppermost* is the *chalk* properly so called, of which there are two principal kinds, viz. the *upper* or soft or common chalk, which abounds in flints in beds, veins, and imbedded masses; and the lower or hard chalk, in which flint is more rarely met with. These chalks also contain iron pyrites and calcareous spar. The fossils are *vertebræ* and *teeth of fishes;* numerous *echinites* and *terebratulites* occur throughout the whole mass; and in the descending order, *ammonites* and *belemnites* first make their appearance in the lower part of the chalk.

#### SUBSECT. 2.—*Plutonian or Igneous Secondary Rocks.*

*Igneous rocks* appear, at different determinate periods, to have broken in among the Neptunian rocks of this class, and also to have forced up through them older rocks of various descriptions, forming mountains, mountain ranges, and groups of mountains. The igneous rocks are porphyry, and sometimes also granite and syenite.

### SECT. IX.—*Tertiary Rocks.*

#### SUBSECT. 1.—*Neptunian Tertiary Rocks.*

The rocks of this class were first pointed out by Werner; but it was not until the publication of the excellent work of Cuvier and Brongniart on the geology of Paris, that their importance was felt and acknowledged by geologists. In the regular succession they rest immediately upon the chalk or uppermost member of the secondary class. Although the rocks are looser in texture than those of the secondary class, yet among them beds occur equally compact with those of the secondary class. They abound in fossil remains of the animal and vegetable kingdoms; although many species are different from the present ones, many of the genera are the same. The following are the Neptunian rocks in the order of their occurrence, from below upwards: 1. Plastic clay. 2. Calcaire grossier, or London clay. 3. Gypsum with bones. 4. Superior marine sandstones and sands, sandstone of Fontainebleau. 5. Upper fresh-water formation.

(1.) *Plastic clay.* This clay is frequently divided into two beds by a bed of sand; the upper bed is more or less mixed with the sand, the lower bed is pure, kneads completely with water, and is infusible in the porcelain furnace. The upper bed abounds in fossil remains; the lower bed contains none. *Jet* and *brown coal*, which are fossilised remains of dicotyledonous and monocotyledonous plants occur, in it. Remains of the *palm tribe* are very frequent; but ferns have not been met with. *Insects* well preserved in *amber* are also met with. The fossil shells are partly fresh-water, partly marine, which are sometimes separate, sometimes mixed together.

(2.) *Calcaire grossier*, or *à cerites* of French authors, the *London clay* of English geologists. This deposit is sometimes separated from the plastic clay by a bed of sand, which occasionally contains pure and solid sandstone, but no petrifactions. Resting upon this sand is a bed of shelly limestone, abounding in green coloured grains of silicate of iron, and which sometimes passes into a kind of sand; it is in this limestone that the *nummulite* shells are so abundant, and which are mixed with corals and numerous shells in a high state of preservation. Immediately above this lies the great bed of true calcaire grossier. It is so compact, that in the Paris basin, where it abounds, it is used extensively as a building-stone. It is the common building-stone in Paris. It contains marine shells well preserved, and also remains of plants. In some districts it is divided into two beds by an interposed bed of *lignite* or *brown coal*, which is intermixed with fresh-water shells. It is interesting to notice, that here a limestone abounding in marine shells is separated into two beds by an interposed mass of coal, filled with fresh-water shells. Around London there is a great deposit of clay abounding in the same shells as occur in the calcaire grossier; thence, for this and other reasons, it is considered as the equivalent of the Paris calcaire grossier. The uppermost part of this formation consists of sand, hornstone, and sandstone, with alternating beds of limestone. It sometimes abounds in *cerites.*

(3.) *Gypsum with bones.* This deposit may be considered as consisting of three stages; a lower, a middle, and an upper. The *lower part*, or that which rests immediately upon the calcaire grossier, consists of gray and white limestone, more or less compact, penetrated in all directions by silica. This silica, when it finds its way into cavities in the limestone, lines them with chalcedony or with quartz crystals. It contains species of the fresh-water genera *Lymnea* and *Planorbis.* The *middle part* is composed of gypsum which alternates with layers of marl. It is in this gypsum that remains of the genera *Palæotherium*, *Anaplo-*

*therium*, of various carnivora, also different species of birds and of fresh-water fishes, likewise the *Tronex*, *Testudo*, and *Crocodilus*, are met with: and of the shells, the most characteristic is the *Cyclostoma mumia*. Here also in the marls occurs that curious kind of opal named *menilite ;* a mineral which in some degree may be considered as characterising this gypsum deposit. In this gypsum is situated the salt of Wielickza. The *upper part* consists of marls, with fresh-water shells of the lymnea and planorbis tribes, remains of fishes, and frequently remains of the palm tribe.

(4.) *Superior marine sands and sandstones.* The *lower part* of this deposit is a green-coloured argillaceous marl with *celestine*, upon which there are marls containing fossil *oysters*. The *middle part* consists of micaceous sands, and sandstones without shells. The *upper part* is sandstone with marine shells.

(5.) *Upper fresh-water formation.* The *lower part* of this deposit consists of sands, marls, and vesicular quartz or millstone (meulière), without shells. The millstone occurs rarely in beds, usually in angular masses in the marls and sands. The *upper part* consists of calcareous marls, limestones, and millstones, containing fresh-water shells. This formation contains of fossil plants, species of *Exagenites*, *Lycopodites*, *Poacites*, *Chara*, and *Nymphea*. It is further characterised by the numerous fossil fresh-water shells of the same genera as occur at present in the neighbourhood, but of different species. The genera are, *Lymnæa*, *Planorbis*, *Potamides*, *Cyclostoma*, *Helix*, and *Bulimus*. The *gyrogonites* of Lamarck, which are small round grooved bodies, are not animal remains, but seeds of the plant *chara*.

M. Desnoyers describes a marine deposit met with in the basin of the Loire, as resting upon the upper fresh-water formation. The deposit appears to be the same as the *crag* of English geologists, and has been lately met with also in Provence.

### Subsect. 2.—*Plutonian or Ignigenous Tertiary Rocks.*

The rough felspathose porphyries, known under the name *trachyte*, which occur in vast abundance in many countries, appear to be of the same age with the tertiary rocks. *Basalt*, a grayish-black compound of augite and felspar, in which the minerals are not distinguishable by the naked eye ; *greenstone* or *dolerite*, a compound, but of a green colour, in which the augite and felspar grains are distinguishable; *wacke*, which is a clayey greenstone ; *amygdaloid*, which is greenstone or wacke with the amygdaloidal structure; and *clinkstone* or *phonolite*, which is a slaty felspar, are found associated with tertiary rocks. Some classes of mountains, as Mont Blanc, and the Scandinavian ranges, are conjectured to have been upraised partly during and partly after the deposition of the tertiary rocks.

## Sect. X.—*Alluvial Rocks.*

Under this head we include the various *calcareous deposits*, peat, clays, loams, sands, gravels, and rolled masses or boulders, which, in the regular succession, rest upon the newest or uppermost rocks of the tertiary class. These deposits have been variously arranged according to their supposed relative antiquity: probably they may be arranged with sufficient distinctness, according to their situation, in the following manner:—1. *Littoral* or sea-coast *alluvium*, as downs. 2. *River alluvium*, that met with on the bottom and sides of rivers. 3. *Lake alluvium*, that on the sides, &c. of lakes. 4. *Spring alluvium*, that formed by springs, as *calc tuffa*, *calc sinter*, *travertine*, *siliceous sinter*, &c. 5. *Rain alluvium*, that deposited by and moved by rain-water. 6. *Plutonian alluvium*, that formed and distributed over tracts of country by the upraising of chains of mountains.

In this alluvium, remains of vegetables and animals are of frequent occurrence. The vegetables, as far as is known at present, are either foreign species or species identical with those of the country where their remains are found. In the older or Plutonian alluvia, neither remains of human industry nor bones of the human species have been found; but numerous bones and skeletons of land quadrupeds.

These quadrupeds are either of extinct species of living genera, as the elephant, rhinoceros, hippopotamus, tapir, bear, and lion; or of living species, as the beaver, rat, ox, deer, sheep, and dog; or species of extinct genera, as mastodon and megatherium.

## Sect. XI.—*Volcanic Rocks.*

These are rocky masses which owe their origin to volcanoes. They are divided into old and new, or ancient and modern.

*Ancient volcanic rocks.* Under this division we include those volcanic rocks connected with volcanoes, which have not been in a state of activity since the commencement of our history. These rocks very much resemble basalt, and have been sent from the interior of the earth in the form of streams or currents. In almost every country where they occur, we find *craters* from whence they have streamed. These dark-coloured basaltic-like rocks, are accompanied with puzzolana and scoriæ, very much resembling those of active volcanoes. Sometimes lighter coloured lavas, named *leucostine*, and which resemble trachyte, occur along with the darker varieties.

*Modern volcanic rocks.* These, as already enumerated and described at p. 213, 214., are lavas, scoriæ, ashes, sands, &c.

# BOOK III.

## GENERAL PRINCIPLES OF GEOGRAPHY UNDER ITS RELATION TO ORGANIZED AND LIVING BEINGS.

In considering the extensive range of subjects which this book embraces, we have arranged them as they successively rise above the scale of inanimate nature.

The first chapter treats of geography, in its relation to botany, or to the distribution of plants over the surface of the globe.

The second chapter considers it in its relation to zoology, or the distribution of animals, including man viewed simply as to his physical condition.

The third chapter views geography in reference to human society, to man in his political, moral, and social condition.

---

## CHAPTER I.

### GEOGRAPHY CONSIDERED IN RELATION TO THE DISTRIBUTION OF PLANTS.

In proportion as our knowledge increases relative to any of the sciences, we find a more intimate relation and connexion between them. Formerly geography was only studied as it regarded the surface of the earth itself, its figure, the constitution of the several regions and countries, their boundaries, &c.; and botany has had too many votaries who devoted their attention almost exclusively to determining the generic and specific names of plants, neglecting the more beautiful and philosophical parts of the science. Of late years, indeed, our systems of geography have, in some instances, contained a meagre catalogue of the vegetable productions of the different regions, but nothing that could give the least information with respect to the laws of their general distribution: and now that some of the most able naturalists and philosophers of our day have, by their labours, thrown new light upon this interesting subject, we should feel that our work would ill merit the character which we hope it may obtain with the public, were we to omit a notice of it. At the same time, the limits of our publication will permit us to give only a sketch of what indeed must be considered as still in its infancy; and those who have most devoted their attention to botanical geography will most readily join with Mirbel in declaring that "we are even yet far from having arrived at that period when it will be possible to write a good history of this subject. What we do know of climates and of vegetation, is little, in comparison with what we have yet to learn; and hence it would be rash in us to form an estimate of what we do not know by what we are already acquainted with. The surest way is to confine ourselves to collecting and arranging facts, leaving, to those who may follow us, the charge of discovering and developing the theory."

To exhibit the present state of botanical science, we shall endeavour to put together the more interesting facts, collected principally from the writings of our most authentic travellers and naturalists; and, devoting this memoir to vegetable geography in its more enlarged and general sense, shall afterwards, in the different countries, under the head of botany, point out some of the most striking and important productions of their respective regions. As the nature of the present work does not permit us to enter minutely into the subject in all its bearings, we shall give a popular view of it, as little encumbered as possible with technical terms.

That certain vegetables are confined to certain districts or limits, depending in a great measure, but by no means altogether, upon soil and climate, must be familiar to the most careless inquirer into the works of nature. In regard to climate, the two extremes are represented by the country within the tropics, and that which approaches the poles. In the one, nature exhibits herself in her most lovely and her most magnificent and exuberant form, and the earth is covered with vegetables which indicate a never-ending summer; whilst in the others a brief summer, a few days of freedom from frost and snow, call into existence a thinly scattered vegetation of small and stunted flowering plants, which scarcely rise above the mosses and lichens that surround them; and the intermediate zones will be found to be occupied by other races, gradually, however, increasing in difference as they approach to one or other of these extremities. The same gradation exists, we know, upon a lofty mountain, situated within the tropics. At its base may be seen those plants which are peculiar to the tropics; and the beauty, the grandeur and perpetual verdure will gradually diminish in the ascent, until a soil and climate be found on the higher summits similar in respect to climate and productions to those in the vicinity of the poles.

In regard to climate and vegetable productions, our globe has been aptly compared, in its two hemispheres, to two immense mountains, placed base to base, the circumference of which at the foot is constituted by the equator, and the two poles represent the summits, crowned with perpetual glaciers.

That almost every country possesses a vegetation peculiar to itself, is also well known; and this is particularly the case with countries whose natural boundaries are formed by mountains, seas, or deserts, even in the same or different degrees of latitude. Europe exhibits a widely different class of plants from that part of North America which lies immediately opposite to it. The botany of Southern Africa has little or no resemblance to that of the same parallels in South America, or to that of New Holland. In Great Britain, some plants are confined to the eastern and some to the western side of the island. In Scotland, the *Tutsane* and the *Isle of Man Cabbage* are never found but on the western side of the country, and the same is the case with the *pale Butterwort* (Pinguicula Lusitanica), both in England and Scotland. Nature has constituted the barrier, for by art they may be cultivated as well on one as the other side of the island.

Botanical geography is constituted by considering plants in relation to their *habitation*, region, or the country in which they grow, and in regard to their locality or particular *station*, and forming a collection of facts, deduced from these circumstances, from which general laws may be derived: nor is this a science destitute of advantages; such, we mean, as are immediately manifest; for there are few, in the present age, who will be disposed to deny that the study of the works of nature, like every thing that can exalt and refine the mind, is highly deserving of our attention. Vegetable geography is intimately connected with horticulture. Our gardens will be better stocked with vegetables and fruits, our forests with trees, our fields with corn, and our pastures with grasses, in proportion to our knowledge of the relation of plants with the exterior elements. Nay, Schouw has justly observed, that a good chart of the distribution of the vegetable forms over any given country will afford a far more correct idea of the productive strength of that country than many statistical tables. The systematic botanist may thence derive benefit; for by it he will be better able to determine whether certain kinds of plants are species or varieties; he will consider that a different local situation produces different effects upon them; that those growing in wet places are less hairy or downy than those growing in dry; that at great elevations plants are more dwarf in their stature, with fewer leaves, but with larger and more brilliant flowers than those found at lesser heights. The station, too, of certain plants, or groups of plants, frequently leads to a discovery of characters diverse from other individuals of other countries with which they had been associated. Thus the *Canadian Strawberry* and the *Canadian chickweed Wintergreen* (Trientalis), though long confounded with the European *Strawberry* and *Trientalis*, are found to be quite distinct. The regions, too, and the limits of those regions, of very important medicinal drugs, are determined by vegetable geography.

### Sect. I.—*Progress of Botanical Geography.*

This branch of science had been, however, for a long time, wholly neglected. Linnæus, indeed, with whom originated so many improvements in botany, besides what related to systematic arrangement, was the first writer who gave stations for plants, as he called them, or rather habitations, or frequently both combined, and this plan has been followed by every succeeding systematic botanist. Yet although these stations or habitations are frequently consulted in the geographical arrangement of plants, they are too vague and uncertain to be generally depended upon; and they must be employed with caution. De Saussure, who so assiduously studied vegetable physiology, was particularly attentive, on that account, to the elevation at which plants grow above the level of the sea; and appears to have been the first to ascertain *that* elevation barometrically. Mr. Young, the celebrated agriculturist, in his *Travels upon the Continent*, determined with considerable accuracy the northern boundaries of several of the most important cultivated plants, the *Olive*, the *Vine*, and the *Maize*; whilst Soulavie, in the south of France, has characterised the limits of them, and of the *Orange* and *Chestnut*. These, and other authors of less note, prepared the way, during the last century, for the more important labours of the present, when the study has begun to rank as a science. Stromeyer described, to a certain extent, the boundaries of the vegetable kingdom, in a work entitled "*A Specimen of the History of Vegetable Geography*," Göttingen, 1800. The work of Kielmann, entitled "*A Dissertation concerning Vegetation in the Alpine Regions*," Tubingen, 1804, was followed by that of Treviranus, named "*Biologie*," which seems to be the first wherein attention was paid to the distribution of plants according to their natural families; the latter author dividing the globe into regions or distinct Floras; and De Candolle, about the same time, partitioned France into regions in the same way, and wrote on the influence of height upon vegetation. To the celebrated Humboldt, however, we are indebted for the most valuable writings on vegetable geography which have first given it the true character of a science. His "*Essai sur la Géographie des Plantes*," in 1807, and his beautiful "*Tableaux de la Nature*," contained his first ideas on the subject; while his celebrated "*Prolegomena de distributione geographica Plantarum secundum cœli temperiem et altitudinem montium*," forming the introductory chapter to the botanical part of his travels; his invaluable "*Memoir on Isothermal Lines and the*

*Distribution of Heat over the Globe*, published in the Mémoires d'Arcueil, and translated into Brewster's and Jameson's Philosophical Journal, vol. iii.; together with his later work on the subject, "*New Enquiries into the Laws which are observed in the Distribution of Vegetable Forms*," likewise inserted in the Edin. Phil. Journal, vol. vi., may be considered as the most important dissertations on a comprehensive scale that have yet appeared. In the mean time, other eminent naturalists, by their well-directed labours, contributed materially to extend the science: Wahlenberg, for example, in his admirable *Flora Lapponica*, and in that of a portion of Switzerland, and of the Carpathian Alps; whilst Von Buch, in his *Travels in Norway*, detailed many curious facts respecting the distribution of vegetables in that climate, and also in his interesting *Voyage to the Canaries*, made in company with Professor Smith. Mr. R. Brown has published memoirs which rank among the most valuable that have appeared on this subject. We particularly allude to his "*Remarks, Geographical and Systematic, on the Botany of Terra Australis*, 1814," and "*Observations on the Herbarium collected by Professor Christ. Smith, in the vicinity of the Congo*, 1818." Dr. Schouw compiled, in 1824, an admirable history of the science, of which some portions have been translated into Brewster's and Jameson's Journals. This valuable work is accompanied by an Atlas of several maps of the world; each exhibiting the geographical extent of certain tribes or families of vegetables, indicated by different colours; so that we see, at one view, upon a plan of the world, the countries in which these plants are found, their boundaries, and their comparative abundance, indicated by the greater or less depth of colour employed. De Candolle, in the "*Nouveau Dictionnaire des Sciences Naturelles*," has given an admirable *résumé* of these writers, and has added much important original information. A somewhat similar plan is adopted by M. Brongniart in the "*Dictionnaire Classique d'Histoire Naturelle*." Mr. Allan Cunningham, both in Mr. Barron Field's "*Memoirs of New South Wales*," and in the second volume of "*Captain King's Survey of the Intertropical Coasts of Australia*," has furnished some excellent remarks upon the distribution of vegetables, especially of the less frequented parts of New Holland. The "*Mémoires du Muséum d'Histoire Naturelle*" contain some important papers on this subject, particularly that of Mirbel, "*Sur la Géographie des Conifères*," a tribe of plants valuable for its economical uses; and his "*Recherches sur la Distribution Géographique des Végétaux phanérogames dans l'ancien Monde, depuis l'Equateur jusqu'au Pôle Arctique*: and, lastly, we shall name a useful little manual, entitled a "*Lecture on the Geography of Plants*," by Mr. J. Barton.

### Sect. II.—*On the Influence of the Elements on Plants.*

In regarding the limits to which certain plants are circumscribed upon the surface of the globe, we shall see that it is with them as with the mighty ocean; they are equally subject to that fiat of the Almighty, "Thus far shalt thou go, and no farther." The Palms, the Tree-Ferns, the parasitical Orchideæ, are ever confined to the tropics; the Cruciferous and Umbelliferous plants almost exclusively to the temperate regions; while the Coniferous plants, and many of the Amentaceous tribes flourish in those of the north; and since these are all affected by physical agents, we must consider, before proceeding any farther, the influences which the *elements* or *exterior agents* exercise upon plants. These M. de Candolle considers to be *Heat, Light, Moisture, Soil, Atmosphere.*

#### Subsect. I.—*On the Influence of Heat.*

Heat is the most obvious and powerful agent in affecting the existence and growth of plants: and of this we have continual experience before our eyes. In winter all vegetation is at a stand, and we can only cultivate those plants which are in a continued state of vegetation, by artificial heat. Plants are nourished either by water alone, or by substances dissolved or suspended in the water. Hence vegetation is arrested when the temperature is below the freezing point; for the water, becoming solid, cannot enter the vegetable tissue. Again, as in the great deserts of many countries, the heat may be so great that the earth is dried up, and cannot part with its nutritive properties. These effects, however, it is but reasonable to suppose, are more remarkable upon the surface of the earth than at a considerable depth: hence it happens that trees which have long tap-roots resist both the extremes of temperature better than those whose roots are nearer to the surface; their fibres penetrate into a soil, whose temperature is greater in winter than that of the outer air, so that the fluids imbibed keep the interior of large trees, as has been ascertained by experiment, at a degree of heat pretty nearly the same as that indicated by a thermometer placed at the roots of such trees. Hence, the greater the thickness of the stem or branch, and the greater the number of layers interposed between the pith (the softest part being the moistest and the most susceptible of cold) and the exterior air, the better are they able to resist the severity of the cold. It is a well-known fact that a shrub or tree as it grows older becomes more hardened against frost. De Candolle relates that at Montpellier the *Pride of India* (Melia Azedarach) when young is destroyed by a moderate degree of cold; but that when it attains a more advanced age, it will endure, in the garden at Geneva, an intensity of atmosphere four times as severe as that which killed the young plant in the south of France.

Again, in proportion as the exterior layers are deprived of sap or watery fluid, and fortified by a deposit of carbon and resinous matter, the more powerfully they withstand the cold. Every gardener and cultivator is acquainted with the fact that in cold and wet summers when the sun and heat have been insufficient to produce good bark upon the new shoots of the fruit-trees, they are liable to be affected by a very moderate frost in the ensuing winter. *Succulent plants* and *Monocotyledonous plants*, in general, which have no distinct bark, are highly susceptible of cold; whilst the *Birch*, which is fenced around with numerous layers of old and dry bark, and the *Fir*, whose bark abounds with resin, endure an intense degree of it without injury. At Fort Enterprise, in North America, lat. 64° 30″, Dr. Richardson has ascertained that the *Banksian Pine* (Pinus Banksiana), the *white*, the *red*, and *black Spruce*, the *small-fruited Larch*, and other Amentaceous trees, bear a degree of cold equal to 44° below zero of Fahrenheit; and in Siberia, lat. 65° 28″, the *common Larch*, the *Siberian Stone Pine*, the *Alder*, *Birch*, and *Juniper*, &c. attain their greatest size, and are not affected by the extremest cold of that severe climate.

Powerful summer heats are capable of causing trees and shrubs to endure the most trying effects of cold in the ensuing winter, as we find in innumerable instances; and *vice versâ*. Hence, in Great Britain, so many vegetables, fruit-trees in particular, for want of a sufficiently powerful sun in summer, are affected by our comparatively moderate frosts in winter; whilst upon continents in the same degree of latitude the same trees arrive at the highest degree of perfection. Even in the climate of Paris the *Pistacia tree* and the *Oleander* will not bear the winter. Yet the winters there are mild in comparison with those which prevail in the environs of Peking, where the Oleander was found by Lord Macartney to remain abroad the whole year; and at Casbin in Persia, where Chardin assures us that the Pistacia nuts, produced in the open air, are larger than those of Syria. On the other hand, the heat of these two countries in summer is infinitely greater than that at Paris; the summer temperature of Peking especially nearly equals that of Cairo, and surpasses that of Algiers. For the same reason, too, the *Weeping Willow* becomes a large tree in England; while in Scotland, where the winters are at least as mild, but where the summer affords much less warmth, this beautiful tree can only be cultivated in highly favoured situations, and even there its vegetation is exceedingly languid: its young shoots, not ripened by the summer sun, are destroyed even by a slight frost.

Hence the influence of temperature upon the geography of plants is pointed out by M. de Candolle under *three* points of view:—1. The mean temperature of the year. 2. The extreme of temperature, whether in regard to cold or heat. 3. The distribution of temperature in the different months of the year.

The mean temperature, that point which it has for a long time been the great object to ascertain, is in reality what is of the least importance in regard to the geography of plants. In a general view, it may be useful to take it into consideration; but the mean temperature is often determined by circumstances so widely different, that the consequences and the analogies to be deduced from them relative to vegetables would be very erroneous.

By attending to the extreme points of temperature, results more limited, but far more exact, are to be obtained. Thus, every locality which, though at only short intervals, affords a degree of cold or heat of certain intensity, cannot but produce plants which are capable of supporting those extreme degrees. When, however, these widely different temperatures recur at very long intervals, man may cultivate in such a country a vegetable which cannot exist in a wild state; either because, when destroyed by the rigour of the season, he restores it by seeds or by plants derived from a more temperate country; or because he shelters it from the inclemency of the air; or, because he is satisfied with the product of the plant, although it should not bring its seeds to perfection. And thus it is that, in the south of Europe, the *Vine*, *Olive*, and *Orange* trees often vegetate exceedingly well for all the purposes for which they are required, though, if left to themselves, they could not propagate themselves, nor sustain the winter. Thus we see a wide difference in the geography of plants, between those in a state of nature, and those individuals whose growth is artificially encouraged by man.

This, indeed, is a subject closely connected with the *acclimatation of plants*, or the power which man is supposed to exert over them in inuring them by degrees to a climate not originally natural to them. This power is, however, denied by very able vegetable physiologists. Mirbel, in particular, declares that he has known many species indeed whose wants have been, to a certain degree, artificially supplied; but not one whose constitution has been changed. "If," he says, "from time to time, exotics mingle themselves with our indigenous tribes, propagate as they do, and even dispute the very possession of the soil with the native inhabitants; this, assuredly, is not the work of man, but it is the *climate* which dispenses this faculty of naturalization." Cultivators, however, maintain that seedlings from *Myrtles*, which had ripened their fruit in Devonshire in the open air, are better able to endure the cold of the climate than those seeds perfected by artificial heat, or that have come from the warmer parts of Europe. It is true, the power of so acclimating itself already exists in the vegetable; but it is man that calls it into action, for naturally the myrtle would never extend itself to these latitudes. Nay, something of the same kind M. Mirbel himself allows, where he says, "When we consider that the *Vine* is cultivated in the plains of Hindostan and Arabia, between the 13th and 15th parallels; that it is cultivated on the banks of the Rhine and Maine, in lat. 51°; in Thibet, at an elevation above the level of the sea of from 9,000 to nearly 11,000 feet, under the 32d degree of latitude; what astonishes and interests us the most is, not that the vine inhabits countries so remote from one another, or that it grows at so great an elevation above the sea, but that it possesses in so eminent a degree the *property of accommodating itself to different climates;* a property, indeed, much more restricted in a great number of vegetables, which extend from the equator to the tropics on both sides, without ever crossing them; for notwithstanding the greater distance between the 23d degree of south latitude and the 23d degree of north latitude, the climatic differences are much less from one tropic to the other than from the plains of Hindostan to the banks of the Maine."

The distribution of heat at different months of the year is what we shall find to be of the most importance in regard to vegetable geography. Some climates are eminently uniform; a certain mean temperature is produced by a mild winter and a moderate degree of warmth in summer. This is frequently the case on the sea-coasts, because the extremes of heat are continually modified by the sea; that vast reservoir of nearly equal temperature, which therefore imparts heat in winter and cold in summer, and enables even tropical plants to subsist in some situations of the temperate zone. Such are the western shores of Europe and America, and a great portion of the southern hemisphere. A similar mean temperature may indeed be produced by a combination of very severe winters and very hot summers, as in the great continents compared with islands, or the shores of those continents; or the eastern side of continents as compared with the western; or the northern with the southern hemisphere; but these two climates, as may be expected, will produce a very different vegetation.

Annual plants, which require heat during the summer to ripen their seeds, and which pass the winter, so to say, in torpidity, in the state of grain, indifferent to the intensity of cold,* abound most in those regions where the extremes are the greatest; whilst the *perennial plants*, which can better dispense with the maturing of their seeds, and which are injured by the severities of winter, affect the temperate climates. Of these, again, those kinds which have deciduous leaves accommodate themselves best to unequal temperatures; whilst the individuals on which the foliage remains, or *evergreens*, give the preference to districts where the temperature is more constantly equal.

Mirbel reckons that there are about 150 or 160 natural groups or families of plants in the Old World, types of all which exist in the tropical parts of it. Beyond these limits, a great number become gradually extinct. In the 48th degree of latitude, scarcely one half of that number appear; in the 65th, not 40; and but 17 in the vicinity of the polar regions. He further estimates, that within the tropics the proportion of woody species, trees and shrubs, equals, if it does not exceed, that of herbaceous, annual, biennial, and perennial plants. The relative number of the woody species to the herbaceous, annual, biennial, and perennial, decreases from the equator to the poles; but, as an equivalent, the proportion of perennial to annual or biennial plants goes on increasing. Near the extreme limits of vegetation these are, at least, as twenty to one.

We must, however, by no means conclude that the same elevation in corresponding degrees of latitude is necessarily suited to the vegetation of the same plants. A number of circumstances may exist to modify the degree of heat at the same elevation. In Switzerland, for example, the elevation of the valley of Untersee is the same as that of Gestein; yet the thermometer, in 1822–3, fell only to 8° below zero in the former spot; whereas at Gestein it fell to 10½°, and at Berne to 16°. The depth of the valleys influences vegetation; the deeper they are, the more intense is the cold on the summits of the surrounding mountains. Thus, the pine does not thrive on the Bragel, at a height of 5100 feet; whereas it succeeds perfectly, at the same elevation, on the Rhetian Alps, the valleys of the Linth, the Muotta, and Kloen being deeper than those of the latter districts. In like manner, in the valley of the Davos, agricultural produce is certain in places much more elevated than the Bernese valleys, because the latter are deeper. The warm winds from Italy have a perceptible power over the vegetation of the contiguous parts of Switzerland; but the degrees of that influence depend upon circumstances. In the valley of the Inn, barley and flax are cultivated with success at an elevation of more than 5400 feet; whereas at Laret, in the valley of Davos, though the height is only 4900 feet, *no* grain will thrive. Yet, these valleys are alike in most respects, and are surrounded by mountains of similar altitudes; they are both sheltered from the north-east wind; their soil is of the same nature;

* Seeds being, in general, furnished with few organs which abound in moisture, are in a degree insensible to the extremes of heat and cold; whence it arises that, in conveying them from one country to another, they pass through a variety of climate uninjured.

out in the valley of the Inn, the warm winds from Italy are intercepted only by a single chain of mountains, whereas two chains lie between Italy and the valley of Davos: and, besides, the latter being of smaller extent than the former, it admits of the reception of less solar heat. In the Oberland of Berne, an increase in height of 2000 feet diminishes the crop one third.*

Subsect. 2.—*On the Influence of Light.*

The influence of the solar light upon vegetation De Candolle considers to be as important as that of temperature; and although it acts less powerfully upon the geographical distribution of plants, it nevertheless merits a particular notice.

Light is that agent which operates in producing the greatest number of phenomena in vegetable life. It determines, in a great measure, the absorption; for plants imbibe less humidity during the night and in darkness. It completely influences the watery exhalations of the green parts of plants; for these parts do not exhale during the night or in obscurity, whilst these exhalations are very considerable during the day, and especially under the direct influence of the rays of the sun. The light affects, in most cases, the decomposition of the carbonic acid; and consequently the deposition of carbon in vegetables, their substance and their growth, the intensity of their sensible properties, and the direction of many organs. It is the principal, and perhaps the only, cause of those singular movements known by the name of the *sleep of plants;* and, lastly, during the absence of light the green parts absorb a certain quantity of oxygen gas. Although these different causes affect all vegetables, yet they are not affected in the same degree.

Light is more equally distributed than heat upon the surface of the globe; but its mode of diffusion induces some very important consequences. In the countries situated under the equator, an intense light, since it acts more perpendicularly, influences vegetables nearly equally, during twelve hours each day, throughout the whole year. In proportion as we recede from the equator and approach the poles, the intensity of the more oblique rays gradually diminishes; but in regard to the distribution of these rays, the light is completely wanting during the winter, when the absence of vegetation indeed renders it nearly useless to plants; and it is continued during almost the whole period of vegetation, in such a manner that its lengthened influence compensates wholly or in part for its want of intensity. Thus we see that, independently of what concerns the temperature, plants which lose their leaves can better exist in northern countries, and that those whose vegetation is continued have need of the southern regions. And another beautiful and just remark is made by De Candolle, in reference to the distribution of light; namely, that those plants whose foliage and flowers maintain habitually and constantly the same position, can live in northern climates, where the light is almost continued in summer; whilst it is in the regions of the south that we find, as might naturally be expected, those species which are remarkable for the alternate closing and expanding, or sleeping and waking, of their flowers, a motion which has an intimate connexion with the alternation of days and nights. Thus we see why it is found so difficult in our country to cultivate many of the tropical vegetables, or, at any rate, to bring them to perfection. M. de Humboldt has proved that it is less owing to the absence of heat than to the want of sufficient solar light that the *Vine* does not ripen its fruit beneath the foggy skies of Normandy; and M. Mirbel has satisfied himself that the uninterrupted action of the sun's rays, during a great number of days, is the cause of the astonishingly rapid developement of alpine plants in high northern regions.† Dr. Richardson, too, states that the sugar-boilers in the Canadian forests observe that the flow of sap in the *Sugar Maple* (Negundo fraxinifolium) is not so immediately influenced by a high mean temperature as by the power of the direct rays of the sun. The greatest quantity of sap is collected when a smart frost during night is succeeded by a warm sunshiny day. Again, Humboldt assures us, that in all places where the mean temperature is below 62° 6′, the revival of nature takes place in spring in that month whose mean temperature reaches 42° 8′, or 46° 4′. At Cumberland House, Dr. Richardson found vernation to begin in May,

* We may here mention a curious fact of vegetation resting upon a basis of ice. The glacier of Roccosecco, which forms one of the branches of the Berneria, has on its summit a valley filled with ice; and on this the avalanches have brought down masses of earth. This earth produces a number of alpine plants, that afford abundant and nourishing food to the flocks of the inhabitants of Samaden. This singular pasture has been used ever since the year 1536.

† "Vegetables," says M. Mirbel, in his *Elémens de Physiologie Végétale,* "when secluded from the light, send out long, thin, and whitish shoots; their substance becomes lax, and without firmness; in fact, they are bleached. The operation of the luminous beams on these organised bodies consists chiefly in separating the constituent parts of water and carbonic acid, which they contain, and in disengaging the oxygen of the latter. The carbonic acid, with the hydrogen and oxygen of the water, produce those gums, resins, and oils, which flow in the vessels and which fill the cells. These juices nourish the membranes, and bring them into the ligneous state; a result which becomes more marked as the light is strongest and its action most protracted. Darkness and light produce, therefore, diametrically opposite effects on vegetation. Darkness, by keeping up the softness of the vegetable parts, favours their increase in length; light, by ministering to their nourishment, consolidates them, and arrests their growth. Hence it follows that a fine state of vegetation, such as unites in just proportions size and strength, must depend, in a measure, on the nicely balanced alternation of day and night. Now, the hyperborean plants spring up at a period when the sun is constantly above the horizon, and the light which incessantly acts upon them confirms and perfects them before they have time to attain a considerable degree of length. Their vegetation is active, but soon over; they are robust, but small."

when the mean temperature was only 49°, nearly 3° below that which Baron Humboldt considered necessary for the evolution of deciduous leaves; but he adds, "*the influence of the direct rays of the sun was at this time very great*, and the high temperature of the last decade of the month compensated for the first." We can imitate the native climes of many of the delicate exotics, as far as regards temperature; and in summer, when the days are long, we see them flourish almost as if they were in their natural situations; but in winter they languish, and often die, especially the more tender species, such as the ***Hedysarum gyrans***, and the *humble plant* (Mimosa pudica). It is evident that they want that distribution of light which is most congenial to them.

Plants, then, are arranged in their different localities, according to the certain quantity of light which they may require. All those with very watery leaves, which evaporate much, which are of a succulent nature, which, having few pores or organs of evaporation, need a stimulus to determine their action, all which have a tissue abounding in carbon, or which contain very resinous or oily juices, or which offer a great extent of green surface, require much light, and are generally found in exposed places; the rest, according as they are more or less distinguished by these properties, exist either under the slight shadow of bushes, or beneath the more powerful shelter of hedges and walls, or of forests; or, as is the case with many ***Fungi***, in caves and darkness. These last are, indeed, destitute of any green colour; but ***Mosses***, ***Ferns***, and even some evergreens, such as the ***Ivy***, flourish best beneath the shade of dense forests, if the trees of those forests have deciduous leaves; and in situations where plants that vegetate only during the summer could scarcely live.

The subject, however, of the action of light upon vegetation, has not yet received the attention which it deserves. Many more observations and experiments are required before we can employ it with certainty in connexion with botanical geography.

### SUBSECT. 3.—*On the Influence of Moisture.*

Water being the vehicle by means of which nourishment is conveyed into the plant, and, indeed, itself yielding a large proportion or even the whole of the nutriment of many vegetables, it follows that this element is not only of the highest importance in vegetable economy, but one of the causes which affects most powerfully the geographical distribution of plants upon the surface of the globe.

Those vegetables, in particular, necessarily absorb a great quantity of water, which have a large and spongy cellular tissue; those which possess broadly expanded soft leaves, furnished with a great number of cortical pores; those having few or no hairs on their surface; those whose growth is very rapid, which deposit but little oily or resinous matter; those of which the texture is not subject to be changed or corrupted by humidity; those, in fine, whose roots are very numerous, generally need to absorb much moisture, and cannot live but in places where they find naturally a large proportion of it. On the other hand, those plants which are of a firm and compact cellular tissue, which have small or rigid leaves, furnished with very few pores, which are abundantly clothed with hairs, of which the growth is slow, and which deposit, during the progress of their vegetation, much oily or resinous matter; those whose cellular tissue is liable to be changed and decayed by too much moisture, and of which the roots are not numerous, require little water, and prefer, for their natural situation, dry places. Great differences, however, are produced, according to the nature of the water that is absorbed; the less it is charged with the nutritive principle, the more necessary is it that the vegetable shall absorb, in a given time, enough to suffice for its support. Again, the more the water abounds with substances which alter its fluidity or transparency, and which, inasmuch as they are solid particles, tend to obstruct the orifices of the pores, or to impede absorption by their viscosity, the less do such vegetables imbibe in a given time.

The very nature even of those substances dissolved or suspended in the water has a great influence upon the topographical distribution or the locality of plants. The matters so dissolved are, 1. Carbonic acid. 2. Atmospheric air. 3. Animal and vegetable substances. 4 Alkaline principles or earths. Those plants whose cellular tissue is found to contain much carbon, such as trees producing hard wood, avoid, more than others, the vicinity of waters which are extremely pure, and which contain but little carbonic acid gas. Plants which exhibit much azote in their chemical composition, such as the ***Cruciferous Plants*** and the ***Fungi***, seek those spots where there is much animal matter in solution. Those, again, which present, when chemically analyzed, a considerable quantity of certain earthy substances, such as silica* in the ***Monocotyledonous Plants***, gypsum in the ***Leguminosæ***, &c. will require it in a greater or less proportion in the soil where they grow; and if it does not exis there naturally, the agriculturist must supply it artificially; and those species which yield,

* This silica, we know, abounds in the grasses, as well as in other monocotyledonous plants; and M. de Candolle observes, that it is in consequence of its existence in the grasses, &c. and of the comparative indissolubility which is the result, that it is preferred by almost all nations of the world for a covering to their houses. The people of the North thus employ straw for that purpose, on the same principle that those of the tropics use the leaves of the palms.

when burned, a more abundant portion of alkaline substances than usual, can only flourish or even live where these matters abound. The species which have need of carbonate of soda will only grow successfully near the sea or saline lakes or springs. Thus the different property of the substances dissolved in the water is evidently one of the many causes which determine the stations of the vegetable species.

Subsect. 4.—*On the Influence of the Soil.*

The influence of soil M. de Candolle considers as perhaps more complicated than that of the preceding agents. He reduces it to the following heads:—

(1.) The soil serves as a means of support to vegetables, and consequently its *consistence* or tenacity ought to possess, in this point of view, a peculiar fitness for sustaining, in a greater or less degree, plants exhibiting very various forms. Thus, soils composed of blowing sand can only serve as a support to vegetables which are of very humble stature and prostrate growth, so that the winds may not overturn them; or to trees, furnished with very deep and branching roots, which may attach them into this moveable matrix. The contrary holds good in regard to very compact soils. Small-rooted plants may thus be firmly enough fixed, and they may subsist; but the very large roots are incapable of penetrating into soils that are very tenacious. The two extremes of these soils present an equally sterile vegetation. Sands which are not sufficiently stationary (as those very remarkable ones on the northern shores of the Moray Frith), water which is subject to very rapid currents, clay of an extremely compact nature, or rocks of great hardness, are equally unfriendly to the growth of plants.

(2.) The chemical nature of the earths or stones of which the soil is composed, affects the choice of vegetables, as regards their flourishing in such situations. But this subject, simple as it appears at first sight, is in reality very complicated. For the different earths act upon vegetation by physical circumstances; as, for example, according as they absorb the surrounding water with more or less facility, retain it with more or less force, or part with it more or less easily. Now, the celebrated Kirwan ascertained by a comparative analysis of earths which were reckoned excellent for the growth of wheat in various countries, that they contain more silica if the climate is more subject to rain, more alumine if the contrary be the case; in short, that the soil, to be good for any given vegetable, ought to have the power of absorbing more moisture in a dry climate, less in an humid atmosphere: whence it is plain that in different localities the same species of vegetable may be found in different soils.

(3.) Every kind of rock has a certain degree of tenacity, and a certain disposition to decompose or become pulverized: whence results the greater or less facility of particular soils to be formed either of sand or gravel, and to be composed of fragments of a nearly determined form and size. Certain vegetables, from causes which we shall presently indicate, will prefer such or such of this sand or gravel; but the peculiar nature of the soil does not act here immediately; thus, when we find calcareous rocks which decompose like argillaceous schist, the same species of vegetation is observed. These two considerations are particularly applicable to lichens.

(4.) Rocks, according to their colour or their nature, are more susceptible of being heated by the direct rays of the sun; and consequently they may, in some degree, modify the temperature of a given place; and influence also, though slightly, the choice of plants capable of succeeding upon them.

But, independently of all these physical causes, it may be asked, whether the *chemical nature of rocks* has any effect upon vegetables? It is generally considered to be so; but it must be allowed that this action has been frequently very much exaggerated. Bory de St. Vincent, indeed, has assured us that calamine, or native carbonate of zinc, in the vicinity of Aix-la-Chapelle, is always indicated, to a certainty, by particular plants; and the fact is confirmed by a little work, since published, called A Flora of the Environs of Spa. The *yellow heartsease*, a small variety of the *common eyebright* (Euphrasia officinalis), the *white Campion* (Silene inflata), a *Sandwort* (Arenaria), a shrubby *Lichen*, a species of *Bromus* (Brome-grass), constitute this poor but constant vegetation. These, however, no doubt, grow in greater abundance and perfection in other soils: the wonder is that they do not altogether perish here; for even the gallinaceous birds, which eat gravel to triturate their food, die from swallowing fragments of calamine. It must be remarked, in reality, that plants do not often live upon pure rock, but among the decomposed matter of that rock; that the rocks, even though very circumscribed, often present very different natures; that vegetable mould is not only formed by the rocks which immediately surround it, but also by the admixture of earthy substances carried by the waters, and transported by the winds, or by the remains of animals and vegetables which have before existed there. Hence it will be understood how the vegetable earths differ much less in themselves, than the rocks which produce them or serve to support them; and that the greater number of plants yield, in most situations, the alimentary earths which are necessary for them. Indeed, after various botanical journeys made through France, M. de Candolle has found nearly the same plants vegetating spontaneously in almost all the different rocky substances. It has been said that the *Box* (Buxus sempervirens) grows only in calcareous soils, and it certainly prefers them: but it is found abundantly in the argillaceous calcareous schistose rocks of the Pyrenees; and it is even seen among the granite of Britany and upon the volcanic parts of Auvergne. The *Chestnut* has been said to avoid a calcareous country; but there are beautiful chestnuts on both sides of the Lake of Geneva, at the foot of the calcareous mountains of Jura and Chablais.

Pure magnesia, M. Carradori has found, by chemical experiment, acts as a poison on most plants: yet M. Dunal, in visiting a portion of the environs of Lunel, where the soil presents a great quantity of almost pure magnesia, found there the same plants as in the surrounding calcareous soil, and the roots flourishing in the clefts of this magnesian rock. Thus we must be careful not to attach too much importance to the nature of the earth, which is frequently acted upon by causes purely physical.

### SUBSECT. 5.—*Atmospheric Influence.*

The atmosphere, taken in its pure state, we know to be composed, at all times, of the same proportions of *azote* and *oxygen;* and in such cases we may suppose its action to be similar upon all vegetables. But the atmosphere also is of different degrees of transparency or density; it holds in solution other matters or substances, which mix with it in certain places, and render it more or less suitable to certain species of plants. In mines, for instance, the quantity of carbonic acid gas, or of hydrogen, may be so great as to preclude vegetation altogether: or to allow only of the growth of such individuals as are very strong and vigorous, or particularly absorbent of these substances. Then, too, the air charged with saline emanations from the sea injures some plants, and on the other hand encourages the developement of such as require carbonate of soda; as may be seen in the valleys of the south of Europe, where maritime plants affording soda may be cultivated at a considerable distance from the ocean, provided that they lie open towards the sea, and are exposed to the winds that blow from it.

We cultivate in our inland gardens, languidly and but for a year or two, many of the *maritime plants*, such as the *Lithospermum.* The *Nitraria Schoberi* is improved by employing salt where it is grown. Many of the *Statices* may be, however, easily cultivated, and one of them, the *common Thrift* (S. Armeria) even succeeds in crowded towns, whence its English name; yet its native country is either on the shores of the sea or in salt marshes, or upon the summits of the highest mountains.

The most general influence, however, exercised by the atmosphere, is its power of containing and parting with moisture, or its hygroscopic action. The atmosphere is habitually charged with moisture; sometimes in such a manner as to be invisible, and then only ascertainable by the hygrometer; at other times visible in a state of vapour or dew; and we find that vegetables in general succeed better in a climate where, at a given degree of temperature, the air is moderately moist, than in another where it is either too much saturated with moisture or too dry. This is a circumstance which cannot well be imitated in the cultivation of plants in the open air: but in our stoves, and especially by the aid of steam, the various degrees of humidity necessary to a vigorous vegetation may be produced to the greatest nicety.

The agitation or movement of the air by winds and other causes exercises some power over vegetation; but we are too little acquainted with this subject to be able to deduce any particular theory from it.

Of all the atmospheric influences, the most difficult to reduce to its proper value is that of *density;* or, what is the same thing, the influence of height or elevation above the level of the sea. This M. de Candolle has made the subject of a memoir in the volume of the Society of Arcueil, and we shall here give his general ideas upon it.

In proportion as we are elevated in the air, the temperature as well as the moisture continues to diminish; a circumstance which appears to depend upon this, that the rare air has more capacity for heat than dense air. The facts that go to prove that the diminution of the temperature upon high mountains is one of the causes which most affect the distribution of vegetables, are the following:—

(1.) The natural situation of each plant at a determined elevation above the level of the sea is so much the greater in proportion as the country is nearer the equator, and less in more temperate regions; that is to say, the farther we recede from the equator, the greater influence has the exposure upon the temperature.

(2.) In temperate climates, as France, for instance, those plants which are but little affected by temperature, and which grow in all its latitudes, are found also at all those elevations where the earth is not covered by eternal snows; from the level of the sea to the summits of the mountains. M. de Candolle has detected about 700 examples of this law; the *common Heath*, the *Juniper*, the *Birch*, &c. grown indifferently at the level of the sea, and at a height of 10,000 feet.

(3.) If plants which, according to their nature, avoid either too high or too low a degree of temperature, yet grow at different latitudes, we may observe that it is at heights where the effect of elevation may compensate that of latitude; thus the native plants of the northern plains will be seen to grow upon the mountains of the south.

(4.) Plants which are cultivated upon a large scale are guided by laws which entirely correspond with the preceding; those which are cultivated in various latitudes will grow indifferently at various heights; those which are only found at certain latitudes will extend no farther than to proportional elevations. The *potatoe*, which succeeds so well in our plains, is cultivated in Peru at an elevation of 10,000 feet above the level of the sea: the *olive*, which nowhere passes 44° north latitude, will not grow at a height exceeding 1250 feet.

(5.) The elevation above the level of the sea, when we compare the temperature of the seasons, establishes effects very analogous to those which result from the distance from the equator; so that there is the more analogy between the results on vegetation in the two cases. *In proportion as we rise in a direct line*, it follows, from the lessened density of the air, that the intenseness of the solar light continues to increase; this effect is represented in the line of distances from the equator, because the perpetuity of light during the continuance of vegetation is so much the greater in proportion as the latitude is more elevated.

(6.) In proportion to the greater height upon the mountains, so will the hygrometer be seen to indicate a less degree of humidity; the same general effect takes place as we recede from the equator towards the poles.

On mountains, covered with perpetual snow, where the plants are constantly moistened with water in a freezing state, those species, to which a warm temperature is unfriendly, will live at inferior heights to those which they brave in the same latitude, when they are not watered from those cold sources.

It would appear therefore, from all these considerations, that the situation or fixed locality of plants at certain heights depends mainly on the fall of the temperature attributable to that elevation. Now, the only purely theoretical point of view, says M. de Candolle, according to which we can comprehend how the rarefaction of the air bears in itself a direct influence upon vegetation, is this; that plants require to absorb a greater or less degree of oxygen gas in their green or their coloured parts. It cannot be doubted that there is a certain point of elevation where the atmosphere becomes too much rarefied to supply the wants of plants; but where this is the case the mountains are always clothed with snow. M. de Humboldt, too, inclines to think that the pressure of the air may act in encouraging and increasing the quantity of evaporation. But we must say that direct experiment is still wanting to confirm these opinions (and this is perhaps unattainable in the present state of science), in order that we may form a conclusive judgment on their value.

### Sect. III.—*Station and Habitation of Plants.*

The station and habitation of plants must next engage a portion of our attention. They are both important: the former implies their situation as regarding local circumstances, and the action of physical causes upon vegetables; the latter implies the geographical position. When we say that such a plant is found in marshes, on the sea-shore, in woods, or upon mountains, in England, in France, in North America; by the marshes, shore, woods, or mountains, we mean what we here term the *station;* and by England, France, or North America, the *habitation:* such is the sense, at least, in which we shall here use the terms; for in systematic botanical writings the meaning is by no means always thus restricted.

The seeds of plants, by varied and beautiful means, *are widely dispersed* by the liberal hand of nature; whilst some, however, fall upon barren ground, or a soil unfit for the nature of that particular vegetable, others take root in situations, both with regard to the earth and surrounding medium, which are in harmony with their growth, and produce, "some thirty, some sixty, and some an hundred-fold." There are, again, tribes which, under these circumstances, increase so prodigiously that they destroy vegetables of a less vigorous growth, and, to the exclusion of others, appropriate to themselves a great extent of the surface of the earth. Such are termed by Humboldt social plants. In this way, and notwithstanding the extreme poverty of the soil, the *Seaside Sedge* (Carex arenaria), the *upright Sea Lymegrass* (Elymus arenarius), and the *Sea-reed* or *Marram** (Arundo arenaria), occupy a prodigious surface of the sandy shores of Great Britain, almost to the exclusion of other vegetation; their long, creeping, and entangled roots serving to bind the sands together, and thus forming a barrier to the encroachments of the sea. Thus it is with the heaths in the same country, where the sterile moors are purple with the blossoms of the heath.

The flowers of the *Gentians* cover, as with a carpet of the most brilliant ultramarine blue, the sides of the alpine hills in Switzerland and the south of Europe. In England the fields are too often red with *Poppies*, and the marshes are whitened with the "snowy beard" of the *Cottongrass*, and the pastures with the blossoms of the *Cardamine pratensis*, so that

* The Celtic name of this plant is *Maraim*. A village upon the sea-coast of Norfolk is named Marham, from the great abundance in which the *Arundo arenaria* grows in its vicinity.

they appear at a distance as if covered with linen laid out for bleaching, whence arises the vulgar English name* of the latter plant. Some of these plants thus living in society are continually striving with their neighbours, till the strongest obtain the victory. Many low perennial and herbaceous vegetables are overpowered by a colony of taller shrubs; such as the *Whin* or *Furze* and the *Broom:* and these in their turns must occasionally give place to trees and shrubs of a larger and stronger growth. Mr. Brown has, however, noticed a curious fact in regard to the *Field Eryngo* (Eryngium campestre,) and the *Starthistle* (Centaurea Calcitrapa), which cover much cultivated ground upon the continent: viz. that these two engrossers are never mixed together indiscriminately, but that each forms groups of partial masses, placed at certain distances from their rivals.

On the other hand, there are plants, which, from the circumstance of their not increasing much by root, or bearing few seeds, or such seeds as from their light and volatile nature are much dispersed, and which are not particular in their choice of soil, do not form groups, but lie scattered (*Plantes éparses, egrenées*, or *rares*, of the French).

The former kind, or "social plants," are those which it will be most important for us to consider in relation to Botanical Geography.

The stations of plants being thus, as we have already mentioned, liable to the influence of physical agents, it becomes necessary to define them by terms which are calculated at once to point out the places and the circumstances in which they grow. This, however, is a task of no small difficulty; for, without swelling the list to an immeasurable length, it will be impossible to define the various local situations of plants. There are many situations which produce only one or two kinds: for example, the snow, in the highest arctic regions to which travellers have attained, has been found to nourish and to bring to the greatest perfection that highly curious vegetable, the *Red Snow* (Protococcus nivalis). The *truffle* (Tuber cibarium) is found entirely hid beneath the surface of the earth. Some *fungi* are detected upon the dead horns and hoofs of animals (no plant exists upon living bodies†), and upon dead chrysalides; and both *fungi* and *mosses* grow on the dung of animals. Paper nourishes the minute *Conferva dendroidea:* the glass of windows, and the glass table of the microscope, if laid by in a moist state for a certain length of time, produce the *Conferva fenestralis.* Wine-casks in damp cellars give birth to the *Racodium cellare:* and Dutrochet has detected living vegetables in Madeira wine and in Goulard water, (a solution of Saturn). These, however, and many others that might be noticed, may be numbered among the extraordinary stations, and they principally affect cryptogamic vegetables. In a popular view of the subject, though we cannot altogether omit the notice of such minute yet curious vegetable productions, we shall mainly direct our attention to the more conspicuous plants; and they may be thus divided. 1. *Maritime* or *saline plants.* These are terrestrial, but growing upon the borders of the ocean or near salt lakes; as the *Saltworts* (Salsolæ) and *Glassworts* (Salicorniæ), &c. Hence these plants abound in the interior of Africa and the Russian dominions, where there are saltpans, as well as on the shores. 2. *Marine Plants.* This tribe is indeed mostly cryptogamic, and comprises the *Algæ, Fuci, Ulvæ,* &c. The phænogamous, or perfect marine plants, are the *Sea-wracks* (Ruppia and Zostera), and a few others allied to them. 3. *Aquatic plants.* Growing in fresh water. Both stagnant pools and running streams in various situations, abound in plants. Some are entirely submerged, but in this case, with the rare exception of the little *Awlwort* (Subularia aquatica), the flowers rise to the surface of the water for the purpose of fructification.‡ 4. *Marsh or swamp plants.* 5. *Meadow and pasture plants.* 6. *Field plants.* This tribe often includes such as, introduced with the grain sown in those districts, are equally placed there by the hand of man. 7. *Rock plants*, which may include the natives of very stony spots, and such as grow upon walls. Walls, although artificial structures, are known to produce many plants in greater perfection than natural rock; yet we must not suppose that any vegetable is exclusively confined to this habitat. The *Holosteum umbellatum* and *Draba muralis* may be cited as examples of this tribe in England; and amongst mosses, the *Grimmia pulvinata, Tortula muralis*, &c. 8. *Sand Plants.* 9. *Plants of dry moors*, where *heaths* (Ericæ) abound. 10. *Plants which attach themselves to the vicinity of places inhabited by man.* Such are the *Dock, Nettle*, &c.; these species follow everywhere the human footsteps, even

* *Lady's Smock.* Such plants were in olden time dedicated to Our Lady the Virgin Mary.

† Schouw, indeed, has a tribe of plants which he calls "*Plantæ Epizoæ,*" *attached to living animals.* Thus, he says, *Fuci* and other *Algæ* are attached to whales, mussels, and barnacles. But in this case the plants manifestly adhere to a dead portion of the animal; like those vegetables which exist upon the outer and dead part of the bark of trees.

‡ Raymond certainly observed, in the Pyrenees, a species of *Crowfoot*, the *Water Crowfoot* (Ranunculus aquatilis,) producing its flower and fruit wholly under water; but upon a closer investigation of the phenomenon, he found that in these cases the calyx enclosed a globule of air, with which this important function of fertilization was performed. The curious aquatic, *Vallisneria spiralis*, has a still more wonderful contrivance for bringing the male and female flowers in contact. The plant is diœcious. The female flower is attached to the parent plant by means of a very long stalk, spirally twisted like a corkscrew, so that when it is in perfection, it rises to the surface by the untwisting of the stalk. The male flowers, upon a separate plant, are almost sessile, borne on a very short straight stem, which never could reach the surface without detaching themselves from the plant. This they do at the proper season; they float upon the top of the water along with the female flowers, scatter their pollen, and die. The female blossoms on the contrary, by the spiral twisting of their stalks, retire, and ripen their seeds under water.

to the huts and cabins of the highest mountains; encouraged, perhaps by the presence of animal substances, and the azote which in such substances is known to abound. 11. *Forest plants*, consisting of such trees as live in society. 12. *Plants of the hedges*, as are many climbing plants, the *Honeysuckle*, the *Traveller's joy*, the *Bryony*, &c. 13. *Subterranean plants.* Those that live in mines and caves, and which, though tolerably numerous and important, are yet mostly cryptogamous. One species, a fungus, yields a pale phosphoric light of considerable intensity. 14. *Alpine or mountain plants*, for it is very difficult to draw the limit, and indeed they will depend much upon latitude. A plant which grows upon a hill of inconsiderable elevation in Norway, Lapland, and Iceland, will of course inhabit the loftiest Alps of the south of Europe. Again, upon mountains that have no perpetual snow lying on them, alpine plants will be found much higher than on such as have continued streams of cold snow-water descending, which affect the state of the atmosphere at much lower regions. 15. *Parasitic plants*, such as the *Misseltoe*, the various species of *Loranthus*, &c., and the most wonderful of all vegetable productions, the *Rafflesia Arnoldii:* these, as their name implies, derive nourishment from a living portion of the vegetable to which they attach themselves. This is the case, too, with many Fungi which subsist upon the living foliage of plants; some exclusively on the upper, others as invariably on the lower side of these leaves; and, lastly, the name of 16. *Pseudo-parasites* has been given to a very extensive tribe, which subsists upon the decayed portions of the trunk or branches of the trees to which they are attached, as many of the *Lichens*, *Mosses*, &c.; or which are simply attached by the surface of their roots to tropical trees, obtaining no nourishment from them, but from the surrounding element. Among this number may be reckoned that numerous and singular family of the *Orchideæ*, called, from their nature and property, "*air plants.*" Greatly as this list might be swelled, we shall find that even here there is a gradation and an approximation of one tribe to another; but these are amply sufficient for our purpose.

We have been able to account in some measure for the stations of plants, affected as these are by local circumstances; but the study of the succeeding part, which refers to their *habitations*, considered in their most extensive scale, for instance, as belonging to certain regions or countries, we shall find to be much more difficult; and we must frequently be content to study and to admire the amazing variety of vegetable forms which the beneficent hand of nature has scattered over the different parts of our world, without being able to account for these important phenomena. In New Holland we find almost exclusively, all the species of *Banksia*, *Goodenia*, and *Epacris*, and the curious *Acaciæ* without leaves, but with petioles so much enlarged as to assume the shape and perform the functions of leaves. At the Cape of Good Hope, the *Fig Marigolds* (Mesembryanthema), the *Stapeliæ*, the numerous kinds of *Ixia*, *Gladiolus*, *Pelargonium*, and *Protea* abound. The *Aurantiaceæ*, the family of plants to which the *Orange* and *Lemon* belong, are of Asiatic origin; as the *Camellia* and *Thea* are of Chinese. Those curious plants, the *Mutisiæ*, the various species of *Fuchsia*, the *Cinchonæ* or *medicinal barks*, the *Cacti*, are all peculiar to South America. If a few of them are found in other countries, such circumstances are of very rare occurrence, and do not overturn the general laws for the exclusive existence of many plants in certain countries. There are in the temperate parts of Europe one species of *Ixia*, one of *Gladiolus*, and in the north of Africa and south of Europe a few kinds of *Fig Marigold.* Within the tropics the genera of plants throughout Asia, Africa, and America, are similar, but rarely are the species the same. This rule nearly holds good on the opposite continents in temperate climates. We find the *Oriental Plane* (Platanus orientalis) in the old world, and the *Occidental Plane* (P. occidentalis) in the new. Even in the two hemispheres, in similar parallels of latitude, the genera of plants have a great affinity: the southern extremity of the great continent of America has many in common with the north of Europe; and the plants of the latter region, transported thither, succeed extremely well.

To what extent plants migrate, unaided by man, it is not easy to say; but that such migration is going on, by various means and causes, cannot be questioned. Islands which lie near to continents, and which evidently appear at one period to have been joined with them, as England for example, although they may contain a vegetation similar to that of the neighbouring continental shores, have always a smaller number of species; and this can only be accounted for by the interruption which straits or seas occasion to the progress of the seeds. The *Field Eryngo* (Eryngium campestre), to which we have already alluded, the *Venus's looking-glass* (Campanula Speculum), and many other plants of France and Germany, seem to stop at the line formed by the sea; yet these, and many other vegetables of France, reach a limit upon the same continent more northern than any part of England.

The migration of plants may be reckoned to be facilitated by the following causes. 1. *Th sea and its currents*, but to a very limited extent; for if the seed be of such a nature tha the water penetrates its integuments and reaches the embryo, life is destroyed. Yet to such a distance are they carried by this medium, that upon the coasts of Britain, of Iceland, and Norway, the seeds of the West Indies are frequently cast, and it is said sometimes even in a fit state for vegetation. 2. *Rivers*, by the continual movement of their waters, convey many plants to a considerable distance from their original place of growth; and the banks of streams are generally adorned with a vegetation of a more varied kind than the districts remote from them. Thus, too, the different species of *Saxifrage* and other alpine plants are, in mountainous regions, brought down from the higher situations, and flourish in the valleys. 3. *Winds*, which waft the light, winged, and pappose seeds to immense distances, and by means of which they are widely dispersed. 4. *Animals*, which, in wandering from place to place, often carry on their coats those seeds which have hooked bristles, &c. 5. *Birds*, which, swallowing berries and other fruits, pass the seeds in a perfect state, and, it is even said, sometimes better fitted for germination than before. In this manner the seeds are often deposited in the places necessary for their growth, and to which they could not otherwise have reached; of which a familiar instance is found in the *Misseltoe*.

Man is however the most active agent in the dispersion of plants, and we must not overlook the important consequences of his influence. Sometimes, indeed, the causes are accidental, but more frequently intentional. The shipwreck of a vessel on the island of Guernsey, having some bulbs on board from the Cape of Good Hope, caused a plant to propagate in the sands upon the shores of that mild climate, to which has been since given the name of *Amaryllis Sarniensis* or *Guernsey Lily*, and a branch of trade of some importance is carried on in the sale of this very root. At Buenos Ayres, a species of *Artichoke* (Cynara Cardunculus) has increased so much by seeds imported from Europe, that Mr. Head, in his amusing "Sketches of a Journey across the Pampas," &c. tells us that "there are three regions of vegetation between Buenos Ayres and the base of the Cordilleras; a space of 900 miles: the first of which is covered, for 180 miles, with clover and *thistles*. This region," the author continues, "varies with the seasons of the year in a most extraordinary manner. In winter, the leaves of the thistles* are large and luxuriant, and the whole surface of the country has the rough appearance of a turnip field. The clover in this season is extremely rich and strong; and the sight of the wild cattle grazing in full liberty on such pasture is very beautiful. In spring the clover has vanished, the leaves of the thistles have extended along the ground, and the country still looks like a rough crop of turnips. In less than a month the change is most extraordinary; the whole region becomes a luxuriant wood of enormous thistles, which have suddenly shot up to a height of ten or eleven feet, and are all in full bloom. The road or path is hemmed in on both sides; the view is completely obstructed; not an animal is to be seen; and the stems of the thistles are so close to each other, and so strong, that, independent of the prickles with which they are armed, they form an impenetrable barrier. The sudden growth of these plants is quite astonishing; and though it would be an unusual misfortune in military history, yet it is really possible that an invading army, unacquainted with this country, might be imprisoned by these thistles before it had time to escape from them. The summer is not over before the scene undergoes another rapid change: the thistles suddenly lose their sap and verdure, their heads droop, the leaves shrink and fade, the stems become black and dead; and they remain rattling with the breeze, one against another, until the violence of the pampero or hurricane levels them with the ground, when they rapidly decompose and disappear, the clover rushes up, and the scene is again verdant."

The strong-scented Everlasting (Elichrysum fœtidum), a native of the Cape of Good Hope, has found a soil and climate equally suited to its growth on the shores of Brest, where it covers a great portion of the sands, to the exclusion of the aboriginal natives of the soil. *Wheat* is supposed to be indigenous to Barbary. The *potatoe*, first found in South America, is now cultivated all over the world. *Rice*, from Asia, is grown to an immense extent in America, &c.; these, and many other plants similarly circumstanced, which we could mention, together with those that adorn our gardens, often owe their wide diffusion to having escaped into uncultivated places, and become to a certain degree naturalised there.

But there are limits to migration, for some of which we can account, and for others we cannot. Even many garden plants, which, escaping by accident, or designedly placed in uncultivated spots so as to appear wild, have only for a time maintained a languid existence, and then have disappeared altogether. Thus we know that the beautiful *Gentianella* (Gentiana acaulis) cannot have a title to a place in the British Flora, nor can some others, which are mere outcasts from gardens. Some plants are wholly confined to particular spots, and can be found nowhere else. The *Tree-Pink* (Dianthus arboreus) grows still on the single rock in the island of Crete, where Prosper Alpinus first detected it; and the *Double Cocoa-nut* of the isle Praslin, one of the little group of islands called the Seychelles, notwithstanding the annual migration of its nuts for many thousands of miles, has never established itself in any other place. Nature has planted the *common Thrift* (Statice Armeria), the *Scurvy Grasses* (Cochlearia anglica and danica), and the *Rose-root* (Rhodiola rosea), in rocky and stony places, upon shores and on the tops of the highest mountains; yet these plants are never found in any intermediate places.

*The visible obstacles to the migration of plants* are—

(1.) *The sea*, which, though we have introduced it as a means of extending the habitations

* From specimens in our Herbarium, we have ascertained that this *thistle* is the *Cardoon* (Cynara Carduncului), introduced no doubt from Europe as an article of food, but now growing wild, useless, and pernicious.

of plants, is yet a far greater impediment, by the injury it does to the seeds, and the difficulty of their being conveyed to distant countries in a sufficiently short time to prevent the natural death of the seed. It must be observed, too, that the greater number of seeds have a specific gravity heavier than that of water when in a living state. The *Double Cocoa-nut*, when found floating, has always lost its vegetative property. The living nut is immensely heavy, and would inevitably sink.

(2.) *Dry and burning deserts.* These, in spite of their oases, which have been happily assimilated to the isles of the ocean, prove a powerful obstacle to the transport of seeds. Thus, those districts of Africa which are separated from one another by the scorching sands of Sahara exhibit a great dissimilarity in their vegetation. The plants of Morocco and the northern parts of Africa have little resemblance to the indigenous growth of Senegal; whilst the affinity of the vegetables brought by Caillaud from Upper Egypt to those collected by Palisot de Beauvois in Oware and Benin would in itself lead to the conclusion that no very great and continued deserts intervene between these far distant countries.

(3.) *Mountain ranges.* The barriers which these present would almost be insurmountable, were it not for the defiles which here and there occur, forming passages for men and animals, as well as for plants. Thus, the plants on the Italian side of the Alps are quite different from those on the Switzerland side; those of the Spanish Pyrenees from those of the French Pyrenees; and it was a subject of peculiar regret to the enterprising Drummond, when he reached the summits of the Rocky Mountains in North America, that his commission did not allow him to penetrate farther into the western side of that great continent, where he found, every step he took, a vegetation very different from what had been presented to him by the eastern side.

A knowledge of the Natural Orders of plants is in no department of botany so important as in treating of their geographical distribution. The system of Linnæus, or the Artificial Arrangement, does not, as we know, regard the habits and affinities of vegetables, but simply and beautifully points out to us, by certain characters, the means of arriving at the knowledge of any given species. The natural method, which owes so much to the labours of Jussieu, Decandolle and Brown, has a higher object in view, that of grouping plants together according to their natural affinities; and by such an arrangement we are often led to other and very important results. The primary divisions of the Natural Method are, first, ACOTYLEDONES, or plants which have no cotyledons to the seed: these are synonymous to the Cryptogamia, and include the *Mosses*, *Lichens*, *Sea-weeds*, *Fungi*, *Ferns*, &c.; secondly, MONOCOTYLEDONES; those whose seeds have one cotyledon, such as the *Grasses*, *Liliaceous Plants*, the *Rushes*, *Sedges*, the *Palms*, *&c.*; and, thirdly, DICOTYLEDONES, or the plants which have two or rarely more cotyledons to the seed, such as our *Shrubs* and *Trees*, and very many *Herbaceous Plants*. Each of these possesses external characters which, though not very easily defined in words, yet cannot fail to strike the observer who devotes his attention, even for a little while, to the subject; and we find that, in a great proportion of instances, they have not only a peculiar station, but that their geographical distribution is different.

The ACOTYLEDONOUS plants increase in number in proportion to the other great classes, as we recede from the equator to the poles; with the exception, however, of the *Ferns*. The latter abound more within the tropics than anywhere else: not, however, so much in open plains as in the sheltered, moist, and hilly countries; so that their maximum is in the mountainous part of the tropics. The island of Martinique afforded to the Abbé Plumier a rich and abundant harvest of ferns; and some isles of small extent are said to have one-third of their vegetation composed of this kind of plants.

Among the MONOCOTYLEDONOUS *Plants*, the *Palms* are exclusively confined to the tropics: the *Liliaceous plants* abound there and in the warm zones; the three families of *Grasses*, *Sedges* (Cyperaceæ), and *Rushes* (Junci), present some important differences in regard to a comparison with the phænogamous or flowering plants. The disparity between these latter and the *grasses* is not great in each of the zones; whilst the two other families, the *Cyperaceæ* and *Junci*, diminish near the equator and increase towards the north. Nevertheless, there are exceptions to this rule; for the *grasses* are very rare upon the coasts of Greenland. In what we have now said, we allude to the grasses, &c. in a wild state; having no reference to those regions where so many of the grass tribe, as the *Wheat*, *Barley*, *Oat*, *Maize*, *Rye*, *Rice*, &c., are found simply in a state of cultivation.

The DICOTYLEDONOUS *plants* are the most extensively distributed, and we must offer some further remarks upon them. The *Compound* or *Syngenesious plants* (Compositæ), as every one knows, form a very extensive natural family. They are diffused throughout the whole earth, but they are most abundant in the temperate and tropical climates. Fewer, however, of them are found in the warm regions of equinoctial America than in the sub-alpine and temperate districts of the same country. At the Congo and Sierra Leone in Africa, in the East Indies and New Holland, they exist in comparatively smaller numbers than in other regions situated in similar parallels, but which afford situations more congenial to their growth. Again, in the frozen zone, in Kamtschatka and Lapland, the relative proportion of plants of this family is one-half less than in the temperate climates.

The *Leguminous plants* (to which the Pea, the Bean, &c. belong, and such as bear papilionaceous flowers,) abound most in the equinoctial regions: they diminish gradually in each hemisphere in diverging from the equator, except indeed in certain countries where particular genera, by the multiplicity of their species, give a peculiar feature to the vegetation, as in Siberia and the vast provinces of Russia, where so many *Astragali* or Bitter-vetches are found.

Mr. Brown has judiciously separated the natural order of *Rubiaceæ* into two groups those with verticillate leaves and no stipules (the *Stellatæ* of Linnæus), to which belong the *Goosegrass* (Galium), *Madder* (Rubia), &c., and which are almost peculiar to the temperate zones; and the true *Rubiaceæ*, with opposite pairs of leaves, and two opposite stipules (which are in fact abortive leaves, and thus show their affinity with the *Stellatæ*), to which belong the real *medicinal barks* (or Cinchonæ), and some other nearly related plants possessing similar virtues: these latter are almost wholly confined to the equinoctial regions.

The two well-known and extensive natural families, the *Umbelliferous* and *Cruciferous plants*, are very rare in the tropics, if we except the mountains. They abound in the south of Europe, and especially about the valley or basin of the Mediterranean.

### SECT. IV.—*View of Botanical Regions.*

To divide the globe into botanical regions or districts will not be difficult, seeing that certain countries possess a peculiar vegetation, and that numerous impediments prevent emigration; seeing, too, that certain forms or tribes are incompatible with certain climates. M. De Candolle has constituted twenty of those regions; but although each is, to a certain degree, peculiar in its vegetable productions, it would require more space than we can devote to such a subject to characterise them. We must, therefore, content ourselves with giving a bare list. 1. *Hyperborean region.* This district includes the northern extremity of Asia, Europe, and America; and gradually merges into the following. 2. *European region;* comprising all Europe, except the part bordering upon the pole, and the southern districts approaching the Mediterranean. To the east it extends to the Altaic mountains. 3. *Siberian region*, comprehending the great plains of Siberia and Tartary. 4. *Mediterranean region;* comprising all the basin of this great inland sea; that is, Africa on this side the Sahara, and that part of Europe which is sheltered from the north by a more or less continued range of mountains. 5. *Oriental region;* thus called relatively to southern Europe, and containing the countries bordering upon the Black and Caspian Seas. 6. *India*, with its archipelago. 7. *China*, Cochinchina, and Japan. 8. *New Holland.* 9. *The Cape of Good Hope*, or southern extremity of Africa, beyond the tropics. 10. *Abyssinia*, Nubia, and the Mozambique Coast (imperfectly known). 11. *Equinoctial Africa;* viz. the neighbourhood of the Congo, the Senegal, and Niger. 12. *The Canary Isles.* 13. *The United States of North America.* 14. *The Western and Temperate Coasts of North America.* 15. *The West Indian Isles.* 16. *Mexico.* 17. *Tropical South America.* 18. *Chili.* 19. *Southern Brazil and Buenos Ayres.* 20. *The Straits of Magellan.*

Many of the productions of these regions will be considered somewhat at large in other parts of this work; and we shall conclude our introductory sketch of Botanical Geography by a notice of Professor Schouw's *Phyto-Geographics* or General Botanical Division of the Globe. This is illustrated by a map, which accompanies this memoir. Unlike M. De Candolle, Professor Schouw characterises the regions by the most remarkable feature of their vegetation, adopting commonly used geographical terms only where he conceives that a certain division of the earth ought to constitute a distinct region, but is not sufficiently acquainted with its productions to determine and define their forms. He makes the characteristic feature of his regions to depend on these facts: first, that at least one-half of the species should be peculiar to that region; secondly, that at least a quarter of the genera should belong exclusively to it, or at least have there a decided maximum, so that their species in other districts might merely be considered as their representatives; and, thirdly, that individual families of plants be either peculiar to the region, or else have their *maxima* there; nevertheless, when this last characteristic is wanting, while the difference in genera and species is very considerable, it may yet be admitted as a region.

Professor Schouw in this manner reckons twenty-two regions:—

(1.) *Region of Saxifrages and Mosses*, or the *Alpine Arctic Flora.*—This corresponds with De Candollé's first region, and comprehends all the countries within the polar circle; namely, Lapland, the north part of Russia and Siberia, Kamtschatka, Russian America, part of British America, Greenland, and Iceland; but Professor Schouw adds to it, with much propriety, part of the Scottish and Scandinavian mountains, as far as they fall within the alpine region, as also the mountains in the southern and central parts of Europe, inasmuch as they are related to the alpine regions. It is characterised by the abundance of *mosses* and *lichens*, the presence of the *Saxifrages, Gentians, Chickweed tribe* (Alsineæ), *Sedges*, and *Willows;* an entire absence of tropical families, a considerable decrease of the peculiar forms of the temperate zone; by the forests of *beech* or *fir*, or else the total want of trees; the scarcity of animals, and the prevalence of cæspitose plants, whose blossoms are large in proportion, and generally of a pale colour.

(2.) *Region of the Umbelliferous and Cruciferous plants.*—This tribe takes in the whole of Europe, except what belongs to the preceding division, from the Pyrenees, the mountains of the south of France, of Switzerland, and the north of Greece, the greater part of Siberia, and the country about Mount Caucasus. Schouw has characterized it by the *cruciferous* and *umbelliferous* plants, because they form a larger portion of the total number than any other kinds, and because it may thus be best separated from the vegetation of North America in the same parallel. It is not easily distinguished from the next region; but it may be said of it, that *Fungi* abound more, that the *Rosaceous* family and the *Crowfoots* (Ranunculaceæ), the *Amentaceous* and *Coniferous* tribes (Pines), form rather a large proportion; that it bears a resemblance to many of the polar forms, especially in the abundance of its *Sedges* (Cyperaceæ); that its meadows are most flourishing, and that almost all the trees are deciduous in winter. In the northern part of this region, the *Cichoraceæ* (a tribe of the Compositæ or syngenesious plants, including the *Endive, Lettuce, Dandelion,* &c.) much prevail; while in its southern division, or in northern Asia, the *Cynarocephalæ* (Artichoke and Thistle tribes), together with the *Butter-vetches* (Astragali), and *Saline plants* (Sea-worts and Glass-worts), seem to have their maximum.

(3.) *Region of the Labiate flowers* and *Caryophylleæ* (to which the *Pink*, the *Catchfly*, the *Sandworts*, &c. belong); or the *Mediterranean Flora.*—This is bounded on the north by the Pyrenees, the Alps of Switzerland and of the south of France, and the north of Greece, and thus includes the three peninsulas of southern Europe, namely, Spain, Italy, and Greece; on the east by Asia Minor and its islands; on the south it takes in Egypt and all the north of Africa as far as the deserts; and, lastly, it includes the Canary Islands, Madeira, and the Azores. It is marked especially by the two families above mentioned, which are much rarer both to the north and south of the countries just enumerated, and in the corresponding parallels in North America. The *Compositæ*, the *Stellatæ* (*Goosegrass, Madder*, &c.), and the rough-leaved plants (*Asperifoliæ*), are here in considerable numbers, as well as in the similar latitudes. A few tropical plants, or individuals allied to them, now appear; one or two *Palms*, the *Laurels*, the *Arum* tribe, the *Terebinthaceæ* (Pistacia, &c.), some tropical grasses and true *Cyperaceæ. Nightshades* (Solaneæ), *Leguminous* plants, the *Mallow* and *Nettle* tribes, and the *Spurges* (Euphorbiaceæ), increase; *Evergreens* are numerous; vegetation never entirely ceases, but verdant meadows are more rare. This region may be subdivided into provinces: of the *Cisti*, Spain and Portugal; of the *Sage* and *Scabious*, the south of France, Italy, and Sicily; of the shrubby *Labiatæ*, the Levant, Greece, Asia Minor, and the southern part of the Caucasian country; and of *Houseleeks* (Semperviva), the Canary Isles, probably also the Azores, Madeira, and the north-west coast of Africa. Many *Sempervivæ*, some succulent plants, *Spurges* and *Cacaliæ*, characterise especially this province.

(4.) *The Japanese region.*—The eastern temperate part of the old continent, namely, Japan, the north of China, and Chinese Tartary, probably forms a peculiar region; but we are too little acquainted with the botany of these countries to admit it with certainty, and still less are we able to define correctly the characteristics of its Flora. Of the 358 genera found in Japan, 270 occur in Europe and the north of Africa, and about the same number in North America; so that its Flora seems to occupy a middle place between those of the old and new worlds. Its vegetation, indeed, approaches more to the tropical than to the European; for we meet with the *Cycas* family, the *Scitamineæ* (to which belong the *Ginger*, *Cardamom*, &c.), the *Bananas*, the *Palms*, the *Anonæ* or *Custard-apples*, and the *Sapindaceæ;* so that there is a considerable affinity, as might be expected from its situation, to the flora of India. The families of the *Buckthorns* (Rhamni) and *Honeysuckles* are found in a relatively considerable number, and they exhibit some peculiar genera; thus, perhaps, this region might be correctly termed that of the *Rhamni* and the *Caprifoliaceæ.*

(5.) *Region of the Asters and Solidagos* (Michaelmas-daisies and golden-rods.)—The eastern part of North America, with the exception of such as belongs to the first or arctic district, comprehends without doubt two regions; for amongst 417 genera in Walter's Flora of Carolina, 117 are wanting in Barton's Flora of Philadelphia. The northern divisions of the United States have, indeed, but few genera which do not occur also in the southern; but this only shows that a similar relation exists here to what takes place between the north and south of Europe. The southern region will include Florida, Georgia, Alabama, Mississippi, Louisiana, and Carolina; the northern contains the other states of North America. What characterises this region is (besides the number of species of the genera *Aster* and *Solidago*), the great variety of *Oaks* and *Firs;* the very few *Cruciferæ* and *Umbelliferæ, Cichoraceæ* and *Cynarocephalæ;* the total absence of the genus *Erica*, and the presence of more numerous species of the allied family of *Vaccinium* (Whortleberries) than are to be met with in Europe.

(6.) *Region of Magnoliæ.*—This, which comprises the southern parts of North America, is separated from the preceding region by the number of tropical forms which here appear, and which show themselves more frequently than on the similar parallels of the old continent (such, for instance, as the *Scitamineæ, Cycadeæ, Anonaceæ, Sapindaceæ, Melastomea, Cacti*, &c.) From the old world, too, in corresponding latitudes, it is still further distinguished by a smaller proportion of *Labiatæ* and *Caryophylleæ;* and by having more trees of broad-shining foliage and splendid blossoms, (the *Magnolias*, the *Tulip-tree*, the *Horse-chestnut*, &c.) and with pinnated leaves (the *Gleditschiæ, Robiniæ, Acaciæ*, &c.)

(7.) *Region of the Cacti, Peppers*, and *Melastomas;* a very extensive region, including the lower districts of Mexico, Guatemala, the West Indies, New Grenada, Venezuela, Guiana, and Peru, perhaps also, a part of Brazil; in short, all intertropical America. The three families here mentioned appear peculiarly to characterise these countries; for the first belongs exclusively to America, and of the other two there exist comparatively few species out of these districts. *Palms*, the *Rubiaceæ*, the *Solaneæ*, (in which are classed the *Nightshades* and *Potatoe*), the *rough-leaved plants* (Boragineæ), the *Passion-flowers* and *Compositæ*, are here very common. It may admit of several provinces, as that of the *Ferns* and *Orchideæ* (in the West India islands); of the *Palms* (the continent of South America.) Brazil ought certainly to constitute a peculiar province, if indeed it be not a distinct region; and the works of Spix and Martius, St. Hilaire, the Prince de Neuwied, &c., will soon enable us to characterise its vegetable forms. The *Melastomæ* and *Palms* appear to belong to the more numerous inmates of this region.

(8.) *Region of the Cinchonæ* (or Medicinal Barks.)—It appears from Humboldt's works that the middle districts (such at least in respect to their altitude) of South America should form a distinct region from that last mentioned, as they differ considerably from the low lands; and the name now proposed seems to be characteristic of their vegetation, at least of Peru and New Grenada, though certainly not of Mexico, where the species of *Cinchona* are wanting.

(9.) *Region of Escalloniæ, Vaccinia* (Whortleberries), and *Winteræ* (Winter's Barks). —These, according to Humboldt, occupy the highest parts of South America. Besides the plants mentioned, there belong to this region many species of *Lobelia, Gentian, Slipperwort* (*Calceolaria*), *Sage*, several European genera of *Grasses, Brome, Festuca* and *Poa*, the *Cichoraceæ*, as *Hypochæris* and *Apargia;* as well as the more strictly speaking alpine plants (*Saxifrages, Whitlow-grasses, Sandworts*, and *Sedges*.) Perhaps also those parts of the high lands where the species of *Oak* and *Fir* flourish belong to the same region, though in all probability they constitute a peculiar province.

(10.) *Chilian region.*—It appears that Chili should form a distinct region; for amongst the genera which appear there, not one half are found in the low districts of South America. Its character, perhaps, most resembles that of the mountainous country in its *Slipperworts, Escalloniæ, Weinmanniæ, Bæa, Bellflowers*, and *Buddleæ;* but yet the difference is scarcely sufficient to constitute it a province. The Flora of this country appears to be essentially distinct from that of New Holland, the Cape, and New Zealand; though an approach to them is observable in *Goodenia, Araucaria* (Chilian pine,) the *Protea* family, *Gunnera*, and *Ancistrum.*

(11.) *Region of arborescent Compositæ* (syngenesious plants with tree-like stems.)—This takes in Buenos Ayres, and in general the eastern side of the temperate part of South America. It has been already remarked, that the Flora of this district of the world agrees to a considerable degree with that of Europe; amongst 109 genera, 70 are likewise European, and 85 in the north temperate zone. On the other hand, it differs considerably from the Floras of the Cape and of New Holland, for the *Proteas*, the *Myrtle tribe*, and the *Mimosas* are either wholly wanting, or are seen but sparingly; and there are no *Epacridæ, Heaths, Irideæ, Mesembryanthema*, or *Geraniums.* Nor can it be compared with the Flora of the north-west coast of America; for amongst 189 genera mentioned, only 35 are found in Chili. The characteristics of this region seem to lie in the great number of *Arborescent Syngenesiæ*, (particularly of the sub-family *Boopideæ*), which, however, do not exclusively appertain to it, but are also seen at the Cape.

(12.) *Antarctic region.*—This includes the countries near the Straits of Magellan. There is a considerable affinity between the vegetation here and what is seen in the north temperate zone; for, amongst 82 known genera from thence, there are 59 of them which have species in the northern hemisphere. The arctic polar forms also appear, such as *Sedges* (Carices), *Saxifrages, Gentians, Arbutus*, and *Primroses.* Some resemblance to the highlands of South America and to Chili is also shown in the *Slipperworts, Ourisia, Bæa, Bolax, Wintera, Escallonia;* to the Cape, in the genera *Gladiolus, Witsenia, Gunnera, Ancistrum, Oxalis;* and to New Holland, in *Proteaceæ* and *Mniarum*,

(13.) *Region of New Zealand.*—This well deserves to be characterised as a separate region, although its vegetation be a mixture of what prevails on the nearest continents, as South America, Southern Africa, and New Holland. It has, in common with South America, *Ancistrum, Weinmannia, Wintera;* with Southern Africa, the *Fig Marigolds, Gnaphalium Xeranthema* (Everlastings), *Tetragonia* (the famous New Zealand Spinach), *Wood-sorrel*, and *Passerina*; and with New Holland, the *Epacris, Melaleuca, Myoporum;* with both the latter, the families of *Proteaceæ* and *Restiaceæ:* some species also are common both to New Holland and Van Diemen's land, for instance *Mniarum biflorum*, *Samolus littoralis*, *Gentiana montana;* the first also a native of the Straits of Magellan.

(14.) *Region of Epacrides and Eucalypti:* comprehending the temperate parts of New Holland, together with Van Diemen's Land.—This region is very marked. The families of *Stackhouseæ* and *Tremandreæ* are quite peculiar to New Holland, the *Epacrideæ* nearly so. *Proteaceæ*, *Acaciæ*, *Aphyllæ*, and the greater number of the *Myrtle* family (especially of the genera *Eucalyptus*, *Leptospermum*, *Melaleuca*): the *Stylideæ*, *Restiaciæ*, *Casuarineæ*, *Diosmeæ*, separate it from other regions. The tropical part of New Holland, according to Brown, can hardly be united to this, but must be either a particular region, whose Flora resembles that of India, or else a province of this latter region.

(15.) *Region of Fig-Marigolds* (Mesembryanthema) and *Stapelias.*—This comprehends the southern extremity of Africa, the Flora of which is distinguished by a high degree of peculiarity. By the families *Proteaceæ*, *Restiaceæ*, *Polygalæ* (Milkworts), *Diosmeæ*, it may be recognised from most others, except New Holland, and from this it is distinguished by the two numerous genera *Mesembryanthemum* and *Stapelia*, and by the family *Ericeæ*, which is here more abundant than anywhere else. Further characteristics of this region may be found in the many *Irideæ*, *Geraniæ*, *Oxalideæ*, and the extremely large proportion of *Compositæ*. On the other hand, there exist in this district, as in New Holland, but very sparingly, those peculiar forms of the northern temperate zones, the *Cruciferæ*, *Ranunculaceæ*, *Rosaceæ*, *Umbelliferæ*, *Caryophylleæ*.

(16.) *Region of Western Africa.*—We are only acquainted with Guinea and Congo, the vegetation of which, as we have already remarked, possesses but few peculiarities, and is a mixture of the Floras of Asia and America, though most resembling the former. The American tropical families of *Cacti*, *Peppers*, *Palms*, *Passion-flowers*, are either absent entirely, or they occur in small numbers. *Leguminosæ* are more numerous than in America. Above two thirds of the genera and some of the species of Guinea are found also in the East Indies. On the other hand, this region approximates to America, in possessing many *Rubiaceæ*, as also in the genera *Schwenkia*, *Elais* (a palm), *Paullinia*, *Malpighia*, and several more which are wanting in Asia, and in several species which it has in common with America. A considerable proportion of *Grasses* and *Sedges* (Cyperaceæ), with the peculiar genus *Adansonia* (the Baobab, which is the largest known tree in the world), belong to the characteristics of this country. The interior of Africa is unknown to us.

(17.) *Region of Eastern Africa.*—Of the coast of this side of Africa and the adjacent islands our knowledge is imperfect. We are tolerably acquainted with the islands of Bourbon and France; of Madagascar we know but little; and of the east coast itself scarcely anything. The Flora of the two first-named islands has a considerable resemblance to that of India. Amongst 290 known genera, 196 of them (equal to two thirds) are found also in India; and of the species, not a few are likewise Indian; many of these, however, may have been introduced by the constant intercourse that takes place between these two parts of the globe. The genera *Eugenia*, *Ficus* (fig), *Urtica* (nettle), *Euphorbia* (spurge), *Hedysarum*, *Panicum*, *Andropogon*, *Sida*, *Pandanus* (screw-pine), *Dracæna* (dragon-wood), *Conyza* are very numerous in species, as are the same genera in India. In *ferns*, these islands are peculiarly rich. Again, their flora differs considerably from the South African; an analogy existing, however, in their possessing single representatives of the Cape genera *Erica*, *Ixia*, *Gladiolus*, *Bleria*, *Mesembryanthemum*, *Seriphium*, and several arborescent *Syngenesiæ*. Still less is the affinity to the extra-tropical parts of New Holland. The similarity is stronger to the tropical portion of that country, of which the flora also approaches that of India. Single genera are all that it seems to possess in common with America; for instance, *Melicocca*, *Ruizia*, *Dodonæa*, *Dichondra*. The following are, perhaps, peculiar to this region, *Latania*, *Hubertia*, *Poupartia*, *Tristemma*, *Fissilia*, *Cordylina*, *Assonia*, *Fernalia*, *Lubinia*, and others. The flora of Madagascar seems very peculiar. It agrees with the islands last mentioned; and several genera are seen nowhere else than in them and Madagascar; for example, *Danais*, *Ambora*, *Dombeya*, *Dufourea*, *Didymomeles*, *Senacea;* several species also are common to both; as *Didymomeles Madagascariensis*, *Danais fragrans*, *Cinchona Afro-inda*. Still, among the 161 known genera from Madagascar, 54 only are found in the Isles of France and Bourbon; so that there might be good grounds for forming a separate region of the first; unless, perhaps, the east coast of Africa should come under the same. With New Holland and the Cape, Madagascar has probably still less in common than the two other islands.

(18.) *Scitaminean region* (of the *Turmeric*, *Zedoary*, *Cardamom*, *Indian-shot*, &c.), or the Indian Flora.—To this appertain India, east and west of the Ganges, together with the islands between India and New Holland; perhaps, also, that division of New Holland which falls within the tropics. The *Scitamineæ* are here in far greater numbers than in America; also, though to a less degree, the *Leguminosæ*, *Cucurbitaceæ*, *Tiliaceæ*. The previously mentioned South American forms are rare, or else wanting. This region should be separated into several provinces; but as yet we know too little to undertake such a division with any degree of certainty.

(19.) *The Indian highlands* ought to form one or perhaps two regions, their vegetation being very dissimilar to that of the lowlands: in the middle region, *Melastomæ, Orchideæ* and *Filices*, appear to prevail; in the higher, the vegetation is more like the European and North Asiatic, and probably the Japanese: these districts perhaps constitute one region with the whole of Central Asia; but of all these countries we shall know much more when the Flora of India by Roxburgh and Wallich is completed.

(20.) *The Flora of the South of China and of Cochinchina* partly resembles that of India, especially in regard to families; but still Loureiro's Flora contains a great many peculiar genera. It is true that perhaps the number of these genera might be reduced; but even then, the vegetation of this tract will probably prove sufficiently peculiar to constitute a distinct region.

(21.) *The region of the Cassiæ and Mimosæ*, which prevail particularly in Arabia and Persia, seems likewise to have a good right to be separated from India, as it is already sufficiently distinct from the Mediterranean region (No. 3.); for, of 281 genera mentioned by Forskäl, 109 only are found in the south of Europe. It is more probable that the Flora of Nubia and part of Central Africa appertains to this region. Abyssinia perhaps forms a distinct region, its elevated parts possessing such a different climate.

(22.) *The islands in the South Sea* which lie within the tropics form perhaps a separate region; though with but a slender degree of peculiarity. Among 214 genera, 173 are found in India; most of the remainder are in common with America; for instance, *Chiococca, Weinmannia. Guajacum.* Of the species which exist equally in them and Asia, are *Zapania nodiflora, Kyllingia monocephala, Fimbristylis dichotoma, Tournefortia argentea, Plumbago zeylanica, Morinda umbellata, Sophora tomentosa.* In common with America, *Dodonæa viscosa, Sapindus saponaria* (soap-berry): with both *Rhizophora Mangle* (mangrove tree): it has also some in common with New Holland, as *Daphne indica* (a species of *Spurge Laurel*). Peculiar families, or such as have there a decided maximum, can scarcely be cited; though, on the other hand, most of the species are peculiar. The *Bread-fruit* is among the characteristics of these islands; though this tree is not confined to the South Seas.

The limit of the present essay does not allow of the intended introduction of the geographical situation of many of the more useful and important plants, which Professor Schouw has so ably delineated; such as that of the *Beech*, the *Vine*, the *Fir tribes*, the *Heaths*, *Corn*, and such fruits or vegetables as are employed as bread: the *Palms*, the *Proteaceæ*, which form so remarkably striking a feature in the Cape of Good Hope and in New Holland; the *Compositæ*, which are perhaps more universally diffused than any other kind of plant; the *Cruciferæ*, to which the *Cabbage*, *Turnip*, *Mustard*, *Scurvy-grass*, &c. appertain; and the *leguminous tribes*, whose seeds (as the *Pea* and *Bean*) are so valuable for man, and whose foliage, as the *Lupine* and *Trefoil*, &c. affords most of the nourishment to cattle. We must endeavour to incorporate these with the vegetation of the various regions where they are found in the greatest abundance.

---

## CHAPTER II.

### GEOGRAPHY CONSIDERED IN RELATION TO THE DISTRIBUTION OF MAN AND ANIMALS.

The geographic distribution of animated beings is a branch of natural history which only of late years has engaged the attention of philosophers. The celebrated Blumenbach was the first, we believe, who generalized the numerous facts connected with the physiology of man, and proved that all the varieties may be referred to certain types of form, equally distinct in their physical structure and in their geographic distribution. But whether from prejudice, or from the varied and comprehensive sphere of zoology, which renders the subject too vast for the power of any one mind, certain it is that animal geography has been almost neglected. Isolated details, relative to particular countries, classes, or families, have been successfully investigated; but no one has yet attempted to generalize these materials, and use them towards the discovery of the laws of creation. An attempt to ascertain the range of particular species simply within a certain district or kingdom, is merely an inquiry into their *local* distribution; but if our views are extended beyond such confines, and we embrace a large portion of the globe, tracing the relations of its animals, with those of the remaining portions, it is then only that we enter upon the comprehensive subject of *geographic* distribution.

The inquiries relative to physical distribution, when directed to the animal world, assume a higher importance than those, however interesting, which regard plants: for not only do animals appear incalculably more numerous than vegetables, but their natural range, dependent on a multiplicity of concurrent causes, appears to be much more distinctly marked.

Plants, indeed, in a great degree, are stationary beings; but nature has wisely provided for their removal and dispersion to the most distant regions, by the diversified structure or tenacious vitality with which the seeds of numerous families are endowed; hence they become transported by various natural causes to distant shores, and, without any assistance from human aid, take root, flourish, and increase, in lands far distant from those which appear to have been their native regions. It is otherwise with animals: they may, it is true, be removed from their birth-place, and even become domesticated and naturalized elsewhere; but, with the exception of those which seem to have been originally destined for the service of man, such naturalization is only effected by artificial means, and by slow degrees, through several generations. If such transported animals be left to themselves, or rather to the natural resources for supporting life peculiar to their new abode, they almost invariably pine and die. Again, plants, from being inferior to animals in the complexity of their structure, are, perhaps, necessarily dependent on fewer causes for retaining the vital energy; their dispersion is, consequently, upon the whole, much more extensive. It may be mentioned, in support of this remark, that out of 600 plants discovered in tropical Africa by Professor Smith, one-twelfth have been ascertained, by Robert Brown, to be natives also of India and South America. Now, if either the vertebrated or invertebrated animals, not aquatic, of Western Africa, were compared in a similar way with those of the parallel latitudes in America and India, the proportion collectively would hardly amount to one in a hundred: indeed, with regard to the vertebrated orders, it is very questionable whether even one species is truly indigenous to tropical Africa and to America; so totally different are the zoological features of these continents, even at their nearest approximation: and yet, in the above number of plants, no less than twenty-two species are enumerated, as common to equinoctial Africa, India, and America. These facts, while they strengthen the belief that zoology is a more favourable field than botany for discovering the laws of natural distribution, lead us to consider the modes by which such inquiries are most beneficially prosecuted.

### Sect. I.—*Modes of investigating the Subject.*

The powerful effect produced on animals by temperature, food, and locality, are known to all: whether as regards the range of any particular species, or the numbers of which it may be composed. The effect of these agencies is indeed so great, that some writers have looked upon them as primary causes, and have imagined that by such laws alone has nature regulated the distribution of the whole animal creation. Very many instances, no doubt, from among the diversities of animal structure, may be urged in support of this theory; but how far it can be reconciled with other and more general facts, which will be apparent on a wider view of the subject, we shall hereafter investigate. It is clear that, by whatever laws Nature may have been guided, numerous exceptions will be found, proportionate to the vast and almost infinite variety she has displayed in her productions. There is, perhaps, no theory professing to explain the laws of Nature, whether on animal distribution or natural affinities, which the wit of man could possibly devise, that might not be supported with great plausibility, by certain facts, presented by those radiating threads of connexion, and those apparent deviations from her general laws, which are everywhere apparent: yet these will frequently be opposed to other facts; and thus it becomes necessary, before determining on which side the preponderance of evidence lies, that we take as wide a survey of the general distribution of animals as the existing state of knowledge will admit. To set out with the belief that the laws of geographic distribution are fully ascertained, and that nothing remains but to make ourselves acquainted with the range of individual species, is a doctrine which can only be compared to those principles of classification insisted upon by the methodists of the last age in natural history, who considered that all the generic groups had been discovered, and that future naturalists had nothing left but to appropriate to them the newly discovered species, in the best manner they could.

Towards the discovery of the natural geography of animals there is, however, another mode of investigation, analogous to what we now pursue, in searching after the true series of their affinities: this is, to lay aside all preconceived theories, and to begin with considering the primary causes of geographic distribution to be, what in truth they really are, totally unknown. We are thus compelled to take a general survey of all the existing animals yet discovered, and now dispersed over the globe; and, from the facts so elicited, endeavour to attain such general inferences as are supported by a preponderance of evidence, furnished by nature herself. By the first method, as it has been truly said, we make nature bend to our own arbitrary theories; while by the second we humbly endeavour to receive her instructions; striving to obtain a glimpse of that stupendous plan which can never be fully understood by fallible and imperfect mortals.

The geographic distribution of man is connected in our survey with that of animals; not so much in compliance with the popular notion, by which the noblest work of God is classed as a genus next to the brute, but because we may fairly presume, from the great diversity observed among the human species, that their variation and dispersion is regulated by some general plan; and that such plan may be analogous to that which is apparent in the distribution of animals. It may be urged, indeed, that such a remarkable coincidence, if proved, might tend to sanction the modern theory of classing man and brutes together; but the only legitimate construction which we think could be fairly drawn from such a fact would be, that there is but one plan of geographic distribution and of creation throughout nature.

Against classing man with quadrupeds we must enter our decided protest. And here we cannot refrain from expressing regret that a naturalist of no ordinary talent has recently adopted this degrading theory, in apparent opposition to his former most just and philosophic views of the subject. He admits "the greatness of the gulf between man and the orang outang;" yet, because they possess certain analogies of physical structure, is it a necessary conclusion that they form one group? (*Linn. Trans.* xvi. 1. p. 22.) This, at least, was not the opinion (as this philosopher candidly admits) of either Aristotle or Ray, whom he justly considers the two greatest zoologists that have ever existed. It has been argued that the natural pride of philosophy withheld such men from classing themselves with brutes; but we are more disposed to think they were influenced by higher considerations. However this may be, there is an innate repugnance, or rather a disgust and abhorrence, in every human mind, enlightened or illiterate, against the admission of such a relationship. Revelation everywhere places MAN, even in his fallen state, in absolute contrast and contradiction with "the beasts that perish." It is not merely a feeling of pride; it is an innate loathing, engrafted in our nature, apparently for the very purpose of teaching us how immeasurably far we are removed from the brutes that have no understanding. Man has fallen, miserably fallen, but this is from the corruption of that pure spirit with which he was created: his form was then, as it is now; nor are we to suppose that *man*, as he came fashioned by his Creator, without sin, was clothed in a different form to that which he now, in a sinful state, exhibits. Are we then to place such a being in a zoological circle, surrounded with apes and baboons? or are material and immaterial natures so closely allied, that they may be classed together?

There is another argument against including man in the zoological circle, furnished by the very theory upon which that hypothesis is built. If the circular system is part of the system of nature, which at this time of day is perfectly demonstrable, every being has two affinities: by the one, it is connected to that which precedes it; by the other, to that by which it is succeeded. Now, before we can bring man within the circle of the Quadrumana, on the strength of his affinity (whether near or remote) to the orang outang, we must show to what class of animals he is connected on the other hand. What then are our double affinities in the vertebrate circle? We may be allied distantly, perhaps, to *Simia*. But where is the second affinity? If this cannot be pointed out, the whole theory, in our estimation, falls to the ground, since the presumed *type* of the animal kingdom contradicts the laws by which creation is supposed to be regulated; man exhibiting a single affinity, and the rest of organised matter a double one. Take him *from* the animal circle,—place him between matter and spirit;—and his double affinities become at once apparent.

A general sketch of the physical peculiarities of man in all his variations will first claim our attention; the regions inhabited by the different races, and the affinities by which they appear connected, will also be briefly noticed. This part of our subject will be conducted on a somewhat different plan from that which we shall pursue in the sequel. The profound researches of Blumenbach and Cuvier, and the acute and patient investigations of Lawrence and Pritchard, have all conspired to produce nearly the same general conclusions on those points to which we shall particularly draw the reader's attention. These conclusions, moreover, demand our fullest confidence, from being founded on as rigid analysis as the nature of the subject will admit. Hence, we have no need, in this place, of entering into details, or of pursuing the same mode of investigation to which we shall have recourse when subsequently treating of animal distribution.

### SECT. II.—*Varieties of the Human Race.*

The varieties of the human race, according to the opinion of the greatest comparative anatomist, may all be included under three primary divisions, between which, in their typical examples, a very marked difference is observed. These M. Cuvier has termed, 1. the fair or Caucasian variety; 2. the yellow or Mongolian; 3. the black or Ethiopian.

The classification proposed by the celebrated Blumenbach, although apparently different, is but a modification of that promulgated by Baron Cuvier. The former considers the Ethiopian type as divisible into three, 1. the American; 2. the Negro; and 3. the Malay. The latter indicates these additional races, but considers their peculiarities as less prominent than those of the two former; he does not therefore admit them among the primary divisions of the human race. Without, at present, offering any opinion upon this question, we shall first take a rapid survey of the peculiarities, physical and moral, of all these groups.

(1) The Caucasian race (*fig.* 70.) is typically characterised by a white skin, red cheeks,

70

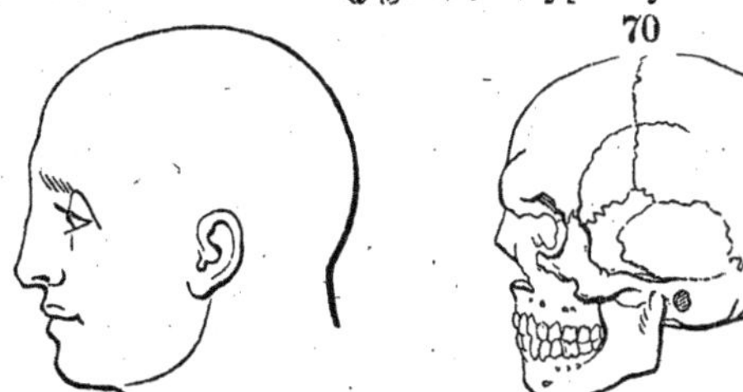
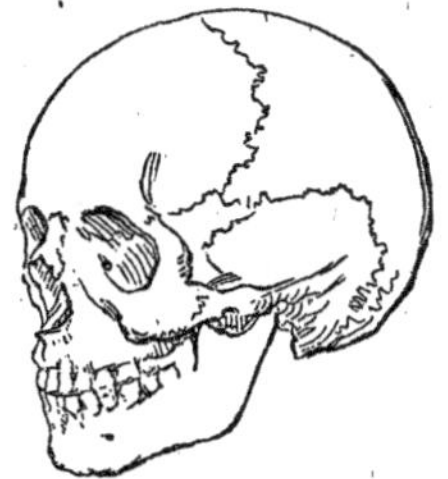

copious, soft, flowing hair, generally curled or waving; ample beard; small, oval, and straight face, with the features very distinct; expanded forehead; large and elevated cranium; narrow nose; and small mouth.

The moral feelings and intellectual powers of this race have been developed in the highest degree of perfection which human nature has ever exhibited. The Caucasian has given birth to the most civilized nations, both in ancient and modern times, and has always exercised dominion over the rest of mankind, when not opposed by a vast superiority of physical strength. The mighty nations of antiquity, and the no less resistless powers concentrated in modern Europe, evince the superiority of this race in all that ennobles the immaterial part of man, and all that renders him formidable to his fellow-creatures; while every age witnesses a progressive but a surprising advance in all those qualities which indicate intellectual endowment.

The original seat of the Caucasian race is supposed, as the name implies, to have been that lofty chain of mountains between the Black and Caspian Seas. This supposition, as Lawrence observes, is in unison with all that can be traced of the original abode of our first parents; and is further confirmed by the natives of these regions being, to this day, the most beautifully formed of all the inhabitants of the earth. From the Caucasian Alps different branches of this race diverge in every direction, as from a common centre; the peculiarities of each being modified, altered, and finally lost, in proportion as they recede from the original seat of their tribe.

Of the branches of the Caucasian race, the most powerful is the Pelasgic, which spreads over the greater part of Europe and Western Asia at its most northern limits, while it blends with the Mongolian race by means of the Fins and Laplanders. From this branch sprang the powerful nations of Greece and Rome, which have been succeeded by the mighty kingdoms of modern Europe. The next is the Syrian, which takes a southerly direction; and includes that portion of Asia formerly inhabited by the Assyrians, Chaldeans, and the ancient Egyptians. The Indian branch, by some thought to be the same with the Pelasgic, passes to the East, and loses itself among the inferior casts of Hindostan. A fourth branch is the Scythian or Tartaric, which spread over the more northern parts of Asia; and gave birth to those wandering and ruthless hordes who, by the physical power of numbers, devastated and finally overthrew the polished empires of Greece and Rome. The wandering and pastoral habits of this tribe have conspired to preserve their peculiarities unmixed with those of the neighbouring nations; except, indeed, in Lesser Tartary, where this branch of the Caucasian race loses itself in the Mongolian.

(2.) The Mongolian variety (*fig.* 71.) has these characteristics:—The skin, instead of

71

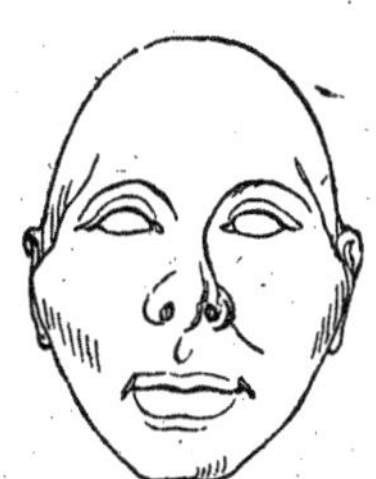
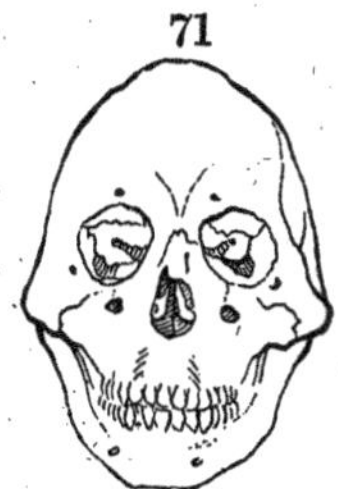
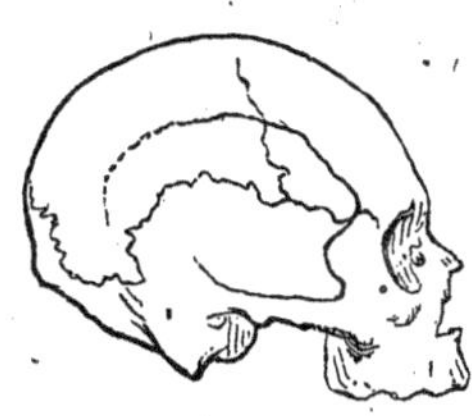

white or fair, is olive yellow; the hair thin, coarse, and straight; little or no beard; broad flattened face, with the features running together; small and low forehead; square-shaped cranium; wide and small nose; very oblique eyes; and thick lips. Stature inferior to the Caucasian. In this race the moral and intellectual energies have been developed in an inferior degree. Tradition, indeed, has assigned to the most powerful nation, the Chinese, a high degree of civilization, at a period when Europe was in a state of barbarism. Yet there are many circumstances which throw considerable suspicion on this fact: and even if it be allowed, a stronger proof could not possibly be produced to show the limited intellectual powers of this race; for while the European Caucasian nations have advanced from rude savages to become masters of the world, the Chinese, after reaching a certain state of civilization, have remained stationary, in every respect, through a long series of ages. Solitary exceptions cannot invalidate the fact; and while we know that, not only in our own times, but so far back as history informs us, neither the sciences, the inventions, nor the improvements of the last three centuries have changed the Mongolian nations from what they then were, we can come to no other conclusion than that they are nationally incapacitated from further improvement. Cuvier supposes that the origin of the Mongolian race may have been in the mountains of Altaï. From thence it has spread over the whole of central and northern Asia, where it is lost among the Esquimaux on the one hand, and the Caucasian Tartars on the other. It further extends to the Eastern Ocean, and includes the Japanese, the Coreans, and a large portion of the Siberians. Its limits to the south appear to extend no farther than to that part of Hindostan north of the Ganges, while the Mongolian features only predominate over those of the Indo-Caucasian in the lower casts of the Eastern Peninsula.

The origin of the Esquimaux and other polaric nations found on the most northern limits of Europe and America, has given rise to great diversity of opinion. Arguments of nearly equal weight, but of opposite tendency, have been employed to show, on the one hand, that the Esquimaux belong to the American variety; and on the other, to prove their structure more in unison with that of the Mongolian. The latter opinion has been supported by Mr. Lawrence; and although we consider the weight of argument to be on this side, it appears not at all improbable that both these suppositions are in part correct. We have before observed, that the characters of each race become less and less apparent, the farther they are removed from their particular type. The proximity of the northern regions of Asia to those of America, renders it highly probable either that their respective inhabitants mingled their races at a remote period, or that the northern Mongolians, whose civilization is supposed to be of so great antiquity, were the first to emigrate, and people the northern regions of America. At all events, it appears certain that the Esquimaux nations unite in themselves many of the characters of two distinct races; and the only theory by which we can reconcile these doubts on their true origin, is that of supposing them to form the link of connexion between the Mongolian and that race which spreads over the remaining portion of the new world. The brief notice we have now taken of the two most powerful races or varieties of the human form is sufficient to show their marked superiority over all others, whether as regards the symmetry or beauty of their physical structure, or the still more striking developement of their moral powers. Hence they both become typical, although in different degrees, of that perfection which the Creator has bestowed upon man, in this his probatory state of existence.

The third primary division or leading variety of the human race, according to the views of the illustrious Cuvier, is the negro or Ethiopian. This, again, presents three variations, considered by Cuvier as secondary, and by Blumenbach as primary. Although these variations are not so great as those between either the Caucasian, the Mongolian, or the African (the latter being considered the type of the Ethiopian variety), still they are sufficiently important to merit a particular specification under distinct names; and they are accordingly termed the American, the Ethiopian, and the Malay varieties.

In the American variety (*fig.* 72.) the skin is dark, and more or less red, the hair black,

72

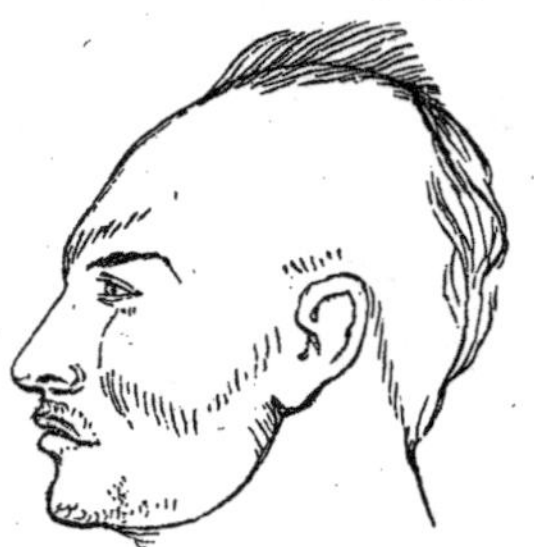
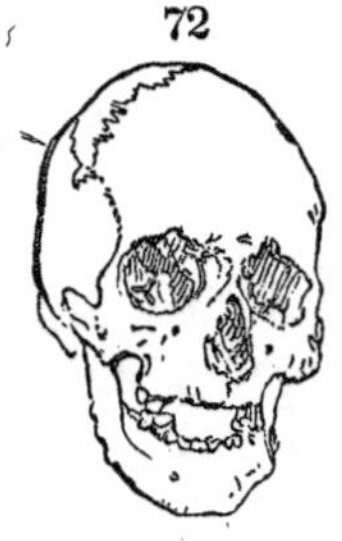
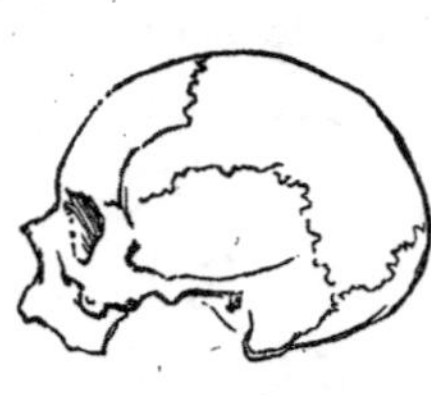

straight, and strong, with the beard small; face and skull very similar to the Mongolian, but the former not so flattened; eyes sunk; forehead low; the nose and other features being somewhat projecting. The moral and intellectual character of this race is in unison with the great difference it presents in outward form from the Caucasian. Like the Mongolian, it has remained stationary; but stopped at a point very much below that to which the Asiatics have reached. The ancient and now extinct empires of Mexico and the Incas may be considered analogous to those of China and India, exhibiting the highest point of civilization to which the two races have ever reached; but farther than this the comparison cannot be carried. Arts, sciences, and all those intellectual endowments which have followed the progress of the Caucasian race, and to a certain extent belong also to the Asiatics, appear to have made little or no progress among the Americans, even in the gorgeous court of Montezuma. When that monarch despatched messengers to bring him an account of the first Spaniards who landed on his territories, so ignorant were the Mexicans of figures or of writing, that their report was made in complicated hieroglyphics, mixed with rude figures of the horses and persons of these unknown invaders. Their idolatrous worship enjoined no moral duties, like those of the superstition of Fo; and its rites were celebrated by human sacrifices of such a revolting nature as to be worthy only of demons. It deserves attention, that while the central portion of America presented in its original inhabitants such a degraded picture of the human mind, the northern nations of the new world, partaking more of the Mongolian aspect, evinced a higher degree of intellect. It is true they were only wandering tribes of hunters, yet they appear to have had a full belief in the existence of one "Great Spirit," and in a blissful immortality for themselves. The American race, blending with the Mongolian to the north, spreads over the whole of the new world; but whether any traces of this type exist beyond these limits, is a question which has not hitherto been investigated.

In the Ethiopian variety (*fig.* 73.), the skin is black; hair short, black, and woolly; skull

73

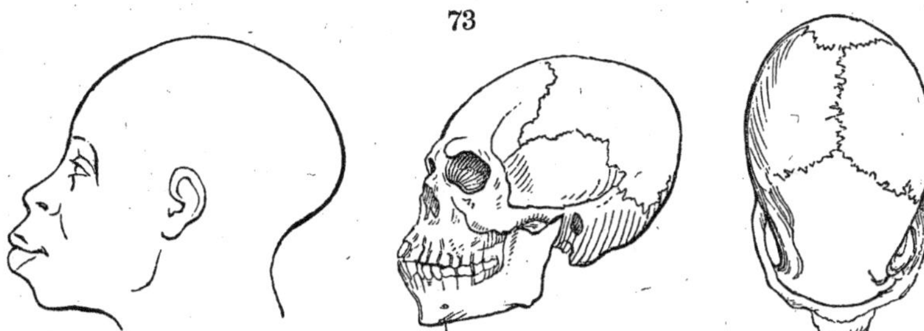

compressed on the sides, and elongated towards the front; forehead low, narrow, and slanting; cheekbones very prominent; jaws projecting, so as to render the upper front teeth oblique; eyes prominent; nose broad and flat; lips (especially the upper one) particularly thick. The African or Ethiopian race has ever remained in a rude and comparatively barbarous state. Their cities are but congregations of huts; their laws, the despotic whim of the reigning chief. Incessantly occupied in war or in the chase, they seek not to perpetuate their ideas. They have no written language, nor even a code of hieroglyphics. Abundantly supplied by nature with every necessary of life, they have retained their character unchanged, after centuries of intercourse with the most enlightened nations. Different branches of this type spread over the whole of the African continent, excepting those parts bordering the north and east of the Great Desert, which are occupied by the Caucasian Syrians, and where all traces of the negro formation disappear.

The Malay variety (*fig.* 74.) varies in the colour of the skin from a light tawny to a deep

74

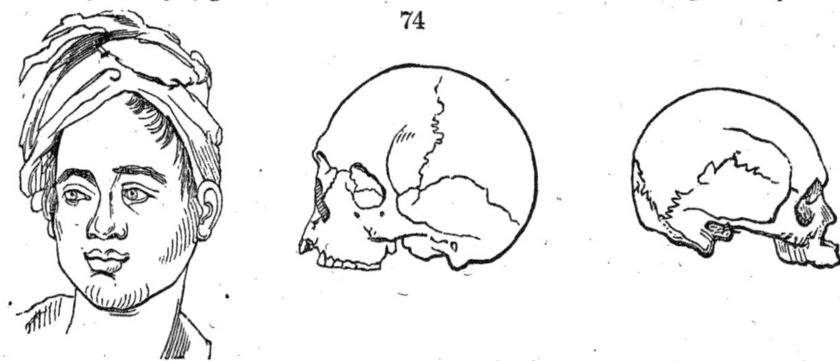

brown, approaching to black; hair black, more or less curled, and abundant; head rather narrow; bones of the face large and prominent; nose full and broad towards the tip. Under this variety, observes Mr. Lawrence, are included races of men very different in organization and qualities. They nevertheless present certain general points of resemblance, which forbid their association with either of the foregoing varieties. Under this head are, therefore, included the inhabitants of Malacca, of Sumatra, and of the innumerable islands of the Indian Archipelago and the great Pacific Ocean. Most of these tribes are stated to speak the Malay language, which may be traced, in the various ramifications of this diversified race, from Madagascar to Easter Island. Their moral character is no less various than their outward form. In such as, by the colour of their skin and their woolly hair, show a general approximation to the African type, the mental powers are little developed. Their language, however, is stated to be peculiar, and they appear to have a copious bushy beard. (*Lawrence*, 489.) Branches of this division of the Malay race spread over the great islands of Sumatra, Borneo, and Andaman; and they appear also to occupy the Molucca and Philippine Islands. They are described as living in the same state of wild and savage barbarity as do the Bushmen of Southern Africa, and such other branches of the Ethiopian variety as appear the lowest in the scale of form and intellect. There is, however, a lighter-coloured and superior race, inhabiting some of the Indian islands, where an oval countenance, longer hair, and finer form, evince a much greater affinity with the Indo-Caucasian type on one side, and a strong analogy to the New Zealanders and Pacific tribes on the other. Proceeding along the same insular chain, we meet with "negro-like men" having curly hair, in the immense island of New Guinea, and in those south-western groups denominated New Ireland, New Hebrides, and New Caledonia. The natives of the vast continent of New Holland show strong indications of the same origin, and of the same untameable barbarism; yet their features are described as not unpleasant, their skin is rather copper-coloured than black, and their hair either curling or straight. The natives of the interior have been described as somewhat more civilized, and as speaking a language different from that used on the coast. In the neighbouring island of New Zealand a considerable change from the black Malayan tribes takes place. The superior castes of these islanders in their persons are tall, active, and well made; their skin is brown, and their long black hair is sometimes straight, sometimes curling. A degree of intellect, superior to all the tribes we have enumerated, accompanies these personal advantages. Retaining many of the barbarous customs of their neighbours, the New Zealanders have, nevertheless, made some progress in the arts of life since their intercourse with Europeans: they believe in a Supreme Being, and in a happy immortality; and evince, in various ways, a desire to improve their condition. The natives of the Friendly Islands have the dark complexion of the New Zealanders, but are a much superior race. They are of the ordinary European stature, though some are above six feet high; their colour is a deep brown, verging in the better classes on a light olive; their features, like those of the New Zealanders, are various, approximating in some respects to them, and also to the true Europeans. Their progress in civilization and in intellectual developement is considerable; as a proof of which, it is mentioned that they have terms to express numbers up to 100,000. The Otaheitians have long been celebrated for their personal beauty: the lower orders, indeed, are of the same brown tint so generally prevalent in the Friendly Islands, but in those of a superior caste this is gradually lost, until we find in the higher ranks a skin nearly white, or at least but slightly tinged with brown; and although the usual colour of their hair is black, yet it is of a fine texture, and frequent instances occur in which it is brown, flaxen, and even red. Their persons are well made, their features sometimes even beautiful, and a blush may be readily observed on the cheek of the women. The harmony of their language, and their simple though refined manners, have been universally remarked. These national characteristics extend to the Society Islands. *Lastly*, The natives of the Marquesas have been described as the finest race in the Southern Ocean: "in form they are, perhaps, the finest in the world." Their skin is naturally "very fair," and the colour of their hair exhibits all the varied shades, (excepting red), which are found in the different tribes of the Caucasian race.

## SECT. III.—*On the Causes of these Varieties.*

The following questions naturally arise from considering these characteristics of the most prominent varieties of the human race; founded as they are on the concurrent testimony of travellers, and generalised by the most eminent physiologists:—1. Whether these races, so dissimilar in their typical peculiarities, have originally proceeded from one, or from distinct stocks? 2. Are they so strongly marked as not to present many and great deviations? and, 3. To what causes are they to be attributed?

In regard to the origin of the human race, there have not been wanting those, who, disbelieving the evidences of the Mosaic history, have attempted to establish the hypothesis that these races have each sprung from different stocks; or, that they are, in fact, so many species. Now, this, at the best, is but an assumption perfectly gratuitous; not only because every record from which it could receive any support is expressly opposed to it, but because it is in direct violation of a primary and universal law of nature: a law by which the lowest being of the animal creation shrinks instinctively from intermixing its *species* with that of another. It has, moreover, been fully ascertained that, however great the variations of the human form may be, such variations among different breeds of the same species of animal are even greater. Unless, therefore, it can be proved that the laws of nature with respect to man and animals are contradictory, we shall, by attaching the least weight to the above theory, openly violate every principle of philosophic reasoning, as well as renounce all belief in revealed religion. On this head the Mosaic records are clear and explicit; and however the sceptic may deny their inspiration, he cannot bring forward, on his side, any testimony of such remote antiquity, or of such generally admitted credibility. As to the second question, it must not be understood that, in arranging the varieties of man under a certain number of divisions, and assigning to each a peculiar character, there does not occur many and very remarkable exceptions in each. So much, indeed, is this the case, that there are not wanting instances of native African tribes having the light skin of Europeans, Caucasians combining the Mongolian with the Malay structure, Americans resembling whites, and Africans with the copper-coloured skin of the American; nay, even in the same island or province, a great diversity both in language and in physical structure, is sometimes apparent, and this between tribes bordering close upon each other; so that, with the exception of a comparatively small portion of each principal race, we find so much diversity in the remaining or aberrant branches—the typical peculiarities become so modified, altered, or evanescent, that it is totally impossible to draw an absolute line of demarcation between them.

This point has frequently been adverted to by a well-known physiologist, who says, "there is no circumstance, whether of corporeal structure or of mental endowment, which does not pass by imperceptible gradations into the opposite character, rendering all those distinctions merely relative, and reducing them to differences in degree. It is concluded, therefore, that every arrangement of these varieties must be in a great measure arbitrary." (*Lawrence's Lect.* p. 472.) Yet, admitting this variation to the fullest extent, it cannot alter the correctness of the principle on which these distinctions are founded. Whatever might have been formerly thought as to the nature of terms employed by naturalists to designate the particular groups of animals, it is now generally admitted that, throughout nature, there are no isolating distinctions, save such as separate species. The characters of every zoological group, of whatever magnitude or denomination, are subject to exceptions equally numerous. The typical peculiarities may, indeed, be prominent; but in proportion to the number of objects which are embraced under any definition, will be the diversity of those imperceptible gradations, those threads of connexion, which shoot out in all directions, and unite not only genera and orders, but the primary kingdoms of the animal and the vegetable worlds. It is, therefore, irrelevant to argue, that, because these divisions are liable to numerous exceptions, and are not always uniform and constant, they are either artificial or objectionable for as we find that all natural groups, both in the animal and vegetable worlds, are subject to the same variations, they are therefore liable to the same objections. In short, if such reasoning is valid, the distinction between plants and animals can no longer be maintained; for it is to this day unsettled at what point the peculiarities of one are lost, and those of the other assumed.

The causes that may have led to these variations in the human species, form the only question of a general nature remaining to be discussed. It has been argued by some writers, that particular climates, food, and modes of life, have gradually operated, through a succession of ages, to produce these effects on the colour, stature, and intellect of different nations. But, however greatly these causes may affect individuals, or even to a certain extent a whole people, they entirely fail when brought to solve our present question; were it otherwise, the same causes would naturally have the same effect on all the inhabitants of a particular region; but such, as is well known, is far from being the case. The negro, under a tropical sun, is black; while an Indian of Para, in the same degree of latitude, is reddish brown. No race produces men more athletic, or more finely formed, than are witnessed among the Gold Coast negroes; yet they inhabit, proverbially, some of the most pestilential districts of Africa. On the other hand, the New Hollanders, and the South African Bushmen, living in a salubrious climate, are described as lean, squalid, and with an appearance scarcely human. It is therefore obvious, that neither the physical nor the moral condition of man can be so affected by climate, or other external agencies, as to produce any great or permanent variation in his form. Indeed, when we consider that such agencies have not produced any physical change in any one nation, within the memory or the records of man, we are tempted to believe that in a general point of view, their influence has been very slight; otherwise, there is no reason to doubt but that the same *natural* causes which operated at one period of time, would still continue to do so at another; and that we should find the descendants of Europeans long since settled in the New World, and in Southern Africa, beginning to assume the red tinge of the American, or the black skin of the Ethiopian. Still less can it be supposed that this departure from one common standard has been effected by civilization, a consequent developement of the mental faculties, or even by diversified modes of life. Man, in remote ages, must have lived pretty nearly the same life in every region; whether as shepherds, hunters, or tillers of the field, their food, habits, and modes of life, must have been simple and regular. Whence comes it, then, that nations which still retain a great portion of what may be conceived their primitive simplicity, do not exhibit a corresponding resemblance in physical structure? If food, raiment, and moral improvement have such a powerful effect in modifying the human frame, it would naturally follow that tribes living nearly in a state of nature would all show a close approximation to one common type; that they would, in short, retain more of the lineaments and characters which must have belonged to our first parents, than if they had deviated from their primitive simplicity; yet the very reverse of this is the fact. The apparent aborigines of every nation are those in which the leading characters of their own tribe are most conspicuous; and which exhibit the strongest contrast to those of others. It is only when they have made some progress in the arts of life, when conquest or commerce has led to a union with other races, that the national characteristics, both personal and mental, give way, and begin either to blend or to be lost in other modifications. These reasons, did they more immediately concern the purposes of this essay, might be much enlarged upon, more particularly as they have been offered by some deservedly eminent writers as a satisfactory solution of the question we are now discussing. Yet, allowing to all these causes the full effect they are known to have produced, we must yet confess they appear to us totally inadequate to explain the origin of the races of man. A writer intimately versed on this subject has well observed, that "external agencies, whether physical or moral, will not account for the bodily and mental differences which characterise the several tribes of mankind." (*Lawrence's Lectures*, p. 431.) We have, in short, now brought the inquiry to a point where human reason is baffled: there is neither history nor tradition to guide us in a research which carries us back to the obscurity of ages; to that remote period when the earth, for a second time, was again peopled, if not by a single pair, yet by the *three* sons of a single family.

We are now to view the question in another light. It has been generally admitted, even by those who reject the Mosaic testimony, that the diversity in the human structure can in no way be accounted for by any known combination of *natural* causes: are we, therefore, to suppose, in a question which concerns the most perfect earthly being made by Omnipotence, that nothing *supernatural* is to enter? that causes which effect the developement not only of the material but of the spiritual essence of man, have been left to chance? Is it not more reasonable to conclude, that, for purposes unknown to us, a supernatural agency *was* employed? and that the immediate descendants of the sons of Noah were as distinctly marked in their outward form as they were in their moral character? The sacred writings, it is true, are not written to answer philosophic inquiries. Those who, in the present age, have been the most profound investigators of nature, discover in every part of creation a symbolic relationship; a mysterious system of types and symbols, which extends from the most complex to the most simple of organized beings: and when we know, for instance, that even the colours of a bird or an insect have a direct reference to such a system, and are employed as typical indications of its station in nature, can it be supposed that such a system does not extend to man? That this will not, in the present infancy of our inquiries, admit of such direct and unanswerable proof as amounts to mathematical demonstration, we do not attempt to deny; but that such a supposition is in harmony with that perfection which belongs to the works of Omnipotence, every reasonable person must admit. Nor are there wanting circumstances which give some degree of sanction to this belief. The curse pronounced upon Canaan as the son of Ham has unquestionably been fulfilled. Learned commentators agree in considering that central Africa was peopled by his descendants, and these have been for ages, and still continue to be, "a servant of servants," to their more favoured brethren. Even their own despotic governments render the subjects but slaves. In them the human form is most debased, the divinity of mind least developed. They still exhibit those leading resemblances which rendered Cain a type of Canaan: with few exceptions, they are, to this day, but "wanderers and vagabonds" on the earth. The blessings pronounced on the two remaining sons of Noah, it has been well observed, are of a very different nature: Shem was more peculiarly favoured than his brother; from his race not only the great patriarchs who typified Christ, but even Christ himself, descended. The peculiarity of the Jewish polity, which preserved the physical peculiarities of their race pure and unmixed through successive generations, leaves us in no doubt that they belong to the Caucasian type, in which, both in structure and intellect, a marked superiority over all the nations of the earth has been universally admitted. The early descendants of Japheth, as is plainly intimated by Moses, were eminently warlike. All writers agree in considering that from the Mongolian race descended those vast and overpowering hordes of barbaric warriors who, at remote periods of time, conquered all Asia, and devastated Europe under Attila, Zingis Khan, and Tamerlane. "It is remarkable," says Dr. Scott, "that the first king of whom we read in authentic history, is Nimrod, the mighty hunter." The same learned writer mentions that there is some ground for believing that the greatest part of Asia (now peopled by the Mongolian race) descended from Japheth. The population of Asia has been frequently mentioned as in an equal ratio to the superiority of its size over Europe, or rather of those countries over which the Caucasian variety has spread. Thus, in every sense, it appears, that the promise to Noah's first son, "God shall enlarge Japheth, and Canaan shall be his servant," has literally and figuratively been fulfilled.

That the three sons of Noah overspread and peopled the whole earth, is so expressly stated in Scripture, that, if we had not to argue against those who unfortunately disbelieve such evidence, we might here stop: let us, however, inquire how far the truth of this declaration is substantiated by other considerations. Enough has been said to show that there is a curious, if not a remarkable, analogy between the predictions of Noah, on the future descend ants of his three sons, and the actual state of those races which are generally supposed to have sprung from them. It may here be again remarked, that although, to render the subject more clear, we have adopted the quinary arrangement of Blumenbach, yet that Cuvier and other learned physiologists are of opinion that the *primary* varieties of the human form are more properly but *three;* namely, Caucasian, the Mongolian, and the Ethiopian. This number corresponds with that of Noah's sons: assigning, therefore, the Mongolian race to Japheth, and the Ethiopian to Ham, the Caucasian, the noblest race, will belong to Shem the *third* son of Noah, himself descended from Seth the *third* son of Adam. That the *primary* distinctions of the human varieties are but *three*, has been further maintained by the erudite Pritchard, who, while he rejects the nomenclature both of Blumenbach and Cuvier, as implying *absolute* divisions, arranges the leading varieties of the human skull under three sections, differing from those of Cuvier only by name. That the three sons of Noah, who were to "replenish the earth," and on whose progeny very opposite destinies were pronounced, should give birth to different races, is what might reasonably be conjectured. But that the observations of those who *do*, and of those who do *not* believe the Mosaic history should tend to confirm its truth, by pointing out in what respect these three races do actually differ, both physically and morally, is, to say the least, a singular coincidence. It amounts, in short, to presumptive evidence that a mysterious, but a very beautiful analogy pervades throughout; and teaches us to look beyond natural causes, in attempting to account for effects apparently interwoven in the plans of Omnipotence.

To reconcile the different theories regarding the number of primary variations in the human form is our next object. The greatest authorities on this subject are Blumenbach and Lawrence, Cuvier and Pritchard. The first two, as already observed, maintain that the primary divisions are five; while the latter, with more show of reason, contend that there are but three, although they readily admit the distinctions assigned to the other two. In what manner, therefore, can these opposite theories be reconciled? To do this, we must revert to a third and very remarkable one, which, although it has hitherto been solely directed to the animal kingdom, will yet be found to exercise a very important influence on the present question: we allude to the circular theory of MacLeay. It is the opinion of this learned naturalist that every group of organised beings divides itself, as it were, into two branches of affinities, which finally uniting again at their opposite extremities, form a circle; and that this disposition of affinities holds good, not only in every group, of whatever magnitude or denomination, but throughout the animal and the vegetable world. It has been further shown that as such a circular arrangement of beings cannot, of necessity, present any absolute or isolated divisions, (for it could not then be continuous and circular), yet, that there may be traced, in each circle, five deviations or varieties of structure; which, however conspicuous in their typical examples, are blended and lost the nearer they approximate to each other. Now, so far as regards the affinities of animals, this circular theory has been demonstrated; but it long remained a matter of doubt what number of *primary* divisions every group contained. Mr. MacLeay considers there are five; and this accords with Blumenbach's arrangement of the human species. M. Cuvier, and Dr. Pritchard, as we have before stated, limit the leading varieties of man to three. In our arrangement of the order Insessores (*North. Zoology*, vol. ii.), one of the most comprehensive divisions in ornithology, we have shown that the primary divisions of every natural group are only *three;* one of which, by forming a circle of its own, includes three of those pointed out by Mr. MacLeay,—thus making the number *five*. Now, this theory, on the natural divisions of birds, rests upon no speculative assumption; it is founded on the most rigorous and minute analysis, and has thus been capable of mathematic demonstration. The question, whether this theory is applicable to one part only of the animal creation, or whether there is presumptive evidence to conclude that it pervades all nature, has been discussed at some length in the "Introductory Observations on the Natural System," prefixed to the same work. In some respects the *trinary* and the *quinary* theory of divisions may be thought virtually the same; and so far as regards our present subject, considered abstractly, this observation may be true. We can analyze a group of insects, of birds, or of other animals, but how are we to analyze the different modifications of man? The thing is utterly impossible. Now, as every true theory must rest upon analysis, our present views on this subject would be purely speculative, did they not so strikingly and wonderfully coincide with those in other departments of nature, into which we can prosecute minute research, and attain logical demonstration. Besides, by supposing that there are *five* principal variations in man, each equally important with the other, we entirely destroy the beautiful analogy between these variations and the sacred writings. But without entering farther upon this question, it will be sufficient for our present purpose to repeat, that, in regard to man, the views of Blumenbach and Cuvier are virtually the same; for if, with the former, we reckon five, there will be two groups more conspicuously typical of perfection, and three others, which, however distinct in many respects, possess several characters in common. If, on the other hand, we follow Cuvier and Pritchard, and restrict the number to three, we have the Caucasian and the Mongolian as the two principal groups, while there is a third, typically represented indeed by the Ethiopian, but still so diversified as to admit of a threefold division, into the American, the African, and the Malay varieties.

That the variation of man has been regulated by similar laws to those which have been traced throughout nature, is a conclusion supported by strong and presumptive evidence; drawn both from the sacred writings, and from inferences in zoological science, which no one has ventured to dispute. In establishing this point, I have studiously confined myself to such facts, connected with the physical history of man, as rest on high and indisputable authority. On a subject so vast and intricate, illustrated by the united labours of the most acute philosophers now living, little that is new could be said, and that little might have been suspected of being brought forward to favour a particular theory. In the preceding sketch of the principal differences in man, we have, therefore, merely condensed the observations and facts detailed in the writings of Blumenbach, Cuvier, Pritchard, Lawrence, and Sumner; rather wishing, that, whatever inferences are drawn from such sources, the facts themselves should rest on testimonies of so much weight.

The order in which these races are here placed leads us to other considerations. Blumenbach is of opinion that the American form is intermediate between the Caucasian and Mongolian; but we have failed to discover any assigned reason for such a disposition, which also seems at variance with the progression of developement. The geographical situation of the two continents, as we have before observed, renders it highly probable that the American variety is more immediately connected with the Mongolian; and the simple fact, that the Esquimaux have been by some considered as of Asiatic origin, while by others they are thought to exhibit more of the American type, is, perhaps, the strongest proof of their intimate relationship to both. Neither does the American race exhibit any direct affinity to the Caucasian; while, on the contrary, both their physical structure and mental developement seem to place them in close approximation to the Africans. For these and subsequent reasons, we have felt no hesitation in adopting the series intimated in the *Règne Animal.* We must now advert to another peculiarity in this arrangement, which renders its similitude to the zoological series still more remarkable. This is the progressive series of affinities, resulting from placing the five leading varieties in the order in which they have been here noticed. The Caucasian and the Mongolian races present the highest degree of civilization, although in very different degrees when compared with each other: the regions they respectively inhabit, in like manner, approximate so closely as not to be divided by water. Yet the configuration of these races is so remarkable, that they cannot be mistaken or confounded. In the third race, comprehending the American, the Malay, and the Ethiopian, very marked deviations from the typical endowments of the two former are manifest. This inferiority is first shown in the American, whose outward form and moral capacity is nevertheless superior to the African. Yet, as nature in the animal kingdom is ever prone to retrace her steps, and to return again to her original type; so we observe that, after exhibiting, in some of the African hordes, the lowest debasement of the human form, and the least capacity for mental improvement, she begins, as Blumenbach observes, in the diversified races of the Malay variety, to show a progressive but a very marked inclination to return through them to the Caucasian type. So strong, indeed, does this appear in many tribes of the South Sea Islanders, not only in the beauty of their forms, but in the advance they are continually making towards intellectual improvement, that every voyager, who has visited their shores, concurs in likening them to Europeans.

The inferences to be drawn from this circular disposition are important, if merely considered in relation to those systems, which, by presupposing a lineal scale in creation, would place the negro in immediate contact with the monkey. Now, without laying any stress upon that primary characteristic of man, a reasoning, thinking, and immaterial soul, of which the body is but a temporary receptacle, we must, before we consent to this hypothesis, get over difficulties which appear insurmountable. That the Ethiopian holds the lowest station among the varieties of his species, is fully granted; but that this admission implies an affinity to the ape, does by no means follow. There may be an approximation: but it is necessary, before we decide on the *degree* of such approximation, that we should examine the relative affinity which the Ethiopian bears to the Caucasian. For if it should appear that the difference between the most perfect and the most imperfect of the human races is unquestionably less than between the latter and the brutes; or, in other words, that the similarities between the negro and the Caucasian are decidedly greater than those between the negro and the ape; we must admit that this latter approximation is too slight to be termed an affinity. If, on the other hand, we consider man only as a material being, he stands so far removed from brutes—the interval between him and them is so great—that it would be a violation of natural affinities, and certainly an insult on his better nature, to class him in the same system. To arrive at a just conclusion on this subject, we must not look so much to any *one* point of comparison, or to mere anatomical analogies, but bring the distinguishing characters of each into direct comparison. Does the negro, it may then be asked, evince a deficiency of those qualities which belong to the Caucasians? we allude not to the natural affections, for these are, in some degree, common to brutes; but in self-privation, compassion, and heroic love of their country. Are they incapable of learning European arts, or of inventing others suitable to their wants or habits? To deny them such qualities would be preposterous; they possess the germs of others infinitely higher, which, under favourable circumstances, have produced expert artisans, skilful physicians, pious divines, and pleasing poets. "I protest especially," observes Mr. Lawrence, "against the opinion which either denies to the Africans the enjoyment of reason, or ascribes to the whole race propensities which would degrade them even below the level of the brute. It can be proved most clearly, that there is no circumstance of bodily structure so peculiar to the negro, as not to be found also in other far distant nations; no character which does not run into those of other races, by as insensible gradations as those which connect together all the varieties of mankind." (p. 428.) To pursue this comparison farther is needless; and to ask whether the least indication of such powers has ever been manifested by the quadrumanous animals would be ridiculous. The learned and eloquent Bishop Sumner forcibly observes, "There is nothing philosophical in the comparison of a being possessed of improvable reason with one that is governed by natural instinct, because there is no just affinity between the talents which are compared." (*Records of Creation*, vol. i. p. 23.) We consider this argument as conclusive. To class man, therefore, in the same zoological division with apes, merely because both have a hyoid bone, is, to our apprehension, as glaring a violation of natural affinities as to arrange bats with birds, because both fly in the air, and possess a crest to their sternum. So far, indeed, from considering man as the type of a zoological order of brutes, we cannot allow that he even belongs to the same system in which they are arranged. It may be, that the deviations of his structure are regulated by those laws which govern the universe; yet, nevertheless, by his nobler qualities (which in fact are his true distinctions) he belongs to a higher order of beings: that he is, in short, a link between matter and spirit; that he carries this evidence, through revelation, within himself; and will hereafter be most assuredly rewarded or punished, according as he suffers his spiritual or his earthly nature to preponderate.

### Sect. IV.—*On the Geographic Distribution of Animals.*

The geographic distribution of animals over the globe, is the next subject of inquiry. In the general outline of the variations in man which has been given above, we have deemed it more important to seek after general results than to enter upon minute details. Our attention has been fixed, not so much on those ramifications which shoot out near the extremities of every branch, and become too indistinct for clear elucidation, but rather to the leading branches themselves, on the nature of which there has been little diversity of opinion.

In the inquiry regarding the geographic distribution of animals, on which we now enter, the same mode will be adopted, but with this difference, that whereas we have hitherto drawn our inferences solely from the facts and general opinions of others, we shall now put aside all theories heretofore promulgated on the distribution of animals, and merely depend on simple facts for the support of those inferences which they may appear to sanction. We shall first briefly notice those principles which have been applied to elucidate the phenomena of animal distribution, and then inquire how far they appear conducive to that end.

That climate, temperature, soil, and food, exercise a paramount influence on the distribution of animals, has been generally believed; and on this assumption naturalists have divided the world into climates, zones, or provinces regulated by degrees of longitude or latitude. Such has been the favourite theory not only of physiologists, but of professed naturalists, whose knowledge of details might have furnished them with insuperable objections against such views. Thus, the celebrated entomologist Fabricius conceived that the insect world could be naturally divided into eight climates: one of which is made to comprehend all those mountains, in every part of the world, whose summits are covered by eternal snow. It is, therefore, not surprising that M. Latreille should consider such a theory as altogether vague in some respects, and arbitrary in others. But will not the latter objection be equally applicable to the distribution which this eminent naturalist has himself proposed for this part of the creation? At least, such is the opinion of one fully competent to judge the question. "A chart of animal geography," says Mr. Kirby, "which is divided into climates of 24° of longitude and 12° of latitude, wears upon its face the stamp of an artificial and arbitrary system, rather than of one according with nature." On much the same principles another theory has been built, by which the earth is divided into seven zoological provinces, or zones, mainly dependent on the respective degrees of latitude they occupy. Now, so far as regards one of these provinces—that comprehended within the arctic circle—this view of the subject, at first sight, appears perfectly just: for there is not only a strong analogy between the groups of animals inhabiting such parts of the two continents as enter into this circle, but there is also an absolute affinity between them; inasmuch as the arctic regions contain not only genera, but numerous species, common to both continents. This theory, however, loses all its force when applied to such divisions as are made to include the tropical regions of Africa, America, and Asia, in one province, and the southern extremities of America and Africa in another. The zoologist immediately perceives that the only relation which these countries bear to each other in their animal productions, is purely analogical; and we are thus compelled to relinquish a theory which appears correct only in one point of view. These and other less eminent writers appear to have erred in the very foundation of their methods. They assume as granted, what has never yet been proved, that temperature exercises a primary influence on animal distribution. Were such the case, it would naturally follow that the animals of such parts of America, Africa, and Asia, as are placed in corresponding degrees of latitude, would be nearly of similar species; or, at least, of the same natural genera. Yet such, as we shall hereafter show, is not the fact. Between the animals of these regions there is, indeed, in very many instances, a strong analogy: such, for instance, as is apparent between the *Trochilidæ* of the New World, the *Cinnyridæ* of Asia and Africa, and the *Melliphagidæ* of the Australian islands. Such, again, is that between the Toucans of America (*fig.* 75. *a*), and the hornbills of Asia (*fig.* 75. *b*). Yet not one species of these birds occur in any two of these countries. Nevertheless it cannot be denied, that the temperature and configuration of a country exercises a powerful influence on the distribution of animals. But these effects are of a secondary nature, and totally fail when employed to elucidate those general principles which appear to regulate the whole system of animal geography. Such agencies, however, may be safely allowed to possess much weight, when we descend to details and investigate the local Fauna of any particular country or district. It has been observed by the celebrated Humboldt, and confirmed by an authority of nearly equal weight, that, with regard to certain tribes of insects, their geographical distribution does not appear to depend solely on the degree of heat or humidity to which they are exposed, or on the particular situation they inhabit; "but rather on local circumstances, that are difficult to characterise." This opinion is in unison with the whole tenor of the facts to which we shall hereafter advert. We must, therefore, agree with Mr. Kirby, and consider that the distribution, not only of insects, but of animals in general, is "fixed by the will of the Creator, rather than certainly regulated by any isothermal lines." (*Introduction to Entomology*, vol. iv. p. 484.)

75

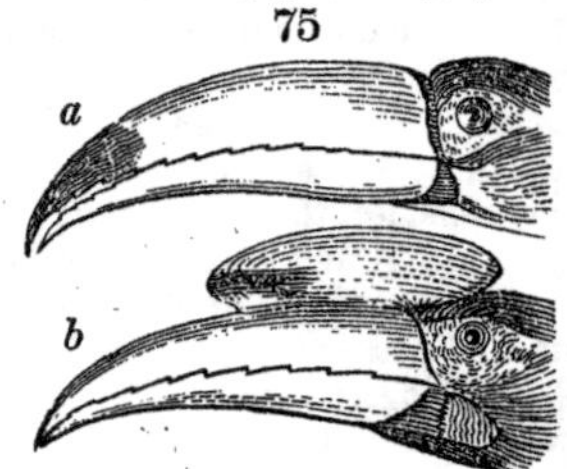


The distribution of animals, in connexion with that of the human race, remains to be considered. From what has been already stated, there appears strong reason to believe, that the variations in the structure of man and of animals are regulated by similar laws; and this supposition will receive considerable weight, should it appear, upon investigation, that those divisions of our globe which have been apportioned to the different varieties of man, are equally characterised by certain peculiarities in their animal tribes. Now, to establish the truth of such a theory, it is necessary to waive all general abstract reasoning, and to draw deductions from known facts. And it is equally obvious that, if such facts are to be collected from the whole animal kingdom, this essay must be extended to several volumes, even admitting that our materials were sufficiently extensive for such a purpose. But the truth is, that the data for such a comprehensive investigation are so few, so meagre, and so unsatisfactory when compared with the diversity and vastness of the subject, that they sink into insignificance. Nor will this appear surprising, if we consider the astonishing number of animals that have been already described by naturalists, or are known to exist in cabinets; setting aside the hosts of species yet unknown, which, in many departments, may possibly amount to double or treble the number we are acquainted with. Yet, as details of some sort must be gone into, it becomes absolutely necessary to select for such a purpose some one department of nature; and the result which might follow, we may fairly presume, would be in unison with those that would attend the investigation of other divisions of the animal world, could they be investigated upon the same principles. Nature, in all her operations, is uniform: and it cannot be supposed that the distribution of quadrupeds, birds, insects, or reptiles, would each be regulated by different laws.

In choosing, therefore, from the animal kingdom some one order of beings for particular investigation, it might be thought that the distribution of quadrupeds would present the best field of inquiry. It possibly might, did not their investigation involve certain points of controversy connected with geology, which, however important, are not so intimately connected with our present object as to render their discussion necessary in this place. The division of reptiles is subject to the same objection, and is not sufficiently extensive for our purpose. The annulose animals, on the other hand, are so numerous that they appear to baffle our inquiries; nor can we hope, while yet in the infancy of geographic natural history, to do more than has been already done by the genius of Latreille. Birds alone remain. It has, indeed, been argued, that no very certain results can attend the study of their distribution; because, from possessing the powers of locomotion, and the instinct of migration, in a high degree, they appear more widely dispersed than any other class of animals. How far this may be true has never, indeed, been made apparent; yet, allowing the assertion its full weight, we may safely conclude, that if, under these disadvantages, any definite notions of geographic distribution can be gathered from the study of such volatile beings, the results would be materially strengthened if found to harmonize with what is already known on the distribution of other orders of animals, which, from their physical construction, are less capable of extending their geographic range. It is here, however, necessary to premise, that in this, as in all other branches of natural history, the accounts and relations of travellers, not in themselves zoologists, must be received with great caution. Unacquainted with those nice distinctions upon which not only the differences of species, but of genera and families, are now known to depend, they perpetually contradict, by a hasty application of well-known names, some of the most acknowledged truths in animal geography. Nor can the facts detailed in the compilations of more scientific writers be always depended upon. The voluminous works of a most industrious and zealous ornithologist of the Linnæan school abound with mistakes of this nature; wherein not only species but genera are said to inhabit countries where they have never been found except in the vague and erroneous narrative of travellers. It is the misfortune of those who complain against the multiplicity, and regret the adoption, of modern divisions, that by so doing they debar themselves from studying the variations of physical structure, and neglect the main clue to enlarged conceptions of zoological science. It is necessary to make these allusions, that the reader may be apprised of our adoption, in this place, of the principal modern genera; and our rejection of many of the localities erroneously given to certain species in the general histories of birds.

### 1. *The Caucasian or European Province.*

The ornithological features of the Caucasian range, or of the regions over which the Caucasian variety of the human species is said to be distributed, will first claim our attention. It has been already shown that this range comprises such portion of Africa as lies north of the Great Desert, nearly the whole of Europe, and a considerable extent of Western Asia. The ornithology of the countries bordering upon this region has been but partially investigated; yet sufficient is known to show that it presents a mixture of those species which have their chief metropolis in other countries. It has been thought that the animals of the arctic circle are so peculiar, as to justify us in considering that region in the light of a distinct zoological province. The objections against this idea have already been alluded to; and they become more forcible when we discover, that on calculating the number of birds, both terrestrial and aquatic, which occur within the arctic circle, they do not amount to more than twenty-two; and that most of these, during the greatest portion of the year, are found in the more northern parts of Britain and America. They probably occur in similar latitudes on the Asiatic continent; but on this point our information is defective.

The swimming birds are known to possess a very wide range; but this is less extensive, perhaps, than is generally imagined. The number of species found on the shores of Europe and Northern Africa, independently of those more peculiar to the arctic circle, is sixty. Of these, two alone have been discovered in the four quarters of the globe; three are common to Europe, Asia, and America; one to Europe, Asia, and Southern Africa; and twenty-seven to Europe and Northern America: thus leaving twenty-seven (or nearly one-half the number of European natatorial species) as peculiar to this zoological division of the world.

Among the Grallatores, or waders, some particular species are so widely dispersed as to suggest the idea that the geographic range of this order is even wider than that of the *Natatores;* and this, generally speaking, may be true. Of the sixty-five species described as natives of Europe, thirteen only occur in America, and two only can be reckoned arctic birds, although several others occasionally frequent those regions. Of the remainder, four occur in Asia; two in Asia and Africa; four in Asia and America; seven in Asia, Africa, and America; and the Whimbrel (*fig.* 76.) (*Numenius Phœpus*) is said to be the same in all the five divisions of the globe. It is consequently among the wading birds that we find those whose range is most extensive; yet, on a general calculation, the number of species peculiar to Europe is considerably greater than those of the *Natatores;* the former being as one to two, the latter nearly as one to four. It thus appears, that, even among birds of the most vagrant habits, the ornithology of Europe is characterised by a decided superiority in the number of its own peculiar species.

76

The Whimbrel.

The rapacious birds, next to the aquatic orders, are thought to be the most widely distributed; particularly the nocturnal species. It is very remarkable, that out of thirteen different owls inhabiting Europe, five only are peculiar to this continent; and two of these more particularly frequent the arctic regions. Of the rest, five occur in America, two in Southern Africa, and one both in Asia and America. The *Falconidæ*, or diurnal birds of prey, in regard to their species, have a more restricted distribution; yet, of these, the eagles enjoy no inconsiderable range. Out of eight discovered in Europe, one is more properly arctic, three have been found in several parts of Africa, and one occurs in America; leaving three only to Europe. It is singular that those rapacious birds which, from the peculiar structure of their wings, have been supposed to enjoy the greatest powers of flight among their congeners, are those most restricted in their geographic limits. This is proved by the fact, that out of eight genuine falcons occurring in Europe and Northern Africa, two only have been discovered in America. It has, however, recently been stated that the Falco peregrinus of Australia is identically the same as that of Europe: neither does Southern Africa, we believe, possess a single European species, or not one of those inhabiting the northern extremity of that peninsula; the *Montagnard* of Le Vaillant, long confounded with the European Kestril, being a decidedly distinct species. Upon the whole, the distribution of the forty-four species of European *Raptores* will stand thus: three are Arctic, eleven are found also in America, two in Asia and Africa, and one in Asia and America; leaving twenty-seven, or more than one-half, peculiar to European ornithology.

77

The Great Bustard.

The Gallinaceous genera are few; and their wide dispersion is decidedly against the theory, that all birds with heavy bodies and short wings are more limited in their geographic range than other terrestrial tribes. This argument has been ingeniously used to account for the very restricted limits within which many of the Indian parrots have been found; one or two species being frequently confined to a particular island. Ornithologists, however, need not be told that the wings of the *Psittacidæ* are peculiarly adapted for strong and vigorous flight; and those who have seen these birds in their native regions cannot fail to have remarked that their flight is *peculiarly rapid;* many genera, in this respect, passing through the air with the celerity of the hawk. The wide dispersion of the *Gallinaceous* order is very evident. The range of the great bustard (*fig.* 77.) extends from one extremity of temperate Europe to the confines of Asia; and the quail, remarkable for its heavy body and short wings, performs two annual migrations, from and to Northern Africa, over Europe and Western Asia. We consider very few of the European Gallinaceous birds as truly arctic; for nearly all the species appear to occur as plentifully beyond those regions as within them. Many of the meridional European birds, as Upupa Epops, Oriolus galbula, Coraceas garrulus, &c., might with equal justice be classed as peculiarly characteristic of Central or Southern Africa. It nevertheless appears that, even among the Gallinaceæ, fourteen out of twenty-seven have their principal seat in Europe. The remainder are thus apportioned: five extend to Western Asia, five to the confines of the great African desert, two are dispersed in Central Asia and Africa, while two only occur in North America.

78

European Kingfisher.

The Fissirostral birds, typically represented by the swallow, are, of all the insectivorous tribes, most conspicuous for their powers of flight. With but one exception, the European Kingfisher (*Alcedo europæa, fig.* 78), they are all migratory: hence we find that most of the species occur beyond the limits of the European Fauna. The proportion of those which appear confined to Europe and Northern Africa is as one to three.

The small Granivorous birds not only present a great diversity in their species, but a considerable preponderance in their numerical amount. Forty-one are included in the European list; two of which, at certain seasons, frequent the polar regions in great numbers, but are nevertheless abundant in all the northern latitudes; seven inhabit North America, and three extend both to Asia and Africa; so that Europe may be considered the metropolis of nearly thirty peculiar species.

The Scansorial birds are few; yet eight out of the fifteen recorded as European are unknown in other regions. It is among the *Insectivorous* and soft-billed birds that we must look for the principal ornithological features of any particular region. The immense family of Humming-birds in the New World, and of Melliphagidæ, or Honey-suckers, in the Australian islands, would alone be sufficient to mark these regions with a distinct zoological character. To what cause we are to attribute the fact that these birds, by no means deficient in the power of flight (which, indeed, in many of them is considerably developed,) should nevertheless be so strictly confined within certain geographic limits, remains unexplained. We can only in this place illustrate the fact. Of eighty-five species belonging to the Linnæan genera of Turdus, Sylvia, Parus, and Muscicapa, eighty-two are strictly European. In this number we of course include those which migrate, at certain seasons, to Northern Africa and Western Asia; for these regions, it must be always remembered, come within the zoological province we are now treating of; yet, if we deduct the number of those which have actually been detected in parts *beyond* the shores of the Mediterranean on one side, and Western Asia on the other, they will amount only to ten; leaving seventy-two as a marked peculiarity in the ornithology of Europe. In further proof of the limited range of these families, it may be remarked, that three only out of eighty-five have been detected in

America; and that the identity of one of these (Parus atricapillus *L.*) with an European species (Parus palustris *L.*) is very questionable.

The Omnivorous birds, as the Sturnidæ, Corvidæ, &c., are the last requiring notice. A few of these appear widely dispersed; but upon the whole, several species, and even peculiar genera, are left to characterise this portion of the world. We may state their number at twenty-one: thirteen of which, or more than one half, habitually reside in Europe; four occur in Northern and Central Africa; one (Pastor roseus T.) inhabits both the table-land of Asia and the deserts of Central Africa; and three have been found in America.

These details, tedious perhaps to the general reader, but interesting to the man of science, it becomes necessary to dwell upon, before any valid deductions can be drawn from the facts they exhibit. In this difficult and somewhat laborious investigation we have been much assisted by the writings of Wilson, Temminck, and Le Vaillant; but more than all by the liberality which throws the magnificent collections of the French Museum open to the use of all scientific inquirers, whatever their object or their nation may be.* It cannot, however, be supposed that, even with greater sources of information, some inaccuracies may not have occurred. Such calculations, in short, from their very nature, can never be perfect; because they are founded upon present knowledge, and *that* is perpetually extending. The most that can be done is to make as near an approximation to the truth as circumstances will admit; and having done this, the result may be entitled to some degree of confidence.

As a general recapitulation of the European birds, we may state the total number, exclusive of a few which occasionally appear at remote intervals as stragglers, at 388. Of these, thirty-one are more peculiar to the arctic regions of Europe, America, and probably of Asia; the proportion being as one to thirteen. Sixty-eight (forty being aquatic) occur also in temperate America; nine are dispersed over four divisions of the globe, to neither of which can they be particularly appropriated; and either one (Numenius Phœpus) or two extend to Australia. With these deductions, the number will thus be reduced to about 280. If from these we abstract such others as may *possibly* have a partial range beyond the limits already defined, the number may be further reduced to about 250; so that, even with this allowance, nearly two thirds of the birds of Europe, Northern Africa, and Western Asia may safely be considered as zoologically characteristic of those countries.

Another character in European ornithology deserves attention. This regards the superior number of generic types which it exhibits, in proportion to the number of species. These genera amount to 108, omitting those which have not been generally adopted, or which, from the modifications of form being but slight, should more properly be termed sections. The proportion which these genera bear to the number of species (estimated before at 388) amounts to more than two to seven; or, in other words, does not give seven birds to two genera. It is further remarkable, that most of these exhibit in their structure the *greatest perfection* of those orders or families to which they respectively belong; and which groups are denominated by naturalists *typical.* True it is that such genera are widely dispersed; but in no division of the world do they appear so numerous, in proportion to the species, as in Europe. This remark not only applies to the typical genera, but is frequently applicable to the number of species they respectively contain. One instance may suffice. The noble falcons, or those to whom the generic name of Falco is now restricted, are generally considered the most typical group of their family: of these, the Kestril (*fig.* 79.) and five others have their metropolis in Europe and Northern Africa. The whole of North America has hitherto produced but four. Le Vaillant enumerates the same number from Southern and Central Africa. Those of Central Asia are not known; but only two have been recently described as peculiar to the vast regions of Australia. Now, if we merely look at these respective numbers, the difference does not appear very remarkable; but when the great inferiority between the Caucasian regions and those of America, Africa, and Australia, *in point of extent*, is taken into the account, it will be immediately seen that the proportion of these eminently typical species in the European regions is particularly great. Among the typical groups of the wading and swimming birds this is still more apparent; so that, if we endeavour to define what is the most striking feature in the ornithology of this zoological province, none is so remarkable as the number of purely typical groups. This peculiarity will be more apparent on looking further into the matter. The total number of birds throughout the world, existing in museums or clearly described in authentic works, may be estimated at 6000. These have been arranged under about 380 genera; but as several of these genera will comprise more than one sub-genus, we will put down 400 as a nearer approximation to

79
The Kestril.

* We have been *officially* informed that, by the laws of the Zoological Society of London, no one can receive permission to make use of their Museum, for general scientific purposes, who is not a member.

correctness: this would leave rather more than fourteen species to each generic group while, if the ornithology of Europe and Northern Africa is alone considered, the proportion is no more than one to three; and even this will be further diminished when those geographic groups among the *Fringillidæ* and *Sylvaidæ*, which are decidedly peculiar to this portion of the globe, are investigated and defined. Now, it is very singular that, in speaking of the leading varieties of the Caucasian race, a writer, whose testimony is no mean authority, observes, "that the tribes among the Caucasians are more numerous than in any other." And again—"Whether we consider the *several nations* or the individuals in each, bodily differences are much more numerous in the highly civilized Caucasian variety than in either of the other divisions of mankind." (*Lawrence*, p. 442. 475.) When we glance over the list of those nations generally supposed to have sprung from this type, we are struck with the justice of these observations. It is the more remarkable, as the regions they occupy are disproportionably small, when compared with those peopled by the Mongolian and Ethiopian races. That there are instances wherein typical forms of higher groups than genera do *not* occur within the European range, is a circumstance which will not materially affect the question. Thus the only European bird belonging to the *Tenuirostres* of M. Cuvier is the European Hoopoe (*Upupa Epops*), which is certainly not a typical example; but this, so far as tribes are concerned, is the only exception to the rule. It is curious, also, that this exception should occur in that division which comprises the smallest and weakest of birds. If we descend to families, there is scarcely one *pre-eminently typical* of its own perfection which is not European. A further objection may possibly be urged, that, although such forms are indeed abundant in this Fauna, they are nevertheless found in nearly every other part of the world; and cannot, therefore, be looked upon as characterising Europe more than any other country: but this will not be a just conclusion, unless it is first shown that the proportion of such types to the total number of European species is not decidedly greater than in any other region. Now the facts we have already stated prove this beyond doubt.

These results, obtained from unquestionable data, are so important to our present inquiry, that their hasty notice would not have been sufficient. The materials for illustrating the ornithology of Europe are naturally more numerous than can be expected for other portions of the globe; and it became very desirable to ascertain how far the ornithology of those regions, occupied by the Caucasian race, presented a peculiarity of character sufficiently strong to show a mutual relationship with the geographic distribution of this variety of man. We are, I think, sufficiently authorised to consider that both are in unison. At least, there are so many singular points of analogy, as to render it highly probable that there exists an intimate relationship between the distribution of one race of mankind and one of the principal geographic divisions of birds.

How far this view of European ornithology would be borne out by an extended investigation of other orders of animals, it is impossible to say. Yet even if our present limits would permit the inquiry, we should have to rely more upon theory than facts. Many of the quadrupeds of Europe have long been slowly but certainly disappearing, in proportion as culture and civilization have advanced; and any conclusions drawn from those which still remain in a wild state would be open to great objections, particularly as the question must necessarily embrace the nature of those no longer existing, but whose bones occur in a fossil state throughout Europe. We think it may fairly be presumed that, in all those convulsions which have agitated our globe, birds have suffered less than any other vertebrated animals. Their fossil remains are few, and of rare occurrence; while extensive deposits of bones and skeletons, belonging to quadrupeds, reptiles, and fish, occur more or less abundantly in almost every region, and attest the wide destruction to which such animals were exposed. It naturally follows that, in tracing the distribution of the feathered creation, we are left unshackled by geological controversy.

The few observations on the Ichthyology, Entomology, and Conchology of the Mediterranean we shall hereafter make, in conjunction with those of Britain, will be found in unison with those features in the geographic distribution of birds we have already traced; and will equally evince the propriety of including the whole under one zoological division. This we propose to name the ***European***. Such a designation is, indeed, somewhat objectionable, inasmuch as it embraces not only Europe, but Northern Africa and Western Asia; yet it will, perhaps, convey more definite ideas than if the name were adopted from the particular race of men belonging to these regions.

### 2. *The Mongolian or Asiatic Province.*

The birds of the Mongolian range will be now adverted to. The typical nations of this variety of man occupy the remaining portion of the vast continent of Asia; while their characteristic peculiarities appear blended with the Malays in the more eastern islands of the Indian Archipelago. The ornithology of such a vast proportion of Asia is as varied as it is remarkable; but the very imperfect nature of the materials hitherto furnished for its elucidation, renders it impossible for us to give those satisfactory data which have beer furnished by writers on the birds of Europe. Naturalists look forward with the greatest interest to the speedy termination of the zoological researches of General Hardwicke, as likely to supply these deficiencies. The vast stores of knowledge which a long residence in the East, and an ardent passion for natural history, have placed at the command of this naturalist, render him peculiarly qualified for such an undertaking.

For our present purpose, minute detail is not, however, essential. Whatever doubts might at first have arisen on the propriety of considering Europe as the centre of an ornithological province, there can be none with respect to Asia. It is in these regions that the chief sea of the typical Gallinaceæ is placed; they abound in China, Thibet, the Indian Peninsula and even extend to those islands which are considered the confines of the Mongolian race. The larger species, arranged in the genera *Pavo* and *Polyplectron*, appear to characterise the more elevated and central parts of the continent; while those of the genus *Gallus* are more numerous in Sumatra, Java, and the adjacent islands. The pheasants of China and Thibet form a no less striking feature in Asiatic ornithology; five species of magnificent plumage are peculiar: one of these, the elegant Silver Pheasant (*Nycthemerus argentatus*) (*fig.* 80.) has been long domesticated in our aviaries. Three other superb species represent a group (*Lophophorus* Tem.), discovered only upon the continent. The whole of these Gallinaceous genera are totally unknown in Africa, Australia, or in the New World. When to these we add the Hornbills (*Buceridæ*), the Sun-birds (*Cinnyridæ*), the short-legged Thrushes (G. *Brachypus*), the short-tailed Thrushes (*Pittæ*), certain groups among the *Psittacidæ*, and many others totally unknown in Europe, Northern Africa, and Western Asia, yet abounding in the Mongolian nations, no further details appear necessary to mark the ornithological peculiarities of Asia, as distinct from those of Europe.

80

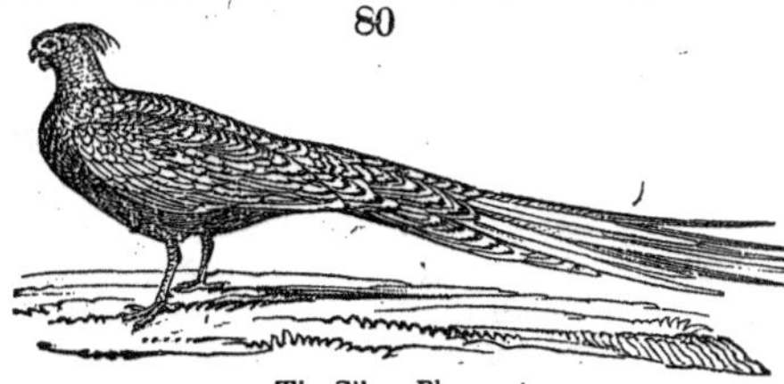

The Silver Pheasant.

From the Asiatic islands it would, perhaps, be more natural if we proceeded at once to notice the Malay or Australian range, as it is here that the Faunas of these divisions of the globe evidently meet. But as this would interfere with the order observed in the early portion of this essay, we shall pass from the northern regions of Asia to those of the New World; particularly as both present a mixed race of men, probably originating from the Asiatic continent.

### 3. *The American Province.*

We proceed to a rapid sketch of American ornithology. It has already been shown that, excepting the Natatorial birds, there are fewer species common alike to Northern America and to Europe than might, perhaps, have been supposed; yet, were the proportion much greater, the circumstance would only prove that nature knows no abrupt distinction. It is not to the remote ramifications which she employs to connect her chain of operations that our attention is to be fixed; for they are too subtile to be unravelled by beings with faculties so limited. But as soon as she quits these inexplicable mazes, and again displays herself in a new but decided form, we may hope to gain some acquaintance with her laws. It is not, therefore, from either extremity of the New World that we must form our opinion on its zoological peculiarities. The ornithology of the Northern latitudes is evidently blended with that of Europe, and in all probability many of these species exist in Northern Asia; those of the more southern parts of America, beyond the Rio de la Plata and Paraguay, are nearly unknown. It is only within the last few years that the provinces, elevated on the Mexican Cordilleras, and now constituting a great republic, have been opened to the naturalist; and although, as yet, but superficially explored, there is perhaps no region in the New World which promises to yield more interesting facts, as connected with the animal geography of that hemisphere. Even the configuration of the continent, at the junction of its two great divisions, is typical of this distribution. It appears as if nature, elevated as on a throne upon this vast table-land, 7200 feet above the level of the sea, had dispensed her forms to the right hand and to the left, retaining immediately around her a typical representation of every group. To the north she has given innumerable flocks of slender-billed insectivorous birds (*Sylvicolæ*, &c.), which annually depart to breed in those more temperate climes. These are accompanied by particular species of Flycatchers, Thrushes, Pigeons and Hangnests (*Icterina*); the two latter in such countless numbers as to darken the air. To Southern America has been more particularly assigned the Macaws, Toucans, Scansorial Creepers (*Dendrocolaptes*), Ant Thrushes (*Myotherina*), Ground Doves (*Chamæpelia*), Tanagers (*Tanagra*), Trogons, Fruit-eaters (*Ampelidæ*), and the numerous and splendid race of Humming-birds. Yet of all these groups, save one (*Ampelidæ*), typical examples are concentrated on the table-land of Mexico. These, moreover, are accompanied by some peculiar forms, not yet discovered in either portion of America, and by species among the natatorial tribes hitherto found only in the more northern latitudes.

The typical Gallinaceous birds begin to show themselves adjoining the equator, nearly in the same parallel of latitude as they occur in Asia: they belong, however to distinct and peculiar types; as the genera Meleagris, Crax, Penelope, Ourax, Phosphea, Ortalida, and Opisthocomus. These find their representatives, for the most part, in the ancient continents, but not one species has been detected beyond the New World. The foregoing remark applies to the two great divisions of the *Simiæ*, or Monkeys, so accurately illustrated by those distinguished naturalists, MM. Cuvier and Geoffroy St. Hilaire.

81

Humming Bird.

The Melliphagous groups of America, at the head of which shine the splendid family of Humming-birds (*fig.* 81.), form the chief peculiarity of its ornithology; other races, scarcely less beautiful, occur in Africa, Asia, and Australia: yet the natural genera are totally distinct. The number of species, and the variety of forms, among the frugivorous birds is another striking feature in the productions of the New World. Under this term we must include the richly coloured Chatterers (*Ampelidæ* Sw.) and Manakins (*Piprinæ* Sw.); together with the whole family of Tanagers (*Tanagrinæ*), Hangnests (*Icterinæ*), and Parrots (*Psittacidæ*). The first four belong solely to this continent, which more than any other abounds in vast forests of lofty trees, affording a perpetual and countless variety of fruits and berries, adapted to nourish all the families of hard and soft-billed frugivorous birds. If we turn to the other orders of vertebrated animals, the *Mollusca*, *Annulosæ*, or *Radiatæ*, each and all conspire to stamp certain peculiar features on the zoology of the New World, and to mark it as a distinct zoological empire.

### 4. *The Ethiopian or African Province.*

The chief seat of the Ethiopian variety of our species is central Africa; while most writers agree in thinking that its northern limits do not pass the Great Desert. The pestilential atmosphere of tropical Africa has been an insuperable bar to the researches of Europeans; and all the ideas that can be formed on the zoology of such regions must be gathered from the partial gleanings made by travellers on the shores of Senegal and of Sierra Leone. The ornithological productions received from these districts evince a total dissimilarity from those of Northern Africa, but intimately accord, both in species and genera, with the ornithology of the south: to this, however, there are several exceptions. The Plantain-eaters (*Musophagidæ*), and the bristle-necked Thrushes (*Trichophorus* Tem.), are among the groups hitherto found only towards Sierra Leone. The Guinea Fowl, as its name implies, is most abundant in the interior of that country, where three species have been discovered. The common Bee-eater, and the Golden Oriole are the only species among the land birds of Western Africa that occur in the European range; and these extend southward to the Cape of Good Hope. The whole extent of Africa south of the desert exhibits, in short, a marked difference in its ornithological groups and species from those belonging to Europe, Northern Africa, and Western Asia. The comparatively few exceptions of birds common to Europe and the Cape cannot diminish the general force of this remark, but merely shows that a few exceptions must never be taken as the groundwork of any particular theory. It is to one of the greatest ornithologists that France, or indeed any other nation, has produced, that we are indebted for the most perfect account of South African ornithology yet published; but it must ever be regretted that this portion of M. le Vaillant's labours terminated abruptly; leaving the Gallinaceous, Wading, and Swimming orders to be completed by some other, who, with equal enterprise and observation, should visit the same regions, and record their manners with the same veracity.

Between the ornithology of Africa and of America there is, within the same parallels of latitude, a very strong analogy, although (in the sense in which we apply the term) there is none of affinity. We know not, in short, a single perching bird common to both continents; although in the rapacious order, which among terrestrial birds are well known to have nearly the widest range, two or three species occur which likewise inhabit both extremities of Africa no less than North America.

The other vertebrated animals, and the insects of Southern Africa, furnish similar results. On examining the large collection of insects formed by Mr. Burchell, in the territories of the Cape of Good Hope, we could not discover one out of many hundreds which was to be found in a much more considerable collection brought by us from South America, although many generic groups, particularly among the Lepidoptera, appeared common to both continents.

Between the faunas of Africa and America the difference is unquestionably striking; yet there are several points of connexion between the ornithology of Africa, Asia, and Australia; and these appear not merely in generic groups, but even in species. The Drongo Shrikes (G. *Edolius*), the Larva-eaters (G. *Ceblepyris*), the typical Fly-catchers (G. *Muscipeta*, C.), the Crab-eaters (G. *Halcyon*), the Grakles (*Lamprotonis*), the African Saxicolæ, the two groups of tropical Finches (*Estrelda Amadina* Sw.), are all genera common to these three regions,—to neither of which, in a geographic division, can they be exclusively assigned. But we need not dwell further on such resemblances, which, after all, are but sc many points of connexion between geographic divisions, sufficiently distinct in their more prominent characters.

### 5. *The Malay or Australian Province.*

The regions peopled by the Malay tribes is the last zoological division requiring elucidation. We have already adverted to the great diversity of tribes comprised under this variety of the human race, and the little authentic information yet collected concerning their origin or history. The zoological results, however, are more definite.

On looking to the Indian Archipelago, as to that region where physiologists concur in thinking that the Malayan form is first apparent, we are told that several of these islands are peopled by two different races of men (*Lawrence*, p. 489. and *Cuvier*, p. 187.); the one frequently confined to the inland tracts, while the other people the maritime districts: their respective origins, however, are so little known, that it is still a matter of doubt which has usurped the territories of the other. (*Marsden's Sumatra*, 326, 327.) We confine these remarks to Sumatra and Java; for with regard to the vast islands of Borneo, Celebes, and those smaller groups to the eastward, we know little or nothing of their productions or of their people.

That the isthmus of Malacca and the adjacent islands exhibit the first indications of a peculiar race of people, is a fact upon which all writers appear to agree; and that we here begin to discern the indications of a new zoölogical region is equally certain: yet it would be altogether rash, with our present limited information, to hazard any theory which would respectively assign to these islands a definite character in its inhabitants or productions. But the zoology of Java and Sumatra have been of late so zealously and ably investigated not only by two distinguished British naturalists,* but by others† sent from France, that we shall in this place attempt to draw some results from their labours. The ornithology of these islands, with some few peculiarities, differs in no very decided manner from that of southern India. In both, the Gallinaceous genera, when they occur, are the same, although some of the Javanese species differ. Of the more typical *Sturnidæ*, common to the Old World, but as yet unknown to the Australian or Oceanic islands, no less than three inhabit Java. To these groups must be added, *Parus, Sitta, Bucco, Cursorius, Clareola, Buceros, Oriolus, Brachypus*, and many other genera characteristic of the ancient continents. The number of typical Scansorial birds within the narrow limits of these two islands is truly remarkable. Eight species of *Picus* are described by Dr. Horsfield, and four or five others; one, the Malacolophus Concretus, *Sw.* (*fig.* 82.), of a remarkably small size, have been sent to France by M. Diard. The total absence of this family throughout the whole Australian range, is a circumstance in itself sufficiently strong to place the ornithology of Java and Sumatra beyond such limits; to which, nevertheless, it approximates very closely.

82

Malacolophus Concretus.

The birds of Java and Sumatra, which indicate an approximation to the Australian province belong to certain genera common to both regions; but unknown in Africa or India: these are, *Pitta, Centropus, Ocypterus, Prinea, Pogardus, Crateropus, Dacelo*, &c. In the Suctorial birds (the *Tenuirostres* of M. Cuvier,) we find in Java an evident departure from the typical form of *Cinnyris* towards the *Melliphagida* of Australia, in the genus *Dicæum;* four of the known species being Javanese, and three Australian. What little is yet known of the birds of New Guinea, and its surrounding islands, exhibits a still greater deviation from the ornithological features of India. These enchanting regions, long the fairy-land of naturalists, remained nearly unknown until visited by learned Frenchmen, to one of whom has been assigned the distinguished honour of giving to the world the fruits of their scientific and important discoveries.‡ It is in these islands that the Melliphagous genera begin to be developed in the most novel forms, and the most sumptuous plumage. The grand *Promerops* of New Guinea can only be likened to the Australian *Ptiloris*. Several *typical Melliphagidæ* are in M. Lesson's collections. To these we can now add two species of genuine *Philedons* (Cuvier), and two of the genus *Vanga*. The group of which the *Muscicapa carinata* (Sw.)§ is the type, displays itself in three new and beautiful birds, accurately described and figured by M. Lesson. The stay of the French naturalists on the coast of New Guinea was comparatively short, and their gleanings of its ornithology could not, from necessity, be otherwise than scanty; yet it is surprising that, among the birds thus procured, so large a proportion should belong to groups hitherto supposed peculiar to New Holland. It is clear, therefore, in a natural arrangement of ornithological geography, that the islands of New Guinea may be safely brought into that division which includes New Holland, New Zealand, and their dependencies: this distribu-

* Sir Stamford Raffles and Dr. Horsfield. † MM. A. Duvaucel and Diard.

‡ M. Lesson, Voyage autour du Monde. § Zoological Illustrations, vol. iii. pl. 147. Zool. Journ. i. p. 306.

tion has, indeed, been generally adopted by geographers, merely from the relative positions of these islands.

On the zoology of New Holland it is scarcely necessary, in this place, to expatiate. All naturalists concur in viewing this insular continent as the chief metropolis of a peculiar creation of animals; whose limits on one side we have already traced, and whose range on the other extends over the innumerable islands scattered in the great Pacific Ocean. The Menura Superba (*fig.* 83.) is the most remarkable gallinaceous bird of this range. The Australian province is thus in full accordance with the distribution assigned to the Malay variety of our species: its connexion with Asiatic zoology is unquestionable; but we have no means of judging into which of the three remaining divisions it blends, at its opposite extremity. Of the birds peculiar to those remote clusters of islands adjoining the north-west coast of America we are completely ignorant; nor are our materials sufficient to furnish even a plausible conjecture on the subject. Whether the Australian province, at its northern limits, unites again with the Asiatic, the American, or the European, must therefore be left to future discovery.

83

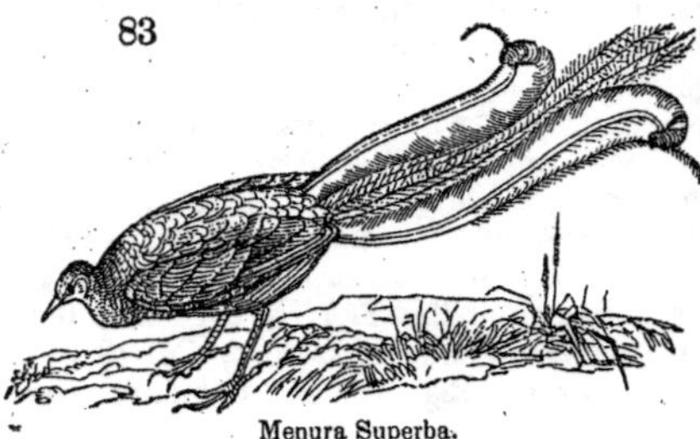

Menura Superba.

We have now completed a general survey of the distribution of birds over the globe. The facts we have stated show the propriety of arranging the whole under five great divisions or provinces, which may be distinguished as the European, the Asiatic, the American, the African, and the Australian: each of these corresponds, with little variation, to the geographic distribution assigned by authors to the different races of man. We must, therefore, now adopt one out of the two following conclusions: either that there is just and sufficient ground for believing that the distribution of man and animals in general has been regulated by the same laws; or, that man and birds have been distributed alike, and all other animals differently. To us, at least, the latter conclusion appears highly improbable; not only as being unsupported by the least shadow of evidence, but as opposed to that harmony in creation, which is more apparent the more it is viewed in all its relations.

### SECT. V.—*General Summary of the Subject.*

In offering these elucidations of a subject so vast in itself, and so important in all its bearings, it will be readily perceived that two different relations between animal groups are alluded to; one we have considered as of affinity, the other of analogy; and as the truth or fallacy of these views will mainly depend on the justness of these distinctions, a few observations upon them appear necessary. Naturalists, in general, have considered those resemblances which exist between certain groups placed in different regions, but in the same parallels of latitude, as indicating affinities; and on this supposition, as before stated, have framed theories by which animal geography has been divided into zones or provinces, limited more or less by certain degrees of latitude. It must be confessed that, upon a superficial view, there are many circumstances which appear to justify such a theory. Confining our attention to that department of nature which we have throughout selected, we shall partly recapitulate our former observations.

The arctic regions, in one sense, may be considered an ornithological zone; for not only the same groups, but the same species are found in such parts of Europe, America, and probably Asia, as enter within its limits. But admitting this to the full extent, let us ask if these regions—by the number, variety, and peculiarity of their animals, are entitled to hold a primary rank with the great geographic groups already mentioned? Is there to be met with among the arctic birds numerous species which are not distributed far beyond such limits? Are there any generic or sub-generic groups which do not occur even towards the central parts of Europe, Asia, and America? These questions which must be answered in the negative, sufficiently prove that the arctic regions do not possess the characteristics of a primary division; they must rather be looked upon as a point of junction, where the ornithology of the three northern continents blends and harmonizes together.

The tropical regions of the Old and the New Worlds have likewise been united in one province. How widely the ornithology of these countries really differs, has been already explained. True it is, that in numerous instances one group typifies another, as in the case of the American Humming-birds (*Trochilidæ*) being represented in the Old World by the Sun-birds (*Cinnyridæ*); and such relationship, in one sense, is certainly an affinity, inasmuch as in the natural system they appear to follow one another; but if we admit such a degree of affinity to be a sufficient guide to a distribution of birds, we must also do the same with regard to the varieties of man, since both appear dispersed upon the same plan. The red Indian of America as certainly represents the black negro of Africa as the latter does the sooty inhabitant of New Guinea; yet no one would think of classing them in the same race, merely because they inhabited countries under similar degrees of latitude. The dispersion of particular groups and of their species, upon the whole, is more in a longitudinal than in a latitudinal direction. This is exemplified in a remarkable manner by the migratory birds, which invariably proceed from north to south, or from south to north. It would, indeed, appear, that if animal distribution is to be regulated by geographic degrees, as accurate notions might result from making the divisions of longitude as of latitude: both, however, would be clearly artificial.

These parallel relations of analogy, which everywhere present themselves in the animal kingdom, nevertheless deserve our greatest attention, as fraught with peculiar interest to the reflecting mind. There are throughout nature so many immediate and remote relations, so many unexplained ties of connexion, that the most careful of her students are perpetually misled in attempting to trace her footsteps. In ordinary cases, the admirable distinction, that has been drawn between affinity and analogy (*Hor. Ent.*) is, perhaps, the best that can be given; yet instances might be named, in which even this is totally inadequate to the end proposed. Natural relations are so complicated, that series of affinities apparently incontestable, will frequently, upon rigid analysis, turn out completely erroneous; proving no more than that nature, however diversified, presents so many points of general resemblance and of connexion, that *partial* harmony will result even from a false combination of parts. Let us not therefore conclude, as is now too generally done, that by synthesis alone we can exhibit the true affinities of nature; that we may henceforward, without hesitation, assign to each of her productions its true station in the scale of being; that we have suddenly, and as if by magic, got full possession of that mighty secret which at once explains her laws, and expounds all that has perplexed the wise and confounded the learned, since science first dawned upon man. That the circular system is the nearest approach yet made to the *true* disposition which pervades nature,—a system which, from the perfections of its Creator, must be replete with order and beauty surpassing our utmost comprehension,—is indisputable, because none other has attempted to explain the relations of parts and the unity of the whole; but farther than this its pretensions must not be carried: it still involves questions of great weight, since by one theory the number of its primary divisions is stated to be *five*, while by another, founded on much more extensive analysis, it is maintained to be *three*. The searcher after truth will give to these his patient investigation, his cool and unprejudiced judgment: he may then hope to make one step nearer to truth; for science, in all ages, has ever remained most stationary when the advocates of any system have been most prejudiced.

It is with these qualifications that the views here taken on the distribution of man and animals are given to the reader. It has been our desire to trace a connexion, and a unity of plan, in both, and to simplify a subject hitherto involved in much intricacy. How far this object may have been attained, it is not for us to determine; but he who draws proofs of a Divine Creator from the harmony and design apparent in his works, has surely not written in vain.

---

## CHAPTER III.

### GEOGRAPHY CONSIDERED IN ITS RELATION TO MAN IN SOCIETY.

Man, when considered not as a mere animal, but as a being endowed with thought, reason, and contrivance, capable of social intercourse and union, must be regarded as the most conspicuous object in the delineation of the globe. These attributes raise him to the first rank in this lower world; and in every region occupied and improved by him, the communities which he has formed become the most prominent characteristic; all other beings are there subordinate and subservient to him. The description therefore which, in the succeeding part of the work, will be given of the different regions of the globe, must be chiefly employed in delineating the aspects which man, as an active and social being, presents. At present, however, it would be premature to enter into the numerous details which this subject embraces. We can do little more than indicate the following general heads, under which it will be treated:—1. Historical Geography. 2. Political Constitution of the different countries. 3. Productive Industry. 4. Civil and Social State of Man. 5. Languages.

### Sect. I.—*Historical Geography.*

A survey of the history of man is necessary for enabling us accurately to understand, and duly to estimate his present condition. Not only inanimate nature, but even the animal and vegetable kingdoms, if left to themselves, would remain constantly in the same situation: the changes and modifications undergone by them have been produced entirely by man's interposition. That improved and civilized form under which he now appears, is the result of a continued succession of changes, which have been taking place from the earliest periods of authentic history. All the revolutions, both of ancient and modern times, have had a greater or less influence in producing the present moral, political, and social condition of man in the more improved quarters of the globe.

### SUBSECT. 1.—*Ancient History.*

Ancient history is generally considered as comprehending the period which elapsed from the earliest authentic records, and particularly from the rise of the great monarchies, to the downfall of the Roman empire. The various forms which government and society assumed during that long period, though they were instrumental in preparing those which have existed in the modern world, did not bear any exact resemblance to them. Through the conquest of Rome by the barbarous nations, with which the first of these eras closed, almost every connexion between them was cut off, except those of record and tradition.

The rise of the great monarchies, Egypt, Assyria, and Babylon, constitutes the first grand epoch in ancient history. It nearly coincides with that of the great commercial republics, Tyre and Carthage. Human society, which had before existed in a very rude and imperfect shape, began to assume a regular, orderly, and even splendid character. All the arts which contribute to man's support and accommodation were carried to a considerable degree of improvement; and the foundation was laid of those intellectual attainments, which were to constitute his highest honour. Alphabetic writing was invented and widely diffused; the arts of painting, sculpture, and architecture, made a considerable progress; there were even formed some elements of science and philosophy. During this period, too, while the world generally was buried in the darkest superstition, a divine revelation, preparatory for another more perfect, having been first communicated to the patriarchs, was more formally disclosed to the legislator of the Jewish nation.

The Persian empire embraced a wider extent of the globe than any that had previously existed, and comprehended those countries which had been most remarkable as the seats of improvement and civilization. Although, however, it thus became instrumental in linking distant nations together, it bore chiefly the character of empty and barbarous pomp, and does not appear to have produced any material advance in knowledge and improvement.

The rise of the Grecian States formed, perhaps, the proudest era in the history of the human race. The constitutions then formed afforded a degree of political liberty, and a developement of the higher energies of the human mind, which could not be attained in extensive empires, subjected to the arbitrary rule of a single individual. The military exploits of the Grecian people, by which they baffled the force of almost the whole known world united under the sway of Persia, were the most splendid that had hitherto illustrated the annals of mankind. Genius was exerted with nearly unrivalled power in every department; the historic page unfolded its utmost degree of energy and beauty; and many sublime lessons of morality were taught by the Grecian sages. The fine arts, poetry, painting, and architecture, reached an eminence which they have scarcely since regained, and in each the purest models were left for future imitation. After Greece had long maintained a glorious defensive war against Persia, her arms were directed to conquest. The reign and triumphs of Alexander, while they subverted her admired forms of civil polity, diffused her language, her arts, her knowledge, over a wide extent of the eastern world, and thus spread a circle of civilization, the traces of which have never been wholly obliterated.

The dominion of Rome, which succeeded and overpowered that of Greece, extended over a still greater variety of countries and people, than had been comprehended under any former empire. Her character, at first stern and austere, was gradually softened; and on arriving at her highest pinnacle of wealth and power, she made at the same time an unrivalled display of the pomp and refinement of polished life. She emulated, without fully equalling, what was most brilliant in the arts and intellectual attainments of Greece. But the most signal service which Rome rendered to the cause of civilization, was by extending its empire over wide regions in northern and western Europe, which had previously been the seat of almost complete barbarism; though they now form the most enlightened and improved portion of the globe.

### SUBSECT. 2.—*Modern History.*

The downfall of the Roman Empire, which marked the commencement of modern history, formed one of the most remarkable and disastrous eras in the destiny of the world. During the fourth and fifth centuries, a succession of barbarous hordes from Germany, Scandinavia, Russia, and even the remotest extremities of northern Asia, poured in upon civilized Europe, and exterminated or reduced to bondage the greater part of its people. All the arts and sciences, which had shed such a lustre on the Greek and Roman name, disappeared, leaving only some imperfect remnants, which were preserved in the depth of monasteries. The empire was partitioned into a number of disorderly little kingdoms, gradually merged into a few great monarchies, which, in their general outline, have continued to the present day. This era was also distinguished, in the East, by the introduction of the religion of Mohammed, and the rise of the Saracen power, which undertook, by force of arms, to diffuse that religion over the world. Its armed votaries overran a great part of Asia, Africa, and even of Europe, and continue still to maintain a powerful influence over the destinies of the human species. For some time, the states formed under this system pre sented a somewhat enlightened aspect, and even revived the expiring lamp of science; but the final issue of Moslem ascendency has been, to diffuse through the world, ignorance, despotism, barbarism, and every principle hostile to human improvement.

The feudal system was established gradually among the barbarous states formed out of the dismembered portions of the Roman empire. The king, or chief, distributed the territory among his nobles or followers, subject only to the condition of military service. These nobles, possessing almost uncontrolled jurisdiction within their own limits, holding at their disposal the services of numerous vassals, took advantage of every interval of weakness in the reign of the sovereign, and rendered his power little more than nominal. They reduced the body of the people to a state of comparative slavery, waged numerous private wars with each other, and practised various robberies and extortions. During this turbulent era, all refined arts and pursuits languished, while, on the basis of ignorance, superstition erected an absolute and tyrannical dominion. The institutions of chivalry, however, which were then formed and gradually improved, introduced a sense of honour, and a dignity and refinement of manners, which have beneficially influenced modern society. This period was also marked by the piratical inroads of the Scandinavians or Northmen, who ravaged all the coasts of Europe, and obtained at least a temporary possession of considerable districts and even kingdoms. It was marked, lastly, by those memorable expeditions into the East, called the crusades, which, though attended with great extravagance, and occasioning much disaster and bloodshed, tended, on the whole, towards the improvement of European policy and social life.

The subversion of the feudal power, accompanied by the revival of knowledge, arts, and industry, formed a most memorable era in the history of mankind. This change, which had been for several ages silently preparing, was carried into complete effect during the fifteenth and sixteenth centuries. The turbulent rule of the great nobles was then broken down, and was succeeded by several extensive but mildly administered monarchies, along with some free and commercial republics, and in one instance a limited constitutional monarchy. The reformation of religion eminently distinguished this period; but being opposed by the violent intolerance of the Catholic church, it gave rise to a series of dreadful and sanguinary struggles. A general activity prevailed throughout the whole sphere of human exertion. The revival of learning, the invention of printing, the extension of maritime enterprise, leading to the discovery of new regions, and of new routes to those formerly known, rendered the age peculiarly eventful and interesting. It derived, however, a somewhat disastrous character from the establishment of the Turkish empire in the East, by which the throne of the Greek emperors at Constantinople was finally subverted, and very serious alarms spread through the whole body of the European nations.

The modern system of polity followed, as the result of the great changes which had taken place in the preceding period. During the seventeenth and eighteenth centuries, when it prevailed, civilization made very remarkable advances. The manners of social life became more polished and refined. The arts and sciences were carried nearer to perfection, and more widely diffused through the great body of mankind. Amicable relations, before unknown, were established between the different nations of Europe; fixed laws were agreed upon for regulating their intercourse; and war, when it did occur, was carried on with greatly diminished ferocity. The system of colonization in the other quarters of the globe was also carried to a vast extent, particularly in America; and though its first establishment was attended with many circumstances of injustice and tyranny, it had the effect of bringing those quarters of the world into a more improved and civilized condition.

The era of political revolution, which commenced towards the end of the eighteenth century, being that which is still in progress, cannot be characterised in so decided a manner. The formation of the great monarchies had delivered Europe from the turbulent sway of the feudal chieftains; yet the almost absolute power with which the sovereign was then invested, was found productive of many evils. The hereditary nobles, exchanging their rural seats for a residence in the great capitals, and indulging in ease and luxury, lost all influence over the body of the people. The diffusion of intelligence and wealth through the middling and, in some degree, even the lower ranks, was followed by a demand, on their part, to be admitted to some share in the administration of public affairs. This spirit, after fermenting for some time, and being diffused by the exertions of many distinguished writers, produced the French revolution, and the extraordinary series of events which have thence arisen. That great crisis did not merely agitate the interior of France, but by exposing it to foreign interference, and then impelling its own rulers to schemes of conquest, it changed for some time, in an extraordinary manner, the aspect of all Europe. Then, however, by a grand re-action, France was driven back within her original boundaries, and the political relations of the Continent were re-established nearly on their former footing. Considerable agitations, however, still prevail in the interior of different kingdoms, and their political constitutions have suffered, and are likely to suffer, material alterations.

SECT. II.—*Political Constitution.*

The political constitution under which any community subsists, forms a most important element in its social condition. Being usually established within certain local boundaries, and accompanied with a similarity in manners, religion, and other characteristic circumstances, it is the leading agent in constituting a country or state. In distributing, therefore, the four quarters of the globe into their smaller portions, the geographer uses chiefly political divisions. He finds states which have made any progress in civilization arranged into kingdoms, empires, and republics. The elements of political power appear to consist of monarchy, aristocracy, and democracy; while the public functions, to be exercised within any state, are the executive, legislative, and judicial.

A kingdom is a state of considerable though not vast extent, governed by a single person, as France, Spain, Prussia. The subjects are usually united by a similarity of language and manners, and pervaded by a national spirit. The power of the sovereign is commonly extensive, though controlled in some instances by national assemblies; and there is almost always a body of nobles possessed of high privileges and immunities.

An empire generally consists of a number of detached kingdoms, which have been united by conquest under one head, as the Turkish, Persian, and Chinese. Being thus formed of an aggregation of different states, empires are usually of very great extent; and as military force has been the instrument of their combination, the sovereigns exercise almost always an unlimited authority. The different members having been brought into union by force only, rarely feel united by any national tie, and remain very dissimilar in manners, religion, and social institutions.

Republics consist of states which own the supremacy of no king or sovereign, but are governed by a senate, an assembly of the people, or by both conjoined. Though these governments have acted a conspicuous part in the history of the world, they have been generally of small extent, consisting, in many instances, of not more than a single city, with a limited circle of territory. Where this form of government has been diffused over a great surface of country, it has consisted usually of a number of states, joined in a federal union. This is remarkably the case with the United States of America, where such a government has been introduced on a scale of greater magnitude than in any other quarter of the globe.

Monarchy, among the elements which compose the political system, holds the most conspicuous place, and is the most generally prevalent. In some cases, the power of the monarch is wholly or very nearly absolute. In a majority of instances, however, it is more or less controlled by the influence of certain powerful and privileged bodies. In some constitutions the power of the monarch is combined with that of aristocratic and popular bodies, which share with the sovereign all the higher functions of government. These are called limited monarchies, and are well adapted for the preservation of a great people in a state of peace and prosperity. This form of government, after being for a long time confined to Britain, is now spreading, though with some difficulty and confusion, over the rest of Europe.

Aristocracy, or the power vested in a distinguished and privileged class, is found existing much less frequently as a distinct and decided form of government, than as an element combined with monarchy and democracy. Venice, perhaps, afforded almost the only example in which aristocracy subsisted for a series of ages pure and unmixed. In monarchies, the aristocracy consists of a body of nobility, possessing various gradations of personal and hereditary titles and rights; while in a republic it is formed into a deliberative body, or senate, exercising or sharing the powers of the state. In mixed monarchies, both these privileges are usually held by the nobles.

Democracy is the name given to the government in which the sovereignty resides in the great body of the citizens. They exercise it, either in a general assembly of the whole nation, or by means of persons elected, during a certain period, to act for the body of their constituents. The former was the mode usual among the ancient republics; the latter is more prevalent in modern times, and is alone compatible with the great extent of territory occupied by the leading republics of the present day. Popular government has been very generally combined in a greater or less degree with aristocracy, though there seldom fails to be an almost incessant opposition between the two parties.

The legislative, among the different functions of the body politic, is justly considered supreme; it establishes the laws and regulations, according to which all public affairs are to be administered, and to which the persons exercising the other functions are bound to conform. Countries in which the legislative as well as the executive power is exercised by one man, form absolute monarchies, where every thing depends upon the arbitrary will of that single individual. A purely aristocratic legislature is commonly felt to be severe and oppressive by the great body of the people. A government cannot be considered as free, unless the various classes of which the nation is composed have a voice in legislative arrangements. Those political systems, however, in which the laws are enacted by the whole body of the assembled people, are fitted only for a single city with a territory of limited extent. Of such a nature and scale were the ancient republics of Greece, and also that of Rome, during the earlier periods of her history. But when the whole of a great people are convened into one place, they form a mere tumultuary crowd, incapable of any regular or effectual exercise of legislative functions. This disadvantage has, among modern nations, been studiously remedied by the representative system, under which the inhabitants of each different district elect an individual understood to possess their confidence, who exercises in their stead the legislative function. Upon this basis have been founded those constitutions that have been considered as exhibiting the most perfect forms of civil polity.

The judicial power provides for the security of person and property among all ranks of individuals composing the political body, and forms thus one of the arrangements most essential to general prosperity and well-being. The institutions for this purpose vary greatly in different nations and stages of society. Among very rude tribes, the individual has only his own strength and that of his kindred to aid in repelling aggression. As society advances, the administration of justice between man and man becomes a leading object of public concern. In the earlier forms of polity, however, the executive and legislative functions are usually blended; the monarch, or his deputy, sits on the tribunal of judgment, and the forms of procedure are exceedingly simple. The parties appear, and plead their cause *vivâ voce;* while the judge decides promptly and on the spot. In the further progress of improvement, it is discovered that this branch of public economy cannot be duly executed, without being entirely separated from the legislative and judicial departments, and made independent of them. Hence arise the different orders, judges, lawyers, and agents, by whom the different stages of procedure are conducted; written and voluminous codes of law are formed, with the view of providing for every particular case. Yet the expense and delay consequent upon these complicated arrangements sometimes cause the society to look back with regret on the simple and expeditious machinery employed by their rude ancestors.

Other important particulars are comprehended in the political state of a society:—the *titles of nobility*, and the badges of honour and distinction among individuals; the *military and naval force* employed in the defence of a country; the *elements* which compose it; and the manner in which these are arranged and directed. The same subject embraces also the *revenue*, its amount, the sources whence it is derived, and the manner in which it is levied and expended.

### SECT. III.—*Productive Industry.*

The industry of a nation is employed in producing the necessaries, the conveniences, the ornaments, and the luxuries of life—all that is comprehended under the name of *wealth*. It forms thus one of the most important constituents of their prosperity and well-being.

The sources of national wealth are usually divided into three; agriculture, manufactures, and commerce: each of these is divisible into several distinct branches, nor can the catalogue be completed without including the two occupations of mining and fishing.

Agriculture, including the means of procuring every part of the produce of land, or what land bears on its surface, is unquestionably the grand source of human subsistence and accommodation. Hence chiefly are derived the materials used in manufacture; the objects, in the exchange of which commerce consists. The modes in which support and the means of enjoyment are obtained from land may be divided into three; hunting, pasturage, and tillage, which last being the only form in which labour is employed upon the ground itself, is more specially considered as agriculture. The collection of the spontaneous fruits of the earth, being confined to a few tribes in the lowest stage of improvement, scarcely requires to be taken into consideration.

Hunting, or the chase of wild animals, to obtain their flesh as food, and their skins as raiment, is the earliest and rudest mode of procuring human support. This employment requires art and contrivance as well as bold adventure; but is usually accompanied with rude and turbulent habits, and, combined with them, constitutes what is called the savage state. As culture advances, and the greater proportion of the soil is devoted to the plough, or to the support of tame animals, its range is greatly limited, and in a high state of cultivation becomes little more than the amusement of the opulent. The chase of the fur-bearing animals, however, still affords one of the most valuable materials of commerce.

Pasturage, or the deriving of subsistence from herds and flocks, tamed and trained so as to be subservient to the use of man, forms a more improved and comfortable occupation than hunting. Peculiar habits of life usually distinguish nations subsisting solely by pasturage. They are often destitute of any fixed abodes, moving from place to place in large bands or encampments, living within their tents in patriarchal simplicity, but towards other nations practising on a great scale war and robbery. These habits constitute what is called the barbarous state, still prevalent among the Arabs, Tartars, and other nations occupying an extensive portion of the earth's surface.

Tillage, or the culture of the soil by the processes of ploughing or sowing, is employed, by all the more improved nations, as the most efficacious means of drawing subsistence from the earth. In proportion to the general improvement which any people have attained, is usually the skill and diligence with which this most important art is practised. The community which derives its chief subsistence from the culture of the soil, merits generally, to a great extent, the character of civilized. Some of the oriental people, as the Hindoo and Chinese, practise this important art with an indefatigable industry applied to every available portion of their soil, which is scarcely to be paralleled elsewhere; but in Europe, and especially in Britain, the use of machinery, the skilful rotation of crops, and various improved processes, render the same measure of industry much more productive. The objects of culture vary exceedingly, and for the most part according to the varieties of soil and climate. Grain, the main staff of human subsistence, forms everywhere the most extensive and important object of tillage. Climate chiefly determines the grain cultivated in any particular region. In the tropical countries it is rice; in the best part of the temperate zone, wheat and barley; in the colder tracts, oats and rye. Of luxuries, wine and oil are the most grateful, and in the most general demand; they have their almost exclusive growth in the warmer tracts of the temperate zone. The delicate fruits, from which they are produced, do not flourish in the excessively luxuriant soil of the tropics. There, however, the fragrant aromatic plants, and those filled with rich and saccharine juices, produce valuable substances, which are eagerly sought after by the natives of less genial climates.

Fishery, by which subsistence and wealth are derived from the waters, forms a peculiar branch of industry, which flourishes in every stage of society. Even the rudest savages, wherever their situation admits, conjoin it with hunting, as a means of affording an immediate supply to their wants. They practise it often with a great degree of diligence and contrivance; but the progress of industry leads to various processes for extending and improving this branch. By the operations of salting and drying, fish is rendered fit to be conveyed as merchandise to the most distant countries. Some of the great maritime nations send large fleets into remote seas, where they find situations favourable to this pursuit. The whale, the cod, and the herring fisheries have, in this manner, been raised to the rank of great national concerns.

Mining, or the extraction of valuable substances from beneath the surface of the earth, can be extensively practised only in a somewhat advanced state of human industry. Yet nature has lodged in these dark repositories objects the most essentially conducive to the use and comfort of man, and others which afford his most brilliant ornaments. Here are found the bright and attractive metals of gold and silver; there the solidly useful ores of iron and copper; here glitter the diamond, the ruby, and the amethyst; there extend vast beds of coal, lime, and freestone. Gold, the most precious of the metals, is often the most easily accessible; but we can scarcely give the name of mining to the operation by which the savage merely collects its grains in the sands of the rivers, or even extracts it by pounding, when mechanically combined with other substances. But metals, in general, when lodged in the bowels of the earth, exist in the form of ore, intimately and even chemically united with other materials, from which they can be separated only by smelting, refining, and other elaborate and even scientific processes. From the toilsome nature of these operations, and from the gloomy depths in which they are conducted, it is often difficult to procure a supply of workmen; hence slaves and individuals condemned for crimes have been employed to a later period in this than in most other species of labour. Whatever skill may be employed in mining, it is necessarily a local occupation, nature having irregularly and almost capriciously distributed its objects over the different regions of the globe. Even the experiments made to discover whether metals are lodged in any particular spot, are often attended with considerable cost, and even peril.

Manufactures may be regarded as a process by which man creates, as it were, a value for himself. He cannot, indeed, make any new substance; he can seldom even alter essentially the quality of that which is furnished to him; but he can altogether change its character and quality, can convert a rude and shapeless substance into one eminently conducive to benefit, convenience, or ornament. The excrescence shorn from an animal, the pod hanging from a shrub, objects in themselves neither useful nor beautiful, are converted into commodious and magnificent robes, adorned with the most brilliant tints. Almost every natural product requires to undergo some change before it is fitted for the use of civilized man. Grain must undergo the process of grinding and baking; the juice of the vine, that of fermentation; even animal food, that of cooking. But the name of manufacture is not given to these processes, nor to any which do not, to a material extent, increase the value of the substances on which they are employed. The various articles of clothing form the principal objects of manufacture; next to which rank stuffs for furniture, metallic implements, and utensils. Manufacturing skill and industry, carried to a certain extent, mark, beyond almost any other circumstance, the advance of a people in arts and civilization. The savage usually employs unaltered the substances with which nature furnishes him. He feeds on the flesh of the animals which he has killed in the chase; he clothes himself in their skins; he consumes in their crude state the roots and herbs which the earth spontaneously affords. Even the nations which subsist by pasturage, and have made, perhaps, a certain progress in agriculture, though they have usually acquired a desire for articles of fine manufacture, prefer to obtain them from more industrious neighbours, in exchange for their own rude produce. The eastern empires, for the consumption of their courts and great men, produce a few articles of exquisite fineness and beauty by mere manual labour, without any capital or any machinery at all costly or complicated. It is among European nations, that the two principles, the division of labour and large capital employed in the construction of the most ingenious machines, have enabled the manufacturer to produce fabrics which, for abundance, elegance, and cheapness, have surpassed those of every other age or nation, and have found their way into all the markets of the globe.

Commerce, the third grand source of national wealth, does not even aim at producing any new article, or altering the texture or quality of that in which it traffics. It merely conveys it from a place in which it is superabundant, to another in which it is wanted. This sometimes confers an exchangeable value on that which previously had none; in every case, where judiciously exercised, it very considerably enhances the value attached to the article which it conveys from one place to another.

The home and the foreign trade form the two great branches into which commerce is divided. The former, in consequence of each of its transactions being on a smaller scale, and affording little scope for brilliant adventure and splendid speculation, attracts, in general, less notice, and is considered of inferior political importance; yet it is proved by Smith to be by much the most extensive, as well as the most conducive to national prosperity. Its basis consists in the exchange between the country and the town, of the grain, cattle, and other raw produce of the one, for the varied commodities framed by the manufacturing industry of the other, or, in countries of great extent, of the raw or manufactured productions of one section for those of another. Home trade is either coasting or inland, the former, where practicable, being preferred for bulky commodities, or those to be conveyed between distant parts of a kingdom; much of the interior commerce also passes along rivers and canals. Foreign trade has no limits but those of the habitable globe; and, for reasons similar to those just hinted at in another case, the more distant branches are considered generally as the most brilliant and important; while, in fact, the trade with the countries most closely contiguous, from its quicker returns, ranks highest in real amount and value. Unfortunately, it has been hitherto much fettered by the jealousy and rivalry between neighbouring nations, which make each imagine the prosperity of another to be gained at its expense, and every commodity received from them, to be so much abstracted from its own wealth. Although this illiberal system has somewhat abated, yet the consequence still is, that intercourse with distant colonial possessions is more sure and steady than with any power entirely foreign. The extensive capitals now possessed by some European powers, especially Britain, enable them to carry on the most extensive commerce with countries situated at the greatest distance, and even at the opposite extremity of the globe. In the interior, also, of the great continents, there is a foreign trade by land, carried on by caravans, which are so numerous as to resemble armies, and proceed to an immense distance.

The instruments employed in conducting and facilitating commerce, and which are chiefly shipping, roads, and canals, form the most important part of what is called the fixed capital of a country. Under the head of roads, the invention of railways, though yet only in its infancy, promises to facilitate, in a remarkable manner, the interior communications of the countries in which it is employed.

### Sect. IV.—*Civil and Social Condition of Man.*

The population, or the number of individuals, of whom any community is composed, forms, if not the most important, at least the most prominent circumstance in its social condition, and one on which its magnitude, and its place in the scale of nations, intimately depend. The ancient statesmen considered the increase of the numbers of a people as one of the most important of national objects, with a view both to its prosperity in peace, and its strength in war. Some politicians of the present day take a different view of the subject, maintaining that population in all circumstances of tolerable peace and prosperity easily keeps itself on a level with the means of subsistence, has even a tendency to rise higher, and by its superabundance to produce a distressing degree of national poverty: they have suggested schemes for checking the progress of population.

The actual amount of the population in any particular period or country, has been involved in considerable uncertainty. It is only in modern Europe, and in the United States of North America, and there very recently, that general or careful enumerations have been made. But in all the other quarters of the globe, the estimates are formed upon very vague observation, founded on the density with which, on a superficial view, the districts appear to be peopled.

A national character is found to pervade every community. The particulars have been often exaggerated, fancifully delineated, and rashly and indiscriminately applied to individuals; but to a certain extent such a variation may be always traced between one people and another. The grand distinction, founded upon the progress of arts, letters, knowledge, and refinement, is into savage, barbarous, and civilized: the first being marked by the total absence of these improvements; the second, by the possession of them in only an imperfect and progressive degree; the third, by their having arrived at a certain maturity. The savage state prevails among the natives of America, and the islanders of the South Sea; the former, however, being now in a great measure supplanted by European colonists. The barbarous state is general throughout Africa, and extends over a great part of Asia. The civilized state is found in the great empires of Eastern Asia, and in a higher degree, as well as under different characters, among the nations of Europe, and their widely-spread colonies. In these last, too, civilization appears to continue in a progressive and advancing state, while over the rest of the world it is nearly stationary.

The religion professed by any people is a remarkable and most important feature in their social condition. Religious opinions do not come directly under the cognizance of the geographer; but he is called upon to mark this, as a particular in which nations strikingly differ from each other. The inhabitants of the earth may, in regard to religion, be divided into three great classes,—Christian, Mahomedan, and Pagan. The first, as to numerical amount, does not exceed the second, and still falls short of the third; but the nations professing it, have acquired such an ascendency in arts, social improvement, and political power, while their colonies have filled, and are multiplying over all the lately savage and unoccupied portions of the globe, that in all probability this faith will, in a few generations, be more widely diffused than any other. The Mahomedan nations, though in numbers they perhaps equal the last mentioned, and though they occupy a large proportion of the most fertile regions of the globe, are yet sunk into such a state of slavery and degradation, and so decidedly surpassed by the Christian people, that their sway is not likely to endure above two or three centuries. Of the Pagan religions, much the most numerous, and the only civilized, professors, are those attached to the kindred creeds of Brahma and Boodh, established, the one over the greater part of Hindostan; the other in China, and other continental kingdoms, and insular territories of Eastern Asia. From their peculiar habits, and the immutable nature of their institutions, they are likely to adhere to these systems with greater pertinacity than the votaries of superstition in Africa, the South Sea, and other quarters, where the train of belief and observance, however fantastic, is of a slighter and looser texture.

The progress of knowledge forms a most conspicuous chapter in the history of the human species: it follows generally that train of civilization which we have already delineated. In surveying different communities, various particulars connected with this subject are highly deserving of the attention of the geographer. Among these we may mention the most eminent philosophers, men of science, and authors who have flourished in any nation,—the institutions formed for the promotion and advancement of science,—the degree in which knowledge is diffused throughout the community,—the establishments formed for public and private education.

The fine arts,—which are intimately connected with the more elevated and intellectual part of man's nature, and of which the successful cultivation confers glory on a people, and polishes and improves their manners,—merit to be considered similarly, and under the same general heads, as their intellectual attainments.

There are various points of minor importance, which yet are distinctive and characteristic of a people, and excite thus a just and natural curiosity. Such are the amusements in which they chiefly delight, the peculiar costume in which they are attired, the species of food on which they subsist, and the liquor by which they are exhilarated, as well as the mode in which these articles are prepared for their use.

## SECT. V.—*The Languages of the World.*

On the subjects now enumerated, it has been judged sufficient to indicate their nature, and the light under which they will be treated, reserving the details for the succeeding part of the work, when they come to be considered successively in reference to the various regions of the globe. But there is one subject into which it will be expedient, even at the present stage, to enter more particularly.

Language is one of the strongest characteristics by which nations are distinguished from each other; at the same time the dialects spoken by different communities, even when most widely dissimilar, display in many cases relations and alliances indicative of a common origin. There exist over the world classes of languages, each of which comprehends the speech of numerous people, and forms a tie between them, marking early relations and connexions. Language thus acquires a character especially geographical, illustrating the origin and families of nations, and the connexions between different countries. It will then be advantageous to consider, in a large and comprehensive view, first, the languages spoken generally over the globe, and then those which prevail in its different quarters.

The languages by which the nations of the earth are distinguished, and from which are derived the *names*, not only of its principal features, natural and artificial, but of its different regions, and of the *places* contained in them, constitute an important department of geography. When we contemplate those names in maps, a little reflection suffices to convince us that most of them are to be regarded, not as mere arbitrary or fortuitous appellations, but as terms of definite meaning, or as significant memorials of the people by whom they were imposed; and, in tracing those of ancient origin through the mutations they have undergone, we are compelled to summon history to the aid of geography, for the purposes of explaining them with reference to the great events which have, from time to time, altered the political, civil, and social condition of the nations composing the great family of mankind. Thus, without adverting to the rise, growth, and extinction of kingdoms and empires in Asia, we may observe, that the series of revolutions which ended in the overthrow of the Roman empire, and the foundation of the existing system of Europe on its ruins, is in nothing more remarkable than in the change which it contributed to produce in the greater part of the world, through the migration of nations; a change so absolute, that it has served to mark the distinction between ancient and modern history, ancient and modern geography, and ancient and modern languages. Of this change the geographer, equally with the historian, is at every step of his investigations reminded. *France*, for instance, commemorates in her modern name that branch of the Germanic family of nations who prevailed in *Gaul;* yet she retains, not less in her topographical vocabulary than in her language generally, unequivocal traces of Roman dominion; and we recognise, though strangely curtailed, the imperial appellations *Augustodunum* and *Aureliana,* in *Autun* and *Orleans.* Italy and Spain, preserving a semblance of their ancient names, exhibit similar instances of disfigurement in those of particular places: *Forum Julii* and *Cæsar-Augusta* survive in *Friuli* and *Saragossa;* but the Trasimene suggests a less classic reminiscence as the lake of Perugia; nor can the Betis and the Durias be recognised under the more sonorous names, the Guadalquivir and the Guadalaviar (the *great river* and the *white river*), conferred on them by the Arab conquerors of Spain. Appellatives, also derived from languages little known, whether ancient or modern, are liable to mutilation from the varying orthography of travellers; and we can no longer wonder at the confusion caused by voyagers in this particular, when we call to mind the difference not only between foreign and vernacular names, but between their written and oral expression; as when a German spells his native country Deutschland, and pronounces it Teytshland; or a Persian writes for Persia *Irān*, and pronounces it *Eeraun.* But the different idioms of the human race claim our attention from far higher considerations than the mere naming of places or of countries; for geography, considered as an auxiliary to what has been emphatically called "the proper study of mankind," is principally valuable as combining, with a description of the earth, a view of the different branches of the great human family by whom such vast portions of it have been "replenished and subdued."

Ethnography is the term which has been employed to designate this branch of geographical science. It distinguishes nations by their languages, and professes to class them in kingdoms, families, genera, species, and varieties; but this systematic arrangement is as yet far from being completed. Of the numerous languages that are or have been spoken on the earth, many are so imperfectly known that it is difficult to determine to what family they belong. For this and other reasons it has been deemed expedient by a modern writer, who appears to have collated the labours of his predecessors on the subject,* to adopt a geographical arrangement, and consider languages in their relation to the five great divisions of the globe; the *Asiatic*, the *European*, the *African*, the *Oceanic*, and the *American.* It is obvious, however, that the ethnographical and geographical limits of a nation and its language may be widely different; the Spanish and the British, for instance, extend ethnographically to the remotest regions of both the Indies. Adopting this arrangement, not only as most convenient in regard to a branch of knowledge still in its infancy, but as most suitable to a *geographical* treatise, we shall proceed, without pausing to discuss the merits of any particular theory, to offer, in this and subsequent parts of the present work, such a succinct view of the known languages of mankind as its just proportions will allow.

The distribution of languages into Shemitic, Hamitic, and Japhetic, according to the scriptural account, seems however entitled to some notice, as being well warranted in relation to the early languages of the world, if we can reconcile our thoughts to an affinity of languages after their confusion, and the consequent dispersion of the human race. It has been placed in a striking point of view by the able author of the "History of Maritime and Inland Discovery," in Dr. Lardner's *Cabinet Cyclopædia;* and a brief sketch of his observations may be useful as an introduction to an account of languages more strictly geographical.

On reference to the sacred records, we find that in the order in which the generations of the sons of Noah are given, Japheth takes precedence of Ham and Shem, and is called the elder. This the learned writer we are now citing has not noticed; he has taken the names in the order which long and universal usage has sanctioned.

"The family of Shem," he observes, "comprised the pastoral nations which were spread over the plains between the Euphrates and the shores of the Mediterranean, from Ararat to Arabia. The Hebrews themselves were of this stock; and the resemblance of their *lan-*

* Balbi, Atlas Ethnographique du Globe. Paris, 1826.

*guage* with the Aramean, or ancient Syrian, and with Arabic, sufficiently proves the identity in race of what are called the *Shemitic* nations. There is no difficulty in assigning to each of the sons of Shem his proper situation. Elam founded the kingdom of Elymeis; Assur, that of Assyria; and Aram, the kingdom of Aramea or Syria, a name still clearly preserved in that of Armenia. From Arphaxad were descended the Hebrews themselves, and the various tribes of Arabia; and this close affinity of origin was always manifest in the *language* and in the intimate correspondence of the two nations. Some of the names given by Moses to the children of Shem are still used in Arabia as local designations: thus there is still in that country a district called Havilah; and Uzal, the name given to Sana by the sacred historian, is not quite extinct.

"The descendants of Ham," continues this learned writer, "constituted the most civilized and industrious nations of the Mosaic age. The sons of that patriarch were Cush, *Mizraim*, Phut, and Canaan. The name of *Ham* is identical with *Cham* or *Chamia*, by which Egypt has in all ages been called by its native inhabitants; and *Mizer* or *Mizraim* is the name by which the same country, or more probably the Delta, is still known by the Turks and Arabians." [We may add, that it is the name by which, in the original Hebrew, Egypt is called in the admonition that precedes the decalogue.] "The land of Phut appears to signify Libya in general; and the name Cush, though sometimes used vaguely, is obviously applied to the southern and eastern parts of Arabia. The names of Saba, Sabtah, Raamah, and Sheba, children of Cush, have long survived in the geography of Arabia. The posterity of Canaan rivalled the children of Mizraim in the early splendour of arts and cultivation. Though the Canaanites, properly speaking, and the Phœnicians, were separated from each other by Mount Carmel, yet, as the same spirit of industry animated both, they may in a general sense be considered as one people. The Phœnicians possessed the knowledge of the Egyptians, free from superstitious reluctance to venture upon the sea. Their local position naturally engaged them in commercial enterprise. Their chief cities, Tyre and Sidon, had reached the highest point of commercial opulence, when the first dawn of social polity was only commencing in Greece."

To Japheth, "the Japetus of the Greeks," this writer concurs with others in ascribing the superiority over the sons of Noah, if not in the number of his descendants, in the extent of their possessions. All the Indo-Teutonic nations, stretching without interruption from the extremity of Western Europe, through the peninsula of India, to the isle of Ceylon, he considers as belonging to this common ancestor. The Turkish nation also, occupying the elevated countries of central Asia, boasts the same descent. Their own traditions accord with the Mosaic history; and indeed the affinities of language, which are still evident among all the nations of the Japhethian family, fully confirm the relation of the sacred writer; yet the meaning assigned to the patriarch's name in the Sanscrit language, *Yapati*, "lord of the earth," tells for nothing unless we can suppose the name Japheth to be thence derived.

To Gomer, the eldest of Japheth's sons, is ascribed, on the authority of Josephus, the distinction of being ancestor of the Celts. Magog may have been the founder of some Scythian nation. Madai is recognised as the ancestor of the Medes. The posterity of Javan and Tubal, and Meshech and Tiras, may be traced from Ararat, always called Masis by its inhabitants, through Phrygia into Europe. Tubal and Meshech left their names to the Tibareni and Moschi, Armenian tribes, whose early emigrations appear to have extended into Mœsia. In like manner the Thracians may have owed their origin to Tiras.

That the progeny of Japheth peopled Europe, seems apparent on another ground, which we shall explain, after mentioning the remaining branches of his posterity. Ashkenaz, the son of Gomer, is thought to be that Ascanius whose name so frequently occurs in the ancient topography of Phrygia, and from whom, probably, the Euxine, at first the *Axine*, Sea derived its appellation. "In Togarmah," observes this writer, "we see the proper ancestor of the Armenian nation, and it is even asserted by the Turks."

"*Javan was the Ion of the Greeks, the father of the Ionians.* In the names of his sons we find fresh proofs of the consistency of the Mosaic history. In Elishah we see the origin of Ellis or Hellas. The name of Tarshish is supposed, with little foundation, to refer to Tarsus in Cilicia. Kittim is said to mean Cyprus; and Dodanim, or Rodanim, is understood to apply to the island Rhodes." Here we may remark, that the sacred text contains a most important record relative to the descendants of Japheth: "By these were the *isles* of the Gentiles divided in their lands, every one after his *tongue* after their *families*, in their *nations*." Now, if the Oriental latitude of expression be allowed in this instance, the *isles* of the Gentiles must include not only the ISLES of the Mediterranean and other European seas, but the PENINSULAS of *Asia Minor*, of *Greece*, of *Italy*, and of *Spain*.

To the Phœnicians must be partly ascribed the discovery of those territories collectively called "The isles of the Gentiles," and the earliest intercourse with them. Unfortunately those early navigators have left no records of their discoveries; and the little we know of their enterprises is derived from Scripture, and from the scattered notices of the Greek and Latin authors. They were, as elsewhere observed, the pilots of Solomon's fleet; and as often as the fleets of Egypt are mentioned by ancient historians, we find them manned and guided by Phœnicians. Their commercial enterprises had contributed to augment the wealth of that kingdom, which had attained a high degree of social order and economy seven hundred years before the Greeks became acquainted with the use of money. The numerous colonies which they planted along the shores of the Euxine, the Mediterranean, and the Atlantic, beyond the Straits of Gibraltar, attest the extent of their early voyages. Those of Utica, Carthage, and Gades, or Cadiz, were founded between twelve and eight hundred years before the Christian era; but the seas of the west were probably explored for ages before settlements were formed at such a distance from the parent state. Their geographical knowledge, even in the fabulous times of Greece, probably embraced as large a portion of the earth as that of the Romans in the time of Augustus; but, with the caution characteristic of a mercantile people, they forbore to communicate that knowledge to the rest of mankind. The silence of these descendants of Ham leaves us in uncertainty as to the progress of those of Japheth in peopling the *continent*, the *peninsulas*, and the *isles* of Europe. In still deeper mystery is involved the descent of the negro tribes of Africa from the father of Canaan. Having thus briefly characterized the Shemitic, Hamitic, and Japhetic races, we leave to the consideration of the curious the theories that have been framed upon them in respect to the different idioms of mankind, and revert to the geographical arrangement which we propose to adopt.

Separating all the known languages of the globe into five grand divisions, we name them the *Asiatic*, the *European*, the *African*, the *Oceanic*, and the *American*, according to the part of the world in which they are spoken. Then tracing, according to the best authorities, the several languages by their affinities, we class those which appear to be sister idioms in one group, assigning to it a distinctive name; as the *Mongolian* family, the *Celtic* family or the *Sanscrit* family, conformably, in most cases, to the name of the principal people of each of those families. But here a difficulty arises from the variance between geographic and ethnographic limits. Several nations included in one of these groups have dwelt from time immemorial at once in Asia, Africa, and Europe; others in regions partly European, partly Asiatic: to which part of the world then must the family be assigned to which those nations belong? Two reasons influence the decision; the historical importance of the people, and its mass, or relative number, as may be better understood from one or two examples.

That the Chaldeans, the Assyrians, the Arabs, the Hebrews, and other nations of the great Shemitic family, were from the earliest times inhabitants of Western Asia, we know from the writings of Moses, with which the results of the most eminent philologers and mathematicians wonderfully agree. These nations, therefore, belong unquestionably to Asia; and the comparison of the Gheez and Amharic vocabularies having demonstrated an indisputable affinity between them and the people of Abyssinia, who speak the idioms comprehended in the branch called Abyssinian, the languages of the latter also are classed in the Asiatic branch, though in all epochs, even anterior to historical tradition, those nations have dwelt in Africa.

The great mass of the Malay people occupies almost all the isles of the Indian Archipelago, those of Polynesia, and some of Australia. Hence we regard the Malay family as Oceanic, and class all the people characterized by this idiom as belonging to that great ethnographical group. Thus, besides the Malays of the peninsula of Malacca, whose settlement in the extremity of Asia is of no remote date, this division includes the Si Deïa or Formosans of Asia, and the Madecasses of the African isle Madagascar.

The Uralian nations belong equally to Europe and Asia; because, from the little we know of them, they have inhabited, time out of mind, the north-east and east of Europe, and the north-west and west of Asia. Following the demarcation prescribed by M. Malte Brun, we find that the great mass of the Uralian or Finnish nations belongs to Europe. We therefore regard the Finnish family as European, and class among them all the ancient and modern nations who, from striking analogies in their respective idioms, seem to belong to them.

The Esquimaux have from time immemorial extended over all the north of the New World; while the sedentary Tchutchhis, who speak a language evidently related to the idioms of those American tribes, occupy only the extreme north-east of Asia. The Tchutchhis we therefore consider as American colonies, and, following the precedent of Balbi, re-unite them as such to the other nations of America who form the family of the Esquimaux.

Under a perfect ethnographical arrangement, the languages of the Indo-Germanic nations, extending from Ceylon and the Ganges to the extreme west of Europe, and even to Iceland, would form, not a single family, but rather an ethnographic kingdom divided into six families.

In subsequent parts of this work, the languages of the earth will be considered as divided into five principal branches; the *European*, the *Asiatic*, the *African*, the *American*, and the *Oceanic*.

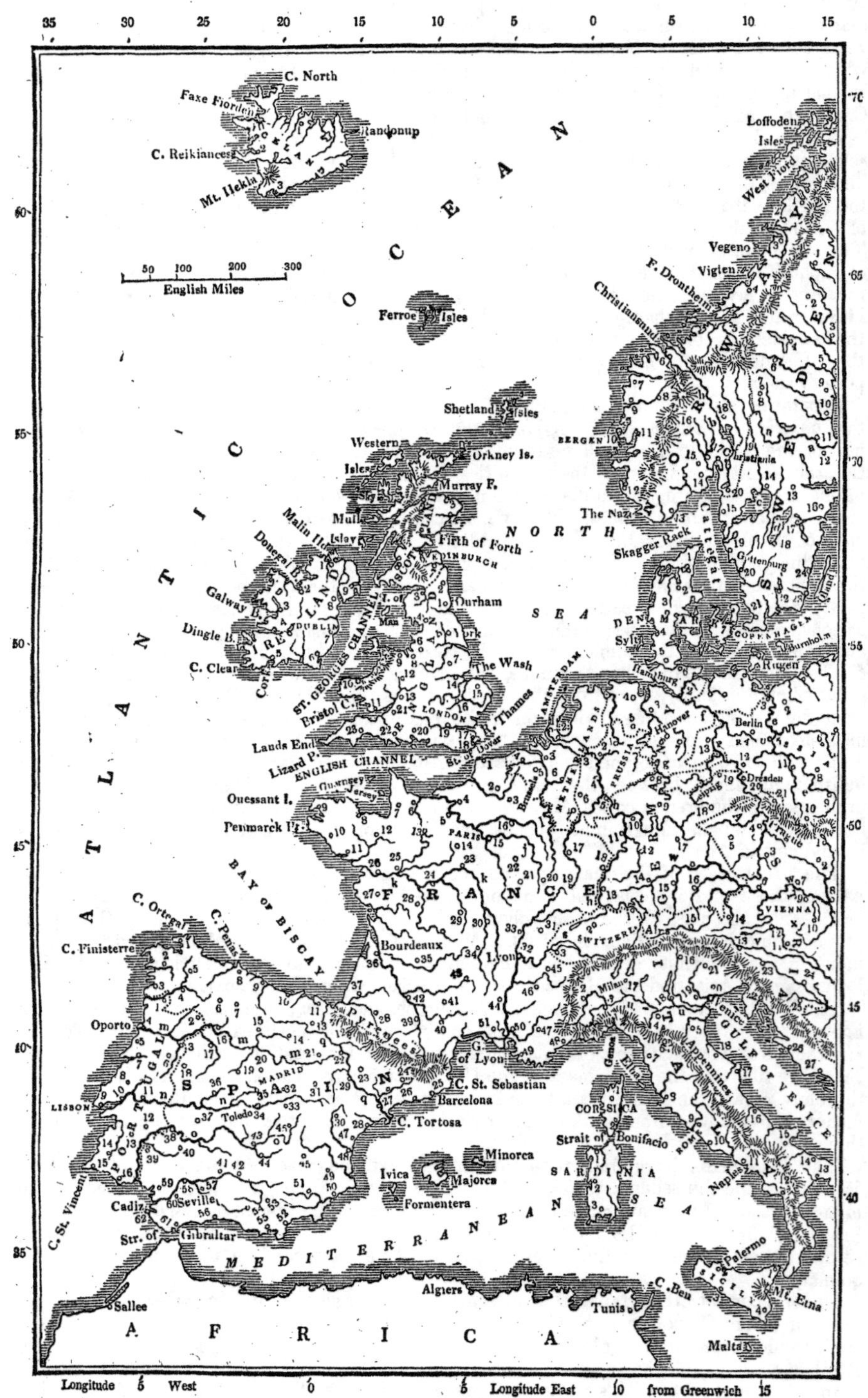
35 30 25 20 15 10 5 0 5 10 15
C. North
Faxe Fiorden
Randonup
C. Reikiances
Mt. Hekla
ATLANTIC OCEAN
50 100 200 300
English Miles
Ferroe Isles
Loffoden Isles
West Fiord
Vegeno
Vigten
F. Drontheim
Christiansund
Shetland Isles
Western Isles
Orkney Is.
Murray F.
Mull
Islay
Malin Head
Donegal B.
Galway B.
Dingle B.
C. Clear
Cork
IRELAND
DUBLIN
Firth of Forth
EDINBURGH
SCOTLAND
I. of Man
Durham
York
The Wash
ST. GEORGES CHANNEL
Bristol C.
LONDON
R. Thames
ENGLAND
Lands End
Lizard P.
ENGLISH CHANNEL
St. of Dover
Guernsey
Jersey
Ouessant I.
Penmarck Pt.
BERGEN
NORWAY
SWEDEN
Christiania
The Naze
Skagger Rack
Cattegat
Gottenburg
NORTH SEA
DENMARK
Sylt
COPENHAGEN
Bornholm
Rugen
Hamburg
Hanover
Berlin
PRUSSIA
NETHERLANDS
AMSTERDAM
Brussels
Dresden
Leipzig
Prague
GERMANY
VIENNA
PARIS
FRANCE
Bourdeaux
Lyon
G. of Lyon
SWITZERLAND
Alps
Milan
Venice
Genoa
GULF OF VENICE
Appennines
ITALY
ROME
Naples
BAY OF BISCAY
C. Ortegal
C. Penas
C. Finisterre
Oporto
PORTUGAL
LISBON
SPAIN
MADRID
Toledo
Pyrenees
C. St. Sebastian
Barcelona
C. Tortosa
Seville
Cadiz
Str. of Gibraltar
C. St. Vincent
Minorca
Majorca
Ivica
Formentera
CORSICA
Strait of Bonifacio
SARDINIA
MEDITERRANEAN SEA
Palermo
SICILY
Mt. Etna
Malta
C. Bon
Tunis
Algiers
Sallee
AFRICA
70 65 60 55 50 45 40 35
Longitude 5 West 0 5 Longitude East 10 from Greenwich 15

ARCTIC OCEAN
North C.
Sviatoi C.
WHITE SEA
LAPLAND
SWEDEN
FINLAND
Gulf of Bothnia
Aland
Gulf of Finland
BALTIC SEA
STOCKHOLM
Gottland
Riga
ST. PETERSBURG
MOSCOW
Smolensk
Tchernigov
Kiev
Warsaw
Lublin
Dantzic
PRUSSIA
RUSSIA
Wilna
Minsk
Pskov
Tver
Jaroslav
Kazane
Viatka
Perm
Archangel
L. Onega
L. Ladoga
Imandra L.
Ural Mts.
Oufa
R. Volga
Oural R.
R. Don
ASTRAKHAN
CASPIAN SEA
ASIA
Carpathian Mts.
BUDA
AUSTRIA
TURKEY
Sophia
Adrianople
CONSTANTINOPLE
BLACK SEA
CRIMEA
Sea of Azov
Cherson
GREECE
Gulf of Venice
Corfu
C. Leuca
MOREA
Athens
ARCHIPELAGO
Cerigo
Candia
Cyprus
MEDITERRANEAN SEA
ASIA MINOR
50 100 200 300
English Miles
Longitude East 30 from Greenwich

# PART III.

## GEOGRAPHY CONSIDERED IN RELATION TO THE VARIOUS REGIONS OF THE GLOBE.

In the second part of this work, the principles of geography have been treated of as founded upon a general survey of the globe. The most extensive portion of our task still remains. We must delineate the leading objects of nature, art, and human life, as they appear successively in each different region into which the earth is divided.

Five great general divisions of the earth are now usually recognized:—1. Europe. 2. Asia. 3. Africa. 4. America. 5. The extensive and numerous islands of the South Sea, to which the French give the name of Oceania, the English those of Australasia and Polynesia, to which we may add the islands of the Polar Sea. Each of these will form the subject of a separate book.

---

# BOOK I.

## EUROPE.

Europe is the smallest in extent of the four great continents, and yet we may pronounce it the most important of all the divisions of the globe. Asia, indeed, was the cradle of civilization and knowledge; but her empires soon became, and have ever since continued stationary; while Europe has carried the sciences, arts, and refinement, with almost unin

---

*References to the Map of Europe.—West Part.*

ENGLAND.
1. Durham
2. Morpeth
3. Carlisle
4. Kendal
5. York
6. Manchester
7. Lincoln
8. Chester
9. St. Asaph
10. Cardigan
11. Llandaff
12. Worcester
13. Gloucester
14. Peterborough
15. Norwich
16. Cambridge
17. Canterbury
18. Dover
19. London
20. Manchester
21. Bristol
22. Poole
23. Exeter

SCOTLAND.
1. Thurso
2. Inverness
3. Banff
4. Aberdeen
5. Perth
6. Edinburgh
7. Selkirk
8. Ayr

IRELAND.
1. Londonderry
2. Sligo
3. Galway
4. Limerick
5. Cork
6. Wexford
7. Dublin
8. Drogheda
9. Belfast

NORWAY.
1. Saltdalen
2. Selnes
3. Rys Vand
4. Sœvug
5. Drontheim
6. Romsdal
7 Forde
8 Ardat
9 Loerig
10 Bergen
11. Tondal
12. Stavanger
13. Christiansand
14. Tonsberg
15. Kongberg
16. Goel
17. Christiania
18. Faaldberg
19. Tongsinger
20. Fredrickshall

SWEDEN.
1. Tarna
2. Tasjo
3. Liden
4. Ostursund
5. Sundswall
6. Hede
7. Tara
8. Sarna
9. Hudiksvall
10. Soderhamn
11. Husby
12. Sala
13. Orebro
14. Carlsbad
15. Oville
16. Nykoping
17. Linkoping
18. Jonkoping
19. Gottenburg
20. Folkenberg
21. Malmo
22. Christianstad
23. Kalmar
24. Emin

DENMARK.
1. Aalborg
2. Wiborg
3. Veile
4. Ripon
5. Sleswick
6. Kiel
7. Copenhagen

ICELAND.
1. Holar
2. Bessested
3. Sandfall

PRUSSIA.
1. Colberg
2. Stargard
3. Stettin
4. Berlin
5. Frankfort
6. Posen
7. Gnesna
8. Lissa
9. Breslau
10. Glatz
11. Sagan
12. Torgau
13. Magdeburg

AUSTRIA.
1. Olmutz
2. Brunn
3. Tabor
4. Prague
5. Pilsen
6. Lintz
7. Krems
8. Presburg
9. Vienna
10. Sopron
11. Gratz
12. Bruck
13. Villach
14. Saltzburg
15. Hall
16. Brixen
17. Milan
18. Mantua
19. Padua
20. Venice
21. Belluno
22. Rimini
23. Laybach
24. Agram
25. Carlstadt
26. Zara
27. Spalatro

ITALY.
1. Genoa
2. Turin
3. Alessandria
4. Parma
5. Bologna
6. Florence
7. Leghorn
8. Orbetello
9. Rome
10. Nettuno
11. Naples
12. Policastro
13. Taranto
14. Bitonto
15. Foagia
16. Pescara
17. Ancona
18. Pesaro

GERMANY.
1. Stralsund
2. Hamburg
3. Bremen
4. Oldenburg
5. Osnaburg
6. Hanover
7. Brunswick
8. Cassel
9. Fulda
10. Darmstadt
11. Wurms
12. Heilbronn
13. Freyburg
14. Ulm
15. Augsburg
16. Munich
17. Nuremburg
18. Hof
19. Leipzig
20. Dresden

SWITZERLAND.
1. Constance
2. Berne
3. Geneva

WEST PRUSSIA.
1. Munster
2. Wesel
3. Cleves
4. Cologne
5. Coblentz
6. Pruym

NETHERLANDS.
1. Amsterdam
2. Rotterdam
3. Antwerp
4. Ghent
5. Brussels
6. Liege
7. Luxemburg

FRANCE
1. Calais
2. Amiens
3. St. Quintin
4. Rouen
5. Evreux
6. Caen
7. St. Lo
8. St. Brieux
9. Brest
10. Quimper
11. Vannes
12. Rennes
13. Alencon
14. Chartres
15. Paris
16. Soissons
17. Metz
18. Strasburg
19. Epinal
20. Chaumont
21. Chatillon
22. Troyes
23. Orleans
24. Tours
25. Angers
26. Nantes
27. La Roche
28. Poitiers
29. Gueret
30. Moulins
31. Lons
32. Lyons
33. Macon
34. Clermont
35. Perigaux
36. Bordeaux
37. Dax
38. Pau
39. Toulouse
40. Alby
41. Rodez
42. Agen
43. Aurillac
44. Privas
45. Chamberry
46. Grenoble
47. Digne
48. Draguinon
49. Toulon
50. Avignon
51. Nismes

SPAIN.
1. Ferrol
2. Santiago
3. Vigo
4. Orense
5. Lugo
6. Astorga
7. Leon
8. Oviedo
9. Lanes
10. Santander
11. Bilboa
12. Pampeluna
13. Vittoria
14. Burgos
15. Palencia
16. Zamora
17. Salamanca
18. Ciudad Rodrigo
19. Avila
20. Segovia
21. Soria
22. Tudela
23. Huesca
24. Ago
25. Barcelona
26. Tarragona
27. Lerida
28. Peniscola
29. Saragossa
30. Teruel
31. Utrilla
32. Guadaxara
33. Huete
34. Toledo
35. Madrid
36. Placentia
37. Truxillo
38. Badajoz
39. Moura
40. Zafra
41. Cordova
42. Andufar
43. Ciudad Real
44. Torrenueva
45. Alvacete
46. Ville de Canas
47. Murviedro
48. Valencia
49. Villencia
50. Alfuente
51. Murcia
52. Vera
53. Baza
54. Granada
55. Almeria
56. Malaga
57. Ecija
58. Carmona
59. Huebla
60. Seville
61. Gibraltar
62. Cadiz

PORTUGAL.
1. Molgaco
2. Braganza
3. Almeida
4. Oporto
5. Aveyro
6. Guarda
7. Coimbra
8. Leria
9. Lisbon
10. Obidos
11. Abrantes
12. Evora
13. Alvito
14. Ourique
15. Lagos
16. Faro.

*Rivers and Lakes.*
a Dal, R.
b Moisen, L.
c Wener, L.
d Wetter, L.
e Oder, R.
f Elbe, R.
g Weser, R.
h Rhine, R.
i Meuse, R.
j Seine, R.
k Loire, R.
l Garonne, R.
m Douro, R.
n Tagus, R.
o Guadiana, R.
p Guadalquivir, R
q Ebro, R.
r Rhone, R.
s Geneva, L. of
t Constance, L. o
u Po, R.
v Drave, R.
w Danube, R.

CORSICA.
1. Corte
2. Porto Vecchio

SARDINIA.
1. Sassari
2. Oristagni
3. Cagliari

SICILY.
1. Messina
2. Palermo
3. Sciacca
4. Syracuse

terrupted progress, to the comparatively elevated state at which they have now arrived. All the branches of industry are conducted with a skill and to an extent unattained in any other part of the earth. European vessels carry on the commerce of the most distant regions. The military and political influence of Europe is now of a magnitude with which the most powerful and populous empires of the other continents can no longer be compared. European colonists have now peopled, and are *more* and *more* peopling, all the formerly savage and unoccupied quarters of the earth; and, with the exception of some strongholds of ancient and imperfect civilization, the whole world is, through their influence, rapidly becoming civilized and European.

---

# CHAPTER I.

## GENERAL SURVEY OF EUROPE.

EUROPE is bounded on the north by the Arctic Ocean, and on the west by the Atlantic. On the south, the grand inlet of the Mediterranean divides it from Africa; and the Grecian Archipelago, with its subordinate branch, connected only by a narrow strait, the Euxine or Black Sea, divides it from a great part of Asia. Between the north-east extremity of the Black Sea and the Northern Ocean is an interval of 1400 or 1500 miles of land, forming the eastern boundary of Europe. Had this been known to the ancients, they would perhaps have identified Europe with Asia; but the separation is now too deeply marked, and is defined by too many characters, moral and political, ever to be altered. The absence of sea, the natural and most obvious boundary of a continent, has somewhat embarrassed modern geographers; for even a river limit is here wanting. The chain of the Urals, running from

---

*References to the Map of Europe.—East Part.*

SWEDEN

1. Altengaard
2. Jukas Jervi
3. Gellivare
4 Of Kalix
5. Gorjan
6. Arjeplog
7. Lulea
8. Pitea
9. Lyeksele
10. Lofangers
11. Umea
12. Sanga
13. Upsal
14. Stockholm

RUSSIA.

1. Enare
2. Kola
3. Voronezkaya
4. Panoi
5. Palitza
6. Oumba
7. Ekostrovskayo
8. Kandalskava
9. Sodankyla
10. Kittila
11. Kemitrask
12. Rovamemi
13. Tornea
14. Ajo
15. Uleaborg
16. Krest Novolok
17. Kounte
18. Vigo
19. Andozero
20. Sotkamo
21. Kajana
22. Brakested
23. Carleby
24. Pie Pisjarvi
25. Pielts
26. Kibelirs
27. Purmala
28. Ruovesr
29. Wasa
30. Christinestad
31. Biorneborg
32. Abo
33. Kilkala
34. Tavaftehus
35. Borgo
36. Vyborg
37. St. Petersburg
38. Olonetz
39. Petrozavodsk
40. Povienetz
41. Vasevskaya
42. Onega
43. Archangel
44. Rougt
45. Staroisbische
46. Mezene
47. Labavko
48 Nikilza
49 Ousa
50. Ovinnika
51. Gelova
52. Stchemass
53. Borovskaya
54. Mousleijskaya
55. Pinega
56. Verkouskei
57. Shestdzerskoi
58. Chalchelskaya
59. Karshakovska
60. Makaoovska
61. Krasnobosk
62. Metverskava
63. Yarensk
64. Oust Sisolsk
65. Kai
66. Tcherdin
67. Solikamsk
68. Vilrenskoe
69. Ortova
70. Oova
71. Garshkova
72. Mishamovsk
73. Ivotovska
74. Aksenterskoe
75. Velikoustong
76. Vielsk
77. Pudog
78. Vitegra
79. Bielozersk
80. Kirilov
81. Vologda
82. Tolma
83. Tchuchloma
84. Kologhiv
85. Nikolsk
86. Sergievitza
87. Kotelnitch
88. Slobodskov
89. Viatka
90. Nolinsk
91. Glazov
92. Ochansk
93. Perm
94. Osa
95. Krasharfunsk
96. Birsk
97. Sarapoul
98. Elabouga
99. Malmish
100. Kazane
101. Sviajsk
102. Kozinodemiansk
103 Yaransk
104. Vetlouga
105. Varnavin
106. Semenov
107. Inrevetz Povolskoe
108. Kostrom
109. Jaroslav
110. Ribinsk
111. Posechon
112. Ostiujna
113. Tikvin
114. Yamburg
115. Narva
116. Revel
117. Derpi
118. Luga
119. Novgorod
120. Valdai
121. Ottishkaij
122. Borovitchi
123. Vishnei Volotchoki
124. Ouglitch
125. Petrovsk
126. Kovrov
127. Nizney Novgorod
128. Bouinsk
129. Sinbirsk
130. Singilei
131. Sizzan
132. Kanader
133. Ardotov
134. Potchinki
135. Norovtchat
136. Temnikov
137. Murom
138. Sudogda
139. Kasmov
140. Moscow
141. Pokov
142. Tver
143. Majaisk
144. Zubtzov
145. Bieloz
146. Velikie Luki
147. Cholm
148. Pskov
149. Ostrov
150. Luitzin
151. Valk
152. Penau
153. Riga
154. Mitau
155. Libau
156. Memel
157. Seventziani
158. Vileika
159. Drissa
160. Polotzk
161. Witepsk
162. Veliz
163. Smolensk
164. Dorogobuz
165. Kalouga
166. Kalomna
167. Toola
168. Kiazane
169. Kozlov
170. Tambov
171. Tchembar
172. Penza
173. Petrovsk
174. Volsk
175. Saratov
176. Balashev
177. Novokhopeck
178. Usman
179. Voronez
180. Phatez
181. Livni
182. Krapivna
183. Bolchov
184. Orel
185. Saraz
186. Koslovl
187. Moghilew
188. Rogatchev
189. Sloutzk
190. Borisev
191. Minsk
192. Wilna
193. Grodno
194. Nowograd
195. Warsaw
196. Rawa
197. Vidava
198. Lublin
199. Mienjirietz
200. Brest Litoy
201. Bielsk
202. Kobrin
203. Pinsk
204. Visotzk
205. Ovroutch
206. Mozir
207. Cholmitch
208. Tchernigov
209. N. Bieletza
210. Rilsk
211. Soumi
212. Koursk
213. Oskol
214. Volouiki
215. Bobrov
216. Pavlorsk
217. Zatovskaya
218. Kamishin
219. Ilolinskaya
220. Tzaritzin
221. Tilkha
222. Koslin
223. Sheslibalotchkaya
224. Tcherkask
225. Donetsk
226. Iziuna
227. Charkov
228. Poltava
229. Novomoskovsk
230. Krement
231. Zolotonosha
232. Kozeletz
233. Kiev
234. Padomist
235. Jitomir
236. Rovno
237. Kametz
238. Balta
239. Gaisin
240. Tcherk
241. Novomirgorod
242. Olviopol
243. Novogrigorevsk
244. Aleksandrovsk
245. Ekaterinoslavl
246. Oriekhov
247. Aleshki
248. Chorson
249. Tiraspol
250. Nov Doubasari
251. Billzi
252. Bender
253. Akermann
254. Ismail

PRUSSIA.

1. Sczueryn
2. Konigsberg
3. Heilsberg
4. Marienburg
5. Dantzic
6. Gnesna
7. Culm
8. Thorn
9. Plotsk
10. Posen
11. Sieradz
12. Ratibor

AUSTRIA.

1. Treutsen
2. Schemnicz
3. Eperies
4. Husa
5. Debreczen
6. Agria
7. Hant
8. Buda
9. Solt
10. Pets
11. St. Maria
12. Baces
13. Belgrade
14. Temeswar
15. Arad
16. Bihar
17. Clausenburg
18. Carlsburg
19. Hermanstadt
20. Kuti
21. Tarnopi
22. Stry
23. Sember
24. Lemberg
25. Sandeez
26. Sendomirje
27. Cracow

TURKEY

1. Jassy
2. Bijrlat
3. Adgrad
4. Galatz
5. Ibraila
6. Silistria
7. Bukarest
8. Slatina
9. Crotova
10. Tchernetz
11. Jogodina
12. Usitza
13. Serajevo
14. Mostar
15. Cattaro
16. Novibazar
17. Scopia
18. Nissa
19. Widin
20. Sophia
21. Oreava
22. Nicopoli
23. Shumla
24. Burgos
25. Midieh
26. Constantinople
27. Rodosto
28. Adrianople
29. Cavalla
30. Philippoli
31. Isbar
32. Petolia
33. Salonica
34. Scutari

GREECE.

1. Berat
2. Butrinto
3. Jannina
4. Arta
5. Lepanto
6. Tripolitza
7. Corinth
8. Athens
9. Zeitoun
10. Larissa

*Rivers and Lakes.*

a Dwina, R.
b Mezene, R.
c Pitchova, R.
d Kama, R.
e Viatka, R.
f Volga, R.
g Oka, R.
h Don, R.
i Donetz, R.
j Dnieper, R.
k Dniester, R.
l Pruth, R.
m Danube, R.
n Vistula, R.
o Niemen, R.
p Dwina, R.
q Tchudskoe, L.
r Ilmen, L.
s Ladoga, L.
t Onega, L.
u Puruvesi, L.
v Sego, L.
w Vigo, L
x Top, L
y Imandra, L.
z Enare, L.

north to south, forms so important a feature, that it has been taken as the grand line of division; and is protracted to the Black Sea by means of continuous portions of the great rivers Kama, Volga, and Don.

The form of this continent is singularly broken and varied. While Asia, Africa, and the two Americas are each formed into a vast inland expanse, Europe is split into many distinct portions; peninsulas, large islands, and kingdoms, with extended and winding coasts. This form arises chiefly out of its inland seas, which penetrate farther, and are more deeply embayed, than those of any other part of the globe. Numerous gulfs, scarcely secondary in magnitude and importance, branch out from them. The Mediterranean, which forms, as it were, a little ocean, separating Europe, Asia, and Africa, is connected with the Atlantic only by the celebrated Straits of Gibraltar, twenty miles in breadth. Its great enclosed branches of the Adriatic and the Black Sea penetrate, and render maritime, some of the most inland districts of the continent. In the north, the Baltic, with its great gulfs of Bothnia and Finland, is neither indeed so extensive nor so accessible; but it is of the highest commercial value, as affording a channel by which the rude necessaries, the metals and woods of the north, may be exchanged for the wines, the silks, and other luxuries of the south. The British isles, by their varied configuration, enclose beween themselves and the opposite continent several important seas and channels. We may add, that the mountains and the plains of Europe do not display those immense unbroken groups, or those level and almost endless expanses, which give so vast and monotonous a character to the interior regions of Asia and Africa. In general they are separated into smaller portions, and are happily and commodiously interchanged. They have kept Europe divided into a number of separate nations, holding easy intercourse. Probably, this relative position has been one great cause of that intellectual activity, and those vigorous exertions in all liberal and ingenious arts, which have raised this part of the globe to so high a pre-eminence. The immense inland plains of Russia and Poland, presenting an aspect wholly Asiatic, remained, even after the civilization and improvement of all western Europe, sunk in the deepest barbarism, from which they are but slowly and with difficulty emerging.

### SECT. I.—*Natural Features.*

The surface of Europe, as we have observed, is very diversified. Its mountains do not reach that stupendous height, nor stretch in such unbroken chains, as those of Asia and America: nevertheless, we may trace pretty distinctly two highlands, the northern and southern, and an intermediate lowland. The southern highland comprises the most elevated mountains of the continent, the Alps and the Pyrenees, connected together by the low chain of the Cevennes. Inferior branches from the Pyrenees extend through the Spanish peninsula; while from the Alps branch forth the Apennines, which range through all Italy, and spread their lower slopes over the greater part of southern Germany. The extremity of the Julian Alps, and the mountains of Dalmatia, connect the range with the great Turkish chains of Hæmus and Rhodope; parallel to which, though with a large group intervening, stretches the circuit of the Carpathian mountains. North of this, the great European lowland comprises the largest part of France, the south of England, the Netherlands, Northern Germany, all Poland, and the greater part of Russia. In the extreme north of Europe the mountainous character again prevails. The Dofrines reach through Scandinavia; while the north of England and nearly all Scotland is covered with mountains of secondary magnitude. Of all the European mountains the Alps are by much the highest, and perhaps may rank fourth to the Himalaya, the Andes, and Caucasus, among the mountain chains of the globe. Mont Blanc and Monte Rosa exceed 15,000 feet above the sea. The numerous other summits of this chain exemplify all the descending grades of elevation. The Apennines vary from 3000 to 6000 feet; but Ætna, at their utmost extremity, is nearly 11,000. The most elevated of the Pyrenees rises somewhat above that height. The Spanish summits are in general of the level of the Apennine, except the Guadarrama, which exceeds 8000 feet, and the Sierra Nevada, which equals the Pyrenees. The Thracian chains have not yet been subjected to survey; but they doubtless exceed those of Greece, which ascend to 6000 or 7000 feet. The Dofrines, notwithstanding their snowy and terrible aspect, are not of first-rate elevation. The great Norwegian chain does not quite reach 9000 feet; Ben Nevis is only 4300 feet; and none of the English mountains reach that altitude.

The rivers of Europe are numerous, but none of them of the very first magnitude. The two largest flow through the great eastern plain, a semi-Asiatic region, and terminate in distant and interior seas, where they contribute little to commercial intercourse. The Volga, which alone can come into rivalry with the great rivers of Asia, passes the Asiatic limit, where it spreads into the great interior expanse of the Caspian. The Black Sea absorbs the other rivers from the great plain of Russia and Poland: it receives also the noble stream of the Danube, which belongs indeed to the central region of Europe; but directing its lower course through barbarous and uncultivated regions, and terminating in this distant receptacle, it conduces only in a secondary degree to the distribution of wealth and plenty through the continent. Western Europe is too much broken into separate portions, and crossed by high mountain barriers, to allow to its rivers a length of more than from 400 to 600 miles; and they have usually their entire course through a single country,—the Rhine, the Elbe, and the Oder, through Germany; the Loire, the Rhone, and the Garonne, through France; the Po through Italy; the Ebro, the Douro, the Tagus, and the Guadalquivir, through Spain. The northern rivers of Britain and Scandinavia, restricted to a still narrower field, seldom accomplish so long a course as 200 miles. Yet, though Europe does not present the grand rivers which distinguish the greater continents, it is on the whole happily and commodiously watered. Almost every part of it enjoys the benefit of river communication; it is neither overspread by the dreary swamps of America, nor the sandy deserts which render uninhabitable so great a part of Asia and Africa.

The lakes of Europe are numerous, chiefly enclosed within its mountain regions; but few of them are of sufficient magnitude to rank as inland seas. Those alone entitled to this distinction are the Ladoga and the Onega, which, forming a sort of continuation of the Gulf of Finland, and being situated in bleak and frozen regions, minister very little to internal intercourse. Finland is covered with similar lakes. The Wener and Wetter of Sweden rank next in magnitude, and, surrounded by immense woods and iron mines, possess considerable beauty and value. Switzerland, with its Italian border, is the chief lake-region of Europe: its waters, particularly those of Geneva and Lucerne, enclosed between the loftiest snowy pinnacles of the Alps, present scenes of grandeur and beauty almost unrivalled; but they are not on such a scale or so situated as to afford any important inland navigation. Those of England and Ireland are merely small picturesque features. Those of Scotland are larger and more numerous; and a chain of them, having been connected by a broad canal, was expected to form a great naval route across the island.

The European soil is distinguished for productions, perhaps surpassing in value those of any other quarter of the globe. It does not, indeed, possess that brilliant luxuriance of vegetation which adorns the equatorial regions of Asia and America. But corn and wine, the most substantial and most agreeable articles of human diet, are nowhere produced on so great a scale or in such high perfection. Grain, of one description or another, is raised over its whole surface, excepting in the extreme north; wines throughout all its southern kingdoms. In hemp, flax, and wool, those staple materials of clothing, Europe is equally preeminent. Silk, another valuable commodity, it produces copiously, though not so as to be independent of supplies from India and China. Cotton is the only great material which the immense manufactures of Europe derive almost entirely from foreign regions. If we except the horse and the camel, for which Asia is renowned, Europe contains the most valuable as well as the most numerous breeds of domestic animals. Its northern forests produce the finest timber in the world, with the exception of the teak; and its iron, the most useful of metals, surpasses that of the rest of the world: but all the more precious substances, gold, silver, pearls, jewels, exist in an extent so limited as scarcely to be deserving of mention. The cultivation of the soil is carried on with much greater diligence than in any countries except in the south-east of Asia, while in science, skill, and the extent of capital employed upon it, European agriculture is quite unrivalled.

In manufacturing industry, this quarter of the world has, within these few centuries, far surpassed all the others of the globe. Asia, indeed, has long boasted some fabrics of extraordinary beauty,—silks, muslins, carpets, and porcelain,—which are not yet altogether equalled; but the looms and workshops of Europe now yield a variety of fine and beautiful fabrics, in such profusion, and at so cheap a rate, as to place them within the reach of almost every class of society. This continent thus clothes all the young nations which have issued from her own bosom, and which fill nearly two entire quarters of the habitable earth.

Commerce, on so great a scale as to connect together the distant quarters of the world, can hardly be said to exist out of Europe. European vessels are found in the utmost bounds of Asia and America, in the snowy regions of either pole, and crowding the ports of the Austral continent. There is not now a place on earth, however remote, affording any scope for the employment of commercial capital, which is not immediately filled with the same promptitude as if it had been situated in the heart of Europe. The ships of that continent exceed those of all the others in number and dimensions: they are also the most skilfully constructed, and navigated by the only seamen who are qualified to guide a vessel across the great oceans. All these observations are liable to one exception: the new American states are beginning to form a commercial and maritime system, modelled on that of Europe—a system which may one day surpass the original.

## Sect. II.—*Inhabitants.*

The population of Europe, though more closely calculated than that of any other quarter of the globe, is yet far from being ascertained on data that are very precise. In regard to some districts, and in particular to the whole of the Turkish empire, no census has ever been instituted; in others, the computation is founded only on the number of houses; and in some, ten, twenty, and thirty years have elapsed since any was attempted.*

* See the Table at the close of this book.

The people of Europe are divided chiefly into three great races, which differ, to a very marked degree, in language, political situation, and habits of life. These are the Sclavonic, the Teutonic, and a third which Hassel calls the Romish, as occupying the chief of those countries which once composed the Western Empire.

The Sclavonic races cover the greater extent of Europe, since they occupy the whole of the eastern plain bordering on Asia. The people have a resemblance to those of that continent; and were considered almost as beyond the social and political pale of Europe, till within the last half century. They have now forcibly thrust themselves into the European system, and rank among its most influential members. The Sclavonic people consist of about twenty-five millions of Russians, ten millions of Poles, Lithuanians, and Letts, and about ten millions of other races, known under the names of Windes, Tcheches, Slawakes, Croats, Morlachians, which have found their way into eastern Germany, Hungary, and Illyria. Without wishing to consider intellectual and moral qualities as necessarily belonging to any particular race exclusively, we may notice it as a fact, that the Sclavonians are, in both respects, less improved than other Europeans. They have only some infant forms of art and literature, which have sprung up from the imitation of those of the eastern nations. They are generally subjected to absolute monarchy, and the greater part of them are only beginning to emerge from the degrading condition of personal slavery. All the habits of life which connect them with polished society have been recently and studiously imported from the west, and are still intermingled with deep remnants of barbarism. The majority profess that superstitious form of Christianity acknowledged by the Greek church. Yet they are a brave, enterprising, and persevering race, and have established themselves as a ruling and conquering people, in reference to all the contiguous nations of Europe and Asia.

The Teutonic race occupies generally the centre and north of Europe; besides Germany, their original seat, they have filled the greater part of Scandinavia, the Netherlands, and Great Britain, and may be reckoned at upwards of fifty millions. Under the limitations above stated, we may describe the Teutonic people generally as brave, hardy, intelligent, and industrious, though somewhat blunt and unpolished. All the sciences, and even the arts, both useful and ornamental, have been carried among them to the highest perfection; yet they are accused of wanting some of the graces and *agrémens* which embellish the courts and fashionable circles of the south, by whom they are treated as semi-barbarians. A great majority of the Teutonic nations are Protestants; and that profession is in a great measure confined to them, and to the nations in the other parts of the world who have sprung from them.

The race called Romish, which comprehends the modern inhabitants of France, Italy, and Spain, has only a very imperfect claim to that title. The Teutonic nations, in conquering these countries, poured into them a vast mass of their own population: but Roman manner and the Roman language had taken such deep root in countries which once constituted the main body of the western empire, that the latter forms still the chief basis of the dialects spoken in this part of Europe. The Romish were the most early civilized of the modern nations. They have carried the polish of manners and the cultivation of the elegant arts to a higher pitch than any other known nation. In solid energy and intelligence, they scarcely equal the Teutonic nations. The Roman Catholic is the ruling religion in all these countries, and has among them her metropolitan seat.

Certain interesting and antique races inhabit the rude and mountainous extremities of Europe. The *Celts* were the most numerous people, and at a period of high antiquity, the possessors of all western Europe. Subdued and disarmed by the Romans, they rapidly declined when the falling empire could no longer protect them, and became the helpless victims of that mighty torrent of barbarous invasion which poured in from the remotest extremities of Europe and Asia. At this dreadful period they sought or found a refuge, partly in Ireland and the Highlands of Scotland, where they exist under the name of Gael; partly in Wales and Britany, where they are called Cymri; and partly in the north of Spain, where they are termed Basques. Having retained their condition unaltered during so many ages, they cherish a fond attachment to antiquity, and trace their pedigree higher than any of the Romish or Teutonic nobles. They have a traditional poetry celebrating the exploits of their ancestors, to which they are fondly attached; but in general they have, in the rapid progress made by the more modern races, been left somewhat behind; though individual emigrants have raised themselves to eminence in every department. Hassel calculates the Gael at 3,720,000, which, from the last census of Ireland, must be much too low; the Cymri at 1,610,000; the Basques at 630,000. The *Greeks*, once the most illustrious of all the races, no longer plant their colonies along the shores of the Mediterranean, but still occupy their old seats, and are spread through different parts of the Turkish empire. Depressed by two thousand years of slavery, they had ceased to display those high attributes which excited the admiration of mankind; but the prospects of independence which they have now opened for themselves, afford some hope that they may regain their place in the scale of nations. Their number may be about 2,100,000. The *Jews*, that singularly interesting people, are spread through all Europe, but especially the eastern countries, Poland.

Russia, and Turkey. They are supposed rather to exceed 2,000,000. The *Gipsies*, in an humbler sphere, are strangely scattered over all Europe to the supposed number of 340,000; a wild, roaming, demi-savage race, of unknown origin, but probably Asiatic rather than Egyptian.

Several Asiatic nations have penetrated by conquest or migration into the east of Europe. These are chiefly Tartars, whom Hassel estimates at 3,250,000 heads. The most prominent branch is that of the Turks, the ruling people in the Ottoman empire, though they form in a few districts only a majority of the population. It seems doubtful, however, if all the Tartars who wander over the southern steppes of Russia can be considered as Asiatic in their origin. The Magyars, who, to the number of 3,000,000, prevail in Hungary and Transylvania, appear to be also Asiatic, or at least to have sprung from that most eastern border of European Russia, which can scarcely be distinguished from Asia.

The religion of Europe is almost entirely monotheistic. A mere handful of pagans, the Samoiedes, are found in its north-eastern extremity, on the shores of the Icy Sea. Europe is almost entirely Christian; and the small population of Mahomedans who have found their way into it consist of Asiatic races, Turks and Tartars. The Jews, however generally diffused, have nowhere a national church, nor are they in any nation fully identified with the body of the people. The Christians of Europe are divided into three great churches, the Greek, the Latin or Roman Catholic, and the Protestant.

The Greek or Eastern church, which was that of the Constantinopolitan empire, was severed from the Latin by the great schism in the ninth century, caused by some abstruse questions respecting the nature and person of Christ. It is still professed by the modern Greeks, is the established religion of Russia, and has votaries in Hungary and all its appendant territories. Hassel reckons its numbers at 32,000,000; Malte-Brun at 50,000,000—a strange discrepancy. We should think the former much nearer the truth, though perhaps somewhat under it. This religion having been long prevalent among unenlightened and degraded nations, has become encumbered with empty pomp and childish ceremonies; and many of its clergy are ill-informed and of irregular lives.

The Roman Catholic religion, which reigned so long with supreme sway over Europe, embraces still a numerical majority of its people. In Italy, Spain, France, and the dominions of the house of Austria, it is dominant and almost exclusive. It still holds attached to it a large portion of the smaller states of Germany, and of the Cantons of Switzerland. The greater part of Ireland and of Russian Poland continue attached to it, without regard to the opposite systems supported by the state. That intolerance which gave birth to so many struggles in attempting to extirpate the Protestant faith, has been greatly mitigated, and, except in Italy and Spain, all professions enjoy an almost complete toleration. The number of Roman Catholics seems to be fairly estimated at between 90,000,000 and 100,000,000. The absolute authority of the Pope in matters of faith and worship, auricular confession, the prohibition of the Scriptures in the vulgar tongue, and a splendid ritual calculated to dazzle the eyes of the multitude, form the peculiar characters of the Roman Catholic system. The monstrous pretensions once advanced to excommunicate and depose kings, and to grant indulgences to commit crime, seem now to be generally withdrawn.

The Protestant or Reformed religion raised its standard early in the fifteenth century, and made most rapid progress, especially in the north of Europe. It sought to purge Christianity from the superstitious observances which had enveloped it during many ages of darkness; to introduce a more spiritual and simple form of worship; to break up the institutions devoted to celibacy; to deny human authority in matters of doctrine, and rest it solely on the foundation of Scripture. It had to maintain a dreadful struggle against the Romish see, which armed in its cause all the great monarchs of Europe; and in France and Bohemia, after taking deep root, it was nearly extirpated. It has been finally established, however, in Great Britain, in the Netherlands, the north of Germany, and the Scandinavian peninsula. Notwithstanding its numerical inferiority, it now ranks among its votaries the most powerful, the most opulent, and the most intelligent nations of Europe and the globe. Its rejection of human authority, and direct appeal to the Scriptures, have caused it to be split into numerous sects and divisions. The most prominent is into Lutherans and Calvinists; the Lutherans retaining still many of the Romish rites and doctrines, to which, in every point, the Calvinists place themselves in the most decided opposition. The English church may be considered a sort of medium between the two, inclining nearer to the Lutheran. In the Protestant countries, numerous smaller sects have asserted the right of private judgment, on which the Reformation was founded. Among these are the Anabaptists, chiefly in Germany, the Netherlands, and England, whom Hassel perhaps underrates at 240,000; Methodists and Quakers in Britain, estimated at 190,000; the Moravian brethren in Germany, 40,000. The Unitarians have an established church in Transylvania, comprising 40,000 souls, and are diffused, openly or secretly, through the other European countries, especially Britain.

In learning, art, science, all the pursuits which develope the intellectual nature of man, which refine and enlarge his ideas, Europe has far surpassed every other continent. The empires of Southern and Eastern Asia alone have an ancient traditional literature, of which the remains are yet preserved. But, besides being now in a very decayed state, it never included any authentic history, sound philosophy, or accurate knowledge of nature. An extravagant though sometimes poetical mythology, proverbial maxims of wisdom, and a poetry replete with bold and hyperbolical images, compose almost its entire circle. The science of Europe has been employed with equal success in exploring the most distant regions of the universe, and in improving the condition of man in society. Astronomy, which elsewhere is a mere mass of superstition and wild conjecture, has here not only delineated with perfect precision the situation and movements of the heavenly bodies, but has disclosed numberless systems of worlds, of which without her aid the existence could never have been suspected. Chemistry, which was formerly a mere collection of empirical receipts and chimeras, is become a mighty science, which analyses the most secret operations of nature, and discovers important, and before unknown, substances. A similarly sound and comprehensive character marks her attainments in physical science, and in every branch of natural history. In regard to poetic fancy, although some natural flights may be found among the rudest tribes, and though the Orientals possess a peculiar vein of learned and studied ornament, it is in Europe, during either ancient or modern times, that the polished and classic models of poetical composition have been exclusively produced.

The invention of printing, and the consequent general diffusion of information among all classes, are features especially European. By their means, in its enlightened countries, the essential branches of knowledge are now placed within the reach of the humblest classes, and even the highest branches are not absolutely beyond their attainment. The endowments for the support of learning are very extensive, founded in a great measure during the middle ages, and bearing some stamp of the then infant state of literature; but they are now adapting themselves to modern improvements. The extensive and extending institutions for the instruction of the lower orders have produced a general diffusion of intelligence, to which in the other parts of the world, if we except America, there is nothing analogous.

The political state of Europe is also peculiarly fortunate. Elsewhere, with rare exceptions, a turbulent anarchy prevails, or vast empires are subjected to the absolute sway of a single despot. It is in this continent only that the secret has been found of establishing a regular and constitutional liberty, in which the extremes of tyranny and licentiousness are equally avoided. Even the absolute monarchies are generally administered with mildness, according to legal forms, and afford to the bulk of the people a tolerable security of person and property. The European states have also established among themselves a balance of power, which sets bounds to the encroachments of any particular state, and has repeatedly rescued the whole continent from the imminent danger of universal subjugation. The military and naval power has been raised to a height, to which none of the other continents can offer any effectual resistance. A great proportion of them has now been conquered, occupied, or colonised by Europe; and if the whole is not reduced under this condition, it is only through distance and extensive deserts that many great countries still preserve their independence.

The geology of Europe will be more advantageously treated of under its respective countries.

## SECT. III.—*Botany.*

The botany of Europe presents some general characters, which it may be important to notice. In the preliminary observations, we have given a very general and rapid sketch of the vegetable geography of the globe, taken in its more enlarged sense. We must now survey it in its subordinate divisions; and the plan which we have prescribed to ourselves, is, in the first instance, under the great principal divisions of the earth, to mention the more striking vegetable features; and then, under each respective country, to give a more particular statement of the plants belonging to it which deserve notice, either from their extreme abundance, their rarity, their peculiar properties and qualities, or some circumstance of general interest.

The nature of the present publication only allowing us to consider, in a very general way, the vegetable productions as connected with their geographical distribution, we cannot devote much space to what concerns the primary divisions. The artificial boundaries of Europe, especially to the east and to the south, are of that nature that many of what might otherwise be ranked among its more striking botanical features are gradually blended into those of Asia on the one hand, and of the north of Africa on the other. Local circumstances, as we have already seen, affect the presence or absence of certain plants, to an extent more than equal to that of any artificial geographical arrangement. Temperature, which has so powerful an effect upon them, varies in a regular progression upon a lofty mountain; but it is not so in all situations, and with the same regularity, especially on the great continents, upon the plains and low grounds. "Sometimes," says the eloquent Mirbel, "a chain of mountains forms a barrier against the freezing winds of the north,* and receives and

* In one spot, in the extreme south of Sweden, facing the sea, and backed by lofty hills, *olives* have succeeded r the open air, and ripened their fruit; while, at the distance of six Swedish miles northward, the inhabitants clothe themselves with furs in the winter, to protect themselves from the severity of the cold.

refracts upon the plants the heat which it derives from the solar rays; sometimes a parching sirocco from the south raises the temperature; in some places, the winters are tempered by the proximity to the sea; whilst at other times all these causes combined, produce a climate so mild, that, to judge of its geographical position only by the indication of the thermometer, we should suppose its latitude to be much nearer the tropics than it actually is. Again, continued plains of vast extent, exactly on a level with the sea, are of rare occurrence; and if there be but an elevation of 1000 or 1100 feet, it suffices to produce a considerable reduction of temperature. This, in its turn, obtains an influence over the vegetable creation; it changes the line of the progress of plants in their migration; it arrests them, and limits their boundaries. Sometimes the northern species proceed southward towards the tropics; sometimes those of the south migrate northwards; and sometimes groups belonging to both of these tribes exchange countries, passing one another; each about to establish colonies in privileged stations, in the midst of a vegetable population to which they are no less strangers by their physiognomy than by their temperament."

86

Borassus. Date Tree. Dwarf Palm.

We shall here confine, as much as possible, our observations to a table, by M. Mirbel, of the phænogamous (or flowering) plants of Europe; to which have been added, for reasons already alluded to, part of those of Asia and of Northern Africa. He divides the northern hemisphere into imaginary belts or zones; the *equatorial*, the *transition temperate*, the *temperate*, the *transition frozen*, and the *frozen zones*. The *temperate transition*, where European vegetation commences, is limited, to the north, by the disappearance of the *Olive;* the *temperate zone* by the cessation of the Oak; and the *frozen transition* by that of the Fir (*Pinus sylvestris*) in the west, and of the Spruce (*P. Abies*) in the east. The *frozen zone* is divided into two bands; the *lower* or *southern*, and the *upper* or *northern*. Both are entirely destitute of trees; but in the *first* band are many shrubs and suffruticose plants:* whilst in the *second* scarcely any thing is found but small herbaceous plants; and these cease where the line of perpetual snow commences.† Here, too, another important fact must be considered,—that, in the frozen or arctic regions, almost exactly the same flora is exhibited in Europe, Asia, and America.

In the extent of country to which the following table is more peculiarly applicable, the Dwarf Palm (*Chamærops humilis*), and the Date Tree (*Phœnix dactylifera*), (*fig.* 86.), are the plants that have the nearest approximation to a tropical vegetation, and which are, of course, the most southern. The plant which is found the nearest to the pole, and which, there is every reason to believe, ascends to it, is the *Palmella nivalis* (*Hooker*), *Red Snow* (*fig.* 87.) of arctic navigators, belonging to the Cryptogamic family, and which will be more especially noticed hereafter. In speaking of vegetation, however, generally, and except the contrary is otherwise expressed, the Cryptogamic plants are not taken into account; partly because we are at present but imperfectly acquainted with their extent or limits, and partly because they are not of such general interest.

87

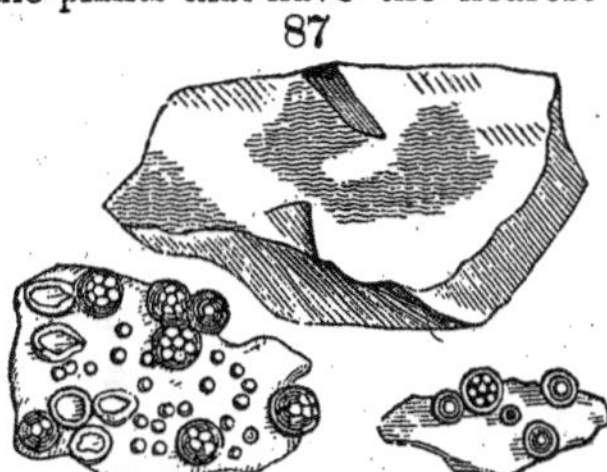

Red Snow.

* The shrubby or suffruticose plants of the southern band of the frozen zone, are fifteen willows: the Dwarf Birch (*Betula nana*), the Humble Birch (*B. pumila*), the White Birch (*B. alba*)—this last is only found on the southern coasts of Greenland; the Hoary Birch (*B. incana*), the Juniper (*Juniperus communis*), the Trailing Azale (*A. procumbens*), the Blue Menziesia (*M. cærulea*), the *Ledum palustre* and *L. latifolium*, the Lapland Diapensia, the Downy Whortleberry (*Vaccinium pubescens*), the Marsh Whortleberry (*V. uliginosum*), the Red Cowberry (*V Vitis Idæa*), the Cranberry (*V. Oxycoccos*), the Glaucous Kalmia, eight species of Rhododendron, the Alpine Arbutus, the Crowberry, the Common Heath, the Shrubby Potentilla, and the Rowan Fir (*Pyrus aucuparia*), on the southern shores of Greenland.

† Almost the only shrubby plants of the northern band of the frozen zone, are the little Arctic Willow (*Salix polaris*), the reticulated Willow (*S. reticulata*), and the four-sided Andromeda (*A tetragona*).

## COMPARATIVE TABLE

Of the phænogamous vegetation of a part of the *Temperate Transition Zone* (Palestine, Syria, Asia Minor, and the Caucasian regions; a portion of the north of Africa and the south of Europe being comprised in this zone) of the *Temperate Zone* (Central Europe as far as the Ural Mountains and the Caspian Sea, and parts of Tartary bordering upon that sea); of the *Transition Frozen Zone* (Northern Europe, Siberia, and Kamtschatka); and all the *Frozen Zone* (Polar Regions) of the Old and New World. Extracted from M. Mirbel's table, in the *Mem. du Muséum d'Hist. Nat. de Paris.*

| Names of Natural Families. | Temperate Transition Zone. | | Temperate Zone. | | Frozen Transition Zone. | | Frozen Zone. | | Amount of Species of each Family of the Four Zones. |
|---|---|---|---|---|---|---|---|---|---|
| | Number of Species of each Family. | Relative Proportion of the Families to the whole of the Species of this Zone. | Number of Species of each Family. | Relative Proportion of the Families to the whole of the Species of this Zone. | Number of Species of each Family. | Relative Proportion of the Families to the whole of the Species of this Zone. | Number of Species of each Family. | Relative Proportion of the Families to the whole of the Species of this Zone. | |
| Reed-Maces, Typhinae, and Arums, Aroideae... | 22 | 0.002 | 10 | 0.002 | 8 | 0.003 | - - | - - | 25 |
| Grasses, Gramineae, | 503 | 0.061 | 246 | 0.061 | 134 | 0.062 | 37 | 0.088 | 617 |
| Sedges, Cyperaceae, | 195 | 0.023 | 275 | 0.069 | 90 | 0.042 | 33 | 0.071 | 265 |
| Restio, Restiaceae, | - - | - - | - - | - - | 1 | - - | - - | - - | 1 |
| Rushes, Junceae, | 40 | 0.004 | 42 | 0.010 | 27 | 0.012 | 11 | 0.026 | 52 |
| Water-Plantains, Alismaceae, | 28 | 0.003 | 30 | 0.007 | 19 | 0.008 | 2 | 0.005 | 33 |
| Asparagus, Asparageae, | 28 | 0.003 | 11 | 0.003 | 8 | 0.003 | - - | - - | 31 |
| Colchicums, Colchicaceae, | 12 | 0.001 | 9 | 0.002 | 4 | 0.001 | 2 | 0.005 | 16 |
| Lilies, Liliaceae, | 180 | 0.021 | 78 | 0.020 | 38 | 0.018 | 1 | 0.002 | 207 |
| Narcissus, Narcisseae, | 40 | 0 004 | 11 | 0.002 | - - | - - | - - | - - | 42 |
| Iris, Irideae, | 51 | 0.006 | 26 | 0.006 | 17 | 0.008 | - - | - - | 70 |
| Orchis, Orchideae, | 106 | 0.012 | 54 | 0.013 | 42 | 0.016 | 5 | 0.012 | 128 |
| Frogsbit, Hydrocharideae,<br>Pondweed, Naiades, | 13 | 0.001 | 8 | 0.002 | 6 | 0.002 | - - | - - | 14 |
| Balanophoreae | 1 | - - | - - | - - | - - | - - | - - | - - | 1 |
| Palms, Palmae, | 3 | - - | - - | - - | - - | - - | - - | - - | 3 |
| Pines, Coniferae, | 34 | 0.004 | 12 | 0.003 | 9 | 0.004 | 1 | 0.002 | 38 |
| Amentaceous, Amentaceae, | 106 | 0.012 | 63 | 0.015 | 46 | 0.021 | 20 | 0.045 | 178 |
| Elms, Ulmaceae, | 8 | 0.001 | 3 | 0.001 | - - | - - | - - | - - | 9 |
| Nettles, Urticeae, | 20 | 0.002 | 9 | 0.002 | 6 | 0.003 | - - | - - | 21 |
| Spurges, Euphorbiaceae, | 103 | 0.011 | 38 | 0.009 | 11 | 0.005 | - - | - - | 112 |
| Birthwort, Aristolochiae, | 16 | 0.002 | 2 | - - | 2 | 0.001 | - - | - - | 16 |
| Sea Buckthorn, Eleagneae,<br>Sandal-wood, Santalaceae, | 8 | 0.001 | 10 | 0.002 | 3 | 0.001 | - - | - - | 12 |
| Daphne, Thymeleae, | 30 | 0.003 | 8 | 0.002 | 4 | 0.001 | - - | - - | 32 |
| Laurel, Laurineae, | 1 | - - | - - | - - | - - | - - | - - | - - | 1 |
| Buckwheat, Polygoneae, | 63 | 0.007 | 46 | 0.011 | 36 | 0.016 | 9 | 0.021 | 86 |
| Goosefoot, Chenopodeae, | 104 | 0.011 | 126 | 0.031 | 47 | 0.022 | - - | - - | 166 |
| Amaranth, Amaranthaceae, | 17 | 0.002 | 5 | 0.001 | 2 | 0.001 | - - | - - | 18 |
| Plantain, Plantagineae, | 65 | 0.007 | 24 | 0.005 | 12 | 0.005 | 3 | 0.007 | 73 |
| Thrift, Plumbagineae, | 57 | 0.006 | 21 | 0.005 | 17 | 0.008 | 1 | 0.002 | 71 |
| Marvels, Nyctagineae, | 3 | - - | - - | - - | - - | - - | - - | - - | 3 |
| Globularia, Globulareae, | 10 | 0.001 | 3 | 0.001 | - - | - - | - - | - - | 10 |
| Primrose, Primulaceae, | 65 | 0.007 | 56 | 0.0014 | 30 | 0.013 | 11 | 0.025 | 109 |
| Butterwort, Lentibulariae, | 10 | 0.001 | 8 | 0.002 | 9 | 0.004 | 2 | 0.005 | 14 |
| Figwort, Scrophularinae, | 298 | 0 036 | 150 | 0.007 | 93 | 0.043 | 23 | 0.054 | 365 |
| Nightshade, Solaneae, | 78 | 0.010 | 38 | 0.009 | 10 | 0 004 | - - | - - | 92 |
| Gentian, Gentianeae, | 41 | 0 005 | 50 | 0.013 | 36 | 0.016 | 4 | 0.009 | 83 |
| Swallowwort, Apocyneae, | 22 | 0.003 | 8 | 0.002 | 3 | 0.001 | - - | - - | 25 |
| Acanthus, Acanthaceae, | 4 | - - | - - | - - | - - | - - | - - | - - | 4 |
| Polemonium, Polemoniaceae, | 1 | - - | 1 | - - | 2 | 0.001 | 2 | 0.004 | 3 |
| Bindweed, Convolvulaceae, | 48 | 0.005 | 11 | 0.003 | 7 | 0.003 | - - | - - | 52 |
| Borage, Boragineae, | 192 | 0.023 | 80 | 0.020 | 48 | 0.022 | - - | 0.005 | 252 |
| Labiate, Labiatae | 431 | 0.052 | 135 | 0.033 | 77 | 0.036 | 1 | 0.002 | 473 |
| Vervains, Verbenaceae, | 4 | - - | 1 | - - | 1 | - - | - - | - - | 4 |
| Jasmine, Jasmineae, | 19 | 0.002 | 2 | - - | - - | 0. - | - - | - - | 19 |
| Heaths, Ericineae,<br>Rhododendrons, Rhodoraceae, | 37 | 0.004 | 28 | 0.007 | 32 | .0015 | 27 | 0.063 | 61 |
| Ebony, Ebenaceae, | 2 | - - | - - | - - | - - | - - | - - | - - | 2 |
| Bellflowers, Campanulaceae,<br>Cardinal-flowers, Lobeliaceae, | 128 | 0.015 | 56 | 0.014 | 16 | 0.007 | 3 | 0.007 | 146 |
| Compound, Synathereae, | 1168 | 0.142 | 520 | 0.131 | 223 | 0.104 | 41 | 0.097 | 1450 |
| Teasels, Dipsaceae, | 80 | 0.010 | 35 | 0.008 | 11 | 0.005 | - - | - - | 94 |
| Valerians, Valerianeae, | 40 | 0.005 | 20 | 0.005 | 6 | 0.003 | - - | - - | 48 |
| Madders, Rubiaceae, | 112 | 0.014 | 64 | 0.016 | 23 | 0.010 | - - | - - | 140 |
| Honeysuckles, Caprifoliaceae, | 27 | 0.003 | 19 | 0.005 | 13 | 0.005 | 2 | 0.005 | 34 |
| Umbelliferous, Umbelliferae, | 368 | 0.045 | 182 | 0 045 | 74 | 0.030 | 3 | 0.007 | 443 |
| Saxifrages, Saxifrageae, | 70 | 0.008 | 49 | 0.013 | 31 | 0.014 | 26 | 0.059 | 94 |
| Purslanes, Portulaceae, | 13 | 0.001 | 8 | 0.001 | 5 | 0.002 | - - | - - | 16 |
| Knawels, Paronychiae, | 31 | 0.004 | 14 | 0.003 | 2 | 0.001 | - - | - - | 32 |
| Houseleeks, Crassuleae, | 80 | 0.009 | 36 | 0.009 | 15 | 0.007 | 4 | 0.009 | 91 |
| Currants, Ribesiae, | 6 | 0.001 | 7 | 0.001 | 8 | 0.003 | - - | - - | 12 |
| Prickly Pears, Opuntiaceae, | *1 | - - | - - | - - | - - | - - | - - | - - | 1 |
| Fig-Marigolds, Ficoideae, | 8 | 0.001 | 1 | - - | 1 | - - | - - | - - | 9 |
| Gourds, Cucurbitaceae, | 10 | 0.001 | 5 | 0.001 | - - | - - | - - | - - | 13 |
| Willow-herbs, Onagrariae, | 24 | 0.003 | 23 | 0.005 | 18 | 0.008 | 6 | 0.014 | 26 |
| Myrtles, Myrtaceae, | 3 | - - | - - | - - | - - | - - | - - | - - | 3 |
| Lythrum, Salicariae, | 19 | 0.002 | 11 | 0.003 | 7 | 0.003 | - - | - - | 21 |
| Roses, Rosaceae, | 200 | 0.024 | 152 | 0.038 | 108 | 0.050 | 28 | 0.061 | 295 |
| Leguminous plants, Leguminosae, | 975 | 0.119 | 283 | 0 070 | 155 | 0.072 | 16 | 0.038 | 1168 |
| Sumachs, Terebinthaceae, | 16 | 0.002 | 2 | - - | - - | - - | - - | - - | 16 |
| Buckthorns, Rhamneae, | 30 | 0.003 | 13 | 0.003 | 5 | - - | - - | - - | 35 |
| Coriaria, Coriareae, | 1 | - - | - - | - - | - - | - - | - - | - - | 1 |
| Rue, Rutaceae, | 36 | 0.004 | 6 | 0.001 | 2 | 0.001 | - - | - - | 39 |
| Woodsorrels, Oxalideae, | 5 | - - | 3 | - - | 2 | - - | - - | - - | 5 |
| Balsams, Balsamineae, | 1 | - - | 1 | - - | 1 | - - | - - | - - | 1 |
| Geraniums, Geraniaceae, | 70 | 0.009 | 28 | 0.008 | 12 | 0.007 | - - | - - | 76 |
| Vines, Ampelideae, | 1 | - - | 1 | - - | - - | - - | - - | - - | 1 |
| Azedarach, Meliaceae, | 1 | - - | - - | - - | - - | - - | - - | - - | 1 |
| Horsechestnut, Hippocastaneae, | 1 | - - | - - | - - | - - | - - | - - | - - | 1 |
| Maple, Acerineae, | 9 | 0.001 | 5 | 0.001 | 2 | 0.001 | - - | - - | 10 |
| St. John's Wort, Hypericineae, | 39 | 0.004 | 12 | 0.003 | 5 | 0.002 | - - | - - | 41 |
| Orange, Aurantiaceae, | 2 | - - | - - | - - | - - | - - | - - | - - | 2 |
| Linden, Tiliaceae, | 3 | - - | 4 | 0.001 | 1 | - - | - - | - - | 5 |
| Mallow, Malvaceae, | 55 | 0 005 | 13 | 0.003 | 6 | 0.003 | - - | - - | 60 |
| Flax, Lineae, | 30 | 0.003 | 17 | 0.004 | 4 | 0.003 | 1 | 0.002 | 35 |
| Pinks, Caryophylleae, | 352 | 0.046 | 180 | 0.045 | 125 | 0.058 | 35 | 0.080 | 535 |
| Frankenia, Frankeniaceae, | 8 | 0.001 | 2 | - - | - - | - - | - - | - - | 8 |
| Milkworts, Polygaleae, | 16 | 0.002 | 7 | 0.002 | 5 | - - | - - | - - | 22 |
| Sundews, Droseraceae, | 5 | - - | 4 | 0.001 | 4 | 0.002 | - - | - - | 5 |
| Violets, Violeae, | 18 | 0.002 | 24 | 0.006 | 19 | 0.009 | 2 | 0.005 | 39 |
| Gum Cistus, Cistineae, | 150 | 0.018 | 21 | 0.005 | - - | - - | - - | - - | 154 |
| Caper, Capparideae, | 35 | 0.004 | 4 | 0.001 | - - | - - | - - | - - | 35 |
| Cruciferous plants, Cruciferae, | 540 | 0.065 | 252 | 0.063 | 140 | 0.065 | 50 | 0.118 | 717 |
| Fumitory, Fumariae, | 22 | 0.003 | 12 | 0.003 | 16 | 0.007 | 1 | 0.002 | 37 |
| Poppy, Papaveraceae, | 31 | 0.004 | 15 | 0.004 | 6 | 0.003 | 2 | 0.005 | 40 |
| Waterlily, Nymphaeaceae, | 5 | 0.001 | 5 | 0.001 | 3 | 0.001 | - - | - - | 7 |
| Berberry, Berberideae, | 6 | 0.001 | 2 | - - | 2 | 0.001 | - - | - - | 8 |
| Moonseed, Menispermeae, | 1 | - - | - - | - - | 1 | - - | - - | - - | 2 |
| Ranunculus, Ranunculaceae, | 192 | 0.023 | 126 | 0.031 | 116 | 0.054 | 21 | 0.050 | 272 |
| | 8103 | | 3982 | | 2129 | | 438 | | 10,292 |

* This solitary Cactus is introduced from America.

In the temperate transition zone, out of 8193 species, 1262 have been ascertained to be woody, and 6898 herbaceous; and of these latter 3861 are known to have perennial, and 2373 annual or biennial roots.

In the temperate zone, out of 3982 species, there are 357 woody, and 3625 herbaceous; of which 2610 are understood to have perennial, and 944 annual or biennial roots.

In the frozen transition zone, out of 2129 species, are 193 woody plants, and 1936 herbaceous; of which 511 are supposed to have perennial, and 363 annual or biennial roots.

In the frozen zone, of the 438 species, 46 are woody, and 392 herbaceous; of which 371 are estimated to have perennial roots, and only 15 annual or biennial roots.

We have already stated that in the frozen or polar region the vegetation is very similar throughout the north of Europe, Asia, and America; which may in part arise from its limited extent, and from the continents approaching comparatively so near to each other. There must necessarily, too, be a greater equality of temperature than in the other zones; the vegetation everywhere appearing nearly upon a level with the sea. In Greenland, Schouw estimates that there is hardly one-sixth of the plants that are not equally found in Lapland. Of the genera of Greenland only two are not found in Lapland (*Streptopus* and *Coptis*), and both occur in North America. We shall, by-and-by, notice how analogous is the vegetation discovered during Captain Parry's arctic voyages to that both of the European and American continents, in corresponding latitudes. Even in Kamtschatka, one half of the plants found by Wormskiold are European; and of the genera only eight or ten are not European; and they are North American. But, as we proceed from the Arctic Regions to the south, we find the vegetation gradually becoming more and more dissimilar between America and Europe; except, indeed, when the high mountains in the respective countries are examined, and then the resemblance again appears. Pursh, whose flora comprises, to a very limited extent, the plants of the arctic or sub-arctic regions, or of the lofty mountains of North America, but is principally confined to Canada, and to those districts of the United States whose latitude corresponds pretty nearly with that of the more temperate parts of the European continent, has about one-seventh of his species only European; and if the doubtful natives, those *probably* introduced from the Old World, be taken into account, only one-tenth: out of 716 genera of North American plants, 480, or two-thirds, also occur in Europe, or in Northern Africa.

Schouw estimates the most striking disparities between the vegetation of the western parts of the Old World, and the eastern parts of the New, to be as follows:—

1. The *Cruciform* (*fig.* 88. *a*) and *Umbelliferous families* (*b*): those of the *Pinks* (*c*) and *Labiate* flowers (*d*) are much the most numerous on the old continent. The first, in North America, may be estimated at $\frac{1}{27}$, in Europe at about $\frac{1}{20}$; and the other families may be classed in the following proportions:—

| | North America. | France. | Denmark. |
|---|---|---|---|
| Umbelliferous - - - - - - - | $\frac{1}{34}$ | $\frac{1}{21}$ | $\frac{1}{23}$ |
| Pink Family - - - - - - - | $\frac{1}{34}$ | $\frac{1}{23}$ | $\frac{1}{21}$ |
| Labiate flowers - - - - - - | $\frac{1}{36}$ | $\frac{1}{23}$ | $\frac{1}{25}$ |

2. Of the family with *Compound flowers* (*Compositæ*), the groups of the Endives (*e*) (*Cichoraceæ*), and of the Artichokes and Thistles (*Cynarocephalæ*), are more abundant in Europe; whilst, on the other hand, North America possesses such a number of species of Michaelmas Daisy (*Aster*), and Golden Rod (*Solidago*), that they constitute one-third of the compound flowers of that country, forming a striking feature in the vegetation of the United States, and carrying the preponderance in favour of North America.

3. The family of Bellflowers (*f*) (*Campanulaceæ*) abound most in the Old World; that of the Cardinal Flowers (*Lobeliaceæ*), in the New.

4. Not a single species of Heath (*g*) is found in the new continent; while, in the old, immense tracts are covered with them; but their places are taken in America by the Whortleberries (*Vaccinia*).

5. Both in North America and in Europe, the forests are constituted by the families of

the Cone-bearing (*Coniferæ*) and Amentaceous (*Amentaceæ*) trees; but in America they far exceed those of Europe in respect to the number of species.

6. In North America we find the types or representatives of many tropical families; as, for example, of the ***Cactuses***, ***Scitamineous plants***, the Sago (*Cycadeæ*), the Custard Apples (*Annonaceæ*), the ***Sapindaceous***, and the ***Melastomaceous*** plants: these are wholly wanting in similar latitudes in the Old World; and in regard to many others, which are common to both countries, such as the Palms, Laurels, Swallowworts (*Asclepiadeæ*), Sumachs, Cassias, and Mimosas, they are more abundant, and generally reach a higher northern latitude, in North America than in the Old World. In Europe, again, there are fewer arborescent plants; for, according to Humboldt, while North America has 137 trees whose trunks reach the height of 30 feet and upwards, Europe possesses only 45 of that character.

Siberia, bounded as it is on the side of Europe by the Ural Mountains, differs from the latter country in a much less degree; and it is mostly in North American genera that this difference lies; as in the presence of the genus ***Phlox***, ***Mitella***, ***Claytonia***, &c. and in the predominance of the tribes of Michaelmas Daisy (*Aster*), Golden Rod (*Solidago*), Meadow-Sweet (*Spiræa*), and especially of the Milkvetches (*Astragalus*) and Wormwoods (*Artemisia*), as well as (on account of the numerous saline lakes) the ***Goosefoots*** and ***Saltworts***.

In the southern hemisphere, the vegetation is very different from that of Europe in the corresponding degrees of latitude. In Southern Africa, Thunberg enumerates 118 species which are analogous to those of Europe; which would probably be found considerably to exceed the truth, if the species were accurately examined. Mr. Brown assures us that the Alpine Catstail Grass (*Phleum Alpinum*) and the Moonwort Fern (*Botrychium lunaria*) exist in the Banksian herbarium, which were gathered in the extreme parts of South America: and the same accurate writer observed 45 European phænogamous plants in Terra Australis, of which 23 are dicotyledonous and 21 monocotyledonous, and 121 acotyledonous or Cryptogamia; namely, 2 of the Fern family, 25 Mosses, 14 Hepaticæ, 38 Lichens, 10 Fungi, 12 Algæ.* The very general distribution of plants of this class over the surface of the globe, we have before, indeed, had occasion to notice.

### SECT. IV.—*Zoology*.

The zoological features of Europe, although sufficiently important to render this continent a primary division of geographic natural history, are neither so extensive nor so varied as those of more genial regions. We have already shown the propriety of including within this range the southern parts of Africa bordering the Great Desert; while the western provinces of Asia appear to partake both of the European and the Oriental zoology. It might be imagined that such a division, including countries suffering by the extremes of cold and heat, would present animals of the most diversified nature: but such is by no means the case, at least to any great extent. The chief seat of this zoological province appears to be on the southern side of Central Europe, towards the Alps, or those countries lying between the latitudes of 40° and 50° N.; as within these parallels the greatest proportionate number of species appear to be found. It may, however, be more natural to consider this zoological region as presenting three minor divisions: 1. The arctic; 2. The central; and, 3. The southern.

The *arctic* division will include Greenland, the islands of Spitzbergen and Iceland, and a considerable part of Norway, Sweden, and Northern Russia. The *central* division may be said to commence towards the northern limits of Scotland, and to reach the shores of Northern Italy; or, more properly, to about the 45th degree of north latitude. The *southern* range includes the whole of the Mediterranean countries, Northern Africa, and Asia Minor.

The animals more particularly belonging to the arctic circle are few in species. Those dreary and inhospitable regions afford but little sustenance to ruminating quadrupeds, or to insectivorous land birds; while the intense cold is as inimical to vegetation as to the production of insects. Yet these undisturbed solitudes are instinctively chosen by multitudes of marine animals, as secure retreats from the interruption of man, for breeding and providing for their young. The polar seas abound with innumerable water-fowl; they congregate and build among the rocks, whose surface they almost cover by their numbers.

89

British Herring.

Of the Herring, (*fig.* 89.) Pennant was among the first naturalists who believed that the countless myriads which annually visit the northern shores of Europe, migrated from the Arctic Ocean. The account given by this eloquent writer is so interesting, that we shall repeat it nearly in his own words:—"The great winter rendezvous of the herring is within the arctic circle. There they continue for many months, in order to recruit themselves after the fatigue of spawning; the seas within that space swarming with insect food in a degree far greater than in our warmer latitudes. Thus renovated, this mighty army begins to put itself in motion in the spring. They appear

* Of the 121 acotyledonous plants it may be observed, that all, except one, the Marsilea quadrifolia, are found in Great Britain.

off the Shetland Isles in April and May: these are only the forerunners of the grand division, which comes in June; and their appearance is marked by certain signs, and by the numbers of birds which follow to prey upon them: but when the main body approaches, its breadth and its depth are such as to alter the appearance of the very ocean. It is divided into distinct columns, of five or six miles in length, and three or four in breadth; and they drive the water before them with a kind of rippling. Sometimes they sink for ten or fifteen minutes, then rise again to the surface, and, in bright weather, reflect a variety of splendid colours, like a field of the most precious gems."

The zoology of arctic Europe has received much less attention than that of Northern America; we must, therefore, be somewhat concise on this head. Among the few original writers who have treated on the fauna of arctic Europe, the learned and acute Otho Fabricius, many years a resident in those dreary regions, deservedly ranks foremost. He enumerates thirty-two species of *Mammalia* as natives of Greenland, nine of which belong to the genera of Walrus and Seal (*Trichecus* and *Phoca*), and fifteen to the cetaceous order; thus leaving but eight species of terrestrial quadrupeds, a proportion at once explained by the wild and desolate nature of these regions. The number of birds, comprehending such as are occasional visiters, amounts to fifty-two. Seven of these are rapacious, and five are referable to the families of Warblers and Finches (*Sylviadæ* and *Fringillidæ*); the remainder, with the solitary exception of the Ptarmigan (*fig.* 90.), or *Lagopus mutus*, belong to the wading and swimming orders, to whose nourishment and increase the arctic solitudes are particularly congenial. Nevertheless, by far the greater number of these birds occur abundantly in more southern latitudes; and many extend their flight to the warm shores of the Mediterranean. Those species, in fact, which habitually live within the arctic circle, as if by preference, are remarkably few, and offer no good foundation to ground a belief that these regions constitute one of the primary groups in animal geography.

90

Ptarmigan.

The zoology of Central Europe may be said to commence towards the 60th degree of northern latitude, where a sensible change in the number and species of animals may be perceived; vegetation assumes a marked and decisive character; and those animals which depend for their support both on the produce of the earth and on the insect world are greatly increased, at once in number and in species. Vegetables furnish nutrition to insects, and seeds to birds: the former, again, become the prey of the latter; and thus the supplies of nature are nicely and accurately balanced, with a just regard to the preservation of all her creatures. The dark pine forests of Norway, Sweden, and Lapland are the most northern boundaries of the Woodpeckers; one of which (*Apternus tridactylus* Sw.) is remarkable for having but three toes to its feet (*fig.* 91.), and is more peculiarly a native of these high latitudes. The insectivorous and omnivorous tribes begin, also, to be common; while the wading and natatorial birds diminish in numbers, though not in species; for as they congregate at certain seasons in the polar seas, so during winter they disperse themselves on the shores of Great Britain and the Continent. We have no very precise information as to the extreme northern range of those birds whose chief metropolis is in Central Europe; and we are still deficient in a Fauna Scotica.

91

Three-toed Woodpecker.

Most of the Arctic birds occur on the northern shores of Scotland, the islands of Orkney and Shetland, and on the coasts of Norway, Sweden, and Denmark. Müller, in his *Zoologia Danica*, enumerates 57 species of *Mammalia*, and 131 of birds, as natives of that kingdom. Among the former, 3 only are marine, and 14 are *Cetaceæ*: while the land birds amount to 87, exclusive of 26 belonging to the rapacious genera of Eagles, Falcons, and Owls. On comparing these numbers with those of the Greenland fauna, we observe, on the one hand, a considerable diminution of marine *Mammalia*, and a very large addition to the list of terrestrial birds; this latter circumstance is easily accounted for,—they are not formed to endure extreme cold; and being dependent upon insects and seeds for their support, their dispersion is naturally limited by the facilities afforded by nature for supporting life. Proceeding to those countries which lie towards the centre of Europe, there is a gradual augmentation of animal life: we may even trace this change in the local distribution of the animals peculiar to the British islands. Many species, in every department of zoology, are common in the southern and western counties of England, which are totally unknown in the northern counties and in Scotland. Even among the domesticated races, a greater developement of structure under a more genial climate is apparent in the horse, the sheep, and the ox of Britain, when compared to those of the islands and mountains of Scotland; while among birds the gallinaceous genera, which, in the former climates, breed and live at all seasons in the open air, are reared and preserved with difficulty in countries farther north; of these the peacock and Guinea fowl may be cited as examples.

The southern part of central Europe is, then, the field best calculated for studying the peculiarities of European zoology. Commencing with the existing quadrupeds, we may remark, that while two species alone appear to inhabit the cold regions of Denmark, there are thirteen described as natives of France and the adjacent kingdoms, seven of which have been enumerated among British quadrupeds. The great white Bear, which is perhaps more truly an arctic animal than any other, disappears on the southern shores of the Polar Sea, and is replaced in temperate Europe by the common brown species. Of this genus there are, according to Cuvier, but two recent species belonging to Europe, the brown (*fig.* 92.) and the black bear. Others imagine, with some show of reason, that there are more; as the varieties from the first are very remarkable. The second is the black bear of Europe, differing from that of America in many important points of structure: only one living example appears to have been seen and dissected; and this, having died in confinement, afforded no clue to a knowledge of its haunts or manners.

92

Brown European Bear.

The Wolf and the Fox, under different varieties or species, appear generally distributed over Europe: to these we must add the Lynx and the Wild Cat, as the only true rapacious or carnivorous animals that have been appropriated to this division of the globe. The Lynx, once common in central Europe, is now only known in some parts of Spain, the Apennines, and in the northern kingdoms. The wild cat is still said to be a native of Britain, and is spread over other kingdoms on the Continent. A recent author includes among the "extinct animals" of Britain the hyæna and tiger whose bones have been found in the caves of Kirkdale, as forming part of the modern geographic distribution of animals. This hypothesis lies open to many and great objections. If such formidable and terrific carnivorous animals have existed in Europe since the last revolution of our globe, what others constituted their prey? Their food being flesh alone, what were the other races of quadrupeds destined by nature to furnish them with subsistence? These questions must be first considered, before we can assent to an opinion so confidently advanced. Whatever might have been the character of European zoology before the deluge, certain it is, that in its present state it exhibits that harmony and consistency which peculiarly marks a wise provision for all created things. As the number of European *Mammalia* is so disproportionably small, when compared with those of Asia, Africa, and America, so are the species which are to keep their own class under subjection feeble and few; and this law is not only apparent among quadrupeds, but is equally observable in every other division of animals. Now, as birds are much more numerous, we find that in addition to the natural enemies in their own class, there is a group of quadrupeds more particularly destructive to the feathered tribes. These are the *Mustelæ*, or Weasels; few perhaps in species, but important in their numbers, and in their powers of destruction. No less than eight species inhabit different parts of Europe. Like the monkeys of the tropics, many of them climb trees and suck eggs; and by thus destroying birds in every stage of life, from the egg to the adult, are peculiarly adapted to prevent an undue increase of numbers.

On the granivorous quadrupeds it may be observed, that although the woods of Europe are deficient in that variety of pulpy fruits so abundant in tropical countries, and upon which the numerous monkeys, bats, and other animals of those regions principally live, yet there is a great diversity of nuts and grain. Hence we find a proportionate number of small quadrupeds, whose subsistence entirely depends upon these bountiful supplies of nature: under this head may be enumerated the Hedgehog, Squirrel, and the various Mice, of which seven species belong to Europe. The Beaver (*fig.* 93.) is found in the vicinity of the Rhone, the Danube, the Rhine, and other of the larger European rivers. If naturalists are correct in considering this to be identical with the American beaver, it is one of the very few instances of the same species of animal inhabiting the temperate parts of the old and new continents. The black bear of Europe was long confounded with that of America; and a similar difference may possibly exist between the beavers of the two continents.

93

Beaver.

The different species of Mice, &c., now arranged under many genera, form an important part of European zoology; as will appear from the following list, furnished by Mr. Griffith from the valuable *Mammalogie* of M. Desmarest:—

| | | | |
|---|---|---|---|
| Arvicola amphibius | Water Rat. | Mus musculus | House Mouse. |
| —— arvalis | Field Mouse. | —— messarius | Harvest ditto. |
| —— fulvus | Fulvous ditto. | —— minutus | Small ditto. |
| —— argentoratensis | Strasburg ditto. | —— agrarius | Setnic ditto. |
| Georychus Norvegicus | The Lemming. | —— soricinus | Shrew-like ditto. |
| —— terrestris | Land ditto. | —— dichrurus | Partycoloured Rat. |
| Mus sylvaticus | Field Mouse. | —— islandicus | Iceland ditto. |
| —— campestris | Plain ditto. | | |

The Hamsters, remarkable for their cheek pouches, and belonging to the same natural family as the mice, have their chief metropolis in Siberia; yet one species (*Cricetus vulgaris*) extends to central and northern Europe. The Marmots (*Arctomys Marmotta, Bobac*) are likewise nucivorous, and occur on the mountains of central and northern Europe, together with the *Spermophilus citillus*, or Soulisk of the Germans. Of the Hare, four species are European, the snowy, the common, the calling, and the rabbit; and these complete the list of European *Glires*.

Among ruminating quadrupeds, the Elk and Reindeer are well-known inhabitants of the northern countries; the latter giving place to the Fallow-deer, the Stag, and the Roebuck, in the midland parts of Europe. In the lofty mountains and inaccessible precipices of the Alps and Pyrenees, the Chamois, Yzard, and Ibex still live in partial security, notwithstanding the daring intrepidity of their hunters. The Musmon is another European quadruped deserving particular notice, as being generally considered the origin of all our domestic breeds of sheep. It appears still to exist in a state of nature among the high mountains of Corsica and Sardinia; and although now extirpated upon the continent, is well ascertained to have formerly been common in the mountains of Asturia in Spain. Lastly, it appears incontestable that the ox, one of the most valuable of nature's gifts to man, originally existed in a wild state over the whole of Europe, but whether as a distinct species or mere variety is still uncertain. The white ox of Scotland is a peculiar breed, still preserved in some few parks of the nobility, and will be noticed hereafter. But a much larger race, distinguished by Hamilton Smith under the name of the Fossil Urus (*Griff. Cuv.* iv. 414.), although, probably, in existence long after the invasion of Cæsar, is now only known, like the elk of Ireland, by its gigantic bones.

From this brief enumeration of the European quadrupeds it will be perceived that their numbers are too few, and their original dispersion too obscure, to allow of any correct notions being formed as to their natural distribution. With regard to the origin of our domestic animals, and the several races, breeds, or varieties that have apparently sprung from them, the reader must be referred to the writings of F. Cuvier, and the extensive researches of Hamilton Smith, whose acquaintance with the order of ruminating animals, more particularly, is, perhaps, superior to that of any other living zoologist.

The ornithological features of the zoological province to which Europe belongs, have already claimed our attention. We shall, therefore, now merely notice a few circumstances connected with the ornithology of central Europe. On the highest summits of the Alps, and in the vast forests which clothe their sides in Hungary, Switzerland, and the Tyrol, are found all the four species of European Vultures: only one of these, *Vultur fulvus* (*fig.* 94.), appears to have a range in countries farther north; yet all are distributed over the southern kingdoms, and two are again met with on the northern limits of Africa and western Asia. The Iceland or gyr Falcon, long supposed to be peculiar to the high northern latitudes, is now considered the same with the *Falco candicans* of the northern parts of Germany. The wide geographic range of the rapacious order has already been adverted to; nor do we find any species besides the Vultures which serve to mark the ornithology of central Europe. The forests of Germany, Austria, Switzerland, and France appear to contain all the European Woodpeckers, which, notwithstanding their wide dispersion, are but thinly and partially scattered in the northern and southern kingdoms.

94

Fulvous Vulture.

The range of the small insectivorous birds, or warblers, requires much investigation; nor are we at this moment aware of any species in Germany which does not occur in France or towards northern Italy. The few gallinaceous birds of Europe are nearly all found towards its centre, although the different species of grouse seem to affect the more northern latitudes. The warm covering of feathers which protects their feet, is peculiarly adapted as a defence from the intense cold of the polar regions. The Bustards, on the contrary, occupy the middle regions of Europe, and extend latitudinally from the confines of Asia to the shores of the Atlantic. The Bee-eater (*Merops apiaster*), the Roller, the Hoopoe, and the Golden Oriole, in their annual migrations from Africa, visit all the central parts of the Continent, but become progressively scarce as we advance northward.

In the third portion of the European range, we comprehend the south of France, the whole of Spain, Italy, and Turkey, together with the coasts and islands of the Mediterranean Sea bordering Asia Minor, and Northern Africa.

On the geographic range of the quadrupeds more peculiar to these countries, little can be said; as the materials to be gathered from the relations of travellers unacquainted with zoology are generally most imperfect. There is no evidence of the great northern ruminating animals, such as the Elk and the Reindeer, being found wild in any of the countries which border the Mediterranean Sea, although a small species, probably the fallow deer or the roebuck, is represented as still to be met with in the extensive forests of Calabria. The Porcupine, now wild in those countries, is supposed, (but with a slight show of reason,) to have been introduced from Africa; but for what purpose we are uninformed. The Buffalo is domesticated in Greece and Turkey, and some parts of southern Italy; where it is sometimes, though rarely, used for draught.

The ornithology of the countries bordering upon the Mediterranean presents many interesting peculiarities. The vultures, which are seldom found northward of the Alps, occur more frequently as the climate becomes warmer. This tribe appears to follow the course of the Apennines in Italy, and of the higher mountains of Spain and Greece, from whence they extend their range to Asia Minor and northern Africa. The Imperial Eagle (*Falco imperialis* Tem.) is chiefly found in southern Europe, while the Golden Eagle is much more numerous in the colder latitudes. The gigantic Owls of the polar regions are here unknown; but two or three horned species, of diminutive size, follow the migratory troops of smaller birds in their annual journeys across the Mediterranean. Two of these small owls have not yet been described. In the extensive family of the warblers, many appear peculiar to Italy, Spain, Sicily, and Sardinia; and in the latter island there has recently been discovered a second species of European Starling (*Sturnus unicolor* Tem.) (*fig.* 95.) The grouse of northern Europe are rarely, if ever, seen. But two species of bustard (*Otis Tetrao* and *Houbara*) seldom met with farther north, are common in Spain, Italy, and Turkey. Here also we first meet with the African and Asiatic genera *Cursorius* and *Hemipodius;* birds which delight in the dry and arid plains of those continents, where they run with amazing swiftness. The rocky and uncultivated wastes of Spain, Turkey, and Asia Minor, furnish two species of rock grouse (*Pterocles*) long confounded with that northern genus, of which it is the representative in warm climates. The beautiful Wall-creeper, with its bright rosy wings, although rare in other parts of Europe, is not uncommon in Italy; while the Golden Oriole, the Bee-eater, the Hoopoe, and the Roller, four of the most beautiful European birds, are so abundant in the two Sicilies during the spring and autumnal migrations, that they may occasionally be seen hanging in the poulterers' shops of Naples and Palermo. The union of the African, European, and Asiatic ornithology on the coasts of the Mediterranean is further apparent among the water-birds. The Pelican, the Spoon-bill, and the Flamingo, are still to be met with in these countries; although, from their large size attracting the sportsmen, they are never seen in any considerable numbers.

95

Sturnus Unicolor.

The European reptiles are too few to afford any material illustration of animal distribution. The most remarkable forms and the greatest numerical proportion occur in southern Europe, particularly in Italy and Greece, and the islands of Sicily and Malta: some of these, as the Gecko, or house lizards of Naples and Sicily, belong to genera not met with farther north, but common on the opposite shores of Africa and Asia Minor.

The fish and other marine animals of the Spanish and Portuguese coasts bordering on the Atlantic have not been well investigated, and our slight acquaintance with them is insufficient to give us any correct idea of their nature; but on entering the Mediterranean, we find, at Gibraltar, many of those peculiar to much more southern latitudes. Spain and Portugal cannot be said, like England, France, or Holland, to have national fisheries; but no sooner do we pass Gibraltar, than these natural sources of prosperity and plenty are again opened to the industry and support of man. The enormous shoals of Anchovies, (*fig.* 96.) annually employ, in their capture and preparation, a great number of persons: and the exportation of this highly flavoured little fish, to all parts of the world, creates an important branch of permanent commerce. The Herring and, we believe, the Pilchard, are not unknown in the fish-markets of Sicily and Malta; but, notwithstanding their abundance in northern Europe, they are scarce in the Mediterranean, and never seen in any considerable numbers. The tunny fishery is peculiar to Sicily, although there is very little doubt that the same fish frequents the shores and islands of the Peloponnesus; yet the total disregard of the Turks to all sources of national wealth blinds them to this, and to every other advantage which Nature has placed within their grasp. The Ichthyology of southern Europe is certainly of a more marked and peculiar character than any other department of European zoology. Of nearly 150 species observed in the Mediterranean Sea, not more than one-third belonged to the Ichthyology of Great Britain and northern Europe.

96

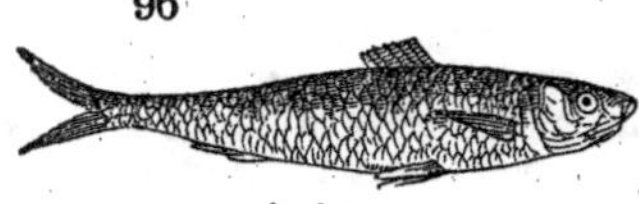

Anchovy.

The Turtle of the Mediterranean is that described by authors under the name of *Testudo carella:* writers have uniformly copied each other in asserting that this is the same as the Loggerhead Turtle of the West Indies; and that its flesh is coarse, rank, oily, and not edible. The accuracy of both these statements may be questioned. Whatever may be the qualities of the West Indian Loggerhead, we know, from personal experience, that the flesh of the Mediterranean species is delicious. We were once becalmed off the Isle of Elba, and in one morning captured a sufficient number of small turtle to supply the cabin table for a week. They made exquisite soup; and although one of the company was ill, it arose from repletion. We omitted to draw and describe the animal, from a belief that it was the Hawk's-bill Turtle, the only species described as inhabiting the Mediterranean; the figure given by Gottwold (*fig.* 97.) has been considered, by Dr. Shaw, as representing the *Testudo caretta.*

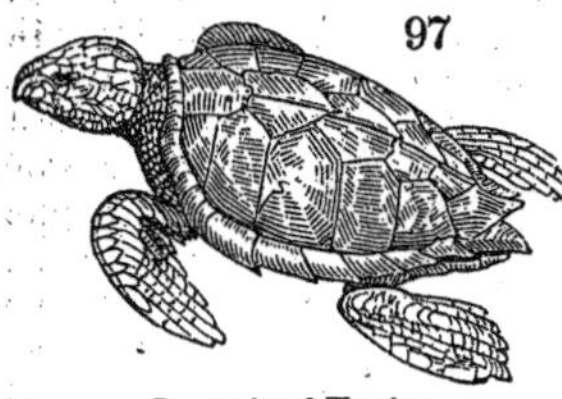
97

Loggerhead Turtle.

Of European insects, a bare enumeration of the genera would alone fill a volume; and in the half-artificial, half-natural, arrangement in which our entomological systems at this moment remain, it is impossible to form any precise idea even on the natural distribution of the families. As we approach the provinces of southern Italy and the Peloponnesus, we find many genera which more properly characterise Western Asia and Africa; while, in Sicily and Malta, the geodephagous groups, particularly the Linnæan *Carabii*, are diminished; apparently in species, but certainly in numbers. It is in these countries that the Ants, those universal scavengers of nature in tropical countries, begin to appear in almost every situation, and to perform those offices which in more temperate regions have been assigned to the *Geodephaga*, *Brachelytra*, and *Necrophaga* among coleopterous insects. Most of the northern Butterflies (*Papiliones* Sw.) are common even in Sicily, where, notwithstanding a dissimilar vegetation and a more heated atmosphere, we find only three or four species unknown to the British fauna: among these, the *Gonepteryx Cleopatra* (*fig.* 98.) or Cleopatra's Butterfly, much resembles a British species, but has the middle of the anterior wings of a rich orange.

98

Cleopatra's Butterfly.

The Radiated animals of the Mediterranean are particularly numerous; the many harbours, coves, and sub-immersed rocks, sheltered from those violent commotions which agitate the mighty Atlantic, afford them secure protection, and contribute to their rapid increase. Their investigation, hitherto much neglected, offers a wide field for the discoveries of naturalists who can study them in their native seas. Numerous species of Sea Anemone, or animal flowers, unfold themselves in the crevices of the rocks; one of these (*fig.* 99.), ornamented with rich purple, is particularly common on all the shores of Sicily.

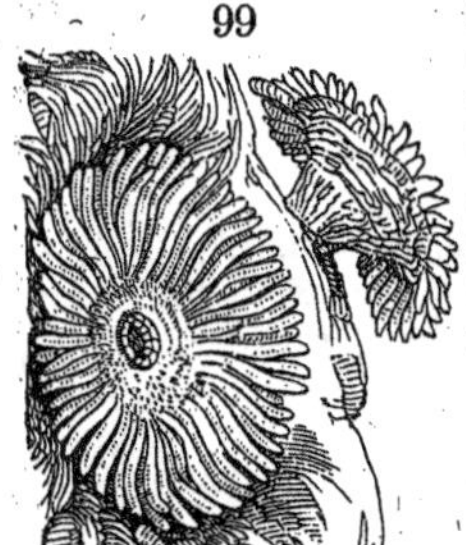
99

Animal Flowers.

The tubular and cellular polypes, whose habitations are termed corals and corallines, are generally abundant in warm latitudes. Among these a vast number of species occurs on the shores of Sicily, Italy, and the Greek islands, which do not inhabit the British coasts. Sicily, for many ages, has been celebrated for its fisheries of the true red coral (*fig.* 100.); and it still affords employment at certain seasons to many fishermen: but the produce of the old grounds of late years has materially diminished, through want of care and due preservation. The Bay of Naples likewise produces this beautiful substance, but the pieces usually found are small, and in no great abundance.

100

Red Coral.

The Molluscous animals or shell-fish of southern Europe are in great variety; and are much prized by all classes, as general articles of food. It is no uncommon thing to see from twelve to fifteen different sorts of shell-fish, none of a small size, exposed in the principal market at Naples; and we have been assured that double this number are not unfrequently served at the tables of the higher ecclesiastics and nobility of Tarentum during Lent, that city being highly celebrated for its shell-fish. The *Solen strigilatus* (*fig.* 101.) is abundant at Naples, and considered most delicate food.

101

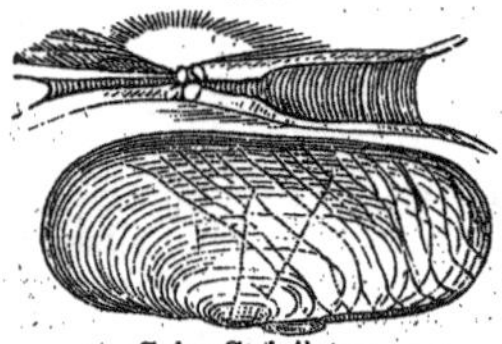

Solen Strigilatus.

On comparing the conchology of the Mediterranean with that of Britain, there does not appear so much difference as at first might have been imagined; nor are we aware of more than three or four genera in those southern latitudes of which examples have not been found in the British seas. Yet, on descending to species, the difference is much greater. Perhaps two-thirds or three-fifths of the Mediterranean shells have been found in the Channel, and on the western or other coasts of Britain. The remaining portion indicate a strong affinity with the conchology of India and the Red Sea on one hand, and that of Africa, towards Senegal, on the other. The fluviatile species are most numerous in central Europe, where the heat of summer is less calculated to dry up those small pools and shallow streams, in which most of these univalve mollusca delight to dwell. The fluviatile bivalves are few; but are of species which seem peculiar to the European range. Independently of those common alike to Britain and the Continent, there are others in France and the south of Europe (*fig.* 102). *Unio littoralis* (*a*) and the true *U. batava* (*b*) are common in the Seine; and we have received another shell from near Gibraltar, which we suspect to be a new species, intermediate between the latter and *ovatus;* we name it provisionally *Unio intermedius* (*c, c*).

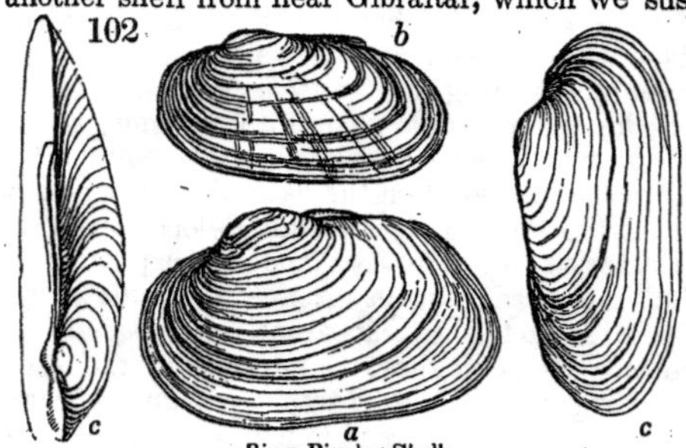

River Bivalve Shells.

The Cephalopoda, or cuttle-fish of the Mediterranean, though not of many species, are sometimes found in prodigious numbers, and frequently grow to an enormous size. The zoology of the Black and Caspian Seas is very little known.

The phosphorescence of the Mediterranean is at times so brilliant, that it excites the admiration of all voyagers; it therefore deserves to be particularly mentioned. This phenomenon, is entirely produced by various marine animals. Spix, the Bavarian naturalist and traveller, in his passage down the Mediterranean, caused several buckets to be filled with this luminous water; and the following results attended his experiments:—

These luminous animalcula adhered to whatever was wetted with the water, and continued to shine thereon; the buckets, when shaken, appearing full of luminous particles. The water, examined by a microscope, was filled with little bodies, some roundish, some oblong, and generally about the size of a poppy-seed; each of these had, at one end, a small navel-like opening, encircled by from six to nine delicate filaments which float within the bladder, and with which the animal seems to attach itself to other bodies, and to seize its nourishment. In the inside of these bladders there were many other small darker points, crowded together on one side, or here and there some larger ones, which might be either the remains of smaller animals which they had swallowed, or their own spawn. These globular animalcula (which Spix considers to be of the nature of Medusæ) have been named by Péron and Lechenault *Arethusa pelagica*, and by Savigny *Noctiluca miliaris.* They swim in greater or less numbers at night, but in the sunshine they appear to the naked eye like little drops of grease. When put into a vessel they soon die and fall to the bottom; when they come near together, they appear involuntarily to attach each other, so that they form whole groups. The same phenomenon is sometimes observed in the day-time, when the sky is dark, which rarely happens: as these animals are seldom found in water taken up in the day-time, it is probable they then sink to the depths of the ocean, and only return near the surface towards night. (*Spix, Trav.*)

Other luminous bodies resemble balls as large as a nut; and every wave striking a ship, when filled with these animals, lights up all surrounding objects. Besides these, there are sometimes insulated luminous bladders, like fiery balls, a foot in diameter, which rise singly above the water; and the striking of two waves together produces a shallow bluish streak of light, resembling the reflection of lightning on the water. (*Spix, Trav.* i. 44. 47.)

The quadrupeds of Europe, according to the most recent distribution of the species (*Griff. Cuv.*), under the modern divisions, comprise about ninety species, arranged under the following genera and sub-genera. To these must be added the fish-quadrupeds, or Cetaceæ, chiefly inhabiting the high northern latitudes:—

| | | | | | | | | | | | |
|---|---|---|---|---|---|---|---|---|---|---|---|
| *Bats.* | | Sorex | 8 | Lutra | 1 | Myoxus | 2 | Hystrix | 1 | Taurus | 2 |
| | | Mygale | 2 | Canis | 1 | Mus | 8 | Lepus | 3 | | |
| Rinolphus | 2 | Talpa | 1 | Vulpes | 3 | Cricetus | 2 | Lagomys | 2 | *Marine.* | |
| Plecotus | 1 | Ursus | 2 | Felis | 1 | Gerbillus | 1 | Cervus | 3 | Phoca | 1 |
| Vespertilio | 13 | Meles | 1 | Lynx | 1 | Aspalax | 1 | Antilope | 1 | Trichecus | 1 |
| | | Gulo | 1 | Castor | 1 | Arctomys | 3 | Rupricapra | 1 | Otaria | 1 |
| *Land Quadrupeds.* | | Putorius | 4 | Arvicola | 4 | Sciurus | 2 | Capra | 1 | Mirounga | 1 |
| Erinaceus | 2 | Martes | 2 | Georychus | 1 | Pteromys | 1 | Ovis | 1 | | |

The genera of European birds, in reference to our former remarks on the geographic distribution of animals, deserves particular attention. Those marked * are typical of families or sub-families; those † include sub-genera, or subordinate variations of structure to which we shall not attach a distinct patronymic name; either because the higher groups have not been sufficiently analysed, or because these subordinate forms have been mistaken for genera. Decided stragglers are excluded; other genera, of uncertain rank, are not marked. The typical genera of the wading birds have not yet been ascertained.

*Rapacious Birds.*

* Vultur *Auct.*
* Gypætos *Stor.*
Neophron *Sav.*
Pandion *Sav.*
Haliætus *Sav.*
Aquila *Ray.*
Aster
Accipiter
* Falco
† Buteo
† Circus
† Strix

*Fissirostres.*

Caprimulgus
* Hirundo
Cypselus *Ill.*
* Merops
Coracias
* Alcedo

*Dentirostres* Cuv.

* Muscicapa
* Lanius
* Merula *Ray.*
Cinclus
* Oriolus
* Saxicola
Erythæca *Sw.*
Phœnicura *Sw.*
* Philomela *Sw.*
† Curruca *Bech.*
* † Sylvia *Lin.*
* † Parus *Lin.*
Accentor *Bech.*
Budytes *Cuv.*
* Motacilla *Lin.*
† Anthus *Bech.*
* Bombycilla *Bris.*
* † Alauda
* † Emberyza
* Carduelis
Pyrgita *Cuv.*
* † Fringilla *Sw.*
* Pyrrhula *Cuv.*
* Sturnus
* † Pastor *Tem.*
Nucifraga *Bris.*
* † Corvus
* Garrulus
Fregilus *Cuv.*
* Coccothraustes *Bris.*
Corythus *Cuv.*

*Climbers.*

* Cuculus
Dryotomus *Sw.*
Dendrocopus *Sw.*
Apternus *Sw.*
Chrysoptilus *Sw.*
* Sitta *Lin.*
* Certhia *Lin.*
Tichodroma
Troglodytes
* Upupa *Lin.*

*Gallinaceous Birds.*

Tetrao *Lin.*
Lagopus *Ray.*
Lyurus *Sw.*
* Columba *Lin.*
* Phasianus *Lin.*
* Perdix *Lin.*
* Coturnix *Tem.*
Pterocles *Tem.*
* Otis *Lin.*

*Waders.*

Balearica *Bris.*
Grus *Ant.*
Ardea *Ant.*
Phœnicopterus *Lin.*
Platalea *Lin.*
Tantalus *Lin.*
Ibis *Ant.*
Numenius *Bris.*
† Tolanus *Bech.*
Recurvirostris
† Limosa
Scolopax
† Machetes *Cuv.*
† Phalaropus
Phæopus *Cuv.*
Glareola
Rallus
Crex *Bech.*
Gallinula *Bris.*
Porphyrio *Bris.*
Fulica
Hæmatopus
† Calidres *Illiger.*
Tachydromus *Ill.*
Strepsilas *Ill.*
† Tringa, *L.*
Vanellus *Bris.*
† Charadrius *Lin.*
Œdicnemus *Cuv.*
Himantopus *Bris.*

*Swimmers.*

* † Anser
* † Anas
* † Mergus
† Cygnus
Podiceps *Lath.*
Colymbus
† Uria
Mormon *Ill.*
† Alca
Halicus *Ill.*
Dysporus *Ill.*
* Pelecanus *Lin.*
* Sturna *L.*
Thalassidroma *Vig.*
* Larus *L.*
Lestris *Ill.*
Procellaria *L.*
Puffinus *Ray.*

## Sect. V.—*Languages.*

Europe, considered in regard to its languages, comprehends the whole globe, through those immense colonies which have been founded by the nations of this continent in every other quarter of the world.

The European languages, ancient and modern, form six families:—1. The family of the *Iberian* languages; 2. That of the *Celtic* languages; 3. That of the *Thraco-Pelasgic* or *Græco-Latin* languages; 4. The family of the *Germanic* languages; 5. That of the *Sclavonic* languages; 6. The family of the *Uralian* languages, commonly called the *Finnish* or *Chudic.*

### Subsect. 1.

The Iberian or Basque family has been divided into the two following branches:—1. Ancient languages long extinct, under which are classed the idioms spoken by the Iberians in the greater part of the Spanish peninsula, in southern Gaul, and in some parts of Italy and its three great islands. 2. Ancient languages still living; of which the only one remaining is the *Escuara* or *Basque*, formerly spoken in a large portion of Spain and of southern Gaul, and now spoken only by the *Vascongados* or *Basques* in the Spanish provinces of Biscay and Navarre, and in some parts of the south of France. The Basques are the descendants of the ancient Vascones. Their language, which resembles no other European idiom, though it has adopted several Latin and some German words, appears to have a certain affinity to the Shemitic languages, and, in its conjugations, some analogy to the languges of America.

### Subsect. 2.

The Celtic family exhibits, like the Basque, two branches:—1. Ancient languages long extinct, among which are classed the idioms spoken by the numerous Celtic nations in Gaul, in Belgium, in the British Isles, in parts of Germany, Italy, and also Galatia in Asia Minor. 2. Ancient languages still living, of which there are two: 1. The *Gallic, Gaelic* or *Celtic Proper*, spoken in *different* dialects by the descendants of the true Celts, in a large portion of Ireland, in the Highlands of Scotland, in the Hebrides, and in the Isle of Man. 2. The Cambrian or Celto-Belgic, formerly spoken by the Cymri or Belgæ in Belgium and Britain, and now confined to a part of England and France. In this language are distinguished three principal dialects: the *Welsh*, spoken and written by the people of that name descended from the ancient Britons; the *Cornish*, formerly spoken throughout Cornwall, but extinct since about the middle of the last century; and the *Bas-Breton*, called also by French writers the *Celto-Breton*, spoken in the part of France formerly called Lower Bretagne, by the descendants of those British fugitives who, in the fifth century, sought refuge and settled in Armorica. The *Bas-Breton* has many sub-dialects and varieties.

### Subsect. 3.

The numerous family of the Græco-Latin languages may be divided into four branches: I. The *Illyrian;* II. The *Etruscan;* III. The *Hellenic;* IV. The *Italic*, including the Latin, the Romaic or Romano-Rustic, the modern Italian, the French, the Spanish or Castilian, the Portuguese, and the Valaque or Wallachian.

I. The Thraco-Illyrian branch includes all those Thracian and Illyrian nations once seated in Asia Minor west of the river Halys, and in Europe all over its eastern portion, from Noricum, occupied by Celtic tribes, to the mouths of the Danube and the Dnieper, and even beyond. Of those nations, long extinct, or confounded with others, the principal were the Phrygians, the Trojans, the Bithynians, the Lydians, the Carians, the Lycians, the Cimmerii, the Tauri, the Thracians properly so called, the Mæsi, the Getæ, the Macedonians, the ancient Illyrians, among whom were the Dalmati and the Istri, the Pannonians or Pæones, the Veneti, and the Siculi. In this branch, according to M. Malte-Brun, may be not improperly placed—

The Albanian, spoken in Albania and other countries by the *Skipatar*, named Arnauts by the Turks, and generally known under the name of Albanians. They form the principal population of Albania, and are scattered throughout European Turkey, especially in Roumelia, Bulgaria, and Macedonia; others on the Slavonic military confines of the Austrian empire, and others in various parts of the kingdom of the Two Sicilies. This *Scyp*, or Albanian language, according to M. Malte-Brun, appears to be formed of one-third of ancient Greek, especially the Æolic dialect, one-third Latin, and one-third of an idiom not yet ascertained, probably the Illyrian. The Albanians have three different alphabets: one sacred or hieratic, now fallen into disuse; another, the Greek alphabet; a third, the modern Italian or Latin.

II. The Etruscan, (we are here reminded of the *Osci* and *Heterosci*, quasi *Etrusci?*) spoken by the Etrurians, called also Tyrrhenians by the Greeks. This nation, according to some, appears to have been a mixture of Rhætian Celts with the Aborigines of Italy. The Etruscan alphabet was the same with the primitive alphabet of the Greeks; it had sixteen letters, and was written from right to left.

III. The Pelasgo-Hellenic, including the idioms in ancient times spoken by the famous *Pelasgi* and *Hellenes*, long since incorporated with other nations. The people of early origin who may with probability be classed under this branch are, the Pelasgi, the Leleges, and other tribes enumerated by ancient geographers among the population of Greece and its isles, especially the Græci, originally a small community of Thessaly, but remarkable for having given name to the whole of that celebrated nation, whose language was—

The Hellenic, or ancient Greek, formerly spoken in Greece and its dependencies, and at a later period in a great part of Sicily, Lower Italy, Asia Minor, Egypt, and its dependencies, in part of Gallia Narbonensis, and in other districts bordering on the Mediterranean.

During the Macedonian empire the Hellenic was spoken at all the courts of the descendants of Alexander, and by persons of distinction in all the countries subject to the Macedonians. In a subsequent age, it was studied by all the most distinguished subjects of the Roman empire, and was the prevailing idiom in the East until the fall of Constantinople, at which period it was studied with renewed ardour in the West. In this language, 270 years before Christ, was written the famous version of the Hebrew Scriptures called the Septuagint; in this language also was the Gospel promulgated by the Apostles; and it thus became for ever sacred. It appears not the least wonderful among the dispensations of Providence, that the light of Christianity should have been originally diffused under the most powerful empire and in the most cultivated language of the ancient world, and that it should prevail notwithstanding the power of the one, and the learning and philosophy for which the other was so proudly distinguished. The literature of the Greeks, comprehending some of the finest productions of the human mind, is, perhaps, the richest in the world, and presents an unparalleled series of eminent writers, extending from the age of Homer to the middle of the fifteenth century. The language is one of the most flexible, harmonious, and copious that have ever existed; its grammatical forms are almost identical with those of the Latin, to the formation of which it has greatly contributed, but in many essential points it is superior, and especially in the unlimited faculty of making as many compounds as can be required. M. Malte-Brun distinguishes in the ancient Greek two different idioms:—1. The *primitive Hellenic*, which he subdivides into three principal dialects—the Arcadian, the Thessalian, with the ancient Macedonian, and the Œnotrian, transported into Italy and mingled with the Latin; 2. The Hellenic of the historical times, divided into four principal dialects and several varieties.

The Romaic, or the modern Greek, spoken by the Greeks of our own times, especially in the Morea, in Livadia, Thessaly, the isle of Candia, the Archipelago, part of Albania, Macedonia, Roumelia, Thrace, Asia Minor, Cyprus, and by the Greeks established in Wallachia, Moldavia, Syria, and Egypt. The Romaic is also spoken by the inhabitants of the Ionian Isles, by considerable numbers of Greeks in the Austrian and Russian empires, and some hundred of Mainotes in Corsica, near Ajaccio. It is divided into two principal dialects, the Romanic and the Æolo-Dorian, each including various sub-dialects.

IV. The Italic branch, so called, as including the languages of the aborigines of Italy, which form the stem of the modern idioms comprised in this branch. Those *aborigines* were, the Euganei, the Ausones, the Lucani, the Brutti, the Piceni, the Marsi, the Latini the Sabines, and the Samnites. From a mixture of the three last idioms, primarily with the original Hellenic, afterwards with the old Æolian and ancient Doric, was formed, as M. Malte-Brun inclines to think, the language spoken by the Romans, and called the Latin language. The languages included in that branch are,—

The Latin, which was the written and current language of the higher classes in Italy and throughout the Roman empire. It was very different from the *lingua plebeia* or *rustica*, spoken in the rural districts of the peninsula, and by the lower classes in Spain, Gaul, and the other provinces. Its grammatical forms are similar to the Greek, though less perfect. Latin literature, formed on that of Greece, is very rich in all branches of knowledge, and, together with the Greek, is the source from which flows the literature of the modern nations of Europe. Its most brilliant epoch was the Augustan age. In this language St. Jerome wrote the Vulgate, or Latin translation of the Bible which is used in the Romish church. The overthrow of the Roman empire in the fifth century gave birth to a corrupt Latin, mingled with a great number of barbarous words, and named low Latin, which, until the fourteenth, was, almost exclusively, the written language throughout the West. In the two succeeding centuries, Latin literature again flourished, especially in Italy; but it was only to contribute to the improvement of modern languages, which being diligently and successfully cultivated, the Latin was restricted to works of erudition alone. Its phraseology has had a marked influence on that of the most polite nations of Europe. It is now a dead language, except in Poland and Hungary, where some educated persons speak it in ordinary life with considerable purity, and with the continental pronunciation, of course almost unintelligible to English travellers, who cannot or will not relinquish the Saxon diphthongal sounds of the vowels A, I, and U, the chief causes of their embarrassment. Latin is no longer employed except in the Catholic liturgy, in medicine, in the diplomacy of the court of Rome, and partially in the literature of all the civilized nations of Europe. The alphabet, of twenty-three letters, having been improved in its characters by the Italians and French, is used by all the people of Europe, except the Greeks, the Russians, and some other nations who have particular alphabets. This same Latin alphabet, with the Gothic forms it assumed under the pen of the writers of the middle ages, is used by the Germans and Danes, and by the Bohemians, and other Slavonic nations; and, according to some authors, its capital letters, truncated and squared to facilitate the inscription of them in wood or stone, constitute the Runic alphabet, formerly used in the north of Europe.

The Romana, or Romana Rustica, spoken in the brightest ages of Rome by the lower classes in the south of the empire, excepting Greece, and some other counties. After various modifications more or less considerable, it appears still to subsist among the vulgar dialects spoken throughout a great part of Spain, France, Switzerland, and some districts of Italy. The chief of those dialects, according to M. Champollion Figeac, are the following, classed with reference to those four regions:—In Spain, Sardinia, and the Balearic Isles, the Catalan, the Valencian, the Majorcan. In France, the Languedocian, the Provençal, the Dauphinois, the Lyonnais, the Auvergnat, the Limousin, and the Gascon. In Switzerland, the Romanic, or Celto-Romanic, (frequently called Romance, Khurwelsh, and Rhætish,) the Valaisan in the Valais. In the states of the king of Sardinia are spoken the Savoisian; and the Vaudois in the vales of Lucerne, Perosa, and part of Piedmont. To these might be added the jargon called *lingua Franca*, in which Catalan, Limousin, Sicilian, and Arabic are the principal ingredients. The Romance literature is also called that of the Troubadours. From the mixture of this language with the different Germanic, Slavonic, and other idioms, were formed, in the tenth century, the following languages:—

The Italian, spoken by the Italians in almost all Italy, in the isles geographically connected with that peninsula, and in various Alpine territories; also frequent in Dalmatia and the isle of Tino; very common at Constantinople, and in several mercantile towns of the Ottoman empire. The *written* language, which is nowhere *generally* spoken, is common with all well-educated Italians, and differs considerably from the vulgar tongue, which is subdivided into a great number of dialects. The principal of these are, the Piedmontese and Genoese; the Milanese, or Lombard proper; the Low Lombard; the Bolognese, the Bergamasc; the Venetian, the Friulian, the Tyrolean, the vulgar Tuscan; the Roman; the Sabine and Abruzzan; the Calabrian and Apulian; the Tarentine; the Neapolitan; the Sicilian, and the Sardinian.

The French language, spoken by the French almost throughout the north of France; by the Walloons and Flemings in various Netherlandish provinces; by the Swiss, in several of their cantons; by the people of Jersey and Guernsey; also in some parts of the Austrian and Russian empires, and of the Prussian monarchy; by the French colonists in Asia, Africa, and America. The following are the principal dialects:—the *Picard*, the *Flemish*, the *Norman*, the *Walloon* or *Rounchi*, the *vulgar French*, the *Breton French*, the *Champénois*, the *Lorraine*, the *Burgundian*, the *Franche-Comté*, the *Neufchâtelain*, the *Orléannois*, the *Angevin*, and the *Manceau*. To these might, perhaps, be added the jargon spoken by the negroes and creoles in the French West Indies.

The Spanish or Castilian language, spoken by the Spaniards in the greater part of Spain, and, with some variation and admixture, by their descendants in Oceania, Africa, and America; also by the numerous Spanish Jews established in the Ottoman empire, and in other states of Europe, and of North Africa; in the isle of Trinidad belonging to the crown of Great Britain; in some parts of Florida and Louisiana; and in the eastern part of Hispaniola or St. Domingo. This language is also common to all the inhabitants of the towns of Spain where the Basque and Romance languages are spoken. The written and polished language is almost identical in its grammatical forms with the Romance and the Portuguese; and differs little from the Italian; it is very rich and harmonious, notwithstanding some guttural and aspirate sounds taken from the Arabic, from which it has borrowed many words. It is singular to remark, that the *German* is characterised by similar gutturals or aspirates. The reigns of the emperor Charles V. and of his son Philip II. were the golden age of Spanish literature; after which it fell into decay, but partially revived under the Bourbon kings Philip V. and Charles III. Of the dialects, which differ little from each other, the following are the principal:—the dialect of Toledo; that of Leon and the Asturias; the Andalusian; the Murcian; the Galician, or Gallego; and the Transatlantic, spoken in America; where, next to the English, the Spanish language is spoken by the greatest number of inhabitants.

The Portuguese language, spoken by the Portuguese in Portugal and the Azores, and, with some differences, by the Portuguese Jews settled in Hamburg, Amsterdam, the Tyrol, and other parts of Europe, Asia, and Africa; also by the descendants of the Portuguese in their Asiatic, African, Oceanic, and American colonies. The Portuguese is as rich and concise as its sister languages; it has borrowed some words from the Arabic and the French; to the French it seems indebted for the soft sound of *g*, and for the nasal syllables; it is sonorous, soft, and unimpeded by the aspirates and gutturals of the Spanish; but the frequency of hiatus, and of the modern nasal *ao*, equisonant with the French *am* or *an*, injure the harmony of the language. Its origin, like that of the Spanish, is dated in the eleventh century; and it had attained its maturity in the sixteenth. The Portuguese literature, which Camoens illustrated with one of the finest epics in existence, is as varied and rich as the Spanish, though less known. It revived in the memorable reign of Joseph. The language may be said to exhibit no differences of dialect; there are only varieties: those which differ most from the written language are, the Minho, Algarve, and Azores varieties in Europe; the Brazilian in America; those of Congo and Mozambique in Africa; and of Goa and Macao in Asia. Some, however, regard as a dialect of the Portuguese, the jargon called *lingua geral*, spoken along the east and west coasts of Africa, also along the coasts of Ceylon and the Indian peninsula. In Africa, as well as in Asia, it presents the phenomenon offered by the *lingua Franca* in the Mediterranean, and attests the power formerly held by the Portuguese in those regions.

The Valac or Wallachian, spoken by the Rumanje or Roumouni, better known as Valacs, a people apparently descended from the ancient Roman colonists settled in Dacia and Thrace, and the Slavonic and other nations dwelling there. Its literature is very meagre. Among its numerous dialects the more remarkable are the Roumounic or Valac proper, spoken in Wallachia, Moldavia, and Bessarabia; the Hungarian Valac, the Macedo-Valac, and the Kutzo-Valac, spoken in various sub-dialects, in several parts of European Turkey, south of the Danube.

### SUBSECT. 4.

The family of the Germanic languages next claims our notice. Without entering into the history of the Germanic nations, which rivals in importance that of the Græco-Latin, we may class these different idioms, according to M. Malte-Brun's theory, in four branches; the *Teutonic*, the *Saxon* or *Cimbric*, the *Scandinavian* or *Normanno-Gothic*, and the *Anglo-Britannic*.

The Teutonic branch, which comprises the idioms of the various ancient nations and tribes recognised as German by the Roman historians and writers; as the Bastarnæ, the Suevi, the Marcomanni, the Hermonduri, and the Franci, presents the following idioms:—

The ancient high German (*alt hoch Deutsch*), formerly spoken in different dialects throughout South Germany, Switzerland, Alsace, Hesse, Thuringia, Wetteravia, and a great part of the countries once subjected to the Franks. It has been extinct for several centuries: its three principal dialects were, the Francic, and the Alemannic, which are of contemporary origin, and contain the most ancient productions of that language, and the *Middle* High German, which succeeded them. The *Francic* or *Tudesc* was the language of the Franks: it was spoken at the court of the Merovingian and Carlovingian sovereigns, until Charles the Bold; after whose reign it gave way to the old French in France, but continued to be the court language in Germany until the times of the Hohenstaufen. The Middle High German is the language in which were composed the numerous works of the Suabian, Bavarian, Austrian, and Swiss writers, and several other authors in Middle and Lower Germany, from the eleventh to the fifteenth centuries. Its finest productions are dated in the period of the Hohenstaufen, from 1136 to 1254, called also the *Minnesänger*, the trouveurs and troubadours of Germany. The Nibelungen-lied, the finest epic in this language, is supposed by Winter to have been composed in 1290, by Conrad of Würtzburg.

The German, called also *neu hoch Deutsch*, in which distinction must be made between the written and the spoken language. The latter is divided into a great number of very different dialects, subdivided into several sub-dialects and varieties. The written language is nowhere spoken by the people; it was formed at the period when Luther, rejecting the *Middle High* and the *Middle Low German*, adopted in preference the dialect of Misnia or Meissen, which had begun to be written much later. This Misnian dialect, ably employed by that great man and his numerous followers, soon became, as the language of books and of good society, common to all well-educated Germans, and also ranked as the learned language of the north and great part of the east of Europe. The literature of Germany, in regard to the quality of its productions, rivals those of France and England, and surpasses them in abundance. The German is the richest in words of any language in Europe; and this distinction it owes to the great number of its monosyllabic roots, with which it creates new terms *ad infinitum*, by derivation and composition. Its principal dialects are, the Swiss; the Rhenish; the Danubian, with its four sub-dialects, the Bavarian, the Tyrolean, Austrian, and Bohemo-Hungaro-Silesian; and the Franconian, or Mittel-Deutsch. To these, on the authority of Adelung, we may add two others, remarkable for the strange admixture of words totally foreign; these are, the ***German Jewish;*** and the Rothwelsh, spoken by the Jenish or Jauner, who are generally reported to be thieves and vagabonds. It contains a multitude of terms and expressions quite different from German.

The Saxon, or Cimbric, which comprises the idioms anciently spoken by the Cimbri; also by the Angli, who, with the Jutes and Saxons, afterwards made so great a figure in northern history; the Bructeri and Chauci, the Menapi, the Tungri, the Batavi, the Frisones, and other nations of less note, the ancient Saxons, and probably the Longobardi. This branch includes the four following idioms:—

The ancient low German (***alt nieder Deutsch***), called also the ancient Saxon, after the people who spoke it. This language, now extinct, was current throughout Lower Germany and the Netherlands, except in the countries occupied by the Frisones and the Angli. About the commencement of the seventeenth century it wholly ceased to be written. Its principal dialects are, the ***Saxon proper***, or idiom of Lower Saxony; the ***Eastern Saxon***, spoken in various sub-dialects in Prussia, and the ***Westphalian***, or Western Saxon.

The Frisic, formerly spoken along the coast, from the Rhine to the Elbe, by the Frisones, and their allies the Chauci, the ancestors of the present Frisians, who are now far from numerous, and speak a language very different from the ancient Frisic, being mixed with other idioms. Its three principal dialects are, the Batavian Frisic, the Westphalian Frisic, and the North Frisic, or Cimbric.

The Netherlandish, or modern Batavian, has two principal dialects, the ***Flemish***, and the Hollandish, or, as it is commonly called in this country, the ***Dutch***. The Flemish is spoken in the southern provinces of the kingdom of the Netherlands, excepting those where German and French are spoken. It was the written and oral language of the seventeen provinces once subject to the Counts of Burgundy. After their extinction, and under the Spanish rule, the Flemish idiom gradually gave way in the north to the Dutch, in the south to the French language. The ***Dutch*** is spoken in different varieties in the seven provinces of the North, and in some bordering districts of the South: with certain changes and admixtures it is also spoken, or at least understood, in the various settlements founded by the Dutch in Africa, Oceania, and America, and in several places in Ceylon, India, and the peninsula of Malacca; in South Africa; at the Cape of Hope; and on the American continent in Guiana. Some descendants of Dutch settlers also in the United States retain their native language. It was only in the sixteenth century that this vulgar idiom of the province of Holland, in some degree polished and improved, became the national language of the Dutch. It is a mixture of ancient Francic, Frisic, and low German.

The Scandinavian, or Normanno-Gothic, comprises the idioms formerly spoken by the Jutes, the Goths or Gutæ, and other less considerable nations of pure Gothic race. There are five different idioms in this branch:—

The Mœso-Gothic, formerly spoken by the Goths established in Mœsia. According to Grimm, this is the richest of the Germanic languages in grammatical forms: it has not less than fifteen declensions, with 120 cases, and sixteen conjugations. The Mœso-Gothic has been dead many centuries. Its most ancient productions are, the famous ***Codex Argenteus*** of Upsal; and other fragments of the translation of the Bible, made between the years 360 and 380, by Bishop Ulphilas. The Mœso-Goths appear to have been the first to embrace Christianity of all those nations who overthrew the Roman empire.

The Normannic, called by Grimm the ***Alt-Nordisch***. It is the language of the Edda, of the Voluspa, and other poems of uncertain date, and was generally spoken throughout Scandinavia in the eighth, ninth, and tenth centuries.

The Norwegian, ancient Norwegian, Norrœna tunga, not to be confounded with the modern Norwegian or Norsk, which is only a dialect of the Danish. Its principal dialects are, the Icelandic, the Norwegian proper, the Dalska, or Western Dalecarlian, the Jämtlandish, and the Norse, spoken in the Shetland Isles.

The Swedish (***Svenski***), spoken by the Swedes throughout the greater part of the Swedish monarchy; also in the principal towns of Finland and the isle of Runoe, in the Russian empire. It has two principal dialects, the Swedish, and the modern Gothic, subdivided into several sub-dialects and varieties.

The Danish, spoken by the Danes in Denmark, and in their Asiatic, African, and American settlements; also by the higher classes in the Feröe Isles, and in Iceland. It has two principal dialects, each having several sub-dialects and varieties: the ***Danish proper***, which includes the insular Danish, the ancient sub-dialect of Bornholm, the modern Norwegian, and the idiom of Scania. The ***Jutlandish***, or modern Jutic, including the Normanno-Jutic, the Dano-Jutic, and the Anglo-Jutic.

The Anglo-Britannic (not to be confounded with the *British*, which is *Welsh*), comprises only two idioms.

The Anglo-Saxon, formed by a mixture of the idioms spoken by the Angli, the Saxons and the Jutes, who, invited by the Britons against the Picts, finally took possession of the country, where their language was successively preserved in three dialects, until the eighth century. During the invasions and temporary ascendency of the Danes, it was so modified as to become *Dano-Saxon*, or rather this may be called a dialect of the Anglo-Saxon. For several centuries this language has been totally dead.

The English, spoken in England, in the east and south-east of Scotland, in part of Ireland and of Wales; in the Shetland Isles, in the isles of Jersey and Guernsey, in the British colonies of Asia, Oceania, Africa, and America. It is the national language of the United States of America. It is also cultivated and spoken by a great number of persons of different nations in all parts of the world on account of its literary, political, and commercial importance: the two latter considerations render it very current in the kingdom of Hanover, in the Ionian Isles and Malta, in Portugal and Brazil, and in the republic of Hayti. The English language is a mixture of the Anglo-Saxon and the Neustrian French or Franco-Norman, with some Celtic words, and a few of ancient British origin. It has imported largely from the Greek and Latin, as knowledge and culture advanced in the nation. If the number of words in the language be taken at thirty-eight thousand, those of Saxon or northern origin will be found limited to about eight thousand, the rest being principally Greek and Latin derivatives. Copious and energetic, the English language is the simplest and most monosyllabic of all European idioms; and it is that also of which the pronunciation differs most from the orthography. It did not become the language of the state until the reign of Edward III., since which time it has rapidly improved. Towards the commencement of the seventeenth century may be dated its regular developement, and in the beginning of the eighteenth it took its fixed and invariable form. The English language occupies one of the most eminent places in European literature; it is comparable with any of them in elegance, and perhaps, surpasses them all in energy. It is no less graceful than concise; its poetry is at once manly and harmonious; and, like that of the cognate languages of the north, is admirably adapted to depict the sublimities of nature and pourtray the stronger passions: as the language of political and parliamentary eloquence, *it is without a rival.* Of the number of its dialects it might be difficult to speak with precision: foreign philologers distinguish four as the principal:—the *English* proper; the *Northumbrian English*, called also Dano-English from the great number of Danish words retained in it, and spoken in various sub-dialects in Yorkshire, Lancashire, Cumberland, and Westmoreland: the *Scottish* or *Anglo-Scandinavian*, including the *Lowland Scottish*, with the Border language; and lastly the *Ultra-European English*, prevalent in the English colonies and in the United States. It has been observed that the English language is spoken by the *greatest number* of the inhabitants of the New World.

### SUBSECT. 5.

The family of the Slavonic languages is widely diffused. From the neighbourhood of Udina in Italy, from Sillian in the Tyrol, and from the centre of Germany to the remotest extremities of Europe and of Asia, and even to the north-west coast of America, are nations of Slavonic origin to be found; the tract of country over which they hold sway amounting to about a sixth part of the habitable surface of the globe. These nations exhibit almost all the varieties of the human race, both physical and moral, if not from the most exalted, at least to the most degraded.

The Slavonic languages, so far as is at present known, may be regarded as forming three branches:—1. The Russo-Illyrian. 2. The Bohemo-Polish. 3. The Wendo-Lithuanian.

(1.) The RUSSO-ILLYRIAN is so called from its chief people, the Russians, and from the general appellation Illyrian given to most of the nations who speak Servian or Croate. The languages comprised in this branch are:—

The Slavonic, Servian, Serbe, or Illyrian, called also by some authors *Rutena*, spoken in different dialects by the more southern Slavi, generally denominated Illyrians. They dwell in the Austrian and Ottoman empires, excepting a small number, settled as colonists in south Russia. The dialects differing most from each other, and from the ancient Slavonic, are the *Servian* or *Serblin*, with various sub-dialects; the *Italiano-Slavonic*, spoken on the coast of Dalmatia; the *Uskoke*, spoken by the wandering tribes in Servia, Bosnia, Dalmatia, Croatia, Maritime Hungary, and Carniola. It is mixed with many Turkish words. Lastly, the *Bulgarian*, spoken in Bulgaria, in the Ottoman empire.

The Russian, Ruski, or modern Russian, spoken throughout the Russian empire by the Russians, who are the ruling nation; also spoken in a great part of Gallicia and part of Hungary in the Austrian empire. Since the reign of the Czar Peter, when the Slavvenski was abandoned for the Ruski, it became the language of literature and of business throughout Russia. It has the following dialects, which differ little from each other, the *Valiki-Ruski* or Russian of Great Russia; the *Malo-Ruski*, or Russian of Little Russia; the *Suzdalian*, the *Olonetzian*, and the Rusniac.

The Croate, spoken by the Croates or Khorbates, who delight to call it the *Illyrian.*

The Wende or Winde, spoken by several Slavonic nations subject to the Austrian empire, and known by different names in the countries they inhabit. In the Wende appear to be distinguished three principal dialects, the Carniolan, the Carinthian, and the Styrian.

(2.) The Bohemo-polish, named from its two principal nations, the Bohemians and the Poles. The languages belonging to this branch are the *Bohemian* or *Chekhe*, including the Bohemian proper, and certain idioms, bearing the character of principal dialects, and spoken in the Austrian empire.

The Bohemian proper, or Chekhe, is spoken in several very different sub-dialects by the Chekhes or Czecks, better known by the appellation of Bohemians. The dialect of Prague is the most elegant and pure. The others are the *Slowac*, the *Hannac*, the *Straniac*, the *Passekarsk*, the *Sallashac*, and the *Szotac.*

The Polish is spoken by the Poles, called in the middle ages, Lechen or Liachy. They form more than three-fourths of the population of the present Russian kingdom of Poland, almost the whole population of the province of Cracow, and of the western part of Gallicia, in the empire of Austria. They also form three-fourths of the population of the grand duchy of Posen, two-thirds of that of West-Prussia, and part of that of Silesia. The Polish is also the national language of the nobility and part of the commonalty in all the countries formerly belonging to the kingdom of Poland, and is spoken by thousands of colonists in Russia. Its principal dialects are those of Great Poland, of Little Poland, of West Prussia, of Mazovia, of Polish Silesia, of the Geralys or highlanders, belonging to part of the Carpathians in Gallicia. The preference given in Poland to the Latin, long retarded the progress of this national language.

The Serbe or Sorabe, spoken until the fourteenth century by the Serbes, or Sserske. It has two dialects; the Upper Lusatian, and the Lower Lusatian.

(3.) The Wendo-Lithuanian, called also the *Germano-Slavonic.* This branch comprises the following idioms:—

The Wend, spoken until the fourteenth century in different dialects throughout the north of Germany, from Holstein to Pomerania, by various nations, as the *Wagrians*, the *Polabes*, the *Wilzians*, the *Obotrites*, the *Rugians*, and the *Pomeranians.* Since the fourteenth century it has been extinct, with the exception of the *Linonish*, improperly called the *Polabish* dialect, which subsisted in some districts, until the latter half of the eighteenth.

The Prucze or ancient Prussian, formerly spoken in eleven very different dialects, by tho tribes forming the powerful nation of the Pruczi, dwelling between the Vistula and the Pregel. It is almost entirely extinct.

The Lithuanian or Littauish, formerly spoken by those powerful nations the Lithuanians and Kriwitschi, and now current only among the common people; as the higher classes speak Polish, with Russian or German, according to their different countries. Its principal dialects have been thus classed:—The *Lithuanian proper*, the *Samogitian*, the *Kriwitsh*, and the *Prusso-Lithuanian.*

The Lette, Lettwa, Lettonian, or Lettish, spoken by the Letts or Lettons, forming the bulk of the population in the government of Mitta, a large part of that of Riga, a small portion of that of Witepsk in Russia, and of the province of East Prussia. It has five principal dialects, subdivided into a multitude of very different sub-dialects. The former, according to Mr. Watson, are, the *Lette proper;* the *Semgallian* or *Sengallish;* the *Letto-Livonian* or *Lieflandish;* the *Seelian*, spoken by the Seeles in Courland: the *Wende* by the Wendes, in the north-east of that duchy, particularly in the neighbourhood of Windau. This language abounds with German phrases and expressions.

The Slavonic nations employ five different alphabets:—1. The Cyrilian, invented by St. Cyril in 865, called also the Servian or Ruthenian. 2. The *Glagolitic*, *Slavonic*, *Krukowitza*, or *Divinica*, called also that of St. Jerome. 3. The Russian alphabet of the Czar Peter, which is the Cyrilian modified by that emperor: it has thirty-five letters, and is in use throughout the Russian empire. 4. The Sorabes, Bohemians, and Slavo-Silesians use the *German* alphabet or character. 5. The other Slavonic nations, as the Poles, Lithuanians, Lettes and Wendes, use the *Latin* or *Roman* letters. To these five alphabets may be added the *Runic Wend*, the Greek alphabet, adopted, according to Karamsin, by those Slavi who, in the eighth century, settled in Peloponnesus; and lastly, the *Bulgarian*, imitated from the Glagolitic, and used by the Bulgarians.

### Subsect. 6.

The family of the Uralian languages, also called the Finnish or Chudic, completes the ethnographic division of Europe.

From the north-west coast of Norway to the long chain of the Urals, and beyond those mountains to near the Yeniseï in the centre of Siberia, in another direction from the Leitha to the Seret, and from the Carpathians to the Danube, nations of Uralian race live among other nations, and retain the manners, habits, and language of their forefathers. In marking the gradations among the people composing this family, we may consider the Hungarians and the Ostiaks as exhibiting the two extremes in a moral as well as physical respect, notwithstanding the great affinity of their respective languages.

The Uralian family includes four branches, according to Klaproth; but some languages not included in them may be separately considered as a fifth.

The Finnish, or Germanised Finnish branch, includes the four following languages:—

(1.) The Finnish proper, or Sumenkieli, spoken by the Suomi, better known as the Fins or Finlanders. Its principal dialects are, the Finlandish, the Tawastian, the Carelian or Kyriala, the Olonetzian, and the Watailaiset.

The Esthonian spoken by the Esthonians or Esthen, whose ancestors were formidable pirates, and who now form the most numerous part of the population of the government of Reval, and of the circles of Pernau and Dorpat in that of Riga. Its two principal dialects are that of Reval and that of Dorpat.

The Lapponian, spoken by the Sames, better known as the Lappons or Laplanders, inhabiting the northern extremity of Europe, partly under the monarchy of the Swedes, and partly under the Russian empire. This language, which is said to have more affinity with the Hungarian than with the Finnish, has a great number of very different dialects, which nave been classed under the *Lappo-Norwegian*, the *Lappo-Swedish* (western and eastern), the *Lappo-Russ*, spoken in the circle of Kola, in the government of Archangel. Through the beneficent care of the Swedish government, at the close of the last and the beginning of the present century, the Laplanders have been reclaimed from idolatry, and have begun to enjoy the blessings of Christianity and civilization.

The Livonian, spoken formerly by the *Lives* or *Liven*, who gradually abandoned this idiom for the Lettish, in consequence of which it is become nearly extinct.

(2.) The Wolgaic branch includes the languages spoken along the Wolga and its tributaries. They have a strong admixture of Turkish, and may rank under two classes, the Cheremisse and the Morduine, including as dialects the Mokshau and the Ersan.

(3.) The Permian branch includes two languages, the *Permian proper*, spoken by the Komi or Permians, and the Syrenes or Syranes; and the *Wotieque*, spoken by the Udi or Wotiaks scattered among the governments of Wiatka, Oremburg, and Kasan. They are all Christians, and the most industrious people of Uralian race in the Russian empire, except the Fins and perhaps the Esthonians.

(4.) The Hungarian branch includes the following languages:—

The Hungarian or Magyar, spoken by the Magyars or Hungarians. They form about a third of the population of Hungary, and almost a fourth of that of Transylvania; several thousands also of this people are settled in the Bukowine in Gallicia, and about forty thousand in Moldavia, under the Turkish sway. The Hungarian, according to Czaplovicz, has four principal dialects:—1. The *Paloczen*. 2. The dialect of the *Magyars beyond the Danube*. 3. That of the *Magyars of the Theiss;* and 4. That of the *Szekler*, living in Transylvania, in the Bukowine, and in Moldavia. The Hungarian language is very harmonious; and is mixed with many foreign words, especially Slavonic, German, and Latin.

The Wogoule, spoken by the Mansi or Manskum, more known as the Woguls, and called Wogoulitshe by the Russians. They are almost all Christians, and live principally as hunters and fishermen, scattered over the government of Saratow, in the high valleys of the Ural, in that of Perm, and in that of Tobolsk, between Kourjan and Beresow. Klaproth distinguishes in it four dialects, that of Chiasow, those of Werchoturia, and Cherdin, and that of Beresow in the government of Tobolsk.

The Ostiak, or Obi-Ostiak, which is not to be confounded with the Yeniseï family. The *As-jachs* or *Ostiaks* of the Obi, who speak this language, are mostly Christians; some are still idolaters. The principal dialects are those of *Beresow*, *Lumpokol*, *Wass-i-gun*, and *Narym*. Under the branch still uncertain are ranked the *Hunniac*, the *Awar*, the *Bulgarian*, and the *Chazar*.

---

## CHAPTER II.

### ENGLAND.

The British islands, placed nearly in the north-western angle of Europe, command peculiar advantages, no less for natural strength in war, than as an emporium of commerce in peace: on the southern side, they are almost in contact with France, Holland, and Germany, for ages the most enlightened and flourishing countries of the civilized world; on the east, a wide expanse of sea separates them from the bleak region of Scandinavia; on the west, they overlook the Atlantic Ocean, whose limit in another hemisphere is the coast of America; while, in the extreme north they may be almost said to face the unexplored expanse of the Polar Sea. Exclusive of the northern insular appendages, they may be considered as

Yelli I.
Unst
Fetlar I.
SHETLAND ISLANDS
Whalsay I.
Foula
Bressay I.
Fair I.
Papay
Nth. Ronaldshay
Westray
Sanday
ORKNEY ISLANDS
Mainland
Hay Wass
Pentland
Sth. Ronaldshay
Firth
Duncansby Hd.
C. Wrath
The Minch
Lewis
WESTERN HEBRIDES OR ISLES
St. Kilda
North Uist
Benbecula I.
South Uist
Barra
Mingalay
Little Minch
Rum I.
Eig I.
Coll I.
Tirree
Mull
Jura
Oransay
Islay
Murray Firth
Banff
Kinnairds Hd.
Aberdeen
Arbroath
Firth of Forth
Berwick
Holy I.
Newcastle
R. Tees
Whitby
Flamborough Hd.
Spurn Hd.
R. Humber
THE WASH
Harwich
M. of the Thames
LONDON
Strait of Dover
Calais
Malin Hd.
Rathlin
Tory I.
N Arran
Tillen Hd.
Donegal B.
Achil I.
Galway B.
S. Arran I.
Mal B.
R. Shannon
Dingle B.
Kenmare R.
Mizen Hd.
Cork
Cork Har.
Dublin
Wicklow
Carnsore Pt.
I. of Man
Walney
Solway Firth
Morecambe B.
R. Dee
IRISH SEA
Anglesey
CHANNEL
ST. GEORGE'S
Cardigan B.
St. Brides B.
Milford Haven
BRISTOL CHANNEL
Lundy I.
Lands End
Scilly Is.
Lizard Pt.
Start Pt.
Portland Bill
I. of Wight
Portsmouth
Beachy Hd.
ENGLISH CHANNEL
Alderney
Guernsey
Sark
Jersey
C. de la Heve
Seine R.
Dieppe
Rouen
Caen
St. Lo
Evreux
Bas I.
I. Brehat
Ouessant
St. Brieux
FRANCE
NORTH SEA
ATLANTIC OCEAN
SCOTLAND
ENGLAND
WALES
IRELAND
10 20 40 60 80 100 120
English Miles
Longitude West from Greenwich

situated between the fiftieth and fifty-ninth degrees of north latitude, and between the second degree of east and the tenth of west longitude. They are geographically divided into two islands of unequal magnitude, Great Britain and Ireland: Britain, again, is divided into two unequal parts: England, which, including Wales, contains 57,960 square miles; and Scotland, which contains 30,500. The three, though united into one kingdom, respectively exhibit peculiarities which characterise them as distinct countries. It will, therefore, be requisite to describe each separately, commencing with England, the seat of empire and legislation. The chapter which treats of England will afford the proper place for many details, particularly of a political nature, which are alike applicable to the two sister countries.

---

*References to the Map of the British Islands.*

ENGLAND.

1. Alnwick
2. Rothbury
3. Morpeth
4. Blythe
5. Newcastle
6. Hexham
7. Billingham
8. Carlisle
9. Cockermouth
10. Egremont
11. Ravenglass
12. Ulverston
13. Kendal
14. Keswick
15. Penrith
16. Appleby
17. Aldstone
18. Darlington
19. Durham
20. Sunderland
21. Stockton
22. Stokesley
23. Guisborough
24. Whitby
25. Pickering
26. Thirsk
27. North Allerton
28. Hawes
29. Ripon
30. Kendal
31. Lancaster
32. Garstang
33. Poulton
34. Bradford
35. Skipton
36. Knaresborough
37. Leeds
38. York
39. New Malton
40. Billington
41. Scarborough
42. Great Driffield
43. Hornsea
44. Hedon
45. Kingston on Hull
46. Barton
47. Grimsby
48. Ravendale
49. Saltfleet
50. Thedlethorpe
51. Boston
52. Alford
53. Horncastle
54. Lincoln
55. Gainsborough
56. Ashby
57. Doncaster
58. Sheffield
59. Pontefract
60. Manchester
61. Preston
62. Liverpool
63. Chester
64. Newcastle
65. Newport
66. Stafford
67. Burton
68. Derby
69. Ashbourn
70. Chesterfield
71. Mansfield
72. Alfreton
73. Nottingham
74. Melton Mowbray
75. Grantham
76. Newark
77. Sleaford
78. Spalding
79. Lynn Regis
80. Wells
81. Cromer
82. Yarmouth
83. Beccles
84. Harleston
85. Norwich
86. Reepham
87. East Dereham
88. Diss
89. Thetford
90. Ely
91. March
92. Peterborough
93. Oundle
94. Stamford
95. Harborough
96. Leicester
97. Coventry
98. Tamworth
99. Lichfield
100. Birmingham
101. Bridgenorth
102. Shrewsbury
103. Plynlimmon
104. Ludlow
105. Tenbury
106. Leominster
107. Bromford
108. Tewkesbury
109. Worcester
110. Alcester
111. Warwick
112. Evesham
113. Towcester
114. Northampton
115. Wellingborough
116. Thrapston
117. Huntingdon
118. Bedford
119. Cambridge
120. Mildenhall
121. Bury St. Edmund's
122. Framlingham
123. Aldborough
124. Ipswich
125. Sudbury
126. Harwich
127. Colchester
128. Coggeshall
129. Royston
130. Bishop's Stortford
131. Hertford
132. St. Albans
133. Aylesbury
134. Winslow
135. Buckingham
136. Woodstock
137. Burford
138. Gloucester
139. Hereford
140. Ross
141. Cotford
142. Bristol
143. Melksham
144. Malmesbury
145. Cirencester
146. Swindon
147. Hungerford
148. Kennet
149. Abingdon
150. Oxford
151. Wallingford
152. Thame
153. Windsor
154. Uxbridge
155. Kingston
156. Croydon
157. Greenwich
158. London
159. Chelmsford
160. Maldon
161. Maidstone
162. Canterbury
163. Margate
164. Ramsgate
165. Dover
166. Rye
167. Hastings
168. Seaford
169. Battle
170. East Grinstead
171. Reigate
172. Horsham
173. Brighton
174. Arundel
175. Pulborough
176. Guildford
177. Godalming
178. Petworth
179. Chichester
180. Portsmouth
181. Southampton
182. Whitchurch
183. Andover
184. Salisbury
185. Lymington
186. Poole
187. Shaftesbury
188. Bath
189. Uxbridge
190. Wells
191. Glastonbury
192. Ilchester
193. Taunton
194. Porlock
195. South Barnstaple
196. Bideford
197. Torrington
198. Launceston
199. Bodmin
200. St. Agnes
201. Penzance
202. Falmouth
203. Tregony
204. Tavistock
205. Plymouth
206. Modbury
207. Dartmouth
208. Ashburton
209. Chumleigh
210. Tiverton
211. Exeter
212. Sidmouth
213. Honiton
214. Lyme Regis
215. Dorchester
216. Weymouth

*Rivers.*

a Tyne
b Tees
c Derwent
d Swale
e Wharfe
f Aire
g Don
h Trent
i Ouse
j Thames
k Avon
l Severn
m Dee

WALES.

1. Flint
2. St. Asaph
3. Denbigh
4. Aberconway
5. Bangor
6. Beaumaris
7. Holyhead
8. Caernarvon
9. Llan Haiarn
10. St. Mary's
11. Harlech
12. Bala
13. Corwen
14. Montgomery
15. Dinasmowd
16. Towyn
17. Aberystwith
18. Rhainder
19. Bault
20. Tregarron
21. Llanbear
22. Cardigan
23. Newport
24. Fiscard
25. St. David's
26. Pembroke
27. Caermarthen
28. Cwyrgryg
29. Brecon
30. Monmouth
31. Uske
32. Chepstow
33. Newport
34. Cardiff
35. Landaff
36. Llantrissent
37. Swansea

*Rivers.*

a Towey
b Tievy
c Dee

SCOTLAND.

1. Durness
2. Tongue
3. Reay
4. Thurso
5. Wick
6. Dunbeath
7. Helmsdale
8. Dornoch
9. Tain
10. Portinleik
11. Ullapool
12. Poolew
13. Torridon
14. Loch Carron
15. Dingwall
16. Beauly
17. Inverness
18. Grantown
19. Nairn
20. Elgin
21. Inveraven
22. Cullen
23. Banff
24. Huntley
25. Turreff
26. Frasersburgh
27. Peterhead
28. Newburgh
29. Aberdeen
30. Stonehaven
31. Bervie
32. Tulloch
33. Braemar
34. Fort Augustus
35. Gleneig
36. Arasaig
37. Appin
38. Fort William
39. Perth
40. Dunkeld
41. Blair Athol
42. Brechin
43. Montrose
44. Forfar
45. Arbroath
46. Dundee
47. St. Andrews
48. Anstruther
49. Kinross
50. Inverkeithing
51. Clackmannan
52. Muthill
53. Stirling
54. Inverary
55. Oban
56. Dumbarton
57. Greenock
58. Paisley
59. Irvine
60. Hamilton
61. Glasgow
62. Falkirk
63. Linlithgow
64. Whitburn
65. Peebles
66. Edinburgh
67. Haddington
68. North Berwick
69. Dunbar
70. Berwick
71. Kelsoe
72. Jedburgh
73. Hawick
74. Ashkirk
75. Biggar
76. Moffat
77. Sanquhar
78. Lanark
79. Kilmarnock
80. Ayr
81. Girvan
82. Ballintrae
83. Stranraer
84. Port Patrick
85. Wigton
86. Kircudbright
87. New Galloway
88. Monihive
89. Dumfries
90. Langholm
91. Annan

*Rivers.*

a Spey
b Don
c Dee
d Tay
e Clyde
f Ken
g Nith
h Annan
i Tweed

IRELAND.

1. Belfast
2. Antrim
3. Larne
4. Glenarm
5. Ballycastle
6. Ballymoney
7. Coleraine
8. Tubbermore
9. Strabane
10. Londonderry
11. White Castle
12. Raphoe
13. Lifford
14. Letterkenny
15. Killybegs
16. Donegal
17. Ballybofy
18. Omagh
19. Pomeroy
20. Clogher
21. Dungannon
22. Armagh
23. Lurgan
24. Donaghadee
25. Portaferry
26. Downpatrick
27. Strevoy
28. Newry
29. Dundalk
30. Monaghan
31. Cavan
32. Callahill
33. Enniskillen
34. Churchill
35. Sligo
36. Drumeirn
37. Ballymore
38. Colooney
39. Ballina
40. Killala
41. Ballyglass
42. Claggan
43. Newport
44. Westport
45. Kumor
46. Ballinrobe
47. Castle Barr
48. Kilcolman
49. Tuam
50. Elphin
51. Roscommon
52. Leitrim
53. Longford
54. Moynalty
55. Carrickmacross
56. Dunleer
57. Drogheda
58. Balbriggan
59. Dublin
60. Screen
61. Trim
62. Maynooth
63. Naas
64. Tullamore
65. Mullingar
66. Athlone
67. Eyrecourt
68. Ballyforan
69. Newton Bellew
70. Loughrea
71. Ornmore
72. Ougntera
73. Galway
74. Gort
75. Innistymon
76. Kilrush
77. Clare
78. Ennis
79. Limerick
80. Portumn
81. Nenagh
82. Killaloe
83. Thurles
84. Roscrea
85. Durrow
86. Ath
87. Kildare
88. Carlow
89. Tullow
90. Baltinglass
91. Blessington
92. Togher
93. Wicklow
94. Gorey
95. Ballycanoe
96. Enniscorthy
97. Wexford
98. Fethard
99. Waterford
100. Thomas Town
101. Kilkenny
102. Carrick on Suire
103. Clonmel
104. Ballyporeen
105. Tipperary
106. Killmallock
107. Askeyton
108. Ballylongford
109. Tralee
110. Castle Ford
111. Killarney
112. Kenmare
113. Castletown
114. Bantry
115. Castletown
116. Kinsale
117. Cork
118. Killady
119. Tuchgeela
120. Mallow
121. Rathcormuck
122. Kildorery
123. Lismore
124. Youghall
125. Dungarvan
126. Tramore

*Rivers.*

a Ban
b Carlingford
c Boyne
d Barrow
e Nore
f Suire
g Blackwater
h Shannon
i Suck.

### Sect. I.—*General Outline and Aspect.*

England is bounded on the south by the English Channel, interposed between its coas and that of France; on the east by the German Sea, on the north by Scotland, from whicl it is separated by the Tweed, the Cheviot hills, and the Frith of Solway; on the west by th Irish Sea and St. George's Channel: the promontory of the Land's-End, forming its south western extremity, faces the vast expanse of the Atlantic.

The greatest dimension of England is from south to north, between the Lizard Point 49° 58′ N., and Berwick on Tweed, 55° 45′ N.; four hundred miles in length. The point of extreme breadth are the Land's-End (*fig.* 104.), in 5° 41′ W., and Lowestoffe, in 1° 44′ E. forming a space of about 280 miles. Ther is no point, however, where a line of thi extent can be carried across the island, an the northern part does not on an averag exceed one hundred miles in breadth.

104

Land's-End.

The surface of England is of a diversifi ed character; the eastern districts are i general level, and there are several direc tions in which hundreds of miles may b travelled without seeing a hill. Along th western side of the island are large tracts not only hilly, but sometimes rising even t mountain grandeur. Such are the countie of Cumberland and Westmoreland, the bleak ridge of Ingleborough, extending like a spin through the north of England: of the same character are Derbyshire, the whole principalit of Wales, and a great part of Devon and Cornwall. These tracts exhibit all the varieties o mountain scenery: in Cumberland, encircling little plains filled with beautiful lakes; i Wales, enclosing narrow valleys through which the rapid mountain stream dashes; in Der

---

*References to the Map of England.—North Part.*

NORTH SERIES.
1. Berwick
2. Meldrum
3. Belford
4. N. Charlton
5. Alnwick
6. Whittingham
7. Uswayford
8. Elsdon
9. Rothbury
10. Warkworth
11. Morpeth
12. Blythe
13. Clifton
14. Stamfordham
15. Kirk Harle
16. Harlington
17. Bellingham
18. Buttershaugh
19. Shillburn
20. Kennel
21. Bewcastle
22. Longtown
23. Brampton
24. Haltwhistle
25. Simonburn
26. Hexham
27. Hickley
28. Newcastle
29. North Shields
30. Tynemouth
31. South Shields
32. Sunderland
33. Shotton
34. Durham
35. Chester-le-Street
36. Lanchester
37. Wolsingham
38. Stanhope
39. Acton
40. Aldstone
41. Crossgill
42. Kirk Oswald
43. Lasonby
44. Hutton
45. Carlisle
46. Orton
47. Wigton
48. Abbeyholme
49. Maryport
50. Workington
51. Cockermouth
52. Ireby
53. Keswick
54. Matterdale
55. Penrith
56. Clifton
57. Appleby
58. Milburn
59. Brough
60. Slackholm
61. Middleton
62. Eggleston
63. Barnard Castle
64. Staindrop
65. West Auckland
66. Bishop Auckland
67. Sedgefield
68. Hartlepool
69. Seaton Carow
70. Guisbrough
71. Whitby
72. Stokesley
73. Raunton
74. Yarm
75. Darlington
76. Croft
77. Rokeby
78. Bowes
79. Reeth
80. Kirkby Stephen
81. Orton
82. Mardale
83. Ambleside
84. Seathwaite
85. Whitehaven
86. Egremont
87. Ravenglass
88. Whitbeck
89. Ulverston
90. Hawkshead
91. Kendal
92. Fawcolt
93. Millthorpe
94. Sedbergh
95. Hawes
96. Askrigg
97. Middleham
98. Richmond
99. Catterick
100. Bedale
101. Burneston
102. Thirsk
103. North Allerton
104. Helmsley
105. Kirby Moorside
106. Snainton
107. Cloughton
108. Scarborough
109. Filey
110. Hunmanby
111. Bridlington
112. Kilham
113. Driffield
114. Sledmere
115. Wintringham
116. New Malton
117. Garraby
118. Stillenham
119. Coxwold
120. Easingwold
121. Aldborough
122. Knaresborough
123. Ripon
124. Masham
125. Whernside
126. Grassington
127. Arncliffe
128. Settle
129. Ingleton
130. Kirkby Lonsdale
131. Hornby
132. Lancaster
133. Garstang
134. Slaidburn
135. Clitheroe
136. Colne
137. Paythorne
138. Skipton
139. Thurcross
140. Otley
141. Harewood
142. Ripley
143. Wetherby
144. Tadcaster
145. Cawood
146. York
147. Pocklington
148. Middleton
149. Market Weighton
150. Beverley
151. Brandsburton
152. Hornsea
153. Aldborough
154. Hedon
155. Pattrington

SOUTH SERIES.
1. Poulton
2. Blackpool
3. Kirkham
4. Preston
5. Chorley
6. Blackburn
7. Burnley
8. Halifax
9. Keighley
10. Bradford
11. Dewsbury
12. Wakefield
13. Leeds
14. Pontefract
15. Snaith
16. Selby
17. Howden
18. Burton
19. South Cove
20. Hull
21. Barton
22. Grimsby
23. Ravendale
24. Caistor
25. Glanford Bridge
26. Kirton
27. Brumby
28. Crowle
29. Thorne
30. Doncaster
31. Budsworth
32. Barnesley
33. Penistone
34. Huddersfield
35. Meltham
36. Ashton-under-Line
37. Manchester
38. Rochdale
39. Bury
40. Bolton
41. Leigh
42. Wigan
43. Ormskirk
44. Formby
45. Liverpool
46. Prescot
47. Newton
48. Warrington
49. Knutsford
50. Altringham
51. Stockport
52. Disley
53. Chapel in the Frith
54. Tideswell
55. Castleton
56. Sheffield
57. Dronfield
58. Rotherham
59. Worksop
60. Blyth
61. Retford
62. Gainsborough
63. Willoughton
64. Wragby
65. Market Rasen
66. Louth
67. Saltfleet
68. Sutton
69. Alford
70. Burgh
71. Wainfleet
72. Spilsby
73. Horncastle
74. Tattershall
75. Dunston
76. Navenby
77. Lincoln
78. Thorney
79. Tuxford
80. Newark
81. Mansfield
82. Bolsover
83. Chesterfield
84. Alfreton
85. Matlock
86. Wirksworth
87. Winster
88. Buxton
89. Lognor
90. Leeke
91. Horton
92. Macclesfield
93. Congleton
94. Talk
95. Nantwich
96. Middlewich
97. Northwich
98. Tarporley
99. Chester
100. Holt
101. Wrexham
102. Mold
103. Flint
104. Ruthin
105. Denbigh
106. St. Asaph
107. Abergeley
108. Aberconway
109. Llanrwst
110. Pentre Voelas
111. Tremadoc
112. Bangor
113. Beaumaris
114. Amlwch
115. Llanerchymedd
116. Holyhead
117. Caernarvon
118. Bwich Mawr
119. Pwllheli
120. Crickieth
121. Harlech
122. Arrennig
123. Llanuwch-Uwyn
124. Bala
125. Corven
126. Llangollen
127. Ellesmere
128. Wem
129. Whitchurch
130. Malpas
131. Drayton
132. Eccleshall
133. Stone
134. Newcastle-under-Line
135. Burslem
136. Cheadle
137. Uttoxeter
138. Ashborne
139. Derby
140. Belper
141. Nottingham
142. Bottesford
143. Grantham
144. Sleaford
145. Folkingham
146. Donnington
147. Boston
148. Burnham Market
149. Castle Rising
150. Fakenham
151. New Walsingham
152. Holt
153. Cromer
154. N. Walsham

ISLE OF MAN
1. Ramsey
2. Peel
3. Douglas
4. Castletown

*Rivers.*
a Till
b Aln
c Coquet
d Wensbeck
e Blyth
f Tyne
g Wear
h Tees
i Esk
j Rye
k Derwent
l Ouse
m Swale
n Ure
o Wharf
p Air
q Calder
r Don
s Rother
t Derwent
u Dove
v Trent
w Ankholm
x Witham
y Conway
z Clwyd
a* Dee
b* Weaver
c* Mersey
d* Ribble
e* Lune
f* Derwent
g* Eden

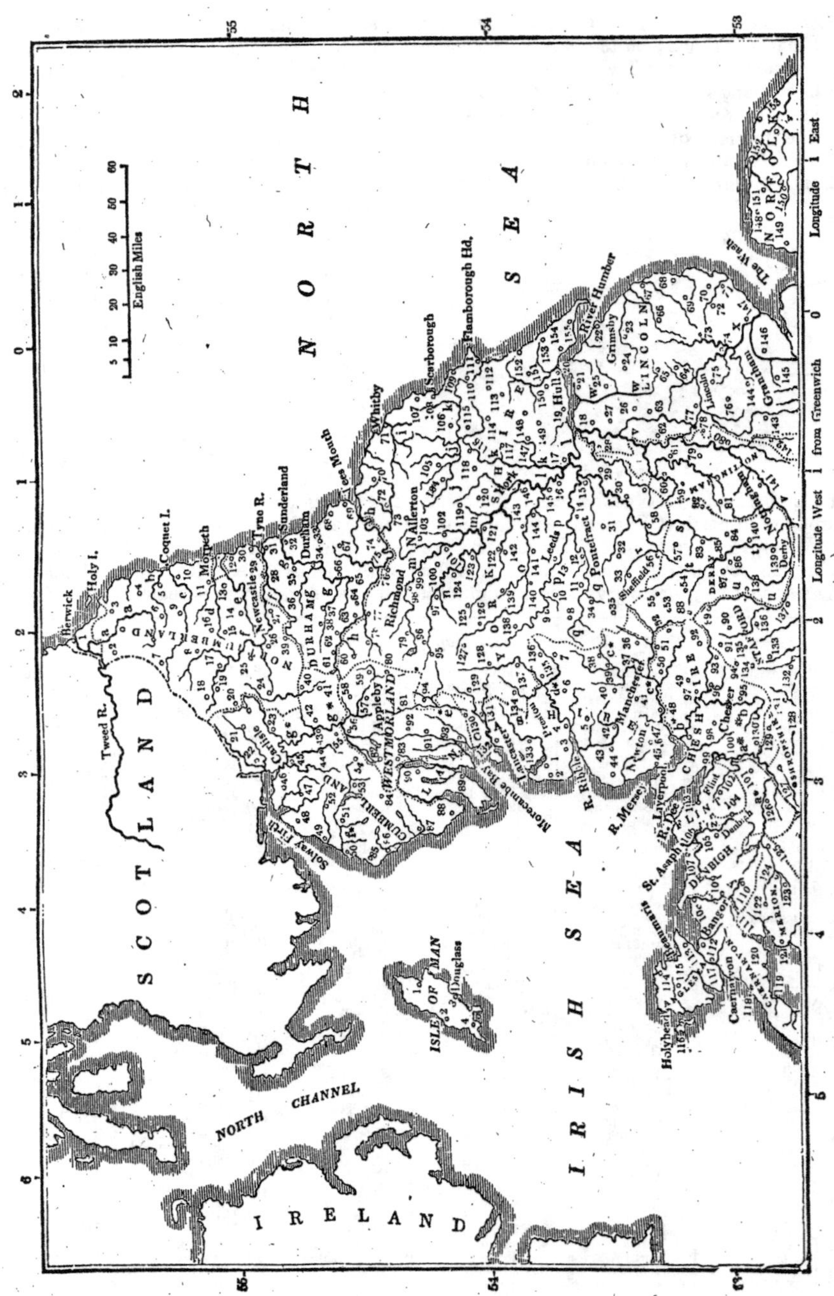
SCOTLAND
NORTH SEA
IRISH SEA
IRELAND
NORTH CHANNEL
ISLE OF MAN
Douglas
English Miles
Tweed R.
Berwick
Holy I.
Coquet I.
Morpeth
Tyne R.
Newcastle
Sunderland
Durham
Tees Mouth
Whitby
Scarborough
Flamborough Hd.
River Humber
Grimsby
Hull
York
Leeds
Pontefract
Sheffield
Manchester
Liverpool
Chester
Lancaster
Morecambe Bay
Solway Firth
Carlisle
Appleby
WESTMORLAND
DURHAM
Richmond
N. Allerton
R. Ribble
R. Mersey
R. Dee
St. Asaph
Flint
Denbigh
Bangor
Caernarvon
Holyhead
Beaumaris
Lincoln
Grantham
Nottingham
Derby
The Wash
Longitude West from Greenwich
Longitude East

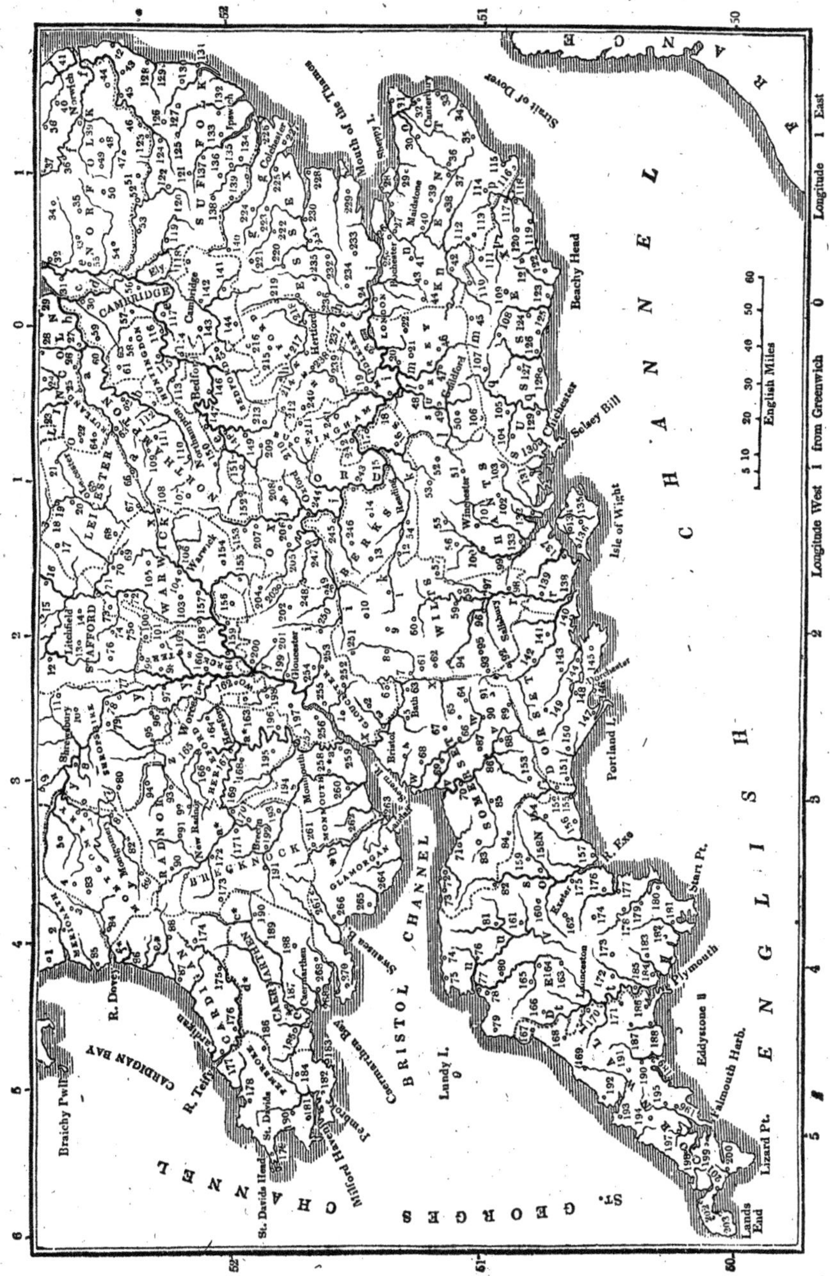
Mouth of the Thames
Strait of Dover
Beachy Head
Selsey Bill
Isle of Wight
Portland
Start Pt.
Plymouth
Eddystone
Falmouth Harb.
Lizard Pt.
Lands End
Lundy I.
BRISTOL CHANNEL
ENGLISH CHANNEL
ST. GEORGES CHANNEL
CARDIGAN BAY
Braichy Pwll
St. Davids Head
Milford Haven
Pembroke
Caermarthen Bay
Swansea B.
GLAMORGAN
R. Dovey
R. Teify
R. Exe
English Miles
Longitude West 1 from Greenwich
Longitude 1 East
CAMBRIDGE
LONDON
Canterbury
Maidstone
Chichester
Salisbury
Winchester
Dorchester
Gloucester
Oxford
Hertford
Bedford
Warwick
Lichfield
Shrewsbury
Cambridge
Colchester
Ipswich
Norwich
Exeter
Launceston

byshire, presenting rocky scenery in every picturesque and fantastic shape; while in Devonshire low broad steeps overshadow wide and beautiful vales.

With one exception, the most important rivers of England traverse the breadth of the kingdom: rising among the western hills, and flowing toward the German Ocean, they do not attain that length of course which the extent of its territory in another direction would have admitted. Though deficient, however, in magnitude, they are numerous, commodious, and valuable; flowing through broad vales and wide-spreading plains.

The Thames, though not the longest, deserves to be ranked as the first of British rivers. It originates from a number of rivulets on the borders of Wilts and Gloucestershire, which,

---

*References to the Map of England.—South Part.*

NORTH SERIES.
1. Tallybout
2. Dolgelly
3. Dinasmowddy
4. Hendre
5. Llanfyllin
6. Pool
7. Llanfair
8. Shrewsbury
9. Oswestry
10. Wellington
11. Newport
12. Stafford
13. Cannock
14. Lichfield
15. Abbot's Bromley
16. Burton
17. Ashby de la Zouch
18. Kedgworth
19. Loughborough
20. Mount Sorrel
21. Melton Mowbray
22. Oakham
23. Corby
24. Bourn
25. Stamford
26. Market Deeping
27. Crowland
28. Spalding
29. Holbeach
30. Wisbeach
31. Islington
32. Lynn Regis
33. Narborough
34. Litcham
35. Swaffham
36. East Deerham
37. Foulsham
38. Aylsham
39. Norwich
40. Wroxham
41. Yarmouth
42. Lowestoft
43. Beccles
44. Loddon
45. Bungay
46. Harleston
47. New Buckingham
48. Wymondham
49. Hingham
50. Watton
51. East Harling
52. Thetford
53. Brandon
54. Methwold
55. Downham
56. Ely
57. March
58. Ramsey
59. Thorney
60. Peterborough
61. Norman Cross
62. Oundle
63. Rockingham
64. Uppingham
65. Leicester
66. Market Harborough
67. Lutterworth
68. Hinckley
69. Nuneaton
70. Atherstone
71. Tamworth
72. Coleshill
73. Sutton Coldfield
74. Walsall
75. Birmingham
76. Wolverhampton
77. Bridgenorth
78. Broseley
79. Much Wenlock
80. Bishop's Castle
81. Montgomery
82. Newtown
83. Llanfair
84. Machynlleth
85. Towyn
86. Aberystwith
87. Aberllowyn
88. Sputty Ystwith
89. Llanidloes
90. Rhayadergwy
91. Llandegley
92. New Radnor
93. Knighton
94. Clunn
95. Ludlow
96. Cleobury Mortimer
97. Bewdley
98. Kidderminster
99. Stourbridge
100. Harlesowen
101. Bromsgrove
102. Droitwich
103. Henley in Arden
104. Warwick
105. Coventry
106. Leamington
107. Daventry
108. Rugby
109. Rothwell
110. Northampton
111. Kettering
112. Thrapston
113. Kimbolton
114. St. Neot's
115. Huntingdon
116. St. Ives
117. Willingham
118. Newmarket
119. Little Barton
120. Bury St. Edmond's
121. Stow Market
122. Ixworth
123. Diss
124. Eye
125. Debenham
126. Wingfield
127. Framlingham
128. Southwold
129. Dunwich
130. Saxmundham
131. Aldborough
132. Woodbridge
133. Ipswich
134. Hadleigh
135. Whatfield
136. Bildeston
137. Needham
138. Lavenham
139. Sudbury
140. Haverhill
141. Linton
142. Cambridge
143. Caxton
144. Royston
145. Potton
146. Bedford
147. Olney
148. Newport Pagnel
149. Fenny Stratford
150. Towcester
151. Buckingham
152. Brackley
153. Bandbury
154. Kineton
155. Shipston upon Stour
156. Campden
157. Stratford on Avon
158. Alcester
159. Evesham
160. Worcester
161. Pershore
162. Upton
163. Ledbury
164. Bromyard
165. Leominster
166. Weobly
167. Hereford
168. Thruxton
169. Hay
170. Talgarth
171. Llyswen
172. Builth
173. Landulas
174. Tregaron
175. Llampeter
176. New Castle Emlyn
177. Cardigan
178. Newport
179. St. David's
180. Haverford West
181. Milford
182. Pembroke
183. Tenby
184. Narberth
185. St. Clear's
186. Lanvernach
187. Caermarthen
188. Landebie
189. Langadoe
190. Landovery
191. Trecastle
192. Brecon
193. Crickhowell
194. Abergavenny
195. St. Weonard's
196. Ross
197. Mitcheldean
198. Newent
199. Gloucester
200. Tewkesbury
201. Cheltenham
202. Northleach
203. Stow in the Wold
204. Moreton in the Marsh
205. Charbury
206. Woodstock
207. Dedington
208. Bicester
209. Winslow
210. Aylesbury
211. Wendover
212. Ivinghoe
213. Leighton Buzzard
214. Luton
215. Stevenage
216. Baldock
217. Hatfield Bishop
218. Hertford
219. Bishop's Stortford
220. Dunmow
221. Thaxted
222. Braintree
223. Coggeshall
224. Halstead
225. Colchester
226. Harwich
227. St. Osyth
228. Bradwell
229. Rochford
230. Maldon
231. Chelmsford
232. Ingatestone
233. Horndon
234. Romford
235. Chipping Ongar
236. Epping
237. Enfield
238. St. Alban's
239. Watford
240. Berkhampstead
241. Amersham
242. Marlow
243. Wallingford
244. Oxford
245. Abingdon
246. Wantage
247. Whitney
248. Burford
249. Lechlade
250. Cirencester
251. Malmesbury
252. Wotton under Edge
253. Minchinhampton
254. Stroud
255. Berkeley
256. Blackney
257. Monmouth
258. Usk
259. Chepstow
260. Newport
261. Merthyr Tydvil
262. Llantrissent
263. Llandaff
264. Cowbridge
265. Pyle
266. Neath
267. Abernant
268. Pontardylais
269. Kidwelly
270. Penrice

SOUTH SERIES.
1. Thornbury
2. Chipping Sodbury
3. Bristol
4. Wrington
5. Pensford
6. Marshfield
7. Bradford
8. Chippenham
9. Calne
10. Wotton Bassot
11. Marlborough
12. Hungerford
13. Lambourne
14. E. Ilsley
15. Reading
16. Wokingham
17. Maidenhead
18. Windsor
19. Uxbridge
20. Kingsto
21. Ewell
22. Croydon
23. London
24. Woolwich
25. Gravesend
26. Rochester
27. Chatham
28. Sheerness
29. Faversham
30. Canterbury
31. Margate
32. Sandwich
33. Deal
34. Dover
35. Hythe
36. Wye
37. Ashford
38. Smarden
39. Lenham
40. Maidstone
41. Wrotham
42. Tunbridge
43. Sevenoaks
44. Westerham
45. E. Grinstead
46. Reigate
47. Dorking
48. Ripley
49. Guildford
50. Godalming
51. Alton
52. Odiham
53. Basingstoke
54. Newbury
55. Whitchurch
56. Andover
57. Ludgershall
58. Amesbury
59. Stonehenge
60. Devizes
61. Trowbridge
62. Westbury
63. Bath
64. Bruton
65. Shepton Mallet
66. Glastonbury
67. Wells
68. Axbridge
69. Blackford
70. Bridgewater
71. Whatchet
72. Minehead
73. Portlock
74. Combe Martin
75. Ilfracombe
76. Barnstaple
77. Appledore
78. Bideford
79. Hartland
80. Torrington
81. South Molton
82. Dulverton
83. Wiveliscombe
84. Wellington
85. Taunton
86. Longport
87. Somerton
88. Ilchester
89. Milborn Port
90. Castle Cary
91. Wincaunton
92. Shaftesbury
93. Mere
94. Warminster
95. Hindon
96. Wilton
97. Salisbury
98. Downton
99. Romsey
100. Stockbridge
101. Winchester
102. Bramdean
103. Petersfield
104. Midhurst
105. Petworth
106. Haslemere
107. Horsham
108. Cuckfield
109. Uckfield
110. Tunbridge Wells
111. Wadhurst
112. Goudhurst
113. Cranbrooke
114. Appledore
115. New Romney
116. Lydd
117. Rye
118. Winchelsea
119. Hastings
120. Battle
121. Hailsham
122. E. Bourne
123. Seaford
124. Lewes
125. Brighton
126. N. Shoreham
127. Steyning
128. Worthing
129. Arundel
130. Chichester
131. Havant
132. Fareham
133. Southampton
134. Newtown
135. Newport
136. Yarmouth
137. Lymington
138. Christchurch
139. Kingwood
140. Poole
141. Wimborn Minster
142. Blandford
143. Beer Regis
144. Wareham
145. Corfe Castle
146. Melcombe Regis
147. Weymouth
148. Dorchester
149. Cerne Abbas
150. Bridport
151. Lyme Regis
152. Axminster
153. Chard
154. Honiton
155. Colyton
156. Sidmouth
157. Exmouth
158. Silverton
159. Collumpton
160. Crediton
161. Chumleigh
162. Crockernwell
163. Oakhampton
164. Hatherleigh
165. Sheepwash
166. Holsworthy
167. Stratton
168. Jacobstow
169. Camelford
170. Launceston
171. Callington
172. Tavistock
173. Stanford Spiney
174. Moreton Hampden
175. Exeter
176. Chudleigh
177. Newton Bushel
178. Ashburton
179. Totness
180. Dartmouth
181. Kingsbridge
182. Modbury
183. Plympton Earl
184. Plymouth
185. Saltash
186. St. Germans
187. Liskeard
188. Looe
189. Fowey
190. Lostwithiel
191. Bodmin
192. St. Minver
193. Padstow
194. St. Michael
195. Grampound
196. Tregony
197. Truro
198. Redruth
199. Penryn
200. Helston
201. Marazion
202. St. Ives
203. Penzance

*Rivers.*

a Welland
b Nen
c Old Bedford
d Old Ouse
e Ouse
f Wenson
g Coln
h Lea
i Thames
j Charwell
k Kennet
l Wey
m Mole
n Medwa
o Stour
p Rother
q Arun
r Avon
s Exe
t Tamer
u Taw
v Perrot
w Axe
x Avon
y Severn
z Tome
a* Wye
b* Taaf
c* Towey
d* Teifi
e* Ystwith
f* Dovey

uniting at Cricklade, form a stream which is about nine feet broad in summer, and is called the Thame. Near Oxford it receives the Charwell and the Isis, assuming on its junction with the latter river the compound name of Tamesis, which has been abbreviated into Thames. After a course almost southward to Reading, it winds northward through the wooded vale of Henley and Maidenhead, and thence by the castellated heights of Windsor. Its course to London is by Chertsey, Hampton, Twickenham, and Richmond, among the magnificent woods and palaces of this paradise of England. Near Teddington its current is slightly acted upon by the extreme ebb and flow of the tide, which rises higher in this than in any other river of Europe. It divides the capital into two unequal parts, having on its northern bank the cities of London and Westminster, and on its southern the borough of Southwark. Below London Bridge it is navigable for vessels of large burthen; its ample channel, and the spacious docks connected with it, are there constantly filled with forests of masts, and seem to contain, as it were, the wealth of the world. It winds its way to the ocean through a country presenting few objects of interest, except the vast naval establishments situated on the south bank of the river. Woolwich claims particular attention, not only on account of the royal dockyard, and the national depôt of artillery, but for its military academy, which ranks as the first in the empire. The estuary of the Medway, opening into the river from Kent, affords commodious sites for the naval stations of Chatham and Sheerness. The entire course of the Thames is about 220 miles.

The Trent, with its tributary, the northern Ouse, traverses the whole midland territory of England, and several of its principal manufacturing districts, to which it affords a communication with the eastern, and by canals with the western, ocean. It rises among the low Staffordshire hills, and at Burton, it becomes navigable for vessels of moderate size. Receiving the Dove and Derwent, which, after dashing through the rocky recesses of Derbyshire, have already subsided into peaceful streams, it passes Nottingham, and at Gainsborough becomes navigable for steam-boats, and other vessels of larger burthen. After a farther course of about thirty miles, it flows into the Humber, already rendered a broad estuary by the Ouse, which has collected the principal streams of Yorkshire. The Ouse, formed by the confluence of the Aire and the Swale from the uplands of the North Riding, is subsequently augmented by the Wharfe. The Aire, with its tributaries the Calder and Don, enable it to communicate with all the great manufacturing towns of the West Riding, and the confluence of the Derwent from the East Riding renders it equal in magnitude to the Thames. The Ouse, with its branches, forms one of the most useful and least beautiful of English rivers. It winds a sluggish course through manufacturing districts and rich arable fields without any diversity of scenery. The Humber, formed by the junction of the Trent and Ouse, resembles an arm of the sea; and its trade contributes mainly to the commercial prosperity of Hull.

The Severn is the only great stream which runs from north to south for a considerable part of its course. Rising in Wales, near the foot of Plinlimmon, it flows through the vales of Montgomery; and, after winding round Shrewsbury, directs its course to the southward, through some of the richest and most beautiful plains of England, passing by the cities of Worcester, Tewkesbury, and Gloucester. In commercial importance it also ranks high, since it flows through Colebrook Dale, and other principal seats of the iron trade; while the tracts on its lower course have for ages been distinguished for the manufacture of fine woollens. Its navigation is not free from obstructions, but much has been done to obviate these disadvantages, and to connect the Severn by canals with the other great rivers. In approaching Bristol, it receives the Wye, which, rising in Wales, flows through scenery that renders it the most picturesque of English rivers. The Severn then expands into the estuary of the Bristol Channel, the seat of a commerce once second only to that of the metropolis, but now surpassed by that of Liverpool.

The other rivers of England are small; the Eden, the beautiful river of Cumberland, forms the Solway; the Mersey of Lancashire, with its tributary the Irwell, is important, for the mass of commodities which it conveys from the great manufacturing districts to Liverpool; the southern Ouse, combines with the Witham of Lincolnshire in forming that broad, shallow, marshy estuary called the Wash, through which is exported a considerable quantity of grain from the agricultural districts; the Tyne and the Tees in the north of England are the channels of extensive trade; the Tyne, in particular, which carries down the product of the vast coal mines of Newcastle.

The lakes of England occur principally in the counties of Cumberland and Westmoreland, which are denominated the country of the lakes. These, of which Windermere, the largest, is only twelve miles long and one broad, have been raised to distinction by the taste of the age for picturesque beauty, rather than as geographical features of the country. Their number, which is considerable, entitles them to notice; and a description of them will accompany that of the districts to which they belong.

### Sect. II.—*Natural Geography.*

This subject will be treated under the heads of Geology, Botany, and Zoology.

### SUBSECT. 1.—*Geology of England.*

While in Scotland the prevailing formations belong to the *primitive* and *transition* classes, in England the deposits that most abound are the *secondary, tertiary,* and *alluvial.* Hence it is that Scotland appears lofty and rugged, when contrasted with the hilly, flat, and low land of England. To enable our readers to form a general conception of the geognostical structure of England, we shall consider the mineral formations in the following order:—I. *Primitive and Transition.* II. *Secondary.* III. *Tertiary.* IV. *Alluvial.*

I. *Primitive and Transition.* These rocks are principally confined to the more moun tainous parts of England, and appear most abundantly, in Cumberland and some neighbouring counties; in Wales; and in Cornwall and Devon.

(1.) *Cumberland district.* This district is bounded to the west and the south by the Irish Sea and Morecombe Bay; towards the north it descends into the plain of the new red sandstone, within the basin of the Eden; and on the east it is bounded by the central carboniferous chain of the north. Within these limits there are two sets of rocks, viz. Plutonian and Neptunian; the more central parts being Plutonian, and the others Neptunian. The order in which they occur, is as follows:—

1. Granite and Syenite. They form the *geognostical axis* of all this region, and extend from the centre of the Skiddaw range to the neighbourhood of Egremont. There is a fine display of the granite in the bed of the Calden, where it is intersected by veins of quartz, and contains, besides other minerals, molybdena, tungsten, wolfram, and phosphate of lime.

2. A series of crystalline slaty deposits, forming the centre of the Skiddaw region, extending across Cromac lake, and by the foot of Ennerdale, as far as Denthill, is composed of gneiss, mica slate, hornblende slate, and chiastolite slate. In some parts of Skiddaw and Saddleback the curious mineral named *chiastolite* occurs: veins of quartz and galena occur in Thornthwaite, Newlands, Loweswater, and other places; a copper-mine was formerly worked in Newlands. The *salt springs* of Borrowdale issue from these rocks.

3. Deposit of clay slate.

4. An enormous formation of a green felspathose slate, intimately associated with porphyry, like that of Snowdonia in Wales, and the Needle's Eye in Scotland. The famous graphite or black-lead mine of Borrowdale is situated in the upper end of the valley of that name, where the graphite occurs in irregular veins associated with calc spar, brown spar, and quartz. The graphite is in nests in these veins, and the veins are contained in a Plutonian rock, viz. felspar porphyry, which is in some places amygdaloidal. Some nests of graphite have afforded 3000*l.* worth of that mineral.

5. Greywacke, with subordinate beds of limestone enclosing organic remains. A gryphæa and turritella occur near to Kirby-Lonsdale; a pecten, plagiostoma, trigonia, and patella near to Keswick. On the north side of the geognostical axis the Neptunian formations are repeated, with the exception of the greywacke series, which is probably buried under the old red sandstone and mountain limestone; and on this northern side, notwithstanding its less extensive developement, there is a group of mountains, almost entirely composed of *diallage rock*, and other minerals; of which, it is said, no trace occurs in the south. These occupy the place of the green felspar slate and porphyry series of No. 3. of Wales, afterwards to be noticed; and seem to be in the precise place of the serpentine of the Lizard in Cornwall. Further, there is on the west side of Cumberland another formation of granite and syenite, which underlies, traverses, and overlies the clay slate, No. 3., and is considered the great centre of elevation of the region. It never overlies, it is said, the mica slate, chiastolite slate, &c.; but is probably connected with veins of syenite, and other detached masses of crystalline rock, which do not belong to the ordinary rocks of superposition. A range of transition limestone extending from Mellam in Cumberland to the neighbourhood of Wasdale Head in Westmoreland, nearly across the whole region we are now describing, is finally cut off by a protruding mass of granite, newer than the limestone.

(2.) *Wales, including the Isle of Anglesea.* The Neptunian and Plutonian rocks in this extensive district are arranged as follows:—1st, *Granite* rising among the clay slate strata in the Isle of Anglesea. 2dly, A group of slaty rocks consisting of mica slate, chlorite slate, and quartz rock. These appear upheaved by the subjacent granite. They occur in the Isle of Anglesea. In this island are the great Mona marble and Paris copper mines, in which the ore is common copper pyrites. The Mona marble, a beautiful compound of marble and serpentine, occurs among these rocks. 3dly, A great group containing a very large proportion of felspathose rocks and porphyries. Of these the district of Snowdonia is probably the lowest portion. Some of the slates of the Snowdon range contain organic remains, principally of shells, some of which appear referable to the genus *Producta.* 4thly, A vast deposit of clay slate. 5thly, Greywacke, which forms the uppermost or newest member of the great series of deposits. Connected with these series are great beds of limestone. Fossil organic remains are met with in this series, and much more abundantly than in the deeper-seated slates. *Corals* of various kinds, *crinoid* animal shells, and *crustacea* occur among these rocks, in a fossil state. Of *fish*, the remains of bones, teeth, and the defensive fin-bones named *ichthyodorulites*, are met with. In the lists of organic remains of these slates we find extinct genera, and genera that still exist: and, judging from the nature of the remains, we infer that some of the animals were inhabitants of deep, others of shallow, seas. The organic remains in greywacke rocks are rare, and form a very small proportion to the extent of the rock.

(3.) *Cornwall and Devon.* In this district of England the rocks of the primitive class are arranged in the following order:—1st, *Granite.* There are four great projecting masses of granite rising through the bounding slaty strata: they send arms or veins among the Neptunian strata, and have upraised and variously modified them. The granite is traversed by contemporaneous veins of granite, and also encloses contemporaneous masses and veins of a compound of quartz and schorl, named *schorl-rock.* It is also traversed by veins of porphyry, called *elvan.* 2dly, Resting upon, or adjacent to, the granite there is a vast deposit of clay slate, named, in the county, *killas.* It abounds in ores, hence is sometimes named *metalliferous slate.* Where in the vicinity of granite, there is interposed gneiss or mica slate, or both; and in many parts it contains subordinate beds of greenstone, felspathose slate, &c. 3dly, Apparently above the preceding slates there occurs, in two places, a formation of *serpentine*, which, in the Lizard, contains *diallage rock*, *talc slate*, *hornblende slate*, and *mica slate*, and appears to occur below the greywacke. 4thly, *Greywacke.* This, which appears to form a great mass, is the uppermost and newest member of the stratified series. It contains considerable beds of limestone, including various organic remains.

*Mines in Cornwall and Devon.* Cornwall and Devonshire present three principal mining districts. The part of Cornwall situated in the vicinity and to the southward of Truro, the neighbourhood of St. Austle, and the neighbourhood of Tavistock. The first of these districts is the most important of the three, from the number and richness of its mines, in which copper, tin, and lead are obtained. The ores of copper, which are principally copper pyrites and gray copper, form regular veins, having a direction nearly from E. to W. in the rock named *killas;* and sometimes in the granite which projects amongst the slaty strata. The tin occurs principally in veins, which, like the preceding, traverse the killas and granite. They have also, very often, a direction nearly from E. to W.; they have a different inclination from that of the copper veins, which intersect and interrupt them, and which are, consequently, newer. The tin also occurs in contemporaneous masses and veins, and disseminated through the granite. Some veins afford, at the same time, copper and tin; but most of them produce only one of these metals in any quantity. There are also in Cornwall *cross veins*, that intersect the veins both of copper and tin; these contain argentiferous galena, native silver, and ores of silver. Near to Tavistock there are veins of copper, tin, and lead. Mines of antimony occur at Huel Boys in Devonshire, and at Saltash in Cornwall. The tin and copper ores of Cornwall are accompanied with arsenical pyrites, which is turned to profit by manufacturing oxide of arsenic from it.

II. *Secondary Rocks.* The rocks of this class form the largest portion of the surface of England, and the districts composed of them are generally flat or hilly; never assuming the mountainous character, unless where the old red sandstone or mountain limestone appears. We shall now describe the different formations in the order in which they occur, beginning with the deeper-seated or oldest (the old red sandstone), and finishing our view with an account of the newest, or chalk.

(1.) *Old red sandstone.* This sandstone, which is distinguished from those newer in the series by its greater hardness and red colour, occurs in greatest abundance in Herefordshire and Brecknockshire. Smaller portions occur in the Cumberland district, the Isle of Man and the Isle of Anglesea.

(2.) *Mountain limestone, metalliferous limestone,* or *carboniferous limestone.* This rock is generally grey coloured; sometimes, however, it exhibits various tints when it is worked as an inferior kind of marble. Its fracture is compact, lustre glimmering, and opaque or translucent on the edges. Its structure is sometimes *oolitic*, as is the case in the vicinity of Bristol. Veins of calcareous spar frequently traverse it, and occasionally contribute to the beauty of the varieties used as marble. Sometimes remains of the encrinus are so abundant in it, that it is named *encrinal limestone.* Its name *carboniferous* is from its sometimes occurring along with coal, as that of *metalliferous* from its, in some districts, abounding in ores. It abounds in organic remains of various genera of *corals*, *radiaria*, and *shells;* also some genera of *crustacea* and *fishes.* These bear a strong resemblance to the fossils of the transition limestone in the greywacke districts. Derbyshire, Northumberland, and Cumberland afford fine displays of this formation.

*Mines in mountain limestone.* The mountain limestone forms several mountainous districts in England and Wales; in which there are three districts rich in lead mines. The *first* of these comprehends the upper parts of the valleys of the Tyne, the Wear, and the Tees, in the counties of Cumberland, Durham, and York. Its principal mines are situated near Aldston Moor in Cumberland. The veins of sulphuret of lead or galena, which form the principal object of the works, traverse alternately beds of limestone and sandstone. They are remarkable, from the circumstance that they suddenly become thinner and poorer on passing from the limestone into the sandstone; an arrangement probably connected with some electro-magnetic action. There is also a copper mine S. W. of Aldston Moor. The ore is common yellow copper pyrites, which is associated with galena in a vein of great extent, and which does not seem to belong to the same formation as the other veins in this county. The iron mines of Ulverston are in this district. The ore is red hematite, which traverses the limestone in the form of veins; some of which are said to be 30 yards wide. Near Whitehaven great masses of reniform hematite alternate with red beds of mountain limestone. The *second metalliferous district* is situated in the northern part of Derbyshire, and the contiguous parts of the neighbouring counties. The districts called Peak and Kingsfield are the richest in ore. The blende, associated with the lead, is worked as an ore, and zinc is obtained from it. A vein of copper pyrites occurs at Ecton in Staffordshire, on the borders of Derbyshire. The Derbyshire veins have been long famous on account of the beautiful minerals they produce, especially *fluor spars*, and also from the interruption which the metalliferous veins experience on meeting with trap rocks, called *toadstone*, which occurs alternately with the limestone. The *third metalliferous district* is situated in Flintshire and Denbighshire, which form the N. E. part of Wales. It is the most productive next to Aldston Moor. Besides lead, it furnishes also calamine or true ore of zinc. The mines are situated partly in the mountain limestone, partly in various rocks of older formation. To the S. W. of this district there are also lead mines in Shropshire: like the preceding, they occur partly in mountain limestone and partly in older rocks. They yield a great annual return of lead. Some mines of galena and of calamine are mentioned as occurring in the Mendip hills to the south of Bristol; but they appear to be now abandoned. Many beautiful and interesting minerals are met with in these mines. Of the vein stones, quartz, in Cornwall, is the most abundant; while it is fluor spar and calcareous spar in Derbyshire; in Yorkshire heavy spar or sulphate of barytes; and in Cumberland, heavy spar and fluor spar.

(3.) *Coal formation.* This, which is the most important of the secondary deposits, follows in the regular succession the mountain limestone, on which it therefore rests. The lower beds of this deposit sometimes alternate with the upper strata of the mountain limestone. The rocks of which it is composed are *shale*, *sandstone*, *clay ironstone*, *indurated clay*, and *coal*, alternating in various ways with each other. The shale, sandstones, ironstones, and clays contain numerous fossil remains of extinct species of plants, rarely of animals, the animal remains occurring principally in the limestone. No country of the same size in the world affords so much coal as England, and nowhere has its natural and economical history been so well examined as in this island. Messrs. Conybeare and Phillips arrange the different coal districts in the following manner:—

1. *Coal district north of the Trent*, or grand Penine chain.—1. Northumberland and Durham. 2. North of Yorkshire. 3. South York, Nottingham, and Derby. 4. South of Derby. 5. North Stafford. 6. South Lancashire. 7. North Lancashire. 8. Cumberland and Whitehaven. 9. Foot of Crossfell.

2. *Central coal district.*—1. Ashby de la Zouch. 2. Warwickshire. 3. South Stafford or Dudley. 4. Indications near the Lickey hill, &c.

3. *Western coal district*, divided into, 1. *North Western* or *North Welsh.*—1. Isle of Anglesea. 2. Flintshire.

4. *Middle western* or *Shropshire.*—1. Plain of Shrewsbury. 2. Colebrook-dale. 3. The Clee hills and South Shropshire. 4. Near the Abberley hill.

5. *South Western.*—1. South Wales. 2. Forest of Dean. 3. South Gloucester and Somerset.

These different districts are accurately described in Conybeare and Phillips's *Geology of England and Wales.*

*Changes of the coal fields from the British Channel to the Tweed.* The great coal fields in England experience a great change of structure in their range from the Bristol Channel to the valley of the Tweed: these changes we shall now enumerate, using the view given by Sedgwick. In the various coal basins on the Bristol Channel, the limestone strata are developed only in the lower, and the coal beds in the upper, part of the series; and the two members are separated by nearly unproductive deposits of millstone-grit and shale The arrangement in Derbyshire is nearly the same; there, however, the millstone-grit is more varied, and is of very great thickness, and subordinate to the great deposit of shale, and, here and there, very thick masses of a peculiar argillaceous sandstone, disposed in a tabular manner. On the re-appearance of the carboniferous limestone, at the base of the Yorkshire chain, we still find the same general analogies of structure; enormous deposits of limestone form the lowest part, and the coal fields the highest part of the whole series; and, as in the former instances, we also find the millstone-grit occupying an intermediate position. The millstone-grit, however, becomes a very complex deposit, with several subordinate beds of coal; and is separated from the great inferior calcareous group (the *scar* limestone), not merely by the great shale and shale-limestone, as in Derbyshire, but by a still more complex deposit, in some places not less than 1000 feet thick; in which five groups of limestone strata alternate with great masses of sandstone and shale, abound in impressions of coal plants, and three or four thin beds of good coal extensively worked for domestic use.

In the range of the carboniferous chain from Stainmoor, through the ridge of Crossfell to the confines of Northumberland, we have a repetition of the same general phenomena. On its eastern flanks, and superior to all its component groups, is the coal field of Durham. Under the coal field, we have, in a regular descending order, the millstone-grit, the alternations of limestone and coal measures nearly identical with those of the Yorkshire chain, and at the base of all is the great *scar limestone.* The scar limestone begins, however, to be subdivided by thick masses of sandstone and carbonaceous shale, of which we had hardly a trace in Yorkshire; and gradually passes into a complex deposit, not distinguishable from the next superior division of the series. Along with this gradual change is a great developement of the inferior coal beds alternating with the limestone; some of which on the north-eastern skirts of Cumberland, are three or four feet in thickness, and are now worked for domestic use.

The alternating beds of sandstone and shale expand more and more as we advance towards the north, at the expense of all the calcareous groups, which gradually thin off and cease to produce any impress on the features of the country. And thus it is, that the lowest portion of the whole carboniferous system, from Bewcastle Forest, along the skirts of the Cheviot Hills, to the valley of the Tweed, has hardly a single feature in common with the inferior part of the Yorkshire chain; but, on the contrary, has almost all the most ordinary external characters of a coal formation. Corresponding to this change, is also a gradual thickening of carbonaceous matter in some of the lower groups. Many coal works have been opened upon this line; and near the right bank of the Tweed (almost on a parallel with the great *scar limestone*) is a coal field, with five or six good seams, some of which are pretty extensively worked. The beds of sandstone, shale, and limestone, forming the base in the carboniferous system in the basin of the Tweed, are often deeply tinged with oxide of iron; and have been compared sometimes with the new, sometimes with the old, red sandstone: to the new red sandstone they have no relations; "and I would rather compare them," says Sedgwick, "especially as the old red sandstone of the north of England seldom exist but as a conglomerate, and is seen in that form on the flanks of the Cheviot Hills, with the red beds of mountain limestone and sandstone, which, both in Cumberland and Lancashire, sometimes form the base of the whole carboniferous series."

These coal fields are traversed and variously deranged by great *faults;* interesting descriptions of which, particularly those in the northern fields, have been published by Messrs. Phillips and Sedgwick.

The coal strata, or *metals* as they are sometimes called, are in some parts of England affected by Plutonian trap rocks, but in a very inferior degree to what takes place in Scotland. The principal trap rock is greenstone, which appears in the form of *overlying* masses, as at Clee Hill and at Dudley; in the form of intersecting tabular masses or *dikes* (veins), as in Northumberland and Durham. Sometimes the trap mass has been forced between the strata, when it has the character of *a bed*, or these bed-like masses may be some of the rocks of the coal formation softened and recrystallised *in situ* by heat from below. The great *whin sill* of Northumberland, and the toadstone beds of Derbyshire, are examples of these *trap beds.* The strata near the trap frequently appear changed, the clays hardened, the limestone rendered crystalline and magnesian, the coal charred, and the sandstone hardened, &c.; and these strata are either moved from their original position, or are unchanged.

Although rather foreign to our subject, we may, as an illustration of the importance of the coal formation to England, mention the quantity of iron manufactured, and of coal consumed, in the carboniferous district of Wales. The quantity of iron, according to Mr. Forster, annually manufactured in Wales, has been calculated at 270,000 tons. Of this quantity a proportion of about three-fourths is made into bars, and one-fourth sold as pigs and castings. The quantity of coal required for its manufacture on the average of the whole, including that used by engines, workmen, &c. will be about 5½ tons for each ton of iron; the annual consumption of coal by the ironworks will, therefore, be about 1,500,000 tons. The quantity used in the smelting of copper ore imported into Wales from Cornwall, in the manufacture of tin-plate, forging of iron for various purposes, and for domestic uses, may be calculated at 350,000, which makes altogether the annual consumption in Wales, 1,850,000 tons.

(4.) *Magnesian limestone formation.* The upper part of the coal formation has sometimes a red colour with an arenaceous and conglomerated character. Above or resting upon it we have the magnesian limestone deposit. This deposit extends through Yorkshire and Durham. Its lower part is said to be separated from the coal formation by a deposit of sand and sandstone, with occasional red marl and gypsum. The magnesian limestone itself consists in its lower part of a *bituminous marl slate*, abounding in fossil fishes of the genus *Palæothrissum;* the middle and upper parts being a yellowish small granular or glimmering magnesian limestone. The organic character of this limestone approaches nearly to that of the mountain limestone already described. It contains *Productæ*, which, however do not occur higher in the series; also *Spiriferæ*, a tribe found as high as the oolite.

(5.) *Variegated or new red sandstone, with the red variegated marl deposit.* As the shell limestone is wanting in England, the variegated sandstone and the red and variegated marls come together, and may here, therefore, be viewed as one formation. They rest immediately upon the magnesian limestone, but of the two sets the marl appears in general to be the uppermost or newest. The sandstone is of a looser texture than that of the old red sandstone deposit, has a red or variegated colour, and the strata are generally horizontal. The marls are red or variegated in colour. In these sandstones and marls, beds and great masses or nodules of gypsum occur, as in Derbyshire, Staffordshire, &c. All the *salt mines* in England are situated in this deposit. At Northwich there is an extensive deposit of solid *rock salt*, forming two beds, together not less than 60 feet in thickness. These beds are supposed to form large insulated masses of this mineral, extending in length about a mile and a half, and in breadth about 1300 yards. The *salt works* at Droitwich in Worcestershire are also in this red marl deposit. Iron-sand and iserine are said to occur in this sandstone on the banks of the Mersey opposite Liverpool; and in other places sulphuret of copper, gray oxide of cobalt, and black oxide of manganese occur in the sandstone or its marls. It forms the surface of vast tracts extending with little interruption from the northern bank of the Tees in Durham to the southern coast of Devonshire. We find a tract in the great plain in the centre of England of about 80 miles in length and sixty in breadth, principally covered with this deposit; *several islands* of the *older rocks*, however, rising, in various places, through it. These are, 1st, the syenite, greenstone, and slate district of Charnwood forest in Leicestershire; 2dly, the coal district surrounding Ashby de la Zouch in the same county; connected with which are several patches of the carboniferous magnesian limestone, and a patch of millstone-grit at Stanton-bridge on the Trent; 3dly, the coal-field of Warwickshire; 4thly, the coal-field in the south of Staffordshire, with the transition limestone on which it rests; 5thly, the lower and northern range of the Lickey hill, near Bromsgrove in Worcestershire, which exhibits strata, probably of transition quartz rock. Some *trap rocks* occur in this formation at Upton Pyne, a village five miles north of Exeter, and at other points near that town.

(6.) *Lias and oolite formation.* This great formation occupies a zone having nearly 30 miles in average breadth, extending across the island from Yorkshire on the north-east, to Devonshire on the south-west. It is eminently remarkable on account of the number and variety of fossil organic remains which it contains, and its wide distribution not only in England, but also in many other parts of the world. In this formation, at Stonesfield, the first or earliest remains of mammiferous animals were found. Crocodiles and many vast and strangely organised reptiles occur in this deposit, with a vast variety of shells, many *radiaria*, and also corals. Fishes are also met with in a fossil state, but by no means so frequently as reptiles. Fossil plants of various tribes also occur, and thus add to the organic variety of this remarkable formation: they belong to the *Algæ*, *Equisetaceæ*, *Filices*, *Cycadeæ*, *Coniferæ*, and *Lilia*. Beds of coal, generally of an indifferent quality, occur in different parts of the country in this deposit.

(7.) *Wealden clay and Purbeck stone.* This formation, which lies immediately upon the oolite, consists of limestones, sands, and clays abounding in fossil organic remains, principally of terrestrial and fresh-water plants and animals, marine species being rare. In the lower part of this formation, in the neighbourhood of Weymouth, there is a bed of black earth, called the *dirt bed*, containing, in a silicified state, long prostrate trunks of coniferous trees, and stems of *Cycadeoideæ*. These trunks lie partly sunk into the deep black earth, like fallen trees on the surface of a peat bog, and partly covered by the incumbent Purbeck limestone. Many trunks of trees also remain erect, with their roots attached to the black soil in which they grew, and their upper part in the limestone; and show that the surface of the subjacent Portland stone was for some time dry land, and covered with a forest; and probably in a climate such as admits the growth of the modern *Zamia* and *Cycas*, remains of these genera being found here. This forest has been submerged; first, beneath the fresh waters of a lake or estuary, in which were deposited the Purbeck beds, and sands and clays of the Wealden formation (amounting together to nearly 1000 feet), and subsequently beneath the salt water of an ocean of sufficient depth to accumulate all the great marine formations of green sand and chalk that rest upon it.

(8.) *Chalk formation with green sand.* This great deposit consists principally of chalk, with less extensive subjacent beds of green sand and tuffaceous chalk. It stretches, with little interruption, from Flamborough Head on the coast of Yorkshire, to near Sidmouth on the coast of Devonshire; forming a range of hills often of some hundred feet high, and of which the most precipitous face is generally on the north-west side. From this long range several ranges shoot toward the east and south-east. Chalk does not often bear the character of a level or flat country; but, on the contrary, is subject to perpetual undulation of surface, the hills being remarkable for their smooth rounded outline, and the deep hollows and indentations on their sides.

The upper part of this formation, through a great part of England, is characterised by the presence of common gun-flint, arranged in thin beds or in variously-shaped masses, disposed more or less in parallel lines. In the lower part of the formation the flints become less and less abundant, and at length entirely disappear. This arrangement, however, is not always to be observed, for in some places the lower chalk abounds in flints. In the chalk formation, the upper and middle parts are of chalk, while the lower and under are of sands, sandstones, and clays. The upper part may be considered an original deposit, the matter derived from the interior of the earth; the lower of a mechanical and alluvial nature. Chalk abounds in fossil remains of animals, and also contains fossilised plants. Corals in great variety, radiated animals, particularly echinites, are in vast numbers; shells of all the grand divisions and in great variety add to the zoological interest of the formation, which is further heightened by the fossil crabs, fishes, and reptiles, occasionally met with in it. The plants are *Confervæ, Fuci, Zosteræ, Cycadeæ,* with dicotyledonous wood perforated by some boring animal. The formation, as it occurs in England, appears to have been variously elevated and depressed at different times by some subterranean actions; but, as far as we know, it does not anywhere occur in contact with trap or other Plutonian rocks.

III. *Tertiary rocks.* Hitherto, in England, these deposits have been found only in what are called the *London basin* and the *Isle of Wight basin;* two spaces conjectured formerly to have had the basin shape, but now more or less filled with tertiary rocks; an opinion, however, which the late observations of Professor Buckland have shown to be less plausible than has been generally believed. The boundary of the first of these supposed basins may be stated, generally, as a line running from the inner edge of the chalk, south of Flamborough Head, in Yorkshire, nearly south, till it crosses the Wash, then south-west to the upper part of the valley of the river Kennet, near Hungerford, in Wiltshire; and thence trending south-east to the south of the Thames, and the north-west angle of the Isle of Thanet: in all these directions the boundary line is formed by the chalk hills; on the east side, the boundary is the coast of the German Ocean. The boundaries of the Isle of Wight basin may be stated as follows:—on the north, a few miles south of Winchester; on the south, a little north of Carisbrook in the Isle of Wight; on the east, Brighton; and on the west, Dorchester. It is everywhere circumscribed by chalk hills, excepting where broken in by the channel between the Isle of Wight and the main land. The different members of the tertiary series met with in England, are named *Plastic clay, London clay, Bagshot sands,* the *Freshwater formations* of the Isle of Wight, and the *Crag.—Plastic clay.* This deposit consists of a plastic clay with gravel beds, alternating with beds of sand (sometimes in a state of sandstone) and clay. Its organic remains are principally marine shells, with layers of lignite or brown coal.—*London clay.* This is a bluish or blackish clay, sometimes so much impregnated with carbonate of lime as to form a kind of compact marl. Layers or nodules of septaria (a calcareous concretion) frequently occur in it. It is the great clayey deposit on which London is built. It has been bored to a depth of 700 feet, without reaching its bottom. The highest point it attains is the summit of High Beach in Essex, being 759 feet above the sea. It abounds in fossil organic remains from the animal as well as from the vegetable kingdom. Crocodiles, turtles, fishes, and crabs have been observed; but these are few in number compared with the host of fossil shells. These shells are often very beautifully preserved, frequently retaining the appearance of recent species. There are very few genera of recent shells which have not some representative in this formation, but the specific character is usually different; on the other hand, but few of the extinct genera, so frequent in the older formations, occur in this. The Isle of Sheppey, formed of London clay, affords a vast variety of fossil fruits and seeds, very few of which agree with any known seed-vessels; many of them are conjectured to belong to tropical plants, some to the cocoa-nut and spice tribes. Fragments of wood pierced by a shell animal, resembling the *Teredo navalis,* are met with; a fact which shows that the wood may have floated about in the sea.—*Bagshot sands.* These rest upon the London clay; they consist of sand, with greenish-coloured clay, variously coloured marls, containing grains of green sand, and fossil trochi and pectinites.—*Freshwater formations of the Isle of Wight and Hampshire.* The Freshwater strata of the Isle of Wight are divided into two deposits by a rock characterised by the presence of marine remains, and named the *upper marine formation,* from being a supposed equivalent to the sands which intervene between the two freshwater deposits of Paris. The *lower freshwater* deposit of Binstead, near Ryde, consists of a limestone formed of fragments of freshwater shells, white shell marl, siliceous limestone, and sand. One tooth of an *Anaplotherium* and two teeth of a *Palæotherium* have been found in the lower marly beds of the quarries at Binstead. In the same quarries several rolled fragments of pachydermatous animals, and the jaw of an animal allied to the musk-deer tribe. In Colwell Bay the upper part of this deposit contains a mixture of freshwater and marine shells.—The *upper marine formation.* This deposit of calcareous beds abounds with freshwater shells in the lower part, but in the upper part we find marine shells; hence it is conjectured to have been formed in an estuary.—*Upper freshwater formation.* This consists principally of yellowish white marls. The organic remains are either freshwater or land. The geological history of the tertiary deposits in England has not yet been placed in direct connexion with that of similar deposits on the continent of Europe. No trap or granite rocks have hitherto been met with in England in any way connected with the tertiary strata.

IV. *Alluvial rocks.* Nearly the whole of England is more or less covered with alluvium, or débris of previously existing rocks: thus it occurs on mountain ridges, and on the sides and bottoms of valleys; it is spread over plains, fills up, wholly or partially, fissures in rocks, and caves, and caverns, and forms beaches and other accumulations of greater or lesser extent on the sea coast. It varies in age, from the oldest called *diluvium*, which stands in immediate connexion with the *crag* or upper tertiary deposit, to the newest, those forming at present through the agency of the atmosphere, springs, lakes, rivers, and the waves and currents of the ocean. It encloses numerous remains of plants and animals, either more or less mineralized, or simply bleached: those of the oldest deposits appear to be of animals, and sometimes of plants, which are apparently extinct; while the newer enclose remains only of living animal and vegetable species. Although our limits do not allow us to enter into details on this very important and curious department of geology, we may remark, that the characters and modes of distribution of these alluvia are, in many instances, intimately connected with risings and depressions of the land; and consequently with apparent sinking and rising of the waters of the ocean, and the violent agitations sometimes induced in the great mass of the ocean, and also in lakes, by changes in the level of the solid parts of the globe.

### SUBSECT. 2.—*Botany.*

The botany of the different parts of the British empire is so similar, that we propose to treat under one head that of England, Scotland, Ireland, and their adjacent islands.

Extending through eleven degrees of latitude, Great Britain includes a considerable variety of climate, but everywhere, more or less tempered by the surrounding ocean; so that, in no part of the island, except on the mountains, or high table-lands, can the temperature be compared to similar latitudes, upon the European, much less upon the American continent. Yet, from its proximity to the former, the vegetation is, with few exceptions, similar to that of the adjacent districts of Europe. Although in consequence of the unfavourable summers, the frequent obscurity of the sun, the damp and foggy atmosphere, it is not possible, without artificial heat and protection, to bring many of the fruits of more favoured climates to perfection; yet the mildness of the winter renders it easy to introduce and to naturalise plants of much more southern latitudes: so that the gardens, parks, shrubberies, and even forests, are adorned with the most varied vegetation, producing the most beautiful flowers, or the most valued timbers.

On the *extreme southern coast of England and Ireland*, the native vegetables of the warmer temperate zone are successfully grown in the open air, and come to considerable perfection. In the south of Devonshire, the orange and lemon trees are loaded with fruit of the finest kind, trained, indeed, to a wall, but without protection, or only provided with it during a very short portion of the winter months; the Lemon-scented Vervain (*Lippia citriodora*, formerly called *Verbena triphylla*, becomes quite a tree, without any artificial protection; the American Agave, the creeping Cereus, the Prickly Pear, myrtles from the south of Europe; the Tea, Camellias and other Chinese and Japanese plants, thrive well in the open air, as well as the Magnolias, and many other trees, from the southern states of North America, whose native latitudes lie many degrees nearer to the tropics.

The only two floras of Great Britain, which are so complete as to demand particular attention, are Sir J. E. Smith's *English Flora*, and Gray's *Arrangement of British Plants*, the former classed according to the Linnæan system, extending, however, only to the end of the class Polygamia, and the first order of the class Cryptogamia Filices. Gray's *Flora* includes the whole of the British vegetables, arranged according to the natural method, and is the only one that approaches, however deficient it may still be, to any thing like a catalogue of our present state of knowledge of the Cryptogamia. Among the Phænogamous plants however, Mr. Gray has included a great number that are only known in a state of cultivation, as has been done by De Candolle, in his *Flore Française*, and many other continental botanists. We have, therefore, deemed it convenient thus to give a list of the plants, according to each of these authors; and the increased number in the columns of species according to Mr. Gray, will be thus easily accounted for.

A LIST of the Number of Species of British Plants, arranged according to the Classes and principal Families to which they belong; exhibiting the relative proportion which these latter bear to the whole of the respective Classes.*

| Names of the Natural Families. | Species in Smith's *English Flora.* | | | Proportion of Natural Orders to Phænogamous, per Smith. | Species in Gray's *Arrangement of British Plants.* | | | Proportion of Natural Orders to Phænogamous, per Gray. | Average Proportion of Natural Orders to Phænogamous Plants. | A LIST of the Species of Scottish Plants.† Species. | | | Proportion of Natural Orders to Phænogamous Plants. |
|---|---|---|---|---|---|---|---|---|---|---|---|---|---|
| Fungi | – | – | – | – | – | 800 | – | 1 to 2 | 1 to 2 | – | 974 | – | 1 to $1\frac{1}{9}$ |
| Algæ | – | – | – | – | – | 400 | – | 4 | 4 | – | 465 | – | $2\frac{1}{3}$ |
| Lichenes | – | – | – | – | – | 400 | – | 4 | 4 | – | 260 | – | $4\frac{1}{6}$ |
| Hepaticæ, by Hooker | – | 90 | – | $16\frac{1}{10}$ | – | 97 | – | $16\frac{3}{5}$ | $16\frac{7}{9}$ | – | 73 | – | $14\frac{3}{7}$ |
| Musci, by Hooker | – | 290 | – | $5\frac{1}{5}$ | – | 290 | – | $5\frac{6}{10}$ | $5\frac{4}{10}$ | – | 264 | – | $4\frac{1}{7}$ |
| Filices | – | 58 | – | 26 | – | 58 | – | $28\frac{1}{5}$ | $27\frac{1}{10}$ | – | 48 | – | $22\frac{1}{2}$ |
| ACOTYLEDONES | – | – | – | – | – | – | 2045 | $\frac{4}{5}$ | $\frac{4}{5}$ | – | – | 2084 | $\frac{2}{5}$ |
| Gramineæ | 121 | – | – | $12\frac{1}{2}$ | 170 | – | – | $9\frac{3}{5}$ | 11 | 94 | | | |
| Cyperaceæ | 92 | – | – | 17 | 91 | – | – | 18 | $17\frac{1}{2}$ | 66 | | | |
| Junceæ and Restiaceæ | 32 | – | – | 47 | 33 | – | – | $49\frac{1}{2}$ | $48\frac{1}{4}$ | 28 | | | |
| Glumaceæ | – | 245 | – | $6\frac{1}{8}$ | – | 294 | – | $5\frac{1}{2}$ | $5\frac{3}{4}$ | – | 188 | – | $5\frac{7}{9}$ |
| Orchideæ | – | 37 | – | $40\frac{2}{3}$ | – | 33 | – | $49\frac{1}{2}$ | 45 | – | 19 | | |
| Monocotyledones cæteræ | – | 73 | – | – | – | 89 | – | – | – | – | 53 | | |
| MONOCOTYLEDONES | – | – | 355 | $4\frac{1}{4}$ | – | – | 416 | $3\frac{9}{10}$ | 4 | – | – | 260 | $4\frac{1}{6}$ |
| Coniferæ | – | 4 | – | 376 | – | 7 | – | 234 | 305 | – | 3 | | |
| Amentaceæ | – | 78 | – | $19\frac{1}{4}$ | – | 72 | – | $22\frac{3}{4}$ | 21 | – | 56 | | |
| Euphorbiaceæ | – | 16 | – | 94 | – | 16 | – | $102\frac{1}{4}$ | 98 | – | 7 | | |
| Scrophul. and Orobancheæ | – | 52 | – | $28\frac{1}{2}$ | – | 55 | – | $29\frac{4}{5}$ | $29\frac{1}{4}$ | – | 37 | – | 1 to $29\frac{1}{4}$ |
| Labiatæ and Verbenæ | – | 56 | – | $26\frac{4}{5}$ | – | 69 | – | $23\frac{3}{4}$ | $25\frac{1}{4}$ | – | 39 | – | $28\frac{1}{5}$ |
| Boragineæ | – | 23 | – | 1 to $65\frac{1}{3}$ | – | 23 | – | 1 to $71\frac{1}{8}$ | 1 to $68\frac{1}{5}$ | – | 18 | | |
| Ericineæ and Pyroleæ | – | 22 | – | 67 | – | 22 | – | $74\frac{1}{3}$ | $70\frac{2}{3}$ | – | 18 | | |
| Campanulaceæ | – | 14 | – | $107\frac{1}{3}$ | – | 15 | – | 109 | $108\frac{1}{6}$ | – | 9 | | |
| Compositæ | – | 137 | – | 11 | – | 144 | – | $11\frac{1}{3}$ | $11\frac{1}{6}$ | – | 105 | – | $10\frac{1}{3}$ |
| Rubiaceæ | – | 21 | – | $71\frac{1}{2}$ | – | 19 | – | 86 | $78\frac{3}{4}$ | – | 16 | | |
| Umbelliferæ | – | 64 | – | $23\frac{1}{2}$ | – | 69 | – | $23\frac{3}{4}$ | $23\frac{5}{8}$ | – | 44 | – | $24\frac{3}{5}$ |
| Rosaceæ | – | 81 | – | $18\frac{1}{2}$ | – | 81 | – | $20\frac{1}{5}$ | $19\frac{1}{3}$ | – | 52 | – | $20\frac{4}{5}$ |
| Leguminosæ | – | 66 | – | $22\frac{4}{5}$ | – | 69 | – | $23\frac{3}{4}$ | $23\frac{1}{4}$ | – | 43 | – | 25 |
| Malvaceæ | – | 6 | – | $250\frac{1}{2}$ | – | 6 | – | $272\frac{2}{3}$ | $261\frac{1}{2}$ | – | 5 | | |
| Caryophylleæ | – | 59 | – | $25\frac{1}{2}$ | – | 60 | – | $27\frac{3}{10}$ | $26\frac{4}{10}$ | – | 45 | – | 24 |
| Cruciferæ | – | 71 | – | $21\frac{1}{8}$ | – | 73 | – | $22\frac{5}{7}$ | $21\frac{7}{10}$ | – | 56 | – | $19\frac{1}{3}$ |
| Ranunculaceæ | – | 36 | – | $41\frac{3}{4}$ | – | 42 | – | 39 | $40\frac{3}{8}$ | – | 25 | | |
| Dicotyledones cæteræ | – | 342 | – | – | – | 378 | – | – | – | – | 245 | | |
| DICOTYLEDONES | – | – | 1148 | $1\frac{1}{3}$ | – | – | 1220 | $1\frac{1}{3}$ | $1\frac{1}{3}$ | – | – | 823 | $1\frac{3}{10}$ |

It must be remarked, that in *Cyperaceæ*, *Junceæ*, *Salix*, *Saxifraga*, *Rosa*, *Rubus*, and some others, the *species* are not formed on the same rules as in Smith's *English Flora*; and therefore, before drawing a parallel between these orders in Scotland, and in the whole of Britain, a considerable number of species ought to be added. To make this comparison, then, about twenty species may be added to the *Monocotyledones*, and about fifty (say forty-seven), to the *Dicotyledonous* plants, making these two, 280 and 870; whence the Monocotyledones of Scotland are to the whole of those in the British dominions as one to one and a quarter, or as four to five; and the Dicotyledones as eight to eleven.

Ireland possesses a flora which partakes of the nature of those of England and Scotland. A list of the phænogamous plants has been recently published by Mr. J. T. Mackay, of the Dublin College Botanic Garden. It exhibits a much poorer vegetation than its sister island, including only 934 species; of which there are, 41 Filices; 211 Monocotyledones, and 682 Dicotyledones. So that the proportion of Filices to Phænogamous plants is as 1 to $21\frac{3}{4}$; Monocotyledones to Phænogamous plants, 1 to $4\frac{1}{4}$; Dicotyledones to Phænogamous plants, 1 to $1\frac{1}{3}$. The proportion of Irish Monocotyledones to British Monocotyledones (according to the species of Smith) is as 1 to $1\frac{2}{3}$, or as 3 to 5: of Irish Dicotyledones, 1 to $1\frac{2}{3}$, or as 3 to 5.

* Drawn up by G. A. W. Arnott, Esq. of Edinburgh.

† The proportions in the Cryptogamia will be found probably much more correct for Scotland than those given in the British table are for the whole of Britain; owing to the researches made in that tribe by Dr. Greville, and Captain Carmichael; particularly by the latter in the Fungi and Algæ; the discoveries of that gentleman alone in those two groups, in one small district (Appin) in the west highlands of Scotland, amount to more species than were previously described as inhabiting the whole of the British dominions.

Few, indeed, of the species of plants now enumerated as natives of England, Scotland and Ireland, and the adjacent isles, can be considered as exclusively belonging to these countries. For though there are many which are not referred to as species in the works of other authors, yet they are, for the most part, among such families as are not well understood, and about which there will always exist a difference of opinion; as among the Grasses, Willows, Brambles, &c.

Many plants reach their northern limits in the south of England and Ireland. We must particularly mention the Strawberry Tree (*Arbutus Unedo*, *fig*. 107.), which forms so charming a feature in that most beautiful of all scenery, the Lake of Killarney. Some have, indeed, supposed that it was introduced into Ireland by the monks of Mucruss Abbey, at

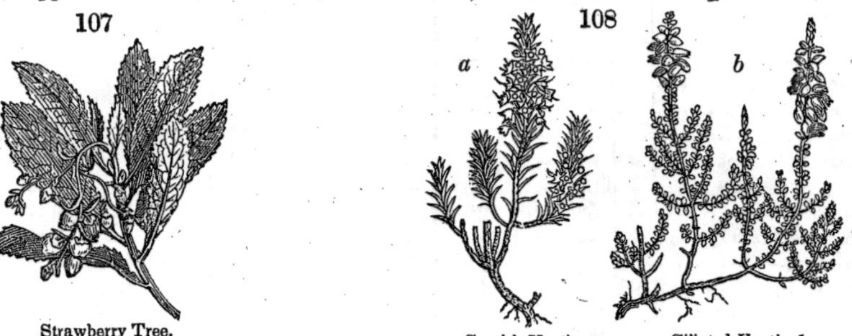

107 Strawberry Tree. 108 Cornish Heath. Ciliated Heath.

some very remote period. Its appearance is, however, altogether that of an aboriginal native, coming to a great size,* perfecting its bright scarlet berries, which are disseminated over the rocks and islands in every direction. The *Erica vagans*, or Cornish Heath (*fig*. 108. *a*), is found nowhere in Britain except Cornwall; and the same may be said of the newly-discovered *E. ciliaris* (*b*), and the following, of great beauty or rarity: *Lobelia Dortmanna*, *Phyteuma orbicularis* and *P. spicata*, *Sibthorpia europæa* and *Isnardia palustris*, are quite southern plants in the British dominions.

The Water-Soldier (*Stratiotes aloides*); the Water Violet (*Hottonia palustris*); the small Maidenhair Grass (*Briza minor*); the Sweet Violet (*Viola odorata*); several Mulleins; the Primrose-peerless (*Narcissus poeticus* and *biflorus*); the common Snake's Head (*Fritillaria meleagris*); the Agrostis setacea, the Star of Bethlehem (*Ornithogalum pyrenaicum*); the two species of Squill (*Scilla autumnalis* and *bifolia*); the Mountain Spiderwort (*Anthericum serotinum*); the Solomon's Seal (*Convallaria polygonatum*); and Sweet Sedge (*Acorus Calamus*); the Yellow-wort (*Chlora perfoliata*); the Mezereum (*Daphne Mezereum*); the Flowering Rush (*Butomus umbellatus*); the Yellow Marsh Saxifrage (*Saxifraga Hirculus*); though on the Continent a very arctic plant, the Clove Pink (*Dianthus caryophyllus*); and D. prolifer; several Catchflys (*Silene*); Euphorbias, Cistuses, Anemones, the Traveller's Joy (*Clematis Vitalba*); the Ground Pine (*Ajuga Chamæpitys*); the Wood-Sage (*Teucrium Scorodonia*); the crested and field Cow-wheat (*Melampyrum cristatum* and *arvense*); some Orobanches, the Vella annua, Draba aizoides, and Iberis amara, some Fumitories (*Fumaria solida*, *lutea*, and *parviflora*); the yellow and crimson Vetchlings (*Lathyrus Aphaca* and *Nissolia*); the Vicia hybrida, lævigata, and bithynica, Hippocrepis comosa; Orchis Morio,† pyramidalis, ustulata, fusca, militaris, tephrosanthos, hircina; Aceras anthropophora, Herminium monorchis; all the species of Ophrys, Epipactis rubra, Malaxis Loeselii; the beautiful and rare Lady's Slipper (*Cypripedium Calceolus*); the Birthwort (*Aristolochia Clematitis*); the Roman Nettle (*Urtica pilulifera*); the Xanthium strumarium and Amaranthus Blitum; the Spanish Chestnut Tree (*Fagus castanea*); and Misseltoe (*Viscum album*); the Sea Buckthorn (*Hippophae rhamnoides*); and White Poplar (*Populus canescens*): these are some among the most striking of the British plants, which do not reach the middle of the kingdom, and fail below the south of Scotland.

The most interesting of the Scottish plants are, principally, such whose types are found on the continent of Europe, in high northern latitudes, or in the extreme arctic regions of both Asia and America; such as Veronica fruticulosa, saxatilis, and alpina, several alpine grasses, and other glumaceous plants; such as Phleum alpinum and Alopecurus alpinus, Eriophorum alpinum; Juncus castaneus, arcticus, and biglumis; and Luzula arctica, Primula scotica (*fig*. 109. *a*), the Myosotis alpestris (*d*), Azalea procumbens, Gentiana nivalis (*c*) Sibbaldia procumbens, Convallaria verticillata, Epilobium alpinum, Arbutus alpina, Pyrola uniflora (*b*), Saxifraga nivalis and rivularis, Stellaria scapigera (the latter is exclusively

* Mr. Mackay measured a trunk of this fine evergreen tree on Rough Island, nearly opposite O'Sullivan's Cascade, which, in 1805, was 9½ feet in girth, at a foot from the ground.

† On the authority of Lightfoot, indeed, this plant, so abundantly found in England, is given as a native of Scotland: but no living botanist, that I am aware of has ever seen it there.

British), Arenaria rubella and fastigiata, the Cherleria sedoides, Lychnis Viscaria and alpina, Spergula saginoides, Potentilla opaca, Nuphar Kalmiana, Ranunculus alpestris, Ajuga pyramidalis, Cardamine bellidiflora, Orobus niger, Astragalus uralensis and campestris, Erigeron

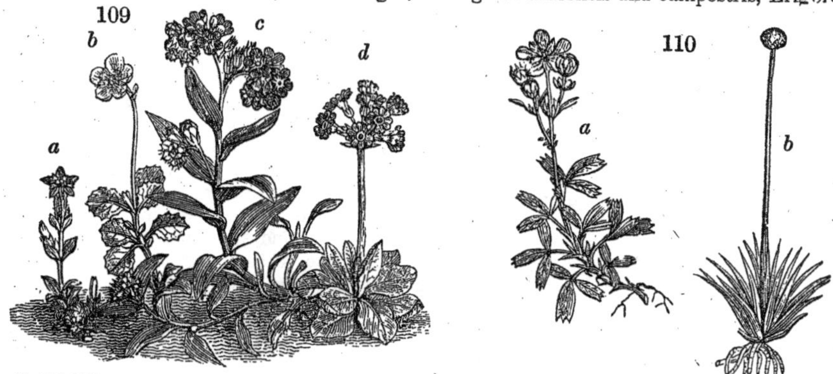


*a*, Scottish Primrose. *b*, Rock Scorpion Grass. *c*, Single-Flowered Water-Green. *d*, Small Alpine Gentian.

*a*, Trifid-Leaved Cinquefoil. *b*, Jointed Pipewort.

alpinum, Corallorhiza innata, Achillæa tomentosa, Goodyera repens; the most alpine Carices and Salices, and the Dwarf Birch (*Betula nana*).

There are two plants which deserve particular notice, as natives of Great Britain, and found nowhere else in Europe; but these are again met with in North America; the one is Potentilla tridentata (*fig.* 110. *a*) abundant in arctic America and upon the Rocky and White Mountains, the other the Eriocaulon septangulare (*fig.* 110. *b*). This latter genus is mostly tropical, or a native of the warm temperate zones in America, the East Indies, and Australia. The only exceptions to this rule are the Eriocaulon pellucidum of Michaux, and the plant in question; the former being found in North America as high as Canada; and, upon examination, the two species prove identical. In these instances, the Eriocaulon and the Potentilla seem to have overcome many obstacles in their migration, and to have reached their eastern boundary. The Eriocaulon is confined to a few lakes in the Hebrides, where we have been surprised in the month of September at the high temperature of the water, which probably never freezes; and in some spots in the south and west of Ireland: the Potentilla is only found on one hill in Angusshire.

It is worthy of remark, that the genus Pedicularis, which is so numerous in species, in the eastern and southern parts of Europe, almost wholly disappears in Britain; for, notwithstanding the vast numbers of it which are found in Siberia, the South of Russia, Switzerland, extending even to the Pyrenees, and Germany, Great Britain possesses but two, which are equally abundant upon the Continent; and although almost wholly an alpine genus, the British mountains possess not one really alpine species. It would appear that the climate is peculiarly unsuited to their nurture: for in North America, in the same and especially in still higher northern latitudes, they again become abundant.

Ireland exhibits a few striking peculiarities in some of its vegetable productions. Besides the Strawberry tree (*Arbutus unedo*) already mentioned, it can boast of Pinguicula grandiflora (*fig.* 111. *a*), a beautiful flower, native of France and the Pyrenees; Menziesia poli-

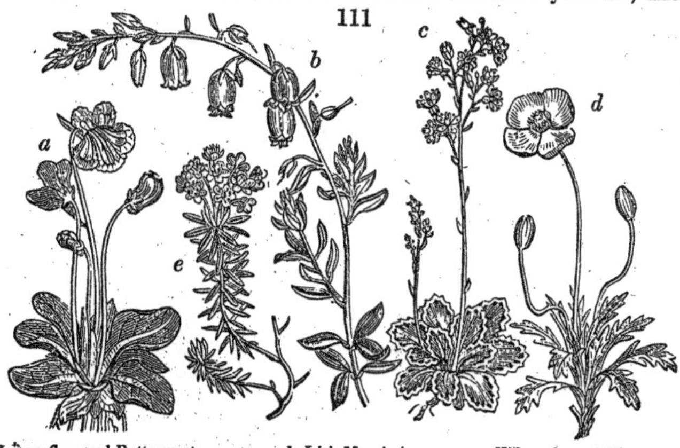


*a*, Large-flowered Butterwort. *b*, Irish Menziesia. *c* Kidney-leaved Saxifrage *d*, Naked-stalked Yellow Poppy. *e*, Marsh Ledum.

folia (*b*), a species belonging to the latter country and to Spain, and found in a wild state in no other parts of the world; it is, too, a most lovely one: also St. Patrick's Cabbage (*Saxifraga umbrosa*) and the London Pride (*S. Geum*, *c*) and their varieties, which are scarcely known to exist but in Switzerland and the Pyrenees; Arenaria ciliata, a native of the mountains on the continent of Europe; and to these rarities have lately been added by Professor Giesecké, the Yellow Poppy (*Papaver nudicaule*, *d*), and the Ledum palustre (*e*,) both of them peculiarly arctic productions, and plentiful on the northern extremity of America and Greenland; and with these we must be permitted to number, though Cryptogamic plants, the Trichomanes brevisetum (*fig.* 112. *b*), which scarcely grows anywhere else in the world but in Madeira and in Yorkshire (if it be not now extinct in the latter habitat), the Adiantum Capillus Veneris (*a*), whose only locality in the British dominions is the west of Ireland, and one spot in Wales, but which is frequent in the south of Europe, and even in the tropical parts of America; and two mosses, Hookeria latevirens, and Daltonia splanchnoides, entirely peculiar to Ireland.

112

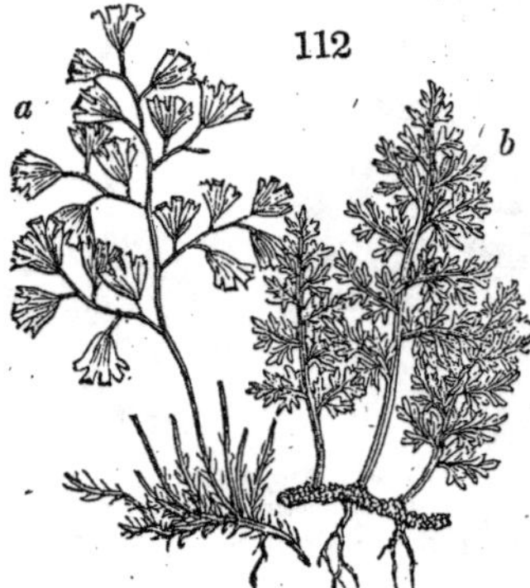


*a*, True Maiden-Hair.
*b*, Short-styled Bristle-Fern.

That country also possesses three remarkable vegetable productions, now pretty generally distributed in gardens and shrubberies throughout the kingdom, and universally known by the names of the Irish Broom, Irish Furze, and Irish Yew. The former we believe to be the Spartium patens of Linnæus, a Spanish species, with very hairy pods; and it is, probably, not wild in that country. The Irish Furze has an appearance very different from that of the European or Dwarf Furzes (*Ulex europæus* and *nanus*), having very erect short branches, and closely placed spines; so that the whole plant has a remarkably dense and compact habit, appearing almost as if it were kept close clipped with shears. It blossoms rarely, but we have seen both flowers and seed-vessels, which do not differ in any material point from those of Ulex nanus. In some gardens it is called U. europæus var. strictus; but Mr. Mackay considers it to be quite a distinct species, and he has called it, in his "Catalogue of the Indigenous Plants of Ireland," Ulex strictus. Still, the only stations for this plant are in the Marquess of Londonderry's park and shrubberies, at Mount Stewart, county of Down, where there are some very large bushes; but whence it came, no one can tell. This would, however, be a very valuable plant to the agriculturist; for, it has been planted (it increases readily by cuttings) in dry hilly pastures in the north of Scotland, and in the early spring throws up an abundant crop of succulent shoots, which are greedily eaten by sheep, when there is little or no grass to support them.

113

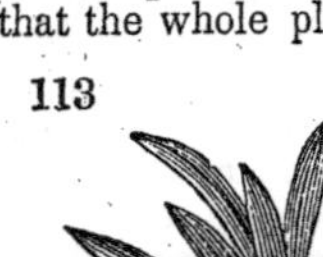

Irish Yew

The third Irish botanical curiosity is the Irish Yew (*fig.* 113), Florence-Court Yew, as it is called in that country, from its being first discovered at Florence Court, the seat of Lord Enniskillen. Mr. Mackay does not consider it to be wild; but Mr. Hervey, in the *Agricultural Magazine* for October, 1828, says, that it is an undoubted native, and plentiful in the neighbourhood of Antrim, where there are trees at least a century old. It is distinguished by its upright branches, which give the whole plant somewhat the habit of a Cypress; by the leaves growing, not in a distichous manner, but from all sides of the stem: the drupe or berry, too, is of a different form from that of the common Yew.

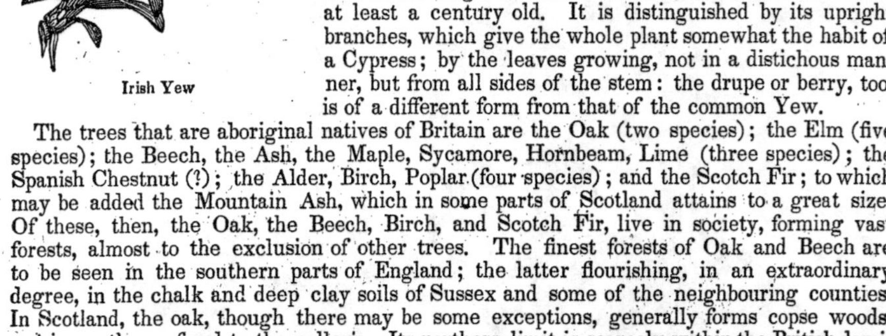

The trees that are aboriginal natives of Britain are the Oak (two species); the Elm (five species); the Beech, the Ash, the Maple, Sycamore, Hornbeam, Lime (three species); the Spanish Chestnut (?); the Alder, Birch, Poplar (four species); and the Scotch Fir; to which may be added the Mountain Ash, which in some parts of Scotland attains to a great size. Of these, then, the Oak, the Beech, Birch, and Scotch Fir, live in society, forming vast forests, almost to the exclusion of other trees. The finest forests of Oak and Beech are to be seen in the southern parts of England; the latter flourishing, in an extraordinary degree, in the chalk and deep clay soils of Sussex and some of the neighbouring counties. In Scotland, the oak, though there may be some exceptions, generally forms copse woods, and is mostly confined to the valleys. Its northern limit is scarcely within the British dominions. It extends to lat 60°, on the continent in Russia, and 64° in Norway; and if in Scotland oaks are not found in the extreme north, it is rather owing to want of shelter and of suitable soil, than to any other circumstance.

The Pine, (*Pinus Sylvestris, fig.* 114.) constitutes noble forests among the mountainous districts of North Britain, filling the valleys, and ascending, probably, to the height of 2500 feet upon the hills, among the northern Grampians, and exhibiting individual specimens of great size and beauty.

114
Scotch Fir.

Of the fruit trees which are successfully cultivated in the open air, the number is limited. In the south, exclusively, or, perhaps, as far as the centre of the kingdom, under favourable circumstances, the Vine, the Fig, the Quince, the Mulberry, Chestnut, Walnut, and Medlar may be advantageously planted. The Apple, Pear, the Plum of various kinds, the Peach, Nectarine, and Apricot; all, according to soil, exposure, and other local circumstances, ripen their fruit in the open air, if afforded the protection of a wall, as high north as Inverness, and some of the most hardy ones much higher; but the want of sun must ever be a hindrance to the thorough perfecting of good fruit in the north of Scotland.

Of the various kinds of Corn, which are used as food for man or cattle, Wheat, Barley, Bere, Bigg, Oats, and Rye are the universal crops; and these all succeed in situations not too much elevated above the level of the sea, as far to the northward as Inverness, beyond which the wheat becomes a very uncertain crop; and even considerably south of Inverness, to the north of the Forth and Clyde, in lat. 56°, the cultivation of wheat is almost wholly confined to the eastern side of the country, the west being the district for pasture.

In regard to the height at which certain plants will grow above the level of the sea, the southern and midland parts of Great Britain do not contain mountains upon a sufficiently lofty scale to render their investigation particularly interesting. The northern parts of England possess mountains of upwards of 3000 feet; and as Winch's "Essay on the Geographical distribution of Plants throughout the Counties of Northumberland, Cumberland, and Durham," of which the lat. 55° may be considered the medium, embraces a very great protion of this very country, which, from its situation, may, in point of climate, be considered as intermediate between the more northern and southern floras of Great Britain, we select from his work what concerns the more valuable and more striking vegetable productions.

The Oak, in lat. 55°, attains a large size in the valleys; it ascends the hills, but gradually becomes of stunted growth in Weardale and Teesdale, to the elevation of 1600 and 1700 feet.

The Common Elm (*Ulmus Campestris*) is not indigenous north of the Tees; its place being taken by the Wych Elm (*U. montana*), which skirts the mountains at a height of 2000 feet.

The Beech and Aspen flourish beautifully in the low sheltered spots, but do not climb the hills to equal heights with the oak. The White and Black Poplars (*Populus alba* and *nigra*) are doubtful natives of the north of England, as of Scotland; though the White Poplar is remarkable for withstanding the north-easterly winds, which are so destructive to vegetation in the counties of Northumberland and Durham. The Lime, (*Tilia Europæa*), the Chestnut (*Castanea vesca*), and the Hornbeam (*Carpinus Betulus*), stand in the same predicament.

Holly trees are among the chief ornaments of the woods in Durham, Northumberland, and Cumberland, as is the Yew (*Taxus Baccata*). The Birch (*Betula alba*) is not found on the mountains at a greater elevation than the Sycamore (*Acer Pseudo-platanus*), which in the subalpine regions seems to be as vigorous, and to attain as great a size as it does near the sea-coast. The Mountain Ash (*Pyrus aucuparia*) is found on the hills; the White Beam (*Pyrus Aria*) may be traced from the High-Force of the river Tees to the coast, the Alder (*Alnus glutinosa*) and the Guelder Rose (*Viburnum Opulus*) accompany the streams; and the Hazel, Black Cherry (*Prunus Cerasus*), Bird Cherry (*Prunus Padus*), the Spindle-tree (*Euonymus europæus*), the Raspberry (*Rubus idæus*), and the common Elder, (*Sambucus nigra*), are found in all the woods from the sea-shore to those situated on an elevation of 1600 feet: but the common Maple (*Acer campestris*) occurs only in the hedges, in some parts of the flat country.

The Ash tree (*Fraxinus excelsior*), the White Thorn (*Mespilus Oxyacantha*), the Crab tree, or Wild Apple (*Pyrus Malus*), and Black Thorn (*Prunus spinosa*), abound throughout the district in question. The Bullace (*Prunus insititia*) is rare: and the Plum-tree (*Prunus domestica*), Pear (*Pyrus communis*), Red currant (*Ribes rubrum*), the Berberry (*Berberis vulgaris*), and Gooseberry (*Ribes Grossularia*), though of frequent occurrence, appear not to be original natives of the soil. But the Rock Currant (*Ribes petræum*), the Acid Mountain Currant (*Ribes spicatum*), Alpine Currant (*Ribes alpinum*), Black Currant (*Ribes nigrum*), and Privet (*Ligustrum vulgare*), are indigenous, and not unfrequent.

The Furze (*Ulex europœus,*) attains to an elevation of 2000 feet in sequestered spots, accompanied by the Bramble. Juniper may be traced from the coast to the height of 1500 feet. The Cloudberry (*Rubus Chamæmorus*), the Bearberry (*Arbutus Uva Ursi*), and Sand Willow (*Salix arenaria*), attain the same elevation; while the Dwarf Willow (*Salix herbacea*), but without its usual attendant the Reticulated Willow (*S. reticulata*), reaches to the tops of the loftiest mountains, upwards of 3000 feet above the level of the sea.

Coarse Grasses, Sedges, and Rushes too often cover the wet moors with a scanty and almost useless vegetation. To the agriculturist the different Heaths are scarcely more acceptable; but they are unquestionably among the most beautiful of the native plants, and their abundance and the vast extent of ground which they clothe, give a peculiar character to very many parts of Great Britain, especially in the North. In the districts in question, the common Heather (*Calluna vulgaris*), the Fir-leaved Heath (*Erica Cinerea*), and the Cross-leaved Heath (*Erica Tetralix*), the latter, however, less fragrant, and preferring moist situations, flourish in various situations, from 1000 to 3000 feet above the level of the sea, but never in calcareous soil, which circumstance occasions the striking difference between the heaths of Durham and Northumberland, and the Yorkshire Wolds as they are called, where the substratum is chalk.

The most considerable elevation to which the cultivation of wheat extends in the north of England does not exceed 1000 feet above the level of the sea. Oats grow at nearly double that height; but in unfavourable years the sheaves may often be seen standing among the snow, which not uncommonly covers the tops of the mountains in October, and is never later in falling than the middle of November. The limits of Barley and Rye are between those of wheat and oats; but Bigg, a more hardy kind of grain than either of the former, is no longer cultivated. Turnips, though of small size, and Potatoes, grow at the same height as Oats. On the soil of the moors being ploughed for the first time, and lime applied, White Clover (*Trifolium repens*) comes up in abundance.

### SUBSECT. 3.—*Zoology of Great Britain.*

The *Zoology* of the United Empire might be treated of under the three kingdoms of which it is composed, were our materials sufficiently ample to mark the peculiarities of each. But although every year witnesses an accession of new species to the British fauna, no attempt has yet been made to generalise these discoveries, with reference to the geographic range of groups or species. The zoology of Ireland has been sadly neglected, and we are still without a Fauna Scotica. We must therefore consider the natural history of Britain in the aggregate; noticing such species as more particularly belong to the northern and the southern extremities.

Of Quadrupeds, the most recent catalogue contains sixty living species, including the whale tribe; besides those which progressive civilisation, and the effects of the chase, have now extirpated from the islands. Nine species of Bats have been detected, four of which have as yet been found only in the southern and western counties: two belong to the division of horse-shoe bats, so named, from their nostrils being furnished with a complicated membrane, like a horse-shoe; an appendage which is probably intended to act as a sucker to assist the animal in retaining its prey. The Vespertilio murinus, or common bat, has been so far tamed as to take flies out of its master's hand, carefully throwing aside the wings. The woods and heaths still shelter the Hedgehog (*fig.* 115.), a harmless and a most useful animal in destroying snails, slugs, and worms; but persecuted by the vulgar for a long list of imaginary and nonsensical properties. These prejudices have been extended to the Mole, whose little hillocks form the best top-dressing, as a sensible farmer once assured us, to poor lands, that can possibly be given: their soft fur has long been mixed with that of the Beaver, in the making of hats. Allied to the Mole, in general conformation, are the Shrew Mice, of which two species are natives, the common and the Water Shrew (*Sorex araneus* and *fodiens*): both these appear to be widely distributed. Of true Mice there are three distinct sorts: the Common or House Mouse, the Field Mouse, and the Harvest Mouse; the latter being as destructive to the farmer as the first is to the housewife. The Brown and the Black Rat infest dwellings, and are equally injurious: the latter is known by the tail being longer than the body; whereas, in the Brown Rat, both these parts are equal. The pretty little Dormouse (*Myoxus avellanarius*), like the Squirrel and Jerboa, eats its food in an erect attitude, sitting on its haunches, and using its forefeet as hands. The Water Rat

115

Hedgehog.

and Short-tailed Mouse of Pennant (now placed in the genus *Arvicola*) occur in England: but the former is stated not to have been found in the northern islands; the latter is a most destructive little animal in gardens, where it grubs up seeds, particularly peas, just after they have begun to germinate. A few years back, the short-tailed mouse suddenly appeared in immense numbers in the New Forest, and notwithstanding every artifice employed to stop their ravages, they destroyed many thousands of young trees, and devastated whole acres of young plantations.

The *Badger* is a nocturnal feeder, sleeping in its hole during the day, yet, when attacked, is remarkably quick in its motions, and successful in its defence. If undisturbed, it is harmless and inoffensive, chiefly subsisting upon vegetables, although it will likewise devour frogs and slugs. The *Otter* has become much less frequent than formerly; it was once considered as a beast of chase, as old game-books mention otter hounds particularly trained for hunting this animal. It feeds entirely upon fish, which it dives after with great celerity; and, unless pressed by extreme hunger, invariably leaves the tail extremity untouched. The legs are very short; and the toes being connected together by a membrane, gives to the animal the power of swimming very rapidly.

The rapacious or carnivorous quadrupeds of Britain are very few, and from their small size too insignificant to inflict much personal injury upon man. The *Bear* and the *Wolf* have long been extinct in Britain, and the Fox might have shared the same fate, had it not been preserved as a beast of the chase since the extirpation of more formidable game. Pennant mentions three varieties of this animal found in Wales and other mountainous parts of Britain: — 1. The *Milgri*, or Greyhound Fox, is the largest, tallest, and boldest, and is distinguished by a white tag or tip to the tail. 2. The Mastiff Fox, which is less, but more strongly built. 3. The *Curgi*, or Cur Fox, of a still smaller size, and having the tip of the tail black. (*Brit. Zool.* i. 87.) The varieties do not appear, however, to have fallen under the actual observation of subsequent naturalists.

The Ferret tribe comprehends the Polecat, Weasel, Stoat or Ermine, the Common Marten, and the Pine Marten.

The Polecat (*Putorius vulgaris* Cuv.), called also the Fitchet, Fitchew, or Foumart, measures, with the tail, about twenty-three inches. Its fetid smell is proverbial. Although included in the list of British quadrupeds, it appears, according to Strabo, to have been imported from the north of Africa. Like all its congeners, its habits are sanguinary; for it will destroy and suck the blood of many victims, before it attempts to carry off their bodies. The well-known Ferret is considered only a variety of this species. The Weasel is much smaller, and although repulsive from its odour, is yet an elegant-shaped animal. It feeds on mice and small birds, but will occasionally attack animals of a much larger size. Few persons suspect that the skins they see nailed against farm out-houses frequently belong to an animal whose fur, in another state, forms a most elegant and expensive ornament to female dress. This animal, despised in one state, and valued in another, is the Stoat (*fig.* 116.), the pest of the farmer, and the destroyer of his poultry. In the temperate and

116

Stoat.

117

Pine Marten.

southern parts of Europe, its fur is yellowish-brown above, and pale yellow beneath; yet so soon as its geographic range enters on the more northern countries, as Russia, Norway, and Siberia, these colours vanish, leaving the fur of a pure white in every part but the tail, which is tipped with deep black; and in this state the skin is called ermine. In Scotland the animal, during winter, is frequently found in an intermediate stage of summer and winter clothing. Although small, it will attack large rats, and has been known to pursue a young hare by the scent.

The Common or Beech Marten (*M. Fagorum* Ray) seems to prefer dwelling near habitations, choosing the shelter of out-houses and farm-buildings, as convenient retreats for carrying on its depredations among poultry, of which it is a great devourer; it also breeds occasionally in the hollows of trees.

The Pine Marten (*M. Abietum* Ray, *fig.* 117.) is rather larger, and is further distinguished from the last in having the throat and breast yellow, instead of white. It is wild and solitary; shunning mankind; and only dwells in thick woods and forests, principally those composed of pines. It climbs with great facility; preys upon birds and their eggs, and also upon squirrels; the female generally making use of the nest of one of her victims for the rearing of her own young. The skin of this is much more prized than that of the common Marten, and appears to have been formerly, at least in Scotland, a lucrative article of commerce.

The Wild Cat closes our list of these small but ferocious indigenous animals. Its manners are similar to those of the lynx, and Mr. Pennant justly calls it the British tiger. In its savage state it appears to be much larger than the ordinary domestic cat; and the teeth and claws, for the size of the animal, are tremendous. It is still found, although rarely, in the mountainous and woody parts of Great Britain. Formerly they appear to have been much more numerous, and to have been considered a beast of chase. The best authorities agree in considering this species, common to the forests of Europe, as the origin of our domestic breed, the usual varieties of which are well known. Another, which seems peculiar to Cornwall, is without any visible tail, and is stated to be an hereditary variety. (*Cuv.* ii. 489.)

To enumerate the varieties of the Dog now domesticated in Britain would be tedious, particularly after the luminous manner in which this subject has been treated by Pennant (*Brit. Zool.* i. 70.). Britain has been famous for her dogs from remote antiquity. The British mastiffs were held in such estimation by the Romans, that their emperors appointed an officer in the island, with the name of *Procurator Cynegii*, whose business was to transmit thence such as would prove equal to the ferocious combats of the amphitheatre. Strabo also mentions that the mastiffs of Britain were in great repute, being trained for war, and used by the Gauls in their battles.

The Bloodhound, during the troubled periods of English history, was in high estimation, and much used to track the footsteps of robbers and marauders; but the breed is now extinct. A remarkable variety of the Greyhound, more peculiar to Ireland (hence called the Irish Greyhound or Wolf Dog), is nearly lost, a few couples alone having been preserved in one of the parks in that island. The Terrier is the best house guard; while the Shepherd, the Water, and the Newfoundland dogs are probably the most sagacious.

Of ruminating animals now existing in a state of nature, there are but three; the Stag or Red Deer, the Fallow Deer, and the Roebuck. It would appear, however, that the first two are not indigenous to these islands. Mr. Pennant writes—"We have two varieties of fallow deer, which are said to be of foreign origin: these were introduced by King James I. out of Norway, which he visited for his intended bride, Anne of Denmark. He first brought some into Scotland, and from thence transported them to his chases of Enfield and Epping, to be near his palace of Theobald's." The only memorial of this palace is probably preserved in the name of Theobald's Road. M. Cuvier, indeed, expresses a doubt whether the stag was originally European; but Major Hamilton Smith, with much better reason, considers the Fallow Deer (*Cervus Dama*) as indigenous to Europe; adding, that it is still found wild from Sweden to Gibraltar, and from Ireland to Constantinople. The Stag (*Cervus Elaphus*) seems to be unquestioned as an indigenous species; and although the wild breed is yearly diminishing in numbers, it is still found in Gloucestershire, the north-west part of Devon, and in some of the remote districts of Scotland. Pennant, by some unaccountable mistake, has placed the Stag and the Fallow Deer as varieties of one species.

The Roebuck (*Cervus capreolus* Ham. Smith) is much less than the two preceding, and is, indeed, the smallest of European deer. It is remarkably graceful and active, habitually preferring the sides of elevated woods or forests. As he leaves a strong scent, nature has given him peculiar sagacity to perplex his pursuers: he begins, after a forward dash, bv doubling over his track, to mislead the hounds, and then by some great bounds he springs forward to a cover, where he lies down to let the chase pass. The roebuck is now become very scarce in Britain, and was equally so in Scotland, but we are told it has re-appeared of late years in Fifeshire, in consequence of the increased plantations. (*Brit. An.* p. 26.)

The Ox is the only remaining animal of this order which claims a place among the indigenous quadrupeds. We have before observed, that in remote ages, a gigantic race of oxen was numerous throughout Europe; and that, although now extinct, there is reason to believe that the colossal species mentioned by Cæsar, as existing in his time, was of this race, now only known by its fossil bones. These remains lie scattered through the whole of temperate Europe, in the same strata with the lost species of Elephant, but that the race was preserved to a much later period is proved by similar bones occurring in more recent formations, as in peat mosses, drained lakes, marshes, and beds of sand. The wild races, of inferior size, belonging to this species, may probably, as Major Smith observes, even now exist in Asia. However this may be, it appears certain that the real Urus was found wild in the Vosges mountains, and in the forests of Ardennes and Germany; while its existence in England is incontestably proved by Fitz-Stephen, who speaks of the *Uri silvestres*, which in his time (that is, about 1150) infested the great forests—round London!

The only existing breed of wild oxen now known, is the white Urus, or *Urus scoticus* of Ham. Smith. Its skull agrees with the fossil breed in being "square from the orbits to the occipital crest, somewhat hollow at the forehead, and the horns showing a peculiar rise from their root, at the side of the above crest, upwards, and then bending outwards, then forward and inward: no domestic race shows this turn." The true *Urus* was further dis tinguished by a mane, which is still observed about two inches long, in old bulls of the Scottish race (*fig*. 118.). When this breed was exterminated from the open forests is not known; but it was confined to parks long before the Reformation. The colour is entirely white, with the muzzle wholly black. Their manners are singular: upon perceiving a stranger, they gallop wildly in a circle round him, stop and gaze, toss their heads, and show signs of defiance; this is repeated several times, each circle being made smaller, till they approach sufficiently near to make an effective charge. The cows conceal their young eight or ten days: and when one of the herd is wounded or enfeebled, the others gore it to death. The breed is still preserved at Chillingham Castle, near Berwick-upon-Tweed, Wollaston in Nottingham, Gisburne in Craven, Limehall in Cheshire, and at Chartley in Staffordshire.

118

Wild Scottish Ox.

The domestic Ox (Bos Taurus), considered by some as a variety, and by others as a distinct species from the last, is supposed by Hamilton Smith to have been first domesticated by the Caucasian nations of western Asia. It is stated to have fourteen ribs, whereas those of the *B. Urus* are but twelve; a distinction sufficiently important to sanction the belief of a specific difference. Whether or not this parent of our domestic races ever existed in these islands in a state of nature, is very doubtful. The various breeds for which Britain has long been justly celebrated will be noticed under the head of domestic animals.

The marine and cetaceous mammalia are few, and are not very generally dispersed. Two species of seal have been noticed by Pennant. The Piked Whales (*Balænoptera musculus* and *boops*), the Razor-back Whale, and several others of the great northern cetacea, wander near the Hebrides and Orkney islands, and occasionally visit the shores of Northumberland and Yorkshire. The Porpoise and the Grampus have a wider range, and large shoals roam unmolested near all the coasts.

*Exterminated native animals.* In every country the increase of civilization and agriculture is marked by the progressive diminution and final extirpation of the larger quadrupeds, particularly of such as are injurious to man. Among those which history clearly informs us were once living in Britain, the most remarkable are the Bear, the Wolf, the Beaver, and the wild Boar. To the writings of Pennant and Hamilton Smith we are indebted for the following notes on these lost inhabitants of our forests.

It appears that Bears, in the time of Plutarch, were transported from Britain to Rome where they were much admired. They appear to have been extinct in Britain long before Queen Elizabeth's time.

*Wolves.* It seems to have been a vulgar error that the wolf was extirpated in Britain by the salutary edicts of King Edgar, who accepted their tongues and heads as tribute, or as a commutation for certain crimes: for in the reign of Edward I. these animals had again increased to such a degree, that officers were appointed to promote their destruction, and lands were held by hunting and destroying them. Wolves infested Ireland many centuries after their extinction in England; some having been killed so late as 1710. In Scotland, the last on record was destroyed in 1680.

The Beaver was still an inhabitant of the Welsh rivers in 1188, as is attested, according to Pennant, by Giraldus Cambrensis; but even at that remote period they must have considerably diminished, as the historian only mentions their being found on the river Teivi. Local names of other waters in the principality attest their existence in other places. Fossil remains of this species are stated to have been found in beds of marl, under peat moss in Berkshire; and similar bones have occurred in Perthshire and Berwickshire.

The Wild Boar, from which have sprung the domestic breeds of swine, must be reckoned among indigenous quadrupeds, although now extinct in Britain. William the Conqueror punished those who killed the Wild Boar, the Stag and the Roebuck, by the loss of their eyes. Fitz-Stephen affirms that the vast forest, which in his time stood on the north side of London, was the retreat of Stags, Fallow Deer, Wild Boars and Bulls. At a more recent period, Charles the First turned out Wild Boars in the New Forest; but they were destroyed during the civil wars.

*Fossil quadrupeds.* The splendid discoveries that have resulted from the investigations of Buckland, Mantell, Conybeare, and other eminent geologists, have opened a field of research, which in Britain had long been overlooked or neglected. Without entering into the question whether these fossil remains belong to animals which did or did not at some period inhabit the spots wherein their bones have been found, it is sufficient to confine ourselves to simple facts. The remains of the cave bear of Dr. Buckland occur in several caverns, and are sufficient to prove the living animal must have equalled a horse in size. The Kirkdale and Plymouth caves abound with the bones of an extinct hyæna, somewhat resembling in its osteology that now existing in South Africa; with these have been found the bones of a tiger, which must have been as large as the Bengal species. The tusks, teeth, and other fragments of an extinct species of elephant, totally different from those now in existence, have been detected in marl clay, &c. joined with those of two other gigantic quadrupeds, a rhinoceros and hippopotamus; while the jaw of a marsupial animal, unknown among the existing race of beings, has been found in the Stonesfield slate quarries (*fig.* 119.)

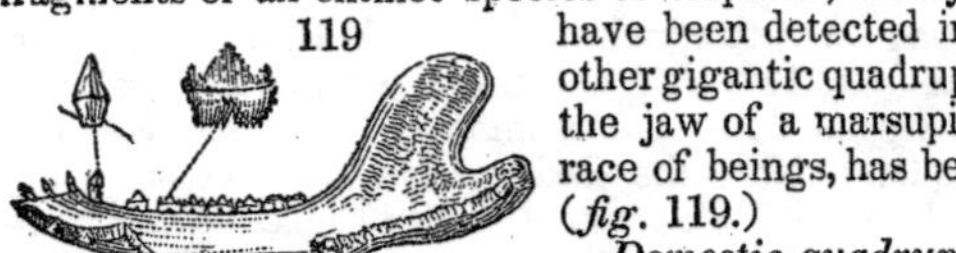

119

Jaw of Marsupial Animal.

*Domestic quadrupeds.* No nation, perhaps, has been more solicitous to improve their originally poor breeds of domesticated quadrupeds than the British; and hence their present superiority over most of those on the Continent. Under this head we commence with the ruminating animals, as the ox, the sheep, and the goat, so essential in supplying food and clothing to man; while the horse, the ass, and the dog assist him in his labour, or protect his property.

The principal breeds of oxen more peculiar to Great Britain have been arranged by Major Hamilton Smith under nine divisions. Of these, three belong to England, three to Scotland, two to Wales, and one to Guernsey.

The long-horned or Lancaster breed (*fig.* 120.), as the name implies, is remarkable for long horns; they have firm thick hides, long close hair, large hoofs, and give in proportion less milk, but more cream. They are of various colours, but are in general finched, that is, with a white streak above the spine, and a white spot inside the houghs. The improved Leicester is a slight variety, originally bred near Coventry.

120

The long-horned Ox.

The short-horned breed includes those that are named the Holderness, Teeswater, Yorkshire, Durham, and Northumberland. This has been the most improved, producing usually twenty-four quarts of milk per day, and three firkins of butter per season. Their colour varies, but is generally red and white mixed; called by the graziers fleeked.

The middle-horned includes the Devon, Hereford, and Sussex breeds: they are active, hardy, and much esteemed for draught: but although they fatten early, do not milk so well as the last. The pure Devons are of a high red colour, without spots, a light dun ring round the eye, fine in bone, clear neck, thin faced, and the tail set on high: the north Devon is most esteemed for eating. The Sussex and Hereford are larger, the ox weighing from 60 to 100 stone.

The Scottish breeds may be arranged under the Polled, the Highland, and the Fifeshire.

The Polled Galloway is the most esteemed: it is straight in the back, the hair soft, the colour black or dark brindled, and the size not large. They travel well, and reach the London markets without deterioration. The Suffolk Dun is a variety of this race. The Highland race includes several varieties, the most valuable ones being the West Highland, Argyle, or Skye, and the Kyloe from the Hebrides. The Norlands is another variety, with coarse hides, long legs, and of a narrow make. The Orkney or Shetland are very diminutive: an ox weighing about 60 lbs. a quarter, and a cow 40 lbs. Their colours are various, and their shapes bad; but they give an abundance of excellent milk, and fatten rapidly. The Fifeshire appears an improved breed of the Highlands, crossed with the Cambridgeshire; they are black, spotted with gray; the horns small, white, and very erect: a variety occurs in Aberdeenshire.

The Welsh have two breeds: the first is large, dark brown, with some white; the legs long and slender; the horns white, and turned upwards: these, next to the Devon, are the best in yoke, and are a cross of the long-horned: the second is lower, well formed, black with little white, and are good milkers. The Alderney or Guernsey race is proverbially small: their colour is mostly yellow or light red; marked with white about the face and limbs, and with crumpled horns. The true breed is known by being yellow within the ears, and at the root of the tail and its tuft.

Respecting draught Oxen, we cannot refrain from here inserting an excellent and judicious remark of Pennant. "It is now," observes this sensible writer, "generally allowed, that, in many cases, oxen are more profitable in the draught than horses: their food, harness, and shoes being cheaper; and should they be lamed or grow old, an old working beast will be as good meat, and fatten as well, as a young one." (*Brit. Zool.* i. 28.)

The Sheep is scarcely inferior in utility to the ox: and the breeds now cultivated in Britain, taking all their qualities into consideration, are perhaps the most valuable in the world. It is a curious fact, that the famed Merino sheep of Spain originated from the English breed, sent to that country by Edward IV. as a present to King John of Arragon. (*Bak. Chron.* p. 206.) Major H. Smith estimates the present annual value of wool shorn in England, at five millions sterling.

The British sheep, according to Mr. Culley, may be arranged under fourteen different breeds, and some others might also be enumerated. These may be classed under two prin cipal divisions; those derived from the ancient race being furnished with horns, while the others in general have none.

Of the horned breeds, the most ancient is the black-faced (*fig.* 121.), still met with in some heathy parts of Yorkshire, and the adjacent northern counties: the wool is coarse and shaggy. The Norfolk and Suffolk sheep, also, have the horns large and spiral, with the face black, but the wool is short and fine: they have a voracious appetite, and a restless disposition. In the Dorset the face is no longer black, but both sexes are usually horned. This breed is remarkable for producing lambs at almost every season, and is therefore highly valuable for supplying the London markets with house lamb. The Wiltshire is a much larger variety, having no wool on the belly. The Hertfordshire is a fine productive variety, with short tails. The Exmoor comes from Devonshire: it is small, the wool long, and the face and legs white. Scotland furnishes three breeds of horned sheep; the Dun-faced, the Shetland, and the Hebridean.

121

The Black-Faced Sheep.

122

The Hereford Sheep.

The hornless race may be divided into nine breeds. The Lincoln has long wool and a white face: in the Teeswater the wool is shorter and lighter, and the legs longer. The Dishley, or new Leicester, is distinguished by a clean head, and the excellency of its flesh. The Devonshire Nots, like the three preceding, are long-woolled; they have white faces and legs, thick necks, short legs, and large bones. The short-woolled hornless breeds are the following:—The Hereford (*fig.* 122.) have very fine wool, which grows close to their eyes, the legs and face being white: the store sheep of this country are called Collings or Rylands. The South Down, principally cultivated on the chalky downs of Sussex, have the face and legs gray, and are highly esteemed for the table. The Cheviot have the head bare and clean, and are sometimes spotted with gray or dun; the fleece is very short and fine. The Hardwicke is peculiar to the rocky districts of Cumberland, and is speckled on the face and legs.

The Goat, which in some parts of Italy supplies the only milk and butter known to the inhabitants, is of little utility in a country abounding in sheep and oxen. But to the Welsh mountaineers it is a valuable animal: the suet will make excellent candles; the meat is little inferior to venison, and those who have habitually feasted upon mountain kid, know how superior its flavour is to lamb.

The Horses of Britain, improved as they have been by the most sedulous care, next to the Arabian, are the finest in the world. The British breeds, originally but ill adapted for the saddle, have progressively improved; and the crossing of the indigenous kind with those of other countries has produced four principal classes of horses,—the Racer, the Hunter, the Roadster, and the Dray Horse; to these may be added the Poney, one of the original breeds.

The Ornithology of Great Britain, after the general observations already made on that of Europe, will be here but briefly dwelt upon. The native birds may be arranged under three natural divisions:—1. the rapacious; 2. the perching; and 3. the walking, running and swimming orders.

The rapacious birds, as in all other countries, are the smallest in number, but the most formidable in strength. Among these the Golden Eagle (*Aquila chrysaëtos, fig.* 123.) is the largest known in the British islands: this noble bird weighs twelve pounds, and is still found among the highest of the Welsh and Cumberland mountains; it is said also to breed in Orkney. The Erne or Sea Eagle is somewhat smaller, and is principally confined to the maritime rocks of Wales and North Britain. The Falcon tribe is more numerous in species; but the destruction to which they are doomed by game preservers has long been diminishing their numbers: some species are almost extirpated, and nearly all are now become rare.

123

Golden Eagle.

The Osprey (***Pandion Haliætus***), or Fishing Eagle, is now seldom met with. The two species of Henharrie (***Circus cyaneus*** and ***cinerascens***) were first discriminated by Montagu. The Owls are similar to those of the Continent, but the great Snowy Owl has only of late years been detected in the north of Scotland as a native bird. The Eagle or great horned Owl is of the same size; the former hunting by day, the latter by night. The Barn or White Owl is known to every farmer, and appears to be distributed over the whole habitable globe.

The toothed-bill or perching birds (*Dentirostres* Sw.) are those furnished with a notch to their bill, by which their food is held firm before it is swallowed. Some are formed to climb, others to hop on the ground, and a few catch their food (like the swallows) upon the wing. They are united to the rapacious order by the shrikes or butcher-birds, so called from their singular custom of impaling insects and small birds upon the thorns round their nests. Three species of these birds are known in Britain. The melody of the Blackbird and Song-thrush need not be eulogised; and during spring and summer the woods and hedges are enlivened by numbers of warblers, or small insectivorous birds, which visit them in the breeding season: among which the Nightingale is most conspicuous. Large flocks of Finches, and similar hard-billed birds, feast, in winter, upon the red berries of the black and white thorn; while Crows, Starlings, and Fieldfares devour prodigious quantities of slugs, worms, and other animals noxious to the farmer. The Woodpeckers, Creepers, and Titmice prey only upon those insects prejudicial to trees; the Swallows, during summer, join with the warblers in keeping within due bounds the myriads of insects, which would otherwise increase to an alarming extent.

The entire-billed birds (*Curtipedes* Sw.) are those which have no notch at the end of their bill, and never seek their food among trees: they are united to the former by the Pigeons, and comprise the gallinaceous, wading, and swimming tribes. Among the first Britain possesses the Partridge, Grouse, and Quail, but more particularly the Great Bustard, the largest of the European gallinacea: its weight is about 25 lbs., and its flesh excellent. To enumerate the wading and swimming birds would far exceed our limits: they visit the coasts principally in winter, and depart in spring.

The exterminated birds are very few; for although some, as the Egret (*fig.* 124.) and the Crane, are no longer common in Britain, yet individuals are sometimes met with, showing that man and not nature has scared them from their hereditary range. Perhaps the only extirpated species is the cock of the wood, or capercaillie grouse (*Tetrao Urogallus* L.), a noble bird of game, weighing near thirteen pounds; once common in the fir forests of Scotland, but which has not been seen, it is said, since 1760.

124

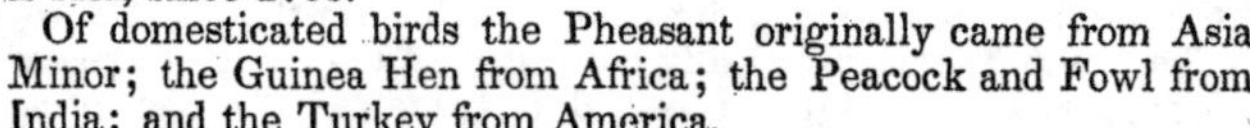

Egret.

Of domesticated birds the Pheasant originally came from Asia Minor; the Guinea Hen from Africa; the Peacock and Fowl from India; and the Turkey from America.

The fishes, both marine and freshwater, are numerous: most are edible, and many highly esteemed. Whale, and other cetacea, are mostly confined to the northern shores: but those of the west are famous for the herring and pilchard fisheries. The John Doree is as remarkable for its grotesque form as for its exquisite flavour. The Turbot, Cod, Sole, &c. are well known. The chief river fish are the Salmon, Trout, and Char; and these are principally furnished by the northern counties. The salmon fisheries are highly important, and have long engaged the attention of the legislature: the eggs of one fish will often exceed 15,000. The Char is confined to the lakes of Cumberland and Westmoreland; those of Windermere are the best, and when *potted* become a great delicacy. The Herring and Sprat supply the poor, during winter, with a wholesome dish; while the citizens of London consider another species, called the White Bait, as possessing a peculiarly fine flavour. The Anchovy is not unknown in some of our estuaries; and even the Flying-fish has occasionally wandered to the Welsh coast.

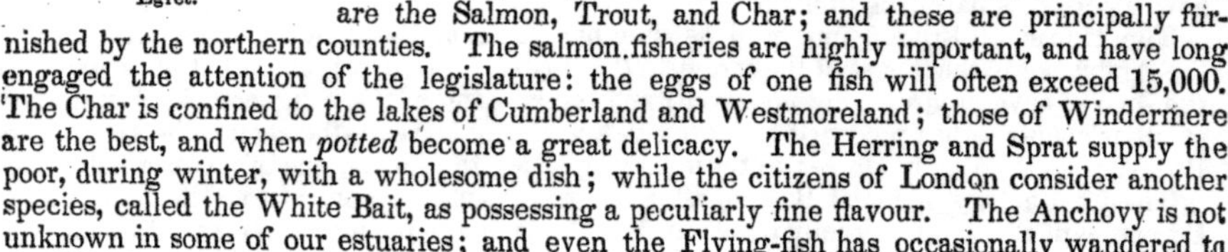

The reptiles of Britain, known in a living state, are very few. Besides the Warty Eft (*Lacerta palustris* Lin., *fig.* 125.) there are two other water lizards, and probably as many

125

Warty Eft.

126

Common Viper.

species inhabiting the land. Of the Frog and Toad two sorts of each occur. The snakes and the blind-worm are harmless; the Common Viper (*fig.* 126.) being the only venomous reptile: yet this species varies so much in its colours, that naturalists have described it under several names. The Great or Gigantic Frog of Pennant is only a variety of the common toad.

*Extinct reptiles.* The researches of geologists have brought to light the remains of such gigantic and extraordinary reptiles, that, but for such indubitable proofs, their existence might be thought fabulous. At the head of these we may place the *Megalosaurus*, resembling both a lizard and a crocodile, whose probable length was near 40 feet! The *Ichthyo saurus*, uniting the characters of a lizard with the snout of a dolphin, the teeth of a crocodile, the fins of a turtle, and the vertebræ of a fish, is scarcely less wonderful. The *Plesiosaurus* is still more extraordinary; for with the fins of a turtle, it had the head of a lizard, and a long neck, formed like the body of a serpent. Lastly, the remains of several distinct species of crocodiles have been discovered in similar strata. All these attest the existence, at some unknown period, of a stupendous race of aquatic monsters, which have long been swept away from the existing animal creation.

Among the radiated animals, vast shoals of transparent *Medusæ* wander about the coast during summer, and are frequently by a sudden change of wind cast up on the beach in great numbers. But the deep recesses of the ocean frequently give to the nets of the fisherman animals still more singular. The Black Line Worm, or Sea Long Worm (*Linnæus longissimus* Sow., *fig.* 127.), whose mouth is hardly a quarter of an inch wide, is said, by the fishermen, to measure twelve fathoms in length: it is soft, and so fragile, that the entire animal seems not yet to have been procured.

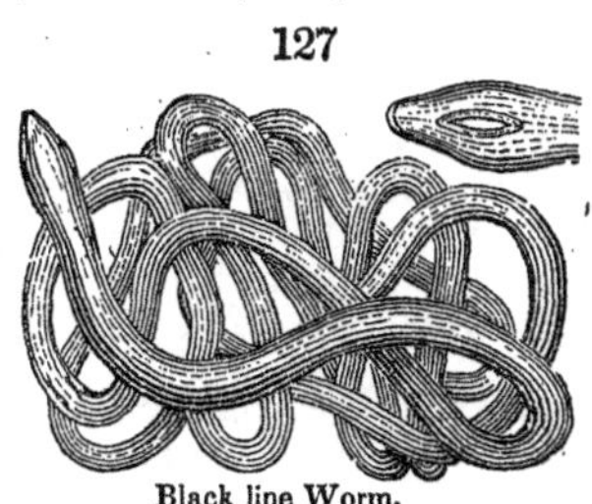

Black line Worm.

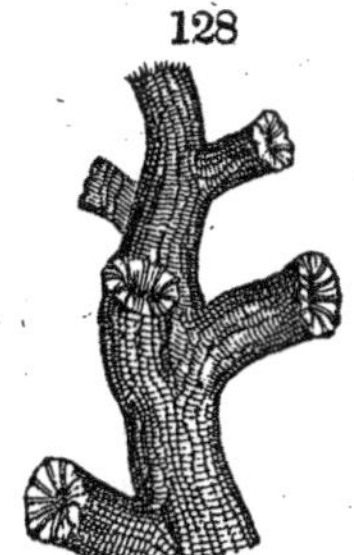

May-blossom Coral.

Ellis was the first to make known the true nature of those plant-like productions generally termed corallines. Of Corals, the British seas afford few native species; the largest and most elegant is the May-blossom coral (*Caryophyllia ramea*), (*fig.* 128.), common in the Mediterranean, and occasionally found upon the Cornish coast: it is cinnamon-coloured; and retains, for many years, a slight scent, like that of hawthorn.

The Conchology of Britain, in the number and interest of its species, compensates for its deficiency in large or richly coloured objects. The beautiful varieties of *Pecten opercularis* are, nevertheless, frequently variegated with the most lovely tints of yellow, orange, pink, and deep red; they also afford a nutritious food to the lower classes. The most celebrated edible shell-fish is the oyster, well known and highly prized by the luxurious Romans; and every one is acquainted with the superior excellency of those from Colchester and Milton. Fluviatile shells, in a country so humid and watered as Britain, are more abundant than towards the south of Europe. Most of the rivers produce Unio pictorum (*fig.* 129. *a*), and Unio ovatus (*b*): Cyclas cornea (*d*) is generally found in the same situations. The ponds and stagnant waters are frequently covered with Lymneus palustris (*e*), ovatus (*g*), and Planorbis corneus (*l*); while the large Duck-mussel (*Anodon anatinus*) (*c*) burrows in the

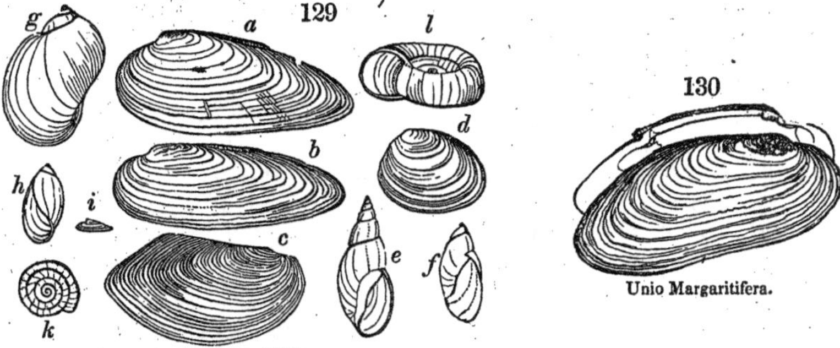

Fluviatile Shells.

Unio Margaritifera.

muddy bottom, A little fragile shell, Succinea amphibia (*f*), crawls upon rushes and aquatic plants; and Physa fontinalis (*h*), Ancylus lacustris (*i*), and Planorbis vortex (*k*) prefer clear shady streams and ditches overhung with wood.

Native pearls were reckoned by the Romans among the productions of Britain. They are the produce of a fluviatile bivalve shell, the Unio margaritifera, (*fig.* 130.), still common in many of the northern counties; but it was on the banks of the Welsh rivers that the British pearl fishery was chiefly carried on.

*Insects.* Considering the nature of the climate, it may excite surprise, that more than 10,000 different species have actually been found to inhabit Britain. Yet the bee may be reckoned the only insect whose services are immediately and obviously beneficial to man. Among the butterflies, are many of great beauty; while Eurymus Europome, or the Clouded Sulphur (*fig.* 131.), is considered one of the rarest British insects.

131

Clouded Sulphur

132

Red Grouse.

*Scotland.* The zoology of Scotland exhibits many arctic animals as common inhabitants, which are only known as rare visitants to the western shores of England; in other respects, it does not materially differ from that of South Britain. The northern islands give shelter to innumerable wild fowl, and to many peculiar land birds, as the Ptarmigan and the Golden Eagle. The great horned or Eagle Owl, is found to breed in Orkney. The Highlands are famous for an abundance of Grouse, the red species (***Lagopus scoticus***, *fig.* 132.) being the only bird peculiar to Great Britain.

The domestic animals are of a small size; in other respects, they are highly valuable. The polled or hornless cattle, with the Highland and the Fifeshire, have already been noticed. The ***Kyloe*** breed are so named, because in their progress to the south from the Hebrides, they cross the kyloes or ferries in the main land and Western Islands. (*Ham. Smith.*) The same writer considers that the sheep of this kingdom spring from three principal breeds: the first is generally named dun-faced sheep; they are a small, horned race, said to have been originally imported from Denmark or Norway, and are still found, with slight variations, in the North of Scotland and the isles. In Kincardineshire, this breed is known by its yellow face and legs, and by the dishevelled texture of its fleece, which is in part coarse, and in part remarkably fine wool; its flesh also is delicate and highly flavoured. The Shetland breed carry a very fine wool, in three different successions yearly, two of which resemble long hair more than wool, and are called Fors and Scudda. The wool is of various colours. The Hebridian sheep is the smallest animal of its kind; its horns are usually short and straight, the face and legs white, the tail very short, and the wool of different colours.

The Highland Ponies and Shetland Ponies (*fig.* 133.), notwithstanding their diminutive size, are greatly esteemed for their activity and strength.

133

Highland Pony.

134

Scottish Greyhound.

Among the numerous breeds of dogs, there appear to be three more particularly found in Scotland: the true Shepherd's Dog, or Colly, is still preserved, unmixed, in many of the sheep districts: the Shetland Hound, approaches in character to the Greenland Dog; while the Scottish Greyhound (*fig.* 134.), common in the Highlands, is possessed of great sagacity, strength, and swiftness.

The Zoology of Ireland has been much neglected; nor are we prepared to show what peculiarities belong to its natural history. The Irish Wolf Dog, called also the Irish Greyhound, has generally been thought peculiar to this island; but others consider it the same breed as the French mâtin (***Canis laniarius*** L.) It is a noble animal, standing near four feet in height, and seems to have been mainly instrumental in clearing the country of the numerous wolves which once over-ran it. The cattle and sheep are inferior to those of Britain. Yet Ireland exports vast quantities of salted provisions, besides the supplies furnished to the navy and shipping interests. The remains of the Fossil Elk (*fig.* 135.) are of frequent occurrence in beds of shell marl, beneath peat. Its antlers measure from the extreme tip of each, no less than ten feet ten inches, and from the tip of the right horn to its root, five feet two inches. Remains of the same animal have been also found in England, and a very perfect specimen in the Isle of Man. The Irish shores furnish the conchologist with several native shells, seldom seen on the British coasts, particularly the Isocardia cor, or Heart Cockle (*fig.* 136.).

135

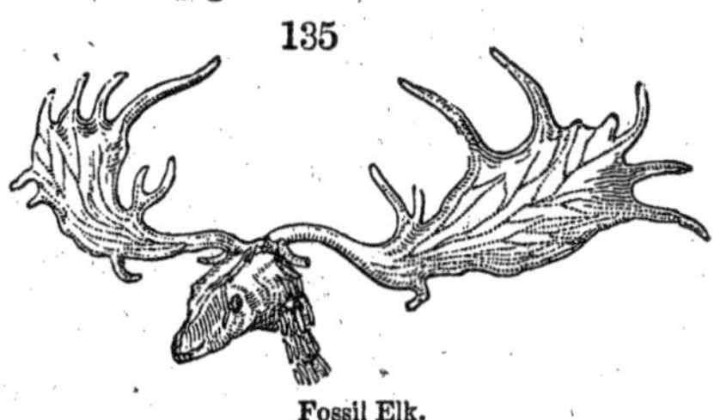

Fossil Elk.

136

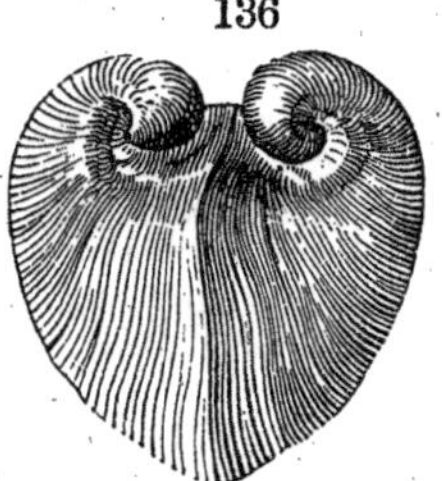

Heart Cockle.

Sect. III.—*Historical Geography.*

Britain was originally peopled from Gaul, by inhabitants of the Celtic race. For a long time it appears to have been noticed only as a country supplying tin; a rare and useful metal, not then found in any other part of Europe, or in Western Asia. To obtain this valuable mineral, the coasts of Britain were at an early period sought by the ships of various mercantile states, especially the Carthaginians; and the *tin* of Tarshish, mentioned by Ezekiel, was doubtless brought from the mines of Cornwall.

Britain was invaded by the Romans, about fifty-five years before the Christian era. Of the thirty tribes of barbarians among whom the country was then divided, the most considerable were the Belgæ in the west, the Brigantes in the north, the Silures in South Wales, the Iceni in Norfolk and Suffolk, and the Cantii, who occupied Kent and part of Middlesex. The latter had made some progress in agriculture and the arts of civilized life; but the other inhabitants derived their subsistence from flocks and herds, clothed themselves in skins, and painted their bodies. The precarious authority of the chiefs derived support from the influence exercised by the Druids, in one of the most terrible forms of superstition that ever enslaved the human mind. Besides the ordinary implements of war, they had armed chariots, which they managed with surprising dexterity; and they were united in a species of political confederacy, of which Cassivelaunus was the head. They could not, however prevent the landing of Julius Cæsar, but that conqueror was prevented by more urgent affairs from prosecuting an enterprise of which the difficulties were not likely to be compensated by its glory. In the reign of Claudius the hardihood of Caractacus, and the heroic desperation of Boadicea, failed of exciting an effectual resistance to the disciplined legions of Rome, whose victorious progress was continued during the reign of Nero. In that of Domitian, the Roman dominion was extended by the wisdom and valour of Agricola, who defeated the Caledonians under Galgacus, at the foot of the Grampians; and the only part of the island which remained unsubdued was the region which lies north of that natural rampart.

The Britons now subjected to the Roman empire were compelled to cultivate the habits and arts of peace: but when that empire, weakened, distracted, and verging to its decline, was compelled to withdraw its protection from its distant provinces, the Scots and Picts, emerging from their mountain fastnesses, then broke in, and committed dreadful devastations among their unwarlike neighbours. The Romans had recourse to the expedient of frontier walls; first, one between the Forth and Clyde, called the Wall of Antonine, and afterwards a similar rampart between the Tyne and Solway, called the Wall of Severus. About the middle of the fifth century, the Roman forces were finally withdrawn, and the Britons were left to depend entirely on their own resources.

The Saxons were called in as allies, about forty years after the dissolution of the Roman government. These hardy adventurers, originating from the north of Germany, and occupying the line of coast from the mouth of the Rhine to Jutland, had long infested by their piracies the neighbouring parts of Britain and Gaul. They eagerly accepted an invitation to a country so superior to their own. In the year 450, 1600 men under Hengist and Horsa, arrived in Britain, and obtained an easy victory over the Scots and Picts. The success of the two brothers attracted numerous bands of their countrymen; and in the course of a century, colonies arrived from the mouths of the Elbe, the Weser, and the Rhine, chiefly composed of three valiant tribes, the *Jutes*, the *Old Saxons*, and the *Angles*. From allies, they became formidable enemies to the Britons; whom, after a long and sanguinary struggle of one hundred and fifty years, they compelled to retire into Wales and Cornwall.

Thus was established the Heptarchy, or Seven Saxon Kingdoms in Britain: viz. 1. Kent; 2. Sussex, including Surrey; 3. East Englas, including Norfolk, Suffolk, the Isle of Ely, and Cambridgeshire; 4. Wessex, including all the southern counties from Berkshire to Cornwall; 5. Northumberland, including all the northern counties of England, and the southern counties of Scotland to the Frith of Forth; 6. Essex, including Essex, Middlesex, and part of

Hertfordshire; 7. Mercryc, or Mercia, the largest division, including the midland districts of England to the confines of Wales.

About the year 800 these small states were united into one kingdom, under the name of England, by Egbert, king of Wessex. The Anglo-Saxon dynasty derived its chief lustre from Alfred, one of the wisest and most virtuous monarchs that have appeared in any age or country. He delivered his country from the thraldom of the Danes; but in the course of the ensuing century, however, they regained the ascendency; and in 1017, Canute, king of Denmark and Norway, added England to his dominions. It was held successively by his sons, Harold and Hardicanute; but on the death of the latter, it was restored to the Saxon dynasty, and Edward the Confessor ascended the throne.

The conquest by William of Normandy, in 1066, overthrew for a time the liberties of the people of England. Claiming the crown by virtue of a pretended grant from Edward the Confessor, and acquiring it by victory over Harold II., himself an usurper, to the prejudice of Edgar Atheling, the rightful heir, he maintained by tyranny a dominion gained by fraud and violence. One of the consequences of the acquisition of the English crown by William was to convey to the kings his successors certain claims on the French territory, which led to long, expensive, and sanguinary wars.

Henry the Second, surnamed Plantagenet, son of Geoffry of Anjou, who married Matilda, daughter of Henry I., in the right of his father, was master of Anjou and Touraine; in that of his mother, of Normandy and Maine; in that of his wife, of Guienne, Poitou, Saintonge, Auvergne, Perigord, Angoumois, and the Limousin. To these states he afterwards annexed that of Bretagne. The possession of provinces composing above one-third of the French monarchy, and superior in opulence to the rest of the territory, rendered this vassal more powerful than his liege lord, and contributed to provoke that rivalry which for ages existed between England and France. Henry the Second acquired the sovereignty of Ireland; Edward the First annexed Wales to his dominions, and for a time subjugated Scotland. The contending claims of the houses of York and Lancaster for the crown of England, after a civil war of nearly sixty years, were adjusted by the marriage of Henry the Seventh with Elizabeth, daughter of Edward the Fourth. Among the memorable events that occurred under the Plantagenets, may be noticed the signature of Magna Charta, extorted by the barons from King John; the rise of the House of Commons in the reign of Henry the Third; and the reformation of the church, commenced by John Wickliffe, in 1369.

The reign of Henry the Seventh was signalized by the overthrow of the feudal sway, and by the introduction of the modern system of polity. The emancipation of the kingdom from papal dominion was effected by his successor. In the reign of Elizabeth, the most strenuous exertions were made to strengthen the maritime power of England, and extend her commercial intercourse. The result of these measures was to raise the nation to a very prosperous and flourishing condition, and to overturn the lawless domination of the nobles, substituting for it, however, an authority almost absolute on the part of the sovereign.

The union of the two crowns on the accession of James the Sixth of Scotland to the throne of England, terminated those animosities which had proved alike injurious to both countries. The despotic conduct of Charles the First led to a struggle in which he lost both his crown and his life. In the interregnum which ensued under the Commonwealth, the vigilant, energetic, and decisive policy of Oliver Cromwell exercised a commanding influence over every cabinet in Europe. Charles the Second suffered England to lose the ascendency which she had attained, and the infatuated conduct of James the Second led to the revolution of 1688, from which epoch to the present time, the industry, commerce, and wealth of Great Britain, rapidly rose to a height unparalleled in any other nation, ancient or modern; but her political power sustained various fluctuations. She acquired in the East and in the West two empires, each far more extensive than her own territory. That in the East she retains and is continually extending; that in the West, having become independent, is her rival in commerce, and manifests a disposition to dispute, at no distant period, her maritime supremacy. Among the memorable transactions and events of this period may be ranked the union with Scotland in 1707; that with Ireland in 1801; the Scottish rebellions in 1715 and 1745; the Irish rebellion in 1798; and a series of wars with France, occurring at intervals rarely exceeding eight or ten years. The contests arising from the French revolution were distinguished by the most brilliant naval achievements, and afterwards by successes which raised the military glory of England to a level with her maritime renown, rendering her influence paramount among the states of Europe.

## SECT. IV.—*Political Geography.*

The constitution of Great Britain centres in the laws by which the country is governed, and in the union of powers by which the laws are made and the government is administered. The *legislative* power is vested in the Parliament, consisting of the KING, an hereditary sovereign; the LORDS, an hereditary aristocracy; and the HOUSE OF COMMONS, consisting of members chosen by the people from among themselves, and therefore said to represent the commons of the realm. The *executive* power is entrusted to the king.

Of the three estates of the realm thus composing the legislature, the King is the highest: he is the head or chief of the parliament: and except in extreme cases, a parliament cannot be held unless convoked by him, nor can it except by him be dissolved or prorogued. His *assent* is requisite to give the force of law to any measure proposed by either of the two houses, and agreed upon by them. Propositions of laws, or *bills* as they are technically called, may be brought forward in either house; all money bills *must* take their origin in the House of Commons; but only in one instance can the king initiate an act of parliament, and that is, an act of grace, for the pardon of persons after a rebellion, or for the release of insolvent debtors.

The King is not supposed to hold his throne by divine right, or in virtue of any indefeasible hereditary claim. The nation, by its supreme council, has dictated certain rules of exclusion with regard to the succession, of which the most important is, that the sovereign shall maintain the Protestant reformed religion, and, either at his coronation or on the first day of the first parliament, shall repeat and subscribe the declaration against popery. On the death or demise of the king, his heir becomes instantly invested with the kingly office and regal power.

By a constitutional fiction accordant with the feudal policy, all lands are held mediately or immediately from the crown. Thus the king is entitled to all lands left by the subsiding of the sea; and estates may revert to him by escheat, from the commission of crime by their possessors. He is sovereign in all seas and great rivers; he alone has a prerogative to erect beacons and lighthouses; he is entitled to all royal mines of gold and silver, and is entrusted with the coinage. All persons born in his dominions are his subjects, and owe to him an allegiance which they can neither renounce nor transfer to any foreign prince. He is supreme head of the church within his dominions; and as patron paramount of all the benefices in England, he has a right to present to all dignities and benefices of the advowson of archbishoprics and bishoprics during the vacancy of their respective sees. He is the fountain of justice, and has an undoubted prerogative in creating officers of state, ministers, judges, and other functionaries. To him, as *parens patriæ*, belongs the care of all who are unable to take care of themselves; he has an original right to superintend the disposal of charities; and in all such cases the application is to the Court of Chancery. He has, in certain cases, the high prerogative of pardoning, and likewise that of issuing special proclamations for the prevention of offences. The power of making war or peace is lodged singly in the king. He is held to be incapable of doing wrong, and if an unlawful act be done, the minister instrumental in that act is alone obnoxious to punishment. By virtue of his prerogative the king may make grants and letters patent, conferring various rights and privileges. Lastly, the king cannot be attainted, and is never a minor; though when the crown has devolved to a very young heir, it has been thought prudent to appoint a regent, or council of regency. The same expedient has been adopted when, by reason of grievous illness, the exercise of the royal functions has been interrupted.

All supplies granted by parliament are given to the king; but of these the largest proportion belongs to the public or its creditors; that which pertains to the king in his distinct capacity, called the *Civil List*, is the provision for the support of the honour and dignity of the crown. On the commencement of the reign of William IV., the civil list was entirely new-modelled, being limited to the personal expenses of the sovereign, and the maintenance of his state; while the branches of administration hitherto defrayed out of it were charged upon the Consolidated Fund. The sum of 510,000*l.* was granted, under the following heads:—

| | |
|---|---|
| Privy purse, King's, | £60,000 |
| Queen's, | 50,000 |
| Maintenance of royal establishment, | 171,000 |
| Salaries in the departments of Chamberlain, Steward, Master of the horse, home secret service, &c. | 154,000 |
| Pensions, | 75,000 |
| | £510,000 |

Thus the royal prerogative is counterbalanced by the control which the representatives of the people in parliament exercise over the public purse. The king has the prerogative of commanding armies and equipping fleets; but without the concurrence of his parliament he cannot maintain them. He can confer appointments to offices; but without his parliament he cannot pay the salaries. He can declare war; but without the aid of parliament he cannot carry it on. He has the exclusive right of assembling parliaments; but by law he must assemble a parliament every three years. Though head of the church, he cannot alter the established religion, or call individuals to account for their religious opinions. He cannot create any new office inconsistent with the constitution or prejudicial to the subject. He has the privilege of coining money; but he cannot alter the standard. He has the power of pardoning offenders; but he cannot exempt them from making compensation to the injured parties. Even with the military power he is not absolute, since it is declared in the Bill of

Rights that a standing army without the consent of parliament is illegal. The king himself cannot be arraigned; but if any abuse of power be committed, those who were either the advisers or the instruments of the measure may be impeached and tried before the House of Lords; in which case it is of no avail to plead the king's command, or to produce his pardon. A dissolution of parliament does not abate an impeachment, neither can the royal authority interpose to stay or suspend its course. Other restraints on the prerogative exist in the uncontrolled freedom of speech in parliament, secured by the Bill of Rights, and in the important provisions by which, during the reign of George III., the independence of the judges was established.

The House of Lords is composed of the lords spiritual and temporal of England; sixteen temporal peers of Scotland; one archbishop, three bishops, and twenty-eight temporal peers of Ireland. The roll of the lords spiritual and temporal forming the House of Peers, in the session of 1833, exhibits 426 lords, including the Catholic peers of England. They are thus distinguished:—

| | | | | | |
|---|---|---|---|---|---|
| Royal dukes | 4 | Earls | 109 | Peers of Scotland | 16 |
| Archbishops | 3 | Viscounts | 18 | of Ireland | 28 |
| Dukes with English titles | 21 | Bishops | 27 | | |
| Marquesses | 19 | Barons | 181 | Total | 426 |

The Lords Spiritual are, for England, two archbishops and twenty-four bishops; and for Ireland, one archbishop and three bishops; the English hold their seats for life, the Irish by rotation. The archbishops rank above all dukes except the princes of the blood; the bishops next below viscounts.

The Lords Temporal are not limited in number, it being the prerogative of the king to raise to the peerage any of his subjects whom he thinks deserving. They consist of dukes, marquesses, earls, viscounts, and barons. The sixteen peers of Scotland are, by the articles of union, elected by the peers of that country from among themselves: the election is renewed for every parliament. The Peers of Ireland are, as established by the act of union, four lords spiritual sitting by rotation of sessions, and twenty-eight lords temporal elected for life by the peers of Ireland. As a supreme court of judicature, the House of Lords exercises jurisdiction in civil causes upon appeals or writs of error from the inferior courts; and in criminal questions, when brought before them, by presentment of the House of Commons, in the form of an impeachment.

All members of parliament have the privilege for themselves and their menial servants of being freed from arrests or imprisonment for debt or trespass; but not from arrests for treason, felony, or breach of the peace. The peers have other privileges peculiar to themselves. In all cases of treason, felony, or misprision of felony, a nobleman is tried by his peers; but in misdemeanours, he is tried like a commoner. In judicial proceedings, a peer gives his verdict not upon oath, but upon his honour; he answers also to bills in chancery upon his honour; but when examined as a witness in the inferior courts or in the high court of parliament, either in civil or criminal cases, he must be sworn. Slander against a peer subjects the offender to very heavy punishment, being branded by the law with the term *scandalum magnatum*. Every peer, by license from the king, may make a proxy to vote for him in his absence, a privilege which cannot be held by a member of the lower house. All bills which may affect the rights of the peerage, are, by the custom of parliament, to originate in the House of Peers, and to suffer no changes or amendments in the lower house.

The House of Commons, as a distinct branch of the legislature, is the peculiar boast of the British constitution. In the earliest times of which any record exists in English history, there appear to have been assemblies of the nation, convoked to deliberate on occasions of great emergency; but it was not until (A. D. 1266) after the overthrow of Simon Montfort, earl of Leicester, that the people were regularly summoned by the king to send representatives to the great council of the nation. The crown, little apprehensive of the formidable character which the House of Commons was afterwards to assume, favoured all the steps of its early progress, hoping by those means to counterpoise the overbearing sway of the great barons, and at the same time to obtain supplies of money from the growing wealth of the people. The decline of the feudal system had for some time favoured such a course of policy. Baronies escheated by forfeiture or for want of issue had been subdivided; hence arose a class of men called minor barons, holding by knight's service; and these being too numerous and too poor to be all called to parliament, and to rank with the greater barons, were allowed to sit by representatives. Of these *knights*, each *shire* was summoned to send two; writs to that effect being addressed to the sheriffs of the several counties. The Cinque Ports probably about the same period sent their *barons*, and the cities and boroughs their *burgesses*. In early times these representatives appear to have considered attendance in parliament as a hardship rather than an advantage. It was expensive, and, from the imperfect police then established, often insecure; and the summons, being always the prelude to a demand for money, was by no means welcome. With the granting of supplies, however, was necessarily combined the right of petition, of stating grievances, and demanding guarantees; and these could not, by a sovereign pressed by various exigencies, be always denied.

The election of the Commons never rested on any principle of universal or even general suffrage, excepting perhaps that of knights for each shire. As the kings, however, could only attain their objects by assembling the most powerful and influential of the people, they endeavoured to make an equal distribution of the right of election, so far, at least, as related to property and influence, at the time when such a measure was adapted to countervail the preponderance of the barons. In after-times, when seats in parliament came to be appreciated as conferring a desirable privilege, and as constituting a powerful check on the prerogative of the monarch, it would have been irregular to have allowed to the king an arbitrary selection; and all parties adhered to the rights conferred on them by early gift or long usage. This permanence of the elective franchise, amidst the local changes that ensued in the course of ages, gave rise to some very striking anomalies. Manchester, Leeds, and several other towns, which within the last century have become the commercial capitals of the kingdom, did not send a single representative; while places once important, but now dwindled into insignificance, returned each two members. Cornwall, at a period when the rest of the kingdom was poor and rude, enjoyed an abundant source of opulence in its tin mines, and retained a number of chartered boroughs, beyond all proportion greater than those of any other county. The places holding the right of election were in many instances so small, that what is called the patronage of them was easily acquired; and that patronage of course involved the advantage of nominating one or both candidates for the representation. These were called close boroughs, or, more reproachfully, rotten boroughs. Another anomaly consisted in a number of what were called treasury boroughs, the nomination of which rested with the administration. With the view of remedying these defects, the Reform Bill was passed, in 1832, after long discussion and opposition. By this bill fifty-six of the smallest boroughs were entirely disfranchised, and thirty were reduced from two members to one, while Weymouth and Melcombe Regis were reduced from four to two; a reduction was thus made of 144 members. In the room of these, twenty-two large places,—Manchester, Birmingham, Leeds, Sheffield, Greenwich, Sunderland, Devonport, Wolverhampton, Bolton, Blackburn, Bradford, Brighton, Halifax, Macclesfield, Oldham, Stockport, Stoke-upon-Trent, Stroud, and four districts of the metropolis, viz. Marylebone, Finsbury, Tower Hamlets, and Lambeth,—received each the right of electing two members; while twenty smaller towns,—Ashton-under-Line, Bury, Chatham, Cheltenham, Dudley, Frome, Gateshead, Huddersfield, Kidderminster, Kendal, Rochdale, Salford, South Shields, Tynemouth, Wakefield, Walsall, Warrington, Whitby, Whitehaven, and Merthyr Tydvil,—acquired the right of nominating one member each. At the same time twenty-seven counties acquired the power of sending each two additional members, and seven that of sending one additional member.

The representation of Great Britain now stands as follows:—

| | | | |
|---|---|---|---|
| English members for | counties | 143 | |
| | universities | 4 | |
| | cities and boroughs | 324 | |
| | | | 471 |
| Welsh members for | counties | 15 | |
| | cities and boroughs | 14 | |
| | | | 29 |
| Scotch members for | counties | 30 | |
| | cities and boroughs | 23 | |
| | | | 53 |
| Irish members for | counties | 64 | |
| | university | 2 | |
| | cities and boroughs | 39 | |
| | | | 105 |
| | Making in all | | 658 |

The qualifications requisite for a member of the House of Commons, in respect to property, are these:—A person to be eligible as a member for a county must have a freehold or copyhold, or must have been mortgagee in possession at least seven years, of a clear estate of the value of 600*l.* per annum; and to be eligible for a city, borough, or other place, except the universities, of the value of 300*l.* per annum. The person so qualified is also to be of mature age, and must take the oaths imposed as indispensable to a member of the legislature. Among the persons who cannot sit in the House of Commons are judges, clergymen, persons holding certain offices under the crown, and persons having pensions under the crown during pleasure or for any term of years; sheriffs of counties, and mayors and bailiffs of boroughs, are ineligible in their respective jurisdictions; but a sheriff of one county is eligible as knight for another.

The qualifications required in electors differ, as they relate to counties or to boroughs. In the election of county members every member must have a freehold of the clear yearly value of forty shillings, over and above all rents and charges payable out of and in respect of the same, and must have been in the actual possession of it for twelve calendar months, unless it came to him within that time by descent, marriage settlement, devise, or promotion to a benefice in the church, or to an office. To these freeholders the new bill has added all persons holding property to the amount of ten pounds on copyhold, or on lease of not less than sixty years; and also those occupying lands or tenements for any period, at a rent of not less than 50*l.* per annum.

The qualifications of electors for cities and boroughs were, previous to the present act, extremely various. The right of voting in different places resided variously in the freeholders, the corporations, the burgage tenants, and sometimes in the whole body of resident householders. The new act, however, admits only the simple qualification of occupying a house rated at not less than 10*l.* per annum. Those, however, who were freemen under the former system are still entitled to vote, although not possessed of the 10*l.* qualification, provided they reside within the borough.

The mode of proceeding to an election for a county and for a borough is nearly the same. On a dissolution of parliament, writs, pursuant to a warrant from the king, are issued under the great seal, addressed to the sheriffs of counties, directing them to summon the people to elect two knights for each county, and one or two burgesses for each borough. To supply a vacancy while parliament is sitting, the warrant for the writ proceeds from the House of Commons. A certain day after, the date or *teste* of the writ is fixed for the election to commence; and on that day the candidate or candidates are put in nomination, at the place appointed, in the presence of the returning officer. In a county election, the sheriff or the under-sheriff is the returning officer; in a city or borough, the mayor or bailiff. If there be rival candidates put in nomination, the returning officer calls on the voters for a decision by a show of the hands, after which the friend of any candidate, if dissatisfied, may demand a poll. The poll was formerly taken at only one place, and might last for fifteen days; but under the new act, the cities and counties are divided into districts, with separate booths, or polling-places, appropriated to each. The poll is allowed to continue only for two days, which must be successive, and it must close at four o'clock in the afternoon of the second day. Poll clerks attend, to record the names of the voters, and their accuracy is watched by inspectors nominated on each side. The returning officer who presides must, if required, oblige the candidates to swear to their qualifications. At the close of the election, or on the following day, the returning officer declares the names of the persons who have the majority of votes; and, unless a scrutiny be demanded, he forthwith makes his return.

The duration of a Parliament has, for more than a century, been extended to the term of seven years, from that of three, to which it was formerly limited. The king, however, has the power of dissolving parliament at any time; he can also prorogue it at any time and for any period; and, as such prorogation concludes the session, it puts an end to all bills or other proceedings depending in either house, which must in the next session be again instituted, as if they had never been begun. Either house, or both houses, may adjourn of their own accord, and, at their meeting again, may take up the bills and other proceedings in the state of advancement in which they were left. A session of parliament usually commences in January or February, and continues until June or July.

At the commencement of every session committees of the whole house are appointed; one called the *Committee of Supply*, to consider the amount required by the crown for the service of the army, navy, ordnance, and other departments; and the other the *Committee of Ways and Means*, to devise modes of raising, by taxes or loans, the sums which the house have granted. In this committee of ways and means, the chancellor of the exchequer, in an exposition technically called the *Budget*, demonstrates to the house in detail that the sums voted are sufficient to justify the committee in imposing such taxes, or sanctioning such loans, as are then recommended. When the two committees are closed, the House of Commons pass a bill in which the grants made in the committee of ways and means are recapitulated, and directed to be applied to the services voted by the committee of supply specifying the particular sums granted for each service.

Parliament have the sole right of making, altering, and amending all the laws of the kingdom, and by their authority alone can taxes be imposed or levied. An annual vote of the House of Commons is requisite to maintain the land and sea forces at the degree of strength which is every year fixed and determined upon. By these and other privileges, the annual meeting of parliament is secured without any express stipulation to that effect. By withholding these annual votes they may testify their disapprobation of the measures of government, and even compel it to change its ministers; indeed, the principle has now become indisputable, that the minister who cannot rely on a majority of votes in parliament is disabled from conducting the affairs of the nation.

The Privy Council is composed of persons, appointed by the king, who are bound by oath to advise their sovereign to the best of their judgment with all the fidelity and secrecy which their station prescribes. The king with the advice of his privy council publishes proclamations binding on the subject; but they are to be consonant to, and in execution of, the laws of the land. The power of the council is, to inquire into all offences against the government, and to commit the offenders to safe custody for trial in some of the courts of law; but persons so committed are entitled to their *habeas corpus* as much as if they had been committed by an ordinary justice of the peace. The privy council is a court of appeal in plantation and admiralty causes, which arise out of the jurisdiction of the kingdom, as also in cases of idiotcy and lunacy. When questions arise between two colonies respecting the extent of their charter, "*the king in council*" exercises original jurisdiction in them, on the principles of feodal sovereignty; he also determines, on the same principle, the validity of claims to an island or province founded upon grant from the king or his ancestors. But from all the dominions of the crown excepting Great Britain and Ireland, an *appellate* jurisdiction, in the last resort, is vested in the *privy council.* The judicial authority is exercised in a committee of the whole privy council, who hear allegations and proofs, and make their report to *his majesty* in council, by whom judgment is finally given. The dissolution of the privy council depends on the pleasure of the king, who may at his own discretion discharge any member, or the whole of them, and appoint another council. It continues six months after the demise of the crown, unless sooner determined by the successor. Any natural-born subject of England is capable of being a member of the privy council, taking the proper oaths for security of the government and test for the security of the church. A privy counsellor, if he be only a private gentleman, is styled *right honourable*, and takes precedence of all knights, baronets, and the younger sons of all barons and viscounts.

A cabinet council is not, strictly speaking, recognised by the constitution, but by usage it is regarded as a body selected by the sovereign to conduct the business of the state; and the members composing it are held to be the responsible advisers of the crown. The cabinet council usually consists of those ministers of state who exercise the most important functions of the executive authority; their number and selection depend only on the king's pleasure; and each member receives a summons for every attendance. Though this body, as constituting what is essentially *the government*, be composed principally of officers of state; yet a privy counsellor selected by the king as a member of his cabinet council, may hold his seat as such, without accepting any particular office. The officers of state are those enumerated in the following lists:—

*Officers of State forming the Cabinet.*

| | |
|---|---|
| First Lord of the Treasury. | Secretary of State for Colonies and War. |
| Lord Chancellor. | Chancellor of the Exchequer. |
| Lord Privy Seal. | First Lord of the Admiralty. |
| President of the Council. | Master-general of the Ordnance. |
| Secretary of State for the Home Department. | President of the Board of Control. |
| Secretary of State for the Foreign Department. | Chancellor of the Duchy of Lancaster. |

*Officers of State not of the Cabinet.*

| | |
|---|---|
| Lord Chamberlain. | Vice-President of the Board of Trade. |
| Lord Steward. | Postmaster-General. |
| Master of the Horse. | Lieutenant-General of the Ordnance. |
| Secretary at War. | First Commissioner of the Land Revenue. |
| Treasurer of the Navy. | Attorney-General. |
| President of the Board of Trade. | Solicitor-General. |
| Paymaster of the Forces. | |

*Ireland.*

| | |
|---|---|
| Lord Lieutenant of Ireland. | Vice-Treasurer. |
| Lord Chancellor. | Attorney-General. |
| Commander of the Forces. | Solicitor-General. |
| Chief Secretary. | |

That officer of state who holds the appointment of First Lord of the Treasury, is by eminence the minister. In the event of a change of ministry, the person who is directed by the king to form another, receives an implied offer of that high office, and is generally placed at the head of the administration. The first lord of the treasury, that is, the first of the five lords commissioners for executing the office of lord high treasurer, possesses most of the powers formerly held by the lord high treasurer, and is sometimes, though not invariably, chancellor and under treasurer of the exchequer. The revenue applicable to the general purposes of the state is, with a trifling exception, derived entirely from taxes. In the course of the last century it increased to an amount unparalleled in the history of any other country; but in consequence of the wars in which Great Britain was engaged with little intermission until the year 1815, it did not keep pace with the expenditure, and an enormous debt was gradually contracted, the interest on which occasioned a correspondent increase of taxation.

Since 1817, *a deduction* has been made of about *sixty* millions from the principal of the debt, and about *five* millions from the annual charge on its account. This diminution has been principally effected by taking advantage of the fall in the rate of interest since the peace, and offering to pay off the holders of different stocks, unless they consented to accept a reduced payment.

The system of funding by which the debt has been rendered national, rests on the principle of assigning for the amount of a loan, an equivalent amount of nominal capital, bearing interest charged on the national revenue in half-yearly payments called dividends, or of terminable annuities also payable half-yearly. Annuities granted for an indefinite period are called *redeemable debt*, being redeemable at the option of government when at par; those granted for a limited period are called *irredeemable* debt; they exist only for a certain number of years, and a portion of the capital is annually absorbed in the interest. The funds are respectively designated according to the rate per cent. they bear; and the share which a public creditor holds in any of them, being transferable by sale under the name of *stock*, they constitute a kind of circulating capital.

The rate of interest granted on certain portions of the national debt, though nominally lower than that of five per cent. allowed by law, has been rendered advantageous to the lender by being charged on a larger amount of nominal capital than the sum borrowed Loans have been made in funds at four and five per cent., but the greater part has bee made in a fund bearing three per cent. interest on the nominal capital, and commonly calle the *three per cent. consolidated annuities.* The prices of these and other annuities consti tuting the *redeemable* debt are rated according to the money value of one hundred pound on such stock; terminable annuities according to the number of years' purchase which they are supposed to be worth.

Particular taxes were, at an early period of the funding system, appropriated to defray the interest of different descriptions of debt; but in the year 1786, the whole were collected into one fund, called the *Consolidated Fund.* The particular branches of revenue included in it were the *customs* (with the exception of a certain amount applicable to other public services), the *excise*, the *stamps*, the *land* and *assessed taxes*, and the *post-office.* To this fund are applicable moneys arising from other resources, specified in the annual accounts.

The following statement shows the progress of the *national debt*, from the Revolution to the present time:—

| | Principal. | Interest. |
|---|---|---|
| | £ | £ |
| Debts at the Revolution in 1689 | 664,263 | 39,855 |
| Excess of debt contracted during the reign of William III. above debt paid off | 15,730,439 | 1,271,087 |
| Debt at the accession of Queen Anne, in 1702 | 16,394,702 | 1,310,942 |
| Debt at the accession of George I. in 1714 | 54,145,363 | 3,351,358 |
| Debt at the accession of George II. in 1727 | 52,092,238 | 2,217,551 |
| Debt at the peace of Paris, in 1763 | 138,865,430 | 4,852,051 |
| Debt at the commencement of the American war in 1775 | 128,583,635 | 4,471,571 |
| Debt at the conclusion of the American war in 1784 | 249,851,628 | 9,451,772 |
| Debt at the commencement of the French war in 1793 | 239,350,148 | 9,208,495 |
| Debt contracted during the French war | 608,932,329 | 24,645,971 |
| Total funded and unfunded debt, 5th January, 1817, when the English and Irish Exchequers were consolidated | 848,282,477 | 33,854,466 |

A sinking fund for the gradual reduction of the debt had been formed by Sir Robert Walpole in 1716, but had been so frequently encroached upon, that in the course of half a century, it had not extinguished above fifteen millions. Its revival formed part of the financial arrangements of Pitt in 1786. Out of the aggregate of the taxes applicable to the consolidated fund, government then pledged itself, that one million annually should be paid to the commissioners for the reduction of the national debt. To this annual million were added the amount of government annuities as they successively expired, and the interest of such stock as was annually redeemed. In 1792, Pitt obtained an act of parliament, declaring, that besides a provision for the interest of any loan that might be thenceforward contracted, taxes should be imposed for a sinking fund of one per cent. on the capital stock created by it, which should be exclusively employed in the liquidation of such particular loan; and that no relief should be afforded to the public from the taxes which constituted the one per cent. sinking fund, until a sum of capital stock, equal in amount to that created by the loan, had been purchased by it. That being accomplished, both the interest and the sinking fund were to be applicable to the public service. It was calculated that, under the most unfavourable circumstances, each loan would be redeemed in forty-five years from the period when it was contracted. The provisions in this act, and in the former act of 1786, were altered by subsequent enactments; but, by an act passed in 1813, those alterations were rescinded; and it was provided first, that, as a sum equal to the debt of 1786, and bearing an interest nearly equal to the interest of that debt, was then vested in the hands of the commissioners, the debt of 1786 should be declared discharged as soon as the interest of the debt redeemed should become fully equal to that debt; the sums appropriated to its interest and sinking fund applied to the charge of future loans, and no new taxes imposed for interest and sinking fund of those loans, till the same should amount to a sum equal to the interest of that considered as released. Secondly, that, instead of applying the one per cent. sinking fund on each loan to the separate discharge of that loan, the whole funds of that kind united should be applied to the discharge of the first contracted loan, and successively to the redemption of all the loans contracted since 1792; the whole sinking fund created in 1786, or subsequently, being continued for the redemption of all debts then existing or to be created. The system established by this act continued until March, 1823, when an act of parliament was passed, directing that on the 5th of April of that year, all payments out of the consolidated fund to the commissioners for the reduction of the national debt should cease, all stock in their names be cancelled, and that in future the annual sum of five millions shall be payable quarterly to the commissioners, and set apart for the reduction of the debt, not to be infringed upon until the accumulation of this sum shall amount to one hundredth part of the debt then existing: at present, however, the sinking fund is declared to be the excess of income over expenditure, whatever that may be. In 1830 it amounted to 2,792,707*l.* 14*s.* 0$\frac{7}{8}$*d.*

On the consolidated fund are likewise charged the annuities for forty-five years, created in the year 1822, for the purpose of apportioning the burden occasioned by the military and naval pensions and civil superannuations (collectively called the *Dead Weight*), amounting to 5,000,000*l.*, into equal annual payments. The original intention was to contract with parties who might be willing to engage to pay into the exchequer within forty-five years the sum wanted, for a fixed amount of annuity for forty-five years; but no capitalists being found to accept these terms, it was agreed, instead of assigning the fixed annuities to any corporate body, or to private individuals, that they should be vested, namely, 2,800,000*l.* terminable at the end of forty-five years, and charged upon the consolidated fund, in trustees appointed by parliament; payable at the exchequer half yearly (viz. October 10. and April 5.), and to cease in April, 1867. In March, 1823, a portion was sold to the Bank of England by the trustees, on condition that the bank should undertake the payments to be made in pursuance of the act, from the 5th of January, 1823, to the 5th of January, 1868, upon the transfer to the bank of an annuity of 585,740*l.*, to commence from the 5th of April, and to continue for the term of forty-five years. The total amount of payments undertaken to be made by the bank in consideration of the said annuity is 13,089,419*l.*

Besides the funded debt, there is generally *a considerable amount in exchequer bills, navy bills, and ordnance bills, denominated the unfunded or floating debt.* Exchequer bills are issued in consequence of acts of parliament, for obtaining part of the money required for public service. They are sometimes granted on the credit of supplies for the current year, and the produce of the annual taxes is in this way often anticipated. Sometimes they are charged on the supplies of the following year; and in time of war, a large sum to be thus raised is generally authorised by a vote of credit previous to the rising of parliament. New exchequer bills are often issued in discharge of former ones; and it has frequently been found necessary to *fund* them, by granting capital in some of the stocks on certain terms, to such holders as are willing to accept them. Exchequer bills are issued for 100*l.*, 500*l.*, 1000*l.*, and upwards, but none for less than 100*l.*; and they bear interest at two-pence a day for every 100*l.* After being in circulation they are received in payment of taxes or other debts due to government, and sometimes they are paid off pursuant to previous notice by advertisement. The daily transactions between the bank and the exchequer are chiefly carried on by bills of 1000*l.* each, which are deposited by the bank in the exchequer, to the amount of the sums received by them on account of government; they remain in the exchequer as pledges or securities, of course bearing interest until the advances on which the bank first received them are paid off.*

*Number of persons deriving incomes from the funds.* It appears from the regular returns, that in 1830 (and the number has not sensibly varied since), 274,823 dividend warrants were issued to persons deriving incomes from the funds. The number of persons dependent upon the funds for support is, however, much greater than appears upon the face of this account: for the dividends upon the funded property belonging to public establishments, are paid upon single warrants, as if they were due to so many private individuals.

The customs and excise form the two main branches in the collection of the revenue; the former relating to goods imported, the latter to those produced and manufactured within the country. Among the accommodations to trade, established by Mr. Pitt, is the *bonding system*, by which the goods of merchants are warehoused under the joint custody of the proprietor and of government; payment of duty not being demanded until a sale is effected. This has been also extended to British spirits.

The navy is the force on which Great Britain mainly relies for maintaining her own independence and her ascendency over foreign nations. By it she has acquired the sovereignty of the seas, and the advantages, which that sovereignty confers, of securing her possessions in the most distant quarters of the globe, of protecting her commerce, and sustaining the exertions of her armies during war. During the most active period of the last maritime war, the number of seamen in employment amounted to 140,000; and there were in commission 160 sail of the line and 150 frigates, with 30,000 marines. The estimate for 1831

* See Statistical Tables, at end of Chap. IV.

comprehended 22,000 seamen and 10,000 marines. The pay of these men amounts to 1,081,000*l.*; their subsistence, to 603,000*l.*; which, with the cost of stores, and allowance for wear and tear, raised the regular current expense to nearly 2,000,000*l.* The building and repair of vessels, the charges of the dock-yards, pay of officers connected with the navy, and a variety of other items, amounted to about an equal sum. These charges, with 1,688,000*l.* in half pay and pensions, made up the sum of 4,657,000*l.* as the entire navy estimate for the year 1831.

The military force of the nation, at the close of the French wars, amounted to 200,000 regular troops, exclusive of about 100,000 embodied militia, a large amount of local militia and volunteers, to which might also be added a number of regiments employed in the territories of the East India Company, and in its pay. After the peace of 1815 a rapid reduction of the military establishment was effected. The militia were disembodied; the regular force was reduced, and in 1835 the estimates were for 81,271 men, independent of 19,720 employed in India, and paid out of the land revenue of that country. The charge for these forces was 5,784,808*l.*; but about half of this sum consisted of half-pay, retired allowances, pensions, and other charges consequent on the former immense establishment.

The laws of England, established during ten centuries of legislation, constitute the most extensive system of jurisprudence ever constructed. The municipal law is divided into two kinds, the *unwritten* or common law; and the *written* or statute law. The common law derives its force from immemorial usage; and its evidences exist in the records of the several courts of justice, as well as in books of reports and judicial decisions. It includes not only the system by which the ordinary courts of justice are guided and directed; but certain portions of the ancient civil and canon laws which are used in the ecclesiastical courts, the military courts, the court of admiralty, and the courts of the two universities. The written laws are those made by the king, lords, and commons, in parliament assembled; they are judicially called *Statutes*, and are either *declaratory* of the common law, or *remedial* of some of its defects. The statutes are also distinguished as either general or special, public or private.

The high court of parliament, independently of its legislative functions, is the supreme court of judicature in the kingdom. The House of Lords exercise jurisdiction in civil causes, upon appeals or writs of error from the inferior courts, and in criminal questions, when brought before them by presentment of the House of Commons, in the form of an impeachment.

The high Court of Chancery, in which presides the Lord High Chancellor, has two distinct tribunals: the one ordinary, being a court of common law; the other extraordinary, being a court of equity. From the ordinary or legal court issue all original writs that pass the great seal, all commissions of charitable uses; as also of bankruptcy, idiotcy, and lunacy; for such writs it is always open to the subject. In the extraordinary court, or court of equity, the chancellor exercises a most extensive jurisdiction, determining causes beyond the reach of the ordinary tribunals, and others in which reason and justice require that the rigorous application of the rules of common law should be mitigated. These decisions emanate from the judgment of the lord chancellor alone. An assistant judge, called Vice-chancellor of England, has power to hear and determine all causes depending in the court; all his decrees are valid and effectual, subject, however, to *reversal* by the lord chancellor, and not to be enrolled until signed by him; nor are they to discharge, reverse, or alter any decree of the lord chancellor or of the Master of the Rolls. The Master of the Rolls, who ranks next to him in dignity, and holds his office for life, acts in a judicial capacity as assistant to the lord chancellor, and also hears and determines causes on certain appointed days; but his orders and decrees cannot be enrolled until signed by the lord chancellor, who has the power to discharge or alter them. The masters in chancery are twelve in number, including the Master of the Rolls, who is their chief, and also including the Accountant-General. They are assistants and associates of the lord chancellor and the master of the rolls, and sit with them in court by turns, two at a time. In 1826 the property of suitors in chancery amounted to more than 40,000,000*l.* The masters make up their accounts with the Accountant-general, and pay into the Bank of England all moneys remaining in their hands, to be placed to his account. He merely keeps the account with the bank, the governor and company being answerable for such moneys.

The Court of King's Bench is the supreme court of common law in the kingdom, and takes cognisance both of criminal and civil causes: the former in what is called the crown side or crown office; the latter in the plea side of the court. It is also a court of appeal, into which may be removed, by writ of error, determinations of all the courts of record in England. The court consists of a chief justice, and three *puisné* judges.

The Court of Common Pleas takes cognisance of all civil actions depending between subject and subject. Many questions, however, may, by legal contrivances, be brought into this or into the Court of King's Bench at the option of the parties. The Court of Common Pleas consists of a chief justice, and three *puisné* judges.

The Court of Exchequer has jurisdiction both in law and equity. In it are tried all questions relating to the revenue, and, by fictions of law, various civil actions and personal suits. The judges are four; a chief baron and three *puisné* barons.

Trial by jury, an institution coeval with the origin of the constitution, and justly valued by the people as the bulwark of their liberties, is employed in all cases between the crown and the subject, in all criminal cases, and in all those for which damages are awarded. The jury in England consists of twelve persons, whose verdict must be delivered by their foreman as unanimous, or, in the technical phrase, as *agreed upon.*

Courts of Assize and Nisi Prius are auxiliaries to the superior courts at Westminster for the trial of causes in every county in England, twice a year in most counties, once a year in others. The counties are comprised in six circuits: 1st, the Home Circuit; 2d, the Midland; 3d, the Norfolk; 4th, the Oxford; 5th, the Northern; and 6th, the Western Circuit. These circuits are supplied by the twelve judges, two being appointed to each. In these courts, the senior or superior judge generally sits on the crown side for the trial of criminals, and the junior or inferior judge on the *nisi prius* side, for the decision of cases of property.

A Court of General Quarter Sessions of the Peace, held in every county once in every quarter of a year is the most important of the minor tribunals. Its jurisdiction extends to all felonies and trespasses; but capital felonies are usually remitted to the assizes. The sheriff's tourn is also a court of record, held twice a year at some place within the county. The court-leet or view of frank-pledge is a court of record held once a year, within a particular hundred, lordship, or manor, before the steward of the leet. It is the King's court granted by charter to the lords of those hundreds or manors. In aid of these, and other institutions tending to the maintenance of order and tranquillity throughout the country, subordinate magistrates are appointed in each county, under the name of justices of the peace. They hold special commissions from the king, and are empowered to suppress riots and affrays, to take securities for the peace, and to commit felons and inferior criminals. Their jurisdiction is enforced by constables and other subordinate officers.

## Sect. V.—*Productive Industry.*

The productive industry of England, at this moment, far surpasses that of any other country, either ancient or modern. Her fabrics clothe the most distant nations; her vessels traverse alike the polar and equatorial seas. The downfall of the feudal power; the civil and social advantages which the people acquired under the last Henries; and, above all, the spirit of enterprise diffused among them under Elizabeth, gave a great impulse to commerce and industry. It was not, however, till the era of the Revolution, that the nation entered upon that grand career of prosperity, in which she has ever since proceeded with accelerated activity.

Agriculture, as the greatest and most essential source of human wealth and comfort, must always claim pre-eminence over the other branches of human industry. For two or three centuries the English tenantry have been an independent and substantial race. Such had been the progress of agriculture, that, even in the middle of the last century, England had become a regular grain-exporting country. Still, fifty years ago, the practice of this important art was comparatively cumbrous, costly, and unproductive. Since that time, nobles and statesmen have vied with each other in their zeal for the promotion of agriculture. Prizes, exhibitions, and other institutions calculated to excite a spirit of improvement, have been established on a great scale. Even royal patronage was extended to this most useful of arts, and a board was formed under public auspices for its promotion. An extraordinary impulse was also given by the scarcity at the close of the eighteenth century; when the continental ports were closed, and grain rose to an unprecedented price, from which it has since been reduced, indeed, but not to its former rate. The old routine system was, after that crisis, broken up, and every exertion made to augment the products of the soil. Commons were enclosed, marshes drained, grasses of the most useful species cultivated, and every process that multiplied experiments had proved to be advantageous, introduced. Particular attention was bestowed in improving the breed of cattle and sheep; and for the accomplishment of this purpose, the best species were imported from abroad. At the same time, economical farming was greatly studied; the disproportionate number of horses and oxen was reduced; and machinery, particularly the threshing-machine, came into general use. Thus a great augmentation took place in the produce of the soil; still greater in the profit of the farmers, and much the greatest in the rent of the landlord, which, in many instances, was more than tripled. The reduced prices, however, which have ultimately been the result of this augmented production, have, at last, rendered it difficult to suppor the great advance in this last particular.

The natural fertility of England is not equal to that of the countries in the south of Europe. Her pastures, however, are richer; and her soil is capable of yielding all the valuable kinds of grain in abundance, and of good, if not superior quality. These natural advantages, improved by her extraordinary industry, raise the agricultural products of Eng land to a much greater amount than those of any other country in Europe.

The surface of England is thirty-seven millions of acres. About half a million is occupied by roads; and if we also make allowance for waters, natural and artificial, &c., we may probably have to deduct two millions from the part which forms the proper subject of agriculture. Of this, half is under the plough, and half devoted to pasturage; upwards of three millions are in wheat; about three millions in oats and beans, and between two and three millions in barley. About 300,000 cwt. of hops, of the value of £200,000, and 4,400,000 gallons of cider, are annually produced.

The manufactures of Britain, still more than even the immense products of her agriculture, have astonished the world, and raised her to a decided superiority over all other nations. This distinction she has attained, not so much by their extreme fineness; for, as to this particular, France excels not only in silks and cambrics, but even in woollens; and British porcelain does not equal that of Dresden. But she stands unrivalled in the immensity of useful and valuable products, calculated for the consumption of the great body of mankind; and above all in the stupendous exertions made in contriving and constructing the machinery by which they are produced.

The woollen manufacture is the old staple of the country. As soon as England began to exercise any kind of industry, her first aim was to manufacture her own wools, instead of leaving this operation in the hands of the Flemings. The fabric began in Kent and Sussex; but soon spread, and fixed itself in the interior districts; that of coarse woollens in the West Riding of Yorkshire, and that of the finer cloths in Gloucestershire and Wiltshire. In 1800, the total value of the fabrics was 20,000,000*l.*, of which not much less than half was exported. In the course of the century it has continued increasing, though not with the same rapidity as some other fabrics. The quantity exported has not, however, been augmented in proportion. In 1802, it exceeded 7,000,000*l.*; but in 1832 was only 5,240,000*l.* This manufacture, however, depending chiefly upon home consumption, is less liable to vicissitude than those which have their principal market in foreign countries.

The wool is partly produced in Britain, partly drawn from abroad. English wool is divided into long and short. The former was long considered as exclusively adapted to worsted stuffs; but the recent improvements in machinery have enabled the manufacturer to produce these stuffs almost equally well from shorter wool. The short wool is fitted for cloth and hats; but all that is produced in England is of secondary fineness. Efforts were made, about the close of the last century, to introduce the merino breed from Spain, and not without success; but the flesh being bad, the farmers gave it up, and, devoting themselves to the improvement of the carcase, have allowed the wool even to degenerate, though the increased quantity is supposed to indemnify them. The best short wool is that of Sussex (Southdown) and Norfolk; the best long wool that of Lincoln. The number of short-woolled sheep throughout England, in 1828, amounted to about 14,850,000, that of long-woolled to 4,150,000; and the produce was 264,000 packs of long, and 120,000 packs of short wool; to which might be added 69,000 packs of lamb's wool, and 9000 for Wales; making in all 463,000. The defect of English wool renders it necessary to import a large quantity from abroad. The fleece chiefly valued is that of the merino, long confined to Spain: and Spanish wool, in the early part of this century, was introduced to the extent of 6,000,000 lbs. annually, but in 1827 it fell short of 4,000,000 lbs., and in 1832 did not exceed 2,626,000 lbs. It has been supplanted by the wool of Saxony, and other parts of northern Germany, where the merino breed has been introduced and propagated with the greatest success. The importation from Germany, which in 1810 was only 778,000 lbs., was in 1830 so high as 26,073,000 lbs., though in 1832 only 19,832,000 lbs.: New Holland and Van Diemen's Land in that year furnished 2,377,000 lbs. of very fine wool; and the supply is increasing. The entire import amounted in 1830 and 1831 to about 32,000,000 lbs.; in 1832 to only 28,140,000 lbs.

The annual value of the woollen manufacture appears to be about 20,000,000*l.* sterling, and the persons employed between 400,000, and 500,000. There were exported, in 1832, 396,661 pieces of cloth; 23,453 pieces napped coatings, duffels, &c.; 40,984 pieces of kerseymeres; 34,874 pieces baize; 1,800,714 stuffs or worsted; 2,304,750 yards flannels; 1,681,840 yards blanketing; 690,042 yards carpeting, &c. There were exported also 4,199,000 lbs. of British wool, and 2,204,000 lbs. woollen yarn.

The cotton manufacture is of much more recent introduction, and for a long period the progress of this branch of industry was slow. In 1760, the value of the fabric was only 200,000*l.* In 1767, James Hargreaves, a common Lancashire weaver, invented the spinning jenny, by which at first 8, and finally 120 spindles were moved by a single spinner. Hargreaves became exposed to the persecution of the working people employed in this operation; was obliged to flee to Nottingham; and died in poverty. Richard Arkwright, a barber of Nottingham, invented the water-twist, or "perpetual twist," spinning frame, in which the whole process was performed by the machine, and the workmen had only to supply the material and watch its progress. Samuel Crompton, in 1775, produced the machine called the *mule*, a combination of the two preceding, which it soon superseded both in the finer and more valuable articles.

That machinery should weave as well as spin, was necessary to consummate the triumph of art. This was accomplished by the Rev. Mr. Cartwright, a clergyman of Kent, who invented a machine by which cloth was woven; but the first trial was unsuccessful as to profit, and an impression long prevailed that cottons could be woven cheaper by the hand. Within the last few years, however, the system of power-loom weaving has been adopted to an immense extent; it is estimated that there are in Britain 80,000, absorbing 10,000,000*l.* of fixed and 5,000,000*l.* of floating capital, employing 160,000 operatives, and working up 124,800,000 pounds of cotton.

The steam-engine, the moving power, the greatest of all these discoveries, remains to be mentioned. Machines moved by horses and water, originally employed in manufacturing and other processes, were cumbrous, expensive, and often unmanageable. The steam-engine, brought to perfection by Watt, became at once the moving power of all this machinery, and the principal cause to which its vast results may be attributed.

The cotton wool imported into Britain, which in 1781 little exceeded 5,000,000 lbs., rose in 1809, to 93,000,000; in 1817, to 126,000,000; and in 1832, to 288,000,000. The finest is that called Sea Island, a name given to what is grown on the coast of Georgia and Carolina. The bowed Georgia, produced in the interior, is not of equal value. Next to the Sea Island rank the West India and Brazil. Of the quantity imported in 1831, there came from the United States, 219,333,000 lbs.; from Brazil, 31,695,000; from the East Indies, 25,805,000; from the West Indies, 2,401,000; and from Egypt, 7,714,000 lbs. The consumption of printed cottons has diminished in England, silk being preferred as an ornamental dress, and the use of cotton, printed or dyed previously to weaving, having become prevalent. The demand abroad, however, is still extensive, so that the amount of pieces printed is about 4,500,000, giving employment to 100,000 persons.

The produce of the cotton manufacture is 34,000,000*l.* annually. Of this 18,000,000*l.* is paid in wages to 800,000 persons employed in its different branches; and allowing for those who are dependent upon them, and for the subsidiary employments, it affords subsistence to not much fewer than 1,400,000 people. The value of cotton manufactures exported in 1831 was 13,282,000*l.*; of twist and yarn, 3,975,000*l.* They were chiefly of the following descriptions:—Calicoes, cambric muslins, dimities, &c., 299,597,000 yards; lace, gauze-net and crape, 48,164,000 yards; cotton and linen, mixed, 1,668,000 yards; velvets and velveteens, 404,000 yards; counterpanes and quilts, number, 23,000; hosiery, shawls, handkerchiefs, &c., 536,000 dozen; tapes, bobbins, &c., 99,000 dozen; thread, 1,105,000 lbs.; twist and yarn, 48,098,000 lbs.

The working in metals is also one of the branches in which England has attained to a most decided pre-eminence. About the middle of the sixteenth century it rose to the rank of a staple; and within the last half century it has greatly increased in importance. Sheffield, perhaps the original seat of the trade in England, is still distingnished for the most solid and useful articles, knives, grates, and their appendages, agricultural implements, &c.; while Birmingham adds to these utensils a variety of small articles, ornaments, and toys, which, though minute in detail, amount to a vast value in the aggregate. Each of these two great cities forms, as it were, the centre of a large circle of population, all employed in the same manner. The number of persons employed in the product and manufacture of metals is estimated at 350,000, and the entire produce at 17,000,000*l.* The export of hardware and cutlery in 1831 amounted to 16,799 tons, value 1,620,000*l.*; in 1832, it was 15,294 tons; value, 1,433,000*l.*

The silk manufacture was of late origin in England; but it was considerably improved by the revocation of the edict of Nantes, which drove a number of French weavers into that country. It is established in a quarter of the metropolis, called Spitalfields, where it employs about 25,000 men: at Macclesfield, Manchester, Coventry, and in other parts of the country, the number occupied in it may amount to 40,000. The entire value of the manufacture was estimated some years ago at 4,000,000*l.*; and may now, probably, be between 5,000,000*l.* and 6,000,000*l.* Notwithstanding the removal of the prohibitory duties on the importation of foreign silks, the British manufacture has maintained its ground, and gone on increasing. The importation of raw and thrown silk in 1832 was 4,224,000 lbs.: of which 1,814,000 lbs. were from the East Indies and China; 1,006,000 lbs. from France; 564,000 lbs. from Italy; and 458,000 lbs. from Turkey. The exports amounted in 1832 to 525,000*l.*, chiefly to North America and the West Indies.

In the manufacture of earthenware and porcelain, England has of late made vast advances, and brought its various products to a high degree of beauty and elegance. Burslem in Staffordshire had, for centuries, been noted for its fabrication of a coarse kind of ware; but it was reserved for Mr. Wedgwood to carry this art to perfection by a combination of elegance and cheapness. Fine white clay from the south-western counties, and ground flint, are the chief materials of this celebrated ware, which bears the name of its inventor. The white ware of Derby and the porcelain of Worcester, though on a smaller scale, are still finer productions. The latter is composed of a mixture of 13 different materials, and each cup passes through 23 hands. Earthenware pays no duty, so that its amount cannot be officially ascertained; the export, however, has diminished from nearly 700,000*l.* in 1815–16 to only 490,000*l.* in 1832.

Hides are imported from all quarters of the world; the entire quantity in 1824 was 300,000 cwt., value 700,000*l.* In 1830 only 225,000 cwt. were imported. In that year the hides tanned or otherwise manufactured amounted to 46,800,000 lbs., value 3,900,000*l.*; and as the value of the finished article is supposed to be three times that of the material, this value will amount to nearly 12,000,000*l.* The shoes made in England are estimated at 6,800,000*l.* and the whole manufacture employs about 250,000 persons.

Beer, glass, soap, and candles are branches of production which employ a large capital and numerous workmen, and yield a yearly amount of great value. In London the quantity of malt liquor annually brewed is 1,700,000 barrels, of which 38,000 are exported. This is chiefly *porter*, a liquor peculiarly appropriate to London, and for which she is famous throughout the world. In all England, there were brewed, in 1829, about 7,400,000 barrels, of the value of upwards of 22,000,000*l.*; without including 1,500,000 barrels of table-beer. *Candles.*—In 1829, the manufacture amounted to 110,000,000 lbs., which would make a value of 3,208,000*l.* *Soap.* — The manufacture, in 1829, was 100,000,000 lbs. which would amount to 3,175,000*l.*

The linen manufacture is that in which England is most deficient; for though she is supposed to produce the value of 1,000,000*l.* a year, this does not supersede the necessity of large imports from Scotland and Ireland. Of late, the elegant *manufacture of lace* has been carried to great perfection by means of bobbinet frames. By this manufacture a value of 160,000*l.* in silk and Sea Island cotton is wrought into lace, estimated at 1,890,000*l.* and employing 208,000 persons. *Distilled liquors or spirits*, too, though they produce a revenue of 2,000,000*l.*, are neither equal in quality nor amount to those of the sister countries of Scotland and Ireland, whose produce, if it had not been excluded by national jealousy, would probably by this time have driven that of England out of the market. The quantity distilled in 1831 and 1832 averaged 7,350,000 gallons.

Mines form one of the most copious sources of the wealth of England. The useful metals and minerals, those which afford the instruments of manufacture and are subservient to the daily purposes of life, are now drawn from the earth more copiously there than in any other country. Her most valuable metals are iron, copper, and tin; her principal minerals are coal and salt.

Iron, the material of so important a class of manufacture, abounds in England, particularly in Wales, Staffordshire, and Derbyshire. While it was supposed, however, that the blast furnaces could be composed only of charcoal, the limited supply of wood depressed the produce, and in the middle of the last century, the iron made in England from fifty new furnaces did not exceed 17,000 tons. It was then found, however, that, furnaces filled with coke might be heated to the same degree as those of charcoal, and the inexhaustible supply of coal might be employed in bringing the iron mines into value. Hence, the increased production has been astonishingly rapid. In 1796, it amounted to 125,000 tons; in 1806, to 250,000 tons; in 1830, it was 680,000 tons, worth 5,100,000*l.*; and which the additional labour of forming it into bar iron may raise to 6,300,000*l.* The export amounted in 1832 to about 150,000 tons, worth 1,120,000*l.* It is exported chiefly in the forms of bar iron, to the amount of 74,024 tons; bolt and rod iron, 6938; pig iron, 17,566; cast iron, 12,495; hoops, 9417; nails, 4347, &c.

Copper, also, has risen to importance in the course of the last half century. It is found chiefly in Cornwall, to the amount, in 1832, of 11,947 tons, and is carried thence to Swansea, to be smelted with the coal of North Wales, which itself produced 1320 tons of copper. The total produce is 14,449 tons, which, at 90*l.* per ton, will be 1,300,410*l.*

Tin, a rare and peculiar metal, is found only in Cornwall and part of Devon. So early was it known, that we find the British Islands first recognized by its name, and it is enumerated among the articles with which the Carthaginians supplied the markets of Tyre. As Cornwall, with the exception of the Indian island of Banca, is the only tract known to produce tin in large quantities, there is a considerable export to most countries of Europe, particularly France and Italy. The annual produce of the mines amounts to 83,000 cwt.; of the value of 115,000*l.*

Lead is found in Cumberland, Derbyshire, and Northumberland, to the supposed amount of about 16,000 tons annually; which, at 20*l.* per ton, will be worth 320,000*l.* In 1833, the British lead exported was 13,898 tons.

Coal, the most valuable of all the mineral substances from which Britain derives her prosperity, exists in almost inexhaustible quantities in the counties of Northumberland, Derby, and Stafford, and in that of Glamorgan in South Wales. It fuses the metals, produces the steam which sets the machinery in motion, and is, indeed, instrumental in bringing almost every substance into a useful and merchantable form. By superseding also the necessity of extensive plantations for fuel, it enables a much greater proportion of the soil to be devoted to cultivation. The Northumberland and Durham field has been estimated at 732 square miles, the South Wales field is 1200; which, allowing for the average depth, will, it is calculated, be sufficient to supply all England for 1700 or 2000 years. At all events, it seems certain that she is secure for many centuries against any deficiency. The quantity shipped from Durham and Northumberland is stated at 3,300,000 tons; and the whole employed as fuel, and in the manufactories and mines throughout England (adding 700,000 exported to Ireland), at not less than 15,500,000 tons. The mines on the Tyne employed 8491 persons underground, and 3463 above; those on the Wear, about three-fourths of this number: the conveyance of these coastwise employs 1400 vessels and 15,000 men; while, in London, 7500 whippers, lighter-men, factors, agents, &c. are engaged in landing and distributing it. Taking into view the whole of Great Britain, Mr. M'Culloch considers that the coal trade will give occupation to not less than 160,000 persons. In 1829, the total quantity shipped was 6,224,125 tons; of which, 5,014,132 were sent coastwise; 840,246, to Ireland; 128,893, to the British colonies: 356,419, to foreign countries.

Of salt, Britain possesses an immense supply. The finest and most valuable kind is the rock salt, drawn from mines and from brine springs in the county of Chester. The salt is refined by being boiled along with the brine of the springs, and is then called white salt. The annual produce is 15,000,000 bushels, of which about 10,000,000 are exported, chiefly to North America, the Netherlands, and Russia.

The commerce of Britain, like her manufacturing industry, is now completely without a rival. The exports of Britain consist almost wholly of her manufactured produce. Cotton takes the precedence of all others. In 1830, the quantity exported, including twist and yarn, was valued at about 15,000,000*l.* sterling; being two-fifths of the whole exportation. They are sent to every country, but most especially to those from which the raw material is imported. The United States take an immense quantity; the West Indies and Brazil import largely; the market in the independent states of South America is daily enlarging, and they make their way in increasing quantities even into the East Indies. In Europe, Portugal and Italy are extensive markets; and though studiously excluded from Spain, large consignments are sent to Gibraltar, evidently with a view to clandestine introduction. Germany takes a great quantity both of manufactured goods, and of yarn and twist for her own manufactories. The woollen manufacture has a different and less extensive range. The United States, the greatest market, take three-eighths of the whole; after which rank the East Indies, Russia, Portugal, and Germany. The wrought metals find a great variety of markets. Of bar iron, 7000 tons, and copper 50,000 tons, go to the East Indies. Ireland takes 7000 tons of bar, 700 of cast, and 2300 of wrought iron. The West Indies take largely both iron and copper.*

Among the imports, a large portion consists of raw materials, brought in vast quantities to be manufactured, in many instances for the use of the regions from which they come. Under the head of manufactures, we have enumerated the principal of these articles, and the countries from whence imported. They are chiefly cotton, wool, silk, and hides; to which may be added, bark, ashes, and barilla; cochineal, indigo, madder, and other dyeing stuffs. Although grain and provisions are now produced in sufficient quantity for internal consumption, there is much want of the raw produce of uncultivated land. Under this head a prominent rank may be assigned to timber and naval stores. Fir and oak timber, and staves, are brought chiefly from North America; masts, deals, and deal ends, from Norway and Russia; oak plank from Prussia.

The import trade of consumption is, after all, the most extensive: it consists chiefly in obtaining from southern regions, and those warmed by tropical suns, the accommodations and luxuries which cannot be matured under a less genial sky. Wine would have been introduced to a very great extent, had not its exclusion been made a prime object of fiscal regulation. This, however, has been so potently applied, that the use of wine has not increased in any proportion to the general wealth of the nation; and it has been forced from the nearest and best wines of France, to the less palatable produce of Spain and Portugal. Brandy, also, still accounted the finest of spirituous liquors, forces itself, to a certain extent, into the circle of imports. But the saccharine and aromatic products of the tropical plains form the basis of an immense commerce, which even the adherents of the mercantile system cherish, under the idea that much of it is carried on with English colonies. The leading articles are sugar, tea, coffee, tobacco, and spices. Notwithstanding the immense cotton manufacture of Britain, the piece goods of India, by their peculiar excellence, still find their way into the country.

The shipping by which so extensive a trade is carried on, must necessarily be very extensive. In 1663 it was only 95,000 tons. It rose in 1701 to 273,000; in 1751, to 609,000; in 1792, to 1,186,000. The vessels belonging to the British empire at the end of 1834, were 25,055, of 2,716,000 tons, and navigated by 168,061 men. The entries and clearances for the coasting trade, in 1832, amounted each to 8,500,000 tons. Besides these, in the same year, 4546 foreign vessels, comprising 639,979 tons, and navigated by 35,399 men, entered the ports of Great Britain.*

* See Statistical Tables, at end of Chap. IV.

The fisheries do not seem to have been so much cultivated in Britain, as the hardy enterprise of the nation might have led us to expect. The whale fishery was considered so valuable, both for its products, and as a nursery for seamen, that, till 1824, a bounty was granted in proportion to the tonnage of the vessels employed. They have found their way to the antarctic polar sea, in search of an oil which, though not superior for burning, is better adapted to the purposes of manufacture, than that drawn from the arctic regions. This fishery, within the last twelve years, has considerably diminished both in amount and in the value of its products, owing to the use of gas, the greater cheapness of rape-oil for manufacture, and also to a larger part of the trade being engrossed by Scotland. In 1829 there sailed from England only 41 vessels, of 13,766 tons burden; which brought in 4912 tuns of oil, and 289 tons of whalebone. The following year was still more deficient, owing to the disasters encountered by the vessels engaged in the fishery.

Of the fisheries in the British seas, that of Herrings, the most important, belongs almost entirely to Scotland. Next to this ranks that of Pilchards, on the coast of Cornwall and part of Devon. The fish is found there in such immense shoals, that it forms the chief food of the people during the greater part of the year, and is also largely salted for exportation. The value annually taken is reckoned at 50,000*l.* or 60,000*l.*

The interior navigation of England is justly regarded as one of the prime sources of her prosperity. Till the middle of last century, the making of canals did not enter into the system of English economy. In 1755 was formed the Sankey canal, a line of twelve miles, to supply Liverpool with coal from the pits at St. Helen's. The example then set by the Duke of Bridgewater gave a general impulse to the nation. Since that time, upwards of 30,000,000*l.* sterling have been expended in this object. Twenty-one canals have been carried across the central chain of hills, by processes in which no cost has been spared; all the resources of art and genius have been employed; every obstacle, however formidable, which nature could present, has been vanquished. By locks, and by inclined planes, the vessels are conveyed up and down the most rugged steeps; they are even carried across navigable rivers by bridges. When other means fail, the engineer has cut through the heart of rocks and hills a subterraneous passage. Of these tunnels, as they are called, there are said to be forty-eight, the entire length of which is at least forty miles.

The Duke of Bridgewater formed the plan of opening a communication between Manchester and his extensive coal-mines, at Worsley. The obstacles were so great, both from nature and art, that the attempt must have proved abortive, had he not been seconded by the genius of Brindley, who, from a common millwright, raised himself to be the first engineer of the age. The canal was carried through vast excavations, made partly in the interior of the mine itself; it was led by aqueducts over a succession of public roads, and over the river Irwell by a magnificent bridge, which left space for vessels with their sails spread to pass beneath. By deep cuttings, and by artificial mounds, in some places supported upon piles, a level of upwards of fifty miles was completed. The Duke expended, in this undertaking, his whole fortune, amounting to 350,000*l.*; and its failure would have left him destitute: but, as it immediately enabled him to reduce the price of coal in Manchester to one half, the trade in a short time yielded twenty per cent. upon his outlay, and rapidly produced an immense income.

The Grand Trunk Canal, an undertaking on a still greater scale, formed under the patronage of the Marquess of Stafford, by a course of ninety miles through Staffordshire, connects the Trent with the Mersey, Liverpool with Hull, and the eastern with the western coasts. It gave animation to the trade of all the districts through which it passed, particularly that of the Potteries, and served as a basis for various canals and railways branching from it. From a point near the commencement of the Grand Trunk, the Ellesmere canal has branched far into Wales, and conveys to Liverpool the mineral and agricultural produce of that principality. From its eastern termination, large branches have been extended to Derby, to Nottingham, to Grantham, and other considerable towns.

The Leeds and Liverpool Canal, by a more northerly line of one hundred and twenty miles, connects the Mersey with the Aire, a tributary of the Ouse, and thus enables Liverpool and Hull to communicate by another line across the great cloth-manufacturing districts. An important branch of this canal is carried to Lancaster, and on to Kendal.

From the vicinity of London the Grand Junction, at an expense of two millions, was carried by a line of ninety miles to the neighbourhood of Coventry. Near Daventry, the Grand Union strikes off, and joins the Grand Trunk, thus securing for London an inland communication with Liverpool, and with all the great manufacturing cities of the West. A great system of canals was formed round Birmingham, of which one result was to connect the Grand Trunk with the Severn, and thus to form a connexion between all the four great rivers of England, and all its commercial and manufacturing cities. A canal had already been formed from Coventry to Oxford. That of the Thames and Severn joined these two main rivers at the highest navigable point of the former. The Gloucester and Berkeley is a lateral canal to the Severn, by means of which Gloucester is connected with the Bristol Channel by a direct line. The principal canals to the south of the Thames are the Kennet and Avon canal, and the Berks and Wilts canal, through which a communication is formed from the Thames near Abingdon to the cities of Bath and Bristol. The total length of canals in Great Britain, excluding those under five miles, is 2581 miles.

Railways form another contrivance, by which the conveyance of goods is wonderfully facilitated, by causing the wheels to roll over a smooth surface of iron. Railways were at first used only on a small scale, chiefly in the coal-mines round Newcastle, for conveying the mineral from the interior to the surface, and thence to the place of shipping; and it is reckoned that round that city there is an extent of about three hundred miles of these railways. They were gradually employed on a greater scale, particularly in Wales, where the county of Glamorgan has one twenty-five miles long, and in all two hundred miles of railway. The railway between Manchester and Liverpool extends thirty-one miles, and is carried over sixty-three bridges, thirty of which pass over the turnpike road, and one over the river Irwell. The entire cost was about 820,000*l.*; but the intercourse has been so extensive as to afford an ample remuneration. The Cromford and High Peak railway is carried over the high mountainous district of Derbyshire, connecting the two canals which bear these names. Its length is thirty-three miles, carried over fifty bridges, and rising to a level of 992 feet above the Cromford canal. The entire expense has not exceeded 180,000*l.*

The common high roads of the kingdom are also an object of high importance to trade and general intercourse. Half a century ago most of them appear to have been in a miserable state, but they are now, perhaps, the best in the world, chiefly through the application of the turnpike system, under which they are made and repaired by tolls levied upon the travellers, and administered by county trustees. There are a few cases where roads are to be carried through poor provinces, or form grand lines of national communication, in which government judges it expedient to assist, or even to undertake the entire construction of them. In 1823, the turnpike roads extended in all to 24,531 miles in length. The amount of tolls was 1,214,000*l.*, burdened with a debt of 5,200,000*l.*

Bridges, in a country intersected by numerous and often broad rivers, necessarily attracted a great share of attention; and the ingenuity and wealth of England have been employed in making extensive improvements in this branch of architecture. Southwark Bridge is the most complete of any yet formed of iron. This species of bridge has the advantage of being lighter, and of requiring much fewer arches than those of stone. A still more daring form has been given to this material by bridges of suspension, formed by iron chains stretched across, and supported by fixed points on each side. This construction, on a certain scale, has existed in China from the earliest ages. The Americans were the first to adopt it of any western nation. The greatest undertaking of this kind yet executed is the Menai Bridge (*fig.* 137.), over the strait which separates Wales from Anglesea. Arches of masonry on each side, at the distance of five hundred and sixty feet, are united by a bridge of suspension, composed of iron chains.

137

Menai Bridge.

## Sect. VI.—*Civil and Social State.*

The population of England in former times was imperfectly known, being calculated only from very vague surveys and estimates. In 1377 the results of a poll-tax were given as 2,300,000; but from the many evasions to which such a census would give rise, that number was probably below the truth. In the reign of Elizabeth, during the alarm of a menaced Spanish invasion in 1575, a pretty careful survey was made, the result of which gave 4,500,000. At the time of the Revolution, the increase appeared to be about a million.* From the commencement of the present century decennial enumerations have been made, of which the following are the results:—

| | Population, 1801. | Increase per cent. | Population, 1811. | Increase per cent. | Population, 1821. | Increase per cent. | Population, 1831. |
|---|---|---|---|---|---|---|---|
| England | 8,331,434 | 14⅔ | 9,551,888 | 17⅞ | 11,261,437 | 16 | 13,098,338 |
| Wales | 541,546 | 13 | 611,788 | 17 | 717,438 | 12 | 805,236 |
| Army, Navy, &c. | 470,598 | ...... | 640,500 | ...... | 319,300 | ...... | 277,017 |
| Total | 9,343,578 | 27⅔ | 10,804,176 | 34⅞ | 12,298,175 | 28 | 14,180,591 |

* *Population of the British Empire and Colonies.*

| | |
|---|---|
| Great Britain and Ireland | 24,311,834 |
| North American Colonies | 1,300,000 |
| West India " | 800,000 |
| African " | 300,000 |
| Asiatic " | 1,000,000 |
| Australian " | 95,000 |
| East India Company | 123,000,000 |
| Total | 150,806,834 |

[Am. Ed.]

*Proportion of deaths, marriages, &c. to the population.*—Among the facts that attest the improved condition of the people of England since 1770, the extraordinary diminution in the rate of mortality is one of the least equivocal. In 1780, the deaths in England and Wales amounted to about 1 in 40 of the population; in 1790, to about 1 in 45; in 1811, to 1 in 52; and at an average of the five years ending with 1830, 1 in 54. The improvement has been particularly conspicuous in the great towns; and is to be ascribed to the more comfortable situation of all classes, the greater attention paid to cleanliness, &c. The proportion of marriages to the population has recently declined. In 1760, there was 1 marriage for every 116 individuals; in 1780, 1 in 118. During the five years ending with 1810, it was as 1 to 122; and during the five years ending with 1830, it was as 1 to 129. But this decrease is to be ascribed wholly to the greater prevalence of moral restraint, the proportion of illegitimate births not having increased. The number of births to a marriage in England is about 4. Consumption is the most fatal disease.

The national character of the English exhibits some very bold and marked features. Of these the most conspicuous is that love of liberty which pervades all classes. The liberty for which the English have successfully contended, includes the right of thinking, saying, writing, and doing most things which opinion may dictate, and inclination prompt. The knowledge that the highest offices and dignities in the state are accessible to all, redoubles their activity, and encourages them to perseverance. It is but little more than a century since they began to be distinguished as a manufacturing and commercial people, yet they have already outstripped other European nations in mechanical ingenuity, in industry, and in mercantile enterprise. The enormous increase of capital, and the substitution of machinery for human labour in most of their manufactures, seem likely at no distant period to produce a total change in the condition of British society. Much of its tone is given by the landed gentry; a numerous body, whose estates, though generally considerable, are not enormous: while, on the Continent, landed property is usually in one or other of two extremes; either divided into minute portions, or partitioned into a few princely domains. The English gentry, unlike their continental neighbours, reside during the greater part of the year at their country-seats; appearing in London and at court only for a few months in the spring. In this class, and indeed among the English in general, an uncontrolled temper, elevated by the feeling of independence, often impels individuals into extremes both of good and evil. Nowhere exists a purer spirit of patriotism; nowhere break forth more violent excesses of faction. In no country of Europe, perhaps, are there so many men who act steadily upon principle; yet in none exists, at the same time, so large a proportion of individuals living in habitual and open violation of all principle, and frequently in contempt of legal ordinances. Domestic life is cultivated by the English more sedulously than by any of the continental nations; the sanctity of marriage is more carefully guarded; and chastity in the female sex more strictly observed. In its minor features, the English character has undergone various changes. The vices of drinking and swearing, once so prevalent, are happily no longer fashionable. Horse-racing, hunting, and rural sports, are carried to excess by some of the country gentlemen; and the more barbarous practice of boxing still has cultivators. Perhaps the most estimable quality of the English is their love of justice; the source of all honourable dealing among the higher classes, and of what is emphatically called *fair play,* in the transactions of humbler life. The principle, that a man's word should be his bond, is acted upon most rigorously where the greatest interests are at stake; as on its observance more than on that of any law that has been or can be devised, the commercial and financial prosperity of the country depends. The English are the most provident people in the world. More than a million of individuals are members of friendly societies, and the deposits in savings banks exceed 13,000,000*l.* The great extension of life insurance affords another proof of this laudable disposition. The English also deserve to be called a humane people, zealous, both from feeling and from principle, for the promotion of every thing that tends to the welfare of their fellow-creatures. Crime in England has undergone a considerable change. Highway robbery, so prevalent towards the beginning and middle of last century, is now nearly unknown, and all sorts of crimes and violence have been materially lessened. On the other hand, there has been a very rapid increase, particularly within the last twenty years, of crimes against property. A material change has recently been effected in the criminal law of England, by the abolition of an immense number of capital punishments.

***Provision for the Poor.*** A compulsory rate has been levied on all kinds of fixed property, for the support of all impotent, poor, and unemployed persons, ever since the reign of Elizabeth. In 1700 the rates amounted to about 1,600,000*l.*, and, notwithstanding the increase of population and taxation in the interval, they were little more than 2,000,000*l.* at the close of the American war. In 1795 several ill-considered changes were made in the mode of granting relief, and the pernicious practice of eking out wages by contributions from the rates was then also adopted. From this period, down to the termination of the late French war, the progress of the rates was very rapid, so that they amounted to 9,320,000*l.* in the year 1817–18. They have since been reduced, but they still amounted in 1831–32 to 8,509,000*l.* The abuses arising out of the practice of paying wages out of rates are not inherent in the system. They were engrafted upon it so late as 1795, and may, and it is to be hoped will, be entirely removed. A reform of this sort would of itself take nearly a third part from the rates. [By the act of 14th August, 1834, which provides for the appointment of three poor-law commissioners, with power to make rules and regulations for the management of the poor and he administration of the poor laws, these abuses have been reformed.—AM. ED

The English are, in general, a people soberly religious, though the nation, among its other excesses, has presented striking displays of infidelity and fanaticism. The Church of England was established in the reign of Queen Elizabeth, when the reformation was completed which had been begun in that of Henry VIII. It is an integral part of the constitution, having for its head the king, who, as head of the church, nominates to vacant bishoprics and certain other preferments, constitutes or restrains ecclesiastical jurisdictions, inflicts ecclesiastical censures, and decides *in the last resort* in all ecclesiastical causes, an appeal lying ultimately to him in chancery, from the sentence of every ecclesiastical judge. In respect to its church government, England is primarily divided into two provinces or archbishoprics, Canterbury and York. Each province contains various dioceses or seats of suffragan bishops, Canterbury including twenty-one, and York three, besides the bishopric of Sodor and Man, which was annexed to it by Henry VIII. Every diocese is divided into archdeaconries, of which the whole number amounts to sixty, each archdeaconry into rural deaneries, which are the circuits of the archdeacon's and rural dean's jurisdiction; and each deanery into parishes, towns or villages, townships, and hamlets. The principal church of each see is appropriately called the *cathedral* church; it is possessed by a spiritual body corporate, called a dean and chapter, who are the council of the bishop, but derive their corporate capacity from the crown. Chapters are usually composed of canons and prebendaries; the maintenance or stipend of a canon as well as of a prebendary being a *prebend.* Prebendaries are distinguished into simple and dignitary. A simple prebendary has no cure, and nothing but his revenue for his support; a dignified prebendary has always a jurisdiction annexed, which is gained by prescription. The archdeacon has authority in the bishop's absence to hold visitations, and under the bishop to examine clerks previous to ordination, and also before institution and induction. He has also power to excommunicate, to impose penances, and to reform irregularities and abuses among the clergy, and has charge of the parish churches within the diocese. Below the archdeacon and the ecclesiastics composing the chapter, no member of the Church of England is entitled to the appellation of dignitary. The inferior orders constitute what is called the parochial clergy. The principal *person* of a parochial church is entitled either rector or vicar, that title, which is really more appropriate and honourable, having become corrupted by vulgar misuse. The revenues of the church of England are very extensive; and considering the different offices and gradations of its members, very variously distributed. The rental subject to tithe has been stated, in returns made to parliament, at 20,000,000*l.* Besides the tenth of this amount, that is to say, the *tithe*, the clergy have other funds, which are supposed to raise their entire income to upwards of 3,000,000*l.* The Episcopal revenues are of various amounts; that of the see of Durham is estimated at 30,000*l.* per annum, and is usually considered the largest. The lowest, that of Landaff, falls short of 3000*l.* The prebends enjoyed by canons and prebendaries are some of them very ample; those which exceed 1000*l.* a year are called golden prebends. Those dignitaries are also competent to hold livings as rectors and vicars. The salaries of curates were formerly in many cases extremely small; but, by a legislative provision and by funds allotted out of the public revenue, most of them have been augmented in proportion to the value of the benefice and its population; 80*l.* a year is the lowest stipend, and, if the living be worth 400*l.* per annum, the bishop may allow the curate of such living 100*l.* a year, whatever be its population.

In her intellectual character, England may be justly considered as standing proudly eminent. Bacon, Boyle, Locke, Newton, Davy, with a long train of coadjutors, have disclosed to mankind perhaps a greater sum of important truths than the philosophers of any other country. Strong, clear, sound sense appears to be the quality peculiarly English; and her reasoners were the first to explode those scholastic subtleties which, having usurped the name of philosophy, so long reigned in the schools. It was their merit to discover and establish true philosophy, and apply it to objects of real interest and utility.

In works of imagination, the genius of the English is bold, original, and vigorous. In the drama, Shakspeare stands unrivalled among ancient and modern poets, by his profound and extensive knowledge of mankind, his boundless range of observation throughout all nature, his exquisite play of fancy, and his irresistible power in every province of thought and feeling, the sublime and the pathetic, the terrible and the humorous. In epic poetry, Milton is acknowledged by common consent to stand first among the moderns. Spenser and Dryden are alike eminent, the one for sweetness, the other for versatility; while in correctness of taste, and the polished harmony of numbers, Pope has no rival among the poets of any modern nation.

In historical writing, England has many illustrious names, among which that of Gibbon deserves an honourable place. In oratory, some of her statesmen have acquired great renown, though the general taste both in the senate and at the bar seems to delight rather in plain sense and in cogency of argument, than in those elaborate, ornate, and declamatory flights by which the great speakers of antiquity acted on the imagination and passions of their hearers.

The institutions for public education in England are extensive and splendidly endowed.

The two universities of Oxford and Cambridge are not only the wealthiest but the most ancient in Europe. They enjoy among other privileges that of returning each two members to parliament, and of holding courts for the decision of causes in which members of their own body are interested. They were of ecclesiastic origin; but they have long been considered as lay corporations. Their resources have been augmented by the munificence of sovereigns, and of opulent individuals. The establishments composing them are distinguished into colleges and halls; the latter being academical houses not incorporated or endowed, though they have had considerable benefactions, which are dispensed to the students in exhibitions limited to a stated period. Oxford has nineteen colleges and five halls; Cambridge has thirteen colleges and four halls, which last, however, possess the same privileges as the former. Each university is under the government of a chancellor, high steward, vice-chancellor, and other officers; the persons who preside over the different establishments as masters, wardens, rectors, principals, or provosts, bear the general denomination of heads of colleges, and each college has a number of fellowships to which large emoluments and easy duties are attached. They possess also extensive patronage in church livings, and a number of exhibitions or scholarships. These, though of considerable value, are not supposed adequate to defray the expense of a residence at a university, which, at the lowest, is calculated to amount to 150*l.* a year. On the books of each university are the names of many members who have long ceased to reside; but, exclusive of these, the number actually resident at Oxford may be stated at 3000, and those at Cambridge amount to considerably more. Students, according to their proficiency in learning, are entitled to the degrees of bachelor and master of arts, bachelor and doctor in divinity, and bachelor and doctor in the faculties of physic and law. The time required by the statutes to be occupied in study before each student can be qualified for taking those degrees is three years for a bachelor, and about four years more for a master of arts; seven years after that he may commence bachelor of divinity, and then five years more entitle him to take the degree of doctor in divinity. In law, a student may commence bachelor after six years', and in physic after five years' standing. Only one year's attendance and the hearing of a single course of lectures are required as preparatory for entering into holy orders, the lowness of the inferior church livings, and the expense of residence, rendering it difficult to exact more from the greater number of candidates for ordination. The qualifications for a bishop include the degree of doctor in divinity.

The mode of instruction is by private tutors, who teach classical literature and the mathematics, the latter branch of study being particularly cultivated at Cambridge. The public examinations are conducted with great diligence, and excite emulation. The lucrative fellowships may sometimes tempt their possessors to indulge in luxurious ease; but to those who are seriously disposed to study, they afford facilities for research hardly attainable in any other sphere.

Two educational establishments, the London University and King's College have been recently instituted in London.

Of the public schools of England, the most distinguished are those of Westminster, Eton, Winchester, and Harrow. Although originally founded as charity-schools, yet being now appropriated to the education of boys of the first families, the habits formed in them are very expensive. Greek and Latin are almost exclusively taught there by masters eminently qualified; and Englishmen of education generally excel in the knowledge of both languages.

For boys of the middle rank, and those destined for commercial pursuits, there are numerous private academies.

Colleges for the particular study of law and equity have long been established in the metropolis, under the names of inns of court and inns of chancery. The principal of these are the Middle and Inner Temple, Lincoln's Inn, and Gray's Inn. Before any person can be admitted to practise as an advocate, he must be regularly entered in, and be a member of, one of the inns of court for five years, and must have kept his commons in such inn, twelve terms. In favour of those who have taken a degree of master of arts or bachelor of laws at an English university, three years are sufficient to be a member of the inn. After complying with these conditions, and paying the regular fees, the student may be called to the bar without having been required to make any public demonstration of his proficiency or ability.

Of primary schools for the great body of the people, there formerly existed a considerable number; but the deficiency of them, at present, is greatly to be deplored. The metropolis, indeed, contains several, of which the most considerable is Christ-church Hospital or the Blue-coat School, in which about 1100 children are maintained and educated. The number of charitable foundations in different parts of the country amounts to 3,898, yielding an income of 65,395*l.* Of these, however, many give also board and lodging, so that their advantages can extend to only a small number; others have been neglected, and left exposed to those abuses to which old establishments are generally liable. So greatly was the influence of these institutions on the great body of the lower orders diminished, that within the last 30 years the larger proportion of labouring people were unable to read. The evils arising from want of education among them have, at length, been strongly felt; and very great exertions have been made, chiefly by the benevolence of private individuals, to remedy the defect.

Of the scientific institutions of England the foremost is "the Royal Society of London for improving Natural Knowledge." In its infancy it owed much to the protection of Oliver Cromwell; and having survived the Commonwealth, was incorporated by royal charter, in 1663. The Society publish an annual volume under the name of *Philosophical Transactions.* The Society of Antiquaries traces its origin to the reign of Queen Elizabeth, but was not incorporated until 1821. It has published a series of volumes entitled *Archæologia.* Several private societies have been formed for the cultivation of particular branches of knowledge, by the union of individuals distinguished for their attainments in or devotion to those branches. Besides these and other institutions in the metropolis, most of the great provincial towns, as Manchester, Bristol, Derby, Liverpool, and Newcastle, have formed literary and philosophical societies, which have made some important contributions to science and literature in their Transactions.

The principal public libraries have owed their origin to the spirit and enterprise of private individuals; the Bodleian Library at Oxford was the bequest of Sir Thomas Bodley, and was enriched by successive donations. The British Museum derived its first treasures from the collections of Sir Robert Cotton and Sir Hans Sloane; but has acquired, through purchase by parliament, the Harleian and Lansdowne MSS., the libraries of Major Edwards and Dr. Burney, and several valuable collections of coins and minerals. It has also been enriched by the entire collection of George III., presented to the nation by his successor. With this accession, the library, which previously consisted of 125,000 volumes, has been augmented by one-half. The Museum is also very rich in specimens of natural history, particularly of mineralogy.

Institutions of a highly useful character have sprung from the general desire of knowledge which marks the present age. Their object is to communicate knowledge to the commercial classes, as well as to persons who have not opportunities for a regular course of study; and the chief means employed for this purpose are a library, a reading-room, and courses of lectures. Of these establishments are the Royal Institution, the London Institution, &c.; and all the great cities and towns have now their public libraries.

Of the Fine Arts, that of painting has been greatly neglected in England. Portrait painting, indeed, always met with encouragement; yet Vandyke, the leader in this branch of art, was a foreigner. It was only toward the close of the last century that Reynolds formed a style decidedly English, and of distinguished excellence.

The Royal Academy, under the immediate patronage of the king, consists of forty artists, including the president, while a number of others are attached in expectancy as associates. There are four professors, viz. of painting, of architecture, of anatomy, and of perspective, who annually read public lectures on the subjects of their several departments. To the schools of this academy free admission is given to all students properly qualified for receiving instruction, and there is an annual exhibition of paintings, sculpture, and architectural designs, to which all artists may send their works for admission, if approved by the committee appointed to judge them. The splendid collection of paintings formed by the regent duke of Orleans was imported entire, and the greater part of it now embellishes the gallery of the Marquess of Stafford. The nobles of Italy, also, on the devastation of that country were obliged to strip their palaces of these valued ornaments, and to dispose of them at low rates to English speculators. From those sources were formed the Grosvenor, the Angerstein, and many other private collections. On the death of Mr. Angerstein, in 1824, his collection was purchased by parliament, and made the basis of a national gallery, which has since received considerable additions both by purchase and bequest.

In the other departments of the fine arts, music, sculpture, and architecture, the English have been far excelled by the continental nations; in engraving, they have produced some distinguished names.

The publishing and selling of books form one of the principal branches of her productive industry. Periodical literature has a very extensive circulation. In the metropolis nearly sixty magazines and reviews are published, of which the monthly value has been estimated at 6000*l.* Another important characteristic of the national spirit may be remarked in the immense circulation of newspapers, notwithstanding a heavy stamp-duty. There are in London eight daily morning papers, and five daily evening papers; seven papers published thrice a week; and upwards of forty weekly papers. Of the latter species of newspaper, every provincial city has two or three, and every town of consequence has one. The number of stamps issued for the London newspapers in 1832 was 21,432,882. The produce of the duty in that year was 490,451*l*,

The favourite amusements of the English are those which combine the advantages of air and exercise. The stage, though eminently rich in dramas, and supplied with actors of high talent, is not the habitual resort of the people. In former times hunting was almost the sole business of life among the English squires; and though their tastes are now much varied. this original pastime, in all its forms, continues to be eagerly followed. By the nobility and gentry, horse-racing is supported with equal ardour, and no country rivals England in the high excellence to which she has brought the breed of animals employed in this diversion. The races of Doncaster, of York, and above all of Newmarket, are attended by the most distinguished persons in the country for rank and opulence; and other race-courses attract great multitudes of miscellaneous spectators. Among the common people boxing matches present a similar occasion of laying wagers. Bull-baiting was put down only by statute. Of the national out-door games, those of cricket and tennis deserve especial commendation, from their tendency to enliven the spirits and invigorate the frame.

In their habits and modes of ordinary life, the English may be called a domestic people, especially when compared with the French. In common with other northern nations, the English retain a taste for fermented or distilled liquors, which, however, has been in a great measure corrected and subdued among the higher and middle classes. Beer and porter constitute the staple drink of the great body of the people; but malt spirit of a cheap and very pernicious kind is consumed in great quantities by the lowest orders, especially in the metropolis, where it is rapidly accelerating their degeneracy. Among the middle classes the wines of Spain, Portugal and Madeira are in general use; but the cellars of the rich are stored with the choicest products of the French vineyards. Convivial excess, so long the reproach of the English, has become comparatively rare.

## SECT. VII.—*Local Geography.*

England and Wales are divided into counties or shires. Wales, until the time of Edward I., was an independent principality, but is now an appendent territory, of very inferior magnitude. It has still, however, its own courts of judicature, and retains some national peculiarities. The number of counties in England is forty, and in Wales twelve; making in all fifty-two. The following statistical table, gives a general view of the extent, population, employment, and wealth of each county:—

| Counties. | Square Miles. | Houses, 10*l.* and upwards. | Rental of Houses. | Population, 1831. | Income in 1814–15, arising from | | | | Poor Rates, 1830. | Cities and Towns. |
|---|---|---|---|---|---|---|---|---|---|---|
| | | | | | Land. | Trade. | Offices. | Mineral Produce | | |
| | | | £ | | £ | £ | £ | £ | £ | |
| Bedford....... | 430 | 723 | 12,619 | 95,383 | 364,276 | 94,796 | 1,481 | ..... | 96,994 | Bedford........ 6,959 |
| Berks ........ | 744 | 3,713 | 83,572 | 145,289 | 719,889 | 299,703 | 3,217 | ..... | 129,533 | Reading...... 15,595<br>Windsor...... 7,103<br>Newbury...... 5,959 |
| Bucks ........ | 748 | 1,894 | 35,655 | 146,529 | 662,872 | 222,981 | 1,998 | ..... | 158,483 | Buckingham.. 3,610<br>Aylesbury .... 5,021 |
| Cambridge.... | 686 | 2,645 | 49,781 | 143,955 | 705,371 | 239,687 | 5,109 | ..... | 115,163 | Cambridge.... 20,917<br>Ely........... 6,189 |
| Chester (*a*) ... | 1,017 | 1,784 | 92,854 | 334,410 | 1,114,927 | 289,309 | 4,207 | 26,608 | 144,102 | Chester....... 21,363<br>Macclesfield .. 23,129 |
| Cornwall..... | 1,407 | 2,852 | 48,117 | 302,440 | 922,258 | 230,112 | 3,233 | 77,986 | 121,202 | Launceston... 2,231<br>Falmouth..... 4,760 |
| Cumberland .. | 1,497 | 2,400 | 42,040 | 169,681 | 737,438 | 179,752 | 3,447 | 46,297 | 58,850 | Carlisle....... 20,006<br>Whitehaven .. 11,393 |
| Derby (*b*).... | 1,077 | 2,287 | 45,633 | 237,170 | 883,370 | 210,583 | 2,908 | 43,000 | 108,303 | Derby ....... 23,627 |
| Devon.. ..... | 2,488 | 12,397 | 237,000 | 494,168 | 1,924,912 | 754,444 | 9,471 | 32,800 | 250,713 | Exeter....... 27,932<br>Plymouth..... 40,651<br>Devonport .... 34,883 |
| Dorset........ | 1,129 | 3,051 | 57,868 | 159,252 | 726,263 | 241,634 | 4,002 | ..... | 104,822 | Weymouth ... 7,655<br>Poole......... 6,459<br>Sherborne .... 4,075 |
| Durham (*c*)... | 1,040 | 4,269 | 69,471 | 253,827 | 885,580 | 253,631 | 3,771 | 52,300 | 100,646 | Durham ...... 10,135<br>Sunderland ... 17,060 |
| Essex (*d*)..... | 1,525 | 6,284 | 139,806 | 317,233 | 1,584,108 | 603,935 | 8,630 | 52,248 | 320,541 | Colchester .... 16,167<br>Harwich...... 4,297<br>Saffron-Walden 4,762 |
| Gloucester (*e*). | 1,122 | 9,080 | 251,974 | 386,904 | 1,315,723 | 367,243 | 2,897 | ..... | 201,402 | Gloucester .... 11,933<br>Bristol........ 59,074<br>Tewkesbury .. 5,780<br>Cirencester ... 5,420 |
| Hereford ..... | 971 | 1,794 | 30,424 | 110,976 | 629,156 | 61,851 | 2,790 | .... | 70,000 | Hereford...... 10,282 |
| Hertford...... | 602 | 3,490 | 70,299 | 143,341 | 583,657 | 262,989 | 4,319 | ..... | 115,092 | Hertford ...... 5,247 |
| Huntingdon .. | 345 | 945 | 16,791 | 53,149 | 325,694 | 68,401 | 4,156 | ..... | 50,092 | Huntingdon .. 3,267 |
| Kent (*f*)... . | 1,462 | 16,129 | 347,110 | 479,155 | 1,687,442 | 1,686,228 | 19,342 | ..... | 399,686 | Canterbury ... 13,649<br>Deptford and Greenwich.. 44,348<br>Maidstone .... 15,387 |

(*a*) Nantwich - - 4,886 | (*c*) Gateshead - 15,177 | Stockton - - 7,763 | (*e*) Cheltenham 22,942 | Deal - · 7,268
(*b*) Chesterfield - 5,775 | Bishop Wearmouth 14,462 | South Shields 9,074 | Stroud - - 8,607 | Margate - 10,339
Matlock - - - 3,262 | (*d*) Chelmsford 5,435 | (*f*) Rochester 9,891 | Ramsgate - [illegible],985

TABLE—*continued.*

| Counties. | Square Miles. | Houses, 10*l.* and upwards. | Rental of Houses. | Population, 1831. | Income in 1814-15, arising from Land. | Trade. | Offices. | Mineral Produce. | Poor Rates, 1830. | Cities and Towns. |
|---|---|---|---|---|---|---|---|---|---|---|
| | | | £ | | £ | £ | £ | £ | £ | |
| Lancashire (*a*) | 1,806 | 28,406 | 795,832 | 1,336,854 | 3,139,043 | 2,292,079 | 39,020 | ..... | 413,529 | Manchester.. 182,812<br>Liverpool.... 165,175<br>Lancaster ... 12,613<br>Wigan ...... 20,774 |
| Leicester (*b*) .. | 816 | 3,357 | 62,748 | 197,003 | 951,908 | 319,607 | 5,827 | ..... | 152,594 | Leicester .... 39,306 |
| Lincoln ...... | 2,787 | 4,026 | 78,694 | 317,244 | 2,096,611 | 373,671 | 6,550 | ..... | 228,952 | Lincoln ..... 11,843<br>Boston ...... 11,240<br>Stamford .... 5,837 |
| Middlesex .... | 297 | 116,279 | 5,143,340 | 1,358,541 | 5,763,373 | 15,255,245 | 1,174,865 | ..... | 779,125 | Part of London and Westminster. |
| Monmouth ... | 516 | 1,688 | 31,572 | 98,130 | 298,981 | 102,571 | 437 | 9,200 | 32,089 | Monmouth .. 4,916 |
| Norfolk (*c*) ... | 2,013 | 5,333 | 97,067 | 390,054 | 1,516,651 | 523,010 | 16,505 | ..... | 338,867 | Norwich..... 61,116<br>Yarmouth .... 21,115 |
| Northampton ...... | 965 | 2,237 | 40,327 | 179,276 | 947,578 | 185,204 | 1,421 | ..... | 173,018 | Northampton 15,351<br>Peterborough 5,553 |
| Northumberland (*d*) | 1,809 | 6,140 | 120,424 | 222,912 | 1,291,412 | 436.404 | 5,763 | 59,900 | 88,035 | Newcastle ... 42,260<br>Berwick ..... 8,920 |
| Nottingham .. | 774 | 3,597 | 71,396 | 225,320 | 751,626 | 314,501 | 2,073 | ..... | 106,707 | Nottingham . 50,680<br>Newark ..... 9,557 |
| Oxford ....... | 742 | 3,628 | 61,869 | 151,726 | 790,866 | 312,809 | 4,815 | ..... | 151,235 | Oxford....... 20,649 |
| Rutland...... | 200 | 241 | 4,621 | 19,385 | 138,216 | 30,938 | 799 | ..... | 12,872 | |
| Salop ........ | 1,403 | 3,402 | 63,091 | 222,503 | 1,083,701 | 279,932 | 4,861 | 26,205 | 99,665 | Shrewsbury.. 23,492<br>Wenlock .... 17,435<br>Bridgenorth . 5,298<br>Ludlow ..... 5,253 |
| Somerset (*e*) .. | 1,549 | 16,568 | 512,909 | 403,908 | 2,308,723 | 1,329,265 | 13,827 | 20.100 | 209,566 | Bath ........ 38,063<br>Bridgewater . 7,897<br>Taunton .... 11,139 |
| Southampton....... | 1,533 | 9,362 | 198,321 | 314,313 | 1,240,547 | 923,713 | 10,751 | 8,700 | 239,122 | Southampton 19,134<br>Portsmouth.. 50,309<br>Winchester.. 8,712 |
| Stafford (*f*)... | 1,196 | 6,122 | 108,507 | 410,485 | 1,200,324 | 536,720 | 10,826 | 48,600 | 171,578 | Stafford...... 6,956<br>Newcastle ... 8,192<br>Lichfield..... 6,499 |
| Suffolk ....... | 1,566 | 3,573 | 61,909 | 296,304 | 1,151,304 | 453,484 | 11,972 | ..... | 299,684 | Ipswich ..... 20,201<br>Bury St. Edmund's .... 11,436 |
| Surrey ....... | 811 | 33,865 | 964,438 | 486,326 | 1,589,701 | 1,564,532 | 21,023 | ..... | 321,304 | Southwark .. 91,501<br>Guildford .... 3,916 |
| Sussex (*g*) .... | 1,461 | 6,818 | 202,837 | 272,328 | 919,350 | 372,058 | 4,610 | ..... | 289,051 | Brighton .... 40,634<br>Lewes....... 8,590<br>Chichester ... 8,270 |
| Warwick (*h*).. | 984 | 9,368 | 190,602 | 336,988 | 1,269,756 | 669,369 | 12,966 | 16,950 | 192,303 | Birmingham. 146,986<br>Coventry .... 27,070<br>Warwick.... 9,109 |
| Westmoreland...... | 722 | 1,039 | 21,120 | 55,041 | 299,582 | 52,575 | 1,184 | ..... | 32,044 | Kendal ...... 10,015 |
| Wilts ........ | 1,283 | 3,622 | 68,577 | 239,181 | 1,215,619 | 376,070 | 6,981 | 3,100 | 220,931 | Salisbury .... 9,876 |
| Worcester (*i*) . | 674 | 4,872 | 100,826 | 211,356 | 820,020 | 273,303 | 1,137 | 3,800 | 97,178 | Worcester ... 18,610 |
| York (*k*)...... | 6,013 | 20,189 | 415,539 | 1,371,296 | 4,700,424 | 1,719,886 | 24,416 | 62,200 | 586,126 | York ........ 26,454<br>Leeds........ 123,393<br>Hull......... 36,293<br>Sheffield..... 59,111 |
| N. Wales. | | | | | | | | | | |
| Anglesea..... | 402 | 220 | 4,080 | 48,325 | 94,760 | 3,998 | ........ | ..... | 19,196 | Beaumaris... 2,497<br>Holyhead.... 4,282 |
| Caernarvon (*l*).... | 775 | 538 | 7,982 | 65,753 | 131,212 | 20,641 | 220 | ..... | 23,440 | Caernarvon.. 7,642 |
| Denbigh (*m*) .. | .... | 856 | 14,411 | 83,167 | 312,576 | 19,677 | 305 | ..... | 41,139 | Denbigh ..... 3,786 |
| Flint (*n*)....... | .... | 176 | 3,375 | 60,012 | 175,115 | 11,666 | 795 | 15,400 | 25,513 | Holywell .... 8,969 |
| Merioneth.... | .... | 292 | 4,578 | 35,609 | 112,516 | 7,261 | 68 | ..... | 16,760 | Dolgelly ..... 4,087 |
| Montgomery . | .... | 605 | 7,971 | 66,485 | 212,083 | 18,748 | 794 | ..... | 38,665 | Welshpool... 5.255 |
| S. Wales. | | | | | | | | | | |
| Brecknock.... | .... | 460 | 7,599 | 47,763 | 161,989 | 22,783 | 560 | ..... | 20,928 | Brecknock... 5,026 |
| Cardigan (*o*) .. | 726 | 74 | 999 | 64,780 | 146,816 | 13,727 | 282 | ..... | 20,685 | Cardigan .... 2,795 |
| Caermarthen . | 926 | 570 | 8,363 | 100,655 | 282,091 | 30,320 | 5,361 | ..... | 37,957 | Caermarthen 9,955 |
| Glamorgan (*p*)... | .... | 1,712 | 31,268 | 126,612 | 372,603 | 103,203 | 3,149 | 55,900 | 42,301 | Swansea .... 13,694 |
| Pembroke (*q*) . | .... | 740 | 12,701 | 81,424 | 220,241 | 45,348 | 1,531 | ..... | 28,308 | Pembroke .... 6,511 |
| Radnor....... | .... | 174 | 2,202 | 24.651 | 101,956 | 3,429 | 40 | ..... | 15,298 | Radnor.. . 1,989 |

(*a*) Bolton - - 41,195
Salford - - 40,786
Rochdale - - 35,735
Preston - - - 33,112
Oldham - - 32,381
Pilkington - 11,006
Crompton - 7,004
Blackburn - 27,091
Toxteth Park 24,067
Chorlton Row 20,569
Warrington - 16,018

Bury - - - 15,086
Chorley - - 9,282
Prescot - - 5,055
(*b*) Loughborough - - 10,800
(*c*) Lynn Regis 13,370
(*d*) Tynemouth 10,182
North Shields 6.744
Hexham - - 6,042
Morpeth - - 3,890
(*e*) Wells - - 6,649

(*f*) Wolverhampton - - - 24,732
Bilston . - 14,492
(*g*) Hastings - 10.097
Rye - - - 3,715
(*h*) Leamington 6,209
Kenilworth - 3.097
(*i*) Dudley - - 23.043
Kidderminster 14,981
Hornbridge - 6,148
Evesham - 3,991

Droitwich - 2,487
(*k*) Whitby - 11,725
Scarborough 8.760
Beverley - - 8,302
Doncaster - 10,801
Huddersfield 19,035
Halifax - 15,382
Bradford - - 23.233
Barnsley - - 10,330
Ripon - - 5,080
Pontefract 4,832

(*l*) Bangor - 4,751
(*m*) Wrexham 5,483
Llangollen - 3,630
(*n*) Mold - - 8,086
Flint - - - 2,216
(*o*) Aberystwith 4,128
(*p*) Merthyr Tydvil - - - 22.083
Cardiff - - 6.187
(*q*) Haverfordwest 3,915
Tenby - 2,128

The topographical details of England may be distributed under the following *subsections*:—1. Southern counties; 2. Eastern counties; 3. Midland counties; 4. Northern counties; 5. Western counties.

### Subsect. 1.—*Southern Counties.*

Under this head, Kent, Surrey, Sussex, Berkshire, Hampshire, Wiltshire, and Dorset, the counties south of the Thames, and along the Channel, will be comprehended. This fine district is, in general, of a level character; but is traversed, however, by ranges of low hills or downs, which give to it a varied and picturesque aspect. Chalk is a predominant feature in its soil; and, on the coast, forms those bold cliffs, which characterise the southern boundary of Britain. Many tracts are under high cultivation, yielding, in perfection, the usual agricultural products, with others of great value, peculiar to this district; particularly hops, in Kent, and part of Sussex and Surrey. A prominent feature consists of large expanses of downs, composed of chalky soil, scarcely fit for the plough, but pastured by vast flocks of sheep.

Kent, the largest and finest of these counties, holds a conspicuous place in English annals. The men of Kent have been noted as a race peculiarly stout, hardy, and courageous. In the west are extensive wealds, presenting still many finely wooded districts; also large marshy tracts, interspersed, however, with dry cultivated portions, in which the best grain in the kingdom is raised. The interior around Maidstone and Canterbury forms almost a continued garden, supplying fruits for the markets of London; and above all, hops, that essential ingredient in the staple beverage of the English nation.

Canterbury, the chief place in Kent, is one of the most ancient and venerable of the English cities. It is the ecclesiastical metropolis of the kingdom, the residence of its primate; who, as such, places the crown on the sovereign's head, and ranks next in dignity to the royal family. Its cathedral (*fig.* 138.) is of early origin and of vast extent; while revered through the Catholic world as the shrine of the murdered Becket, it was visited by crowds of pilgrims, and enriched with offerings; but of these treasures it was stripped by Henry VIII. Canterbury is built in the form of a cross, and intersected by branches of the Stour. Manufactures of cloth, silk, and cotton were early introduced, and still subsist, though they cannot bear a comparison with those of the great towns of the interior and of the north.

138

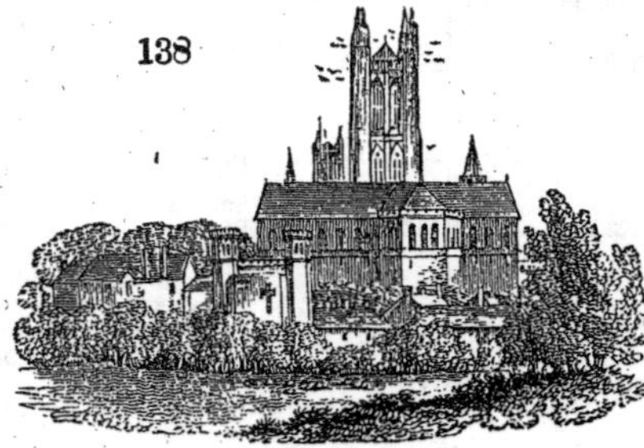

Canterbury Cathedral.

Maidstone and Tunbridge are among the agreeable inland towns in Kent. The former, of great antiquity, has one of the most elegant parochial churches in the kingdom. It is the chief market for hops; and has some manufactures, particularly of paper. Tunbridge Wells, situated five or six miles from the town of Tunbridge, have long been a place of public resort. The springs are considered efficacious in cases of debility and certain chronic disorders. The town has also a thriving manufacture of Tunbridge ware, consisting of various wooden ornaments, snuff-boxes, children's toys, &c.

But the chief places of Kent are maritime, the most ancient being those called the *Cinque Ports.* At an early period, they were considered the most important stations for the defence of the kingdom, and were bound to furnish and equip fifty-seven vessels, each manned with twenty-one sailors; in return for which, their citizens held the rank of barons, and sent two members to parliament from each port. Their greatness is now departed, and some of their harbours have been filled up by sand.

The Kentish Cinque Ports are Dover, Sandwich, Hythe, and Romney. The first is still a place of considerable note. The spacious castle on a commanding eminence, the white and towering cliffs, present to the approaching mariner an imposing spectacle. As the main channel of communication with France, it maintains twenty-seven packets in constant service. Romney and Hythe are of little maritime importance. Sandwich on the east coast, yields in importance to its nominal dependencies, Deal, Margate, and Ramsgate. Deal derives its prosperity from the vicinity of that fine anchorage, the Downs, where the outward-bound fleets of England usually remain for a certain period, when they obtain supplies and refreshments from Deal. Margate is crowded, though not fashionable; and the establishment of steam-packets allows daily intercourse with the metropolis. It likewise carries on some trade

139

Dover Castle.

with the Baltic, and supplies the metropolis with grain and fish. Having risen within the last half century, it is built with regularity, and contains twelve marble baths, into which the sea-water is admitted for those who prefer that mode of bathing. Ramsgate, situated on the isle of Thanet, possesses the advantage of a smooth and extensive beach. Considerable improvements have been made in the harbour at the expense of government, with the view to its yielding protection to vessels navigating this coast, where the dangerous shoals of the Goodwin Sands have often proved fatal.

Deptford, Woolwich, Chatham, and Sheerness, are grand establishments for the construction of ships of war. Deptford contains also the Victualling Office. Woolwich is the depôt of artillery, and the theatre of all the operations connected with its construction and preparation. Here is also the Royal Military Academy, in which an hundred young men of respectable family are trained in all the branches of knowledge necessary for the engineering department; and who, after a strict examination, are appointed to commissions in the service. Chatham is the grand magazine of naval stores. The rope-house is 1128 feet long, in which cables 101 fathoms in length, and upwards of two feet in circumference, are constructed. Twenty forges are constantly employed in the fabrication of anchors, some of which are five tons in weight. This important post, with the exception of Portsmouth, is now the strongest in Britain. Sheerness, on the Isle of Sheppey, is a smaller station, chiefly employed in the repair of shattered vessels.

Greenwich, about two miles below Deptford, is celebrated for its superb hospital (*fig.* 140.) for disabled and superannuated mariners. This edifice was begun by Charles II., on a design of Inigo Jones, as a royal palace. It remained unfinished, until the reign of William III., when it was converted into a naval hospital. It was enlarged by the addition of three wings, enriched by donations, and by a tax of 6*d*. a month from every seaman, and it now supports 3000 boarders, and pays pensions to 5400 in different quarters of the kingdom. In Greenwich park stands the celebrated observatory, furnished with the best instruments that can be obtained for perfecting astronomical observations. The recorded observations of Flamsteed, of Halley, of Bradley, and of Maskelyne, rank among the most important contributions to astronomical science.

140

Greenwich Hospital.

At Gravesend, near the mouth of the Thames, the vessels employed in foreign commerce, both in going up and down, must stop and undergo an examination. Rochester, with an ancient cathedral, contains in its vicinity numerous seats, among which may be particularly noted Cobham Hall. Lee Priory is also remarkable for its works of art; and Knowle Park forms a magnificent structure of great extent.

Sussex extends about forty miles along the Channel. It is covered to the extent of 170,000 or 180,000 acres with noble oaks which are sought for the use of the royal navy. The Sussex sheep are peculiarly valued both for mutton and wool.

The capital is Chichester, an ancient little city with a cathedral. Winchelsea, Rye, and Hastings are Cinque Ports, which have lost their ancient importance; but Hastings, from its fine views of land and sea, attracts numerous visitants during the summer. Brighton, the gayest of all the southern watering-places, from being a large fishing village, rapidly rose to be an elegant town. Its extensive lawn called the Steyne, sloping towards the sea, forms an agreeable promenade. The Pavilion, or palace built by George IV., and the chain pier are among the objects of note.

The rough downs and bleak heaths of Surrey contrasted with its numerous fine parks and wooded districts, give to its scenery a striking and picturesque character. Southwark is in Surrey; but it is too entirely a part of London to be treated separately from the rest of that capital. Along the southern bank of the Thames are Kew, with its palace and fine gardens, containing plants from every quarter of the world; Richmond and its hill, which commands a magnificent view of the Thames winding among wooded parks and palaces. Camberwell, Clapham, and other villages in the vicinity of the capital, are entirely composed of the villas of opulent citizens, and the *seats* are numerous. At St. Anne's Hill, a beautiful villa on the Thames, Fox passed the latter years of his life in literary retirement.

Berkshire contains extensive sheep pastures; and a great expanse of its eastern border is occupied by forests; yet more than half its extent consists of fine arable land. The sheep fair of Ilsley is the most considerable in the kingdom, the annual number sold averaging two hundred and fifty thousand. The hogs also of this county are in high repute. Berkshire is remarkable for its manufactures of copper, which is brought from Swansea to the annual extent of six hundred to one thousand tons.

Reading, the capital of Berkshire, is remarkable in history, as several parliaments were held there, and a siege was sustained during the civil war. It still enjoys some prosperity, through the export of the produce of the fertile surrounding district.

Windsor, from the beauty of its site, on an eminence near the Thames, and the magnificence of its royal castle (*fig.* 141.), forms a commanding feature in the prospect for many

141

Windsor Castle.

miles around. William I. constructed here a fortress of considerable size; but the whole structure was re-modelled by Edward III. Since it ceased to be important as a place of strength, it has been occupied as a palace; and is the only one, in fact, suitable to the dignity of the monarch. The noble terrace walk 1870 feet in length, commands a finely varied and extensive prospect. George III. completely repaired St. George's chapel, and partly restored the north front of the upper ward; but in consequence of his illness, the improvements were suspended for eleven years. George IV. resumed them on a scale commensurate with the importance of so venerable an edifice; and large sums of money were voted by parliament for this national purpose. The royal apartments contain an extensive collection of paintings, among which are some fine portraits by Vandyke, and some historical pictures by Guido, Correggio, Carlo Dolci, and Leonardo da Vinci. The chapel of St. George is considered one of the finest specimens of the ornamented Gothic in the kingdom. The choir in particular is of admirable workmanship, and adorned with banners of knights of the garter ranged on each side. It includes also the tombs of many of the English princes, particularly their late majesties, and the Princess Charlotte; and some of its windows are painted after the designs of Reynolds. To the south of the palace extend Windsor Great Park, and Windsor Forest, grand features, first formed by William the Conqueror. Even after the considerable abridgment that has taken place, the domain is still fifty-six miles in circumference, containing within its range some noble timber. Parts of it were devoted by George III. to his favourite pursuit of experimental farming.

The other towns of Berkshire are small; at Newbury, two obstinate battles were fought in 1643 and 1644. Maidenhead (formerly Mainhithe), on the Thames, is beautifully encircled with villas.

Hampshire contains extensive remains of those grand forests which once overspread so great a part of England. The principal is the New Forest, bordering on the Channel and the bay of Southampton. From this tract of about 92,365 acres, William the Conqueror drove out the inhabitants, and demolished the parish churches, that the royal sports might be carried on undisturbed. The forests of Bex, Holt, Alice, &c., containing upwards of 30,000 acres, belong also to the crown. The wood is chiefly oak and beech; the former with a short thick trunk and strong crooked branches, rendering it of excellent service as knee-timber for the navy, while the masts and acorns feed hogs of vast size, weighing sometimes eight hundred pounds, and producing the best bacon in the kingdom.

Winchester is one of the most ancient and venerable cities in England. During part of the Saxon period, it was the metropolis. It had at one time upwards of ninety churches and chapels, with colleges and monasteries attached to them. Being frequented on account of its fairs, and chosen as one of the staples for wool, it became at one period the seat of a very extensive commerce. After the Norman conquest, when London became the royal residence, the decline of Winchester commenced, and was accelerated by the removal of the wool trade; but above all by the dissolution of the monasteries, in the time of Henry VIII. It now owes its importance to its rank as an episcopal city, and a county town in which assizes are held alternately with Southampton. Its venerable cathedral (*fig.* 142.) has been the work of successive ages. It was founded under the Saxon kings, enlarged by William of Wykeham under Edward III., and completed by Bishop Fox, in the sixteenth century, when extensive additions were made to it in the highly ornamented and pointed English style; of which several of the specimens here preserved are reckoned the finest in the kingdom. The college, or rather school, founded by Bishop Wykeham is also a magnificent edifice, and is one of the four great classical schools to which the distinguished youth of England resort. Southampton now surpasses Winchester, and is a flourishing town, at the head of the bay called Southampton Water. It carries on a considerable trade with the south of Europe, and regular packets sail from it to Havre de Grace.

142

Winchester Cathedral.

Portsmouth is the grand arsenal for equipping the powerful navies of Great Britain. The harbour is formed by a considerable bay, with a commodious entrance, perfectly landlocked, and sheltered from every wind, affording secure anchorage all round; and capable from its dimensions of containing the whole British navy. The Isle of Wight forms at its eastern extremity the safe and magnificent road of Spithead, the principal rendezvous of the national fleets. The place has been strengthened by fortifications, till it has become the strongest and most finished fortress in the empire, and is considered absolutely impregnable. Portsmouth itself is situated on an island about fourteen miles in circumference, separated from the land only by a narrow channel. The suburb of Portsea, on the same island, begun only a century ago, has now outgrown the original town, and contains the principal dockyards. Here are carried on, upon a gigantic scale, all the operations subservient to building, equipping, and refitting ships, and supplying the navy. The sea-wall of the dockyards extends nearly three quarters of a mile, and encloses an area of one hundred acres: the forge, where anchors of huge dimensions are formed; the ropery, above a thousand feet long; the spacious dry docks; the endless range of warehouses; the gun-wharf, the armoury, are objects which astonish by their immensity.

Christchurch is noted for a fine ancient church; Beaulieu for the ruins of its venerable abbey; Andover, Basingstoke, and Romsey are considerable towns.

The Isle of Wight is about twenty-three miles in length, and thirteen in breadth; divided by a channel of only a few miles from the coast, on which are the bays of Portsmouth and Southampton. It is traversed by a ridge of chalky downs, in which are fed about forty thousand fine-woolled sheep of the Dorsetshire breed. On the north are luxuriant meadows supporting valuable breeds of horses and cattle; while on the south are fine arable plains, yielding grain much beyond the consumption of the island. The island is celebrated for its striking and peculiar scenery; the grand views of land and sea enjoyed from its high open downs; the deep and dark ravines of its southern shore, and the bold romantic cliffs which it there presents to the expanse of the English Channel. One of the most conspicuous features is the range of coast called the Undercliff. This district presents the appearance of a series of gigantic steps rising from the shore, to the summit of the great perpendicular wall. The *chines*, or chasms, with torrents bursting through them, are also characteristic features.

The western part of the Isle presents the rugged and pointed cliffs, called the Needles, and a range of magnificent white cliffs, rising perpendicularly to the height of 500 or 600 feet. These precipices are inhabited by gulls and puffins, the eggs of which are taken by the islander, suspended in a basket, which is fixed by a rope to the summit. The eastern shore presents the Culver Cliffs, a range of precipices which, in grandeur and ruggedness, are not surpassed by any other on the island.

The castle of Carisbrook is an ancient edifice, in which Charles I. was for some time imprisoned. The towns, Newport, Yarmouth, Cowes, and Ryde, are small.

Dorset consists of open chalky downs, fit only for sheep, which are here of a breed called the Southdown (*fig.* 143.), peculiarly fine both as to carcase and wool. The fleece is very short and fine; the mutton fine in the grain, and of an excellent flavour. The number of sheep is estimated at 800,000, producing 2,790,000 pounds of wool. The islands of Purbeck and Portland are valuable for the production of fine freestone.

143

Southdown Sheep.

Dorsetshire has no remarkable towns. Dorchester, the capital; Poole, with an excellent harbour; and Weymouth, finely situated for a bathing-place, are the principal.

Wiltshire is a fine county; the chalk hills here terminating, form the table-land, termed Salisbury Plain; a naked, undulating surface, which affords pasturage for sheep. The northern part of Wiltshire, watered by the Thames, is chiefly underwood and pasture and supports a valuable breed of cattle, from whose milk is made the excellent cheese bearing the name of the province. Wiltshire is a manufacturing county. The produce is of the finest description; superfine broadcloth, kerseymeres, and fancy articles; fine flannels at Salisbury, and at Wilton the carpets which bear its name.

Salisbury, the capital, is a handsome and well-built town. The streets are spacious and regular, crossing each other at right angles, and kept clean by streams of water, from the river Avon. The pride of Salisbury is its cathedral (*fig.* 144.) completed in 1258, which is considered the most elegant and finished Gothic structure in the kingdom. It has also the loftiest spire, rising to the height of four hundred and ten feet.

144

Salisbury Cathedral.

Wiltshire has a number of thriving little towns, in which fine woollen manufactures are carried on with activity: Devizes, Marlborough, Chippenham, Malmsbury, Warminster, Wilton, &c. Most of them are adorned with fine old churches.

Stonehenge (*fig.* 145.), in Salisbury Plain, a remarkable monument of antiquity, is supposed to be the remnant of a temple of the Druids. "It consists," says Mr. Sullivan, "of the remains of two circular and two oval ranges, having one common centre. The outer circle is one hundred and eight feet in diameter, and in its perfection consisted of thirty upright stones. The upright stones are from eighteen to twenty feet high, from six to seven broad, and about three feet thick; and being placed at the distance of three feet and a half from each other, are joined at the top by imposts or stones laid across. The inner circle is somewhat more than eight feet from the inside of the outward one, and consisted originally of forty smaller stones; of which only eleven are standing." In the interior of all are two oval ranges, supposed to be the principal part of the work, composing the cell or adytum. The stones that form it are stupendous, some of them measuring thirty feet in height. The whole number is computed to have been originally one hundred and forty.

145

Stonehenge.

No county is adorned with so many fine seats as Wiltshire. Wilton House contains the finest private collection of ancient sculpture in the kingdom. Corsham House and Longford Castle contain celebrated collections of pictures. Wardour Castle is distinguished for its grand terrace; Stourhead for the romantic beauty of the grounds: Longleat is a superb seat.

### SUBSECT. 2.—*The Eastern Counties.*

Under this title are comprehended the counties of Essex, Suffolk, Norfolk, Cambridge, Huntingdon, and Lincoln. The surface of this division is flat and unvaried. Its sluggish streams unite in the shallow marshy estuary of the Wash; a great proportion of its waters, however, never reach that receptacle; but, spreading and stagnating over the land, form the Fens, a tract which is not unproductive to the husbandman, but sends forth pestilential vapours, subjecting the inhabitants to attacks of fever and ague. The district contains wide portions of good arable land, which are well cultivated by skilful farmers with large capitals; and is noted for its breeds of cattle, and for the products of butter and cheese.

Essex, situated along the north of the Thames, is, perhaps, the richest of the English counties. It is diversified by gentle undulations, which do not interrupt the careful culture given to its rich alluvial soil. Its wheat, with that of Kent, is reckoned the best in England; but the districts near the metropolis are chiefly in pasture, or artificial grass, for supplying calves to the London market, or for fattening the cattle brought up from the north.

Chelmsford, the county town, is a small regularly built place, with a handsome town-hall. Colchester, the ancient Camelodunum, contains a strong castle, said to have been founded by the Romans. It is supported by a manufacture of baize, and by the oyster fishery. Harwich, a seaport with a deep and spacious harbour, is the place where the government packets, in time of peace, sail for Holland and Germany. Many villas have been erected in this county, in consequence of its vicinity to the metropolis.

Suffolk is bordered by only a small portion of eastern coast. The greater part of it is capable of good cultivation, and is carefully tilled. The county is almost purely agricultural, there being neither trade nor manufactures of any importance.

Among the towns of Suffolk, Ipswich is considerable, though its employment is confined to sending down the Orwell malt and grain, the produce of the county. Bury St. Edmund's, an ancient town, is rendered venerable by some fine old churches. Lowestoff, the most easterly point of England, is a noted seat of the herring fishery.

Norfolk, though inferior in fertility to the two counties now described, has, by its industry, rendered itself more flourishing than either. The soil generally is a light sand, scarcely fit, originally, for any thing but sheep; beneath, however, is a bed of rich soapy marl, which the farmers, with great labour, dig out, and spread over the ground. The light sandy loam thus formed is peculiarly favourable to the growth of barley, in which grain two-thirds of the country is laid out. Norfolk has extensive manufactures; producing various ornamental fabrics of silk and worsted. The ports carry on a considerable export of grain, and a spirited fishery.

Norwich is the finest city in the east of England. The chief industry of Norwich, however, consists in manufactures. Towards the end of the sixteenth century, a large colony of Flemings settled there, and established the fabric of woollens, which soon reached an unprecedented height. The light and ornamented forms became the staples; bombasines, crapes, fine camblets, and worsted damask. In its general structure, it has the defects of an old town, the streets being narrow and winding, though those recently built are in a more improved style. The cathedral (*fig.* 146.), founded in the eleventh century, ranks among the finest ecclesiastical edifices in the kingdom. Its style of architecture is the Saxon, of that broad and massive character which prevailed before the introduction of the pointed arch and the light ornamental style. The castle, placed in the centre, is more ancient still, since antiquaries refer it to the reign of Canute. Its style is Saxon; the keep remains entire.

146

Norwich Cathedral.

Yarmouth, by commerce and fishery, has attained a prosperity almost equal to that of Norwich. Situated at the mouth of the Yare, it is the chief channel by which the manufactures of that city are transported to foreign parts. A more important resource is its herring-fishery, which employs six thousand seamen, and produces annually upwards of fifty thousand barrels. Its quay, upwards of a mile long, is said to be second only to that of Seville. Yarmouth is also much frequented as a watering-place.

Lynn Regis is a flourishing seaport on the Wash, at the mouth of the Ouse, which, with its tributaries, brings down the agricultural produce of many rich counties.

*Seats.*—Norfolk contains several of the most superb seats in England. Holkham, built by Lord Leicester on a design of Inigo Jones, and particularly noted for a gallery room, is richly adorned with sculpture and paintings, and has also a very extensive library. Houghton is a magnificent seat.

Cambridgeshire presents a considerable variety of surface. Its northern district, called the Isle of Ely, intersected by the lower channels of the Ouse and the Nen, exists almost in an intermediate state between land and sea. Drainage, however, to a great extent has been effected, and many tracts have been converted into fine meadow, or made to yield large crops of oats, though the danger of inundation can never be wholly averted. The classic stream of the Cam or Granta, in descending to join the Ouse, waters a valley called "the Dairies," where some good cheeses and long rolls of excellent butter are prepared for the tables of the Cambridge students. The southern and western districts, encroached upon by the downs from the south, are only fit for the pasture of sheep.

The capital of Cambridge is the seat of one of the two great universities. There are thirteen colleges and four halls, in which the masters, tutors, and students, not only teach and are taught, but are lodged and boarded. Some of the largest of these endowments are stated to be for "poor and indigent scholars;" but are filled with the sons of opulent families, who cannot live there but at a very considerable expense. Yet the resort continues to increase, and the existing colleges are insufficient to contain the applicants, who must often wait several years previously to admission. These colleges are large, and generally fine and handsome buildings; yet they do not produce the same noble and imposing effect as those in the sister university. There are, however, two structures such as its rival cannot match. The first of these is the chapel of King's College, (*fig.* 147.), built between the reigns of Henry VI. and Henry VIII. Its interior has been called matchless; the roof is of the most perfect workmanship, and its support without pillars has been viewed as an architectural mystery. But the most striking characteristic is the prodigious blaze of painted glass, on each side, from twelve brilliantly tinted windows fifty feet high, giving to the fabric the appearance of being walled with painted glass. The other is Trinity College, particularly admired for its library, two hundred feet long, designed by Sir Christopher Wren, and perhaps the most elegant library-room in the kingdom. The hall is also the largest in Cambridge; and the roof is ornamented with fine specimens of old wood-work. Its chapel is marked by a beautiful simplicity, and contains Roubiliac's statue of Sir Isaac Newton, supposed the best resemblance that exists of that great man.

147

King's College Chapel.

The principal library contains 100,000 volumes, many of which are scarce and valuable. Trinity college, in its ornamental hall, has 40,000. Earl Fitzwilliam, from his seat near Richmond, presented lately a handsome library, some fine pictures, and a large collection of engravings. The botanic garden is inferior to none in the kingdom, except those of Kew and Liverpool. The collection of valuable manuscripts and antiquities is likewise extensive. Since the university was adorned by the immortal name of Newton, mathematics and natural philosophy have been the ruling pursuits; and, notwithstanding the lustre reflected on it by Milton, as well as by Bentley and Porson, it has left to Oxford the foremost place in classical knowledge.

At Newmarket, *horse-racing* has chosen its most favourite ground. This town lies amid bleak hills, that have, however, a sufficient extent of level heath to make the finest course in the kingdom. It consists of one long street, chiefly filled with inns and coffee-houses for the reception of the sporting world, who crowd thither in the appropriate seasons, which are April, July, and October. The bustle is then immense. "Trains of horses," says Dr. Spiker, "were led up and down the streets. Excellent equipages, gigs, curricles, landaus, flew past us and past each other with the swiftness of an arrow. Horses were prancing about with their riders; jockeys were carrying bridles to and fro: in short, all was life and bustle." The course is covered with turf, whence the pursuit of horse-racing itself is usually designated *the turf*. Close to the goal is drawn on rollers a small wooden house, in which sits the *judge*, usually an experienced groom, who decides which is the winner. The stand is an open raised house for ladies and other curious spectators; but men of real business crowd round the betting post, immediately behind the judge, where they remain closely wedged together, "and nothing is heard but the continual cry of twenty, thirty, forty, two hundred pounds on such a horse."

The small city of Ely rises like an island amidst the surrounding fens, and displays a magnificent cathedral. Wisbeach, a thriving town on a navigable branch of the Ouse, combines a prosperous trade with some spirit of literary enquiry.

Huntingdonshire lies to the eastward of Cambridge; the two are governed by the same sheriff, chosen alternately in each. Huntingdon is entirely agricultural; the pastures are peculiarly rich, and adapt it for producing the famous Stilton cheese. Huntingdon, the county town, though small, has an antique and respectable appearance. St. Ives is a large village on the Ouse.

Lincolnshire occupies the eastern coast from the Wash to the Humber. The southern territory, called, from that circumstance, "Holland," comprises more than half of the Bedford level, or fen country, and is naturally an almost continuous swamp; but a great extent of it has now been drained, and produces fine pasture land, and excellent crops of oats. The rearing of live stock forms the chief occupation; and Lincoln has breeds of every description that are held in high estimation. The sheep, which amount to upwards of 2,000,000, produce the long wool, which, from the length of its staple, is chiefly fitted for worsted, baize, and other fabrics. Rabbits, almost innumerable, are bred in the upper districts; and the unreclaimed fens, during the wet season, swarm with teal, ducks, geese, and aquatic game of every form and description, with which London and many other parts of England are chiefly supplied from this county. Manufactures have entirely deserted it; even its own wool, since the late inventions in machinery, is no longer spun or carded within itself. The Trent, during all its course through this county, is navigable for large vessels, and artificial channels unite its streams, particularly the Foss Dyke, between the Witham and the Trent. Foreign commerce, however, is much limited by the increasing sand-banks, by which the coasts and harbours are obstructed.

The city of Lincoln was, during the middle ages, one of the most conspicuous and splendid capitals of England. The cathedral (*fig.* 148.) still holds the first rank among religious edifices. From a distance its three towers appear conspicuous; two of them 180, and one 300, feet high, and ornamented with various pillars and tracery; and as the structure stands on a hill, in the midst of a vast surrounding flat, it has the most commanding site in the county. When plundered by Henry VIII., it was found to contain an extraordinary treasure, in gold and silver, pearls, diamonds, and other precious stones. Lincoln, supported only by its county trade, and by the remaining opulence of the cathedral, now holds a moderate rank among provincial towns. Its fifty churches are reduced to eleven; and the fragments of the others are dispersed throughout the town, many ordinary houses being adorned with Gothic arches, doorways, and windows.

148

Lincoln Cathedral.

Boston, on the Witham, carries on the trade of Holland, or southern Lincolnshire. It exports the grain, and affords a great market for cattle; and has thus doubled its population. A fine Gothic church attests the early prosperity of Boston.

Subsect. 3.—*Central Counties.*

Under this term we comprehend that part of the interior which is bounded on the south and south-west by the two divisions already described; on the north and north-west by Yorkshire and Lancashire; and on the west by the counties of Salop, Worcester, and Gloucester.

In a description of this portion of the country, London claims a distinct and separate notice. As the metropolis of the united kingdom, it is the seat of legislation, jurisprudence, and government; the principal residence of the sovereign, at which affairs of state are transacted, and relations maintained with foreign courts; the centre of all important operations whether of commerce or finance, and of correspondence with every quarter of the globe. London, in its comprehensive sense, includes the city and liberties of London, the city of Westminster and its liberties, the borough of Southwark, and the parishes and precincts contiguous to those three component parts of the metropolis. Its extent, from Poplar in the east to Belgrave-square in the west, is nearly eight miles; its breadth, from Islington in the north to Walworth in the south, exceeds five miles. The circumference, allowing for inequalities, is computed at thirty miles. The buildings, streets, squares, and other spaces, including that taken up by the river Thames, winding from the eastern to the western extremity, about seven miles on an average breadth of a quarter of a mile, occupy an area of eighteen square miles.

By a more convenient topographical arrangement, London has been divided into six grand portions: 1st, the City, which may be termed the central division; 2d, the western division, including Westminster; 3d, the north-west division, including the district north of Oxford-street and west of Tottenham-court-road,—these two last mentioned divisions constitute the west-end of the town; 4th, the northern division, comprising the whole district north of Holborn and the City from Tottenham-court-road on the west to Shoreditch and Kingsland-road on the east, including St. Pancras, Somers-town, Pentonville, Islington, Hoxton, and Kingsland; 5th, the eastern division, including the whole district east of the city and of Shoreditch; 6th, the southern division, comprising the borough of Southwark, and the mass of buildings extending from Rotherhithe to Vauxhall, and ranging southward for more than two miles. The divisions north and south of the Thames communicate by five bridges,—London Bridge, Southwark Bridge, Blackfriars, Waterloo, and Westminster bridges. The port of London extends from London Bridge to Deptford, a distance of about four miles, with an average breadth of from four hundred to five hundred yards. Its divisions are the Upper, Middle, and Lower Pools, and the space between Limehouse and Deptford. Connected with it are certain spacious docks, which will be hereafter noticed.

The population of London, according to the returns in 1831 of the census in 1830, is thus stated:—

| | Persons |
|---|---|
| City of London within the walls | 57,695 |
| ——— without the walls (including the Inns of Court) | 67,878 |
| Borough of Southwark | 91,501 |
| City of Westminster | 202,080 |
| Parishes within the bills of mortality | 761,348 |
| Adjacent parishes not within the bills | 293,567 |
| Total | 1,474,069 |

The north division of London, as viewed from the most central and elevated point, rises gently from the Thames, and extends to the foot of a range of hills on which are situated the villages of Hampstead and Highgate. On the east and west are fertile plains extending at least twenty miles, and watered by the winding and gently flowing Thames. On the south, the distant view is bounded by the high grounds of Richmond, Wimbledon, Epsom, Norwood, and Blackheath, terminating in the horizon by Leith Hill, Boxhill, and the Reigate and Wrotham Hills. Shooter's Hill is a conspicuous object to the eastward; and, in a more northerly direction, parts of Epping Forest and other wooded uplands of Essex.

So early as the reign of Nero, London had become a place of considerable traffic, as appears from Tacitus, the earliest of the Roman historians who mentions it by name. The Romans fortified it with a wall, and made it one of their principal stations. At the beginning of the third century, it is represented as a great and wealthy city, and considered to be the metropolis of Britain. In the end of the sixth century, it became the capital of the East Saxons, whose king, Sebert, is reputed the founder of the cathedral church dedicated to Saint Paul, and of the abbey and abbey church of Westminster. After the union of the seven kingdoms, Egbert, in 833, held here his first *wittenagemote*, or council: but London was not constituted the capital of England until its recovery from the Danes by Alfred. William of Normandy, whose interest it was to conciliate the citizens, though he built the fortress called the Tower, to keep them in awe, confirmed the privileges and immunities which they had enjoyed under Edward the Confessor. Notwithstanding several visitations of fire and pestilence, London continued to increase, especially after the accession of the Tudors, when the overthrow of feudal vassalage, and the more frequent resort to the capital, caused an augmentation so rapid as to alarm the government. The dissolution of monasteries, of which London contained so large a proportion, accelerated this increase, while it gave an impulse to industry and commerce. In the reign of Elizabeth, the influx of strangers driven from the Netherlands, by the persecutions of the Duke of Alva, heightened the alarm, and the queen was even induced to issue the absurd decree that no more dwelling-houses should be built: a prohibition which did not retard the growth of the city. In 1636, the refinements of Paris and Madrid were emulated in London by the introduction of hackney coaches and sedan chairs.

The reign of Charles II. includes the most memorable epoch in the history of London. In 1665, a plague swept away 100,000 persons. In September, 1666, broke out that great and awful fire which destroyed 400 streets, 13,000 houses, and 89 churches. For the rebuilding of the city, an admirable plan was presented by Sir Christopher Wren, the architect: the difficulty of reconciling conflicting interests, allowed it to be but very partially adopted. He rebuilt the cathedral of St. Paul and most of the parish churches in the Grecian style, and the front of Guildhall in the original Gothic. Instead of wood and plaster, the chief materials of the former city, the new buildings were of brick, in the substantial though heavy style then in vogue. There were no flagged footpaths; the streets were ill-paved: and as there was no system of drainage by sewers, and no distribution of pure water by pipes, they were in some places far from endurable. The city, however, gained by the change, though with the sacrifice of many interesting memorials of its ancient state, and of its most glorious times.

Westminster, though founded in the time of the Saxons, and chosen at an early period as a royal residence, did not at first keep pace with London. The abbey and its church, founded by Sebert, were rebuilt by the architects who reared so many splendid fabrics of Gothic masonry in the reigns of Henry III. and Edward I. The celebrated hall was built by William Rufus in 1097 and 1098, and it underwent a thorough repair in that of Richard II. On the dissolution of monasteries, Henry VIII. converted this religious establishment into a college, and afterwards into a bishopric. Westminster thus became a city, and has ever since retained that rank by courtesy, though it never had but one bishop, having been transferred by Edward VI. to the see of Norwich.

The city of Westminster is comprised in the united parishes of St. Margaret and St. John; the liberties include seven other parishes, St. Martin's in the Fields, St. James's, St. Ann's, St. Clement Danes, St. Mary's le Strand, St. George's Hanover Square, and St. Paul's Covent Garden, with the precinct of the Savoy and that of St. Martin's le Grand. Several of the parishes westward of Temple Bar had each its church and contiguous village, communicating with each other by roads and footpaths. The Strand was originally a high road connecting London with Westminster by the village of Charing. After the Restoration, the west end of the town rapidly increased; and its inhabitants, affecting superior refinement of manners, claimed to be considered as a distinct class of beings from the industrious merchants east of Temple Bar. By degrees, as the vacant ground was built upon, the two cities and their suburbs were united; and at length the distant villages of Mary-le-bone and St. Pancras became integral parts of the metropolis. A splendid quarter, now occupied by the most fashionable part of the community, has been built to the west of St. James's Park and the new palace. The villages surrounding London, formerly at some distance,-

on the east, Stepney and Limehouse; on the south, Peckham, Camberwell, Brixton, Clapham; on the west, Brompton and Knightsbridge; on the north, Hackney, Hoxton, Islington, Highgate and Hampstead,—being now joined to the metropolis by continued ranges of streets, may be considered as integral portions of it. The population within a radius of eight miles from St. Paul's, which is all virtually London, does not fall short of 1,800,000.

The growth of London, as a port, was at first by no means rapid. In 1832, besides boats and other craft not registered, there belonged to the port of London 2669 ships, of the burthen of 565,174 tons; manned by 32,786 men and boys. In the same year, the gross customs duty collected in the port of London amounted to 9,434,854*l.* The port of London has already been described as extending from London Bridge to Deptford, a distance of four miles; the average breadth being fully a quarter of a mile. Even these limits were far from affording adequate accommodation to the shipping; and the example of improvement exhibited by Liverpool at length roused the merchants of London to form companies for constructing docks, with commodious quays and warehouses. The *West India Docks*, stretching across the isthmus forming the Isle of Dogs to the Middlesex side of the river, were opened in 1802. They consisted originally of an import and export dock, the former containing about 30 and the latter about 25 acres of water, exclusive of basins. To these have recently been added the south dock, formerly the City Canal. The warehouses at the West India Docks are of vast extent, and are, in all respects, most commodious. The *London Docks*, also of very great extent, are situated at Wapping. The tobacco warehouse belonging to them is the largest and finest building of its kind in the world. It covers a space of near 5 acres! The vaults underneath the ground are 18¼ acres in extent, and have stowage for 66,000 pipes of wine! There are also the *St. Katharine's Docks*, adjoining the Tower; the *East India Docks*, at Blackwell; and the *Commercial Docks*, on the Surrey side of the river.

Southwark, the third great portion of the metropolis, (more commonly called the *Borough*, and as such returning two members to parliament,) is situated on the south bank of the Thames. The Borough was governed by its own bailiffs until Edward VI. granted Southwark to the city of London for a sum of money; after which it became one of the city wards by the name of Bridge Ward Without. It is much frequented by agriculturists from Kent, Surrey, and Sussex; and is the principal hop-market in the kingdom. Numerous streets in every direction connect it with the surrounding villages; and by the five magnificent bridges it communicates with every quarter of London and Westminster.

London, is well built, well paved, well lighted, and abundantly supplied with water. Foreigners who visit it for the first time soon discover that utility, not ornament, is the main characteristic of the town, and that business, not amusement, occupies the minds of its inhabitants. The main streets are spacious; and all the streets have the advantage of flagged foot-pavements on each side. The houses are of brick; and though in the most populous streets discoloured by smoke, have by no means a gloomy appearance. The charm of London, as a great city, is its variety. Those who dislike the narrow streets of the city, shady in summer, and sheltered from cold winds in winter, may delight in the spacious streets and squares of the west end; those who desire to contemplate what Dr. Johnson called "the full tide of human existence," may visit Cheapside, Fleet Street, or the Strand: Bond Street is the resort of gaiety and fashion; and Regent Street, for architectural effect, is one of the grandest streets in Europe. Great improvements have been made on the north side of the Strand from Charing Cross to Burleigh Street, by taking down an immense mass of small and old houses, partly in narrow streets and courts, and erecting others of large dimensions and forming wide and handsome streets. Here also has been erected the elegant and commodious structure of Hungerford Market. Another improvement is that of opening a line northward from Bridge Street, Blackfriars, through the site of Fleet Market and across Clerkenwell, to Islington: it is intended that a parallel line should extend from Waterloo Bridge across the Strand, past the portico of Covent Garden Theatre, and into the northern district of the metropolis.

149

St. Paul's.

St. Paul's Cathedral (*fig.* 149.), the masterpiece of Sir Christopher Wren, is the finest specimen of modern architecture in the kingdom, and, after St. Peter's at Rome, may rank as the finest ecclesiastical structure in Christendom; but it is so surrounded with buildings that the beauty of its exterior cannot be appreciated. The style, which is Grecian, unites grandeur of design with justness of proportion. The interior of St. Paul's is too bare of ornament; but the defect is partly supplied by marble monuments of various degrees of merit.

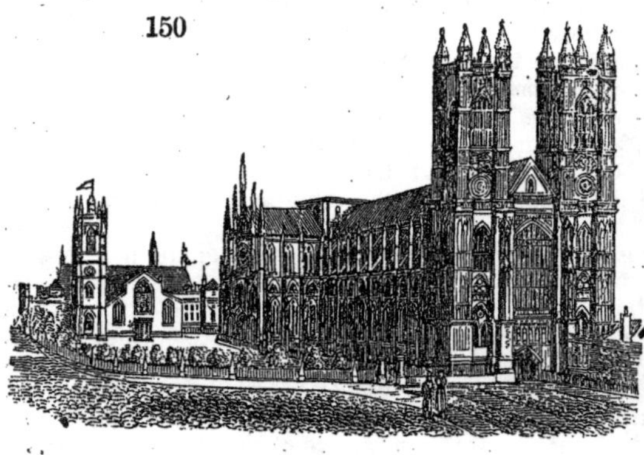
150
Westminster Abbey.

Westminster Abbey (*fig.* 150.) is a noble specimen of Gothic architecture. The interior is grand in design and rich in detail, and the interest which it excites is enhanced by the numerous monuments of kings, warriors, statesmen, philosophers, and poets, which it encloses. The chapel built at the western extremity by Henry VII. in honour of the blessed Virgin, is in the richest style of the later Gothic, and its exterior has been skilfully renovated.

Among the parish churches of the metropolis, that of St. Stephen's, Walbrook, is distinguished for the fine proportions and finished elegance of its interior. The stately portico of St. Martin's, Charing Cross, excites universal admiration; next to which may rank that of the new church of St. Pancras; the steeple of which is constructed on the model of the Temple of the Winds at Athens. The other public buildings are too numerous to be described, and a bare mention of them would give little satisfaction. The principal inns of court, and their subsidiary inns, are remarkable rather for plainness than magnificence of architecture. The pile called Somerset House (*fig.* 151.) would have a grand effect if its eastern wing were completed; and this desideratum is partly supplied by the buildings assigned to "King's College, London." The Banqueting House at Whitehall is a memorial of the fine taste of Inigo Jones; and its ceiling is decorated with an allegorical painting from the pencil of Rubens, which is still exposed to view, though the apartment has been converted into a chapel. Westminster Hall, of which the portal has been rebuilt in the original style, is reputed the longest hall in Europe unsupported by pillars. It is 276 feet long by 76 broad. Within it, on coronation festivals, 10,000 persons have dined. On its south side are entrances to the new law courts, the King's Bench Common Pleas, Exchequer and Chancery, with an additional court for the vice-chancellor. The House of Peers is a spacious and lofty chamber, decorated with tapestry representing the defeat of the Spanish armada. The subordinate apartments and passages are of recent construction and of a dignified elegance. The House of Commons, originally a chapel dedicated to St. Stephen, retains, perhaps, too much of that character in its front and side galleries, the seats rising on either hand beneath them, and the speaker's chair exactly in the place where a pulpit might have stood. The house was altered and enlarged, to admit the accession of members consequent on the union with Ireland.* The Bank of England, a building of great extent; the Royal Exchange; the East India House, in Leadenhall street; the Tower, which has still an arsenal and a garrison, being the depository of the regalia of the United Kingdom; the Trinity House, and the New Mint, both situated on Tower Hill; the new Post Office, in St. Martin le Grand; the new Palace in St. James's Park, &c. deserve mention.

151
Somerset House.

152
The Monument.

The Monument (*fig.* 152.) is one of the most conspicuous ornaments of the metropolis. The pedestal is 42 feet, the shaft of the column 120 feet, the cone at the top with the blazing urn of gilt brass 40 feet, making the total height of the monument 202 feet. It was erected by Sir Christopher Wren, to commemorate the fire of London, in 1666.

* The Parliament Houses were burnt down in 1834.

The bridges of London attract attention by their beauty and utility. Until the year 1740, the only one existing was *London Bridge*, built in the twelfth century, with arches so narrow, unequal, and ill-placed, as to form a sort of breakwater, occasioning a *rapid* or *fall* of the stream, highly dangerous to boats and barges. The new London Bridge (*fig.* 153.) com-

153

New London Bridge.

menced in 1824, and opened in 1831, has taken its place. The bridge consists of five semi-elliptical arches; the centre arch 152 feet span, with a rise above high water mark of 29 feet 6 inches; the two next the centre arch, 140 feet span, rise 27 feet 6 inches; the two abutment arches, 130 feet span, rise 24 feet 6 inches. The length of the bridge from the extremities of the abutment is 928 feet, within the abutments, 782 feet. The roadway is 53 feet between the parapets; of this width, the footways occupy 9 feet each, and the carriage-way 35 feet. Southwark Bridge leads from Queenhithe to Bankside, Southwark. Of its three arches of cast iron, the central one is 240 feet span; the others 210 feet each. The piers and abutments are of stone, the rest of the work iron: this is the most stupendous bridge of these materials in the world. Blackfriars Bridge, built between the years 1760 and 1769, has 8 piers and 9 elliptical arches; length 995 feet. Waterloo Bridge (*fig.* 154.), of granite,

154

Waterloo Bridge.

has nine arches, each 120 feet span; the piers are 20 feet thick. Westminster Bridge has fourteen piers supporting thirteen large and two small arches. The width of the middle arch is 76 feet; that of the two next, 72, that of the last, 52. Waterloo Bridge is the finest piece of masonry in Europe: the expense exceeded 1,000,000*l*. These immense works, with the exception of London Bridge, have all been accomplished by associations of private individuals.

The municipal institutions of London have received from time such modifications as were requisite to improve them. The city is divided into twenty-five wards, the Borough, as Bridge Ward Without, making the twenty-sixth. Each has for its magistrate an alderman chosen for life: and those persons collectively form the Court of Aldermen. The chief magistrate, styled Lord Mayor, is elected annually, from the Court of Aldermen, by the great body of freemen called the Livery. The Common Council is an elective body representing the several wards.—These public bodies form a sort of parliament, the court of aldermen ranking as peers, that of common council as the commons. The military force of the city formerly consisted of the Train Bands; but under an act passed in 1794, two regiments of militia are raised by ballot, each consisting of 2200 men. No troops can enter the city, nor can its own militia depart from it, without permission of the lord mayor. His power is very great; and though his office be elective, his authority does not cease on the demise or abdication of the king, as that of the commission officers does: and in such cases the Lord Mayor of London is said to be the principal officer of the kingdom. There are two sheriffs, one for London and one for Middlesex; but they make but one officer; and if one of them dies, the office is at an end until a successor to him is chosen. The next officers in rank are, the Recorder, the Chamberlain, and the Common Sergeant.

The police of the metropolis has not been brought to a very high degree of efficiency, but is continually undergoing improvements. There are eleven offices: the Mansion House; the Guildhall; Bow Street; Queen Square, Westminster; Marlborough Street, High Street, Mary-le-bone; Hatton Garden; Worship Street; Lambeth Street, in Whitechapel; High Street, Shadwell; Union Street, Southwark; and Wapping New Stairs, for offences connected with the shipping and port. The Bow Street Police Office is wholly under the direction and management of the Secretary of State for the Home Department. All the magistrates belonging to it are in the commission of the peace for the counties of Middlesex, Surrey, Kent, and Essex, this being the chief police office of England. Subject to its authority is the body of foot and horse patrole by which the roads within ten miles of the metropolis are watched and guarded during a considerable part of the night. In another department of police a most important change has been effected by substituting for the nightly watch appointed by different parishes without concert or co-operation, a CONSTABULARY POLICE FORCE, regularly organized, and subject to officers appointed by the Home Secretary of State. The men are maintained by rates levied on the different parishes, and are on duty night and day, in successive divisions, relieving each other like gendarmes.

The gaols and prisons cannot be passed without notice. The King's Bench prison, in Southwark, is under the particular authority of the Court of King's Bench. The liberties, or *rules*, comprehend an area three miles in circumference, within any part of which debtors may reside on paying certain fees. The Fleet Prison, chiefly for debtors, is situated on the east side of Farringdon Street. Whitecross-street prison was erected in 1817, for the reception of such debtors as were liable to be confined in the city gaols of Newgate and the Compter. Newgate, a place of confinement for prisoners before and after trial, has been placed under new regulations through the efforts of benevolent persons anxious to render it a place of reform. Bridewell, Blackfriars, though a prison, is usually ranked among the hospitals. The Middlesex House of Correction, in Coldbath Fields, has long been the terror of delinquents, through the double punishment of incarceration and hard labour. The Penitentiary at Milbank is destined for the reception of convicts selected from those sentenced to transportation or to confinement on board the hulks for a certain term of years. They are confined here to hard labour for a shorter term, part of which is remitted if they behave well. Tothill-fields Bridewell is a large pile of building, finished in 1833. A new House of Correction has been erected at Brixton, in Surrey.

The charitable institutions of London would require a volume for their description. Chelsea and Greenwich hospitals are asylums provided by national gratitude to support the aged or infirm who have devoted their best days to the service of their country by land and sea. St. Bartholomew's and St. Thomas's hospitals are assigned to the maimed and diseased, Bridewell Hospital to the correction of the idle, and Christ's hospital to the support and education of the young and helpless. For the cure of diseases, and for the relief of accidental injuries, there are various institutions; such are the London, Middlesex, St. George's, and Westminster hospitals; St. Bartholomew's, St. Thomas's, and Guy's, are also celebrated as schools of surgery; the hospitals of Bethlehem and St. Luke's are appropriated to insane patients: there are sixteen medical charities for particular purposes, as the Ophthalmic Institution, the Small-pox Hospital, the Vaccine Society, &c.; fourteen lying-in hospitals and charities; schools for the indigent blind, and for the deaf and dumb; the Philanthropic and Humane Societies, the Refuge for the Destitute, the Foundling Hospital, the Magdalen Asylum, the Female Penitentiary, &c. To the class of charitable foundations belong also the alms-houses of the various city companies.

The most distinguished schools of the metropolis are, Christ's Hospital, the Charter-house, Westminster, St. Paul's, and Merchant Tailor's schools. For the acquisition of the higher branches of knowledge, an important provision has been made in the establishment of the London University, and in that of the institution called King's College, London.

Of the scientific and literary associations of the metropolis, the most considerable are the Royal Society, the Society of Antiquaries, the Society for the Encouragement of Arts and Manufactures, the Royal Institution for facilitating the introduction of useful Inventions and Improvements, the London, and the Russel Institutions. The College of Physicians, and the Royal College of Surgeons, decide on the admission of members to practise in each of those professions. For the cultivation of sciences connected with them, four eminent societies exist, and lectures are established at various theatres of anatomy and hospitals. Of institutions for particular branches of knowledge, the more eminent are the Linnean, the Geological, the Horticultural, the Geographical, and the Zoological societies. As a national repository of literature, of antiquities, and of objects belonging to natural history, the British Museum, elsewhere described, is daily rising in public estimation.

London is the principal literary emporium of the kingdom. Almost all books of import ance are there printed and published; and thence distributed over the kingdom; forming a considerable branch of commerce. The annual value sold is estimated at from 1,000,000*l.* to 2,000,000*l.* sterling. Being also the centre of intelligence relative to public affairs, the metropolis gives circulation to a prodigious number of newspapers and periodical journals. Some of the newspapers circulate upwards of 8000 a day; and by the profit derived from such extensive sale, and from advertisements, they are enabled to maintain complete and costly establishments for obtaining early political intelligence, and for reporting trials and parliamentary proceedings. The number of single papers, published annually in London, as calculated from the stamp returns, exceeds 16,000,000.

The manufactures of the metropolis are too miscellaneous to be particularised; indeed, London may be called a commercial rather than a manufacturing city. The most considerable is the Spitalfields silk manufacture, which, however, has for years remained stationary, while that of other parts of the kingdom has been rapidly extending. In household furniture the artisans of London take the lead both in the design or fashion of the articles, and in the excellence of their construction. The same may be said of coaches, carriages, and harness, of watches, of gold and silver plate, and of jewellery. Of articles of consumption, the peculiar product of London is *porter*. In 1823–4, the quantity brewed was 1,168,000 barrels, including a comparatively small quantity of ale; and almost the whole of which was produced by eleven great establishments. The distilleries of British spirits are very extensive.

The foreign trade of London has, since the peace, continued nearly stationary. The vicinity of Liverpool to the manufacturing districts, and her more easy and frequent intercourse with Ireland, give her considerable advantages. But, on the other hand, the vast population of London and of the basin of the Thames, her proximity to the Continent, the immense wealth and connexions of her merchants, will most probably suffice to ensure her predominance. The charges on vessels frequenting the Thames, though within these few years very heavy, are now extremely moderate.

The inland trade of London is very extensive, as appears from the number of arrivals by all the great roads of the metropolis, and by the Regent's Canal, extending from the Thames to the basin at Paddington, a sort of internal port, communicating with the principal canals of the kingdom. Sixty-four mail-coaches and a great number of steam-packets maintain a constant communication between the London General Post-Office and the cities and towns in Great Britain and Ireland. The regulated speed of the mails is eight miles an hour, including stoppages.

London is the great money market of the empire. The Bank of England, founded i 1694, has become the greatest bank of circulation and deposit in Europe. Its usual issue amounts to about 20,000,000*l.* sterling; it advances about 10,000,000*l.* sterling to government, and discounts bills to the value of about 3,000,000*l.* Though some of its privileges are curtailed by the late act, this is compensated by the regulation which makes its notes a legal tender. The Stock Exchange is the place where purchases and sales are effected by brokers, at a commission of one-eighth per cent. on the amount of stock purchased or sold. The establishment consists of a certain number of brokers, about thirteen hundred, elected annually by ballot, and bound in a certain sum to the observance of certain regulations, which are superintended and enforced by a committee. None but members are admitted on the stock exchange; and no stock-broker can, by the regulations, become a dealer, and subject himself to the operation of the bankrupt laws. If he becomes a bankrupt, he is designated a scrivener. The property bought and sold in this market, between the hours of ten and four, is sometimes enormous. The Insurance Companies are about twenty in number, of which only three are incorporated by charter. Of other joint-stock companies, for purposes immediately connected with London, the principal are the Water and Gas Light Companies.

As the seat of legislation and jurisprudence, London is necessarily the resort of the principal persons in the kingdom during the session of parliament, which usually continues from Christmas to midsummer; and as that period includes three of the four law terms, the afflux of strangers is increased by those who are interested in any proceedings before the courts.

The town mansions of the nobility and gentry are not so remarkable as their country residences for architectural beauty; but some of them are celebrated for their treasures of literature or art. The grounds of St. James's Park, Hyde Park, and Kensington Gardens, emphatically called the lungs of London, and the fine enclosure of the Regent's Park, are destined for the recreation of the public.

Middlesex may be regarded as the dairy and garden of London. Its soil is mostly a poor gravel; but, by the application of manure, it is fitted for kitchen gardens to the extent of nearly three thousand acres; the same extent of fruit gardens, and about half that extent of nurseries, whence the greater part of England is supplied with choice plants and exotics. But the largest portion of Middlesex is in grass, partly for the support of 10,000 cows, which supply London with milk, and partly for furnishing it with hay, that of Middlesex being said to be made in a superior manner to any other in the kingdom. Great profits have been derived from that species of clay which is convertible into brick. Large tracts have yielded 4000*l*. an acre; and after this clayey substance has been pared off, the soil has been easily restored, by manure, to the uses of agriculture.

Hampton Court (*fig*. 155.), built by Cardinal Wolsey, and enlarged by Sir Christopher Wren, forms one of the largest of the English palaces. Here are many fine pictures, among which are seven of the cartoons of Raphael, regarded as the masterpieces of that renowned painter. Bushy Park, the seat of William IV. while Duke of Clarence, is surrounded with magnificent woods. Chiswick, the villa of the Duke of Devonshire, and Osterley Park, both in this vicinity, contain fine paintings. Syon House is the seat of the Duke of Northumberland. But the chief ornaments of Middlesex are the villas of the wealthy citizens of London. At Twickenham, barbarous hands have demolished Pope's villa. Strawberry Hill is a light fantastic fabric, built by Horace Walpole. The villas which cover the hills of Hampstead and Highgate command beautiful prospects.

155

Hampton Court.

Hertford, Bedford, Buckingham, Oxford, Northampton, Leicester, consist generally of a vast plain, varied by gentle undulations; the air is healthy and pure; the agriculturists are careful and laborious. The horses and black cattle of Leicestershire are famous throughout the kingdom. Bedford and Berks have some fabrics of shawls, straw hats, and bone lace. Silk and woollen hosiery have found their way into Leicester and Oxford shires, and Coventry has for centuries been renowned for its silk manufacture.

Oxford justly claims the first rank among the midland cities. Its university, the most richly endowed in Europe, and the nursery of so many great men; the numerous and extensive edifices connected with it, arranged in such a manner as to produce a truly noble effect, render it one of the most interesting places in England. The visiter, as he passes along either of the two main streets (*fig*. 156.), beholds at every step some antique and majestic structure; even the houses of private individuals, presenting the aspect of ornamented cottages rising one above the other, have a better effect than the usual mechanical lines of street. This beautiful city is supported almost entirely by the university, which is of great antiquity, and the principal buildings which now ornament it were built between the times of Henry VI. and Elizabeth. Oxford, in the reign of Charles I., was a place of considerable political importance; parliaments were summoned to meet there, and the king maintained it long as his last strong-hold. It has nineteen colleges and four halls, in which reside above three thousand persons, of whom about a third are maintained out of the funds of the colleges; and many, under the character of masters, fellows, and other functionaries, enjoy liberal incomes.

156

High Street, Oxford.

The Bodleian Library is the most extensive in England, after that of the British Museum. In the spacious quadrangle which contains this library are also the public schools; a large gallery of portraits having reference to the university; the Arundel marbles, and the Pomfret statues, which, though much mutilated, present some fine specimens of ancient sculpture. The Radcliffe Library is the finest library room in Oxford; but it labours under a deficiency of books. Christ-church is an ample and venerable edifice, adorned with some fine old painted glass. In an adjoining apartment is the collection of pictures bequeathed by General Guise, which contains some specimens of unquestioned excellence. New College chapel attracts admiration by its fine series of paintings on glass, executed by Jervis after the designs of Sir Joshua Reynolds. All-Souls College, Magdalen College, and Queen's College, display architectural beauties of no common order.

Woodstock has a gay aspect; to the interesting features in English history and romance it adds the solid benefit of a large manufacture of leather gloves. Buckingham and Daventry are small antique towns. Newport Pagnell, in Bucks, forms a sort of centre of the lace trade. Bedford carries on some manufactures of this description; and being situated in a rich valley, watered by the Ouse, has a considerable stir in transmitting its produce. The industry of Dunstable is attested by the straw hats which bear its name. Hertford is a small provincial capital, chiefly remarkable for the college which the East India Company have founded, for the education of the civil servants whom they send abroad: St. Alban's is venerable for its antiquity, and its cathedral. Northampton, a place of considerable name in English history, a well-built town on the Nen, with a market-place which has been reckoned the finest in the kingdom, has a manufactory of boots and shoes for exportation, and of lace. It is a great centre of the inland travelling between London and the north; and the trade in horses has always been carried on in great fairs at this place. Leicester is a still more important provincial capital. It is a place of note in English history, and attests its ancient importance by some fine old churches; but it had fallen into considerable decay, till it was revived by the prosperity of the surrounding country, chiefly in consequence of the introduction of new breeds of stock into fine pastures. Leicester has also a large fabric of woollen stockings, in which it is only excelled by Nottingham, and which, under favourable circumstances, employs seven or eight thousand persons. Oakham, the capital of Rutlandshire, is a very small town.

The seats of this extensive district, though not so thickly planted as in the southern, are yet numerous. Foremost stands Blenheim (*fig.* 157.) that proud monument of a nation's gratitude to its long unrivalled hero. Its exterior displays that minuteness of detail and general heaviness, which characterise the designs of Vanbrugh: some of the apartments, however, are of almost unequalled grandeur; particularly the great hall, fifty-three feet by forty-four, and sixty high; and the library, one hundred and eighty feet by forty-three. The woods, also, the lake, and the general disposition of the grounds, are greatly admired. The gallery of pictures is one of the very finest in the kingdom, containing some of the best works of Rubens, Vandyke, and Titian. Stowe, the seat of the Duke of Buckingham, is celebrated as the most elaborate and splendid example of the species of gardening called classical, in which an attempt is made to present nature herself in an ornamented form. Her own proper ornaments, of wood, water, hill and plain, are heightened by the introduction of temples, ruins, statues, inscriptions, and other objects calculated to excite lofty and poetical ideas. Modern taste rejects many of these accessories, as breaking in upon the idea of simple nature, to which it seeks to make the nearest possible approach; yet, a space of four hundred acres, filled with groves, temples, and meandering streams, must present many beautiful sites. "The rich landscapes," says Walpole, "occasioned by the multiplicity of temples and obelisks, and various pictures that present themselves as we shift our situation; occasion surprise and pleasure, sometimes recalling Albano's landscapes to our mind, and oftener to our fancy the idolatrous and luxurious vales of Daphne and Tempe." The house also is handsome and richly ornamented, and contains some fine paintings. Woburn Abbey, where the house of Russel, by princely shows and festivals, have thrown a new lustre on British agriculture, is a magnificent edifice. The stables, experimental farm, and other appendages of the most useful of arts, excite the admiration of every farmer and even amateur; nor is this residence deficient in the lighter embellishments of painting and statuary. Althorp, near Northampton, is adorned with many rare and valuable works of art; but it is in London chiefly that Earl Spencer keeps his library, the first in the kingdom. Opposite to Stamford is Burleigh, a noble old residence of Cecil, Elizabeth's minister. It contains a fine library of books and manuscripts; and the Exeter family have enriched it with a collection of paintings, generally supposed to be the most extensive in England. Near Oakham, is another Burleigh *on the hill*, once the seat of the gay revels of Buckingham. It has a noble terrace in front, and contains a good library, with some curious paintings. On he border of Leicestershire and Lincolnshire, stands the Duke of Rutland's proud castellated edifice of Belvoir. From a lofty height it overlooks a vast extent of country, including the vale of the same name, one of the richest and most beautiful in England. The collection of paintings is of great value.

157

Blenheim.

Warwick is a noble county. Its woodlands, the remains of the wide ancient forest of Arden, are still extensive, and a great part lies in fine natural grass. Pasturage predominates greatly over agriculture, occupying nearly two-thirds.

Warwick, an ancient and well-built town, still preserves a portion of its prosperity by the manufacture of woollens. Coventry is a large old town, built very irregularly, and many of the houses exhibiting the uncouth architecture of a distant period. Its ecclesiastical monuments, however, are of importance. St. Michael's is a very light and elegant structure, with a spire rising to three hundred feet. The fabric of silk, introduced more than a century ago by the French refugees, has made a most rapid progress, so that in 1819 it employed 2819 looms. In the making of watches, also, this city now rivals London. Leamington, though its spa is mentioned by Camden, never became a scene of crowded resort, till the beginning of this century; yet so great since that period has been its attraction, that it has risen from a mere village to be a flourishing place. There are both hot and cold baths; and the waters are used either for drinking or bathing. Leamington now possesses, on a handsome scale, baths, inns, a theatre, an assembly-room,—all the accommodation for the sick and the gay. Stratford, a considerable town on the Avon, to which the muse has given a deathless name, is the birth-place of Shakspeare; the poetical pilgrim here beholds the genuine tomb of the poet, and the site of the house chosen by him for his final residence; though the house itself a barbarous hand has demolished. Birmingham is in Warwickshire, but as it is the capital of the iron country, which is almost wholly in Staffordshire, we shall class it with the great towns devoted to the working of that material.

There are two castellated seats in this county, Kenilworth and Warwick, both of almost matchless grandeur; but the former presents only the picturesque remains of its pristine state (*fig.* 158.). Founded in the reign of Henry I., it was extended and adorned by John of Gaunt; and remained with the princes of the house of Lancaster till wrested from them by the triumph of the house of York. It continued thenceforth a royal appanage; and was bestowed by Elizabeth on her handsome favourite, Leicester, whose residence here, and the splendid fêtes and romantic incidents connected with it, have been so happily worked up by the greatest romance writer of the age. At the close of the civil wars, it was given up wholly by Cromwell to his soldiers for plunder, and was reduced to the totally fallen state in which it now appears. The walls were indeed entire, but completely naked and roofless; and the visiter who stands at the interior foot of the tower can trace only by chimneys, and other slight marks, the successive apartments rising above each other till they are terminated by the dome of the sky. Kenilworth exhibits the feudal age in its total downfall; but the traveller has only to proceed a few miles in order to see it entire and in full glory. This is the proud mansion once inhabited by the king-making Earl of Warwick (*fig.* 159.). It was built by the Earl of Warwick, who, in the fourteenth century, distinguished himself at the battles of Cressy and Poitiers. Edward IV. seized an opportunity of annexing it to the crown. It was afterwards bestowed by King James on Lord Brooke, who spent a large sum in restoring it from a state of decay; and the late earl repaired it so judiciously, and made his additions in such harmony with the original pile, that he may be considered almost the creator of the edifice in its present state. The entrance, cut through a rock, and opening at once on three of the loftiest towers, has an effect truly striking. The interior is equally grand and interesting. First is a passage or corridor upwards of 300 feet in extent, seen from end to end, and along which the state apartments are arranged. The grand hall, 62 feet long, is wainscoted with oak, hung with armour, and maintained in full feudal keeping.

158

Kenilworth Castle.

159

Warwick Castle.

Staffordshire has a somewhat bleak and uninviting aspect; the farms are smaller, and improvements less advanced than in the other midland counties, but its mineral stores are immense. The region of coal is supposed to be about 50,000 acres in extent, and cannot be exhausted for ages. Besides its economical uses, this mineral is the main basis of the works and manufactures of the county, and of all those in the north-west of England, which, but for this ample supply of fuel, could never have attained their present astonishing height. Iron, the most useful of metals, exists in equal abundance; and since the discovery that it could be worked with coke, iron works have been established on an immense scale. The whole district from Wolverhampton to Birmingham may be called a Cyclopean land, where furnaces without number are continually pouring out fire and smoke. The clays afford the material of the pottery, which forms the other great Staffordshire manufacture. It is long since some coarse vessels were made at Burslem; but Mr. Wedgwood raised this fabric to the highest perfection, and rendered it an object of national importance. Not content with the native materials, he imported the finest white clays and best flints from the southern counties; and formed that variety of articles called Wedgwood's ware, applicable to all purposes of use and ornament, and superior in some respects to the best porcelain. Hence has sprung up a range of villages forming a district called the Potteries, of which Burslem is the centre, and which contain about 60,000 inhabitants.

The principal cluster of large towns in Staffordshire consists of those in the southern quarter which are employed in making iron, and manufacturing it into various forms. Of this district Birmingham is the capital; and at the remotest periods iron is mentioned as its staple, but the grand impulse given was early in the last century, when John Taylor, the founder of the wealthy family of that name, Matthew Boulton, Esq., and other individuals, by the spirit of their undertakings, and by their liberal patronage of skill and ingenuity in every line, contributed greatly to the establishment of the manufacturing fame of the town. Mr. Boulton, having secured the celebrated Mr. Watt, established, in conjunction with him, at Soho, near Birmingham, their immense manufactory, in which talent, science, capital, experience, united every thing which could raise hardware articles to perfection. Pre-eminent above all is the steam-engine, which Mr. Watt, its great improver, not only applied to the use of his works here, but constructed for the rest of England. The copper coinage executed at Soho by steam-power for the use of government has been greatly admired. Under the impulse of such an example, the citizens of Birmingham soon produced their standard articles of a cheapness and excellence which defied all competition. The articles manufactured in Birmingham consist, in a great measure, of such as, individually, appear unworthy of being named, yet astonish and dazzle by their magnitude, when half the world is to be supplied with them; such as pins, buttons, nails, paper trays, filigree, and toys. There are not wanting, however, fabrics of greater magnitude, taken even singly, such as that of fire-arms, &c. During the last war, the gunsmiths of Birmingham met the demand with such energy, that, on one occasion, they delivered to government 14,000 muskets in a week. Of ponderous machinery, none, perhaps, is more interesting than that of the metal rolling-mills. Birmingham is commodiously built, with suitable churches and other edifices, but without any thing prominent in architecture, or any antique monuments. The town can boast of enlightened citizens, under whose auspices letters and the arts have been cultivated with ardour. The institutions for the education of the poor are not, perhaps, surpassed by any in the kingdom for extent and efficacy.

The other great manufacturing towns, almost all in Staffordshire, are *Wolverhampton*, a very populous place, of considerable antiquity, with a fine old church; but indebted for its present greatness to the making of locks and keys in a manner superior to any town in the world. *Wednesbury* has a fine old Gothic church; but its main boast at present is, the making of all the hard materials of coach harness in an unrivalled manner. *Walsall* flourishes by the making of every thing connected with saddlery; *Dudley* by its nails: but it has also a castle of some note in history, commanding a view of seven counties.

The nominal capital, Stafford, is yet to be noticed; an ancient but small town, of neat appearance, ornamented with the usual county buildings. The Grand Trunk Canal, however, passing by it, has given an impulse to its industry; and it carries on a considerable manufacture of boots and shoes. Newcastle-under-Line, and Tamworth, are both considerable towns on one of the great London roads.

Lichfield is a more elegant and interesting place. Its most prominent object is the cathedral, of high antiquity, the finest part of which was built in 1140; some particular portions are equal to any thing of the kind in Britain: such are the portico, richly adorned with sculpture; the choir; and St. Mary's chapel. The society fixed there by this richly endowed establishment, together with the neatness of the town, and its pleasant situation, have induced many of the gentry in this quarter to make it their residence. These circumstances have contributed to give to Lichfield that intellectual character which is so conspicuous, and has made it almost the literary metropolis of south-western England. The birth and early education of Johnson and Garrick are alone sufficient to immortalise it. Lichfield enjoys high privileges as a city, having a district of some extent round it considered a county of itself.

Derbyshire, in its natural features, is perhaps the most remarkable of any county of England. Except in the lower and southern districts on the Trent, the whole county is traversed by ranges of rugged and rocky hills, penetrated by vast excavations, and separated by narrow valleys. Lead is abundant, chiefly in the form of galena. Iron is also worked very plentifully. This county is also celebrated for the variety and beauty of its calcareous substances, particularly the kind called Blue John (fluor spar), which, by the skilful application of a gentle heat, is made to exhibit the most brilliant colours. Lastly, there are numerous hot springs variously impregnated; and the county contains two of the most remarkable watering-places in the kingdom, Matlock and Buxton.

In proceeding to Castleton, the traveller passes through the Winyats, or gates of the winds, a narrow road of about a mile in length, between precipices a thousand feet high, dark, rugged, and perpendicular. At the end of this road opens on one side Mam Tor, or the Shivering Mountain, 1300 feet high; on the other the High Peak crowned with the ruins of a Saxon fortress; and at its foot, the wonder of wonders, "the Peak Cavern." (*fig.* 160.) This is a huge gulf, 42 feet high and 120 long, at the foot of perpendicular cliffs. The visiter is thence guided through a succession of dark cavernous apartments, and is ferried along a subterraneous river; above which the rocks rise so close, that he must lie flat on his face. At the end of somewhat above 2000 feet the cavern terminates, or, at least, becomes no longer passable. Elden Hole is a fissure near Buxton, which descends perpendicularly to an unknown depth. A line of 2652 feet has been let down without finding a bottom. Poole's Hole, near Buxton, is chiefly remarkable for the petrifactions with which it is filled.

160

Peak Cavern, Derbyshire.

On descending into the Low Peak, a milder grandeur presents itself. The most rugged chains of Derbyshire are interspersed with beautiful valleys; but none equals that of Matlock, where the banks of the Derwent are bordered by extensive woods, interspersed with the boldest and most varied forms of rock. Dovedale (*fig.* 161.) is a wilder scene, where the river Dove is hemmed in by perpendicular rocks, of forms so bold, and covered with such variety of trees and shrubs, that this has sometimes been deemed the most picturesque spot in England.

161

Dovedale.

Derby, the capital of this county, on the Derwent, is handsome and well built, and has extensive manufactures. Silk, introduced at the commencement of the last century, has continued to flourish. Porcelain is also manufactured here; and what is called its white ware is considered almost unrivalled. A considerable number of workmen are employed in cutting and polishing marble; and the Derbyshire spar is fashioned into a variety of beautiful forms.

The watering-places in Derbyshire have the next claim to notice. Matlock contains mineral springs, efficacious in consumptive and rheumatic complaints. Buxton, in the High Peak, surrounded by naked mountains, attracts a much greater multitude; and its waters are considered very powerful in rheumatism, gout, and other diseases. The Duke of Devonshire has here constructed a superb crescent, occupied by inns, shops, ball-rooms, and every thing that can contribute to the accommodation and gaiety of the visitants.

Of seats, Chatsworth has sometimes been considered the finest in England. It was built by William first duke of Devonshire, in 1702; and is 191 feet square, of the Ionic order, richly ornamented both within and without. Keddlestone House has a fine Doric front, 360 feet long, considered one of the finest architectural features in England. Hardwicke Hall was long the residence of the unfortunate Mary; the furniture and the portraits remain, in many respects, in the same state as during her residence.

Nottingham is watered by the broad stream of the Trent, its tributaries, and numerous canals. The Vale of Belvoir, to the south-east, ranks with the richest tracts in the island. The north-western part contains the remnant of the great forest of Sherwood, famed for the revelries of the merry outlaw Robin Hood. Being covered, also, in a great measure, with the ornamented grounds of noblemen of high rank, it is called the "dukeries." The manufactures of hosiery in this county, Leicester and Derby, employ 33,000 frames and 73,000 operatives, producing in cotton 880,000*l.*, worsted 870,000*l.*, silk 241,000*l.* The lace trade employs 150,000 embroiderers in this county.

Nottingham is a large town, boldly and picturesquely situated upon the Trent. Its streets are arranged along the face of a hill so steep, that the ground floors of the street behind, in some instances, rise higher than the roofs of those in front. The rocky materials of this hill are so soft and yielding, that they are cut to a great extent into cellars and warehouses. The making of stockings has always been the staple of Nottingham. They are worked on frames, which, in the middle of last century, scarcely exceeded 1200, and at present amount to 10,000. The lace trade recently added is of very great importance. There are stated to be 1240 machines in the town, and 1070 in the neighbourhood; and the lace sold in its market is valued at 130,000*l*. Nottingham has also a great inland trade by the Trent and canals connected with it.

Newark is noted for its castle, and for a parish church, said to be the finest in the kingdom.

Nottinghamshire may boast some splendid seats. Worksop Manor, built by the Duke of Norfolk, contains fine portraits of the Howard family. Clumber Park is fitted up in a magnificent style by the Duke of Newcastle, with a very valuable collection of pictures. Welbeck Abbey, a seat of the Duke of Portland, is noted for its fine stables. Newstead Abbey had been stripped of its fine furniture and paintings before it came to the late Lord Byron.

### Subsect 4.—*The Northern Counties.*

The northern counties of England may be described, generally, as reaching from the Humber and the Mersey to the Scottish border. They include the wide extent of *Yorkshire*, divided into three ridings, and of *Lancashire*, *Durham*, *Northumberland*, *Cumberland*, and *Westmoreland*. The eastern portion is interspersed with large bleak tracts of mountain, moss, and moor. Its ports carry on a thriving trade in coarse, bulky, and useful commodities. The south-western, comprising Lancashire and the west riding of Yorkshire, by the vast produce of its manufactories, leaves far behind it every other district in the world. The north-western, or the country of the Lakes, has a higher degree of picturesque beauty than any other part of England.

The counties of Northumberland and Durham are hilly and elevated; and their chief wealth is subterraneous. A species of coarse coal, mixed with lead, everywhere abounds; and the lead is exported to the extent of from five to ten thousand tons. But within this mineral region there is enclosed a smaller one, reaching from the mouth of the Coquet to the Tees, a length of about fifty miles, and having its greatest breadth of about twenty miles upon the Tyne. Within this tract are found uninterrupted beds of that valuable coal with which London is wholly supplied, and of which great quantities are either sent to other parts of the kingdom, or exported.

Newcastle was famed at an early period in the military annals of England. It formed a leading point in the wall of Hadrian and in that of Severus. Robert, son of the Conqueror, built here a castle of immense strength, more than two miles in circuit, which served long as the main bulwark against Scottish invasion. Scarcely a trace of it now remains; and the occupations of Newcastle are entirely changed. Both banks of the river, down to Tynemouth, form an immense wharf, to which, by railways and steam wagons, coals are conveyed from the contiguous pits. In 1830, the quantity exported was 867,513 chaldrons, about 2,300,000 tons. Newcastle carries on very extensive manufactories, particularly that of glass. There are thirty-one works on the Tyne, which in some years have produced glass to the value of 500,000*l*. In shipping it is second only to London, having belonging to it, in 1832, 1077 vessels, of the burthen of 220,784 tons. Foundery, pottery, weaving, are not on a very great scale. Newcastle is now, on the whole, a well-built town, though some of the streets are inconveniently steep: it is highly ornamented by the spire of St. Nicholas, considered by the best judges as one of the finest specimens of the Gothic. It possesses a literary society, which has published valuable transactions; and an antiquarian society, destined particularly to receive the Roman coins, &c. which are frequently dug up on this line. The large town of Gateshead, on the opposite side of the river, though placed in Durham, is really part of Newcastle, and raises its population to 57,000.

A continued range of great commercial towns cluster thick around Newcastle. Near the mouth of the Tyne are North Shields and South Shields, on opposite sides of the river; the latter being in the county of Durham. They carry on with activity the coal trade, and the others proper to Newcastle; particularly ship-building and the making of ropes and sails. Tynemouth, at the immediate opening of the river into the ocean, displays, on a bold promontory, a castle, a light-house, and a fine old abbey; they form a striking and romantic scene, which contrasts with those immediately above. At the mouth of the Wear, are Sunderland and Wearmouth,—the one a very great, and the other a considerable port. Their prosperity is supported by the same great trade of coals, of which in 1832 they sent 600,000 tons to the port of London, two-thirds of that which comes down the Tyne. They carry on also the same manufactures, particularly ship-building, in which Sunderland is supposed to exer a greater activity than any other place in the kingdom. The bridge there has long been celebrated: it consists of one arch of iron framework thrown across the river, 200 feet span, and 100 feet high, allowing very large vessels to pass under without lowering their sails. "Nothing," says M. Dupin, "can be more striking than this view of the two cities, and the bridge that unites them; that majestic arch drawn against the sky, which allows large vessels to pass under its vault with their sails flying." He afterwards adds, in regard to these ports generally: "It is an admirable thing, within an extent of coast which a man may walk over on foot in three or four hours, to see two great rivers receive 16,000 vessels, and send them away loaded with the produce of their banks. On the same narrow space are six flourishing towns, containing a population of 85,927 persons, all devoted to commerce and industry."

Durham is handsomely built, though on very uneven ground; its grand ornament is the cathedral, reared in the eleventh century, which is perhaps unrivalled as to its situation, ranging along the summit of a precipitous rock eighty feet high above the Wear, which winds along its base. The see of Durham is the richest in England; and the cathedral, besides a dean, twelve prebendaries, and two archdeacons, has attached to it about sixty spiritual servants of various ranks.

The number of smaller towns in those counties is still considerable. In Durham, Stockton near the mouth of the Tees carries on the trade of that river; in 1832 it carried 173,000 tons of coal to London, and has also the Baltic trade, and the manufacture of sailcloth and other naval materials. Hexham, on the Upper Tyne, is the capital of interior Northumberland, and of the grand ancient scene of border debate. Morpeth has a weekly market for the cattle brought up from Scotland.

162

Alnwick Castle.

The seats are chiefly great baronial castles, at the head of which stands Alnwick (*fig.* 162.). This proud keep of the Percies covers five acres, and is defended by sixteen towers. An expense of 200,000*l.* has been incured in converting the interior from a feudal castle into the most splendid of modern mansions. Warkworth Castle, another seat of the Percies, retains its antique character. Lumley, the feudal castle of the Earls of Scarborough, presents entire its august and formidable front. Raby Castle, Howick, Lambton Hall, and Bishop Auckland, are fine seats.

Yorkshire is next in order: its eastern division resembles the two counties just described; while the western forms part of the great central seat of English manufacture. The Yorkshireman has a character of his own, marked by shrewdness, simplicity, good humour, and a species of drollery; so that the London comic stage is considered incomplete without one of his representatives. The North Riding consists, to a great extent, of moorlands; the hills of which rise often to a considerable height. These dreary tracts spread over the whole Riding, so that culture can exist only in the valleys. The East Riding, which extends to the Humber, is traversed also by a range of high wolds, which, though rugged, have not been able to resist the energies of British industry. These Ridings present to the German Ocean high and often precipitous rocks, of which Flamborough Head, nearly 500 feet high, forms one of the boldest features in English landscape. The West Riding is composed chiefly of a wide, flat, fertile plain, traversed by the Aire, the Calder, and other navigable rivers, which convey its produce to the eastern, and, by means of canals, to the western sea. In this tract is placed the immense manufacturing district of Yorkshire; in its extreme west is the district of Craven, the most rugged and mountainous of all England; for here rise Ingleborough, Wharnside, Pennigent, each to the height of nearly three thousand feet. There is scarcely a county in which the spirit of agricultural improvement has been so active as in Yorkshire; and vast tracts of waste and common land have been reclaimed and rendered productive.

Hull, the principal port, is the fourth commercial city in England, only surpassed by London, Liverpool, and Bristol. It carries on a most extensive export of goods brought by the interior system of rivers and canals. It is the principal of the whale-fishery ports; though this branch has lately declined. During the nine years ending with 1818, the average number of vessels fitted out from Hull for the whale fishery amounted to $53\frac{4}{9}$; while in 1830, it sent out only 33. In 1832, it owned 557 ships, carrying 68,892 tons, and there entered its port 1279 vessels, of the burden of 192,661 tons. The Old Dock, completed in 1778, the Humber Dock in 1809, and the Junction Dock in 1829, contain a space of twenty-three acres. *Goole*, on the Ouse, a little above its junction with the Humber, is beginning to share with Hull in the exportation of woollens. Though a few years ago a mere village, and still in 1831, containing only 1670 inhabitants, it has two spacious docks, and in 1829 the customs exceeded 40,000*l.*, and the declared value of exports amounted to 625,000*l.* Goods sent from Leeds or Wakefield by rivers or canals can be embarked at Goole in the course of twelve hours.

Whitby is a very ancient town, with the remains of a fine abbey built soon after the Conquest. Its modern importance is derived from large mines of alum. The export of their produce forms a considerable trade, to which Whitby soon added the other branches prevalent on this coast, and became second only to Hull.

Scarborough, romantically situated on a promontory between two rocks overlooking the sea, is the chief watering-place of the north of England.

York, the capital, is the first object that strikes us as we proceed into the interior of the North and West Ridings. This celebrated city, though so much eclipsed by several that are only of to-day, still boasts a dignity superior to them, and to almost any other in England. Eboracum was a distinguished Roman station; for some time York disputed with London the distinction of being the capital of England; and when obliged to give up this claim, continued the unquestioned metropolis of the north, till the creative powers of trade raised up rivals to it in the north-west. The houses are high, and the streets narrow; yet, altogether, York is a handsome, respectable-looking old city. It boasts one feature of almost unrivalled beauty,—its cathedral. (*fig.* 163.) On the exterior all the richness and elegance of Gothic ornament has been lavished, particularly upon the western front and the large window in the eastern. But the interior is without a rival in the empire; its effect is altogether sublime: its numerous windows of painted glass shed a dim, solemn, religious light, in accordance with the character of the edifice. The chapter-house is of singular elegance and magnificence; and, though of great extent, has its roof supported by a single pin. The choir of this splendid edifice suffered severe injury from a fire kindled by the hands of a maniac; but by great exertions has been fully repaired. The remains of the ruined abbey of St. Mary, and those of several of the twenty-three churches of York, are also deserving notice. There are likewise some elegant modern edifices, particularly the assembly room, the county hall, guildhall, the mansion-house, and the museum of the Yorkshire Philosophical Society. York is still a gay town, visited by many of the northern gentry, particularly at the time of its races. It carries on some inland trade by the Ouse, which passes through it.

163

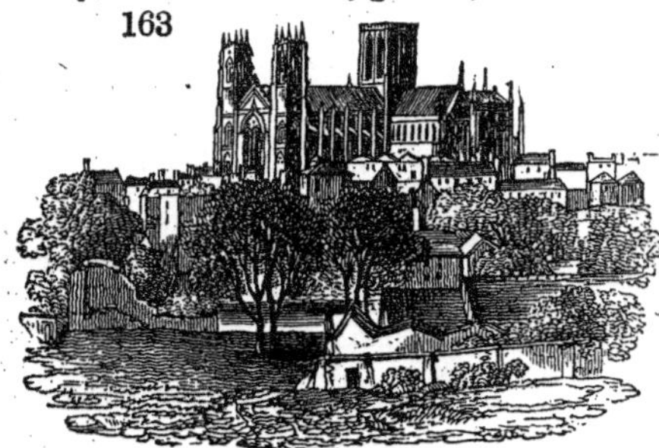

York Cathedral.

Doncaster is much frequented during the time of its races. Pontefract is surrounded by a great extent of garden and nursery ground, the produce of which is sent to a considerable distance. Scarcely a vestige remains of that immense and powerful keep, covering seven acres, in which Thomas of Lancaster, Richard II., and many other fallen chiefs and statesmen, were immured. The parliament, during the civil wars, having taken it after three successive and arduous sieges, caused it to be completely demolished.

Leeds is the capital of western Yorkshire, and, in a commercial sense, of the whole county. Although it was of some note even in early times, its present greatness is modern, and of the most rapid growth. The population, which in 1775 was only 17,117, amounted in 1831 to 123,393; being thus nearly quintupled. A peculiar activity and spirit of enterprise has been observed among the manufacturers of Leeds: it was, doubtless, greatly favoured by the vast extent of inland navigation, which seemed to centre here, connecting it with the capital, with both seas, and with the counties to the south, from which it derives inexhaustible supplies of fine coal. The woollen manufacture is not carried on wholly in large towns; the cloth is wrought to a certain state of forwardness in the numerous villages, thence sent into Leeds, where it is purchased and worked up into a saleable state. The cloths are sold in weekly markets, held in the cloth halls, the most remarkable feature in Leeds. That for mixed cloths was built in 1758, that for white cloth in 1775. They form quadrangular edifices round an open area, and are divided into stands, of which in the first hall are 1800, and in the second 1210. These are let at a moderate rent to the owners of the cloth, who, on the ringing of a bell, occupy their stands, and though the market remains open only an hour, goods to an immense value are often disposed of. Although the staple of Leeds and of Yorkshire be common cloth, yet other branches are in some degree included, as sail-cloth, cotton, carpets, and superfine cloths. Mr. Drinkwater states the persons employed in the mills for wool at 5290; worsted, 702; flax, 2434; cotton, 80; silk, 158; in all, 8664; of whom 5318 are males, and 3346 females; to which may be added 1814 in the suburb of Holbeck. The town of Leeds is mostly well built, with several broad and spacious streets; and the theatre, the new court-house, and the commercial buildings, finished in 1829, are elegant structures. Kirkstall Abbey, three miles distant, presents, in a beautiful situation, the most complete specimen of the architecture of the 12th century that is extant. The people of Leeds have formed a literary and philosophical society, and an institution for the promotion of the fine arts; for the purpose of which a very handsome and commodious edifice has been erected: meritorious exertions have also been made for the education of the poor.

Of the other towns of the clothing district, which cluster round Leeds, *Wakefield*, beautifully situated on the Calder, has a cloth market, on a smaller scale, resembling that of Leeds, and also great grain and cattle markets. *Halifax*, and the whole district about twenty miles round it, has been converted from a desert into a populous and prosperous scene, containing altogether 110,000 inhabitants. Its staples are what are properly called stuffs; shalloons, serges, baize, moreens, kerseys; and it has lately embraced a considerable share of the cotton manufacture. Huddersfield is also a very thriving town, employed nearly in the same branches; and its market hall is supposed, next to that of Leeds, to present the greatest show of woollens in the kingdom. Bradford and Keighley are large towns, which carry on to a great extent the manufacture of worsted: besides which, Bradford has great iron founderies in its neighbourhood.

In the southern part of this riding, the manufactures of iron and cutlery take the place of those of woollen; and flourish to such an extent, that they are second only to the great iron district around Birmingham. Sheffield is the capital of this district. It early derived importance from the fabrication of arms, but it has reached a much higher degree of greatness since it betook itself to the more useful fabrics of knives, forks, razors, snuffers, scissors, combs, buttons, saws, sickles, and various instruments of husbandry. The art of plating goods with silver is carried to a vast extent. The silver is soldered upon the copper; and the articles are wrought by the hand or stamped. The cutlers of Sheffield keep many hundred patterns of knives, of which some are of the value of seven or eight guineas, containing twenty-eight blades within the handle; while others, after passing through a multitude of different hands, are sold for a penny each. The rapid growth of Sheffield commenced about the year 1750, when the river Don was rendered navigable to within a few miles of the town. Since that time its advance has been steady; new branches having been constantly adding, and the former ones extending. The houses are chiefly modern, and well built; and the town makes a tolerable appearance, notwithstanding the smoke of the forges in which it is involved. The military barracks erected here form an extensive pile of building. The infirmary is considered equal to any in the kingdom; and great credit is due to Sheffield for the excellence of the schools which it maintains for the education of the lower orders. It supports also many public charities; has a literary society, a mechanics' institute, and a library.

Barnsley produces wire, nails, and other articles, but derives its chief importance from the linen manufacture. Rotherham has a great foundery for cannon. The first iron bridge was constructed here at the works of Messrs. Walker; and they have since executed those of Sunderland, Staines, and Yarm. Rotherham, being in a fine country, has also a great corn and cattle market.

The superb seats which adorn Yorkshire are so many, that to enumerate even the most distinguished can with difficulty suit our limits. Castle Howard is a magnificent pile, noted for its classical collection of sculpture and painting. Duncombe Park is admired for the noble view obtained from the terrace in front, and for the ruins of Rivaulx Abbey, situated in a beautiful vale at a little distance; Studley Royal, an almost unrivalled specimen of an ornamental park, encloses within its precincts, Fountain's Abbey, one of the grandest of monastic remains, covering several acres. Wentworth House is generally considered the noblest mansion in the north. The principal front extends upwards of 600 feet, forming a centre and two wings, in the middle of which is a fine Corinthian portico.

Lancashire, situated beyond the hilly border of York West Riding, forms the capital or central seat of manufacture for Britain, and even for the world. Its soil and climate are unfavourable; the upland tracts being rocky and barren, and the coast too low and flat, while the moisture from the Atlantic is injurious to the growth of the finer kinds of grain. But coal traverses in large beds the south and south-eastern parts of the county; and being conveyed by short canal lines to all the great towns, affords cheap and abundant fuel for the steam-engines and other grand manufacturing apparatus. Canal navigation, which originated in Lancashire, has been carried to a greater extent there than in any other part of the kingdom. Besides those smaller canals which connect all the great thriving towns, it has the Lancaster Canal running north and south through nearly its whole extent, and into Westmoreland as far as Kendal; and the still more important line of the Leeds and Liverpool Canal; while, in the southern border, the Grand Trunk connects it with London and the whole centre of England. A most important additional communication has recently been opened by the railway, elsewhere described, by which Liverpool and Manchester, so far as respects personal conveyance, are brought almost into contact.

Manchester, the centre of British industry, and the manufacturing capital of the empire, is favourably situated on the Irwell; though this stream, navigable for barges, scarcely makes any figure beside the vast artificial lines formed from its waters. Although the cotton manufacture is now widely diffused throughout England, Manchester continues the centre of the trade; receiving and distributing the raw material, collecting the produce worked up in numerous towns and villages, and transmitting it to the various markets. From the middle of the last century she has advanced with amazing and accelerated rapidity; and the system of inland navigation having afforded copious channels by which the material can be introduced and the manufactured article exported, every obstacle to the absorption of the whole into this centre was removed. Its manufacture embraces the finer muslins and other delicate fabrics, with the plain and useful forms of dimities, fustians, velveteens, checks, shirtings ginghams, diapers, cambric muslins, figured muslins, calicoes for printing, and various fancy goods. The different cotton fabrics generally denominated Manchester goods, are not all manufactured within the town itself, but in the neighbouring towns and districts; and, after being bleached, and some of them printed, are sent in a finished state to Manchester to be sold; the chief *market days* being Tuesdays and Saturdays. Thus Marseilles quiltings, cambric muslins, calicoes for printing, bed quilts and counterpanes, checks, fustians, and shirtings, are brought in from the surrounding towns and villages. A vast deal of yarn is also spun for exportation. Manchester has extensive establishments for printing and dyeing; also, for constructing and keeping in repair steam-engines, as well as other machines employed in manufacture. Even iron founderies are necessary to supply the materials. Other important branches have recently been added. Manchester now rivals Macclesfield and Norwich in the manufacture of silks, and Nottingham in that of lace. In 1832, there were at work in the townships of Manchester and Salford, 96 cotton mills, 16 silk, 4 woollen and worsted, and 2 flax mills. The number employed in cotton factories amounted to 20,585; of whom, 5361 were male and 7035 female adults; 4286 male and 3903 female children. The wages paid to them per month were 40,333*l.*, making about 9*s.* 9*d.* of average weekly earnings to each individual. There were 7174 mule spinners, earning 15,106*l.* per month, averaging 10*s.* 6*d.* each per week; 1497 spinners of a higher class, earning 8491*l.* per month, or 1*l.* 8*s.* 4*d.* each per week. Piecers' scavengers 2944, earning 3287*l.* per month, each weekly 5*s.* 6*d.* In the power looms, women receive 8*s.* to 12*s.*; men, 13*s.* to 16*s.* 10*d.*; dressers, 28*s.* to 30*s.* per week. Manchester is not an elegant town; some parts of its interior are narrow, crowded, full of warehouses and factories in huge masses. The entrances, however, have been made handsome; and, in the extremities of the town, streets of elegant houses have been built for the accommodation of the opulent merchants. It has one handsome Gothic collegiate church of the fifteenth century, and several more modern, that are creditable to the taste of the town, as the Exchange, which includes a news-room and a good library; the Infirmary (which in one year received above 12,000 patients); the Town Hall, which contains one of the most splendid public rooms in Europe; and the Royal Institution for the Promotion of the Fine Arts. The prison called the New Bailey is an immense structure,—the inmates of which are classed and provided with employment to a considerable extent. Manchester is remarkable for its charitable institutions; hospitals of different kinds; and schools for the education of the poor. Cheetham's Hospital, maintaining eighty poor children, has a library of 18,000 or 20,000 volumes, containing rare and valuable works. In 1781, a literary and philosophical society was formed at Manchester, and produced several valuable volumes of Transactions, enriched by the contributions of Percival, Ferriar, Dalton, Henry, and other eminent gentlemen there resident. In 1774, the population of the whole parish was 41,000; the amount of 142,000 for 1831 by no means comprehends all that may be considered Manchester. The large towns and villages which have sprung up within its parish form really its suburbs, and raise the entire population to 270,000. Of these, the most important are Salford, immediately contiguous, and now raised to the rank of a borough; and Chorlton Row, which in 1801 contained 675 inhabitants; in 1831, 20,565.

Huge towns, resembling cities, devoted to the cotton manufacture, are found in every direction round Manchester. To the north are *Blackburn* and *Bolton;* the former chiefly employed in the branch of printed calicoes, which are supposed to be produced to the annual value of 2,000,000*l.* A great advantage is derived from the Leeds and Liverpool Canal passing close by it. Bolton is a town anciently of some strength, but now supported entirely by industry. Some of the greatest improvements in the cotton manufacture, have been made by Arkwright and Crompton, residents in this place. Preston, a flourishing seat of manufacture, elects two members on a basis of almost universal suffrage. Wigan is a large town, which adds to those of cotton and linen some manufactures of brass and pewter. Bury, very near Manchester, besides extensive cotton works, has some of woollen. Oldham was early a place of some consequence, carrying on a large fabric of hats; but the introduction of the cotton manufacture has caused it to make an astonishing progress, so that in thirty years it has nearly trebled its population, and the parish, including Pilkington, Crompton, and other towns, contains 67,500 inhabitants. There are here now 65 cotton mills and 140 steam-engines, almost all erected during the present century.

Some large towns employed in other manufactures than those of cotton lie on the borders of Lancashire. Rochdale, near the western point of Yorkshire, and in character a Yorkshire town, has for its staple woollen stuffs and flannels, of which 8000 pieces are made weekly; fifty-seven steam-engines are employed here, and about 84,000 lbs. of cotton yarn spun in the week. Warrington, on the Mersey, which is navigable for vessels of eighty tons from Liverpool, in Henry VIII.'s time was superior to Manchester; but it is now left far behind. Its staples of sailcloth and coarse linens have been exchanged for cotton, to which it adds glass and pins. Prescot is noted for the making of watch-wheels, springs chains, &c. several of which have been invented and improved by its workmen. Near it, at St. Helen's, is a great manufactory of plate glass, employing 300 persons.

Liverpool, the commercial capital of Lancashire, is, if possible, a still grander object, and far surpassing indeed every other seaport, with the exception of the metropolis. Nothing can be more remarkable than the contrast of its present state with its humble origin. In the sixteenth century, it is described as a small place with only a chapel, having no parish church within four miles. It had then 138 inhabitants, and two or three ships, whose aggregate tonnage was 223 tons; and in a petition to Elizabeth, about the year 1578, it is styled, "her majesty's poor decayed town;" it continued gradually to increase during the seventeenth century, till, in 1700, it was constituted a parish, and had 5000 inhabitants. Since that time it has advanced with rapid and accelerated steps; in 1730, it had 12,000; in 1760, 26,000; in 1800, 56,000 inhabitants; but the most rapid growth has been between 1811 and 1821, when it rose from 94,376 to 141,487. The increase to 165,000 in 1831 appears less rapid; but in fact, the population during this period has overflowed into the adjacent villages, and swelled them into large towns; Toxteth-park increased from 2069 in 1801, to 24,067 in 1831; West Derby, Kirkdale, Everton, form in fact the suburbs of Liverpool, and, added to it, make an amount of 203,000. There must always have been a considerable port at the mouth of the Mersey; but this estuary, in its natural navigation, could never come in competition with the Humber or the Severn. When, however, its disadvantages as a seaport were partly removed, by the formation of docks,—and, much more, when it became the basis of a canal system reaching eastward to the German Ocean, and southward to the Thames,—Liverpool could communicate with an immense interior circle. It derived benefit, above all, from the cotton manufacture established, on such an extensive scale, in the country immediately behind; the materials of which were brought to Liverpool from the opposite side of the Atlantic, and the finished fabric thence exported, partly to the same quarter. At the same time Liverpool imported, for a great part of England at least, articles of consumption from America and the West Indies. It found also a most extensive employment in bringing grain and provisions from Ireland, and returning salt, coals, and pottery. The merchants of Liverpool, meanwhile, were most active in improving these circumstances, particularly by the construction of that immense line of docks, which M. Dupin has described with such admiration. A dock, or space enclosed all round, and fed with sluices, in which the vessels while they receive or discharge their cargoes are kept regularly afloat, without being exposed to swell, tide, or current, is an obvious improvement upon the best natural harbour. The expense, however, is great; and it was not till 1710 that Liverpool began the first dock in Britain, called the Old Dock, which has recently been filled up. Twenty years were employed in its completion; and a still longer time in that of the next, or the Salthouse Dock. The others were, however, constructed on a more extensive scale, and with greater rapidity:—George's (II.) Dock; the King's Dock, for Greenland ships and tobacco; the Queen's Dock, directly for the Baltic and North American trade. On a still larger scale have been constructed the Prince Regent Dock, opened in 1821, and the Clarence Dock, in 1830. The Brunswick Dock, for the accommodation of vessels with cargoes of timber, nearly completes the present plan, when the whole area of water in the docks will exceed 90 acres. In 1832, there belonged to this port 853 registered vessels, of the burthen of 166,028 tons. The customs paid at the port amounted, in 1765, to 269,000*l.*; in 1810, to 2,675,000*l.*; and in 1832 they had risen to 3,925,062*l.* The following are the leading articles of import in the year 1830:—792,350 bags of cotton, 510,000 hides, 42,000 hogsheads of sugar, 8000 hogsheads of tobacco, 300,500 barrels of flour, 7800 casks and 7300 barrels and bags of coffee, 27,000 casks of palm oil, 900 seroons and 1430 chests of indigo, 12,000 puncheons of rum, 31,200 bags of rice, 22,500 barrels of American ashes, 42,500 barrels of tar, 51,000 barrels of turpentine, 6200 tons of logwood, 5650 logs of mahogany. The dock duties, which in 1800 were only 23,379*l.*, amounted, in 1832, to 170,000*l.* In 1832, the ships entered inwards were 10,266, tonnage 1,361,000; outwards, 8717 ships, tonnage 1,218,645. Of this, 610,000 tons were from foreign parts, chiefly the United States and British America, the rest coasters, of which 386,000 were from Ireland. The value of agricultural produce from that country amounted to 4,444,000*l.*

Liverpool has numerous lines of packets to all the principal foreign ports. Every month four sail to New-York, two to Philadelphia, one to Boston, two respectively to Rio Janeiro, Genoa and Leghorn, and to Lisbon; one every three weeks to Oporto. The New-York packets are first-rate vessels containing splendid accommodations for passengers, and the value of goods conveyed in one of them has been known to exceed 140,000*l.* Trading vessels also are continually sailing to the above and to all other commercial places throughout the world. An almost daily communication is maintained by steam packets with Dublin, Belfast, Glasgow, Whitehaven, and all ports of any consequence in Ireland, and on the western coast of England. The solid construction of its docks; the powerful iron gates by which they are enclosed; the long covered ways where the goods may be landed without injury from the inclemency of the weather; the immense magazines, some rising to the height of 12 or 13 stories,—all denote a gigantic industry and a magnificence which spares no sacrifice to attain objects of public utility. The inhabitants of Liverpool have generally shown the same spirit in their other arrangements as in those connected with trade. The town is well lighted with gas. The public building have an elegant and classical character, almost peculiar to Liverpool. The Town-Hall (*fig.* 164), is a fine Grecian edifice, ornamented with a superb cupola and appropriate statues. The Exchange forms behind it an elegant square, in the midst of which is a sculptural composition by Westmacott, representing Nelson and his victories. The new edifice erected for a market is, perhaps, the most spacious and commodious of any employed in the kingdom for that purpose. There are also several elegant modern churches, one formed of cast-iron. The finest view of Liverpool is obtained from the sea, where the vast height and extent of the exterior dock wall, the forest of masts above, and the town behind, make a most imposing appearance. The charitable institutions are administered on a great scale, and with activity. Foremost stands the Blind Asylum, the first established in England, which receives inmates from all parts of the kingdom. The infirmary is in a very spacious and airy situation; and, among the other institutions common to great towns, the Strangers' Friends' Society distinguishes itself by its generous exertions. The English mercantile towns generally show a zeal to combine intellectual pursuits with those of wealth; but none, perhaps so successfully as Liverpool,—one of whose merchants, while carrying on an extensive business, produced works which rank him among the most classical English writers. Although this example be single, it is connected with a general spirit, which displays itself in the liberal procedure of several individuals; in the Lyceum and the Athenæum; two public libraries and literary institutions, supported by subscription; and in a botanic garden, which ranks as the first that was formed, and at least the third as to eminence, in the kingdom. Both the Athenæum and the botanic garden owe their foundation to the public spirit and the munificent example of Mr. Roscoe, who had also the magnanimity to exert his powerful talents for the abolition of the slave trade, in a town long devoted to that traffic.

164

Town Hall, Liverpool

Lancaster, the county town, is handsomely built of a beautiful free-stone; the Town-hall and some other buildings are handsome; but the castle (*fig.* 165.) forms one of the grandest monuments of the feudal age. Its vast extent; its commanding site; the greatness of all its features, even now, when three of its seven towers are fallen into ruin; produce the most powerful impression. It has been converted into a well-arranged prison for the county. Lancaster, though its river, the Lune, is not navigable for vessels of more than 250 tons, possesses 73 sail. It builds some ships, makes sailcloth, and manufactures, upon a small scale, some cotton fabrics. About a mile from it, the Lancaster Canal is carried over the Lune by a very noble aqueduct bridge.

165

Lancaster Castle.

The counties of Cumberland and Westmoreland, or the country of the Lakes, form a bold and peculiar region, presenting a striking contrast to those recently surveyed; being enriched neither by natural wealth, nor by human industry. Wide ranges of high and rocky mountains, enclosing long lakes and narrow vales, afford scanty space for the plough. A great proportion of these fells and moors is absolutely barren; in the more favoured spots the herbage is often scanty; and even the arable tracts are, in general, fit only for the coarser grain of oats. But the multitude of mountains crowded together, their bold, perpendicular, and often projecting forms; the pleasing though not extensive lakes, and soft pastoral valleys, which they enclose, render this the most beautiful country of England, and the favourite resort of all the admirers of the picturesque and sublime.

Three divisions are distinctly seen in these counties, reaching from north to south. I. A plain eastward of the mountains, through which the high road runs by Kendal and Carlisle to London. II. The mountains and lakes, occupying the larger portion of their surface. III. A sea-coast, containing some harbours of importance.

The first part consists of a plain, which, though narrow, is in many places fertile; and contains some large towns. In the northern part is "merry Carlisle," long distinguished in the border annals, and the scene of interesting events in the contest of 1745. Carlisle being a military post of the first consequence, its castle and walls were considered a model of strength, according to the ideas of the middle ages; the cathedral is an ancient edifice, still nearly entire, in the heavy Saxon style. Carlisle has of late begun to carry on some manufacture, chiefly cotton; also woollen, linen, and a few minor articles, A canal connects it with the Solway, and enables it to employ some shipping. Eastward from Carlisle is the great debateable line; and near Brampton is Naworth Castle, that powerful station where Lord William Howard undertook to bridle the license of the border. Yet, however strong, it forms rather a dark border keep, than a display of feudal grandeur. Lord Howard's apartments, which, with their books, furniture, and armour, remain almost undisturbed, are separated by four strong doors from the rest of the castle; and secret passages lead to every part, and to the dungeons beneath. Farther south is Kendal, the chief town of Westmoreland; a considerable place, with an old manufactory of woollens bearing its name, and some of cotton and leather. Burton and Kirby Lonsdale are small neat towns on the border of Lancashire.

The second division comprises the country of the Lakes, forming the peculiar characteristic of the country, and chiefly distinguished by its scenery. Ullswater, (*fig.* 166.) divided into three reaches. The mountains are numerous, steep and lofty, not broken or impending, but of a bold and swelling form. The two highest in the region are Helvellyn, and the square rocky mass of Stone Cross Pike, rearing their almost perpendicular forms to an amazing height above the wooded hills which cluster round them. Opposite rises the immense precipitous steep of Place Fell; and the whole produces a scene of solemn and simple grandeur. At Patterdale, though the features be grand, the beautiful predominates. From the meadows bordering the lake, the numerous glens branching off, with the scattered abodes of the shepherds and dalesmen, present one of the sweetest of alpine pastoral scenes. Keswick or Derwentwater (*fig.* 167.) is of equal grandeur, but a quite different aspect. The mountains preserve no regular form, but are broken, shattered, impending, shooting into a thousand fantastic shapes; and though they do not produce the same grand unity of effect, astonish by a continual change of scenery. In the wooded cliffs and waterfall of Lodore (*fig.* 168.), and on the rocks of Borrowdale, nature seems to have sported her wildest fancies. Yet exquisite beauty is here mingled with horrors, particularly in the views of the lake from the south, with Skiddaw behind; and in a lovely rural vale, which runs along its northern border, and is seen to peculiar advantage from the road to Ambleside. Windermere (*fig.* 169.), is of much wider extent; not shut in by mountainous cliffs, but bordered by wooded and ornamented hills. Around its northern banks, however is ranged an amphitheatre of very high mountains, which, with their varied summits, form a sublime background to all its landscapes. These are generally grand, open, diffusive, and extended. The other lakes, Coniston, Grasmere, Buttermere, Cromack, Wastdale, Enner

166

Ullswater.

167

Keswick Lake

168

Lodore Waterfall.

169

Windermere Lake.

dale, have attractions for the admirers of nature. In this district, the only places to which the name of towns could be given are Keswick on Derwentwater, and Ambleside on Windermere; and even these are only large villages, supported by the resort of travellers, and by some persons of distinction who are induced to reside there by the beauty of the neighbourhood.

The third division consists of the sea-coast. The most considerable port is Whitehaven, which has become flourishing in consequence of the immense coal mines found and worked in its immediate vicinity. Some of them have a depth of 320 yards, supposed to be greater than any other in the world; and some extend several miles beneath the sea. The total quantity worked is estimated at 100,000 chaldrons, chiefly exported to Ireland: besides which, Whitehaven has pushed its trade to Africa, America, and the West Indies; and carries on much ship-building.

Subsect. 5.—*Western Counties.*

The western counties form the last division of England Proper, comprising the counties south of the Mersey, which form the western boundary of England. This extensive line has scarcely any character which can be said generally to apply to it. We mention *Cheshire*, *Shropshire*, *Hereford*, and *Monmouth*, as bordering on Wales, and the last three partaking somewhat of its rude and romantic character; *Worcester*, *Gloucester*, and *Somerset*, occupying the fine valley of the Severn,—a region filled with commerce and cultivation, and containing several great cities; lastly, Cornwall and Devon, the extreme corner of England, but marked by a mild climate, rich mines, and a surface agreeably diversified.

The soil of Cheshire is generally fit for all the purposes of agriculture, particularly in the valley of the Dee: but the dairy is the branch pursued with peculiar success; and it produces the cheese which, bearing the name of the country, equals in richness, though not in delicacy, any other in Britain. There are valuable mines of coal, and some of iron; but the mineral substance of which Cheshire chiefly boasts is salt. The pits were discovered about a century and a half ago, at Northwich, Middlewich, and Nantwich, and have proved of the highest importance to the nation, at once for internal consumption, for the curing of fish, and for exportation.

Chester is, perhaps, the city in Britain which bears the most venerable character of antiquity. The very name implies a Roman camp, the form of which is still preserved in the direction of its principal streets. The effect is heightened by the mouldering red stone, of which its most ancient edifices are built. The principal streets have a very peculiar structure. The lower story, which has been hollowed out of the rock, consists of shops, above which is a paved way covered by the projecting upper story; but the middle part of the house appears thus retired from the open street behind this species of arcade. The arrangement is neither very elegant nor very convenient. The castle of Chester presents a very complete specimen of early military architecture; connected with it is a range of handsome Grecian buildings, containing the barracks, county hall, and county gaol. The cathedral displays considerable grandeur, and has a very elegant chapter-house. The improvements on the Dee enable vessels of 300 tons to come up to Chester, which has 62 vessels, of above 4000 tons; yet its trade with Ireland has been transferred to Liverpool.

Of the other towns, the most remarkable are those near which the salt mines are situated, particularly Northwich. There are fourteen pits of rock salt, and between thirty and forty of brine salt. The rock salt is hard and brown; the pits, after being dug to a certain depth, are excavated horizontally, leaving a portion of the salt for a roof. They thus form apartments, often of more than an acre in extent; and the reflection of lights from the mineral, like that of numberless precious stones, produces a magical effect. Stockport and Macclesfield have flourished greatly in consequence of the introduction from Lancashire of the cotton manufacture, to which Macclesfield adds some branches of that of silk.

Among the seats are Eaton Hall, a magnificent Gothic edifice, which Earl Grosvenor has erected at an expence, it is said, of 400,000*l.*

Shropshire, or Salop, consists chiefly of a wide plain watered by the Severn. On its eastern border it shares to a great extent in the mineral wealth of Staffordshire, coal and iron. These are carried on in a remarkable manner at Colebrook; a deep-wooded vale on the Severn, here traversed by the first iron bridge erected in the kingdom. This county is also interesting to the student of English history; many spots having been the scenes of remarkable events, on which the destinies of the kingdom have depended.

Shrewsbury, the capital, is particularly rich in memorable recollections. Being the strongest fortress on the western marches, it became a rendezvous of the royal army, both for overawing the Welsh, and for northern expeditions; many of the streets are narrow, winding, and irregular, and the old and new buildings too closely intermingled; only a small part of the castle remains; St. Mary's church is elegant and entire. The free school, founded by Edward VI. and Queen Elizabeth, has produced several eminent teachers and pupils. Shrewsbury is praised for its house of industry, and for the arrangement of its county gaol.

Ludlow, an ancient town, was frequently the residence of royalty, and the regular station of those powerful officers the Lords Presidents of the Marches. The castle, placed on a wooded rock overhanging the Terne, was considered one of the strongest places in the kingdom. In its vicinity occurred many of the most distinguished events in the contest between the houses of York and Lancaster. It was afterwards dismantled; yet remained a splendid private mansion, in which Milton's "Comus" was first performed, and where Butler wrote a part of his "Hudibras." It is now entirely roofless and covered with ivy, but still adorns the town, which is well built and pleasantly situated.

Hereford and Monmouth, two demi-Welsh counties, fill the interval from Shropshire southwards to the Bristol Channel. Being traversed by the Wye, the most picturesque of the English rivers, they vie in beauty with almost any part of the kingdom. The chief industry is in the rearing of fruit, and the whole country is as it were covered with orchards: hence Hereford draws its staple production of cider and perry, in peculiar abundance and perfection. The crop is precarious; but in a good year the produce of an acre will be from eighteen to twenty-four hogsheads, sometimes of such fine quality, that it will sell from the press at 20*l*. a hogshead. The western district of Hereford produces also a large quantity of hops, and has one of the finest breeds of cattle in the kingdom, both for draught and feeding. The breed of sheep, called Ryeland (*fig.* 170.), besides the excellence of their flesh, bear the very finest wool in the kingdom. Monmouth is not so fertile: its chief wealth is mineral, coal being most abundant; and iron works are established to such an extent, that they have been known to produce a thousand tons in the week.

170

Ryeland Sheep.

Of the towns, Hereford bears venerable marks of antiquity, particularly its cathedral, notwithstanding the fall of its principal tower. Ross, once the residence of Mr. Kyrle, celebrated by Pope as "the Man of Ross," is a beautiful village, considered as a sort of centre of the picturesque scenes of the Wye.

171

Tintern Abbey.

The towns of Monmouthshire are small. The capital has a limited trade along the Wye; but its situation, in a delightful country, has attracted the neighbouring gentry. There are still remains of its once powerful castle, and of a Benedictine priory. A few miles from Monmouth is Tintern Abbey (*fig.* 171.), the most picturesque, perhaps, of all the English monastic remains. This arises, not merely from its extent and beauty, although these be great: but from its roofless and ruined state, whence the walls, both within and without, are overgrown with luxuriant ivy, and decaying art and nature are blended together. In another direction is Ragland castle, the seat of the dukes of Beaufort (*fig.* 172.), and considered one of the strongest of the ancient fortresses; but, after the gallant defence made by the marquess of Worcester for Charles I., "Cromwell," says Gilpin, "laid his iron hand upon it, and shattered it to ruins; to which it owes its present picturesque form." Chepstow, at the mouth of the Wye, is a neat town, and carries on some trade. It is chiefly interesting, however, from the remains of its castle, one of the most striking of all the mighty fortresses of Wales. Five or six large towers still remain, with the outer walls of a magnificent chapel.

172

Ragland Castle.

Worcester and Gloucester occupy the lower valley of the Severn, which there becomes a river of the first magnitude. This valley is broad, smooth, and fertile, yet nowhere degenerates into a dead unvaried level. Worcester has, on the west, the Malvern Hills, some of whose summits rise to the height of nearly 1500 feet. Gloucestershire, again, has to the east the Cotswold Hills, more rugged, though not so elevated; while to the west are the rugged remains of the Forest of Dean. Worcestershire has, besides, the valley of the Lower Avon and of Evesham, famed for their beauty and fertility. The vales of these fine counties are fitted for produce of every description,—grain, fruits, pasturage, with some preference of the two latter. Gloucester is particularly distinguished for its dairies, which produce that rich cheese well known under its name. The best, or double Gloucester, is produced in the vale of Berkeley, situated along the lowest part of the course of the Severn. Both counties have flourishing manufactures, though not on the vast scale of the northern districts. Gloucester, in particular, has a very extensive fabric of fine woollens, carried on through numberless villages, in what are called "the Bottoms," a range of territory along the lower part of the Cotswold Hills. Its scarlet and blue woollens are in particular repute.

Worcester is a considerable and very handsome city, the principal streets being spacious and regular, with many good houses, and presenting a general air of neatness and comfort. It is of high antiquity, the cathedral (*fig.* 173.) having been founded in the 7th century, though the present structure was almost entirely erected in the 13th and 14th centuries. It is of great extent, simple and august, without the rich ornament which distinguishes some others. It contains the tomb of King John, one of the most ancient in England; also that of Prince Arthur. Worcester is chiefly noted in history for the great battle in which Cromwell totally routed the Scots army, and compelled Charles II. to quit England as a fugitive. The city has lost its woollen manufacture; but has still one of porcelain, the finest in the kingdom. Fifteen different materials are used, chiefly white granite, and steatite from Cornwall; and every piece passes through twenty-three hands before it is brought to perfection. Gloves are also made; and there is a considerable trade up and down the Severn.

173

Worcester Cathedral

Kidderminster is large and flourishing, in consequence of a very extensive manufactory of carpets. Droitwich is noted for its salt springs. They are covered with a deep stratum of gypsum: and for a long time the salt was made only from the brine which penetrated this bed; but, about a century ago, it was bored through, when the brine rushed up in vast quantities, and a large salt river was found to flow beneath. Thus the salt can now be procured in any quantity, and supplies a great part of England.

Gloucester is also an ancient and fine city, though not quite so large as Worcester. It bears, in the arrangement of its streets, the marks of having been a Roman station. It was formerly also, a place of great strength. The manner in which it frequently baffled the utmost efforts of Charles I. was one of the circumstances which contributed most to the downfall of the royal cause. The most conspicuous feature at present is the cathedral, built in the Saxon and Norman styles, between the 11th and 13th centuries. The beautiful lightness of its tower; its east window, said to be the largest in the kingdom; and its whispering gallery; attract peculiar notice. The gaol, built at an expense of 40,000*l.*, afforded one of the first applications of the beneficent principles of Howard. Pins are the chief manufacture of Gloucester; and, small as the article is, the sale is so great as to render the amount it returns considerable. Its trade has been much obstructed by the bad navigation of the Severn; but since the parallel line of the Berkeley Canal has just been completed, by which large ships can come up from the Channel, Gloucester is placed almost on a footing with Bristol.

Cheltenham, by the fame of its waters, and its attractions as a place of fashionable resort, has become a greater and more crowded place than Gloucester. The waters are at once saline and chalybeate; and, being thus both tonic and aperient, are efficacious in indigestion, biliary affections, and similar disorders. Cheltenham now ranks second only to Bath, both as a resort for invalids and a gay rendezvous of the fashionable world.

There are other interesting towns in Gloucestershire. Tewkesbury has in close vicinity the "Bloody Meadow," on which was fought the great battle which finally crushed the fortunes of the house of Lancaster. Placed at the junction of the Severn and Avon, it is a venerable old town, containing the Abbey church a remnant of that grand monastery, of which the superior, being a mitred abbot, sat in the House of Peers. Cirencester, a town of great historical name, covers only part of its ancient site, but contains one of the finest parochial churches in the kingdom. Stroud is the centre of the woollen manufacture carried on, not in itself, but in the surrounding valleys, and raising the population of the parish to 42,000. Bristol we shall consider as belonging to Somerset.

Of the seats the most interesting is Hagley, the grounds of which Lord Lyttelton adorned with classic taste. Near it is the interesting spot of the Leasowes, embellished by Shenstone with all the taste of a poet. Berkeley Castle is a grand castellated edifice, almost as old as the Conquest, and the scene of Edward II.'s death; retaining still its antique character.

Somerset has vales almost as extensive as those of Gloucester, yet it is crossed by long ranges of those rugged hills which pervade all the extreme west of England. The most easterly are the Mendip Hills, rich in mineral stores; farther west are the Quantock Hills, while on the borders of Devon lies Exmoor Forest, the most elevated of all these tracts—its highest point Dunkerry Beacon, being 1668 feet high. The prevailing husbandry is pasturage, chiefly of rich natural grass; and, besides a number of cattle sent to the London markets, the dairy is a great branch of industry. Chedder cheese is considered equal to any in England; and a great quantity of what is called Gloucester is produced in Somerset. The orchards are extensive, and cider and perry nearly as abundant as in the counties on the Severn. The Mendip Hills yield excellent coal, lead of fine quality, and calamine. The manufactures are considerable, both woollen and linen; the former chiefly of the finer sorts; the latter, mostly dowlas, tickens, and sail-cloth.

Bristol, since we have attached it to Somerset, must hold the first place. This city ranked long as second to the metropolis in commercial importance; but in the course of the last century, it has remained nearly stationary in extent and population, though not in wealth. In 1736, it had 80,000 inhabitants; in 1821, 87,771; but in 1831, with its suburbs, 104,886. It has still a very extensive trade, chiefly with Wales, Ireland, and the West Indies. Nor does its spirit seem abated; since, in 1809, it completed, at an expense of 60,000*l.*, a series of extensive improvements, by which the rivers Avon and Frome were spread out into vast basins, for the commodious reception of vessels. The manufactures of Bristol are very considerable; its glass-works are twenty in number; its brass founderies the most extensive in the kingdom; to which it adds shot, pottery, &c. In 1832 there belonged to it 296 ships, of the burthen of 46,567 tons. The amount of customs, in 1831, was 1,168,978*l.*, chiefly from duties on West India produce; and there entered its port 2547 vessels, of the burthen of 625,000 tons. It has still the remains of a magnificent cathedral, and the beautiful church of St. Mary Redcliffe, with many interesting monuments. The old interior of Bristol is ill-built and inconvenient; but the merchants in the new quarters of the city have reared some handsome streets and squares. Bristol has wells, considered very efficacious, especially in consumptive complaints. Visiters chiefly resort to the beautiful village of Clifton, about a mile distant, amid the romantic rocks of St. Vincent. Bristol stands conspicuous for its beneficent institutions, in which those for education stand prominent. Chatterton, Southey, and Coleridge were natives of Bristol.

The name of Bath (*fig.* 174.) implies the circumstance to which from the earliest ages it has owed its importance. The Romans made it one of their principal stations, and built

174

Bath.

splendid baths, of which the remains have been discovered. Near the middle of the last century, it became very distinguished as a scene of fashionable residence, and continued to increase till recently, when its attraction was shared by Cheltenham and some newer places of resort. It became the most beautiful, we may nearly say the only beautiful, city in England. The houses, built of a fine freestone, while those of almost all the other great towns are of brick, have a decidedly superior aspect; and several of the streets, as Great Pulteney Street, the Crescent, the Parades, &c., being not only composed of fine houses, but formed on a regular plan, may vie with the finest in Europe. The city, moreover, rising by a gentle ascent from the Avon, large portions of it may often be seen at once in the most advantageous points of view. The pump-room, the assembly-room, and every structure raised for the sick or the gay, are unequalled in splendour. Bath has a Gothic cathedral one of the latest built, and on a small scale, but the most highly ornamented in the kingdom; the chief beauty is in the west front.

Other venerable and interesting cities are found in Somersetshire. Wells is chiefly distinguished by a cathedral (*fig.* 175.), which ranks with the finest in England. The western front, built in the 13th century, is one of the most splendid specimens existing of the light and highly ornamented Gothic. In the interior, a chapel dedicated to the Virgin is much admired; the rest is Saxon, and heavy. About two miles distant is Wookey Hole, a natural cavern; the aperture, at first, merely allows one man to pass; but it soon opens into a succession of large apartments, filled with spars, concretions, petrifactions of the most fantastic forms. A subterraneous river prevents farther advance. Glastonbury contains the small remains of the most extensive monastery in the kingdom; which, with its various gardens and offices, covered sixty acres, supported 500 monks, and enjoyed a revenue of 25,000*l*. Even the church attached to it rivalled the greatest of the English cathedrals. Bridgewater and Taunton are towns of note in history, which carry on some trade and manufactures. Wellington gives a title to the greatest commander of the age, in whose honour a pillar is there erected. Frome is a large and flourishing town, employed in the woollen manufacture.

175

Wells Cathedral.

Devonshire is traversed by ridges of hills, low, broad and flat, which, seen from a height, appear often as one uninterrupted plain; but on minuter inspection are found separated by deep valleys called *coombs*, walled in by the steep sides of the hills. This structure produces many sequestered and romantic sites; it renders, however, many of the roads steep and circuitous, and in some places scarcely passable. The forest of Dartmoor, an extensive district on the west of the county, is of a character peculiarly rugged, broken into fantastic summits, and the valleys chiefly under wood or lying waste. On the other hand, the Vale of Exeter, and what are called the Hams, in the southern districts, are distinguished for fertility, which is rather heightened than injured by the moderate inequalities of the surface. Grain, cattle, sheep, potatoes, excellent cider, are raised according to the situation, and are all generally good. The cattle are of a very superior breed, both for feeding and draught. Devonshire does not rank high as a manufacturing county; yet woollens are made to some extent in Exeter and several other places. Fishing is carried on with spirit and success, both in the sea and in the rivers; of which last, the Exe and the Tamar are the principal. The Western Canal, joining the two channels, passes chiefly through Devonshire.

Exeter, the capital, is an ancient and pleasantly situated town, near the mouth of the Exe. In consequence of its advantages for education and society, many of the gentry from different parts of the county have made it their residence. Its manufacture and export of serges and kerseys have declined, but are still considerable; the East India Company taking them to the annual value of 400,000*l*. The cathedral holds a high rank among ecclesiastical antiquities. Some part of it is traced to the ninth century; but the greater proportion belongs to the thirteenth and fourteenth. The painted east window, and the bell of 12,500 lbs. weight, the gift of Bishop Courtenay, are particularly noticed. Some modern embellishments have been added.

Plymouth is the most important of the towns of Devonshire, and one of the great naval arsenals of Britain. The main and central depôts lie at Portsmouth and on the Thames; but it is important that the fleets should have this exterior station, where they may rendezvous, and receive their final equipment and supplies before leaving the Channel; where also, when exhausted, they may put in and refit. The Plym and the Tamar, at their junction, form an estuary of nearly two miles broad, composing a harbour, or rather a series of harbours, capable of containing 2000 vessels in a state of perfect security. In that of Hamoaze, on the Tamar, 100 sail of the line may be safely moored. Catwater, the port at the mouth of the Plym; and Sutton Pool, immediately adjoining the town; are both excellent and extensive. Plymouth Bay forms also an excellent roadstead, though exposed to the heavy swell which came in from the Atlantic. To remedy this, government undertook that stupendous work the Breakwater, a mole formed by immense stones heaped upon each othe stretching across the entrance, and at a certain distance from either shore (*fig.* 176.). The

176

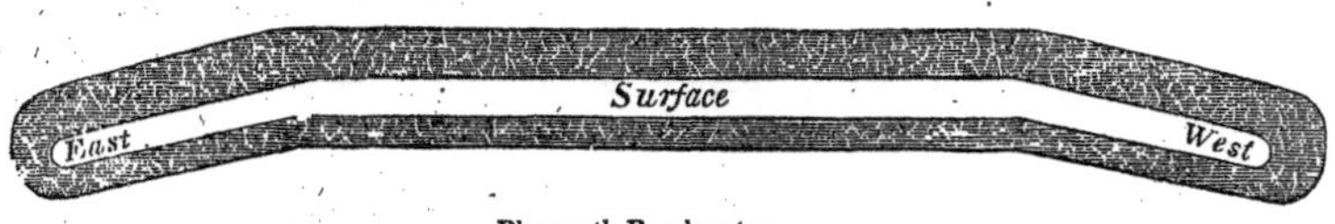


Plymouth Breakwater.

estimated expense was 1,170,000*l.*; and the quantity of stone, 2,000,000 tons. It has completely answered expectation; and, in proportion as it has advanced, has rendered the roadstead more secure. As the approach was also rendered dangerous by the Eddystone rocks, a light-house has, after much difficulty and several unsuccessful trials, been erected there by Mr. Smeaton, sufficiently firm to withstand the furious assaults of the Atlantic waves to which it is exposed. Plymouth is now divided into two nearly equal parts—Plymouth and Plymouth dock, at the mouth of the Tamar, recently called Devonport, and raised to the dignity of a separate borough. The dock-yard is most superb; 3500 yards in length and from 1000 to 1600 in breadth. All the establishments connected with it, the ropery smithy, saw-pits, mast-houses, as also the victualling departments, are on the most extensive scale, yet conducted in the most regular order. Plymouth is not, on the whole, a well-built town: but it contains some handsome edifices; as the government-house; the theatre, chiefly of cast-iron; the public library, &c. The charitable institutions are numerous.

Barnstaple is a sort of capital of North Devon, situated on a rich plain, and retaining a few manufactures. Dartmouth carries on some foreign trade; while between it and Teignmouth is Torbay, where, sheltered from the heavy gales that blow up the Channel, the British fleet can ride safely at anchor.

Cornwall is a peninsula of a triangular form, bounded by Devon, and the sea. The hills form a bleak central ridge, terminating in the rugged and obtuse point called the Land's End. But some of the narrow valleys wear the aspect of smiling fertility. In some secluded spots the climate is so genial, that the myrtle and other shrubs peculiar to the south of Europe flourish in the open air. Cornwall has from the earliest ages been renowned for its mineral products. These are principally tin and copper; it also yields some lead. These metals occur in the granite chain, extending eastward as far as Dartmoor in Devon; but at present the principal mining district is that between the Land's End and St. Austel. The most celebrated are the tin mines of Palgooth,* about two miles west of that town: in these there are no fewer than fifty shafts, of which twenty or thirty are constantly in use. The principal vein of ore, which is about six feet thick, runs from east to west, and dips to the north with an inclination of about six feet in a fathom. The ore is of the vitreous kind, but rarely found in crystals; the colour for the most part grayish-brown; the *country* of the ore is a gray killas. The water is carried away. Steam power has been substituted for that of horses in moving the machinery employed for raising, washing, and stamping the ore; after which last operation it is carried to the smelting-house. Tin cannot be sold until it is assayed and stamped with the duchy seal; for which purpose meetings are usually held four times a year. The annual produce is estimated at 20,000 or 25,000 blocks, each block weighing from 2¾ to 3¾ cwt., and valued on the average at ten guineas. *Grain tin*, which is obtained from stream ore, is deemed superior in value to the common metal, and has been procured to the amount of 2000 or 2400 blocks annually. The annual produce of copper is about 13,000 tons, estimated at 1,300,000*l.* The lead mines are not much worked. The tinners are in many respects a distinct body of men; they have a court and parliament of their own. The stannary laws, by which the mines and the operations connected with them are regulated, do not appear to have undergone any change since the reign of Charles II. The mines give employment to about 16,000 men.

The pilchard fishery affords another source of wealth to Cornwall. The pilchards appear annually in vast shoals about the middle of July; and are taken in large nets of a peculiar form, called *seans*, each sean managed by three boats, containing eighteen men. After lying salted in store for six weeks, the fish are packed in hogsheads, so closely that the whole contents, when turned out, appear in a compact state. The oil expressed from them is so considerable in quantity as to have become an article of trade. The quantity annually exported from the Cornish coast may be worth 50,000*l.* including the receipts for oil. The number of persons employed in this fishery is about 5000.

The towns of Cornwall are small. Launceston, situated on the Tamar, extends up the side of a hill, on the summit of which are the remains of a small fortress called *Castle Terrible*, where a vigorous stand was made to sustain the sinking fortunes of Charles I. Truro is a neat thriving town, the trade of which consists in a considerable export of tin. Penzance, near the Land's End, from the mild salubrity of its air, has been found highly beneficial to persons of delicate constitutions, particularly of a consumptive tendency; and those who take up their residence at Penzance, are agreeably surprised by the lovely scenery in its neighbourhood. Falmouth, the westernmost of the fine harbours on the Channel, is the principal packet station for Lisbon, the Mediterranean, and the West Indies.

### Subsect 5.—*Wales.*

Wales is a territory which, though united to England by early conquest, still retains the title of a separate principality, and possesses a national aspect. The verdant and extensive

* Dr. Maton's Observations on the Western Counties.

plains of western England here give place to the lofty mountain, the deep valley, the roaring torrent, and the frightful precipice. Wales has rivers and torrents without number which roll through its mountain valleys, and whose banks, adorned with verdure and cultivation, combine in the most striking manner with the lofty and varied summits which tower above them. The loftiest mountains are in North Wales; its valleys are deeper and narrower; and it presents more strikingly all the characteristic features of Welsh scenery. In South Wales, on the contrary, the valleys are broader, more fertile, and fuller of towns and villages; they often even expand into wide plains, still encircled by a mountain boundary. Agriculture, in such a country, labours under many disadvantages, and is carried on too often upon the old system of infield and outfield. Manufactures are nearly confined to the article of flannel, which has always been a fabric of the Welsh, in which they still excel their Yorkshire rivals. It is to mining, however, that the industry of Wales has been chiefly attracted, by the profusion of mineral wealth which nature has lodged in the bowels of its mountains. The lead of Flint, Caernarvon, and other counties of North Wales, the copper of Anglesey, and above all, the iron of Glamorgan and other counties in the British Channel, are objects of extensive importance. Coal is found almost everywhere, and is employed either for domestic purposes, or in fusing and refining the metallic ores.

The Welsh are a Celtic race, the descendants of the ancient Britons, who, in these mountain recesses, sought refuge from the destroying sword of the Saxons, which so completely dispossessed them of the low country of England. They could not resist the overwhelming power of Edward I., who annexed Wales to the English crown. In order to hold it in subjection, however, he was obliged to construct, not only on its frontier, but in its interior, castles of immense extent and strength. Yet they did not prevent formidable insurrections, in one of which Owen Glendower maintained himself for years as an independent prince. Within the last 300 years, the Welsh have been as peaceable as any other subjects of the empire. They have retained, of their feudal habits, only venial failings. Among these is national pride, through which the genuine Cambrian holds his country and his nation superior to all others; and regards the *Sasna* or Saxon as a lower race of yesterday. With this is connected, in a high degree, the pride of pedigree; even the humblest Welshman tracing his origin far above any lowland genealogy. Strong ties of friendship subsist between the landowners and their tenants: manifested, on one side, by indulgence and protecting kindness; on the other, by a profound veneration for the representatives of the ancient chiefs of their race. The Welsh have many superstitions, mixed with much genuine religious feeling. They are hardy, active, lively, hospitable, kind-hearted; only a little hot and quarrelsome. Their English neighbours complain that they have not yet attained that pitch of industry and cleanliness in which the former place their pride.

North Wales comprises the counties of *Caernarvon*, *Merioneth*, *Montgomery*, *Denbigh*, and *Flint*, with the island of *Anglesey*. The characteristic feature of this division consists in the very elevated chains of mountains which cross it from north to south, facing the Irish Channel. The chief is Snowdon (*fig.* 177,) which raises its head to the height of 3700 feet; yet it is only the most elevated of a crowd of summits, many of which rear their peaks almost as high. They cover a great part of the county of Caernarvon, at the northern part of which they present to the Bay of Beaumaris the lofty steep of Penmanmawr, whose broken fragments threaten to bury him who travels the difficult path which has been formed along its almost perpendicular sides. Merioneth is chiefly covered with inferior, but lofty and rugged mountains, till towards the southern extremity, they tower into Cader Idris, the second summit of Wales. It is everywhere steep, craggy, and precipitous. Lastly, in the heart of Montgomery, towers the huge mass of Plinlimmon, with a crowd of attendant mountains.

177

Snowdon.

The vales which intervene between these heights diversify bleak and barren regions, otherwise calculated to inspire only impressions of dreary sublimity. The most extensive is that of Clwyd, in the county of Denbigh, where the mountain chains gradually sink. It is about twenty miles in length, and four or five in average breadth; and presents a more brilliant picture of fertility, heightened, doubtless, by contrast, than almost any other spot in the island. The narrower vales, however, present more of picturesque beauty, particularly that of Llangolen, where the Dee, winding through cultivated and pastoral scenes, overhung by high rocks and cliffs, presents at every step a varying landscape. The island of Anglesey is generally level, and its scenery presents few striking features, except the rocks of its western shore. It has happened, fortunately for the improvement of this formidable range of territory, that it lies on the highway from London towards Dublin; and with the view of facilitating the intercourse between the kingdoms, government, at the national expense, has formed one of the finest roads in the world; among the principal features of which is the iron suspension-bridge, formed across the arm of the sea, called the Menai Channel. The chief centre of the flannel manufacture is in Montgomery and Merioneth. The lead mines of Holywell and the copper mines of Anglesey possess an importance scarcely inferior to those of South Wales.

178

Caernarvon Castle.

Caernarvon is a handsome, well-built town. Its chief ornament is the castle, a stately edifice (*fig*. 178.), built by Edward I. to curb the spirit of the newly subdued Welsh. It encloses an area of two acres and a half; the towers are of stupendous magnitude, and crowned by light and beautiful turrets. To the south of Caernarvon is the steep ascent of Snowdon, whence a view of astonishing extent is commanded; though only to be seen in those fortunate days when the veil of mist, which usually wraps it, has been dissipated. On its declivity is the wild and rocky lake of Llanbieris, with the ruined castle of Dolbadern overhanging its banks. Nearly at the opposite extremity of the county is Conway; a poor town, but containing the walls of a still more magnificent castle (*fig*. 179.), also erected by Edward I. The interior is in a state of total ruin; but the view, from a little distance, of its eight mighty towers, ranging along the summit of a lofty rock, which overlooks the Bay of Beaumaris, presents an image of grandeur which scarcely any other castellated structure in the kingdom can rival. About midway between those two castled sites is Bangor, a pleasant little town, on the high road to Holyhead and Dublin. Here, and at Penryn, is a great shipment of slates, brought from the steep sides of the neighbouring mountains.

179

Conway Castle.

Merioneth has a few large villages, each enclosed by a circuit of lofty and almost inaccessible mountains. Bala is supported by a small manufacture of knit gloves and stockings, and by the vicinity of the largest of the little lakes of Wales, which has clear water and abounds in fish. Dolgelly, about midway between Snowdon and Cader Idris (*fig*. 180.), is seated in the very heart of all the grandest scenery of Wales. On the coast, the castle of Harlech, built also by Edward, bears marks of great strength.

180

Cader Idris.

Montgomery, though its centre is occupied by the "huge Plinlimmon," whence branches shoot out in every direction, is yet, on the whole, of a milder aspect. The town of Montgomery is small, pleasantly situated on the declivity of a hill, crowned with the ruins of a once noble castle. Welshpool is an ill-built straggling town, but has a great market for flannels; and communicates by a canal with Chester and Ellesmere. Near Montgomery is Powis Castle, which dates from the twelfth century, and was long one of the proudest fortresses in Wales: it is still a superb modern seat.

In proceeding to Denbigh and Flint, we come to broader valleys, and hills gradually diminishing down to the level plain of western England. Denbigh, a pleasant, ancient little town, is crowned by a castle, seated on a high rock, looking down to the vale of Clwyd, proverbial for its smiling fertility. In the valley of the Dee, is Wrexham, noted for its fairs, in which Welsh flannel is the staple commodity. But the chief ornament of Denbigh is Llangollen Vale, on the upper Dee, where the mixture of culture and wildness produces the most striking variety of scenery. Among its leading features are the ruined castle of Dinas Bran, crowning the steep summit of one of the principal hills; and the remains of the Abbey of Valle Crucis. This last is situated in a valley connected with that of Llangollen, enclosed by lofty mountains verdant to the summit, and sprinkled with trees. The edifice has been in the simplest style of Saxon architecture; but the situation renders it one of the most picturesque spots in England. Chirk has near it a castle, one of the most perfect of the many with which Wales is adorned. Near it also is the fine aqueduct of Pont-y-Cysilte, by which Mr. Telford has conducted the Ellesmere Canal over the Dee, resting on 18 piers, 1007 feet in length, and 126 feet above the level of the river.

Flint is rich in lead and other mineral stores. The county town of Flint, and its castle, have entirely lost the importance they possessed when they were the prison of Richard II.; and the glory of Caerwys, the ancient scene of musical and poetical contest, has entirely passed away. Holywell, besides its extensive lead mine, carries on works in brass and copper, and even some cotton fabrics. Here the sacred well of St. Winfrede, from which it derives its name, is beneficially applied to the purposes of industry. The lead mine of Llan-y-Pander is the most extensive in the kingdom, and employs four vast steam-engines in clearing off the water. Mold is a pretty large town, in the centre of a rich plain of the same name. St. Asaph attracts notice by its neat cathedral.

The Island of Anglesey is generally a naked and gloomy flat. It was anciently the central seat of druidical superstition, still attested by the *cromlechs*, or large, flat, stone tables supported by rude pillars, which are more numerous here than in any other part of Britain. Its importance has rested almost entirely upon its copper mines, but of late they have become unproductive, and the annual amount is only from 750 to 950 tons. Beaumaris, the capital, is a neat little town. Much more importance attaches to Holyhead, now the main point of communication between England and Ireland. To render it such, government has constructed a noble road from London across the most rugged part of North Wales, and also made an admirable harbour. The neighbouring coast is very bold, and the promontory, called the Head (*fig.* 181.), consists of immense masses of precipitous rocks, hollowed into deep caverns. The town itself has been rapidly extended and improved.

181

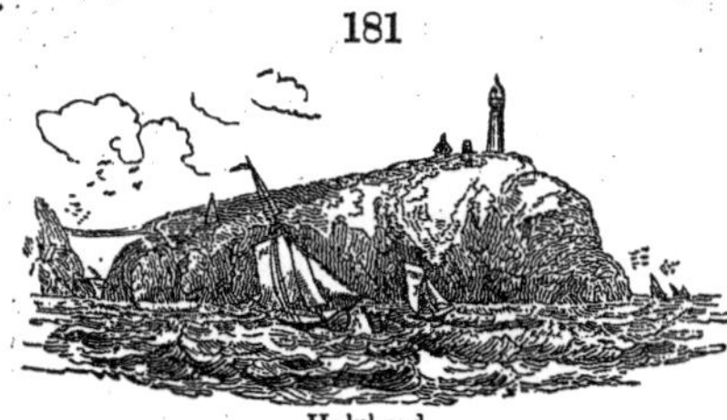

Holyhead.

South Wales comprises the counties of Radnor, Cardigan, Brecknock, Caermarthen, Pembroke, and Glamorgan. It presents scenery equally romantic with that of North Wales, mingled with a greater degree of softness and cultivation; and its agricultural and mining products are of considerably greater value.

Radnor is composed of bleak ranges of mountains, in some parts almost impassable; the greater part is only fitted to afford pasture for sheep, the wool of which is valuable. New Radnor, once a fortified city, is dwindled into a village.

Cardigan includes some of the boldest features of Welsh scenery. The domain of Hafod, in particular, has been covered with extensive plantations, so happily disposed as to render it almost a scene of enchantment. At a few miles' distance is "the Devil's Bridge;" an arch thrown over a deep and narrow rocky chasm, overgrown with wood, at the bottom of which rolls the Mynach, after rushing down three lofty cascades; forming altogether the grandest scene of the kind in the kingdom. The lead mines of Cardiganshire are extensive, though the want of fuel has caused the working of many of them to be discontinued. Cardigan is a small old town, which carries on a considerable coasting trade, having nearly 300 small vessels belonging to it. There is great resort to Aberystwith, an agreeable bathing place; its trade also is considerable.

Brecon, or Brecknock, is mountainous and rugged, but has some fertile lands in the valleys of the Uske and the Wye. Brecon, an ancient town on the Uske, amid lofty mountains, has the remains of a castle, which was once strong, and held by Buckingham, the favourite and afterwards the victim of Richard III.

Caermarthen includes an ample proportion of bleak and barren hills, intermixed with large fertile valleys. There are abundance of coal, and some iron works on the Glamorgan border. The capital, situated on the Towey, which admits to it vessels of 300 tons, is one of the most flourishing and best built towns in Wales.

Pembroke consists of a peninsula branching out between the Irish and British channels, it presents merely an undulating surface, rising at most to elevations of 200 or 300 feet. Its breed of cattle is in high repute, and its indented coasts contain some of the finest harbours in Britain. Two Roman roads cross this county, which is also rich in druidical and feudal monuments. The ancient city of Pembroke is strikingly situated on an almost insulated neck of land on the bay of Milford Haven, the highest part of which presents the vast remains of its castle, one of the most magnificent structures of Wales or England. The town contains some ancient churches. The large bay composing Milford Haven forms the most capacious and secure harbour in Britain. Hence government have been induced, at the new towns of Milford and Haberstone, on its northern shore, to form dock-yards and establish packets for the south of Ireland. St. David's, the ecclesiastical capital of South Wales, is now only a large dirty village, adorned, however with venerable ancient structures.

Glamorgan is the finest county in South Wales, and, as to wealth, superior to any other in the principality. Its coast, along the Bristol Channel, and for some miles inland, is level, and fertile in the extreme. Thence the ground rises into hills of continually increasing elevation, till, on the frontier, they rise to the height of upwards of 2000 feet, and unite with the Brecon chains. From these heights descend numerous streams, which, in their progress to the sea, produce all the varieties of ravines, wooded vales, falls, and cataracts; which, with the beauty of the plains below, and the fine views over the Bristol Channel, render Glamorgan equal in picturesque beauty to any other county in Wales. The crops of every description of grain are ample; and there are good breeds both of cattle and sheep.

But these objects are trifling, when compared with the mineral treasures of Glamorgan. It forms the centre of a vast field of coal and iron, from which branches extend into the neighbouring counties. Since it was found that iron could be smelted with coke, the working of this metal has prodigiously increased, and the town of Merthyr Tydvil, near which it is most abundant, has grown from a mere village to be the most populous place in Wales. In consequence also of the abundance of fuel, the copper ore dug out in Anglesey, Cornwall, and Ireland, is brought hither to be smelted and refined. The plating of iron with tin is also an extensive occupation. The iron is reduced by rollers to the requisite thinness, and is then cut by scissors into plates, which afterwards require little more than simple immersion into the smelted tin. The coal, besides its essential use in these various works, is in itself a most extensive object of exportation, amounting in some years to 300,000 tons. The rivers of Glamorgan are very imperfectly navigable; but this defect has been supplied by industry. From Neath, Cardiff, and Swansea, canals reach far into the interior; and their benefits being extended by railways, a channel has been opened for conveying to the sea the produce even of the most interior mines. Cardiff ranks as the county town, but is now much surpassed by others. Yet it carries on a considerable trade; having a commodious harbour, and being connected by a canal with the interior works at Merthyr Tydvil. It is now much surpassed by Swansea, which has risen to its present importance by immense works in iron and copper, and by the exportation of coal; which is furnished in such abundance, that a large vessel may enter at one tide and go out loaded at the next. Its pleasant situation on a fine bay has also made it an extensive resort for sea-bathing, and led to the erection of many elegant buildings. Swansea has thus risen into a sort of capital of South Wales; yet it is not so large as Merthyr Tydvil has been rendered by the extensive iron works in and round it. There are near it seventeen furnaces, in one of which 11,000 tons of pig iron and 12,000 tons of bar iron are produced annually. Caerphilly, a thriving little town, with some manufactures, deserves notice chiefly from the remains of its immense castle (*fig.* 182.), which present a most stupendous scene of ruins. It is stated to have been a mile and a quarter in circumference, and capable of containing a garrison of 20,000 men. Llandaff, the only nominal city in the county, is only a village, the seat of the least richly endowed bishopric in Wales. The cathedral, however, is a fine ruin.

182

Caerphilly Castle.

The small islands attached to England are unimportant. Man, thirty miles in length by twelve in breadth, is nearly equidistant from each of the three kingdoms. It comprises a considerable extent of level territory; but rises in the interior into high mountains, among which Snowfell, nearly 2000 feet high, stands conspicuous. Man ranked long as an independent sovereignty, held by the Earls of Derby, and is celebrated for the gallant defence made by the countess of that name for Charles I. It descended afterwards to the Duke of Athol, from whom the sovereignty was purchased, in 1765, by the British government, with a view to the prevention of smuggling, and to the establishment of a free trade. The natives are a Celtic race. Castletown, the capital, is the neatest town in the island; and in its centre, Castle Rushen, the ancient palace of the kings of Man, rears its gloomy and majestic brow. Douglas, however, as being the spot in which the whole trade circulates, is now of superior importance, and has attracted a great number of English settlers.

The Scilly isles, situated at some distance from the western extremity of Cornwall, are tenanted by 2000 poor inhabitants, who raise a little grain, but depend chiefly upon fishing, pilotage, and the making of kelp.

Jersey, Guernsey, and Alderney, with Sark, form a group naturally French, and originally part of the patrimony of the Norman kings, which the naval superiority of England has enabled her to retain. They enjoy certain privileges and immunities, founded on this distinction, as laid down by Coke, that, "though parcel of the dominion of the *crown* of England, they are not, nor ever were, parcel of the *realm* of England." The climate is mild and agreeable, and the soil generally fertile. *Jersey*, the finest of the group, is so abundant in orchards, that cider forms the chief object of exportation. St. Helier, the capital of Jersey, is a handsome town.

---

## CHAPTER III.

### SCOTLAND

The place which Scotland holds as part of Great Britain, has already been exhibited in the introduction to the chapter on England. We shall now describe in detail this important, though secondary, member of the empire.

#### Sect. I.—*Geographical Outline.*

Scotland is bounded on the south by England, from which it is separated by a line drawn along the Tweed, the Cheviot Hills, and thence to the Solway Frith. On every other side it is bounded by the Atlantic, the Northern and the German oceans. The length of Scotland, from the Mull of Galloway (*fig.* 183.), in about 54° 40′ to Dunnet Head, Caithness, in 58° 40′, is 280 miles. The greatest breadth, from Buchan-Ness to a point on the opposite shore of Inverness is 130 miles. This breadth varies little in the interval between the friths of Forth and Moray; but to the south of the former, the average breadth scarcely exceeds 100, and to the north of the Moray Frith, 40 or 50 miles. The entire extent of Scotland is 29,600 square miles.

183

Mull of Galloway.

Scotland, in its general outline, consists of two great and perfectly distinct parts: the Lowlands and the Highlands. The former comprehends all Scotland south of the friths of Forth and Clyde; for the pastoral hills of the southern and western borders, less elevated than the northern mountains, and inhabited by a different race, are not considered as forming any tie between these and the Highlands properly so called. Immediately north of the Clyde, the highland ranges begin to tower in endless succession; but on the east coast, the Lowlands extend beyond the Forth and northward through the counties of Fife, Forfar, Kincardine, and Aberdeen; though these last are closely encroached upon by the mountain territory. The lowland district also extends round the northern promontory of Aberdeen, and along the borders of the Murray or Moray Frith, which contain as level tracts of territory, and enjoy as mild a climate, as any part of Scotland. This level tract does not comprehend quite the half of the country; even the Lothians, and still more the western provinces, are hemmed in by low ridges of bleak tablelands, covered, in a great measure, with heath and moss. The arable lands are almost solely comprised in broad flat valleys, chiefly along the friths, called *straths* or *carses.* Several of these are much famed for fertility, a blessing but partially bestowed even on the best districts of Scotland.

The Highlands, which comprise the whole west and centre of northern Scotland, form a region of very bleak and rugged aspect. A chain of long and lofty ridges extends from south-west to north-east, not reaching, however, the German Ocean or the Moray Frith, but leaving between them the level interval of the northern lowland. These mountains usually dip, almost perpendicularly, into the lakes and seas on which they border; and even the interior valleys are on so high a level, that in this climate they admit only in scattered patches the culture of the coarser kinds of grain, particularly oats and bigg. These mountains, particularly the great Grampian barrier, which extends across from Ben Lomond to Blair-Athol, lock in closely with each other, and can be entered only by formidable and easily defended passes. The consequence has been, that they have preserved within their recesses a primitive people, who, in dress, language, and the whole train of their social ideas, differ essentially from the Lowlanders, and have retained antique and striking characteristics, both physical and moral, that are obliterated in almost every other part of Great Britain.

The Isles comprise the third part of Scotland. On the east, indeed, and even on great part of the south-west coast, only a few bold and naked rocks rise perpendicularly from the ocean. But the western highlands are bordered by the Hebrides, an extensive range of large islands, some of which are separated from the continent by such narrow channels, that they may almost be considered as forming part of it. Again, the northern extremity of Scotland is prolonged by the two ranges of the Orkney and Shetland islands, in a continuous line with each other, but at some distance. These islands are rocky and bare, exposed

NORTH SEA
Hoy Waas
Pentland
South Ronaldshay
Firth
Stroma
C. Wrath
Farout Hd.
Whiten Hd.
Strathy Hd.
Butt of the Lewis
LEWIS
Barvas
THE MINCH
L. Inchard
L. Assynt
Rumone
L. of Stornaway
L. Shell
L. Seaforth
L. Broom
SUTHERLAND
CAITHNESS
Thurso
Dornoch Firth
Dornoch
CROM
Ben Wivis
Murray Firth
Cromarty
Spey Bay
Troup Hd.
Kinnairds Hd.
Banff
Elgin
Pt. of Aird
Rona I.
Raasay I.
Scalpa I.
SKYE
Inverness
NAIRN
ELGIN
BANFF
ABERDEEN
New Aberdeen
KINCARDINE
Bervie
Montrose
INVERNESS
Rum
Eig
Muck I.
Coll I.
L. Lochy
Grampian Mts.
FORFAR
Forfar
Arbroath
Bell Rock
MULL
PERTH
Tay R.
Firth of Tay
Cupar
Fife Ness
Kinross
KINROSS
FIFE
Firth of Forth
Scarba I.
Colonsay
ARGYLE
Inverary
Lomond
B. Lomond
Stirling
STIRLING
Clackmannan
DUMBARTON
Glasgow
LINLITH.
EDINBURGH
Edinburgh
Haddington
HADDINGTON
St. Abbs Hd.
BERWICK
Berwick
JURA
ISLAY
Sound of Jura
Gigha I.
Mull of Oe
Cantire
ARRAN
Kilbrannan Sd.
Firth of Clyde
RENFREW
Lanark
LANARK
PEEBLES
SELKIRK
Selkirk
ROXBURGH
Ayr
AYR
Turnberry Hd.
Rachlin
Mull of Cantire
DUMFRIES
Dumfries
KIRCUDBRIGHT
Wigtown
WIGTOWN
Kirkcolm Pt.
Port Patrick
Luce Bay
Wigtown B.
Solway Firth
Isle of Man
Carrickfergus
Belfast L.
Belfast
IRELAND
NORTH CHANNEL
ENGLAND
10 20 30 40
English Miles
Longitude West from Greenwich

to excessive moisture and the perpetual storms of the Atlantic. The population bears, in language and features, the marks of a Scandinavian origin; dating from the period when the piratical rovers of the north made extensive inroads on the western states of Europe.

Among the Scottish mountains, the most considerable are the Grampians, a name which is given very generally to all those which cover the surface of the Highlands, but applied more particularly to the chain running across the counties of Perth and Argyle, and comprising Ben Lomond, Ben Ledi, Ben More, Ben Lawers, and others of that elevated ridge which directly face the low country of Stirling and Perth. Several of these mountains exceed the altitude of 4000 feet. Ben Nevis rises to the height of 4315 feet. On the borders of Inverness and Ross-shire, Ben Wyvis, and some others, are of nearly equal elevation. The south of Scotland is also very hilly; but its heights are seldom more than 2000 feet, green and pastoral. The most remarkable are the boundary chain of the Cheviot, celebrated in the annals of early feud, hunting, and border warfare. The Lowthers, a steep high ridge, including valuable lead mines; the pastoral hills of Ettrick and Yarrow; and Criffel and Cairnsmuir, in Galloway, form important objects: the lower ranges of the Pentland and Lammermoor border the Lothians.

The rivers of Scotland are not so much distinguished for their length or magnitude, as for the pastoral scenery through which they wind their early course, and for the magnificent estuaries which they form at their junction with the sea.

The Forth rises near the foot of Ben Lomond, flows east towards Stirling, near which it is swelled by the larger stream of the Teith; whence, after many windings through the beautiful plain overlooked by Stirling castle, it opens into the great frith on which the capital of Scotland is situated.

---

*References to the Map of Scotland.*

NORTH PART.
1. Dunnet
2. Cannesby
3. Freswick
4. Wick
5. Ulbster
6. Easkay
7. Thurso
8. Brachry
9. Strathy
10. Farr Kirk
11. Riviegill
12. Tongue
13. Inch Keanloch
14. Loch Eriboll
15. Gradey
16. Drumacray
17. Scourie
18. Colesreme
19. Inver Bagasly
20. Loch Naver
21. Loch Baden
22. Achnahoe
23. Latheron
24. Berrydale
25. Helmsdale
26. Clyne
27. Achintran
28. Dalmor
29. Lairg
30. Tulloch
31. Loch Slim
32. Assynt
33. Stoir
34. Dorney
35. Cannahoulish
36. Ullapool
37. Portinlick
38. Bra
39. Golspie
40. Dornoch
41. Tarbat
42. Cromarty
43. Tain
44. Invergordon
45. Kincardine
46. Kildrimore
47. Ben Wyvis
48. Lochbroom
49. Loch Fuir
50. Tinafidine
51. Melveg
52. Erridale
53. Gairloch
54. Loch Maree
55. Loch Fannich
56. Loch Luichard
57. Kiltearn
58. Fortrose
59. Fort George
60. Nairn
61. Forres
62. Elgin
63. Rothes
64. Fochabers
65. Cullen
66. Marnoch
67. Portsoy
68. Banff
69. Turreff
70. Aberdour
71. Frasersburgh
72. Strichen
73. Peterhead
74. Cruden
75. Ellon
76. Rothie
77. Meldrum
78. Cusalmond
79. Kinnethmont
80. Achindore
81. Huntley
82. Kinnacoil
83. Aberlour
84. Grantown
85. Edenskille
86. Dymer
87. Cairmichyle
88. Inverness
89. Dares
90. Obriachan
91. Kilmuir
92. Beauly
93. Mucrich
94. Kilnacrow
95. Attadale
96. Torridon
97. Vonebane
98. Applecross
99. Killilan
100. Glen Shiel
101. Affarie
102. Dundragan
103. Loch Ness
104. Bellaloin
105. Aberarder
106. Aviemore
107. Kincardine
108. Abernethy
109. Achenraw
110. Strathdon
111. Towie
112. Cluny
113. Kintore
114. Inverury
115. Foveran
116. Fintray
117. Old Aberdeen
118. New Aberdeen
119. Stonehaven
120. Ternan
121. Birse
122. Balmoral
123. Braemar
124. Inch
125. Invernahaven
126. Laggan
127. Fort Augustus
128. Loch Garry
129. Loch Lochy
130. Clunes
131. Loch Arkeg
132. Rosary
133. Ruddroch
134. Loch Morrey
135. Arasaig
136. Sminasary
137. Loch Sheil
138. Cromer
139. Strane
140. Ben Nevis
141. Fort William
142. Aberarder
143. Loch Laggan
144. Dalwhinnie
145. Etrish
146. Clachay
147. Clova
148. Mennuir
149. Craigour
150. Glenbervie
151. Bervie
152. Montrose
153. Brechin
154. Lunan
155. Oathlaw
156. Glenisla
157. Moulin
158. Blair-Athol
159. Dalnacardoch
160. Shechallion
161. Loch Rannoch
162. Loch Ericht
163. Loch Treag
164. Kinlochmore
165. Corriherich
166. Aryhoulan
167. Scarnadale
168. Langall
169. Liddesdale
170. Kinlochaline
171. Morven
172. Ardnamurchan

SOUTH PART.
1. Appin
2. Ardchattan
3. Glencoe
4. Loch Etive
5. King's House
6. Fingar
7. Ben Lawers
8. Killin
9. Loch Tay
10. Kenmore
11. Aberfeldy
12. Amubrie
13. Dunkeld
14. Blairgowrie
15. Cupar-Angus
16. Meigle
17. Arbroath
18. Muirdrum
19. Dundee
20. Kilmeny
21. Cupar
22. Newburgh
23. Perth
24. Crieff
25. Comrie
26. Loch Earn
27. Craggan
28. Loch Voil
29. Loch Lochart
30. Glenurchay
31. Cladick
32. Kilmore
33. Ardmaddy
34. Craignish
35. Kilmartin
36. Inverary
37. Strachur
38. Kilmorish
39. Ben Lomond
40. Lock Katrine
41. Loch Lubnaig
42. Doune
43. Williamstown
44. Muchart
45. Forteviot
46. Kinross
47. Falkland
48. St. Andrew's
49. Anstruther
50. Leven
51. Kinghorn
52. Dunfermline
53. Clackmannan
54. Airth
55. Stirling
56. Dumblane
57. Milton
58. Campsie
59. Loch Lomond
60. Tarbat
61. Kilmodan
62. Gilphead
63. Acbahoish
64. Carnmore
65. Killarraw
66. Kilchenzie
67. Southend
68. Campbellton
69. Suddale
70. Gorton
71. Skipness
72. Ruban
73. Greenock
74. Kilbirnie
75. Dumbarton
76. Paisley
77. Renfrew
78. Glasgow
79. Bothwell
80. Airdrie
81. Whitburn
82. Falkirk
83. Linlithgow
84. Borrowstownness
85. Edinburgh
86. Dalkeith
87. Musselburgh
88. Haddington
89. North Berwick
90. Dunbar
91. Scateraw
92. Bunkle
93. Dunse
94. Paxton
95. Eccles
96. Gordon
97. Channelkirk
98. Lauder
99. Middleton
100. Linton
101. Peebles
102. Carnwath
103. Lanark
104. Hamilton
105. Eaglesham
106. Stewarton
107. Dalry
108. Irvine
109. Ayr
110. Mauchline
111. Kilmarnock
112. Strathaven
113. Douglas
114. Crawfordjohn
115. Crawford
116. Culter Fell
117. Galashiels
118. Melrose
119. Selkirk
120. Kelso
121. Yetholme
122. Hownam
123. Southdean
124. Jedburgh
125. Hawick
126. Bedford Green
127. Kirkpatrick
128. Sanquhar
129. Kirkconnel
130. Ochiltree
131. Dalrymple
132. Girvan
133. Ballintrae
134. Balloch
135. Garry
136. Minihive
137. Dunscore
138. Penpont
139. Lochmaben
140. Westerkirk
141. Langholm
142. Gretna Green
143. Annan
144. Dumfries
145. Caerlaverock
146. Douglas
147. Urr
148. Loch Ken
149. Newton Stewart
150. Craighach
151. New Luce
152. Stranraer
153. Portpatrick
154. Maidenkir
155. Ardwell
156. Glenluce
157. Mochrum
158. Whitehorn
159. Wigton
160. Laurieston
161. Kirkcudbright
162. Colvend

*Rivers.*
a Naver Water
b Thurso Water
c Oikel
d Orrin
e Nairn
f Findhorn
g Spey
h Doveran
i Don
j Dee
k Esk
l Tay
m Earn
n Forth
o Tweed
p Annan
q Nith
r Ken
s Ayr
t Clyde

SKYE ISLE.
1. Dig
2. Uig
3. Totnacrach
4. Snizort
5. Stein
6. Roag
7. Bracadale
8. Drumah
9. Gillan
10. Broadford
11. Kyle

MULL ISLE.
1. Kilninian
2. Tobermorie
3. Keallan
4. Aros
5. Achnacraig
6. Cambus
7. Moy
8. Fidden

JURA ISLE.
1. Leaghall
2. Lagg

ISLAY ISLE.
1. Sanaig
2. Kilchoman
3. Bolsha
4. Askaig
5. Bowmore
6. Kildalton
7. Kintra

ARRAN ISLE
1. Oran
2. Corrie
3. Kilbride
4. Kilmory

The Clyde rises on the borders of Dumfries-shire; flows for a considerable space through a wild pastoral valley; and descends, by a succession of most picturesque cascades, into the lower region of Lanarkshire. After passing through a tract which may be denominated the garden of Scotland, it enters Glasgow, becomes a broad stream, and expands into a winding frith, not so broad as the Forth, but the scene of a much more active trade.

The Tweed rises from the same chain as the Clyde, and running eastward, waters the most beautiful and classic of the pastoral districts of Scotland, in whose verse Tweed is the favourite name. Of similar fame are its tributaries, the Yarrow, the Gala, the Teviot; swelled by whose waters it forms, on reaching Berwick, a capacious harbour.

The Tay rises in the central Highlands, descends into the lowlands of Perthshire, and after winding beautifully round the city of Perth, expands into the Frith of Tay, and forms the harbour of Dundee.

The Spey has a longer course than any other; but, rising in the midst of the Perthshire highlands, and rolling northward through the wild recesses of Athol and Braemar, its line is comparatively obscure. The other rivers of Scotland are of subordinate rank; the Dee of Aberdeen, the Esk of Montrose, the Nith and Annan of Dumfries, the Ayr and Irvine of Ayr.

Lochs form a characteristic feature of Scotland; many of them are long arms of the sea, running up into the heart of the mountains. Among these, Loch Lomond is pre-eminent. The traveller admires its vast expanse, its gay and numerous islands, its wooded promontories and bays, and the high mountain barrier at its head. Loch Katrine, in a smaller compass, presents a singular combination of romantic beauty. Loch Tay, enclosed by the loftiest of the Grampians, presents alpine scenery on the grandest scale; while at Inverary, Loch Fyne unites the pomp of art with that of nature. The long chain of Lochs Linnhe, Lochy, and Ness, stretching diagonally across Scotland, comprises much fine scenery, and has afforded facilities for making a navigable communication between the German and Atlantic oceans.

### Sect. II.—*Natural Geography.*

This section will contain Geology only, as the Botany and Zoology of Scotland were described along with that of Great Britain in general, under the head of England.

#### Subsect. 1.—*Geology of Scotland.*

Scotland may be divided geologically into the following great districts:—1. Southern; 2. Middle; 3. Northern; 4. Insular.

(1.) *Southern division.* This division includes that part of the country bounded on the south by the northern frontier of England; and on the north and west, by the comparatively flat country between the Forth and the Clyde. It is traversed from St. Abb's Head on the east coast to Portpatrick on the west coast by a high land, named the *great southern high land of Scotland,* in which are situated the highest mountains in this division of Scotland. This lofty range sends out branches in different directions, many of which reach the sea-coast, while others terminate in the lower and flatter parts of the country that lies around them. Although abundantly supplied with rivers, the southern division contains but few lakes, in this respect forming a striking contrast with the middle and northern divisions. The mountainous regions are composed of transition rocks, while the lower and flatter consist principally of secondary and alluvial formations.

I. *Transition rocks.* The predominating rocks of the Neptunian class are greywacke, with subordinate beds of clay slate, flinty slate, and transition limestone; the Plutonian species are granite, syenite, porphyry, serpentine, and trap; by far the most abundant rock is the greywacke, in which the principal lead-mines in Scotland, those of Leadhills and Wanlockhead, are situated. They have been worked from an early period, and during a long course of years have yielded to the proprietors a very rich return. Of late years, owing to the disturbed state of the world, their prosperity has been interrupted. Copper ores have been raised in Galloway, but not in considerable quantity; and the same may be said of the sulphuret of antimony, formerly mined at Glendinning in Dumfries-shire.

II. *Secondary rocks.* Scotland is distinguished from England by the smaller number of its secondary formations, and their more limited distribution; the southern division contains a greater proportion than the middle or northern; and hence approaches more nearly to England in a general geognostic point of view. The following secondary formations have been observed:—1. Old red sandstone. 2. Mountain limestone. 3. Coal formation. 4. New red sandstone. 5. Various trap and porphyry rocks.

1. *Old red sandstone.* This formation skirts the transition chains of mountains lying immediately upon the greywacke, &c. It is well exposed in the Pentlands, the upper part of the river district of the river Clyde, in the course of the river Tweed, in various points in Dumfries-shire, &c. In the districts where it occurs, it is frequently quarried as a building-stone.

2. *Mountain limestone.* The beds of limestone in the lower part of the coal formation

in the neighbourhood of Edinburgh, and the beds of limestone upon which the coal formation rests in other quarters, as in Dumfries-shire, belong to the mountain limestone.

3. *Coal formation.* This important deposit occupies considerable portions of East, Mid, and West Lothian, and extends westward to Glasgow. It forms extensive tracts in Ayrshire; in Dumfries-shire; and in Berwickshire. The coal mines in the Lothians and around Glasgow are the most productive in Scotland. The annual quantity of coal brought into Glasgow is 561,049 tons; of which 124,000 are exported. It may also be noticed, as connected with coal, that in Glasgow, during twenty-four hours in the winter months, the gas company make upwards of 500,000 cubic feet of gas from coal; and during the same period in the summer months, about 120,000. The pipes extend to more than 100 miles through streets. The great iron-works at Carron are supplied with the ore from which the iron is obtained, from the coalfields of this and the middle division of Scotland. The ore or stone, which is an argillaceous carbonate of iron, occurs in beds and embedded masses, and principally in the slate of the coal deposit. The admirable building-stone around Edinburgh and Glasgow is a sandstone which occurs in beds in the coal formation.

4. *New red sandstone.* This formation in the regular succession rests upon the coal formation, in which position it is to be seen in the neighbourhood of Cannoby in Dumfries-shire.

5. *Trap and porphyry rocks.* These ignigenous masses occur in many parts: they abound, for instance, all around Edinburgh; forming part of the Calton Hill, Castle Hill, Salisbury Craigs, Arthur Seat, the Pentlands, &c.: the beautiful conical hill named North Berwick Law, the Bass Rock, the Isle of May, Traprain Law, are also formed of trap and porphyry rocks. Renfrewshire and Ayrshire also abound in splendid and interesting displays of trap and porphyry. In many parts of the country these rocks are used as building-stones, and the greenstone of the trap series affords an admirable material for road-making. The splendid causeways and roads around Edinburgh are of greenstone.

III. *Alluvial rocks.* In various parts of the country there occur deposits of old alluvium, or what is called *diluvium*; and everywhere the modern alluvium, or that daily forming meets the eye.

(2.) *Middle division.* This division of Scotland is bounded to the south by the southern division; on the north by the Moray Frith and the great chain of lakes extending from Inverness to Fort William and the Linnhe Loch. It is traversed in a north and south-westerly direction by the Grampian range of mountains, which extends from the Mull of Cantyre to Stonehaven in Kincardineshire, and to the rocky northern coasts of Aberdeenshire and Banffshire. The country in general falls rapidly to the west of this great mountain range, and comparatively gently to the eastward of it: hence the western acclivity is steep and short, the eastern gentle and long. On the eastern acclivity and the low lands connected with it are situated the Sidlay, Ochil, and Campsie hills, forming a pretty continuous range; and Kellie Law, Largo Law, the Lomonds, and the Saline Hills in Fifeshire, forming a less continuous and lower range of hills. Water is abundantly distributed over this district, in the form of rivers, lakes, and springs. Lakes, which are so rare in the southern division, are here abundantly distributed, and exhibit many beautiful and splendid scenes. Of these lakes the most considerable are the following: Loch Lomond, Loch Tay, Loch Ness, and Loch Awe. The rocks are more varied in this than in the southern division; magnificent displays of primitive, transition, and secondary formations present themselves to our attention.

I. *Primitive and transition rocks.* The Neptunian kinds are granite, gneiss, mica slate, clay slate, talc slate, chlorite slate, quartz rock, greywacke, limestone: the Plutonian rocks are granite, syenite, porphyry, trap, and serpentine. The Neptunian rocks generally range from north-east to south-west; most frequently dip under an angle of about 45°; and are variously upheaved, broken, and disturbed by the Plutonian rocks. They are principally confined to the Grampian high land and its branches. The most remarkable granite and syenite districts are Cairngorm, Benachie, Aberdeen, Peterhead, Ben Cruachan; and Ben Nevis conjoins along with its slaty Neptunian strata, granite, syenite, and porphyry. In some quarters the limestone is raised as marble, as in Glen Tilt; but more frequently it is burnt into quicklime. The clay slate quarries of Luss, on the banks of Loch Lomond; those of Balachulish, in Argyleshire; and the slate quarries in the interior of Aberdeenshire, are of considerable extent, and employ many workmen. There were formerly lead-mines in the neighbourhood of Tyndrum, where the lead glance, or sulphuret of lead, was disposed in veins in quartz rock and mica slate.

II. *Secondary rocks.* These are, old red sandstone, mountain limestone, coal formation, and new red sandstone, and probably the lias formation: these strata are variously intermingled with trap and porphyry rocks.

1. *Old red sandstone.* This rock, in some parts of the country, as in the vicinity of Stonehaven and near Blair-Gowrie, exhibits magnificent cliffs of conglomerate. It forms the principal rock in the great tract of country included between lines drawn from Stonehaven by Blair-Gowrie, Comrie, Callender, Dumbarton, Stirling, Kinross, Dundee, Arbroath,

Montrose, and Bervie. It appears again near Inverness, and on the banks of Loch Ness. In many localities there are extensive quarries, the sandstone being used as a building-stone, and as a pavement-stone. The Kinguddie sandstone and the Arbroath pavement-stone, from old red sandstone localities, are well known.

2. *Coal formation.* The coal formation in the middle division of Scotland has not been met with farther north than Fifeshire. The counties of Fife, Clackmannan, and Stirling, abound in coal; of these counties, Fife is that which contains the greatest fields of this valuable mineral.

3. New red sandstone occurs apparently in some points on the east coast, and also on the north coast between Cullen and the Cromarty Frith.

4. *Lias formation.* Near to Banff there are beds of clay, which, from the organic remains contained in them, may turn out to belong to this formation.

5. *Plutonian rocks.* These are various traps, as greenstone, amygdaloid, trap tuffa, and basalt; and porphyries, having a basis of claystone or clinkstone. The famous headland the Red Head, on the east coast, exhibits a fine display of Plutonian rocks, connected with the red sandstone. Bervie Head and the vicinity are interesting from their porphyry rocks. The trap rocks of Montrose are famous on account of the agates they afford. Kinnoul Hill, at Perth, is composed of amygdaloid, tuffa, and other rocks of the trap series, and abounds in agates. The Ochil Hills are principally composed of trap and porphyry; and trap rocks abound in the Campsie range. The Fifeshire hills, viz. Kellie Law, Largo Law, the cones of the Lomond, and the Saline Hills, are of trap. These various traps and porphyries have, as is generally the case, broken and changed more or less the Neptunian strata with which they are intermingled.

III. *Alluvial rocks.* These have the same general characters as those met with in the southern division. In a few districts, however, as near to Peterhead, and in the vicinity of Banff, there are numerous *chalk flints.* These, by some, are considered as alluvial, and foreign to Scotland; while others are of opinion that they are remains of the chalk formation, formerly distributed in some of the tracts where the flints are found.

(3.) *Northern division.* This division is bounded on the south by the chain of lakes which forms the northern limit of the middle division, and on the north, the east, and the west, by the ocean. The high land ranges throughout its whole length, from south-west to north-east. The western acclivity is steep and short; the eastern comparatively gently inclined and long. Rivers, springs, and lakes are numerous. The whole of this division, nearly, is composed of primitive and transition rocks, the secondary occurring principally along the east coast and a small extent of the north-west coast.

I. *Primitive and transition rocks.* The Neptunian species are disposed in strata that often range from south-west to north-east, are of gneiss, mica slate, clay slate, quartz rock, talc slate, limestone, and greywacke. The Plutonian rocks are less abundant than in the middle and southern divisions of Scotland; and are granite, syenite, porphyry, and trap. The only mines are those at Strontian, where the ore is lead glance, or sulphuret of lead, in veins traversing gneiss. The mineral in which the *Strontian earth* was first found occurs in these mines, along with other curious minerals, of which the cross-stone is the most interesting.

II. *Secondary rocks.* The formations of this class are both Neptunian and Plutonian. The Neptunian are old red sandstone, new red sandstone, lias, and oolite; the Plutonian, trap and porphyry.

1. *Old red sandstone.* Much of the county of Caithness, and some tracts on the east coast, and a few points on the west, are composed of this formation.

2. *New red sandstone.* The county of Caithness affords examples of this deposit, which is remarkable on account of the beds of *fossil fishes* it contains.

3. *Lias and oolite.* This formation occurs on the east coast of Sutherland. The coal mines at Brora are situated in this deposit; the coal is, however, of indifferent quality.

4. The Plutonian rocks are not frequent, and consist principally of trap and porphyry.

III. *Alluvial rocks.* These exhibit the same characters as in the middle and southern divisions.

(4.) *Insular division.* This may be subdivided in the following manner:—1. Forth Islands; 2. Clyde Islands; 3. Hebrides; 4. Orkneys; 5. Shetlands.

(1.) *Forth Islands.* The Bell Rock is of a red sandstone, having the same characters as that on the neighbouring coast at Arbroath. The other islands are principally composed of trap rocks, occasionally associated with clinkstone porphyry, and rocks of the coal formation. (2.) Clyde Islands and the Cumbrays are composed of secondary rocks; the Neptunian rocks are chiefly old red sandstone, which is traversed and overlaid by different kinds of trap rocks, of which there are magnificent displays in these islands. The southern part of Bute is almost entirely composed of rocks of igneous origin, belonging to the trap series; the middle, of old red sandstone; the northern of clay slate, mica slate, quartz rock, and trap. Arran affords highly illustrative examples of Neptunian and Plutonian rocks of the primitive and transition classes, viz. clay slate, mica slate, greywacke, as Neptunian deposits; and granite, as a Plutonian rock. The junctions of the granite, of which there are two formations, with each other and with the Neptunian slates, are most instructive. Reposing on these rocks is a deposit of the old red sandstone, on which rests the coal formation; and the whole are covered, more or less completely, with new red sandstone. These Neptunian secondary rocks are traversed in all directions by Plutonian rocks of the porphyry and trap series, affording an admirable study to the geologist. Alluvial deposits occur all round the coast, and covering, more or less deeply, the bottom and sides of valleys. Both old and new alluvium are met with in Arran. The Craig of Ailsa, which is 900 feet high, is composed of secondary syenite, in several cliffs disposed in magnificent columns, and traversed by veins of secondary greenstone, &c.

(3.) The Hebrides or Western Islands form two groups; the one, ranging immediately along the coast, the *Inner Hebrides;* the other, lying beyond, to the westward, the *Outer Hebrides.*

*Inner Hebrides.* Gigha, Isla, Jura, Colonsay, Oronsay, Scarba, and the Slate Isles, are principally composed of Neptunian primitive and transition strata, having frequently a north-east and south-west direction; and variously disposed, from the slightly inclined to the vertical position. The rocks are mica slate, quartz rock, talc slate, chlorite slate, hornblende slate, clay slate, limestone, and greywacke. These are traversed by, and intermingled with, Plutonian rocks of the trap and porphyry series. The clay slate is extensively quarried in the isle of Eisdale, one of the Slate Islands. In *Isla* there is a great deposit of limestone, in which formerly lead-mines were worked. *Iona, Tiree,* and *Coll* are principally composed of gneiss, mica slate, quartz rock, hornblende rock, with occasional intermixtures of granite and syenite, and all traversed, more or less frequently, by veins of trap rock. *Mull,* with the exception of two or three points, which are composed of granite, gneiss, and mica slate, is composed of secondary trap and porphyry rocks, with occasional intermixtures of lias limestones, and lias coals. The usual alluvial deposits appear in different parts of the island. *Staffa,* which is composed of basalt, amygdaloid, and trap tuffa, has been long celebrated on account of its splendid columnar basaltic cave, the Fingal's Cave of travellers. *Eigg* is principally composed of trap rocks, occasionally intermingled with lias limestones. The Scure Egg is a remarkable columnar ridge of pitchstone porphyry, presenting the most splendid display of the natural columnar structure to be met with anywhere in the British islands. *Canna* is entirely composed of secondary trap rocks; and *Rum,* a wild, rugged, and hilly island, besides red sandstone, which forms a prominent constituent part, also contains many varieties of trap, some of which are remarkable from their containing agates, bloodstone, opal, &c. *Skye,* the largest of the Inner Hebrides, exhibits great variety of scenery and of geological arrangement. The *southern part* of the island is composed of primitive and transition rocks, principally of the Neptunian series; namely, mica slate, clay slate, chlorite slate, hornblende rock, quartz rock, greywacke, and limestone. The *middle part* affords magnificent displays of Plutonian rocks, as syenite, porphyry and trap, which are frequently observed intermixed with lias limestone, which in many places is seen converted into marble through the agency of those ignigenous rocks: the *northern division* of the island is principally composed of various trap rocks, often abounding in zeolite and other curious minerals, and intermingled with lias limestone and coal. The alluvium here exhibits its usual characters. *Rasay.* The southern and middle parts of this island are of secondary formation, principally of old red sandstone and lias sandstone; the northern extremity is of primitive rocks, principally gneiss. *Rona.* This island, which appears formerly to have been a part of Rasay, is entirely of primitive formation, the prevailing rock being gneiss, with subordinate mica slate, quartz rock, hornblende rock, &c., traversed by splendid veins of granite.

*Outer Hebrides.* This group, which lies in a north-east and south-west direction, consists of the following islands; viz. Lewis, Harris, North Uist, South Uist, and Barra. The whole range of islands is nearly of primitive formation, and the predominating rocks, which are gneiss and mica slate, range generally from north-east to south-west. The following rocks, which are generally subordinate to those just mentioned, viz. quartz rock, clay slate, chlorite slate, hornblende rock of various kinds, limestone (?), serpentine, with masses and veins of granite, syenite, and porphyry, present many interesting phenomena.

(4.) *Orkney Islands.* This group of islands is distinguished from all others that lie around the coasts of Scotland, by the uniformity of its structure and composition. With the exception of a small extent of transition rocks near Stromness in the island of Pomona, the largest of the Orkneys, that island and all the others are composed of the old red sandstone, with some rare appearance of secondary trap.

(5.) *Shetland Islands.* This very interesting group of islands exhibits great variety in its geognostical structure and composition. *Mainland.* With the exception of a band of old red sandstone extending from the line of Sumburgh Head to Rovey Head, on the east coast the whole of this island is formed of primitive rocks. The Neptunian strata are gneiss, with subordinate mica slate, clay slate, quartz rock, limestone, and hornblende rocks; the Plutonian rocks, which frequently alter and upraise the Neptunian strata, are granite, syenite, porphyry, greenstone, and epidotic syenite. *Yell* is almost entirely composed of gneiss, variously intersected by veins of granite. *Unst* is composed of gneiss, mica slate, talc slate, chlorite slate, and limestone, which are variously intermixed with serpentine and diallage rocks. Hermaness, the most northern point of the British dominions in Europe, is composed of gneiss; while the Land's End of Cornwall, the most south-westerly cape of Britain, is formed of granite. Unst and the neighbouring island of Fetlar abound in chromate of iron. Hydrate of magnesia, grenatite, precious garnet, and other beautiful minerals, occur in this island. *Fetlar* is composed of serpentine as the predominating rock, with diallage rock, gneiss, mica slate, chlorite slate, and quartz rock. *Whalsey* is composed of gneiss. *Bressay*, *Noss*, and *Mousa* are composed of old red sandstone. *Barra* and *House* are composed of gneiss and mica slate, with subordinate limestone; *Papa Stour* is a mass of porphyry. In *Foula* the predominating rock is old red sandstone; at one point there is a limited display of primitive rocks of granite, gneiss, mica slate, and clay slate.

## SECT. III.—*Historical Survey.*

To the Greek and Roman writers, Scotland was not known as a distinct country. Albion, or Britain, was viewed as one region, parcelled out among a multitude of different tribes. Agricola first penetrated into that part of Britain, which we now call Scotland. He easily over-ran the low country, but encountered the most obstinate resistance when he approached the Caledonians, who appear then to have held all the northern districts. An obstinate battle, the precise place of which has never been ascertained, was fought at the foot of the Grampians. All the rude valour of Caledonia could not match the skill of Agricola and the discipline of the Roman legions. The whole open country was abandoned to the invaders, whose progress, however, was stayed by what they termed the Caledonian forest, under which they seem to have vaguely comprehended the vast pine woods of Glenmore, and the steep barrier of the Grampians. Their military occupation, however, is attested by the formation of numerous camps, of which that of Ardoch, (*fig.* 185), ten miles north of Stirling, is the most extensive and complete. The Romans endeavoured to resist the incursions of the natives, by rearing at different periods, two walls, one between the Forth and Clyde, and the other south of the low country of Scotland, between the Solway and the Tyne. The northern tribes, however, continued their inroads, now chiefly under the name of Picts, who seem clearly to have been the same people with the Caledonians. In the fifth century Britain was abandoned by the Romans, and over-run by the Saxons, who occupied the eastern part of the south of Scotland, as far as the Forth.

185

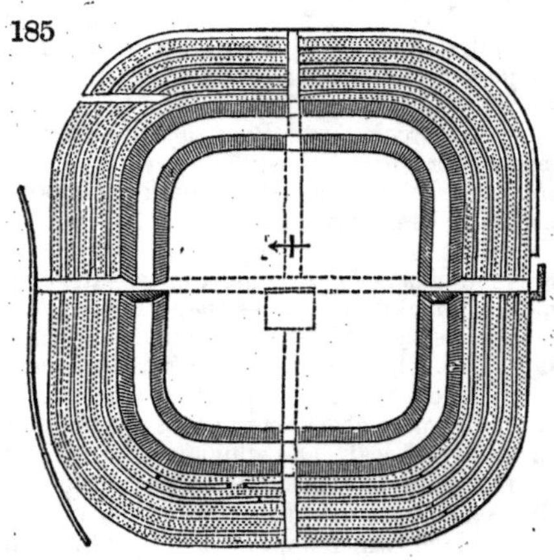

Camp at Ardoch.

The western part was formed into the kingdom of Strathcluyd. It flourished for about 300 years, and was rendered illustrious by the name and exploits of Arthur and his knights, whose power from 508 to 542, is represented by tradition as having been predominant over the south of Scotland and the north of England. The capital and bulwark of this kingdom was Alcluyd, called afterwards Dun Briton and Dumbarton, seated on an insulated precipitous rock at the mouth of the Clyde. The Strathcluyd Britons, closely pressed by their Saxon neighbours, endeavoured to defend themselves by a lengthened *fosse*, of which the traces have been supposed to remain in the Catrail or Picts'-work Ditch, drawn across the counties of Selkirk and Roxburgh. Such feeble defences could not support a sinking monarchy; in 757, Alcluyd was taken by the Saxons, and the kingdom subverted.

The Scots, before this time, had come from Ireland, their original seat, which, in the fourth century, was often called Scotland. Even before the departure of the Romans, the Scots, joined with the Picts, are mentioned as the ravagers of defenceless Britain. They appear at one time to have been driven back into Ireland; but in 503 they again landed in Cantyre, and during the next four centuries, spread gradually over the kingdom. At length under the victorious reign of Kenneth, which commenced in 836, they wrested the sceptre from Wred the Pictish king, and established supreme sway over the whole of that country, which, from them, was ever afterwards called Scotland.

The Scoto-Saxon era, as Mr. Chalmers calls it, is memorable rather for an insensible change, than for any sudden revolution. After the subversion of the kingdom of Strathcluyd, by the Saxons, that people had colonized and filled the whole south; and the Scottish kings, though of Celtic origin, having established themselves in this more fertile part of their territories, soon began to imbibe the spirit of its occupants. From this or other causes the whole lowlands of Scotland is in language and manners Teutonic, and the Gael or Celts were again confined within their mountain boundary.

An era of disputed succession arose out of the contending claims of Bruce and Baliol, after the death of Margaret of Norway. Edward I., availing himself of this dissension, succeeded in introducing himself under the character of an arbiter, and having established Baliol on the throne by an armed interference, sought to rule Scotland as a vassal kingdom. The result was a struggle, calamitous to Scotland, but which, however, placed in a conspicuous light the energy and heroism of the nation, and brought forward the names of Wallace and Bruce, ever afterwards the foremost in her annals. The result was glorious; the concentrated force of the English was finally defeated in a pitched battle at Bannockburn; they were compelled to renounce their ambitious pretensions, and allow the kingdom to be governed by its native princes.

Under the turbulent and unfortunate sway of the Stuarts, Scotland continued for several centuries without any prominent revolution, though with a continual tendency to internal commotion. This dynasty, from their connexion with the French and English courts, had acquired the idea of more polished manners, and habits of greater subordination as due from the nobles. Such views were ill suited to the power and temper of a Douglas, and many other powerful chieftains, through whose resistance the attempts of the monarchs were followed with disaster, and often with violent death. The introduction of the reformed religion especially, in open opposition to the court, which granted only a reluctant and precarious toleration, was unfavourable to the crown, and fatal to a princess whose beauty and misfortunes have rendered her an object of enthusiasm to the gay and chivalric part of the Scottish nation.

The union of the crowns, by the accession of James VI. in 1603, to the English throne, produced a great change, in itself flattering to Scotland, whose race of princes now held sway over all the three kingdoms. The struggle between presbytery and prelacy gave rise to a conflict which still powerfully influences the temper and character of the Scots. The efforts of the presbyterians, acting under the bond of their League and Covenant, first enabled the English parliament to rear its head, and had a great effect in turning the scale of contest against the crown. The Scots revolted, however, at the excesses of the independents, and endeavoured to rear again, on a covenanted basis, the fallen crown of the Stuarts. These brave but unsuccessful efforts were ill requited by an embittered persecution against all the adherents of presbytery, till the Revolution finally fixed that system as the established religion of Scotland.

The union of the kingdoms, in 1707, placed Scotland in that political position which she has ever since maintained; and, by allaying internal contest, and opening a free trade with the sister kingdom, this union has produced results highly beneficial, although the devoted attachment of her mountain tribes to the exiled Stuarts repeatedly impelled them to attempt to replace that house on the throne; attempts which, at one critical moment, spread alarm into the heart of England.

### Sect. IV.—*Political Constitution.*

The political system of Scotland being now almost completely incorporated with that of England, little is to be added to the statements given under the head of the sister kingdom. A few peculiarities, however, may be deserving of notice.

The representation allowed to Scotland at the union was somewhat scanty. It consisted, for the House of Commons, of forty-five members, fifteen from the boroughs, and thirty from the counties. The members were elected, not by the burgesses, but by the magistrates, who themselves were appointed chiefly by their predecessors in office; thus constituting close boroughs, in which a party having once obtained a majority might keep it *in perpetuum*. In county elections, the right of voting was attached to the possession of lands held immediately of the crown, and of the valued rent of 400*l.* Scots. But the feudal superiority which entitled to vote was separable from the actual possession of the property. The original proprietor, who, perhaps, had a number of these *votes* on his estate, might either sell or distribute them among his friends, so as to multiply his own elective influence. The freeholders of Scotland amounted to not quite 3000, of whom a certain number, for the reason stated, had no actual property in land. The peers of Scotland are represented by sixteen of their number, elected at the commencement of each parliament. There are, besides, upwards of twenty who are British peers, and sit in their personal right.

By the Reform Bill of 1832, the power of returning members to the House of Commons is vested in the following cities and burghs:—

| | Members. |
|---|---|
| Edinburgh | 2 |
| Glasgow | 2 |
| Aberdeen | 1 |
| Paisley | 1 |
| Dundee | 1 |
| Greenock | 1 |
| Perth | 1 |
| Leith, Portobello, Musselburg | 1 |
| Kirkwall, Wick, Dornoch, Dingwall, Tain, Cromarty | 1 |
| Fortrose, Inverness, Nairn, Forres | 1 |
| Elgin, Cullen, Banff, Inverary, Kintore, Peterhead | 1 |
| Inverbervie, Montrose, Arbroath, Brechin, Forfar | 1 |
| Cupar, St. Andrew's, Anstruther Easter and Wester, Crail, Kilrenny, Pittenween | 1 |
| Dysart, Kirkaldy, Kinghorn, Burntisland | 1 |
| Inverkeithing, Dunfermline, Kinross, Queensferry, Culross, Stirling | 1 |
| Renfrew, Rutherglen, Dumbarton, Kilmarnock, Port Glasgow | 1 |
| Haddington, Dunbar, North Berwick, Lauder, Jedburgh | 1 |
| Linlithgow, Lanark, Falkirk, Airdrie, Hamilton | 1 |
| Ayr, Irvine, Campbellton, Inverary, Oban | 1 |
| Dumfries, Sanquahar, Annan, Lochmaben, Kirkcudbright | 1 |
| Wigton, New Galloway, Stranraer, Whithorn | 1 |
| | 23 |

These members are returned by the inhabitants paying rent to the value of 10*l.* and upwards. The counties continue each to elect a member, except that only one in conjunction is returned by Elgin and Nairn, one by Ross and Cromarty, and one by Clackmannan and Kinross. The power of voting, too, is attached to the possession of actual property yielding 10*l.* of yearly rent.

The judicial administration of Scotland has always continued distinct from that of the sister kingdom. The supreme court, or Court of Session, consisted until lately, of fifteen members, sitting together, and deciding in all civil causes, while six of these constituted a Justiciary Court for the trial of criminal cases. The trial by jury was employed only in the Justiciary Court, and in revenue questions, which are tried before the Court of Exchequer. But the supreme court is now divided into two chambers, one of six and the other of seven members. Trials by jury, in civil cases, have been introduced, and are now carried on, like others, under the direction of the Court of Session. The Court of Exchequer, which consisted of five barons, the Consistory and the Admiralty Courts have been abolished, and their jurisdiction transferred to the Court of Session.

The revenue of Scotland has been hitherto collected separately from that of England, and by separate boards for each branch; but, under recent regulations, the whole has been placed under the direction of boards resident in London, and the systems have been in a great measure incorporated together. In the year ending 5th January, 1831—

| | £ |
|---|---|
| The Scottish excise was | 2,395,490 |
| Customs | 1,357,000 |
| Stamps | 526,000 |
| Assessed taxes | 292,000 |
| Post office | 201,000 |
| | 4,771,490 |

## Sect. V.—*Productive Industry.*

Scotland has always ranked as a poor country; and, for a long time, natural obstacles were enhanced by moral impediments. The Scots showed an aptitude to embark in all schemes of turbulence; but indolence, and dislike of plain hard work, might be recognized as a national characteristic. Since the age arrived, however, when industry came into honour, and when improved processes were studiously applied to all the useful arts, the Scots have entered with peculiar spirit and intelligence into this new career; and in its prosecution have been more successful, in some respects, than their southern neighbours.

The agriculture of Scotland has to contend with obstacles which must be manifest, when we look at its rugged aspect, and its vast hills and morasses. Forty years ago, moreover, the progress of Scotland in this primary art was generally behind that of the rest of the empire. As soon, however, as the great system of agricultural improvement was adopted throughout the kingdom, the Scottish farmers not only shared in it, but carried it farther than those of England. The farmers of the Lothians, of the Carse of Gowrie, and even of the district on the Moray Frith, made a complete reform in the whole train of agricultural operations. They brought extensive tracts of common and waste under cultivation, reduced the number of cattle and improved the breed, cultivated the artificial grasses, dismissed superfluous hands, and adopted the use of machinery, of which the most important, the threshing machine, was of Scottish invention. The consequence was, that considerable fortunes were made by successful farmers, and that rents were in almost every instance trebled, and in some cases raised to eight or ten times their former amount. In the mountainous districts, also, a new system was introduced, which proved more profitable to the landlord. The numerous little farms hitherto held by tenants or vassals, were thrown into extensive sheep-walks. Considerable depopulation, in the agricultural districts, was the consequence; a great proportion of this brave and warm-hearted race were forced to quit their native glens, to which they were fondly attached, and to seek support, either in the great manufacturing towns, or in settlements formed on the other side of the Atlantic.

The cultivated lands of Scotland, and the amount of its produce, after all these improvements, are still limited. Of the 18,944,000 acres, its computed extent of land, only 5,043,000 are under regular cultivation, and not more than 1,800,000 under grain. Of these only 140,000 produce wheat, though this is considered the most profitable crop, and is raised of good quality, where the soil and climate admit. Oats, a hardy plant, is the staple produce of Scotland, and the food of its rural population: it covers 1,260,000 acres. Barley occupies 280,000 acres, being raised chiefly for distillation; but in the higher districts it is the ruder species called *bear* or *big*. The chief exportable produce consists in cattle and sheep, which are sent in numbers to the English markets. The sheep are not equal to the fine English breeds, but the mutton of the Grampians and Cheviots is of exquisite flavour.

The manufacturing industry of Scotland has, within the last century, advanced with prodigious rapidity, being quite equal, compared with the extent and population of the country, to that of England. Woollen, the grand original staple of England, has never obtained more than a very partial footing in Scotland. Linen, with other products of flax, is the original staple of Scotland. It was throughout the country a household manufacture, and for household use. Flax, in almost every family, was diligently spun into yarn, which was then sent out to be woven and bleached. The coarser kinds of linen still form the staple of the eastern counties, though Dunfermline excels in fine sheeting and diaper. The linen made in Scotland was estimated, in 1810, at 26,457,000 yards, value 1,265,000*l.* The increase in the manufacture has since been so great, that in 1831, Dundee alone exported more than 57,000,000 yards! By far the greater proportion of the raw material is imported, very little hemp or flax being grown either in Scotland or England; almost all the former, and more than half the latter, is brought from Russia, the rest of the flax from Holland, Flanders, and Germany.

The cotton manufacture, though of comparatively recent introduction, has, in Scotland, no less than in England, risen to be the first in point of magnitude. Glasgow and Paisley produce fabrics carried to an extreme degree of fineness. The muslin of Paisley is one of the most delicate fabrics existing. The printing of cottons, particularly shawls, is also carried on to a greater proportional extent in Scotland than in England. The total quantity of cotton wool spun in Scotland in 1832, amounted to 24,500,000 lbs. of the value of about 4,000,000*l.*

Distillation of spirits from grain has been long a characteristic branch of Scottish industry; and in the highland districts, the quality of the article has been carried to very great perfection. It has been much cramped by fiscal restrictions, which have, of late, been almost entirely abolished. In the first seven years of the present century, the quantity paying duty averaged 2,000,000 gallons; it then gradually approached to 4,000,000; but in 1824, upon the reduction of the duty, it suddenly increased to above 5,000,000, and in 1830 it rose to 6,070,000.

Scotland has various other ordinary manufactures, and generally supplies itself with all the common necessaries of life. The ale of Edinburgh and of some Scottish towns enjoys reputation even out of Scotland. In 1829, there were brewed in Scotland 110,000 gallons of strong beer, and 229,000 of table beer. *Glass* is made to the extent of nearly double the consumption of the country; the surplus being exported, chiefly to Ireland. *Salt*, which does not exist in a mineral form, is largely extracted from sea-water by boiling; and though not equal in quality to English rock salt, nor fit for use in the fisheries, its cheapness recommends it for common culinary purposes. Candles, soap, starch, leather, paper, are produced in quantity sufficient for the supply of the inhabitants. In 1829, the produce was 5,731,000 lbs. tallow candles; 12,721,000 lbs. hard soap, and 2,332,000 lbs. soft soap; 812,000 lbs starch; 6,002,000 lbs. hides; 7,162,000 lbs. paper.

The mineral wealth of Scotland is chiefly of an humble and useful description. Its mountains are not metalliferous. In Lanark and Dumfries is a large deposit of lead mixed with silver, which, together with some smaller mines in the Hebrides, is supposed to yield 136,000*l.* in the former metal, and 10,000*l.* in the latter. Ironstone occurs extensively in the upper coal districts. In 1825, the annual production of pig iron in Scotland was 29,200 tons, which is not, however, sufficient to supply the founderies at Carron and elsewhere. Those at Carron are considerable, the casting being chiefly of ordnance, grates, and culinary vessels. Coal, lime, and stone, compose the solid mineral wealth of Scotland. The great coalfield extends in a diagonal line of 100 miles along the friths of Clyde and Forth; beginning south of the former, and ending north of the latter. It is immensely rich in coal of pretty good quality, though not equal to the best English. A large quantity is exported to Ireland. Lime is furnished abundantly, both for building and manure. Freestone, chiefly on both sides of the Forth; granite, in Aberdeenshire; slate, in the Hebrides and Argyleshire, afford excellent materials for building.

The fisheries form a considerable branch of industry in Scotland; the herring, cod, and haddock abound on various parts of its shores. The Dutch long monopolised the great northern herring bank; and, by a superior mode of cure, obtained a preference in all markets. The British government, however, has for some time made great exertions for the promotion of the Scottish fisheries; and there has been a wonderful increase in the quantity caught, and a corresponding improvement in the processes of cure. The former, which in 1815 was only 160,000 barrels, had risen in 1830 to 329,000, of which 237,000 were exported. In the same year, 63,500 cwt. of cod were cured in a dried state, and 5400 cwt. in pickle; of the former, 23,000 were exported. Salmon, taken in all the considerable rivers, and kept fresh by being packed in ice, chiefly supplies the London market. The whale fishery in Greenland and Davis's Straits has for some time been prosecuted by Scotland with increased activity. In the nine years ending in 1818, she sent at an average only 40 ships: in 1830, she sent 47; the produce of which was 5613 tuns of oil. Kelp was in extensive demand during the late war; but the repeal of the duty on salt, and the reduction of the duty on barilla, have ruined this branch of industry.

The relative foreign commerce of the principal ports of Scotland is exhibited in the following Table:—

| | Tonnage in 1830. | Produce of Customs in 1829. | | Tonnage in 1830. | Produce of Customs in 1829. |
|---|---|---|---|---|---|
| | | £ | | | £ |
| Aberdeen | 46,200 | 52,400 | Inverness | 7,300 | 2,000 |
| Bo'ness | 9,100 | 5,400 | Irvine | 13,300 | 4,400 |
| Dundee | 26,000 | 68,000 | Leith | 14,800 | 6,800 |
| Glasgow | 41,100 | | Montrose | 26,300 | 44,400 |
| Grangemouth | 24,300 | 25,000 | Perth | 16,100 | 9,000 |
| Greenock | 36,200 | 431,000 | Port Glasgow | 6,800 | 248,600 |

Commerce, till the union of the crowns, and even of the kingdoms, could scarcely be considered as existing in Scotland; but it has since been cultivated with great ardour and enterprise. One branch of commercial intercourse is that with her opulent sister kingdom. In England she finds a market for cattle, her chief agricultural surplus; for her wool, such as it is; for her sail-cloth and other coarse fabrics from flax and hemp; for part of her fine calicoes and muslins, &c. In return, she receives almost all the woollen cloth, and a great part of the silk consumed by her; hardware and cutlery of every kind; tea and other East India goods; and through this channel a part of all the foreign luxuries which she requires. The trade with Ireland is chiefly supported by the exchange of coal and iron for oats and cattle. That with the Baltic, particularly Russia, is very active; the eastern part of the kingdom deriving thence the hemp and flax, which form the material of her staple manufacture; also timber, iron, and the other bulky and useful staples of that trade. Having few articles of her own with which this market is not already stocked, the payment is made chiefly in bullion and colonial produce. The flourishing trade carried on from the west coast with America and the West Indies, is supported by the export of cottons, linen, wearing apparel, and other commodities; and by the import of cotton, sugar, rum, and the various luxuries of those fertile regions. The Mediterranean trade is not neglected; and since the opening of that to India, Greenock has adventured into it with considerable success.

The roads, which half a century ago were almost impassable, are now, through all the Lowlands, little inferior to those of England. After the rebellion of 1745, government constructed excellent roads into the heart of the Highlands as far as Inverness; and in 1803, a body of commissioners was appointed by government, for improving the roads of the north of Scotland. They proceeded upon the principle, that half the expense must in every case be defrayed by the county proprietors, and in eighteen years good roads were formed into the remotest tracts of Inverness, Skye, Ross, and even to the farthest point of Caithness.

Artificial navigation meets with peculiar obstructions from the ruggedness of the surface, and hence canals have never become very numerous. The "Great Canal," admits vessels of considerable size to pass from the Frith of Forth to that of Clyde, and thus unite the German and Atlantic oceans. Branches to Glasgow and to the fine coal-field at Monkland have been advantageously opened. The Union Canal, completed at an expense of nearly 400,000*l.*, connects the Great Canal, near its eastern point, with Edinburgh, by a line of thirty miles through a country very rich in coal and lime. The Caledonian Canal, uniting the chain of lakes which crosses Scotland diagonally through the counties of Inverness and Argyle, allows even ships of war to pass, from the east coast, into the Atlantic, without encountering the perils of the Pentland Frith and Cape Wrath. It was finished in 1822, at an expense of nearly 1,000,000*l.* sterling, entirely defrayed by government. The gates of the locks are of iron; the expense of each lock was 9000*l.* The locks are twenty-three in all, eight of which, looking down from Loch Eil, where it opens into the western sea, are called by sailors the "stair of Neptune." The canal is fifty feet broad; length twenty-two miles, with forty miles of lake navigation.

### Sect. VI.—*Civil and Social State.*

Of the population of Scotland an estimate was first attempted in the year 1755, when it was computed to be 1,265,380. The reports of the clergy for the "Statistical Account," between 1792 and 1798, gave 1,526,492; which was raised by the government enumeration of 1801 to 1,599,000. The census of 1811 gave 1,805,000; which was raised by that of 1821 to 2,093,456. In 1831, it was 2,363,842.

In point of disposition, the Scots are a grave, serious, and reflecting people; but bold, enterprising, ambitious, and imbued with a deep-rooted determination to pursue the objects of their desire, and repel those of their aversion. Under these impulses, they quit, without much regret, a land which affords few opportunities of distinction, and seek, either in the metropolis and commercial towns of England, or in the most distant transmarine regions, that wealth and fame which they eagerly covet; yet, amid this distance and these eager pursuits, their hopes and affections remain fixed on the land of their nativity; and they usually seek to spend the evening of their days in Scotland. The Scots appear naturally brave; a quality which is particularly observable among the highland tribes, and by which they rendered themselves formidable, first under Montrose, and afterwards in the rebellion against the house of Hanover. Since they were conciliated by the wise measures of Pitt, they have crowded into the British army, and formed some of its bravest regiments. Among the lower classes, crimes against the order of society are of comparatively rare occurrence, and there is less necessity for capital punishment; there is also less of extreme dissoluteness among the higher ranks. Among the Scottish females, in particular, the obligations of the marriage tie are much more seldom disregarded; and if the other sex too often abuse the license which public manners are supposed to allow, they are at least obliged to observe some outward appearances. The pride of birth is still prevalent, particularly among the highland clans; and it is accompanied with a general ambition to rise above their original station, and a propensity, with that view, to spend their moderate wealth rather in outward show than in solid comfort. The sister nations accuse the Scots as selfish, yet Scotsmen raised to power have not shown any backwardness, either in the general offices of humanity, or to promote the prosperity of their country and countrymen.

To their religious duties the Scots people have always shown an exemplary attention. In catholic times, the Romish church in Scotland enjoyed more influence, and had acquired a much greater proportion of the national wealth, than in England. But they entered upon the cause of reform with an ardent zeal, which left behind it that of all their neighbours. After a desperate struggle, on which, for nearly a century, the political destinies of the kingdom depended, they obtained their favourite form of presbytery, the most remote from that pompous ritual, for which they have entertained the most rooted abhorrence. The principle of presbytery consists in the complete equality of all its clerical members, who have each a separate parish, of which they perform all the ecclesiastical functions. The title of bishop, so long connected with wealth and power, has been rejected, and that of *minister* substituted. In the management of the poor, and some church functions, the minister is assisted by a body of lay members called *elders*, who constitute the *kirk session.* The government of the church consists in *presbyteries* formed by the meeting of the ministers of a certain district, with lay members from each session, the last of whom, however, attend only occasionally. A *synod* is formed by the union of several presbyteries; and the *General Assembly* is composed of deputies, partly clerical and partly lay, from each presbytery and borough. They meet every year, and an appeal lies to them upon every subject; but the laws of the church, though proposed in the Assembly, can be passed only by a majority of presbyteries, after being debated in each. The king sends a *Commissioner*, who is present at the debates of the Assembly, and seems even to claim a right of constituting and dissolving it; but this is denied by the church itself, which acknowledges no human head, and accounts itself and the state as powers entirely independent.

The nobles availed themselves of the downfall of the catholic establishment, to appropriate nearly the whole of the immense income with which it had been endowed. They took at first not only the lands, but the tithes; and even when obliged to make a provision for the presbyterian clergy out of the latter, they retained part, valued often at a very low rate, but subject to be called upon if needed. Thus the Scots clergy have enjoyed only such incomes as enabled them, with strict economy, to maintain their place in the middle rank of society. When even this became impossible under the increased expense of living, augmentations were granted out of the *tiends*, or valued tithes; and where these were exhausted, the legislature have come forward, and raised the lowest stipend to 150*l.* a year. No body of clergy have maintained a fairer character, or more efficiently performed their important duties, than those of the Scottish church.

The dissenters from the Scottish church consist chiefly of persons zealously attached to presbytery, and who have *seceded* because they considered its principles as not maintained in sufficient purity within the establishment. Their chief complaint is against the system of patronage exercised by the landed interest, who present generally to the vacant parishes. Two great bodies, into which they were formerly divided on the subject of the burgher oath, have, since the abolition of that test, been united into what is called the *Associate Synod.* A considerable proportion, especially of the higher ranks, is attached to episcopacy, either as it was established in Scotland under the Stuarts, or as it now exists in England; indeed, an union has been recently formed between these once separate branches. None of the other sects, independents, baptists, methodists, &c. are numerous; and the Roman catholics consist chiefly of emigrants from Ireland, though their form of religion still prevails in some of the remote highland districts.

Literature, soon after its revival in Europe, was cultivated in Scotland with peculiar ardour. Even in the age of scholastic pursuits, Duns Scotus and Crichton were pre-eminently famed throughout the Continent. When the sounder taste for classical knowledge followed, Buchanan acquired the reputation of writing Latin with great purity. Letters were almost entirely suppressed during the subsequent period, marked by a conflict between a licentious tyranny and an austere religious party, who condemned or despised the exertions of intellect and the creations of fancy; and literature lay dormant till the middle of the last century, when Scotland, with a church and universities alike poorly endowed, produced as illustrious a constellation of writers as had been called forth by the most lavish patronage in the great European capitals. We shall only mention, in history, Robertson and Hume; in moral and political philosophy, Hume, Reid, Smith, Ferguson, Kames, Stewart, Brown; divinity, Blair, Campbell, Macknight; poetry, Home, Thomson, Beattie, Burns; physical science, Gregory, Black, Playfair, Leslie. In the present generation, the most popular of fictitious writings, and one of the most able periodical works known in modern times, have issued from the Edinburgh press.

The universities of Scotland have been a powerful instrument in supporting her literary fame. Though not richly endowed, the fees of well-attended classes afford a liberal income, and have enabled them to attract the most learned among the clergy; while, in England, a wealthy church draws eminent scholars from the universities. The students live generally in the towns, without any check on their private conduct, or even any obligation to attendance, except what arises from the dread of the refusal of a certificate at the close. The chief exertion of the professors is bestowed on their lectures, by which they hope to attract students to their class and seminary. The more diligent combine with them examinations and exercises, but not on the same systematic and searching plan as in England; and the degrees are conferred, in many instances, with culpable laxity. A much greater proportion of the people receive a college education than in England. The church exacts an attendance of eight years; four for languages and philosophy, and four for divinity: the faculty of medicine requires also several years; and the gentry and higher grades of the middle ranks in general consider an attendance on the elementary classes as an essential part of education.

The public libraries are not rich. That belonging to the advocates or barristers of Edinburgh contains upwards of 100,000 volumes, among which there are ample materials, both printed and in manuscript, for elucidating the national history. The university library is half as large; and those of Glasgow, King's College Aberdeen, and St. Andrew's, are highly respectable. Each of these universities can claim a copy of every new work.

Scotland has a native music, simple and pathetic, expressive of rural feelings and emotions, to which she is fondly attached. Golf and foot-ball are the only amusements that can be deemed strictly national. Skating, and *curling*, or the rolling of smooth stones upon the ice, are also pursued with great ardour during the season that admits of those amusements. The recreations of the higher ranks are nearly the same as in England. Dancing is practised with peculiar ardour, especially by the Highlanders, who have favourite national steps and movements.

The Highlanders retain the remnants of a national costume peculiar to themselves; the tartan, a mixture of woollen and linen cloth, adorned with brilliant stripes variously crossing each other, and marking the distinctions of the clans; the kilt, or short petticoat, worn by the men, the hose fastened below the knee, which is left bare; and the bonnet, which in another shape is also still worn by the shepherds of the border.

In regard to food, the Scots, in general, are temperate. Even the rich attach less importance than their southern neighbours to the gratifications of the palate. The peasantry, previously to the rise of wages, which took place about thirty years ago, were content with the hardest fare. Neither wheaten bread nor animal food formed part of their ordinary diet. Oatmeal, not accounted in the south of England an article of food for human beings, was prepared here under the forms of cakes or porridge, and constituted the chief means of subsistence. To this was occasionally added barley broth, with greens or *kail*, the chief produce of their little gardens. The Scots have some dishes which they cherish with national enthusiasm, and among which the *haggis* holds the foremost place. This is a mixture of oatmeal, fat, liver, and onion, boiled up in the bag which composed the stomach of the animal. They have, moreover, hotch-potch, and other soups, the merit of which has been acknowledged by English palates.

## Sect. VII.—*Local Geography.*

The following is a table of the extent, population, and rental in the different counties of Scotland, derived from agricultural reports and parliamentary returns:—

| Counties. | Square Miles. | Acres under Cultivation. | Rental in 1812. | Houses in 1821. | Population in 1831. | Towns, with Population in 1831. | | | |
|---|---|---|---|---|---|---|---|---|---|
| | | | £ | | | | | | |
| Aberdeen | 1,960 | 451,000 | 301,000 | 27,579 | 177,651 | Aberdeen | 58,019 | Peterhead | 6,698 |
| Argyle | 3,129 | 270,000 | 207,000 | 16,059 | 101,425 | Campbellton | 9,472 | Inverary | 2,133 |
| Ayr | 1,039 | 325,000 | 369,000 | 17,842 | 145,055 | Ayr<br>Irvine | 7,606<br>5,200 | Kilmarnock | 18,093 |
| Banff | 645 | 123,000 | 85,000 | 8,971 | 48,604 | Banff | 3,711 | Cullen | 1,593 |
| Berwick | 442 | 137,000 | 286,000 | 5,803 | 34,048 | Dunse | 3,469 | Lauder | 2,063 |
| Bute | 161 | 29,000 | 20,000 | 2,205 | 14,151 | Rothesay | 4,819 | | |
| Caithness | 687 | 92,000 | 32,000 | 5,319 | 34,529 | Thurso | 4,679 | Wick | 9.850 |
| Clackmannan | 48 | 23,000 | 39,000 | 2,145 | 14,729 | Clackmannan | 4,266 | Alloa | 6,379 |
| Dumbarton | 228 | 54,000 | 63,000 | 3,536 | 33,211 | Dumbarton | 3,623 | | |
| Dumfries | 1,253 | 232,000 | 264,000 | 12,248 | 73,770 | Dumfries | 11,606 | Sanquhar | 3,268 |
| Edinburgh | 354 | 145,000 | 713,000 | 19,077 | 219,592 | Edinburgh<br>Dalkeith | 136,303<br>5,586 | Leith<br>Musselburgh | 25,853<br>8,961 |
| Elgin | 473 | 121,000 | 66,000 | 6,668 | 34,231 | Elgin | 6,130 | Forres | 3,895 |
| Fife | 467 | 209,000 | 378,000 | 18,944 | 128,839 | Cupar<br>Kirkaldy | 6,493<br>5,034 | St. Andrew's<br>Dunfermline | 5,621<br>17,068 |
| Forfar | 888 | 369,000 | 326,000 | 16,812 | 139,606 | Dundee<br>Forfar | 45,355<br>7,949 | Montrose<br>Arbroath | 12,055<br>6,660 |
| Haddington | 272 | 139,000 | 213,000 | 6,230 | 36,145 | Haddington | 5,883 | Dunbar | 4,735 |
| Inverness | 4,0[illegible] | 244,000 | 172,000 | 17,055 | 94,797 | Inverness | 15,324 | | |
| Kincardine | 380 | 92,000 | 88,000 | 5,894 | 31,431 | Bervie | 1,137 | | |
| Kinross | 72 | 27,000 | 24,000 | ..... | 9,072 | Kinross | 2,917 | | |
| Kirkcudbright | 821½ | 168,000 | 192,000 | 6,441 | 40,599 | Kirkcudbright | 3,511 | | |
| Lanark | 942 | 271,000 | 616,000 | 47,016 | 316,819 | Glasgow<br>Lanark | 202,426<br>7,672 | Hamilton | 9,503 |
| Linlithgow | 120 | 57,000 | 91,000 | 3,302 | 23,291 | Linlithgow | 4,874 | | |
| Nairn | 195 | 37,000 | 12,000 | ..... | 9,354 | Nairn | 3,266 | | |
| Orkney and Shetland | 1,280 | 46,000 | 20,000 | 9,176 | 58,239 | Kirkwall | 3,065 | Lerwick | 2,750 |
| Peebles | 319 | 24,000 | 60,000 | 1,750 | 10,578 | Peebles | 2,750 | | |
| Perth | 2,588 | 580,000 | 512,000 | 26,718 | 142,894 | Perth | 20,016 | Dumblane | 3,228 |
| Renfrew | 225 | 72,000 | 234,000 | 10,490 | 133,443 | Paisley<br>Port Glasgow | 57,466<br>5,192 | Greenock<br>Renfrew | 27,571<br>2,133 |
| Ross and Cromarty | 2,885 | 170,000 | 111,000 | 13,638 | 74,820 | Dingwall<br>Cromarty | 2,124<br>2,901 | Tain | 3,078 |
| Roxburgh | 715 | 206,000 | 242,000 | 6,587 | 43,663 | Kelso<br>Hawick | 4,939<br>4,970 | Jedburgh | 5,647 |
| Selkirk | 263 | 10,000 | 41,000 | 1,081 | 6,883 | Selkirk | 2,833 | | |
| Stirling | 489 | 195,000 | 207,000 | 8,984 | 72,621 | Stirling | 8,340 | Falkirk | 12,743 |
| Sutherland | 1,754 | 63,000 | 28,000 | 4,654 | 25,518 | Dornoch | 504 | | |
| Wigton | 451½ | 101,000 | 131,000 | 5,819 | 36,218 | Wigton<br>Portpatrick | 2,337<br>2,239 | Stranraer | 3,321 |

In treating of Scotland in detail, we shall divide it into three constituent parts:—1. The Lowland counties; 2. The Highland counties; 3. The Islands.

### Subsect. 1.—*The Lowland Counties.*

The whole of the south of Scotland, though diversified by elevated ranges of hills, is always considered as belonging to the Lowlands. It presents, however, three districts of opposite character:—1. The agricultural counties along the German Ocean and the Frith of Forth; 2. The southern pastoral counties; 3. The manufacturing counties of the west.

The agricultural district of southern Scotland consists of the counties of Berwick (formerly the Merse), of *Haddington, Edinburgh*, and *Linlithgow* (fully as familiar under the appellations of East, Mid, and West Lothian), and of Stirling, which touches westward on the highland boundary. Even of this range, the cultivated part is closely hemmed in by Lammermoor, a low, broad, moorish ridge, which fills all the eastern interior, and has even a considerable extent along the shore of the German Ocean.

The cultivated part of Berwickshire consists of the Merse, extending chiefly along the Tweed, and reaching to the sea. Above it is Lauderdale, or the Valley of the Lauder, which is fitted chiefly for grazing, and touches closely on the heaths of Lammermoor. Berwick-upon-Tweed, though its harbour be indifferent, is the chief channel for exporting the valuable produce of the Merse, to the annual amount, it is said, of 80,000 bolls of grain. The strong wall and deep ditch, which once defended Berwick, still remain, though neglected; and large barracks have been erected. Greenlaw, the seat of county business, and Lauder, the only borough, are but small places in the upper district. Dunse, in the agricultural tract, is the most thriving. Coldstream, a large village on the Tweed, is noted as the scene of Monk's retirement. In the western part of Berwickshire is Dryburgh Abbey, a fine old Gothic edifice, in which rest the remains of Scott.

Haddingtonshire, or East Lothian, runs along the Frith of Forth, between which and the range of Lammermoor extends a plain about twenty miles in length and twelve in breadth, perhaps the largest in Scotland, and all under high cultivation. Edinburgh is chiefly supplied with wheat from the market at Haddington, which is considered one of the first in the country. The towns are of secondary importance. Haddington is supported only by the market and by its court for legal proceedings. Dunbar has a little trade and fishery. Its castle, the ruins of which extend over a promontory of broken rocks, stretching out into the sea, forms a truly grand object. The Bass, "that sea rock immense," which rises to the height of 400 feet, forms a perpendicular precipice, on which build crowds of that rare species of sea-fowl called Solan goose. Their young, whose down is of some value, are taken by the perilous exertions of fishermen, suspended by ropes from the top of the cliff. There are still some remains of the fortified prison which was in ancient times reserved for state offenders, and in which some of the most eminent covenanters were confined for several years. On the shore immediately opposite, crowning a perpendicular cliff, appears Tantallon, a strong castle of the Douglases, now in a ruinous state. Prestonpans, a long dirty village, has some manufactures of salt and vitriol.

Mid Lothian, or Edinburghshire, is penetrated by a branch of the Lammermoor, and by the long range of the Pentlands: and, at the distance of a few miles south from Edinburgh, a general high level begins, which is favourable only to the production of oats and barley. There are no manufactures of any consequence, the county being entirely supported by the metropolis and its appendages.

Edinburgh, the capital of Scotland (*fig.* 188.), is a city of no very high antiquity. The Castle Hill, indeed, whose rocky and precipitous sides support on the summit a level space

188

Edinburgh.

of some extent, accessible only by a narrow ridge at one point, must always have been of importance in a military age. It is named in the Pictish annals under the title of Castrum Puellarum, which is supposed to have originated from the custom of placing the princesses and ladies of rank to be educated there, as in a place of security. In the tenth century, mention is first made of the town of *Edin;* but David I., in the twelfth century, founded the abbey and palace of Holyrood; and, under the sway of the Stuarts, Edinburgh became the capital of Scotland. Edinburgh is built upon three ridges, running from east to west, and separated from each other by deep ravines. The Old Town, which, till the last half century, formed the whole of Edinburgh, is situated on the middle ridge, extending nearly a mile of gradual descent from the Castle to the palace of Holyrood. To secure the protection afforded by this site, the houses were crowded into the very smallest possible space, they are raised six or seven stories on the side facing the street, which from the acclivity of the ground, gives to that facing the ravine a height of ten or even fourteen stories. From this central street, there descend on each side *closes* or lanes about six feet broad, and sloping very abruptly. The Cowgate, a poor street, inhabited by small tradesmen, extends along the bottom of the ravine, and terminates in a spacious *Grass-market*, completing old Edinburgh. Although it contains many excellent houses, it is now occupied only by the inferior orders of tradesmen, who occupy spacious apartments at very low rents. The wealthy citizens have migrated to two towns, built on the opposite sides of the Old Town; one on the south side, or St. Leonard's Hill, occupied by citizens of the middle class, those connected with the university, or such as are fond of retirement; the other, called properly the New Town, is on the north; and comprises the residence of almost all the opulent and fashionable classes. Being built on a regular plan, and of fine freestone, it forms one of the most elegant towns in Britain.

The beauty of Edinburgh is enhanced by its situation; being overlooked on one side by the eminence of the Castle, and its ancient towers, and on the other by a range of bold hills, the highest of which is called Arthur's Seat. The lowest, the Calton Hill, round which walks of easy access have been formed, commands a fine view of Edinburgh, the Frith of Forth, and its surrounding shores. The general effect, rather than that of any particular edifices, constitutes the merit of Edinburgh. Of antique structures, there is nothing very fine, except the large hospital for boys, erected from the funds bequeathed by George Heriot, the celebrated goldsmith. The great cathedral of St. Giles has been admired almost solely for its spire, and Holyrood Palace, a comparatively modern structure, for its little ancient chapel. The former has been now externally rebuilt on a very handsome plan, and the latter has undergone a thorough repair. Four miles south, in a very commanding situation, are the remains of Queen Mary's pleasant country palace of Craigmillar. The Register Office, the new College, and new High School are elegant structures; but the National Monument, on the Calton Hill, begun on the model of the Parthenon, is stopped for want of funds.

The inhabitants in 1801, including Leith, were 82,560; in 1831, they had increased to 162,156. The principal support is derived from the law; the professors of the university, and private lecturers, &c. constitute a considerable number; and genteel families are attracted from every part of Scotland by the opportunities of education and agreeable society. Edinburgh is a city eminently scientific and literary, and has even become known under the appellation of the "modern Athens." Connected with these pursuits, an extensive trade in printing and publishing books is carried on by some enterprising individuals. There are few manufactures, with the above exception. A great quantity of ale is brewed, which has attained to a high reputation; and there are in the neighbourhood some considerable distilleries. Shawls are manufactured equal to any in the empire. There are extensive banking establishments, both public and private, and considerable fortunes have been made in that branch of commerce.

The University of Edinburgh, founded in 1581, has risen to great fame, both as an institution for teaching, and a nursery for eminent men. The medical school, in particular, attracts students from all the three kingdoms. The annual number of students at the University exceeds 2000. They are lodged in the town, and are not subject to any personal discipline, except that of attendance on the lectures. Edinburgh has its Royal Society for physical and literary researches, its Antiquarian and Horticultural Societies, an Institution for the promotion of the Fine Arts, and an Academy for Painting.

Leith is the port of Edinburgh, and carries on a considerable import trade for the supply of that capital and all the interior country, for which purpose she carries on a constant intercourse with London and other ports on the eastern coast. Her intercourse with the Baltic is very extensive; and that with the West Indies considerable. The harbour of Leith is not good; but large sums have been expended in the construction of an extensive range of docks for the accommodation of its shipping; and of a pier stretching far into the sea, so as to enable vessels to enter at all times of the tide, with a breakwater opposite. The roads, at the distance of about a mile, afford excellent anchorage. Leith, originally a collection of dirty lanes, is now everywhere skirted by excellent streets, and ranges of villas, erected by the opulent inhabitants for their private residence. In 1832 there entered its port 334 vessels, tonnage 46,200.

Besides these great towns, Mid Lothian contains only some large pleasant villages. Portobello is the principal bathing place of Edinburgh. Musselburgh has a good turf, which has supplanted Leith sands for the annual Edinburgh races. The valley of the Esk contains the finest scenery in the Lothians. Roslin chapel, though not on an extensive scale, exhibits some exquisite specimens of Gothic sculpture; and the ruins of the castle bear marks of great strength. All the south and west of this county consists of wild, hilly, and pastoral scenery, in the heart of which is a pleasingly retired spot, chosen by Ramsay as the scene of his *Gentle Shepherd.*

Linlithgow or West Lothian consists, in its upper part, of a bleak table-land; in its lower, of an extensive, fertile, and highly cultivated plain. It abounds with coal, freestone, lime, and marl. The Union Canal passes through this county. The towns are small; but Linlithgow still retains somewhat of the aspect of grandeur suited to a once royal residence. The palace, (*fig.* 189.) situated on a hill behind the town, and overlooking a beautiful little lake, forms one of the grandest ancient edifices in the kingdom. There is also a Gothic church of some beauty.

189

Linlithgow Palace.

Stirling, an extensive and beautiful county, the link between the Highlands and Lowlands, extends for thirty-five miles along the Forth. It encloses several of the richest *carses* in Scotland: but the greater part is hilly and pastoral, while many of the lower grounds consist of fine meadows, adorned by the beautiful meanderings of the Forth. It even encroaches on the Highlands, since its western extremity includes Ben Lomond. This county is traversed by the celebrated Roman wall between the Forth and Clyde, usually ascribed to Antoninus, though from the account of Tacitus, it would appear to have been first formed by Agricola. It seems to have reached from near Dumbarton to Carriden, rather more than thirty-six miles. Stirling is also crossed by the great canal between the Forth and Clyde.

The town of Stirling can boast a situation as noble and commanding as any in Scotland. The view from its castle, which includes entire the principal range of the Grampians, the meadows or links through which the Forth winds, and a part of thirteen counties, is generally considered the finest in the country. The main street, like that of Edinburgh, descends gradually down the ridge of the hill on which the castle stands (*fig.* 190.). This fortress, in feudal times, was accounted one of the bulwarks of the kingdom; and Stirling was the frequent seat of royalty, and the scene of many of the most memorable and tragic events in Scottish history. The town owes its present limited prosperity chiefly to its carpet manufacture and other branches of industry. Falkirk is a larger town, situated in a broad and beautiful *carse*, through which the Forth flows. The three great annual *trysts* exhibit an immense show of highland cattle and sheep brought up for the supply of the southern districts. Near Falkirk is Carron, accounted only a village, but the seat of the greatest iron-works in Scotland, in which, during war, 2000 men were employed. It particularly excels in grates, and in that species of artillery first cast here, and hence denominated carronades. Grangemouth, at the connecting point of the great canal with the Frith of Forth, derives from this situation a considerable trade.

190

Stirling Castle.

The next district, including the counties of Roxburgh, Selkirk, Peebles, Dumfries, and part of Lanark, may most properly bear the appellation of pastoral Scotland. It is covered with long ranges of hills, from one to two thousand feet high, clothed with pasturage to their summits. This is the region of Scottish poetry. It was amid these scenes that Thomson and Scott caught that inspiration which has rendered their poetry the delight of their country. The chief occupation in this tract is sheep-farming.

The towns in this tract are generally small and agreeable. Kelso is one of the most beautiful in Scotland, being surrounded by ornamented villas and extensive woods. The abbey is not without grandeur; and the ruins of the castle of Roxburgh are striking. The village of Melrose is only distinguished by its abbey (*fig.* 191.), founded by David I., in the twelfth century, and the finest edifice ever erected in the south of Scotland. The profusion of the ornaments, and the beauty of the sculptures, which remain nearly entire, have rendered it the study of the painter and the theme of the poet. Selkirk and Peebles, capitals of their respective little counties, are only pleasant villages, bordering on the great pastoral vales of Ettrick and Yarrow. Dumfries, a well-built, gay-looking city, is a sort of southern Scottish capital, and it has been so distinguished from an early period; but no traces remain either of the castle, or of the monastery in which Cumming fell by the hand of Bruce. The town carries on some trade by the Nith, which admits vessels of one hundred and twenty tons, and it has two great annual markets for the cattle from the west; but it is chiefly supported by the gentry who make it their residence. Annan is agreeably situated at the mouth of the river of that name. A small spot, famed in the annals of gallantry, is Gretna Green, close on the English border; whither fly many a fond matrimonial pair, to escape the jealousy of parents and guardians. On the bleak northern boundary is Wanlockhead; and nearly contiguous to it Leadhills, in Lanarkshire. Wanlockhead yields annually lead to the amount of about 15,000 bars, of nine stones each; and Leadhills about 18,000.

191

Melrose Abbey.

*Seats.* The Duke of Buccleugh has numerous seats in the district, of which the chief is Drumlanrig Castle (*fig.* 192.), a magnificent edifice, on the Nith, and surrounded by extensive parks and plantations. Among many others round Kelso, is Fleurs, the splendid seat of the Roxburgh family. Abbotsford, from the many additions made by its illustrious proprietor, has become a striking and picturesque object.

192

Drumlanrig Castle.

The three counties of Ayr, Wigton, and Galloway compose what is called the West of Scotland. They are chiefly under pasture, and the cultivators are mainly occupied in the rearing of cattle. The range of mountains which separates Ayr and Galloway is almost as elevated as any in Scotland; but the upland country of the latter is, in general, diversified only with steep rocky eminences of two or three hundred feet high. In Ayr, too, though the southern district of Carrick be very mountainous, the middle one of Kyle has a level coast; while Cunningham, the most northerly, consists almost entirely of a fertile plain. Both counties, from the boundary line of mountains, are watered by fine rivers; in one, the Ayr, the Doon, and the Irvine; in the other, the Dee and the Cree. The Ayrshire breed of horses, called also the Clydesdale, is highly esteemed; and generally supplies the markets in the east of Scotland; but the little active breed called galloways are now become scarce. The kine of Ayrshire are valued chiefly for the dairy. The Galloway bullock produces beef of a peculiar excellence. The northern division of Ayr participates to a certain extent in the flourishing manufactures of Lanarkshire. It has immense beds of valuable coal, which not only serve for the supply of the inhabitants, but are exported to Ireland in such quantities as to form the chief trade of this county. To facilitate the transport, the Duke of Portland has formed a fine harbour at Troon, and has connected it by a rail-road with Kilmarnock.

Ayr, at the point where the rivers Doon and Ayr fall united into the sea, forms a sort of capital for the gentry of a considerable part of Scotland. It was the principal scene of some great historical events in the time of Wallace and Bruce; and was carefully fortified by Oliver Cromwell; but the bar at the mouth of the harbour has been unfavourable to its progress. It exports, however, chiefly to Ireland, a considerable quantity of coal, brought by railways. The town is irregularly built, but has one handsome principal street. Its theatre, its academy, and some charitable institutions, are on a greater scale than the size of the town might lead us to expect. The ports of Troon, Saltcoats, and Ardrossan send large quantities of coal to Ireland; whence they receive grain for the supply of the great interior towns. Saltcoats, which has sprung up within the last century, is also noted for the manufacture of salt; and Ardrossan is now a watering-place of increasing resort. Largs, the celebrated scene of the defeat of Haco, the last Danish invader, attracts many visiters by the extreme beauty of its situation. In the interior of Ayrshire is Kilmarnock, its largest and most thriving town. The manufacture of various woollen stuffs, and fabrics of leather; and latterly branches of the cotton weaving from Glasgow, place it high in the list of Scottish manufacturing towns.

Galloway is almost entirely a rural district. Its capitals, Wigton and Kirkcudbright, are pleasant country towns, and the latter, having a good harbour, has, of late, considerably increased. Portpatrick, the nearest point of Great Britain to the Irish coast, is the main channel of communication between Scotland and Ireland; for which purpose an improved harbour has lately been constructed, and regular packet-boats are established.

The counties of Lanark and Renfrew constitute the valley of the Clyde, the grand theatre of Scottish commerce and industry. Lanarkshire, or Clydesdale, is divided into three regions, of widely different character; the upper valley is altogether a rude pastoral region. Below Tinto, the banks of the Clyde assume a softer and gayer character, exhibiting a succession of gardens and orchards. Below Hamilton comes the flat district around Glasgow, which supplies that city with inexhaustible stores of excellent coal.

Glasgow is the commercial capital of Scotland, and in population ranks as the third town in the island. Tradition ascribes its origin and erection into a bishopric to St. Mungo, in the year 560. Its rapid rise commenced with the union, which opened to it the trade with America and the West Indies, hitherto monopolised by the English ports. In 1718, for the first time, a vessel from the Clyde sailed across the Atlantic. By the middle of the century, the merchants of Glasgow imported more than half the entire amount of tobacco which came into Great Britain; and to them the French farmers-general chiefly looked for their supply of this important article.

Their intercourse also with the West Indies, which had hitherto been very limited, was now carried on to a vast extent. A still greater source of wealth was opened at home. Glasgow had, in the course of the century, become a great manufacturing city, employing her industry on the old staple of linen of the finer descriptions, as cambrics, lawns, gauzes; also in the making of stockings and of shoes for exportation; but its product in these branches never exceeded 400,000*l.* But when cotton was extensively introduced into Britain, Glasgow devoted herself entirely to this new manufacture. She became the rival of Manchester; and, if circumstances did not allow her to obtain so great a share of the manufacture, she produced some finer fabrics, and was as prompt in availing herself of every improved process; immense fortunes were realized, and an annual value of nearly 4,000,000*l.* sterling produced. Glasgow was one of the first places which adopted the invention of power looms, and she has now 10,000 of these, and 32,000 worked by the hand. In 1830, the number of persons receiving parochial aid was only 5000, not quite one-fortieth part of the inhabitants, and the sum expended on the poor was only 17,287*l.*, although

Glasgow is now the largest town in Great Britain, London and Manchester excepted. The harbour is at the Broomielaw, where there is an extensive quay along the Clyde; but so great are the obstructions to its navigation, that Glasgow depends chiefly for imports on Greenock and Liverpool. In 1832 there entered its port only 79 vessels, of 8154 tons. Glasgow is a handsome and well-built town. Its original streets of Argyle and Trongate are broad and spacious; and several handsome squares have been built within the limits of the city; but the fashionable residences are now almost exclusively in the west, where, along a range of somewhat elevated ground, a number of elegant and spacious streets have been erected. Gorbals, Calton, Bridgeton, Hutchesontown, Tradeston, and Anderston, are the principal suburbs, and form the manufacturing part of the city. The public edifices deserve admiration. The cathedral (*fig.* 193.), one of the finest in Scotland, is a massive structure, with a wooded hill adjoining, on the top of which a monument has been erected to the memory of John Knox. The modern edifices are also handsome; the Lunatic Asylum, the Assembly-rooms, the Infirmary, the Roman Catholic chapel, the new Exchange Reading-rooms, &c. deserve mention. The bridewell is esteemed the most perfect in Scotland, both in point of construction and management. Glasgow is not a mere commercial town; its university, founded in 1450 by Bishop Turnbull, has been adorned by a long succession of illustrious teachers, of whom Simson, Hutcheson, Reid, Smith, Millar, are sufficient to ensure its celebrity. It is at present attended by 1400 students, and its name stands as high as at any former period. The library contains 30,000 volumes. The Museum bequeathed by the late Dr. Hunter, is rich in anatomical preparations, shells, insects, fossils, as well as in coins and medals. An elegant Grecian edifice has been erected for its reception. Auxiliary to the University is the Andersonian Institution, founded with the view of communicating to the commercial classes a knowledge of the elements of physical science; for which purpose it has been found highly efficacious. The intellectual spirit of the citizens is also proved by three libraries, and a botanic garden, all supported by public subscription.

193

Glasgow Cathedral.

Paisley, though in Renfrewshire, may be considered next, in order to connect together the great seats of manufacture. This town anciently derived its distinction from its ecclesiastical character. The abbey founded in 1160, was in a great measure demolished at the period of the Reformation. Several of the windows, however, still afford fine specimens of the ornamented Gothic; and the nave was left so far entire, that it has since served as a place of worship. Paisley was a small town until the middle of the last century, when it contained little more than 4000 inhabitants. Soon after, its manufactures, which were already begun, made most rapid advances. Down to the year 1783, they consisted chiefly of linen, fine thread, gauzes, both of linen and silk, and other delicate and elegant fabrics. On the introduction of cotton, the manufacturers of Paisley, like those of Glasgow, cultivated this branch almost exclusively, preferring its most elegant species. Muslin, the finest of all the productions of the loom, became the staple of Paisley. In 1805, there were 20,500 persons employed in weaving muslin, the entire produce of whose labours was rated at 1,250,000*l.* Since that time, the population having increased one-half, the productive industry has not, probably, advanced in a less proportion. By the improved navigation of the Cart and a canal, this town has communication with the Clyde, and the canal from Glasgow likewise, destined for Ardrossan, has been carried as far as Paisley. The county gaol and bridewell form one of the finest structures of the kind in the kingdom; the town-hall and several of the churches are very handsome. The operative weavers of Paisley are equal in intelligence to any class of the same rank elsewhere; and this spirit has led to the formation among them of a number of book societies, reading rooms, and subscription libraries.

Greenock is entirely a commercial and maritime station; it is the only great western port of Scotland, but by far the larger proportion of the vessels belong to Glasgow. The principal trade consists in importing the produce of the West Indies, to which is added a very extensive herring fishery, and a share of the cod fisheries of Newfoundland and Cape Breton. The sum of 90,000*l.* has been lately expended in the improvement of the harbour, which can now contain 500 sail, and a handsome custom-house has been built by government. In 1832 there entered this port 282 vessels, tonnage 78,131. Greenock is not an elegant town; but the hills behind it command a noble view of the river, and of the mountains of Argyle on the opposite coast.

Port Glasgow, about three miles higher than Greenock, and a much smaller port, continues subservient to Glasgow, receiving such vessels belonging to that city as are too bulky to ascend the Clyde; in this capacity, its trade is very considerable. Here was built the first dock in Scotland, in front of which a spacious quay extends along the Clyde, for the accommodation of those vessels which do not require to enter the basin. Renfrew, the capital of the county, is an old town, which has not shared in the prosperity of its neighbours. The inhabitants, however, receive a little employment from the manufacturers of Glasgow.

The banks of the Clyde above Glasgow, whose vicinity forms only a small part, however important, of the extensive county of Lanark, are still to be surveyed. First occurs Bothwell (*fig.* 194.), one of the principal seats of the Douglases. Here Edward I. placed the chief garrison, which was intended to hold Scotland in subjection. It is now a bold and striking ruin, rising above the river banks. A little above is Bothwell Bridge, so noted as the disastrous scene of the rout of the covenanting army. Farther up is Hamilton, a pleasant handsome town in a fine country: it is supported by the residence of the family of Hamilton, and by a branch of the cotton manufacture. From Hamilton the road leads through a range of orchards, and the most beautiful scenery, to Lanark. This town, though bearing the name of the county, is only a large straggling village; but about a mile distant is New Lanark, noted for the extensive cotton manufactory established by the late Mr. Dale, and lately conducted by Mr. Owen. Whatever may be thought of the speculative tenets of the latter gentleman, the attention paid to the behaviour and comforts of those employed presented, certainly, in many respects, a model worthy of imitation. But Lanark has a still greater attraction in the falls of the Clyde, Boniton, Corra, Stonebyres, situated above and below it, at about two miles' distance from each other. Their height does not exceed eighty or ninety feet; but the mass of water, with the grandeur of the rocky walls and hanging woods, render them one of the finest examples of this description of scenery.

194

Bothwell Castle.

The northern Lowlands, beyond the Forth, form a belt of about twenty miles in breadth, reaching the shores of the Moray Frith. The coast is generally level and fertile; but a great part of the interior is bleak and moorish. This district contains, however, several cities and seaports of considerable magnitude and importance.

Fife was formerly distinguished as the centre of Scottish industry; and one of its cities forms the ecclesiastical capital of Scotland. All the foreign commerce of the country was carried on in its ports; and less than two centuries ago its rental amounted to a tenth part of that of the whole kingdom. Since Scotland has ceased to be agitated by war, Edinburgh and the opposite side of the Forth have attracted all these advantages; and the numerous seaports on the northern coast of the Forth, have dwindled into fishing villages. Fife is, in general, a level country, yet diversified by a few hills of considerable elevation, as the Lomond Hills, and Largo Law. A great part of the interior is bleak and unproductive; and farming is less advanced than in the Lothians; the spinning and weaving of flax is carried on chiefly for domestic use, unless at Dunfermline, where there is a large fabric of fine sheeting and diaper. The western coast abounds in coal, and in fine limestone, which is exported to a very great extent. The county town is Cupar, a place of moderate size, neat, with some stir of gaiety. A greater interest attaches to St. Andrew's from its former greatness, from the remarkable scenes there acted, and from its splendid edifices, of which fragments still remain. It is seated on a bold coast, facing a wide bay of the German Ocean; and has two fine, broad, parallel streets, of which one is now almost deserted. The castle and cathedral (*fig.* 195.) have been demolished; but a high square tower, and a gable of the chapel of St. Rule, still attest the elegance of the latter structure. The university contains a school of theology and philosophy, but has no classes in law or medicine. Founded under the auspices of Buchanan, it can boast many eminent professors and pupils; though, from its almost insulated situation, it does not attract so great a concourse as Edinburgh. Kirkaldy has some foreign trade, and a considerable linen manufacture. Dunfermline, anciently the most flourishing town in Fife, was a place of importance, and the frequent residence of royalty. Malcolm Canmore founded here an abbey, which became one of the richest and most spacious in the kingdom; it has been nearly demolished, yet its ruins evince its former splendour; and part of them has been appropriated as the parish church. On a contiguous spot, the tomb of Bruce was lately discovered. Dunfermline is distinguished by an extensive manufactory of damask, diaper, and other fine linen cambrics, which employ 1500 looms, and yield an estimated annual produce of 120,000*l.*

195

St. Andrew's Cathedral.

Kinross, the capital of the county of the same name, is a pleasant little town, chiefly noted for its situation on the shores of Lochleven. This is a little lake, of considerable beauty, having, on an island in its centre, a castle, (*fig.* 196.), anciently of great strength, and noted in history, even before it acquired the romantic interest derived from the imprisonment of Mary, and her adventurous escape. Only a square turreted building and one of the walls of the chapel now remain. On another island are the traces of a very ancient and considerable priory.

196

Lochleven Castle.

Clackmannanshire is a pleasant little county, with a considerable extent of fine carse land, and great quantities of coal and lime. The town of Clackmannan is distinguished for the beauty of its situation. Close to it is an ancient tower, built by Robert the Bruce. Alloa, two miles farther down, is a thriving little place, in whose vicinity are mines of coal, of which about 35,000 tons are annually exported.

Forfar, more usually termed *Angus*, is of somewhat rough aspect, the western border being encroached upon by lower branches of the Grampians, while the Sidlaw Hills, a range of considerable height, traverse the centre. Between those is a portion of the great valley of Strathmore, which is here fertile and beautiful, as is also the plain between Sidlaw and the coast. Its prosperity depends chiefly upon manufactures, commerce, and fishery.

Dundee, the largest town in Forfarshire, ranks fourth in Scotland as to population and wealth. It was of early importance and strength, deriving its origin from Malcolm Canmore, and it obtained a fatal celebrity through the sieges, by Edward I.; by the Marquis of Montrose; and by Monk, who gave it up to indiscriminate pillage. Dundee, however, has recovered from these disasters, and is become one of the most flourishing commercial towns in Scotland. Her staple employment consists in the importation of flax and hemp, and working them into coarse linens, sailcloth, &c. There have been exported in one year 100,713 pieces of Osnaburg, 148,377 of sheeting, 81,754 of sailcloth, with bagging, sacking, dowlas, and other fabrics, of the entire value of about 1,500,000*l.*; four-fifths of which were made in Dundee itself. Dundee has belonging to her, 270 vessels of 33,000 tons; and in a single year a tonnage of 212,000 has entered the port. The harbour has been greatly enlarged by wet docks and other additions; and a railway opens a communication into the valley of Strathmore. The population, exceeding 45,000, shows a remarkable increase since 1821 when it was only 30,500. Dundee is agreeably situated on an eminence above the Tay; the old streets are narrow and steep, but new and handsome ones are built and building in every direction; and the vicinity is adorned with elegant villas. There is an academy, distinguished by the scientific attainments of some of its teachers.

Arbroath carries on upon a smaller scale, the same branches as Dundee; and is adorned with the ruins of a magnificent abbey. Montrose is prettily situated at the mouth of a river, bearing, in common with many others, the name of Esk. Its trade and industry are considerable; and it has a safe harbour. A number of the neighbouring gentry have been attracted by its agreeable situation, which renders it the most fashionable place in the county. Forfar, the county town, situated in the valley of Strathmore, is chiefly supported by the business of the courts; there is also a manufacture of brown linens. The village of Glammis is distinguished by the magnificent castle (*fig.* 197.) in its vicinity.

197

Glammis Castle.

Kincardine is closely hemmed in by the Grampians on the west: it contains, however, in its southern district, the termination of the great valley of Strathmore, which is here called the "How of the Mearns;" and forms a tract equally fertile and delightful. The northern part consists chiefly of mountains and moors of the most bleak and dreary aspect. The coast is of great extent, and very bold, presenting in many parts high precipitous cliffs, covered with innumerable flocks of sea-birds; on one of these are the extensive remains of the castle of Dun

198

Dunnottar Castle.

nottar, (*fig*. 198.), considered formerly as impregnable, where the regalia of the kingdom were at one time deposited. Stonehaven, the county-town, carries on some trade, and has a manufacture of brown linen.

Aberdeen is a large and important northern county. It has a very considerable line of coast, both to the east and to the north, and extends, with increasing breadth, far into the interior. There it forms Mar, or Braemar, a highland district, one of the most elevated in the kingdom, some of the mountains rising to above 4000 feet, and containing extensive forests of ancient pines, with large flocks of wild deer, in the deep glens or valleys. From the heights of Braemar descend the Dee and the Don, the first of which forms some very picturesque falls in its early course. Even the Lowland districts are in general bleak and moorish, adapted only to the cultivation of inferior species of grain, and the rearing of cattle. The old staple fabric of knitting worsted stockings has been greatly injured by the cheapness with which these are now produced elsewhere by the aid of machinery; but other woollen branches, together with those of linen and cotton, the latter to a considerable extent, have been introduced. The beautiful rock crystals called *cairngorms*, and also the topaz and the beryl, are found in the mountains of Braemar; and the fine granite which abounds near Aberdeen, yields 12,000 tons to be annually shipped to London and elsewhere. The fisheries also constitute a leading occupation. That of salmon in the Don and Dee, and the whale-fishery, are extensive branches; and from the German Ocean, haddocks, cod, ling, turbot, and shell-fish, are taken in great quantities.

Aberdeen, "the Queen of the North," and the largest city beyond the Forth, is situated between the Dee and the Don. Old Aberdeen is situated near the Don, whose entrance is obstructed by a natural bar, which renders this harbour inadequate for the town. The mass of population has settled on the banks of the Dee, the narrow entrance of which opens into a basin, forming an excellent harbour. It had, however, a bar at its mouth, liable to continual increase by the sand blown from the beach which extends along the coast; a mole of 1200 feet in length has been carried out into the sea, and a channel has been formed, by which vessels of 700 tons may enter. New Aberdeen is a handsome city, especially the principal street, composed of a long range of new and good houses, built of its fine granite. Its commerce, manufactures, and fishery are those of the county, all these branches centering in Aberdeen. This city is now the principal ship-building port in Scotland, possessing, in 1832, 355 ships of 41,671 tons burden. The old town has rather the aspect of a village, if we except the detached houses of the professors of the university, and a range of villas, the opulent tenants of which have been attracted by the agreeable situation. It is adorned by the fine old edifice of King's College, from which rises a square tower, with a light and elegant crown. This seminary was founded in 1494; the salaries are moderate, but the bursaries for poor schools are very extensive. Attached to it is a library of considerable value. Marischal College, founded by the Earl Marischal, nearly a century later, is situated in the heart of New Aberdeen. It is not so well endowed as King's College; but has an excellent cabinet of natural philosophy, and a well-furnished observatory.

Peterhead, an improving place, much frequented for sea-bathing and for a mineral water in its vicinity, has two natural harbours. It sends thirteen ships to the whale fishery, and carries on that of herrings with considerable spirit. To the south is a range of precipitous cliffs, called the Bullers of Buchan, against which the waves dash with perpetual fury.

Three counties, Banff, Moray or Elgin, and Nairn, occupy the southern shore of the Moray Frith. The interior districts border on the loftiest highlands; but the coast, only diversified by gentle hills, constitutes the ancient province of Moray, which the early Scottish writers describe with admiration as the most fruitful part of Scotland, and as enjoying fifteen days more of summer than any other district. Its rivers afford ample fisheries of salmon, which is exported to the computed annual value of 25,000*l*. The herring fishery also is prosecuted with considerable success.

Elgin is an ancient town, situated on the Lossie, and has a tolerable harbour; but its chief distinction rests on its cathedral, which, even in ruin, may dispute with Melrose the glory of being the finest Gothic edifice in Scotland; in 1568 the privy council ordered its leaden roof to be taken off for the payment of the army, and from that time it gradually decayed. In a neighbouring valley are also the remains of the fine priory of Pluscardine. Banff is a somewhat larger and more thriving place, situated at the mouth of the Deveron; carrying on some linen manufactures, and a considerable herring fishery. Nairn is a neat little county town, possessing some industry, and frequented for sea-bathing.

### Subsect. 2.—*The Highland Counties.*

The Highlands of Scotland comprise somewhat more than half the surface of the kingdom. They include the whole region north of the Forth and Clyde, except the belt on the eastern coast, between the friths of Forth and Moray, which has just been described. This region consists altogether of continuous ranges of lofty mountains, which on the borders leave between them some of the fine and broad valleys, called *straths*, but in the interior only the deep and often rocky intervals called *glens*. They are peopled by a race totally distinct from the Lowlanders. These mountaineers wear a costume, already described, quite peculiar to themselves; they speak a Celtic dialect, deep, strong, and guttural, bearing no resemblance to the Teutonic speech of the Lowlands and of England. They have ever maintained that valour, which, under Galgacus, set bounds to the career of Roman conquest, and preserved their mountains untouched by the invader; and they have since been converted from formidable foes into gallant defenders of the rest of the empire. Down to the year 1745, they acted in clans, led by hereditary chiefs, to whom they were entirely devoted, and who exercised over them a paternal but absolute sway. The spirit of clanship led them to attach themselves strongly to the hereditary right of the Stuarts, of which, under Montrose, they gave powerful proofs, which had nearly turned the tide of war in its favour. Afterwards, in 1745, they suddenly invaded England; and, in the absence of the army in Flanders, struck alarm into the dynasty of Hanover. The issue of that contest broke entirely the independence of the highland chiefs. A number were either brought to the scaffold, or sent into exile; military roads were made, and forts erected in the heart of their territory; they were deprived of their feudal privileges; even the national dress was prohibited, on account of the recollections it was calculated to excite. After the first alarms, however, had subsided, the British government adopted the plan of conciliation. Pitt conceived the idea of forming the highlanders into national regiments, allowing even a limited use of the appropriate dress; and they have since ranked with the bravest and most distinguished troops in the British army. Out of the forfeited estates and other funds voted by government, vast sums have been expended on the Caledonian Canal, roads, bridges, and other great works for the improvement of this rude territory. The *lairds*, deprived of their absolute power, and attracted by the gaieties and luxuries of cities, soon accustomed themselves to view their estates only as "material capitals, to be worked according to the great principles of political economy." The multitude of little spots, divided among vassals, in whose numbers they placed their strength, were thrown into large sheep-farms; and the tenants were driven out to seek a home wherever they could find it. Some migrated to the lowland cities, and a great proportion went to America; yet, in consequence of the advance of commerce and fisheries, even the highland counties augmented their population during this period, though not in the same proportion as the Lowlands. Between 1801 and 1821, it increased from 434,000 to 512,000. There is one great manufacture, generally diffused throughout this region, which tends rather to disturb the peace than to improve the condition of the community; this is whiskey, which the people prepare in small stills from their *bere*, or coarse barley, and give it a flavour superior to any other spirit made in England or Scotland.

The Highlands are composed of two great districts,—the west and the north. The former comprehends the shires of Dumbarton, Argyle, Bute, and part of Perth; the latter embraces the counties of Inverness, Ross, Sutherland, &c. The Hebrides, or Western Isles, belong to the counties of Bute, Argyle, Ross, and Inverness.

Perth is a noble and extensive county, forming the link, as it were, between the Lowlands and Highlands; in its different parts uniting the beauty and fertility of the one with the grandeur of the other. The former qualities are conspicuous in the *carse* of Gowrie; a broad sloping plain, on the north bank of the Tay, profusely covered with orchards and cultivated fields. The upper part of Strathearn, also, between Perth and Crieff, varied with gentle hills, cultivated valleys, and the windings of two great rivers, may almost be called the garden of Scotland. As we proceed to the north and west, the Grampians gradually swell, and at length are found occupying the whole interior of the county, in a line from north-east to south-west, and comprehending the mighty summits of Ben Lawers, Benmore, Bengloe, Schehallion, Ben Voirlich, Benledi, Benvenue; all from 3000 to upwards of 4000 feet high. Within their recesses they enclose the three large lochs, Tay, Earn, and Katrine. These lakes, varied with woods and verdure, exhibit in many parts scenes of great grandeur and beauty. In the lowlands of Perth, agriculture is carried to great perfection; the highland tracts, on the contrary, are in general fit only for pasturage. They are, however, covered with the remains of ancient forests, to which the great proprietors have been making very extensive additions. The towns of Perthshire participate in the different national manufactures: the bleachfields and printfields are numerous; but this can in no view be generally regarded as a manufacturing county.

Perth is well built, and, as to situation, one of the most beautiful cities in the kingdom. The view of it from the north, in particular, in the heart of a finely wooded plain, with the Tay winding round it, and the Hill of Moncrieff rising above, is almost without a rival in the kingdom. Perth might, for a long time, be considered the capital of Scotland. It was the frequent residence of the kings. Parliaments and General Assemblies met there oftener than in any other place; and, in the civil contests, the possession of Perth was considered of vital importance by the contending parties. At present it has declined to a rank decidedly provincial; and its commerce, once considerable, has been almost wholly transferred to Dundee. It has linen and other manufactures, which produce an annual value of about 200,000*l.*; while its advantageous site, and the excellent education afforded by the grammar school and academy, attract a number of the neighbouring gentry, and render it gay and fashionable.

The other towns of Perthshire are small, but distinguished for the grand and picturesque scenery amid which they are situated. Dunkeld, in this respect, is generally considered the pride of Scotland; the finely wooded and rocky hills through which the Tay meanders, with the valleys and glens opening on every side, produce a diversity of landscape scarcely equalled elsewhere. The late Duke of Athol, whose spacious domains cover this part of Perthshire, was most active in respect to plantations, since those of Dunkeld alone cover 11,000 acres; and the whole number of trees planted by the duke amount to 30,000,000. A route of twenty miles, directly north, passing opposite to the fine mountain village of Logierait, and through the bold pass of Killikrankie, leads to Blair, also part of the Athol territory, and one of the most picturesque spots in Scotland. Its striking features consist in the lofty mountain Bengloe, the glens of the Tilt and the Garry, and the picturesque rocky falls of the Bruar (*fig.* 199.). Westward is Loch Rannoch, surrounded by extensive forests of fir, and overhung by Schehallion, on whose lofty summit Dr. Maskelyne performed some of his operations for the measurement of the earth. Out of it flows the Tumel, a rapid stream, which forms some romantic cascades. From the Tumel, a military road leads to Loch Tay, the largest of the lakes, and surrounded by the loftiest mountains of Perthshire. Ben Lawers, with a chain of attendant mountains, overhangs it from the north; while Benmore shuts it in on the west; and perhaps there is no lake in Britain enclosed by so grand a circuit. The sides of the mountains are somewhat naked; but the grounds of Taymouth, at the head of the loch, form a rich foreground.

199

Fall of Bruar.

Farther south is the vale of Strathearn, at one end of which, Crieff, a thriving little town, looks up on the windings of the river, and the vast mountains from amid which it issues. Loch Earn, a small lake, is bounded on the south by grand ranges of very lofty mountains.

The upper valleys of the Forth and the Teith have some very remarkable scenery. On the Allan, is Dumblane; a pleasantly situated little town, with the remains of a fine cathedral; Callender, overhung by Benledi, is chiefly frequented as the key of Loch Katrine, situated about ten miles to the westward, and approached by a narrow road along the small lakes of Venachoir and Achray. The scenes of beauty and grandeur which adorn the eastern extremity of this lake, the mighty cliffs of Benvenue, the wild wooded glen of the Trosachs, and the beautiful little island in the centre of the scene, have obtained celebrity from the muse of Scott. Farther south, the Forth, rising from Ben Lomond, rolls through a pastoral mountain valley, once the seat of the power and the scene of the adventures of the outlaw Macgregor. It forms several little lakes, of which Loch Ard is the largest and most beautiful.

The county of Inverness is purely highland, presenting range after range of mountains, of which Ben Nevis, Cairngorm, and several others, are the most elevated in the United Kingdom. The intervals between them are filled either by long lakes, or by narrow glens, the level space of which does not usually exceed a mile in breadth. The principal one, called the Great Caledonian Glen, reaches from Inverness in an oblique direction across the kingdom, filled with an almost unbroken chain of lakes,—Loch Ness, Loch Oich, Loch Lochy, and Loch Linnhe; which last opens by the Sound of Mull into the western sea; a continuity which facilitated the formation of the Caledonian Canal. In the east, the district along the upper course of the Spey, bearing the name of Strathspey, comprises an unusual extent of level land. Only about a fortieth part of the county is capable of cultivation; but that fortieth, composed of *haugh* or alluvial land, on the rivers, or the lakes, is extremely fertile. The greatest branch of industry consists in the rearing of black cattle, sheep, and goats. Game of all kinds abounds, and there are still considerable remains of the great Caledonian forest, composed chiefly of fir.

Inverness, the gay capital of the Highlands, is of a very different character from that of the wild region over which it holds a sort of dominion. Seated on a bay, at the head of the Moray Frith, it partakes in a great measure of the mild and fertile character of its shores, and stands at some little distance from the awful ranges of mountains by which it is enclosed.

After suffering a considerable decline from its ancient importance, it has, within the last thirty years, nearly tripled its extent and population. In general, a considerable polish of manners is observable; and it has been remarked that the English language is spoken in greater purity than in any other part of Scotland; a circumstance which has been ascribed to the residence of English officers after the battle of Culloden. Inverness has a town house, infirmary, assembly-rooms, and theatre. Manufactures of hemp, flax, and tartan have been established. The views, both of sea and land, in its vicinity, are almost unrivalled.

Inverness-shire has scarcely another place which can make much pretension to the name even of a village. Ben Nevis, usually considered the loftiest mountain in Scotland and in the United Kingdom, is 4370 feet above the level of the sea; the view from the summit is very extensive, embracing a great portion of the Hebrides. To the east of Loch Ness, the rivulet of Fyers or Foyers (*fig.* 200.), forms the greatest waterfall in Scotland; the lower or principal fall descends from a height of 212 feet; but the stream is not very copious.

200

Fall of Fyers.

Argyle, commonly called the Western Highlands, is a wide and irregular territory, stretching into long promontories, and indented by deep arms of the sea, so as to form a coast of very great extent. In general the shore is bordered by high hills, and the interior covered with ranges of rugged mountains. Its industry is almost entirely pastoral; herds of black cattle and vast flocks of sheep are fed on the sides of its mountains. The herring of the west coast, and especially of Loch Fyne, enjoys a high reputation. The county is chiefly tenanted by Campbells, who were wont to rally round the Maccallummore, a designation of their chief the Duke of Argyle, with all the ardour of kindred and national attachment.

201

Dumbarton Castle.

Dumbarton is mostly a part of the same district; yet it has a lowland strip extending along the northern banks of the Clyde. In the western part are the Great Canal, joining the Clyde at Dunglass; and the wall of Antoninus, called by the Scottish vulgar "Graham's dike." The approach to Dumbarton affords one of the most striking prospects in Scotland; and its castle (*fig.* 201.), the ancient and mighty hold of the Britons, towering on the summit of a perpendicular rock, still maintains its importance as a fortress. Dumbarton has a large manufactory of crown glass, which is exported to foreign parts; and on the banks of the Leven there are extensive printfields.

Loch Lomond (*fig.* 202.) is celebrated for the expanse of its waters, and the many beautiful islands with which is studded. From its foot, bordered by cultivated hills and ornamented villas, to its mountain head, there is a continued transition from beauty to grandeur, and at the central point of Luss they are remarkably united. The numerous and beautiful islands, and the long wooded promontories stretching into the water, with the majestic form of Ben Lomond in the background, produce a combination of landscape which perhaps no other spot in Britain can equal.

202

Loch Lomond.

On turning the head of Loch Long at Arrochar, the view opens on the romantic valley of Glencoe, enclosed between two ranges of mountains rising almost perpendicularly to an amazing height, and leaving between them only a narrow vale, through which a rivulet flows. The vale of Glenfinglas is then passed, whose high sloping sides covered with innumerable flocks inspire pleasing pastoral images, and at the termination of which appears the grand estuary of Loch Fyne.

Inverary, the capital of the Western Highlands, is situated near the head of Loch Fyne

Its environs are not mountainous; but its noble castle (*fig.* 203.), surrounded by wooded hills and wide lawns, with the lofty mountains which shut in the distant view, render it a magnificent and delightful spot. The town is small and neat, without any employment, except the herring fishery. About ten miles below Inverary, the Crinan Canal joins Loch Fyne to the western sea, and has made Lochgilphead a place of some consequence.

203

Inverary Castle.

The interior and the western coast of Argyleshire are in many respects interesting. Parallel to Loch Fyne, at the distance of ten or twelve miles, is the long line of Loch Awe; an interior lake, over whose head towers Ben Cruachan, the loftiest summit in Argyle. The castle of Kilchurn, rising on one of the islands, produces a highly picturesque effect. Beyond this, Loch Etive, a narrow arm of the sea, stretches far into the interior. Climbing the high mountains at the head of Loch Etive, we come to Glencoe, which in terrific grandeur surpasses perhaps every other spot in Great Britain. This effect is produced by its bold and broken mountain forms, its spiry rocks, and black precipices; at the bottom of which, in a deep chasm or ravine, flows the rivulet of Coe. This stream is the Cona of Ossian, believed the favourite haunt of that celebrated Caledonian bard. The vale has also a gloomy recollection attached to it, from the massacre of 1691. Emerging from this scene, the traveller is cheered with the gay aspect of Loch Leven, which presents much pleasing highland scenery, while the hills round the ferry of Balachulish afford valuable quarries of slate. From Balachulish, along the broad expanse of the Linnhe Loch with which the great Caledonian chain terminates, extends Appin, a beautiful district, diversified with fine woods, rich pasturage, and more culture than is usual in Argyleshire. On the opposite side of the Linnhe Loch is a peninsular district called Ardnamurchan, separated only by a narrow sound from the Island of Mull. The district of Strontian contains lead-mines of some value. Crossing the Linnhe, and passing Lismore, a long, level, and fertile island, we find Lorne, separated by Loch Creran from Appin, to which it is even superior in beauty and fertility. Near the opening of Loch Etive into the sea, tradition places Beregonium, the reported capital of the Picts in the third century; and near it is found Dunstaffnage (*fig.* 204.), once the scene of Scottish regal pomp, now a ruin, crowning a cliff along the western sea. The long peninsula of Cantyre stretches far out into the sea, being visible from the Irish coast of Antrim. The Macdonalds, lords of the Isles, long held sway over it, till they were driven out by the earls of Argyle. Campbelltown, near its southern extremity, is a thriving port, now the largest on this coast, and serving in particular as a general rendezvous for the herring fishery.

204

Dunstaffnage Castle.

The three extreme counties, Ross, Cromarty, and Sutherland, form the most remote and northerly portion of the Highlands, and, Caithness excepted, of all the mainland. The south-eastern border of the friths of Moray, Cromarty, and Dornoch contains some fine land, and several thriving towns; the rest is a continued range of rock, mountain, heath, forest, and loch, similar to Inverness, but still wilder. The lochs which indent the western coast are large and numerous, particularly Loch Carron, Loch Terridon, and Loch Broom; and they have generally grand mountain boundaries. Cape Wrath, the north-western point of Scotland, is a lofty pyramidal rock, standing in front of a vast range of broken cliffs, and breasting the whole wide expanse of the ocean. On the northern coast is Loch Eribol, a wide inlet, bordered by limestone rocks, perforated by caves of great extent and remarkable form. Sutherland presents numerous *Duns*, or ancient forts of peculiar structure, of which the most remarkable is Dun Dornadilla (*fig.* 205.), situated on the lofty sides of Ben Hope, not far from Loch Eribol.

205

Dun Dornadilla.

Cromarty, the capital of the little county of the same name, stands at the foot of its own frith; while Dingwall, the county town of Ross, is situated at the head. Cromarty is a considerable fishing station. On the south side of the Dornoch Frith is Tain, and on the north is Dornoch, an ancient town, of whose cathedral some part still remains.

Caithness forms the north-eastern angle of Scotland: it is scarcely a highland county, only the Paps of Caithness rising to the character of mountains. Its surface is moist, bleak, and bare, filled with little lakes, and covered with extensive moors. The chief branch of industry is the herring fishery. Kelp is also made from the sea-weed thrown on its shores. Thurso, the county town, is an improving place, in the midst of a cultivated country. Its bay affords a safe roadstead, peculiarly valuable for ships, which, in rounding the north of Scotland, must pass through the Pentland Frith, rendered dangerous by its violent and rapid currents. Wick, the grand rendezvous of the herring fishery, owes to this advantage a very rapid increase. The north-eastern point of Caithness and of Scotland bears the familiar appellation of John o'Groat's house; though there is not the vestige of a house to correspond to this title, which is founded on a mere traditionary story.

### SUBSECT. 3.—*Scottish Islands.*

The islands appendent on Scotland, form one of its most conspicuous features. Though neither rich nor fertile in proportion to their extent, they exhibit a great variety of bold and striking scenery, and are peopled by a race whose habits of life and forms of society are peculiar to themselves. They may be divided into the islands at the mouth of the Clyde; the Hebrides, or Western Islands; and the Northern Islands, or those of Orkney and Shetland.

The islands of the Clyde are chiefly Bute and Arran, with the smaller ones of the Cumbrays and Ailsa. Bute is of beautiful aspect, with a climate accounted the mildest in Scotland, and for that reason resorted to by invalids; a considerable part of the surface is arable and well cultivated. Rothsay is a pretty town, much frequented for sea-bathing, and enriched by a considerable herring fishery. Arran presents much bold alpine scenery, the central mountain of Goatfield rising to nearly the height of 3000 feet, while the glen of Sanox at its base has the highest character of savage and romantic grandeur. Lamlash, the principal town, possesses an excellent harbour. Ailsa, off the Ayrshire coast, is a rock 900 feet high, with lofty basaltic cliffs, formed into columns several hundred feet in height.

The Hebrides, or Western Islands, stretch far into the Atlantic. Their general aspect is highland, with rude rocks and mountains, deep and dark valleys, large expanses of peat-moss, hill pastures, and scanty harvests; the mountains ascend rather in single peaks than in long ranges; and the rocky cliffs which face the sea assume, in many places, columnar forms of peculiar grandeur. The climate is moist; yet milder than on the mainland. The earliest inhabitants seem to have been Celtic. About the eleventh century, they were conquered, together with Man, by Harold Harfager, and were governed for several centuries by a Norwegian dynasty, after which they owned the nominal sovereignty of the Scottish kings, but fell really under the sway of the Macdonalds, lords of the Isles. Their territory including a great part of the west coast of Scotland, formed a considerable power, till it fell partly under the dominion of the Scottish crown, and was partly divided among a number of petty chiefs, whose feuds deform the subsequent pages of Hebridean history. At present these islands may be considered as retaining more of highland habits and feelings, than any part of the mainland.

The Hebrides may be divided into two main ranges. One of them consists of the large islands of Islay, Jura, Mull, and Skye, with several minor attendants, which are nearly contiguous to the west coast, and separated from it only by narrow straits and sounds; the other is composed of North and South Uist, Harris, Lewis, which are considerably out at sea, and are classed, with no very strict propriety, under the general appellation of Long Island.

Islay contains a good deal of level and fertile territory, which induced the lords of the Isles to make it their residence; good crops of barley, oats, and even wheat, are raised; and the black cattle, which form the main export, are held in great estimation. Jura is separated from Islay only by a sound, the opposite sides of which correspond so exactly as to suggest the idea of their having been disjoined by some violent shock; it is one continued tract of brown and rocky mountain pasture; all the inhabitants, if collected, would scarcely people a large village. Scarba consists of a single conical mountain broken into rocky precipices, and forming a striking object. Between Jura and Scarba is the perilous strait of Corryvrekan, a whirlpool noted for shipwreck. Colonsay and Oronsay form one long island, the channel between them being passable at low water. The former has a verdant appearance; at Oronsay are the remains of a priory, ranking as the finest in the Highlands next to that of Iona.

Mull is a large, rough, stormy island, with winding and deeply indented shores, separated by a long narrow sound from the Argyleshire coast. The shores are almost everywhere rocky and precipitous; the two once mighty holds of Duart and Aros crown rocky cliffs on its eastern shore. The great keep of the former, with its walls nine feet thick, encloses an area of thirty-six feet by twelve. Black cattle, black-faced sheep, celebrated for their delicate mutton, kelp, and herrings, are exported.

Staffa, a large rock, about a mile and a half round, and encircled by cliffs, which nowhere exceed in height 144 feet, contains the Cave of Fingal (*fig.* 206.) Almost all the rocks of the island are basaltic and columnar; but here they are arranged so as to produce the most singular and magnificent effect. An opening, sixty-six feet high and forty-two wide, formed by perpendicular walls terminated by an arch at the top, admits into a natural hall, more than two hundred feet long, and bounded on each side by basaltic columns rising in regular symmetrical succession. Two other caves, the Cormorants' Cave and the Boat's Cave, present similar scenes. Of the columnar rocks, which extend over a great part of the island, many are bent and twisted in a remarkable manner.

206

Fingal's Cave.

Iona (*fig.* 207), a small island near Staffa, excites the deepest interest by the venerable ruins which attest, in this secluded corner, the early existence of religion and learning, at a time when the rest of the kingdom was buried in barbarism. St. Columba, about the middle of the sixth century, founded here a monastery, and made it a centre whence he endeavoured to diffuse the light of Christianity. This religious establishment was enriched and extended, and a nunnery was afterwards instituted under the same auspices. The Culdees, or followers of Columba, appear to have rendered very great services to Britain, and even to the whole North. Teachers were often drawn from among them for seminaries in England; and they undertook missionary expeditions to Norway, and even to Russia. They taught, in a great measure, the principles of primitive Christianity, rejecting both the vows of celibacy, and the ceremonies of the Romish church. Iona, however, at length became Roman catholic, and continued to flourish till the Reformation, when its monks were dispersed, and its edifices demolished. The cemetery also remains, in which, according to tradition, were buried forty-eight kings of Scotland, eight of Norway, four of Ireland, and one of France. Allowing the scepticism of Dr. Macculloch as to this magnificent list, it appears confirmed, from the ornaments on the tombs, that many of the West-Insular chiefs chose this as a sacred spot, where their ashes might repose. The ruins are extensive. The cathedral is 164 feet long and 34 broad; and near it is a chapel sixty feet long. The style of architecture is early and rude; and the sculptures, though pretty numerous, are, with a few exceptions, grotesque in design and execution.

207

Iona.

Skye, the most northerly of this inner chain, is the largest of the group. It is forty-five miles long; but its shores are so winding, and so penetrated by lochs, that it may be said to form a cluster of peninsulas. Ranges of rocky mountains, many of them 3000 feet high, cover almost the entire surface, and the high rocks with which it is everywhere bordered, display objects of striking and romantic grandeur. In Strathaird, near the southern point, is the celebrated spar cave; it is about 250 feet from the entrance to the extremity; but a great part of the passage is gloomy and rocky, and only in its most interior part do the stalactites begin to branch out into that variety of intricate and brilliant ornaments which make the cave so beautiful. The great body of the island is a hilly moorland, barren, brown, and rugged; the peaks being generally from 500 to 1000 feet high; but some points are level and arable. The exportation of cattle, with that of a considerable quantity of kelp, forms the chief trade of the island; large quantities of herrings are also taken, and cured by fishermen, who carry on this branch of commerce on a small scale. The property of Skye is almost shared between the family of Lord Macdonald who claims descent from the ancient lords of the Isles, and that of Macleod. Duntulm, the almost ruined seat of the Macdonalds, and the Macleods' castle of Dunvegan, a magnificent pile, founded in the thirteenth century, are on the north-west coast. On the east is Rasay, masked by long lofty cliffs of fine sandstone, which have on their tops green and cultivated farms. To the south-west is Rum, a wild and rugged mass of mountains, surrounded by shores scarcely accessible, and involved in almost perpetual tempest. On the east of Rum is Egg or Eigg, which contains several large caves.

*Long Island* is the general name given to the exterior chain of the Hebrides, which consists of five large and many smaller islands; so closely contiguous that the whole may be considered as one island. It is a strange mixture of bogs, rocks, lochs, and sands; its pastures are chiefly occupied with cattle destined for the markets of the mainland; and large quantities of kelp are produced, which yield considerable profit.

*Lewis* is the largest of all the Hebrides, being upwards of eighty miles from north-east to south-west, and, at some points, more than twenty in breadth. Of its inhabitants, those occupying its most northern point, called the Butt of Lewis, appear to be Danish, the remnant of that colony who once ruled the island. The people are industrious in cultivating their rude soil, and in the fisheries which have rendered Stornoway, the capital of Lewis, a place of some consideration. *Harris*, a peninsula on the southern point of Lewis, consists of a mass of rugged rocks, which project in long promontories into the sea, giving to the shore a very picturesque aspect. The arable patches are small, and in such inaccessible sites that they can be cultivated only by the spade. Sheep are more numerous than black cattle, being better adapted to this rugged surface. *North and South Uist*, with *Benbecula*, exhibit the general aspect of Long Island, of whose length they compose about eighty miles. The cattle are small, and not exported in very large quantities. The most flourishing branch of industry is kelp, of which they yield annually about 2500 tons. *Barra* is distinguished for the industry of its fishermen, who carry their cargoes through the Crinan canal to the Greenock market. About half a mile from the southern shore is Chisamil, the castle of the Macleans, now partly in ruin, but of such extent as to have been capable of containing 500 men.

*St. Kilda* is the remotest point of the Hebrides; small and solitary, far out in the Atlantic, whose waves dash continually against its perpendicular cliffs. It is about three miles long, girt on all sides by a wall of rock, which at one point is about 1300 feet high; Conoxhan, the loftiest hill on the island, being there cut down perpendicularly from the summit to the base. "Dizzy heights, from which the eye looks down over jutting crags; a boiling sea below, without a boundary; dark cliffs beaten by a foaming surge, and lost in the gloom of involving clouds; the mixed contest of rocks, ocean, and sky," are the scenes which characterise St. Kilda. On the top of the rocks is a green and somewhat fertile surface, on which are fed sheep of the Norwegian breed, with short tails and coarse wool, but whose mutton is delicious; there are a few cows, and a little very fine bear is grown. But the favourite food of the natives is drawn from the face of the perpendicular cliffs, which in fearful and dizzy height overhang their shores. Suspended by a rope, they step from point to point, and take the eggs or young of the solan goose, puffin, cormorant, petrel, and others of the numerous species which breed on their sides.

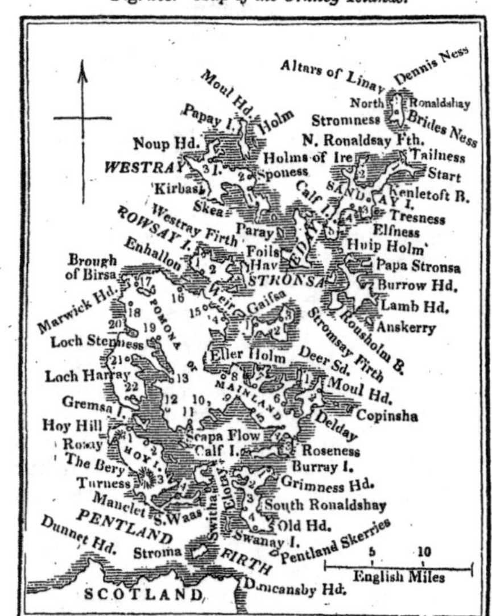


*Fig. 209. Map of the Orkney Islands.*

The *Orkneys* form a group of about thirty in number; but Pomona or Mainland contains nearly as much ground as all the rest put together. Nothing can be more irregular than their form; the deep sounds by which they are penetrated, and the narrow straits which separate them from each other, cause a complete intermixture of land and sea. These straits are rendered dangerous by numerous currents and eddies from the two oceans which rush in from opposite sides.

---

*Reference to the Map of the Orkney Islands.*

NORTH RONALDSHAY.
1. Holland.

SANDAY.
1. Taftsness
2. Savil
3. Maykirk
4. Cross and Burness
5. Stove

WESTRAY.
1. Newark
2. Spoonsay
3. Pyrawall.

ROWSAY.
1. Saveskeel
2. Westside.

SHAPINSHAY.
1. Wallness
2. Kirkbuster
3. Holland.

POMONA or MAINLAND.
1. St. Andrew's
2. Sandside
3. Holm
4. Poplay
5. Galnip
6. Sabo
7. Kirkwall
8. Firth
9. Scapa
10. Wank
11. Orphir
12. Chestron
13. Turnston
14. Rendall
15. Woodwick
16. Burgar
17. Birsa
18. Marwick
19. Kirkness
20. Holorow
21. Sandwick
22. Stromness.

HOY
1. Hoy
2. Bring
3. Air
4. St. Walby.

SOUTH RONALDSHAY.
1. Cara
2. Kirk
3. Berwick
4. Brough.

The Pentland Frith, in particular, between Orkney and the Mainland, is a most formidable passage. The opposing currents keep the channel in a state of perpetual ebullition, and produce at several points, violent whirlpools. Orkney is in general low, bleak, boggy, and bare; though its western islands face the Atlantic with some very bold and rugged cliffs. About a twelfth part is cultivated in a rude manner with the plough; a somewhat larger portion is under regular pasture; the rest is moor and waste. The cattle, though small, are of a good breed; and about 50,000 sheep, almost in a wild state, roam through the commons. The fisheries are not extensive; kelp is the staple commodity for export: it has averaged annually 2500 tons, employing 3000 men. There is some coarse woollen, and of late there has been some linen manufacture. As most of the vessels destined for Hudson's Bay and the whale fishery, and many of those which, from the east coast, sail to all parts of the world, pass by the north of Scotland, the ports of the Orkneys are frequented, and a market is afforded for their provisions.

The topographical details of Orkney do not possess any peculiar attraction. Kirkwall, however, bears marks of the periods when it was a Danish capital, and a residence of the sovereign Earls of Orkney. There is a large and massive cathedral, in some parts very elegantly ornamented; also ruins of a king's palace, an earl's castle, and a bishop's palace. The town has of late been considerably extended and improved, and it has a good natural harbour. Stromness has one of the best harbours in the kingdom, and is the favourite resort of vessels which seek on this coast for shelter and refreshment. Near Stromness is that remarkable remnant of antiquity the "standing stones of Stennis," which in magnitude and singular character almost rivals Stonehenge. Shapinshay, Stronsay, Rowsay, Eday, Westray, Papa, and Sanday, are small islands stretching to the north-east. Burra and South Ronaldshay are towards Caithness; and to the west the long island of Hoy, which presents a series of bold and rugged promontories.

*Fig. 210. Map of the Shetland Islands.*

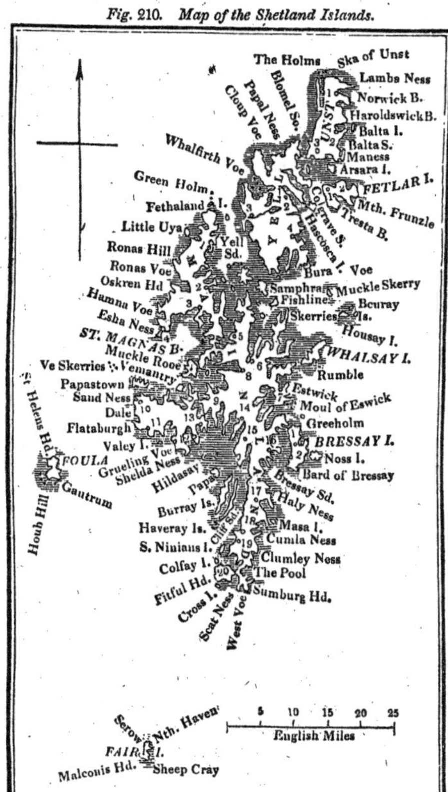


The Zetland or Shetland islands, called by the natives Hialtland, form one of the extremities of Europe, encircled by the illimitable extent of the Arctic and Atlantic oceans. Placed thus far north, and amid so wide a waste of waters, the climate of Zetland is cold, bleak, swept by furious winds, and deluged by torrents of rain. The surface is rugged, without being mountainous; it is everywhere penetrated by long lagoons with flat shores, called *voes*, by which even the largest islands are so intersected, that there is scarcely a spot in them two miles distant from the sea. The extensive mosses, and the trunks of trees dug out of them, prove that a vast expanse was once covered with natural forests; but these are now totally eradicated, and the violence of the winds and sea-spray has rendered abortive every attempt to replace them, so that the aspect of the country is now completely naked, scarcely producing even a shrub. The coasts are peculiarly steep, rocky, and bold, the rocks being hollowed into deep caverns, and broken into precipices and cliffs of the most varied forms. The aspect of these shores, against which the waves of the great surrounding ocean dash with almost perpetual fury, is equally grand and terrible. The

*References to the Map of the Shetland Islands.*

UNST.
1. Norwick
2. Vesgarth
3. New Kirk.

YELL.
1 Windhouse
2. Manse
3. Sandwick
4. Queya.

MAINLAND.
1. Skea
2. Olaberry
3. Orbusta
4. Stenness
5. Sutherhouse
6. Deal
7 Brough
8. Jagon
9. Berfild
10. Melby
11. Mucklure
12. Culswick
13. Sandsteng
14. Brak
15. Dingwall
16. Lerwick
17. St. Paul's
18. Maywick
19 Bigtown.
20. Quendal.

BRESSAY
1. Gardis
2. St. Andrews

author of "The Pirate" draws a most lively picture of these "deep and dangerous seas of the north, their precipices and headlands, many hundred feet in height—their perilous straits, and currents, and eddies—long sunken reefs of rock, over which the vivid ocean foams and boils,—dark caverns, to whose extremities neither man nor skiff has ever ventured,—lonely and often uninhabited isles, and occasionally the ruins of ancient northern fastnesses, dimly seen by the feeble light of the arctic winter." The dangers of the navigation, however, are considerably mitigated by the spacious and commodious havens, formed by the deep bays and *voes*, or by the sounds and channels, between different islands.

The Shetland Islands contain about 20,000 acres of arable land, and nearly as many of good meadow; but this comprises little more than a twentieth part of the surface, all the rest consisting of waste or common, on which the horses, cattle, and sheep are turned out, to find pastures as best they may. The horses are of a very small size, with a huge mane, but active and hardy. The cows are equally diminutive, and give very little milk, but both the milk and the flesh are of good quality. The sheep are most numerous of all, being reckoned at seventy or eighty thousand; they are stunted, like the other animals, and their wool is very scanty; but some of it is peculiarly fine, affording the material of almost the only manufacture of Shetland,—that of knit hosiery, of a texture close, soft, and warm. The greatest branch of Shetland industry, however, is the cod and ling fishery. All the coasts abound with these fish; and, within the last few years, a particularly rich and extensive bank has been discovered to the westward. At the proper season, fleets of boats issue from all the bays and *voes*, to the *haaf* or deep sea-fishery, which is carried on, not without peril, at the distance of from twenty to thirty miles from the coast. The fishermen are supplied by the landlords with boats and implements, on condition of their delivering to them the fish at a stipulated rate; and as their farms are held at will, they are in a state of vassalage more complete, perhaps, than any other class in the United Kingdom.

The annals of Shetland are Norwegian. These islands, according to the earliest tradition, were peopled from Norway. In the ninth century they were conquered by Harold Harfager, or the Fair-haired, the most powerful and formidable of all the sea-kings of the north. The Norwegian sway extended for several centuries over all the Scottish islands; but in the Shetlands it was undisputed, till the cession of them, along with those of Orkney, as the dowry of a princess of Norway married to James III., in the end of the fifteenth century.

Lerwick, the capital, is a thriving village, ill and irregularly built, but improving. The opposite island of Bressay forms Bressay Sound, one of the finest harbours in the world, and the rendezvous of all the vessels destined for the north and the whale fishery. Off Bressay is the Noss (*fig.* 210.), a small high island, with a flat summit, girt on all sides by perpendicular walls of rock. The communication with Bressay itself is maintained by strong ropes stretched across, along which a cradle is run, in which the passenger is seated. The promontories of Sumburgh and Fitful Head, at the southern extremity of the Mainland, are also distinguished by the boldness of their aspect and the perils with which they threaten the mariner. The number of the Shetlands has been variously estimated, according to the gradations of islets and rocks included; but only about forty are inhabited. Of these, Yell, and Unst, stretching northwards from the Mainland, are alone of any magnitude. The last, though the most northerly, is rather the most fertile of any, and distinguished by its numerous caves. Adjacent to Yell is Fetlar; on the east of the Mainland are Whalsay and Bressay; to the west, Burray, Housa, Frondray, Papa Stour, Muckle and Little Rooe, all so close as to be little more than peninsulas. Considerably out at sea, Foula, a small rocky islet, faces the Atlantic, with high cliffs covered with numberless flocks of sea-fowl.

210

Noss Holm, Shetland.

---

## CHAPTER IV.

### IRELAND.

**Ireland** is a fine extensive island, situated to the west of England, and forming one of the three grand portions of the United Kingdom.

#### Sect. 1.—*General Outline and Aspect.*

The greatest dimension of Ireland is from Cape Clear, in 51° 19′, to Malin Head, in 55° 23′ N latitude; making about 280 miles. The utmost breadth, if reckoned from the mos easterly point of the county of Down (opposite Bur Island) to Dunmore Head in Kerry, will be 218 miles; but it is nowhere so broad under the same parallel of latitude. The island, according to Beaufort, contains more than 30,000 English square miles, or nearly 20,000,000 acres; but, till the survey be completed, precision on this subject cannot be attained.

The surface of Ireland cannot on the whole be called mountainous; its central districts composing one vast plain, which crosses the kingdom from east to west. It is, however, diversified by ranges of mountains, superior in extent, and, with the exception of those of Wales, equal in elevation, to any in England. Wicklow, in the vicinity of Dublin, may be classed as an alpine region. On the borders of Leinster and Munster, the Slieve-Bloom, the Knockmele Down, and the Galties, form long and lofty ranges, commanding an extensive view over the wide plains that stretch beneath them. All these, however, are much surpassed by the extreme south-west county of Kerry, which presents a complete chaos of lofty and rocky summits. The most elevated are those which enclose the beautiful and finely wooded lakes of Killarney, Mangerton and Macgillicuddy's Reeks, the last of which is considerably more than 3000 feet high. At the opposite or north-eastern extremity of Ireland, Antrim presents to the Scottish seas a barrier of rocky cliffs, less lofty, but of a very bold and peculiar character; precipitous, and formed into long columnar ranges; a phenomenon which the Giant's Causeway exhibits on a greater scale than any other spot in the known world. The Mourne mountains, a lofty granite range in the south of the county of Down; those of Carlingford, which extend into the county of Armagh; with considerable ranges in Tyrone, Derry, and Donegal, may dispute the pre-eminence with those of the south. In Connaught there are also some considerable detached mountains, of which Croaghpatrick in Mayo has been reckoned by some to exceed even Macgillicuddy's Reeks; but Ireland has no extended table-lands, like those which cover a considerable part of England. The most elevated part of the Bog of Allen, in that central point where the rivers divide, is not more than 270 feet above the level of the sea.

The Shannon is without a rival in the three kingdoms. It rises far in the north, from Lough Allen in the province of Connaught, and has a course of 170 miles, throughout the whole of which it is more or less navigable, the only obstruction which existed having been removed. Below Limerick it expands into an estuary about sixty miles in length, by which the largest vessels have access to that city. The Barrow is also an important river, which runs southward through the greater part of Leinster, receives from the west the Nore and the Suire, and finally forms the harbour of Waterford. The Boyne, so celebrated for the victory gained on its banks; the Foyle, which, after passing Londonderry, forms Lough Foyle; the Bann, which passes through Lough Neagh, and affords a flourishing salmon fishery; and the Blackwater, which terminates in the bay and port of Youghal, are also deserving of mention. The other rivers are rather numerous than of long course; but they almost all terminate in wide estuaries and *loughs*, which diffuse through Ireland the means of water communication, and afford a multiplicity of spacious and secure harbours.

Lakes or loughs are a conspicuous feature in Ireland, where this last name, like the similar one used in Scotland, is in many instances applied to arms of the sea. Lough Neagh is the largest lake in the United Kingdom, covering nearly 100,000 acres. Its banks are flat, tame, and in many places marshy and inundated. Lough Erne, also in Ulster, is divided into two reaches, the united length of which is about thirty miles, while its circuit includes a great variety of rich and ornamented scenery. Lough Foyle, Lough Swilly, and Belfast Lough, are properly bays. The Shannon forms several lakes, of which Lough Ree is the principal; and the whole of its course downwards from Limerick resembles more a lough or bay than a river. Connaught has several extensive lakes. That of Killarney, in the south, is famed, not for its extent, but for the singular grandeur and beauty of its shores. A fuller description of this and some others now mentioned will be found under the local section.

### Sect. II.—*Natural Geography.*

The Botany and Zoology of Ireland, having been treated under the head of England, this section will be confined to Geology.

#### Subsect. 1.—*Geology of Ireland.*

The geology of this part of the empire is not so well known as that of Great Britain. The following sketch will enable our readers to form a general conception of the geognostical structure of those parts of the island which have been already surveyed; viz.—1. North of Ireland; 2. Connaught coal district; 3. East of Ireland; 4. South, and part of the west of Ireland.

(1.) *North of Ireland.* This district, limited by Dundalk Bay on the south-east, and by Lough Foyle on the north-west, is marked by three distinct systems or groups of mountains, one of which occupies the more southern counties, while the more northern are divided between the two others.

1st system. The *Mourne mountains.*—The Mourne mountains form a well-defined

Gigha I.
Cantire
Arran
Kilbrannan Sound
Mull of Cantire
Rathlin I.
Giants Causeway
Glenegad Hd.
Malin Hd.
Tory I.
Bloodyfarland Pt.
NORTH CHANNEL
Port Patrick
Carrickfergus
Nth. Is. of Arran
Londonderry
Foyle
Donegal
Donegal Bay
Killala B.
Sligo B.
Sligo
Killala
Broad Haven
Enniskea Is.
Achil I.
Clew B.
Clare I.
Enniskurk
Entisbofin I.
Birterbuy B.
Kilkerran B.
Galway Bay
Sth. Is. Arran
Clogher
Armagh
Monaghan
Louth
Dundalk Bay
Erne L.
FERMANAGH
Enniskillen
Leitrim
Cavan
Trim
Dublin
Dublin Bay
Roscommon
Mullingar
Philipstown
Kildare
Wicklow
Maryborough
Carlow
Kilkenny
Clare
Limerick
Lough Hd.
Mth. of the Shannon
Tralee
Dingle Bay
Tipperary
Waterford
Wexford
Wexford Har.
Carnsore Pt.
Saltee Is.
Youghal Hr
Cork Har.
Courtmacsherry Har.
Clonakilty Har.
Baltimore Har
Mizen Hd
Bantry Bay
Kenmare R.
ATLANTIC OCEAN
ST. GEORGES CHANNEL
English Miles
10 20 30 40 50 60
Longitude West from Greenwich
10 9 8 7 6
55 54 53 52 51

group, extending from Dundrum Bay to Carlingford Bay, in the southern extremity of Down. Slieve Donard is the highest summit of this group, and rises about 2654 feet above the level of the sea. The north-west of the main group, the Fathom Hill, Slieve Girken, or the Newry mountains, and Slieve Gullen, are situated in the south-east of Armagh; and the Ravensdale and Carlingford mountains, in the north of Louth, may be considered as its appendages. Granite, which is the prevailing rock of these mountains, contains beautiful rock crystals, also felspar and mica crystals, topaz and beryl. To the north of the Mourne mountains Slieve Croob, composed of syenite, and Slieve Anisky, of hornblende rock, form an elevated tract, dependent upon, but placed at some distance from, the main group. Hornblende rock, greenstone, and porphyry are said to be abundant on the skirts of this granite district. The Plutonian granite and syenite hills rise through strata of transition rocks, which are greywacke, greywacke slate, transition clay slate, and transition limestone. The Plutonian rocks bear but a small proportion in superficial extent to those of the transition class, the latter advancing west and north into Cavan, and to Belfast Lough and the peninsula of Ards. The points of the coast of Scotland, directly opposite the peninsula of Ards, present in the neighbourhood of Portpatrick, and through the great alpine band which traverses the south of Scotland, and terminates on the east coast of St. Abb's Head, the same transition rocks. Hence it is probable that the great southern high land of Scotland was formerly joined with the transition hills of the Mourne mountain group by a ridge of land extending across the Channel from Scotland to Ireland. In this district, there are some patches of mountain limestone and of old red sandstone.

2d system. *Primitive chain of Londonderry.*—This mountain group rises at the distance of about 30 miles to the north-north-west of the external chains of the first system, including the counties of Londonderry and Donegal. One of the highest points in this district is Sawell, said to be 2257 feet above the level of the sea. This great tract of country is principally composed of mica slate, with various subordinate beds, as limestone, quartz, &c. On the eastern bank of the Roe, these mica slate hills and mountains are succeeded by a range of secondary hills covered by a great platform of secondary trap, and forming a part of the third system of hills, afterwards to be described. These newer rocks repose upon and con-

---

*References to the Map of Ireland.*

NORTH PART.
1. Newtonglens
2. Ballycastle
3. Clough
4. Rasharkan
5. Ballymany
6. Coleraine
7. Garvagh
8. Giant's Sconce
9. Ballykelly
10. Muff
11. Ballynally
12. Malm
13. Carn
14. Burnfoot
15. Osnakill
16. Rathmullin
17. Gortyhock
18. Dungloe
19. Convoy
20. Stranorlan
21. Raphoe
22. Londonderry
23. Lifford
24. Strabane
25. Clady
26. Maghera
27. Swatteragh
28. Kells
29. Glenarm
30. Ballycorry
31. Carrickfergus
32. Crumlin
33. Antrim
34. Randalstown
35. Moneymore
36. Cookstown
37. Frederickstown
38. Newton Stewart
39. Besebell
40. Derg Bridge
41. Ardrea
42. Tillen
43. Killybegs
44. Inver
45. Donegal
46. Ballyshannon
47. Garrison
48. Churchill
49. Cassidy
50. Kesh
51. Omagh
52. Glogherny
53. Ballygawley
54. Blackwater
55. Dungannon
56. Kingsmills
57. Maze
58. Belfast
59. Holywood
60. Donaghadee
61. Gray Abbey
62. Portaferry
63. Downpatrick
64. Killinchy
65. Hillsborough
66. Dundrum
67. Rathfriland
68. Loughbrickland
69. Lurgan
70. Armagh
71. Newtown Hamilton
72. Monaghan
73. Augher
74. Clogher
75. Five Mile Town
76. Donough
77. Lisnaskea
78. Callowhill
79. Enniskillen
80. Largay
81. Stridock
82. Sligo
83. Dunatra
84. Bunro
85. Killala
86. Battiglass
87. Inver
88. Clogan
89. Ballina
90. Foxford
91. Swineford
92. Balcarra
93. Ballymote
94. Leitrim
95. Ballingmore
96. Belturbet
97. Cavan
98. Drum
99. Ballybay
100. Castle Blaney
101. Jonesboro
102. Newry
103. Narrow Water
104. Kilkeel
105. Carlingford
106. Dundalk
107. Louth
108. Lurgan
109. Clogher
110. Ladyrath
111. Nobber
112. Moynalty
113. Ballyborough
114. Stradone
115. Bally Jamesdu
116. Roesduff
117. Jamestown
118. Elphin
119. Carrick on Shannon
120. Tulsk
121. Ballyhadireen
122. Ballihaunts
123. Kilkelly
124. Kilcolman
125. Beartree
126. Ballinvary
127. Newport
128. Castlebar
129. Westport
130. Killery
131. Claggan
132. Bunowen
133. Cong
134. Ballinrobe
135. Hollymount
136. Kilmainmore
137. Blenwell
138. Dunmore
139. Glanamoddy
140. Ballintober
141. Roscommon
142. Tarmanbarry
143. Longford
144. Kenagh
145. Edgsworthstown
146. Johnstown
147. Mullingar
148. Clonmellon
149. Trim
150. Summerhill
151. Navan
152. Skryne
153. Drogheda
154. Naut
155. Swords

SOUTH PART.
1. Kilkerran
2. Inveran
3. Sunna
4. Killameen
5. Galway
6. Headford
7. Beldare
8. Athenry
9. Monivia
10. Tuam
11. Castle Blackney
12. Ballinasloe
13. Ballinamore
14. Knockroughry
15. Athlone
16. Maystown
17. Moat a Grenogue
18. Ballimore
19. Philipstown
20. Tyrrel's Pass
21. Ballydemot
22. Longwood
23. Cloncurry
24. Clane
25. Maynooth
26. Raloath
27. Rathcoole
28. Dublin
29. Killgobbin
30. Inniskerry
31. Wicklow
32. Donard
33. Blessington
34. Naas
35. Old Kilcullen
36. Kildare
37. Portarlington
38. Mountmelick
39. Birr
40. Bangher
41. Eyre Court
42. Portumna
43. Aughrim
44. Loughrea
45. Carnamart
46. Gort
47. Killany
48. Killfenora
49. Innislymon
50. Ennis
51. Clare
52. Talla
53. Scarriff
54. Killaloe
55. Nenagh
56. Burresakan
57. Roscrea
58. Rathdowny
59. Ballynakill
60. Maryborough
61. Athy
62. Carlow
63. Stratford
64. Baltinglass
65. Rathville
66. Tinchely
67. Rathdrum
68. Arklow
69. Gorey
70. Ferns
71. Clonegall
72. Burris
73. Old Leighlin
74. Kilkenny
75. Urlingford
76. Killenaule
77. Burrisleagh
78. Toomevara
79. Silver Mine
80. Newport
81. Limerick
82. Bridgetown
83. Six Mile Bridge
84. Paradise
85. Clanderlagh
86. Kilrush
87. Dunbegg
88. Ballyheigh
89. Lixnaw
90. Millstreet
91. Ballylongford
92. Listowell
93. Abbyreale
94. Glynn
95. Ardagh
96. Askeaton
97. Kiddogh
98. Brures
99. Patrick's Well
100. Bruft
101. Cullen
102. Tipperary
103. Cappagh
104. Golden Bridge
105. Cashel
106. Fethard
107. Ballypatrick
108. Knocktopher
109. Innistioge
110. Thomaston
111. New Ross
112. Enniscorthy
113. Killane
114. Ballymartin
115. Taghmon
116. Wexford
117. Duncornuck
118. Clonmines
119. Whitechurch
120. Waterford
121. Kilmacow
122. Kilmacthomas
123. Clonmel
124. Ballynamult
125. Cahir
126. Ballyporeen
127. Araglin
128. Kilworth
129. Ballyhooly
130. Doneraile
131. Mallow
132. Liscarrol
133. Newmarket
134. Cas Island
135. Abbey Odorne
136. Tralee
137. Lispole
138. Dingle
139. Cahir
140. Aghart
141. Glanliagh
142. Milltown
143. Kenmare
144. Killarney
145. Shinagh
146. Mill Street
147. Macromp
148. Cork
149. Fermoy
150. Ratcormuck
151. Lismore
152. Dungarvan
153. Aglish
154. Youghal
155. Cloyne
156. Carlisle Fort
157. Passage
158. Camden Fort
159. Kinsale
160. Innishannon
161. Inchigeelagh
162. Dunmanaway
163. Glengarr
164. Garinish
165. Bantry
166. Dunmanus
167. Baltimore
168. Skibbereen
169. Leap
170. Timolcague

*Rivers, &c.*
a Foyle, R.
b Bann, R.
c Mayola, R.
d Newry Canal
e Boyne, R.
f Liffey, R.
g Slaney, R.
h Barrow, R.
i Nore, R.
j Suire, R.
k Blackwater, R
l Lee, R.
m Bandon, R.
n Flesk, R.
o Shannon, R.
p Carnamart, R
q Moyne, R.
r Suck, R.
s Moy, R.
t Deel, R.
u Munree, R.

ceal the mica slate in the eastern part of Derry, but the mica slate again emerges from beneath this covering, after an interval of about 30 miles, on the north-east coast of Antrim, and rises into hills, which break down abruptly towards the coast between Tor Point and Cushenden Bay. The mica slate rocks on this part of the Irish coast may be considered a continuation of those that occur on the opposite coast of Scotland at the Mull of Cantyre, or, on a more general view, as a continuation of the great Grampian range, which may, in this way, be said to extend from the north-east coast of Scotland to the western shores of Ireland, on the coasts of Donegal. In the eastern part of Tyrone, which intervenes between the transition mountains and the mica slate mountains, a coal formation occurs associated with that kind of limestone which is usually found below coal in Great Britain. The position of this coalfield offers another analogy with Scotland, where the space between the southern and northern mountains is principally occupied by rocks of the coal formation.

3d system of mountains. *The Trap group.*—This group may be described as separated into two chains, bounding on the east and west the trough or valley through which the river Bann flows from Lough Neagh to the ocean. The eastern chain lies in the county of Antrim, being comprehended between the valley of the Bann and the North channel. It presents an abrupt declivity towards the sea, falling with a gentle slope towards the west, in which direction the beds composing its mass incline. Knock-lead, in the northern extremity of the chain, is the highest summit: it rises 1820 feet above the level of the sea; but the basis of this hill is occupied to the height of 500 feet by primitive mica slate rock, leaving only 1320 feet for the thickness of the secondary strata peculiar to this system. Diris Hill, near the southern extremity of the chain, is wholly composed of secondary strata, and attains an elevation of 1475 feet. The western part of the chain included between the Roe and the Bann forms the exact counterpart of the former; but the strata here dip nearly in a contrary direction, viz. towards the north-east; the fall of the hills being gradually in this direction, while they front the west and south with abrupt and precipitous cliffs. Cragnashoack, at the southern extremity, rises 1864 feet above the sea, and is the highest summit of the group. The geological nature of this third system is very different from that of the two former; all the principal formations belonging to the secondary class of rocks. These rocks are partly Plutonian and partly Neptunian. The Neptunian rocks are generally covered with an enormous mass of secondary trap, which appears to attain its greatest thickness on the north; the trap cap of Beny-Avenagh, the most northern summit of the western chain, measuring more than 900 feet: the average depth of this superimposed mass may therefore be estimated at 545 feet, and its superficial extent at 800 square miles. The trap rocks are greenstone, basalt, amygdaloid, wacke, and red bole; occasionally associated with them, forming isolated tracts, as in the Sandybrea district, there are porphyries of different kinds, as pitchstone and pearl-stone porphyries. The amygdaloid and also some of the other rocks of this series contain calc spar and white calcedony, semiopal, felspar, and steatite, or serpentine. The basalt contains olivine. Iron pyrites is a mineral frequently disseminated in the greenstone. Wood coal occurs in seams varying from two inches to four or five feet in thickness, alternating with trap rocks, near Ballentoy; also in the cliffs of Fortnoffer on the east of the Giant's Causeway, at Killymoris near the centre of the trap area, and at Portmaoc, and other places on the eastern shore of Lough Neagh.

*Veins of trap.* Trap veins exhibit many interesting phenomena, particularly in their passage through chalk, which they sometimes convert into a kind of marble. They traverse not only the Neptunian strata, as chalk, lias, and coal formation, but also trap itself. The most interesting and splendid displays of the trap rocks occur at the Giant's Causeway and Fairhead, so well known to travellers; and the cliffs of Kenbaan exhibit very interesting displays of the commingling of the trap and chalk.

Underneath and sometimes intermingled with this vast mass of trap are the following Neptunian formations:—*Chalk*, which is frequently very compact, and sometimes, as where in immediate contact with the Plutonian rocks, changed into a granular limestone resembling marble: the average thickness does not amount to more than 200 feet. Underneath the chalk occurs the deposit known under the name *mulatto stone*, the *green sand* of English geologists, lying upon the *lias limestone*. Underneath the lias occur beds of *red and variegated marl*, *variegated sandstone* with gypsum, and from these issue *salt springs*. These four formations, which, together with the trap, form the whole mass of the hills belonging to the third system, cannot be estimated as possessing a less average thickness than from 800 to 1000 feet. The whole system appears at the north-eastern and south-western extremities to repose upon the *coal formation* and its accompanying rocks, and these on the transition or primitive rocks.* Coal occurs in Tyrone, at Coal Island and Dungannon, and in Antrim, near Ballycastle. Of these, the collieries at Ballycastle, which occupy an extent of not less than one English mile along the coast, are the most considerable. They have been long wrought, and were once in a more prosperous state than at present, as

* Patches of *old red sandstone* occur on the east coast between Ballygelly and Glenarm Bay; and also on the same coast to the southward of Gerron Point.

they used formerly to send from 10,000 to 15,000 tons of coal to the market yearly; whereas now the quantity exported does not amount to more than 1500 or 2000 tons. The coal of these districts is almost entirely what Berger calls slate coal. In one of the works, however, in Coal Island, a bed of cannel coal, six feet thick, is said to have been wrought.

The most remarkable minerals of the alluvial kind found in this part of Ireland are the fossil woods of Lough Neagh, a sheet of water 132 feet above the level of the sea, about nineteen miles six furlongs long from N. W. to S. E., and forty-five feet deep at its centre. The wood is silicified, and in some specimens one extremity will be petrified, while the other remains in a ligneous state. The oak, the holly, and the hazel appear to have been the trees thus affected. It occurs in alluvium in the neighbourhood of the lake.

(2.) *Connaught Coal District.* This district occupies a portion of the counties of Roscommon, Sligo, and Leitrim, in the province of Connaught, and part of the county Cavan in the province of Ulster. Lough Allen, situated near the head of the river Shannon, forms a basin in the centre of the district.

A range of primary mountains, varying in breadth from three miles to a quarter of a mile, extends from Foxford in the county of Mayo, to Colooney in the county of Sligo, and terminates two miles to the north-east of Manor-Hamilton, which may be viewed as the base on which the newer formation of this part of Ireland rests. This range of country is principally composed of mica slate, with some subordinate rocks. Benbo Mountain, near Manor-Hamilton, 1403 feet above the sea, may be cited as exhibiting an interesting display of the various primitive rocks. The summit, and about 800 feet immediately below it, are composed of a fine granular granite: the granite is covered on both sides of the mountain with gneiss, dipping in the direction of its declivity at an angle of 50°. At the base of the mountain, mica slate, with garnets, hornblende rock and hornblende slate, are seen. Large blocks of beautiful syenite, also of serpentine with embedded garnets, were found in a stream at the base of the mountain near Lurganboy. The western side of Benbo is traversed by a vein of copper pyrites, which was formerly wrought, but apparently to no great extent. Veins of iron pyrites also occur there.

Resting upon these old rocks in many places, we observe the first or old red sandstone formation. A tract of this sandstone extends in Roscommon from west to east, from Derrynaslieve to Cashcarrigans, and in greatest breadth in a southerly and northerly direction, from Leitrim to the neighbourhood of Drumshambo. Resting upon this sandstone, forming the base of the coal district, and encircling it, is the mountain or carboniferous limestone. This limestone exhibits the usual character of the formations. The coal formation rests upon the limestone, and is the uppermost or newest of the secondary deposits met with in this part of Ireland. The external aspect of this coal district is described as being hilly and dreary, and as extending in greatest length in a north and south direction, from Down Mountain to Keddue, about sixteen miles, and in greatest breadth from the hills above Swadlinbar to Killargy, sixteen miles. The area of the whole coal country within the edge of the limestone is about 114,000 Irish acres; exclusive of Slieve Russel, which is detached from the great district by the limestone valley of Swadlinbar. The rocks which form the coral series in the Connaught coal district are similar to those met with in other coalfields. Besides coal, which is the *black bituminous species*, the formation contains sandstone flag, slate clay, bituminous slate, clay ironstone, and fire clay. Some kinds of the coal afford in the 100 parts, 71.42 carbon, 23.37 bitumen, and 5.21 gray ashes. *Iron-works.* The beds of clay ironstone that occur in all parts of the Connaught coal district appear, at an early period, to have attracted the attention of miners; and works, on a small scale, called *bloomeries*, were carried on in various parts of the adjoining country, as long as any wood remained to supply them with charcoal, but they have since been given up.

(3.) *East of Ireland.* This district extends nearly 100 miles from north to south, and between sixty and ninety miles from east to west, comprehending about a third part of the island. It is bounded on the east by the Irish Channel, on the south and west by the mountains which confine the Suire and the Shannon, and on the north by the clay slate hills of Louth and the mountain limestone hills of Meath, the clay slate hills of Cavan and the mountain limestone of Longford, and by a line produced from thence to the bay of Galway. In the landscape of Ireland there is one very remarkable feature, which cannot fail to strike every observer: in traversing most parts of the island, we meet with ranges and groups of bold mountainous and hilly tracts, in some degree isolated, while the interval between them is generally occupied by a surface that appears nearly level, when viewed on the great scale, but which is found, on a nearer view, to present a gently waved outline: a considerable expansion of the plain occupies the central counties of Ireland, and extends across the island from Dublin Bay on the east, to Galway Bay on the west; and in general, where a similar plain surface occurs, the immediately subjacent rock is mountain limestone; to the abundance of which mineral, next to the mild temperature and general moisture of the climate, the soil of Ireland is probably more indebted for its superior fertility than to any other cause

In this district mountainous and hilly tracts arise above the surface of the limestone plain, on the east, the south, the west, the centre, and the north. The eastern chain extends from the north side of Dublin Bay to the confluence of the Barrow with the Suire on the south. The highest point is Lugnaquilla, which is 3070 feet above low-water-mark in Dublin Bay. It consists almost wholly of primitive and transition rocks, of which the following species occur: granite, mica slate, quartz rock, clay slate, greywacke, trap and porphyry. Metalliferous minerals are wanting on the west side of the granite chain, but abound on the east side. In the granite and mica slate districts there are veins of galena or lead glance; of these the most considerable are in Glenmalur; in the clay slate tract eleven different metallic substances have been met with, viz. gold, silver, copper, iron, lead, zinc, tin, tungsten, manganese, arsenic, and antimony.

Native gold occurs in the Ballinvalley streams at Croghan Kinshela: and in 1801, regular mining was commenced, but did not lead to any important results; and after a time the working was given up. The gold of Croghan Kinshela occurred in grains and masses from the smallest size to lumps of considerable weight; one piece weighed twenty-two ounces. The gold was found in alluvium, accompanied with other metallic substances, as magnetic iron ore, iron glance, red iron ore, brown iron ore, iron pyrites, *tinstone*, wolfram, gray manganese ore, and fragments of quartz and chlorite. In some specimens the gold was observed ramified in slender threads through the wolfram, and in others incorporated with iron ochre: some of the gold was crystallized in octahedrons, and also in the elongated garnet dodecahedral form. Native gold was also found in Croghan Moira mine, about seven miles distant from the former mountain, but in small quantity.

The copper mines of Cronbane and Tigrony, in this district, are situated in clay slate and quartzose clay slate. The ores, which are copper pyrites and black copper ore, are associated with iron pyrites, and rarely with galena; and auriferous silver occurs in beds in the slaty strata. In the twelve years ending in 1811, the produce of the mines was 19,342 tons 13 cwt. of ore; yielding 1046 tons 10 cwt. of copper. The mineral waters flowing from the mines are impregnated with blue vitriol or sulphate of copper. These waters are received into tanks, in which the muddy particles are allowed to subside. The clear waters are then passed into pits filled with plate and scrap iron, which occasions a precipitation of the copper.

The other tracts of this district are composed of secondary rocks, more or less deeply covered with diluvial and alluvial deposits. The secondary rocks are *old red sandstone*, *mountain limestone*, (or as it is called in Ireland, Irish limestone,) and the *coal formation*. Of these formations the mountain limestone is by far the most abundant; indeed, with the exception of the counties of Derry and Antrim in the north, and Wicklow in the east, there is no county in the island in which it does not prevail more or less. The coal formation occurs in the *Leinster coal district*. The sandstone, slate, ironstone, clay, and coal, which constitute the series, alternate with each other, and the whole rests on the mountain limestone, and is frequently disposed in the basin shape. The coal of this district is *glance coal*, the blind coal of miners, the anthracite of French geologists, the Kilkenny coal of some authors (so named because the town of Kilkenny is situated in this coalfield).

The most interesting alluvial phenomena are those exhibited by the limestone gravel, the granite blocks, and the vast peat bogs. The great limestone field abounds in hillocks and ridges of limestone gravel. Sometimes these ridges appear like regular mounds, the work of art, forming a continued line of several miles in extent. That which passes by Maryborough, in the Queen's County, is a remarkable instance of this kind; and similar mounds, hillocks, and ridges occur also in the counties of Meath, Westmeath, Kildare, Carlow, and other portions of the limestone field, in which the limestone gravel and sand frequently exhibit a stratified arrangement, the alternate beds being very distinct from each other. The inequality of surface thus produced, seems to have occasioned the formation of those extensive tracts of peat bog which cover so considerable a portion of the limestone plain of Ireland.* The natural course of springs and streams being obstructed, stagnant lakes and pools of water were formed; thus promoting the growth of those aquatic reeds, grasses, and rushes, which, by their constant increase and decay, appear to compose the mass of the bogs of Ireland. In this manner it is conceivable that shallow lakes may in process of time have become entirely filled with peat; and that peat bogs may thus have gradually acquired a convexity of surface, or at least that greater declivity by which their borders are distinguished. The average depth of these bogs is commonly from sixteen to twenty-five feet, but the extreme depth observed is forty-seven feet. In the same manner we may conceive the gradual growth of peat bog to have successively extended from the higher regions to the flanks, and thence to the feet, of mountains. That fallen forests were not the primary origin of these peat bogs seems evident from the circumstance that two and even three successive growths of trees have been observed at different depths in a section of the same bog. In these instances, the trees lie horizontally, frequently crossing each other, and either attached to their roots or broken over; and in the latter case the stumps usually stand erect where they grew. The prostration of trees, however, may to a certain extent have acted

* Peat is estimated to extend over a tenth of the whole island.

as an auxiliary in promoting the growth of peat bogs; and this prostration appears in general to have taken place either from natural decay, or from trees possessing little hold of a wet spongy soil having been overturned by storms. This may partly account for trees of all ages being found in the bogs of Ireland, whether these bogs be situated in plains, or form the immediate cover of high mountain tracts. The universal destruction of the forests of Ireland is principally to be attributed to the general introduction of iron furnaces, as the most profitable mode of consuming the timber, then a material esteemed of little value; and hence the almost total neglect of copsing those tracts in which the woods had been felled. The marl beds, so frequently met with in these peat bogs, are curious in a zoological view, from their occasionally containing remains of that splendid animal the fossil elk. But the remains of the extinct species occur also in the gravel; and the late Mr. Edgeworth observed the remains of the red deer in the same marl as that which contained the extinct species.

(4.) *South of Ireland.* Under this division we comprise the counties of Cork, Kerry, Clare, Waterford, Tipperary, and part of Galway.

This mountainous, hilly, and diversified region is chiefly composed of chains having generally a direction from east to west, and attaining their greatest elevation in the mountains of Kerry, where Gurrane Tual, one of Macgillicuddy's Reeks, near Killarney (the highest land in Ireland), is 3410 feet above the sea. The rocks in this elevated county are chiefly of the transition class: they decline gradually towards the north, and finally pass under the old red sandstone and mountain limestone of the midland counties. The following may be considered a general estimate of the geognostical relations of the south of Ireland:—

*Transition rocks.* In Kerry, the transition strata range from east to west, and dip to the north and south, with vertical beds in the axes of the ranges: the strata, as they diminish in inclination on each side, form a succession of troughs. The rocks are chiefly Neptunian, the Plutonian being comparatively rare. The Neptunian are either simple or compound; the simple are *clay slate*, *quartz rock*, *hornstone*, *Lydian stone*, and *limestone:* the compound are, *greywacke*, *greywacke slate*, *sandstone*. The Plutonian rocks are *greenstone* and *porphyry*. Organic remains occur in the limestone, slate, and greywacke, but more frequently and abundantly in the limestone than in the other rocks. In Kenmare these fossils consist of a few bivalves, and some crinoidal remains; and these also are most numerous in the Mucruss and Killarney limestones. At the foot of the Slievemeesh range this limestone includes asaphus caudatus, calamine macrophthalma, with orthoceratites, ellipsolites ovatus, ammonites, euomphalites, turbinites, neritites, melanites, and several species of terebratula, spirifer, and producta. Near Smerwick harbour similar organic remains are abundant in slate and greywacke, together with hysterolites, and many genera of polyparia.

*Transition coal.* All the coal of the province of Munster, except that of the county of Clare, is referable to the transition class. At Knockasartnet, near Killarney, and on the north of Tralee, there are three beds of glance coal, alternating with strata of greywacke and slate. In the county of Cork this glance coal is more abundant, particularly near Kanturk, extending from the north of the Blackwater to the Allord. The ravines of the latter river, and various other defiles, expose clay slate, greywacke, talc, and sandstone, in nearly vertical strata ranging from west to east. This transition tract extends to the river Shannon on the north-west. As the strata range from west to east, in a series of parallel narrow troughs, they exhibit great variety of inclination, dipping rapidly either to the north or south, and becoming horizontal between the ridges. The glance coal is raised in sufficient quantities for the purpose of burning the limestone of the adjacent districts.

The coal and the strata with which it is accompanied abound with impressions of equisetæ and calamites, and afford some traces of fucoides. Beds of glance coal also occur in the county of Limerick, on the left bank of the Shannon, north of Abbeyfeale, and at Longhill; and on the right bank of the river at Labbasheada. The transition rocks of Kerry and Limerick extend into Cork and Waterford.

*Mines.* Copper mines occur in limestone in Ross Island in the lake of Killarney. In the county of Cork, there are copper mines at Allihies, Audley, and Ballydehol; and others, producing lead, at Doneen and Rinabelly. The mine at Allihies is one of the richest mines in Ireland; it was discovered in 1812, and yields more than 2000 tons of copper ore annually. The ore occurs in a large quartz vein, which generally intersects the slaty rocks of the country from north to south, but in some places runs parallel to the strata. It is remarked that all this portion of the county of Cork indicates a very general diffusion of cupreous particles, so much so that in the year 1812, there existed a cupriferous peat-bog on the east side of Glandore harbour, forty or fifty tons of the dried peat producing when burnt one ton of ashes, containing from ten to fifteen per cent. of copper. The lead-mines of Doneen and Rinabelly are in slate.

*Coal formation of Clare.* The transition clay slate of this county is bordered by a zone of old red sandstone, to which succeeds, in ascending order and conformable position, the mountain limestone and coal formation, both of which occupy flat and undulating hills, and the strata are nearly horizontal. The best sections are seen in the cliffs on the west coast, where bituminous shale, slate clay, sandstone, and sandstone flag, rest upon limestone. Coal, however, is of rare occurrence, and when found, is of indifferent quality.

As in every other part of Ireland, the district abounds with alluvial deposits. In regard to the distribution of the older of these, or the diluvium in the south of Ireland, it is remarked, —1. That boulders, gravel, and sand, derived from the transition rocks, are distributed along the borders and sides of the mountains in Kerry. 2. In a small district of Limerick and Tipperary, situated between the Gaultees and Slieve-na-muck, the rolled masses consist not only of portions of contiguous rocks, but contain also porphyry, which is not to be found *in situ* near the vicinity of Pallis Hill. 3. In the peninsula of Nenville, near Galway, the surface of the mountain limestone is strewed over with numerous boulders of red and gray granite, syenite, greenstone, and sandstone, which must apparently have been conveyed from the opposite side of the bay of Galway.

### SECT. III.—*Historical Geography.*

The earliest inhabitants of Ireland, from which the native race now existing has sprung, appear, by the language still spoken, to have been Celtic. The Romans, in occupying Britain, could not fail to acquire much information relative to Ierne, Hibernia, or Ireland; and accordingly we find that the map of that country by Ptolemy is less defective than the one which he gives of Scotland. About the fourth century, we find Ireland bearing the name of Scotland, from the leading people on its eastern shore, who afterwards passing into Argyle, and making themselves masters of all Caledonia, communicated to it the name of Scotland, finally withdrawn from the country to which it originally belonged.

The Danes, during the height of their power, from the ninth to the twelfth centuries, possessed almost the whole eastern coast of Ireland, making Dublin their capital. Before this time Ireland had been converted to Christianity, and a number of celebrated monasteries had been founded, the tenants of which were distinguished, even over Europe, for their piety and learning.

The English sway commenced in 1170. Richard Strongbow, earl of Pembroke, as a private individual, formed the first settlement; but Henry II. soon assumed the title of "lord of Ireland." The range of dominion was long restricted to a portion of the kingdom enclosed within what is called the English pale, without which the Irish remained still under the rule of their native chieftains. Henry VIII. assumed the title of "king of Ireland," but without any material extension of his authority over that kingdom.

The Irish massacre was a dreadful outrage, to which attachment to popery and zeal for national independence united in impelling a proud and fierce people. Forty thousand English settlers are supposed to have perished, and the rest were driven into Dublin. Cromwell, however, afterwards crossed the Channel, and made cruel reprisals; he took the principal fortified towns, and reduced Ireland under more full subjection than ever. Yet the disposition of the people remained the same; and when James II. was driven from the English throne, he was received with enthusiasm in Ireland, and became for some time its master. The battle of the Boyne, followed next year by that of Aughrim, decided the fate of the empire, and more especially of Ireland, which then felt for the first time the miseries of a conquered country. The estates of many principal native proprietors were confiscated; the Catholics were deprived of all political privileges; they were rendered incapable of holding any office or employment in the state; they were debarred even from holding land, from devising property, and from exercising other important functions of civil society. Under these severities they pertinaciously retained their political attachments together with their religious creed; and a continual ferment prevailed, which broke out from time to time into partial rebellions.

The gradual emancipation of Ireland commenced at the period of the American war. Till that era England had denied to her the right of trading directly with any foreign nation; and had compelled her to export and import every commodity through the channel of Great Britain. The extremity, however, to which Britain was reduced enabled the Irish to place themselves in a formidable attitude; and by forming armed associations, and adopting other threatening measures, they induced parliament to grant them free trade with all nations. From this time also the most obnoxious of the restrictions on the Catholics were gradually repealed or fell into disuse; and before the end of last century, they had obtained almost every political privilege, except that of sitting in parliament, and of holding the very highest offices of state. The propriety of conceding these also became one of the leading questions which long divided the public mind.

A very formidable rebellion broke forth in spite of these concessions. The French revolution, which caused a general ferment in Europe, was intensely felt throughout Ireland. A society was formed of "United Irishmen;" and secret meetings were held, having in view the entire separation from England, and the formation of the kingdom into an independent republic. The vigilance of government, and the failure of the French in their attempts to land a force of any magnitude, prevented matters from coming to the last extremity till 1798, when a violent insurrection arose in four of the counties nearest Dublin. The rebels, though zealous and brave, being without discipline, were routed in successive encounters with much inferior bodies of regulars and militia; and being unsupported by French aid were completely put down in a few months. The exasperation, however, produced by the tragical events of this short period continued long to rankle in the minds of the Irish, and to aggravate the evils under which they laboured. To soothe this irritation, another expedient was employed, which materially affected the situation of Ireland.

The difficult and reluctant *union of the two kingdoms* was effected in 1800 by Mr. Pitt. Ireland gained thus considerable commercial advantages; and, from the example of Scotland, it was hoped that a gradual tranquillity would be the result. This expectation has not yet been fulfilled. The peasantry of the south, inflamed by national jealousy, by religious animosity, and by the severe privations under which they labour, have continued, if not in open rebellion, at least in a state of turbulence constantly tending towards it; and their discontents have been increased by the indiscreet zeal of the Protestant party.

The bill for Catholic emancipation, so unexpectedly introduced, in 1828, by the Duke of Wellington, and carried after such a violent ferment of parties, has made a remarkable change in the political constitution of Ireland. The political disabilities under which the Catholics had hitherto laboured have been finally removed. They are made admissible to the highest offices of state, with the exception of that of lord chancellor; an exclusion decided upon, not so much on account of the dignity of that office, as the extensive church patronage attached to it. Roman Catholics are also made admissible to sit in both houses of parliament, and to every other political privilege enjoyed by their fellow countrymen.

## Sect. IV.—*Political Geography.*

The political evils under which Ireland labours will sufficiently appear from the foregoing survey of her history. From the earliest times she has been in the situation of a conquered country, without ever becoming reconciled to the yoke, or assimilated to the ruling nation. Within the last two centuries, her devoted adherence to a religion which had been renounced by her rulers, has had a most fatal tendency, which we may however hope to see much mitigated by the healing measures that have now been adopted. In consequence, also, of repeated scenes of rebellion and forfeiture, by much the greater part of the lands are in the possession of English and Protestant proprietors, who, having no natural influence over the occupiers of their estates, hold their place only by the hated tenure of dominion and law. Being connected with the country by no natural ties, and attracted by the superior brilliancy of the English and French capitals, most of them quit Ireland, and become habitual *absentees.* When the Scottish Highlanders arrayed themselves against the government, they acted under the influence of a few leading chiefs, whose interests and passions afforded a lever by which the people could be moved. But the Irish people, deprived of any such guidance, chose their leaders from among themselves, or from those who courted their favour by fostering all their national propensities. Secret associations, party badges, mysterious names, have exerted an influence over their minds, the extent and nature of which it is impossible to calculate.

Ireland, like Scotland, has been united to England; yet it retains somewhat more of the aspect of a separate kingdom. A lord lieutenant still displays a portion of the state and exercises some of the functions of royalty. He has not only a household establishment, but a chancellor, a secretary, and other ministers of state. The courts of justice, and the different orders of magistracy, are nearly on the same footing as in England; yet they have not the reputation of exercising their functions with quite the same dignity and impartiality. The violence of party spirit acts upon judges, and still more upon juries; and in the country, the absence of great proprietors, and the want of any middling class, render it difficult to find materials for a respectable and effective magistracy. Ireland sent to the Imperial parliament 100 members of the House of Commons, of whom 36 were for cities and boroughs, and 64 for counties, which latter sent two members each. The large proportion of this latter class was expected to render the representation more respectable; but, unfortunately, the low qualification required, amounting only to 40*s.*, enabled the great proprietors to split votes among their numerous little tenantry to such an extent as almost to produce universal suffrage. The very system of letting farms on leases for lives, which confers the right of voting, extended that right to almost every tenant. This could scarcely be said to confer the real right of suffrage, as the dependence of the tenants was almost always such as to enable the landlord to dictate their vote; though in late elections, the influence of the priests was in several counties successfully exerted. To remedy these evils, the same act which removed the disabilities of the Catholics, raised the qualification of freeholders in Ireland from 40*s.* to 10*l.* a year, and thus reduced them to less than a third of their former number. Many also of the principal boroughs, as Belfast, Wexford, Cashel, Sligo, Dundalk, Enniskillen, were entirely close, the members being chosen by twelve self-elected burgesses; while, in others, the whole ground on which a borough stood belonged to the nearest great proprietor. The consequence was, that an oligarchy, formed by the possessors of those vast properties into which the greater part of Ireland is divided, held an almost unlimited sway over the country. Previous to the union, the influence of the three houses of Beresford, Ponsonby, and Foster was such, that the aid of one, and, if possible, two of them, was necessary for carrying on the measures of government. That influence, however, has been on the decline, and there is no prospect of its renewal.

The Reform Bill gave to Ireland only five additional members, and it made no material change in the returning boroughs; but, by placing the election in the hands of all householders paying 10*l.* annually, it rendered those nominations open which had formerly been made by the small number of individuals composing the corporation.

The naval and military force of the empire in general defends Ireland. There is a commander of the forces resident in Dublin; acting, however, under the orders, not of the lord lieutenant, but of the British commander-in-chief. The number of regular troops stationed at different points is always considerable.

The revenue levied in Ireland has never borne the same proportion to her natural resources as that of England. The rates in all the principal articles of consumption have been lower. The tax on hearths, however, was found very oppressive; as it required inquisitorial visits, and affected the lowest of the people. This and all the other assessed taxes were so irregularly levied, that, notwithstanding the discontent excited by them, they did little more than cover the expenses of collection. For this reason, by a motion of the chancellor of the exchequer, they were entirely remitted. In 1800 the revenue was 2,684,000*l.* and the debt 25,662,000*l.* At the union, the stipulation was made that Ireland should pay two-seventeenths of the whole expenditure of the empire; this arrangement has led to a continual increase both of debt and revenue. In 1811 the former amounted to 77,382,000*l.*, and the latter to 3,906,900*l.* In 1830 the revenue was 3,548,822*l.*, and in 1835 it amounted to 4,400,953*l.* The particulars for the latter year were:—

| | | | |
|---|---|---|---|
| Customs | £1,744,764 | Stamps | £470,286 |
| Excise | 1,966,531 | Postage, &c. | 219,372 |

The public expenditure in 1830 was as follows:—

| | | | |
|---|---|---|---|
| Charges of funded debt | £1,178,454 | Army | £986,209 |
| Civil list, &c. | 584,969 | Miscellaneous | 747,689 |

The national debt of Ireland in 1817, when it ceased to form a separate item in the public accounts in consequence of the consolidation of the British and Irish exchequers, was 134,602,769*l.*

For local and patriotic objects in Ireland, very considerable sums are allowed out of the public revenue. Of these, for the year 1832, there appear the following:—

| | | | |
|---|---|---|---|
| Schools and Education | £30,000 | Female Orphan House | £1,833 |
| Protestant Charity Schools | 3,000 | Roman Catholic College | 8,928 |
| Foundling Hospital | 26,314 | Royal Dublin Society | 5,300 |
| Four other Hospitals | 10,045 | Belfast Academical Institution | 1,500 |
| House of Industry | 21,192 | Nonconforming and other Ministers | 24,224 |
| Richmond Lunatic Asylum | 1,388 | Public Works | 33,564 |
| Hibernian Marine Society | 950 | Dunmore Harbour | 7,500 |

### Sect. V.—*Productive Industry.*

Ireland, in this respect, has long presented a painful spectacle; a great proportion of her people being involved in extreme and squalid poverty. The Irish do not want enterprise, or even industry; but various causes have combined to degrade them in the scale of improvement. Among these the conduct long held by Britain must be considered as prominent; thus, after other expedients had proved ineffectual, it was prohibited to export woollens to foreign countries. Similar measures were taken with regard to glass, hops, and every branch in respect to which any rivalry was apprehended. There was one article, however, the production of a large surplus of which could by no means be avoided. This was black cattle and sheep; but the value of these was effectually cut down by the prohibition to import them into England, the only accessible market. Under these regulations, all the exertions of Ireland to better her condition were cramped, and while Britain was making the most rapid advances, Ireland continued in the same state of depression. However, in consequence of her spirited efforts at the end of the American war, and of the embarrassments of the British government, the most odious and pernicious of these restrictions were repealed. Further advantages were obtained at the time of the Union; and at present, every exertion is making to place the two countries in a state of perfect reciprocity. The consequence has been, that in the course of forty years, Ireland has made a rapid progress in industry and commerce; yet some of her greatest evils are so deeply seated, that they have scarcely yet begun to give way to the influence of a more auspicious system.

Agriculture has been long in a backward and very depressed state. The farms were, for the most part, small, managed by the farmer himself and his family, destitute of capital with wretched implements, and with a pertinacious adherence to all the obsolete practices of a rude age. The best soils exhausted a great portion of their strength in throwing up weeds, which no effective measures were taken to extirpate. The system also of infield and outfield was strictly adhered to, the ground being heavily cropped as long as it would yield any thing, and afterwards of necessity allowed two or three years to recruit. Although these defects still exist to a considerable extent, yet in all parts of the country, but particularly in the east and north, improved practices and implements are beginning to be introduced.

The Irish tenures are long, some of them perpetual, in which case they may be considered as property, the rent being a mere trifle; a lease of thirty-one years and three lives is very common. These long leases are attended with scarcely any of the benefits which might be naturally expected. As the farmer commences usually without any capital, trusting for the payment of the first year's rent to the produce of his farm, he almost always falls more or less into arrear, and thus lies at the mercy of his landlord. This would be less pernicious, were it the landlord himself with whom he had to deal; but the landlords of Ireland, holding usually properties of immense extent, and being mostly resident out of the country, cannot or will not undertake the task of dealing with this impoverished multitude of small tenants. They devolve it upon the intermediate agents and *middlemen*. The latter, a class peculiar to Ireland, take a large extent of ground, which they let out in small portions to the real cultivator. They grant leases, indeed; but as the tenant, from the circumstances above mentioned, soon comes under their power, they and the agents treat him with the greatest harshness, exact personal services, presents, bribes; and draw from the land as much as they possibly can, without the least regard to its permanent welfare. This system, while it crushes the tenant, is not less injurious to the landlord, into whose coffers there often passes less than one-half of the sum paid by the tenant. The only use to which the latter turns his long lease is to divide and subdivide the lands among his children, till the share of each affords only the most miserable aliment, and an overgrown population is fixed upon the farm. An attempt to let land on a different footing can only be effected by the ejection of more than half its existing occupants, who in that case are apt to fly to violent and revengeful courses, so that even a partial endeavour to introduce such improvements has been a main cause of the existing disturbed state. Another injurious mode is that of partnership leases, in which a number of persons take a farm jointly, and make it a sort of common property. Each is allowed to put upon it a certain number of *collops;* the collop consisting of one horse, two cows, or twelve goats. A degrading stipulation is often introduced into leases, by which the occupant is bound to work for his landlord either without wages, or at a rate lower than ordinary.

Tithe is one of the evils of which the Irish cultivator most grievously complains. Although it must in all cases fall ultimately on the landlord, yet to take from the cabin of the peasant the pig which he has reared, or the handful of potatoes which he has raised for the support of his family, is an act peculiarly discouraging and irritating. The exemption of grass lands tends also to discourage tillage. Measures taken by parliament to promote the commutation of tithes, have been attended with considerable success; and by a late act arrangements are made by which the church rates, instead of being taken out of the farmer's produce, are paid by the landlord out of his rent.

The extent of country, and the objects of culture in Ireland, vary considerably from those of the sister kingdom. Its superficial extent is computed at 12,000,000 Irish, or 19,278 760 English acres. Of this, notwithstanding the considerable amount to be deducted for mountain, lakes, and bogs, Mr. Young calculates that there is a greater proportion of productive land than in England. The soil of Ireland is shallow, consisting most generally of a thin sprinkling of earth over a rocky ground; but the copious moisture wafted from the sea, by which it is everywhere surrounded, produces a quick and rapid vegetation, and in particular a brilliancy of verdure, not equalled perhaps in any other region of Europe. Such a country is of course highly favourable to pasturage; and as this pursuit is suited to the imperfect stages of culture, the rearing of live stock has been long the main staple of Irish husbandry. Its luxuriant plains are depastured by vast herds of black cattle; and from this source is derived the very large quantity of salted provisions shipped from the southern ports. The number of oxen and cows annually killed for this purpose was reckoned at 18,000. This trade has considerably decreased since the peace; but the export of live cattle is extensively carried on. Great facilities have been lately afforded for it by the steam packets. The dairy is also a great branch of industry in Ireland. None of its cheeses, indeed, have acquired a reputation; but butter of excellent quality is made and largely exported. Another species of live stock is an essential article to the economy of an Irish cultivator. The pig usually shares his cabin, and is fed, like himself, on potatoes. It is too great a luxury to be killed for his own consumption; but is sold and driven to the ports to be salted for exportation. Sheep are bred extensively on the mountain tracts, which are unfit for rearing any other stock. In many places they are bred for the wool and milk. In this last respect, however, goats are more productive; and they are reared in immense quantities in the mountain districts in the north. The Irish horses are small, hardy, and capable of doing much work upon little food. Poultry are fed in great numbers in and around all the cabins the interior of which they are admitted to share; a practice extremely favourable to their increase. Great quantities of geese are kept for the sake of the feathers, which are cruelly plucked from the animals alive. The produce of grain is also large, notwithstanding the imperfect processes employed in cultivating it. Wheat and barley were little raised till of late, when both the culture and export of the former have been greatly extended. Still the main objects are oats and potatoes; the former as the subject of a large export, the latter as the staple food of a considerable body of the people. The Irish boast of the potatoe, as if it were nowhere else produced in equal perfection. Compared with grain of any kind, it certainly affords the means of supporting a greater population upon a given extent of ground. The scope, however, which it affords for the multiplication of the people in miserable circumstances, is generally considered by the political economists as one of the causes of the present distress in Ireland. Flax is also a valuable product of Irish husbandry, affording the material of the linen manufacture. According to a return made to the trustees in 1809, the extent sown was 76,749 acres; in addition to which, the various little scattered patches raise the number probably to about 100,000 acres, supposed to produce at an average about 30 stones per acre; which, at 10*s.* 6*d.* per stone, would make the entire value about 1,500,000*l.*

There is a want of trees in Ireland. The immense forests which some centuries ago covered a great proportion of its surface, have fallen and been converted in a great measure into moss or bog. The bogs of Ireland present an extensive obstacle to cultivation. They are estimated by the parliamentary commissioners at 2,330,000 English acres. From them, indeed, fuel is supplied to many districts, yet the draining of a large portion would be certainly desirable; and the commissioners seem to think that, from their generally elevated position, this might be done with great facility and advantage. The great quantity of water beneath these bogs causes often a singular phenomenon, that of moving bogs. Bursting the surface, the bog inundates the surrounding lands, spreading desolation and barrenness through its whole course, which in one instance extended no less than twenty miles.

In respect to manufactures, the state of Ireland cannot be described as flourishing; a misfortune for which she may accuse the oppressive policy of England. One species of fabric, however, she has been allowed and even encouraged to cultivate, and it has attained to a very considerable magnitude.

The linen manufacture was first introduced by the Earl of Strafford, who brought flax-seed from Holland, and workmen from France and the Netherlands. His attainder, and the subsequent troubles, suspended the undertaking; but it was revived by the Duke of Ormond, who established near Dublin a colony from Brussels, Jersey, and Rochelle, and gave lands on advantageous terms to those willing to embark in the business. After the Revolution, the English parliament created a board for the promotion of the linen manufacture, and granted bounties both on the raising of flax and the export of linen. These exertions met with great success; and the manufacture has become general throughout Ireland, and particularly in Ulster. The following, according to a late parliamentary report, was the reputed value of brown or unbleached linens sold in the markets of Ireland in the year 1824:—

| | |
|---|---|
| Ulster | £2,109,309 |
| Leinster | 192,888 |
| Munster | 110,421 |
| Connaught | 168,090 |
| Total | £2,580,708 |

The mode of conducting this manufacture is, however, in several respects, very rude and imperfect. It is generally practised by individuals holding little spots of ground, the culture of which they combine with that of weaving. The same person, or at least the same family, in many cases raises the flax, dresses it, spins it into yarn, and weaves it into cloth. There is too much anxiety to obtain the greatest possible quantity of yarn out of a given quantity of flax, without regard to the quality; and the sorting of the yarn, so that it may be of an uniform texture, suited to the kind of linen intended to be woven, is almost wholly neglected. In some instances, however, it is worked to a most extraordinary degree of fineness. Anne M'Quillin, in the county of Down, could spin 105 hanks to the pound, which would reach 214 English miles. Exertions have lately been made to introduce mill-spinning, which, it is supposed, would generally improve the quality of yarn, though it could not produce it of such extreme fineness as some of that spun by the hand. Twenty years ago the mill could not produce above fifteen cuts to a pound; now it can make nearly fifty.

The export of linen from Ireland, in the year 1824, amounted in all to 49,491,037 yards, of which 46,466,950 were to Great Britain; and 3,024,087 to foreign parts. The real value of the whole was 2,412,858*l.* Of that sent to Great Britain, 31,314,533 yards were retained for home consumption; the rest were re-exported to the same quarters as Scotch linen. This great manufacture is chiefly supported by its own growth of flax. Ireland, however, imports 25,000 tons of hemp from abroad, and 3300 from Britain; also about 7500 tons of linen yarn; of all which materials the value falls short of 45,000*l.*

Distillation is another branch of industry characteristic of Ireland, but by no means attended with the same happy effects. It has hitherto been carried on chiefly in defiance of the revenue and government, and has given birth to a vast system of contraband, equally destructive of morals and of public order. All the mountains, bogs, and deep valleys of the north and west abound with illicit stills, in spots where the most diligent search can scarcely discover them; and where detected, they can scarcely be seized without the aid of an armed force. When the troops are seen advancing, concerted signals are made, and the small light stills are soon conveyed to a distant quarter. The farmers and proprietors encourage illicit distillation as the most ready mode of affording a market for their grain. The quality of the spirit was long much superior to that produced by the legal distillers, owing to restrictions imposed on the latter; so that, in selling, it was considered the highest recommendation that it "never paid duty." The most rigorous laws were enacted in vain, for they only rendered the people concerned in this practice more desperate and determined. Of late, however, the duty, as in Scotland, has been reduced and free exportation permitted. The effect has been remarkable; the quantity of spirits paying duty, which from 1818 to 1822 varied from 3,000,000 to 4,000,000, rose in 1824 to 7,800,000, and in 1832 to 8,657,000; thus warranting a presumption, that the contraband fabrication of this article has been greatly diminished.

The killing and salting of beef and pork for sale forms a great branch of Irish commerce. The beef is packed in three different forms, called planter's beef, India beef, and common beef; the first two, having the coarse pieces taken out, and charged 4*s.* additional per cwt. While the export of salt beef has diminished, that of pork has of late been much extended.

The cotton manufacture, since 1822, has spread through Ireland in a very surprising manner, particularly in the counties of Antrim, Down, Louth, and part of Dublin. The coarser linen fabrics are disappearing before it, and proceeding to the westward and southward, retaining still an equal hold of the kingdom in general. More recently this fabric has rather declined, and linen has regained the ascendency.

The other manufactures are not of primary importance. A great quantity of wool is, indeed, worked up by the peasantry into frieze, linseys, and flannels, for their domestic use; but the only fabrics on a great scale, which are those of broadcloth at Carrick-on-Shannon, and of flannels at Kilkenny, are on the decline. Breweries have been established in the principal towns, and are rather in a flourishing state.

In the distribution of minerals, Ireland has by no means been neglected; but some unpropitious circumstances have prevented any of them from being turned to great account. Of these impediments the most material is the want of a sufficient supply of good coal. The fuel of Ireland is in general either coal imported from England and Scotland, or the turf dug out of its immense bogs; but the latter has not yet been found applicable to the fusion of metals. From these causes the veins of iron ore, which are very extensively diffused through the island, have not yet been turned to any important use. The copper, also of fine quality, which is found in the counties of Wicklow and Cork, must be sent over to Swansea to be smelted. The lead, however of Wicklow is worked to a considerable extent with imported coal.

Fishery is a branch of industry for which the extended shores and deep bays of Ireland would be peculiarly adapted. Nor do the inland waters, the rivers and lakes, less abound in the species of fish appropriate to them. The diligence of the Irish in taking fish for immediate consumption is considerable, being urged on by the frequent abstinence from other food which their Catholic profession enjoins. Their trout and salmon are distinguished both for size and taste: the salmon are caught by weirs, stake-nets, and other contrivances, but with so little precaution that their number has been sensibly diminished. The curing of fish has made very little progress, when compared with the opportunities which the coasts of Ireland afford; and Ireland cannot come into competition with Scotland.

*Commerce.*—The manufactured products of Ireland are quite inconsiderable; she has, however, great facilities for the production of raw materials; and it is in all respects more suitable for her, as well as for England, that she should direct her efforts to this department, and import manufactured articles from Britain, than that she should attempt to enter into an unequal competition with the latter in manufacturing industry. In 1825 the restraints on the intercourse between Ireland and Great Britain were mostly abolished; and owing to this circumstance, and to the establishment of a regular intercourse by steam packets between Liverpool, Glasgow, Bristol, and the principal towns on the east and south coasts of Ireland, the trade between the two countries has been vastly increased. Owing to the circumstance of this intercourse being now placed on the footing of a coasting trade, no account has been kept later than 1825, of the reciprocal imports and exports of each, except in the case of corn.

In 1829, the imports from foreign parts were valued at 1,669,406*l.*; in 1831, they were 1,552,228*l.*; in 1832, they were 1,348,828*l.* The exports in 1831 were 608,938*l.*; in 1832 they were 452,775*l.* Within the last few years there has been a most extraordinary increase in the quantity of grain and live stock imported from Ireland into Great Britain. The former, on an average of 1830 and 1831, amounted to 543,618 quarters of wheat, and 1,563,593 quarters of oats and oatmeal. In 1832, there were imported into Liverpool alone, 338,649 quarters of wheat, value 948,217*l.*; 325,720 quarters of oats, 309,434*l.*; 14,486 quarters of barley, 24,626*l.*; 69,624 cows, 765,864*l.*; 149,090 pigs, 484,542*l.*; 74,260 sheep, 129,955*l.*; 24,077 lambs, 24,077*l.*; 169,817 loads of meal, 203,780*l.*; 177,252 sacks of flour, 407,679*l.*; 10,771 bales of bacon, 64,626*l.*; 292,830 firkins, 15,861 half firkins, and 10,348 coolies of butter, 819,141*l.* These, with some minor articles, made up a value of 4,444,500*l.* The imports into London, Bristol, and other ports, may be presumed to be as much more, and perhaps the whole may not fall short of 10,000,000*l.* sterling.

The following table exhibits the relative foreign commerce of the principal ports of Ireland in the year 1824. We add the ships and tonnage belonging to and the amount of customs on each, which a recent report enables us to bring down to 1829:—

| Entered at | Tonnage Entered. | | Belonging. | | Paid. |
|---|---|---|---|---|---|
| | British. | Foreign. | | | |
| | Tons. | Tons. | Ships. | Tonnage. | Customs. |
| Belfast | 19,123 | 11,992 | 247 | 25,000 | 259,000 |
| Cork | 15,025 | 13,976 | 256 | 17,000 | 196,000 |
| Drogheda | 890 | 420 | 30 | 2,300 | 12,000 |
| Dublin | 24,306 | 10,467 | 289 | 24,000 | 669,000 |
| Galway | 546 | 2,020 | 19 | 800 | 4,800 |
| Limerick | 5,223 | 3,489 | 39 | 1,800 | 85,700 |
| Londonderry | 3,293 | 5,479 | 32 | 4,300 | 74,000 |
| Newry | 6,705 | 7,612 | 161 | 8,000 | 55,000 |
| Sligo | 1,085 | 2,463 | 20 | 1,200 | 1,600 |
| Waterford | 7,600 | 3,137 | 76 | 7,000 | 116,000 |
| Wexford | 1,409 | 232 | 135 | 6,700 | 4,800 |

The shipping of Ireland is small, compared with that of the sister island. On the 31st December, 1830, she had 1424 vessels; the tonnage of which was 101,820, navigated by 7794 men and boys. In 1832 there were built twenty-five ships, of 1909 tons. There were entered inwards, in 1831, 14,499 ships, of 1,420,382 tons; outwards, 9801 ships, 1,073,545 tons. Of this were employed in trade with Great Britain, 13,584 ships, and 1,262,221 tons, inwards; 9029 ships, 921,128 tons, outwards; in foreign trade, 915 ships, 158,161 tons, inwards; 772 ships, 152,417 tons outwards.

Canals have been undertaken in Ireland on an extensive scale, but with only a small portion of the expected benefit. This seems partly owing to the excessive magnitude of the plans, and partly to the prevalence of jobbing. The two chief undertakings are the Grand and the Royal canals, both proceeding from Dublin into the interior. The former, commenced in 1756, has, by large advances from government, been completed, at an expense of upwards of 2,000,000*l.* It is carried across Kildare and King's County to the Shannon, near Clonfert. This distance is eighty-seven miles, which, with a branch to the Barrow at Athy, one westward to Ballinasloe, and several others, makes an entire length of 156 miles. The Royal Canal, of nearly the same dimensions, reaches from Dublin through Meath and Longford, nearly eighty-three miles, to Tarmonbarry, on the Shannon. The expense was 1,420,000*l.*, while the tolls, in 1831, amounted only to 12,700*l.*

The roads of Ireland have long been excellent. Any person may present a memorial to the grand jury of the county, showing the necessity of a new road, and if this presentment be approved, the work immediately proceeds. Government has established mail-coaches to all the principal towns, and, since the rebellion, has made fine military roads into the interior of Wicklow; but stage-coaches and other means of conveyance are indifferent.

### SECT. VI.—*Civil and Social State.*

The population of Ireland, from its great amount and rapid increase is considered as one of the chief causes of the severe poverty which presses upon the body of the people. Till the census of 1821, the data upon which it was calculated were conjectural. Between 1712 and 1726, upon a calculation from the number of houses, at six to a house, it was represented as varying from 2,000,000 to 2,300,000. Calculations founded on the produce of the hearth duty gave in 1754, 2,372,000; and in 1788, 4,040,040. In 1812, it was estimated at 5,937,000. In 1821, a census gave 6,801,000. That of 1831 amounted to 7,767,401, of whom 3,794,880 are male, and 3,972,521 female.

The Irish character presents very marked features, many of which are amiable, and even admirable. Hospitality is an universal trait, and is enhanced by the scantiness of the portion which is liberally shared with the stranger. The Irish are brave, lively, merry, and witty; and even the lowest ranks have a courteous and polite address. They are celebrated for warmth of heart, and for strong attachments of kindred and friendship, which leads them, out of their scanty means, to support their aged relations with the purest kindness. Benevolence is a distinguishing feature of the higher ranks. They are curious, intelligent, and eager for information. With so many good qualities, it were too much to expect that there should not be some faults. They are deficient in cleanliness; have little taste for conveniences or luxuries; and are destitute of that sober and steady spirit of enterprise which distinguishes the English. The love of fighting seems to be a general infirmity. The fairs, which, in every town and village of Ireland, are regular and of long duration, afford the grand theatres, first of unbounded mirth, and ultimately of bloody conflict. The Irish do not fight single-handed, but in bands, and on a great scale. On receiving a supposed injury they go round to their companions, friends, and townsmen, and collect a multitude, with which they make a joint attack on the objects of their wrath. The other blemishes of the Irish are rather frailties than sins. They are represented as vain, talkative, prompt to speak as well as act without deliberation: this disposition, with their thoughtless gaiety, betrays them into that peculiar blunder called a *bull*, which their neighbours have so long held forth as a national characteristic.

The ecclesiastical state of Ireland has been one of the chief causes of its unsettled condition. The native Irish did not share in any degree the reformation so unanimously adopted in England and Scotland. When, therefore, the English church was introduced as the established religion, it threw out, as dissenters, the bulk of the Irish population. Even of the protestant part, a large proportion introduced as colonists from Scotland, were attached to the presbyterian form.

[From a parliamentary paper, it appears that, in 1835, there were,—

| | | per cent. |
|---|---|---|
| Roman Catholics, | 6,427,712 | 80¾ |
| Members of Established Church, | 852,064 | 10½ |
| Presbyterians, | 642,356 | 8 |
| Other Protestants, | 21,808 | ¼ |
| | 7,943,940. | |

Although there is here some slight inaccuracy, yet this statement serves to show very nearly the proportion of the different sects. The places of worship are stated in the same paper to be,—

| | |
|---|---|
| Roman Catholics, | 2105 |
| Established Church, | 1544 |
| Presbyterians, | 452 |
| Others, | 403 |

In 41 benefices there was *no* member of the Established Church.—*Am. Ed.*]

The Roman Catholic clergy receive no stipend from government, but are entirely supported by their flocks. They are formed, however, into a regular hierarchy, at the head of which are four archbishops; Armagh (the primate), Tuam, Cashel, and Dublin. Under them are twenty-two bishops, with a vicar-general, dean, and archdeacon in each diocese. The number of Catholic priests has been stated at 1400, besides several hundred friars. Their income arises less from any fixed allowance, than from dues, offerings, and presents; and the bishops, to make up their incomes, receive from the parish priests a portion of what they have collected. Mr. Wakefield has attempted an estimate, according to which, Christmas and Easter offerings amount to 337,000*l.*; marriages produce, in licenses, fees, and collections, 78,500*l.*; christenings, 12,500*l.*; burials, 12,500*l.*; in all, 440,500*l.* According to Archbishop Curteis, the income of a bishop is about 500*l.* a year; that of a priest varies from 100*l.* to 400*l.* Although a *congé* is asked from the pope, the real election to vacant places rests with the clergy themselves; but as their incomes depend entirely on the favour of their hearers, they are subject to a necessity of choosing popular priests, which is not felt by the established Catholic churches. Hence the influence of the priests, always so remarkable under the Catholic system, exists in Ireland to an extent perhaps unequalled. On the other hand, many, especially among the bishops, are remarked for their exemplary life, and for the diligent discharge of their functions. They are even sometimes instrumental in preventing riot, in discovering theft, and procuring restitution. The recent admission of Roman Catholics to all political privileges, though it does not make any change in the condition of the clergy, has been hailed by the body in general with peculiar satisfaction. It is hoped that it will either make them more friendly to the established government, or diminish their influence in estranging from it the minds of the people.

The Presbyterians, as already observed, are nearly confined to Ulster, where they are the most numerous sect. The synod of Ulster is formed into a sort of establishment, consisting of 201 congregations, besides which there are 110 congregations in communion with the Scottish seceders. The ministers receive a royal gift of 14,000*l.* annually, which affords from 50*l.* to 100*l.* to each. The Presbyterians form the most industrious, thriving, and intelligent portion of the people; yet a great proportion have imbibed republican ideas, and they emigrate to America more readily than any other class.

The Established Church of Ireland is in union with that of England, and every way similar. It consists of four archbishoprics and eighteen bishoprics; but by an act recently passed, two archbishoprics are to be converted into bishoprics; and ten bishoprics are to be abolished.* The entire revenue of the Irish church has been ascertained to exceed 150,000*l.* for the bishoprics, and 715,200*l.* for other benefices. The lands belonging to the bishops are of far greater value; but in consequence of being let on old leases renewed from time to time on payment of fines, and never coming to a termination, the rent derived from them was greatly under the real value. It is proposed now to offer these leases to the present incumbent, in perpetuity, on payment of six years' purchase of their estimated value, which, it is calculated, will produce about 3,000,000*l.* A tax, moreover, varying, according to the amount of income, from five to fifteen per cent., is to be laid on all livings above 200*l.*; and its produce to be applied to the augmentation of the poorer livings, and the building of glebe houses and of new churches. Hence the parochial tax, called the vestry cess, or church rate, amounting to about 90,000*l.* a year, is no longer to be levied.

The literature of Ireland in modern times, cannot boast any very distinguished pre-eminence; yet she has maintained her station in the literary world. In wit and eloquence, indeed, she has excelled both the sister kingdoms. In the former quality, Swift and Sheridan shine unrivalled; and in the latter, Burke, Grattan, and Curran have displayed daring and brilliant flights. In her graver pursuits, Ireland has not been so happy; though Usher attained the first eminence in theological learning, and Berkeley was the author of a highly ingenious system of philosophy.

The Irish establishments for education are scarcely adequate to the magnitude of the country. There is only one university, that of Dublin, founded by Elizabeth on the model of those of England, but not on so great a scale. Of it and of other Irish literary institutions, an account will be found under the head of Dublin. As the constitution of this university is strictly Protestant, and does not allow the teaching of Catholic theology, the students of that faith must have been all educated abroad, had not government endowed for their use the College of Maynooth. It is supported by a revenue of about 9000*l.* a year, and contains a president, vice-president, and eleven professors, all with moderate appointments. The students receive board and education; and the whole annual expense of each is not supposed to exceed 20*l.* The students of the north resort chiefly to Glasgow for theology, and to Edinburgh for medicine; though there has been an attempt to obviate this necessity by the formation of an institution at Belfast.

The education of the poor in Ireland is a subject which excites the deepest interest in all the friends of that country. It appears that by the 8th of Henry VIII., every clergyman, on his induction, becomes bound to keep or cause to be kept an English school. This act, however, is either obsolete, or so far evaded that only 23,000 children are now taught in these parochial schools. The greatest effort at Irish education, however, is that made by the Charter Schools, instituted in 1733, which, by parliamentary grants and private benefactions, have enjoyed an income of 30,000*l.* a year. But this sum, which might almost furnish schools to the half of Ireland, is spent upon 2000 boys, who receive board as well as instruction. Although the act recites no other object than instruction in the English tongue, proselytism has become almost the sole aim. The Hibernian Society, the Baptist Society, and that for discountenancing vice, support schools to a very considerable extent. The Kildare Street Society, established in 1812, founded numerous schools, in which they endeavoured to induce the Catholics to attend by renouncing all attempts to gain proselytes; but from the entire Scriptures being read in these schools, and other alleged causes, the Catholics were supposed to view them with jealousy. The allowance made to this society was therefore withdrawn, and a new plan instituted, in which the moral and literary is separated from the religious education, and is communicated to the youth of both religions during four or five days in the week, while, in the remaining period, religious instruction is expected to be administered by the clergy of the respective churches. Extracts only from the Scripture, approved by the leading Catholic clergy, are read in the common

* The new arrangement, when completed, will be as follows:

| | Income. |
|---|---|
| Armagh (with Clogher, Archb.) | £13,170 |
| Meath | 5,221 |
| Derry (with Raphoe) | 8,033 |
| Down (with Connor, and Dromore) | 5,896 |
| Kilmore (with Ardagh and Elphin) | 7,478 |
| Tuam (with Killala and Achonry) | 5,020 |
| Dublin (with Glandclagh and Kildare) | 9,321 |
| Ossory (with Leighlin and Ferns) | 6,650 |
| Cashel (with Emly, Waterford, and Lismore) | 7,354 |
| Cloyne (with Cork and Ross) | 5,009 |
| Killalo (with Kilfenora, Clonfert, and Kilmacduagh) | 4,532 |
| Limerick (with Ardfert and Aghadoe) | 5,369 |
| Total | 82,953 |

[Am. Ed.]

schools. Local funds, to a certain extent, are required to be contributed. Although this system has met with many opponents, yet, in the beginning of 1833 there had been established under it between 500 and 600 schools, calculated for the education of about 90,000 scholars. In 1824, the number of schools in Ireland was 11,823, and scholars 560,549. Of these scholars 394,742 paid for their own instruction, and among this number were 307,000 Catholics, who thus showed no small ardour in obtaining the benefits of knowledge.

The following table, from parliamentary documents, shows the number of pupils receiving public instruction in the years specified.

| | Males. | Females. | Total. |
|---|---|---|---|
| 1821 | 265,606 | 129,207 | 394,813 |
| 1826 | 349,912 | 209,927 | 568,964* |
| 1834 | 84,645 | 60,876 | 145,521 |

The fine arts do not appear to have attained any great excellence in Ireland. Her best painters have sought for patronage in the British metropolis; and the attempts to establish an annual exhibition in Dublin have not succeeded. The Irish harp and native Irish melodies enjoy considerable reputation. The ecclesiastical structures have not that splendour and richness which so strongly mark many of those in England; but the modern edifices, especially in Dublin, display a taste as well as magnificence which render that capital almost pre-eminent.

In funerals, marriages, and similar solemnities, the Irish retain several old national customs. The practice of hired howling women at funerals, called *ululates*, is very prevalent; a considerable sum is paid to those employed, though, in cases of necessity, they howl gratis. A still more unfortunate custom is that of the wakes, where thirty or forty neighbours assemble, are entertained with meat and drink, and indulge in every sort of *fun*. Marriages in many parts of the country are marked by some real, or at least apparent, violence; the bridegroom collects a large party of friends, seizes and carries off the seemingly reluctant bride. Alluding to this custom, her going to her husband's house, even in ordinary cases, is called the "hauling home." This is not prompted by any peculiar shyness on the part of the fair sex; on the contrary, the mothers, with whom the affair chiefly rests, display even a feverish anxiety that their offspring should not remain long in a state of single blessedness. The fair sex are treated among the higher ranks with a gay and romantic gallantry; among the lower almost as slaves, being subjected to the most degrading labour.

Amusement forms a copious element in the existence of an Irishman. Ample scope is afforded to the Catholics by their numerous holidays, and the Protestants vie with them in this particular. The fairs afford a grand theatre for fun of every description. The chief bodily exercise is hurling, which consists in driving a ball to opposite goals; to this are added horse-racing, cock-fighting, cudgelling, leaping, and dancing; to say nothing of drinking and fighting. The conversation of the Irish is distinguished by loud mirth, seasoned with a good deal of humour, by singing, and telling long stories. Thus employed, even the poor will often sit up to a late hour.

The houses of the Irish, if we except those of the rich, or in towns, which are formed after the English model, are mere hovels formed of earth, taken out of the ground on which they stand; whence the floor is reduced at least a foot below the outer level, and becomes a receptacle for all the superfluous moisture. This is the more incommodious as it has no boards, and the bed no frame; nor is the latter raised from the ground, being merely straw spread upon the floor. This humble mansion is shared by all the living creatures, which the family are able to muster; cows, pigs, geese, and fowls; which are rarely separated by any partition from the other tenants.

No compulsory provision exists in Ireland for the support of the poor; a circumstance to which we are inclined to ascribe much of their distressed state, as well as of the backward state of the country in general. Not being obliged to contribute any thing to their support, the landlords and occupiers have, generally speaking, manifested great indifference to the condition of the peasantry. Few among them have hesitated to allow their estates to be subdivided into minute portions to advance their political interests, or to obtain an increase of rent. But it is abundantly certain that they would have paused before venturing on such a course of proceeding, had they been made responsible, in all time to come, for the paupers they were thus introducing upon their properties.

The dress of the Irish peasantry consists chiefly of the native wool, worked rudely up into frieze or linsey; for they seldom can afford to wear the fine linen which they fabricate. But the most prominent feature of this attire among the lowest class, is its lamentable deficiency; in many instances it covers little more than half of the person, and presents an image of extreme poverty. When this deficiency does not exist, the Irishman loves to display the extent of his wardrobe; when going to a fair, he puts on all the coats he has, though the season be midsummer.

The food of the Irish peasant is no less scanty than his dress and habitation. It is almost

* Including 9,125 not ascertained.

wholly comprised in the potato, without any other vegetable (for he is a stranger to the luxury of a garden), and only in favourable circumstances is it accompanied with milk. This food, however, is sufficient to preserve him in full health and vigour. In the north, the use of oatmeal in the form of cakes and pottage has been derived from Scotland.

### SECT. VII.—*Local Geography.*

Ireland is divided into four provinces, or rather regions: Leinster in the east, Munster in the south, Connaught in the west, and Ulster in the north. This is independent of the minuter English division into counties, a number of which are comprised in each of the four provinces. These last, indeed, when Ireland was ruled by native governments, formed separate kingdoms. They are still distinguished by marked boundaries, by a different aspect of nature, and by a considerable variation of manners and customs.

The following table exhibits the leading provincial statistics of Ireland. The population statements differ considerably from those hitherto published; but they have been furnished by Mr. Porter, of the Board of Trade as the result of the latest and most accurate digest of the returns for 1831.

| Provinces and Counties. | Square Miles. | Improved Acres. | Unimproved Acres. | Estimated Annual Value. | Houses in 1821. | Population in 1831. | Cities and Towns, with their Population. | | | |
|---|---|---|---|---|---|---|---|---|---|---|
| *Leinster.* | | | | £ | | | | | | |
| Dublin..... | 221 | 237,819 | 10,812 | 250,211 | 35,740 | 380,167 | Dublin ..... | 204,155 | | |
| Louth...... | 173 | 191,345 | 14,916 | 164,765 | 21,302 | 124,846 | Drogheda .... | 17,365 | Dundalk..... | 9,256 |
| Meath..... | 512 | 561,527 | 5,600 | 510,414 | 27,942 | 176,826 | Trim ........ | 2,470 | | |
| Wicklow... | 486 | 400,704 | 94,000 | 296,822 | 17,289 | 121,557 | Wicklow .... | 2,046 | Arklow...... | 3,808 |
| Wexford... | 535 | 545,079 | 18,500 | 395,134 | 29,159 | 182,713 | Wexford..... | 8,326 | | |
| Longford... | 209 | 192,506 | 55,247 | 151,595 | 18,987 | 112,558 | Longford .... | 3,783 | New Ross . | 4,475 |
| | | | | | | | Enniscorthy . | 3,557 | | |
| Westmeath | 361 | 313,935 | 55,982 | 251,063 | 23,015 | 136,872 | Mullingar ... | 4,100 | Athlone ..... | 11,362 |
| King's Co. | 440 | 394,569 | 133,349 | 317,019 | 22,564 | 144,225 | Philipstown . | 1,931 | Birr ........ | 5,406 |
| | | | | | | | Tullamore ... | 5,517 | | |
| Queen's Co. | 367 | 335,838 | 60,972 | 277,767 | 23,105 | 145,851 | Portarlington | 2,877 | Maryborough | 2,677 |
| Kildare | 369 | 325,988 | 66,447 | 255,082 | 16,478 | 108,424 | Athy ........ | 3,693 | Naas ........ | 3,073 |
| | | | | | | | Kildare ...... | 1,516 | | |
| Kilkenny .. | 469 | 417,117 | 96,569 | 437,693 | 29,789 | 193,686 | Kilkenny .... | 23,741 | | |
| Carlow .. | 214 | 196,833 | 23,030 | 164,895 | 13,028 | 81,988 | Carlow ..... | 8,035 | | |
| | 4,356 | 4,113,260 | 635,424 | 3,472,460 | 278,398 | 1,909,713 | | | | |
| *Ulster.* | | | | | | | | | | |
| Down...... | 544 | 502,677 | 108,569 | 489,123 | 59,747 | 352,012 | Newry...... | 10,013 | Downpatrick | 4,123 |
| | | | | | | | Donnaghadee | 2,795 | | |
| Antrim .... | 605 | 483,106 | 225,970 | 569,159 | 48,028 | 325,615 | Belfast...... | 53,000 | Carrickfergus | 8,706 |
| | | | | | | | Antrim...... | 2,485 | Lisburn..... | 4,684 |
| Londonderr. | 479 | 372,667 | 136,038 | 310,962 | 34,691 | 222,012 | Londonderry. | 9,313 | Colerain..... | 4,851 |
| Donegal ... | 1,061 | 520,736 | 644,371 | 349,501 | 44,800 | 289,149 | Ballyshannon | 3,831 | Lifford...... | 976 |
| Fermanagh | 440 | 320,599 | 101,952 | 259,291 | 22,585 | 149,763 | Enniskillen.. | 2,399 | | |
| Cavan ..... | 478 | 421,462 | 30,000 | 307,741 | 34,148 | 227,933 | Cavan ...... | 2,322 | | |
| Monaghan . | 280 | 309,968 | 9,236 | 212,581 | 32,378 | 195,536 | Monaghan ... | 3,738 | | |
| Armagh.... | 283 | 267,317 | 42,472 | 178,955 | 36,260 | 220,134 | Armagh ..... | 8,493 | | |
| Tyrone .... | 724 | 550,820 | 171,314 | 528,065 | 47,164 | 304,468 | Omagh ...... | 2,095 | Dungammon. | 3,243 |
| | 4,894 | 3,749,352 | 1,469,922 | 3,205,378 | 359,801 | 2,286,622 | | | | |
| *Munster.* | | | | | | | | | | |
| Clare ...... | 744 | 524,113 | 259,584 | 441,293 | 35,373 | 258,322 | Ennis ....... | 6,701 | | |
| Kerry...... | 1,012 | 581,189 | 552,862 | 344,616 | 35,597 | 263,126 | Tralee....... | 7,547 | Killarney.... | 7,014 |
| | | | | | | | Dingle....... | 4,988 | | |
| Cork....... | 1,638 | 1,068,803 | 700,760 | 1,203,926 | 114,459 | 810,732 | Cork ........ | 107,016 | Bandon...... | 10,179 |
| | | | | | | | Kinsale...... | 7,068 | Youghal..... | 8,969 |
| | | | | | | | Fermoy...... | 3,702 | Mallow...... | 4,114 |
| Waterford . | 410 | 353,247 | 118,034 | 295,364 | 23,860 | 177,054 | Waterford ... | 28,821 | Lismore ..... | 2,330 |
| Tipperary.. | 867 | 819,658 | 182,147 | 886,539 | 55,297 | 402,563 | Clonmel ..... | 15,590 | Cashel....... | 6,548 |
| | | | | | | | Tipperary ... | 6,348 | Carr.-on-Suir | 7,466 |
| | | | | | | | Roscrea...... | 5,239 | | |
| Limerick... | 604 | 588,842 | 91,981 | 629,932 | 42,409 | 315,355 | Limerick .... | 66,554 | | |
| | 5,275 | 3,935,852 | 1,905,368 | 3,801,670 | 306,995 | 2,227,152 | | | | |
| *Connaught.* | | | | | | | | | | |
| Leitrim.... | 400 | 266,640 | 128,167 | 210,187 | 21,762 | 141,524 | Carrick-on-Sh. | 1,673 | | |
| Sligo....... | 386 | 257,217 | 168,711 | 227,443 | 27,059 | 171,765 | Sligo ........ | 9,283 | | |
| Mayo ...... | 1,235 | 871,984 | 425,124 | 550,018 | 53,051 | 366,328 | Castlebar .... | 5,404 | | |
| Galway.... | 1,546 | 955,713 | 476,957 | 868,794 | 58,137 | 414,684 | Galway...... | 33,120 | Tuam ....... | 4,571 |
| | | | | | | | Ballinasloe .. | 1,811 | | |
| Roscommon | 541 | 453,455 | 131,063 | 379,628 | 37,399 | 249,613 | Roscommon . | 3,015 | | |
| | 4,108 | 2,805,009 | 1,330,022 | 2,236,070 | 197,408 | 1,343,914 | | | | |
| | *18,633 | 14,603,473 | 5,340,736 | 12,715,578 | 1,142,602 | 7,767,401 | | | | |

### SUBSECT. 1.—*Leinster.*

Leinster is the richest and most cultivated of the four great divisions, and, as containing the seat of government, the most important theatre of political events. Though the surface be level to a great extent, it is not destitute of considerable ranges of mountains. These

[* This is the Irish mile of 40 to a degree. The area has already been stated to be 30,000 English square miles. —AM. ED.]

include almost the whole county of Wicklow, whose bold and picturesque summits are seen even from Dublin. In the interior, the long range of Slieve-Bloom stretches towards the borders of Munster. A considerable part also of the midland counties is covered by the great bog, which crosses the whole centre of Ireland. After all deductions, however, there remains a large extent of level land, fit either for tillage or pasturage. This is the part of Ireland where wheat is grown to the greatest extent, oats being elsewhere almost the only grain; and its rich pastures supply the capital with cattle and the products of the dairy.

Leinster comprises the counties of Dublin, Kildare, King's county, Queen's County, Wicklow, Carlow, Kilkenny, Wexford, Meath, Westmeath, Longford, and Louth.

The county of Dublin owes its distinction almost exclusively to its containing the capital of Ireland. The city of Dublin disputes with Edinburgh and Bath the reputation of being the most beautiful city in the empire. If the brick of which the houses are built impair the effect of the general range of its streets and squares, its public buildings, composed of stone, surpass in grandeur and taste those of any of its rivals. There is no period of Irish record in which Dublin was not an important place. It is mentioned by Ptolemy under the name of Eblana. The Danes, in the ninth century, made it their capital, and enclosed it with a wall about a mile in length, the course of which may still be traced. As soon as the English began to establish themselves in Ireland, its proximity induced them to make it their head-quarters; it grew with the improvement of Ireland and the extension of the English sway, but all its splendour has arisen within the last sixty or seventy years. The numerous streets and squares formed during that period have been built on a regular plan, and contain several superb mansions, which once belonged to the principal nobles. The squares are particularly admired; that of St. Stephen's Green is nearly seven furlongs in circuit; Merrion Square, which contains the splendid mansion of Leinster House; Rutland Square, in the interior of which are the gardens of the Lying-in Hospital; and Mountjoy Square, are also spacious and finely laid out. Of the streets, the finest is Sackville Street, 170 feet wide, and adorned with many splendid mansions. To the west is the old town, now bearing marks of decay, and still farther west is the tract called "the Liberty," as being out of the jurisdiction of the magistrates. It is inhabited only by the lowest orders, and exhibits scenes of filth and wretchedness not to be paralleled in any city of the sister island. A room fifteen feet square is frequently let to three or four families; and one house was ascertained to have lodged 108 persons. Dublin has been "shorn of its beams" since the Union; when the nobles and gentry, no longer called to attend parliament, transferred their own residence to the metropolis of the empire, and their Dublin mansions have been converted to humbler purposes. The Castle, the residence of the lord lieutenant, is extensive; but its architectural beauty is almost confined to a modern Gothic chapel. The cathedral of St. Patrick (*fig.* 212.), and Christ Church have a venerable aspect; but they can rank only secondary to the fine structures in the English cities. The splendid structure, formerly the parliament-house of Ireland, and now the national bank (*fig.* 213.), was built between 1729 and 1739; but an eastern front was added in 1785, and a western front shortly after. The portico is 147 feet in length, supported by lofty Ionic columns; the whole covering an acre and a half of ground. The Royal Exchange (*fig.* 214.), forms a square of 100 feet, and its principal front has a richly decorated portico of six Corinthian columns. The Four Law Courts, situated on the north bank of the river (*fig.* 215.), form

212

St. Patrick's Cathedral.

213

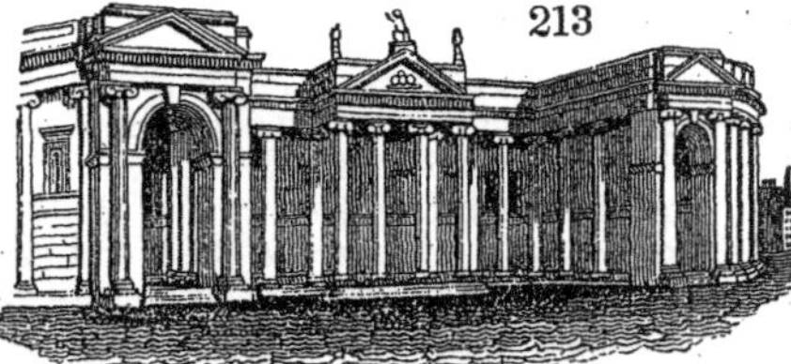

Bank of Ireland, Dublin.

214

Exchange, Dublin.

215

Four Courts, Dublin.

also one of the noblest structures in Dublin: it consists of a square of 140 feet, presenting a front of six Corinthian pillars, supporting a circular lantern and magnificent dome. The quay is ornamented by the Custom-house, of which the front is entirely of Portland stone, embellished with a Doric colonnade, and extending 375 feet. The Post Office, in Sackville Street, is extensive and magnificent, with a front of 223 feet, adorned with an Ionic portico of Portland stone; the main structure is of granite. In the centre of Sackville Street, is the monument erected to Nelson; an object by no means ornamental. The inns of court, the theatre, the half-finished Roman Catholic metropolitan chapel, and several other churches and chapels, with many of the hospitals, may be mentioned as adding to the architectural splendour of Dublin. All the usual associations for the relief of distress are supported on a liberal scale, and great zeal is shown in favour of all institutions for the promotion of knowledge. Trinity College was founded in 1593; and its students amount to 1600. There are 25 fellowships, and the livings in the gift of the university, which are considerable in number and value, are offered to the fellows in the order of seniority. The gradations of rank, amongst the fellows in Trinity College, are indicated by a different dress and table. The library contains 100,000 volumes; but its other collections are not equal to those of the Dublin Society. Usher, Swift, Berkeley, Chandler, Leland, Parnell, Burke, Grattan, Curran, with other distinguished characters, are mentioned as pupils of this seminary. The buildings of the College are on a large scale, divided into three quadrangles, for the accommodation of the fellows and pupils. The front towards College Green extends 300 feet, and is adorned with columns of the Corinthian order. The library forms a fourth quadrangle, built of hewn stone, with a rich entablature; and the principal room, 210 feet long and 41 feet broad, is elegantly fitted up. At a short distance from town is a botanic garden. The Royal Dublin Society, incorporated in 1749, for the promotion of husbandry and the useful arts, has a botanic garden; a museum of natural history; a school for drawing, with models; and teachers in all these departments. The Royal Irish Academy, incorporated in 1782, has published many volumes of Transactions. The Dublin Institution has been formed on the model of that of London, and a city Library established. Although a great literary spirit prevails in Dublin, there are few books printed there, and the art of printing is in a backward state. The works of Irish authors issue from the London presses. Dublin has very little foreign trade; but she has a considerable trade with England, particularly with Liverpool. The bay is spacious, and has good anchorage; but the entrance is beset with formidable sand-banks, particularly those called the North and South Bulls, which cannot be passed by large vessels at low water; so that vessels embayed at that time of the tide, and attacked by strong easterly gales, can scarcely escape being driven upon one of them. To avert these evils, a double wall has been constructed three miles in length, composed of enormous blocks of granite, dovetailed into each other, the interval filled with gravel; and a light-house erected at the end. Another pier of great extent has been built at Dunleary, now Kingstown, on the southern side of the bay, which is connected by a railway with the capital. To these advantages Dublin unites that of being placed at the termination of the Grand Canal on the south, and the Royal Canal on the north, which penetrate by different lines to the Shannon and the interior of Ireland. In 1829, Dublin paid the sum of 660,000*l.* of duty on imported goods, while that paid at all the other ports of Ireland amounted only to 910,000*l.* The environs are celebrated for their beauty. The vast number of villas and villages which cover the adjacent districts, and are rendered conspicuous by the ground sloping down to the bay; the foreground of the Dublin mountains, and the picturesque summits of those of Wicklow in the background, render the situation striking and delightful. To the west, Phœnix Park, a royal demesne of several miles in circumference, affords an agreeable promenade, and has lately been adorned with an obelisk, 210 feet high, in honour of the Duke of Wellington. The rest of the county contains only villages, and the interior possesses few interesting objects. The shores of the bay, however, include many striking sites; and the view from the Hill of Killiney is almost matchless.

Wicklow is in general composed of bog, forest, and mountain, and contributes little to the wealth of Ireland. It is, however, celebrated for picturesque beauty. Its coast, diversified by hills, broken into glens, and richly wooded, is almost covered with the seats of the gentry and opulent citizens of Dublin. These variegated and embellished grounds, having on one side the expanse of the Irish Channel, and on the other the lofty mountains in the interior, produce a number of beautiful sites. The demesne of Powerscourt is pre-eminent, the waterfall (*fig.* 216.), descending 360 feet down a steep hill, amid vast hanging woods. The interior of the county presents features of a very different description; glens between lofty mountains, naked and desolate. Among these is Glendalough (*fig.* 217.), which is surrounded by a most majestic circuit of mountains, and contains some remarkable ecclesiastical monuments attributed to St. Kevin, a great patron saint of Ireland in the seventh century. One of his disciples founded at Glendalough a little city, long celebrated as a seat of religion and learning Only its site can now be traced; but there are distinct remains of seven churches, among which the cathedral and St. Kevin's kitchen are the most entire. Loughs Dan and Brav situated in the bosom of the wildest mountains, and enclosed by dark and lofty rocks, present nature under an aspect the most rudely sublime. Wicklow has veins of copper and lead: gold was collected in one year to the value of 10,000*l.*; but the vein was soon exhausted. The towns of Wicklow and Arklow, though well built, are inconsiderable; yet the latter, at the mouth of the Ovoca, has a little trade, and was once the residence of the kings of Ireland. It was the scene of a memorable action in 1798, when the insurgents, above 30,000 strong, were defeated by a small British detachment.

216

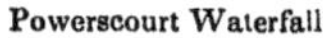

Powerscourt Waterfall

217

Glendalough

Wexford, to the south of Wicklow, is separated from it by a range of mountains; but the interior contains a great deal of level land, in which agriculture is pursued with greater diligence, and the tenantry are more comfortable, than in most other parts of Ireland. Barley is a prevailing crop. The woodlands also are extensive and valuable. Wexford is a place of some consequence, with a harbour much obstructed by sand; yet it carries on some traffic. Some woollens are made both at Wexford and Enniscorthy. New Ross, in the western part of the county, is a flourishing town, on the Barrow, which admits of large ships coming up to its quay.

Kilkenny, a fine and extensive county, separated from Wexford by the Barrow, is watered not only by that river, but by its tributaries the Nore and the Suire. These streams carry off the superfluous moisture, and prevent the formation of bog or marsh to any extent. Kilkenny, being chiefly level, or intersected only by hills of moderate height, is composed almost entirely either of arable or fine pasture land. The latter is employed in extensive dairies, but the system of cultivation is still imperfect. Kilkenny, the capital, advantageously situated on the Nore, is partly built of the marble of the surrounding quarries. Its cathedral is one of the finest in Ireland, and the castle, with its remaining gates and bastions, exhibits indications of that strength which enabled it to hold out against Cromwell longer than any other city in Ireland. At present Kilkenny flourishes by inland trade, and by a manufactory of blankets and other woollens. The foreign trade of the county is carried on by Waterford.

Carlow is encompassed by mountains, which however enclose a champaign tract of great beauty and fertility, equally fit for tillage and pasture, and producing the best butter in Ireland. The town of Carlow is a considerable place, distinguished by an abbey and castle, both of great antiquity. The town has a manufactory of coarse woollens, and carries on a considerable trade down the Barrow. An extensive Catholic seminary has lately been founded here.

Queen's County and King's County form a table-land of moderate elevation. Part of the great chain of bogs crosses these counties, and renders a large proportion of them unproductive, though it supplies them with cheap and abundant fuel. The remaining surface is highly fertile. Queen's County is situated along the heads of the Barrow and the Nore; King's County reaches to the Shannon; and both communicate by canals with Dublin. Portarlington, on the borders of the two counties, is a well-built place, with good schools, and the residence of a considerable number of gentry. Tullamore, on the great canal, and Birr or Parsonstown, are the most thriving towns in King's County.

Kildare, with the exception of about a sixth part of bog, forms a plain of the finest arable soil, well cultivated, and whence the capital is chiefly supplied with grain. The Grand and Royal Canals, which both cross its northern border, afford the means of ready conveyance to Dublin. Kildare-town, presenting a lofty round tower and some other vestiges of past importance, is only supported by the races held on the curragh of Kildare, an expanse of several thousand acres of the very finest turf. Naas and Athy are larger towns, and the castle of the former bears testimony to the period when it was the residence of the kings of Leinster. In this county is Maynooth, a small town containing the college established by government for the education of the Roman Catholics.

Meath is one of the most favoured counties of the kingdom in respect to soil. Its rich pastures support vast herds of black cattle, which supply the markets of the capital, and are exported to England. The products of the dairy are abundant, though not of very superior quality. Trim, where the assizes are held, is a small town; Navan and Kells are larger.

Louth, though the smallest in area of any Irish county, is one of the first in point of natural and acquired advantages. An active spirit of improvement has brought almost every part of its excellent soil under cultivation. Its linen manufacture produces chiefly dowlas and sheetings, with some cambric. Louth presents many samples of the earthen mounds called *raths*. Dundalk, the capital of the county, is ancient, populous, and flourishing. It has been the theatre of important historical events; but its lofty towers and castles are now demolished, and have given place to comfortable dwellings. The town consists chiefly of one large and broad street, whence many lanes are seen diverging. It is the only place in Ireland where the cambric manufacture has been introduced, and continues to flourish. Drogheda, at the mouth of the Boyne, was of still greater importance as a military station, being considered one of the keys of Ireland. In the great rebellion of 1641, it stood a long siege, but was afterwards taken by Cromwell, who punished its resistance by a most barbarous massacre of the garrison. In 1690, two miles above Drogheda, was fought the battle of the Boyne, that memorable field which established the civil and religious liberties of the empire. The fortifications are of obsolete structure, and are commanded on several sides. The place has an excellent harbour, and extensive commerce in grain brought down the river in considerable quantities for exportation; in return for which, coals and other commodities are imported.

Westmeath and Longford, reaching westward as far as the Shannon, consist chiefly of a very extensive plain considerably encumbered with lakes, bogs, and morasses, and subject in part to the overflowing of the Shannon, but including fertile tracts of great extent. Athlone, the largest inland town of Ireland, is situated partly in Westmeath and partly in Roscommon. It is memorable for its resistance to General Ginkle in 1691, previous to the battle of Aughrim, and is still considered an important military station. It is divided by the Shannon into two parts united by a bridge. With this exception, these provinces contain only small country towns and large villages. Mullingar, in Westmeath, has a considerable trade. Longford is the capital of the county of that name.

### SUBSECT 2.—*Munster.*

Munster includes the south and south-west of Ireland, and, though not the most extensive division of the kingdom, is one of those which presents the boldest and most striking features. Most of the great mountain chains of Ireland traverse Munster; among which are conspicuous the Galties and the mountains of Kerry, which encircle Killarney; so that, notwithstanding the almost boundless plains of Limerick and Tipperary, and the level character of a great part of Cork, it may be considered as a mountainous region. It has manufactures, though not on so great a scale as those of the north; and its commerce is very considerable, chiefly in the export of salted provisions. The Catholic religion prevails, with little intermixture of that of the English church. Munster is divided into larger and less numerous portions than Leinster; its counties are Tipperary, Waterford, Cork, Kerry, Limerick, and Clare.

Tipperary, extending over almost the whole frontier of Leinster, is crossed by a long chain of mountains called variously Slieve-Bloom, the Devil's Bit, and other uncouth names; and on the south it includes part of the Galties. On the north a small portion of the great central bog extends across the county; but one district, along the upper course of the Suire, bears the appellation of the Golden Vale. The sheep and horned cattle are of excellent quality. There are manufactures, chiefly for domestic use; and some coal, similar to that of Kilkenny. Clonmel, the county town, is one of the most considerable in the interior of Ireland: it stood a long siege against Cromwell, who after its reduction demolished the strong walls and castles by which it was defended. It is a well-built town, with four streets crossing each other, and carries on a brisk inland trade. Cashel is a large and handsome city, the seat of an archbishop, to whose residence a considerable library is attached. In ancient times, it was the capital of the kings of Munster, of whose palace some remnants may still be traced. Noble fragments remain of the ancient cathedral, majestically seated on the summit of a precipitous rock. The choir and nave, 210 feet long, are strewed with the remains of its rich ornaments. Here was deposited the Lia Fale, or fatal stone, on which the kings of Munster were crowned. The structure is now abandoned to decay, and a modern cathedral of fine Grecian architecture has been substituted. Cashel contains remains of other monastic edifices, of which Hore Abbey, on the same rock with the cathedral, is a magnificent specimen, still almost entire.

Waterford is a mountainous county, and only a small portion is under cultivation: the chief branch of rural industry is the dairy, and great quantities of butter are salted for exportation. Waterford, its capital, one of the principal sea-ports of the empire, being placed at the confluence of the Barrow and Suire, the second and third rivers of Ireland, enjoys a most extensive intercourse with the interior. The quantity of beef, pork, butter, and grain exported to England, in 1831–2, was valued at 2,065,861*l.*; of which bacon was 547,000*l.*; butter, 538,000*l.*; wheat and flour, 566,000*l.*; oats, 128,000*l.*; live pigs, 117,000*l.* The southern packet communication with England is carried on from Waterford to Milford Haven Within these few years, seventy vessels have been fitted out for the Newfoundland fishery Waterford enjoys the benefit of a deep and spacious harbour, and a fine quay half a mile long. Its ecclesiastical monuments are of considerable magnitude, and it has an elegant modern cathedral, with other fine public edifices. Twenty miles to the west, on a small bay, is Dungarvan, the largest fishing town in Ireland; and its antiquity is attested by a castle and several monastic remains. Lismore, on the Blackwater, is now deserted; but its castle, erected by King John, in 1185, still presents marks of ancient grandeur, and has been lately repaired.

Cork is the largest county of Ireland. On the northern border is the lofty range of the Galties, which present many picturesque features, and command extensive and beautiful prospects; its western border partakes of the mountainous character of the neighbouring districts of Kerry; and the rocky shores and headlands washed by the waves of the Atlantic, are of an awful and terrific character. About a fifth of the county consists of mountain and bog; the rest is only traversed by hills of moderate elevation, enclosing fertile and often beautiful valleys, especially that along the river and bay. The style of culture is altogether Irish; in small farms, by poor tenants, chiefly by the spade, and potatoes the prevailing crop. The manufactures consist of sailcloth, coarse linens and woollens. There are also some extensive distilleries.

Cork, the great southern emporium of Ireland, has a population of 107,000; being, in point of wealth and magnitude, the second city in the island. Its monastic structures, once considerable, have almost entirely disappeared. Its great prosperity is modern, in consequence of the provision trade, of which it has become the chief mart. The river Lee, at its junction with the sea, forms the spacious enclosed bay, called the Cove of Cork, composing one of the finest harbours in the world. In consequence of its convenient situation, the West India bound fleets usually touch there, and take in provisions. The export of salted beef and pork has somewhat diminished since the peace; but that of provisions in general, and particularly grain, has been greatly augmented; and Cork, on the whole, is in a very flourishing and prosperous state. A great part of the old town consists of miserable and crowded alleys; but a number of handsome new streets have been built, and several channels branching from the Lee, which flowed through the city, and were detrimental to the health of the inhabitants, have been filled up. Cork has a literary institution, with the usual appendages of library, lectures, and botanic garden; and it supports the charitable establishments usual in great cities on a liberal scale.

Kinsale, on a fine bay at the mouth of the Bandon, was much more frequented than Cork by the early English monarchs, who bestowed on the place extensive privileges, and viewed it as the key of southern Ireland. It has now, however, sunk under the superior importance of its neighbour; and it is chiefly supported by a fishery. Youghal, at the mouth of the Blackwater, has a good harbour, though obstructed by a bar; and carries on some trade and manufacture.

Kerry presents an assemblage of mountains wild, rocky, and desolate. These are interspersed with valleys and narrow plains which are almost wholly employed in pasturage; and Kerry has a small breed of cows, which yield plenty of excellent milk. Its coast is broken into several very deep bays, particularly those of Dingle, Kenmare, and Tralee. A considerable quantity of herring is caught in these bays. Tralee, the county town, exhibits the remains of a strong castle, once the residence of the Earls of Desmond, when, under the title of Palatine, they exercised the real sovereignty over this part of Ireland; a sway which terminated with their attainder under the reign of Elizabeth.

218

Lakes of Killarney.

Killarney and its lakes, as to scenery, have no rival in Ireland. There is only one body of water, to which, however, the term *lakes* is usually applied; so completely is it divided into three bays united only by narrow straits, and presenting each a different aspect. The lower lake, immediately adjoining Killarney (*fig.* 218.), forms the main expanse of water, and presents all the features on the greatest scale On the eastern shore rise the mountains known by the name of Macgillicuddy's Reeks, the highest of which rises to 3400 feet, the most elevated point in Ireland. On this side also are the mountains of Tomies and Glena, with their immense forests. Near the western bank is the beautiful island of Innisfallen. At the most southern point of the lower lake a much smaller bay branches off from it, through channels formed by Dinis Island. This bay, called Turk Lake, is overhung on one side by the precipitous sides of the lofty mountain of that name, and bordered on the other by the long wooded and winding peninsula of Mucruss. The venerable ruin of Mucruss Abbey (*fig.* 219.) adds greatly to the interest of this part of the scenery. From Dinis Island, a long winding channel of more than two miles leads to the Upper Lake. The scenery seen in this passage is of surpassing grandeur and beauty. The most striking spot is at the Eagle's Crag (*fig.* 220.), a stupendous and rugged cliff, which bursts suddenly on the view, rising in a pyramidal form from the water. Throughout all the rocks of Killarney, but here most particularly, the effect of echoes is most powerful and striking. The Upper Lake, the least extensive but the most sublime, exhibits all the loftiest mountains under the most imposing point of view. Its shores are winding and varied with numerous islands, whose rocky sides contrast with the brilliant green of the arbutus. The ascent of the highest mountains, Mangerton to the north, and Gheran Tual, the highest of the *reeks* to the south-east, discloses awful ranges of rugged precipices and of dark and rocky ravines; and their summits command an astonishing view of the mountain glens and rocky shores of Kerry, and the expanse of the Atlantic, and the distant plains of Cork and Limerick.

219

Mucruss Abbey.

220

Eagle's Crag.

Limerick is one of the finest counties of Ireland. Its borders include some branches from the high mountains of Kerry and Tipperary; but the main body consists of a fertile plain. An alluvial tract, two or three miles broad, along the Shannon, is quite exuberant. That noble river, now expanded into an estuary or bay sixty miles in length, runs along the whole northern border of Limerick.

The city of Limerick, now outstripped by Cork, is the third in Ireland Its situation, in the centre of the grand internal navigation of the kingdom, secures to it an extensive trade; and the largest vessels can ascend to the harbour. Limerick is one of the great marts for the export of grain and provisions; the value of those shipped from it in 1831, having been estimated at 854,600*l.* It was anciently the strongest fortress in Ireland, and has always stood out to the last extremity for the Catholic cause. Ireton, Cromwell's lieutenant, reduced it only after a long siege, aided by a party within the place. In 1690–1, it stood two long sieges, and yielded only upon those advantageous terms called the "capitulation of Limerick." Its capture was considered as closing the contest in support of the Stuarts. At this day, not more than a twelfth part of the population of Limerick is protestant. The spacious monasteries are almost entirely demolished; the streets are narrow, crowded, and gloomy; but since the fortifications were demolished, they have been carefully widened. In a quarter built by Lord Perry, and bearing his name, they are spacious and regular; and the houses, though only of brick, built in the most handsome modern style. The assembly-rooms, theatre, and other modern structures, are elegant and commodious.

Clare county is a wild, hilly, romantic district, abounding with fine creeks and harbours, but without commerce, and with mines of lead, iron and coal, which have not been turned to account. More than half the surface consists of mountain, bog, and waste; its hills, however, support numerous flocks of sheep, the wool of which is of superior quality. The plains on the banks of the Shannon and the Fergus vie in fertility with any in the kingdom. Ennis, the capital, is situated on the banks of the last-mentioned river, by which it communicates with the Shannon. It is considerable, though irregularly built; and its abbey, in the purest style of Gothic architecture, is considered the finest in Ireland.

Subsect. 3.—*Connaught.*

Connaught forms a great peninsula, the most westerly part of Ireland, extending from the Shannon to the Atlantic. This division is of all others the most decidedly Irish, having continued unsubdued long after the English kings claimed the proud title of lords of the island. It still contains fewer English inhabitants; the religion is more universally Catholic, industry and manufactures have made less progress, and all the imperfect agricultural implements and processes are in more general use. Disturbances, however, have never taken place here to so great an extent as in Munster and Leinster. Its shores are penetrated by deep and extensive bays, forming some of the finest harbours in the world. The counties in Connaught are Galway, Mayo, Sligo, Roscommon, and Leitrim.

Galway presents to the sea ranges of steep cliffs, which, with the waves of the Atlantic dashing against them, exhibit a grand spectacle. The interior contains two extensive lakes, and is diversified with hills, though there are few which are not fit for pasturage. The cattle are of good quality, and the flocks of sheep are more extensive than in other parts of Ireland. The fisheries of herring and salmon are considerable. Galway has always been a considerable town, and is still supported by some inland and foreign commerce, by a considerable fishery, by the resort of the gentry to it for sea-bathing, and as the only scene of gay society to be found in Connaught. It was once very strongly fortified both by nature and art; and to obtain the protection of the walls, the streets were made narrow, and the houses high, massive, and gloomy; but they have of late been considerably opened, and suburbs built, of a more gay and elegant description.

Tuam is an ancient, handsome town, of considerable extent, the seat of an archbishopric. Ballinasloe, on the eastern border, holds the greatest cattle fair in Ireland, where the oxen and sheep of the pastoral counties of Galway and Mayo are mustered for the capital. At the mouth of the bay of Galway are the bold and rocky islands of Arran.

Mayo is chiefly elevated and rugged; some of the mountains rising to upwards of 2600 feet; but many of their sides are verdant, and the valleys rich and well watered; so that Mayo is a fine pastoral county. The estates are large, but the farms small, and much subdivided. Mayo contains no town of sufficient importance to return a member to parliament. Castlebar, the county town, is well built, with a linen hall; and the linen manufacture flourishes. Killala, a straggling village, on a bay of the same name, is chiefly noted for the landing effected in 1798, by a body of French troops under General Humbert, who penetrated to Castlebar, but were finally obliged to surrender to Marquess Cornwallis.

Sligo contains a considerable quantity of bog; but the remainder consists of a sandy gravelly soil, well adapted to the production of barley and oats; so that pasturage is not so exclusively the employment here as in the two last-mentioned counties. Salmon is caught in large quantities. The linen manufacture has made considerable progress, and is extending. Sligo, the capital, at the mouth of the river and the head of the bay of the same name, was in early times a considerable place: it has suffered severely in civil contention; yet, by the advantage of a good situation and harbour, it has attained considerable importance and trade. In the vicinity is a remarkable circle of stones, called the Giant's Grave, somewhat resembling Stonehenge.

Roscommon is mostly level, finely watered, and celebrated for rich pastures; but the increase of population and manufactures has caused a great part of them to be lately brought into tillage; it contains some pretty little lakes, among which Lough Key is particularly admired. Roscommon is ancient, and marked by some ecclesiastical antiquities, but it is not now so important as Boyle, pleasantly situated on a river of the same name, over which there are two fine bridges; in its neighbourhood are the ruins of a stately abbey, founded in 1512, the arches of which, forty-six feet in height, are deemed models of Gothic architectural grandeur. Elphin, the seat of a very ancient episcopal see, is only a village.

Leitrim is filled with high mountains, presenting nature under bold features, often heightened by the ruined castles which crown their summits. There are veins of iron, lead, copper, and coal, the last of which has been wrought. There are good pastures in the valleys, and on the sides of the hills; and pretty large quantities of oats are raised. The linen manufacture is extending, and there are some considerable potteries. Carrick on Shannon, the county town, and Leitrim, which gives name to it, are only villages.

Subsect. 4.—*Ulster.*

This part of Ireland presents in many respects a superior character to the other three, its population being more industrious, better instructed, and in more comfortable circumstances. The Presbyterian form of worship, introduced by the Scottish settlers under the reign of James I., is the prevailing one. The linen manufacture, the staple of the country, has here its chief seat, and is carried on almost in every village. The harbours of Belfast, Londonderry, and Lough Swilly, are sufficient for the wants of commerce. The coast of Antrim, in the boldness and peculiar character of its rock scenery, is without a match in any other part of the world. The counties of this province are, Fermanagh, Donegal, Londonderry, Antrim, Down, Armagh, Tyrone, Monaghan, Cavan.

Fermanagh is a somewhat rough county, comprising a large proportion of mountain and bog, but with fertile valleys, in which, besides the usual products of oats and potatoes, flax is cultivated to the extent of about 5000 acres. The waters of all the high grounds flow down into Lough Erne, a noble lake, upwards of twenty miles in length. It is studded with numerous islands, covered with fine woods; long wooded promontories are seen stretching far into the waters; and, though the immediate borders of the lake are not mountainous, lofty distant eminences form the general background to its prospects. Castle Caldwell, Belturbet, and Belleisle are the spots in which its beauties are peculiarly concentrated. The chief town is Enniskillen, delightfully situated on an island, accessible only by two opposite bridges; this site enabled it to make its noble stand against the army of James II.

Donegal includes a great extent of the north-western coast of Ireland, full of deep bays and fine harbours. In its interior, however, it consists almost entirely of mountain, moss, and moor, with only a few productive valleys. It is often called, with some adjoining districts, "the black north of Ireland." Distillation forms an active branch of its industry. Lifford, its small county town, stands on the Foyle, upon the borders of Derry. Ballyshannon, almost at the opposite extremity, is a thriving town, beautifully situated on the channel by which Lough Erne pours its waters into the Atlantic. Raphoe is a celebrated episcopal see, but now only a decayed village.

Derry, or Londonderry, a large and fine county, is crossed by a range of mountains, whose principal peaks are from 1000 to 1500 feet high, and a considerable part of whose surface consists of heath and bog. There are, however, fine valleys, and extensive plains, which are cultivated with some diligence, but according to that system of minute subdivision which is the bane of Irish agriculture. The linen manufacture flourishes in full vigour, chiefly according to the Irish system, among the little farmers and cotters, who combine it with the cultivation of a few acres. Londonderry is a fine city, situated at the point where the Foyle, after traversing a great part of this county and that of Tyrone, falls into the broad basin of Lough Foyle. It is ancient, being the theatre of remarkable events even in the time of the Danes. In 1608, after the attainder of O'Neale, it was granted by James I. to the citizens of London, whence it derived the first part of its name. But its chief distinction was from the siege sustained by the city in 1690–1, against the united forces of Ireland under James II. Londonderry is composed of four main streets crossing each other at right angles, and surrounded still by its old walls in full repair, serving rather for ornament than defence. It has an ancient Gothic cathedral, and some handsome modern edifices. It is now supported by an extensive commerce, for which Lough Foyle, though its entrance is somewhat impeded by a bar, affords a spacious and secure harbour. Its chief intercourse is with the United States and the West Indies, to which it exports the linen manufactured in this part of the country. Coleraine is a well-built town on the Bann, which flows from Lough Neagh, and on which is the most extensive salmon fishery in the island; but the rapidity of the stream obstructs the navigation upwards.

Antrim, occupying the north-eastern corner of the kingdom, opposite the coast of Scotland, is one of the most remarkable districts of Ireland, in regard to natural features as well as to commerce and industry. A great part of the surface consists of rugged mountains, composed chiefly of rock and moss, and even its best soils are scarcely available for agricultural purposes till improved by the use of the lime with which the country abounds. The mountains, where they face the ocean, are broken into vast perpendicular precipices, exhibiting the basaltic columnar form on a grander scale than exists in any other part of the world.

Of these objects, the Giant's Causeway (*fig.* 221.) is the most celebrated and magnificent. Three natural piers or moles, 400 feet in height, here stretch out into the sea, and are visible above the water for about 300 yards. The walls are composed of dark basaltic columns, of the most regular form, and so closely united, that only the blade of a knife can be thrust between them. Each column is distinct from the others, and divided into jointed portions, as perfect as if art had formed them; there being in each part a projection, which is lodged in a corresponding concavity or socket of the one contiguous. The coast eastward of the causeway is composed of a succession of capes, presenting the most sublime scenery; dark precipitous cliffs, rising regularly in gradually retiring strata, and formed into various broken colonnades which might suggest the idea of palaces overwhelmed in ruins.

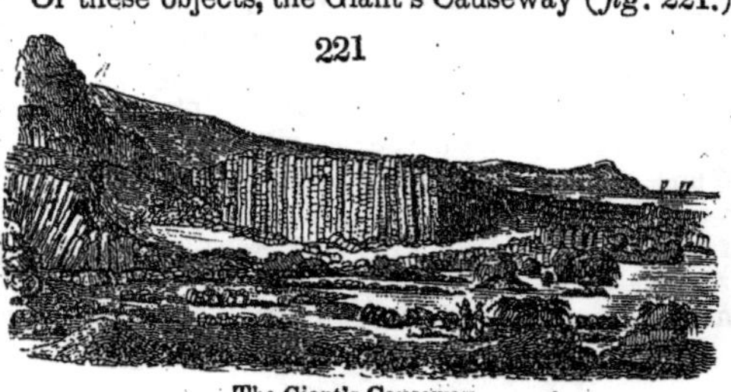
221

The Giant's Causeway.

Other striking features distinguish the coast of Antrim. Conspicuous above all others is

Fairhead, called also Benmore; a promontory which forms nearly the north-eastern point of Ireland. It consists of a vast mass of columnar greenstone, composing a mural precipice rudely columnar, and 250 feet high. At its feet lies a chaos of huge masses of rock, heaped together in the wildest confusion, and forming a scene of ruin the awful grandeur of which has scarcely a parallel. Against this the sea heaves in a solemn majestic swell, the peculiar attribute of the Atlantic waters. Carrick-a-Rede (*fig.* 222.) is a small island composed of a mass of basalt, imperfectly formed into columns, separated from the continent by a chasm of sixty feet. The fishermen, however, have occasion to resort to it with the view of placing nets to intercept the salmon; to reach it, therefore, they have constructed a daring and singular bridge, formed of two strong parallel cables fixed to each side, with planks inserted between them. This slight pontage is subject to violent movements, and, if not judiciously trodden, may precipitate the passenger into the abyss; but the fishermen, accustomed to tread it, carry great loads across without the slightest apprehension. Several of the precipitous cliffs are adorned with the ruins of ancient castles, the grandest of which is Dunluce (*fig.* 223.), whose extensive area covers the long ridge of an almost insulated rock, which presents its perpendicular face to the ocean. The walls enclose the entire surface of the rock, and rise up as a continuation of its precipitous sides. In one place, the rocky base having given way, the apartment above actually overhangs the sea.

222

Carrick-a-Rede.

223

Dunluce Castle.

Belfast, the grand emporium of the north of Ireland, has risen to greatness by rapid steps. Carrickfergus, by means of peculiar privileges, monopolised all the trade of this part of Ireland, till these privileges were bought up by the Earl of Strafford. The career of competition was then opened to Belfast, and she gradually outstripped all her rivals. In 1660, the town contained about 6500 inhabitants. At present the population is 53,000, exclusive of a large suburb in the county of Down. The linen manufacture is very flourishing at Belfast, and that of cotton is rapidly extending; besides which there are various minor fabrics. Commerce, however, is the main source of its wealth. The linen fabrics of the north are largely exported, along with oats, oatmeal, and salted provisions; the entire value of which, in 1810, amounted to 2,900,000*l.* The duties of customs, which in 1801 were 182,314*l.*, had risen in 1829 to 259,000*l.* Belfast Lough forms a noble and secure bay, and the channel at the mouth of the Lagan has been so deepened by art that vessels drawing thirteen feet water can come close to the wharves. Belfast is mostly built of brick; but several public edifices, recently erected, the Commercial Buildings, the Museum, St. George's Church, &c., are ornamented with pillars of freestone. Belfast has several commercial and literary institutions; and in 1810, the Royal Academical College, a seminary on an extensive scale, was founded.

The other towns of Antrim can boast little more than names known in history. Antrim itself has lost its former importance, though beautifully situated near the great body of water called Lough Neagh, which covers about 100,000 English acres, and borders on five counties,—Armagh, Tyrone, Londonderry, Down, and Antrim. Its flat shores possess little of interest or beauty; and its overflowings have converted into bog about 60,000 acres round it. Carrickfergus, at the mouth of Belfast Lough, is a very ancient town, once the emporium and key of northern Ireland, but it has yielded the palm of commerce entirely to Belfast, and is supported only by being the county town and resorted to as a watering-place. Lisburn is a prosperous town, with a manufacture of damask.

Down is a fine county, penetrated by several large lakes, as those of Strangford and Carlingford. The last of these receives the Newry, which communicates by a canal with Lough Neagh. The Mourne mountains, on the southern border, exceed 2600 feet in height, and form a conspicuous object; but a large extent of the county is level, and a greater proportion is under tillage than pasturage. The combination of farming and weaving exists in a remarkable degree; and the linen fabrics are not only extensive, but some of them very fine. Of late, however, those of cotton have gained a preference in many districts. Down, or Downpatrick, celebrated in tradition as the burial-place of the patron saint, is of moderate dimensions, and its public buildings respectable. Newry is larger and more flourishing. These advantages are owing to its situation in the bay of Carlingford, and its canal communication with Lough Neagh, which enable it to export the linen manufactures and provisions produced in an extensive district. It is ancient, but in 1689 was reduced to ashes by Marshal Berwick; so that it is now quite a new town. Donaghadee, a considerable port, with a large substantial quay, is chiefly remarkable for the ferry between it and Portpatrick, the shortest sea communication with Britain, and by which packets are despatched and live stock in very great quantities conveyed over.

Armagh is also a fine and agreeable county. In general it is only pleasingly diversified with little hills, the bogs are no more than requisite for supplying fuel, and only a small part is left unproductive. Both culture and manufacture are prosecuted with great activity. The linens produced in 1824 were reputed at 568,000*l.*, exceeding a fifth of the produce of the whole kingdom. Armagh, the capital, was celebrated in the early history of Ireland as one of its most extensive and populous cities, and has always been the ecclesiastical metropolis of the kingdom. The Augustine monastery, and the college attached to it, ranked for a long time among the most celebrated institutions in Europe for religion and learning; the latter, it is said, could once boast of 7000 students. Armagh sunk, however, under successive ravages by the Danes, the English, and, finally, the Irish insurgents under O'Neale, and fell into decay; but by good fortune had for its primate Dr. Richard Robinson, to whose munificent exertions is ascribed its revival and its having become one of the prettiest little cities in Ireland. To him Armagh is indebted for the repair of its cathedral, for a library, and an observatory. The linen market is well supported by the flourishing state of the manufacture in Armagh. The only other place of consequence is Lurgan, a thriving manufacturing town.

The three counties of *Tyrone*, *Monaghan*, and *Cavan* occupy a great proportion of the interior of Ulster, and present a very uniform aspect; a considerable extent of mountain and bog, fertile plains, rude cultivation, and the linen manufacture. O'Neale, Earl of Tyrone, was long one of the most formidable enemies of the English power. Omagh is the county-town of Tyrone, but is not so considerable as Dungannon, a large, populous, and handsome place, once the chief seat of the O'Neales; but this powerful castle was demolished by the parliamentary forces. Strabane is also a populous place, finely situated on the Foyle. Monaghan and Cavan are both tolerable county-towns, which alone possess any importance in their respective shires.

---

## FINANCES OF THE UNITED KINGDOM.

### I. *Income for the year* 1834.

| | |
|---|---|
| Customs | £21,118,920 |
| Excise | 16,756,716 |
| Stamps and Hackney Coaches, &c. | 7,462,755 |
| Taxes | 4,667,350 |
| Post Office | 2,319,980 |
| Miscellaneous | 456,118 |
| East India Company | 60,000 |
| Balance on hand | 1,907,190 |
| Repayments | 618,732 |
| | £53,456,571 |

### II. *Expenditure for the year* 1834.

| | | |
|---|---|---|
| *Payments out of the gross Revenue.* | | |
| Drawbacks, Repayments, &c. | £2,204,296 | |
| Charges of Collection, &c. | 3,582,635 | |
| Miscellaneous | 738,810 | |
| | | 6,525,741 |
| *Paid at the Exchequer.* | | |
| Interest and Management of Permanent Debt | | 24,158,879 |
| Terminable Annuities | | 3,653,923 |
| Interest on Exchequer Bills | | 691,294 |
| Russian Loan, raised in Holland | | 190,810 |
| Civil List | | 510,000 |
| Civil, Naval, Military and Judicial Annuities and Pensions | | 502,310 |
| Salaries and Allowances | | 162,930 |
| Diplomatic Salaries and Pensions | | 181,448 |
| Courts of Justice | | 433,610 |
| Mint | | 14,850 |
| Army | | 6,493,925 |
| Navy | | 4,503,910 |
| Ordnance | | 1,068,223 |
| Miscellaneous | | 2,335,590 |
| Advances for Public Works | | 2,014,513 |
| Total Expenditure | | £53,441,955 |

### III. *Public Debt—January* 1834. *Charge for* 1833

| | | |
|---|---|---|
| Funded Debt | £751,658,883 | £27,782,116 |
| Unfunded Debt | 27,906,900 | 779,769 |
| Totals | £779,565,783 | £28,561,885 |

I. Account of the Official and of the Real or Declared Value of the principal Articles of British Produce and Manufacture exported in 1832, 1833, and 1834.—(From the *Annual Finance Book* for 1835, pp. 121—128.)

| Articles. | Official Value.* | | | Declared Value. | | |
|---|---|---|---|---|---|---|
| | 1832. | 1833. | 1834. | 1832. | 1833. | 1834. |
| | L. s. d. | L. s. d. | L. s. d. | L. s. d. | L. s. d. | L. s. d. |
| Brass and copper manufactures | 1,126,246 18 3 | 1,018,284 11 5 | 1,086,594 2 4 | 916,563 1 5 | 884,149 4 9 | 961,823 2 11 |
| Cotton manufactures | 37,206,480 10 4 | 40,133,343 2 3 | 44,266,902 13 0 | 12,675,622 6 6 | 13,782,375 17 6 | 15,302,571 7 1 |
| ——— yarn | 6,726,562 17 6 | 6,279,076 5 8 | 6,802,237 18 9 | 4,722,759 3 6 | 4,704,024 9 1 | 5,211,014 17 8 |
| Hardwares and cutlery | 878,361 17 1 | 966,503 4 7 | 947,476 18 11 | 1,434,431 7 11 | 1,466,361 12 11 | 1,485,233 1 1 |
| Iron and steel, wrought and unwrought | 2,408,183 18 3 | 2,690,253 14 3 | 2,621,672 9 8 | 1,190,747 12 10 | 1,405,034 19 3 | 1,406,872 2 1 |
| Linen manufactures | 2,785,549 13 6 | 3,589,539 0 8 | 3,850,763 14 5 | 1,774,726 13 9 | 2,167,023 7 1 | 2,443,344 18 7 |
| ——— yarn | 5,898 7 8 | 50,125 16 5 | 82,169 10 9 | 8,705 7 0 | 72,006 5 0 | 136,312 11 9 |
| Salt | 353,824 19 2 | 392,053 7 8 | 371,469 19 10 | 149,678 1 6 | 184,175 10 2 | 152,126 14 10 |
| Silk manufactures | 475,165 19 2 | 695,324 0 6 | 533,683 9 7 | 529,990 10 10 | 737,403 17 10 | 637,198 5 4 |
| Soap and candles | 348,286 8 3 | 453,910 17 5 | 382,198 10 0 | 315,644 16 3 | 362,284 19 1 | 263,972 4 11 |
| Sugar, refined | 1,292,489 9 8 | 693,131 14 4 | 1,141,565 14 4 | 1,038,789 16 0 | 563,092 4 3 | 916,391 9 6 |
| Tin, wrought and unwrought | 358,259 10 1 | 371,634 3 4 | 370,115 18 10 | 355,056 9 2 | 369,162 0 2 | 370,382 11 5 |
| Wool, sheep's | 149,991 12 4 | 175,479 12 3 | 81,382 17 10 | 219,650 1 0 | 332,503 17 4 | 192,175 14 1 |
| Woollen and worsted yarn | 122,124 19 8 | 113,191 3 9 | 99,933 11 9 | 235,307 7 6 | 246,204 0 0 | 238,543 15 9 |
| Woollen manufactures | 6,556,294 8 8 | 7,788,842 6 3 | 6,514,703 3 10 | 5,244,558 11 8 | 6,294,432 3 9 | 5,736,870 11 0 |
| All other articles | 4,232,981 1 5 | 4,578,646 12 11 | 4,678,680 1 6 | 5,532,293 11 9 | 6,097,113 0 3 | 6,194,358 1 6 |
| Totals | 65,026,702 11 0 | 69,989,339 13 8 | 73,831,550 15 4 | 36,444,524 18 7 | 39,667,347 8 5 | 41,649,191 9 6 |
| Whereof from Great Britain | 64,582,037 9 7 | 69,633,853 16 1 | 73,495,535 11 3 | 36,046,027 11 5 | 39,305,512 19 8 | 41,286,594 5 6 |
| From Ireland | 444,665 1 5 | 355,485 17 7 | 336,015 4 1 | 398,497 7 2 | 361,834 8 9 | 362,597 4 0 |

II. Account of the Real or Declared Value of the various Articles of the Manufacture and Produce of the United Kingdom, exported to Foreign Countries during the eight years ending with 1834; specifying their Value, the Countries to which exported, and the Value of those annually shipped for each.—(*Papers published by Board of Trade*, vol. iv. p. 227.)

| Countries to which exported. | Exports. | | | | | | | |
|---|---|---|---|---|---|---|---|---|
| | 1827. | 1828. | 1829. | 1830. | 1831. | 1832. | 1833. | 1834. |
| | L. | L. | L. | L. | L. | L. | L. | L. |
| Russia | 1,408,970 | 1,318,936 | 1,435,805 | 1,489,538 | 1,191,565 | 1,587,250 | 1,531,002 | 1,382,300 |
| Sweden | 46,731 | 42,699 | 38,252 | 40,488 | 57,127 | 64,932 | 59,549 | 63,094 |
| Norway | 39,129 | 53,582 | 64,234 | 63,926 | 58 580 | 34,528 | 55,038 | 61,988 |
| Denmark | 104,916 | 111,880 | 95,247 | 118,813 | 92,294 | 93,396 | 99,951 | 94,595 |
| Prussia | 174,338 | 179,145 | 189,011 | 177,923 | 192,816 | 258,556 | 144,179 | 136,423 |
| Germany | 4,654,618 | 4,394,104 | 4,473,555 | 4,463,605 | 3,642,952 | 5,068,997 | 4,355,548 | 4,547,166 |
| Holland | 2,104,561 | 2,142,736 | 2,050,014 | 2,022,458 | 2,082,536 | 2,789,398 | 2,181,893 | 2,470,267 |
| Belgium | | | | | | | 886,429 | 750,059 |
| France | 446,952 | 498,938 | 491,388 | 475,884 | 602,688 | 674,791 | 848,333 | 1,116,885 |
| Portugal, Proper | 1,400,044 | 945,016 | 1,195,404 | 1,106,695 | 975,991 | 540,792 | 967,091 | 1,600,123 |
| Azores | 26,687 | 27,940 | 31,244 | 23,629 | 41,638 | 77,920 | 54,430 | 63,275 |
| Madeira | 39 916 | 39,802 | 40,283 | 38,444 | 38 960 | 28,038 | 33,411 | 38,455 |
| Spain and the Balearic Islands | 225,414 | 301,153 | 861,675 | 607,068 | 597,848 | 442,926 | 442,837 | 325,907 |
| Canary Islands | 48,821 | 38,152 | 50 010 | 42,620 | 33,282 | 21,053 | 30,507 | 30,686 |
| Gibraltar | 1,045,266 | 1,038,925 | 504,163 | 292,760 | 367,285 | 461,470 | 385,460 | 460,719 |
| Italy and the Italian Islands | 1,942,752 | 2,176,149 | 2,202,030 | 3,251,379 | 2,490,376 | 2,361,772 | 2,316,260 | 3,282,777 |
| Malta | 200,949 | 239,458 | 224,010 | 189,135 | 134,519 | 96,994 | 135,438 | 242,696 |
| Ionian Islands | 37,196 | 41,078 | 30,465 | 56,963 | 50,883 | 55,725 | 38,915 | 94,498 |
| Turkey and Continental Greece (exclusive of the Morea) | 531,704 | 185,842 | 568,684 | 1,139,616 | 888,654 | 915,319 | 1,019,604 | 1,207,941 |
| Morea and Greek Islands | | 335 | ....... | 9,694 | 10,446 | 10,149 | 25,914 | 37,179 |
| Egypt (Ports on the Mediterranean) | 53,624 | 35,302 | 59,305 | 110,227 | 122,832 | 113,109 | 145,647 | 158,877 |
| Tripoli, Barbary, and Morocco | 8,201 | 13,745 | ....... | 1,138 | 426 | 751 | 2,350 | 14,823 |
| Western Coast of Africa | 155,759 | 191,452 | 244,253 | 252,123 | 234,768 | 290,061 | 329,210 | 326,483 |
| Cape of Good Hope | 216,558 | 218,049 | 257,501 | 330,036 | 257,245 | 292,405 | 346,197 | 304,382 |
| Cape Verd Islands | 76 | 5,856 | 240 | 1,710 | 215 | ....... | 146 | 530 |
| St. Helena | 41,430 | 31,362 | 45,531 | 38,915 | 39,431 | 21,236 | 30,041 | 31,615 |
| Isle of Bourbon | 127 | 35,188 | 16,341 | 10,042 | ....... | ....... | ....... | 7,091 |
| Mauritius | 195,713 | 185,972 | 205,558 | 161,029 | 148,475 | 163,191 | 83,424 | 149,319 |
| Arabia | ....... | ....... | ....... | ....... | ....... | ....... | ....... | 250 |
| East India Company's Territories and Ceylon | 3,662,012 | 4,256,582 | 3,659,218 | 3,895,530 | 3,377,412 | 3,514,779 | 3,495,301 | 2,578,569 |
| China | 610,637 | ....... | ....... | ....... | ....... | ....... | ....... | 842,852 |
| Sumatra and Java | 120,747 | 189,200 | 255,885 | 162,102 | 285,296 | 150 606 | 471,712 | 410,273 |
| Philippine Islands | 65,926 | 300 | 4,721 | 71,220 | 39,513 | 102,284 | 185,298 | 76,618 |
| New South Wales, Van Diemen's Land, and Swan River | 339,958 | 443,839 | 310,688 | 314,677 | 398,471 | 466,238 | 558,372 | 716,014 |
| New Zealand, and South Sea Islands | 172 | 2,487 | 845 | 1,396 | 4,752 | 1,576 | 936 | |
| Ports of Siam | ....... | ....... | ....... | 10,467 | ....... | ....... | ....... | 19,742 |
| British North American Colonies | 1,397,360 | 1,691,044 | 1,581,723 | 1,857,133 | 2,089,327 | 2,075,725 | 2,092,550 | 1,671,069 |
| British West Indies | 3,583,222 | 3,289,704 | 3,612,085 | 2,838,448 | 2,581,949 | 2,439,808 | 2,597,589 | 2,680,024 |
| Hayti | 257,931 | 248,328 | 297,709 | 321,793 | 376,103 | 543,104 | 381 528 | 357,297 |
| Cuba and other Foreign West Indies | 649,378 | 569,728 | 672,176 | 618,029 | 663,531 | 633,700 | 577,228 | 913,005 |
| United States of America | 7,018,272 | 5,810,315 | 4,823,415 | 6,132,346 | 9,053,583 | 5,468,272 | 7,579,699 | 6,844,989 |
| Mexico | 692,800 | 307,029 | 303,562 | 978,441 | 728,858 | 199,821 | 421,487 | 459,610 |
| Guatemala | 1,943 | 6,191 | ....... | ....... | ....... | ....... | 3,700 | 30,366 |
| Colombia | 213,972 | 261,113 | 232,703 | 216,751 | 248,250 | 283,568 | 121,826 | 199,996 |
| Brazil | 2,312,109 | 3,518,297 | 2,516,040 | 2,452,103 | 1,238,371 | 2,144,903 | 2,575,680 | 2,460,679 |
| States of the Rio de la Plata | 154,895 | 312,389 | 758,540 | 632,172 | 339,870 | 660,152 | 515,362 | 831,564 |
| Chili | 400,134 | 709,371 | 818,950 | 540,626 | 651,617 | 708,193 | 816,817 | 896,221 |
| Peru | 228,466 | 374,615 | 300,171 | 368,469 | 409,003 | 275,610 | 387,524 | 299,235 |
| Isles of Guernsey, Jersey, Alderney, and Man | 320,959 | 329,428 | 319,996 | 344,036 | 324,634 | 317,496 | 335,934 | 360,665 |
| Totals | 37,181,335 | 36,812,756 | 35,842,623 | 38,271,597 | 37,164,372 | 36,450,594 | 39,667,347 | 41,649,191 |

* The rate at which all articles of export and import are officially valued was fixed in 1696, but an account of the real or declared value of the exports is also prepared; there is, however, no such account of the imports, and therefore their official value alone can be given.

III. Account of the Quantities of the Principal Articles of Foreign and Colonial Merchandise imported into, exported from, and retained for Consumption in the United Kingdom, with the Nett Revenue accruing thereon during the Years ended 5th January, 1834, and 1835.—(*Papers published by Board of Trade*, vol. iv. pp. 12-19.)

| Description of Merchandise. | Quantities imported. | | Quantities exported. | | Quantities retained for Consumption. | | Nett Revenue. | |
|---|---|---|---|---|---|---|---|---|
| | 1833. | 1834. | 1833. | 1834. | 1833. | 1834. | 1833. | 1834. |
| | | | | | | | L. | L. |
| Ashes, pearl and pot, - - - - - - - cwts. | 169,729 | 94,134 | 11,395 | 6,136 | 166,422 | 89,960 | 1,505 | 1,326 |
| Barilla and alkali - - - - - - - - - —— | 214,523 | 193,971 | 2,458 | 3,233 | 219,503 | 180,490 | 16,703 | Gross rev. 17,754 |
| | | | | | | | Drawbacks & repayments | 4,460 |
| | | | | | | | | 13,293 |
| Bark for tanning or dyeing - - - - - - - - - - - - - —— | 852,201 | 849,300 | 354 | 1,132 | 854,279 | 849,561 | 26,674 | 28,276 |
| Coffee, viz. :— | | | | | | | | |
| British plantation - - - - - - - - - lbs. | 18,833,830 | 22,089,123 | 194,980 | 768,946 | 20,941,194 | 22,224,073 | | |
| East India and Mauritius - - - - - — | 6,218,299 | 9,951,141 | 3,996,097 | 6,303,562 | 1,799,319 | 1.558,604 | 591,241 | 614,434 |
| Foreign plantation - - - - - - - - - — | 9,373,980 | 9,824,847 | 11,158,501 | 8,177,972 | 1,471 | 2,418 | | |
| Totals - - - - - - - | 34,426,109 | 41,865,111 | 15,349,578 | 15,250,480 | 22,741,984 | 23,785,095 | | |
| Cocoa - - - - - - - - - - - - - - - - - lbs. | 4,608,718 | 2,984,894 | 2,351,877 | 2,205,316 | 1,268,287 | 1,173,795 | 12,026 | 11,779 |
| Husks and shells - - - - - - - - - - - — | 515,688 | 404,039 | - - - - - - - | - - - - - - | 449,168 | 443,786 | | |
| Cotton wool from foreign countries, viz. :— | | | | | | | | |
| United States of America - - - - - — | 237,506,758 | 269,203,075 | | | | | | |
| Brazil - - - - - - - - - - - - - - - - — | 28,463,821 | 19,291,396 | | | | | | |
| Turkey and Egypt - - - - - - - - — | 987,262 | 865,167 | | | | | | |
| Other foreign countries - - - - - - — | 1,696,108 | 2,260,852 | | | | | | |
| Cotton wool from British possessions, viz. :— | | | | | | | | |
| East Indies and Mauritius - - - - — | 32,755,164 | 32,920,865 | | | | | | |
| British West Indies, the growth of - - - - - - - - - - - - - - - - — | 1,653,166 | 1,672 211 | | | | | | |
| British West Indies, imported from - - - - - - - - - - - - - - - — | 431,696 | 624,314 | | | | | | |
| Other British possessions - - - - - — | 162,862 | 47,545 | | | | | | |
| Total quantities - - - - - - | 303,656,837 | 326,875,425 | 17,363,882 | 24,461,963 | 293,682,976 | 302,935,657 | 473,011 | 373,812 |
| Indigo - - - - - - - - - - - - - - - - - lbs. | 6,635,436 | 4,155,296 | 3,664,814 | 3,928,226 | 2,323,300 | 2,447,827 | 29,781 | 32,056 |
| Lac dye - - - - - - - - - - - - - - - — | 326,894 | 708,959 | 52,811 | 88,234 | 435,572 | 393,474 | 1,170 | 1,057 |
| Logwood - - - - - - - - - - - - - - tons. | 26,080 | 21,054 | 7,045 | 4,548 | 17,595 | 14,026 | 3,492 | 2,942 |
| Madder - - - - - - - - - - - - - - - - cwts. | 61,397 | 72,004 | 756 | 1,527 | 72,186 | 70,951 | 14.730 | 7,207 |
| Madder roots - - - - - - - - - - - - —— | 56,662 | 80,297 | 27 | - - - - - - - | 60,549 | 75,271 | 3,721 | 1,892 |
| Flax and tow, or codilla of flax and hemp - - - - - - - - - - - - —— | 1,129,633 | 811,722 | 18,202 | 19,569 | 1,112,190 | 794,272 | 4,728 | 3,405 |
| Currants - - - - - - - - - - - - - - - —— | 142,539 | 192,786 | 10,554 | 12,967 | 140,445 | 163,523 | 311,063 | 242,180 |
| Lemons and oranges - - - - - - - - chests | 351,951 | 266,323 | 5,294 | 1,460 | 319,147 | 254,783 | 69,392 | 57,434 |
| Raisins - - - - - - - - - - - - - - - - cwts. | 158,324 | 213,729 | 36,127 | 27,635 | 137,692 | 147,467 | 149,195 | 122,272 |
| Hats of straw - - - - - - - - - - - - - No. | 25,723 | 16,550 | 56,093 | 23,956 | 21,469 | 11,487 | 6,092 | 3,260 |
| Plaiting of straw - - - - - - - - - - - lbs. | 22,223 | 45,372 | 2,801 | 2,832 | 22,079 | 25,470 | 18,768 | 20,915 |
| Hemp undressed - - - - - - - - - - - cwts. | 527,459 | 673,811 | 32,170 | 19,672 | 512,623 | 666,096 | 2,110 | 2,844 |
| Hides, untanned, viz. :— | | | | | | | | |
| Buffalo, bull, ox, cow, or horse hides - - - - - - - - - - - - - - cwts. | 296,300 | 437,291 | 29,366 | 56,127 | 265,861 | 342,718 | 39,027 | 51,769 |
| Hides, tanned, viz. :— | | | | | | | | |
| Buffalo, bull, ox, cow, or horse hides - - - - - - - - - - - - - - - - lbs. | 65,702 | 80,262 | 10,460 | 4,964 | 48,578 | 40,339 | 532 | 517 |
| Leather gloves - - - - - - - - - - - - - pairs | 1,436,472 | 1 697,944 | - - - - - | 22,638 | 1,411,215 | 1,603,828 | - - - - - - - | 29,952 |
| Molasses - - - - - - - - - - - - - - - cwts. | 717,934 | 678,382 | 1,332 | 2,078 | 643,886 | 507,980 | 289,623 | 228,621 |
| Oil— | | | | | | | | |
| Olive - - - - - - - - - - - - - - - - galls. | 1,891,918 | 2,318,142 | 397,367 | 234,930 | 1,368,217 | 2,225,227 | 45,743 | 46,365 |
| Palm - - - - - - - - - - - - - - - - cwts. | 267,194 | 270,669 | 19,738 | 20,412 | 216,225 | 264,806 | 27,043 | 23,606 |
| Train, spermaceti and blubber - - tuns | 32,876 | 25,334 | 2,083 | 3,727 | 31,242 | 21,462 | 1,761 | 1,559 |
| Saltpetre and cubic nitre - - - - - cwts. | 165,746 | 359,488 | 20,737 | 68,276 | 160,235 | 215,963 | 4,184 | 5,992 |
| Flax and Linseed - - - - - - - - bushels | 2,179,135 | 2,210,237 | 652 | 7,523 | 2,222,967 | 2,211,968 | 13,923 | 13,890 |
| Silk— | | | | | | | | |
| Raw - - - - - - - - - - - - - - - - - lbs. | 2,785,109 | 3,643,512 | 66,187 | 207,007 | 4,417,027 | - - - - - - - | 15,900 | 13,860 |
| Waste and knubbs - - - - - - - - — | 649,451 | 1,012,951 | | | 267,472 | - - - - - - - | 292 | 450 |
| Cassia Lignea - - - - - - - - - - - - — | 1,297,710 | 2,066,836 | 1,341,546 | 1,680,350 | 77,067 | 100,182 | 1,778 | 2,196 |
| Pepper - - - - - - - - - - - - - - - - — | 8,729,552 | 7,675,340 | 3,997,027 | 6,391,247 | 2,228,393 | 2,457,020 | 111,174 | 122,852 |
| Pimento - - - - - - - - - - - - - - - — | 4,844,978 | 1,396,773 | 2,810,384 | 1,799,143 | 330,245 | 323,751 | 6,894 | 6,726 |
| Sugar, viz. :— | | | Raw. | | | | | |
| West India - - - - - - - - - - - - - cwts. | 3,655,621 | 3,844,243 | 366,550 | 598,744 | | | | |
| East India and Mauritius - - - - - — | 737,653 | 697,141 | Refined. | | 3,651,804 | 3,741,579 | 4,414,302 | 4,559,392 |
| Foreign - - - - - - - - - - - - - - - - — | 346,018 | 202,030 | 245,698 | 401,044 | | | | |
| Tallow - - - - - - - - - - - - - - - - - — | 1,115,427 | 1,397,407 | 39,245 | 19,068 | 1,090,765 | 1,160,180 | 171,605 | 182,998 |
| Tea - - - - - - - - - - - - - - - - - - — | 32,057,832 | 33,643,980 | 254,460 | 1,181,005 | 31,829,619 | 34,969,651 | 3,444,102 | 3,589,361 |
| Timber, viz. :— | | | | | | | | |
| Battens and batten ends - - - - - - — | 10,597 | 13,360 | 60 | 88 | 12,384 | 13,560 | 116,215 | 129,774 |
| Deal and deal ends - - - - great hund. | 55,798 | 67,105 | 1,098 | 860 | 57,291 | 62,808 | 521,494 | 601,914 |
| Masts 6 and under 8 inches in diameter - - - - - - - - - - - - - - No. | 9,169 | 10,223 | 484 | 269 | 8,756 | 9,595 | | |
| Masts 8 and under 12 inches in diameter - - - - - - - - - - - - - - — | 3,136 | 3,853 | 213 | 210 | 3,209 | 3,612 | 10,449 | 8,108 |
| Masts 12 inches and upwards - - lds. | 4,416 | 4,470 | 465 | 86 | 4,833 | 3,791 | | |
| Oak planks - - - - - - - - - - - - - — | 2,381 | 2,739 | 19 | 1 | 2,549 | 2,616 | 10,149 | 10,442 |
| Staves - - - - - - - - - - - - - gt. hund. | 63,896 | 86,855 | 3,081 | 2,634 | 65,480 | 83,186 | 43,386 | 36,756 |
| Fir, 8 inches square and upwards, loads | 466,694 | 489,466 | 910 | 624 | 481,523 | 493,200 | 437,629 | 440,300 |
| Oak, ditto - - - - - - - - - - - - - —— | 27,622 | 26,494 | 42 | 32 | 27,236 | 26,854 | 33,775 | 33,075 |
| Unenumerated, ditto - - - - - - - - —— | 32,484 | 41,769 | 90 | 34 | 33,111 | 40.352 | 8,308 | 10,170 |
| Wainscot logs, ditto - - - - - - - - —— | - - - - - | 3,031 | - - - - - - - | - - - - - - - | - - - - - - - | 3,269 | - - - - - - - | 8,867 |
| Tobacco, viz. :— | | | | | | | | |
| Unmanufactured - - - - - - - - - - lbs. | 22,082,579 | 38,517,861 | 8,060,562 | 12,980,951 | 20,502,971 | 21,048,324 | | |
| Manufactured or segars - - - - - - — | 386,609 | 959,882 | 210,914 | 273,360 | 143,856 | 145,385 | 3,140,085 | 3,223,648 |
| Snuff - - - - - - - - - - - - - - - - - — | 3,864 | 164 | 2,359 | 10,303 | 138 | 161 | | |
| Wool, sheep and lambs' - - - - - - - —— | 38,046,087 | 46,455,232 | 442,696 | 807,362 | 39,066,620 | 40,840,271 | 137,855 | 131,319 |
| Wine, viz. :— | | | | | | | | |
| Cape - - - - - - - - - - - - imp. galls. | 454,394 | 484,298 | 16,436 | 5,568 | 545,191 | 524,081 | 75,975 | 72,048 |
| French - - - - - - - - - - - - - - - —— | 275,366 | 363,376 | 99,540 | 128,506 | 232,550 | 260,630 | 63,165 | 71,131 |
| Portugal - - - - - - - - - - - - - - —— | 2,226,733 | 4,213,427 | 243,577 | 296,538 | 2,596,530 | 2,780,303 | | |
| Spanish - - - - - - - - - - - - - - - —— | 3,368,530 | 3,446,563 | 732,306 | 688,024 | 2,246,085 | 2,279,853 | 1,491,078 | 1,562,341 |
| Madeira - - - - - - - - - - - - - - - —— | 301,057 | 372,698 | 209,194 | 173,910 | 161,042 | 150,369 | | |
| Other sorts - - - - - - - - - - - - - —— | 817,761 | 885,754 | 312,245 | 346,575 | 426,372 | 485,308 | | |
| All sorts - - - - - - - - - —— | 7,443,841 | 9,766,116 | 1,613,298 | 1,639,121 | 6,207,770 | 6,480,544 | 1,629,219 | 1,705,529 |

IV. Account of the Shipping employed in the Trade and Navigation of the United Kingdom in 1834; specifying the Number and Tonnage of Vessels entering Inwards and clearing Outwards (including their repeated Voyages), and the Number of their Crews; separating British from Foreign Vessels; and distinguishing the Navigation with each Country.

| Countries. | Inwards. | | | | | | Outwards. | | | | | |
|---|---|---|---|---|---|---|---|---|---|---|---|---|
| | British. | | | Foreign. | | | British. | | | Foreign. | | |
| | *Ships.* | *Tons.* | *Men.* | *Ships.* | *Tons.* | *Men.* | *Ships.* | *Tons.* | *Men.* | *Ships.* | *Tons.* | *Men.* |
| Russia | 1,519 | 297,013 | 13,568 | 228 | 59,166 | 2,725 | 1,082 | 217,375 | 9,941 | 132 | 38,826 | 1,732 |
| Sweden | 103 | 15,353 | 764 | 183 | 35,910 | 1,731 | 101 | 15,278 | 770 | 125 | 22,174 | 1,051 |
| Norway | 63 | 6,403 | 398 | 618 | 98,303 | 5,139 | 44 | 4,177 | 283 | 642 | 107,809 | 5,406 |
| Denmark | 47 | 5,691 | 276 | 657 | 53,282 | 3,138 | 335 | 56,703 | 2,667 | 817 | 86,720 | 4,696 |
| Prussia | 193 | 32,021 | 1,506 | 557 | 118,111 | 5,081 | 155 | 25 609 | 1,216 | 425 | 88,396 | 3,817 |
| Germany | 701 | 115,278 | 5,502 | 544 | 45,471 | 2,552 | 719 | 117,964 | 5,669 | 586 | 48,865 | 2,721 |
| Holland | 1,011 | 137,546 | 6,684 | 646 | 67,230 | 3,667 | 877 | 120,584 | 5,847 | 597 | 64,214 | 3,891 |
| Belgium | 407 | 40,875 | 3,265 | 371 | 43,683 | 2,260 | 373 | 34,051 | 2,896 | 332 | 36,369 | 1,893 |
| France | 1,565 | 128,017 | 12,168 | 1,403 | 74,382 | 9,207 | 1,574 | 131,941 | 12,361 | 1,202 | 66,459 | 7,682 |
| Portugal, Proper | 514 | 59,0[illegible]5 | 3,492 | 36 | 4,539 | 322 | 508 | 61,618 | 3,832 | 90 | 16,833 | 895 |
| Azores | 165 | 12,338 | 753 | ..... | ..... | ..... | 165 | 12,493 | 848 | 2 | 261 | 26 |
| Madeira | 14 | 2,475 | 160 | ..... | ..... | ..... | 20 | 3,432 | 197 | | | |
| Spain and the Balearic Islands | 427 | 45,254 | 2,588 | 34 | 3,862 | 288 | 341 | 36,799 | 2,176 | 52 | 8,492 | 500 |
| Canary Islands | 36 | 3,830 | 198 | 1 | 104 | 6 | 34 | 3,711 | 196 | 1 | 92 | 8 |
| Gibraltar | 28 | 3,720 | 207 | ..... | ..... | ..... | 94 | 11,734 | 648 | 6 | 1,151 | 64 |
| Italy and Italian Islands | 387 | 58,142 | 3,218 | 63 | 14,380 | 799 | 473 | 71,076 | 3,943 | 60 | 12,947 | 703 |
| Malta | 8 | 1,063 | 67 | 1 | 156 | 9 | 80 | 12,022 | 645 | 6 | 984 | 61 |
| Ionian Islands | 62 | 8,469 | 462 | ..... | ..... | ..... | 42 | 5,753 | 306 | | | |
| Turkey & Continental Greece | 134 | 18,688 | 1,012 | 1 | 298 | 15 | 140 | 20,789 | 1,166 | 1 | 292 | 14 |
| Morea and Greek Islands | 16 | 2,311 | 121 | ..... | ..... | ..... | 10 | 1,158 | 69 | | | |
| Egypt | 6 | 1,124 | 57 | ..... | ..... | ..... | 24 | 5,067 | 299 | 1 | 260 | 14 |
| Tripoli, Barbary, & Morocco | 33 | 4,014 | 209 | ..... | ..... | ..... | 20 | 2,534 | 141 | 1 | 322 | 16 |
| Coast of Africa, from Morocco to the Cape of Good Hope | 137 | 32,313 | 1,763 | 5 | 452 | 48 | 151 | 35,533 | 2,091 | 4 | 640 | 35 |
| Cape of Good Hope | 27 | 5,566 | 330 | ..... | ..... | ..... | 47 | 9,145 | 530 | | | |
| Eastern Coast from the Cape of Good Hope to Babel Mandel | 1 | 138 | 7 | | | | | | | | | |
| Isle of Bourbon | ..... | ..... | ..... | ..... | ..... | ..... | 1 | 195 | 14 | | | |
| Cape de Verd Islands | ..... | ..... | ..... | ..... | ..... | ..... | 3 | 892 | 39 | | | |
| St. Helena and Ascension | 2 | 362 | 19 | ..... | ..... | ..... | 12 | 2,158 | 119 | | | |
| Mauritius | 75 | 20,909 | 1,073 | ..... | ..... | ..... | 33 | 9,192 | 490 | | | |
| Arabia | ..... | ..... | ..... | ..... | ..... | ..... | 2 | 587 | 28 | | | |
| East India Company's Territories, Singapore & Ceylon | 186 | 75,461 | 4,638 | ..... | ..... | ..... | 197 | 90,833 | 5,829 | | | |
| Sumatra | ..... | ..... | ..... | ..... | ..... | ..... | 1 | 279 | 21 | | | |
| China | 30 | 29,308 | 2,649 | ..... | ..... | ..... | 16 | 8,887 | 632 | 4 | 1,476 | 64 |
| Java | 5 | 1,901 | 99 | 2 | 584 | 31 | 11 | 2,766 | 161 | 4 | 1,623 | 76 |
| Philippine Islands | 6 | 1,586 | 85 | 1 | 372 | 18 | 3 | 728 | 46 | | | |
| Ports of Siam | ..... | ..... | ..... | ..... | ..... | ..... | 1 | 337 | 20 | | | |
| New South Wales | 42 | 12,400 | 672 | ..... | ..... | ..... | 90 | 29,567 | 1,756 | | | |
| British Northern Colonies | 1,905 | 524,606 | 23,270 | ..... | ..... | ..... | 1,880 | 503,393 | 23,315 | | | |
| British West Indies | 918 | 246,605 | 13,387 | ..... | ..... | ..... | 900 | 246,609 | 13,836 | | | |
| Hayti | 13 | 1,928 | 113 | ..... | ..... | ..... | 49 | 7,728 | 454 | 2 | 391 | 23 |
| Cuba, and other Foreign West Indies | 35 | 7,152 | 359 | 5 | 1,367 | 54 | 87 | 16,755 | 960 | 11 | 3,236 | 146 |
| United States | 281 | 94,658 | 4,078 | 402 | 204,529 | 8,417 | 387 | 133,754 | 6,217 | 546 | 220,913 | 9,261 |
| Mexico | 35 | 6,893 | 366 | 2 | 490 | 23 | 29 | 5,502 | 314 | 2 | 490 | 24 |
| Guatemala | 2 | 272 | 17 | | | | | | | | | |
| Colombia | 36 | 7,459 | 414 | ..... | ..... | ..... | 18 | 3,820 | 203 | | | |
| Brazils | 140 | 29,371 | 1 515 | 3 | 508 | 26 | 176 | 41,154 | 2,101 | 3 | 854 | 42 |
| States of Rio de la Plata | 52 | 10,120 | 526 | ..... | ..... | ..... | 48 | 9,206 | 513 | 3 | 820 | 41 |
| Chili | 27 | 6,341 | 358 | 4 | 1,074 | 55 | 28 | 6,532 | 385 | | | |
| Peru | 15 | 2,768 | 167 | ..... | ..... | ..... | 11 | 2,176 | 135 | | | |
| The Whale Fisheries | 107 | 34,161 | 3,993 | ..... | ..... | ..... | 99 | 33,014 | 4,275 | | | |
| Isles of Guernsey, Jersey, and Man | 2,380 | 146,543 | 10,103 | 37 | 5,652 | 286 | 2,141 | 122,365 | 8,841 | 2 | 249 | 14 |
| Greenland (Ice) | 7 | 802 | 51 | ..... | ..... | ..... | 2 | 231 | 16 | | | |
| Foreign parts (not distinguished) | ..... | ..... | ..... | ..... | ..... | ..... | 5 | 1,169 | 47 | 164 | 20,669 | 913 |
| Totals | 13,903 | 2,298,263 | 126,727 | 5,894 | 833,905 | 45,897 | 13,639 | 2,296,325 | 129,504 | 5,823 | 852,827 | 45,829 |

# CHAPTER V.

## DENMARK.

**Denmark** is an ancient kingdom, formerly very powerful, holding sway over the surrounding regions, and, as a predatory state, the terror of all Europe. Though now reduced to the secondary rank, her situation renders her of importance in the general system of the Continent.

### Sect. I.—*General Outline and Aspect.*

Denmark consists mainly of an extensive peninsula, shooting out from the north-west corner of Germany, and a cluster of large islands to the east of the peninsula. The northern shores of Denmark approach close to the southern point of the Scandinavian peninsula, bounding the great interior sea of the Baltic. She commands the only channel by which the countries around this sea can transmit their products to the rest of Europe; a circumstance which gives her some consideration as a maritime state, at the same time that the toll she imposes on ships passing and repassing the Sound, is productive of revenue. The Danish peninsula is termed Jutland; and the islands in the interior of the Baltic, interposed between Jutland and Scandinavia, are Zealand, Funen, Odensee, and a few others of smaller note. Denmark holds also the German territories of Sleswick and Holstein; with Iceland, the Faroe Islands, and some settlements on the coast of Greenland, remnants of her former maritime power.

The extent of the dominions of a country broken into such a variety of detached portions can with difficulty be estimated. The only compact mass consists of Jutland, Sleswick

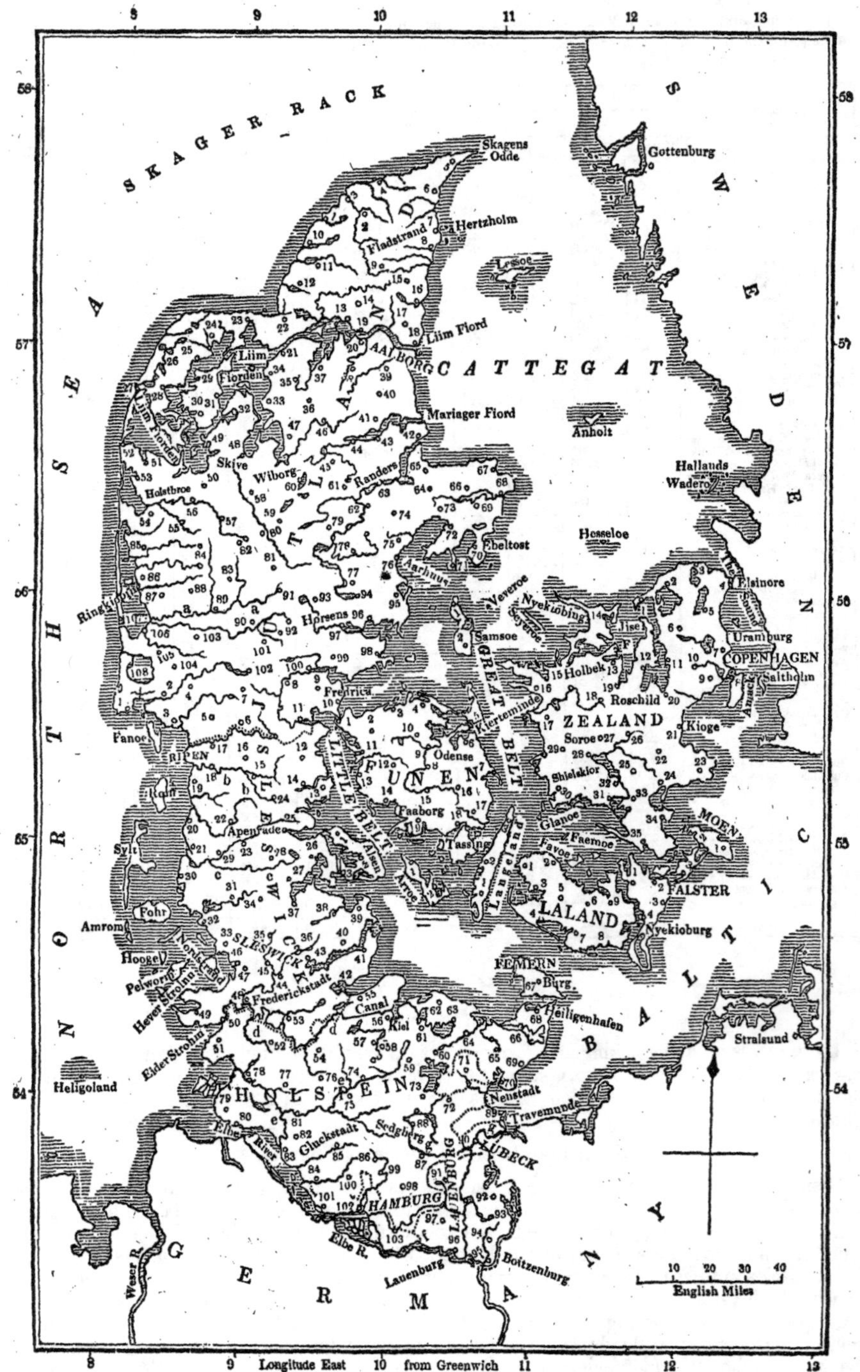
SKAGER RACK
Skagens Odde
Gottenburg
SWEDEN
Hertzholm
Fladstrand
Lessoe
Liim Fiord
Liim Fiorden
AALBORG
CATTEGAT
Mariager Fiord
Anholt
Skive
Wiborg
Randers
Holstbroe
Hallands Wadero
Hesseloe
Ebeltost
Aarhuus
Veveroe
Nyekiobing
Elsinore
Ringkiobing
Horsens
Samsoe
GREAT BELT
Uraniburg
COPENHAGEN
Saltholm
Holbek
Roschild
Fredrica
Kiertemunde
ZEALAND
Kioge
Fanoe
RIPEN
Odense
FUNEN
Soroe
Shielskior
LITTLE BELT
Faaborg
Tassing
Glanoe
Femoe
MOEN
Apenrade
Sylt
Alsen
Arroe
Langeland
Favoe
FALSTER
LALAND
Nyekioburg
Fohr
Amrom
SLESWICK
Hooge
Pelworm
Nordstrand
Hever Strohm
FEMERN
Burg
Frederickstadt
Canal
Kiel
Heiligenhafen
BALTIC
Elder Strohm
Stralsund
Heligoland
HOLSTEIN
Neustadt
Travemunde
Gluckstadt
Sedgberg
LUBECK
Elbe River
HAMBURG
LAUENBURG
Elbe R.
Lauenburg
Boitzenburg
Weser R.
GERMANY
NORTH SEA
English Miles
Longitude East from Greenwich

and Holstein; bounded on the west and north by the North Sea or German Ocean; on the east by the sounds which form the entrance of the Baltic; on the south by the Elbe. This tract lies generally between 53½° and 57½° north latitude, and 8° and 11° east longitude. We have thus a length of 280 miles, and a breadth of 120. The total area of the Danish monarchy, is about 22,000 square miles.

The surface of Denmark is nearly flat; forming, with the exception of Holland, the lowest part of the great plain of Northern Germany. The islands, in particular, in many places, rise only a few feet above the level of the sea. The soil, as in the rest of this plain, is frequently sandy and marshy; the climate humid, though not liable to those severe frosts which prevail in the interior of Scandinavia. Hence it affords good pasturage, and its soil is favourable to the growth of the coarser species of grain.

The waters of Denmark consist chiefly of its numerous sounds and bays; the Skager-rack, which comes in from the North Sea, and separates Jutland from Norway; the Categat, which, running southward nearly at right angles to the Skagerrack, separates that peninsula from Sweden; the Sound, a narrow strait at the extremity of the Cattegat, between Zealand and Sweden, and which forms the main entrance into the Baltic. The insular and peninsular character of her territory gives Denmark an extent of coast which certainly does not fall short of 600 miles; and there is said to be no part of the land more than ten miles distant from the sea. This structure leaves no room for the formation of any rivers of the least consequence, except the Eyder in Holstein, and the canal of Kiel, by which an important communication is formed between the ocean and the Baltic. Jutland contains a number of shallow but extensive lakes, closely bordering on the sea, with which they in many places communicate, and may hence be regarded as bays.

## Sect. II.—*Natural Geography.*

### Subsect. 1.—*Geology.*

*Denmark.* The geology of this low and flat country has not been completely ascertained. As far as is known at present, it contains neither primitive nor transition rocks: the only secondary deposits are Weald clay, and the various members of the chalk formation; both of which are generally covered up with tertiary soils; which, in their turn, are as deeply covered

---

*References to the Map of Denmark.*

NORTH PART.
1. Lykenshuus
2. Hioring
3. Harshals
4. Toersted
5. Skagen
6. Aalbek
7. Fladstrand
8. Sœbye
9. Bottergaard
10. Blokhuus
11. Tolstrup
12. Thuse
13. Byslet
14. Biersted
15. Vaar
16. Altz
17. Ulsted
18. Hals
19. Sundbye
20. Aalborg
21. Logstor
22. Kollerup
23. Kiorup Præstegaard
24. Kolbye Herrugaard
25. Tisted
26. Forbye
27. Agger
28. Visbye
29. Sundby
30. Rested
31. Nykiobing
32. Hierk
33. Strandbye
34. Malle
35. Gundersted
36. Aars
37. Bisley
38. Elleshoy
39. Kongsley
40. Siem
41. Vive
42. Sodringholm
43. Mariager
44. Hobroe
45. Isindum
46. Boldrup
47. Ulbierg
48. Skive
49. Kaas
50. Borbeirg
51. Lemvig
52. Harboe Ore
53. Nees
54. Ulborg
55. Vringelberg
56. Holstbroe
57. Hodsager
58. Sorup
59. Knudstrup Over
60. Wiborg
61. Skierne
62. Laurberg
63. Randers
64. Horning
65. Oersted
66. Ulstrup
67. Gierild
68. Greenaae
69. Alboge
70. Ebeltost
71. Helgenaes
72. Agrie
73. Thorsager
74. Hornslet
75. Skeibye
76. Aarhuus
77. Dover
78. Dallerup
79. Midstrup
80. Agerskov
81. Engisvang
82. Sunds
83. Arenburg
84. Noromme
85. Sondervang
86. Rinkioping
87. Dijberglund
88. Herningsholm
89. Faurgaard
90. Brandholm
91. Snee
92. Give
93. Grendstrup
94. Scanderborg
95. Tvenstrup
96. Haldrup
97. Horsens
98. Aastrup
99. Engum
100. Veile
101. Ringgive
102. Greene
103. Oddam
104. Frostrupgaard
105. Lundage
106. North Bork
107. Haureig
108. Kiergaard

SOUTH PART.
1. Hoe
2. Varde
3. Jerne
4. Hodde
5. Giording
6. Folding
7. Vaarbase
8. Odsted
9. Smidstrup
0. Frederica
11. Colding
12. Christiansfelde
13. Aaroe
14. Hadersleben
15. Gram
16. Hyam
17. Hiortland
18. Ripen
19. Reisbye
20. Ballum
21. Hoyer
22. Lygum Kloster
23. Hoist
24. Schrudstrup
25. Apenrade
26. Gravenstein
27. Holebul
28. Ucke
29. Tonder
30. Embsbull
31. Leck
32. Ockkolm
33. Bredstedt
34. Medelburg
35. Jorl
36. Arenholt
37. Flensborg
38. Steerup
39. Gelting
40. Kappel
41. Windemark
42. Eckernforde
43. Sleswick
44. Hollingstede
45. Treya
46. Husum
47. Mildsted
48. Frederickstadt
49. Garding
50. Tonningen
51. Weslingburen
52. Tellingstedt
53. Rendsburg
54. Barloch
55. Schnelm
56. Kiel
57. Rumor
58. Reesdorf
59. Preetz
60. Ploen
61. Stesen
62. Krokan
63. Dransan
64. Lutgenburg
65. Halendorf
66. Oldenburg
67. Burg
68. Heiligenhafen
69. Gromniz
70. Neustadt
71. Eutin
72. Sarau
73. Schamersdorf
74. Neumunster
75. Wildenscharen
76. Ostersted
77. Gribbom
78. Meldorf
79. Marne
80. Brunsbuttel
81. Itzehoe
82. Krempe
83. Gluckstadt
84. Uetersen
85. Barmstedt
86. Hohenhorst
87. Oldesloh
88. Sedgberg
89. Travemunde
90. Lubeck
91. Labenz
92. Sterley
93. Gudow
94. Greven
95. Boitzenburg
96. Lauenburg
97. Stunau
98. Wolhorn
99. Lemsal
100. Pinneberg
101. Wedel
102. Hamburg
103. Bergedor

*Rivers.*
a Skiern
b Gielst
c Widaw
d Eyder
e Stor
f Elbo
g Trave

LAALAND.
1. Fredericksdal
2. Raunsholt
3. Nakskov
4. Skibbelunde
5. Ryde
6. Marieboe
7. Rodbye
8. Nyested
9. Saxkioping

FALSTER.
1. Onslev
2. Slubbekioping
3. Karleby
4. Nyekioping

MOEN.
1. Mondemark
2. Steege
3. Phanefiord

ZEALAND.
1. Tomnaerup
2. Ramlos
3. Gillelye
4. Elsinore
5. Fredensborg
6. Slangerup
7. Lyngbye
8. Copenhagen
9. Golstrup
10. Ballerup
11. Gylling
12. Krobbesholm
13. Holbek
14. Nyekioping
15. Egemark
16. Callundborg
17. Giorlov
18. Undlose
19. Aagerup
20. Roschild
21. Kioge
22. Ottestrup
23. Tryggevelde
24. Ruholte
25. Glumsoe
26. Ringsted
27. Soroe
28. Antvorskov
29. Slagelse
30. Shielskiov
31. Saltoeslot
32. Vallensved
33. Nestved
34. Proestoe
35. Wordingborg

SAMSOE.
1. Nordbye
2. Selveg

FUNEN.
1. Middelfarth
2. Indslov
3. Bogensee
4. Bederslov
5. Kierteminde
6. Ronkebye
7. Nyborg
8. Bellinge
9. Odense
10. Broebye
11. Hunsbye
12. Oersted
13. Assens
14. Dreslette
15. Sallinge
16. Risling
17. Gudbier
18. Svendborg
19 Faaborg

ALSEN.
1. Nordburg
2. Augustenburg
3. Sonderburg

ARROE.
1. Soebye
2. Kioping

LANGELAND.
1. Humble K
2. Rudkiobing
3. Stoense

with diluvium of sand, and calcareous loam; which latter are occasionally concealed by newer alluvial deposits.

*Iceland.* This island, so far as is known to geologists, is entirely composed of ignigenous rocks. These are of two classes; viz. Plutonian and volcanic. The Plutonian formations are *greenstone*, and its accompanying rocks, and *basalt*, with its associated tuffas, amygdaloids, &c. Of all the rocks of the trap series, amygdaloid is that which contains the greatest variety of minerals; and of these the zeolites and calcareous spars are the most interesting and beautiful. The volcanic rocks exhibit the usual characters, and in Iceland are spread around in vast abundance.

*Faroe Islands.* This small insular group consists of seventeen large inhabited islands, and of many smaller, with and without inhabitants. In none of the inhabited islands are the most elevated summits lower than 1000 feet; the highest land is in the island of Osteroe, which rises to fully 2,800 feet above the level of the sea. The two prevailing rocks are *greenstone* (dolerite) and *claystone*. The greenstone is sometimes basaltic, sometimes porphyritic, or amygdaloidal. The claystone is red, yellow, brown, and green. It alternates with the greenstone, in beds of varying thickness. The beds of greenstone and claystone of the group all incline or dip towards a central point of the group, rendering it probable that the islands are but portions of one whole. The upper surface of the greenstone is slaggy, showing that the mass had been in a state of igneous solution. There are two principal varieties of greenstone; one porphyritic, with crystals of glassy felspar, the other without the porphyritic structure. In some of the islands there are beds of *pitchcoal*, associated with fire clay, slate clay, and sphærosiderite, resting upon the trap, and covered by it. The beds of greenstone and slate clay are often traversed by veins or dikes of basaltic and porphyritic greenstone, which, however, do not appear to occasion any change in them; but the greenstones are changed in position and direction by the invasion from below of a conglomerated rock, a kind of trap tuffa. The trap rocks of the Faroes have been long celebrated, on account of the splendid zeolites they afford: some species of this beautiful family appear to be daily forming. The chloropœrite, peridote, and precious opal are also productions of this insular group.

### Subsect. 2.—*Botany.*

*Denmark* and *Sweden*, *Norway* and *Lapland*, the *Faroe Islands*, and *Iceland*,—the latter giving a name, indeed to a plant equally common in the other countries, Lichen islandicus, or Iceland Moss, (*fig.* 224.),—may be considered under one head, so far as regards their vegetable productions; for it is difficult to draw an exact line of demarcation, and even of these the very nature of our work does not allow us to treat much at large: this is the less to be regretted, because the classical works of Linnæus and Wahlenberg are in the hands of every botanical student; and they contain a mine of valuable information in the *Flora Lapponica* and *Suecica* of both these authors, and a fund of interesting and delightful narrative in the *Lachesis Lapponica* of the great Swedish naturalist. The various writings of Œder, Vahl, and Hornemann afford much useful matter relative to the plants of Denmark. The vegetation of a great portion of these countries may be considered the same as that of the more northern and mountainous parts of Great Britain. Yet as the northern regions of the continent of Europe present an alpine and arctic vegetation, in a much more perfect degree than islands, we should scarcely do justice to our subject, did we not offer some remarks on the distribution of the vegetable productions of a portion of that more interesting and extreme northern European territory; namely Lapland. The natural boundaries of this country are formed by some low mountains, about 500 feet in height, at a distance of from five to eight Swedish miles from the extremity of the Gulf of Bothnia. They present no naked summits, but are covered with forests of Spruce Fir* (*fig.* 225.): these may be considered as the last subalpine range in northern Europe. Commencing in the south-east, a little beyond the lake Kemistrask, in lat. 67°, it tends towards Upper Tornea, and near to Ofover Calix in the west; stretches south to Edifers, in Lulea; and reaches its southernmost point at the Tafvelsjon, in Umean Lapland, lat. 64°. This mountain chain exhibits Calla palustris (*fig.* 226.), (a plant of a poisonous family, closely allied to the Arum maculatum or Wake-robin, and to the Caladium esculentum of the tropics; and, as with them, a kind of bread called Missenbröd, or the bread of famine, is made by the Laplanders from the roots); Sweet gale*, common Speedwell*, Ox-eye*, Meadow Fescure-grass*, and Carex stellulata*. The Birch* there produces its leaves in the beginning of June.

224

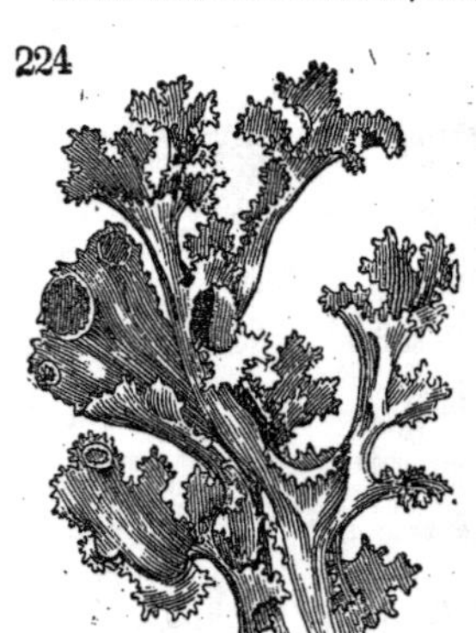
Iceland Moss.

* The names marked with an asterisk are those of plants found also in Britain.

The inferior and woody district of Lapland has its upper limit at Sondankyla in Kemean Lapland, between Kengis and Munoniska in Tornea, at Jockmock in Lulea, and at Falstrak, in Umean Lapland; and it yields, besides the Spruce Fir, the Meadow Trefoil, the Lysimachia thyrsiflora*, Lily of the Valley*, and White Water Lily*, which grow abundantly Some plants which are peculiarly subalpine begin to appear, as Tofieldia palustris* and Serratula alpina*.

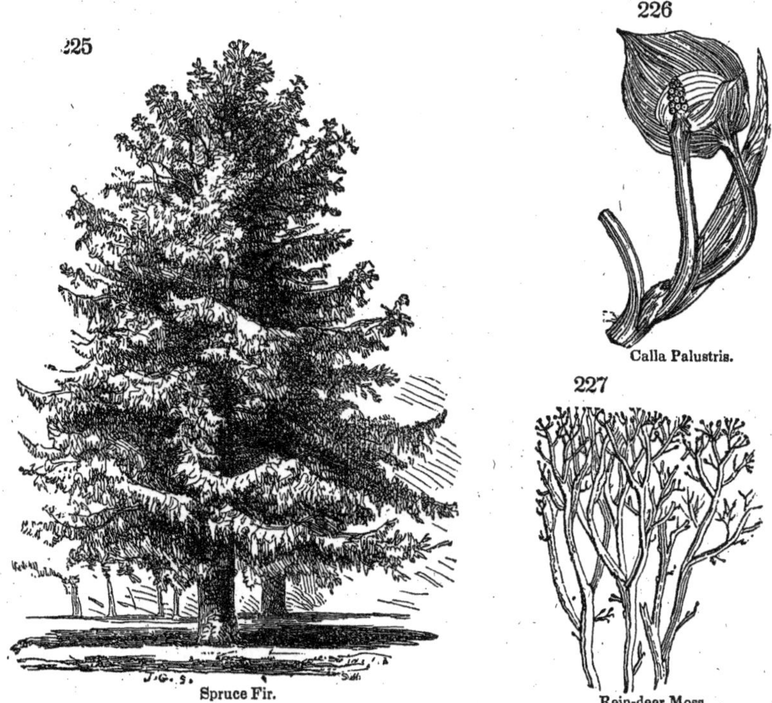


Spruce Fir.

Calla Palustris.

Rein-deer Moss.

The upper woody district is distinguished by the absence of the last-mentioned plants; but the forests of spruce still abound. Where the Spruce ceases, in places of warm exposure, the upper limit of this region is indicated. Its boundary in Kemean, Tornean, and Pitean Lapland, is more distinctly marked, because the country is flatter, and destitute of deep valleys; but in such situations, in Lulea and Umea, the Spruce Fir approaches nearer to the Alps, and the sides of the mountains are covered with it. There its utmost northern limits are found to be at Kyro, near the great lake of Enare, in lat. 69° north. Here, too, is the most northern boundary of many well-known plants, such as Trifolium repens*, Festuca rubra*, Rumex aquaticus*, the Yellow Water Lily*, and several other aquatics. Many alpine plants commence, as Salix glauca*, extending south to the middle of this region, Salix hastata*, confined to the north, and Bartsia alpina*, with Lychnis alpina*, on the banks of the streams. The culture of barley still succeeds; but scarcely beyond this line.

The subalpine mountains in this region are very dry and remarkably gravelly and stony; abounding in that plant which Linnæus has so beautifully described, in his *Flora Lapponica*, as the main support of the Rein-deer, and consequently of the Laplander, Lichen Rangiferinus* (*fig.* 227.), or Rein-deer Moss. Ill could the Laplander subsist without the supplies afforded by that useful animal; it is his sole wealth. Almost the only winter food of this serviceable animal is the moss, which the deer are so fond of, that though it is commonly buried at that season under a great depth of snow, yet, by scratching with their feet, and digging with their antlers, they never fail to get at it. In short, without this lichen, both the reindeer and the Laplander must perish. "Thus," adds Linnæus, "things which are often deemed the most insignificant and contemptible by ignorant men, are, by the good providence of God, made the means of the greatest blessings to his creatures." Linnæus assures us that this lichen grows so luxuriantly in Lapland, as to be found sometimes a foot in height.

But as the hills scarcely rise to the limits of perpetual snow, about 200 or 300 feet higher than the woods are found, they are fertile in such plants as flourish in a dry and barren soil, viz., Menziesia cærulea*, Arbutus alpina*, Juncus trifidus*, Lycopodium alpinum*, Azalea procumbens,* and, though rarely, Diapensia lapponica. Here the Lichen tartareus (*fig.* 228.) or Cudbear, abounds, and is, both here and in Sweden and Norway, collected and exported to the dye-manufacturers. Wahlenberg distinguishes by the term "Regio subsylvatica," or partially wooded region, that where the Scotch Fir grows, but not the Spruce. This is more contracted than the other regions, and more difficult to be defined. It is not unfrequently eight Swedish miles broad in northern Lapland; in Kemea extending to nearly 70° of lat. Before the Scotch Fir ceases, the Carex globularis disappears, and, in the more northern parts, Prunella vulgaris. Within the Fir region, the beautiful Pedicularis lapponica appears scattered through the woods; Viola bifolia, and Thalictrum alpinum* following the course of the streams; Salix lanata,* with its splendid golden catkins, at the margins of marshes and springs, and also Ranunculus lapponicus. The cultivation of barley scarcely succeeds, and the colonists are miserably poor. The Birch comes into leaf at the summer solstice. The lakes and rivers have an elevation of about 1000 feet above the level of the sea. The subalpine region still yields the Birch* (*Betula alba*), though other trees will not grow. Its upper boundary is marked by the dwarf stature of these, where they scarcely attain a height of six feet. The Aspen* (*populus tremula*) and the Bird-cherry (*Prunus Padus*) cease before the Birch: the Sorbus Aucuparia,* or Mountain Ash, extends as far. The Birch always in Lapland reaches to a much greater elevation and more northern latitude than the Scotch and Spruce Firs. Its limits are more easily determined; yet, on a geographical map, they are with difficulty expressed, because the Birch ascends to the alpine regions, circumscribes all the mountains, and penetrates all the lesser valleys: thus it extends almost to lat. 71° in Western Finmark, and stops but little short of the North Cape. The dry portion of this region is again the habitation of the Lichen rangiferinus, and of Azalea procumbens,* Luzula spicata,* and Juncus trifidus.* On the borders of Russia, the Birch as well as the Scotch Fir extend even to the Northern Ocean.

228

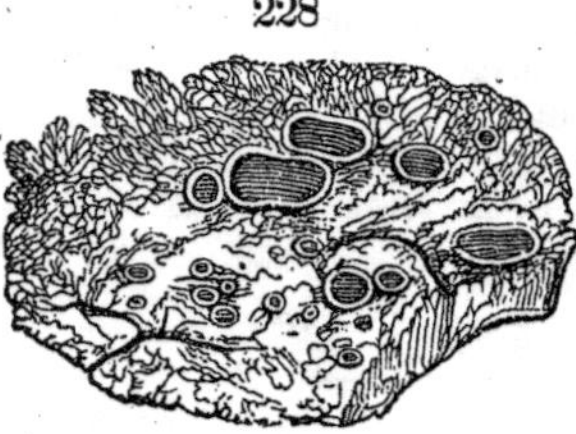

Cudbear.

The lower alpine region, or the Lower Alps, commence where the Birch ceases to exist, and where the snow, not of perennial duration, except in caves and hollows, melts before the middle of July. There the Diapensia lapponica, Silene acaulis,* and Andromeda hypnoides are found. The Salix myrsinites* and Dwarf Birch still grow erect. Nearly the same vegetation as is met with on the Lower Alps exists upon the maritime alps of Finmark, to the most northern promontory, with this difference only, that the steep and precipitous rocks harbour more moisture and snow, and the affinity is greater with the alpine range in the higher mountains, which retain the snow during the whole summer, the partial melting of which creates a moist and even a boggy soil. Here, therefore, are seen the little Dwarf Willow* (*fig.* 229.) (*Salix herbacea,*) Ranunculus glacialis and nivalis, Pedicularis hirsuta and flammea, Stellaria biflora, Erigeron uniflorum;* plants eminently alpine, and peculiar to those situations.

229

Dwarf Willow.

Beyond these is the region of perpetual snow. Towards the Norwegian Ocean, another form of the alps presents itself; lofty mountains without any plains, circumscribed with very narrow zones, which Wahlenberg defines as *the more elevated sides* of the alps, reaching nearly to the limits of perpetual snow, consequently always irrigated with snow-water: they nourish a few, and those marshy, plants. The Ranunculi (Crowfoots) principally abound.

The lower, or less elevated, sides of the alps, generally destitute of perpetual snow, yield the Dwarf Birch* in the moister spots; and, on the drier, Andromeda hypnoides, the Alpine Speedwell*, Juncus bifidus*, and the Procumbent Azalea.*

The bases of the alps are where the Birch grows, but no Pines. Among the Birches, scarcely six feet high, the Purple alpine Saxifrage*, with Saxifraga nivalis and cernua, abound in the moist and precipitous places, and, in those that are more dry, Aspidium Lonchitis. The lower portion of this zone affords tall birches, such as are found in the more northern regions, only in the inmost recesses of the deep bays, and, beneath them, Aspidium Filix Mas*, Osmunda Struthiopteris, the Blue Alpine Sowthistle*, and the Red Currant.*

The maritime alps include the islands and promontories; so exposed to the winds that they derive their alpine character more from their peculiar situation than from their elevation above the level of the sea: and so bare are they of trees and shrubs, that even the Juniper will not succeed there. They are almost equally destitute of the more alpine shrubs, such as Andromedas; but they are adorned with succulent alpine plants, such as Saxifraga oppositifolia*, Silene acaulis*, and Dryas octopetala. Near the shore occur some productions of the alps of the south of Europe, such as Erigeron alpinum*, Sedum villosum* and Gentiana involucrata, which in Lapland are found nowhere inland. The Norwegian alps nourish numerous annual plants; but the dryer ones of Sweden, remote from the sea, are remarkable for the little alpine shrubs, particularly Azalea lapponica, which scarcely occurs in Norway; Salices alone, such as S. myrsinites*, occupying their place.

The subalpine spots and valleys are marked by the presence of the Pine; but the most extended Fir forests are only found at the heads of the deep inlets of the sea, in narrow ravines, sheltered by the loftiest mountains. These valleys enjoy a much milder climate than all the rest of Lapland: there are found the Convallaria verticillata*, Campanula latifolia* and Fragaria vesca*, in abundance; but no alpine plants will grow, except the Starry Saxifrage* (*Saxifraga stellaris*) along the margins of the rills.

A more interesting account of the vegetation of Lapland, at different elevations, is published by Sir J. E. Smith, in the Appendix to the ***Lachesis Lapponica*** of Linnæus. It is translated from the Swedish of Dr. Wahlenberg; his "Observations made with a view to determine the height of the Lapland Alps." (1.) On approaching the Lapponese mountains (*Fjäll*), we first reach the line where the Spruce Fir ceases to grow. This tree had previously assumed an unusual appearance; that of a tall slender pole, covered from the ground with short, drooping, dark branches: a gloomy object in these desolate forests! The Arctic Raspberry* (*fig.* 230.) (***Rubus arcticus***) had already, before we arrived at this point, ceased to bring its fruit to maturity. With the Spruce we lose the Cinnamon Rose (***Rosa cinnamomea****), and the Twin-leaved Solomon's Seal (***Convallaria bifolia***), &c.; and the borders of the lakes are stripped of their ornaments of Reeds (***Arundo Phragmites****), Lysimachia thyrsiflora*, Galium boreale*, and Carex globularis. Here is the true station of the Arctic Coltsfoot (***Tussilago nivea***). The last beaver-houses are seen in the rivulets; and no pike nor perch is to be found in the lakes higher up. The boundary of the Spruce Fir is 3200 feet below the line of perpetual snow, and the mean temperature 37° of Fahrenheit.

230

The Arctic Raspberry.

(2.) Scotch Firs* (***Pinus sylvestris***) are still found, but not near so tall as in the lower country. Their stems here are low, and their branches widely extended. Here are seen the last of Ledum palustre*, Salix pentandra*, Veronica serpyllifolia*, &c. The bogs have already a very sterile ppearance. Near the utmost boundary of the Scotch Fir grows Phaca alpina. Higher up, hardly any bears are to be met with; and the fruit of the Bilberry* does not ripen well. The Gwiniad and Grayling, two species of the Salmon tribe, soon after disappear from the lakes. The upper limit of this zone, at which the Scotch Firs cease, is 2800 feet below the line of perpetual snow, and the mean temperature about 36° Fahrenheit. A little short of this point, or about 3000 feet before we come to perpetual snow, Barley will not ripen; but small farms, the occupiers of which live by grazing and fishing, are met with as far as 400 feet higher; for instance, Naimaka in Enontekis, and so far also potatoes and turnips grow large enough to be worth cultivating.

(3.) Beyond this, the dwarf and stunted forests consist only of Birch.* Its short, thick stem, and stiff, widely-spreading, knotty branches, seem prepared to resist the strong winds from the Alps: its lively light green hue is delightful to the eye, but evinces a weakness of vegetation. The birch forests soon become so low, that they may be entirely commanded from the smallest eminence. Their uppermost boundary, where the tallest of them do not equal the height of a man, is 2000 feet below the line of perpetual snow. This zone is therefore much wider than the preceding. Long before its termination, the Alder* (***Alnus incana***), the Bird-cherry* (***Prunus Padus***), and the Aspen (***Populus tremula****), were no more to be seen. A little before the Birch ceases, we miss the Mountain Ash*, which for some time had not presented us with any fruit; the Arctic Bramble* (***Rubus arcticus***) was already likewise barren; the Ling* (***Erica vulgaris***), Aconitum Lycoctonum, &c. Where the birch forest becomes thinner, the reflection of the heat from the sides of the mountains is the strongest. Here, in many spots, we find the vegetation of Sonchus alpinus*, Struthiopteris, and Aconitum Lycoctonum remarkably luxuriant. The dryer spots now become covered with the Iceland Moss* (***Lichen rangiferinus***): Tussilago frigida and Pedicularis sceptrum-carolinum extend to the utmost boundary of the Birch. Thus far only the Char (***Salmo alpinus***) is found in the lakes, and higher up all fishing ceases.

(4.) All mountains above this limit are called Fjäll (alps). Near rivulets, and on the margin of bogs only, is found a little brushwood, consisting of Salix glauca*, whose gray hue affords but little ornament to the landscape. The lower country is covered with the dark-looking Dwarf Birch* (***Betula nana***), which still retains its upright position. A few Juniper bushes*, and some plants of Salix hastata*, are found scattered about. Every hill is covered with Arbutus alpina*, variegated with Andromeda cærulea*, and the Wintergreen*

(*Trientalis europæa*). The more boggy ground is decorated with Andromeda polifolia* in its greatest beauty, and Pedicularis lapponica. On the sides of the mountains, where the reflected heat bears most power, grow Veronica alpina*, Viola biflora*, Pteris crispa*, and Angelica archangelica.* This zone extends within 1400 feet of the line of perpetual snow. The glutton (*Mustela Gulo*) goes no higher than this. The berries of the Cloudberry (*Rubus Chamæmorus*) still ripen here, but not at a greater elevation.

(5.) Now no more brushwood is to be seen. The white Salix lanata* is not above two feet high, even about the rivulets, and Salix myrsinites* is of still humbler growth. The Dwarf Birch* occupies the dry spots, and creeps entirely upon the ground. The hills are clothed with the rather brown than green Azalea procumbens*, and A. lapponica, which give this zone its most peculiar feature. Verdant spots between the precipices, where the sun has the greatest power, produce Lychnis apetala*, Erigeron uniflorum*, Astragalus leontinus and montanus, with Ophrys alpina. In boggy places, Aira alpina*, Carex ustulata*, and Vaccinium uliginosum* are observable. The only berries, however, which ripen at this degree of elevation are those of the Crowberry* (*Empetrum nigrum*); but these are twice as large as what grow in the woodlands, and better flavoured. The upper boundary of this zone is 800 feet below the line of perpetual snow. The Laplanders scarcely ever fix their tents higher up, as the pasture for their reindeer ceases a very little way above this point. The mean temperature is about 34° Fahrenheit.

(6.) Next come the snowy Alps, where are patches of snow that never melt. The bare places between still produce a few dark shrubby plants, such as the Crowberry*, destitute, however of fruit; Andromeda tetragona and hypnoides, and Diapensia lapponica. Green precipices, exposed to the sun, are decorated with the vivid azure tints of Gentiana tenella and nivalis*, and Campanula uniflora, accompanied by the yellow Draba alpina. Colder and marshy situations, where there is no reflected heat, produce Pedicularis hirsuta, and Dryas octopetala.* This zone reaches to within 200 feet of the limits of perpetual and almost uninterrupted snow.

(7.) Beyond it, the eternal snows begin to cover the ground, and we soon arrive at a point where only a few dark spots are here and there to be seen. This takes place on the alps of Quickjock at the elevation of 4100 feet above the sea; but nearer the highest ridge, and particularly on the Norway side of that ridge, at 3100 feet. Some few plants with succulent leaves are thinly scattered over the spongy brown surface of the earth, where the reflected heat is strongest, quite up to the line of uninterrupted snow: these are Saxifraga stellaris*, rivularis*, and oppositifolia*; Ranunculus nivalis and glacialis; Rumex digynus*, Juncus arcuatus*, and Silene acaulis. The mean temperature, at the boundary of perpetual snow, is 32½° of Fahrenheit.

(8.) Above the line of perpetual snow, the cold is occasionally so much tempered, that a few plants of Ranunculus glacialis, and other similar ones, may now and then be found in the clefts of some dark rock rising through the snow. This happens even to the height of 500 feet above that line. Farther up, the snow is very rarely moistened, though some umbilicated Lichens (*Gyrophoræ*), &c. still occur in the crevices of perpendicular rocks, even 2000 feet above the line of never-melting snow. These are the extremes of vegetation, where the mean temperature seems to be 30° Fahrenheit. The Snow Bunting (*Emberiza nivalis*) is the only living being that visits this elevated spot.

SUBSECT. 3.—*Zoology*.

The native Zoology, in conjunction with that of Norway, has been ably illustrated by the celebrated Danish naturalist Müller, and shows that the fauna of those kingdoms is much richer than their northern and ungenial climate would lead us to imagine. The total number of land quadrupeds, including the domestic species, is forty-one. Among these we find the lynx, the glutton, the beaver, the leming, and the flying squirrel; together with four of the largest deer inhabiting Europe; namely, the elk, the stag, the rein-deer, and the fallow-deer.

The Elk (*Cervus Alces*) (*fig.* 231.) of Europe is not the same with the Moose-deer of America: it is found in Europe between latitude 53° and 65°: in size it is higher than a horse; and, to support the enormous weight of its horns, sometimes nearly fifty pounds, its neck is short, thick, and very strong. Its movements are rather heavy: it does not gallop, but ambles along, the joints cracking so much at every step, that the sound is heard to some distance. During winter it chiefly resides in hilly woods; but in summer it frequents swamps and the borders of lakes; often going deep into the water, to escape the stings of gnats, &c., and to feed without stooping. With its enormous horns it turns down branches of trees, to feed upon the bark, with great dexterity; and these are also used as shovels, to get at pasture when covered with snow. The young are so simple and fearless, that they will

231

The Elk.

suffer themselves to be taken by the hand. An unusually large elk, killed in Sweden, is said to have weighed 1200 lbs. These animals do not now appear to be employed in any domestic office.

The Wolverine, or Glutton, is one of those animals whose history has long been shrouded in fiction and romance. It is only now that its true habits have been given to the world, by that enterprising traveller, Dr. Richardson. The Wolverine of America, generally considered the same with the European Glutton, feeds chiefly upon beasts that have been accidentally killed; but it will hunt smaller animals, as meadow-mice, marmots, &c. and occasionally attack disabled animals of a larger size. In its gait it resembles the bear; and, although not fleet, is very industrious. Mr. Graham observes, that it does more damage to the small fur trade than all the other rapacious animals conjointly; as it will follow the martin-hunter's path round a line of traps extending sixty miles, and render the whole unserviceable, merely to get at the baits. Yet it flies from the face of man, and may be killed with a stick. Its total length is not more than two feet and a half.

The Birds, according to Müller, amount to 232 species: the greater part of these are common to the northern countries of Europe; but the Mocking Jay (*Corvus infaustus* Lin.) (*fig.* 232.), and the Nutcracker (*Nucifraga caryocatactes*) are unknown in Britain and more southern latitudes: the bill of the latter is shaped much like that of a woodpecker, and is said to be used for breaking the shells of nuts: whence its name. The species of fish, from the maritime nature of the region, are numerous.

The Mocking Jay.

*Domestic animals.* It appears that the breeds called the lesser and greater Danish Dogs are much more common in other countries than in that from which they have been named. The horses and cattle are of very large-sized breeds, generally called the Holstein. The greatest number of oxen seem to be bred in Jutland: they are fattened, during summer, in the rich marshes of Holstein, and driven, in the autumn, to Hamburg.

### Sect. III.—*Historical Geography.*

During the early period of the middle ages, the swarms of pirates sent forth by Denmark spread desolation and terror to the remotest extremities of Europe. Canute king of Denmark even ascended the English throne in 1017. Denmark, at the same time, carried on frequent wars against the contiguous districts of Germany and Poland, and often held sway over large portions of them. But her most brilliant era was the reign of Margaret of Waldemar, surnamed the Semiramis of the North, who, by her courage, popularity, and address, succeeded in effecting the union of Calmar, which placed on her head, and on that of her nephew Eric, the crown of the three northern kingdoms of Denmark, Sweden, and Norway.

The decline of Denmark began in the thirteenth century, under the violent and tyrannical reign of Christian I. The sanguinary course by which he sought to punish an insurrection of the Swedes roused all the dormant spirit of that brave people, who found a deliverer in Gustavus Vasa, and were finally freed from the Danish yoke. During the two following centuries, Sweden, led to victory by a succession of heroic monarchs, rose to the highest pitch of military glory; while Denmark, always defeated, was stripped of many of her most important territories, and sunk into the rank of a secondary state. Still she successfully cultivated maritime commerce and shipping, and obtained some valuable possessions in the East and West Indies.

In the great crisis produced by the conquests of Napoleon, Denmark was thrown into an unfortunate predicament. Placed, as it were, at the point of collision between France and Russia, she could with difficulty escape being crushed between them. Circumstances of peculiar hardship threw her into the arms of France, to whose cause she adhered, and at the great contest which ended in the downfall of Napoleon, she became a victim. First, she was deprived of Norway, that it might be ceded to Sweden, and that Russia might retain Finland. Denmark received in return Swedish Pomerania as an inadequate compensation. Next, she was required to exchange Pomerania for Lauenburg, a territory of still inferior extent and value; but, as it borders on Sleswick and Holstein, it has rendered her dominion more compact, and extended her frontier to the Elbe, so that she is perhaps rather a gainer by the exchange.

### Sect. IV.—*Productive Industry.*

The agriculture of Denmark is conducted under considerable disadvantages both of climate and soil. The climate, though not subject to severe frost or intense cold, is chill and damp; and the land consists in a great measure of sand and marsh. Every part of the kingdom, however, is capable of some cultivation, and occasional tracts of luxuriant fertility occur Such are the islands of Zealand Laaland, and Falster; and, in a still greater degree, the sea-coast of Sleswick and Holstein; for the interior is arid and sandy. The industry of the peasant in Denmark Proper suffers many severe checks; he has been but recently emancipated from personal bondage, and is still subjected to many feudal usages. Life-leases, under which the payment is made in produce or personal services, are common. The proprietors are generally embarrassed, and unable to expend much on the improvement of their lands. The farmers of Holstein and Sleswick carry on the process of cultivation with great skill and activity. The chill moisture of the climate is less favourable to the cultivation of wheat than of barley, rye, and oats; all of which afford a large surplus for exportation. The rearing of cattle is also an extensive branch of industry, though too little attention has been paid to the improvement of the breeds, unless on the west coast of Sleswick, on whose moist and rich meadows is produced what bears a high reputation under the name of "Hamburg beef." Over all Denmark, the produce of the dairy forms the basis of a large export trade.

The manufactures of Denmark are extremely rude, and consist chiefly in working up the flax and wool of the country in a coarse form for domestic use. A great proportion also of the wool is exported. Government have employed great efforts to raise Denmark to the rank of a manufacturing country; and some fabrics in the different kinds of cloth, brandy, sugar-refining, &c., have, under its patronage, been set on foot in the large towns; but these are all languishing, and with difficulty support foreign competition.

The commerce of Denmark is in a more active state than the other branches of industry; though it is still not such as to give her a prominent place among the powers of Europe. The basis consists in the exportation of its raw produce. The grain exported from Jutland and the islands, at an average of seven years to 1827, amounted to 29,000 quarters of wheat; 141,000 quarters of rye; 190,000 quarters of barley; 43,000 quarters of oats. The rye was chiefly exported to Norway, to be used as bread-corn, and the barley to be employed in distillation. The value of these articles amounted, in 1825, to $2,300,000. That of butter and cheese exported was, in the same year, $1,300,000. Holstein and Sleswick, called the duchies, exported at an average also of seven years, 78,000 quarters of wheat; 55,000 of rye; 75,000 of barley; 130,000 of oats. The value of butter, cheese, and salted meat, is still greater. Denmark, from its situation between the northern and middle states, has a considerable carrying trade of the bulky articles produced by the former; and has also a good deal of ship-building. Both the whale and herring fisheries are likewise carried on to some extent.

## SECT. V.—*Political Geography.*

The constitution of Denmark, originally founded on the basis of the most complete feudal independence, to the extent of rendering the monarchy itself elective, underwent a complete change in 1660, when Frederick III. had the address to obtain an act by which the crown was declared hereditary, and himself invested with supreme and absolute power. The sway of the Danish princes has, however, been exceedingly mild and popular, and their despotic power exerted in a manner beneficial to the people, as it limited the oppressive rights exercised by the nobles. These, however, continue to be extremely obnoxious; and it is only within a very few years that the body of the people were emancipated from a state of personal slavery. The nobles are few in number, consisting only of one duke, nineteen counts, and twelve barons. The king himself presides at the supreme national tribunal.

The revenue amounts to from about $7,500,000 to $8,000,000. There is a nominal debt of $75,000,000; but the interest paid upon it is small.

The military and naval establishments are on a scale suited to a greater country than what remains of Denmark. The army is kept up to nearly 40,000 regular troops and 60,000 militia. The navy has not recovered from the severe shock which it received during the last war: at present it consists of six ships of the line, six frigates, and four corvettes, besides smaller vessels. The sailors being all registered, no difficulty is ever found in manning the navy.

## SECT. VI.—*Civil and Social State.*

The population of the Danish dominions in 1832, amounted to 2,049,000; of which 1,540,000 were in its ancient domain of the islands Jutland and Sleswick; 404,000 in Holstein; 40,000 in Lauenburg; 51,000 in Iceland; 14,000 in Greenland and the Faroe Islands.*

*National character.* The Danes are generally quiet, tranquil, and industrious. The inhabitants of the towns, who are chiefly engaged in trade, have a great share of the patient, thrifty, and persevering habits of the Dutch. The peasantry, poor and oppressed, are beginning, however, to raise their heads; and the nobles, no longer addicted to those rude and

* The Danish colonies are Christiansborg and other stations in Guinea, with 44,000 inhabitants; Santa Cruz St. Thomas, and St. John in the West Indies, with 47,000; and Tranquebar and factories on the Coromandel coast, in the East Indies, with 60,000.—AM. ED.

daring pursuits which rendered them once so formidable, live much in the style of opulent proprietors in other European countries.

The Lutheran religion was early and zealously adopted in Denmark, to the extent, indeed, of granting toleration to no other; but the liberal principles now diffused throughout Europe, have made their way fully into that country. Science was at one era somewhat brilliantly patronised in Denmark. The observatory at Orienbaum was the theatre of many of the most important modern observations; and Tycho Brahe ranks as one of the fathers of modern astronomy. Œlenschlager and other writers have introduced a school of poetry and dramatic literature, founded upon that of the modern German. The government has bestowed a laudable attention on the general education of its people, and has even passed a law, requiring every child, of a certain age, to be sent to school. The schools, on the plan of mutual instruction, amounted, in 1829, to 2500, and more were in progress; there are also 3000 grammar and parish schools.

### Sect. VII.—*Local Geography.*

The local divisions of continental Denmark present little variety in consequence of the uniformity of its surface, and the small number of considerable cities. Its divisions are Zealand and the other islands; Jutland, Sleswick, Holstein, Lauenburg; with the remote territories of Iceland, Greenland, and the Faroe Islands.

*Zealand* is a flat, fertile, and extensive island, separated from Funen by the Great Belt, and from Sweden by the Sound. Including the capital, and chief seats of trade, it forms the most important part of the Danish dominions.

*Copenhagen*, (*fig.* 233.), (in Danish, Kiobenhafn, or the "merchant port,") the capital of Denmark, is situated on the east coast of Zealand, with the island of Amak oppposite to it, and several little lakes in its vicinity. Its walls enclose a circuit of five miles, a great part of which, however, is covered with open spaces, and with the harbour and docks. The houses, with a few exceptions, are built of brick, plastered over, and painted in different colours. The number of inhabitants is about 115,000; the houses are lofty, and contain many families in each. The city is divided into three parts; the old town, which contains the greater part of the population; the new town, in which are all the finest edifices; and the port, or Christian's Haven. In the midst of the principal square is the bronze statue of Frederick V., weighing 45,000 lbs. This square, with the adjoining one called the King's Mark Place, surrounded by the palace of Charlottenborg, the theatre, the principal hotel, and other stately buildings, forms the handsomest part of Copenhagen. The cathedral was destroyed during the bombardment by the English, and is left in ruins; but the Frue Kirke is an elegant Grecian edifice, 215 feet by 180, with a Doric portico, and for which Thorwaldsen is preparing statues of the apostles and evangelists. The palace of Rosenborg, though now unoccupied, contains an extraordinary display of jewels, precious stones, and porcelain. The collections in science and art are equal to those of the greatest capitals. The king has a library of 400,000 volumes, with numerous manuscripts illustrative of the history and literature of the North, as well as those brought by Niebuhr from the East; an extensive museum of northern antiquities: a gallery of pictures, comprising some fine specimens of the greatest masters, and a numerous collection of engravings. The University of Copenhagen, a highly respectable institution, has a valuable library of about 100,000 volumes, and an excellent collection of northern manuscripts. The arsenal is said to equal that of Venice in beauty, and to surpass it in extent. The mint throws off 200 pieces in a minute.

233

Copenhagen.

The other towns in Zealand and the islands are of comparatively small magnitude. Roschild, the ancient capital of Denmark, which contained once thirty convents and thirty churches, is now remarkable only for its Gothic cathedral, in whose vaults are deposited the remains of the kings of Denmark. Several of the monuments are fine. Elsinore, with its castle of Cronborg, is important from its situation on the Sound, which being commanded by the castle, the government is enabled to levy what are called the Sound dues. The passage to Helsinborg, in Sweden, may be made in half an hour. Elsinore, from its favourable situation and good roadstead, carries on a considerable commerce, and contains, among its inhabitants, many British, Jews, and even Mahometans. It has a handsome cathedral, with some fine tombs. Population 7000. At Cronborg is shown the chamber in which the unfortunate Matilda was confined. This castle commands a noble view over the sea, the islands, and the opposite coast of Sweden. The terrace from which these are viewed recalls to the English reader the first scenes of Hamlet, the tradition of whose story is still prevalent here. Soroe, in the interior, surrounded by a fine country, has a noble academy; and contains the tombs of Eric, Canute, and other princes. Odensee, the capital of Funen, has a college, and is rather a thriving town, with manufactures of woollen and soap. Nyeborg, in Funen, and Corsoer in Zealand, derive some importance from their situation on the passage of the Great Belt; and Middelfarth, in the former island, from the passage of the Little Belt.

The towns of Jutland are of small interest, and have been little observed, with the exception of those which lie on the high road from Hamburg to Copenhagen. Aalborg, near the northern extremity, is the seat of one of the four bishoprics; and, being situated on a narrow arm of the sea, with a good harbour, carries on some trade. Aarhuus, on the eastern coast, is the seat of another bishopric; and, being in the midst of a fertile country, exports some grain. Population, 5,000. Colding derives some importance from its vicinity to the passage of the Little Belt. Wiborg and Ripen are also deserving of mention.

In Sleswick, the city of that name is agreeable, though irregularly built. Its cathedral, with numerous monuments of ancient dukes, is viewed with interest. Flemsborg, on a deep and winding *haaf*, or bay, with an excellent harbour, possesses a much greater commercial importance, while it carries on the communication with the Baltic: it has 15,000 inhabitants. Tonningen, on the other side, near the mouth of the Eyder, communicates with the countries situated round the German Ocean; and, by the canal of Holstein, it has now a water communication with the Baltic.

Holstein, the most southern province of Denmark, ranks as a part of the German empire, to which it once belonged, and gives to the king of Denmark a vote in the diet. Reaching to the Elbe, and being more in the commercial circle, it has a considerably brisker trade than the northern or peninsular territory. Altona, a few miles below Hamburg, is a repetition of that city on a smaller scale; having 25,000 inhabitants, busily employed in the commerce of the Elbe, in ship-building, and in several manufactures. Gluckstadt, about twenty miles lower, though inferior in extent, is a handsome and regular town, with considerable naval establishments. Kiel, on the eastern or Baltic coast, has an excellent harbour, and derives importance from its situation at the extremity of the canal which connects the eastern and western seas. It contains an university. Lauenburg, a level tract, intersected with several small lakes, though it rounds the Danish borders, does not possess much importance, either in itself or its little capital, with 3,000 inhabitants.

Iceland, an appendage of the Danish crown, unimportant in a political view, but interesting from its physical and moral aspect, is situated in the Northern Ocean, on the border of the arctic circle, and at the farthest verge of the civilized world. It is a large island, 220 miles in length, and 210 in breadth; containing about 40,000 square miles. Iceland belongs, by its situation, to the polar world; and the mountain chains, from 3000 to 6000 feet high, with which it is everywhere intersected, give it a still more severe and stern character. Barley is the only grain that can be raised, and this only in patches; cabbages, and a few other imported vegetables, may be produced, but by no means in perfection. The dependence of the inhabitants is chiefly upon the abundance of fish which the surrounding seas afford; so that the interior, comprising about half of the island, is a desert of the most dreary character.

The mountain phenomena of Iceland are very striking. According to Glieman, the jokuls, or hills covered with ice, rise to the following heights: Oerefe, 6240 feet; Snafell, 4572; Findfall, 5368; Hecla, 5210; Eyafiall Oester, 5794. All these mountains are, at the same time, glaciers capped with ice which never melts; but these glaciers consist not, like those of Switzerland, of great masses sloping down from upper regions of the mountains to the valleys; they are the snows of winter melted and frozen where they fall. Beneath this mantle of ice and snow burns a perpetual fire, which in every part of the island bursts forth in the most strange and fearful phenomena. Hecla (*fig.* 234.), with its flaming volcano, is the most celebrated; but its eruptions, of which six have occurred in the course of a century, are at present suspended. There are six other volcanoes, which, in the course of a century, have emitted twenty eruptions.

234
Hecla.

The Geysers form a phenomena strikingly characteristic of Iceland, and rank with the most extraordinary that are produced on any part of the globe. They consist of fountains, which throw up boiling water, spray, and vapour, to a great height into the air. The eruptions are not continuous, but announce their approach by a sound like that of subterraneous thunder; immediately after which, a column of water, accompanied with prodigious volumes of steam, bursts forth, and rushes up to the height of fifty, sixty, ninety, or even a hundred and fifty feet. The water soon ceases; but the spray and vapour continue to play in the air for several hours, and, when illuminated by the sun, produce the most brilliant rainbows. The largest stones, when thrown into the orifice, are instantly propelled to an amazing height, and remaining often for some minutes within the influence of the steam, rise and fall in singular alternation. Stones thrown into the fountain have the remarkable effect of acting as a stimulus to the eruption, and causing it to burst from a state of tranquillity. The basin of the Great Geyser (*fig.* 235.), is of an oval form, with diameters of fifty-eight and sixty-four feet. Every spot around the Geysers is covered with variegated and beautiful petrifactions. Leaves, grass, rushes, are converted into white stone, preserving entire every fibre.

235

Great Geyser.

The Sulphur Mountains, with their caldrons of boiling mud, present another phenomenon which the traveller beholds with the utmost astonishment. These consist chiefly of clay, covered with a crust, which is hot to the touch, and of sulphur, from almost every part of which, gas and steam are perpetually escaping. Sometimes a loud noise guides the traveller to a spot where caldrons of black boiling mud (*fig.* 236.), largely impregnated with this mineral substance, are throwing up, at short intervals, their eruptions. That on the Krabla, observed by Mr. Henderson, had a diameter equal to that of the Great Geyser, and rose to the height of thirty feet. The situation of the spectator here is not only awful, but even dangerous; standing, as Sir George Mackenzie observes, "on a support which feebly sustains him, over an abyss where fire and brimstone are in dreadful and incessant action."

236

Caldron of Boiling Mud.

The civil and social state of Iceland presents features no less interesting. It was discovered about the year 840, by Nadod, a Danish pirate. After its settlement it became a little independent republic; and the arts and literature, driven before the tide of barbarism, which then overwhelmed the rest of Europe, took refuge in this remote and frozen clime. Iceland had its divines, its annalists, its poets, and was for some time the most enlightened country then perhaps existing in the world. Subjected first to Norway, in 1261, and afterwards to Denmark, it lost the spirit and energy of an independent republic. Yet the diffusion of knowledge, even among the lowest class, which took place during its prosperous period, still exists in a degree not paralleled in the most enlightened of other nations. Men who seek, amid the storms of the surrounding ocean, a scanty provision for their families, possess an acquaintance with the classical writings of antiquity, and a sense of their beauty. The traveller finds the guide whom he has hired able to hold a conversation with him in Latin, and on his arrival at his miserable place of rest for the night, is addressed with fluency and elegance in the same language. "The instruction of his children," says Dr. Holland, "forms one of the stated occupations of the Icelander; and while the little hut which he inhabits is almost buried in the snow, and while darkness and desolation are spread universally around, the light of an oil-lamp illumines the page from which he reads to his family the lessons of knowledge, religion, and virtue."

The Faroe Islands compose a group in the Northern Ocean, between 61° 15′ and 62° 20′ N. lat., to the N. W. of Shetland, which they resemble. The principal are Stromsoe, Osteroe, Suderoe, and Norderoe, with the smaller islands of Nalsoe, Vagoe, and Sandoe. Their only wealth is produced by the rearing of sheep, fishing, and catching the numerous birds which cluster round the rocks. With the surplus of these articles they supply their deficiency of grain. Thorsharn, on Stromsoe, is the only place that can be called a town.

## CHAPTER VI.

### SWEDEN AND NORWAY.

SWEDEN and NORWAY, now united into one kingdom, form an extensive region, stretching from the utmost verge of the temperate zone far into the frozen range of the arctic circle. Along the north and west stretch the wide shores of the Frozen Ocean, so far as yet known. The south-west point of the kingdom borders on the North Sea or German Ocean. The Baltic and the Gulf of Bothnia enclose it on the south and east; so that it forms an immense peninsula. The isthmus by which it is joined to Russia is above 200 miles broad, but so closely barred by mountains and frozen plains, that the kingdom is nearly inaccessible, except by sea.

### SECT. I.—*General Outline and Aspect.*

This kingdom is of vast extent. Its length, from the extreme point of Scania to the North Cape, is 1550 miles. Its breadth, from the extreme points of the provinces of Stockholm on the east, and Bergen on the west, will little exceed 350 miles. Its area is 297,000 square miles. Of this large territory, scarcely a half can be considered as belonging to the civilized world. The Laplander, who derives his whole subsistence from the rein-deer, can hardly be included within the pale of civilized society. Even the southern districts have a rugged and repulsive aspect, when compared to almost any other European state. Forests of tall and gloomy pine stretch over the plains, or hang on the sides of the mountains; the ground for five months in the year is buried under snow; cultivation appears only in scattered patches, and was long quite insufficient to furnish bread to the inhabitants.

The mountains consist chiefly of the dark and lofty chain of the Dofrines, which were for ages a barrier between the two separate and hostile states of Sweden and Norway, but are now included within the united kingdom. It commences near Gottenburg, on a low scale, and becomes much more elevated in passing through Norway, where some of its pinnacles exceed 8000 feet. Chains of secondary elevation run through Lapland; but, in approaching the North Cape, they again rise as high as before, and face the polar seas with cliffs of prodigious magnitude.

The rivers are numerous, Sweden being a country profusely watered; but, as they rise in the Dofrines, and traverse the divided breadth of the peninsula, they seldom attain any material length of course. The largest is the Dahl, which crosses Dalecarlia, and falls into the sea at Geffle, after a course of 260 miles. The most important as to navigation are those which form the outlet to the lakes, particularly the Gotha, reaching from the lake Wener to Gottenburg. The Glomme and the Dramme are pretty considerable rivers, running from north to south, and down which considerable quantities of timber are floated. Lapland pours a number of large streams into the head of the Gulf of Bothnia; but these are usually chained in ice, and at no time can be subservient to the purposes of agriculture or navigation.

Lakes form the grand depository of the surplus waters of Sweden. The Wener bears almost the character of an inland sea, and the completion of the canal of Trölhätta, by enabling its coasts to communicate by the Gotha with Gottenburg, has given them almost the full advantages of a maritime site. The Wetter, though equal in length, covers not nearly so great an extent of ground. Mäler, or Malar, is a narrow, winding loch, or, more strictly, a bay, running sixty miles into the interior from Stockholm, to whose environs its variegated and rocky shores give a beautiful wildness. Small lakes, enclosed between hills, are of very frequent occurrence, both in Norway and Sweden.

### SECT. II.—*Natural Geography.*

#### SUBSECT. 1.—*Geology.*

(1.) GEOLOGY OF SWEDEN.—I. *Primitive rocks.* Granite occurs in the mountains of Jämtland, in Herjeadalen, in Lulea Lappmark, in Pitea Lappmark. It occurs also in the plains, without any covering of other rocks, as in Upland, Westmanland, Sudermanland, and a part of East and West Gothland. It passes into gneiss and syenite. Gneiss occurs in many places in Sudermanland, East Gothland, &c., with beds of copper and iron ore. Mica slate abounds not only in the principal, but also in the subordinate chains, and contains the greater number of the metalliferous beds met with in Sweden. It often alternates with vast beds of *primitive limestone*, *quartz*, &c. In the high mountain ridges, the strata of this rock are generally disposed at an angle of 45°; while in the subordinate chains they are vertical. In many places it abounds in garnets, when it is known under the name *noorka*, or *murkstein*, the *garnet rock* of geologists. Clay slate occurs sparingly: *talc slate*, in several quarters, occurs in considerable abundance. Porphyry occurs only in Smaland, where the basis is a quartzy hornstone (*halleflinta*) with embedded crystals of felspar, and grains of quartz. Primitive limestone occurs generally in the secondary mountain chains, but seldom in the neighbourhood of the central chains. It is mixed up with hornblende tremolite, quartz, serpentine, garnet, magnetic ironstone, and mica. It is often metalliferous, containing galena, copper, and iron pyrites. Serpentine, with the exception of masses in some metalliferous beds, seldom occurs pure: it is often mixed with limestone, when it occurs in primitive limestone. Quartz rock occurs either pure, and in whole mountains, as in Dahlsland, Smaland, and many other places; or it alternates with mica slate, as in Dahlsland, and also in the metalliferous beds of Persberg and Klacka. The limestone of Danemora contains mica slate. It also occurs in veins in granite and mica slate, &c. Porphyritic quartz, a granite rock, with embedded grains and crystals of felspar, occurs in Smaland, Tornea Lappmark, &c. *Primitive trap.* Of this interesting group of rocks, the following kinds are met with; viz. hornblende rock, hornblende with felspar, and hornblende with mica.

II. *Transition rocks.* Conglomerate and sandstone, which, in some places, are covered with transition limestone, occur in Jämtland, Tornea Lappmark, Angermanland, Dalecarlia, Schönen, islands in the Lake Wetter, East and West Gothland, Nerika, Dalarnia. Transition porphyry: in the parish of Elfdal, in Dalarnia. The basis is of the nature of hornstone. It rests upon transition sandstone, and is covered by syenite, porphyry, and transition greenstone. Greywacke slate lies upon sandstone, and is covered by transition limestone. It sometimes contains coal, and then passes into a kind of shale. It also contains fossil remains of marine animals. Transition limestone occurs in Gothland, Œland, Schönen, East and West Gothland, Nerika, Dalarnia, and Jämtland. In the regular succession, it lies immediately upon alum slate, but in Gothland directly upon sandstone. It is seldom covered by other rocks, excepting in West Gothland, where it is covered by clay slate and greenstone. It contains many different petrifactions, as orthoceratites, ammonites, anomites, echinites, corallites, and entrochites. Its colour is commonly gray, or bluish gray, and reddish brown, often varied with veins of a green colour. Transition trap is the youngest rock of the transition class in Sweden. In Elfdal it rests upon porphyry; upon transition clay slate and alum slate in Kennekulle, Billengen, the Hunne and Halleberge, and others, in West Gothland.

III. *Secondary rocks.* The mountain chain around Helsingborg, in Schönen, is composed of secondary sandstone. It contains beds of slate clay, bituminous shale, and black bituminous coal. This sandstone, which belongs to the black bituminous coal formation, is covered with other secondary deposits, as limestone, the age of which is not well known. The only one of these newer secondary deposits, the geognostical history of which has been made out, is *Chalk.* This interesting formation occurs at Limhamn, near to Malmo. It encloses balls of common flint, and, at its lower part, passes into a more solid chalk and secondary limestone.

IV. *Tertiary rocks.* The tertiary deposits seem to occur in some points of the land not far distant from the sea-coast; but they have not been carefully explored.

V. *Alluvial rocks.* Many tracts more or less deeply covered with gravel, sand, and clay, occur in Sweden.

*Mines.* The mines of Sweden have been long celebrated all over the world, and have been frequently described by travellers. *Gold and silver mines.* The Adelfors mine, which formerly yielded thirty or forty marks of gold annually, now furnishes only three or four; those of Fahlun, where copper predominates, return annually four marks of gold and fifty marks of silver. The silver mine of Sahla, which, during the reign of Queen Christina, yielded annually 20,000 marks of silver, does not at present afford annually more than 2000 or 3000 marks. *Copper mines.* The most considerable copper mines are those of Fahlun, which is also known under the name of *Kopparberg.* The mines of Atwidaberg, in East Gothland, furnish about a sixth part of all the copper which the Swedes obtain annually from mines; those of Fahlun yield more than the half of the copper raised in Sweden. The ore at Fahlun is copper pyrites, disposed in an immense irregular-shaped mass, in mica slate: 10,200 quintals of copper are yielded by it annually. *Iron mines.* The greatest iron mines are those in the province of Upland: of these the most important are those of Skebo, of Œsterby, not far from Danemora, of Gimo, of Ronaes. Iron is mined as far north as Gellivara, which is 200 leagues to the north of Stockholm. The island of Uto, on the east coast of Upland, also affords a considerable quantity of iron. The whole mines afford annually 1,800,000 quintals of iron. *Cobalt mines.* The principal mines of this metal are those of Tunaberg, near to Nyköping, and at Awed, in East Gothland. These mines afford excellent cobalt, but the quantity is not great. *Coal mines.* Coal mines have been worked for some time in Scania, two leagues from Helsinborg, and are affording a considerable return. *Sulphur and vitriol.* The pyritical minerals of Dylta afford annually 1050 quintals of sulphur, and those of Fahlun about 100 quintals of the same substance. The vitriolic waters of Fahlun afford annually about 600 quintals of green vitriol, or sulphate of iron, and a small quantity of blue vitriol, or sulphate of copper. *Alum.* The annual produce of alum is about 42,600 quintals. *Quarries.* Sweden possesses, besides its regular mines, also valuable quarries of granite, porphyry, and marble. The porphyry quarries of Elfdal are the

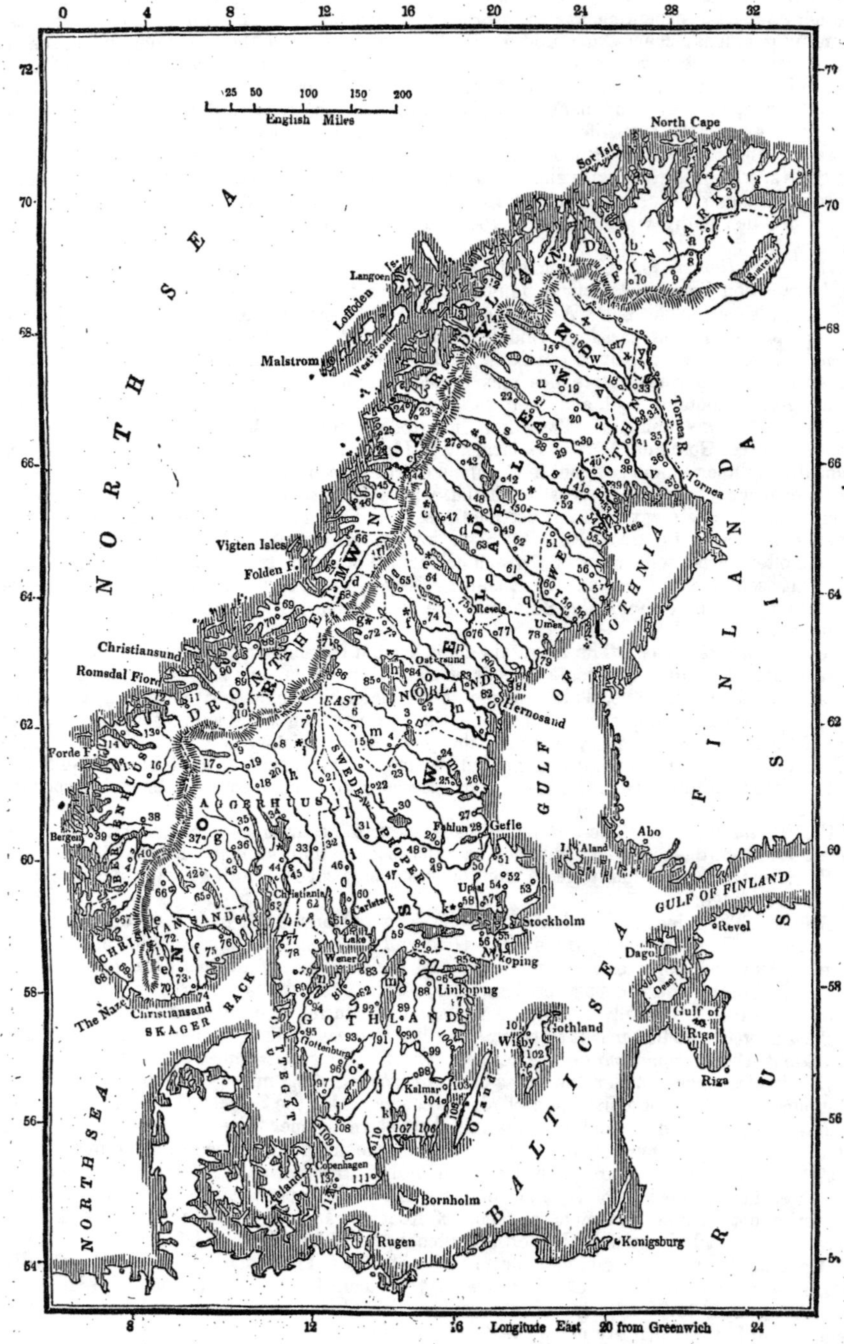
English Miles
North Cape
Sor Isle
Langoen Is.
Loffoden
Malstrom
West Fiord
Vigten Isles
Folden F.
Christiansund
Romsdal Fiord
Forde F.
Bergen
Christiania
Christiansand
The Naze
SKAGER RACK
CATTEGAT
NORTH SEA
NORTH SEA
GULF OF BOTHNIA
GULF OF FINLAND
BALTIC SEA
FINLAND
RUSSIA
FINMARK
LAPLAND
WEST BOTHNIA
NORLAND
SWEDEN PROPER
GOTHLAND
Tornea R.
Tornea
Pitea
Umea
Ostersund
Hernosand
Gefle
Fahlun
Upsal
Stockholm
Abo
Aland
Revel
Dago
Oesel
Gulf of Riga
Riga
Koping
Linkoping
Gothland
Wisby
Kalmar
Oland
Gottenburg
Carlstadt
Wener
Copenhagen
Zealand
Bornholm
Rugen
Konigsburg
Longitude East 20 from Greenwich

largest and most celebrated in Europe. Nearly all the fine modern works in porphyry are in the porphyry of Elfdal.

(2.) Geology of Norway and Lapland.—I. *Primitive rocks.* These wild but highly interesting countries are principally composed of primitive and transition rocks; secondary rocks occur but rarely, and alluvial deposits are not so abundant as in many other less extensive regions. *Granite* is a rare rock in Norway and Lapland, and may be considered one of the least abundant rocks in Scandinavia. The granite frequently appears in veins traversing the primitive stratified rocks, or running parallel with beds or strata; and sometimes it can be seen spread over the surface of mica slate, as at Forvig, or irregularly associated with clay slate and diallage rock, as in the island of Mageroe. *Gneiss* seems to be by far the most frequent and abundant rock in Scandinavia, all the other primitive rocks appearing to be in some degree subordinate to it. *Mica slate* rests upon and alternates with the gneiss, but is far from being so generally distributed as that rock. *Clay slate* along with the mica slate is not of frequent occurrence. *Quartz rock, various hornblende rocks*, and *limestone*, occur in beds subordinate to the gneiss and mica slate. *Gabbro*, or *diallage rock*, one of the most beautiful of the older rocks, occurs in great quantity, connected with clay slate, in th island of Mageroe, and other parts of Norway.

II. *Transition rocks.* This class contains, besides *greywacke, alum slate*, and *limestone* (which contains much tremolite), and other rocks well known to mineralogists as members of this class, the following:—1. *Granite*, which sometimes contains hornblende. 2. *Syenite*, which contains a beautiful *Labradoric* variety of *common felspar*, and numerous crystals of the gem named zircon. 3. Porphyry, and, associated with it, various trap rocks allied to basalt and amygdaloid.

III. *Secondary rocks.* The great primitive land of Scandinavia continues onward to the extreme northern point of Norway; but in this high latitude some new formations make their appearance among the older. The sandstone quartz of Alten has been known since the publication of the travels of Von Buch. On the East, towards the Russian dominions, there is a considerable tract which differs more from the primitive formations than the sandstone quartz of Alten does. *Sandstone* and conglomerate extend across the subjacent gneiss in a horizontal position. These rocks probably belong to the *old red sandstone.*

IV. *Alluvial rocks.* Old alluvium occurs on the coast, and in the interior in many of the valleys, and the new everywhere in greater or less quantity.

*Mines.* The only *silver mines* in Norway are those of Köngsberg, situated in mica slate, which formerly afforded rich returns, but of late have yielded no profit. The *gold mine* of Edswold, and the mines of *lead* and *silver* in Jarlsberg, have been but feebly worked. The *copper mines* are principally situated in the northern division of the kingdom. The most considerable, near Ræraas, were discovered in 1644. They have afforded considerable quantities of copper: in 1805, the annual return was 7860 quintals of copper. The other mines of copper are from 15 to 20 leagues of Drontheim, at Quikne, Lækken, Selboe, and in the district of Christiania, at Fredericksgave or Foledal. The principal *iron mines* are those of Arendal and Krageroe, in southern Norway. The mine of Laurwig, near the town of that name,

---

*References to the Map of Sweden and Norway.*

NORTH PART.
1. Kiberg
2. Nisseby
3. Tana
4. Lababije
5. Hammerferst
6. Altengaard
7. Joksby
8. Alsapahta
9. Peiviaskanta
10. Kautokeino
11. Kollojaures
12. Finland
13. Ofoden
14. Ankenes
15. Kurravaara
16. Ragisvari
17. Soppero
18. Stranvo
19. Gellivare
20. Ripas
21. Quickjock
22. Ruotivare
23. Saltdalen
24. Liones
25. Slipfies
26. Selsnes
27. Silbojock
28. Rindijaur
29. Waimat
30. Lulea
31. Oras
32. Sopijenfri
33. Pulla
34. Bajala Kengis
35. Pello
36. Upper Tornea
37. Tornea
38. Kalix
39 Ranea
40. Harads
41. Tvara
42. Arjeplog
43. Hytta
44. Henne
45. Dolstad
46. Hogholm
47. Tarna
48. Sorsele
49. Lomsele.
50. Arvids
51. Norsio
52. Gumdtrasken
53. Lulea
54. Pitea
55. Albyn
56. Burtrask
57. Lofanger
58. Umea
59 Nyby
60. Jekrosele
61. Lycksele
62. Raska
63. Busele
64. Ormsjo
65. Gaddedett
66. Foldereid
67. Strom
68. Olderness
69. Honstad
70. Holmset
71. Undersuker
72. Kallsjon
73. Folinge
74. Strom
75. Asele
76. Junsele
77. Amund
78. Nordmaling
79. Parviken
80. Ressele
81. Nordingra
82. Hernosand
83. Fors
84. Ostersund
85. Mariæby
86. Herndal
87. Drontheim
88. Leinsvig
89. Garberg
90. Hevne

SOUTH PART.
1. Sundswall
2. Bracke
3. Lanss
4. Sveg
5. Lindsalls
6. Hede
7. Sorrag
8. Tyldal
9. Lessoe
10. Opdal
11. Romsdal
12. Orskoug
13. Sondelv
14. Stavum
15. Forde
16. Sognedal
17. Lom
18. Ringebo
19. Ovam
20. Grotte
21. Engedal
22. Asbyn
23. Hegen
24. Linsdel
25. Arbra
26. Soderhamn
27. Hamrange
28. Gefle
29. Fahlun
30. Mora
31. Malung
32. Dunby
33. Grusel
34. Moe
35. Flathen
36. Flaa
37. Hoel
38. Kleiven
39. Bergen
40. Aarevig
41. Odden
42. Tussungdal
43. Nore
44. Christiania
45. Fryksande
46. Narens
47. Norrbarke
48. Tuna
49. Hedmora
50. Ferneb
51. Lofsta
52. Lena
53. Waddo
54. Upsal
55. Stockholm
56. Mariafrel
57. Enkoping
58. Westeras
59. Orebro
60. Philipstad
61. Carlstad
62. Holmedal
63. Moss
64. Tonsberg
65. Ovamen
66. Ranland
67. Selsoe
68. Egersund
69. Bakke
70. Christiansund
71. Langoe
72. Valle
73. Mokland
74. Arendal
75. Sando
76. Holden
77. Frederickstad
78. Frederickshall
79. Uddevalla
80. Wenerborg
81. Lidkoping
82. Skara
83. Mariestad
84. Ragna
85. Nykoping
86. Norkoping
87. Westerwick
88. Linkoping
89. Saby
90. Ekesjo
91. Jonkoping
92. Hjo
93. Oreryd
94. Garchem
95. Gottenburg
96. Ketsjoy
97. Halmstad
98. Notteback
99. Morlundo
100. Misterhult
101. Wisby
102. Nass
103. Rumpekulla
104. Calmar
105. Borgholm
106. Carlscrona
107. Carlshamm
108. Lalholm
109. Landscrona
110. Christianstad
111. Borum
112. Falsterbo
113. Malmo

*Rivers.*
a Tana
b Alten
c Rannens
d Namsen
e Torris
f Nidelven
g Reina
h Glommen
i Klar
j Laga
k Morrins
l Dahl
m Ljusne
n Nijurunda
o Indal
p Angermana
q Umea
r Windel
s Pitea
t Lulea
u Lina
v Kalix
w Tornea
x Lainio
y Muonio

*Lakes.*
a* Horn
b* Stora
c* Ave
d* Umea
e* Walgomas
f* Apunus
g* Kalls
h* Stors
i* Foemund
j* Miosen
k* Maler
l* Hjelmar
m* Wetter
n* Wener
o* Bolmen

affords annually 26,000 quintals of bar-iron and 6000 quintals of cast-iron. The establishment of the same kind at Moss affords annually 10,000 quintals of iron in bars and cast. The same annual quantity is afforded by the mines of Bærum, Bolvig, Ulfoss, Eidfoss, Egeland, Naes, Dikkemarken Fossum, and Oudalen. Lastly, the mines of Hassel, Froeland, Lessoe, and Mostmarken, furnish from 3000 to 5000 quintals of iron annually. The annual produce of the iron mines of Norway is estimated by a well-known statistical writer at about 150,000 quintals. The mines of *cobalt*, which are worked at Modum and Fossum, are extensive but not deep. In the year 1792 they yielded 2817 quintals of ore. There is a mine of *plumbago* and *black lead* at Engledal. The mines of *alum*, which are worked in the mountain of Egeberg, near to Christiania, afford not only a sufficiency for the consumption of the Danish states, but also a considerable quantity for exportation. Norway possesses quarries of *granite*, *marble*, *millstone*, *whetstone*, *slate* and *clay*. Granite is exported to Holland; the marble and other minerals supply the Danish states.

### SUBSECT. 2.—*Botany.*

The Botany of these countries has been noticed under that of Denmark.

### SUBSECT. 3.—*Zoology.*

The Zoology of Sweden, the native country of the celebrated Linnæus, is so well known to naturalists, by the writings of that great man, that to them the subject is familiar. Nor does it present any thing very different in its general character from that of Denmark. The bleak and inhospitable regions of Norway and Lapland, to which nature has denied the rich and verdant pasturage of Britain, and the consequent abundance of grazing animals, are, however, the chief metropolis of the Rein-deer, whose diversified qualities are beautifully adapted for supplying such deficiencies.

The Rein-deer (Rangifer Tarandus *H. Smith*) (*fig.* 238.) forms the sole riches of the Laplander, and its care is almost his only occupation. According to the season, he migrates to the sea shore, the plains, or the mountains. The rich often possess 2000 head; and the poorer seldom less than 100. The adult male, in a wild state, is even larger than a stag; but the domesticated races are somewhat smaller: the sight and scent of these creatures are astonishing, and guide them with wonderful precision through the most dangerous passes and in the darkest stormy nights of an arctic winter. To this sagacity the Laplander trusts his life with confidence; and accidents rarely happen: they draw his sledge with such amazing rapidity, that in twenty-four hours a pair of Rein-deer have been said to perform a journey of 100 miles. In a wild state they are gregarious; and, when domesticated, evince an excessive attachment to each other. During summer they are much tormented by a species of gad-fly; but the old account of the glutton falling upon them from a tree, and then devouring them, is now considered fabulous. During life this useful animal supplies its master with labour and milk; and, when dead, every part becomes serviceable, the skin for clothing, and for boots; the horns to make utensils; the sinews for thread, and the flesh for food: the intestines are also used; and the tongue is a well-known article of commerce.

238

The Rein-Deer.

The Birds are not numerous, and, with few exceptions, differ not from those of Denmark and the other northern kingdoms. The Iceland Falcon (*Falco islandicus*) (*fig.* 239.) rarely wanders to more temperate climes; and a gigantic Owl (*Strix lapponica* Lin.) is a peculiar inhabitant of the dreary solitudes of Lapland: to these we may add two other species; the large Ural Owl, and the Great Snowy Owl. These formidable birds prey upon numerous ptarmigans and grouse, great numbers of which inhabit the confines of the arctic circle. The Curruca suecica *Sw.* or Blue-throated Reed Warbler, one of the most elegant birds of Europe, is not peculiar, as its name would imply, to Sweden, being common in France and Switzerland.

239

Iceland Falcon

The insects of Sweden, during its short summer, are very numerous; and many, enumerated by Acerbi, very beautiful; but, in autumn, nearly the whole country is terribly infested by Musquitoes, these tormenting little animals being beyond calculation more numerous in high northern latitudes than in the woods of tropical America.

## Sect. III.—*Historical Geography*

The early history of Scandinavia is deeply involved in fable and uncertainty. Ptolemy and Pliny, the best informed of ancient geographers, seem to distinguish it from "Great Germany," off the coast of which they represent Basilia, or Baltia, as a large island, though not nearly approaching to the real dimensions. The Goths were found in early possession of Sweden, and its southern provinces have been denominated Gothland; but the question, whether they were the native possessors, or entered it as conquerors, is one which can scarcely be now decided. Scandinavia has been called the "storehouse of nations;" and "the blue-eyed myriads from the Baltic coast" are supposed to have been among the most numerous of those who spread war and desolation throughout Europe. Dr. Clarke ridicules this idea, as inapplicable to a country of unbroken forests, and a slowly advancing population, making the first essays of agriculture; yet, though the population could never be great, the simple and pastoral habits of the people might dispose emigrants to seek subsistence with the sword in happier climates.

Scandinavia, first, by a series of formidable expeditions, made a figure in history at the end of the ninth century. Harold Harfager, or the Fair-haired, the first of the great sea-kings of the North, having united the formerly independent districts of Norway under his sway, undertook triumphant expeditions against Shetland, Orkney, and the Hebrides. For several centuries the Danes and Norwegians held full possession of those islands; gave a king to England, and formed a permanent establishment in Normandy. The defeat of Haco in Scotland, and of Harold III. in England, during the eleventh century, put an end to this maritime dominion: and the northern nations, notwithstanding their immense supply of naval stores, have never since attained to more than a secondary rank among the maritime powers.

The union of the kingdoms of Scandinavia, in 1388, under Margaret, called the Semiramis of the North, forms a memorable era. Immediately, however, after the death of that able princess, the Swedes began to struggle for independence. But their repeated attempts to establish a separate kingdom were always defeated, till the cruel and tyrannical reign of Christian II. drove matters to extremity, and brought on a new revolution.

Gustavus Vasa, in 1520, hoisted again the national standard in the province of Dalecarlia, and, in three years subsequently, entered Stockholm in triumph. After a long struggle, the Danes were compelled to recognise the independence of Sweden.

The reign of Gustavus Adolphus formed a glorious era for Sweden. The Protestant religion having been established under Gustavus Vasa, Sweden began to be looked to as its support when assailed by a formidable confederacy. In 1630, Gustavus took the field at the head of only ten thousand Swedes; but around this gallant band rallied all the Protestant powers of Germany. The splendid victory of Breitenfeld humbled the house of Austria, and re-established the civil and religious liberties of the empire. Even after his fall, in the glorious field of Lutzen, his generals continued to wage that desperate war of thirty years, which was necessary to compel the Catholic league finally to renounce its pretensions. Sweden, at the peace, obtained Pomerania, and other important possessions in Germany; and continued, till the end of the seventeenth century, to exercise a powerful influence on the affairs of Europe.

The victories and reverses of Charles XII. threw a wild and romantic lustre around Sweden, which terminated, however, in the loss of her station and greatness. Being defeated at Pultowa, by the Czar Peter, and driven to seek shelter from the Turks at Bender, he was obliged to purchase peace by the sacrifice of Livonia, and others of his finest provinces. The influence of Sweden was thenceforth confined within its own barren limits, and it ranked with difficulty as a power of the second order. The only remarkable change in the course of the century was produced by the revolutions of 1772 and 1789, when Gustavus III. succeeded in converting the government into an absolute monarchy, though in other respects his reign was advantageous to Sweden.

The election of Bernadotte, one of Bonaparte's commanders, to fill the throne, left vacant through the rash conduct of the legitimate monarch, made a great change in the relations of Sweden. To conciliate his new subjects, he restored in full plenitude the representative constitution, which had been reduced to a mere shadow. Having joined the confederacy against his former master, he received Norway in compensation for the loss of Finland, and had thus a more compact and defensible territory. The Norwegians exclaimed, not without reason, against this compulsory transference; yet Denmark had deprived them of their free constitution, which they now regained, and had in so many respects depressed the country, with the view of concentrating every thing at Copenhagen, that the connection now terminated has been considered the bane of Norway.

## Sect. IV.—*Political Geography.*

The constitution of Sweden is one of the few in Europe, which has always preserved some portion of that representative system which had been formed in remote ages. Towards the close, indeed, of the last century, it was reduced by Gustavus III. to little more than a form. Bernadotte, however, an elected monarch, without any national claim, was obliged to court the favour of the nation, and, with that view, to re-establish the rights of its ancient diet. This is now rather an antique and cumbrous form of legislature, consisting of four orders; the nobles, the clergy, the peasants, and the burghers; who sit and vote in separate houses.

Of these houses, that of the nobles consists of about 1200 members; the head of each family being, by inheritance, its legal representative. They are divided into three classes:—*herra*, counts, barons, &c.; *reddar*, knights; and *sivena*, or gentlemen who, though without any title, have received letters patent of nobility. The house of clergy consists of the archbishop and all the bishops; while the rest of the ecclesiastical body is represented by deputies. The burghers are chosen by the towns, every freeman who pays taxes having a vote: they form an independent body, partly, perhaps, because the honour of a seat is not eagerly contested. The peasants do not exactly correspond to our idea of that term: they consist of a body of little proprietors, or *lairds*, who cultivate their own ground, and who are numerous in Sweden. Their allowance of a dollar a day is provided by a subscription among their constituents; and, in some cases, two or three districts must combine to furnish out one deputy. The nobles have bestirred themselves much to keep down the attempts made by this class to rise in society. They have procured regulations, according to which no person could sit in the house who allowed himself to be called *Herr* (or Mr.), or who wore a coat of fine cloth. Notwithstanding all their efforts, however, this house, and that of the burghers, are daily increasing in strength.

In the division of powers, the royal prerogative is ample. The king appoints to all offices civil and military, and he is obliged to convoke the diet only once in five years, and to continue its sittings three months; but he may make the meetings more frequent, and longer. He has also a negative upon the laws proposed by the diet. In regard to the diet itself, the division rests with a majority of the houses; but if they be two against two, the balance is struck by the committee of state, a body composed of a certain number of members from each. No tax can be levied, or loan obtained, without the consent of the diet.

The *storthing* of Norway, restored by Bernadotte, is possessed of much higher privileges than the Swedish diet. It assembles more frequently, and at its own time, without any control from the king; and it allows to him only a suspensive *veto*, obliging him to accept any project which has been three times presented by the storthing. These rights having been once granted, Bernadotte, who found them pressing somewhat hard against his prerogative, has in vain made several attempts to abridge them. A highly republican spirit prevails in Norway, and the influence, and almost existence, of the nobles is nearly annihilated.

The revenue of Sweden arises from a poll-tax; the produce of the royal demesnes, duties on exports and imports, mines and forges, distilled spirits, and some monopolies. The whole produce is about $5,000,000 a year, exclusive of lands assigned to soldiers and sailors, and by which these classes, in time of peace, are chiefly supported. The *military force*, is at present,—

| | Sweden. | Norway. | Total. |
|---|---|---|---|
| Infantry | 26,221 | 9,642 | 35,863 |
| Cavalry | 4,580 | 1,070 | 5,650 |
| Artillery | 2,400 | 1,278 | 3,678 |
| Landwehr | 83,368 | 10,000 | 93,368 |

The troops are raised by conscription: they only receive pay when on actual service; remaining, at other times, in the provinces, where they employ themselves in cultivating lands assigned to them for their support.

### SECT. V.—*Productive Industry.*

Sweden seems doomed by nature to be a poor country. Her most southern districts are beyond the limits of that zone, in which alone the finer and more valuable kinds of grain, and the richer fruits, come to maturity. Her scanty harvest consists solely of rye, bigg, and oats, scarcely accounted as food in more favoured climates. Scandinavia is described generally as one unbroken boundless forest, varied only in its aspect by little patches of cultivated land.

Agricultural industry till of late had not done much to remedy natural deficiencies. According to the valuable statistical details collected by Dr. Thomson, the arable land in Sweden amounts to 1,818,450 English acres, which is only a sixty-second of the entire surface, or, throwing out the Norrland deserts, a thirty-second. Of this, 1,363,000 acres are returned as under cultivation. But the average size of a Swedish farm is only twenty-seven and a half; the annual average of grain sown on each farm does not amount to a Winchester bushel; and the annual produce of the whole country was only 5,700,000 spanns, or about 71,000 quarters. Hence Sweden was obliged to import grain to a great extent; and such is the scarcity, that the peasantry often grind the bark or even wood of the fir-tree into flour a nutriment equally scanty and unwholesome. These statements are given in 1812; since which time we find it mentioned that agriculture has made a very rapid progress; that improved processes have been introduced from other countries; and that, in the most southern provinces, a great extent of moving (and before entirely barren) sand has been rendered solid, and covered with plantations and grain. The consequence has been, that in 1827, Sweden even exported 39,000, and, in 1828, 164,000 tons of grain of every description. Every farm has a tract of forest of about 1000 acres attached to it, on which cattle are fed: these are reported as only amounting to 403,000 horses, 1,475,000 cows, and 1,212,000 sheep. The most valuable product of land is formed by the vast forests with which nature has covered the whole country. The trees over all Scandinavia are small, and consist chiefly of the birch, the pine, the spruce and Scotch firs. Wooden inclosures (*fig.* 240.) of a peculiar form, are universally employed. The poplar and the willow are also indigenous. The timber of these trees, as well as the tar, pitch, and turpentine, drawn from them, forms the chief objects of Scandinavian exports. Those on the hills of Norway are in much demand for masts. According to M. Hegelstamm, not more than the 115th part of the surface of Norway is under cultivation, chiefly in oats; a space which might be greatly extended; yet the annual production is stated at 2,650,000 tons.

240

Swedish Mode of Inclosure.

The manufactures of Scandinavia are inconsiderable, unless we should class their mines as such. Even in the common trades the work is lazily and ill performed, and charged at a high rate, which renders this the most expensive country in Europe for those who live luxuriously. It is a curious fact that some great merchants in the western towns send their linen to be washed in London.

The mines of Sweden are peculiarly rich in important products. Its iron, found chiefly in primitive rocks, is the finest in the world, and is widely diffused. In 1812, there were 176 mines; 624 smelting-houses; 764 forges; producing in all 1,293,411 cwt. of iron. The exportation, in 1821, amounted to 340,000 skippund, and in 1824 had risen to 373,000, of which 345,000 were in bars, and 28,000 in ruder forms. There are also some valuable mines in the southern provinces of Norway. A most extensive deposit of copper occurs in the province of Dalecarlia, particularly at Fahlun. Gold occurs at Adelfors, in Sweden, to no great amount; but the silver mines of Köngsberg, in Norway, are the richest in Europe. The metal occurs in masses, of which there was once found one weighing 600 lbs. There are also lead mines of some importance at Scola, and in other parts of Sweden.

Fishery appears a pursuit peculiarly appropriate to the extensive coasts of Scandinavia. Yet the Swedes are not much addicted to it, probably because the Baltic during a great part of the year is frozen. Gottenburg had once a herring fishery, now nearly lost, the shoals having taken another direction. The Norwegian fishery is considerable, though bearing only a small proportion to the almost unlimited opportunities afforded by its wide seas, and its deep and commodious bays. Its chief theatre is far to the north, off the Isles of Loffoden. The season lasts only for seven or eight weeks in the year, when fishermen crowd thither from all quarters. Codfish is the chief object: it is cut into pieces, and spread on the rocks to dry, whence it receives the names of stockfish and clipfish. According to Mr. Brooke, the number taken in a year was 700,000, which may be worth nearly $600,000; they are sent chiefly to Germany, Spain, and Italy. The roes are also salted and barrelled for exportation also the fish oil to the amount of about 30,000 barrels.

The commerce of Scandinavia is greater than its unimproved agriculture and total want of manufactures might lead us to suppose. But nature has gifted these bleak regions with an almost inexhaustible store of timber and iron, two of the prime necessaries of human life; the main implements in ship-building and in the construction of houses, machinery, and furniture. These articles are indeed also the produce of North America; and Britain, which affords the best market, has lately sought to favour her colonies in that quarter by a great inequality of duties. Yet the superior quality of the Scandinavian commodity always secures it a sale. The entire exports of Norway are estimated by Dr. Clarke at 1,800,000*l.* sterling; but we believe that this is very much beyond the mark. The commerce of Sweden is not on so great a scale; her surplus timber being not nearly so ample, though her iron is superior. She has suffered much injury from the absurd prejudices of the peasantry, who obtained the prohibition of colonial produce, and of almost all foreign articles of consumption; and though these were regularly imported, and in daily use, the trade was greatly fettered by being carried on only as contraband. In 1828, however, commercial treaties were concluded on a more liberal footing. The total number of merchant vessels belonging to the different towns of Sweden, in 1829 was 1178, of the burthen of 61,000 tons.

## SECT. VI.—*Civil and Social State.*

The population of Sweden, according to the latest census, made in 1825, amounted to 2,771,252; of whom 20,499 were nobles; 13,977 ecclesiastics; 66,604 citizens; the remainder belonged to the class of peasants. Of these, 1,332,970 were males, and 1,438,282 females; 2,489,973 resided in the country, 281,279 in the cities. This was a rise of 186,562 since 1820.*

The population of Norway, by a census made in November 1826, amounted to 1,050,132; of whom 105,021 inhabited cities, 934,414 the country. This was a rise of 164,662 since 1815.

The national character of the Swedes is usually painted under favourable colours. Their honesty is described as proverbial; and Dr. Clarke considers the contrast between them and the Russian people, in this respect, as most striking. Highway robbery, though it has been known, is exceedingly rare; and charity boxes, which are often set up on the public roads, have never been plundered. "The nation," says Mr. James, "has its singularities: there exists something of a reciprocity between the moral and political constitution of Sweden. Rigidly ceremonious, they make their stiff and measured courtesies the essentials rather than the forms of life; and seem, in a stranger's eye, a people cold in their nature as the very snows they dwell upon. Their characteristics, a passive courage, not unmixed with indolence; a pride not free from ignorance; a disposition that is not ill-humoured, from having no humour at all, from indifference, from apathy. But a Swede is never in extremes; even these traits are not deeply marked; and if we review the more favourable side of his character, we shall find in him an undaunted spirit of perseverance, and an honest love of freedom, to which the feelings of every one do homage." The same writer mentions a cold-blooded obduracy, connected, perhaps, with a sanguinary turn of mind, displayed in those frequent assassinations which have stained the pages of Swedish history. The manners of the higher ranks, in consequence, perhaps, of political connexion, have been studiously formed on the French model, which does not accord very happily with the somewhat rude simplicity of the Swedes, who find it easier to imitate the frivolity and dissipation of that people, than their easy and careless grace. Several habits are enumerated as prevalent even among the higher classes in Scandinavia, which seem to negative its pretensions to any high pitch of refinement. Among these are, spitting even on handsome carpets, blowing the nose with the fingers, and recording games on the table with chalk.

The religion of Sweden is Lutheran, and the church Episcopal. This country, which stood long at the head of the great Protestant confederacy, is animated with an ardent zeal for the reformed religion. The Catholics, till of late, scarcely enjoyed common toleration, and they are still excluded from the diet and the higher offices of state. The Swedish people are commended for their regularity in performing the duties of their religion: at the same time it has been remarked that the dissenters from the established church are much fewer than in other Protestant countries; which has been imputed to the want of any peculiar fervour upon the subject. The wide extent and thin population of the northern districts must often render the provision for their religious instruction very defective. The diocese of Tornea, in Lapland, is 750 miles in circumference; and, what is more blameable, the small number of clergy employed are not required to understand the language of the natives. The income of the largest bishopric in Sweden is about $5000 a year.

In science, the Swedes, considering their poverty and remote situation, have made a very distinguished figure. Gustavus Adolphus favoured the interests of literature with a degree of ardour not generally known. Of the spoils of places conquered by him, he set a particular value upon books which he transmitted to Sweden, in order to form the foundation of several large libraries. The Swedes cultivated with peculiar ardour botany and mineralogy, which some of their countrymen mainly contributed to raise to the rank of sciences. In botany, the name of Linnæus is yet without a rival; and Cronstadt and Bergman were in their day little inferior, though they now yield to Werner and other great names which have arisen in other countries. Bergman and Scheele made also large contributions to chemistry, which is still ably pursued by Ekeberg, Berzelius, and Afzelius. Although history and poetry have been cultivated, they have not produced any writers whose reputation has spread throughout Europe. From the limited sphere of the Swedish language, few works of science are written in it, or translated into it: hence the literati of Sweden are particularly well versed in the languages of foreign nations. One of the subjects in which Sweden may most justly exult is, the general spread of education among the lower orders, which seems to equal or exceed that which Scotland enjoys; and to this may probably be in a great measure ascribed their generally meritorious conduct. Norway is not nearly so literary a country as Sweden; Dr. Clarke even states that there is not in the whole country a single bookseller's shop. This was in a great measure owing to the jealousy of Denmark, which would not allow an university to be founded even in Christiania, which used to be a rival to that of Copenhagen.

* The only Swedish colony is St. Bartholomew in the W. Indies, with about 9000 inhabitants.—AM. ED.

Yet Norway can boast of literary names; Holberg, Pontoppidan, Vahl the botanist, Torfæus, and Snorro Sturleson, the old historians. A vein of bold and rude poetry is cultivated with peculiar ardour; and Dr. Clarke exhibits a roll of names unknown to Europe, whose claims to distinction appear to be somewhat justified by a specimen given to us by Mr. Wilson.

Of the learned establishments of Sweden, the most eminent is the university of Upsal, the chief nurse of all the great men who have distinguished her literary records. This celebrated seat of northern learning was founded in 1478, by Steno Sture, was enlarged by Gustavus Vasa and Gustavus Adolphus, but reached its highest eminence in the last century, when it was adorned by Linnæus, and all the men of science who have been distinguished as reflecting glory on Sweden. Since that time its lustre has been somewhat diminished, though statements on this subject vary considerably. The professors have salaries of about $500 a year; and are left thus almost wholly dependent on their students, who live in private lodgings. They attend what and whom they please; and their exertions are not stimulated or tried by any public examinations. The mineralogical collection is one of the most complete in Europe; and the library contains 50,000 volumes. Its most precious treasure is the Codex Argenteus, a manuscript of the four Gospels, written in silver characters, and supposed to date as far back as the fourth century. The garden of Linnæus has been neglected for a larger one lately founded, but which scarcely corresponds to the botanical fame of Upsal. The royal library at Stockholm is still more extensive. It is particularly rich in manuscripts, in sagas, and other historical works, and in original drawings by the great masters. This collection is open to the public. The Swedish academy of sciences, founded in 1739, by learned private individuals, has published above 100 volumes. It is considered one of the most distinguished in Europe, and the greatest men in other countries have viewed it as an honour to be enrolled among its members. In the college of mines are preserved copious specimens, drawn from a country so rich in metallic productions. The cabinet of models, presenting the various mechanical contrivances employed through the different parts of Sweden, is also considered very interesting.

The fine arts in Sweden have been cultivated amidst considerable difficulties. The opera is conducted with splendour and taste; Lergell, as a sculptor, has been ranked second to Canova, and even called the Michael Angelo of the North. Breda in portrait, and Fulerantz in landscape, enjoy reputation.

The habitations of Scandinavia are very simple and uniform. "Having," says Dr. Clarke, "once figured to the imagination a number of low red houses, of a single story, and each covered with turf and weeds, a picture is presented of the oppidan scenery of Sweden." The houses, however, are well finished within, and elegantly furnished; and by means of stoves, double windows, and close doors, they are kept comfortably warm, even during the most rigorous winter. Swedes have even complained that they suffered much more from cold in London than in their native city.

The dress is described by Dr. Clarke as equally uniform with the habitations. "A skull-cap, fitting close to the crown, edged with a little stiff lace, the hair being drawn as tight and straight as possible beneath the cap from all parts of the head, as if to start from the roots; add to this, a handkerchief thrown over the cap when they go out; a jacket; short petticoat; stockings of coloured or white woollen; and high-heeled shoes:" this is the general costume of the Swedish women. Mr. Wilson thus describes the dress of the representatives of that class of peasants:—"White worsted stockings, half-boots extending above the calf of the leg, yellow leather small-clothes with knee-buckles, a short brown coat and waistcoat, and a plain handkerchief tied round their necks." The annexed cut (*fig.* 241.) may give an idea of the attire and aspect of the Norwegian peasantry. In winter these garments must be reinforced to the utmost ability of the wearer, as a fence against the excess of the cold. The peasantry wear a sheepskin cloak, with the wool towards the body, and close fur caps. Dr. Clarke mentions as a travelling dress, thick yarn stockings covered by stout leather boots, and over these again boots made of the hides of rein-deer, with the hair on the outside, and doubly lined with sheepskin covered with black wool. The people wear, besides, fur caps on the head, bearskin pelisses over the body, besides several flannel waistcoats, and on the hands, gloves of sheepskin covered by double gloves of fur and wool. Yet these accumulated guards are insufficient to prevent the feeling of the most intense cold, which, in those not duly fenced against it, sometimes produces death, and frequently a frost-bitten limb.

241

Norwegian Peasants.

## SECT. VII.—*Local Geography.*

This section naturally divides itself into three subordinate parts:—1. *Sweden;* 2. *Norway* and 3. *Lapland;* which, though accounted partly Swedish and partly Norwegian, has a distinct character of its own.

### SUBSECT. 1.—*Sweden.*

Sweden is formed into three great divisions: Svealand, or Sweden Proper; Gotaland, or Gothland; and Nordland, or Norrland. In the following statistical table, the extent and arable produce are from materials collected in 1812; since which time cultivation has been greatly extended; but the population is from the census of 1825.

| | Arable Ground, Tunnlands. (1 3-4 acre.) | Being to the whole as 1 to | Number of Farms. | Operative Farmers. | Grain produced in Spanns. (1-20th bushel.) | Population. |
|---|---|---|---|---|---|---|
| *Nordland.* | | | | | | |
| Norrbotten | 8,080 | 2,151 | 522 | 22,824 | 37,570 | 40,624 |
| Vesterbotten | 10,530 | 1,465 | 694 | 23,870 | 56,576 | 44,911 |
| Vester Norrland | 22,780 | 220 | 1,563 | 36,812 | 103,509 | 72,237 |
| Jamtland | 10,720 | 917 | 945 | 20,281 | 48,348 | 39,122 |
| | 52,110 | 915 | 3,724 | 103,787 | 245,998 | 195,894 |
| *Sweden.* | | | | | | |
| Stockholm | 71,416 | 22 | 4,056 | 58,649 | 316,987 | 103,095 |
| Upsala | 84,364 | 13 | 3,548 | 48,657 | 285,356 | 81,897 |
| Vesteros | 55,515 | 27 | 2,852 | 49,063 | 211,100 | 88,618 |
| Nyköping | 54,011 | 24 | 3,276 | 59,791 | 225,006 | 106,793 |
| Orebro | 46,223 | 36 | 2,774 | 61,720 | 198,279 | 109,254 |
| Carlstadt | 82,473 | 42 | 1,708 | 92,592 | 377,514 | 163,372 |
| Stora Kapparberg | 51,547 | 129 | 1,792 | 79,313 | 240,781 | 129,388 |
| Gefleborg | 28,367 | 140 | 2,089 | 50,024 | 153,996 | 96,736 |
| | 473,916 | 45 | 22,096 | 499,809 | 2,009,017 | 879,153 |
| *Gothland.* | | | | | | |
| Linköping | 104,061 | 21 | 5,458 | 94,194 | 360,044 | 182,280 |
| Calmar | 66,121 | 34 | 3,347 | 83,404 | 230,566 | 160,720 |
| Jonköping | 53,684 | 40 | 3,905 | 76,115 | 233,346 | 129,996 |
| Kronoberg | 37,695 | 48 | 2,837 | 56,010 | 175,229 | 102,709 |
| Blekinge | 21,715 | 27 | 1,089 | 31,522 | 139,143 | 85,314 |
| Skaraborg | 143,192 | 12 | 4,804 | 89,910 | 425,864 | 159,614 |
| Elfsborg | 73,808 | 37 | 4,209 | 102,715 | 334,282 | 187,021 |
| Gottenborg | 42,458 | 22 | 2,783 | 66,409 | 215,757 | 146,691 |
| Halmstadt | 43,983 | 23 | 2,922 | 47,485 | 167,120 | 85,657 |
| Christianstadt | 89,344 | 13 | 3,002 | 79,331 | 306,027 | 145,380 |
| Malmohus | 222,609 | 4 | 4,033 | 95,637 | 548,334 | 192,199 |
| Gothland | 30,064 | 20 | 1,098 | 17,560 | 83,523 | 38,151 |
| | 928,734 | 20 | 39,487 | 840,262 | 3,204,184 | 1,625,632 |
| Stockholm city | ........ | .. | ...... | ........ | ........ | 79,473 |
| Total | 1,454,760 | 62 | 65,309 | 1,443,858 | 5,702,835 | 2,771,252 |

Sweden Proper occupies the centre of the kingdom, and includes the capital, and the great mining districts. It consists of an immense plain, covered by almost boundless forests, intermixed with patches of cultivation; only a few hills of moderate height breaking its vast uniformity. Three great lakes, like inland seas, the Wener, the Wetter, and the Malar, form almost a continuous chain across its centre. Besides these, there is an immense number of smaller lakes, especially towards the north, communicating by river channels with the greater. These lakes do not display the grandeur which belongs to those of Switzerland; but their wide and winding shores, broken with rocks, and fringed with a profusion of wood, present many romantic scenes.

The division into provinces, of Sweden Proper, as well as of Gothland, as given in the preceding table, was made recently by government, and is the only one upon which statistical details have been collected. But there is another and earlier division, which remains still fixed in the Swedish mind; and corresponds, in fact, both to the aspect of nature and to the peculiarities in the people. These are Sudermanland, the province which contains the capital, and is situated on the south side of the lake Malar; Upland, a high territory on the northern side of that lake; Westmanland, to the west of Upland; Nerike, a beautiful little region, completely enclosed between the three great lakes; Warmeland, to the north of the Wener, covered with a multitude of little lakes; and, lastly, Dalecarlia, called also Dalarne, or the Plains, a province which, of all others, presents the most striking and peculiar features. It is, above all, distinguished by the energetic character of its peasantry, whose exertions at one time reared the fallen monarchy, and who continue to form its most powerful defence. They still hold as a maxim, that one Dalecarlian is equal to two of any other Swedes. Their diet is poor in the extreme, consisting in a great measure of bark-bread, yet their health and vigour do not suffer; and a number of them, who were quartered as troops at Stockholm, were affected with fevers in consequence of the repletion caused by eating wheaten bread. The memory of the great Gustavus Vasa, the founder of the Swedish monarchy, is cherished in this province with the utmost warmth; and many memorials of him are preserved in different places.

Stockholm (*fig.* 242.), with which we shall commence our details, is finely situated, at the junction of the extensive and beautiful lake of Malar, or Mäler, with the sea. It stands partly on some small islands, and two peninsulas, presenting a view as beautiful and diversified as imagination can conceive. Innumerable craggy rocks rise from the water, partly covered with houses, and partly planted with wood; while vessels of all forms and descriptions are seen passing to and fro. White edifices, consisting of public and private palaces, churches, and other buildings, rising from an expanse of waters, produce an effect of incomparable grandeur. When the lake and sea are frozen, they are covered with sledges of all kinds, and exhibit one of the gayest scenes imaginable. If external appearance were alone to be relied on, Stockholm might be deemed the most magnificent city in the world. This impression is not sustained by any beauty or convenience in the interior. Except the great square of Norden Malm, the streets, though of very considerable length, are neither broad nor handsome. There is no foot pavement; the houses are lofty, all whitewashed, and the shops are extremely poor. The different families reside in separate floors or stories, one above another, the ground-floors being usually occupied as shops. The royal palace, however, begun by Charles XI., and finished by Gustavus III., may vie with any structure of the kind in Europe. It is in the Grecian style, quadrangular, four stories high, built of brick only, but faced with stone-coloured cement. Its situation, facing the quay, and commanding a view of all parts of the city, adds greatly to its beauty. It contains some fine specimens of sculpture and painting, curiosities connected with Swedish history, and a range of small apartments embellished by Gustavus III. in a fanciful manner. This palace, with the finest buildings of the city, stands on one of the islands. The kings of Sweden have in the country other palaces: that of Drottningholm is a handsome stuccoed building, roofed with copper, and having side wings; but the gardens are barbarously laid out in the old fashion, with trees and hedges clipped into fanciful shapes.

242

Stockholm

Nyköping is the only tract of Sweden Proper which is south of the lakes. The town of that name, though small, has an air of magnificence. The houses are of wood painted yellow.

The provinces of Westeros, Orebro, and Carlstadt, along the north side of the lakes, reach across the kingdom. Enköping, on a branch of the Malar, is the first town which occurs westward from Stockholm, but it is not of great consequence. Westeras, on the same lake, has more commercial importance, as a link between the capital and the northern and western provinces. There is only one principal street, about two miles in length; the houses are only of one story, and often roofed with turf. It is the see of the richest bishopric in Sweden. The cathedral is a simple edifice; but one of the most elegant in Sweden, adorned with a very elegant porphyry monument erected to Eric IV., who died by poison in 1577. Next comes Köping, small and poor; but celebrated as having been the residence of Scheele. It lies at the extreme interior point of the Malar. Quitting that lake, and proceeding southwest, we come to Arboga, a beautiful little town on a river which falls into that lake, and near a canal which connects it with the lake Hjelmar. A steam-packet, established by an Englishman, now enables it to communicate with the capital. Nearly due west is Orebro, a more considerable town, and the occasional place of meeting for the Swedish diet. It is reckoned the fifth town in Sweden, containing about 4000 people, and the streets are broad and spacious, though the houses, as elsewhere in Sweden, are low, and of painted wood. The stadthus, or governor's residence, which includes also the prison, is a huge shapeless edifice. The church, which forms also the place of meeting for the diet, is an ancient structure, originally Gothic, and built of stone, but patched with brick, and in various styles. Proceeding westward, we enter Carlstadt, or, as anciently called, Warmeland, a region entirely of mines, forests, and lakelets, and bounded on the south by the extended shores of the Wener lake. Carlstadt is situated near the point where this lake receives the Clara, a considerable river, which traverses these wooded regions, and down which immense quantities of timber are floated; advantage for this purpose being taken of the floods to which i is occasionally subject. One company from Gottenburg has saw-mills, at which are annually cut upwards of 50,000 planks. Carlstadt is a place of from 2000 to 3000 people, presenting the ordinary aspect of Swedish towns. It collects the vast produce of the mines and forests of Warmeland, and transmits them across the Wener to Wenersberg, whence they find their way to Gottenburg. Considerably in the interior is Philipstadt, in the very heart of the iron mines, by which it is supported.

The most remarkable are those of Persberg (*fig.* 243.), a few miles to the eastward. They are thirteen in number, dug into a mountain entirely composed of veins and beds of iron ore. Dr. Clarke, after having, in the course of ten years' travel, inspected many of the principal works of this kind in different countries, declares, that he had never beheld any thing equal to this for grandeur of effect, and for the tremendously striking circumstances under which human labour is here performed. In the wide and open abyss, suddenly appeared a vast prospect of yawning caverns and prodigious machinery. Immense buckets, suspended by rattling chains, were passing up and down; ladders were scaling all the inward precipices; upon which the work-people, reduced by their distance to pigmies, were ascending and descending. The clanking of chains, the groaning of the pumps, the hallooing of the miners, the creaking of the blocks and wheels, the trampling of horses, the beating of the hammers, and the loud and frequent subterraneous thunder from the blasting of the rocks by gunpowder, in the midst of all this scene of excavation and vapour, produced an effect that no stranger could witness unmoved.

243

Persberg Mine.

Dalecarlia, or Dalarne, extends to the north-east of Warmeland. It is covered with an extraordinary profusion of mosses and fungi, so that it is termed by Dr. Clarke the supreme court of the cryptogamia. We have already remarked the peculiar character of the people, who preserve entire the dress, habits, and the daring energy of the ancient Swedes. The most important branch of productive industry consists in the mines, particularly the great copper mine at Fahlun (*fig.* 244.). It is immediately adjoining to the town, and consists of an enormous conical mass with the top downwards. The bottom of the cone, being the top of the mine, was the first worked; and the galleries being made through it without due precaution, the whole fell in, producing an immense open crater which still remains. Regular staircases of easy descent traverse this immense crater or basin, from its outer lip to the lowermost point, whence arise vast volumes of smoke and vapour, giving it the appearance, on a greater scale, of the Neapolitan Solfatra. It is divided into no less than 1200 shares or sections, among which the ore is divided immediately on being brought up, and it is then smelted on a small scale by the different individuals. The ore is not rich. In 1600, this mine is said to have yielded 8,000,000 pounds of copper; in 1650, 5,500,000; but at present only 1,120,000 pounds. The workmen have now reached the bottom, or the surface of the cone, and are still working through the ground, in the fond hope of coming to the top of another cone, reaching downwards. Unless this chimera should be realised, the mine, it is said, will, in a few years, cease to be productive. Fahlun is a regularly built but old-fashioned and dirty town, subsisting solely by the mine. It has two churches, one covered with copper, but this has not a handsome appearance, the colour of that metal being converted into a whitish green soon after exposure to the weather. Near Fahlun is the house where Gastavus Vasa lay concealed, the proprietor of which has studied to preserve in its pristine state this asylum of the Swedish king. His chamber, bed, and clothes are still shown; his shirt of worsted mail fitted similar to those made by the Circassians, and his other weapons.

244

Fahlun Mine.

Sala, which is properly in Westmanland, may be mentioned here as another mining town on a smaller scale, neat, regular, but ill-paved. The only important mine is one of galena, which yields 2000 marks of silver, and 32,000 pounds weight of lead. There is also a copper mine, which produces little; and one of iron, which is not considered worth the expense of working.

Upland, coinciding nearly with the modern Upsala, is an interesting province, extending from a part of the lake to the river Dal. It is flat, but diversified with numerous little round knolls, which, with the small lakes and the numerous fine forests, render it picturesque. It contains Upsala, the seat of the great northern university, and Danemora, the most valuable of the iron mines.

Upsala, or Upsal (*fig.* 245.), is the place in Sweden most venerable for its antiquity. It was long the residence of the kings, and has always been the chief seat of religion and learning. Even in pagan times it was the residence of the highpriest of Odin; and in 1026, Everinus, a bishop from England, was placed there, for the purpose of converting the natives to Christianity. The cathedral is the largest and finest ecclesiastical monument in Sweden, a country not eminent for such structures. The exterior is indeed only of brick, and there is an injudicious mixture of the Gothic with the Doric towers. But the interior is very striking, adorned with a double row of fourteen fluted columns, a magnificent altar, and above all by many monuments of the kings and heroes of Sweden. Particular notice is attracted by that of Gustavus Vasa, and the three Stures, successively regents of the kingdom, who, in that station, earned the title of fathers of their country. The shirt of mail of Margaret, the Semiramis of the North, is also kept as a warlike relic. Upsala contains also a palace founded by Gustavus Vasa, now half burnt down. It is at present supported solely by the university, of which an account has already been given. It is destitute of all trade or industry. It is therefore small, but very regular and neat, having a large square in the centre, where all the streets converge.

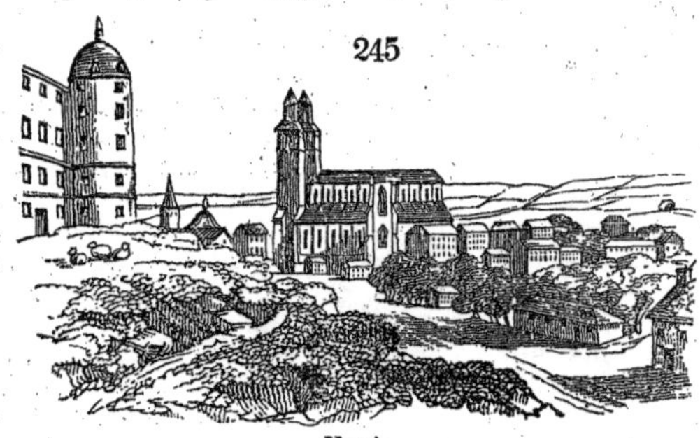
245

Upsala.

The mine of Danemora is situated near the small town of Osterby. Swedish iron is the best in the world, and the iron of Danemora is the best in Sweden. Dr. Thomson was told at Sheffield, that cast steel could not be made with any other. Danemora was first wrought as a silver mine, but this was soon exhausted. The iron then began to be wrought, and soon established the high character it now holds. The great opening is fifty fathoms deep, and the mine has been wrought thirty fathoms lower down. The ore is blasted with gunpowder. At short intervals are heard tremendous explosions, like the discharge of the heaviest artillery, which are echoed through the caverns, and shake the earth like a volcano, while volumes of smoke burst forth after each crash. From the mouth of the cavern enormous masses of iron are raised up by machinery. The mine belongs to a number of private individuals, who have erected a steam-engine at an expense of 36,000 rix-dollars. The produce is estimated at 4000 tons. There are twenty-seven other mines in the province of Upsala.

Gothland, or Gotaland, the southern division of the kingdom, forms a large peninsula, with a wide circuit of shores. It enjoys a considerably milder climate, and is the only part of the kingdom where wheat is raised in any considerable quantity. It is here also that the recent improvements in agriculture have been chiefly observable. There is thus more land in cultivation, and trees will not grow in the immediate vicinity of the coasts; so that Gothland is not so thoroughly covered with wood, as the provinces to the north of the lakes. If we except the capital, this division contains almost all the sea-ports and naval arsenals; and consequently engrosses nearly all the foreign commerce of the kingdom.

The modern and official divisions of Gothland have been exhibited in the statistical table. The ancient divisions are into Eastern and Western Gothland, divided from each other by the long line of the lake Wetter; Smaland, an extensive but barren tract, to the south of that lake; and Scania, or Schönen, the southern peninsular extremity of Sweden, a better peopled, and better cultivated district than any other in the kingdom.

Eastern Gothland comprises chiefly the modern provinces of Nyköping and Linköping. The town of Nyköping is agreeably situated at the extremity of a small bay of the Baltic, and though small has an air of magnificence; but it carries on little or no trade. It is now much outstripped by Norköping, the largest of all the *köpings* (i. e. markets), and the fourth town in Sweden. Norköping lies upon the large river Motala, which communicates between the lake Wetter and the Baltic, and which is here broken into numerous rocky channels. The chief branch of industry consists in the manufacture of broadcloth, which is produced so fine as to sell at twenty-seven shillings per ell, of one yard and three quarters broad. The breed of sheep in the neighbourhood has been considerably improved by the introduction of merinos. The town is regularly built, of neat wooden houses. Linköping is another provincial capital, handsomer in its aspect, though much smaller, than Norköping. The cathedral, rebuilt four hundred years ago, is one of the finest ecclesiastical structures in the kingdom, and near it is a very handsome theatre.

The district of Smaland has for its chief town Jonköping, situated at the extremity of the Wetter, and commanding grand and beautiful views over that immense lake, which has here a wide border of low but finely wooded rocks. The town has been entirely rebuilt since 1790, when it was burnt to the ground. Though built chiefly of wood, like other Swedish towns, it contains many good and commodious houses, the residence of wealthy inhabitants, who have been attracted by the amenity of the site. A high court of appeal for this part of Sweden is established here. About ten miles distant is Tuberg, a long round-backed hill, composed wholly of one unbroken mass of fine magnetic ironstone. It presents such a colossal mass as in Hausmann's opinion must continue to afford a source of riches to the remotest posterity. The upper bed, 370 feet thick, has been wrought for 250 years. It is merely blasted with gunpowder, when the fragments fall to the bottom, and are conveyed to neighbouring furnaces. The ore is not very rich, the proportion of pure iron varying from 21 to 32 per cent.; but it is very tractable, and free from any hurtful ingredients. The hill, though only 400 feet high, commands an almost boundless view over the vast wooded flats of Smaland. This district contains also a considerable quantity of bog iron ore of inferior quality, and some copper mines.

The sea-coast of Smaland, consisting of the modern provinces of Calmar and Bleking, is of a naked and unpromising aspect, but contains some havens of importance. Calmar is noted in Swedish history as a strong fortress, and still more because in one of the apartments of its castle was signed the celebrated treaty which united the three crowns of the north on the head of Margaret. Carlscrona is the chief naval arsenal and one of the largest towns in Sweden. It is built on three small islands connected with each other and with the coast by long wooden bridges, while other islands serve for the erection of works for the defence of the harbour. These are square batteries of stone, well mounted with ordnance, which appear formidable enough, though probably not capable of coping with a ship of the line. Separate establishments exist for the large vessels, and for the flotilla; but one of the most remarkable features consists of the covered docks, partly excavated out of the vast masses of solid rock. The want of tides in the Baltic is supplied by sluices, which open into the port, and are emptied again at pleasure. Carlshamn is a smaller town, romantically situated, like a cluster of nests, on the tops of cliffs. During war it enjoyed a considerable proportion of the neutral trade, which it has since lost. Christianstadt is a fortress of considerable celebrity, the capture of which formed the first military achievement of Gustavus Adolphus. Some fragments of the fortifications remain, and the approach to them is defended by an extensive swamp which surrounds the place.

Scania begins here, a flat and fertile peninsula, forming the most southern part of Sweden. There are numerous German residents in Scania, supposed to have sought refuge there during the Protestant persecution in Germany; and some Scotch farmers have also sought to introduce an improved system of agriculture. In the centre of Scania is Lund, the seat of the second university in Sweden, containing 30,000 volumes, a good observatory and botanical garden, and a noble cathedral in the Norman style of architecture. Malmo, formerly one of the Hanseatic towns, is the chief seat of trade. Helsenving and Ystadt, neat little ports, are the chief places of embarkation for Denmark and Germany. All these towns command magnificent views of the Sound, enlivened by the crowds of shipping that are continually passing.

Having turned the southern point of Sweden, we come to the coast of West Gothland, situated on that great gulf of the German Ocean called the Cattegat. Being the part of the kingdom nearest to the great states of Europe, it carries on a principal part of the commerce of Sweden. Laholm and Halmstadt are ports of some consideration, in the gloomy and heathy province of Halland, but almost the whole of the western commerce of Sweden centres at Gottenburg.

Gottenburg is built in the interior of a bay set round with rugged and naked rocks, and the whole country round is sterile and desolate. It is supported by its situation at the mouth of the Gotha, the broadest and most navigable of the rivers of Sweden, which by means of the canal of Trölhätta affords a full communication with the great interior lake of Wener, and the opportunity of bringing down those immense stores of wood and iron produced around its shores. The prosperity of Gottenburg was also greatly promoted by the French anti-commercial system, under which this port remained one of the few channels by which British goods could force their way into the Continent. It is a very handsome city, built entirely of stone, the use of wood having been prohibited since the last great conflagration, the second which had occurred in the course of ten years. A magnificent church, lately built, is constructed, in a great measure, of stone imported from Scotland. The principal street, which is long and wide, has a canal running through it; the others strike off from it at right angles. The principal merchants are Scotch, who live in a style of great magnificence.

West Gothland presents still some other striking features. Among these rank foremost the cataracts and canal of Trolhätta. Above the former the river is a mile broad; but being confined between two lofty rocks, it pours down its waters with prodigious force. The descent, however, is only a hundred feet in the course of two miles, making thus a rapid rather than a fall; the water rushing along with inconceivable rapidity, boiling up, and covered with foam. The noise is prodigious, and clouds of vapour are thrown up. These cataracts opposed a complete obstruction to the navigation of the Gotha, which the kings of Sweden expended immense sums in endeavouring to overcome; but their works were too imperfect to resist the impetuosity of the current. At length, in 1793, the enterprise was taken up by a company of private merchants, who in seven years brought it to a happy completion. The canal is twenty-four feet wide, and eight feet deep. It extends only two miles; but being cut through a granite rock, sometimes to the depth of one hundred and fifty feet, it proved a work of very great labour. Wenerborg, at the junction of the Gotha with the Wener, is the channel by which the products of the interior are brought down the river; yet it does not derive from this trade much prosperity or importance. Uddevalla and Stronstadt, are small sea-ports, with some trade and fishery, but they have suffered since the herrings deserted the coast. Skara and Fahlkoping are places of some consequence in the interior of West Gothland.

*Norrland* forms a third division, which, if considered as including Lapland (and it is so considered politically), would be much more extensive than all the rest of the kingdom put together. It is, however, our intention to reserve for a particular section the vast and peculiar region known under the name of Lapland. Norrland, in a restricted sense, comprises the four provinces named in the table, but is better known under the divisions of Jamtland, Angermanland, Medelpad, and Helsingland. Jamtland, where it borders on Norway, includes some of the highest mountains, several of them rising to 6000 or 7000 feet. The rest of Norrland is flat, and the climate moist and variable, like that of Jamtland, but colder. Wheat scarcely ripens beyond Sundswall; near to the northern border, barley and rye ripen with difficulty. Almost the only fruits are cherries and gooseberries. The land under cultivation did not, in 1812, exceed 52,000 acres, which is, in proportion to the whole, only as 1 to 915. Yet the people are industrious; and Von Buch observed a greater air of prosperity here than in the rest of the kingdom. The woods which cover almost the whole country, are infested by numerous herds of wolves. Of the entire population, amounting to 159,100, only 6318 live in the towns, which of course must be very unimportant. Sundswall and Hernosand are, however, sea-ports of some little consequence, as is Umea; but this last properly belongs to Lapland.

### Subsect. 2.—*Norway.*

This extensive portion of the Swedish monarchy, recently, by compulsion, but in all likelihood permanently, united, comprises a very long line of maritime territory, facing the boundless expanse of the Northern Ocean. Throughout its whole length, in an oblique line parallel to the sea, runs the chain of the Dofrines, presenting many bold and lofty summits covered with perpetual snow. Sneehatta, the highest, is 8100 feet. These mountains throw out numerous chains, sloping downwards to the sea, which form romantic valleys and deep and winding bays. Norway produces some corn, not nearly sufficient, however, for its own consumption; but exports large quantities of timber and fish, receiving, in return, those commodities of which it stands most in need.

The southern Norwegian provinces of Aggerhuus, Christiania, and Christiansund, include a considerably greater proportion of level territory than the others. They have the great range of mountains to the north and west, and are not separated from Sweden by these natural barriers. Through these provinces flow southward into the bay of Christiania the Drammen and the Glommen, the two greatest rivers of the North, and bring with them an immense quantity of timber, which is cut into deals, and exported to all parts of Europe. The export of iron is also considerable.

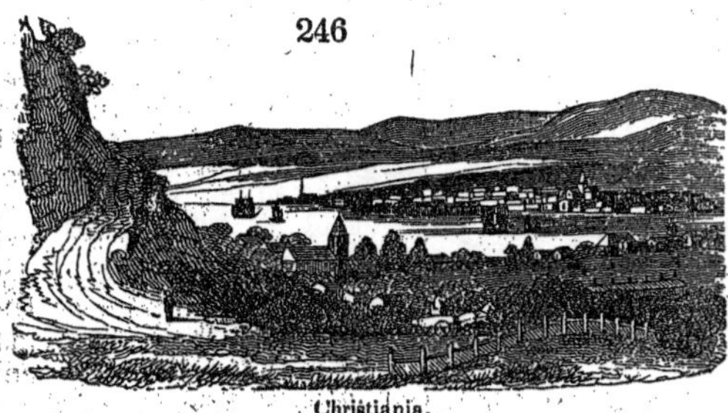
246
Christiania.

*Christiania*, (*fig.* 246.), capital of all this district, with a population of 20,581, now ranks as the capital of the whole kingdom. It is situated at the head of a long interior bay or fiord, and enjoys a situation which Von Buch considers as altogether wonderful. The bay, its islands, the crowds of sails spread among them, with the view of majestic hills rising over hills in the distance, appeared to him equalled only on the lake of Geneva, which, however, has not the vessels and islands. Christiania is chiefly supported by the trade in deals; and those cut in its saw-mills are considered, by the traders in this article, to be superior to all others. Some of its merchants, particularly the Ankers, maintain the state of princes, and are considered equal in wealth and liberal views to any in Europe. Christiania comes more into contact than Bergen with the more advanced countries of Europe, and has adopted almost exclusively the improvements which distinguish them. The buildings are regular, and mostly of stone; so that in the course of 200 years, while other Scandinavian towns have been repeatedly reduced to ashes, Christiania has suffered only slight injury from fire Since the union with Sweden, it has received an university, with two professors, who have moderate incomes, chiefly derived from grain.

There are other havens of some importance in this southern tract of Norway. On the western coast of Christiania fiord, the two, Bragenæs and Stromsoe, unite in forming what is called Drammen, at the mouth of the important river of that name. Tonsberg, at the bottom of the same side, is a town of some ancient celebrity, but now a good deal decayed. On the eastern side of the same bay is Moss, watered by a stream, turning twenty saw-mills, by which an immense quantity of deals are prepared for exportation. Frederickshall, an ancient and still important frontier town, is beautifully situated in an interior bay, winding among mountains. Near it is the strong fortress of Frederickstadt, the scene of the death of Charles XII. The pass of the Swinsund (*fig.* 247.), on the immediate frontier, presents one of the most romantic and picturesque scenes in Scandinavia. Christiansund, the most southern province of Norway, has a capital of the same name, the fourth town in the kingdom, which, from its situation on the Skagerrack, is visited for shelter and supplies by numerous vessels entering and leaving the Baltic. The interior from Christiania, though it includes Hedemarken, and other large pastoral valleys, and though its communications are facilitated by the large lake of Miosen, does not contain a single town. That of Hammer attests its former magnificence, by the remains of a palace, and of several churches now restored. The whole of this territory is hemmed in on the west and north by the gigantic ranges of the Doverfield and Fillefield, which separate it from Drontheim and Bergen.

247

Swinsund Ferry.

The province of Bergen is rude, rocky, and mountainous, consisting of the slope downwards to the sea of the highest part of the Dofrine range. The town of Bergen, (*fig.* 248.), at the head of a long interior bay, was formerly accounted the capital, and contains a population of 18,511. Its commerce, which is considerable, is founded on the exportation, less of the produce of the country behind it, than of the northern fishery at Daffoden, of which the produce is brought to Bergen by numerous barks. Its merchants had long the monopoly of this, and still retain much the greatest share. They are chiefly Dutch, and send a vessel weekly to Amsterdam for a supply of the garden stuffs which their own soil does not yield. Bergen is built of large masses of wooden houses, amid rocks, and has suffered severely by fire.

248

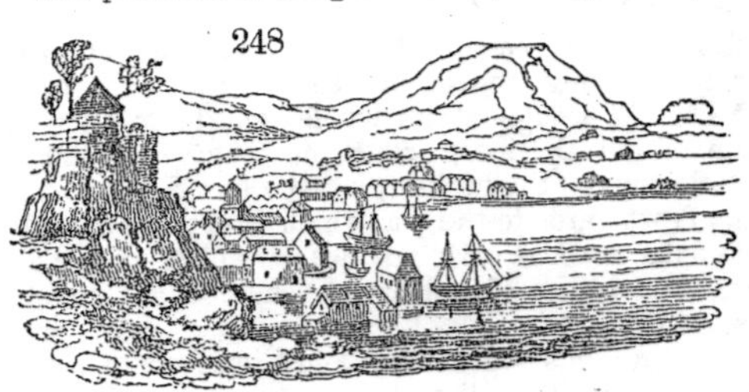

Bergen.

The province of Drontheim, to the north of Bergen and Christiania, and separated from them by vast mountains, corresponds in latitude with the Swedish Jamtland. The capital (*fig.* 249.), of the same name, is situated on the shore of a winding fiord, but subsists less by foreign commerce than by the internal communication between numerous valleys and districts to which it forms a central point of union. Of these valleys, that of the Guldal is the most extensive and beautiful, and singularly celebrated in Swedish story and tradition. Here, it is boasted, dwelt the mighty Haco, the noble and wise Olaf Tryggvason. The society of Drontheim is always

249

Drontheim.

held forth as representing under the happiest light, the genuine Norwegian character; its warmth of kindness, and generous hospitality. Dr. Clarke praises chiefly its truly Norwegian simplicity; but Von Buch considers it as marked by more refined taste, more graceful and attractive manners, than the society of Christiania. In no district of Norway is there said to be such a feeling of patriotism and public spirit. Drontheim is built wholly of wood, and has in consequence been seven times burnt to the ground; yet the houses are handsome, and ornamented with taste. There is a spacious palace, built wholly of this material, and partaking its imperfection. Drontheim also contains the remains of a cathedral, the largest edifice in the country, and to which the whole population of the North came once in pilgrimage. The environs are very beautiful, with numerous country-seats, and lofty snow-crowned hills in the distance. Christiansund is also a small sea-port and fishing town in this province.

Beyond Drontheim commences Norrland, a district rather than a province, the name being vaguely applied to all the north of Scandinavia. Relatively to Norway, it is marked by an increasing intensity of cold; the mountains, even at 3000 feet high, being capped with perpetual snow, and vast table-plains or fields remaining covered with it during the whole summer. Grain, even of the coarsest descriptions, ripens only in a few favoured spots. The spruce fir gradually disappears, and shelter is necessary to allow the Scotch fir and the birch to spring up. The climate, however, is somewhat milder than that of regions under the same latitude on the Baltic; so that, while the ports of Stockholm and Carlscrona are shut during several months of the year, those of Norrland remain continually open. Yet in this dreary region occurs a busy scene of human action and existence. The numerous islands, and the deep bays between them and the land, afford spots to which shoals of fish come from the farthest depths of the North Sea to deposit their spawn. During the whole year, the herring affords a regular occupation to the Norrland boatman; but from February to April, the shoals, migrating from thence, and from all the surrounding coasts, crowd to the Loffoden Islands, the central seat of the northern fishery. These islands form a chain parallel to the land, and separated by narrow channels through which the tides of the Northern Ocean rush with tremendous rapidity. The sea flows as in the most rapid rivers, and the name of stream is employed:—Malström, the famous whirlpool, Grimström, Sundström, which, when the tide is high, produce the effect of a mighty cataract. Waves are seen struggling against waves, towering aloft, or wheeling about in whirlpools; the dashing and roaring of which are heard many miles out at sea. The produce of the fishery, which has been rendered much more abundant by the introduction of large nets instead of hooks, is conveyed to Bergen in a great number of little barks. The Danish government endeavoured to form at Stromsoe a commercial depôt for the produce of Norrland; but in this bleak situation it has not flourished. The Russians come with numerous vessels from Archangel, bringing meal and provisions, which they give in exchange for the fish caught.

### Subsect. 3.—*Lapland.*

The vast region of Lapland is divided from the rest of Scandinavia by a line drawn across it nearly coinciding with the Polar Circle, so as to render it almost entirely an arctic region. It consists partly of great chains of mountains, some of which are 4000 feet high, while other extensive tracts are level. Through these roll the Tornea, the Lulea, the Pitea, and other rivers of long course, and navigable for the few boats which have any occasion to pass along them. The Laplanders are a peculiar race, short, stout, brown, with black hair, pointed chin, and eyes rendered weak by exposure to the smoke and snow. They are divided into the mountain or wandering Laplanders, and those who dwell in what are called villages; but Kautokeino, which forms a sort of Lapland capital, when visited by Acerbi, was found to contain not more than four families and a priest. The swift-footed rein-deer, which they train to draw them in sledges over the snow, form their riches; the flesh and milk of these animals compose their food, and the skins their furniture. The tents of the Laplanders (*fig.* 250.) are formed by six beams of wood meeting nearly at top, covered with cloth, a flap of which, left between two of the beams, serves as the door. The floor is spread with rein-deer skins, having the hair upwards, and which thus serve for either lying or sitting, the tent being too low to stand in, except in one place. A stone frame is made in the middle, for the fire; and there is a hole at the top, to which the smoke

250

Mountain Laplander's Tent.

must find its way; but this it does not effect till it has thickly impregnated the whole tent with its fumes; which, however, are valued as affording a protection in winter against the cold, and in summer against the swarms of musquitoes with which, during a period of short and extreme heat, the air is infested. The herds of rein-deer vary from 300 to upwards of 1000, according to the wealth of the possessor. All day they wander over the hills, and in the evening are driven, not without some occasional resistance, into an enclosed park, where they are milked. Each yields only about a tea-cupful of milk; but rich, aromatic, and of exquisite taste. Linnæus mentions nineteen farms in which milk is prepared for food; but cleanliness does not preside over their cookery; and the use of the hand, without knife or fork, to carry every thing to the mouth, and of the tongue to lick the dishes, prevents an European from joining these meals with any relish. The Laplanders travel from place to place, and move their families, usually at the beginning of winter and summer, in sledges made in the form of a boat, and drawn by rein-deer (*fig.* 251.). These animals are tamed and trained with considerable difficulty, and they are sometimes restive; but, in general, they bound over hill and dale with surprising celerity. The natives have also a species of snow-shoe; not a broad flat board, like that of America, but somewhat in the form of a skate, with which they glide rapidly along the surface of deep snow, and even up and down the steep sides of the hills (*fig.* 252.).

251

Laplanders Travelling.

252

Laplander descending a Snow-Flake.

Their dress is carefully contrived for the purposes of warmth. The under part, or shirt, is composed of sheep's skin with the wool inwards; while the exterior coat is formed by the skin of the rein-deer, or some other animal, having the fur outwards. They add fur gloves, and a woollen pointed red cap (*fig.* 253.).

The entire population of Lapland, spread over a surface of 150 miles square, is stated by Dr. Thomson not to exceed 60,000, or one inhabitant to every three square miles. Even this scanty measure is supported only on the sea-coasts by a supply of fish. The parish of Kautokeino, in the interior, extending 200 miles in length and 96 in breadth, was reported to Acerbi as containing not more than ninety families, of whom twelve only are fixed. The Laplanders are a harmless race, among whom great crimes are unknown. Only one murder has been heard of in twenty years; and the absence of theft is proved by that of bars, bolts, and other safeguards. They do not show that open hospitality and warmth of heart, for which rude nations are so often celebrated. They are cold, shy, mistrustful, and difficult to treat with, at least unless tobacco or brandy be brought in as mediators. They were formerly very superstitious; and the Lapland witches were famous for their empire over the winds, which they enclosed in bags, and sold to the mariner. The magic drum

253

Mountain Laplander.

254

Laplander with Magic Drum.

(*fig.* 254.) and the enchanted chain (*fig.* 255.) are still in occasional use. Yet the Laplanders have been converted to Christianity, and are attentive to its duties, coming often from vast distances to attend divine service, though the instructions are conveyed to them only through the broken medium of an interpreter.

255.

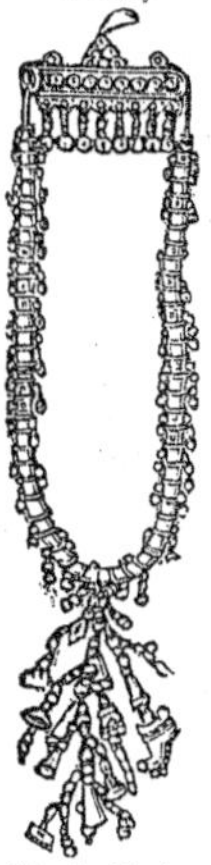

Magic Chain.

The sea-coast of Lapland presents a continuation of the same bold and rocky features which distinguish that of Norway. Here, too, the fishery is carried on with activity. It is chiefly in the hands of a Finnish race, called Quans, who have pushed across Lapland, and exert an activity unknown to the natives of that region. The Russians from Archangel, also, not only bring their meal to exchange for fish, but carry on the fishery themselves to a great extent. In July and August they cover with their small three-masted vessels all the fiords and sounds, and throw out lines that are sometimes two miles long, and contain 600 or 700 hooks; so that their vessels are filled with the utmost rapidity. The government has founded, on the large island of Qualoe, the town of Hammerfest, the most northern in the world, and destined as a rival to Archangel; but the settlement has never taken root in this ungenial climate, and continues also, with one exception, to be the smallest that exists. On the other side of the North Cape, on the extreme frontier, the fort of Wardhuus, defended by twenty men, forms the only barrier to prevent the Russians from taking possession of the whole country. Mageroe, the most northerly of the islands, consists of steep rocks rising perpendicularly from the sea, and ascended as if by stairs. In a rocky recess stands Kielvig, with four or five families, on a level spot, barely affording a site for the houses, and exposed to the perpetual war of the elements. The tempests here rage with such fury, that it is often impossible to leave the house without danger of being blown into the sea. At the northern point of this island is formed by the North Cape the grand boundary of the European continent, facing the depths of the Polar Ocean. It consists of an enormous mass of naked rock, parted by the action of the waves into pyramidal cliffs, down which large fragments are continually falling.

---

## CHAPTER VII.

### HOLLAND AND BELGIUM.

The Netherlands, comprising now the two kingdoms of *Holland* and *Belgium*, form a maritime territory, which, situated almost in the centre between the north and the south of Europe, and penetrated by the Rhine and its tributaries, possesses great natural advantages for industry and commerce. It has, accordingly, from a very early period of modern history, ranked as one of the most prosperous and flourishing parts of Europe. The union of the Batavian and Belgic Netherlands into one kingdom, though in fact only a renewal of that which subsisted at a former period, was suddenly terminated, in 1830, by a revolution of the Belgians. The separate existence, however, of Holland and Belgium being yet recent, and the statistical information respecting them having for a number of years been collected with reference always to the entire Netherlands, they will be still treated most advantageously in combination. It may be sufficient to observe, that, since the revolution of 1830, Belgium has been erected into a separate monarchy, through the mediation of the five great powers of Europe; and the crown, with their consent, has been conferred on prince Leopold, formerly of Saxe-Coburg.

### Sect. I.—*General Outline and Aspect.*

Holland and Belgium may be regarded as a large corner or segment cut off from France and Germany, which form round it a species of irregular arc. Arbitrary lines, drawn conformably to treaties, mark all except its maritime boundaries; for, though several of the greatest rivers of Europe cross its territory, none of them have any limitary character. The maritime boundary, which, like the inland, extends from north-east to south-west, is the North Sea, or German Ocean, which is formed here into a species of large gulf by the opposite coast of part of the English Channel. Holland is also penetrated by the deep inlet of the Zuyder Zee. The whole territory extends between 49° 30′ and 53° 34′ N. lat., and 2° 30′ and 7° 12′ E. long.; making about 280 miles in length, and 220 miles in breadth. The entire extent, according to the best calculations, amounts to 24,870 square miles, or 15,900,000 English acres.

In respect to surface, this country includes the lowest portion of the great low land of the European continent. The northern parts, composing the new kingdom of Holland, are mostly below the level to which the bordering sea rises during high tides or swells. Hence originated an imminent danger of inundation, till the Dutch constructed those mighty dikes, by which the sea is excluded, and which form so extraordinary a monument of their industry. Holland is humorously described by Butler as a country that draws fifty feet of water." The Belgic provinces are also flat, but not lower than the surface of the sea, nor much exposed

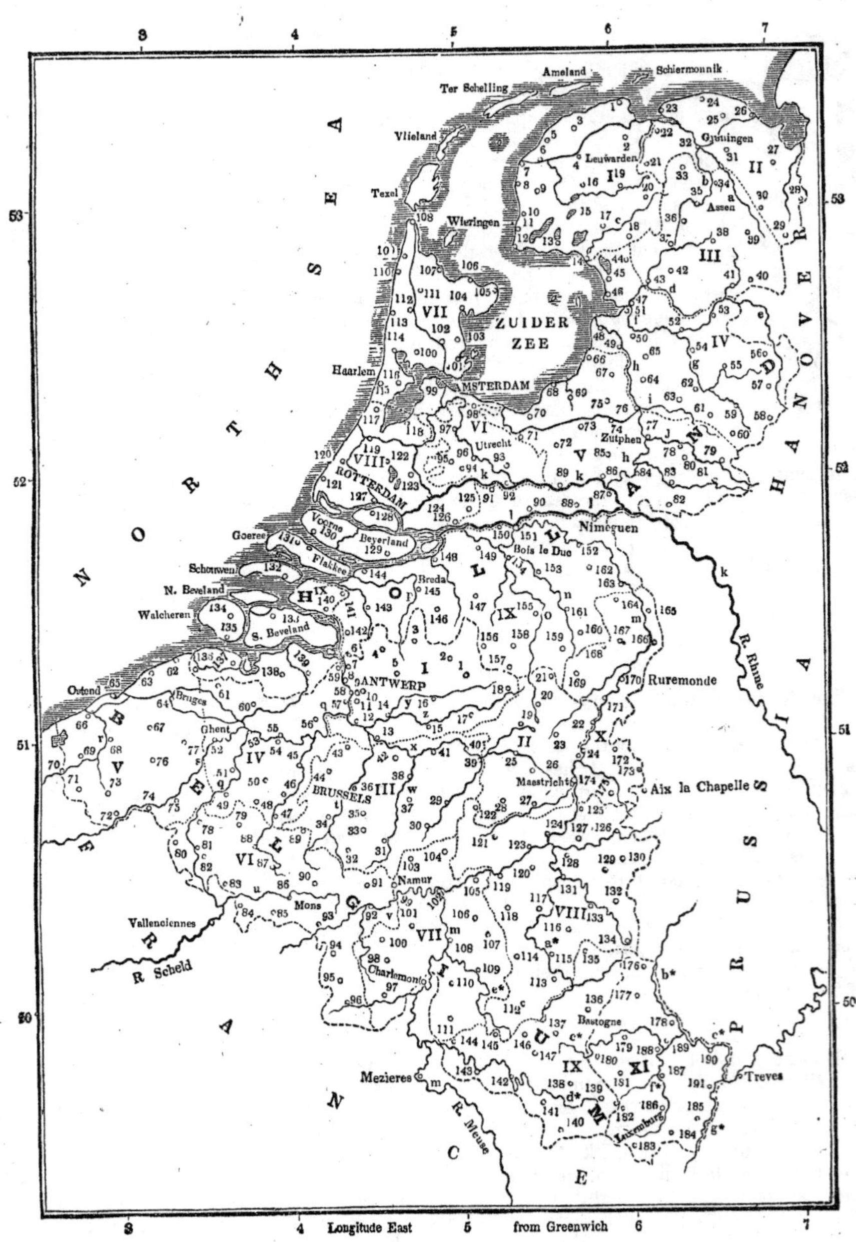
NORTH SEA
ZUIDER ZEE
HOLLAND
BELGIUM
FRANCE
HANOVER
PRUSSIA
Ameland
Schiermonnik
Ter Schelling
Vlieland
Texel
Wieringen
Leuwarden
Groningen
Assen
Haarlem
AMSTERDAM
Utrecht
Zutphen
ROTTERDAM
Voorne
Beyerland
Goeree
Flakkee
Schouwen
N. Beveland
Walcheren
S. Beveland
Nimeguen
Bois le Duc
Breda
Ruremonde
R. Rhine
ANTWERP
Ostend
Bruges
Ghent
BRUSSELS
Maastricht
Aix la Chapelle
Namur
Mons
Vallenciennes
R. Scheld
Charlemont
Bastogne
Mezieres
R. Meuse
Treves
Luxemburg
Longitude East from Greenwich

to river inundation. In the south-eastern district of Liège and Namur, branches of the Rhenish mountains render the surface irregular, and sometimes hilly, particularly in the tract forming part of the ancient forest of Ardennes.

Several rivers, which rank among the greatest in Europe, and are derived from distant sources, pass through this territory; and, separating into numerous channels, form broad estuaries at their entrance into the ocean. They all unite in the channel of the majestic Rhine; yet, by a singular fortune, this great name is not retained by the main branch of the river, which, in turning to the westward, receives the name of Waal, and afterwards that of its important tributary the Maese, under which designation it flows into the sea below Rotterdam. The Yssel, another considerable branch, runs northward into the Zuyder Zee; while the name of Rhine is retained by another, comparatively a rivulet, which passes through the provinces of Gueldres and Utrecht. The Maese or Meuse is the only great river which has the larger part of its course through the Netherlands, traversing the interior of Belgium from south to north. Its main tributaries, the Sambre on the west, and the Roer on the east, have only a portion of their course through Belgium. The Scheldt has not nearly so long a course; but this river, and its tributaries, the Lys, the Dyle, the Dender, and the Neethe, water the most improved districts, and visit the greatest cities of Belgium. When united under their main branch, they form a broad navigable channel, opening into an estuary, which affords to Antwerp the means of carrying on an extensive maritime commerce.

---

*References to the Map of Holland and Belgium.*

HOLLAND.

I. *Friesland.*
1. Paasens
2. Buitenpost
3. Dobkum
4. Leuwarden
5. St. Jacob
6. Franeker
7. Harlingen
8. Kornwurt
9. Bolsward
10. Workum
11. Hindelopen
12. Stavoren
13. Sloten
14. Kuinder
15. Terkappel
16. Grouw
17. Schoot
18. Noordwelde
19. Beestor Zwang
20. Donkerboek

II. *Groningen.*
21. Marum
22. Grypskerke
23. Zoltkamp
24. Uskert
25. Loppersum
26. Delfzyl
27. Winschoten
28. Fort Bourtange
29. Ter Apel
30. Ter Maarsch
31. Kolhom
32. Groningen

III. *Drenthe.*
33. Roon
34. Gasteren
35. Assen
36. Smilde
37. Dieverburg
38. Westerborg
39. Odoorn
40. Schoonebeek
41. Koevorden
42. Ruinen
43. Meppel

IV. *Overyssel.*
44. Steenwyk
45. Blockzyl
46. Vollenhoven
47. Swartesluis
48. Kampen
49. Hattem
50. Zwoll
51. Genemuiden
52. Ommen
53. Hardenberg
54. Den Ham
55. Almelo
56. Ootmarsum
57. Oldenzaal
58. Enschede
59. Delden
60. Haaxbergen
61. Goor
62. Ryssen
63. Holten
64. Wesepe
65. Heyno
76. Deventer

V. *Guelderland.*
66. Elburg
67. Posthuis
68. Harderwyk
69. Leuvenum
70. Nykerk
72. Barneveld
73. Kootvyk
74. Apeldoom
75. Vaasen
77. Zutphen
78. Lochem
79. Borkulo
80. Ruerlo
81. Biedevort
82. Heerenberg
83. Deutichem
84. Doesburg
85. De Woest Hoef
86. Arnheim
87. Huissen
88. Herveld
89. Wageningen
90. Thiel
91. Kuilenburg

VI. *Utrecht*
92. Wyk
93. Venendaal
94. Isselstein
95. Montfoort
96. Utrecht
97. Nieuwersluis
98. Naarden
71. Amersfoort

VII. *North Holland.*
99. Amsterdam
100. De Koog
101. Monnikendam
102. Purmerend
103. Edam
104. Hoorn
105. Enkhuisen
106. Medenblick
107. Kolhorn
108. The Helder
109. Calandsoog
110. Petten
111. Broek
112. Alkmaar
113. Egmondaan Zee
114. Beverwyk
115. Zandvoort
116. Haarlem

VIII. *South Holland.*
117. Lisse
118. Leimuden
119. Leyden
120. The Hague
121. Gravezande
122. Wilsveen
123. Gouda
124. Schoonhoven
125. Leedam
126. Gorcum
127. Rotterdam
128. Charloi
129. Stryen
130. Helvoetsluys
131. Goeree

IX. *Zealand.*
132. Zierikzee
133. Goes
134. Veere
135. Middleburg
136. Sluys
137. Biervliet
138. Axel
139. Hulst
140. Tholen
141. Steenbergen

IX. *North Brabant.*
142. Bergen op Zoom
143. Rozendaal
144. Williamstad
145. Breda
146. Chaam
147. Tilburg
148. Geertruidenberg
149. Heusdon
150. Bommel
151. Fort St. Andries
152. Grave
153. Vechel
154. Bois le Duc
155. Houvel
156. Reusel
157. Luiks Gestel
158. Eerzel
159. Leende
160. Asten
161. Helmont
162. Wanroy
163. Verlingbeck

X. *Limburg.*
164. Velten
165. Peterwerth
166. Venlo
167. Helden
168. Meyel
169. Weert
170. Ruremonde
171. Wessen
172. Oirsbeeck
173. Roilduc
174. Maestricht
175. Gulpen

XI. *Luxemburg.*
176. Wies Wampach
177. Clervaux
178. Vianden
179. Eschdorf
180. Martelange
181. Nider Pallen
182. Luxemburg
183. Esch
184. Frisange
185. Canach
186. N. Anwen
187. Morsch
188. Ettelbruck
189. Diekirch
190. Echtenach
191. Grevenmacheren

BELGIUM.

I. *Antwerp.*
1. Arendonck
2. Turnhout
3. Minderhout
4. Goring
5. Oost Malle
6. Sant Vliet
7. Fort Lillo
8. Fort St. Philip
9. Antwerp
10. Bergenhout
11. Berchem
12. Boom
13. Mechlin
14. Lier
15. Vosdoncken
16. Herenthals
17. Gestel
18. Lommel

II. *Limburg.*
19. Helck Teren
20. Peer
21. Hamont
22. Maseyck
23. Asch
24. Reckem
25. Hasselt
26. Bilsen
27. Tongres
28. Manshoven

III. *South Brabant.*
29. Tirlemont
30. Incourt
31. Moustier
32. Nivelles
33. La Belle Alliance
34. Halle
35. Waterloo
36. Brussels
37. Vlanden
38. Louvain
39. Haerlen
40. Diest
41. Aerschot
42. Ecluse
43. Donderzeel
44. Asche

IV. *East Flanders.*
45. Alost
46. Ninove
47. Grammont
48. Parieke
49. Oudenarde
50. Leeuwerghem
51. Dencnock
52. Deinse
53. Ghent
54. Weteren
55. Caleken
56. Hamme
57. Burcht Town and Fort
58. Tete de Flandres
59. Doel
60. Envelde
61. St. Laurens

V. *West Flanders.*
62. Cuooke
63. Blankenburg
64. Bruges
65. Ostend
66. Nieuport
67. Thorout
68. Dixmuide
69. Loo
70. Roustbrugge
71. Poperinghe
72. Warneton
73. Ypres
74. Menin
75. Courtray
76. Rousselaere
77. Thielt

VI. *Hainault.*
78. Pottes
79. Depret
80. Temp Leuve
81. Tournay
82. Fontenoy
83. Peruvels
84. Quivrain
85. Sars
86. Mons
87. Lens
88. Ath
89. Enghien
90. Roeulx
91. Gosselies
92. Charleroi
93. Merbes le Chateau
94. Beaumont
95. Ransse
96. Chimay

VII. *Namur.*
97. Marienbourg
98. Philipville
99. Ligny
100. Thil Baudian
101. Graux
102. Namur
103. Gembloux
104. Eghezee
105. Andennes
106. Nattore
107. Pessoulx
108. Dinant
109. Jambeline
110. Beau Raing
111. Gedinne

VIII. *Liege.*
112. St. Hubert
113. Beausainte
114. Marche
115. Marcourt
116. Grand Menil
117. Tohogne
118. Mieraij
119. Huy
120. Neuville
121. Omal
122. Landen
123. Flemalle
124. Liege
125. Vise
126. Limburg
127. Heron
128. Baufays
129. Spa
130. Solvastre
131. Douflame
132. Stavelot
133. Thession
134. Vieil Salm

IX. *Luxemburg*
135. Trailles
136. Bastogne
137. Neuville
138. Chau de Bologne
139. Arlon
140. Virton
141. Belle Fontaine
142. Perensart
143. Bouillon
144. Orchimont
145. Anloy
146. Recogne
147. Neuf Chateau

*Rivers.*
a Schuyten
b Hoorn
c Kuinder
d Reest
e Dinkel
f Vecht
g Regge
h Yssel
i Chipbeech
j Berkel
k Rhine
l Waal
m Meuse
n Great Aa
o Dommel
p Merk
q Scheldt
r Yperlee
s Lys
t Senne
u Haine
v Sambre
w Dyle
x Dermer
y Little Lethes
z Great Lethes
a* Ourt
b* Our
c* Sure
d* Semoy
e* Lesse
f* Alsette
g* Moselle

The only considerable lake in Holland is Haerlem-Meer, a wide shallow expanse; which, however, was of great service to the Dutch during their grand struggle for independence, by giving them the means of laying the surrounding country under water. There are several smaller lakes of the same character in Friesland.

## SECT. II.—*Natural Geography.*

### SUBSECT. 1.—*Geology.*

The higher parts of this country are composed of *strata of transition slates* and *quartzes* more or less inclining to sandstone, generally directed from N. E. to S. W., and traversed by numerous veins of quartz. These slates are *clay slate*, *whet slate* or *hone*, *drawing slate* or *black chalk*. Resting upon the transition rocks occur various secondary deposits. The first formation is the old *red sandstone*, upon which rests the *mountain limestone*. Associated with these rocks are various slate clays, and beds of *anthracite* or *glance coal*. Mines of *brown iron ore*, or hydrate of iron, and of *red iron ore*, or oxide of iron, occur among these rocks. A great field of the *coal formation*, resting upon this mountain limestone, extends from Aix-la-Chapelle to Douay. The coal formation in this tract of country forms a series of irregular basins, of which the most considerable are those of Liège and Charleroi, which are separated from each other by a small ridge of limestone. The chief rocks of these coal-basins are sandstone, slate, clay ironstone, and coal. The most important coal mines are those in the neighbourhood of Mons and Charleroi; but the mines of Liège are remarkable on account of the difficulties the miners meet with in their workings; the number of beds of coal being reckoned as high as eighty-three by M. Dumont. From Aix-la-Chapelle by Maestricht and Brussels, the country is composed of chalk, with occasional displays of green sand, gault and Shanklin sand, rising from under it.

The tritonian or lower tertiary rocks form in the Netherlands a very considerable basin, in which is situated the city of Brussels. It is composed principally of sands, ferriferous sandstones, white sandstones, flint, limestone, and clayey marl. These tertiary deposits are observed more or less deeply covered with *diluvium;* and at the mouths of the Scheldt, Meuse, and Rhine, there are vast deposits of river *alluvium*, which alluvium forms also the islands of Zealand, and the greater part of Holland.

### SUBSECT. 2.—*Botany.*

The *Botany* of this country is noticed under that of Germany.

### SUBSECT. 3.—*Zoology.*

The Native Zoology offers nothing peculiar. The Dutch horses (*fig.* 257.) are only valuable for draught: those of Friesland, Berg, and the country of Juliers, are the best; but their feet are generally large, they eat much, and have little endurance. This race appears to have been derived from Denmark, and to have produced the Holstein, which was the parent of the old unimproved English breeds of horses. The Flemish sheep are of a breed common to France and the Netherlands, being in general hornless, high on the legs, and derived from an intermixture with the Barbary long-legged sheep. The Dutch oxen are of an immense size, sometimes weighing 2000 pounds.

257

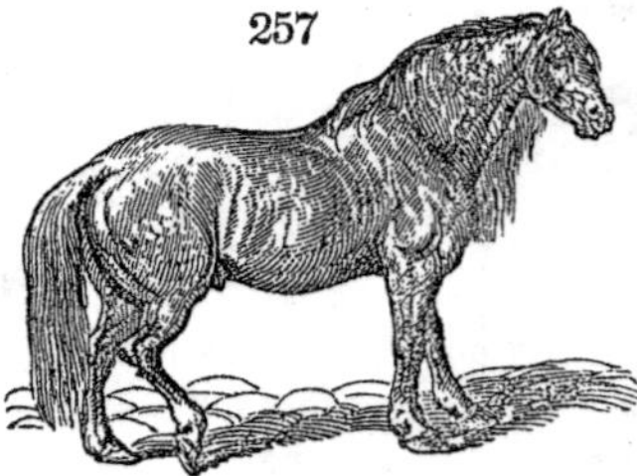

Dutch Horse.

## SECT. III.—*Historical Geography.*

The Netherlands formed, in ancient times, the principal part of Gallia Belgica. The Belgæ were the rudest, the bravest, and the fiercest of the three nations of Gaul. A desperate struggle was maintained before they yielded to the genius of Cæsar, and the superior discipline of the Roman armies. At length the country within the Rhine was reduced to the condition of a Roman province; but the Batavi the ancient Hollanders, united themselves to Rome rather as allies than subjects.

During the middle ages the Netherlands passed through a series of vicissitudes. So early as the era of Charlemagne, they had acquired distinction in the pursuits of industry; and some of their fabrics were sent by that monarch to the caliph Haroun Alraschid, as specimens of the arts and industry of Europe. When the empire of Charlemagne fell to pieces, these states were divided into a number of separate principalities, all successively united, by marriage contract or inheritances, under the sway of the house of Burgundy. It was at this time that the Flemish provinces rose to the highest pitch of manufacturing and commercial prosperity. They received all the raw materials of France and England, countries then rude and agricultural, and returned them in a manufactured state. Ghent alone is said to have employed 40,000 looms; though this is most probably much exaggerated. Bruges first, and then Antwerp, formed the grand depôt for the commerce of the northern and middle states of Europe.

The house of Austria, by the intermarriage of Maximilian I. and Mary, the heiress of Burgundy, succeeded to the rich dowry of the Seventeen Provinces. They formed one of the chief sources of the power of Charles V., who transmitted them, with Spain and his Italian dominions, to his son Philip II.

The Reformation was early introduced into the Netherlands, and had a most powerful influence upon their destiny. Being suited to the sober and thinking habits of a manufacturing population, it was soon embraced by a majority of the people, who were thus placed in direct collision with the fierce and gloomy bigotry of Philip II. The Inquisition being introduced, in its most unrelenting severity, with a view to the suppression of the new doctrine, drove the people into open rebellion; and a contest of fifty years' duration arose, the most fierce, bloody, and important in its consequences, of all those to which differences of religion have given rise. The duke of Alva, who boasted that, during his government in the Low Countries, 18,000 persons had perished on the scaffold, was, however, unable to subdue the independent spirit and determined enmity to Spanish dominion which he had been instrumental in kindling. The more moderate conduct of his successors, and, above all, of Alexander Farnese, succeeded in re-establishing the Spanish sway over the Belgic provinces which were not defended by any natural barriers. Even the Dutch were reduced to the disastrous necessity of opening their dikes, and allowing a great part of their territory to be inundated. Their courage and perseverance, however, the great talent of the first two princes of the house of Orange, and the aid afforded by Elizabeth, enabled them finally to achieve their independence. The union of Utrecht, when they constituted themselves into an independent state, by the title of the Seven United Provinces, was concluded in 1597.

From this period the destiny of the United Provinces, called more commonly by the name of Holland, the chief province among them, was entirely different from that of Belgium. They speedily attracted many of the manufactures, and all the commerce, which had raised the Flemish cities to prosperity. The Dutch conquered from Portugal, at that time under the dominion of Spain, the finest of her possessions in the East Indies; obtained a temporary footing in Brazil; and rendered Amsterdam the centre of a flourishing trade with India: they carried on the fisheries, especially those of herrings, upon an unprecedented scale; and became the first maritime people in the world. The commercial greatness of Holland presents so remarkable a phenomenon, that we cannot forbear availing ourselves of some part of that luminous illustration of it, which has been afforded by the researches of Mr. M'Culloch. That able writer observes:—

"Between the years 1651 and 1672, when the territories of the republic were invaded by the French, the commerce of Holland seems to have reached its greatest height. De Witt estimates its increase from the treaty with Spain, concluded at Munster in 1643, to 1669, at fully a half. He adds, that, during the war with Holland, Spain lost the greatest part of her naval power; that since the peace, the Dutch had obtained most of the trade to that country, which had been previously carried on by the Hanseatic merchants and the English; that almost all the coasting trade of Spain was carried on by Dutch shipping; that Spain had even been forced to hire Dutch ships to sail to her American possessions; and that so great was the exportation of goods from Holland to Spain, that all the merchandise brought from the Spanish West Indies was not sufficient to make returns for them.

"At this period, indeed, the Dutch engrossed, not by means of any artificial monopoly, but by the greater number of their ships, and their superior skill and economy in all that regarded navigation, almost the whole carrying trade of Europe. The value of the goods exported from France in Dutch bottoms, towards the middle of the seventeenth century, exceeded 40,000,000 livres; and the commerce of England with the Low Countries was, for a very long period, almost entirely carried on in them.

"The business of marine insurance was largely and successfully prosecuted at Amsterdam; and the ordinances published in 1551, 1563, and 1570, contain the most judicious regulations for the settlement of such disputes as might arise in conducting this difficult but highly useful business. It is singular, however, notwithstanding the sagacity of the Dutch, and their desire to strengthen industrious habits, that they should have prohibited insurance upon lives. It was reserved for England to show the advantages that might be derived from this beautiful application of the science of probabilities.

"In 1690, Sir William Petty estimated the shipping of Europe at about 2,000,000 tons, which he supposed to be distributed as follows:—viz. England, 500,000; France, 100,000; Hamburg, Denmark, Sweden, and Dantzic, 250,000; Spain, Portugal, and Italy, 250,000 that of the Seven United Provinces amounting, according to him, to 900,000 tons, or to nearly one half of the whole tonnage of Europe! No great dependence can, of course, be placed upon these estimates; but the probability is, that, had they been more accurate, the preponderance in favour of Holland would have been greater than it appears to be; for the official returns to the circulars addressed in 1701 by the commissioners of customs to the officers at the different ports, show that the whole mercantile navy of England amounted at that period to only 261,222 tons, carrying 27,196 men. (*Macpherson's Annals of Commerce*, anno 1701.)

"It may, therefore, be fairly concluded, that, during the seventeenth century the foreign commerce and navigation of Holland was greater than that of all Europe besides; and yet the country which was the seat of this vast commerce had no native produce to export, nor even a piece of timber fit for ship-building. All had been the fruit of industry, economy and a fortunate combination of circumstances.

"Holland owed this vast commerce to a variety of causes: partly to her peculiar situation, the industry and economy of her inhabitants, the comparatively liberal and enlightened system of civil as well as of commercial policy adopted by the republic; and partly also to the wars and disturbances that prevailed in most European countries in the sixteenth and seventeenth centuries, and prevented them from emulating the successful career of the Dutch.

"Many dissertations have been written to account for the decline of the commerce of Holland. But, if we mistake not, its leading causes may be classed under two prominent heads, viz. first, the natural growth of commerce and navigation in other countries; and second, the weight of taxation at home. During the period when the republic rose to great eminence as a commercial state, England, France, and Spain, distracted by civil and religious dissensions, or engrossed wholly by schemes of foreign conquest, were unable to apply their energies to the cultivation of commerce, or to withstand the competition of so industrious a people as the Dutch. They, therefore, were under the necessity of allowing the greater part of their foreign, and even of their coasting trade, to be carried on in Dutch bottoms, and under the superintendence of Dutch factors. But after the accession of Louis XIV. and the ascendency of Cromwell had put an end to internal commotions in France and England, the energies of these two great nations began to be directed to pursuits of which the Dutch had hitherto enjoyed almost a monopoly. It was not to be supposed that, when tranquillity and a regular system of government had been established in France and England, their active and enterprising inhabitants would submit to see one of their most valuable branches of industry in the hands of foreigners. The Dutch ceased to be the carriers of Europe, without any fault of their own. Their performance of that function necessarily terminated as soon as other nations became possessed of a mercantile marine, and were able to do for themselves what had previously been done for them by their neighbours.

"Whatever, therefore, might have been the condition of Holland in other respects, the natural advance of rival nations must inevitably have stripped her of a large portion of the commerce she once possessed. But the progress of decline seems to have been considerably accelerated, or rather, perhaps, the efforts to arrest it were rendered ineffectual, by the extremely heavy taxation to which she was subjected, occasioned by the unavoidable expenses incurred in the revolutionary struggle with Spain, and the subsequent wars with France and England. The necessities of the state led to the imposition of taxes on corn, on flour when it was ground at the mill, and on bread when it came from the oven; on butter, and fish, and fruit; on income and legacies; the sale of houses; and, in short, almost every article either of necessity or convenience. Sir William Temple mentions that in his time —and taxes were greatly increased afterwards—one fish sauce was in common use, which directly paid no fewer than *thirty* different duties of excise; and it was a common saying at Amsterdam, that every dish of fish brought to the table was paid for *once* to the fisherman, and *six* times to the state.

"In consequence principally of the oppressiveness of taxation, but partly, too, of the excessive accumulation of capital that had taken place while the Dutch engrossed the carrying trade of Europe, profits in Holland were reduced towards the middle of the seventeenth century, and have ever since continued extremely low. This circumstance would of itself have sapped the foundations of her commercial greatness. Her capitalists, who could hardly expect to clear more than two or three per cent. of net profit by any sort of undertaking carried on at home, were tempted to vest their capital in other countries, and to speculate in loans to foreign governments. There are the best reasons for thinking that the Dutch were, until very lately, the largest creditors of any nation in Europe. It is impossible, indeed, to form any accurate estimate of what the sums owing them by foreigners previously to the late French war, or at present, may amount to; but there can be no doubt that at the former period the amount was immense, and that it is still very considerable. M. Demeunier (*Dictionnaire de l'Economie Politique*, tome iii. p. 720.) states the amount of capital lent by the Dutch to foreign governments, exclusive of the large sums lent to France during the American war, at *seventy-three* millions sterling. According to the author of the *Richesse de la Hollande* (ii. p. 292.), the sums lent to France and England only, previously to 1778, amounted to 1,500,000 livres tournois, or sixty millions sterling. And besides these, vast sums were lent to private individuals in foreign countries, both regularly as loans at interest, and in the shape of goods advanced at long credits. So great was the difficulty of finding an advantageous investment for money in Holland, that Sir William Temple mentions, that the payment of any part of the national debt was looked upon by the creditors as an evil of the first magnitude. 'They receive it,' says he, 'with tears, not knowing how to dispose of it to interest with such safety and ease.'

"Among the subordinate causes which contributed to the decline of Dutch commerce, or which have, at all events, prevented its growth, we may reckon the circumstance of the commerce with India having been subjected to the trammels of monopoly. De Witt expresses his firm conviction, that the abolition of the East India Company would have added very greatly to the trade with the East; and no doubt can now remain in the mind of any one that such would have been the case. The interference of the administration in regulating the mode in which some of the most important branches of industry should be carried on, seems also to have been exceedingly injurious. Every proceeding with respect to the herring fishery, for example, was regulated by the orders of government, carried into effect under the inspection of officers appointed for that purpose. Some of these regulations were exceedingly vexatious. The period when the fishery might begin was fixed at five minutes past twelve o'clock of the night of the 24th of June! and the master and pilot of every vessel leaving Holland for the fishery were obliged to make oath that they would respect the regulation. The species of salt to be made use of in curing different sorts of herrings was also fixed by law; and there were endless regulations with respect to the size of the barrels, the number and thickness of the staves of which they were to be made; the gutting and packing of the herring; the branding of the barrels, &c. &c. (*Histoire des Pêches, &c. dans les Mers du Nord*, tom. i. chap. 24.) These regulations were intended to secure to the Hollanders that superiority which they had early attained in the fishery, and to prevent the reputation of their herrings from being injured by the bad faith of individuals. But their real effect was precisely the reverse of this. By tying up the fishers to a system of routine, they prevented them from making any improvements; while the facility of counterfeiting the public marks opened a much wider door to fraud, than would have been opened had government wisely declined interfering in the matter.

"In despite, however, of the East India monopoly, and the regulations now described, the commercial policy of Holland has been more liberal than that of any other nation. And in consequence, a country not more extensive than Wales, and naturally not more fertile, conquered indeed, in a great measure from the sea, has accumulated a population of upwards of two millions; has maintained wars of unexampled duration with the most powerful monarchies; and, besides laying out immense sums in works of utility and ornament at home, has been enabled to lend hundreds of millions to foreigners."

The French revolution produced a movement so great, and with which Holland was in such close contact, that it acted powerfully upon her political destinies. The revolutionary armies, after having defeated those of all the allied powers on the plains of Belgium, advanced into Holland; where, meeting with support from a powerful internal party, they had no difficulty in subverting the dynasty of the house of Orange. In its stead was formed the Batavian republic, virtually united to, and ruled by, the republican government of France. A vigorous attempt, made in 1799, by Britain and Russia, to re-establish the old order of things, was baffled; and no sooner had Napoleon been made emperor of France, than he bestowed Holland, formed into a kingdom, on his brother Louis. This prince, of a mild and amiable temper, was disposed to promote the welfare of the Dutch; but he was allowed only to act as viceroy to his brother, and was obliged to assist in forwarding those measures by which Napoleon, in the vain hope of ruining Britain, endeavoured hermetically to seal all the ports of the Continent against foreign commerce. This system was most distressing to all countries subjected to it; but to Holland it was peculiarly ruinous: that maritime commerce on which her whole greatness had rested, received a blow from which, perhaps, it will never recover.

The kingdom of the Netherlands grew out of the measures adopted by that great coalition which, after a long series of triumphs, totally overthrow the colossal fabric that had been raised by the genius of Napoleon and the bravery of the French. After its fall, Austria might have advanced a claim to the Netherlands, so long a portion of her extended dominion. Being, however, so remote, and so much detached from her other territories, it was likely to prove a dependency inconvenient and difficult to defend. She therefore consented to accept indemnification in another quarter, and to allow Belgium, with Holland, to be formed into a representative kingdom, under the house of Orange; believing it might serve as a barrier against any future encroachment of France. The kingdom of the Netherlands, thus formed, was divided into two distinct parts, Holland and Belgium; but the latter, differing in religion, language, and manners, was always discontented at this union, and considered itself as a subject state. Inspired by the example of France in 1830, the people rose in arms, and, after a short but desperate struggle, succeeded, with the ultimate consent of the great powers, in forming themselves into a separate kingdom, under the name of Belgium. It comprises the provinces of South Brabant, East and West Flanders, Antwerp, Hainault, Namur, Liège, the greater part of Limburg, and a small part of Luxemburg. Holland, besides the ten United Provinces, has nearly all Luxemburg, and a small part of Limburg, containing, however, Maestricht, its largest town.

### SECT. IV.—*Political Geography.*

A limited monarchy was the constitution established for the new kingdom of the Netherlands, and continued, with some modifications in Belgium, in both the parts into which it has been separated.

The legislative power in Holland is vested in the States-General; a popular assembly, modified, however, somewhat differently from those either of Britain or France. Each province, as under the ancient Dutch system, has an assembly of its own, which regulates local affairs, and has even the power of imposing local taxes. It cannot, however, injure commerce by imposing heavier duties on the produce of other provinces than its own. The members of these provincial assemblies are chosen by electoral colleges formed in every great town; not by public meeting, or open election; but by the police officers going from house to house, and collecting billets signed and sealed. The members of the second chamber of the States-General are chosen for three years, one-third of the number being annually renewed. The upper chamber does not consist of hereditary nobles, but of a council of from forty to sixty, named by the king for life. [The Belgian chambers are both elective; the Senate or upper house being chosen for the term of eight, and the Representative chamber for that of four years.—AM. ED.]

The revenue of the kingdom of the Netherlands amounted to about $35,000,000, raised by the usual expedients of land-tax, excise, customs, stamps, post-office, and by a tax on *patents*. These are required to be taken out by all persons exercising trades or professions; and partake of the character of an income tax, inasmuch as their magnitude is determined by the extent of the sales made by the parties during the preceding year.

| Produce of the principal branches of the Revenue of the Netherlands. In Florins. | 1816. | 1826. |
|---|---|---|
| Direct Taxes | 25,363,700 | 28,972,813 |
| Stamps, Registration, &c. | 12,316,266 | 12,501,902 |
| Import and Export Duties and Excise | 22,127,999 | 31,121,666 |
| Warranty on Gold and Silver | 131,786 | 188,908 |
| Posts | 1,066,308 | 1,984,476 |
| Lottery of the Netherlands | 448,952 | 584,448 |
| Lottery of Brussels | 1,475,047 | 1,029,567 |
| High Roads | 1,546,080 | 1,108,823 |

| Principal branches of the Expenditure of the Netherlands. In Florins. | 1816. | 1826. |
|---|---|---|
| King's Household | 2,600,000 | 2,100,000 |
| Great Offices of State | 1,468,635 | 1,065,430 |
| Foreign Affairs | 937,838 | 766,969 |
| Justice | 3,394,511 | 2,191,049 |
| Interior and Waterstaat* | 7,245,910 | 6,159,249 |
| Religions, except the Catholic | 1,264,261 | 1,327,311 |
| Catholic Religion | 1,325,176 | 1,631,413 |
| Education, Arts, Commerce, and Colonies | 3,894,736 | 73,019† |
| Finances | 23,314,342 | 38,707,562 |
| Navy | 6,554,531 | 6,582,842 |
| Army | 27,128,574 | 18,444,535 |

The total average annual produce of the revenue, during this period, was 88,044,152 florins.

The article finances means chiefly the interest of the public debt. This amounted, in 1826, to upwards of four per cent. on a capital of 832,334,500 florins. The debt was almost wholly contracted by the Dutch, principally during their protracted and glorious struggle for independence, and partly during the period that Holland was connected with France.

The total annual average expenditure, during the above-mentioned years, was 98,106,820 florins.

[It has been settled that Holland should assume six-thirteenths of the Netherlandish debt, and Belgium the remaining seven; but the latter has not hitherto paid any part of the interest. The expenditure of the Dutch kingdom in 1833 was 49,385,849 florins, exclusive of 44,000,000 for extraordinaries on account of the war establishments. The former sum includes the interest on the whole debt, amounting to 21,621,484 florins.

The expenditure of Belgium was 73,000,000 francs, comprising no charges on the debt; but nearly three-fifths of this sum was absorbed by the military, which it has been necessary to keep on the war establishment.—AM. ED.]

The military force of the kingdom of the Netherlands was in a somewhat large proportion to its resources. This was supposed to be rendered necessary by the proximity of so great a power as France, whose attack, or at least whose dictation, there might be room to apprehend. The army, before the late changes, amounted to about 62,000 men. The Belgic provinces, having been long the principal theatre of hostility between France and Austria, were guarded by a line of strong fortresses. These had been allowed to fall somewhat into decay; but the allies, having brought their contest with France to a triumphant conclusion, determined to strengthen them as a barrier against the future encroachments of that power; and the large contributions levied upon her were, in a great measure, employed in restoring the fortresses to their original condition. Several of these, however, by an agreement made between the French and English governments, have been recently dismantled. Both powers have kept up large forces since the revolution; but will soon re-

* The expenses of canals, dikes, and navigation in general.

† The charges for education are now included under the head of "interior."

duce them to a regular peace establishment, of which it is impossible at present to give any account.

In naval affairs, Holland, no longer the maritime rival but the close ally of Britain, made only faint attempts to raise her navy from the low state to which it was reduced by the disasters of the revolutionary war.

[It consists, at present, of six ships of the line, sixteen large class and seven small class frigates, thirty corvettes and brigs, four steam vessels, and about eighty armed barks, of five guns, for the defence of the interior waters.—Am. Ed.]

The foreign possessions of Holland, after being entirely wrested from her during the war, were, with the exception of Ceylon, the Cape of Good Hope, Demerara, and Berbice, restored in 1814. In the East Indies, she possesses the Moluccas, the extensive and fertile island of Java, with settlements on Sumatra, Celebes, and Borneo; and some factories on the coast of Malabar and Coromandel. In Africa, she retains El Mina, and other factories on the Gold Coast. Her West India colonies are not, and never were, very considerable, unless as commercial depôts. Both the navy and the colonial possessions, in the separation of the two kingdoms, remain with Holland.

## Sect. V.—*Productive Industry.*

There is no country, perhaps, which in proportion to its extent and original resources, produces so great an amount of valuable and useful commodities as Holland and Belgium.

The agriculture of the Belgic provinces, though, contrary to the usual course, it was founded upon their manufactures and commerce, being exempted from the vicissitudes which befell them, continues to form the most ample source of wealth. The whole territory of Flanders is cultivated like a garden. A great proportion consisted originally of harsh, barren sands, producing nothing but heath and fir; yet by the application of manure these were gradually reclaimed, and brought into their present state of high fertility. The culture of artificial grasses, and especially of clover, is the characteristic process of Flemish husbandry, which it has taught to the rest of Europe. The care of the Flemish farmers in collecting manure was early conspicuous, and as naturally grew out of the use of artificial grasses, and consequent stall-feeding. The use of liquid manure, collected in large reservoirs, is common to this country with China, and not known in any other part of Europe, except, perhaps, Norway. Turf ashes, especially those imported from Holland, are in high estimation, and are said to produce an almost magical effect on the vegetation of clover. In general, the Flemish agriculture is conducted on a careful, economical, antique practice; the farmers not having adopted many modern improvements in the arrangements of husbandry, such as the crossing of the breeds of cattle, and the use of machinery, which have been adopted in England with such happy effect. But this system of agriculture, after supplying the most dense population in Europe with the standard productions of the soil, yields several articles, such as madder, rape, clover, and mustard-seeds, hops, &c., for exportation.

The objects of culture in the Dutch provinces, in consequence of their humid climate, and of the demand for animal food for the great cities, are almost entirely connected with pasturage. Holland is as it were one great meadow, intersected by canals, and traversed by rows and groups of trees. The cattle are stalled in the winter, and fed on hay, turnips, &c.; but in summer they are kept constantly grazing in the open air. The produce of the dairy has been brought to such a state of improvement as to be an object of exportation; Dutch butter enjoys a high reputation, and the cheese is in good repute over all Europe.

Horticulture, which elsewhere is only a recreation, has in the Netherlands attained such importance, as to become a national object. Besides amply supplying its own markets with culinary vegetables, Holland exports them in large quantities to Norway, and other districts, where the growth is prevented by the rigorous climate. Ornamental gardening has been cultivated with peculiar ardour, especially in its floral department. When the tulipo-mania reigned in Holland, it was carried to such an excess, that lots of 120 tulip-roots sold, in 1637, for 100,000 florins; and particular specimens have brought from 8,000 to 10,000. In point of fact, however, these roots formed a kind of imaginary currency, or medium for a systematised species of gambling. They were never actually transferred from one individual to another; but were a sort of stock whose whole value was derived from caprice. The government at length put down this species of gambling, and the prices of tulips fell to their natural level.—Careful enquiries carried on by the government of the Netherlands are considered as having proved that the agricultural capital of the whole country amounted to 10,395,000,000 francs. The following estimate was made of the growth and produce:—

| | Hectares. | Value in Francs. |
|---|---|---|
| Wheat | 350,000 | 154,000,000 |
| Rye | 700,000 | 168,000,000 |
| Buckwheat | 200,000 | 32,000,000 |
| Barley | 280,000 | 84,000,000 |
| Pulse | 110,000 | 48,000 000 |
| Potatoes | 131,000 | 41,000,000 |
| Oats | 300,000 | 84,000,000 |
| Orchards | 54,000 | 3,000,000 |
| Vegetables | 92,000 | 55,000,000 |
| Hemp and flax | 210,000 | 126,000,000 |
| Madder | 30,000 | 21,000,000 |
| Cattle and animals | | 150,000,000 |
| | | 966,000,000 |

Manufacturing industry is the branch in which the Belgic provinces formerly most excelled, and in which their decay has been most conspicuous. Three centuries ago, the linens and woollens of Ghent, Louvain, Brussels, and Mechlin, clothed the higher ranks in all the surrounding countries. Since that time, the fabrics of France and England, have attained such an astonishing superiority, and are at once so cheap, and so well adapted to the taste of the age, that the Low Country manufacturers can with difficulty maintain their ground even in internal consumption. In cottons, especially, they are quite unable to withstand British competition. There are still, however, some fine linen fabrics, laces, lawns, cambrics, in which the manufacturers of Mechlin, Brussels, &c. continue unrivalled, and which, though so much superseded by muslin and Nottingham lace, still enjoy a certain demand throughout Europe. The fine laces have been sold for seventy or eighty Napoleons a yard. The Flemish breweries are also very extensive.

The manufacturing industry of Holland is not on so great a scale as her commerce. The pottery ware of Delft has lost most of its ancient reputation, and even in Holland is superseded by the earthenware of England. The spirit called gin, geneva, or hollands, is produced at Schiedam, Amsterdam, and other towns, of an excellence which is universally acknowledged. The refining of sugar, and the manufacture of snuff, are continued on a great scale, chiefly in Amsterdam and Rotterdam, and the making of tobacco-pipes at Gouda is said to employ 5000 persons. Silk, leather, and woollens, are still manufactured, though not to such an extent as formerly, nor much with a view to exportation. The general value of Dutch and Belgian manufactures has been estimated as follows:—Iron, 46,000,000 francs; copper, 5,000,000; woollens, 80,000,000; linens, 95,000,000; lace, 25,000,000; cottons, 50,000,000; refined sugar, 14,000,000; salt, 10,000,000; spirits, 40,000,000; beer, 110,000,000; tobacco, 28,000,000; oil, 30,000,000; soap, 10,000,000; leather, 28,000,000; earthenware, 4,000,000; bricks, 6,000,000; books, 15,000,000; bleaching, 10,000,000; dyeing, 10,000,000; paper, 8,000,000: in all, 675,000,000 francs.

The commerce of the Netherlands has declined, both absolutely and relatively, but in a less remarkable degree. The causes have appeared in the historical survey. The total suspension of all maritime intercourse with other countries during the subjection of Holland to France, and the conquest of the Dutch colonies by England, rendered it necessary, as it were, to begin every thing afresh at the restoration of peace in 1815. But the large capitals in the hands of the Dutch merchants, their commodious situation in the centre of the most improved states of Europe, the recovery of some of the most valuable of their foreign possessions, and the considerable surplus of native commodities which their country affords for exportation, secured for them, as soon as the ports were open, a considerable trade. Since the peace, it has been continually increasing; and, previously to the late revolution, was more equally distributed than before among the Belgic as well as the Dutch ports. Holland exports, of its own produce, butter, cheese, geneva, tobacco-pipes; of the produce of its fishery, herrings, stockfish, whalebone, whale oil; from its foreign possessions, coffee, sugar, rum, cotton wool, cloves, nutmegs, mace, pepper; with linens, wool, and various articles from Germany and the Baltic. Belgium exports madder, vegetable oils, lace, lawn, and fine linen.

There are no official returns of imports and exports published; but a very able writer in the *Foreign Quarterly Review*, to whose researches we have been much indebted, has given from original sources the following account of the *importation* of the principal articles of merchandise into the Netherland ports during the year 1827:—

| ARTICLES. | PORTS. | | | |
|---|---|---|---|---|
| | Amsterdam. | Rotterdam. | Antwerp. | Middleburg. |
| Coffee, bales | 111,059 | 97,397 | 376,102 | 2,678 |
| Ditto, tons | 2,603 | 1,079 | 3,539 | 117 |
| Sugar, chests | 12,160 | 7,508 | 56,356 | |
| Ditto, mats | 2,927 | 8,145 | 50,939 | 79 |
| Ditto, tons | 18,653 | 3,829 | 4,028 | 2,609 |
| Tobacco of America, tons | 15,205 | 13,934 | 1,331 | |
| Rice, bales | 1,980 | 13,892 | 16,359 | |
| Ditto, tons | 8,412 | 5,301 | 14,935 | |
| Cotton, bales | 12,092 | 19,907 | 22,856 | 152 |
| Indigo, chests | 66 | 476 | 1,332 | |
| Ditto, seroons | 128 | 88 | 611 | |
| Tea, quarter chests | 15,124 | 9,527 | 1,467 | 4,200 |
| Skins, pieces | 9,271 | 34,501 | 215,044 | |
| Pepper, bales | 31 | 5,247 | 21,847 | |
| Wheat, lasts | 12,494 | 1,602 | 26 | |
| Rye, ditto | 7,835 | 5,130 | 96 | |
| Barley, ditto | 878 | 1,412 | | |
| Potash of Russia, puds* | 50,583 | 24,791 | 106,920 | |
| Linseed Oil of do. do | 1,246 | | | |
| Tallow of ditto do | 9,416 | 835 | 1,191 | |
| Hemp of ditto do | 19,110 | 4,555 | 8,372 | |

* A Russian weight of 36 lbs.

The herring fishery, which once formed so ample a source of Dutch wealth, (though in this respect its importance has been greatly exaggerated,) was almost annihilated during the war; and the ground having since been occupied by neighbours and rivals, Holland has been able to recover only a small portion. Instead of 1500 herring busses, in 1818 she sent out only 200. Not more than sixty ships go annually to the whale* and cod fisheries; and, during the late war, the English undertook the task of supplying their own markets with fresh fish; in which business, however, the Dutch still employ about 6000 boats.

For other commercial particulars, M. de Cloet states, that on an average of twenty years, between 1775 and 1795, the number of vessels entered inwards in all the Dutch ports was 4140, and outwards the same; making a total of 8280 a year. The entries inwards, in 1822, for Amsterdam, Rotterdam, and Antwerp, were 4051; which, adding 500 for Harlingen and Dort, becomes 4551. The number outwards for the same three ports was 4045, which we may, with a similar addition, call 4545; making a total of 9096 ships. In 1827, the number entered inwards was 5203, outwards 4548, making 9751 altogether. Taking the average number, however, at 10,000 (instead of 9751), so as to cover the trifling trade of Ostend and Nieuport, and valuing each cargo, with M. de Cloet, at 40,000 francs, a sum moderate enough, the amount of the trade by sea will be 400,000,000 francs. The trade by land with France and Germany, which, in 1814, was estimated at 152,000,000 francs, may now be taken at 160,000,000; so that, if the calculations be at all correct, the annual value of the foreign commerce of the Netherlands is altogether about 560,000,000 francs.

*Mines.* The south-eastern provinces in the neighbourhood of Mons, Charleroi, and Liège, are said to contain 350 mines of coal, employing 20,000 men; but this number, we should think, must be a good deal exaggerated. Turf is the fuel chiefly used, especially in Holland. There are also in the southern district ironworks, supposed by Mr. Jacob to yield about 1000 tons. Clay suited for the manufacture of porcelain is found in Holland, and there are stone quarries in the south.

*Canals* form one of the most remarkable features in the economical arrangements of Holland, and a leading source of her prosperity. From the structure of the country, these are formed with peculiar facility, and it is everywhere intersected with them; every town, every village, being connected by canals of greater or less dimensions. They run through the streets of the cities, enabling vessels to load and unload under the eye of the merchant. When frozen, they serve as highways, on which the Dutch females, heavily laden, convey themselves along on skates with surprising rapidity. In general, from the flatness of the country, and the abundance of water, canals may be made without much exertion of art or skill. There is an exception, however, in the canal of Pannerden, constructed with the view of draining off the superfluous water of the Rhine, by which a great extent of ground was converted into a marsh. It is two miles long, and 200 feet below the level of the sea, the waters being received into three different sets of sluices. It is considered a masterpiece, and completely answered its object. Another, on a most magnificent scale, connecting Amsterdam with the Helder, was commenced in 1819, and finished in 1825, at an expense of 10,000,000 florins. It is 50 miles long, 125 feet wide at the surface, 36 feet wide at the bottom, and 21 feet deep. It is calculated to admit ships of war of 46 guns, and merchantmen of 1000 tons burden. It was constructed to avoid the troublesome navigation to and from Amsterdam through the Zuyder Zee, and the necessity of lightening large vessels before crossing the Pampus.

The canals in Belgium are spacious and commodious, connecting all the great cities, though not nearly in equal number, nor uniting every village, as in Holland.

### Sect. VI.—*Civil and Social State.*

The population of the kingdom of the Netherlands, though not comparable, as to absolute amount, with that of any of the great states, is superior to them all in one highly important particular, that the country contains a greater density of population on the same surface than any other in Europe, or perhaps in the world. This, in the Belgic provinces at least, is the more remarkable, as they are inhabited, not by a manufacturing population, drawing subsistence from agricultural countries, but by a population subsisting exclusively on the produce of the land itself. The census of 1816 gave a total population of 5,491,945: 2,476,159 for the northern provinces; 3,249,841 for those of Belgium; and 225,945 for the duchy of Luxemburg. This gives an aggregate average density of about 212 to the square mile; but the rate rises much higher in certain provinces. Throughout Belgium the proportion is 296 to the square mile; in the province of East Flanders, however, it is as high as 560. In the United Netherlands the average density is only 180 per square mile; and in Luxemburg, which has much of a German character, it is as low as 66. The census of 1825 gives a population of 6,013,578; and some further augmentation has taken place since.†

* [In 1827, only one ship sailed to the whale-fishery from Holland, which in 1680 had out 260 ships manned by 14,000 sailors, engaged in that branch of industry.—Am. Ed.]

† [The population of the two kingdoms in 1833, was 6,536,000, of which 3,791,000 belonged to Belgium, and 2,745,000 to Holland.—Am. Ed.]

The following details with respect to the population of the Netherlands are extracted from the publications of M. Quetelet, one of the ablest statistical writers of the Continent:—

*Table of the Movement of the Population in Holland and Belgium for Ten Years.*

| Provinces | Population. 1815. | Population. 1825. | Births. | Deaths. | Marriages. | Divorces. |
|---|---|---|---|---|---|---|
| Zealand | 111,108 | 129,329 | 55,331 | 42,436 | 10,645 | 27 |
| Guelderland | 264,097 | 284,363 | 90,862 | 59,818 | 19,337 | 13 |
| North Brabant | 294,087 | 326,617 | 100,863 | 69,507 | 20,380 | 1 |
| North Holland | 375,257 | 393,916 | 145,744 | 121,725 | 34,789 | 209 |
| South Holland | 388,505 | 438,202 | 165,741 | 143,850 | 34,942 | 148 |
| Utrecht | 107,947 | 117,405 | 41,038 | 29,928 | 8,982 | 30 |
| Friesland | 176,554 | 202,530 | 65,565 | 38,219 | 15,327 | 46 |
| Overyssel | 147,229 | 160,937 | 51,951 | 37,479 | 11,629 | 13 |
| Groningen | 135,642 | 156,045 | 51.673 | 30,539 | 11,492 | 37 |
| Drenthe | 46,459 | 53,368 | 16,723 | 9,858 | 3,954 | 3 |
| Limburg | 287,613 | 321,246 | 101,781 | 70,549 | 22,960 | 5 |
| Liège | 358,185 | 331,101 | 113,623 | 82,698 | 24,387 | 24 |
| Namur | 164,400 | 189,393 | 58,690 | 34,134 | 12,592 | 8 |
| Luxemburg | 213,597 | 292,610 | 92,242 | 58,695 | 18,740 | 1 |
| Hainault | 488,595 | 546,190 | 183,198 | 118,289 | 39,591 | 27 |
| South Brabant | 441,649 | 495,455 | 169,181 | 119,109 | 36,423 | 5 |
| East Flanders | 615,689 | 687,267 | 218,830 | 162,834 | 43,120 | 0 |
| West Flanders | 516,324 | 563,826 | 191,139 | 141,310 | 37,882 | 6 |
| Antwerp | 291,565 | 323,678 | 101,471 | 70,623 | 23,075 | 2 |
| | 5,424,502 | 6,013,478 | 2,015,646 | 1,421,600 | 430,247 | 605 |

The births and marriages in the Netherlands are proportionally more numerous, while the deaths are about equal to those of France, and exceed those of Great Britain in the ratio of three to two. The account stands thus:—

| | Netherlands. | France. | Great Britain. |
|---|---|---|---|
| 100 births to | 2,807 inhabitants | 3,168 | 3,534 |
| 100 deaths | 3,981 | 4,000 | 5,780 |
| 100 marriages | 13,150 | 13,490 | 13,333 |

There has been a very material increase in the healthiness of the people of the Netherlands, and particularly of Holland, during the last thirty or forty years.

The provision for the support of the poor of the Netherlands is pretty ample, and it is applied with great economy and skill; forming, indeed, an important branch of the public administration. The following table, compiled from authentic sources, by M. Quetelet, cannot fail of being interesting:—

*Charitable Institutions of the Netherlands*

| Nature of Institution. | Number of Institutions. | Individuals relieved. | Expenses of Relief. | Expense for each Individual. |
|---|---|---|---|---|
| | | | Florins. | Florins. |
| Administrations for relieving the Poor at home | 5,129 | 745,652 | 5,448,740 | 7.31 |
| Commissions for distributing Food, &c. | 36 | 22,056 | 82,424 | 3.73 |
| Societies of Maternal Charity | 4 | 1,448 | 13,493 | 9.32 |
| Hospitals | 724 | 41,172 | 4,091,157 | 99.37 |
| Funds for Military Service | 1 | 2,277 | 110,942 | 48.73 |
| Royal Hospital of Messine* | 1 | 156 | 23,290 | 149.30 |
| Poor Schools | 285 | 147,296 | 247,176 | 1.67 |
| Workhouses of Charity | 34 | 6,169 | 406,704 | 65.92 |
| Depôts of Mendicity | 8 | 2,598 | 229,587 | 88.37 |
| Societies of Beneficence for the Colonies | 2 | 8,553 | 353,529 | 41.33 |
| Establishments for the Deaf and Dumb | 4 | 239 | 41,994 | 175.70 |
| Totals | 6,228 | 977,616 | 11,049.036 | Average 11.30 |
| Monts de Piété | 124 | ........... | 4,208,068 | — |
| Savings Banks | 50 | 18,035 | 2,771,608 | Average153.93 |

The national character of the Dutch has been long moulded into the form natural to a highly commercial people; solid, steady, quiet, laborious, eagerly intent on the accumulation of wealth, which they seek rather by economy, steadiness, and perseverance, than by speculation. They carry the virtue of cleanliness to an extreme. Outward decorum of manners, at least, is better observed than among the neighbouring continental nations. Yet the *spiel* houses in the great towns, where the most respectable citizens used to mingle with persons entirely destitute of character, presented in this respect a strange anomaly. But at present these can hardly be said to exist; and are frequented only by the very dregs of the populace. A traveller in Holland will rarely meet with a drunken person; or with a man, woman, or child, in rags. Every class of people seems comfortable, the result of their great frugality and unwearied industry. Were a young sturdy beggar discovered teasing passengers for

* In West Flanders, for the daughters of soldiers invalided or killed in service

alms, he would instantly be sent to the workhouse; where, if he refused to perform his allotted task, he would be compelled to save himself from drowning by working at the pump! Holland is, and always has been, a country of short credit. Bankruptcy is rare. Notwithstanding the invasion of the French in 1795, and the consequent interruption to all sorts of business, the bankruptcies were not comparatively so numerous as in England in ordinary years. The Belgic provinces, long subjected to a foreign yoke, and in constant intercourse with foreigners, seem to have lost in a great measure the original Flemish character, and to present no very distinctive features.

It is not very easy, from the differences of their judicial organization, to compare the state of crime in different countries. In this respect, however, the Netherlands would have nothing to fear from a comparison with France and England. In Holland, the police is excellent, and robberies very rare.

The prevailing religion of Holland is Calvinism, while that of Belgium is almost exclusively Catholic; a difference which contributed not a little to that rooted dislike entertained by the inhabitants of the latter to those of the former. The Dutch have the honour of being the first people who established a system of unrestrained toleration. Even popery, notwithstanding the grounds which the nation had to dread and hate it, was allowed to be professed with the utmost freedom. The government allows salaries, of a greater or less amount, to the clergy of every persuasion, only making those of the Presbyterian ministers higher than the others. The latter retain, besides, the old parish churches, and the exclusive privilege of using bells. They amount to about 1600, and are all paid and appointed by government, which, however, respects the wishes of the leading parishioners. Their salaries are very moderate; 3000 florins in the great cities; 800 to 1000, with house and glebe, in the country. They are divided into moderate and high Calvinistic parties; the former, which are said to be the most numerous, having the command of the university of Utrecht, while that of Leyden is attached to the opposite interest. There are about 300 or 400 Catholic congregations, in general very small. The Armenians or Remonstrants, who originated in Holland, have only about forty or fifty ministers; but their tenets are preached in many of the presbyterian churches. The Anabaptists, called here Mennonists, have about 100 congregations, composed of many opulent and respectable members. The Lutherans have fifty or sixty churches; and the French Protestants about thirty. [By the budget of 1833, 1,330,000 florins were voted for the support of the Protestant worship, and 400,000 for the Catholic.—Am. Ed.]

In Belgium, the Catholic clergy have shown a very rooted spirit of intolerance, with the bishop of Ghent at their head, and vehemently objected to the indulgent treatment of the other sects. The bishop was imprisoned for two years by Napoleon, on account of his obstinacy in this particular. The great possessions of the church, however, have been forfeited, and the clergy receive very moderate salaries from government. The monasteries have been rooted out, and generally also the nunneries, though that of Ghent still retains all its pomp. [There is an archbishop of Mechlin with a salary of 21,000 francs, and the five bishops have each 14,700 francs a year. These, with 64 vicars general and canons, 246 curates, and 4,288 inferior officers, form the body of the Catholic clergy. There are only about 5000 Protestants in Belgium, with 19 ministers, clerks, &c., who are paid by government.—Am. Ed.]

Learning in the Netherlands no longer boasts such names as Erasmus, Grotius, and Boerhaave; but the institutions for its diffusion continue to be very ample. Holland retains its two famous universities of Leyden and Utrecht. The former, which, under Boerhaave, had once the reputation of the first medical school in Europe, is still highly respectable. The professors, who are twenty-one in number, receive salaries of 3000 florins, independent of fees; and this being a better income than any of the ecclesiastical livings, the university draws from the church its most learned members. The medical education, however, cannot be completed unless at Amsterdam, which affords the advantage of hospitals and other accommodations peculiar to a large city. The university of Utrecht is not so considerable as that of Leyden; and that of Groningen is still inferior. In 1833, the number of students was, in Leyden 684; in Utrecht 476; in Groningen, 284.

The universities of Belgium, of which the most celebrated were Ghent and Louvain, were partially stripped of their ample endowments, first by Joseph II., and then by the French, who in their room substituted lyceums, which are now continued nearly on the same footing, under the name of colleges. Only the languages, and some general branches, are taught; education for professional purposes being received in separate appropriate seminaries. Ghent and Brussels have the highest reputation; but the salary of professors in the former does not exceed 1500 francs. The three universities of Louvain, Liège, and Ghent have lately been restored; and in 1827 the first was attended by 678 students; the second by 506; and the third by 404 students. Besides athenæums, which are only colleges on a smaller scale, Holland has primary schools in every village, by which the benefits of education are communicated to the lowest ranks. Belgium is at present very deficient in institutions for popular education.* But at an average of the Netherlands, the proportion of children at school to the entire population, in 1827, was as high as 1 to 9.5; a proportion not exceeded in any European country, with the exception, perhaps, of Prussia.

The fine arts were cultivated with zeal and success in both parts of the Netherlands. Wealthy merchants liberally patronised the arts of design; and the gentry and landholders being induced by the constant wars, of which the Low Countries were the theatre, to live much in towns, acquired more refined tastes than could have been formed in a country residence. Antwerp, during its prosperity, became, in some measure, a Belgic Athens. Yet the Flemish and Dutch painters never attained that grandeur of design, and that pure and classic taste, which were formed in Italy, by the study of the antique, and the refined taste of its nobles. The Flemish school, under its great masters Rubens and Vandyke, displayed, however, may excellences in a degree not inferior to any other in modern times; splendour of colouring, grandeur of composition, and force of expression. The Dutch school has been eminently successful in a lower sphere. Under Rembrandt and his disciples, subjects of common life and vulgar humour were treated with a native force, which, being aided by brilliant effects of light and shade, have rendered this school exceedingly popular, though it has failed in all attempts at high and heroic delineation. The landscape painters have seldom employed their pencils upon the grand scenery delineated by Claude and Poussin; but Berghem, Cuyp, Ruysdael, Hobbima, Vandevelde, and others, have represented, in the most natural and pleasing colours, the pastoral scenery of their country; its meadows, its woods, and the banks of its seas and rivers.

Amusement is far from being a primary object with the Dutch. They have most of the diversions of the neighbouring nations, though they do not follow them with much ardour. A great portion of their time is passed in smoking; the Dutchman having seldom the pipe out of his mouth. The rivers and canals passing through the streets, afford the opportunity of fishing from the windows. The great Flemish kermes, or fairs, though no longer subservient to commerce, exist still as festivals, at which there is a great display of humour and character, such as we find happily illustrated in the works of the Flemish painters. There seems nothing peculiar in the Dutch style of cookery. The peasantry both of Holland and Flanders have their peculiar local costume; as the huge breeches of the men, and the short jacket of the females; but the higher classes dress in the French or German style.

## SECT. VII.—*Local Geography.*

The following, according to recent official statements, are the extent and population of Belgium and Holland, respectively:

| BELGIUM. | | | | | | | | |
|---|---|---|---|---|---|---|---|---|
| Provinces. | Extent in Hectares. | Population in Dec. 1827. | Principal Towns. | | | | | |
| South Brabant. | 328,000 | 499,728 | Brussels | 72,800 | | | Louvain | 18,580 |
| Antwerp | 283,000 | 338,294 | Antwerp | 65,000 | Mechlin | 16,000 | | |
| East Flanders. | 282,000 | 708,705 | Ghent | 81,941 | St. Nicholas | 10,980 | | |
| West Flanders | 316,000 | 575,807 | Bruges | 36,000 | Ostend | 10,500 | Ypres | 15,150 |
| Hainault | 372,000 | 567,300 | Mons | 18,400 | | | | |
| Namur | 347,625 | 194,845 | Namur | 15,100 | Verviers | 10,070 | Spa | 3,000 |
| Liège | 288,000 | 347,625 | Liège | 45,300 | | | | |
| Limburg | 460,000 | 328,234 | Tongres | 4,000 | | | | |
| | 2,676,000 | 3,560,538 | | | | | | |
| HOLLAND. | | | | | | | | |
| Holland, South | 287,000 | 453,818 | Rotterdam | 63,033 | Hague | 45,144 | Leyden | 29,045 |
| | | | Dort | 18,400 | Delft | 13,285 | Gouda | 10,568 |
| Holland, North | 245,000 | 391,586 | Amsterdam | 201,000 | Haarlem | 18,453 | Zaandam | 9,016 |
| | | | Alkmaar | 8,435 | Hoorn | 8,155 | | |
| Zealand | 158,000 | 133,932 | Middleburg | 20,800 | Flushing | 6,380 | | |
| Utrecht | 133,000 | 122,213 | Utrecht | 34,087 | Amersfoort | 9,395 | | |
| North Brabant | 501,000 | 332,551 | Bois le Duc | 13,340 | Breda | 13,000 | Bergen-op-Zoom | |
| Guelderland | 509,000 | 293,396 | Nimeguen | 12,780 | Arnheim | 10,050 | | |
| Drenthe | 326,000 | 59,915 | Assen | 1,100 | | | | |
| Friesland | 263,000 | 200,332 | Leuwarden | 18,380 | | | | |
| Overyssel | 328,000 | 165,936 | Deventer | 9,530 | | | | |
| Groningen | 204,000 | 153,982 | Groningen | 28,851 | | | | |
| Limburg, part of | uncertain. | | Maestricht | 21,000 | | | | |
| Luxemburg | 650,000 | 298,655 | Luxemburg | 10,250 | | | | |
| | 3,654,000 | 2,606,000 | | | | | | |
| | 2,676,000 | 3,560,538 | | | | | | |
| | 6,330,000 | 6,166,354 | | | | | | |

* [In 1832 there were 5,229 primary schools in Belgium, with 370,996 pupils, beside 1,318 in the Athenæums, and 1,788 in the universities. Annual expense, 743,200 francs.—AM. ED.]

Subsect. 1.—*Belgium.*

South Brabant, which nearly coincides with what was formerly the Austrian part of that large province, forms a rich plain in the heart of Belgium, and is the seat of the finest manufactures carried on in that country.

Brussels (*fig.* 358.) is the capital of Belgium. Considered as such, it is small, yet it is one of the gayest and most elegant cities of Europe. Its situation is fine, in a valley watered by the Senne and the canal to Antwerp. The Allée Verte, consisting of three rows of trees bordering the canal, makes a beautiful approach. The market-place and the park are the two great ornaments of Brussels. The former is of great extent, and surrounded by the town hall, one of the most elegant Gothic structures in Europe, adorned with a tower, 348 feet high, and by the old halls of the different corporations. The park forms an extensive range of pleasure ground, interspersed with rows of lofty trees, and pleasing lawns, ornamented with fountains and statues, and it is surrounded by all the most spacious and sumptuous edifices. The church and chapel of St. Gudule are also distinguished for the elegance of their ornaments. Brussels has an academy of painting, attended by 400 or 500 students; and in the palace there is a library of 12,000 volumes, and a small but valuable collection of paintings. It was on the plains of Brabant, near the little villages of Quatre Bras, St. Jean, La Belle Alliance, and Waterloo a few leagues from Brussels, that the fate of Europe was decided in 1815.

358

Brussels.

Another ancient and important city is Malines, or Mechlin (now in the province of Antwerp), still retaining traces of the prosperity derived from the lace bearing its name, which is considered the strongest, though not the finest, made in the Netherlands. Another branch of industry consists in the making of excellent brown beer. The houses are ancient, and very spacious, often constructed in a curious and grotesque manner, and most nicely whitewashed. The tower of the cathedral is highly finished, and rises to the height of 348 feet. The other churches contain many of the masterpieces of Rubens and Vandyke. Louvain is equally fallen from the period when its extensive cloth manufactures and its university, one of the first in Europe, gave it a population of 150,000. It is a large ill-built town, whose bulky walls, seven miles in circumference, are now falling to decay. Its Catholic university, an attendance on which was once required as a qualification for holding any office under the Austrian government, perished in the French revolution, and was replaced by what could only be called a lyceum; but the ancient institution has since been restored. The town hall, enriched by numerous carved figures, and the collegiate church, whose spire, before its fall, at the beginning of the seventeenth century, rose to the height of 500 feet, are the chief ornaments of Louvain.

Antwerp (*fig.* 359.), formerly the port of Brabant, has now a province, to which it gives its name. This territory is situated along the Lower Scheldt, and is covered to a great extent with pleasure-grounds and houses, erected by the rich merchants during the period when Antwerp was in its glory. That city, down to the close of the fifteenth century, was almost without a rival among the commercial states of Europe. In the great struggle which then arose, Antwerp embraced with ardour the reformed cause, in support of which it suffered the most dreadful calamities. In 1576 it was sacked by the Spaniards; and being afterwards wrested from them, surrendered on favourable terms, after being besieged for more than a year, to the Prince of Parma. Subjected to the bigoted and tyrannic sway of Spain, and oppressed by the active rivalry of Holland, it lost all its commerce, and presented the mere shadow of its former greatness. Its renewed prosperity dates from its occupation by the French. Bonaparte made it one of his grand naval arsenals, and erected immense works, in the vain hope of creating a fleet which might rival that of Great Britain. Since the peace, Antwerp, having been placed on an equal footing with the ports of Holland, has availed itself of the advantages of its situation, and regained a considerable commerce. Having a ready navigation into the interior, and com-

359

Antwerp.

municating by canals with the principal seats of manufacture, it is destined by nature to be the chief emporium of Belgium. In 1828 there entered its port 955 vessels. Antwerp is still a noble city, containing numerous stately buildings, both private and public, which include some of the finest specimens of Gothic architecture existing. The cathedral, which occupied 100 years in building, is celebrated over Europe. It is 500 feet long, 230 wide, and 360 high. The spire is 466 feet high, of extreme beauty, and from its summit is obtained a magnificent view of the windings of the Scheldt, with the distant towers of Ghent, Malines, and Breda. The interior is adorned with the greatest masterpieces of Rubens and Vandyke, which, after being carried off to Paris, have been again restored. Numerous fine specimens of the Flemish school are found in the other churches, as well as in private mansions. Antwerp has always been the centre of Flemish art; the birth-place of Rubens, Vandyke, Jordaens, Teniers, and all its greatest masters. Zealous patronage is still bestowed upon the art; an academy is supported, at which 400 or 500 students are almost gratuitously taught: annual prizes are given, and crowns placed on the heads of the successful candidates. This encouragement has called forth some respectable talents, though none, as yet, to rival the fame of the old masters.

East Flanders is chiefly an inland district, and is the part of Belgium in which culture has been carried to the highest perfection. It displays an aspect of uniform luxuriant fertility, resulting altogether from the application of art and capital. Even in journeying along the road, the traveller finds the wheels of his carriage sinking in the sand, while beyond the hedge on each side, the soil consists of the richest black mould. The most fertile district is called the Waes, or St. Nicholas.

Ghent, even in its fallen state, is still one of the noblest of the old cities of Europe. That vast circuit of walls which, according to the boast of Charles V., could contain all Paris within them, may still be traced. It is built on twenty-seven islands, most of them bordered by magnificent quays, and connected by three hundred bridges. The streets, with a few exceptions, are spacious and handsome, and there are many fine old churches: but the great cathedral does not display the architectural grandeur of that of Antwerp, though the interior is rich in the extreme, adorned with numerous pillars of white marble. This and the other churches, as well as the academy, contain numerous paintings by the old Flemish masters. Ghent, though it can no longer send its 40,000 weavers into the field, is still one of the most manufacturing cities of Belgium. Prior to the revolution, its staple was sorted lace; but since the great improvements in the cotton manufacture, several large fabrics have been established at Ghent. The society is good, this being a favourite residence of the old Flemish nobles, and now frequented by a considerable number of English families.

The other towns in East Flanders are Dendermonde, a small but strong place, which has stood repeated sieges; Alost, on the eastern frontier; St. Nicholas and Tokerem, two large villages, of more than 11,000 inhabitants each, in the centre of the Waes, flourishing by means of corn-markets and of some considerable manufactures. Sas-van-Ghent is the centre of the sluices on the canal to the Scheldt, by which the whole country can be laid under water. Hulst is a strongly fortified little town.

West Flanders is a continuation of the same richly cultivated plain which has now been described; yet, being partly mixed with sand and marsh, and exposed to the blighting influence of fogs and sea breezes, it does not display altogether the luxuriant aspect of the Pays de Waes. It has no place comparable to Ghent, yet it comprises an extraordinary number of ancient cities, which still retain a portion of their former prosperity.

Bruges, formerly the residence of the counts of Flanders, and one of the factories of the Hanseatic league, was the greatest commercial city in the Low Countries, and perhaps in the north of Europe, till it was first surpassed by Antwerp, and then, from the same causes, shared its fall. Its situation in the midst of so fertile a country, and its communications by spacious canals with the sea and with the interior, still secure to it a considerable trade. Bruges has the character of an old town, the streets being narrow, and the houses lofty. The town hall is its most conspicuous edifice, and it is adorned also with many noble churches, containing some of the finest works of the great Flemish painters. The invention of painting in oil has been ascribed to this city.

Ostend is an ancient town, early celebrated for its fortifications. The siege by Spinola, which began in 1601, and lasted two years, was one of the most memorable in modern history; and upon its issue the destiny of the Low Countries was considered to depend. But though it ultimately fell, the exhaustion of the Spanish army, and the time which had been afforded to Holland for collecting her energies, prevented its capture from having the ruinous effects anticipated. Under Austrian sway, Ostend, which has one of the few good harbours in Flanders, became the chief theatre of the limited trade of the Belgic provinces. Napoleon restored its fortifications, which were still farther strengthened by the allies. It has not now above a third of its former population, but still carries on a brisk intercourse with England, and has almost the appearance of an English town. In 1828, 574 vessels entered its port.

Other large fortified places, celebrated in the military annals of Europe, are found in West

Flanders. Courtray, Ypres, and Menin have the usual character of Flemish towns. They are large, rather well built, with handsome churches and town halls; fallen from their ancient prosperity, yet retaining considerable manufactures of linen and beer; and having, in the long course of the Low Country wars, been repeatedly taken and retaken. Courtray is noted for the very fine flax grown in its neighbourhood. Oudenarde, the scene of one of Marlborough's victories, Dixmuide, and Furnes, present the same characters on a smaller scale. Nieuport is rather a noted fishing and trading town, surrounded by sluices, by means of which the country can be inundated.

Hainault, to the east of Flanders and the south of Brabant, presents a long range of military frontier to the once hostile border of France. It is watered by the upper courses of the Scheldt and the Sambre; and, instead of presenting the same dead level with Flanders, is varied by gentle undulations, still highly cultivated, yet not with the same extreme care or ample expenditure. In this province are rich mines of coal, a mineral not found in any other part of the Low Countries; and though Hainault never formed any of the great seats of manufacture, it is by no means deficient in this branch of industry.

Mons, Tournay, and Charleroi are the chief towns of Hainault. The description given of the secondary cities of Flanders may apply to them. Mons, called once Hannonia, is very ancient; it is well built, but appears often almost buried under the smoke of the steam-engines employed in working the neighbouring coalmines. It has a very extensive foundling hospital. Tournay, a fine large, old city, with a handsome cathedral, has stood many sieges. Charleroi, besides its military reputation, has that of making very fine nails, with which it supplies all Belgium. In front of Mons is Gemappe, and eight miles east of Charleroi is Fleurus, both celebrated for signal victories gained by the French during the revolutionary war. The large and strong cities of Condé and Valenciennes are now annexed to France.

Namur, to the east of Hainault, presents a striking variety from the tame and flat surface which covers the greater part of the Low Countries. Consisting of the valley of the Meuse, which traverses the whole province from north to south, it contains numerous rugged eminences, which give to it a varied and picturesque character. The banks of the river, from Namur to Liège, overhung by wooded rocks, and opening into deep valleys, abound in the most romantic scenes.

Among the cities, Namur is one of the most ancient in the Low Countries, its origin being traced to the time of the ancient Germans. It lies in a beautiful valley bordered by high mountains, at the confluence of the Sambre and Meuse. The castle, on a high rock, was formerly considered almost impregnable, and stood many sieges, till Joseph II. dismantled, and the French afterwards almost demolished it. The cathedral and the Jesuits' church are fine edifices, and, unlike the other churches of the Low Countries, of Grecian architecture. Namur has in its neighbourhood extensive iron mines, which employ many of the inhabitants; the manufactures of the city consist in working up this metal into fire-arms, cutlery, &c. Ascending the Meuse towards the French frontier, we come to the small fortified towns of Dinant and Charlemont.

The provinces of Liège and Limburg, which are much intermingled with each other, form the eastern frontier of Belgium. They run from north to south along the Meuse, fronting Germany, and are, indeed, half German. On the banks of the Meuse, and in some particular districts, the territory is broken and rocky; but most of it consists of an extended and highly cultivated plain. The eastern district is distinguished by the peculiar richness of its pastures, which produce butter and cheese of great value. Its manufactures, also, especially those of fine woollens, are very flourishing.

Of the cities in these two provinces, Liège, once the seat of a sovereign bishop, is ancient and large, but upon the whole ill built and gloomy; and though some of its buildings are large, they do not display the taste conspicuous in other Belgic cities. The church of St. Paul is, however, admired, as was that of St. Lambert, till it was destroyed during the revolution. Liège has a manufacture of fine woollen cloths, which sell at a high price. The town of Limburg, now included in Liège, has lost much of its population and industry; and a great part of its precincts is in ruins. Spa, situated amid romantic rocks, is one of the most celebrated watering places in Europe. The resort, though much diminished, is still considerable, and composed of persons of distinguished rank. The inhabitants work the beechwood, which grows in the neighbourhood, into a variety of toys, for which they find a ready sale among the visiters. St. Tron and Tongres are ancient towns, the former having a celebrated Benedictine abbey. Eupen, like Verviers, has flourishing manufactures of cloth. Hervé is the chief market for the Limburg cheese, which goes by its name. Stavelot is noted for its leather.

### Subsect. 2.—*Holland.*

The province of Holland is of paramount importance, including all the great cities and principal seats of commerce; so that its name was most usually given to the whole republic. It forms a long narrow strip, almost everywhere enclosed and penetrated by water; on one side it is washed by the North Sea; on the other, by the Zuyder Zee; in its centre it has the large lake called Haarlem-Meer; while the Rhine and the Lech intersect its numerous channels. The whole country is so low, that it is habitable only by means of enormous dikes, which exclude the sea: when these give way, the waters rush in, and inundate the whole territory. The country forms, in fact, one vast well-watered meadow scarcely any where subjected to the plough, though extensive gardens are cultivated, both for use and ornament. But the chief products are cattle, butter, and cheese, for the supply of the population of the cities, and for export.

Amsterdam (*fig.* 360.), the capital of the province and kingdom of Holland, is situated at the point of confluence of the river Amstel with the Y, an arm of the Zuyder Zee. It was a considerable town in the fourteenth century; but it was not until the sixteenth century, when the persecutions of the Spaniards in Belgium proved fatal to the trade and navigation of Antwerp and the southern provinces, that Amsterdam attained to the distinction which she enjoyed till about the middle of the last century, of being the first commercial city of Europe. It is but justice, however, to state that her extraordinary progress depended as much, or more, on the liberal and enlightened policy of her rulers, as on external events. Every individual, whatever might be his country or his religion, was received with open arms at Amsterdam; and acquired, by means of a trifling payment, the right of citizenship, and the enjoyment of all the privileges of a native. All the public institutions were calculated to promote commerce; and at a time when trade and industry in other countries were oppressed by prohibitions, in Holland they were comparatively free. When most prosperous, Amsterdam is supposed to have contained about 240,000 inhabitants; but at present the population is not supposed to exceed 200,000. Being built in a marsh, the foundations of the city are laid on piles; and it is a common complaint that a house costs as much below as above ground. The three principal streets are parallel to each other, and are not easily to be matched for length, breadth, and the magnificence of the houses; many of which, though antique, are splendid, and are kept in the best possible repair. The city is intersected by an immense number of canals, communicating by draw-bridges, and having sluices for the purpose of regulating the level of the water: these canals are for the most part bordered by fine trees. The expenses incurred in keeping the sluices in order, and in clearing the canals and port of mud, are very heavy. The matchless industry and perseverance of this wonderful people, are in nothing so signally displayed as in their works and contrivances for conquering the difficulties incident to their situation, and making the waters, which threaten to overwhelm them, contribute to their comfort. The stadthouse (*fig.* 361.), now the royal palace, is the finest building in the city; and is, indeed, one of the noblest anywhere to be met with: it is of large dimensions, and is adorned with pillars, and with sculptures emblematical of commerce and navigation. Above 13,000 piles are said to have been employed in forming its foundation. The harbour is inconvenient, large ships being obliged to lighten before they can pass the Pampus or bar at the mouth of the Y, and the navigation of the Zuyder Zee is also difficult. To remedy these inconveniences, the large canal to the Helder, already alluded to, has been constructed. The trade of Amsterdam has increased considerably within the last few years; and about 2200 ships now annually clear out for foreign countries. None of the water from the canals is made use of for culinary purposes; the town being supplied with fresh water, conveyed in carts from the Vecht, about five or six miles distant; but most of the houses have cisterns, where the rain-water is collected. There is a national museum of pictures, which contains many fine specimens of the Dutch school. The various prisons and houses of correction and industry at Amsterdam are said to be managed on more approved principles than similar institutions in most parts of Europe. The police is excellent; crimes rare; and no beggars to be seen in the streets. The inhabitants seem vigorous and healthy; but the mortality, though materially diminished within the last thirty or forty years, is still greater

360

Amsterdam.

361

Stadt-House, Amsterdam.

than in most European cities; a consequence, probably, of the humidity of the climate, and of the effluvia arising, in summer, from the canals.

Rotterdam (*fig.* 362.), the second city in Holland, is more conveniently situated for commerce than Amsterdam, having a readier access to the sea; and the Maese on which it is situated, being so very deep as to admit vessels of the largest draught of water to lie close

362

Rotterdam.

363

Statue of Erasmus.

to the quays. Its commerce is rapidly increasing. Its principal exports are geneva and madder; and it carries on the business of sugar-refining on a large scale. It has all the characteristics of a Dutch town; being neat, clean, uniform; the houses high, and built of very small bricks. The canals intersecting it are numerous, deep, and, unless in a few of the most crowded streets, connected by draw-bridges. Rotterdam boasts of being the birthplace of Erasmus; to perpetuate whose memory, she has erected a handsome statue (*fig.* 363.).

364

The Hague.

The Hague (*fig.* 364.), though ranking only as a village, is, in fact, one of the handsomest cities in Europe. The streets and squares are well built, bordered with fine walks and avenues of trees. Neither the old nor the new palace can boast of any splendid architecture; but the former is large, and contains some valuable collections. An avenue of two miles leads to the neat fishing town of Scheveling, whence the dealers are daily seen bringing their commodities in little carts drawn by large dogs.

365

Leyden.

Leyden (*fig.* 365.) is a fine old city, situated in the heart of the Rhineland, where this ancient bed of the river is cut into an infinity of canals, which render this the richest meadow land of Holland. The beer, the butter, and the bread of this district are held in the highest estimation. Leyden, during the war with Spain, was the most important city in Holland, and on the event of its siege the fate of that country was supposed to depend. The Spaniards, by a lengthened and strict blockade, reduced it to the last extremity; while the Dutch could muster no force adequate to its relief. It was then that they formed the magnanimous resolution of breaking down their dikes, and admitting the ocean. It was some time before the full effect was produced; but at length, impelled by a violent wind, the sea rushed in, overwhelmed all the works of the besiegers, and forced them to a precipitate flight. The little fleet of boats which had been prepared for the relief of Leyden, immediately sailed over the newly formed expanse, and triumphantly entered the city. The Prince of Orange offered to Leyden the option of two benefits,—an immunity from taxes for a certain period, or the foundation of a university in the city. The citizens crowned their former glory by choosing the latter alternative, and a university was accordingly founded, which speedily became one of the most eminent schools in Europe; and, though much injured by the numerous rivals which have since sprung up, it continues to maintain a high reputation, particularly as a classical school. Leyden is still a handsome and flourishing town; carries on the woollen manufacture with success, though on a diminished scale; and is a great market for butter and cheese. Haarlem (*fig.* 366.) is another city of ancient importance. In the great struggle for independence, it stood a memorable siege of seven months; when it surrendered upon honourable terms, which were basely violated by the Duke of Alva. Haarlem is still spacious and flourishing, and excels peculiarly in the bleaching of linen and cambric, which it performs for all the neighbouring provinces. The matchless and brilliant whiteness of the Haarlem linens has been imputed to a peculiar quality in the water, but is more probably the result of the extreme skill of the inhabitants, acquired by long practice. Flowers are principally raised for sale in the vicinity of Haarlem. Delft, an ancient gloomy town, was formerly celebrated for the manufacture of the ware which bears its name; but this, as already observed, has been almost entirely supplanted by English earthenware. Dort or Dordrecht, enclosed by branches of the Maese, was the ancient capital of Holland, while the main commerce of that country continued to centre in this its most natural quarter. It still retains very considerable traces of this early importance. The town-hall and great church are magnificent structures. There is a considerable trade in goods coming down the Rhine, particularly floats of timber, so large that one of them has been valued at 350,000 florins. Gouda is a large flourishing village, in a rich country, and carries on an extensive manufactory of tobacco-pipes. It is celebrated for the excellence of its cheese.

266

Haarlem.

North Holland forms a considerable peninsula, almost entirely encircled by the Zuyder Zee and the North Sea, and bordered by sand-hills of some elevation; but the interior is covered with rich pastures, on which are fed large herds of cattle. The ancient and not ungraceful costumes (*fig.* 267.) of the Dutch peasantry are preserved with greater exactness in this sequestered part of Holland, than in any other; and the fishery, for which their situation is peculiarly adapted, is carried on with great activity. Alkmaar is an agreeable town, with a great traffic in butter and cheese, and a manufacture of nets. The most important places in North Holland are the Helder and the Texel, two grand naval stations; the one a strong fort, commanding the entrance of the Zuyder Zee; the other an island opposite, in which the Dutch fleets used to rendezvous, from the facility it afforded for their getting to sea. Along the coast of the Zuyder Zee are the considerable towns of Hoorn and Enkhuisen, and the smaller ones of Edam and Purmerend.

267

Peasantry in Holland.

Zealand is a region more completely enclosed by, and sunk below, the level of the water, than any other part of the United Provinces. It consists of nine islands, formed and environed by branches of the Maese and the Scheldt, as, passing from the state of rivers into friths, they unite with the ocean. The mariner, in approaching, sees only points of the spires peeping above the immense dikes which defend them from inundation. The soil is moist and rich, peculiarly adapted to the cultivation of madder. The damp air, however, and the exhalations from the waters, render these islands unhealthy, and even fatal to foreigners, as was dreadfully experienced by the British troops while quartered at Walcheren; but the natives do not experience the same pernicious effects. Middleburg is a considerable city, with a town-hall and several churches, which afford fine specimens of Gothic architecture. Flushing is an eminent naval station, and has a considerable trade and fishery. The island of Schowen has Zierikzee, the ancient capital of the counts of Zealand; and South Beveland has Goes, or Tergoes, with a considerable trade in salt.

Utrecht, a more inland province than Holland, forms a continuation of the same tract of flat meadow land, interspersed with gardens and country residences. Utrecht, the capital, is a remarkably agreeable city, and being a little elevated, the view from its ramparts and the top of its cathedral over the vast plains and broad waters of Holland is extensive and delightful. The Romans called it Ulpii Trajectum, as commanding an important passage over the Rhine; and in the middle ages it was held by the warlike bishops of Utrecht. In this city was concluded the treaty of confederation, in 1597, by which the United Provinces were constituted, and also the celebrated treaty of 1715, which terminated the long war of the Spanish succession. Amersfoort, pleasantly situated on the Ems, and noted as the birth-place of Barneveldt, has considerable fabrics of dimity and bombazeen, and extensive bleaching grounds. Naarden, a small town, forms the key of all the water communications of Holland.

North Brabant, comprising that which was the Dutch part of the province, is a flat, sandy, marshy tract, not distinguished by either the natural fertility or manufacturing industry so conspicuous in the rest of Holland and Belgium. Forming, however, the barrier by which the Dutch maintained their independence, it contains several of the strongest fortresses in Europe, which have indeed the reputation of being almost impregnable. Breda is one of the most conspicuous. After Prince Maurice of Nassau took it by surprise, in 1590, its fortifications were greatly extended, and the surrounding country, being intersected by rivers and marshes, can be laid under water. It is an agreeable city, commanding from the ramparts a fine view, and both its church and its town-hall are admired Gothic edifices. Bois le Duc, or Herzogenbosch, on the Dommel, so named from an old hunting-wood of the Dukes of Brabant, is a large town, and equally strong. It is so intersected by canals, that eighty bridges are required to cross them; in winter the place is entirely surrounded by water, and can be approached only in boats. Bergen-op-Zoom, farther to the west, is similar as to strength, and was esteemed the masterpiece of the celebrated Cohorn. The disastrous attack made upon it by the British in the last war is well remembered.

The outer provinces of Guelderland, Friesland, Overyssel, Drenthe, and Groningen, which lie between the Zuyder Zee and the Ems, are rather appendages than integral portions of Holland, and form by their situation part of the great level plain of northern Germany. The country is similar to Holland, however, in its aspect and the general state of cultivation, though a somewhat greater proportion of the land is employed in the raising of grain. Friesland has a very fine breed of horses and horned cattle; and the linen manufacture flourishes to a considerable extent. In these provinces, particularly in Guelderland and Overyssel, there is a large extent of sandy and marshy ground, which is not forced into cultivation with the same minute care, as in the central provinces. Much benefit, however, is expected from the pauper colonies lately established there.

The towns of this region are pretty numerous and considerable, though none are of the first class. Nimeguen, in Guelderland, is ancient, strong, and handsome, commanding a noble view over the Rhine. Zutphen is an old imperial city, dreadfully pillaged in 1572 by the Duke of Alva. It has a magnificent church; and the fens around it have been so completely drained, as to render the air no longer unwholesome. Arnheim is a large and beautiful town, at the foot of the hills of Veluwe, and forming a great thoroughfare into Germany. Deventer, in Overyssel, is an ancient member of the Hanseatic league, and has a venerable cathedral. Zwoll, on the Yssel, is strong, large, and well built. Assen, though capital of the new province of Drenthe, is only a village. In Friesland, Leuwarden, on the Ee, is a large and populous town, in a country surrounded and intersected with canals, which enable it to communicate with the sea, and to carry on a considerable trade. Campen, an ancient Hanse town, has lost its importance, the harbour being now choked up. Harlingen, Franeker, Dokkum, Bolsward, are ports on the Zuyder Zee, and manufacturing places of some importance. Groningen, capital of the provinces of the same name, is the most important of all the towns east of the Zuyder Zee. It is well built, and adorned with noble edifices; and its university was once distinguished among Dutch seminaries. Large vessels can ascend the Hunse from the Zuyder Zee.

Luxemburg, an extensive province, though political revolutions attached it to the Netherlands, and now to Holland, forms part of Germany, entitling the king to a vote in the Germanic diet. Its character is every way in decided contrast to the rest of Holland and Belgium. Instead of a dead, rich flat, traversed by navigable streams and canals, Luxemburg presents almost throughout high mountains and woods, forming scenes of savage grandeur, similar, though on a smaller scale, to those of Switzerland. The country is destitute of water communications, is imperfectly cultivated, and does not contain a population of more than sixty-six to the square mile. Its breeds of cattle and sheep are of small size; but, as usual in mountain pastures, of delicate flavour. The horses are active and hardy; and the tract which borders on the Moselle produces valuable wine.

The cities and towns are by no means on the same scale as those in the rest of the kingdom. Luxemburg, the capital, situated on two rocks, whose steep sides form a glacis, while the river Else, at their feet, serves as a wet ditch, is one of the strongest fortresses in Europe. The horse and cattle markets are considerable. Theux has in its neighbourhood mines of a beautiful black marble. Maestricht, the principal town of Limburg, has, along with all the part of that province east of the Meuse, been assigned to Holland. It is large, handsome, and well fortified. Ruremonde and Venlo, also neat towns of some strength, are included in the same district.

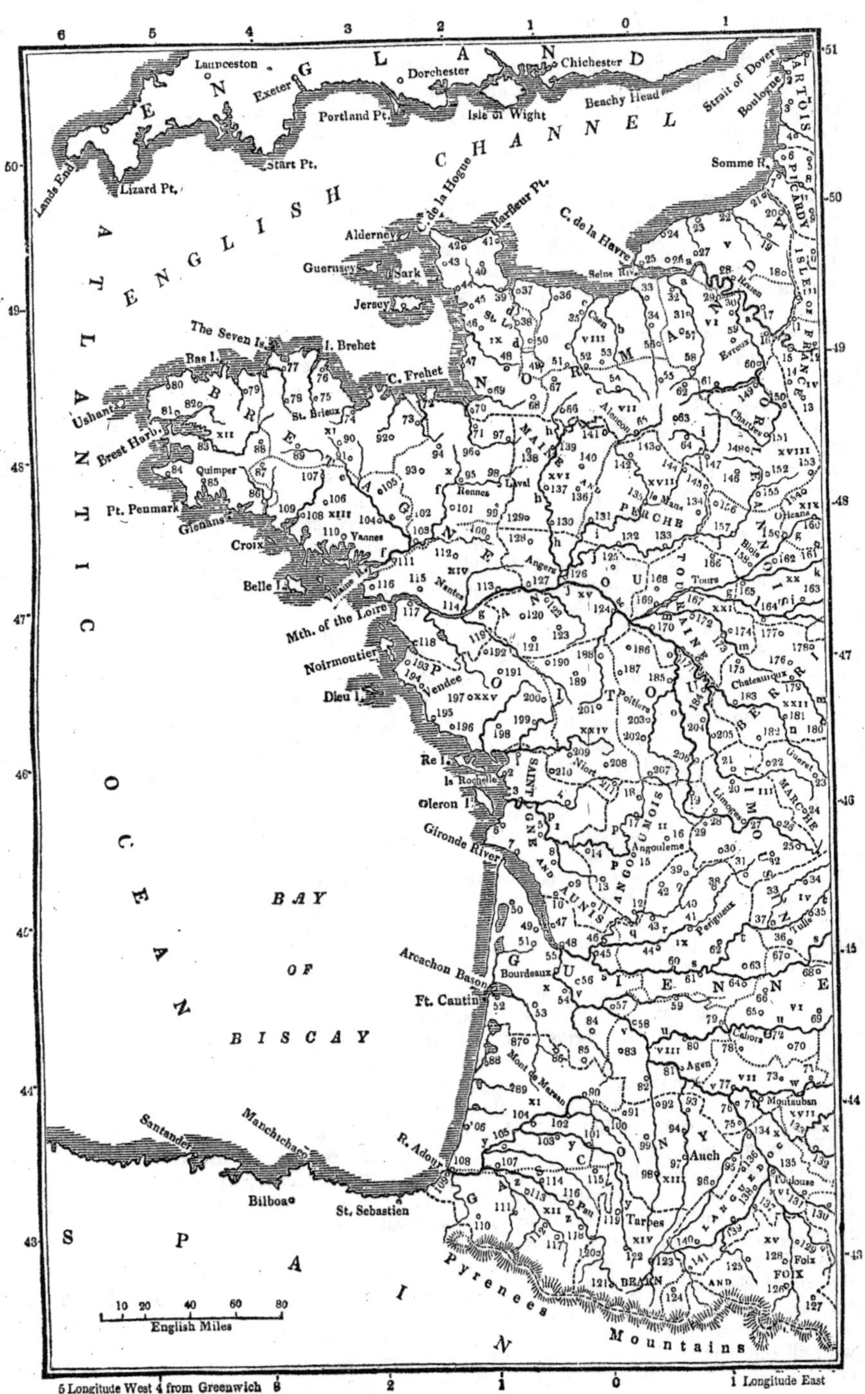
ENGLAND
ENGLISH CHANNEL
ATLANTIC OCEAN
BAY OF BISCAY
SPAIN
Pyrenees Mountains
Launceston
Dorchester
Chichester
Exeter
Portland Pt.
Isle of Wight
Beachy Head
Strait of Dover
Boulogne
Lands End
Lizard Pt.
Start Pt.
C. de la Hogue
Barfleur Pt.
C. de la Havre
Somme R.
Alderney
Guernsey
Sark
Jersey
The Seven Is.
I. Brehat
Bas I.
C. Frehet
Ushant
Brest Harb.
Quimper
Pt. Penmark
Glenans
Croix
Belle I.
Mth. of the Loire
Noirmoutier
Dieu I.
Re I.
Is Rochelle
Oleron I.
Gironde River
Arcachon Bason
Ft. Cantin
Bourdeaux
Santander
Manchichaco
R. Adour
Bilboa
St. Sebastien
Rennes
Laval
Nantes
Angers
Tours
Vannes
St. Brieux
Caen
St. Lo
Evreux
Chartres
Alencon
Le Mans
Orleans
Blois
Poitiers
Niort
Angouleme
Limoges
Gueret
Chateauroux
Perigueux
Tulle
Cahors
Agen
Montauban
Auch
Toulouse
Pau
Tarbes
Foix
Mont de Marsan
BEARN
FOIX
10 20 40 60 80
English Miles
5 Longitude West 4 from Greenwich 3
1 Longitude East

10 20 40 60 80
English Miles
NETHERLANDS
GERMANY
SWITZERLAND
ITALY
MEDITERRANEAN SEA
GULF OF LYONS
Lake of Constance
L. of Neufchatel
L. of Geneva
Gulf of Genoa
Brussels
Namur
Lisle
Mezieres
Metz
Nancy
Epinal
Strasbourg
Colmar
Bale
Rhine R.
R. Rhine
Aare R.
Meuse R.
Moselle R.
Lis R.
Escaut R.
BERN
Geneva
Genoa
Nice
CORSICA
Levant
Porquerolle
Porteros
Toulon
Marseilles
Mths. of the Rhone
Aix
Avignon
Nismes
Montpellier
Perpignan
Aude R.
Carcassonne
ROUSSILLON
Alby
Rodez
Mende
Aurillac
Puy
Privas
Valence
Grenoble
Gap
Digne
Draguignan
Alps
DAUPHINY
LYONNOIS
Lyon
Macon
Bourg
Lons le Saulnier
FRANCHE COMTE
Besançon
Vesoul
Dijon
BURGUNDY
Auxerre
Troyes
Chalons
Rheims
CHAMPAGNE
LORRAINE
ALSACE
Bar le Duc
Chaumont
Laon
Beauvais
PICARDY
Amiens
ARTOIS
Arras
FLANDERS
PARIS
ISLE OF FRANCE
Melun
ORLEANNOIS
NIVERNOIS
Nevers
BERRI
Bourg
BOURBONNOIS
Moulins
MARCHE
LIMOUSIN
AUVERGNE
Clermont
Montbrisson
FOREZ
LANGUEDOC
2 3 4 5 6 7 8 9
4 Longitude East 5 from Greenwich 6
51 50 49 48 47 46 45 44 43

## CHAPTER VIII.

### FRANCE.

FRANCE is a great and powerful kingdom, placed, as it were, in the centre of the civilized world, and for several centuries distinguished by the conspicuous part which it has acted on the theatre of Europe. Its population, military power, central situation, vast resources, and active industry, render it peculiarly deserving of an attentive survey.

---

*References to the Map of France.—West Part.*

NORTH PART.
Province of ARTOIS.
*Department of*
I. Strait of Calais. (Pas de Calais.)
1. Calais
2. Boulogne
3. Samer
4. Montreuil

Province of PICARDY.
*Department of*
II. Somme.
5. Cressy
6. Rue
7. St. Vallery
8. Abbeville
9. Airaines

Province of the I. OF FRANCE.
*Departments.*
III. Oise
IV. Seine and Oise.
10. Grandvillers
11. St. Clair
12. Meulan
13. Rambouillet
14. Houdan
15. Mantes

Province of NORMANDY.
*Departments.*
V. Lower Seine
VI. Eure
VII. Orne
VIII. Calvados
IX. The Channel. (La Manche.)
16. Vernon
17. Andeleys
18. Gournay
19. Neufchatel
20. Blangis
21. Eu
22. Dieppe
23. St. Valery
24. Fecamp
25. Havre de Grace
26. Bolbec
27. Yvetot
28. Rouen
29. Elbœuf
30. Louviers
31. Brionne
32. Pont Audemer
33. Pont l'Eveque
34. Lisieux
35. Caen
36. Bayeux
37. Isigny
38. St. Lo
39. Carentan
40. Valognes
41. Barfleur
42. Cherbourg
43. Les Pieux
44. Barneville
45. Creance
46. Coutances
47. Granville
48. Villedieu
49. Vire
50. Thorigny
51. St. Germain
52. Pont d'Ouilly
53. Falaise
54. Argentan
55. Gace
56. Orbec
57. Bernay
58. Rugles
59. Evreux
60. Ivry
61. Verneuil
62. L'Aigle
63. Mortagne
64. Belesme
65. Alencon
66. Domfront
67. Tinchebray
68. Mortain
69. Avranches
70. Pontorson

Province of BRETAGNE.
*Departments.*
X. Ille and Vilaine
XI. North Coast
XII. Finisterre
XIII. Morbihan
XIV. Lower Loire
71. Antrain
72. St. Malo
73. Dinan
74. St. Brieux
75. Guingamp
76. Paimpol
77. Lannion
78. Belle Ile
79. Morlaix
80. Lannilis
81. Brest
82. Landerneau
83. Chateaulin
84. Andierne
85. Quimper
86. Quimperle
87. Gourin
88. Carhaix
89. Rostrenen
90. Uzel
91. Loudeac
92. Broons
93. Montfort
94. Hede
95. Rennes
96. St. Aubin
97. Fougeres
98. Vitre
99. La Guerche
100. Chateaubriant
101. Cervin
102. Carentoire
103. Redon
104. Maletroit
105. Ploermel
106. Band
107. Pontivy
108. Hennebon
109. L'Orient
110. Vannes
111. Roche-Bernard
112. Nozay
113. Ancenis
114. Nantes
115. Savenay
116. Guerrande
117. Paimbœuf
118. Bourgneuf
119. Clisson

Province of ANJOU.
*Department of*
XV. Mayenne and Loire.
120. Beaupreau
121. Chollet
122. Chalonne
123. Vihiers
124. Saumur
125. Bauge
126. Angers
127. Ingrande
128. Segre

Province of MAINE AND PERCHE.
*Departments.*
XVI. Mayenne
XVII. Sarthe.
129. Craon
130. Chateau Gontier
131. Sable
132. La Fleche
133. Chateau de Loir
134. St. Calais
135. Le Mans
136. Vaiges
137. Laval
138. Juvigne
139. Mayenne
140. Ebron
141. Prez en Pail
142. Frenay
143. Mamers
144. La Ferte Bernard
145. Montmirail

Province of ORLEANAIS.
*Departments.*
XVIII. Eure and Loir
XIX. Loiret
XX. Loir and Cher.
146. Brou
147. Nogent le Rotrou
148. Alliers
149. Dreux
150. Maintenon
151. Chartres
152. Bonneval
153. Toury
154. Arlenay
155. Chateaudun
156. Mondoubleau
157. Vendome
158. Blois
159. Melun
160. Orleans
161. Cosson
162. Chambord
163. Romorantin
164. St. Aignan
165. Chaumont

Province of TOURAINE.
*Department of*
XXI. Indre and Loire.
166. Chateau Regnault
167. Tours
168. Savigne
169. Langeais
170. Chinon
171. La Haye
172. Montbazon
173. Loches
174. Beaulieu

Province of BERRI.
*Department of*
XXII. Indre.
175. Chatillon sur Indre
176. Levroux
177. Valencay
178. Valan
179. Chateauroux
180. La Chatre
181. Argenton
182. St. Benoit
183. Le Blanc

Province of POITOU.
*Departments.*
XXIII. Vienne
XXIV. Two Sevres
XXV. Vendee.
184. La Roche Posay
185. Chatellerault
186. Loudun
187. Moncontour
188. Thouars
189. Bressure
190. Chatillon sur Sevre
191. Pouzange
192. Montaigu
193. Beauvoir
194. St. Gilles sur Vie
195. Sables d'Olonne
196. Talmont
197. Bourbon-Vendee
198. Lucon
199. Fontenay
200. Chataigneraye
201. Parthenay
202. Vivonne
203. Poitiers
204. St. Savin
205. Montmorillon
206. L'Isle Jourdain
207. Civray
208. Melle
209. Niort
210. Mauze
211. Sauze

SOUTH PART.
Province of SAINTONGE AND AUNIS.
*Department of*
I. Lower Charente.
1. Marans
2. La Rochelle
3. Rochefort
4. St. Jean d'Angely
5. Saintes
6. Marennes
7. Royan
8. Pons
9. Jonzac
10. Mirambeau
11. Monlieu

Province of ANGOUMOIS.
*Department of*
II. Charente
12. Aubeterre
13. Barbezieux
14. Cognac
15. Angouleme
16. La Rochefoucauld
17. Mansle
18. Ruffec
19. Confolens

Provinces of MARCHE AND LIMOUSIN.
*Departments.*
III. Upper Vienne
IV. Correze
V. Creuse.
20. Bellac
21. Le Dorat
22. Souterraine
23. Gueret
24. Bourganeuf
25. Eymontiers
26. St. Leonard
27. Limoges
28. St. Junien
29. Rochechouart
30. Chalus
31. St. Yrieix
32. Pierre Buffiere
33. Uzerche
34. Treignac
35. Tulle
36. Turenne
37. Donzenac

Province of GUIENNE.
*Departments.*
VI. Lot
VII. Tarn and Garonne
VIII. Lot and Garonne
IX. Dordogne
X. Bordeaux
38. Thiviers
39. Nontron
40. Brantome
41. Perigueux
42. Mareuil
43. Riberac
44. Mucidan
45. Libourne
46. Coutras
47. Blaye
48. Bourg
49. Medoc
50. Lesparre
51. Castelnau
52. La Tete de Buch
53. Le Barp
54. Castres
55. Bordeaux
56. Creon
57. La Reolle
58. Marmande
59. Castillonez
60. Bergerac
61. La Linde
62. Miremont
63. Sarlat
64. Domme
65. Catus
66. Gourdon
67. Martel
68. St. Cere
69. Figeac
70. Concots
71. St. Antonin
72. Cahors
73. Caussade
74. Montauban
75. Verdun
76. Castelsarasin
77. Moissac
78. Moncuq
79. Fumel
80. Villeneuve-d'Agen
81. Agen
82. Nerac
83. Castel-Geloux
84. Bazas
85. Captieux

Province of GASCONY.
*Departments.*
XI. Landes
XII. Lower Pyrenees
XIII. Gers.
86. Sore
87. Murat
88. Mimizan
89. La Bouliere
90. Roquefort
91. Eauze
92. Condom
93. Lectoure
94. Fleurance
95. Isle en Jourdain
96. Lombez
97. Auch
98. Mirande
99. Vic Ferenzac
100. Nogaro
101. Aire
102. Mont de Marsan
103. St. Sever
104. Monfort
105. Dax
106. St. Vincent
107. Peyrehorade
108. St. Esprit
109. Bayonne
110. St. Jean Pied de Port
111. Mauleon
112. Oleron
113. Navarreins
114. Orthes
115. Garlin
116. Pau
117. Arudi
118. Nai

Province of BEARN AND FOIX.
*Departments.*
XIV. Upper Pyrenees
XV. Arriege
119. Tarbes
120. Argellez
121. Luz
122. Bagneres
123. Sarrancolin
124. Bagneres du Luchon
125. St. Girons
126. Tarascon
127. Ax
128. Foix
129. Pamiers

Province of LANGUEDOC.
*Departments*
XVI. Upper Garonne
XVII. Tarn.
130. Castelnaudary
131. Villefranche
132. Lavaur
133. St. Sulpice
134. Grenade
135. Toulouse
136. St. Lys
137. Muret
138. Rieux
139. Cazeres
140. St. Gaudens
141. St. Beat

*Rivers.*
a Seine
b Dives
c Oure
d Vire
e Oust
f Vilaine
g Loire
h Mayenne
i Sarthe
j Loire
k Beauvron
l Le Cher
m Indre
n Creuse
o Vienne
p Charente
q Dronne
r Isle
s Dordogne
t Vezere
u Lot
v Garonne
w Aveyron
x Tarn
y Adour
z Gave de Pau

## Sect. I.—*General Outline and Aspect.*

France is bounded on the North by the Channel, which separates it from England, and

*References to the Map of France.—East Part.*

NORTH PART.
Province of
FLANDERS.
*Department of*
I. The North.
1. Maubeuge
2. Avesnes
3. Landrecy
4. Le Cateau
5. Cambrai
6. Valenciennes
7. Douay
8. St. Amand
9. Lille
10. Hazebrouck
11. Cassel
12. Dunkirk
13. Gravelines.

Province of
ARTOIS.
*Department of the*
II. Strait of Calais.
14. Ardres
15. St. Omer
16. Aire
17. Fauquemberg
18. Hesdin
19. St. Pol
20. Bethune
21. Arras
22. Bapaume.

Province of
PICARDY.
*Department of*
III. Somme.
23. Doulens
24. Amiens
25. Peronne
26. Roye
27. Montdidier
28. Poix.

Province of
THE ISLE OF
FRANCE.
*Departments.*
IV. Oise
V. Seine
VI. Seine and Oise
VII. Seine and
Marne
VIII. Aisne.
29. Breteuil
30. Beauvais
31. Clermont
32. Noyon
33. Compiegne
34. Crespy
35. Senlis
36. Meru
37. Pontoise
38. St. Denis
39. Luzarches
40. Dammartin
41. Meaux
42. Coulommier
43. Marolles
44. Paris
45. Sceaux
46. Versailles
47. Corbeil
48. Etampes
49. Melun
50. Fontainebleau
51. Nemours
52. Montereau Fault
Yonne
53. Rosoy
54. Provins
55. Chateau Thiery
56. La Ferte Milon
57. Villers Coterets
58. Soissons
59. Laon
60. La Fere
61. St. Quentin
62. Guise
63. Sissonne
64. Vervins.

Province of
CHAMPAGNE.
*Departments.*
IX. Ardennes
X. Marne
XI. Aube
XII. Upper Marne
65. Rocroy
66. Charleville
67. Mezieres
68. Sedan
69. Grand Pre
70. Vouziers
71. Attigny
72. Rethel
73. Asfeld
74. Rheims
75. Courtagnon
76. Valmy
77. St. Menehoud
78. Chalons
79. Epernay
80. Dormans
81. Montmirail
82. Sezanne
83. Vertus
84. Vitry sur Marne
85. St. Remy
86. Ramaru
87. Arcis sur Aube
88. Marsilly
89. Nogent sur
Seine
90. Troyes
91. Chaource
92. Bar sur Seine
93. Clairvaux
94. Bar sur Aube
95. Montierender
96. Vassy
97. Joinville
98. Chaumont
99. Auberive
100. Langres
101. Fay le Billot
102. Bourbonne les
Bains
103. Bourmont.

Province of
LORRAINE.
*Departments.*
XIII. Vosges
XIV. Meurthe
XV. Meuse
XVI. Moselle.
104. Signeville
105. Plombieres
106. Epinal
107. Remiremont
108. Gerardmer
109. St. Dic
110. Rembervillor
111. Mirecourt
112. Neufchateau
113. Gondrecourt
114. Bar le Duc
115. Vaucouleurs
116. Commercy
117. Toulon
118. Nancy
119. Luneville
120. Raon
121. Sarrebourg
122. Chateau Salins
123. Nomeny
124. Gorze
125. Frenes
126. St. Mihiel
127. Vaubecourt
128. Verdun
129. Varennes
130. Estain
131. Montmedy
132. Longwy
133. Briey
134. Metz
135. Thionville
136. St. Avold
137. Sarreguemines
138. Bitche.

Province of
ALSACE.
*Departments.*
XVII. Lower Rhine
XVIII. Upper Rhine
139. Weissemburg
140. Haguenau
141. Bouquenon
142. Saverne
143. Strasburg
144. Molsheim
145. Schelstat
146. St. Marie aux
Mines
147. Colmar
148. Neuf Brisach
149. Mulhausen
150. Altkirch
151. Chann
152. Giromagny.

Province of
FRANCHE-
COMTE.
*Departments.*
XIX. Upper Saone
XX. Doubs
XXI. Jura.
153. Lure
154. Luxeuil
155. Jussey
156. Vesoul
157. Champlitte
158. Dampierre
159. Gray
160. Gy
161. Baume
162. Montbeliard
163. St. Hypolite
164. Le Russey
165. Passavant
166. Ornans
167. Besancon
168. Quingey
169. Dole
170. Poligny
171. Salins
172. Rochejean
173. Neuve
174. Clairevaux
175. Lons le Saulnier
176. Dortan
177. St. Claude.

Province of
BURGUNDY.
*Departments.*
XXII. Ain
XXIII. Saone and
Loire
XXIV. Cote d'Or
XXV. Yonne.
178. Nantua
179. Fort de l'Ecluse
180. Seyssel
181. Belley
182. Poncin
183. Mount Luel
184. Trevoux
185. Chalamont
186. Bourg
187. Macon
188. Port de Vaux
189. Cluny
190. Semur en Bri-
onnois
191. Charolles
192. Bourbon-Lancy
193. M. St. Vincent
194. Tournus
195. Romenay
196. Louhans
197. Chalonne
198. Chalons
199. Nolay
200. Montcenis
201. Antun
202. Saulieu
203. Arnay le Duc
204. Beaune
205. Nuits
206. Dijon
207. Is sur Til
208. Semur
209. Avalon
210. Coulange les
Vinces
211. Auxerre
212. Vermanton
213. Ravieres
214. Montbard
215. Baigneux
216. Chatillon sur
Seine
217. Tonnerre
218. St. Florentin
219. Joigny
220. Villeneuve l'Ar-
cheveque
221. Sens
222. Pont sur Yonne
223. St. Julien.

Province of
ORLEANAIS.
*Department of*
XXVI. Loiret.
224. Courtenay
225. Chatillon
226. Montargis
227. Boyne
228. Pithiviers
229. Combreux
230. Sully
231. Gien.

Province of
BERRI.
*Department of*
XXVII. Cher.
232. Aubigny
233. Sancerre
234. Vierzon
235. Bourges
236. Chateauneuf
237. Chateau Meil-
lant
238. St. Amand
239. Blet
240. Sancergues.

Province of
NIVERNAIS.
*Department of*
XXVIII. Nievre.
241. Nevers
242. La Charite
243. Cosne
244. Clamecy
245. Champlemi
246. Corbigny
247. Chateau Chinon
248. Moulins en Gil-
bert
249. Decize
250. St. Pierre le
Moutier.

Province of
BOURBONNAIS.
*Department of*
XXIX. Allier.
251. Bourbon-l'Ar-
chambault
252. Moulins
253. Donjon
254. Varennes
255. La Palisse
256. Casset
257. Gannat
258. St. Pourcain
259. Herisson
260. Mont Lucon.

SOUTH PART.
Province of
MARCHE.
*Department of*
I. Creuse.
1. Boussac
2. Jarnage
3. Chambon
4. Auzance
5. Aubusson
6. Felletin
7. Courtine.

Province of
LIMOUSIN.
*Department of*
II. Correze.
8. Ussel
9. Bort
10. Egletons.

Province of
GUIENNE.
*Department of*
III. Aveyron.
11. Figeac
12. Livignac
13. Villefranche
14. St. Sernin
15. St. Afrique
16. St. Rome
17. Milhau
18. Rodez
19. Severac
20. St. Geniez
21. Guiolle
22. Entraigues
23. Espalion
24. Ville Contal.

Province of
AUVERGNE.
*Departments.*
IV. Cantal
V. Dome.
25. Mount Salvy
26. Maurs
27. Aurillac
28. Chaudes Aigues
29. St. Flour
30. Massiac
31. Murat
32. Mauriac
33. Seignes
34. Bosso
35. Issoire
36. Ambert
37. Billom
38. Clermont
39. Rochefort
40. Pont Gibaud
41 Montaigu
42. Riom
43. Thiers.

Province of
LYONNAIS.
*Departments.*
VI. Loire
VII. Rhone.
44. L'Hopital
45. Pacudiere
46. Roanne
47. Aigueperse
48. Thizy
49. Villefranche
50. Lyons
51. Iseron
52. Montbrison
53. St. Rambert
54. St. Etienne
55. St. Chamond
56. Brignais.

Province of
DAUPHINY.
*Departments of*
VIII. Isere
IX. Upper Alps
X. Drome.
57. Vienne
58. Peage
59. Cote St. Andre
60. Bourgoin
61. Cremien
62. La Tour du Pin
63. Voiron
64. St. Barraux
65. Grenoble
66. Marcellin
67. La Mure
68. Bourg d'Oysans
69. Briancon
70. Montdauphin
71. St. Bonnet
72. Die
73. Beaufort
74. St. Jean de Roi
75. Isere
76. St. Vallier
77. Valence
78. Crest
79. Montelimart
80. Nions
81. Largu
82. Argencon
83. Gap
84. Embrun.

Province of
PROVENCE.
*Departments.*
XI. Vaucluse
XII. Lower Alps
XIII. Var
XIV. Mouths of the
Rhone.
85. Barcelonnette
86. Colmars
87. Digne
88. Sisteron
89. Forcalquier
90. Sault
91. Vaison
92. Orange
93. Carpentras
94. Avignon
95. Orgon
96. Cavaillon
97. Lambese
98. Apt
99. Manosque
100. Les Mees
101. Riex
102. Castellane
103. Entrevaux
104. St. Auban
105. Vence
106. Antibes
107. Grasse
108. Draguignan
109. Frejus
110. St. Tropez
111. Le Luc
112. Hieres
113. Brignolle
114. St. Maximi
115. Toulon
116. La Ciotat
117. Marseilles
118. Aix
119. Martigues
120. Salon
121. Arles

Province of
LANGUEDOC.
*Departments.*
XV. Gard
XVI. Ardeche
XVII. Upper Loire
XVIII. Lozere
XIX. Herault
XX. Tarn
XXI. Aude.
122. Aigues-mortes
123. Sommieres
124. Nismes
125. Uzes
126. Pont St. Esprit
127. Barjac
128. Alais
129. Genoilhac
130. Villefort
131. L'Argentiere
132. Viviers
133. Aubenas
134. Privas
135. Tournon
136. Annonay
137. St. Agreve
138. Yssingeaux
139. St. Julien de
Chap
140. Le Puy
141. Brioud
142. Langeac
143. Chely d'Ap
144. Jovols
145. Langogne
146. Marvejols
147. Mende
148. Canourgue
149. Florac
150. Meyrueis
151. Le Vigan
152. Anduze
153. Ganges
154. Montpelier
155. Balaruc
156. Pezenas
157. Lodeve
158. Bedarrieux
159. La Caune
160. Alby
161. Castres
162. Puis Laurens
163. Mazamet
164. St. Pons
165. Beziers
166. Narbonne
167. Caunes
168. Carcassonne
169. St. Papoul
170. Fanjeaux
171. Alet
172. Rodome
173. Quillan
174. La Grasse

Province of
ROUSSILLON
*Department of*
XXII. Eastern Py-
renees.
175. Rivesaltes
176. Prades
177. Mt. Louis
178. Prats de Molo
179. Ceret
180. Perpignan.

*Rivers.*
a Rhine
b Moselle
c Meuse
d Aisne
e Escaut or Scheldt
f Somme
g Oise
h Marne
i Seine
j Aube
k Serain
l Yonne
m Loire
n Allier
o Le Cher
p Lot
q Tarn
r Aude
s Rhone
t Durance
u Isere
v Ain
w Saone
x Oignon
y Doubs
z Loue.

by part of the frontier of the Netherlands. On the east it is bounded by Germany, from which it is divided by the Rhine, and by Switzerland and Italy, which lie on the other side of the mighty barrier of the Alps. Its southern limits are the Mediterranean and the broad isthmus filled by the Pyrenees, on the other side of which extends the Spanish peninsula. On the west is the Atlantic, and more especially that vast gulf called the Bay of Biscay. The southern extremity, on the line of the Pyrenees, falls in 42° 30′ N. lat. the northern beyond Dunkirk in 51° 10′, making in length eight and a half degrees of latitude. The breadth may be from 8° 20′ E. long., to 4° 40′ W. long. making thirteen degrees of longitude. This will give dimensions nearly square of 595 miles from north to south, and 550 from east to west. The superficial extent is about 205,000 English square miles, or somewhat above 130,000,000 acres.

The surface of this very extensive territory is in general level, although it borders, and is encroached upon by the greatest mountain ranges of Europe. The Alps cover the full half of its eastern frontier, and their branches extending into Dauphiny and Provence, render them very rugged and romantic regions. The Pyrenees, which rank second among the chains of the Continent, range along the southern border, and cover with their branches Roussillon and Gascony. On the east, where France reaches to the Rhine, are the Vosges and other chains of moderate height, parallel to that river. The only range exclusively French, is that of Auvergne, in the centre of the kingdom, which not only includes all that province where it rises to the height of 5000 or 6000 feet, but stretches by a winding line along the left bank of the Allier to Languedoc, parallel to the coast of the Mediterranean, where it is called the Cevennes. But by far the greater part of France, including the whole north and the whole west, is one widely extended plain, which yields in very high perfection all the fruits and products of the temperate zone.

The rivers of France, though not of the first magnitude, are noble and commodious. Traversing almost every part of the kingdom, they afford ample means of internal navigation; and the broad plains which border on them yield the most luxuriant harvests. The Loire, which is the principal, rises in the south, on the borders of Provence, and flows for some time nearly north, parallel to the course of the Rhone and the Saône, though in an opposite direction. Near Nevers it receives the Allier, which in a parallel and nearly equal stream has hitherto accompanied it; it now gradually bends round into a westerly course, which it follows through the plains of Orleanais and Touraine, the garden of France, till after a course of 700 miles, it falls into the sea a little below the great commercial city of Nantes. The Rhone is not at first a French river: it rises in the heart of Switzerland, amid the eternal snows and glaciers of the Grimsel and the Shreckhorn, and rolls its earliest course beneath the mighty mountain walls of St. Gothard, Monte Rosa, and the Simplon. It now expands into the Leman lake, from whence it emerges near Geneva, where it soon enters France, and rolls direct towards Lyons. At that great city, it receives the Saône, bringing down an ample stream from the Vosges, swelled by that of the Doubs from the Jura. The Rhone, now following the direction of its tributary, turns directly south, and, after a rapid course through Dauphiny and Provence, enters the Mediterranean by several mouths. In this course, the Alps transmit it to the Isère, and the classical stream of the Durance: its entire length may be 500 miles. The Seine, though of inferior magnitude, claims distinction as flowing by the metropolis: it rises on the frontier of Burgundy, and runs almost due north till it receives the parallel and nearly equal Aube, when their united waters flow west and north-west. Before reaching Paris, it receives from the south the Yonne, and from the north, almost under the walls of the capital, its greatest tributary, the Marne. At Paris it is navigable for vessels of considerable burden. Beyond Paris, the Seine makes some extensive windings, and is augmented from the north by the waters of the Oise bringing those of the Aisne. It then passes the fine and flourishing city of Rouen, and, spreading into an estuary, joins the English Channel at the ancient port of Havre. The Garonne has a course of still less extent, though its broad navigable stream, flowing through a magnificent plain, the most productive in valuable wine of any in France, gives it a high commercial importance. It rises near the eastern Pyrenees, and flows northward to Toulouse, where it assumes a steady north-west course, during which, swelled from the north by the Aveyron, the Lot, and the Dordogne, and passing the great haven of Bordeaux, it becomes an estuary, capable of receiving the largest vessels. The Rhine is to France only a limitary river for somewhat above 100 miles; but its great tributaries, the Moselle and the Meuse, rise and have most of their early course within its territory. The important Belgic river, the Scheldt, also rises within the French territory.

France has no lakes, which, in a general view, seem worthy of mention.

## SECT. II.—*Natural Geography.*

### SUBSECT. 1.—*Geology.*

*Primitive and transition districts.* In France there are six districts where the older rocks, or those of the primitive and transition classes, prevail: viz. Western Normandy, with

Britany and Anjou; the northern side of the Pyrenees; the departments of the Lower Alps, Upper Alps, and part of the Isère; Central France, or the table-land of France; central part of the Vosges; and the Ardennes.

(1.) *Western Normandy, Britany, and Anjou.* In this region the rocks are partly Neptunian, partly Plutonian: the Neptunian strata are gneiss, mica slate, clay slate, greywacke, quartz rock, and limestone; the Plutonian rocks are granite, syenite, greenstone, and porphyry.

(2.) *Northern side of the Pyrenees.* On the French side of the Pyrenees the central rocks are of primitive formation, and consist of mica slate, clay slate, limestone, or marble; reposing upon these, and forming the great body of the range, are rocks of the transition class; viz. clay slate, greywacke, and transition limestone.

(3.) *Departments of the Lower and Upper Alps, and part of Isère.* In this mountainous region there are magnificent displays of many of the more interesting formations of the primitive and transition classes.

(4.) *Central table-land or plateau of France.* The centre of France is occupied by a vast table-land or plateau of old rocks, in general granite, which forms the mountains of Burgundy, the Limousin, Aveyron, Ardèche, and the Cevennes. It is more than eighty leagues in breadth from the heights of Limoges; but in proceeding towards the south, it gradually thins off, and terminates in a point which connects it with the Montagne Noire. This latter group of old rocks forms a kind of peninsula, which is separated from the Pyrenees, by a longitudinal basin of secondary and tertiary formations. The acclivities of this central granitic table-land, and some of its hollows, are covered more or less densely with newer rocks of various descriptions. Besides these, there occurs on its eastern part a splendid display of volcanic rocks. The primitive and transition rocks of this table-land are the following; viz. granite, porphyry, talc slate, serpentine, gneiss, clay slate, greywacke, and limestone.

(5.) *Central part of the Vosges.* The oldest rocks in this range of mountains, and which are said to belong to the transition class, are the following: granite, syenite, hornblende rocks, greenstone, red quartziferous porphyry, augitic porphyry, dolomite, diallage rock, serpentine, talc slate, clay slate, greywacke, with anthracite, granular and compact marble or limestone.

(6.) *Ardennes.* That part of this range of mountains included within the limits of France, which belongs to the older part of the geognostical series, is composed of various clay slates, with greywacke, all of which seem to belong to the transition class.

*Secondary districts.* The lower and flatter parts of France which extend from the primitive and transition districts, are composed of secondary and tertiary deposits, more or less covered with alluvial matters; and in some quarters intermingled with volcanic rocks. The secondary formations are arranged in the same order, and exhibit similar relations with those already described in our account of Britain. The mountain limestone and coal formations form, when contrasted with their abundance in Britain, but a small portion of the surface of France; while the new red sandstones, with the series of the Jura limestone, including the oolites, form great tracts of country. Chalk, or uppermost rock of the secondary series, occurs in vast abundance, forming two basins, the one the northern, extending in length from the northern extremity of Artois to the southern limit of Touraine, and in breadth from Havre de Grace to near Bar le Duc. The northern side of the southern basin extends from Rochefort to Cahors, and the southern side ranges along the northern face of the Pyrenees.

*Tertiary districts.* France is remarkable on account of the great extent of its tertiary deposits; of these the following may be considered as the principal ones:—1. That of which Paris forms the central point; which extends towards the north as high as Laon, and southward to Blois; while it stretches across from Pontoise on the west to Epernay on the east. 2. The great southern deposit, which extends from the south side of the river Gironde to the south bank of the river Adour. 3. The south-eastern deposit, which covers part of the Departments of Herault, Gard, Mouths of the Rhone, Var, and Vaucluse. 4. The deposit in the valley of the river Allier, and that in the upper part of the course of the Loire. 5. The great deposit in the course of the Rhine and Saône, extending from about Valence to Dijon. 6. The tract along the Rhine, extending from Basle to the neighbourhood of Carlsrhue.

*Volcanic districts.* True volcanic rocks occur in France only in the great central table-land or plateau; in the Departments of Loire, Upper Loire, Cantal, and Puy de Dôme. The volcanic rocks are basalt and basalt tuffa; trachyte with its tuffa; and lava, with its tuffas, scoriæ, &c. The newest of these rocks are the lavas; while the basalt and trachytes appear of more ancient date, although still not very old, as we find them breaking through rocks of the tertiary class.

*Alluvial districts.* Alluvia of every description occur in France. Diluvium or the old alluvium forms extensive tracts in many quarters of the kingdom, where it contains remains of extant species of animals, of which the most characteristic are those belonging to the order pachyderma, as the elephant, rhinoceros, &c. Diluvium is also found in caves along with bones of extinct animals, particularly of the carnivorous genera; and rents and fissures in strata are sometimes filled up with a diluvium also containing remains of extinct animals, of which the most characteristic are the small herbivora. Bone caves and bone breccia occur at St. Antonin and St. Julien near Montpelier; at Billargues, Vendargues, and Pezenas-Herault; at Anduze and St. Hippolyte, in Gard; at Aix, in the department of the Mouths of the Rhone; at Villefranche and Lauraguais, in the Upper Garonne; and at Perpignan, in the Eastern Pyrenees. This diluvium is covered, to a greater or less depth, with the various well-known kinds of modern alluvium and of vegetable soils.

### *Mines and Quarries.*

*Coal mines.* Coal of various descriptions, as glance, bituminous, and brown coal, are mined in the following departments in France, affording annually but a small return for so vast a country:—Allier, Aveyron, Mouths of the Rhone, Calvados, Gard, Herault, Isère, Upper Loire, Lower Loire, Mayenne and Loire, Moselle, Nièvre, North, Pas de Calais, Puy de Dôme, Upper Rhine, Lower Rhine, Lower Saône, and Tarn.

*Iron mines.* Iron mines, some of them of considerable importance, occur in the following departments:—Ardennes, Charente, Cher, Côte d'Or, Dordogne, Doubs, Eure, Eure and Loir, Forets, Indre, Indre and Loire Isère, Jura, Lower Loire, Upper Marne, Moselle, Nièvre, North, Orne, Upper Rhine, Lower Rhine, Upper Saône, Saône and Loire, and Vosges.

*Mines of silver and lead.* The principal lead mines and silver mines are the following:—

| | Mines of | Quintals of Lead | Marcs of Silver |
|---|---|---|---|
| Finisterre | Poullauen | about 8,000 | 1200 |
| Ditto | Huelgoet | 3,000 | 1600 |
| Lozère | Villefort | 18,000 | 1500 |
| Isère | Vienne | 1,500 | — |

*Copper mines.* These are situated in the following departments:—Upper Alps, Rhone, Rhine and Moselle.

*Mines of manganese.* This metal is mined at Romanèche and St. Micaud, in the department of the Saône and Loire; at Suquet in Dordogne; in the mountain of Tholey in Moselle; at Laveline, near Saint Dier, in the Vosges; and at Saint Jean de Gardonenque in the Cevennes.

*Mines of antimony.* Antimony occurs in the provinces of Charente, Upper Loire, La Vendée, Cantal, Allier, Gard, and Puy de Dôme.

*Mines of vitriol and alum.* The principal mines of sulphate of iron or vitriol are those of Saint Julien de Valgargue, near Alais, which furnishes annually 30,000 quintals; and that of Becquet and of Goincourt, near Beauvais, which in some years affords 15,000 quintals; that of Ural, in the department of Aisne, and of Gersdorf, in the department of Lower Rhine. There are celebrated manufactories of alum at Montpelier, and at Javelle near Paris. Some considerable beds of rock-salt have been discovered at Vic, in the department of Meurthe. One of these is upwards of fourteen yards thick, and another has not as yet been cut through. Although cobalt, arsenic, nickel, and tin also occur in France, no considerable mines of those minerals have been established.

*Quarries.* The most extensive quarries are those of marble, building-stone, slate, gypsum, millstone, and flint. Different kinds of marble are raised at Givet, Brabançon, Mons, Namur, Boulogne sur Mer, Caen, Troyes, Montbar, Cosne, Tournus, Narbonne, Aix, Marseilles, Tarb, and in many valleys in the Pyrenees. There are quarries of excellent building-stone in the departments of La Manche, Calvados, Moselle, Côte d'Or, Yonne, Oise, Seine, Loire, Dordogne, and in many departments in the south. Vast slate quarries are worked in the departments of La Manche, Meuse, Ardennes, Maine and Loire, and at the foot of the Pyrenees. In many other places, and particularly in Champagne, &c., there are quarries and pits of clay for brick and tile-making. The gypsum of the neighbourhood of Paris, the chalk of the departments of Marne and Seine, the talc named *chalk of Briançon*, the millstone or *buhr-stone* of Ferte sous Jouarre, are objects of considerable commercial importance. The departments of Yonne, Cher, and Lower Charente, supply all France and different foreign nations with gun-flints. Among the clays met with in France, that of Forges les Eaux, was formerly in great repute in Holland for the manufacture of pipes; the clay or earth of Belbœuf, near Rouen, is considered an excellent material in the purifying of sugar; and the potters' clay of the vicinity of Beauvais and Montereau, and the porcelain earth or kao-lin of Saint Yrieix, near Limoges, are highly esteemed.

## SUBSECT. 2.—*Botany.*

Having devoted already so great a portion of our space to preliminary remarks upon vegetable geography on its more extended scale, and to that of Great Britain in particular, we must content ourselves with a more limited account of the plants of other countries, otherwise we should greatly overstep the bounds prescribed to us by the nature of the present work. Following the plan here adopted for the arrangement of the different countries, *France* comes next under our notice; and a more interesting field for the geographical botanist does not exist in Europe; not only because of its extent and vast variety of surface the great height of its mountains, and its geological structure; but because, by the labours of its naturalists, especially Lamarck and De Candolle, the vegetable productions of France have been better explored than those of almost any other country in the world. All that we can do here, however, is to notice in general those that are the most interesting, from their utility, their beauty, or some circumstances connected with their history; or as showing how vegetable forms or groups are situated, in regard to their distribution, upon the surface of the earth.

France, extending, as it does, from lat. 42° 30′ to 51° N., or nearly to the latitude of London, and from 9° east longitude, to 5° west, is bounded by the Mediterranean, and the great chain of the Pyrenees on the south; by the Atlantic on the west; by the British Channel and the Netherlands on the north; and on the east by Savoy, Switzerland, and Germany, which form, for its entire length, a vast mountain barrier. Such an alpine region cannot fail to exert a manifest influence on the vegetation of a country; not only because of its own peculiar productions, depending in part on their elevation, and in part on their soil and geological structure, but by their exposure even at the same elevation, on two opposite sides; that of the south will be found to exhibit very different vegetable forms from that of the north; and such mountains often exercise a more powerful influence in limiting the surrounding vegetation, than even seas and rivers.

Lamarck and De Candolle, in a very interesting Botanical Map which accompanies their *Flore Française*, 3d edit., have divided France into five regions:—

(1.) The region of maritime plants, which of course extends everywhere along the coast, from Ostend to Bayonne on the north and west, and from Perpignan to Oueille on the Mediterranean; together with the *Salines* of Dieuze and Château Salins near Nancy, and those of Durkheim and Frankensthal near Mayence in the interior. Thus we find that a vegetation similar to that of the sea-shore exists in the interior, whenever that interior yields a sufficient quantity of marine salt. All the maritime plants of the north of France, according to M. de Candolle (and they have the greatest affinity with those of England), are equally found in the south; but the reverse does not hold good; for a very large proportion of the French Mediterranean plants of the sea-shore grow very sparingly, if at all, upon the shores of the Ocean, principally indeed on the coast of Gascony, and reach no higher than the mouth of the Loire, or at most to the middle of Britany.

(2.) *The region of mountain and alpine plants.* When the French, by their conquests, included the Pyrenees, the Alps, and Savoy within the range of the floras of their own country, this region constituted the very richest of any flora in Europe; for it included a country, not only of considerable extent, but mountains, and in very southern latitudes, many of whose crests rise greatly beyond the line of perpetual snow. As France is now limited, the mountains of the Vosges near Strasburg, and of the Cevennes, and those of Auvergne, whose origin is volcanic, exhibit its most alpine scenery: among the latter, the Puy de Sasi, one of the Monts d'Or, rises to an elevation of 6300 feet above the level of the sea. The Plomb du Cantal is estimated at 6200, and the Puy de Dôme at 5000 feet. If the summits of the Pyrenees and of the Jura be considered as forming the natural barrier of France, as constituting her line of separation from the adjacent territories, she will still possess an exceedingly rich alpine flora in the northern side of the former and the western side of the latter mountains. But the line of demarcation of this region is nevertheless not so distinctly marked as in the preceding region. The valleys exposed to the sun often participate in the vegetation of the southern provinces, while the cooler valleys exhibit a growth which has more in common with the vast plain in the north and centre of France. However, it is undeniable that these same districts do contain a very considerable number of plants which are peculiar to them, and found on almost all the more elevated mountains of France; for whatever differences the chain of the Vosges and the Jura may present from those of Auvergne, the Cevennes, and the Pyrenees in the south, it is allowed that the aspect of their vegetation offers considerable traits of similarity, and that the greater part of the mountain plants are alike found on the different chains.

(3.) A third region, and a very important and interesting one, is that of the *Mediterranean plants:* this, of course, is bounded on the south by the Mediterranean Sea, and stretches inland till you come to the foot of the mountains, or following the course of the Rhone, extending north as far as Montelimart on that river; or it may be said to occupy or constitute the great basin of the mouth of the Rhone.

(4.) A vast region is occupied by the plains, whose vegetation is very uniform. This comprises more than one-half of France, and especially all the plain country situated to the north of the chains of mountains. Many of these plants are found in other regions already indicated; but it wants the species which are peculiar to each of those respectively.

(5.) and lastly—MM. Lamarck and De Candolle indicate an intermediate region, which includes plants partaking of the nature of the plains of the north and the provinces of the south. This occupies a large portion of the south-west of France, and some districts up the valley of the Rhone between Montelimart and Lyons.

The map just alluded to has these different regions represented in different colours, and is attended with this advantage, that, by the slightest inspection, a general idea is conveyed of the prevailing nature of vegetation in any given district. We see that the plants of the southern provinces resemble more those of the north as you advance by the west side of France than by the east; that the floras of Mans on the border of Normandy, and of Nantes upon the Loire, in lat. 47° and 48°, scarcely differ from those of Dax and Agen, between lat. 43° and 44°; whilst on the east side of France, the productions of Dijon and Strasburg vary considerably from those of Montpelier and Aix, situated at nearly similar relative distances from each other. All this is accounted for on the principles we have already laid down, namely, that the stations of plants are mainly influenced by temperature; and that the mean temperature of a place is greatly determined by distance from the equator, and elevation above the level of the sea. According to M. de Candolle, an altitude of 460 feet above the level of the sea affects the temperature nearly to the same extent as a degree of latitude nearer to the north in the eastern hemisphere.

By comparing the western provinces of France with the eastern, we see that the surface of the former is but little raised above the level of the sea; for, even at a considerable distance from the coast, the hills scarcely exceed 300 feet; whilst, on the other hand, upon the western side, in the midst of a mountainous region, the plain has generally an elevation of from 1300 to 1600 feet. This height diminishes, it is true, on the Belgian frontier; but there the temperature is sensibly affected by the second cause adduced, namely, the distance from the equator. Thus, there is nothing but what is conformable to physical laws, in the southern plants having a greater resemblance to those of the north upon the west, than on the east side of France.

But even where the mean temperature is the same, the distribution of plants between these two parts of France may yet be very different, on account of the different degrees of temperature at particular seasons of the year. We have already stated that, the latitudes being the same, maritime countries enjoy a more equal temperature than districts removed from the sea; in other words, that the summers are less warm, the winters less cold: thus, the provinces of the west of France, which are all maritime, experience this degree of uniformity; which cannot take place in the east, being far from the sea, and in the vicinity of the mountains.

Plants now, in what concerns climate, may be divided into two classes: those which suffer from a severe winter cold, but which, during summer, do not require an excess of heat; and those which can endure great severity of cold in winter, but, during summer, require a great proportion of heat. In the first class, M. de Candolle places all those trees which, without being resinous, preserve their leaves, and consequently their sap, through the winter; in fact, the greater proportion of the trees of the south being found, whether indigenous or naturalised, towards the north in the maritime provinces; such as the Live Oak, the Cork Tree, the Kermes Oak, the Strawberry Tree (*Arbutus*), the Bay, the Fig,

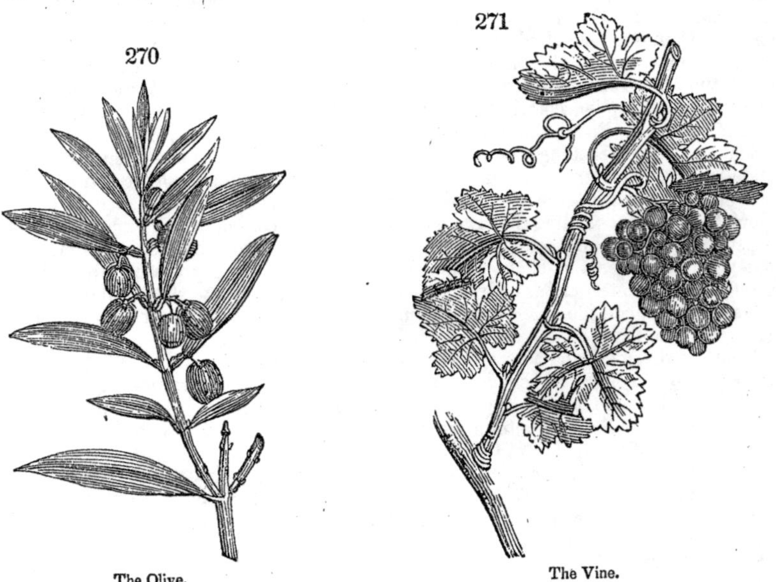

270 The Olive.

271 The Vine.

the Phillyrea, &c. On the other hand, in the second class, that is to say, among such as can brave a great degree of cold, and do so because the movement of the sap is interrupted by the fall of the foliage, is the Vine, &c., and those that avoid cold because the plants, or at least their stems, are annual, such as Maize. It may be readily supposed that the individuals belonging to the second class will flourish better, and become more easily naturalised on the east than on the west coast of France.

Let us apply this law to a peculiarity in regard to the cultivation of those most precious vegetable productions of France, namely, the Olive (*fig.* 270.), the Maize, and the Vine (*fig.* 271.). Mr. Arthur Young, during his travels in France, paid great attention to agriculture and the mode of cultivation adopted there, and published a map of the country, in which he represented, by three nearly parallel lines, the northern limits of the three plants just alluded to, the Olive, the Maize, and the Vine. It excited the surprise of many, that the lines should ascend most to the north on the east side of the country, or, in other words, that the plants in question should grow farther north in the eastern than in the western districts; directly the reverse of what takes place in regard to the aboriginal native productions of the soil. This apparent contradiction is reconciled by the twofold comparison of the physical nature of the east and west of France, and of the character of the plants cultivated, as compared with the wild species.

The nature of the cultivated productions in question forms a striking feature, which cannot fail to arrest the attention of a traveller while journeying through the districts thus appropriated, and forcibly to exhibit their agricultural riches. In the extreme south of France, between a line drawn from Narbonne, in lat. 43° N. and in the meridian of Paris, to a little below Grenoble, he will find the plains, parched and dry as they naturally are, rendered still more melancholy by the lurid green of the olive-groves. Between that line and another drawn from the mouth of the Garonne rather below 46°, to near Strasburg, in the north-west, he will observe, together with the vine, which is by no means wanting in all the southern provinces, fields where the gigantic maize (*fig.* 272.) takes the place of what we usually term bread-corn; again, between it and a line extending from the mouth of the Loire to the Rhine, passing at about an equal distance between the Meuse and the Moselle, he will find, intermingled with vineyards, fertile fields of corn, wheat (*fig.* 273.), oats, and barley; whilst, north of that line, there exists a most perfect similarity in agriculture with that which prevails throughout the greater part of England. Fruit trees of all the kinds that are grown in Britain, here attain a much greater degree of perfection than in that country, because of the increased heat of the summers.

272

The Maize.

Thus, in what concerns a great portion of the territory of France, its vegetable productions much resemble those of the southern parts of Great Britain.

It is not, perhaps, generally known that that most useful root, the Potato, was cultivated in almost every part of Europe before its value was appreciated, and its culture became general, near the capital of France. To England is due the credit of first growing it upon a large scale. Upon the Continent it was introduced between the years 1714 and 1724 into Swabia, Alsace, and the Palatinate; and in 1730 to the vicinity of Berne. In 1774, potatoes were known on the mountains of the Cevennes, where they now constitute a main portion of the food of the people: but it is principally to the famous M. Parmentier that France owes the general use of potatoes. The following anecdote may give some idea of the assiduity with which this philanthropic individual laboured to generalise their culture: it is well attested that he farmed some spots of ground in the vicinity of Paris for this sole purpose, though the prejudice against potatoes was then so strong, that few of the poor persons to whom he offered the roots would accept of them. However, M. Parmentier soon suspected that people occasionally stole his potatoes to eat them: he was well pleased at this, and continued to plant what he hoped would be purloined, rightly concluding that the experience of the thieves would contribute to diminish the established prejudice. After much trouble and many years, he had succeeded in propagating potatoes in several situations, when the dreadful scarcity, the consequence and effect of the revolutionary disturbances, suddenly rendered their cultivation universal; and now they form so constant an article of food, that the common people generally believe them to be aboriginal natives of the country.

The mountains of France exhibit the British alpine plants, with many others that are peculiar to themselves, and which they possess in common with the higher Alps of Switzerland, Savoy, Germany, and the Pyrenees.

Of the intermediate region, as De Candolle terms it, a great portion lying in the south-west of France, embraces a country called the *Landes*, where the shepherd-peasantry whether walking, or at rest during the day, live upon stilts (*xcangues*, in the language of

273

Wheat, Oats, and Barley.

the country): this custom gives them the opportunity of viewing the land around in search of their sheep, for a great extent, of wading through the numerous shallow lakes of water; and by these means it is said they can traverse triple the space of ground they could do by the ordinary mode of walking; when they stop, they support themselves by a long stick behind. In this same district a vast extent of flat land near the ocean, and extending from Bayonne in the south to the Tête de Buch in the north, and for a distance of from four to twelve leagues inland, is occupied by forests of Pine (*Pinus maritima*) (*fig.* 274.): these are called *Pignadas*, and they give a remarkable feature to the Landes, in conjunction with the habits of the people and their dress, the latter consisting entirely of sheep-skins with the hair outwards, little different in outward appearance from the flocks which it is the great object of their lives to tend. The resinous substances of the pine are extracted in immense quantities; in doing which, one man takes care of 3000 trees. The country being so dry, these pignadas are liable to alarming conflagrations; one of them that took place in 1803, continued burning for two months. The mode adopted for extinguishing them is remarkable: when one part of the forest is in flames, it is customary to set fire to another spot, at a greater or less distance, according to the magnitude of the evil; a current of air soon takes place between the burning masses, which drives the conflagration from both sides on the intermediate trees; these are shortly consumed, the fire dies out for want of fuel, and the rest of the forest is preserved.

274

The Pine.

But the Mediterranean region, which we have already mentioned, and whose vegetation partakes of what is found to characterize the whole shores of that vast inland sea, has many plants so different from those of the rest of France, that it would be unpardonable did we not particularise some of them.

Almost everywhere in this region, the soil is described as consisting of the secondary limestone of the Jura, extending to the very brink of the sea, forming arid coasts, often utterly destitute of vegetation, or clothed with Wild Olives and the Aleppo Pine (*Pinus halepensis*), with Evergreen Oak, Pistachio-Nut, Myrtles, and numerous species of Cistus. Here, too, is found one species of Palm, the Chamærops humilis (*Palmetto* or *Dwarf Palm*); but it grows principally in the environs of Nice. At the opposite extremity of the Mediterranean region, namely, about Roussillon and Provence, and there only in the hotter parts, are seen the Indian Fig (*Cactus Tuna*), and the American Aloe (*Agave americana*): the introduction of these is due to the Spaniards, who brought them to Europe from the New World. Schouw regards the Mediterranean shores in general as the kingdom of the Caryophylleæ and Labiatæ; this latter family especially abounds in the south of France, and particularly the genera Phlomis, Teucrium, Thymus, Lavandula, and others, remarkable for their aromatic qualities. In the same places, and always on very stony ground, the elegant Coris monspeliensis excels the heaths of Britain in beauty. The mulberry is cultivated throughout this territory; and among other useful fruits, the Fig, the Jujube, the Pomegranate, the Date, and the Pistachio, all arrive at great perfection. The Orange can scarcely be said to be cultivated without shelter in any part of France. It is grown, however, and somewhat extensively, at the Isles d'Hières, and in the vicinity of Nice, that happy climate which is probably unequalled by any part of Europe. Corn, which is but a secondary article of culture, ripens at a very early period; so much so that it is not unfrequent to carry barley which has been reaped on the coast into the mountains, where the seed is sown, and a second crop is produced the same year. Many plants may be here enumerated which this country possesses in common with Greece and Italy, and even the Spanish peninsula, and which seem to accompany the Olive. Mirbel has drawn up the following list of woody kinds, which inhabit these provinces:—Pinus Pinaster, and Pinea, Juniperus phœnicea and Oxycedrus, Quercus Ilex, Suber and coccifera, Celtis australis, Ficus Carica, Osyris alba, Laurus nobilis, Fraxinus Ornus, Phillyrea latifolia and angustifolia, Jasminum fructicans, Vitex Agnus-castus, Nerium Oleander, Diospyros Lotos, Styrax officinale, Arbutus Unedo, Viburnum Tinus, Tamarix gallica and africana, Myrtus communis, Punica Granatum, Philadelphus coronarius, Cratægus Azarolus, Mespilus pyracantha, Ceratonia siliqua, Cercis Siliquastrum, Rhus Cotinus and Coriaria; Pistacia Lentiscus, Terebinthus, and vera; Rhamnus Alaternus, oleoides, and infectoria; Zizyphus vulgaris, Paliurus australis, Capparis spinosa, Melia Azedarach, Acer monspessulanum, &c.

Hitherto the attention of naturalists in the study of vegetable geography has been directed to those plants that grow upon the surface of the earth: Humboldt alone, in his *Carte Géographique des Plantes*, has indicated the station of some subterranean Fungi, and in a general way has marked the ocean as the habitat of Ulvæ and Fuci (*fig.* 275.). It remained for M. d'Orbigny to describe to a certain extent at least, the Zones and Bands inhabited by the marine Algæ (Sea-Weeds). This he accomplished upon the coasts in the Gulf of Gascony, and particularly on the shores of La Vendée and the Lower Charente, partly by diving to considerable depths in the sea, and partly by means of drag-nets fixed to graduated cords; and the results of his observations are given in the *Mémoires du Muséum d'Histoire Naturelle*, vol. vi. With extracts from this, as we shall scarcely have again the opportunity of touching on this beautiful and interesting tribe of plants, we shall conclude this sketch, already too much extended, of the vegetable geography of France. Maritime plants, says M. d'Orbigny, grow in the most opposite temperatures: every country, every latitude, and every situation possessing some which are peculiar to itself. Still, climate and temperature appear almost alike to many of these productions, which are found by voyagers in every different ocean, while others require particular spots and climes: some few preferring the mouths of rivers, and the brackish waters of salt marshes, where the bitterness of the sea is modified by the admixture of fresh water, and in such situations attaining to an enormous size, as Ulva lactuca var. altissima, while to the greater number of these plants, fresh water proves absolutely destructive.

275

Ulvæ and Fuci.

As for those kinds which grow indifferently everywhere in the sea, they seem to be increased without any attachment to solid bodies, as Fucus natans, &c. Banks of great extent formed by this plant, are often found within the tropics of such dimensions as to retard the progress of navigation. Some individuals among these groups may frequently be seen which bear the appearance of having been originally fixed to rocks, their flattened, disc-like stem yet retaining a portion of such substance. There seems to be ground for the supposition that, though these sea-weeds are capable of living and growing in the water, unattached to any soil, yet that they must primarily spring from some solid body, as no young plants of this kind are ever found between the tropics.

Some of the Algæ prefer the southern sides of rocks, others affect an eastern, western, or northern exposure; but they change their position according to the difference of latitude: those which are found on the southern side in cold climates, being generally seen on the northern in the warm or temperate regions. Certain species live near the surface, and close to the sea-beach: others, at various degrees of depths: the first would seem to enjoy the regular exposure to light and heat which they experience during the turnings of the tide; the second, on the contrary, shun the influences of the atmosphere; and, growing and fructifying in depths where the light can scarcely ever penetrate, they bear, without receiving any injury, both the enormous column of water which constantly presses upon them, and the severe cold which exists in those regions. There are even parasitical *Algæ*, which grow indifferently upon all the others, and some which only affect peculiar species.

Many sea-weeds prefer such spots as are exposed to the fury of the waves and the action of the currents, where they are perpetually floating in an agitated medium: others dwell in the hollows of rocks, or in marine gulfs, where the water is generally calm. The lapse of a few days puts a period to the existence of some kinds, whilst the tempests of successive winters fail to destroy others. The general aspect is apt to change in several individuals, so that, were it not for more stable characters, derivable from their fructification, texture, &c. they might be mistaken for novel species.

A number of the more delicate marine plants are quickly destroyed by a removal from their native place of growth; but the greater proportion, being coriaceous, and insoluble in salt water, live for a length of time in different situations; and it is not uncommon to find, upon our own shores, the *Algæ* of the most distant regions, which have traversed the ocean, and yet remain unchanged in their general appearance. We must thence necessarily infer that it is not all the *Algæ* that are found in any country that may be said to belong to that country.

The proportions of marine plants are as variable as those of terrestrial ones. Some are barely discoverable with the highest magnifiers; while others rise from the various depths of the mighty ocean, and, forming at its surface an angle of greater or less acuteness according to the force and velocity of the currents and the tides, then suffer their long summits to float on the waves, and receive the benign influences of atmospheric light and heat. During the great equinoctial floods, the sea often forsakes, periodically, certain rocks, which are only uncovered at such times. If, during that interval, the sun shines forth, or the north wind blows, many of the minute and delicate *Algæ*, thus exposed, dry up and die; while others, though equally circumstanced, revive immediately upon the return of the genial fluid.

A certain proportion of marine plants are natives of the French seas, while we must refer the accession of many species to the force of the winds, waves, and currents, especially to that which generally goes under the name of *Gulf Stream*, and is called by the French the *Mexican Current*. Almost all the northern *Algæ* grow in the Gulf of Gascony. It is not so with those from the Mediterranean and Southern Ocean; a very small number of them are there seen in a living state, and their almost northern limit never exceeds the mouth of the Loire, or at farthest the rock of Morbihan. Independently of the influence of temperature, this circumstance may be attributed in a measure to the current, which, generally setting in on these shores from north to south, brings the seeds and plants themselves of northern seas to these rocks, while those of southern growth are wafted by the same current to Africa and the Atlantic.

But few are the kinds of sea-weed which prefer any peculiar spot, or show a predilection for one substance above another whereon to fix. Deriving no nutriment from their roots or points of attachment, they need nothing farther than a temporary support; thus, they cling indiscriminately to any solid marine body, equally to granitic and calcareous rocks, to floating or sunken pieces of wood, to the bones of terrestrial or marine animals, to shells, polypi, &c.

Notwithstanding that many highly respectable naturalists have averred that the growth of these plants proceeds with most vigour on such and such substances, on some or other peculiar rock, in the vicinity of rivers, or in the open sea; it has been fully ascertained, by a great number of observations, that marine weeds do grow with equal vigour, though planted upon rocks or substances of very different natures; and that, if we except some few *Ulvæ*, which affect brackish water, those which vegetate in situations where fresh water mingles with the salt, are generally bleached, produce little or no fructification, have a thin and weak texture, and contain but little soda. The qualities requisite for the different uses of which I shall treat hereafter, are only found united in such sea-weeds as grow in pure sea-water, where they have found a spot which is sufficiently tenacious to fix them in that zone of habitation which they prefer.

Some kinds certainly prefer sand or mud; but then their roots become elongated, and strike deep, till they meet with some stone or shell or other body which may serve them as a point of attachment, and offer the requisite degree of resistance.

If the nature of the bottom appears indifferent, in a great measure to maritime plants; it is not so with the level which they select in the ocean, or with the distance of their birth-place from the surface. Every species of maritime vegetable appears to affect, to as great an extent as the terrestrial kinds, certain zones or regions of different depths in the sea; places where the superincumbent weight of water, and the relative proportion of light and caloric are adapted to its peculiar organs. Those individuals which are found towards the centre of their proper zone contain all the elements requisite for their perfect developement, and generally show an active state of vegetation; they are vigorous, they fructify at the season suitable to their degree of immersion, while those which grow at the extreme limit, or out of the bounds, of this same zone, prove languishing, fructify imperfectly, are always covered with marine animals which destroy them, and live but a short time in comparison with their well-situated congeners. The seeds which escape from these plants would appear, by their various specific weights, to gain an equilibrium equivalent to the column of water which they displace, or, in other words, to float in that peculiar zone which the future *Algæ* would prefer to inhabit. Those which become developed either above or below it, are inevitably driven from their spot of nature or of election, by the agitation in the waves at the vicinity of the coasts.

Lower down than a hundred feet from the surface of the sea, (taking a medium between the high and low tides,) it is rare to find living sea-weeds in the Gulf of Gascony, and even these are attached to portions of rock severed from more elevated rocks, and before long they inevitably perish.

It may be observed that the lower we investigate the sea, the fewer will the number of plants appear, and the more numerous the polypi. For instance, below forty feet from the surface of the water, but very few *Ulvæ* are found; beyond sixty feet, no living *Ceramium;* and after having descended to the depth of a hundred feet, not a *Fucus* is to be seen, and the vegetable kingdom wholly ends.

1st Zone, extending from one foot above the medium height of the sea to twenty feet below, is inhabited by Ulva compressa var. β; U. intestinalis, ventricosa, Lactuca var. α; Fucus pygmæus, amphibius, &c.

2d Zone, from five feet below the medium height to thirty feet:—Ulva articulata, Nostoc, bullata, fistulosa, Lactuca var. β, umbilicalis, lanceolata, purpurea, Linza, contorta, serrata, dichotoma, crispa, pavonia, atomaria (?); Fucus vesiculosus, spiralis, ceranoides, serratus, canaliculatus, cæspitosus, laceratus, hybridus, longissimus, pinnatifidus, viridis, arbuscula, fastigiatus, tenuissimus (?), confervoides; Ceramium spongiosum, rupestre, Mertensii, penicillatum, fucoides, nodulosum, gracile, linum; Zostera marina and mediterranea; Diatoma rigidum, flocculosum, &c.

3d Zone, from fifteen to thirty-five feet below the medium surface. Ulva ocellata, palmata, lingulata, polypodioides, caulescens; Fucus longifructus, lumbricalis, bifurcatus, ericoides, barbatus, abrotanifolius, vermicularis, norvegicus, obtusus, asparagoides, Wigghii, verrucosus, helminthocortos; Ceramium simplicifolium, casuarina, cancellatum, coccineum, incurvum, elongatum, polymorphum, forcipatum, filum, capillare, glomeratum, elegans, &c.

4th Zone, from twenty to forty feet below the medium surface:—Ulva Phyllitis, saccharina, digitata, bulbosa, ciliata, edulis; Fucus nodosus, uvarius, furcatus, ciliatus, alatus, plocamium, plumosus, corneus, gigartinus, aculeatus, plicatus; Ceramium verticillatum, equisetifolium, sericeum, scoparium, &c.

5th Zone, from thirty to sixty feet:—Fucus siliquosus var. α, purpurascens, ligulatus, pistillatus; Ceramium coccineum, ægagropilum, &c.

6th Zone, from forty to a hundred feet:—The flattened Fuci; F. siliquosus var. β, loreus, sanguineus, fibrosus, coronopifolius, &c., and Ulva tomentosa, which is, in fact, a polypus.

### Subsect. 3.—*Zoology.*

The zoology of France assimilates less to that of central than of southern Europe. Notwithstanding the narrowness of its separation from Great Britain, it possesses many animals unknown as natives, or even as visiters, of that island. With regard to quadrupeds, this circumstance is not surprising; for any channel of the sea, however narrow, forms an insurmountable obstacle to the wanderings or migration of purely terrestrial species: while others, of a semiaquatic nature are too small and feeble to effect the passage. These considerations, however, are insufficient to explain the limited range of the smaller birds, hitherto found only upon the Continent. The distribution of insects is dependent, in a great degree, upon that of plants; and the numbers of both common in France, but unknown in Britain, are nearly proportionate; on the calculation that has been made of six species of insects to one of plants.

276

The Wolf

Among the wild quadrupeds of France is the wolf (*fig.* 276.), which is still not uncommon in the wooded and mountainous districts: when pressed by hunger, it descends to the farms, and even attacks the inhabitants. The beaver is said still to exist in the southern parts, and probably the wild boar may not be wholly extirpated.

from the existing forests. Bears were once common, while three or four of the smaller quadrupeds appear peculiar to France.

Several interesting and beautiful birds, unknown or but rarely met with in Britain, are here not uncommon; such as the wood-chat (*fig.* 277.), shrike (*Lanius rufus* T.) the grossbeak or hawfinch, the blue-throated warbler, and several others of the same family. In short, from the connection of this country with the central and southern kingdoms of Europe, the ornithologist might probably discover in France more than three-fourths of all the continental birds.

277

The Wood-Chat.

The marine productions of those provinces bordering on the Channel, as may be expected, do not offer any marked difference from those of the British coasts; but on the warm shores of Nice and Marseilles the naturalist meets with numerous productions, indicative of the rich stores of the Mediterranean Sea. The entomology of these southern provinces, in like manner, presents us with many of those more striking insects, which properly belong to the fauna of Italy. The beautiful *Papilio Podalirius* (*fig.* 278.) so rare in England that its existence there is still doubted, is here a common insect. France has long stood foremost in promoting and illustrating the study of nature; and a society comprising some of her most able zoologists is at this moment engaged in publishing a *Fauna Gallica.* An able and indefatigable naturalist, M. Risso, has particularly illustrated the fishes and crustacea of Nice. It was near this place that one of the

278

Papilio Podalirius.

279

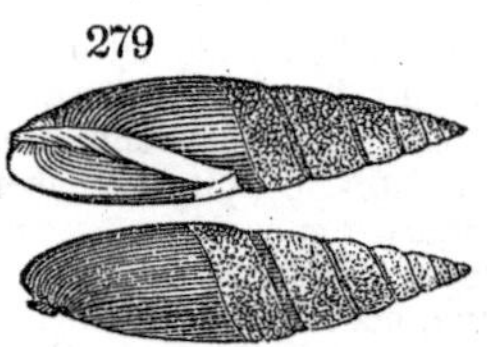

Mitra Zonata.

rarest and most beautiful shells of Europe, the *Mitra zonata* (*fig.* 279.) was fished up by the anchor of a vessel; only one specimen is known to exist in collections.

Among the domestic animals, the French horses are not very excellent; yet those used in the public stages are strong, active, and compactly made; nor have their masters copied the ridiculous and barbarous custom of disfiguring these animals, by cutting off their tails or ears. The stallions of England are much prized, and have been judiciously used to improve the native breeds.

The oxen are of two races; the one called *bœufs de haut crû* are of a middle or small size, with a fierce look, thick hide, and coarse hair; they are principally bred in the mountainous provinces of Gascony, Auvergne, &c. The others are called *bœufs de nature*, and are larger, with a mild aspect, thin hide, and soft hair: they fatten easily, and belong to the plains.

The native breeds of sheep, not in themselves good, have been of late sedulously and successfully improved. The Flemish breed, common both to France and the Netherlands, is generally hornless, with long legs, and is derived from an intermixture with those of Barbary. The *Solognot* are mostly without horns, and the wool is curled only at the ends. The *Berichonne* are likewise hornless, but are known by their long neck: the face is covered with wool; that on the body being fine, white, close, short, and curled. The *Roussillonne* is derived from the merino race; and has very fine wool, the filaments of the piles being twisted spirally. Lastly, the *Ardennoise* is horned, and bears a very fine fleece: this breed likewise extends over part of the Netherlands. (*Ham. Smith.*)

A large and elegant variety of the Domestic Cat is very common in some parts of France; it is nearly double the size of the common cat, and is bearded much in the same manner as the lynx.

## Sect. III.—*Historical Geography.*

The Gauls, the ancient inhabitants of France, and the chief among the Celtic nations, were an active, powerful, and ambitious people. Their emigrant hordes repeatedly crossed the Alps, possessed the whole north of Italy, once sacked the imperial city, and even penetrated into Greece and Asia Minor. Both Switzerland and Belgium were then included as part of Gaul. The people, though still barbarous, had made some steps toward civilisation.

The nobles and Druids enjoyed high power and influence, and had reduced the body of the nation almost to a state of vassalage. They combated with obstinacy, and made a long resistance to the progress of the Roman arms; but being opposed to Cæsar, the greatest of the Roman captains, after a war of twenty years, they were entirely and permanently subjected.

The conversion of Gaul into a Roman province, though it humbled the chiefs and quelled the martial spirit of the people, was attended with many beneficial changes. Peace was established; cultivation and industry promoted; Roman and even Greek literature introduced; and the people finally converted to the Christian faith.

The irruption of the Teutonic tribes, on the decline of the Roman empire, was early felt in Gaul, where the Goths, the Heruli, the Burgundians, and the confederacy called the Franks, overwhelmed and ravaged the whole kingdom, and drove the Celtic population and language into its remote and mountainous corners. From amid a chaos of convulsions, the vigorous hand of Clovis established the undisputed supremacy of the Franks, and founded the monarchy of France.

The reign of Charlemagne, son and successor to Pepin, who from mayor of the palace had occupied the throne, formed the most brilliant period in French history. That eminent and powerful prince not only placed on his head the iron crown of Lombardy, but reduced to his dominion, after a long and obstinate resistance, the intractable tribes of Germany, who had defied the utmost efforts of the Roman eagle. He penetrated also into Spain; but the fierce encounter of the Saracens, and the disastrous adventure of Roncesvalles on his return, completely stopped his career in that direction. Charlemagne, though himself illiterate, made some efforts to rekindle the declining light of science and letters in Europe.

The contests among the successors of Charlemagne were attended with the most violent and bloody convulsions, and with continual changes in the position of the three great kingdoms which composed his empire. At length it fell entirely to pieces. Germany retained the title of empire, and the claim to the dominion of Italy; and in France the Carlovingian dynasty, or that of Charlemagne, having become extinct under Louis Outremer, the throne was seized by the Capets, the most powerful among the noble French families.

Hugh Capet, having in 987 assumed the title of king, the real power attached to which had already been exercised by his father, Hugh the Great, founded the present dynasty. The administration, however, was long marked by a strong feudal character, and a high spirit of independence among the great nobles, of whom the counts of Provence and Britany, and the dukes of Burgundy, ranked altogether as separate and often hostile princes. The feudal age of France was also marked by chivalric and eventful wars with England, which long held several of the finest provinces, and whose king, Henry V., was crowned at Paris; but from that seemingly approaching downfall, the monarchy, through the romantic exploits of the Maid of Orleans, suddenly revived, and became more mighty than before.

The establishment of monarchical power in its plenitude was chiefly effected by the profound and insidious policy of Louis XI., favoured by the circumstances of the age. All France was united under the sway of the kings, who were thus enabled to form great armies, which, under Charles VIII. and Louis XII., overran nearly the whole of Italy. But it was under the gay and enterprising reign of Francis I. that its energies were fully developed. It then, however, came into collision with the house of Austria, whose extensive possessions in Germany, Spain, the Netherlands, and Italy, wielded by a powerful hand, secured to it during this period a decided, though not overwhelming, ascendant.

The civil wars arising out of the persecution of the Protestants agitated France for a very long time, and produced scenes of the most bloody and calamitous description. They lasted for a hundred years; for the popular reign of Henry IV. could scarcely be considered as more than a truce. At length Richelieu, by the reduction of Rochelle, terminated the long struggle of the Protestants for religious liberty, which in France alone, of all the countries where it was maintained upon a great scale, had this fatal issue. At the same time, this daring and despotic minister finally crushed the power and pretensions of the nobles, and formed France into a simple monarchy.

The reign of Louis XIV., during which a single hand wielded all the energies called forth during the prior struggles, exhibited France more powerful than she had been since Charlemagne. The house of Austria, now divided into the German and Spanish branches, of which the latter had become weak and inert, was humbled by repeated blows, which at length almost threatened her existence. France seemed advancing in the career of universal monarchy, when the interposition of England and the victories of Marlborough turned the tide of success, and rendered the last days of Louis humiliating and disastrous. The final issue, however, by which a Bourbon was placed on the throne of Spain, and the consequent family alliance, gave to France an increased weight, especially in the maritime concerns of Europe.

The French revolution was an event attended with awful and mighty vicissitudes, so fresh in the memory of the world, that it would be quite superfluous to attempt to enumerate them. After tearing up France by the roots, and holding all Europe in chains; after exhibiting during twenty years the vicissitudes of republicanism, total anarchy, and pure despotism; at length, by a mighty re-action, it terminated nearly at the point from which it commenced. France, however, obtained checks on the arbitrary power of her monarchs, which, notwithstanding their opposition, she rendered more and more effective. At length Charles X., having rashly attempted to break through all the limits placed on his authority, was driven from his throne, which was filled by Louis-Philippe, head of the collateral line of Orleans, under the title of King of the French.

## Sect. IV.—*Political Geography.*

The political constitution of France, prior to the Revolution, was almost purely despotic The privileges of the nobles consisted nearly altogether in unjust exemptions from taxation, and in *corvées*, or iniquitous and oppressive claims upon the labour of the peasantry. The only very salutary limit to the royal authority consisted in the parliaments, hereditary bodies, by whom the laws were very fairly and honourably administered; and the parliament of Paris had even the important privilege of registering every new tax before it could become legal. The exorbitant powers vested in the sovereign being however inconsistent with the growth of national intelligence and the augmented force of the *tiers état*, a collision took place, the most terrible on record, which ended in the temporary subversion of the throne. When the Bourbons were restored by foreign victories, they felt, and were warned, that France could no longer be governed by the former absolute system; and they bestowed by charter a representative government formed on the admired model of England. The nobles and parliaments, however, had been entirely swept away in the late convulsions, and left no hereditary aristocracy out of which an upper house could be composed. A Chamber of Peers was formed, by the royal appointment, of a body of individuals, many distinguished rather by talents and influence than by birth; and in the number were included some of the most distinguished of Napoleon's generals. Pensions were assigned to support the dignity of the Peers, which was at first hereditary, but by a recent enactment is to continue only for life. The Chamber of Deputies, corresponding to the House of Commons, is chosen by electors united in certain bodies called electoral colleges. These include all persons paying a certain amount of direct taxes; which limits the right of voting to the middling class, and to an entire number throughout France scarcely exceeding 130,000. The number of Deputies is 430. The functions of the French chambers are high. Their annual vote grants all the supplies of the year, and the expenditure of the preceding one is submitted to their rigorous examination. No taxes can be imposed, or loans contracted for, without their concurrence. Their debates are regularly made public, and an arrangement is enacted by law for the convenience of the reporters. Yet the chambers want some of the functions of a British parliament. They cannot fix the amount of the army, unless by limiting the funds to be employed in its maintenance; nor can they call in question the engagements held by government with foreign powers, unless by withholding the funds necessary to fulfil them. The liberty of the press was professedly granted by the charter; but there has been much fluctuation in its exercise; it was even repeatedly made subject to a censorship: even since the last great change, its freedom has not been established on as ample a basis as in Britain.

The administration of justice in France, which, before the Revolution, was still more complicated than in England, has been simplified in a very remarkable degree. The National Assembly early applied themselves to form a new series of codes, which might supersede those vast and voluminous records in which the law was formerly contained. They projected five codes, respectively referring to civil law, civil procedure, commerce, criminal law, and penal infliction. These were completed under Bonaparte, who gave to the whole the name of *Code Napoléon:* it is comprised in a moderate volume, sold for a few francs. All the ancient parliaments and seigniorial authorities being swept away, a new system of jurisdiction has been formed. Of the judicial authorities, the lowest class are the *juges de paix*, who amount to nearly 3000. They have salaries of 800 to 1000 francs, and decide finally on all cases where the question at issue does not exceed fifty francs. Immediately above them are the tribunals *de première instance*, before whom all questions and charges come in the first instance, and who judge finally respecting any property not exceeding 1000 francs. There are 360 of these courts, and the judges are supposed little short of 3000. To them are attached the tribunal of correctional police, which has cognizance of all minor offences. Above these rank the *cours royales*, sometimes called *cours d'appel*, because an appeal lies to them from the inferior courts. They are twenty-seven in number, attached to the chief cities in the kingdom. They consist, in populous towns, of twenty, thirty, and in Paris of fifty members; who, in that case, are divided into several chambers. Attached to them are the *cours d'assise*, or, as we would call them, jury courts, to which all criminal cases of importance are referred by the *cours royales*. A French jury consists of twelve, and a simple majority decides. From the decisions of the cours royales an appeal lies to the *court of cassation*, the highest tribunal, which also exercises a general jurisdiction over the other judicial bodies. All the judges are appointed by the crown, but hold their offices for life

[The following tables from official documents contain important data illustrative not less of the moral history of mankind, than of the state of society in France.

I. Statement of the Number of Persons charged with Criminal Offences before the Courts of Assize, in each year, from 1828 to 1832.

| | 1828. | 1829. | 1830. | 1831. | 1832. |
|---|---|---|---|---|---|
| *Crimes against the Person.* | | | | | |
| Against the State and Public Officers | 178 | 178 | 365 | 618 | 1,088 |
| Murder and Manslaughter | 520 | 528 | 469 | 605 | 641 |
| Parricide | 15 | 14 | 4 | 15 | 23 |
| Infanticide | 99 | 91 | 109 | 86 | 88 |
| Cutting and Wounding | 531 | 456 | 309 | 340 | 342 |
| Assaults upon Women | 167 | 184 | 136 | 115 | 131 |
| " " Children | 157 | 139 | 107 | 103 | 111 |
| Perjury and Subornation of Perjury | 73 | 79 | 71 | 72 | 104 |
| Bigamy | 9 | 11 | 7 | 2 | 6 |
| Other Crimes | 52 | 64 | 52 | 54 | 83 |
| Totals | 1,844 | 1,791 | 1,666 | 2,046 | 2,644 |
| *Crimes against Property.* | | | | | |
| Coining | 29 | 78 | 48 | 105 | 81 |
| Forgery of Commercial Papers | 99 | 102 | 90 | 73 | 88 |
| Other Forgeries | 323 | 332 | 281 | 301 | 327 |
| Robbery and Theft in Churches | 47 | 67 | 47 | 35 | 38 |
| " " on Highways | 188 | 185 | 135 | 123 | 168 |
| " " by Domestics | 966 | 1,215 | 1,016 | 939 | 958 |
| Other kinds of Robbery | 3,592 | 3,245 | 3,280 | 3,481 | 3,352 |
| Fradulent Bankruptcy | 89 | 95 | 84 | 67 | 70 |
| Incendiarism | 96 | 88 | 138 | 122 | 169 |
| Other Crimes | 123 | 175 | 177 | 314 | 342 |
| Totals | 5,552 | 5,582 | 5,296 | 5,560 | 5,593 |
| General Totals | 7,396 | 7,373 | 6,962 | 7,606 | 8,237 |

II. Statement showing the Degree of Instruction of Persons charged with Crimes before the Courts of Assize, in each year, from 1828 to 1832.

| Year. | Unable to read or write. | | | | | Able to read or write imperfectly. | | | | |
|---|---|---|---|---|---|---|---|---|---|---|
| | Crimes against Persons. | Crimes against Property. | Total Accused. | Acquitted. | Convicted. | Crimes against Persons. | Crimes against Property. | Total Accused. | Acquitted. | Convicted. |
| 1828 | 1,009 | 3,157 | 4,166 | 1,539 | 2,627 | 505 | 1,353 | 1,858 | 715 | 1,143 |
| 1829 | 1,063 | 3,460 | 4,523 | 1,696 | 2,827 | 496 | 1,451 | 1,947 | 787 | 1,160 |
| 1830 | 990 | 3,329 | 4,319 | 1,654 | 2,665 | 465 | 1,361 | 1,826 | 766 | 1,060 |
| 1831 | 1,144 | 3,456 | 4,600 | 1,948 | 2,652 | 568 | 1,479 | 2,047 | 1,000 | 1,047 |
| 1832 | 1,333 | 3,416 | 4,749 | 1,883 | 2,866 | 850 | 1,606 | 2,456 | 1,162 | 1,294 |
| Total in Five years. | 5,539 | 16,818 | 22,357 | 8,720 | 13,637 | 2,884 | 7,250 | 10,134 | 4,430 | 5,704 |
| | Able to read and write well. | | | | | Received a degree of Instruction beyond mere reading and writing. | | | | |
| 1828 | 215 | 565 | 780 | 342 | 438 | 36 | 82 | 118 | 77 | 41 |
| 1829 | 185 | 544 | 729 | 325 | 404 | 46 | 124 | 170 | 89 | 81 |
| 1830 | 174 | 514 | 688 | 330 | 358 | 37 | 92 | 129 | 82 | 47 |
| 1831 | 234 | 533 | 767 | 426 | 341 | 98 | 92 | 190 | 132 | 58 |
| 1832 | 292 | 583 | 775 | 373 | 402 | 169 | 88 | 257 | 162 | 95 |
| Total in Five years. | 1,100 | 2,639 | 3,739 | 1,796 | 1,943 | 386 | 478 | 864 | 542 | 322 |

AM. ED.]

*Financial system.* During the period of the Revolution, France shook off the heavy burden of debt which had been a main iustrument in bringing on that catastrophe. Yet the amount of taxes had not exceeded 550,000,000 livres, and the nation was crushed rather by the arbitrary and injudicious modes of levying the imposts, than by their actual amount. Napoleon, to support his continual wars, laid on large additional taxes, chiefly in the form of land assessment, and contracted, a debt of 3,000,000,000 francs. This was augmented by the events of 1815, and the occupation of the French territory by the allied armies at the expense of France. The debt is now expressed in the form of *rentes* or annuities, which in the budget of 1830 amounted to 249,496,000 livres: this, with other funds for which government were responsible, was considered as representing a capital of 4,988,738,000 francs.

The statement of receipt and expenditure for the year 1830 is as follows:—

| RECEIPT. | Francs. |
|---|---|
| Direct Taxes, chiefly on Land | 290,265,819 |
| Registration Stamps, and Domains | 187,225,038 |
| Custom-houses and Salt | 154,231,103 |
| Liquors, Sundry Duties, Tobacco and Gunpowder | 193,081,582 |
| Post Office | 33,469,030 |
| Falls of Timber | 24,060,697 |
| Salt-works | 1,200,000 |
| Gaming-houses | 4,338,888 |
| Royal Lottery | 10,042,799 |
| Coinage | 141,381 |
| Sundry proceeds | 11,585,418 |
| Extraordinary resources | 48,402,241 |
| Deductions on Receipts | 25,900,000 |
| | 983,944,066 |

| EXPENDITURE. | Francs. |
|---|---|
| Civil List | 27,666,666 |
| Chamber of Peers | 799,999 |
| Chamber of Deputies | 600,000 |
| Legion of Honour | 3,655,209 |
| Sinking Fund | 41,665,050 |
| Debt | 276,356,668 |
| Justice | 19,566,020 |
| Foreign Affairs | 8,778,000 |
| Religion and Public Instruction | 38,961,500 |
| Interior | 126,122,716 |
| War | 233,363,817 |
| Marine | 38,527,474 |
| Finance | 22,877,167 |
| Administration of Revenue | 129,072,351 |
| Repayments | 46,300,808 |
| | 1,064,288,445 |

The army of France is no longer that vast and terrible mass, which for so many years held the whole of continental Europe in thrall. The events of 1815 having proved too clearly the attachment of the old troops to their former master, they were nearly all disbanded, and their place supplied by fresh conscription. The government has the power of levying 60,000 men in the year. By a regulation, breathing still the republican spirit, one-third of the officers must be raised from the ranks. The army in the year 1832 was on a very formidable footing. It amounted in all, including 19,036 officers, and 3794 children of soldiers, to 411,816 men. Of these, the infantry consisted of 9505 officers and 264,141 men; the cavalry of 2805 officers and 51,335 men; the artillery of 1190 officers and 32,594 men, besides gendarmerie, engineers, &c.

The French navy, which, in 1791, amounted to seventy-four sail of the line and sixty-two frigates, lost half during the war; and those which remained, having never ventured for many years to stir out of port, lost all their experience and efficiency. At present, it consists of 55 ships of the line, 66 frigates, 30 corvettes, 103 smaller vessels, 17 steam-vessels, numerous armed transports, &c. The French navy is now in a high state of efficiency, and is rapidly increasing.

## SECT. V.—*Productive Industry.*

France, with regard to internal economy, is one of the richest and most flourishing countries in the world. In point of industry she ranks third after Britain and the Netherlands, while she possesses a greater extent and more natural advantages than either of those great seats of commerce and manufacture.

Agriculture is the most flourishing branch, yet is not in so advanced a state as in Great Britain. It has gained greatly by the French revolution, in consequence of the abolition of feudal rights, *corvées*, and tithes. The great possessions of the nobility were then broken up, and during the grand emigration, the farmers, or neighbouring little proprietors and capitalists. were able to purchase at a very cheap rate portions of the forfeited domains. It has become a rage in France for every one to possess a little spot of land; and the division of a man's property among his children, which the law enforces, tends to split it perpetually more and more into minute portions. Travellers have even observed three or four proprietors obliged to join in keeping a common plough. In vineyards and other garden cultures, where nice care and diligence are chiefly requisite, this minute partition seems advantageous. Chaptal even calculates, that a small vineyard cultivated by the proprietor's own hand will yield double the quantity of that which is leased out by a large proprietor. But in corn lands, where a considerable capital, good machinery, strong and well-fed cattle are necessary, the cultivation is thus kept down to a much lower standard than it would otherwise reach. The little occupants, also, are by no means prompt in discovering any improved processes, or in adopting those discovered elsewhere. Artificial grasses, and the rotation of crops which they facilitate, are by no means generally diffused; and an old vicious circle, of wheat, oats, and fallow, is still very generally adhered to. In short, all operations on a great scale, and requiring a considerable outlay, are deficient in France. M. Dupin, in a discourse on the effects of public instruction, in the introduction to his normal course of lectures on geometry, has drawn a striking contrast between northern and southern France. Although the former produces neither the olive, the vine, nor any of the finer fruits, yet it pays of taxes 127,630,000 francs on a surface of 18,690,000 hectares; while the south pays only 125,410,000 francs upon 34,840,000 hectares. Even in the south, the districts least favoured by nature are both the most enlightened and the most industrious; the high Alps, the high Pyrenees, and the departments immediately adjoining to them.

Grain, notwithstanding the imperfection in its cultivation, is produced with such diligence as to yield enough in ordinary years to supply the extensive population of France with food. The only exception is in part of its southern coast, which, when permitted, draws a supply from Odessa. France is not distinguished for any very superior quality of grain, nor is it an exporting country. It seems to have attended less than most other countries of Europe to the culture of potatoes, which are still planted only in gardens, along borders, or in tracts unfit for grain. Maize is mixed with wheat in the southern departments. Chaptal has given the following statement, calculated on an average of twelve years, from 1800 to 1812, of the entire products of this branch of French agriculture:—

| | Hectolitres. | | Hectolitres. |
|---|---|---|---|
| Wheat | 51,500,200 | Barley | 12,576,603 |
| Rye | 30,290,161 | Potatoes | 19,800,741 |
| Maize | 6,302,316 | Oats | 32,066,587 |
| Buckwheat | 8,409,473 | | 160,946,081 |

A more recent estimate, in a memoir read to the Society of Statistics in 1830, makes the average produce of the years 1825 to 1828 amount to 60,553,000 hectolitres of wheat, 114,733,000 of other grains; 46,238,000 of potatoes and chestnuts.

Wine ranks next in importance to grain, and forms a most valuable part of French industry. The wines of France, though not so strong as those of more southern climates, are generally accounted the most delicate in the world. Those of Burgundy and Champagne are without a rival, if we except a few rare specimens of Tokay. The wines of the Garonne do not rank quite so high; but, from their light, safe, and agreeable qualities, are drunk more freely, and exported on a larger scale. The finest and strongest of these wines are cultivated chiefly to supply the consumption of Britain and the other northern nations. The interior consumption of France consists chiefly of the light wines, drunk at table, nearly as our beer. Two elaborate attempts have been made to estimate the produce of the French vineyards; one by Chaptal, in his "General Treatise on French Industry," and the other in the report of a committee of the Chamber of Peers, presented in 1824 by the Duc de Dodeauville. They differ pretty considerably. Chaptal supposes that 1,631,000 hectares are employed in producing wine to the average annual amount of 35,500,000 hectolitres. The table, however, given by the duke, of the produce of each department does not exceed 31,630,000 hectolitres. The difference as to value is still more remarkable. Chaptal, after leaving out a sixth, as made into brandy, estimates the remainder at 678,000,000 francs: he supposes that there are 800,000 worth each 200 francs; 1,600,000 worth 50; gradually descending till he comes to 10,500,000 worth only 7½ francs. Dodeauville does not bring the amount to more than 480,000,000. The highest average value he assigns to the wines of any department is to those of the Oise (champagne), 36 francs; those of the Marne, Yonne, and Côte d'Or (burgundy), 26 to 24; of the Gironde, and Lot, and Garonne (claret), 19 to 21; the rest from 17 to 9. His estimate, however, seems too low; since M. Dupin (*Forces Productives, &c. de la France*) calculates the value, according to the tax paid to government, at 543,155,078 francs. The brandy into which one-sixth of the above produce is made, is, like the wine, the finest in the world, and a grand staple of French trade. Chaptal estimates the value distilled at 40,000,000 francs. M. Dupin states the quantity at 469,817 hectolitres; that of other spirits at 90,000. He calculates also 8,868,218 hectolitres of cider, and 2 965,022 hectolitres of strong beer.

Live stock does not form the most approved part of French husbandry. Chaptal considers that the animals are too few, whether for culture, for use, or for the production of manure; and also that the measures taken to improve the breed have been very partial and defective. The number of horses, including mules, in 1827, was 2,550,000. Of these it was reckoned that 300,000 were employed in riding, posting, the artillery, &c. The stock requires to be kept up by an importation, which in 1809 to 1812 was valued at 3,541,000 francs annually, but according to M. Senac had risen, in 1822 to 1825, to 7,500,000. In return, there is an extensive breeding of mules on the Pyrenean frontier, and they are exported to Spain to the value of 1,400,000 francs. France had in 1812, 214,000 bulls, 1,701,000 oxen, 3,909,000 cows, 856,000 heifers. The importation at that time amounted to only 2,360,000 francs, but in 1825 it was 7,680,000. The exportation is, however, considerable. Sheep are a species of stock very considerable in amount, particularly in the departments bordering on the Alps and Pyrenees, in those which compose the mountain district of Auvergne, and on the pastoral banks of the Eure and the Cher. The number of sheep in 1812 was 766,310 merinos, 3,578,000 mixed, and 30,843,000 native or unimproved. The first introduction of merinos was in consequence of the treaty of Basle, which stipulated that 4000 of these highly prized animals should pass into France. An experience of thirty years has shown that the breed might be preserved and extended in full perfection; but the above statement will show that the diffusion of it is, as yet, very partial. Pure merinos are valued at thirty francs, mixed at twelve francs, and native sheep at only five francs. The number of swine in France is estimated by Balbi, in 1826, at 4,000,000. The ass is considered by M. Senac to be, from the poverty of his owners, in an almost hopeless state of degradation; and the fowls, the bees, and the pigeons to demand a thoroughly improved system of rearing. Chaptal has not attempted to estimate the winged species, but has guessed their entire value at about 51,000,000 francs.

Among the materials of manufacture, the most important is silk, which was at first introduced near Tours, but was soon found to be well suited only to the most southern districts. The amount, according to Chaptal, is about 11,400,000 lbs., and the value 15,440,000 francs; but this is only about two-fifths of the quantity consumed in the manufactures, so that a large importation is necessary from Lombardy. Hemp and flax are cultivated universally, but always on a small scale, every farmer having his little patch for domestic use. It is difficult to estimate these; but Chaptal guesses the value of hemp at 30,000,000 francs, and flax at 20,000,000 francs. Vegetable oils are produced to the supposed extent of 1,300,000 quintals, worth about 75,000,000 francs; yet so great is the quantity consumed in domestic use, and in the different manufactures, that they are imported to the value of nearly twenty-five millions.

There are certain tropical and colonial productions which it was the eager wish of Napoleon that France should cultivate, in order that she might be independent of commerce. One of his favourite projects was the culture of the beet-root, for the extraction of sugar, an article of consumption with which Europeans can least dispense. The admission of colonial and foreign sugars, under reasonable duties, after the overthrow of the continental system, gave a severe check to this spurious branch of industry. To prevent its decline, heavy additional duties were laid on colonial and foreign sugars in 1816 and 1822; and, in consequence of this encouragement, the production of beet-root sugar has been rapidly increasing during the last five years, and is now supposed to amount to about 8000 tons, or 8,960,000 lbs. The art has been a good deal improved; and it is supposed by many that it will, at no distant period, be so much ameliorated that the beet-growers will be able to withstand the competition of the West India planters under the same duties: but any such expectation seems to us to be quite visionary. The entire consumption of sugar in France amounts, at present, inclusive of that from the beet-root, to about 72,000 tons a year; being not much more than a third part of the consumption of Great Britain and Ireland, which amounts to about 190,000 tons. Tobacco, after the removal of the *régie* or royal monopoly, rose to 50,000,000 lbs.; but since the restoration of the régie in 1812, it has fallen to 5,000,000.

Wood is an important article, especially in a country which is nearly destitute of any other fuel. Chaptal estimated the woodlands at 7,072,000 hectares (about 17,500,000 acres); but according to a more recent memorial in 1824, by M. Herbin de Halle, sub-administrator of the forests, it is only 6,521,000 hectares (about 16,000,000 acres). Of this, 1,122,000 hectares belong to the state, 1,896,000 to the communes, 65,969 to the crown, 192,000 to princes of the royal family, and 3,243,000 to private individuals. Woods thus occupy a little more than an eighth part of the soil. The greatest proportion exists in the departments bordering on the Alps and the Pyrenees, and along the Rhine, the Moselle, the Saône, the Marne, and other eastern rivers. Chaptal estimates the value of the annual cuttings at about 141,000,000 francs; but if this be reduced according to M. de Halle's estimate, it will give only 130,000,000. Fruit trees are also of importance, especially chestnuts, cultivated on a large scale in several provinces, and valued by Chaptal at about 10,000,000 francs. He estimates the fruit growing open in orchards at 22,500,000 francs, and that on walls, or in rows as single trees, at 68,750,000. He is afraid that this last will be thought too low; we should rather apprehend an opposite error in this instance, as well as in that of reckoning the herbs which grow in 328,000 hectares of garden ground, at 200,000,000 francs.

On the whole, Chaptal calculates that in the 52,000,000 hectares of which France consists, twenty-three are arable; ten woods, vines, fruit-trees; seven pasturage; the rest waters, roads, buildings, waste. He makes the annual average produce of an acre 28 francs. By this and other estimates, the annual territorial produce comes to about 1,500,000,000 francs. The entire agricultural capital he estimates at 37,500,000,000 francs. M. Dupin, in 1827, reckons the territorial revenue at 1,626,000,000 francs.

The manufactures of France, though they do not present the immense results of those of England, are considerably more productive than those of almost any other nation. Colbert, the celebrated minister of Louis XIV., finding this branch in a very depressed state, compared with its prosperous condition in some neighbouring countries, bestowed on it almost an exclusive attention. Chaptal calculates, that during the Revolution it made still greater progress than agriculture. He regards as almost miraculous the advance made in the cotton and other fabrics. The miracle, however, was wrought solely by the rigid exclusion of British goods; and amid all the boasted proofs of French ingenuity, he is obliged to confess, that when, as minister of the interior, he sought eagerly the means of introducing new manufactures, he could find no effectual expedient, except that of alluring English manufacturers into France, and of copying their processes. However, these prohibitions, which have been continued to a great extent under the royal system, have in fact forced a number of manufactures which could not otherwise have withstood British competition.

Silk has been long one of the most prominent objects of French manufacture. Even the revocation of the edict of Nantes, though it drove many of the most industrious citizens out of the kingdom, left that branch of industry still very flourishing. It suffered more from the dreadful calamities which befell Lyons, its chief seat, during the height of the revolutionary mania. The 15,000 establishments that existed in 1788 for the manufacture of silk, were reduced in 1800 to 3500; but amounted, in 1831, to about 15,000, employing above 21,000 workmen. It is chiefly in cloths that this city excels all others, both as to the brilliancy of the dyes, and the richness and beauty of the stuffs. Nismes excels in taffetas, mixed silk and cotton stuffs, gauzes, and crapes; Tours in furniture stuffs; Avignon in satins, levantines, &c. The Cevennes are famous for bonnets, while almost all the silk ribands are fabricated in the department of the Loire. The entire value of the manufacture is estimated at 125,000,000 francs, of which 30,000,000 is exported.

The woollen manufacture is still more extensive and valuable than that of silk. The woollens of France are either very coarse or very fine; the former are established chiefly in the hilly tracts of the southern border, where the sheep yield abundance of coarse wool, and the shepherds spend the leisure of winter in working it up into serges, friezes, and similar stuffs. On the other hand, at Sedan, Louviers, Abbeville, are manufactured finer cloths than any of those of Britain, though the latter produces a much larger quantity of good and substantial cloth. Although France produces 84,000,000 lbs. of wool, she yet imports to the value of 12,000,000 or 14,000,000 of francs: Chaptal estimates the whole unmanufactured wool at 93,000,000 francs, and the finished work at 238,000,000, of which the exports amount to about 25,000,000.

The making of linen is as widely scattered as the culture of hemp and flax. The coarse cloths are chiefly fabricated by the peasantry, each out of the produce of his own little patch of land. There are, however, large manufactures of plain useful cloth in Normandy and Dauphiné, the latter from hemp; and great quantities of sailcloth are made in the maritime countries. In the departments along the Belgic border there are extensive fabrics of lawns, cambrics, and lace; which last, though not of equal reputation with that of Brussels and Mechlin, forms yet an important object of trade. We may reckon the raw material of hemp at 37,000,000 francs; the finished manufacture at nearly 110,500,000; flax, raw material, 20,000,000, the finished fabric, 75,000,000. The exportation is about 37,500,000, almost wholly of the finest kinds of the manufacture.

The cotton manufacture was established in France during the continental system; and has been propped up since the restoration of the Bourbons by the prohibition of importation from abroad. In 1810 the imports of raw cotton amounted to above 25,000,000 lbs., and during the next ten years they were more than doubled. But the high price of machinery in France, the scarcity of coal, and the want of skill on the part of the workmen, seem to oppose almost insuperable obstacles to the further progress of the manufacture. It is at present in a very depressed state, and the following account shows that it has been nearly stationary during the last ten years:—

*Imports of Cotton Wool into France.*

| | lbs. | | lbs. |
|---|---|---|---|
| 1822 | 61,758,300 | 1827 | 87,185,100 |
| 1823 | 50,953,500 | 1828 | 61,839,600 |
| 1824 | 75,322,200 | 1829 | 72,669,000 |
| 1825 | 61,371 600 | 1830 | 84,825,600 |
| 1826 | 96,052,200 | 1831 | 65,517,900 |

[In 1834, it again rose to 279,674 bales, or about 73,250,000 lbs.; and in 1835, to 314,350 bales, or about 94,000,000 lbs.—Am. Ed.]

Of the secondary objects of manufacture, that of leather is perhaps the most extensive, though not peculiarly French. It is supposed that in France the annual product amounts to 857,000 cow-hides; 110,000 horse-hides, and 2,032,000 calf-skins. There are 31,000 shoemakers in Paris, who make upwards of eight millions of pairs of shoes yearly, not only for the city itself, but the provinces, and even foreign countries. Chaptal reckons the whole produce of tanning, currying, shoemaking, and all processes connected with leather, at 143,000,000 francs. Hard soap was formerly supplied by Marseilles to all France and the colonies, but its produce of 225,000 quintals is now reduced by a third; owing partly to the reduction of the colonial demand, and partly to the more general diffusion of the manufacture. It is thought still to amount to 30,000,000 francs. Starch, including hair-powder, may amount to 18,000,000 pounds. There are sundry little matters of jewellery, trinkets, furniture, perfumery, scented waters, volatile salts, which elsewhere are only petty trades, but which taste and fashion in France raise to the dignity of manufactures, the whole produce of which is reckoned at upwards of 100,000,000 francs. Crystal, glass, and pottery are branches in which the French have recently made great progress; and, from being dependent on foreigners for these articles, are now able to export them. The first two branches are estimated at 21,000,000; porcelain made at Sèvres and other places, at 5,000,000; pottery in imitation of English, a little more; coarse pottery for the lower ranks, 15,000,000.

*Mineral kingdom.* France yields in abundance the most solid and useful of all metals, iron. There are about 400 forges in the kingdom, chiefly in the Pyrenean and Alpine departments, and along the heads of the Marne, the Moselle, and the Saône.

The produce which M. Chaptal reckoned only 81,000,000 kilogrammes, had, according to M. Dupin, risen in 1825 to 161,000,000 (about 161,000 tons), the value of which would be about 75,000,000 francs. Chaptal supposed the workmanship bestowed even on the smaller quantity produced in his time sufficient to raise the value to 200,000,000 francs. Nearly all the copper and lead employed in France is imported from abroad. Salt is extracted on the southern coast from sea-water evaporated by the heat of the sun, and in the north from brine-springs artificially evaporated. During the period when salt, relieved from the old oppressive monopoly, was left entirely free, its production and use rose to the extraordinary height of upwards of 20 millions of quintals. Since the re-establishment of the tax, it has fallen to not quite two millions; upon which there is paid a duty of 45,000,000 francs. This astonishing diminution seems chiefly owing to the disuse of it in agriculture; a circumstance however very injurious to that branch of industry. Other mineral products, with their supposed value, are, alum, 2,500,000; saltpetre, 3,000,000; nitric acid, 6,000,000; muriatic acid, 250,000.

The total value of the products of the mines and manufactures of France is estimated at 2,000,000,000 francs. The particulars are about 450 millions of home raw materials; 225 millions of foreign raw materials; 900 millions of workmanship; 225 millions of general expense, as implements, repairs, lighting, interest of fixed capital; 200 millions for the profit of the manufacturer.

The commerce of France, while all the other branches of industry were thus advancing, has perceptibly declined. It was reduced, indeed, to a state of temporary annihilation by the violent policy of Napoleon, who absolutely lined the coast with troops, that not a single vessel might enter. Thus all the commercial ties of France were broken, every channel closed by which she was accustomed to exchange her commodities with those of foreign countries. Indeed, the anti-commercial spirit seems to have become rooted in the mind of the nation; and when we find even the enlightened mind of Chaptal extolling the prohibitory system, and considering every thing as a source of loss to France which she imports from abroad, there can appear little prospect of any amendment. That writer considers the year 1789 as the most flourishing period of French commerce; when the exports amounted to 18,200,000*l.* sterling, and the imports to 26,500,000*l.* This extraordinary excess of imports, a result, according to old ideas, considered so disastrous, he explains by observing, that the imports include ten millions from the colonies, while the exports thither were only four, and also two millions and a half in gold and silver. Whether this explanation be sound or otherwise, we have no idea that there could be any permanent or extensive difference between the two branches. Chaptal has, with grief, declined to give any record of the feeble efforts at revival made by the French commerce. Since the appearance of Chaptal's work, however, it has considerably improved. In 1827, the import trade was carried out by 3350 vessels, under the French flag, tonnage 353,000, value of cargoes 230,140,000 francs; and by 4439 foreign vessels, tonnage 474,000, value of cargoes 136,041,000 francs. There were, besides, imported by land, goods to the value of 199,621,000 francs; making the imports in all, 565,802,000 francs.

In the same year the export trade was carried on by 3522 French vessels, tonnage 346,000, value of cargoes 235,120,000 francs; and 4141 foreign vessels, tonnage also 346,000, value of cargoes 167,728,000 francs. The exports by land amounted to 156,767,000 francs; making in all, 559,615,000 francs.

The following was the value of the leading articles of import and export:—

IMPORTS.

| | Francs. |
|---|---|
| Raw hides | 8,700,000 |
| Wools | 11,140,000 |
| Feathers | 1,580,000 |
| Silks | 32,270,000 |
| Tallow | 2,500,000 |
| Fruits to plant | 1,220,000 |
| Tobacco | 7,650,000 |
| Vegetable juices | 2,270,000 |
| Oils, not for food | 21,430,000 |
| Medicines | 2,130,000 |
| Wood | 17,000,000 |
| ——, ornamental | 2,900,000 |
| Hemp | 4,210,000 |
| Flax | 56,000 |
| Cotton | 51,910,000 |
| Gems | 8,200,000 |
| Sulphur | 1,290,000 |
| Coal | 8,080,000 |
| Cast-iron | 1,170,000 |
| Copper | 9,110,000 |
| Tin | 2,130,000 |
| Potash | 3,420,000 |
| Indigo | 14,880,000 |
| Horses | 3,360,000 |
| Sheep | 6,400,000 |
| Horned cattle | 2,520,000 |
| Butter | 1,960,000 |
| Eggs | 3,830,000 |
| Grain | 7,150,000 |
| Cheese | 3,140,000 |
| Fruits | 16,200,000 |
| Sugar | 36,000,000 |
| Coffee | 10,000,000 |
| Straw-hats | 4,550,000 |
| Linen, or hemp stuffs, | 15,880,000 |
| Mercery | 2,170,000 |

EXPORTS.

| | Francs. |
|---|---|
| Dye stuffs | 8,300,000 |
| Gems | 2,120,006 |
| Horses | 1,290,000 |
| Mules | 4,840,000 |
| Sheep | 1,420,000 |
| Horned cattle | 2,520,000 |
| Refined sugar | 4,550,000 |
| Wine, ordinary | 41,510,000 |
| ——, liqueurs | 5,720,000 |
| Brandies | 22,970,000 |
| Straw-hats | 2,090,000 |
| Porcelain | 3,680,000 |
| Glass | 2,600,000 |
| French books | 3,140,000 |
| Paper | 3,960,000 |
| Perfumery | 5,390,000 |
| Cloths, wool | 26,920,000 |
| ——, silk | 90,860,000 |
| ——, ribands | 24,380,000 |
| ——, cotton | 46,020,000 |
| ——, linen | 17,370,000 |
| Cambric and lawn | 16,580,000 |
| Plaqué | 3,170,000 |
| Clock and watch-work | 4,240,000 |
| Tabletterie | 3,790,000 |
| Mercery | 6,880,000 |
| Modes | 2,300,000 |
| Made clothes | 6,480,000 |
| Parisian articles | 5,690,000 |

*Mercantile navy.* In 1827, the mercantile navy of France consisted of 14,530 vessels, of the burden of 700,000 tons. Of these there belonged to—

| | Ships. | Tons. |
|---|---|---|
| Bordeaux | 431 | 77,000 |
| Marseilles | 711 | 65,000 |
| Havre | 359 | 62,000 |
| Nantes | 537 | 56,000 |
| Rouen | 254 | 28,000 |
| Dunkirk | 229 | 17,500 |

The interior commerce must be very extensive, though it is difficult to estimate its amount, as, notwithstanding considerable advantages for navigation, the bulk of it is carried on by land. The old medium of *fairs* has been not only preserved, but greatly extended. M. Bottin, upon documents furnished by the minister of the interior, calculates that there are 26,314 fairs in France. Some of these are held on the frontier of a province or kingdom, others round a great cathedral or noted place of pilgrimage; some at the foot of high mountains on the melting of the snows, which have kept the inhabitants imprisoned for several months. Sometimes they open with burlesque representations, as processions of giants, of flying dragons, or monstrous fishes. The fair of Longchamps, held in spring at Paris, those of Beaucaire in Languedoc, and of Guibray in Normandy, are the most extensive.

The canals of France were long entirely undertaken by the government, which carried on these works with some spirit. The earliest was the Canal of Briare, to unite the Seine and the Loire. It is about 38 miles long, 4 feet deep, has 40 locks, and cost 1,000,000 francs. The canal of Languedoc is on a much greater scale, and was considered in its day a stupendous undertaking. It was intended to unite the Mediterranean with the Atlantic, and is 170 miles long, 6½ feet deep, with 100 locks. The cost was 32,000,000 francs, which would have been, at least, doubled had the work been executed in the present day. It was considered the largest canal in Europe, till it was eclipsed by the Caledonian, which is three times as deep, and admits ships of war; whereas the canal of Languedoc has afforded a mere inland navigation, along which pass 1900 vessels of 100 to 120 tons; but it has not, for the most common merchant-vessels, superseded the necessity of going round by the Straits of Gibraltar. The Canal of the Centre, joining the Saône and the Loire by a line of 70 miles, was completed in 1793, at an expense of 10,000,000 francs; but only 5 feet deep. The Canal of Picardy, from the Oise towards Lille, remarkable for its long tunnel near St. Quintin, was completed in 1810, at an expense of 10,800,000 francs. Still, France, in this grand national improvement, remained far behind England, which, by M. Dupin's estimate, made a few years ago, had more than four and a half times as much canalization in proportion to its surface. Very recently, however, France has displayed an extraordinary activity in planning, and a considerable diligence in executing, designs of this nature. This too has been displayed not by government only, but by private associations, asking only aid and advances from the state. Independent of the finished works above stated, twelve great new canals are in progress. These are,—1. The Canal *Monsieur*, joining the Rhine and the Rhone by the Saône and the Doubs; length 180 miles. 2. Of Burgundy, joining the Saône to the Loire by the Yonne, 145 miles. 3. Of Angoulême, making the Somme navigable to Amiens. 4. A lateral canal along the Loire, to avoid the difficulties of its navigation, from Dijon to Briare, 120 miles. 5. From Nantes to Brest, with a view of provisioning the ports of Britany, 220 miles. 6. Of Ille et Rance, joining Nantes to Brest and St. Malo. 7. Of Nivernais, joining the Yonne to the Loire. 8. Of the Duke of Berri, joining the Cher to the Upper Loire. 9. Ardennes. 10. Blanet. 11. Arles. 12. Oise. Several canals, on a still more magnificent scale, have been recently contemplated, and what the French call the *studies* of them are even far advanced; but no part of the works has yet been commenced. Doubts are even entertained if they will repay the immense expense required for their completion. The principal of these are,—1. A maritime canal from Paris to the sea, avoiding the circuitous navigation of the Seine, and admitting ships of large burden to that capital. The estimate is 150,000,000 francs, and 1,500,000 francs for a harbour at Paris. 2. A canal from Paris to Strasburg; which would become, as it were, the French Grand Trunk, and might easily be extended to the Danube. The length would exceed 300 miles. 1. The Pyrenean Canal, from Toulouse to Bayonne, forming a more direct communication from sea to sea than at present. Length, 210 miles.

The roads of France, at least the high roads, have been chiefly supported by government. They are broader, more spacious, more direct, and on the whole of grander aspect, than the English roads; but they have not been kept in such good condition for travelling. Roads have been made and repaired rather for political and military purposes, from solicitation and favour, than for objects of real utility. The system seems to have been, to neglect them as long as possible, till the clamour of the district became irresistible, and then to give them a thorough repair; to which Dupin justly prefers the system of keeping roads constantly in a good state by small repairs as the necessity arises. The French roads, however, have been greatly improved since 1810, and the maintenance of a great proportion of them has been undertaken by the departments; so that they are now divided into royal and departmental. The royal roads, in 1828, extended 8631 leagues, and there was expended on them 199,000,000 francs; but this was chiefly on repairing and extending different parts of them. It was thus divided:—

| | | | Francs. |
|---|---|---|---|
| To maintain | 4205 | leagues, cost | 9,349,000 |
| To repair | 3166 | ditto | 61,051,000 |
| To complete | 814 | ditto | 43,403,000 |
| To open | 446 | ditto | 34,964 000 |
| Works of art | | | 50,696,600 |
| | | | 199,463,000 |

The departmental roads, in 1828, extended 7704 leagues, of which 6040 had been opened, and to complete the remaining 1664 would require an expenditure of 112,000,000 francs.

There are several rail-roads in France, but of no great extent; the principal are that of Andrezieux and Roanne, 50 miles in length; that of St. Etienne and the Loire, 15 miles; and that of St. Etienne and Lyons, 45 miles.

Of the bridges of France several are handsome, as those over the Loire at Orleans, Tours, and Nantes; over the Seine at Paris, Neuilly, and Rouen; over the Rhone and Saône at Lyons; and over the Garonne at Bordeaux. Bridges of suspension have been constructed at Paris in front of the Hôtel des Invalides, and over the Rhone, between Tain and Tournon. These operations have been entirely in the hands of government.

### SECT. VI.—*Civil and Social State.*

The population of France, which in 1780, by the enquiries of Necker, appeared to be 24,800,000, was found by the census of 1791 to amount to 26,363,000; by that of 1817, to upwards of 29,000,000; and by that of 1820-21, to 30,616,000, including Corsica and the army. According to the royal ordonnance of March 15th, 1827, it amounted to 31,851,545. There were in that year 965,634 births; of which 898,329 were legitimate, and 67,305 illegitimate. The births consisted of 498,187 boys, and 467,447 girls. The marriages were 229,613, the deaths 772,428. At an average the proportion of male births in France to female births is as 16 to 15; the marriages are to the population as 1 to 133; the births are to the marriages nearly as 4 to 1; and to the population as 1 to 31.53; the deaths are to the population as 1 to 39.4. The extraordinary improvement since 1780 in the condition of the people is obvious from the fact that at the last-mentioned period the deaths were to the whole population as 1 to 30.2: so that while, in 1780, one individual died annually out of every 30 individuals, in 1832 one only died out of about 39.*

The French national character has very marked features, and has been the object of mingled admiration and contempt to the neighbouring nations. In the eyes of Frenchmen, especially of the old school, *la belle France* is the centre of all that is refined and polished in human existence, and whatever lies beyond its sphere is marked with a deep taint of barbarism; while their rougher neighbours brand them as artificial, effeminate, and fantastic. The art of living in society seems certainly carried to greater perfection than in any other country; and the manners are characterised by a peculiar gaiety, amenity, and courtesy. The polish of the higher ranks seems to have descended even to the lowest circles. "The man who breaks stones upon the road takes off his hat to the woman that leads her cow in a string; the tinker and the shoeblack whip off their hats to each other." A certain openness and kindness of disposition is certainly evinced in the custom of whole families, with married sons and daughters, continuing to dwell under the paternal roof. The Frenchman lives as it were in public: his house, for a part of the day, is open to a large circle of acquaintance. He enjoys society without expense and ceremony. He resorts habitually to the theatre, spectacles, and scenes of public amusement. In more serious points of view, the French possess estimable qualities. Intoxication is a vice confined to the lowest ranks; and swearing is repelled at least as a mark of barbarism. The French are ingenious, acute, active, and intelligent. If they have not what can strictly be called patriotism, they have at least a very strong national feeling. To exalt the glory and promote the influence of France, is the prevailing impulse which actuates the mind of almost every Frenchman. It is, however, alleged, that there is a want of that sterling principle, that openness and integrity, which forms the boast of the English character. Dissimulation and insincerity seem widely diffused through the intercourse of the higher circles. The honesty of the lower classes is, however, remarkable; and the system of higgling in shops, is a consequence of the contracted state of commerce. The deportment of the female sex, however embellished by *tournure*, and the graces, does not accord with our ideas of social and domestic propriety. The young ladies are strictly watched, and held in almost monastic seclusion; but the era of marriage is the signal, if not of positive irregularity, at least of a system of regular flirtation, which we cannot reconcile to the conjugal and matronly character. It is probable, however, that the impression of the general dissoluteness of French manners has been chiefly derived from the opulent circles of the capital; while, as a late writer has observed, Paris and the provinces form entirely separate worlds. Among the peasantry, and even among the trading class in the cities, there appears to be much that is respectable and amiable. The great activity and prominent station of the female sex are everywhere conspicuous: they are seen managing the shops, carrying on great manufactories, and joining in the hardest toils of the loom and the field. It is not at all uncommon upon a farm to see the master sowing, his wife guiding the plough, and a fine girl filling the dung-cart. Such avocations divest the fair sex in the provinces of any great portion of beauty. Indeed, the gay hilarity of the French character does not seem quite so universal as is generally supposed. Travellers in the south, from Arthur Young to those of later date, complain rather of a singular gravity and taciturnity. Mr. Matthews remarks in his "Diary of an Invalid," that a very con-

[* The population in 1833 was 32,500,000.—AM. ED.]

siderable change of manners has taken place since the Revolution. All the distinctions of rank have been cut down like the old trees of the forest, and the new generation, like the coppice, are all on a level. "You will seek in vain," he says, "for that high-bred polish of manners, which has been so much boasted as peculiar to the *haut-ton* of France. A republican spirit prevails, and shows itself in an independent roughness of manner, savouring of sans-culottism."

The Roman Catholic has been the ruling religion in France, ever since the fatal issue of the long struggle for religious liberty. Previously to the Revolution, however, a general scepticism pervaded all the well-informed classes, both as to the Catholic tenets, and as to religion in general. This was doubtless one great cause both of the Revolution and of many of the fatal and disastrous aspects which it assumed. A furious anti-religious fanaticism reigned; all form of public worship was suspended, and even prohibited; the churches were rifled and defaced in a barbarous manner. At this time the vast domains of the church, by which so many dignitaries and so many convents were supported in splendour, were voted the property of the nation, and sold at a low price to supply its necessities. Napoleon had the merit of re-establishing religious worship, and on a very liberal footing; an allowance being made for the support of the Protestant clergy, proportioned to the number who still hold that faith, and who amount to about 1,500,000. As all the former funds however had disappeared, the establishment is supported out of the public revenue, and is frugal, and even scanty, both as to numbers and salary. In 1831, there were four cardinals, ten archbishops, and sixty-six bishops. After the intermediate classes of vicars and canons come the *curés*, or parish priests, amounting to 3000, with incomes of 1000 or 1500 francs; but the chief labour devolves upon 23,000 *desservans*, or acting curates, who starve upon 400 or 600 francs a year with the addition of only some small fees. The whole church expenditure, in 1823, amounted to 1,575,000 livres, but in 1832 was reduced by a third; and the church has been in a somewhat unsettled state. The Bourbons were supposed to aim at restoring it to all its former power, splendour, and privilege; a course viewed with extreme jealousy by the republican party. The high church party endeavoured to remedy the deficiency of the establishment by sending sound missionaries who were listened to by the people with enthusiastic delight. The author of "Four Years in France" mentions one who in departing from a city had his cassock torn off his back, and cut into pieces to be distributed as relics. The liberals deride them as ignorant fanatics; but some travellers who cannot be charged with superstition, report them as displaying a good deal of natural eloquence, and that their doctrines appeared really very edifying, since many persons who had been guilty of thefts, even at remote periods, were induced by them to come forward and make confession and restitution.

The intellectual character of the French has been brilliant, and since the age of Louis XIV. has had a powerful influence, in matters of taste, on the general literature of Europe: that prince, ambitious of glory in every form, extended a munificent patronage to letters and arts. The French Academy, though its endowments were not very splendid, and though intrigue often influenced its admissions, gave a fixed and high place in society to men of letters; who, amid all the frivolity of French character, were received even among the highest ranks with a distinction not accorded to them in any other modern country. The aim of Louis to make the French a sort of universal language was in a great measure successful; it became the established dialect at all the courts, and the chief medium by which the different nations communicated with each other. The departments in which the writers of that age excelled, were chiefly pulpit eloquence, poetry of a light and satirical character, and the drama in a somewhat fettered and artificial form. The writers of the following age took a bolder and more varied flight, and sought to turn the opinion of mankind into new channels upon all subjects. The wit and varied talent of Voltaire, the eloquence of Buffon and Rousseau, the comprehensive views of Montesquieu, and the science of D'Alembert, gave a new turn to the ideas of the thinking world throughout Europe. These writers, with their successors of the same school, had a powerful influence in bringing on this revolution, in the ruins of which several of them were buried. Learning was for some time almost extinguished in France; but as soon as the revolutionary frenzy abated, the National Assembly constituted a new body called the National Institute, round which, under the changed appellations of Imperial and Royal, all the highest names in science have since continued to rally. The French during this period did not shine in poetry or general literature; but in mathematics, physics, and chemistry, the labours of Lavoisier, Laplace, Lalande, Chaptal, and a number of others, have, notwithstanding the powerful rivalry on the other side of the Channel, raised them perhaps to the very first place. Recently France has produced some very eminent historians, and popular poets of a peculiar character; there has been also a remarkable extension of the habits of reading. The periodical sheets printed were in 1814 only 45,000; in 1826, they were 144,000. The most solid and useful branches also are those which have most increased, as appears from the following table, formed by M. Dupin:—

| | No. of Sheets printed. | | | No. of Sheets printed. | |
|---|---|---|---|---|---|
| | 1814. | 1826. | | 1814. | 1826. |
| Theology | 4,974,000 | 23,268,000 | Military Subjects | 441,000 | 1,445,000 |
| Legislative | 1,374,000 | 18,605,000 | Fine Arts | 773,000 | 1,999,000 |
| Sciences | 2,546,000 | 12,160,000 | Belles Lettres | 13,352,000 | 27,704,000 |
| Philosophy | 753,000 | 3,032,000 | History, Travels, &c. | 16,226,000 | 46,545,000 |
| Political Economy | 1,634,000 | 2,097,000 | Varieties, Almanacs, &c. | 3,600,000 | 7,699,000 |

The literary and scientific collections of Paris are the most splendid in Europe: the royal library contains 800,000 printed volumes, 100,000 manuscripts, 5000 volumes of engravings, and 1,000,000 historical documents. There are sixteen other libraries in Paris, containing 800,000 volumes. The Museum of Natural History and the Jardin des Plantes are equally copious in their respective departments. All these are opened to the public in the most liberal manner. The provincial collections are also respectable, though they do not equal those of the minor princes of Germany; and France is, on the whole, less rich in this species of treasure.

Among the establishments for public education in France, the universities, which are twenty-six in number, hold the first rank. That of Paris is perhaps the most celebrated in Europe, and was, even in the dark ages, the grand theatre of those dialectic combats, which then usurped the honours of science. Though destroyed during the fury of the Revolution, it has been re-established on a great scale, and with a larger appointment of professors than any other in Europe; it attracts students from every part of the kingdom, as none of the rest enjoy equal repute, and indeed bear at present only the name of academies. The *Lycées*, now called royal colleges, are an institution of Napoleon; the expense of board and education is from 350 to 750 francs a year; but they enjoy a very unwarrantable monopoly of the right to teach Latin; they were attended, in 1825, by 10,000 pupils. Primary schools intended for the general instruction of the people amounted in 1825 to 22,900, and were attended by 116,000 scholars. Lancasterian schools have since been introduced, and amounted in 1820 to 800, attended by 80,000 scholars. M. Dupin remarks striking local differences in this respect. In the north, 13,000,000 of inhabitants send to school 740,000 children; while in the south, 18,000,000 send only 375,000: even in the south, the proportion is largest in the districts least favoured by nature, the Upper Alps and the Upper Pyrenees; while in Touraine, emphatically called the garden of France, it is only one in 229. All these establishments are under the patronage and control of the government, which grants annually about 5,000,000 francs for their support.*

The fine arts were zealously promoted by the regent duke of Orleans, and by Louis XIV.; and though they never reached the splendour of the Italian or even of the Flemish schools, yet they could boast several masters of the first class; the Poussins and Claude Lorraine, having fixed their residence and even found their scenery in Italy, became half Italian. Le Brun and Le Sueur were the chief artists decidedly French: of whom the former enjoyed the favour of the king, and the chief direction of the great works; but the latter has been pronounced by posterity to be his superior. After this the French school sunk greatly, and was employed in delineating only the artificial forms of court society; but within the last thirty years a new school has sprung up, in which David, Gerard, Guerin, Girodet, and their followers have sought, not without success, to imitate the highest classical models. The French school has produced a series of very eminent engravers; and the names of Desnoyers, Bervic, and Massard still support its reputation, though it no longer surpasses, or perhaps equals, those of England and Italy. The French galleries of art have passed through many vicissitudes: before the revolution they were certainly the first out of Italy. During that convulsion, all the collections of the princes and nobles were put up to sale; the entire Orleans collection was carried to England; the Crozat went to Russia; various minor collections shared the same fate. When the French, however, over-ran Italy and the Netherlands, they were seized with the desire of enriching Paris with treasures of art, and carried off whatever could be removed from among the masterpieces of the Flemish and Italian masters, and of ancient sculpture. Thus was assembled in the Louvre a display of all that is most brilliant in art, such as nothing before existing in the world could have rivalled. But

*[It appears from official documents, that in 1833 the number of children between the ages of two and six years, was 2,744,524, of whom about 250,000 attended infant schools; of those between six and fifteen years, there were 4,987,261, of which 2,449,725 attended the primary schools; and of persons above fifteen, there were 22,966,170, of whom 14,355,856 could neither read nor write;—so that there were nearly 19,400,000 persons above the age of two years, who received no instruction at all. The same papers give the following statements of the schools existing, and of the number required to educate the whole population:—

| | | |
|---|---|---|
| Infant Schools | 1,000 actual number. | 40,000 required number. |
| Primary do. | 30,467 " | 54,284 " |
| Female Working do. | 1,000 " | 20,000 " |
| Adult do. | 2,361 " | 54,840 " |
| Totals | 34,828 | 169,124 |

AM. ED.]

a dire reverse awaited the nation. The allied armies who conquered at Waterloo, and thence advanced to occupy Paris, determined to exact full restitution of all this brilliant booty. The Venus, Apollo, and Transfiguration were sent off for Rome; the Descent from the Cross for Antwerp; and numberless other masterpieces were restored to their ancient possessors. The unseemly gaps thus left were filled up by native productions and others taken from the palaces; and the gallery presents a *coup d'œil* almost as brilliant as ever; the intrinsic value, however, is vastly diminished; though since the purchase of the Borghese collection it still comprises some of the finest specimens of ancient sculpture.

The houses in France under the former régime presented a great variety; for while the mansions of the nobles displayed a profuse splendour and luxury, and might be characterised as palaces, those of the body of the people, compared with the English, were very deficient in neatness and comfort; the rooms being dark, the passages straggling, the floors of stone, the doors and windows by no means well finished. The palaces, however, can no longer be maintained as such by their impoverished owners; and all the fine old châteaus throughout France are converted into barracks, prisons, or manufactories. On the other hand, the habitations of the peasantry, as well as their general condition, appear to be sensibly improved.

Amusement used to form as it were the life of a Frenchman, and was sought for in every various and possible shape; but since the Revolution a very great change has taken place in this respect. Paris still claims to be, as it were, the centre of gaiety to the civilized world. The Parisians go from home in search of amusement much more than their neighbours; almost all their leisure is spent in places of public resort, which are open on terms that render them accessible to all classes. Dancing is an exercise peculiarly French, in which, as to agility, and perhaps grace, they excel most nations. Much of their time is also spent in the open air; and the extensive ranges of gardens in Paris are provided with every recreation suited to the tastes of its citizens. Although many improprieties doubtless mingle with these entertainments, especially in Paris, there is less of intoxication, turbulence, or quarrelling, than in the amusements of the lower orders in England: so far, even as concerns the public places, there are fewer open violations of decorum.

Dress is a particular in which the French long claimed, and were allowed to give the law to the rest of Europe. Paris has been for ages the grand *magasin des modes*. In that capital seems to have originated the system which is termed fashion, and which consists in the continual change, according to a prescribed model, of the form and construction of every part of the human attire. Such light and constant changes, however, while they indicate an inordinate attention to the object, seem as inconsistent with the formation of a pure and elegant taste, as the immutable costumes of our ancestors and of the East. The empire of Paris seems considerably shaken by the extinction of its brilliant societies, and its long separation by war from the other countries; but its influence remains still very considerable in this department.

In the preparation of food, the French equally boast of a refinement and *recherche* superior to that of the other European nations. Instead of plain joints presented in their natural form, French cookery delights in what are called made dishes, stews, fricassees, and ragoûts, which retain few traces of the original material. On the merits of this system various opinions have been entertained; but at present the fashion of this cookery out of France is on the decline, and the time seems past when it was considered a matter of state that the tables of the great should be covered with French dishes.

### Sect. VII.—*Local Geography.*

The local divisions of France, prior to the Revolution, were provinces, thirty-two in number, most of which had formed independent states, and even little kingdoms, when they were merged into the mass of the French monarchy. The National Assembly, however, superseded this division by one much more minute, into departments; which has been retained by the Bourbons, and is the basis of all administrative operations. It is indeed very convenient, being founded upon natural divisions of rivers and mountains: all the departments are tolerably equal as to magnitude, and each has its seat of administration nearly in the centre. All the exclusive privileges and restraints upon internal communication, which were attached to the arrangement into provinces, have been happily removed. Yet these divisions must still be kept in view, not only because they are necessary for the understanding of history, but because they remain rooted in the mind of the nation, and often mark striking differences of race, of manners, and even of language. It would not consist with our limits, or be interesting to readers out of France, to enter into a detailed description of each department; but the following tables will exhibit a very comprehensive view of their respective statistical details. The first exhibits the departments in their relation to the ancient provinces, their extent according to the report of the commission of the Cadastre, their population according to the census of 1827, and their chief cities and towns. The square French league may be reduced to the square English mile by multiplying by 8, or more closely, 7.84.

The following table exhibits both the provinces and the departments as nearly as possible in their relation to each other, with their extent in square leagues, and the population of the capital and principal towns according to the estimate formed by the French government in 1827.

| Provinces and Departments. | | Sq. Lgs. | Population. | Cities and Towns, with their Population in 1827. | | | | | |
|---|---|---|---|---|---|---|---|---|---|
| Flanders | Nord | 283 | 962,648 | Lille | 69,860 | Douay<br>Dunkirk | 19,880<br>24,517 | Valenciennes<br>Cambrai | 19,841<br>17,031 |
| Artois | Pas de Calais | 338 | 648,969 | Arras | 22,173 | Boulogne<br>St. Omer | 19,314<br>19,019 | Calais | 8,854 |
| Picardy | Somme | 395 | 526,282 | Amiens | 42,032 | Abbeville | 19,520 | St. Quentin | 12,351 |
| Normandy | Lower Seine | 300 | 688,295 | Rouen | 90,000 | Havre | 21,049 | Dieppe | 17,077 |
| | Calvados | 281 | 500,956 | Caen | 38,161 | Bayeux | 10,060 | Falaise | 10,303 |
| | Manche | 304 | 611,206 | St. Lo | 8,509 | Cherbourg | 17,066 | Coutances | 9,032 |
| | Orne | 283 | 434,379 | Alençon | 14,071 | Argentan | 6,044 | | |
| | Eure | 293 | 421,665 | Evreux | 9,729 | Louviers | 9,242 | | |
| Isle of France | Seine | 24 | 1,013,373 | Paris | 890,531 | Scéaux | 1,529 | St. Dénis | 5,731 |
| | Seine and Oise | 277 | 440,871 | Versailles | 29,791 | Etampes | 7,867 | | |
| | Oise | 297 | 385,124 | Beauvais | 12,865 | Compiègne | 7,362 | | |
| | Seine and Marne | 301 | 318,209 | Mélun | 7,199 | Fontainebleau | 7400 | Meaux | 7,836 |
| | Aisne | 375 | 489,560 | Laon | 7,354 | St. Quentin | 17,661 | Soissons | 7,483 |
| Champagne | Marne | ... | 325,045 | Châlons | 12,419 | Rheims | 34,862 | Epernay | 5,080 |
| | Ardennes | 256 | 281,624 | Mezières | 4,159 | Sedan | 12,608 | Rocroy | 3,500 |
| | Aube | 306 | 241,762 | Troyes | 25,587 | | | | |
| | Upper Marne | 315 | 244,823 | Chaumont | 6,027 | Langres | 7,180 | | |
| Lorraine | Meuse | 305 | 306,339 | Bar le Duc | 12,520 | ........................ | | Verdun | 9,882 |
| | Moselle | 339 | 409,155 | Metz | 4,276 | Thionville | 5,821 | | |
| | Meurthe | 282 | 403,038 | Nancy | 29,122 | Luneville | 12,378 | Toul | 7,507 |
| | Vosges | 252 | 379,839 | Epinal | 7,951 | St. Die | 7,339 | | |
| Alsace | Upper Rhine | 194 | 408,741 | Colmar | 1,549 | Béfort | 4,803 | | |
| | Lower Rhine | 210 | 535,467 | Strasburg | 49,708 | Saverne | 4,993 | Weissemburg | 6,146 |
| Britany | Ille and Vilaine | 321 | 553,453 | Rennes | 29,377 | St. Malo | 9,838 | | |
| | Côtes du Nord | 375 | 581,684 | St. Brieux | 9,963 | Dinant | 7,175 | | |
| | Finisterre | 350 | 502,851 | Quimper | 10,032 | Brest | 26,655 | Morlaix | 9,761 |
| | Morbihan | 360 | 427,454 | Vannes | 11,289 | L'Orient | 15,310 | | |
| | Lower Loire | 308 | 457,090 | Nantes | 71,739 | | | | |
| Maine and Perche | Mayenne | 261 | 354,138 | Laval | 15,840 | Mayenne | 9,799 | | |
| | Sarthe | 323 | 446,519 | Le Mans | 19,477 | | | | |
| Anjou | Maine and Loire | 365 | 458,674 | Angers | 29,978 | Saumur | 10,314 | | |
| Touraine | Indre and Loire | 321 | 290,160 | Tours | 20,920 | Cherson | 4,406 | | |
| Orléanais | Loiret | 356 | 304,228 | Orleans | 40,340 | Montargis | 6,653 | | |
| | Eure and Loire | 304 | 277,782 | Chartres | 13,703 | Dreux | 6,247 | | |
| | Loir and Cher | 319 | 230,666 | Blois | 11,337 | Vendôme | 6,805 | | |
| Berri | Indre | 354 | 237,628 | Châteauroux | 10,010 | Issoudun | 11,223 | | |
| | Cher | 360 | 248,589 | Bourges | 19,500 | | | | |
| Nivernais | Nièvre | 334 | 271,277 | Nevers | 15,782 | | | | |
| Burgundy | Yonne | 364 | 342,116 | Auxerre | 12,348 | Sens | 8,685 | | |
| | Côte d'Or | 440 | 370,943 | Dijon | 23,845 | Semur | 4,220 | | |
| | Saône and Loire | 290 | 515,776 | Maçon | 10,965 | Autun | 9,936 | Châlons | |
| | Ain | 295 | 341,628 | Bourg-en-Bresse | 8,424 | | | | |
| Franche-comte | Upper Saône | 262 | 327,641 | Vesoul | 5,252 | Gray | 7,203 | | |
| | Doubs | 276 | 254,312 | Besançon | 28,795 | Pontarlier | 4,549 | | |
| | Jura | 254 | 310,282 | Lons le Saulnier | 7,864 | | | | |
| Poitou | Vendée | 341 | 322,826 | Bourbon-Vendée | 3,129 | Fontenay le Comte | 7,493 | | |
| | Two Sèvres | 296 | 288,260 | Niort | 15,799 | | | | |
| | Vienne | 349 | 267,670 | Poitiers | 21,562 | Châtellerault | 9,241 | | |
| Marche, Limousin | Creuze | 265 | 252,932 | Gueret | 3,448 | | | | |
| | Upper Vienne | 290 | 276,351 | Limoges | 25,612 | | | | |
| | Corrèze | 278 | 284,882 | Tulle | 8,479 | | | | |
| Aunis, Saintonge, Angoumois | Charente | 280 | 353,653 | Angoulême | 15,306 | Cognac | 3,017 | | |
| | Lower Charente | 307 | 424,147 | Rochelle | 11,073 | Saintes | 10,300 | Rochefort | 12,909 |
| Auvergne | Puy de Dôme | 409 | 566,573 | Clermont | 30,010 | Riom | 12,736 | Thiers | 11,613 |
| | Cantal | 274 | 262,013 | Aurillac | 9,576 | St. Flour | 6,640 | | |
| Lyonnais | Rhône | 141 | 416,575 | Lyons, with suburbs | 170,875 | Trevoux | 2,452 | | |
| | Loire | 234 | 369,298 | Montbrison | 5,156 | St. Etienne | 30,615 | | |
| Dauphiny | Isère | 420 | 525,984 | Grenoble | 22,149 | Vienne | 13,780 | | |
| | Upper Alps | 275 | 125,329 | Gap | 7,015 | Embrun | 2,300 | | |
| | Drôme | 331 | 285,791 | Valence | 10,283 | Montelimar | 7,589 | | |
| Guienne | Dordogne | 476 | 464,074 | Périgueux | 8,588 | Bergerac | 8,412 | | |
| | Gironde | 517 | 538,151 | Bordeaux | 93,549 | | | | |
| | Lot and Garonne | 242 | 336,886 | Agen | 11,971 | Villeneuve | 9,495 | | |
| | Lot | 263 | 280,515 | Cahors | 12,413 | | | | |
| | Aveyron | 445 | 350,014 | Rhodez | 7,747 | Villefranche | 9,521 | | |
| | Tarn and Garonne | 114 | 241,586 | Montauban | 26,466 | Moissac | 10,115 | | |
| Bourbonnais | Allier | ... | 285,302 | Moulins | 14,525 | | | | |
| Gascony and Bearn | Landes | 459 | 265,309 | Mont de Marsan | 3,088 | Dax | 5,045 | | |
| | Gers | 312 | 307,601 | Auch | 10,844 | | | | |
| | Upper Pyrenees | 233 | 222,059 | Tarbes | 8,712 | Bagnères | 7,037 | | |
| | Lower Pyrenees | 386 | 412,469 | Pau | 11,761 | Bayonne<br>Oleron | 13,498<br>6,423 | Orthes | 6,834 |
| Foix | Arriège | 287 | 247,932 | Foix | 4,958 | | | | |
| Roussillon | Eastern Pyrenees | 205 | 151,372 | Perpignan | 15.357 | | | | |
| Languedoc | Upper Garonne | 339 | 407,016 | Toulouse | 53,319 | | | | |
| | Aude | 306 | 265,991 | Carcassonne | 17,775 | Narbonne | 10,097 | | |
| | Tarn | 290 | 327,665 | Alby | 10,993 | Castres | 15,663 | | |
| | Herault | 315 | 339,560 | Montpelier | 35,842 | Beziers | 16,515 | Soden | 9,842 |
| | Gard | 303 | 347,550 | Nismes | 39,068 | Alais | 10,252 | | |
| | Lozère | 257 | 138,778 | Mende | 5,445 | | | | |
| | Upper Loire | 250 | 285,673 | Le Puy en Velay | 14,998 | | | | |
| | Ardèche | 277 | 328,419 | Privas | 4,109 | Argentière | 2,797 | | |
| Provence | Lower Alps | 275 | 153,063 | Digne | 3,955 | Sisteron | 3,920 | | |
| | Mouths of the Rhone | 226 | 326,302 | Marseilles | 115,943 | Aix | 23,132 | Arles | 19,868 |
| | Var | 368 | 311,095 | Toulon | 30,171 | Draguignan | 8,016 | Grasse | 12,716 |
| | Vaucluse | 167 | 233,048 | Avignon | 31,180 | Orange | 8,864 | Carpentras | 9,750 |
| Corsica | Corsica | ... | 185,079 | Ajaccio | 7,658 | Bastia | 9,527 | | |

The following statistical table exhibits a comparative view of the state of culture and production in the different departments of France. The amounts of grain, cattle and wool are furnished by Chaptal. The wine is drawn from the report presented to the peers by the Duc de Dodeauville, and the forests from the memorial of the sub-administrator, M. Herbin de Halle. The entire annual amount of land revenue is derived from an estimate of the average produce of the arpent in each department, founded upon the Cadastre or general survey of the kingdom. It is furnished by Chaptal:—

| Departments. | Wheat. | Rye. | Oats. | Cattle. | Wool. | Wine. | | Forests. | Land Revenue. |
|---|---|---|---|---|---|---|---|---|---|
| | Hectol. | Hectol. | Hectol. | No. | Kilogrammes, 2 1-5th lbs. each. | Hectolitres, 26 1-2 gallons each. | Average Prices in Francs. | Hectares. | Francs. |
| Ain | 374,000 | 498,000 | 148,000 | 93,000 | 68,000 | 373,000 | 15 | 64,000 | 10,062,000 |
| Aisne | 1,422,200 | 1,040,000 | 566,000 | 84,000 | 1,107,000 | 291,000 | 22 | 103,000 | 27,441,000 |
| Allier | 282,000 | 746,000 | 1,721,000 | 111,000 | 147,000 | 288,000 | 17 | 106,000 | 8,238,000 |
| Alps, Upper | 180,000 | 166,000 | 13,000 | 25,000 | 338,000 | 101,000 | 16 | 74,000 | 3,604,000 |
| —— Lower | 185,000 | 108,000 | 786,000 | 11,000 | 556,000 | 99,000 | 16 | 60,000 | 4,664,000 |
| Ardeche | 108,000 | 394,000 | 39,000 | 54,000 | 384,000 | 77,000 | 18 | 28,000 | 11,767,000 |
| Ardennes | 663,000 | 458,000 | 2,000 | 80,000 | 557 000 | 55,000 | 20 | 150,000 | 12,203,000 |
| Arriege | 162,000 | 189,000 | 224,000 | 54,000 | 222,000 | 117,000 | 15 | 55,000 | 11,618,000 |
| Aube | 469,000 | 631,000 | 147,000 | 45,000 | 168,000 | 572,000 | 17 | 77,000 | 13,685,000 |
| Aude | 1,290,000 | 183,000 | 30,000 | 39,000 | 1,442,000 | 601,000 | 10 | 56,000 | 17,263,000 |
| Aveyron | 312,000 | 433,000 | 278,000 | 71,000 | 620,000 | 291,000 | 14 | 45,000 | 12,462,000 |
| Bouches du Rhone | 387,000 | 13,000 | 120,000 | 2,000 | 595,000 | 590,000 | 14 | 54,000 | 17,263,000 |
| Calvados | 1,152,000 | 228,000 | 249,000 | 99,000 | 304,000 | | | 32,000 | 43,637,000 |
| Cantal | 52,000 | 578,000 | 125,000 | 103,000 | 425,000 | 4,000 | 12 | 30,000 | 10,022 000 |
| Charente | 291,000 | 241,000 | 962,000 | 70,000 | 256,000 | 1,826,000 | 9 | 22,000 | 17,323,000 |
| ——— Lower | 709,000 | 34,000 | 1,211,000 | 67,000 | 211,000 | 1,791,000 | 10 | 38,000 | 26,258,000 |
| Cher | 40,000 | 260,000 | 1,501,000 | 42,000 | 835,000 | 333,000 | 20 | 150,000 | 9,330,000 |
| Correze | 104,000 | 630,000 | 185,000 | 86,000 | 213,000 | | | 13,000 | 9,572,000 |
| Corsica | 104,000 | 14,000 | 2,046,000 | | 104,000 | | | 55,000 | |
| Cote d'Or | 904,000 | 511,000 | 120,000 | 104,000 | 240,000 | 520,000 | 42 | 228,000 | 27.396,000 |
| Cotes du Nord | 416,000 | 523,000 | 24,000 | 163,000 | 136,000 | | | 18,000 | 19,383,000 |
| Creuze | 9,000 | 855,000 | 22,000 | 95,000 | 331,000 | | | 39,000 | 6,929,000 |
| Dordogne | 650,000 | 365,000 | 42,000 | 120,000 | 462,000 | 427,000 | 16 | 67,000 | 14,431,000 |
| Doubs | 265,000 | 138,000 | 30,000 | 104,000 | 53,000 | 139,000 | 18 | 113,000 | 14,464,000 |
| Drome | 552,000 | 223,000 | 277,000 | 10,000 | 963,000 | 251,000 | 18 | 92,000 | 20,749,000 |
| Eure | 1,398,000 | 621,000 | 202,000 | 43,000 | 413,000 | 55,000 | 22 | 97,000 | 27,486,000 |
| Eure and Loir | 1,532,000 | 162,000 | 696,000 | 56,000 | 917,000 | 1,094,000 | 20 | 44,000 | 15,912,000 |
| Finisterre | 282,000 | 479,000 | 444,000 | 200,000 | 46,000 | | | 12,000 | 13,666,000 |
| Gard | 351,000 | 134,000 | 75,000 | 6,000 | 703 000 | 1,041,000 | 10 | 81,000 | 18,213,000 |
| Garonne, Upper | 1,197,000 | 47,000 | 76,000 | 76,000 | 550,000 | 467,000 | 14 | 50,000 | 18,035,000 |
| Gers | 1,011,000 | 115,000 | 115,000 | 81,000 | 190,000 | 1,094,000 | 9 | 11,000 | 10,556,000 |
| Gironde | 415,000 | 333,000 | 46,000 | 89,000 | 438,000 | 2,565,000 | 19 | 90,000 | 18,130,000 |
| Herault | 504,000 | 87,000 | 73,000 | 7,000 | 900,000 | 1,713,000 | 10 | 70,000 | 11,660,000 |
| Ile and Vilaine | 619,000 | 450,000 | 638,000 | 164,000 | 88,000 | 2,000 | 12 | 20.00 | 18,451,000 |
| Indre | 457,000 | 265,000 | 375,000 | 102,000 | 816,000 | 282,000 | 13 | 102,000 | 5,433,000 |
| Indre and Loire | 737,000 | 315,000 | 243,000 | 63,000 | 226 000 | 665,000 | 16 | 73,000 | 16,176,000 |
| Isere | 737,000 | 1,025,000 | 210,000 | 113,000 | 269,000 | 153,000 | 21 | 133,000 | 32,334,000 |
| Jura | 439,000 | 117,000 | 142,000 | 113,000 | 84,000 | 308,000 | 17 | 138,000 | 23,474,000 |
| Landes | 256,000 | 254,000 | 16,000 | 58,000 | 236,000 | 419,009 | 12 | 125,000 | 16.285 000 |
| Loir and Cher | 534,000 | 279,000 | 569,000 | 69,000 | 664,000 | 647,000 | 12 | 66,000 | 16,337,000 |
| Loire | 157,000 | 33,000 | 29,000 | 72,000 | 144,000 | 276,000 | 19 | 36,000 | 11,269,000 |
| Loire, Upper | 220,000 | 630,000 | 108,000 | 50,000 | 339,000 | 88,000 | 14 | 23,000 | 15,786,000 |
| —— Lower | 597,000 | 267,000 | 88,000 | 133,000 | 259,000 | 710,000 | 10 | 37,000 | 15,959,000 |
| Loiret | 612,000 | 227,000 | 853,000 | 72,000 | 533,000 | 693,000 | 16 | 95,000 | 8,743,000 |
| Lot | 500,000 | 159,000 | 40,000 | 54,000 | 482,000 | 240,000 | 17 | 25,000 | 7,936,000 |
| Lot and Garonne | 885,000 | 218,000 | 31,000 | 58,000 | 125,000 | 401,000 | 21 | 25,000 | 17,689,000 |
| Lozere | 57,000 | 35,000 | 16,000 | 33,000 | 721,000 | 14,000 | 18 | 21,000 | 5,578,000 |
| Maine and Loire | 810,000 | 1,125,000 | 144,000 | 161,000 | 317,000 | 493,000 | 16 | 43,000 | 32,426,000 |
| Manche | 977,000 | 122,000 | 184,000 | 150,000 | 390,000 | | | 16,000 | 37,650,000 |
| Marne | 780,000 | 1,118,000 | 864,000 | 63,000 | 336,000 | 422,000 | 26 | 81,000 | 8,991,000 |
| ——— Upper | 535,000 | 124,000 | 685,000 | 81,000 | 159,000 | 509,000 | 14 | 223,000 | 12,626,000 |
| Mayenne | 480,000 | 330,000 | 446,000 | 129,000 | 172,000 | | | 26,000 | 19,414,000 |
| Meurthe | 1,100,000 | 71,000 | 1,094,000 | 75,000 | 136,000 | 688,000 | 13 | 218,000 | 13,151,000 |
| Meuse | 709,000 | 32,000 | 453,000 | | | 546,000 | 16 | 180,000 | 10,393,000 |
| Morbihan | 511,000 | 590 000 | 284,000 | 174,000 | 68,000 | | | 18,000 | 16,631,000 |
| Moselle | 850,000 | 310,000 | 500,000 | 76,000 | 165,000 | 260,000 | 17 | 132,000 | 21,776,000 |
| Nievre | 294,000 | 231,000 | 230,000 | 99,000 | 97,000 | 33,000 | 20 | 182,000 | 10,289,000 |
| Nord | 1,536,000 | 501,000 | 1,178,000 | 172,000 | 744,000 | | | 57,000 | 32,645,000 |
| Oise | 1,217,000 | 756,000 | 1,147,000 | 74,000 | 932,000 | 85,000 | 36 | 88,000 | 26,984,000 |
| Orne | 549,000 | 152,000 | 1,497,000 | 101,000 | 452,000 | | | 59,000 | 20,758,000 |
| Pas de Calais | 2,019,000 | 307,000 | 136,000 | 146,000 | 662,000 | | | 46,000 | 36,117,000 |
| Puy de Dome | 625,000 | 1,022,000 | 59,000 | 104,000 | 846,000 | 310,000 | 22 | 55,000 | 21,665,000 |
| Pyrenees, Lower | 305,000 | 17,000 | 82,000 | 102,000 | 486,000 | 159,000 | 17 | 112,000 | 14,729,000 |
| ——— Upper | 122,000 | 88,000 | 66,000 | 49,000 | 348,000 | 278,000 | 11 | 68,000 | 9,831,000 |
| ——— Eastern | 120,000 | 120,000 | 651,000 | 15,000 | 648,000 | 70,000 | 16 | 49,000 | 8,587,000 |
| Rhine, Lower | 602,000 | 155,000 | 35,000 | 107,000 | 86,000 | 464,000 | 18 | 156,000 | 16,142,000 |
| —— Upper | 500,000 | 109,000 | 297,000 | 49,000 | 182,000 | 347,000 | 14 | 159,000 | 9,720,000 |
| Rhone | 160,000 | 217,000 | 421,000 | 44,000 | 93,000 | 458,000 | 16 | | 10,021,000 |
| Saone, Upper | 593,000 | 194,000 | 178,000 | 93,000 | 121,000 | 78,000 | 20 | 150,000 | 19,137,000 |
| Saone and Loire | 800,000 | 597,000 | 62,000 | 113,000 | 76,000 | 408,000 | 19 | 131,000 | 23,784,000 |
| Sarthe | 487,000 | 377,000 | 300,000 | 108,000 | 193,000 | 148,000 | 15 | 58,000 | 18,770,000 |
| Seine | 88,000 | 79,000 | 189,000 | 12,000 | 68,000 | | | 4,000 | 65,001,000 |
| —— Lower | 1,491,000 | 189,000 | 84,000 | 60,000 | 640,000 | | | 84,000 | 34,290,000 |
| Seine and Marne | 1,361,000 | 244,000 | 243,000 | 78,000 | 1,196,000 | 557,000 | 5 | 73,009 | 27.388,000 |
| Seine and Oise | 1,326,000 | 335,000 | 264,000 | 117,000 | 1,082,000 | 849,000 | 17 | 74,000 | 32,242,000 |
| Sevres, Two | 329,000 | 373,000 | 60,000 | 63,000 | 390,000 | 264,000 | 12 | 39,000 | 12,741,000 |
| Somme | 882.000 | 1,367,000 | 60,000 | 85,000 | 778,000 | 600 | 20 | 55,000 | 28,947,000 |
| Tarn | 840,000 | 650,000 | 1,039,000 | 50,000 | 634,000 | 433,000 | 12 | 42,000 | 12,343,000 |
| Tarn and Garonne | 720,000 | 844,000 | 728,000 | 39,000 | 351,000 | 264,000 | 8 | 11,000 | 10,845,000 |
| Var | 438,000 | 13,000 | 28,000 | 11,000 | 573,000 | 693,000 | 11 | 118,000 | 21.823,000 |
| Vaucluse | 279,000 | 130,000 | 23,000 | 4,000 | 438,000 | 306,000 | 18 | 57,000 | 10.972,000 |
| Vendee | 563,000 | 379,000 | 309,000 | 104,000 | 226,000 | 336,000 | 10 | 19,000 | 10,868,000 |
| Vienne | 517,000 | 297,000 | 72,000 | 42,000 | 381,000 | 435,000 | 11 | 57.000 | 8,630,000 |
| —— Upper | 76,000 | 565,000 | 766,000 | 94,000 | 232,000 | 21,000 | 17 | 22,000 | 8,577,000 |
| Vosges | 507,000 | 168,000 | 1,181,000 | 106,000 | 45,000 | 101,000 | 18 | 216,000 | 7,802,000 |
| Yonne | 401,000 | 439,000 | 613,000 | 57,000 | 174,000 | 907,000 | 26 | 158,000 | 26,444,000 |

The Isle of France, now divided into several departments, claims priority of notice as containing the capital. It is not, strictly speaking, an island; but being situated near the junction of the Oise, the Marne, the Aisne, and the Seine, is intersected by very numerous river channels. It is in general level, fertile, and highly cultivated; and beneath the surface are quarries of gypsum so copious, that the substance is commonly designated "plaster of Paris."

Paris, the capital of France, has also made pretensions to be considered as the general capital of the civilized world. London can, in fact, alone dispute its claim, being more extensive, more wealthy, and the seat of a much more extended commerce; yet the central situation of Paris, the peculiar attractions rendering it the crowded resort of strangers, and its brilliant and polished society, especially under the old monarchy, gave to this city a gayer aspect, and rendered it a more conspicuous object in the eyes of Europe. Paris is not only less populous than London, but in proportion to its population it covers less ground. It forms on both banks of the Seine an ellipse of about four miles in length and three in breadth. The principal streets are long, narrow, bordered by high houses, which, like those of Edinburgh, are each occupied by several families. The streets of shops are further encumbered by the exhibition of the merchandise in front of the doors, a practice only tolerated in the most obscure districts of British cities. Paris thus presents generally a more gloomy and confused aspect than London; nor has it any structure which can match the grandeur of St. Paul's, or perhaps the beauty of Westminster Abbey; yet some of its quarters contain long ranges of superb and stately edifices, which London cannot rival. The palaces of Paris, in particular, far excel those of the rival metropolis. The most distinguished is the Louvre, finished with the utmost splendour in the style that distinguished the age of Louis XIV. Its front, 525 feet long, is a model of symmetry, the effect of which is only injured by the want of space before it. The Louvre is not now occupied as a palace, but as a grand depôt of the objects of taste and art. The gallery, which is more than a quarter of a mile long, and the walls of which are entirely crowded with paintings that are still fine, forms a magnificent *coup d'œil.* The hall of statues is still adorned with some of the finest specimens of ancient sculpture. The Tuileries, which is the present royal residence, was begun at an earlier period than the Louvre, and carried on at successive times; whence it exhibits varied and sometimes discordant features, but is on the whole a noble and venerable edifice, surrounded with fine gardens and avenues. The palace of the Luxembourg (*fig.* 280.), on the south of Paris, and the Palais Bourbon on the west, are edifices of great taste and beauty. The former, now stripped of the famous series of paintings by Rubens, which has been transferred to the Louvre gallery, affords in one part a place of assembly for the Chamber of Peers, and in another apartments for the exhibition of paintings by living artists; while the Palais Bourbon is in part occupied by the Chamber of Deputies. The Palais Royal (*fig.* 281.) is no longer exclusively a palace, but is in part leased out to sundry persons, for purposes partly of business, but much more of pleasure: it is filled with shops, coffee-houses, taverns, gaming-tables, and every form of gaiety and dissipation which can find acceptance in such a city. Notre Dame, the ancient cathedral of Paris, is somewhat heavy and massive, but the interior is richly decorated. The modern church of St. Geneviève, called during the Revolution the Pantheon, was highly extolled during its erection as destined to eclipse both St. Peter's and St. Paul's; and such was the expectation entertained in France, till, the scaffolding being removed and the front thrown open, its inferiority became apparent: however, it is still an edifice of a high class (*fig.* 282.) St. Sulpice is also a modern structure. Paris has no fine streets, nor any of those ample squares which are so great an ornament of London. It boasts, however, of its *places*, which, without having the regular form or dimensions of a square, command admiration by the ranges of noble buildings that surround them. In particular, the *Place Louis Quinze* standing in a central situation among the palaces, presents one of the most brilliant points of view to be found in any city. This capital possesses also great advantages in

280

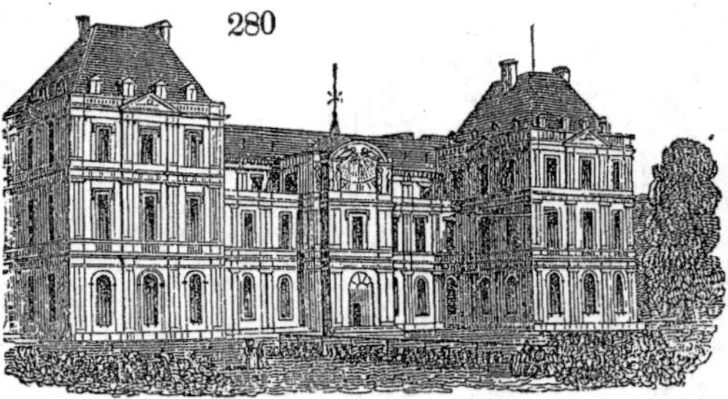

The Luxembourg.

281

Palais Royal.

282

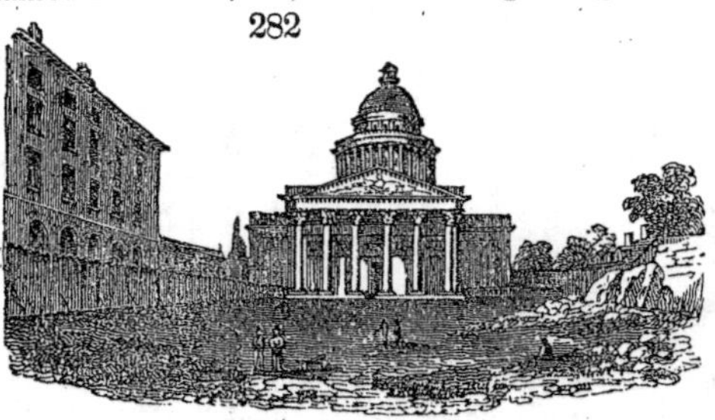

Church of St. Genevieve.

the wide ornamented open spaces which lie in the very heart of the city. The Boulevards, the ancient rampart of Paris, when it was circumscribed within a much narrower compass, are now converted into a walk adorned with rows of trees, and filled with numerous exhibitors and venders of every thing that can conduce to public amusement. The gardens of the Tuileries, and the embellished spot called the *Champs Elysées*, are also open to the public.

The statistics of Paris have been carefully illustrated in a series of interesting works by the Count de Chabrol. The population, in 1821, amounted to 713,966, but has now risen to 890,431. The births, in the three years ended 1821, averaged 24,700; the deaths 22,680; leaving thus 2000 as the annual excess of births. A third of all the births were illegitimate, and of these only a third were acknowledged by the parents. The still-born children were averaged 1365. The average of marriages in the three years was about 6000. In the three years 732 died of small-pox, and only one child out of twenty-five was vaccinated. The violent deaths averaged 350, half of whom were married persons, and the most common cause was domestic chagrin. Drowning was the most frequent mode: 170 persons were drowned annually by accident. The consumption of Paris consisted, in 1823, of 76,689 oxen; 8142 cows; 74,759 calves; 361,946 sheep. The taxes paid in Paris amount to 110,000,000 francs. House-rent amounts to 80,000,000 francs. The number of houses, in 1821, was 27,000, with an average of thirty-four doors and windows in each. The loans made on pledges by the charitable establishment called the *Mont de Piété* amount to 19,500,000 francs, upon 1,000,000 articles, of which 14,500,000 are redeemed. There are fourteen hospitals for the sick, and eight *hospices* for the infirm. The former received annually 42,500, of whom about 40,000 went out cured; the latter 18,500. The annual expense is about 7,000,000 francs. There is besides an office of charity in each of the twelve *arrondissemens*, the aids of which are administered by "sisters of charity," who divide the poor among themselves, make regular lists of them, and pay frequent visits. They make an annual collection in their district, the produce of which is transmitted to the office. The annual distributions made by the offices of charity amount to 1,250,000 francs in money; 747,000 quartern loaves; 270,000 lbs. meat; 19,000 ells of cloth, &c. The manufactures of Paris are considerable. The principal are of works in gold and silver, which employ 7000 or 8000 workmen, and yield a value, according to M. Dupin, above 125,000,000 francs. There are manufactured also, by 2000 workmen, 80,000 gold and 40,000 silver watches, with 15,000 clocks, which may be worth 19,000,000 francs. Sugar refinery is also supposed to produce 20,000,000 lbs., worth 32,000,000 francs. Eighty printing-offices employ 600 presses and 3000 workmen, and use annually 280,000 reams of paper; supposed value 8,750,000 francs. Of the various articles above enumerated, there are exported to the value of nearly 50,000,000 francs. Paris is visited by 12,000 or 13,000 boats, of which 1000 are from the lower Seine, and the rest from the upper. Twenty are steam-boats. The city has 1000 boats of its own.

The environs of Paris are not covered with those numerous villas and country residences which have been constructed to gratify the rural taste of the citizens of London. Immediately beyond the gates they present a flat open corn country. They are chiefly marked by the royal palaces; superb fabrics, the works of successive kings, and on which millions have been expended. The most elaborate and most splendid is Versailles (*fig.* 283.). It was

283

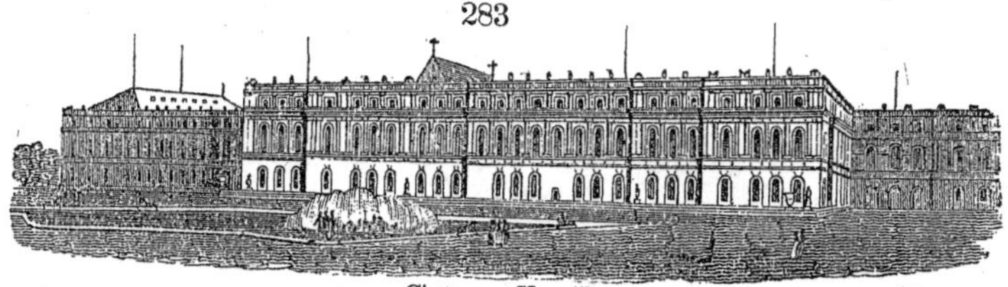

Chateau at Versailles.

begun by Louis XIII. who found it little more than a village; but its chief ornaments are due to Louis XIV., who, during twelve years, expended immense sums in surrounding it with every kind of magnificence. The front is highly elegant, built of polished stone, and approached by three great avenues. The interior consists of spacious apartments embellished in the most costly manner, and many parts of them, and of the staircases, are covered with frescoes executed by eminent French painters. The interior and the gardens are filled with crowds of statues, partly antique and partly the work of French sculptors. Water was at first deficient; but it has been conveyed in such abundance as to be lavished in fanciful and fantastic forms,—fountains, jets d'eau, cascades, with which Versailles is more profusely embellished than any other royal residence. The two palaces, called the Great and Little Trianon, are in the vicinity, and are celebrated, particularly the last, for gardens laid out in the English style. The long residence of the court at Versailles assembled round it a splendid city formed by the courtiers and great nobles, who considered it necessary to have at least a mansion there. Since the tragic scenes of October, 1789, the palace has never been inhabited; though the Bourbons, after their return, placed it in repair. Hence the city has declined in population, and the late mansions of the nobles are in a great measure occupied by English residents. St. Cloud, four or five miles distant from Paris, is particularly admired for its gardens and extensive woods, an excursion to which forms a popular amusement, especially on festival days. It was the favourite residence of Napoleon, whose court was thence called the cabinet of St. Cloud. Fontainebleau is the hunting-seat of the monarchy, being surrounded by a forest of nearly 30,000 acres. The palace, built by successive monarchs, from Francis I. to Louis XV., is chiefly noted for its long and numerous galleries. Among the few towns in this country, Meaux is distinguished not only by the beautiful choir of its cathedral, but by having been the see of the celebrated Bossuet, whose tomb it contains. Melun is a considerable, but ill-built and gloomy, old town.

The northern departments, comprising the provinces of French Flanders, Picardy, and Normandy, compose together an extensive plain, the richest, most flourishing, and most highly cultivated in the kingdom. The farms, though of various size, are generally larger than in the rest of France; the improved English processes are gaining ground, and the introduction of artificial grasses has in a great measure supplanted the routine of wheat, oats, and fallow. This region is also the chief seat of manufactures. These provinces have produced many men of distinguished talent, and knowledge is very generally diffused in them. The Flemings retain their national character, distinct from that of the French; heavy, phlegmatic, industrious, addicted to pretty close drinking and long rustic festivals. The Norman still partakes the adventurous spirit of his forefathers; he loves expeditions and journeys, readily engages in any enterprise, and eagerly pursues it.

The cities throughout all this part of France are large and flourishing. Those of French Flanders, or the *Nord*, rank among the strongest fortresses in Europe, and are the bulwarks of the monarchy. Lille perhaps holds among these the very first place, being considered the master-piece of Vauban. It was reduced by Marlborough only after a long blockade, and is considered in any other way almost impregnable. It is also well and regularly built, and the *Rue Royale* is a very splendid street. Lille has also a very considerable variety both of manufacturing and commercial industry, with institutions both for literature and the arts. Douay is an ancient and strong town on the Scarpe, and enjoys some celebrity as a seat of rather antiquated and scholastic learning. Its university consists of three colleges, now united, one of which is called the English college, and is resorted to from all the three kingdoms as a place of Catholic education. Cambrai is a very ancient and celebrated city, the capital of the Nervii in Cæsar's time, and afterwards of the kingdom of the Franks. Here was concluded, in 1597, the league of Cambrai, which caused the downfall of Venice; and it was the scene of other important diplomatic transactions; but perhaps the name is best known from its having formed the archiepiscopal see of Fénélon. It ranks still as a fortress of the first class, and was one of those held by the army of occupation, after the peace of Paris, in 1815. Valenciennes is another ancient bulwark of the kingdom, which yielded to the allies in 1793, after a long siege; but they did not derive any advantage from their success. It has some fine manufactures of lace, gauze, and cambric.

284

Amiens Cathedral.

In Picardy and the part of the Isle of France bordering on it, there are several large and flourishing cities. Amiens has long been celebrated for its manufacture of coarse woollens, as serges, plush, velvets for furniture, and carpets; also coarse linens. Here was concluded the peace of 1801, between Britain and France. Its cathedral (*fig.* 284.) is one of the most spacious and most highly ornamented in France or in Europe. Abbeville is celebrated as one of the few seats of the manufacture of very fine woollen cloth, which surpasses even the English; it deals most extensively in sailcloth, sheeting, and other coarse fabrics from hemp and flax. St. Quentin, the scene of the great victory of Philip II., enjoys a more humble and useful distinction as one of the most thriving manufacturing places of France. Its manufactures consist in lawns, cambrics, and still more of late in the spinning and weaving of cotton; all which employ in the town and neighbourhood upwards of 50,000 persons. The citizens of St. Quentin display an enterprise and an activity in pushing every new and promising branch of industry, which are not usual in France. A canal is here cut from the Oise to that of Douay, remarkable for its extensive tunnels. Laon is an ancient town, with a stately cathedral. Soissons is distinguished in French history, and its bishop had, second to that of

Rheims, the right of crowning the king of France. It does not now present any striking features. Beauvais is thriving and industrious.

The ports of Picardy and French Flanders are also very deserving of notice. Dunkirk, being the only one which opens into the North Sea, was always considered of great importance. Louis XIV. having definitively obtained this place in 1662, made it one of the strongest harbours in Europe. It soon became so annoying to British trade, that advantage was taken of the triumphs of the war of succession, to require, at the treaty of Utrecht, its entire demolition. By canals and other means, the French contrived always to replace it in an effective state; but by successive treaties, the demolition of the fortifications on the side of the sea was again and again stipulated, till the circumstances of the peace of 1783 obliged England to cease from exacting it. From that time Dunkirk became the main centre of the privateering system. It has also a considerable share of fishery and of the Baltic trade. A memorable era in its history was its siege by the British in 1793. They were compelled abruptly to raise it, and this formed the commencement of a long series of reverses sustained by the allied arms. Dunkirk has a good harbour in the centre of the city, entered by a canal of a mile and a half; it is rather well built, but for want of springs the inhabitants are obliged to use rain-water. The neighbouring territory is low and marshy, only preserved from the inundation of the sea by a ridge of downs, and only cultivated by means of numerous draining canals. Calais is well known as the point of communication with England, which so long held it as the key of France, even after her aims at the entire conquest of that monarchy had ceased. At present, it is chiefly supported by the packet intercourse, its indifferent harbour (*fig.* 285.) unfitting it for any commerce on a great scale. Calais is in a very flat country, intersected by canals, by which it might be even inundated. Boulogne has more maritime importance; though its port, choked with sand, will no longer receive vessels of any size, unless at high tide. It has lost altogether the forced consequence given to it by the construction of the grand flotilla, destined to subdue the British empire, but now abandoned to rot. Its proximity, however, to the coast has rendered it a great resort of English families, who inhabit it to the amount of several thousands. The fishery of herring, mackerel, &c. varies in value from 1,000,000 to 2,000,000 francs.

285

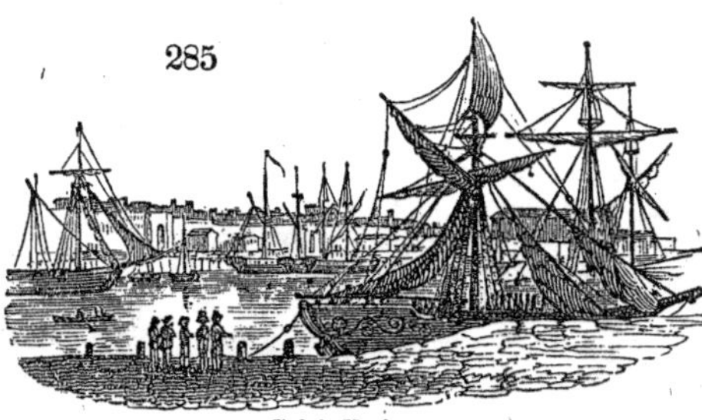

Calais Harbour.

The cities of Normandy are larger and more important than those already described. Rouen is one of the noblest in France. Its manufactures are, perhaps, the most enterprising and industrious in the kingdom, and from their vicinity to England have had peculiar facilities in borrowing her processes. The main staple is cotton-spinning and weaving, which are supposed to occupy two-thirds of the 55,000 workmen, and so to constitute the same proportion of the two millions sterling of manufactured goods annually produced. The cathedral (*fig.* 286.), commenced by William the Conqueror, was considered one of the finest specimens of ecclesiastical architecture in France, till the late disaster, which overthrew a great part of it. The streets are excessively narrow and dirty, though those adjoining to the Seine are agreeable. That river was long crossed only by a pontoon, composed of nineteen large barges, strongly moored together by iron chains; but as this had many inconveniences, a handsome stone bridge has been lately substituted. At Elbœuf, near Rouen, is a manufactory of fine cloth, almost equal to that of Louviers. Caen is a very ancient city, of great historical name, the favourite residence of William the Conqueror, and the frequent head-quarters of the English armies. It is still a considerable place, rather unusually well built for a French town, containing a handsome castle, the only remaining part of its fortifications, and some fine old churches. Its manufactures are numerous, but none of them very eminent, except that of lace, which gives employment to about 20,000 females in this place and the neighbourhood. It is of some eminence as a seat of literature, gave birth to Malherbe and Huet, and has a university of considerable reputation, which, though suppressed during the Revolution, has been restored

286

Rouen Cathedral.

in full lustre. Havre, at the mouth of the Seine, is the port of Paris, and one of the most active seats of French commerce. The custom duties, in 1824, amounted to somewhat above a million sterling, and its trade has since been greatly augmented. The chief fabric of the town and neighbourhood is that of printed cottons. It is a gloomy town, the streets narrow, and the houses often built of a framework of wood filled up with mortar. Dieppe, St. Valery, Fécamp, and Honfleur are very active stations for fishing; which is not, however, carried on with the same energy and adventure as before the Revolution. The immense efforts made to render Cherbourg a naval station of the first rank, have proved nearly abortive. The French government, after the peace of 1783, began to erect a series of cones, with the view of breaking the force of the waves; but these were overwhelmed, and retain no vestige of their original form: they lie under water, a shapeless ruin, which Bonaparte in vain attempted to make the foundation of a regular breakwater. After two millions had been spent in this undertaking, he employed other five millions in forming an interior basin and a wet dock; but all these mighty works remain unfinished.

Britany forms a peninsula distinguished by many marked features from the rest of France: its rude surface, composed in a great measure of forests, marshes, and heaths, enabled it not only to preserve a large portion of its original Celtic population, but to give shelter to fugitives from Britain, whence it received its name. After being long a separate duchy, it was united to France by the marriage of its heiress with Louis XII. It retained, however, down to the era of the Revolution, its feudal states, which assembled every two years. The Bas Breton is a Celtic dialect. The people are very numerous and very poor. The country is divided into small properties or farms, seldom exceeding twelve acres, cultivated by the manual labour of the occupants, according to antiquated and unskilful processes, to which they adhere with the most fixed determination. The peasantry reside in small huts, gloomy, dark, and damp; they are strongly attached to their homes; ignorant and superstitious, but at the same time frank, brave, hospitable, constant in their friendships, and faithful to their word. They are stubborn and hardy, and those on the coast make bold sailors.

Of the cities of Britany, Rennes, the ancient capital of the Rhedones, is the first in dignity, and was the place of meeting for the states, the discontinuance of which has diminished its importance. It is still rather a fine and handsome city, having been regularly rebuilt since a great fire in 1720; and its cathedral of St. Peter is adorned with lofty towers. There is a library of 30,000 volumes, a fine botanic garden, a museum of natural history, and extensive collections in the fine arts. It carries on some trade by the river Vilaine, which admits barges of considerable size. Vannes, the ancient capital of the Veneti, is a much smaller and poorer town, though its vicinity to the sea gives it some commerce and fishery. Morlaix and Quimper are rather good towns in the western departments: but the finest city in Britany is undoubtedly Nantes, which seems almost to belong to the rich provinces on the Loire; it is situated on a hill above that river, twenty-seven miles from its mouth, and has the advantage of delightful walks and environs. Its situation, at the mouth of the greatest river in France, is very favourable to commerce, which was carried on to a vast extent, till ruined by the disastrous influence of Napoleon's continental system; but Nantes is beginning again to rear its head. The West India trade and the cod fishery were the most extensive branches. Much ship-building is carried on for the merchant service, and vessels of 1000 tons are occasionally built. Its manufactures are various, and were formerly extensive, especially sugar refinery, cotton, woollen, and linen cloths, and earthenware. It is connected with the opposite side of the river by a noble bridge, which, uniting five different islands, extends in its entire length more than two miles. In its construction Nantes exhibits the usual faults of old cities; the most agreeable parts are the suburbs, and the islands are thickly planted with trees and houses.

Brest, on the western coast of Britany, is the chief naval station of France on the ocean, as Toulon is on the Mediterranean. It was selected for this purpose in 1631 by Cardinal Richelieu, in consideration of its harbour, which is secure from every wind, and of a spacious roadstead, affording anchorage to 500 ships of war. From Brest issued the fleet which was totally defeated, in 1792, by Lord Howe; and during the whole of the subsequent war between England and France, this port, with the navy which it contained, was held in almost constant blockade. The works of Brest are very strong, and the attempt made in 1694 to carry them by storm, was repulsed with considerable disaster. The town, though modern, having been built in haste, and with a sole view to utility, is crowded and dirty; but within the last half-century there has been built a handsome suburb, called *La Recouvrance.* Brest, besides its naval importance, carries on a considerable fishery.

There are other maritime stations of considerable magnitude in Britany. L'Orient has been made a depôt for naval stores, and strongly fortified; it derived much importance from being the almost exclusive seat of the commerce of the East India Company; but since that trade has been nearly annihilated, this port has greatly declined. St. Malo contains a race of bold and hardy mariners, actively employed in the Newfoundland and other fisheries; and who, in time of war, exercised briskly the trade of privateering. Morlaix carries on a considerable trade with the north of Europe. Quimper, though ranking above Brest, as capital of the department of Finisterre, is now only an old town of little importance.

The provinces on the Loire, in its course from east to west, comprehending Orleanais, Touraine, Anjou, to which may be added those of Maine and Perche, adjoining on the north, are the most central and perhaps the richest in the kingdom. A great part, indeed, especially of Anjou and Maine, is covered with those wide wastes, overgrown with brush-wood and heath, which occupy so much of the French soil. But the banks of the Loire around Orleans are generally considered the garden of France; they consist of unbounded plains, through which the magnificent Loire winds its stately course, and which are variegated with rich meadows, vineyards, gardens, and forests. On this theatre were acted many of the greatest events in the history of the monarchy, particularly its rise from the apparent peril of total subjection, through the inspiring influence of Joan the Maid of Orleans.

The cities of this region are celebrated and magnificent. Orleans, in former times, ranked almost as a second capital: though it exhibits the usual characters of antiquity, it is a superb and beautiful city. A very fine stone bridge of nine arches opens to the *rue royale*, spacious and handsome, which extends to the fine square in the centre; here is placed a statue of Joan, the sculpture of which is not altogether so elegant as might be desired. The cathedral is a very fine edifice, the choir of which was raised by Henry IV. From its steeple is an almost unbounded view over the magnificent plain of the Loire. Situated in the centre of France, and dividing as it were the Lower from the Upper Loire, Orleans enjoys a great transit trade. Blois is almost equal to Orleans in historical celebrity; its ancient edifices, placed on a hill above the Loire, have a most commanding appearance. The castle, on a rock overhanging the river, is an immense and lofty pile, full of windows of all shapes and sizes, balconies, galleries, buttresses, and "a strange incongruous assemblage of buildings destined for ornament in peace and defence in war." All the parts are little; but the whole is so vast as to be almost sublime. In this edifice the states-general once assembled. The glory of Blois has now entirely passed away: its streets are narrow, gloomy, and dismally dirty. Tours, equally ancient, is now much more flourishing; its plain is pre-eminent, even among the other districts on the banks of the Loire. The silk manufacture, first introduced here, has been in a great measure transferred to Lyons, but it still employs 7000 or 8000 persons. Happily for the beauty of the city, a great part of it was consumed 50 years ago, and occasion was taken to build a new street, running its whole length, of fine hewn stone, broad, and on an elegant design; it is, perhaps, the finest in France. It is connected with a bridge of 14 arches, which till of late was considered equally unrivalled; and also with a fine promenade bordered with trees. The metropolitan church was almost entirely demolished during the revolutionary excesses; only two of its lofty spires remain. The beauty and abundance of the country around Tours have attracted such numbers of English residents, that Mrs. Carey was asked on the road what great convulsion was agitating England, that her people were flying from it in such crowds. Saumur, once highly flourishing and industrious, lost two-thirds of its population by the revocation of the edict of Nantes. Angers is a large, old, steep, ill-built town, but has a considerable trade; its monuments have been dreadfully shattered during the Revolution. Le Mans, capital of Maine, on the Sarthe, is very old, but large and clean, with a spacious market-place and some considerable manufactures.

The provinces between the Loire and the Garonne, Poitou, Berri, Limousin, and the Marche, are of diversified and somewhat peculiar aspect: they present none of those boundless plains which characterise France north of the Loire; they are everywhere traversed by valleys and ridges of hills, never rising into mountains, but giving to the country a broken and variegated aspect. This, according to the nature of the soil, is sometimes rude and dreary, sometimes gay and smiling. Mr. Young ranks the Limousin as the most beautiful district in all France, such is the variety of hills, dales, streams and woods which compose its landscape. Mrs. Carey describes Marche, beyond Argenton, as singularly pastoral; the hills covered with sheep, goats, kids, and lambs, the last of which at evening come down bleating, and are received into the houses. Poitou, a part of which is so fatally celebrated under its new name of La Vendée, is a rough country, a great part of which is covered with a forest called the Bocage. All these districts are more productive of cattle than of grain, though they are cultivated by a simple peasantry with hardihood and vigour, but quite in the antique style, and with a strong antipathy to all modern improvements. In Poitou, the proprietors, being small, and residing much on their estates, excited feudal feelings and attachments, that were extinct in the rest of France; hence the formidable war which they waged single-handed in defence of the ancient régime.

The cities in this range of provinces, though ancient, are neither large, nor distinguished by much industry. Poitiers is of high antiquity, and presents some interesting Roman remains; in modern times it is distinguished by the signal victory gained here by the Black Prince. The city is of great extent, but comprises many empty spaces and gardens. Limoges is an ill-built town, with many houses of timber, roofed with tiles, and projecting eaves, but there are several handsome squares and fountains, and the public walks command a beautiful view of the Vienne flowing down a charming valley. Its cathedral, said to have been built by the English during their temporary possession of this part of France, suffered much during the revolution, and has only one tower left standing. Bourges, the ancient Biturgiæ, is very ill-built, but adorned with a fine cathedral, and distinguished for its university, and as the birth-place of Bourdaloue, and of the jesuit, Father d'Orléans. Châteauroux is gloomy, but has a large woollen manufacture.

The two departments of the Charente, watered by the fine river of that name, form a region different in character from those now described; level, and extremely fertile, though in some parts marshy and unhealthful. A great part of the produce of its rich vineyards is at Cognac converted into brandy, which bears an unrivalled reputation, though, probably, the name is applied with a fraudulent latitude to inferior liquors. The yellow tinge so generally given to brandy is the consequence of a local custom at Cognac. Saintes is ancient even as a French city. An ample theatre, an aqueduct, and a triumphal arch of white marble, attest its ancient importance as a Roman city; and the cathedral is said to belong to the age of Charlemagne. But the most conspicuous features of the Charente are Rochelle and Rochefort. The former is renowned as the grand and last bulwark of the Protestant cause; and its reduction, effected by the almost incredible efforts of Cardinal Richelieu, fixed the downfall of civil and religious liberty in France. Though no longer a haven of the first magnitude, its colonial trade, prior at least to the late war, was very considerable. The town is handsome, with broad streets, many of the houses built on arcades, with shops beneath as in Chester. Rochefort has little trade, but is one of the principal French naval stations. It has a secure harbour, with very safe and extensive docks. Being one of the few towns in France that are not much more than a century and a half old, it is built on a regular plan, with broad open streets. Angoulême, in the interior, stands on a rock in the centre of a charming valley, through which winds the silver stream of the Charente. It is a clean well-built town, having a cathedral with five cupolas, and displaying other marks of historical importance. There is a large manufacture of paper.

Guienne is a most important province, which for several ages formed an appanage of the English crown. It consists of a magnificent and highly cultivated plain, watered by the Garonne, whose broad stream here resembles an arm of the sea, and by its ample tributaries, the Tarn, the Lot, and the Dordogne. It is distinguished by various rich productions, but more especially by the wines bearing the name of claret, which, though not quite so rich and highly flavoured as some, are so light and agreeable that a greater quantity is drunk at the tables of the opulent, than of any other. M. Frank, in a late work published at Bordeaux, estimates the entire produce of claret at 250,000 tuns. The wines of the farms Laffitte and Château-Margaux are the most esteemed; but much is sold under these names which has no title to them.

Bordeaux (*fig.* 287.), near the mouth of the Garonne, is one of the grandest emporia in France, and, indeed, in Europe. Situated at the mouth of the Garonne, which here allows the largest vessels to ascend to its port, it exports all the valuable produce of this great southern plain, of which the wines are said to amount to 100,000, and brandy to 20,000 pipes annually. It is engaged also in colonial trade, and in the cod and whale fisheries. Recent travellers remark a greater display of wealth and prosperity in this than in any other of the French commercial cities. Every thing is on a grand scale, and buildings are in progress which, when finished, will leave it without a rival in France. The theatre, designed after that of Milan, is considered a model of architectural beauty. Many of the ecclesiastical structures were founded by the English. A very republican spirit is said to prevail at Bordeaux.

287

Bordeaux.

The other towns of Guienne are not of the first magnitude. Montauban embraced with ardour the Protestant cause, and had a distinguished university, which was suppressed, when the place was taken in 1629, by Louis XIII., and the fortifications razed. This seminary, however, was restored by Napoleon in 1810. Montauban is well-built, of painted brick, with wide and clean streets; and an elevated walk, which commands a most extensive view, reaching to the Pyrenees. Agen is a very dirty ill-built town, but famous for the plums raised in its vicinity. Cahors has some thriving manufactures, and its vicinity produces the *vin de Grave*, which is held in high estimation. Rhodez, on the Aveyron, is a gloomy old town, but the seat of a distinguished bishopric.

Gascony is a large province, extending to the Pyrenees, and consisting chiefly of a wide level surface, of peculiar character, called the *landes*. These are plains of sand, in some places loose and blowing, but mostly covered with pine trees, sometimes affording pasturage for sheep, and more rarely detached tracts fit for cultivation. The Gascons, long an independent people under their dukes, are a peculiar race, fiery, ardent, impetuous, and proverbially addicted to boasting; hence the term *gasconade*. Bayonne, though not very large, is one of the strongest and prettiest towns in France. Situated at the broad mouth of the Adour, it has a considerable traffic in exporting the timber of the Pyrenees and the Landes, and sends also vessels to the cod and whale fisheries. Mont de Marsan, the capital of the Landes, is but a small and poor place.

The Pyrenean departments comprehend some interesting features; Bearn, the little original principality of Henry IV., which he governed with paternal kindness; and Roussillon, which underwent several revolutions, alternately belonging to France and to Spain, before it was finally annexed to the former. Young gives a delightful view of the state of this mountain district. It is divided into a number of small properties, which are well enclosed, well cultivated, each comfortable cottage being surrounded by its garden well stocked with fruit trees; the inhabitants snugly dressed, like Highlanders, in red caps. The subdivision of property, though great, seems not to have gone so far as to lead to misery. Pau is a considerable town, in a romantic situation, and celebrated as the birth-place of Henry IV., whose cradle is still shown in the ancient palace, now converted into a prison. It makes a good deal of linen, and is noted for its excellent hams, which are exported from Bayonne. Tarbes, capital of the upper Pyrenees, and Bagnères, with its mineral hot springs, a place of crowded and fashionable resort, are delightfully situated, affording an approach to the fine valleys of the highest Pyrenees. The slopes of the neighbouring mountains are richly cultivated, and often well enclosed. Roussillon is Spanish as to language and customs; but the magnificent roads effected in defiance of natural obstacles, and the thriving industry of the people, mark the influence of a more active and enlightened government. The extensive fortifications of Perpignan render it a barrier of the kingdom. It is gloomy and ill-built, but has some manufactures.

Languedoc, the ancient Gallia Narbonensis, and afterwards the domain of the counts of Toulouse, is the pride of France in regard to climate, soil, and scenery. The air along its coasts is generally considered the most salubrious in Europe. The plains of Languedoc are celebrated; yet they are encroached upon not only by the Pyrenees on the east, but by the Cevennes, which form their constant northern boundary, and in many places reduce them to a breadth of a few miles. But on the line from Beziers by Montpelier to Nismes, the plain is of much greater breadth, and displays a luxuriant fertility scarcely rivalled in any other part even of this happy region. Every thing flourishes here, even what is most strictly denied to other provinces; not only grain and the vine, but the silk-worm and the olive.

The cities of Languedoc are not of the very first magnitude; but they are handsome and finely situated; and they present some interesting Roman monuments. Toulouse covers a great extent of ground, but it has suffered in consequence of the discontinuance of its parliament, which was one of the most important in France. The cathedral is very large, but not very beautiful; and many of the churches were destroyed during the Revolution. There is an university attended by 1500 students, and two large libraries open to the public. Castres is a well-built, industrious, large town, the birth-place of Rapin and Madame Dacier. Carcassonne still retains some of the bastions and towers of the castle on its hill; but this ancient quarter is almost deserted in favour of the neat pleasant town built beneath. Beziers is ugly and dirty, but has a handsome cathedral, and is important from its site on the canal of Languedoc. Narbonne, though celebrated as a Roman capital, presents few monuments of that people; these are said to have been taken down at the building of the walls. Montpelier enjoys an unrivalled fame for its mild and salubrious air; but late travellers have declared themselves unable to discover on what that renown is founded. It is subject to alternations of heat and cold; cloth pelisses must be worn the whole winter, and fires cannot be discontinued till May. It is, however, an agreeable residence; the public walk commands a view over the Mediterranean and the surrounding country, scarcely equalled in Europe: there is a flourishing medical school, with good practitioners, and a library of 40,000 volumes. Montpelier is not uniformly well-built; but it presents a noble Roman aqueduct a fine cathedral, and other public buildings. Nismes is one of the greatest and most flourishing cities in the south of France. The silk manufacture, as already noticed, flourishes there to a great extent. More than half the inhabitants are Protestant, who, as may be well remembered, were, on the restoration of the Bourbons, exposed to violent outrages on the part of their Catholic fellow-citizens; but these disorders were disavowed by the French court, and have ceased. The city is ill-built, ill-paved, ill laid out; but there is a fine boulevard bordered with trees; and it is particularly illustrious for the magnificence of its Roman monuments. The amphitheatre is nearly entire, and, though rather smaller than that of Verona, from its massive grandeur, and the enormous stones of which it is constructed, suggests the idea of an imperishable fabric. But the edifice called the *Maison carrée*, supposed to have been a temple of Augustus, is that which has excited the admiration of all travellers, from its extreme elegance and graceful proportions, which render it almost a perfect model of architectural beauty. It remains after so many ages quite entire, "as if savage and saint had been alike awed by its superlative beauty." Near Nismes is the Pont du Gard (*fig.* 288.), an ancient bridge, or rather aqueduct, forming one of the most remarkable monuments now extant of Roman grandeur.

288

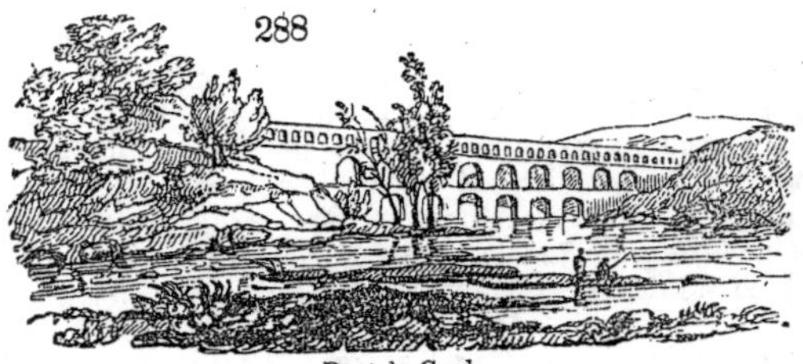

Pont du Gard.

Provence is one of the most celebrated and interesting of the French provinces, first, as the earliest seat of wealth, civilisation, and poetry; next, as containing the ecclesiastical capital, Avignon, near which is Vaucluse, the favourite residence of Petrarch; lastly, as including Toulon and Marseilles, the greatest naval and the greatest commercial city in the kingdom. The classic stream of the Durance, though it crosses the whole region from its alpine boundary to the Rhone, and too often overflows its banks, does not preserve the extensive tracts covered with rude calcareous hills from the evils of aridity. Although, therefore, the products of this province are various, and many of them fine, it does not yield corn sufficient for its own consumption, nor can it boast of extensive manufactures, but depends chiefly upon commerce.

The cities of Provence rank, in all respects, among the greatest and most interesting of the kingdom. Aix is not the largest, but is reckoned the capital, and was formerly the seat of the parliaments of Provence. Its name is contracted from that of Aquæ Sextiæ, given to it by the Romans from the copious warm baths, in whose vicinity numerous medals and inscriptions have been discovered. It is pleasant, airy, well built, in a fine plain encircled by lofty mountains. The *cours* is very beautiful, formed by two rows of trees, with hot fountains bubbling up, at which women are seen washing clothes. Greater celebrity attaches to the name of Avignon, for some time an ecclesiastical capital, and still more illustrious by association with the names of Laura and Petrarch. It is finely situated on the Rhone, with many handsome houses; but the streets are crowded and ill-paved. In the centre rises an insulated rock, separated by the river from a range of hills on the other side, and in which are the remains of the palace of the popes, now converted into barracks and prisons. The cathedral had accumulated immense wealth in silver and other offerings, of all which it was rifled at the Revolution; an event more fatal to Avignon than to any other city, except Lyons. Avignon is surrounded by a wall built only for fiscal purposes, and the Rhone is crossed by a handsome bridge built by St. Benezet in the twelfth century from the produce of alms, and which yields 50,000 francs of annual toll. It would be profane for a traveller to leave Avignon without visiting the tomb of Laura in the church of the Franciscans, and making an excursion to the beautiful fountain of Vaucluse (*fig.* 289.), the scene of inspiration to Petrarch. Arles was, in early times, one of the most important cities in the south of France; under the Romans it was the seat of the prætorian prefect; in the ninth century it was the capital of a separate kingdom, and afterwards the seat of an archbishop, and of thirteen successive councils. It is still a large city, and presents the vestiges of a Roman amphitheatre (of which the interior area is now built upon), once capable of containing 30,000 persons. Tarascon is still a flourishing place, above which rises the ancient castle of the counts of Provence, now converted into a prison. On the opposite bank of the Rhone is Beaucaire, distinguished for its great annual fair, at which are still sold goods of various descriptions to the value of about 7,500,000 francs. Digne and Carpentras are of some importance as capitals of districts.

289

Fountain of Vaucluse.

Marseilles and Toulon, the two great southern havens, form now the most important features of Provence. The commercial fame of Marseilles dates from early antiquity, when it was a Greek colony, and carried on almost all the commerce of Gaul. In modern times it has been the chief centre of the trade to the Levant; and though its prosperity suffered a total eclipse under the régime of Napoleon, it has since regained much of its former splendour. The harbour is spacious and secure, but it is somewhat narrow at the entrance, and shallow. It is bordered by extensive quays of hewn stone, with spacious warehouses; and is filled with all the shipping peculiar to the Mediterranean, among which are galleys, and beautiful pleasure-boats with silk awnings; it is crowded with all the nations of that sea, Greeks, Turks, Jews, Spaniards, Italians, and loaded with the produce of Asia and Africa. It is compared by a late writer to Liverpool: the districts round the port are a nucleus of trade and dirt; but in the exterior, the streets are handsome, airy, and well built. Among other fine public buildings is the *hôtel de ville*, with its magnificent marble staircase. The *cours* is formed by two rows of fine trees bordered by handsome houses, and the central walk is crowded like a fair. The neighbouring plain is finely cultivated, but is bounded by bold and rugged mountains that rise above the range of vegetation. Toulon, though not a seat of commerce, is the chief naval station of France on the Mediterranean. It has two ports, the old and the new: the latter alone receives ships of war, and is bordered by most extensive arsenals, in which 5000 men are constantly employed. This port can contain 200 sail of the line; and without is a very spacious and well-sheltered roadstead. It is defended by two strong forts, which, however, were occupied in 1793 by the British, who, at the end of the year, were obliged to evacuate the place. This was the first occasion on which Bonaparte's military talents became conspicuous. Toulon is a clean, pleasant town, refreshed by streams of water, running through the streets. The adjacent country is wild and romantic, and interspersed with some cultivated valleys.

290

Grande Chartreuse.

Dauphiny is a region completely alpine, the two departments of the Upper and Lower Alps occupying the greater part of its surface. The mountains are chiefly calcareous, and broken into the most picturesque, peculiar, and romantic forms. Young even considers the scenery of Dauphiny, particularly along the Isère, as surpassing that of any other part of the Alps. In one of the most awful recesses of these rocks and wilds, at a distance from all the smiling scenes of earth, St. Bruno erected the monastery of the Chartreuse (*fig*. 290.), of which Gray has drawn so sublime and imposing a picture. There are other scenes emphatically termed the wonders of Dauphiny; as the burning fountain, the grottoes of Sassenage, &c. Although this part of the kingdom cannot be considered as productive, yet great numbers of cattle and sheep are reared on its high slopes by a simple race of men resembling the mountaineers of Switzerland; and even the silk-worm is bred in its lower valleys.

The cities do not require very particular notice. Grenoble is a considerable place, not ill built, with a library of 60,000 volumes, and some other literary establishments. It took a conspicuous part in promoting the commencement of the Revolution, and was also the first town that opened its gates to Napoleon on his return from Elba. Gap is a pretty large but poor old town, in a deep hollow, amid barren mountains. Vienne is a Roman city, and presents a temple, with several other interesting remains of that people. It has also a fine modern cathedral with a very lofty spire. Valence has a military school, at which Bonaparte was educated. Near Tain is produced the celebrated wine called Hermitage.

The Lyonnais is a small territory, penetrated by branches of the Alps, in some places rough and stony, in others finely diversified with hill and dale. Its chief interest, however, centres in the great city which is its capital.

291

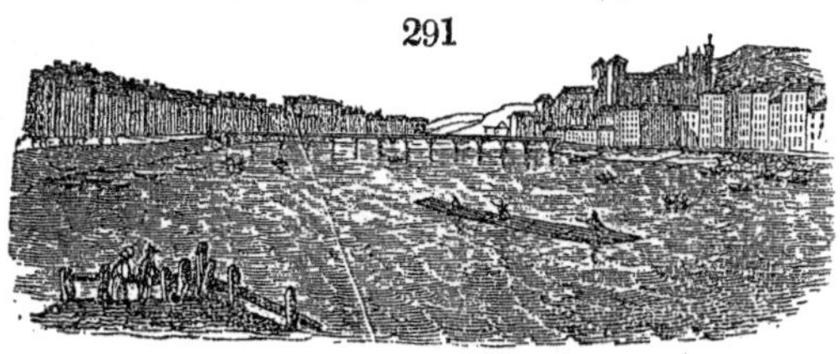

Lyons.

Lyons (*fig*. 291.) is generally considered as the second city in France, and as foremost in regard to commerce and industry. It is on the whole a noble city. The quays along the Rhone are superb; the *hôtel de ville* is held to be second only to that of Amsterdam; the cathedral is highly ornamented in the florid Gothic style; and the squares, especially the *Place de Bellecour*, with its fountains and statues, are nowhere surpassed. On the other hand, the old streets are narrow, bordered by lofty and gloomy walls, and divided by a muddy stream. To turn into them from the quays has been compared to entering subterraneous passages, watered by the sluices of Cocytus. Lyons suffered dreadfully under the sway of the jacobins, who made it a chief theatre of those atrocities that rendered them the horror of mankind. To say nothing of the massacres perpetrated under the appellation of *fusillades* and *noyades*, they studiously broke in pieces all the manufacturing machinery, while with barbarous hands they defaced all the ornaments of the city, filled up the fountains, broke the statues in pieces, and demolished the whole of the cathedral except the walls. Her citizens have made diligent efforts to restore her prosperity, and not without success; still the want of capital and the stagnation of trade are serious obstructions, and cause the evils of poverty among a large population to be severely felt. The Lyonnese have the propensities usually observed in manufacturing places: they dislike the Bourbons, and the sight of an Englishman is wormwood to them.

Auvergne, to the west of the Lyonnais, is the only mountainous and pastoral tract which France has peculiarly its own. It consists of a continuous range of mountains which have evidently been in a state of volcanic action, the country being covered with lava, and the houses built of it. From an elevated and extensive plain rises the great Puy de Dôme, nearly 5000 feet high, with about sixty attendant mountains, called in the country the giantess and her children. The country is diversified with many rugged and precipitous rocks, having castles and even towns built on them. Yet Auvergne is not a barren country. The Puys are mostly covered with herbage, and have large level plains. The natives are laborious, and rear large herds of cattle, which are almost wild; they are even said to beat off the wolf, the low of the animal attacked summoning all the rest to its assistance; but, in return, they cannot be milked unless the calf be on the other side. The people are homely, and very republican; they form themselves into a number of societies, of which the principle is a common table, attended however by the men only. In winter they take up their abode under the same roof with the cattle which occupy each end, and by their heat save fuel which is scarce. Clermont is a considerable town, perched on the top of a hill, and built of lava. It is extremely dirty, and Mr. Young compares several of its streets to channels cut in a dunghill; however, the mountain breezes purify the air. The cathedral, which was fine, was nearly destroyed during the Revolution. In the surrounding country are many curious caverns, petrifying wells, warm springs, cascades, &c. Aurillac also, Riom, and Thiers are elevated towns, commanding striking views of the rocks and cones of this remarkable chain. Towards Puy en Velay, which naturally belongs to Auvergne, the rocks become still more steep and romantic; and among the castles seated in them, Mr. Young especially distinguishes that of Polignac (*fig.* 292.), the form and site of which appears to him so striking, as to cause all the feudal ages, by a sort of magic influence, to rise before the mind. St. Michael's church, in the centre of the town of Puy itself, stands on the top of a very striking, almost precipitous rock, of tower-like form.

292

Castle of Polignac.

Burgundy and Champagne, with the small adjoining provinces of Bourbonnais and Nivernais, form a vast plain extending north of the provinces last described. Burgundy, however, is traversed by branches from the Vosges, forming hilly tracts of moderate elevation. This is the great country of wine, producing the finest in France, and, with very few exceptions, in the whole world. The surface of the wine-district is chiefly red sandstone rock, with very little soil. The vineyards are cultivated by small proprietors, who do not usually hold more than twenty or thirty arpents. It costs 500 francs to plant an arpent in vines, and 30 annually to keep it in repair. Three years elapse before it yields any wine, and six before it yields good wine. Common vineyards sell at 1500 francs an acre; and there are some that sell so high as 10,000. The precariousness of the crop, however, and the want of capital, render this branch of industry a poor employment; and the cultivators of Burgundy are the least flourishing of any in France. Few new vineyards are now laid down; though the capital invested in the old ones is a sufficient reason for keeping them up.

293

Cathedral at Rheims.

Of the chief towns, the first in dignity is Rheims, a noble and ancient city, the ecclesiastical capital of France, where the kings were crowned and anointed. The cathedral (*fig.* 293.) has been considered the most splendid specimen of Gothic architecture existing, though some of its ornaments are not in the purest taste. The Hôtel de Ville is also fine; and the streets, unlike what is usual in old towns, are broad, straight, and well built. Rheims is still the chief mart of that favourite wine called champagne, and from thence the connoisseurs of Paris take care to procure their supplies. Troyes, once celebrated for its great fairs, and noted as having given its name to the Troy weight, ranks as capital of Champagne, and is still a large and flourishing town on the Seine. Châlons sur Marne is also considerable, and, by a seemingly capricious choice, is the capital of the department of the Marne, instead of Rheims. Mezières and Sedan are strong frontier towns; the latter celebrated for its manufacture of fine woollen cloth, as well as for one of arms. Rocroy is only distinguished for the signal victory of 1643, which first established the superiority of the French arms. In Burgundy, Dijon (*fig.* 294.), with its numerous and lofty spires, presents a noble appearance to the approaching traveller; but it has lost much of its ancient importance. Its churches, now too numerous for the place in its reduced state, were dreadfully defaced and mutilated during the Revolution: one has been converted into a market for fish, another into one for corn. The streets, however, are wide and clean. Dijon has a distinguished university, and can boast of giving birth to Bossuet, Buffon, and Crébillon. Autun attracts notice by a temple and other remains, which indicate its importance as a Roman city, also by a fine modern cathedral (*fig.* 295.) Auxerre still flourishes by the excellent wine produced in its neighbourhood, and is adorned with a cathedral and several lofty spires. Châlons sur Saône is a good country town. Sens, the see of an archbishop, and formerly the seat of several councils, presents still some noble monuments in decay. Moulins, capital of the rich plain of the Bourbonnais, though not handsome, is busy and cheerful, having a considerable traffic upon the Seine. Nevers, in Nivernais, is finely situated on the Loire, but is an ill-built and dirty town.

294

Dijon.

295

Autun Cathedral.

The provinces of Lorraine, Franche-comté, and Alsace are less an integral part of France than a series of appendages obtained by conquest chiefly during the reign of Louis XIV. They remain still in many points connected with Germany. They are watered by the Meuse and the Moselle, tributaries of the Rhine; they are traversed by the chain of the Vosges, connected with the Swiss Alps and the Black Forest; their surface is rude and irregular; their wines have the same agreeable acid quality as the Rhenish. Even yet Alsace, both as to language and manners, is altogether German.

The cities are,—Nancy, capital of the dukes of Lorraine, a race of gallant and accomplished princes. It is said to be the most elegant city in France, especially the new town, built in the sixteenth century. The gates appear almost like triumphal arches; the public buildings are numerous; the *place royale* and the adjoining area are superb. The place is lighted in the English manner. Metz is a larger town, and now more important, being one of the strongest of the French fortresses. It is nearly enclosed by the Moselle and the Seille, and entered by successive drawbridges. The usual complement of its garrison is 10,000 men. Metz is celebrated for its long and triumphant defence under the Duke of Guise against the army of Charles V. It is still a flourishing town, with numerous manufactures, and contains a library of 60,000 volumes. Luneville was for some time the residence of Stanislaus, the ex-king of Poland, who considerably embellished it; and it was the scene of Bonaparte's first triumphant treaty in 1801. It is now rather a poor place, having few manufactures. Another strong fortress is Verdun, a name familiar to English ears, as the scene of the detention of their countrymen in 1803. It is well situated on the Meuse. Salins flourishes by means of the salt extracted from the brine-springs, which are found also in other parts of this territory. Besançon, in Franche-comté, was a city of the German empire till the treaty of Westphalia, when it was ceded to the Spaniards, from whom it was wrested by Louis XIV. It is a large and industrious place, particularly distinguished by a manufacture of clocks and watches, introduced towards the end of the last century, and employing about 1800 persons. It has also valuable scientific and literary establishments. Dôle is likewise a very ancient town, once the capital of Franche-comté. Vesoul and Lons le Saulnier are pretty good towns, and capitals of departments. In approaching Switzerland, the country becomes elevated, and the towns occupy picturesque sites. Ornans lies in a deep dell, skirted by green rocky hills, like Matlock. Pontarlier stands on a height having a strong castle which guards the passage into Switzerland. Nantua is placed in a nook between two enormous mountains. On crossing the Vosges appears the rich and fruitful plain of Alsace, more highly cultivated than any other part of the kingdom except French Flanders. Here Colmar, Haguenau, Saverne, Weisemberg, are agreeably situated and rather thriving towns. But by far the most important place in this part of France is Strasburg (*fig.* 296.). It was early celebrated as an imperial city, enjoying extensive privileges, and enriched by the navigation of the Rhine. Its prosperity was still farther promoted in consequence of the zeal with which, along with the rest of Alsace, it embraced the reformed doctrines. Strasburg and Alsace suffered a severe misfortune, by being, in 1689, subjected to France by Louis XIV. Yet the city retained privileges beyond any other in France, and continued to be distinguished both by wealth and intelligence. Its schools were considered second only to those of Paris, till the Revolution, when they were severely injured, and have not yet been fully restored. Strasburg, however, has still valuable institutions, both literary and economical, and is one of the greatest and most flourishing cities of France. Its ancient importance is attested by its cathedral or minster, one of the most splendid existing monuments of the Gothic. Its tower, 470 feet high, is said to be the most elevated structure in the world, with the exception of the Great Pyramid of Egypt.

296

Strasburg.

---

## CHAPTER IX.

### SPAIN.

SPAIN forms the principal part of a very extensive peninsula; the most southern, and also the most western, portion of Europe. It is only connected by an isthmus about a hundred miles broad, traversed by the Pyrenees, a chain holding the second rank among the mountains of Europe. Spain is thus almost insulated from the rest of the continent.

#### SECT. I.—*General Outline and Aspect.*

The boundaries of the Peninsula in general are, on the north, the Bay of Biscay, on the west, the Atlantic; but this coast for more than half its extent is occupied by Portugal, whose interior frontier forms to that extent the western boundary of Spain. The most southern point near Gibraltar is only separated by a narrow strait from the opposite shore of Africa. Eastward from this strait is the Mediterranean, along which the coast winds in a north-easterly direction, gradually receding from Africa, and facing at a great interval the western coast of Italy. From its termination, the Pyrenees stretch across to the Bay of Biscay, and form the lofty limit between Spain and France.

The extent of Spain, north and south, is, from Tarifa Point in the straits, in 36° N. latitude, to Cape Ortegal in Galicia, 43° 46′; about 540 English miles. From east to west, the extreme points of the peninsula are Cape Creus, in Catalonia, 3° 17′ E. longitude, and Cape La Roca, 9° 30′ W. longitude; implying twelve and three quarters degrees, which, in this latitude, amounts to about 560 miles. Thus the Peninsula forms almost a square; allowance being made for the irregularity of its outline; and, the entire extent of Portugal being taken off, Spain is reckoned to contain 183,600 square miles.

The surface of Spain is strikingly irregular. It is traversed by long and lofty ranges of mountains, having plains of vast extent between them and the sea. These mountains may be considered as part of the great range which crosses Europe from the Black Sea to the Atlantic. The Pyrenees common to France and Spain, form a long continuous line of lofty summits, the most central and elevated,* of which is Mont Perdu near the source of the Cinca, which the accurate measurements have fixed at upwards of 11,160 feet. Towards the sea, on both sides, the mountains sink into a more moderate elevation, and the barrier between the two kingdoms is less formidable. This great chain shoots lower branches into

* [The highest point of the Pyrenees is now known to be La Maladetta, 11,424 feet in height. The highest peak of the Sierra Nevada called the Cerro de Mulhacen, is still more elevated, being 11,660 feet above the sea.—AM. ED.]

Catalonia and Navarre, presenting also some striking insulated peaks, among which that of Montserrat is the most conspicuous. From the western extremity of the Pyrenees, a great chain, which has been called the Iberian, reaches almost due south, forming the boundary of the fine plains of Aragon and Valencia. All the other ranges run from east to west. The Cantabrian is nearly a continuation of the Pyrenees: it stretches across the whole north of Spain, covering the provinces of Asturias and Galicia, and leaving only a narrow and rugged plain along the sea-coast. Parallel to this, on the opposite side of a vast plain through which the Duero flows, is another transverse range, bearing in its highest points the names of Guadarrama and Somosierra, and enclosing with its rugged and romantic cliffs the elevated palaces of San Ildefonso and the Escurial. On the opposite side of the Tagus and of the plain of Madrid is another parallel chain, the Sierra of Toledo. It borders the wide elevated plain of La Mancha; on the southern boundary of which is the more celebrated chain of Sierra Morena, the lofty barrier of the rich plains of Andalusia. Beyond these rises another longitudinal chain, of a peculiarly bold and lofty character, called the Sierra Nevada, from the snow which perpetually covers many of its summits; between which and the Mediterranean only a narrow though beautiful plain intervenes. These long and lofty ranges, as observed already, are separated by very extended plains, which, in the interior, are of great elevation, and even Madrid is 2170 feet above the sea: the plains along the Mediterranean, and almost on a level with it, display a profuse fertility, and abound in all the choicest fruits of a southern climate.

The rivers of Spain form as important and celebrated a feature as its mountains. The Tagus and the Duero, rising in the Iberian chain, on the frontiers of Aragon, roll along the two grand central plains, receiving numerous though not very large tributaries from the mountains by which they are bordered. Unfortunately for Spain, they terminate in the somewhat hostile realm of Portugal, and are scarcely navigable above its frontier; so that the commercial benefits arising from them are of little importance. The Guadiana belongs to La Mancha, and on its approach to Portugal forms the boundary of the two kingdoms; but the high tract through which it flows is only distinguished for its rich pastures, and does not render its port of Ayamonte a place of any importance. Beyond the Sierra Morena, the Guadalquivir waters the plain of Andalusia, and has on its banks the noble cities of Cordova and Seville; while Cadiz, not far from its mouth, forms the chief emporium of Spain. Though its navigation is now much impeded, and practicable for large vessels only to Seville, it is the only river in Spain of much commercial importance. The Ebro, which derives from its position a greater historical celebrity than any other, rising in the Cantabrian mountains, nearly crosses the breadth of north-eastern Spain, and separates Catalonia and Aragon from the extensive regions of the interior. Its banks at present afford few materials for trade, except a large quantity of timber. The Guadalaviar and Xucar in Valencia, and the Miño in Galicia, are also rivers of some magnitude.

The mountains of Spain enclose no lakes, their waters finding a ready issue along the vast plains on which they border.

## Sect. II.—*Natural Geography.*

### Subsect. 1.—*Geology.*

The principal mountain chains in Spain differ not only in their external aspect, but also in their internal composition: they appear more as different individuals than as members of a single system. They have this in common with one another, that their nucleus consists, in whole or in part, of primitive and transition rocks; but not only the species, but also the relations of these, vary in the different chains. A great body of granite, which seldom reaches the highest points of the country, and contains subordinate beds of gneiss and other primitive rocks, ranges through the Pyrenees properly so called. It is surrounded by a predominating mass of crystalline slate and of transition rocks, among which the most abundant are clay slate and limestone. On the contrary, on the western continuation, in the Biscayan mountains, the older rocks are not widely distributed, and appear first in Galicia, at the western extremity of the northern mountain chain, where, according to Humboldt, granite, accompanied by crystalline slates, appears again, and in great extent. The principal mass of the mountain chain which separates Old from New Castile is composed of gneiss and granite. In the chain of mountains extending between the Tagus and the Guadiana, according to Link, the principal rock is granite. The long ridge of the Sierra Morena contains principally transition rocks; granite breaks out on its southern foot towards the Guadalquivir. This rock, so frequent in the Iberian peninsula, appears to be wanting in the highest southern chain. The middle mountain ridges consist of mica slate, abounding in garnets, which, in the ridges lying before them, passes into less crystalline mica slate, chlorite slate, and clay slate, which sometimes enclose beds, at times of vast magnitude, of compact limestone, marble, dolomite, and serpentine. On the south coast, newer transition slate and greywacke slate, with beds of flinty slate, lie here and there on the older slate. The basis or fundamental part of the rock of Gibraltar is of these rocks.

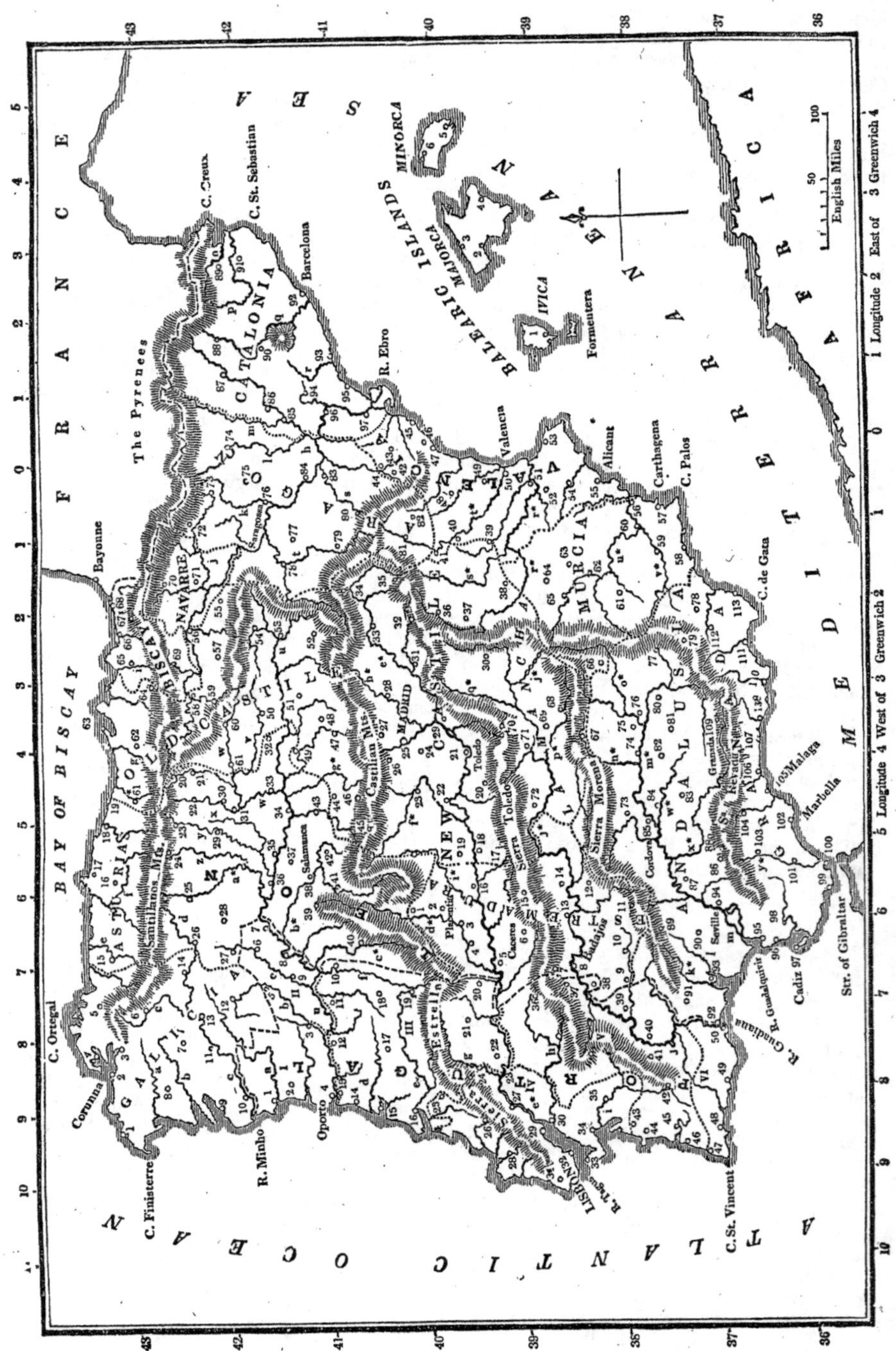
FRANCE
BAY OF BISCAY
Bayonne
The Pyrenees
C. Creux
C. St. Sebastian
Barcelona
R. Ebro
BALEARIC ISLANDS
MINORCA
MAJORCA
IVICA
Formentera
Valencia
Alicant
Carthagena
C. Palos
C. de Gata
MEDITERRANEAN SEA
AFRICA
English Miles
CATALONIA
NAVARRE
BISCAY
ASTURIAS
GALICIA
MURCIA
ANDALUSIA
Saragossa
MADRID
Toledo
Castilian Mts.
Sierra Morena
Sierra Toledo
Sierra Estrella
Salamanca
Caceres
Badajos
Cordova
Seville
Granada
Malaga
Marbella
Cadiz
Str. of Gibraltar
R. Guadalquivir
R. Guadiana
C. St. Vincent
LISBON
R. Minho
Oporto
Corunna
C. Ortegal
C. Finisterre
ATLANTIC OCEAN
Longitude 2 East of 3 Greenwich 4
Longitude 4 West of 3 Greenwich 2

The structure of the chains of mountains corresponds in general with their chief direction. Not only the alternation of the different rocks, but also the direction of the strata, are conformable with the direction of the chains: hence, in the greater part of Spain, the principal direction of the slaty rocks is from S.W. to N.E., or W.S.W. to E.N.E. But the inclination of the strata varies. In the Pyrenees, properly so called, the dip of the strata is conformable with the two acclivities of the range. In the Somosierra and Guadarrama ranges, the principal mass of gneiss dips S.E. towards the granite lying before it. In the Sierra Morena, the predominating dip of the slaty strata is towards the N.W., so that they appear to rest on the granite which breaks from under them. In the Sierra Nevada, the dip of the strata is conformable with the two acclivities of the chain. It is worthy of remark how the curvature of the south coast of Spain obeys the direction of the strata, and how the formation of the far-projecting southern point of the land also stands in connection with the direction of the strata. At the foot of the rock of Gibraltar, the slaty strata run nearly north and south with a rapid dip towards the east. The Gut of Gibraltar is therefore nearly at right angles to the direction of the strata. The rocky wall between the Mediterranean and Atlantic Seas, by this direction of the strata, must have opposed the strongest resistance to the currents. The primitive and transition rocks, in very different places, are rich in ores. The present mines are confined principally to the south-west and south-east parts of Spain. The mighty lead-glance veins of Linares occur in granite; the colossal deposit of lead-glance in the Sierra de Gador, which afforded, in the year 1828, 600,000 cwt. of lead, is distributed in masses (putzen), in a limestone which may be referred to the oldest transition rocks, and the rich mercury mines of Almaden are contained in clay slate. The secondary rocks also assist in forming the principal Spanish mountain chains, but in a different manner. They ascend to a great height on the Spanish side of the Pyrenees; even some of the highest summits are of secondary rocks. The western continuation of the Pyrenean chain consists, in the Biscayan provinces, principally of secondary rocks; and it is probable that the lofty limestone mountain ridges which separate Asturias from Leon are a continuation of the Biscayan secondary formation. On both sides of Somosierra the primitive rocks are

*References to the Map of Spain and Portugal.*

NORTH PART.

*Galicia.*
1. Camarinas
2. Corunna
3. Betanzos
4. Ferrol
5. Mera
6. Lugo
7. La Gesta
8. Santiago
9. Vigo
10. Tuy
11. Ribadavia
12. Ababides
13. Orense
14. La Rua.

*Asturias.*
15. Illano
16. Oviedo
17. Gijon
18. Rivadacella
19. Lanes.

*Leon.*
20. Aguilar de Campos
21. Herrera
22. Saldana
23. Almanza
24. Leon
25. Astorga
26. San Justo
27. La Mezquita
28. Corvijal
29. Mayorga
30. Anusco
31. Palencia
32. Villaconancia
33. Valladolid
34. Tordesillas
35. Toro
36. Zamora
37. Fuentelsauca
38. Salamanca
39. Matilla
40. Ciudad Rodrigo
41. Cespedosa
42. Penaranda
43. Medina del Campo.

*Old Castile.*
44. Arevalo
45 Bonilla
46. Espinar
47. Segovia
48 Pedraza
49. Cuella
50. Lerma
51. Fresnillo
52. Barrona
53. Almazan
54. Soria
55 Arnedo
56. Logrono
57. Najera
58. Frias
59. Brieviesca
60. Burgos
61. Palenzuela
61* Alles
62. Vargas
63. Santander
64. Orduna.

*Biscay.*
65. Bilboa
66. Deba
67. Tolosa
68. St. Sebastian
69. Vittoria.

*Navarre.*
70. Pampeluna
71. Tudela.

*Aragon.*
72. Verdun
73. Jaca
74. Ainsa
75. Huesca
76. Saragossa
77. Garinena
78. Calatayud
79. Luco
80. Montalban
81. Teruel
82. Sarrion
83. Ixar
84. Pina

*Catalonia.*
85. Lerida
86. Balaguer
87. Orgagna
88. Urgel
89. Figueras
90. Cardona
91. Gerona
92. Barcelona
93. Tarragona
94. Cervera
95. Espital
96. Flix
97. Tortosa

SOUTH PART.

*Estremadura.*
1. La Cliva
2. Placentia
3. Galistea
4. Coria
5. Alcantara
6. Caceres
7. El Tersorero
8. Badajos
9. Oliva
10. Xerez
11. Llerena
12. Majacella
13. Merida
14. Acaders
15. Truxillo
16. Almaraz.

*New Castile.*
17. Gaudalupe
18. Azutan
19. Oropesa
20. Talavera de la Reyna
21. Toledo
22. Cayocca
23. El Prado
24. Mostoles
25. Madrid
26. El Escurial
27. El Pardo
28. Guadalaxara
29. Aranjuez
30. La Mota de Belmont
31. Secadon
32. Canavara
33. Valtablado del Rio
34. Hinoiosa
35. Frias
36. Cuenca
37. La Parra
38. Yniesta
39. Requena

*Valencia.*
40. Tuejar
41. Ademuz
42. Forcali
43. Morella
44. Zurita
45. Peniscola
46. Ft. de Sal
47. Oropesa
48. Almedixar
49. Murviedro
50. Valencia
51. Alcira
52. Felipe
53. Denia
54. Xizana
55. Alicante

*Murcia.*
56. Rafat
57. Carthagena
58. Almazarron
59. Totana
60. Murcia
61. Cebegin
62. Hellin
63. Velannera
64. Chinchilla
65. Ayna
66. Chiclana

*La Mancha.*
67. S. Lorenza
68. Almagro
69. Ciudad Real
70. Madridejos
71. Malagon
72. Lehornia

*Andalusia.*
73. Demacar
74. Andujar
75. Linares
76. Baeza
77. Huescar
78. Ablox
79. Oullar
80. Jodar
81. Monasterio
82. Jaen
83. Montilla
84. Bujalance
85. Cordova
86. Ossuna
87. Carmona
88. Ecija
89. Aracena
90. Axiarcollar
91. Almendro
92. Ayamonte
93. Huelva
94. Seville
95. S. Lucar
96. Rota
97. Cadiz
98. Xerez
99. Tarifa
100. Gibraltar.

*Granada.*
101. Guocin
102. Marbella
103. Ronda
104. Antequera
105. Malaga
106. Velez Malaga
107. La Herradura
108. Motril
109. Granada
110. Agra
111. Almeria
112. Purchena
113. Mujacar.

PORTUGAL.

I. *Entre Douro e Minho.*
1. Viana
2. Braga
3. Amarante
4. Oporto.

II. *Tras os Montes.*
5. Cazabranca
6. Braganza
7. Miranda de Vita
8. Aldea
9. Mirandella.

III. *Beira.*
10. Almeida
11. Lamego
12. Alearcal
13. Villanova
14. Feira
15. Aveiro
16. Coimbra
17. Viseu
18. Trancoso
19. Guarda
20. Salvatierra
21. Castello Branco
22. Sardoal
23. Abrantes.

IV. *Estremadura.*
24. Arega
25. Porta
26. Leiria
27. Santarem
28. Obidos
29. Villafranca
30. Benevente
31. Cintra
32. Lisbon
33. Almada
34. Setubal or St. Ubes
35. Alcacerdo.

V. *Alemtejo.*
36. Portalegre
37. Elvas
38. Olivenca†
39. Povoa
40. Serpa
41. Beja
42. Ourique
43. Melides
44. S. Andre
45. Villa Nova
46. Serdao.

VI. *Algarve.*
47. Seyja
48. Lagos
49. Albofeira
50. Castro Marino.

*Rivers of Spain.*
a Tambre
b Ulla
c Minho
d Sil
e Navia
f Nalon
g Besaya
h Ebro
i Durango
j Aragon
k Gallego
l Cinca
m Ribagorzano
n Segre
o Muga
p Ter
q Llobregat
r Francoli
s Martin
t Xiloca
u Douro
v Arlanza
w Arlanzon
x Pisuerga
y Carrion
z Esla
a* Orviego
b* Tormes
c* Coa
d* Zezere
e* Tagus
f* Alberche
g* Eresma
h* Henares
i* Tietar
j* Guadiana
k* Odiel
l* Tinto
m* Guadalquivir
n* Jandula
o* Guadalimar
p* Guadix
q* Giguela
r* Xucar
s* Cobriel
t* Guadalaviar
u* Segura
v* Lorca
w* Guadajoz
x* Genil
y* Guadiaro.

*Rivers of Portugal*
a Luna
b Tamaga
c Saliar
d Vouga
e Mondego
e* Tagus
f Coa
g Zezore
h Loura
i Saldo
j Guadiana.

BALEARIC ISLANDS.

*Ivica.*
1. Ivica

*Majorca*
2. Palma
3. Soller
4. St. Lorenzo.

*Minorca*
5. Mahon
6. Ciudadela.

† Olivenca is within the Spanish limits.

skirted by those of the secondary class; but they are far from the middle and higher parts of the mountain chain. When we follow the road from Madrid to Andalusia, we meet with secondary rocks near the transition clay slate of the passes of the Sierra Morena; but we must descend very low on the south side before we meet with similar rocks. The high mountains of Jaen are formed of secondary rocks. In the northern *vorgebirge* of the Sierra Nevada, between Granada and Guadiz, there are secondary deposits, which are not, however, so considerable and extensive as to reach to the high ridges. Also in the vicinity of Malaga new secondary rocks lie on the foot of older mountain masses; and the ridges of secondary rocks extend from the hills of Ronda towards the southern extremity of Spain. The wonderful isolated rock of Gibraltar is also principally composed of new secondary rock. The distribution of the rock is not confined to the immediate vicinity of the higher mountain chains, but it extends from the one to the other, rises or falls in the intermediate spaces, and forms in this way the widely extended high table-land.

The most important of the Spanish secondary rocks are the following; viz., variegated sandstone and marl, gryphite limestone, and the white limestone or Jura limestone. The first of these exhibits the same relations as in Britain, where it is known under the name of new red sandstone and red marl. The shell limestone, which, in Germany, is enclosed between Werner's variegated sandstone and the younger marl formations, is wanting in Spain, as is also the case in England. The sandstone and marl is rich in gypsum and masses of rock salt. At Vallecas, near Madrid, and in some other places, there rests upon it, in single beds, that rare deposit consisting of *meerschaum*, with nests of siliceous minerals. It is to this formation, which occurs widely spread over the high table-lands of Old and New Castile, that these countries owe the reddish-brown colour of their soil, and the tiresome uniformity of their surface. The lias formation is widely distributed in the northern provinces of Spain. It appears to reach a considerable height on the Spanish side of the Pyrenees. In the Biscayan provinces it exhibits the same characters as the gryphite limestone of the Weser, and is so widely distributed that nearly all the older rocks are covered by it. Here it is remarkably prolific in an excellent iron ore. The immense mass of sparry iron ore, converted by decomposition into brown and red iron ores of Sommorostro, near Bilboa, and which probably forms the ironstone hills mentioned by Pliny in the 34th book of his *Natural History*, belongs to this formation. Probably also the vast beds of coal in the Asturias are subordinate to it. The white Jura limestone, which is one of the most widely distributed formations, is also of great geognostical importance in Spain. It forms, in most places, the immediate cover of the variegated sandstone and marl, and occurs in the north, and also in the south of Spain, in single ridges and great mountain masses. This formation is exhibited in its most characteristic forms in the narrow pass of Pancorbo in Old Castile, in the lacerated mountains of Jaen, and the isolated rocky wall of Gibraltar. Wherever it occurs, its presence is announced by the yellowish-brown colour of the soil with which it is covered.

Some members also of the chalk formation occur in Spain. The sandstone of the rocky ridge of the southern coast, between Cadiz and Gibraltar, and the limestone in the district of Los Barios, bring to our recollection the rocks of the Saxon Switzerland. The first agrees with the German quader-sandstein, the latter with the Saxon planer limestone, an equivalent for impure chalk.

Tertiary deposits occur in different parts of Spain. In the south, particularly near the sea-coast, there is a deposit, filled with marine organic remains, in which calcareous sand and pebbles occur, partly in a loose mass, and partly more or less firmly compacted by means of calcareous cement. Judging from the included petrifactions, among which are beds of oyster-shells, this deposit, on which Cadiz stands, and which, in some places, rises into hillocks and low hills, belongs to the upper tertiary sea-water formation. Probably the tertiary deposit mentioned by Brongniart as occurring in the neighbourhood of Barcelona belongs to the same deposit. That fresh-water limestone occurs in Spain has been sufficiently proved by the observations of Baron Férussac. The deposit very much resembles that so generally distributed in Germany, and is found in different parts of Spain, both in the interior and on the coast, and at different heights. The calcareous breccia, generally with a ferruginous basis, which occurs principally in the south-west, where it is widely distributed, belongs to the latest of the antediluvian deposits. It not only incrusts limestone rocks of different formations more or less thickly, but also fills up rents and fissures in them: thus it abounds among the calcareous rocks of Gibraltar, where it sometimes contains bones of quadrupeds no longer met with there. The formation of the breccia is ascribed to a catastrophe which affected different parts of the coast of the Mediterranean sea. As Professor Hausmann, to whom we owe the preceding details, had not an opportunity of travelling in Murcia, he was not able to confirm or reject the accounts of Spanish geologists, who maintain that it contains true volcanic rocks. The occurrence of other rocks, which are conjectured to have come from below, has been noticed in but few places. Characteristic basalt occurs in Catalonia. The porphyritic and basaltic-looking rocks extending from Cabo de Gata, and from Avila, on the north side of the Guadarrama range, are still problematical. Hypersthene rock has been found by Professor Garcia in the vicinity of Salinas de Poza, in Old Castile, in contact with Jura limestone. Professor Hausmann found, in the mountains of Jaen, near to variegated marl containing masses of gypsum, rocks of greenstone. Col. Silvertop describes tertiary deposits in Granada.

It may not be improper, from Professor Hausmann, to point out the influence of soil and climate on the other departments of nature, as also on the peculiarities and occupations of man. A glance at the whole nature of Spain discovers a threefold principal difference. The northern zone, which extends to the Ebro, differs entirely in its characters from the middle zone; and this again is completely different from the southern zone, which is bounded on the north by the Sierra Morena, and a part of the Ostrandes. The northern zone, which includes Galicia, Asturias, the Biscayan provinces, Navarre, the northern part of Aragon, and Catalonia, is a widely extended mountainous and hilly country. The snow-fields and glaciers of the Pyrenees on the one side; and on the other the north and north-west winds, have a marked influence in lowering the temperature of the atmosphere, and in increasing the supply of water. The increased humidity is favourable for vegetation, which, on the whole, very much resembles that of the south of France; and the variety of rocks containing lime, clay, and sand, and also their frequent alternations, operate beneficially on the soil. The soil everywhere invites to cultivation, and the Catalonians and Biscayans are active cultivators of the ground. The middle part of Spain, to which belongs Old and New Castile, a part of Aragon, Leon, and Estremadura, is not so favourably circumstanced. In general, we rarely meet with either beauty or variety of aspect. The extensive and lofty table-lands, destitute of trees, are dull and tiresome; their uniform and monotonous surface, formed by vast deposits of horizontally disposed secondary strata, is swept across by the wind, and burnt up by the sun's rays. Whichever way the eye turns, it meets with scarcely any thing but wretchedly cultivated cornfields and desert heaths of cistus. Seldom, in general, more in the southern than in the northern districts, plantations of olive-trees afford a meagre shelter, and vary the scenery, although in an inconsiderable degree. Nothing, certainly, has so great an influence on these properties of nature, with which many of the peculiarities and modes of life of man harmonise, than the high situation of the widely extended table-lands, and the uniformity of the rock which forms the support of the soil. It is owing principally to the horizontal stratification, and the want of water, that the great Spanish table-lands are so widely extended, and so little intersected by deep valleys. The rivers, in most cases, carry but little water in comparison with the magnitude of the land, and the number of considerable mountain chains; and it is further surprising how insignificant the waters of most of the Spanish mountain groups are, even when the qualities of the rocks favour the formation of springs. The causes of this great deficiency of water are principally the great dryness of the atmosphere, the inconsiderable cover of snow on the mountains, and its short continuance; the absence of forests, and the want of great moors on the heights, and the comparatively inconsiderable breadth of the mountain ranges. The southern and south-western part of Spain, which comprehends Andalusia, with Granada and Murcia, is very different from that just described. On the opposite side of the Sierra Morena the whole land has a more southern and foreign aspect, a breathing of that African nature, which announces itself not only by the world of plants, but also by the animal world, and man himself. The great difference of climate is produced by the southern situation, the exposure of the acclivity on the south and south-west to the African winds, and the strong reflection of the solar rays from the lofty, naked mountain walls. The mountain ranges are more closely aggregated, the valleys more deeply cut: there is no room for very extensive table-lands, and the more limited ones that occur, as those of Granada, are more amply supplied with water than those in the middle of Spain. Along with this arrangement, there is greater difference among the rocks, and also of their position. The south of Spain, therefore, possesses not only a much higher temperature, one fit for the orange and the palm, but also a more varied and a more favourable soil for cultivation. But these relations would have acted more beneficially if the air had been more humid, and moisture had been everywhere more abundant. The deficiency of moisture is the principal cause not only of the striking meagreness of phenogamous vegetation, on most of the mountain acclivities, but also of the remarkable paucity of lichens and mosses on the mountains on the coast; and in connection with this is the fact, that the weathering of the rocks, and the reforming of the original surface of the mountains, assume there a somewhat different course from what is observed in places which are moister, and provided with a more powerful vegetation.

### Subsect. 2.—*Botany.*

"Oh! Christ! it is a goodly sight to see
What Heaven hath done for this delicious land!
What fruits of fragrance blush on every tree!
What goodly prospects o'er the hills expand!
(But man would mar them with an impious hand).

"European Spain," says M. de Humboldt, "situated in latitudes under which Palm trees (*Phœnix dactylifera* and *Chamærops humilis*) grow upon the plains, presents the majestic spectacle of a chain of mountains, the tops of which shoot up into the region of everlasting snow. By a levelling survey executed with the greatest care, it has been ascertained that in the Sierra Nevada of Granada, the Pico de Veleta rises about 11,385 English feet, and the Mulhacen 11,660 English feet, above the level of the ocean. None of the mountains of the Pyrenees are of so great a height; for Mont Perdu, the loftiest of the Spanish Pyrenees is only 11,168 feet, and the highest of the French Pyrenees only 1722 fathoms. The peak of Mulhacen, in the Sierra Nevada of Granada, wants only 76 fathoms of being as high as the Peak of Teneriffe. Yet even this summit, if situated in the same latitude as the town of Mexico, would not be perpetually covered with snow: for the never-melting snows begin under the equator at 2460 fathoms; under the twentieth degree of latitude at 2350 fathoms; under the forty-fifth, at 1300 fathoms; and under the sixty-second, at 900 fathoms."

Thus circumstanced in regard to climate, and the elevation of its mountains, how greatly is it to be regretted that no country in Europe has been so little investigated in regard to its botanical productions! Enough, however, is known for our purpose, which may be collected from the different travels in, and accounts of, Spain and Portugal, and from the *Recherches sur la Distribution Géographique des Végétaux Phanérogames dans l'Ancien Monde*, already alluded to, by M. de Mirbel. This author considers the whole of this peninsula, with the exception of the northern part of Spain, which forms the shores of the Gulf of Gascony, and which belongs to the temperate zone, as entering into the transition zone. If, therefore, its vegetation has any affinity with that of France, it is only where its mountainous parts, especially the Pyrenees, resemble the mountains of France, and its warm districts are like the extreme south of France. In East Valencia and Murcia, in the south of Andalusia and the Algarves, in Western Alemtejo and South Estremadura, the rich and varied vegetation calls to mind the fertile plains of Syria. In Andalusia, frosts are unknown, and the snow, if it ever falls, melts the moment it touches the soil: so that it is not surprising that, in the cultivated parts, the Spaniards, long famous for their voyages, should have introduced many vegetables from remote parts of the world; thus giving a perfectly tropical appearance to the country.

The *Erythrina Corallodendron*, or Coral tree, with its brilliant scarlet blossoms, the *Schinus Molle*, with its gracefully pinnated foliage, and the *Phytolacca dioica*, are introduced, with many other plants, from South America. Even the bananas are common to the south of the Guadalquivir; as are also the Cayenne Pepper; and, in gardens, the Convolvulus Batatas, or Sweet Potato. Everywhere about the rural habitations of the Spanish peasantry, the Date, the Orange (*fig.* 298.), the Lemon, the Olive, the Pomegranate, the Fig

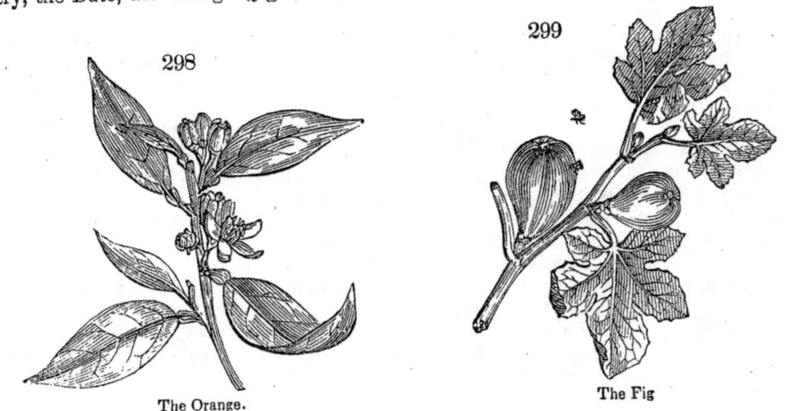
298

The Orange.

299

The Fig

(*fig.* 299.), and the Mulberry, flourish nearly as well as in the native soil. Link notices the trees growing about Lisbon; "they are chiefly," he says, "Olive and Orange trees, Cypress, Judas trees: Elms and Poplars appear too. But of Oaks, Beeches, and Lime, there are none, and very few Willows; so that one may instantly perceive how different is the character of a Lisbon view from that of Germany." The Orange is the most striking of these. for there are many plantations in quintas, where they form compact groves, and also scattered in open spots. These trees require much artificial watering, and they are propagated by seed, and afterwards by grafting upon those seedling trees. In December and January the fruit begins to turn yellow; and at the end of January and in February, before they are ripe and sweet, they are gathered for exportation. Towards the end of March and April the oranges are very good, but they are not in perfection till early in May. In July and August, they are scarce, and over-ripe. At the end of April and May, the new flowers appear, the fragrance of which extends far and wide, and at this time the quantity of glittering fruit embosomed amid the dark foliage, "like golden lamps in a green night," relieved still more by the snowy blossoms, presents an object which continually excites new admiration, though it is one of daily occurrence. One single tree frequently bears 1500 oranges, and examples are not wanting of their bearing 2000, and sometimes, though rarely, 2500. In the provinces, they sell for half a farthing apiece. Figs are exported largely from the city of Faro; they are the most important produce of the Algarve, and are brought down by the country people to the merchants' in immense quantities. They are thrown in heaps in a building prepared for the purpose, where a syrup flows from them, which is used to advantage in making brandy. They are then spread to dry in he sun, in an open situation, where they are left for a few days, in proportion to the heat of the weather; after which they are packed into small baskets made of the leaves of the Fan Palm, and exported. "Greece and the Algarves," M. Link observes, "are the only countries where caprification is practised, for in the latter country are some varieties of Figs, and those very excellent, that fall to the ground immature, unless punctured by gnats." Two ideas prevail respecting the effect of this operation; the general opinion being, that the little insect, on entering the Fig, (which is known by botanists to be a fleshy receptacle, including many, and often only barren flowers,) carries with it, from other figs that it has visited, and from which it comes loaded, the farina necessary for fertilisation: while others maintain, and among them M. Link, that the puncture caused by the insect gives a fresh stimulus and a new movement to the sap or juices of the fruit, thereby not only preventing the fall of the fruit, but rendering it sweeter and better flavoured; and it is certain that many of our common fruits, when pierced by insects, acquire the sweetest flavour. The ancients perfected the figs in the Archipelago by means of an insect, a species of Cynips (*C. Ficus*). In Algarve, besides the cultivated kind, another wild sort is grown; in which the insects abound. These trees are recalled *Fijos de tora;* and branches of them are, at the proper season, broken off, and suspended over those intended to be fertilised, when the little animals come forth, alight upon the fruits, puncture them, and aid their ripening.

Formidable fences are made of the Cactus Tuna (*fig.* 300.), and the Agave americana, or American aloe. The former is often mixed with the Pomegranate, but of itself it constitutes a hedge almost impervious to cattle. In Portuguese it is called, on account of its prickles, *Fijo do inferno:* the flowers are yellow and the fruit esculent; the latter is by no means unpalatable, and is regularly sold in Lisbon. Of the *Agave americana* we have already spoken, and shall, therefore, simply mention here, that its leaves undergo a process by which a valuable thread is extracted, known in Portugal by the name of *Filo da pita.* The largest and most perfect leaves are cut off, laid upon a board, and scraped with a square iron bar, which is held in both hands, until all the juices and pulp are pressed out; the nerves only remaining, when these are found easily separable into threads. Where pasturage is scarce, as in Algarve, the cattle eat the foliage of this plant, if cut into thin transverse slices.

300

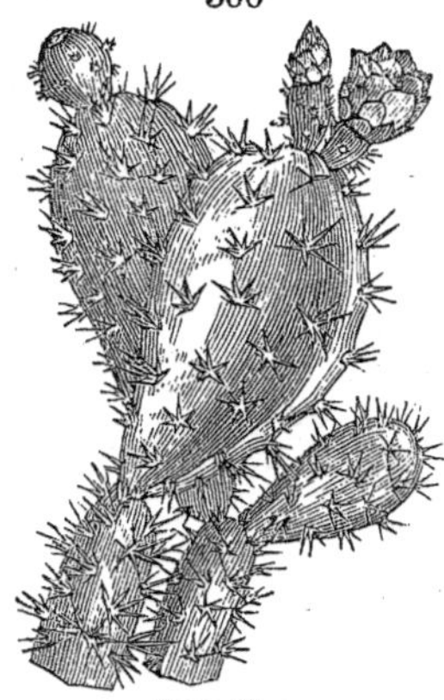

Cactus Tuna.

In La Mancha grows the Esparto grele (*Stipa tenacissima*), of which cords are made, and the foliage is sent in large quantities into Portugal for this purpose. To prevent the careless destruction of these valuable plants, penalties are inflicted on any person who ventures to gather them before the month of May, when they are in perfection.

The Carob tree (*fig.* 301.) Link reckons the most beautiful of European trees. It attains a considerable height, forming, with its large evergreen pinnated foliage, a head of considerable dimensions, and yielding a welcome shade. Among the foliage hang down the numerous long pods, which, when ripe, are used as fodder for cattle, especially the mules, and as meat for swine, though inferior to the acorns of the Evergreen Oak. Before the expulsion of the Moors, the Sugar Cane was cultivated to a considerable extent, and lately it has been re-introduced, at San Lucar, into a garden "d'acclimation," together with Coffee, Indigo, and Gum Arabic. A vast extent of country is covered by the Chamærops humilis (*Dwarf Palm* or *Palmetto*), growing in waste places. This vegetation, in part exotic, follows the coasts of the Spanish peninsula, to the east and to the west. It is diffused in all its luxury in the delicious territory of Valencia, where the agriculture of the Moors is still held in respect. With the species already named, are here cultivated the Aloë perfoliata, Yucca aloifolia, Cassia tomentosa, Melia Azedarach, many kinds of Mimosa, Annona, &c. In the environs of Alicant, the Date harvest is very abundant. This Palm there grows in large plantations,

301

Carob Tree.

and often attains the height of 120 feet. It reaches along the entire coast, to the 40th degree, and perhaps higher. The Agave abounds in the environs of Tarragona, in the 41st degree; and the Olive continues to the shore of France.

In general, the vegetation of the east of the Peninsula differs little from that of the other shores of the Mediterranean. The coasts of the Ocean, on the west, are less hot, according to M. Bory de St. Vincent, than corresponding latitudes on the east sides; so that the southern vegetation does not extend so far to the north. Be this as it may, the Date, the Lemon, the Orange, abound in Algarve and Alemtejo. The Orange grows plentifully in the environs of Oporto, in 41°; and the Olive extends to 42°. A great number of American plants, the seeds having been probably brought in ballast, are mingled, and, as it were, confounded, with indigenous species. Upon the whole, however, the vegetation may be considered as having more in common with that of the Atlantic than with the coasts of the Mediterranean. Link thus pictures the climate of Portugal, and its effects upon vegetation:—"A heat, equal to 96° of Fahrenheit, is not uncommon in this country; and, from comparative observations, it appears that the climate is warmer here than in Brazil, though the heat does not continue near so long. From Midsummer-day to the middle of September, rain is extremely uncommon, and even in the beginning of that month very scanty; the drought often continues much longer. Immediately after the first rains, follow the autumnal flowers, the Meadow Saffron (*Colchica*, two species but little known); Saffron (*Crocus sativus*); the Autumnal Snowdrop (*Leucojum autumnale*); the sweet-smelling Ranunculus bullatus, and many others. These appear in the higher lands around Cintra, where the rains are earlier than in the low parts near Lisbon. Immediately after the autumnal flowers, come the spring plants, owing to which the interval between spring and autumn is scarcely perceptible. In October the young grass springs up, and the new leaves shoot out, rendering it the pleasantest month of the year. In November and December fall heavy rains, with frequent storms. Days of perpetual silent rain are very rare, for in general it comes down in torrents. The brooks round Lisbon, which it was a little while before easy to step over, and which wholly disappear in summer, now rush like torrents down the hills. This swelling of the streams renders travelling difficult at that season, and would retard the operations of war as much in winter as the drought in summer. In January, cold, clear weather often prevails, but becomes milder in February, which is generally a very pleasant month."

The most common vegetables of the plains of Spain are the Cork tree (*fig.* 302.), the Ilex, and Kermes Oak (*fig.* 303.), the Bay tree, the Myrtle, the Philyrea media and angus-

302 Cork Tree. 303 Kermes Oak.

tifolia, Juniperus Sabina, Celtis australis, Pistacia Terebinthus and Lentiscus; Rhamnus Alaternus, and many other species of this genus; Viburnum Tinus, Osyris alba, Paliurus australis, the Strawberry tree, the common and shrubby Jessamines, the Caper plant, and a great number of Cisti (*fig.* 304.) with other shrubs, whose foliage is of an evergreen and coriaceous nature. Immense plains are clothed with Lygeum Spartum, and the running streams are bordered with Bupleurum spinosum and Nerium Oleander.

But it has been justly remarked, that no country in Europe presents a more sorrowful aspect than the interior of the Peninsula. "No man, perhaps, saving a botanist," says Link, "could travel with any pleasure in the barren tracts of Old Castile; but this pursuit can render travelling both instructive and interesting, even in these apparently sterile wastes. Where forests have existed there, they have yielded to the stroke of the axe; and the naked soil remains without any culture. Vast chains of mountains spread out in all directions, and between them are extended the Parameras, more or less elevated plains, frequently as naked as the steppes of Siberia." M. Bory estimates at from 1800 to 2000 feet the elevation of the Paramera which divides the sources of the Douro and the Ebro. In the valleys formed by these rivers and their tributary streams, a vegetation of great beauty is found, partaking of that in the more temperate climates of the north. Here are seen small fields of Maize, and even of Rye and Barley, more rarely of Wheat, surrounded by lofty Oaks, Chestnuts, and Poplars, every tree supporting a Vine, which spreads over it and not unfrequently reaches to the very summit of the highest Oaks.

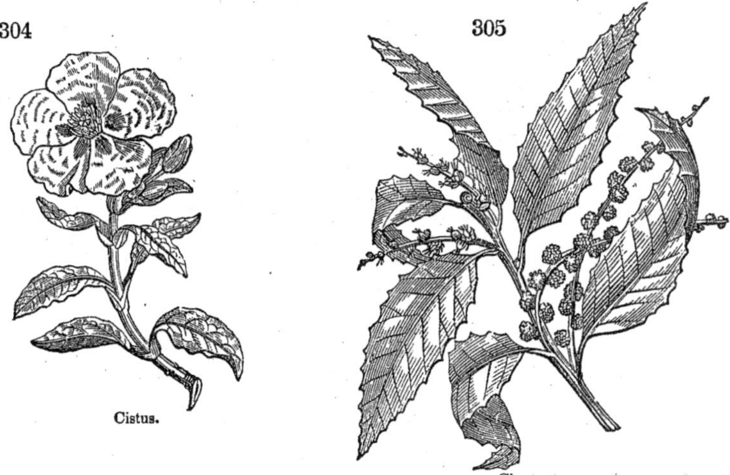

304 Cistus.

305 Chestnut.

The great mass of the forests which have escaped destruction are mostly formed of Evergreen Oaks; among which, besides the other species already enumerated, are found the Quercus Ballota, ægilopifolia, faginea, prasina, crenata, rotundifolia, humilis, &c. The latter does not exceed six inches in height. In the valleys and on the mountains also, grow Tilia europæa (*platyphyllos?*), Fagus sylvatica, Castanea vesca (*fig.* 305.), Taxus baccata, Pinus sylvestris, Fraxinus, Ornus, &c. The commonest forest tree on the plains of the temperate zone, namely the Oak (***Quercus Robur***), inhabits the southern slope of the Pyrenees. It is said that this tree occurs also in some parts of the Peninsula.

The vegetation which prevails on the lofty mountains in the interior of Spain is almost wholly unknown to us. M. Ramond has made some interesting observations on that of the Pic du Midi, one of the highest of the Pyrenees; and has compared the plants of its most elevated summit, estimated at about 10,000 feet, with that of Melville Island, as described by Mr. R. Brown. The similarity is very striking.

| SUMMIT OF THE PIC DU MIDI | | |
|---|---|---|
| *Cryptogamia.* | | |
| Fungi | 0 | |
| Lichens | 51 | |
| Hepaticæ | 1 | |
| Mosses | 6 | |
| Ferns | 4 | |
| | | — 62 |
| *Phænogamous.* | | |
| Cyperaceæ | 3 | |
| Grasses | 7 | |
| Junci | 0 | |
| Polygoneæ | 1 | |
| Plantagineæ | 1 | |
| Plumbagineæ | 1 | |
| Lysimachiæ | 4 | |
| Pedicularinæ | 3 | |
| Labiatæ | 1 | |
| Scrophularinæ | 1 | |
| Boragineæ | 1 | |
| Gentianeæ | 2 | |
| Campanulaceæ | 1 | |
| Cichoraceæ | 3 | |
| Corymbiferæ | 10 | |
| Rubiaceæ | 2 | |
| Papaveraceæ | 1 | |
| Cruciferæ | 6 | |
| Caryophylleæ | 6 | |
| Ficoideæ | 4 | |
| Saxifrageæ | 4 | |
| Rosaceæ | 4 | |
| Leguminosæ | 4 | |
| Amentaceæ | 1 | |
| | | — 71 |
| | | 133 |

| MELVILLE ISLAND. | | |
|---|---|---|
| *Cryptogamia.* | | |
| Fungi | 2 | |
| Lichens | 15 | |
| Hepaticæ | 2 | |
| Mosses | 30 | |
| Ferns | 0 | |
| | | — 49 |
| *Phænogamous.* | | |
| Cyperaceæ | 4 | |
| Grasses | 14 | |
| Junci | 2 | |
| Polygoneæ | 2 | |
| Scrophularinæ | 1 | |
| Ericeæ | 1 | |
| Campanulaceæ | 1 | |
| Cichoraceæ | 1 | |
| Corymbiferæ | 4 | |
| Ranunculaceæ | 5 | |
| Papaveraceæ | 1 | |
| Cruciferæ | 9 | |
| Caryophylleæ | 5 | |
| Saxifrageæ | 10 | |
| Rosaceæ | 4 | |
| Leguminosæ | 2 | |
| Amentaceæ | 1 | |
| | | — 67 |
| | | 116 |

Of these, eight of the Melville Islands *lichens* and one of its *mosses* are found on the summit of the Pic du Midi; five others of the lichens, and one of its two *hepaticæ*, and six of its mosses, grow on the crags of the peak, or in its immediate vicinity.

SUBSECT. 3.—*Zoology.*

The native zoology has been so little investigated, that nothing beyond a meagre list could be furnished of indigenous animals. In the mountains of Asturias the Ibex is not uncommon, and the Alpine Squirrel (*Sciurus alpinus*) is only found in the Pyrenees. In the southern parts, bordering on the African shore, a few species of warblers have recently been found, which are as yet unknown to the rest of Europe. The European Bee-eater (*fig.* 306.) frequents the vicinity of Gibraltar in large flocks during the season of migration.

306

European Bee-Eater.

Among the domesticated animals, the horse and sheep of Spain deserve particular notice, as having been long celebrated throughout Europe. The best horses are generally about four feet six or eight inches high; they have all the fire, docility, grace, and action of the beautiful Arabians of Barbary (generally called Barbs), and there can be no doubt of these noble animals having been introduced by the Moors, and crossed with the native breed: those of Andalusia, Granada, and Estremadura are the most distinguished. At Xeres are found two perfectly distinct races; the one, which possesses the fine qualities above mentioned, is still preserved in all its purity at the Chartreux. The other race is larger, stronger, less elegant, and used for common purposes. Latterly but little care has been bestowed in keeping up the more noble breed, so that fine horses are not so common in Spain as formerly.

The mule, in so mountainous a country, is particularly useful, and, with the ass, is principally used for conveying goods in the interior; the breeds of the latter are very fine, and are hardly excelled by those of Egypt. Spain is still famous for its merino race of sheep (*fig.* 307.). The flocks are kept constantly travelling during the greater part of the summer, but are carefully pent up in winter. This race, subdivided into breeds, is extended over the greater part of Spain; but those of *Cavage*, and *Negrate*, are the best. A third breed, the *Souan*, appears more hardy, and passes the winter in Estremadura, Andalusia, and New Castile: these three constitute the *Transhumante*, or travelling race, to distinguish them from the *Estantes*, or those of a somewhat inferior breed, who do not migrate. The best fleeces are those which appear almost black on their surface, caused by the dust adhering to the peculiar greasy pile; for it is invariably found that such fleeces are of the purest white beneath. The merinos, dispersed by George III. over England, have incalculably improved the native races. By great care and expense on the part of the native graziers, this valuable race has likewise been introduced in the distant regions of Australia with equal success. There is a very large breed of oxen in the country round Salamanca; but the cattle of Spain have been much neglected; the mountaineers deriving all their milk and butter from goats. The spaniel appears to be a breed of dogs originating from this country; and the Spanish pointer is considered to have a greater acuteness of scent than that of Britain.

307

Merino Sheep.

SECT. III.—*Historical Geography.*

The earliest inhabitants of Spain, like those of Gaul and Britain, were of the Celtic race, and from the river Ebro (Iberus) were called Celtiberi. The whole country was by the Greeks called Iberia, and sometimes, from its western position, Hesperia. The people, like those of the rest of Europe, were divided into a number of small tribes, hardy and warlike, who often showed a peculiar attachment to national independence, and obstinacy in its defence.

The Carthaginians were the first civilised people who occupied Spain, which, for several centuries, was considered as theirs. They founded colonies on the most advantageous points, worked its rich silver mines, and easily allured many of its brave but poor inhabitants into their mercenary armies; they were far, however, from having thoroughly subdued the Peninsula, the people of which, on the rise of the Roman power, endeavoured by its alliance to emancipate themselves from the Punic yoke. The siege and fall of Saguntum seemed to have extinguished these hopes, and to have secured the ascendency of Carthage; but the events which marked the close of the second Punic war completely humbled that proud republic, and put an end to its dominion over Spain.

The Romans, by the capture of Numantia in B. C. 134, established their supremacy over Spain, undisputed by any other nation; but the complete subjugation of its inhabitants was a long and arduous task, to which the utmost exertions of Cæsar and his lieutenants were not fully adequate. Spain, however, was at length reduced to a province, divided by Augustus into three parts:—Tarraconensis, the north and east; Bætica, the south; and Lusitania, Portugal. The Spaniards even became civilised and peaceable subjects; so that when Rome, sinking under its own weight, was unable to defend them, they could not resume their early independence, but fell a prey to the Vandals, Goths, and other barbarous hordes that poured in from the north of Europe.

The Goths, in this terrible struggle, finally prevailed; and in 418 a Gothic dynasty was fully established over Spain. These barbarous invaders appear here, as elsewhere, to have expelled or extirpated the native people, whose features and language are recognised only in some of the higher mountain districts. After a sway of three centuries, the Goths were destined to yield to a new people, coming from a remote quarter.

The Arabs, rendered invincible by fanaticism, had over-run all the north of Africa, and established a powerful kingdom in Fez. The vengeance of Count Julian invited them over, and opened the way for them; their immense host covered the plains of Andalusia; Roderick, the Gothic king, was totally defeated. The invaders then over-ran the whole kingdom, with the exception of some mountain recesses, in which a remnant of the Gothic chiefs found shelter; they even passed the Pyrenees, and seemed about to over-run all western Europe. But Charles Martel met them on the plains of Aquitaine; and, after a dreadful battle of three days, they were signally overthrown, and never again attempted to pass the Spanish frontier. Meantime Don Pelayo, and other chiefs of the Gothic race, again raised the national standard in the mountains of the Asturias: then commenced a contest of 700 years, distinguished by numerous heroic achievements and memorable events, which gave to the Spanish character that romantic and adventurous cast which it has never wholly lost. The Arabs or Moors still retained the finest provinces, and the courts of Cordova and Granada were the most splendid and polished in Europe. The Spaniards, however, under a succession of able chiefs and particularly of their great hero the Cid, gained ground: new kingdoms were successively founded; which all merging into those of Castile and Aragon, comprehended the whole of Spain, except the extreme southern kingdom of Granada.*

Spain was again formed into one great kingdom by the union of the crowns of Castile and Aragon, under Ferdinand and Isabella, in 1474, and by the final overthrow and expulsion of the Moors. From this period commences the most brilliant era of her annals. The discovery of America, the conquest of the golden regions of Mexico and Peru, and of other dominions so extensive as to make it a plausible boast that the sun never set on them, threw an almost unrivalled lustre around the Spanish crown. Under Charles V. and Philip II., Spain continued the most powerful kingdom, and her armies the most formidable, of any in Europe. The throne derived even an addition of apparent lustre from the subversion of the popular part of the government, and the conversion of a body of grandees, once the proudest in Europe, to the condition of humble vassals.

The decline of Spain, though its causes had begun to operate, did not become perceptible till after the death of Philip II. A gloomy indolence and degrading superstition now marked her councils; her armies were vanquished by the French under Condé and Turenne; she lost her place and rank in Europe. The trade with her vast colonies, fettered by absurd restrictions, became profitable only to the industrious nations which supplied its materials. The war of the succession drew notice towards this country, and called forth some displays of national energy; but the Bourbon dynasty, which it placed on the throne, soon relapsed into the characteristic indolence, and Spain became little more than a dependency of France. We know not whether to designate as an era, the train of remarkable events which have

---

* The Arabs in Spain, like the Saxons in England, established a lasting memorial of their dominion by engrafting their own language on that of the country which they subdued. Of this, the topography of the Peninsula exhibits innumerable instances. The names of rivers, mountains, towns, and places, were either totally or partially changed, by the victorious invaders; and after the expulsion of their descendants, those names were perpetuated, though with alterations in some instances as arbitrary as those which were made in the ancient topography of the country: thus, the Roman station, *Pax Augusta*, was transformed by the Arabs into *Batalio*, and afterwards by the Spaniards into *Badajoz; Cæsar Augusta*, by an abbreviation less violent, became *Saragossa;* and *Emerita Augusti* was contracted into *Merida.*

The Arabic term *Medina* (city) survives in two eminent instances among the titles of the Spanish nobility: *Medina Selim* (the city of Selim) is recognised in the dukedom of *Medina-Celi;* and the colony probably called New Sidon, is that of *Medina-Sidonia.* From the generic term *guad*, a river, and *velez* or *veled*, a landed estate or district, many names may be explained which at first view appear capricious and arbitrary:—

*Ex.* Guad-al-aviar,.......................................The white river.
Guad-al-quivir,.......................................The great river.
Guad-al-higiara, now Guadalaxara, .............................The river of rocks.

*Velez* and *Veled* are often conjoined with proper names, *Velez Malaga, Veled Vlid*, now Valladolid: thus, Navarre and Leon, their confines never having been occupied by the Arabs, were called by them *Veled Arroum*, the land of the *Romans. Gezira* was applied indifferently to an island or a peninsula; hence *Algezira. Aldea* means what is comprehended under the English term *a farm.* It is of common occurrence in itineraries, as *Aldea del Rio, Aldea Gallega, Aldeas de Fonsso.* From *cántara*, a bridge, we account for the emphatic name *Alcántara. Calánto*, a castle, enters more or less prominently into the composition of various names; as *Caláat Ayat*, the castle of Ayat, is now *Calatayud; Caláat Rabah*, the castle of Rabah, is now *Calatrava; Al Caláat*, simply the castle, is now *Alcalá. Alcazar*, a word of frequent occurrence in Spanish topography, is a fortified house or small castle; *Almeria* is an observatory. See *Description of Spain*, by Gerif Alhedris, in the translation of Don José Antonio Condé, whose *History of the Domination of the Arabs in Spain* is esteemed one of the most masterly works that have appeared in the present age.

occurred between 1808 and 1822. The Spaniards excited the admiration and astonishment of Europe by their daring defiance of the power beneath which the greatest sovereigns had been reduced to the rank of vassals. Their subsequent exploits did not altogether correspond to this beginning. Still, their resistance, considered as that of a people, was, on the whole, obstinate and glorious; it even appeared that there had been formed a body attached to popular government, and eager to redress the political grievances under which Spain laboured. Ultimately, however, the eagerness with which the majority of the nation acquiesced in the system of absolute power, re-established by foreign interference, tarnished its honour, and reduced it again to that imbecile and degraded state in which it had existed for several centuries.

### Sect. IV.—*Political Geography.*

The constitution of Spain, ever since the downfall of her liberties under Charles V., has been the most despotic of any in Europe, except Russia and Turkey. The Cortes, that powerful assembly, whose privileges were greater than those of any other European representative body, have since that period been rarely assembled, and then only partially, on occasions of mere form. The only two bodies which possess any influence, are the council of state and the council of Castile; but as these are entirely under the appointment and direction of the monarch, they form little more of a check upon absolute power, than the Turkish divan.

Two attempts to restore a representative form of government have lately been made, under circumstances which must be familiar to our readers. Unluckily, the leading or liberal party were hurried, on this occasion, into an opposite extreme; adopting the system of universal suffrage, forming themselves into one house, and allowing only a temporary veto to the monarch. This system, which excluded the nobles and clergy, the most wealthy and influential bodies, was from the first decidedly unpopular; and Ferdinand found it easy, first without, and afterwards with, foreign aid, to subvert it, and to re-establish in full plenitude the despotic sway exercised by his predecessors,

[The Cortes were convoked anew in 1834, with some modifications of their ancient organization. The body now consists of two houses; that of proceres or peers, composed in part of hereditary members, in part of members named by the king for life, and the procuradores or deputies, elected by colleges of electors, who are chosen by the principal citizens. The Cortes have extensive legislative powers, but their existence and authority have emanated from the royal will.—Am. Ed.]

The grandees and other privileged orders in Spain are distinguished for their pride beyond any others in Europe. Even Charles V. was baffled in his attempt to retrench the right of wearing the hat in the royal presence. The Spanish nobles impair their fortunes less by extravagance than those of the same rank elsewhere; and as they intermarry only with each other, the number of titles or *hats*, as they are called, continually accumulates upon single heads. The dukes of Medina-Celi, of Alba, of Infantado, of San Estevan, of Ossuna, and some others, hold possessions truly immense, covering whole provinces. They are administered, indeed, in the worst possible manner, being kept in their own hands, managed by tribes of factors or intendants, of whom some nobles keep 300; so that it is truly astonishing that they should sometimes yield $25,000 or $40,000 a year. As these grandees, however, live not on their estates, but in the cities, in secluded pomp, they have lost all their feudal influence, and the ties which united them with the greater body of the people. The *hidalgos*, claiming nobility by descent from the members of great families, are much more numerous, and form, in some provinces, a large proportion of the inhabitants. They are often reduced to great poverty; in which they display that union of pride and indolence which has been supposed characteristic of the Spaniard. Mr. White mentions a species of illustrious birth quite peculiar to this country, consisting in a pure Christian descent, without any mixture of Jewish or Moorish blood, which last is supposed to produce so deep a stain, that no time can efface it. The clergy, moreover, exercise a paramount influence over the minds particularly of the lower orders, and have been the main-spring in all the movements, good or bad, which for a long time past have taken place in the Peninsula.

The revenue of Spain, though levied with little regard to the comfort and well-being of the subject, has never risen to any great amount. Yet she is the only power which ever derived any from her colonies; as the *quinta*, or royal fifth of the mines of Mexico and Peru, after every deduction, brought home considerable treasure; but this source of wealth is now withdrawn. The other taxes were the most ruinous to industry and trade ever contrived by any government. The alcavala, or impost upon each transference of commodities from one hand to another, seems expressly destined to impose fetters upon commerce; while the royal monopolies of salt, lead, powder, tobacco, and other articles in general use, have the usual pernicious effects. Combined with those prohibitory clauses, by which Spain endeavoured without success to prevent her industrious neighbours from supplying the wants of her American colonies, they gave rise to a vast contraband, carried on in almost open defiance of government. Hence the taxation of Spain, though highly oppressive to the nation, yields very little to the crown; being in a great measure absorbed by the support of the individuals employed in its collection, who are said to amount to 16,650. Although, therefore, the entire sum taken from the people has been suspected not to fall short of 12,000,000*l.* sterling, the receipt by government in 1828 did not exceed 5,980,000*l.* The expenditure in that year was for the army, 2,650,000*l.*; navy, 400,000*l.*; marine, 1,445,000*l.*: justice, 145,000*l.*; state, 108,000*l.*; royal household, 505,000*l.* At the same time, Spain is burdened with a debt of 160,000,000*l.* sterling, of which the revenue would be wholly inadequate to defray the interest, had not more than half consisted of the *royal vales*, which do not bear any. Under the constitutional government a considerable addition of debt was incurred, which, however, Ferdinand VII. cleared off by refusing to acknowledge it; while he himself ineffectually attempted to raise a loan to any amount.

The navy, at the commencement of the late war, was at least respectable, and a formidable auxiliary to France. The fatal days of St. Vincent and Trafalgar, and the fruitless expeditions to South America, reduced it to a feeble state. In 1826 it consisted of ten ships of the line, sixteen frigates, and thirty smaller vessels.

The army of Spain, which under Charles V. and Philip was the bravest and most formidable in Europe, has for a century and a half enabled her to rank very low among military nations. It is, however, at present the best organised part of her establishment. According to the author of "A Year in Spain," it consists of 25,000 royal guards, and 55,000 troops of the line and provincial militia, which, being commanded by experienced officers, formed during a period of protracted warfare, possess a considerable degree of efficiency; and their discontent being an object of dread, every effort is made to pay them regularly. The royalist volunteers, amounting to about 300,000 men, formed a band of armed fanatics almost entirely under the command of the priests and monks, and seeking in their favour to lord it both over king and people.

## Sect. V.—*Productive Industry.*

In respect to industry and wealth, Spain, which had every opportunity within and without of becoming the foremost nation of Europe, is, in fact, the poorest and the most uncultivated. The insecurity of property, and the multiplied restraints imposed by an unenlightened government, appear to be the main causes which have paralyzed all branches of industry. The furious bigotry of its monarchs, in particular, led to the most suicidal acts against the public weal. At the commencement of the fifteenth century, the country contained a numerous population of Jews and Moors, who formed its most industrious and wealthy inhabitants, and rendered it the most flourishing kingdom in Europe. The Jews, unless in the alternative of feigned conversion, were expelled from the kingdom by Ferdinand and Isabella, the Moors by Philip III. Although it appears to be upon exaggerated estimates that Spain has ever been supposed to have previously contained 20,000,000 of people, yet it cannot be doubted that the emigration of mercantile communities, with their capital and machinery, must have struck deeply at the root of the national prosperity.

Spanish agriculture, it must be confessed, has some obstacles to struggle against. The territory, as we have had occasion to observe, is traversed in every direction by chains of rugged, and often barren, mountains. Yet these elevated provinces being the seats of comparative liberty and industry, are on the whole the best cultivated and the most populous The great extent and continuity of these chains certainly present serious difficulties to the transport of grain. When government were bringing a supply from Old Castile to the capital, it was found that 30,000 beasts of burden were necessary to carry 2000 quarters. Another great impediment to effective agriculture consists in the habit, partly oriental, partly formed during a long internal warfare, which leads the farmers to crowd into towns, and thus live often at many miles' distance from the fields which they cultivate. In many cases they merely pitch their tents during seed-time and harvest, and at other seasons pay only occasional visits. They are also very poor, destitute of capital, and oppressed by the burden of tithes and other exactions.

The grain produced in Spain is of admirable quality; the wheat of Andalusia bearing a price of ten or fifteen per cent. higher than that of any foreign wheat brought to the markets of Cadiz. But a deplorable defect appears, when it is stated that Spain, a country purely agricultural, does not grow corn for her own use, but makes a regular importation. This, however, according to Bourgoing, amounts only to 2,000,000 fanegas or 400,000 quarters; a small proportion of the entire consumption, which may be estimated at 12,000,000 of quarters. The agriculture of Spain, however, produces three valuable articles; wool, wine, and barilla.

The wool of the merino is of almost unrivalled fineness, though dearly purchased by the system upon which it is produced. Vast flocks, amounting to 20,000, 30,000, or even 60,000, belong to the grandees, convents, and dignitaries of Spain. After being pastured, during summer, on the sides of the mountains of Leon and Old Castile, they descend, in winter, chiefly to the plains of Estremadura. According to the rules of the powerful society of the *mesta*, composed of the above high members, they must pass freely, and be allowed, on payment of a very inadequate rent, to pasture upon all the unenclosed lands, which form the bulk of those in Spain. The entire number of sheep in all these wandering flocks is reckoned at 5,000,000; and there are a great number which remain stationary, and enjoy privileges nearly similar. The annual shearing takes place on a great scale, and with much celebration; and the wool is carefully sorted into three kinds, according to the part of the body from which it is taken.

The wines of Spain are produced on the fine plains of the southern provinces. The most important is the Xeres or sherry, which has come into such general use with the English nation. Mr. Jacob reckons that 40,000 pipes are produced in the plain of Xeres; of which 15,000 are exported, almost the whole to England. Around Malaga is made wine still more valued, though not in such quantity; which, when white, is called *mountain*, when red, *tent* (tinto). The northern and central provinces yield wine only of inferior value.

Barilla, the finest known species of ashes, and highly useful in glass-making, bleaching, and other processes, is procured by burning various species of saline and aromatic plants in the provinces of Murcia and Valencia, and is one of the few articles which other nations can nowhere else procure of equally good quality. Silk and oil, in the Mediterranean provinces, are only limited by the want of culture or demand.

The manufactures of Spain have been of little importance since the expulsion of the Moors. That industrious people introduced the silk manufacture; a branch entirely suited to a country where the material is produced in the greatest perfection; but it is now generally decayed, unless in Valencia, where it was supposed lately to employ 3000 people. The blades of Toledo were once famous over Europe, and the city has still a royal manufactory of swords, though of little importance. The Spanish government has devoted rather an extraordinary attention to manufactures, but unfortunately seeks to promote them by the king becoming himself the producer. He has established a great factory of broadcloth at Guadalaxara, which, having fine materials at hand, is rather thriving. Yet Spain does not supply herself with fine cloth. Other royal works are those of porcelain, at San Ildefonso; paper, in Segovia; cards and tapestry at Madrid: all rather for show than use.

Commerce, for which Spain seemed to have monopolised the most extensive materials, has long been in a state at least as low and depressed as any other branch. It has suffered severely, indeed, from the immense importance attached to it by the government, which actually crushed it to pieces in the attempt to prevent any portion from escaping. To absorb within their own circle the entire treasures of Mexico and Peru, was the first policy of the Spanish sovereigns. The gold and silver of those regions were to be brought exclusively to Spain, never to be taken out of it, and only the produce and manufactures of that country to be sent in exchange. By a sad fatality, the commerce of the colonies was carried on almost entirely by French and English merchants; nearly all the goods exported thither were foreign; and Spain, of all her neighbours, was the most destitute of the wealth accruing from this trade. These colonies, with the exception of Cuba and the Philippines, are now gone, and with them the greatness of Cadiz, which, by the absurd monopoly granted to her, became one of the principal emporia of Europe. The trade of Spain consists now in the export of wines, fruits, brandies, wool, silk raw and manufactured, lead, quicksilver, barilla, and a few other articles, which, according to a very imperfect document, issued by the Spanish government, amounted in 1826 to about 1,584,000*l*. Of this, 241,000*l*. was stated to be to the colonies. Her imports consist of sugar, cocoa, salt fish, spices, wood, rice, butter and cheese, hides, cotton wool, and almost every species of manufactured commodity. They are stated for the same year at about 3,267,000*l*., of which 724,000*l*. was from the colonies.

Internal communication is a particular in which Spain actually labours under natural disadvantages, from the obstructed navigation of its rivers, and its long and steep chains of mountains. These obstacles the government has endeavoured to surmount by vast but ill-executed projects of improvement. They had conceived the plan of a grand canal, which, passing through Asturias, Old Castile, and Aragon, might join the Mediterranean with the Bay of Biscay. Of this mighty undertaking, only two small portions exist; the canal of Aragon, running parallel to the Ebro from Saragossa, and that of Old Castile along the Pisuerga and Carrion by Placencia; but as neither of them makes any approach to the sea, their benefit is very limited. The main roads maintained by government between Madrid and the other great cities are good, and the mails well conducted; but most of the other communications are mere tracks worn by the feet of mules, which are chiefly employed in the conveyance of goods.

### SECT. VI.—*Civil and Social State.*

The population of Spain, according to a census made in 1798, amounted to 10,351,000. It was generally understood, however, that the jealousy of the people, and all the obstacles usually encountered in such undertakings, operated to a peculiar extent in diminishing the amount. The census, in 1787–8, gave only 10,268,000, of which 188,600 were churchmen; and among these, 61,000 were monks, and 32,500 nuns. There were 480,000 hidalgos; 34,000 merchants; 40,000 manufacturers; 271,000 artisans; 907,000 peasants; 960,000 day-labourers; 280,000 domestic male servants. A census was undertaken in 1826, which was not fully completed, but carried so far as to prove that the number of inhabitants must be considerably greater than the above: it is estimated by Minano at 13,732,000, by Hassel at 13,953,000.

The national character of the Spaniard is marked by striking features. The genuine Spaniard is grave, proud, adventurous, romantic, honourable, and generous. It has been insinuated that this is the Spaniard of the sixteenth century, of whom the Spaniard of the present day is only, as it were, the shadow. But though the higher ranks have certainly lost the original stamp, and become frivolous and dissipated, the body of the people, and especially the peasantry, form a very fine race. Even among the former, the late troubles brought forward signal displays of heroism, though, as too often happens in such cases, equally base examples of treachery. In the virtue and wisdom of the best Spaniards, there is apt to be something speculative and theoretical, not applicable to the practical purposes of life; a want of the wisdom of action. In prosperous circumstances they readily give way to supineness and false confidence; but in sudden and overwhelming vicissitudes, which sink the spirit of others, their latent energies are roused, and they display unexpected and surprising resources. Although assassination, which was once the reproach of Spain, is greatly diminished, yet a promptitude to fight and to shed blood, characteristic of all nations imperfectly civilized, is still prevalent. It is accompanied with a readiness to rise in tumultuary insurrections, and an unwillingness to submit to the restraints of discipline. The jealousy which was wont to dwell so deep and dark in the mind of the Spanish husband, has been superseded by a general laxity of morals. The custom is said to prevail, that every married lady should have a *cortejo* or gallant, corresponding to the Italian *cicisbeo;* and though the usage may not be so decidedly criminal as it appears to strangers, it is certainly inconsistent with those habits and feelings which form the felicity of the matrimonial state. In this singular relation, fixed rules are observed, and a certain fidelity is exacted; the jealousy of the husband is assumed by the *cortejo;* and the lady who changes, at least with any frequency, this object of attachment, loses *caste* in the eyes of the public.

The religious state of Spain need only be mentioned to suggest the dark and gloomy features by which it is marked. That bigotry and superstition which the Romish faith contracted during ages of darkness, and which in all other countries is so much abated, retains nearly its full force in Spain. The Inquisition, that frightful tribunal, the disgrace of modern Europe, which here held its central seat, kept alive its fires against all who exercised their reason on a subject connected with the national faith. The order of Jesuits, who have been called the militia of the Romish church, originated also in this country. The Inquisition perished in the late struggle; yet a numerous body still call aloud for its re-establishment; and the most liberal rulers, whom the revolution raised to power, durst not attempt any approach to toleration, or to trench upon the "Catholic religion one and indivisible." This spirit of bigotry and superstition is deeply diffused through the nation, who, if they no longer demand that heretics shall be committed to the flames, never doubt at least of the future tortures to which they are destined. All the childish and absurd customs which marked its prevalence during the dark ages, are preserved nearly unaltered; the processions and exhibitions, in which the events of sacred history are represented, often in a familiar and ludicrous manner; the endless festivals, which impoverish the nation, and favour its natural indolence; and the zeal of multitudes, who are induced by mistaken piety to withdraw themselves from their families and the world. Mr. Blanco White has given a striking account of the artifices by which the young female is led to make the irrevocable sacrifice; the respect and importance attached to her during the period of noviciate; the ceremonies, which resemble those of marriage, even the name of bride being given to her; and the disgrace attached to a retractation. Yet it appears evident, from the same author, that this profession is often deeply sincere; that it aids in producing that strong moral feeling which prevails throughout the nation; that many are even tormented by minute conscientious scruples; and that, with such persons, absolution, founded on false pretensions to penitence, is considered as aggravating the guilt. At the same time, there is a combination of deep devotion and dissolute conduct, which not only rapidly succeed each other, but actually coexist, in a manner never seen in any Protestant society. It may be observed, that amid this thick darkness which covers the nation, a body of men has lately arisen, of active and enquiring minds, who have discerned the errors of the national creed, and have passed to the opposite extreme. They are comparatively few in number, however; and, as already observed, even in their greatest triumph, although they considerably reduced the conventual establishments of Spain, they never durst attempt to introduce the toleration of any form of worship different from the Catholic.

Spanish literature, during the era of the national glory, supported itself at least on a level with that of any other nation in Europe. Spain had, as it were, a literature to itself, scarcely any of the productions of which, if we except the inimitable satire of Cervantes, became familiar to the rest of Europe. During the middle age, she was rich in chivalric romance, the taste for which, however, was banished by the appearance of Don Quixote, a change which some lament, as having led to the decline of the national spirit. The poetry of Spain, roused by so many vicissitudes of internal revolution and transmarine triumph, took a somewhat lofty flight. The *Araucana* of Ercilla, celebrating her conquests in the New World, is named together, though not on a level, with the best modern epics. Garcilasso de la Vega, Villegas, Mendoza, and others, chiefly officers in the army of Charles V., introduced a style formed on the Italian model; and, having the advantage of a noble and sonorous language, worked up their verses to the highest polish. But it is in the drama, that the Spaniards have been chiefly distinguished. Lope de Vega and Calderon, indeed, construct their plots with an entire disregard of the unities, filled with extravagant incidents, and strained and artificial sentiments. But they display an inexhaustible fertility of invention, and often strong traits of character; so that, though they never could be transferred entire to any other stage, they furnished useful hints both to the French and English dramatists. Mariána's History of Spain ranks among classical productions; while Herrera and Solis, though of inferior merit, have produced valuable histories of the Spanish transactions in the New World. To Don Antonio de Solis, the Spaniards are willing to ascribe that inimitable satire on human character and manners, Gil Blas, which must, they say, have been written by a Spaniard and a courtier. As such, he might rejoice that it had amply fulfilled his intentions without compromising his security, and could very well afford to dispense with the fame which redounded to its reputed author, Le Sage. These writers belong to the classic age of Spain, which nearly expired with the seventeenth century; but of late, the intellectual spirit which has spread so actively throughout Europe, has penetrated into Spain, and made vigorous struggles against the night of ignorance and prejudice in which that country was involved. Campomanes, Ustariz, Jovellanos, and Arguelles, have endeavoured to trace the causes which have paralysed Spanish industry, and to discover the means of reviving it; Feyjoò has done much to rouse a spirit of reflection; Yriarte, Isla, and Melendez Valdez, have produced agreeable miscellaneous writings; and Moratin has adopted a more regular drama, formed on the French model. There are extensive public libraries; one, the royal library in Madrid, consisting of 130,000 volumes, with valuable manuscripts, and a rich collection of medals; and others in the great provincial towns; but the prevalence of monkish legends, and the prohibition of many of the most important standard works, greatly limit their value. The universities are numerous, and that of Salamanca once perhaps the most celebrated in Europe; but education being conducted upon obsolete and scholastic principles, and impregnated with the national bigotry, they have long ceased to attract students from any place out of Spain. Some of the younger members were supposed to have embraced novel ideas in regard to religion and government; whence they have become objects of jealousy to the government, which will probably be little anxious to rescue them from that decay into which they were thrown by the events of the revolution.

308

The Guitar.

The fine arts, especially painting, could boast in Spain of a distinguished school, marked by features strikingly national and original. It is characterised by depth, force, great truth of nature, and a warm expression of devotional feeling. Murillo, Ribeira (self-named Spagnoletto), and Velasquez, are those alone whose works are diffused throughout Europe; but by those who have visited Spain, Cano, Juanes, Ribalta, and Morales are mentioned in terms of equal praise. The Escurial and other royal palaces are likewise adorned by some of the finest pieces of Raphael, Titian, and Rubens. This taste seems to have declined with that of literature; and Townshend observed that the nobles set little value on the magnificent collections with which their palaces were adorned. Of late the efforts to revive painting have been considerable, but without producing any artists of much celebrity. The Spaniards are fond of music, but delight rather in detached airs for the serenade and ball, than in that higher class in which the Italians and Germans excel. The guitar (*fig.* 308.) as an accompaniment for song, and the castanets for the national dance. are characteristic Spanish instruments.

The Spaniards have favourite and peculiar diversions. They are most passionately attached to the bull-fight: a large space is enclosed, sometimes the great square of the city, around which the people sit as in an amphitheatre. The bull, being introduced, is first attacked by the *picadores*, or horsemen armed with spears; a desperate conflict ensues; the horse is frequently killed or overturned with his rider, when persons on foot run in, and distract the animal, by holding up different kinds of coloured stuffs. He is next attacked by *banderilleros*, or footmen armed with arrows; and not only their skill, but their dexterity in escape, are the subjects of admiration: at last, when the animal is completely covered with wounds, the *matador* or slayer appears, and closes the scene. Tumultuous applause or hissing from the populace accompanies every part of this savage performance, according to the respective merits of the bull or his assailants. The comparative excellence of different matadores becomes often a party question, and the subject of keenly agitated discussion in the circles of Madrid. Wounds frequently, and death sometimes, are the result to the actors in this exhibition, for whose benefit a priest with holy water is in regular attendance. Not less is the fondness for the dance, particularly under its national forms of the *fandango* (*fig.* 309.), the *bolero*, and the *guanacho*, performed with the castanet in the hands; and the two former especially consisting chiefly in movements expressive of passion, but so little consonant to the rules of decorum, that the indulgence shown to these amusements by the church cannot but be regarded as a matter of surprise.

309

The Fandango.

The dress of the Spaniards is antique, and varies much according to the different provinces; that of the ladies consists chiefly of a petticoat and a large mantilla or veil, covering the upper part of the person. The grandees, and the opulent in general, display a profusion of jewels; the dress of the men is slight, and closely fitted to the body, with the exception of a loose cloak thrown over the whole. The minister, Squillace, under Charles III., having conceived that these cloaks, by concealing the person, served as a cover to deeds of violence, stationed persons at the corners of the streets, who seized the passengers, and forcibly cut down this part of their dress to the legal dimensions; but this measure raised so violent and general a clamour, that the king was forced to appease it by the sacrifice of the minister who had attempted such an obnoxious curtailment.

Both in eating and drinking the Spaniards are temperate; the only noted national dish is the *olla podrida*, in which various meats, vegetables, and herbs are mixed together in a manner which even foreigners admit to be palatable. The pleasures of society are chiefly sought at *tertulias* or evening parties, where only slight refreshment is presented; but *refrescos* or dinner parties are given on a large scale upon very special occasions.

## Sect. VII.—*Local Geography.*

Of the divisions of Spain, the most prominent is into kingdoms or principalities, each of which, at some period of its eventful history, enjoyed an independent existence, though they are now merged into one monarchy. More recently the country has been split into a number of smaller departments or jurisdictions; but the original distinction into kingdoms, being founded upon natural limits, and maintained by feelings and impressions derived from former independence, is still the most interesting. The kingdoms are New Castile, Estremadura, Old Castile, Leon, Galicia, Asturias, Biscay, Navarre, Catalonia, Aragon, Valencia, Murcia, Granada, and Andalusia.

The following table exhibits the divisions and subdivisions of Spain, with the extent and population of each, according to Hassel:—

| | | Square Leagues. | Population. | | | Square Leagues. | Population. |
|---|---|---|---|---|---|---|---|
| New Castile | Madrid | 110 | 298,000 | Asturias | | 3082 | 565,000 |
| | Toledo | 734 | 485,000 | Galicia | | 1330 | 1,585,000 |
| | Guadalaxara | 163 | 153,000 | Catalonia | | 1003 | 1,116,000 |
| | Cuença | 945 | 362,000 | Navarre | | 205 | 288,000 |
| | La Mancha | 631 | 257,000 | Biscay | Biscay | 106 | 145,000 |
| Estremadura | | 1199 | 556,000 | | Guipuscoa | 52 | 136,000 |
| Old Castile | Burgos | 642 | 612,000 | | Alava | 902 | 93,000 |
| | Soria | 341 | 267,000 | Aragon | | 12,322 | 856,000 |
| | Segovia | 290 | 221,000 | Valencia | | 643 | 1,255,000 |
| | Avila | 215 | 153,000 | Murcia | | 659 | 493,000 |
| Leon | Leon | 493 | 311,000 | Granada | | 805 | 1,097,000 |
| | Palencia | 145 | 153,000 | Andalusia | Seville | 752 | 970,000 |
| | Toro | 165 | 126,000 | | Jaen | 268 | 277,000 |
| | Valladolid | 271 | 243,000 | | Cordova | 348 | 325,000 |
| | Zamora | 133 | 93,000 | | | | |
| | Salamanca | 471 | 273,000 | | | | |

With New Castile, the central and metropolitan province, we commence our survey: it consists chiefly of an extensive plain enclosed between two of the long parallel mountain ranges, the Sierra de Guadarrama and the Sierra de Toledo. Along this plain, and parallel to both ranges, the Tagus flows in a deep rocky bed. Beyond the Sierra de Toledo, the district of La Mancha, which we include also in New Castile, extends to a third paralle mounta'n range, the Sierra Morena, dividing it from Andalusia and the southern provinces

The plain of Castile Proper is elevated and naked; and being thus exposed to the sun's direct rays, presents a bare and parched appearance. It includes, however, fertile valleys, producing wine, oil, grain, and fruits of various kinds; but the inhabitants are extremely deficient in every species of industry.

Madrid (*fig.* 310.), the capital of Castile, and of "all the Spains," stands on several low hills on the immense Castilian plain, which on the north appears bounded by the high distant range of the Guadarrama, but on every other side has no visible termination. A small rivulet, the Manzanares, flows past the city, and falls into the Tagus. Madrid is a superb but some

310

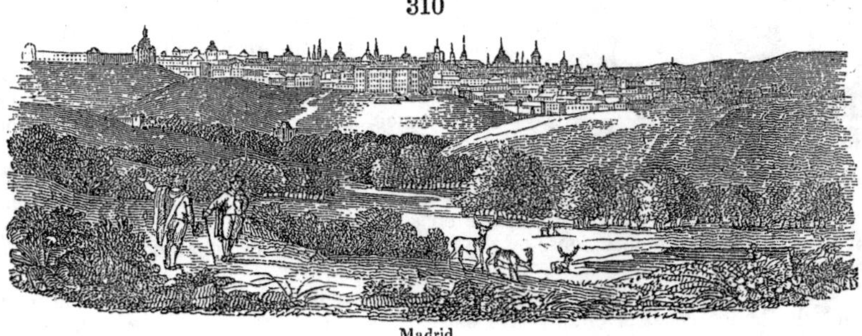

Madrid.

what gloomy capital; the houses are high, well built of good stone, not defaced by smoke, the streets are well paved, and have broad footpaths. The main street of Alcala, long, spacious, and bordered on each side by a row of princely houses, attracts particular admiration. The Prado, a wide public walk, bordered by trees, and connected with gardens all open to the public, is equally conducive to ornament and pleasure. There are many public fountains, supplied with pure, light, and salubrious water, filtered through beds of gravel and sand, from a distance of seven or eight leagues. The gates built by Charles III. are uncommonly beautiful, particularly that of Alcala; but in a miserable wall which might be battered down by a three-pounder in half an hour. The royal palace, built by Philip V., is a spacious and magnificent structure, though the taste displayed in it is a subject of controversy. It contains numerous fine paintings, which do not equal, however, those of the Escurial. The Retiro, with its fine gardens, was defaced by the French, who made it a military post; an extensive and costly menagerie is now forming within its precincts. The museum of statuary and painting, a new and elegant building, has recently been enriched with some of the finest pictures from the royal palaces. The cabinet of natural history, supported by the government, is also a handsome structure, and its contents valuable. The environs of Madrid are not remarkable for beauty; they are much broken into hills and hollows; so that, of the 200 villages situated in them, only three or four can be seen at once. Population, 201,000.

Toledo, even in its present decay, excites an interest equal or superior to Madrid. Once the proud capital of Spain, it has a commanding site on a lofty rock, almost insulated by the Tagus. A position so strong rendered it a grand national bulwark during the long ages of internal warfare, but occasioned its desertion during peace, when it was felt as extremely inconvenient, the streets being so steep that a carriage can scarcely drive safely through them. Its manufactures of wool and silk, which are said once to have employed nearly 40,000 men, have disappeared; and government has in vain attempted to revive that of swords, of which those formerly manufactured at Toledo were valued above all others. Its population of 200,000 has been reduced to 25,000; and it presents a mere mass of narrow, deserted, winding, and dirty streets. Toledo, however, still exhibits two grand monuments; the Alcazar or palace, and the cathedral. The former is a noble and extensive pile, in a pure style of architecture, and the granite columns of the Corinthian order which adorn the inner court are particularly admired. The grand staircase and spacious gallery, no longer crowded with guards and courtiers, are now dirty, deserted, and silent. The edifice, though neglected and decaying, still wears a stately and imposing aspect; "and its handsome front, immense quadrangle, and elegant colonnade, declare it to have been the pride and ornament of a happier period." The cathedral is also one of the grandest edifices in the Peninsula. It was originally a mosque, built in a grand style; but its simplicity has been much impaired by tasteless additions, and by the profusion of gilding, relics, and statues, with which its interior has been filled. It retained its wealth and splendour, however, till the late war when its treasures became the prey of the invader, and its six hundred ecclesiastics were dispersed, leaving only a few to perform the sacred functions.

Two other considerable towns in New Castile are Guadalaxara, to the east of Madrid, where the government has established a manufacture of fine cloth on a great scale; it is of course an ill-conducted and unprofitable concern; yet it supports the population of 12,000 or 14,000 in a degree of comfort not usual in Spanish towns: and further east, Cuença, the capital of a mountain district of the same name, interposed between Valencia and the plain of Castile. It is a small ancient city, distinguished by a cathedral and some other monuments.

La Mancha, sometimes reckoned a separate province, is the most southern part of Castile from which it is separated by the Sierra de Toledo. It is an immense table-plain, intersected by different ridges of low hills and rocks, without a tree except a few dwarf evergreen oaks; or an enclosure, except mud walls round the villages. All this vast tract of open country is cultivated, and produces corn or vines: its wine, especially that of Val de Peñas, enjoys a high repute. Its name, however, is chiefly familiar to the public as having given an appellation to the celebrated hero of Cervantes. The names of Don Quixote and Sancho Panza are familiar to the district; and the dress of the peasantry presents still an exact model of that of the doughty squire. There are a number of large villages; and Ciudad Real, the capital, is well built in a fine plain, though it has lost much of its former prosperity. Almagro and Ocaña are also pretty considerable towns.

Estremadura forms a continuation to the west of the same plain as New Castile, traversed like it by the Tagus, and bounded by the same ranges of mountains. It is a fine, wide, wild province, diversified by rugged mountains, deep valleys, and almost boundless plains. The depopulation generally complained of in Spain seems more remarkable here than in any other province; and vast tracts may be passed without seeing a human habitation. This seems chiefly owing to the pernicious laws of the Mesta, which assign it almost entirely for the occupation of the merino flocks, when they descend from the mountains of Leon. Estremadura, therefore, forms a vast pastoral district; only a small proportion of its surface being necessary to furnish grain for its scattered population. Yet the Romans made it one of the chief seats of their dominion; and no part of the Peninsula exhibits more striking works and monuments of that great people. The Estremenos also retain much of the antique Spanish aspect and character; and no province, during the late crisis, made more striking displays of patriotic energy.

The cities are no longer considerable. Badajos, the capital, a strange corruption of the Roman name Pax Augusta, is a considerable and strong town, but much shattered by the successive sieges it sustained in the late war from Soult and Wellington. Merida, the ancient capital of Lusitania, excites more interest, from the striking remains which it presents of Roman magnificence. The amphitheatre, baths, a lofty triumphal arch, three votive altars, and a handsome stone bridge, are all magnificent monuments, and in wonderful preservation. Truxillo, an old city, of small extent, was the birth-place of Pizarro, whose splendid mansion is still to be seen, adorned with barbarous trophies of his conquest. Almaraz is distinguished chiefly by the very noble modern bridge adjoining to it. Talavera de la Reyna, once splendid but now decayed, has acquired recent lustre from being the theatre of one of the greatest battles fought during the peninsular war. In the extensive plain north of the Tagus are the two pleasant little cities of Coria and Placencia; the latter of which was the scene of the singular monastic retirement of Charles V. In the mountains separating this part of the province from Leon is a rocky region, of the most savage and desolate character, called Batuecas.

Old Castile is situated on the opposite side of the chain of mountains which forms the northern boundary of New Castile. It presents a high variegated table-land, separated on the north by the Cantabrian chain from Asturias. Some parts are rugged; but it is, upon the whole, a fertile well-watered region, traversed by the Duero in its early course. There are many tracts of rich pasturage, and others equally fitted for the growth of corn. It is, however, one of the provinces in which the marks of decay are most striking. The capitals are neglected and ruinous; large portions are left uncultivated; and of the fine manufactures of cloth from the merino wool, only a remnant is now supported by the aid of government. Castilian pride and indolence have fixed here their old and central seat: the hidalgos belonging to Old Castile amount to 146,000, a much larger proportion than in any other province.

Burgos, the once magnificent capital of the kings of Castile, and the highest in rank of any city in the kingdom, is dwindled into a poor place, not containing above 10,000 inhabitants. Amid its gloomy and decayed streets, however, towers the cathedral, one of the finest specimens of Gothic architecture existing in Europe, and the form of which bears a considerable resemblance to that of York minster. The strong ancient castle, which had fallen into decay, was so far re-established by the French, that it successfully stood a long siege from the Duke of Wellington.

Of the other towns of Old Castile, Segovia presents some interesting monuments of Roman and Moorish grandeur. Its aqueduct (*fig.* 311.), of 159 arches, nearly half a mile long, and in one place 94 feet high, is a stupendous Roman work, ranked by Swinburne above the Pont du Gard. The Alcazar, or royal castle, was erected by the Moors on a rock overlooking a wide range of country. After it came into the possession of the Christians, it was employed as a state prison, and is now a military school. Five centuries ago, Segovia had very extensive manufactures of fine cloth; but these, notwithstanding the honour of having the king for a partner, have dwindled to a very small amount. Population 15,000. Avila, capital of a small province of the same name, is a city of ancient distinction; and its massy walls, its towers, its Alcazar, and the dome of the old cathedral, render it imposing at a distance; but it is in a state of wretched desertion. The attempt to establish manufactures of cloth and cotton has not been successful. Soria, near the site of the ancient Numantia, on the right bank of the Duero, near its source, is a tolerable country town, capital of one of the smaller provinces into which Old Castile has been subdivided.

311

Aqueduct of Segovia.

The palaces of the Escurial (*fig.* 312.) and San Ildefonso are striking objects in Old Castile. The "royal monastery" of the Escurial was founded by Philip II. on a plan entirely congenial to his gloomy mind. It unites the characters of a palace and a convent; and has the form of a gridiron, the instrument of the martyrdom of St. Lorenzo, to whom it is dedicated. Attached to it is the Pantheon, a classic and somewhat profane structure, in which, however, are interred all the crowned kings and queens of Spain since Charles V. The wealth of the Spanish monarchs has been continually employed in adding new ornaments to this favourite residence, which is considered by the nation as the eighth wonder of the world; and large volumes have been filled with descriptions of it. The church and the great altar have scarcely a rival for magnificence and grandeur of effect. The library is not extensive, but contains manuscripts, especially Arabic, that are of great value. The collection of paintings, it is probable, yields only to that which covers the walls of the Vatican. Besides select productions of Murillo and other masters of the Spanish school, it contains several of the greatest works of Raphael, Titian, and others of the first Italian masters. The environs are wild and naked in the extreme, without shelter from the cold blasts of winter, or the intense heats of summer. On the opposite declivity of the same mountains, looking towards the north, San Ildefonso, without any pretensions to equal magnificence, is finely surrounded by woods, gardens, and beautiful jets d'eau. Aranjuez stands in quite a different situation, on the lowest plain of Castile, at the junction of the Tagus and the Xarama. It is chiefly admired for its magnificent woods and gardens; the former carried in long and spacious avenues, the latter containing in profusion the finest native and exotic plants.

312

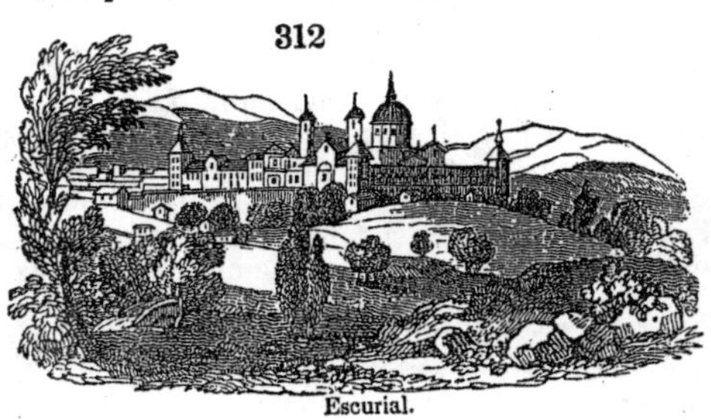

Escurial.

Leon forms a continuation of the plain of Old Castile, along the lower course of the Duero, and bounded by the same ranges of mountains. For several centuries it was the seat of a kingdom, comprising the chief Christian power in Spain, until it was united to that of Castile. It is almost entirely within the domain of the *mesta*, and thus devoted principally to pasturage. The consequent depopulation has been very great; insomuch that, according to Townshend, the bishopric of Salamanca, which once contained 748 townships, is now reduced to 333. The vast extent of open plain which forms the centre of this province has been found highly favourable to an invader who possessed superior cavalry; such as the Moors once, and more latterly the French.

The cities of Leon are almost solely interesting from the traces which they present of ancient grandeur. Leon itself, by its highly ornamented cathedral, its nine convents, and its ancient palace, testifies the remote period when it was the seat of royalty; but a heterogeneous assemblage of dirty streets filled with beggars, splendid churches, and half-ruined family mansions, are all that it now presents. Salamanca, by its university, has acquired a much greater fame. This seminary, one of the first in Europe, was founded in 1200, and extended during the same century by Alfonso the Wise, celebrated for the progress which astronomy made under his auspices. From the medical knowledge of Avicenna, Averroes, and other Arabian sages, it derived a character superior to those of the other monkish universities during the middle ages. Salamanca, however, remained stationary in the fourteenth century; and, while sound science was spreading through the rest of Europe, continued to occupy its students with dogmatic theology, and with the worship of Aristotle and Aquinas. Its students, once reckoned at 16,000, have been reduced to less than 2000. Salamanca is crowded with sacred edifices, to enrich which, all the four corners of the world have been made to contribute; and on days of high festival the display of silver and precious stones was altogether dazzling. The cathedral and principal square are very magnificent, but the streets are narrow and gloomy. Captain Sherer, in 1813, found Salamanca quite a deserted city; only a few of the old professors and youthful students still lingered in the colleges, or paced the spacious aisles of the elegant cathedral. Of the latter, some, as appears from Mr. White, notwithstanding the antiquated course of instruction, had adopted modern and liberal ideas, and in the late crisis obeyed the call of their country and of liberty. The French having made Salamanca a military position, a great part of the place was levelled or battered down; and subsequent events have not been favourable to its restoration. We must not, however, dismiss Salamanca without noticing the new lustre it has derived from giving name to one of the most splendid of Wellington's victories.

Valladolid has a great name in history. Charles V. made it his capital, and it continued to be the residence of the Spanish court until Philip IV. removed it to Madrid. In these splendid days Valladolid was supposed, perhaps with some exaggeration, to contain 200,000 inhabitants, now reduced to a tenth of that number. Yet it covers a very large space of ground; and the numberless spires, domes, and turrets of its sacred edifices give it still the appearance of a large metropolis. Its university is attended by 2000 students, and taught by forty-two professors and fifty doctors. After a very marked period of decay, Valladolid experienced lately a considerable revival. Its environs are particularly healthy and agreeable.

Several other large decayed towns attest the former grandeur of Leon. Zamora and Toro, both on the Duero, are capitals of two of the small provinces. Benavente is distinguished by its castle, which has been described as one of the grandest monuments of the age of chivalry; and Tordesillas was a royal residence in the reign of Charles V. Astorga, once capital of the Asturias, and one of the bulwarks of the Peninsula, has lost its strength and magnitude. Palencia is also a small capital, pleasantly situated on the Carrion, having a little inland trade. Ciudad Rodrigo is a national barrier on the Portuguese frontier, still kept up as a strong fortress, which sustained successive sieges during the peninsular war.

Galicia, separated by its mountain boundary from Leon, forms the north-western corner of the Peninsula. It is entirely a highland and alpine region, broken into rugged rocks and narrow passes, though with valleys of great fertility and of peculiar beauty interspersed. The Gallegos are industrious; and the country is better peopled than many of the more favoured regions of the Peninsula. They are hardy and enterprising, and often leave this barren territory to seek employment in the cities of Spain and Portugal, where, like the Scottish highlanders, they act chiefly as porters and servants. The shores and ports of Galicia are celebrated in naval history, forming as it were the outer coasts of Europe, beaten by the waves of a tempestuous ocean, and where fleets from the distant quarters of the globe often made their first appearance in Europe, and met with hostile fleets on the watch for them.

The interior towns of Galicia have for their capital, St. Jago de Compostella, the most celebrated shrine of the Peninsula, supposed to contain the body of St. James, its patron. In the chapel dedicated to him is his statue, two feet high, of pure gold, illuminated every night by 2000 wax tapers. Twenty-two other chapels have been enriched by the offerings of pilgrims from every part of the Peninsula, whose numbers have diminished. Lugo presents the poor remains of an ancient city surrounded by a wall and towers, once of great strength, but now mouldering into ruin. Orense, a little city, formerly celebrated for its hot springs, and Tuy, a strongly situated fortress, are on the Portuguese frontier.

Of the seaports of Galicia, Vigo had the greatest reputation, several great naval actions having been fought near it; particularly that of 1702, when the whole fleet of Spanish galleons was sunk or taken by the English. It has one of the finest harbours in Spain; which, however, since Ferrol became the chief naval station, is only employed for a limited coasting trade. Corunna on the Groyne is now the most trading place in the province, and packets sail from it to England and America. It is a steep, dirty, but well-paved town, of no strength, being commanded by the neighbouring heights. Population 23,000. Ferrol, since 1752, has been made the chief naval station of Spain. Its harbour, besides being one of the safest and most spacious in Europe, has the advantage of being accessible only by a narrow winding passage which can be rendered almost impassable by a chain of forts. A considerable city has been formed, and very extensive docks and arsenals built; but since the extinction of the Spanish navy, these have of course fallen into considerable neglect. Population 13,000.

The Asturias form a long narrow strip between the Bay of Biscay and the Cantabrian mountains, which extend along its whole length. It is celebrated in history as the sacred retreat in which the hero Pelayo raised again the national standard, after it seemed for ever trampled under foot by the Saracen invaders. Since the fourteenth century the Asturias have given the title of prince to the heirs of the Spanish throne. The province is approached only by narrow ravines and passes, through which torrents dash, and which are overhung by steep cliffs and luxuriant woods. There are, however, a number of valleys, and the whole plain of Oviedo is distinguished both for fruitfulness and beauty. Instead of wine, a good deal of tolerable cider is made and exported: amber, jet, and coal abound, but the last strongly impregnated with sulphur. The Asturians are brave and proud, boasting that their country was never conquered, even by the Romans; and more than a third part of the population is composed of hidalgos.

Oviedo, the only large town, has more magnificence than its situation might lead us to expect: the cathedral in particular, long the only shrine secure from the rage of the invader, afforded an asylum to many pious treasures scattered through the Peninsula. These, however, consist chiefly of relics, valuable only to devout and believing eyes. Among them are the rod of Moses, the mantle of Elias, the olive-branch borne aloft in entering Jerusalem; thorns from the sacred crown; the milk of the blessed Virgin, &c. Oviedo is still a considerable town, with a rich bishopric, and many religious houses, of which the principal is a convent of Benedictine nuns. Population 10,000. Gijon, though with a costly and not very complete harbour, carries on all the little trade of the province. Avila and Santillana are large villages, giving their name to districts. Santander and Santona are sea-ports of some little consequence, in the district of Montana, on the borders of Biscay.

Biscay is a small, high, rugged province, on the western slope of the Pyrenees. Streams descending from its numerous heights, combine in forming the channel of the Upper Ebro. The Basques are a peculiar race, preserving the only remnant which revolutions have left in the Peninsula, of Celtic language and aspect. Under the name of Cantabria, this region presented a barrier even to Roman conquest; and though the Saracens penetrated through it into the plains of France, it is still boasted that they never could reach the mountains of High Cantabria. The Basques, amid the general slavery of Spain, have still preserved some portion of their original rights. They have a cortes of their own; and the taxes, levied by provincial authority, are presented to the sovereign in the form of a free gift. Every native Biscayan is an hidalgo or noble, scarcely owning a superiority of birth in the proudest Castilian. With all this they are excessively industrious; the mountain declivities are cultivated as high as the plough can reach; and while the finest plains of Castile are nearly a desert, Biscay's rude vales are covered with a numerous population.

The cities in such a district cannot be large: yet Bilboa, the capital, situated on the Ybaizabal, which admits large vessels up to the town, is one of the most commercial places in Spain, with 15,000 inhabitants. Most of the merino wool from the plains of Castile is brought hither for exportation. Biscay Proper contains also Orduña, a neat little city, and numerous villages. Guipuscoa is another district, lying more to the east, and in closer contact with France. Its capital is St. Sebastian, an indifferent port, but a neat, tolerably large city, and so strongly fortified as to be considered one of the four keys of the kingdom; the others being Pamplona, Barcelona, and Figueras. Fontarabia, close to the frontier, has a great name in history, but little else is now left. The small village of Irun stands on the immediate bank of the Bidassoa, whose broad clear stream, descending from the Pyrenees, forms the boundary between two rival and long hostile nations. More in the interior, and on a lower level, is the district of Alava, having for its capital Vittoria, a somewhat well-built modern town, and celebrated as the theatre of the complete victory there gained by the Duke of Wellington over the French army under Joseph Bonaparte, which was thence finally expelled from the Peninsula.

Navarre is a small province or kingdom, lying immediately beneath the highest and steepest Pyrenees. Eight very difficult passes penetrate through them into France, but scarcely any one passable for the artillery and train of an army. The principal is that of St. Jean Pied de Port; on the French side of which is Roncesvalles, or Roncevaux, celebrated in history, and still more in romance, for the disaster which there befell Charlemagne and his knights. For many centuries it formed a separate little kingdom connected with France, until Ferdinand the Catholic succeeded in annexing to Spain all the part south of the Pyrenees. Navarre retains, however, privileges and customs peculiar to itself, and its governor bears the title of viceroy. The population is active, hardy, and brave. The bands of guerrillas under Mina proved the most formidable irregular force with which the French had to contend in the Peninsula. Pamplona, or Pampeluna, the capital, the foundation of which is ascribed to Pompey, is one of the chief bulwarks of the Peninsula, and one of the strongest fortresses in Europe. It was reduced by the Duke of Wellington, and by the French, in their last invasion, after a long blockade. There are also Tudela and Calahorra, ittle towns on the Ebro. Pampeluna has 10,000 inhabitants.

Aragon, south from Navarre, is an extensive province, extending along the greater part of the course of the Ebro; whence it reaches on one side to the Pyrenees, and on the other to the chains which shut in the Castiles and Valencia. A great part of it is rugged and barren; though other tracts in the central plains, and along the rivers, are very susceptible of culture. Aragon, during the middle ages, was a powerful kingdom, comprising Catalonia and Valencia, forming the half of Christian Spain, then divided between it and Castile. Even after the union of the crowns under Ferdinand and Isabella, it still enjoyed its constitution and its cortes, which exercised higher prerogatives, and kept the power of the kings under stricter limitations, than any similar assembly in Europe. Of these it was deprived by the unfortunate issue of the civil war under Charles V., and more completely by the Bourbon succession, after Aragon had espoused the cause of Charles of Austria. The peasantry of this province are a fine body of men, stout, brave, and honest. Culture and population are generally in a backward state; yet the canal of Aragon, conducted parallel to the course of the Ebro, though it has not yet reached the sea, according to its destination, has given a considerable impulse to the agriculture of the district through which it is led.

Saragossa, or Zaragoza, the capital of Aragon, is a large and celebrated city, situated amid a fine plain, on the banks of the Ebro and of the canal of Aragon. From Augustus, who enlarged and improved it, the city was called Cæsar-Augusta, corrupted into Saragossa. It is not well built, the streets being narrow and crooked; but there are several open market-places, and some very splendid religious edifices. The principal is that dedicated to the Virgin, under the title of "Our Lady of the Pillar;" an object of the most profound veneration to the citizens, and enriched by offerings from every part of Spain. The church of St. Engracia is also filled with relics and gifts; and each of the forty convents of Saragossa has its peculiar boast. A stone bridge, and the finest wooden bridge in Europe, are thrown over the Ebro. The university has 2000 students, but not much literature. Saragossa has earned an immortal name by her heroic resistance against the unprincipled invasion of Napoleon, in 1808. Without walls, except an old one of earth, which could not resist for an hour an attack conducted on modern principles; without army, arms, or artillery, it maintained a long and finally successful conflict with the French, in their first invasion. Afterwards, when assailed by an immense and overwhelming force, the flower of the French armies, without hope of relief, it made a mighty resistance; and it was only by mining operations, blowing up successively house after house, that the French finally became its masters, after having reduced it to a heap of ruins. Population 43,000.

Aragon has some other small ancient towns, ranking even as cities; Jaca and Huesca on the northern frontier among the Pyrenees, both episcopal seats; Daroca and Calatayud in the plain bordering on Castile; the former enclosed with large ruined fortifications, the latter industrious, and surrounded by a smiling country.

Catalonia, to the east of Aragon, is one of the finest and most extensive provinces of Spain. It presents a remarkable variety of surface, from the steep and rugged heights of the higher Pyrenees, to the elevated valleys of Upper Catalonia, and the luxuriant though not very extensive plains that border on the Mediterranean. The Catalans redeem to a great extent the Spanish national character, uniting with its loftiness and energy a spirit and an activity which are elsewhere wanting. They have been always commercial, industrious, and fond of liberty. After bearing successively the yoke of the Romans, the Goths, and the Saracens, Catalonia was long ruled by counts of French descent, whose posterity extended their sway over Aragon, and finally over the whole Peninsula, in which this principality merged. The Catalans, however, bore more impatiently than other Spaniards the loss of their privileges; and during the war of the succession, on receiving a pledge for their restitution, espoused with extraordinary ardour the cause of the Archduke Charles. Even after its unfortunate issue, when deserted by Britain and all the other powers, they made a last dreadful struggle, which ended, however, in the loss of all those rights for which they had so nobly contended. In the last two wars, Catalonia acted a most conspicuous part; maintaining an unremitted resistance to France, notwithstanding the close vicinity of that kingdom, and in the late constitutional struggle making efforts, both for and against liberty, much greater than any other province.

Barcelona is, after the capital, the largest city, and at the same time the most industrious and flourishing, of all Spain, containing 150,000 inhabitants. It is situated about the centre of the Catalonian coast, and draws its subsistence from a fertile and extensive plain behind. It is said to have been originally a Carthaginian town, founded by Hamilcar Barcas; but rose to little distinction under the Romans, who made Tarraco the capital of all eastern Spain. It was not till the twelfth century that Barcelona began to be distinguished for its commercial spirit. It suffered severely during successive wars, particularly that of the succession; but in the course of the last century, the exertions of its patriotic governor, the Marquis of Mina, enabled it to retrieve all its losses, and become more prosperous than ever. The port is artificial, formed by solid and convenient moles, but has a bar at its entrance, which excludes vessels drawing more than twelve feet of water. It carried on a great and various traffic; had woollen, silk, and cotton manufactories, all on a considerable scale; about a thousand vessels annually entered its port; and the whole amount of exports was reckoned by Laborde at 1,750,000*l.* According to the latest account, however, by the author of "A Year in Spain," the late disasters and misgovernment have caused a great declension in the above branches of manufacture; and instead of the ranges of tall masts assembled within its mole, there are to be seen only a paltry assemblage of fishing-boats and feluccas. The ecclesiastical edifices of Barcelona are handsome, particularly the cathedral, though not of so grand a character as those in some other parts of Spain. The convent of the Dominicans has a singular series of ornaments, the sentences of five hundred heretics decreed by the Inquisition, and under each sentence a representation of the sufferer, whom the demons, in various shapes, are torturing and devouring. The walls of Barcelona are strong, but its chief dependence is upon the citadel of Montjuich, which commands it, and is considered almost impregnable, though the Earl of Peterborough took it by surprise. At the close of the war of the succession, when Barcelona was besieged by the Duke of Berwick, a terrible and almost frantic resistance was made in the streets, not by troops, but by priests, students, tradesmen, and even women: the consequences were terrible. Bonaparte, in 1808, obtained by treachery and threats the cession of this and the other keys of the kingdom; but in the late invasion, its resistance against Moncey was most gallant.

There are several other large, ancient, and strong towns in Catalonia. Tarragona, the Roman capital of the east of Spain, has fallen into great comparative decay, and has but 12,000 inhabitants. It is situated on a rocky peninsula, and presents many traces of Roman antiquity, as of the palace of Augustus, the amphitheatre, and an extensive aqueduct. More recently, the harbour has been improved, and some new streets built; and in the war of 1808, the fortifications were restored, and the city made a brave defence against Marshal Suchet, who at length carried it by storm, with circumstances of great cruelty. Tortosa is also a considerable and ancient city near the mouth of the Ebro, which is there broad and navigable. It made a distinguished figure during the wars with the Moors, chiefly through the exploits of its heroines, to commemorate whose valour a military order was instituted by Raymond Berenger. Its position on the river affords scope for a considerable trade; and during the last war its fortifications were restored by the Spaniards. It contains 16,000 inhabitants. Between the two last-mentioned cities has arisen, within the last half century, Reus, a large, flourishing, industrious town, carrying on various manufactures, particularly of brandy and leather. Population 25,000. All these are on the coast west of Barcelona. To the east the chief place is Gerona, a large gloomy town, in a fine situation. It is well fortified; and its resistance, protracted for more than half a year, to the unremitted efforts of Bonaparte's generals, formed one of the most glorious events of the peninsular war. Rosas, a little town, prettily situated in a fine bay, exports cork and other timber. In the interior, Lerida, distinguished as a Roman station under the name of Ilerda, is a large and strong town, situated in a most delightful country on the banks of the Segre. A considerable stand was made here by the patriotic armies during the French invasion. Mequinenza, at the junction of the Segre with the Ebro, is also an important military post. Cervera, the seat of a considerable university, and Igualada, are pretty large interior towns, supported by the produce of the rich vales in which they are situated. But the most striking feature in all Catalonia is the single, lofty, and precipitous mountain of Montserrat (*fig.* 313.). It consists of a crowd of conical hills piled over each other, broken into steep walls of white and variously tinted limestone cliffs, the interstices of which are filled with evergreen and deciduous trees and plants. The Benedictine monastery, an ancient and remarkable structure, stands on a cleft at the top of a high rock, where space is scarcely left for the edifice, while far beneath roars the Llobregat. Numerous hermitages pitched on the top of precipices, or in cavities hewn out of the rock, increase the singular and romantic appearance of the scene. This mountain, in the last war, was converted into an almost impregnable military position. On the highest of all the Catalonian vales, which is extensive, and rich in grain, stands Urgel, a small episcopal see, and a strong military post, the roads being almost impassable to artillery.

313

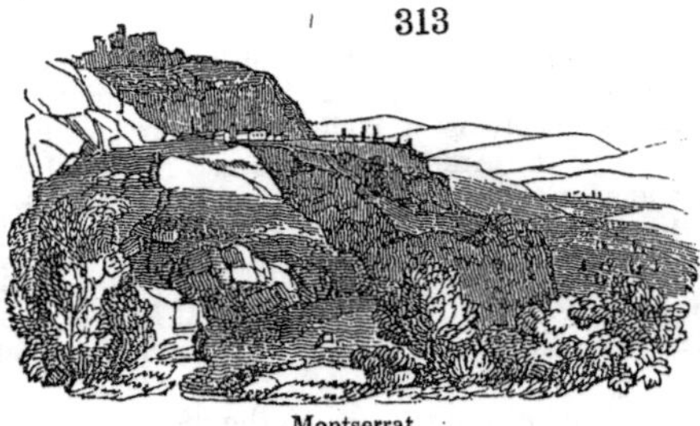

Montserrat.

Valencia, beginning from the border of Catalonia and Aragon, occupies an extensive coast running from north to south, and is the first of the southern provinces. The plain ranks as the garden of Spain, and almost of Europe. The fields of corn; the yellow green of the mulberry plantations, the pale hue of the olive; the woods, villages, and convents, thickly scattered over this great expanse, with numberless slender steeples, present, when united, an inimitable landscape. The country is finely watered by the Xucar, the Guadalaviar, and other rivers, numerous though not of long course. A great extent of artificial navigation was formed by the Moors, and is still kept up, though not in a very complete state. The province yields, in abundance, the usual products, corn, wine, oil, silk; with rice enough to supply the greater part of Spain, and barilla for exportation. The Valencians are very industrious, and of a gay disposition. Colonies from the south of France, introduced by the first Christian conqueror, brought with them a portion of the spirit of that nation.

Valencia, at the mouth of the Guadalaviar, is one of the largest and most flourishing towns of the kingdom. It is of Roman origin, but its fame dates from the eleventh century, when it was conquered by the Cid from the Moors, and ruled as a fief by that greatest of the Spanish heroes. It was the scene, however, of a long-continued contest; and its final annexation to Christian Spain did not take place until a century and a half later. The lofty walls and towers of Valencia are now nearly demolished, and in the war of liberty neither it nor the province made any very conspicuous figure. The silk manufacture is one of the most extensive in Spain, though checked by an absurd prohibition against the exportation of its produce. In a levy during the late war, exemption was granted to upwards of 3000 silk-weavers, that the trade might not be interrupted. There are also manufactures of woollens and paper. The Grau, or port of Valencia, is only an indifferent roadstead, and the commerce not nearly equal to that of Alicant. The city, though large and rich, is not handsome; the streets being narrow and winding, and bordered by high old houses. The churches and convents are of course numerous, and many of them richly ornamented, but none very prominent in architectural beauty. They are adorned, however, with numerous pictures by some of the most eminent Spanish painters, natives of Valencia; Juanes, Ribalta, and others, whose works are unknown in this country, but are admired by those who have visited Spain. The religious festivals of Valencia are celebrated with a childish pomp, in some degree disused in other parts even of this country. On these occasions, all the most memorable events and most illustrious characters in scripture history are represented either by figures in wickerwork, or by citizens fantastically attired. The exhibitions of this kind, amounting annually to a hundred and fifty, give great occasion to idleness and dissipation; yet the attempts to reduce their number have been hitherto unsuccessful. Population 66,000.

Alicant, situated at the bottom of a bay on the southern frontier, ranks high as an industrious and commercial town. Its prosperity is modern, chiefly owing to the refuge which its lofty castle afforded from the dreadful irruptions of the Barbary corsairs. Even since this danger ceased, Alicant has continued to be a fortified town; and none of the invading armies in the late war were able to obtain possession of it. About 1000 vessels annually enter its port, and are laden with barilla, raisins, and a small quantity of wine and brandy. The import from England consists chiefly of salt-fish, the great article of consumption in Catholic countries. The herring and other fisheries are carried on with considerable activity on this coast. They are encouraged by the government, but with an absurd limitation to a body of enrolled fishermen, amounting to about 16,000. Population 25,000.

Among other important towns may be mentioned Elche and Orihuela, large and flourishing places, in the very finest part of the plain of Valencia. Segorbe and Liria are pleasant interior towns towards the frontier of Aragon. San Felipe, under the name of Xativa, made a distinguished figure in the war of the succession; when, after being demolished, it was rebuilt by Philip V. under its present name. Denia and Gandia in the south, and Peñiscola in the north, are sea-ports on a smaller scale. But all these places yield in ancient fame to Murviedro, occupying the rocky site of the ancient Saguntum, the siege of which formed the commencement of the career of Hannibal. The long resistance of this powerful and unfortunate city forms the first of the many remarkable sieges which have distinguished the Spanish annals, ancient or modern. The Romans restored and made it a great colony, and the Moors erected a range of fortifications on the summit of the hill; so that its mountain site is now covered with ruins of various dates and descriptions. Half-way up the eminence, the outline of a theatre capable of containing 9000 persons may still be traced; and a few ropemakers plying their trade alone break the silence of this august ruin. Murviedro is a small town still fortified, though the resistance made by it in the last war was not formidable.

Murcia is a small province, partly bounded on the south-east by the coast, which here changes its direction from southerly to westerly. Its vale is almost without a rival for beauty and fertility, even in southern Europe. Its natural fruitfulness is greatly aided by the numerous canals of irrigation which the Moors drew from the river Segura. These advantages are little improved by the present inhabitants, who are noted as exhibiting, in a peculiar degree, all the blemishes of the Spanish character; its pride, its bigotry, and its laziness. Even the song and the dance do not inspire gaiety in its vales, as in all the rest of Spain; almost the whole time of the people being spent in eating, sleeping, and making cigars. A sullen and vindictive spirit is said to lurk under this outward apathy. Few Murcians have made a figure in literature, in the arts, or in public life.

The cities of Murcia, if we except its port of Carthagena, do not merit particular notice The capital, bearing its name, is an irregular, ill-built, ill-paved large town, with 36,000 inhabitants. The ecclesiastical edifices, however, are very costly, and the front of the cathedral, according to Mr. Townshend, produces a splendid effect with its sixteen Corinthian columns of marble, and thirty-two images as large as life. The interior does not possess equal elegance, but is chiefly distinguished by the proportion of gold, silver, and jewels, not to mention the relics, which are accounted by the faithful as of much superior value. Lorca is a large town, built with some elegance, and surrounded by fine promenades. Population 40,000. It had extensive fabrics of silk and saltpetre, which were reviving, when a singular accident arrested their progress. A speculative individual had collected all the waters of the neighbourhood into an immense reservoir, whence he supplied them to the cultivators for purposes of irrigation; but this receptacle, not being fully secured, burst at one point, destroyed part of the suburbs of Lorca, desolated a great extent of country, and reached even Murcia. Totana, a populous village, is enriched by the copious production of barilla in its neighbourhood. The castle of Almanza (*fig.* 314.), picturesquely seated on a height, is noted as the spot near which, in 1707, was fought the celebrated battle which decided the Spanish succession in favour of the house of Bourbon.

314

Almanza.

Carthagena, situated in Murcia, though scarcely belonging to it, forms one of the few great Spanish emporia, and contains 37,000 inhabitants. This celebrated capital of ancient Spain was founded by Asdrubal; and when captured by Scipio, in the year of Rome 550, was considered one of the most opulent cities in the world. It was nearly destroyed by the Vandals, but was restored by Philip II., and has ever since continued to flourish. It enjoys one of the finest ports in Europe, consisting of a bay sheltered by high mountains from almost every wind. The staples are the same as at Alicant. The revenue, raised by a small though impolitic duty on the export of barilla, amounts to 25,000*l.* The fishery is also considerable. There are few Murcian residents, and the trade is carried on chiefly by English, French, and Italian houses. The streets are wide, and the houses agreeable, with terraced roofs, commanding a view of the sea; but neither here nor at Alicant are there any structures, even ecclesiastical, at all worthy of notice.

Andalusia, taken in its most comprehensive sense, is the largest of the Spanish provinces, and, we may add, the finest and most remarkable, both as to nature and art. The Guadalquivir, with numerous and large tributaries, waters its whole extent. Its mountains, covered in many places with perpetual snow, are the loftiest, its valleys the most fruitful, in Spain. Andalusia, indeed, comprises four celebrated kingdoms; Granada, Seville, Cordova, and Jaen, and contains great capitals founded by the conquering Moors, which were the seats of science and splendour, when the greater part of Europe was plunged in rudeness and barbarism.

Granada, which is sometimes called Upper Andalusia, was the central seat of Moorish power and magnificence. Even amid the general decline of that power in Spain, Granada was still supported by the multitudes who resorted thither from the subdued provinces. Its fall, in 1492, was considered the most deadly blow which Islamism ever received; and in all the mosques prayers are put up every Friday for its restoration. Granada presents a wonderful combination of all that is most wild and sublime, with what is most soft and beautiful in natural scenery. South from the capital rises the Sierra Nevada, covered, as its name imports, with perpetual snow to a great depth. Mulhacen, the most elevated peak, is 11,660 feet above the sea; while the line of perpetual snow begins at about 10,000 feet. The Alpujarras, a lower range, are cultivated with considerable diligence, by descendants of the Moors, a remnant of whom found refuge here, amid the general proscription of their race and nation. The Vega or plain of Granada, watered by numerous streams descending from the high regions, displays nature in her utmost pomp and beauty.

The city of Granada is in the heart of the Vega, beneath the loftiest heights of the Sierra Nevada. This city still displays ample monuments to attest the period when it was the great western capital of the Moslem world. Nothing can exceed the beauty of its approach. "The rich and populous country well supplied with trees, the clear rivulets descending from the mountains, and artificially contrived to intersect it in every part; the splendid city extending in a half-moon from the river, on the gradual ascent of a hill; the streets rising above each other; the profusion of turrets and gilded cupolas; the summit crowned with the Alhambra; the background composed of the majestic Sierra Nevada, with its summit covered with snow; complete a scene to which no description can do justice." Mr. Jacob, who thus describes the scene, considers it not too much to have travelled two hundred miles of bad road to see it. The interior, as in most Spanish and especially Mohammedan cities, does not correspond to the approach. The streets are narrow, the walls high and gloomy; many quarters are now deserted; and marks of decay and splendid poverty are everywhere visible. Its population, once comprising 400,000 souls, is now reduced to 80,000. But the eye of the curious traveller is soon attracted towards the Alhambra (*fig.* 315.), the ancient palace and fortress of the kings of Granada. It is the noblest specimen existing of Moorish architecture; and nothing perhaps in Europe, out of Italy and Greece, can come into competition with it. The site is fine, resembling that of Windsor, on a hill above the river. Its exterior structure, however, is the reverse of beautiful: a huge heap of ugly buildings huddled together, without the least seeming intention of forming one habitation; the walls only gravel and pebbles daubed over with plaster. On entering the threshold, however, the visiter seems transported into a fairy scene. He passes through a range of apartments; the baths, the Court of the Lions; the Hall of the Abencerrages (*fig.* 316.); the Golden Saloon, or

315

The Alhambra.

316

Hall of the Abencerrages.

317

Gate of the Sanctuary of the Koran.

Hall of the Ambassadors; the Gate of the Sanctuary of the Koran (*fig.* 317.); the Tower

318

Mosaic Pavement.

of the Two Sisters; with others, in which the various resources of Oriental pomp are displayed, along with all that can refresh the eye or the sense in a sultry climate. The courts are all paved with marble, and surrounded with marble pillars, in a pure and beautiful taste; and the walls and pavement are profusely ornamented with gilded arabesque and mosaic (*fig.* 318.), the colours of which, by an art which seems to have been lost with the Moors, are as brilliant as when they were first laid on, five hundred years ago. Water is made to spout into the air, or, in smooth sheets bordered with flowers, refreshes the interior of the apartments. After the expulsion of the Moors, Charles V. built on part of its site a new palace, the external architecture of which was much superior; but it was never finished. The Generalife is another Moorish palace, in a more elevated and finer situation; but its interior splendour, though great, is quite eclipsed by that of its neighbour. The cathedral, though it must yield to these Moorish structures, is yet of considerable extent and beauty. Granada is the seat of one of the two high courts of chancery, and of other tribunals of high jurisdiction. It retains a certain proportion of its former immense silk manufactures, with some of woollen and leather; and a considerable number of persons are employed in extracting the nitre with which the neighbouring soil is copiously impregnated.

Malaga has in modern times attained a greater importance, and is reckoned the third port in the kingdom, ranking next to those of Cadiz and Barcelona. The chief foundation of its trade is the fine wine called Malaga or *mountain*, produced in the numerous hills behind it. It is raised at very great expense, and only upon the declivities which have an exposure to the sun. The country produces also very fine raisins and other fruits; and anchovies, caught and cured on the coast, have been sold to the annual extent of 20,000 quintals. Malaga is the only great Spanish port of which the exports have always exceeded the imports. Malaga has a very secure though not extensive harbour, formed by artificial moles. It lies in a deep bay on a little plain overhung by lofty and craggy cliffs, which at a distance appear quite naked, but on approaching, every crevice is found to be filled with vines. This situation renders the heat very severe, and has aided in exposing the inhabitants to the destructive ravages of pestilential fever. The streets are close, narrow, and dirty; but the cathedral is a very noble pile, and contains paintings by great Spanish masters. Population 52,000.

Other very considerable towns occur in Granada. Five leagues to the east of Malaga is Velez-Malaga, most delightfully situated in a plain diversified by numerous gentle hills, clothed to the summit with vines, while the plains below wave with luxuriant harvests of grain. Farther east are the small ports of Motril and Almeria; the latter ancient, and celebrated in the history of the Moors, under whom it was highly prosperous and flourishing. Near it is the rock of Filabres, 2000 feet high, composed of a single block of white marble; and beyond it stretches into the sea the bold and huge promontory of Cabo de Gata. Guadix, Baza, and Purchena, are considerable interior towns, in the eastern part of this province, seated in valleys enclosed by the numerous ranges of hills which intersect it. Santa Fé, two leagues west of Granada, is remarkably exposed to earthquakes, which have split its cathedral in two, and laid open the cells of one of the convents; yet the citizens still inhabit and keep it in repair. Alhama is strikingly situated amid a circuit of precipitous rocks, through which dashes a rapid stream. It is frequented for the salubrity of its air, and for its medicinal springs and baths. Antequera is very ancient; filled with Roman and Moorish monuments, and still large; the adjacent country is very fertile, and distinguished for the variety both of its vegetable and mineral productions. Population 20,000. Ronda, (*fig.* 319.) capital of a wide mountain district, is singularly situated on a rock with perpendicular cliffs and broken crags, through a deep fissure in which the river flows, and surrounds the city on three sides. It is crossed by a stupendous bridge 110 feet in diameter, and 280 feet in height. Stairs of 350 steps lead down to the river, and gardens have been formed on some level projecting points of the precipice. The mountaineers of Ronda are an honest, active, hardy race; and so healthy as to make it a proverb, that "at Ronda a man is a boy at eighty." The vicinity of Gibraltar gives them great opportunities for smuggling, which they carry on in large bands, and in open resistance to government, without, however, incurring any imputation on their general loyalty.

319

Ronda.

The kingdom of Seville, west of Granada, is a still finer region, and perhaps superior to any other in the Peninsula. Its plains are the most productive in wine, oil, and fruits; the noble river Guadalquivir conveys its products to the sea; and Seville and Cadiz are, in some respects, superior to all other Spanish cities.

Seville (*fig.* 320.) is situated in the midst of a fertile and delightful plain, and near the mouth of the Guadalquivir, which formerly admitted vessels of large size: it was a great city from the earliest period. By the Romans it was celebrated under the appellation of Hispalis: its foundation was ascribed to Hercules; and, with the neighbouring colony of Italica, it formed the capital of Bætica. Under the Moors it became an independent kingdom; and if it be true that, on its capture by Ferdinand the Catholic, 400,000 Moors marched out at one of its gates, it must indeed have been an immense city. Notwithstanding the depopulation thus occasioned by bigotry and treachery, it soon became more splendid than ever, in consequence of becoming the emporium of the wealth which flowed in from the western hemisphere. Its manufacturing industry was then also very flourishing. By a return made to government in 1601, Seville was said to contain 16,000 silk looms, giving employment to 130,000 workmen. It frequently received an increase of splendour by becoming a royal residence. Since the above period, Seville has not only declined with the gradual decline of Spain, but has suffered by the filling up of the channel of the Guadalquivir, which has rendered it navigable only for small ships, and has transferred to Cadiz the commerce of America. Seville is now a solemn, inert, gloomy city, with 91,000 inhabitants. Like other Spanish places, particularly those of Moorish origin, its streets are narrow, winding, and dirty; but it contains some splendid public edifices. Foremost stands the cathedral, the largest ecclesiastical structure in the Peninsula, 420 feet long within, and 373 broad; but the most striking feature is its tower, originally erected by the learned Geber or Guever, and used as an observatory, but raised by the Christians to the height of 350 feet. Many of the convents also are very splendid, and previous to the late invasion by the French contained numerous works of the greatest Spanish artists, of whom Seville was the chief nurse. There was, above all, a splendid collection of the works of Murillo, the prince of these artists, and a native of Seville. Of these treasures the city has been in a great measure despoiled by the ravages of the invader; Marshal Soult, in particular, had in his collection numerous masterpieces of Murillo, by which the convents of Seville were formerly adorned. Seville has still 2500 silk looms; and government maintains a cannon foundery and a tobacco manufactory. The Exchange and the Marine Academy are also handsome edifices.

320

Seville.

Cadiz (*fig.* 321.) is, in an equal degree with Seville, the boast of Spain. In the commercial annals of the world no city is of higher antiquity. Tartessus, occupying a site in its vicinity, was one of the earliest and most flourishing Phœnician colonies. Afterwards Gadeira, or Gades, was recognised by the Greeks and Romans as one of the chief European emporia. In modern times, when commerce did not form part of the European system, Cadiz declined into a secondary rank; and the intercourse with America was at first nearly monopolised by Seville. The circumstances which transferred it from that city to Cadiz took place early in the last century, when the latter rose to be the chief theatre of Spanish commerce. It enjoyed for some time the entire monopoly of the American trade; and even when, in 1778, it was thrown open to the whole kingdom, it had taken such deep root in Cadiz as to frustrate all competition. In 1784, when the entire imports from America were 12,630,000*l.* that city, for its share, had 11,280,000*l.*; and of the whole exports, amounting to 4,300,000*l.*, it had 3,600,000*l.* Notwithstanding severe shocks, in consequence of political revolutions, and the war with England, it always revived, and derived a temporary greatness from becoming the capital of the constitutional government. It received, however, its mortal blow by the separation of the colonies. The merchants, deprived thus of almost their only employment, have been reduced to the funds already accumulated, and have in a great measure retired from the confined situation of Cadiz to the pleasant sites and villages which are scattered round the bay. The city is situated on a small neck of land, at the point of the long Isle of Leon. It does not boast any remarkable structures, but the whole is elegantly built in regular squares, and streets with a square court in the centre and an awning over it. Population 53,000.

321

Cadiz.

Gibraltar (*fig.* 322.), though no longer Spanish, forms also a striking and important feature in this province. This rock is celebrated from the earliest antiquity as one of the two "Pillars of Hercules," which guarded the entrance into the Mediterranean; though Mount Calpe, on the opposite side, is considerably loftier. In 1704, Sir George Rooke and Sir Cloudesley Shovel carried this fortress by a *coup de main;* since which time Spain has vainly attempted to regain possession of it. Her grand effort was towards the close of the American war, when the fleets of France and Spain rode masters of the sea. A combined attack was made on the 13th of September, 1782, by the two powers, with fifty sail of the line, 30,000 troops, and ten mighty floating batteries, which were expected to demolish all opposed to them. They kept up a tremendous fire from ten in the morning till midnight, at which time smoke and fire were seen rising from the batteries which before next morning were reduced to ashes, with a dreadful destruction of the assailants. No subsequent attempt has been made; nature, in fact, has rendered Gibraltar almost impregnable. The rock is precipitous on all sides, and is connected with the continent only by a narrow neck of marshy ground. The western front alone towards the sea is in any degree accessible; and this is defended by batteries cut in the solid rock, and by other works so extensive and so well planned as to bid defiance to any future effort. Gibraltar has one handsome street, the houses of which are built in the English style, with trees and flowers skilfully planted in scanty fragments of soil. The rest of the town is close, crowded, and dirty, inhabited by about 20,000 people, chiefly Moors and Jews, the latter of whom have sought refuge here in great numbers from Spanish bigotry, and have four synagogues. The expense of maintaining Gibraltar is considerable: but it forms an important naval station, a depôt for the commerce of the Mediterranean, and a channel for introducing into Spain great quantities of goods, declared contraband by the jealous policy of that country.

322

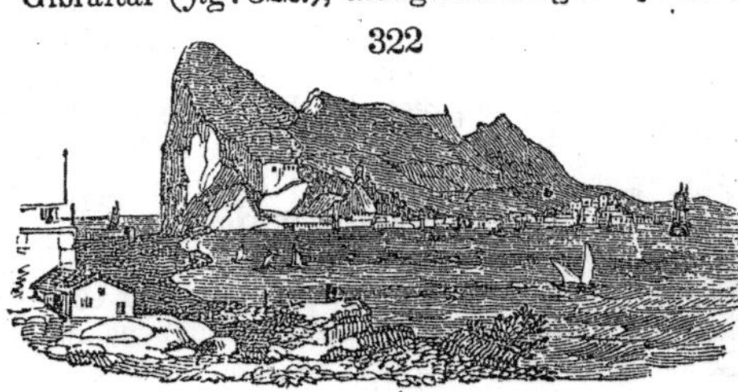

Gibraltar.

Among other places of some importance is Tarifa, the most southern point of Spain, and even of Europe, and the probable place of the landing of Tarik, with the Saracen army destined for the conquest of that country. Seated on an almost insulated rock, it is still a fortress of some strength. Algesiras, on the opposite side of the bay, has grown up as a small rival to Gibraltar; its population consists chiefly of smugglers and adventurers. In the interior is the flourishing and populous town of Xeres, situated in a wide region of vineyards, producing the wine called Sherry, the consumption of which is so general in this country. Mr. Jacob supposes the entire produce to be 40,000 pipes, of which 15,000 are exported, one half to Britain. Ecija, a large town, was famous as a scene of contest between the Christians and Saracens, and afterwards as the head quarters of a most formidable band of robbers; but its walls are now in ruin. Lebrija and Carmona are ancient towns, containing Roman monuments of considerable grandeur. The districts to the north and west of the Guadalquivir are mountainous and rugged; though Huelva and Moguer, at the mouth of the Tinto, and Ayamonte, at the mouth of the Guadiana, derive some importance from their situation, and carry on a little fishery.

Cordova (*fig.* 323.), on the upper part of the course of the Guadalquivir, is another kingdom of Andalusia, deriving its chief interest from the celebrated capital of the same name. Corduba, founded by the Romans, was not only a provincial capital, but the seat of an university, which could boast the great names of Seneca and Lucan. It displayed, however, a far higher pomp, when, after the Saracen conquest, it became the first capital of the Mohammedan empire in Spain. Under Abdelrahman and Almansor, it is represented as containing 1600 mosques, and nearly 1,000,000 people. Admitting a certain exaggeration, its past greatness is clearly attested by the vast and now almost empty circuit enclosed by its walls, in a great measure filled with palm trees and gardens, and by the astonishing remains of its mosque. This vast edifice presents nothing very striking in its exterior, which is in a great measure hid by the surrounding streets. But when the stranger enters any one of its nineteen gates, he is astonished and bewildered by the endless labyrinth of columns which stretch before him in every direction (*fig.* 324.). These columns have almost defied the attempts to number them; by one writer they have been estimated at 1400, but are generally

323

Cordova.

stated as exceeding 400, dividing the mosque into nineteen aisles, and producing a perpetual and surprising change of scene to the visiter. The edifice, however, though it astonishes by its immensity, does not equal in elegance those erected during that more refined age when Granada became the capital. The Christians have converted it into a church, and erected in the centre a choir of great beauty, but quite out of harmony with the Saracenic part of the structure. Cordova, though its days of splendour are long departed, still enjoys delightful environs, producing a breed of horses the finest in Spain, of which a splendid stud was lately kept by the government. There is also some remnant of its once extensive manufactures, particularly of that fine species of leather called from it Cordovan. The population is 57,000.

324

Interior of Mosque at Cordova.

Jaen ranks as a fourth kingdom, though it cannot enter into any rivalry with those already described. Its capital, of the same name, however, though little known, from its detached situation, is still a large city, the see of a bishop. Andujar is a considerable place, with a very ancient castle, at the entrance of the defiles of the Sierra Morena; and to the north of it is Baylen, where the Spaniards gained that signal victory which caused the surrender of Dupont and his army. In the upper part of this tract are the settlements of La Carolina, where an expanse of rude mountain waste has, by German and other colonists, been converted into a productive territory.

The Balearic Islands, Majorca, Minorca, and Iviça, with the minor ones of Cabrera and Formentera, form an appendage to Spain of some importance and celebrity. The Balearian slingers are celebrated in the military annals of antiquity; but the islands in general followed the political fate of Spain. Majorca, the largest, about forty miles in length, and thirty in breadth, possesses very considerable natural advantages. Several mountain chains, varying from 1500 to 4500 feet high, penetrate its centre, and defend it both from the excess of the heat and the violent action of the sea-breezes. Its summits are somewhat arid, but the intervening valleys are thickly clothed with olive trees; and corn and the vine grow luxuriantly, though with imperfect culture, on the plains below. Oranges and citrons flourish so abundantly in the northern district, that 20,000 mule-loads of them are exported to France and Catalonia. M. Cambassedes values the entire produce of the isle, in 1820, at 53,000,000 reals, about $3,000,000. Of this, about 34,000,000 are in grain and pulse, 5,000,000 in oil, and 2,500,000 in wine, 1,500,000 in fruits, 3,000,000 in hops, and 2,000,000 in sheep. Palma, the capital of Majorca, is a considerable town, slightly fortified, inhabited chiefly by the nobles, who possess the greater part of the isle, and have rarely sufficient activity or curiosity to visit their estates. In no Spanish city are indolence and superstition more prevalent. There are thirty convents, some of which enjoy a revenue of $10,000 a year. Processions and religious festivals, celebrated often with great tumult, form the chief amusements. In these it is customary to deck up figures of Judas, with tablets containing the enumeration of his crimes, among which that of being "chief of the liberals" was lately included! Population 34,000.

Minorca is a much smaller island, more barren, covered with bare and rocky mountains, and destitute of any trees at all lofty, the growth being prevented by the violent winds from the sea. But it is distinguished for one of the finest harbours in Europe, Port Mahon, which being strongly fortified, has been a subject of eager contest to the maritime nations. Having been taken by England in the Succession War, it was recovered by the French in 1756, notwithstanding Byng's attempt to relieve it. After several other vicissitudes, it remained with Spain. The harbour is extensive, possesses deep water, and is sheltered by hills on each side from every wind. The town has nothing of a Spanish aspect; the streets being broad, the houses small but neat, the people a stirring and active race, who scarcely allow themselves to be called Spaniards. During the late French war, being protected by the English navy, they made considerable wealth by privateering. Ciuidadella, though of smaller extent, is the nominal capital, and the residence of the nobility. Iviça, or Iviza, is a small isle, of rugged surface, which forms one immense mountain, shooting up into a variety of summits. The island is thus refreshed by cool breezes and numerous streams, and yields readily all the productions of this climate, particularly figs. In the quarter called Las Salinas, salt is evaporated by the heat of the sun, and exported to the extent of 15,000 tons.

### [Sect. VIII.—*Republic of Andorra.*

This little republic, with a territory of hardly 200 square miles, and a population of about 15,000 souls, has been overlooked by the author of this work. It occupies a valley on the southern side of the Pyrenees, situated between the Maladetta and the Moncal, and lying between Foix in France and Urgel in Spain. Beside Andorra, the capital, a town of 2,000 inhabitants, it contains five villages, which export iron and timber. It is governed by a Syndic, who presides over the council of the valley, and by two Viguiers, appointed the one by the king of France, and the other by the bishop of Urgel.—AM. ED.]

---

# CHAPTER X.

## PORTUGAL.

PORTUGAL has by political causes alone been separated from Spain. There is no physical peculiarity by which the two kingdoms are distinguished. On the contrary, all the grand natural features of Spain are prolonged into Portugal, and become Portuguese.

### SECT. I.—*General Outline and Aspect.*

The boundaries of Portugal are the Atlantic Ocean on the west throughout its whole extent, and also on the south; on the north the Spanish kingdom of Galicia; and on the east those of Estremadura and Leon. The greatest dimension is from north to south, or from 37° to 42° 10′ north latitude, and it extends from 6° 15′ to 9° 30′ west longitude. Its surface is 38,800 square miles.

The mountains of Portugal may be considered as prolongations of those of Spain, chiefly of the chains of Guadarrama and Toledo, and those in the north of Galicia. Those ranges, seldom rising to the first magnitude, cover almost the whole country, leaving between them many picturesque and fertile valleys. There are only two extensive plains, one on the south of the Tagus, and the other between the Mondego and the Douro.

The rivers of Portugal consist chiefly of the spacious terminations of the greatest streams of Spain in their progress to the ocean. The Douro forms the great maritime emporium of Oporto, and the Tagus that of Lisbon. The Guadiana, also, in its lower course, flows along the eastern frontier of Portugal. The Minho, a much smaller stream, comes down from Galicia; and the Mondego, alone, is entirely Portuguese, flowing nearly across the breadth of the kingdom.

### SECT. II.—*Natural Geography.*

#### SUBSECT. 1.—*Geology.*

This kingdom has the same general geognostical structure and composition as Spain. The mountainous parts of the country are generally of gneiss, mica slate, and other Neptunian primitive strata, occasionally intermingled with Plutonian rocks of granite and porphyry. Secondary formations of limestone occur in the Sierra d'Estrella, and in the vicinity of Cape St. Vincent, and all around Lisbon and at Cape St. Vincent the strata are of rocks of the tertiary class, more or less intermingled with trap rocks.

*Mines.* It appears that the Carthaginians wrought tin mines in this part of the Peninsula. It is asserted that there were formerly mines of tin stone in the granitic mountains of the neighbourhood of Viseu, in the province of Beira, at the place called Burraco de Stanno. Lead ores were worked in the last century, not far from Mogadouro, on the banks of the Sabour, in the province of Tras os Montes, and near Longroiva, on the banks of the Rio Prisco. Near Mogadouro, mines of graphite or plumbago occur. Iron mines also occur in the same country, near Felguiera and Torre de Moncorvo. They supply the iron forge of Chapacunha. Two very old establishments of the same kind occur in Portuguese Estremadura, one in the district of Thomar, the other in that of Figuero dos Vinhos. They are supplied by mines of red oxide of iron, situated in the frontier of that province and of the province of Beira. There is a deposit of cinnabar at Couna. The mountains of the neighbourhood of Oporto everywhere present indications of copper and of other ores. In Portugal, as in Spain, the sands of rivers were washed for the gold they contain; and it is said in this way large quantities of the precious metal were collected. At present there is but one gold mine in Portugal, at a place called Adissa, in the district of St. Ubes. Its annual produce is trifling: in the year 1815 it was 41 lbs. of pure gold; 1816, 18 lbs.; 1817, 11 lbs.; 1818, 12 lbs.; 1819, 13 lbs.; 1820, 12 lbs.; and in 1821, 18 lbs. Beds of coal occur at Vialonga, to the N. N. E. of Oporto; and there is a mine of coal at Cabo de Buarcos in the province of Beira.

#### SUBSECT. 2.—*Botany.*

The botany of Portugal is included under that of Spain.

#### SUBSECT. 3.—*Zoology.*

The zoology cannot be very different from that of Spain; but no documents have appeared to illustrate either the one or the other. The horses are rather small, and altogether infe rior; but the mules are fine, and nearly equal to those of Spain. Improvement, however, is neglected; nor have the indolent Portuguese profited by crossing their sheep from the merinos of Spain. A long-legged race of swine is common to both kingdoms, and furnishes excellent hams.

### Sect. III.—*Historical Geography*

The Carthaginians and Romans who occupied the Peninsula, did not recognise Portugal as a distinct country. Their Lusitania included a part of Spain, and did not comprise the whole of Portugal: Merida, in Estremadura, was its capital. Portugal, like Spain, submitted successively to the formidable irruptions of the Goths and of the Moors.

The existence of Portugal as a distinct kingdom dates from the commencement of the twelfth century. At that time, Henry, duke of Burgundy, having married the daughter of the duke of Castile, obtained as her dowry the northern part of Portugal, which had been rescued from the Moors. The capital, at that time, was Porto or Oporto, whence the modern name of the kingdom appears to be derived. His successors gained a series of conquests, and obtained possession of Lisbon and the southern provinces, carrying their conquests to the frontier of Seville.

The fifteenth century, and the reigns of John and Emanuel, formed the true era of the greatness of Portugal, when it outshone all the other kingdoms of Europe. Confined on the land side within narrow limits, it opened for itself a vast career of maritime discovery and conquest. Spain, indeed, shared this pursuit; but her first acquisitions were made by private individuals, partly foreign, with only faint assistance from the government; while the Portuguese expeditions were planned, fitted out, and all the resources for them supplied by the government. Their flag, at one time, floated victorious over all the eastern seas; while in the west, by the possession of Brazil, they came into some competition with Spain.

A disastrous eclipse of the Portuguese monarchy took place in the sixteenth century, in consequence of the rash and romantic expedition undertaken by king Sebastian into Morocco, where he himself and the flower of his troops were cut off. Hereupon Philip II. of Spain, a powerful and ambitious prince, raised a claim to the succession, which the superiority of his arms enabled him to secure. Portugal, with all her eastern and western possessions, then became an appanage to the crown of Spain. The connection was every way unfortunate. Not only did she lose her political and civil liberty, but many of her finest foreign possessions were wrested from her by the Dutch, the spirited and active enemies of Philip.

The restoration of the monarchy, in 1640, was still more sudden than its fall. The deep-rooted indignation of the people was combined into an extensive conspiracy, which, having been concealed to the last moment, burst forth at once: the Spaniards were driven out, and the duke of Braganza raised to the throne, under the title of John IV. Yet Portugal did not thus achieve any revival of her ancient glory. The new monarch soon re-established absolute power: a sluggish and indolent character pervaded all the departments of government: its foreign possessions were lost or neglected; and Portugal continued a stranger to all the improvements and energies which raised Britain and France to the first place in the system of Europe. Yet, during this period, the elevation of the Bourbons to the Spanish throne, led to a very intimate alliance between England and Portugal, the natural foe of Spain. It was cemented in 1803, by a commercial treaty, in which Portugal secured an exclusive market for her wines, while Britain obtained a market for her woollens, and an arrangement by which the gold of Brazil might find its way into her ports.

The recent convulsions of the Peninsula have been very amply shared by Portugal. Regardless of the neutrality which she had strictly maintained, Bonaparte, by a most unprovoked aggression, sent Junot, in 1807, to take possession of Lisbon. The king did not attempt a vain resistance, but sailed for Brazil, and established his court at Rio de Janeiro. The British arms, and the glorious achievements of Wellington, drove the French out of this part of the Peninsula, and finally out of the whole. Afterwards Portugal imitated the example of Spain in compelling her monarch to grant a representative constitution; but again, by a counter-revolution, she re-established an absolute monarchy. More recently, on the death of the late king, Don Pedro proclaimed the separation of Brazil from Portugal, reserving the former to himself, but granting to the latter a charter, the observance of which was made the condition of holding the throne.

### Sect. IV.—*Political Grography.*

Portugal, after the downfall of the feudal system, and especially after her subjection to Philip II. became one of the most absolute of European governments. The Marquis of Pombal and one or two more enlightened men found their way into the ministry; but, in general, measures were as ill conducted as possible, and corruption prevailed in every department of the state. The course of justice was equally polluted; and, no adequate salaries being allowed to the judges, they were under an almost irresistible temptation to accept bribes.

The pride of the nobles was nearly as great as in Spain, without being accompanied by the same lofty sentiments. They are divided into two branches, the *titulados* and the *hidalgos*, and have held the peasantry in a subjection little short of slavery.

The army of Portugal, prior to the revolution, though composed nominally of 30,000 men, was in a most inefficient state, not through want of physical courage or discipline in the men, but from the incapacity of the officers, and the general defects of the military system. When the French, however, had been driven out of Portugal, an army of 40,000 men was levied, and disciplined by British officers, under the superintendence of Lord Beresford; and thus prepared, the Portuguese acted, during the eventful war which followed, in a manner that would not have disgraced any troops in Europe. The army is still maintained; and though the new government will not brook British command, yet, under its influence, Portuguese officers of merit have been formed.

The navy, which was never considerable, was carried out with the royal family to Brazil, and has never been restored.

### Sect. V.—*Productive Industry.*

The industry and commerce of Portugal, which presented so brilliant an aspect during her era of prosperity, have sunk lower than those of almost any other European nation.

Agriculture did not, until very lately, experience any of the improvements which have become general in the rest of Europe. The plough is composed of three pieces of wood awkwardly put together, and imperfectly aided by the clumsy machinery of wheels. Though generally very fertile, this country did not produce a third of the grain necessary for the supply of its inhabitants. Of late some improvement has taken place, especially by the introduction of potatoes; and the dependence upon foreign supply has been considerably diminished. The chief object of attention is the vine, which, with the olive and other fruit trees, is cultivated with the utmost diligence in the valleys and on the sides of the hills, in the elevated province of Entre Douro e Minho. Here is produced abundantly the port wine, which forms the main basis of Portuguese trade, and finds so copious a market in Britain. The entire produce is estimated at 80,000 pipes. Of white wine Portugal produces about 60,000 pipes; but this is of inferior quality, and chiefly consumed at home. Sheep are bred on the hills, to a pretty large extent; but not so abundantly as in Spain, neither is their wool so fine.

The manufactures of Portugal scarcely deserve to be named. Little is known beyond the working of their wool for domestic use by each family or neighbourhood; all their finer fabrics are imported. According to a late observant traveller, ignorance, or at least an imperfect knowledge of the commonest arts, is conspicuous among the Portuguese. Their carpenters are the most awkward and clumsy artisans that can be imagined, spoiling every thing they attempt; the wood-work even of good houses being finished in a manner that would scarcely be tolerated in the rudest ages. Their carriages of all kinds, their agricultural implements, locks, keys, &c. are ludicrously bad. Working in gold and silver plate forms almost the only exception; cambrics also are well made in some places; and a few other local objects might be enumerated.

Of mines and fisheries, the former is not at all cultivated, though great materials for it are said to exist; but in the absence of trial this may be only conjecture. Fish of the finest kinds, particularly tunny and sardinias, are caught in considerable quantity for immediate consumption; but the salt which the kingdom so abundantly produces is not used for preserving them; and a large import of salted fish is still necessary to meet the wants of a population so rigidly Catholic.

The commerce, which formed the greatness of Portugal, when her ports interchanged the products of the East and the West, is now a mere shadow. The loss of her Indian possessions, and the separation of Brazil, have reduced her to the common routine of export and import. The staple of the former is port wine, for which the market of England was secured first by favouring duties, and now seemingly by an established predilection. The wine is raised almost solely for the English market, and all of the best quality is bought up by English merchants residing at Oporto.

Another staple export of Portugal is *salt*, evaporated by the heat of the sun in the bay of St. Ubes, or Setubal, which seems as if expressly formed for that purpose. It is carried off chiefly by the English, to be employed in curing fish destined for the Portuguese market: the annual amount is estimated at 100,000 tons. There is also a considerable surplus of wool, of which 1,000,000 lbs. weight have been imported into England in one year; but as it is not so fine as that of Spain, the duty imposed by the British landholders has greatly checked the importation. In return, Portugal takes grain, salt-fish, and a variety of manufactures, chiefly from Britain; but as her imports cannot much exceed the exports, she cannot afford a very copious market.

The internal communications of Portugal consist of the several noble rivers which traverse her territory, and which are navigable throughout. The intercourse by land is rendered very difficult by chains of mountains extending in the same direction. Nothing has been attempted on any important scale, either to improve these advantages, or to amend the defects; so that travelling is worse in Portugal than in any other European country.

## Sect. VI.—*Civil and Social State.*

The population of Portugal, according to the last census, which was taken in 1798, amounts to 3,683,000; calculating at the somewhat high estimate of five to a family. According to more probable estimates it now amounts to 3,530,000. Upon a surface of 38,800 square miles, this gives a density of about ninety-one to the square mile, which is remarkable, as exceeding that of Spain nearly in the proportion of three to two. The exemption from the *mesta*, and the high cultivation of the province of Entre Douro e Minho, appear to be the redeeming circumstances in her case.

No nation, as to character, owes less to the opinion of the world, than the Portuguese. They are described as indolent, dissembling, cowardly, destitute of public spirit, and at the same time fierce and deeply revengeful. In Spain it is said, strip a Spaniard of his virtues, and he becomes a good Portuguese. From a late minute inspection, however, the peasantry (*fig.* 325.) have been pronounced to be a fine people; and, on repeated occasions during the late war, they displayed energies not unworthy of their ancestors, in an age when their glory resounded throughout both hemispheres. Almost all, however, that floats on the surface is base and degenerate. There cannot be a doubt that this may be greatly ascribed to priestcraft, to the stupifying influence of a sluggish and tyrannical government, and to the general corruption which has pervaded all the branches of administration.

325

Portuguese Peasantry.

The established and exclusive religion is the Catholic, in its extreme and most degrading excess; and the body of the people are almost entirely under the thraldom of the priesthood. The burning of Jews continued till within the last half-century. The physiognomy of a large proportion of the people shows their descent from this hated race, whose tenets many, it is probable, still cherish in secret. There are, in Portugal, about 550 religious houses, of which 150 are nunneries* (*fig.* 326.). The number of two archbishops and thirteen bishops is not so disproportionate.

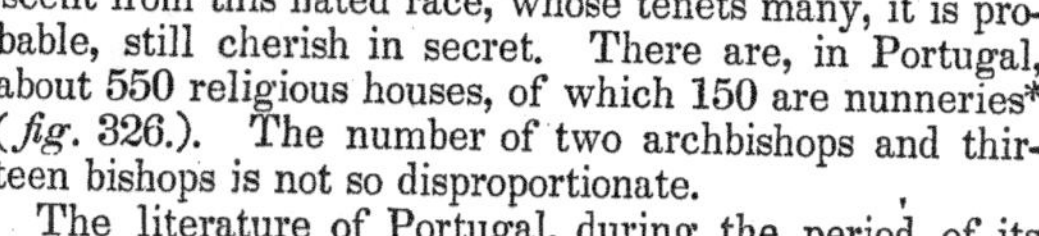

326

Friar and Nun.

The literature of Portugal, during the period of its glory, was by no means contemptible. The genius and fate of Camoens spread his name throughout Europe, and entitled him to rank among the few modern epic poets. By the students of Portuguese literature, however, Saa Miranda and Antonio Ferreyra are reckoned scarcely second to him; and Rodriguez Lobo held the nation long enchanted by the sweetness of his pastorals. At the same time Di Barros, Castanheda, and Faria y Sousa, recorded, in magnificent though somewhat inflated historical narrative, the mighty exploits of their countrymen in the African and Indian seas. The subjection to Spain gradually divested Portuguese literature of its manly and energetic character. The muse of history was silent; poetry assumed the form only of the sonnet, and Gongora infected it wholly with a strain of false and meretricious ornament. The house of Braganza for some time did little for knowledge; but in the beginning of the last century, the Conde de Ericeyra introduced the French literature, and founded a royal academy. In the course of the century, Barros Pereyra, Antonio da Lima, Manuel da Costa, a Brazilian, Correa Garcas, and Paulino Cabral, a bishop, made not unsuccessful efforts to revive the ancient Portuguese poetry, and to introduce that of Italy. Portugal has two universities. That of Coimbra, founded at Lisbon in 1290, was transferred to Coimbra in 1308. It enjoys some celebrity, is divided into eighteen colleges, and is still attended by several hundred students; but the course of study is of that obsolete description which prevailed during the middle ages. A smaller university was founded at Evora in 1578.

For the minor particulars of amusement, dress, food, &c., reference may be made to Spain, as Portugal has no peculiarities that are more than provincial.

## Sect. VII.—*Local Geography.*

Portugal is divided into the following six provinces, several of which, like those of Spain, in reference to events in their past history, are sometimes called kingdoms:—

* [The religious houses, monasteries, and nunneries, were suppressed in 1834.—Am. Ed.]

| Provinces. | Extent in English Acres. | Population. | Principal Towns, with their Population. |
|---|---|---|---|
| Estremadura | 5,450,880 | 826,860 | Lisbon, 260,000; Setubal, 15,000; Santarem, 8,000. |
| Alemtejo | 5,848,320 | 380,480 | Elvas, 10,000; Evora, 9,000 |
| Algarve | 1,536,000 | 127,613 | Faro, 8,000; Tavira, 9,000. |
| Beira | 4,994,600 | 1,121,595 | Coimbra, 15,000; Lamego, 9,000; Viseu, 9,000. |
| Entre Douro e Minho | 1,927,040 | 907,965 | Oporto, 70,000; Braga, 14,000; Viana, 8,000. |
| Tras os Montes | 3,007,760 | 318,665 | Braganza, 4,000. |

Estremadura occupies a great extent of coast, both to the north and south of the Tagus, without ever penetrating very deep into the interior. It presents a rocky, varied, and picturesque surface. It is chiefly important, however, as containing Lisbon, the capital.

Lisbon (*fig.* 327.) is situated near the mouth of the Tagus, which may here be almost considered an arm of the sea, since not only the tide flows up, but the water is salt, and the swell often tempestuous. The approach to it presents a more magnificent spectacle than that of perhaps any other city of Europe. Lisbon rises direct from the water, crowning the sides and summits of several hills; which, according to the Portuguese, are seven in number, like those of Rome. The palaces, convents, and churches, which crown this amphitheatre of buildings; the dazzling whiteness of the houses; the light appearance of the windows and balconies; the tasteful arrangement of plants, shrubs, and flowers on their roofs and terraces; the golden orange groves which adorn the suburbs, and the stately specimens of Indian or American botany which are scattered through the scene, produce an effect that cannot be described. The noble harbour, also, crowded with vessels; the numerous pilot and fishing-boats, with their large, handsome lateen sails, ascending or descending the river; and, nearer the shore, hundreds of small neat boats, with white or painted awnings, finely vary the scene. The moment, however, that the stranger lands, and enters the place, he finds that he has been imposed upon by a brilliant illusion; and the gay and glittering city is found to resemble a painted sepulchre. The streets are narrow and ill paved; the houses gloomy, with here and there a latticed window; filth and nuisances assault him at every turn. Lisbon does, indeed, appear to be the dirtiest and most noisome city on the face of the earth. In passing through the streets, a stranger encounters at every turn the most disgusting effluvia. Every species of vermin destined to punish indolence and slovenliness, the mosquito, the scolopendra, and a species of red ant, multiply to an extraordinary degree. Nor is Lisbon found, on inspection, to exhibit that architectural beauty which it promises on a distant view. It might have been expected, among forty churches and seventy-five convents, built by a superstitious people, that there would have been some signal display of this kind; but this is not found even in the cathedral. The defect seems partly owing to the mean taste of the Marquis of Pombal, who ordered them to be all built on a line with the street, to preserve a dull uniformity. Two handsome squares, however, have been formed, the Commercial and the Roscio, which are connected by well-built streets; but the absence of trees, or even shrubs, and the blinding sand that drifts through them, combine to produce a disagreeable effect. Lisbon derives an awful interest from the ruins still left of the great earthquake of 1755, the most dreadful catastrophe which ever befell a modern European city. Six thousand houses were thrown down, 30,000 inhabitants killed; and a conflagration kindled which spread a still wider destruction. The ruins are the more dismal, as they portend similar disasters, which the earth, still heaving from time to time, perpetually threatens. Meantime, Lisbon displays one very grand feature; the aqueduct, to the construction of which, though it conveys the water only half a mile, peculiar obstacles were presented. It is carried in one place through a tunnel, and in another over a defile 230 feet deep, by arches, which are said to be the highest in the world. The width of the centre arch is 107 feet. It was built in 1738, by Manuel de Maya; and is of such solidity that it withstood the shock of the great earthquake, which only caused the keystone to sink a few inches.

327

Lisbon.

The vicinity of Lisbon presents some beautiful sites and palaces. Cintra is the most striking, consisting of an immense mountain, partly covered with scanty herbage, partly with broken, huge, and varied piles of rock, elsewhere presenting thick groves of cork, elm, oak, hazel, and other trees. It includes many lovely and fantastic spots; but the view from it is naked and dreary. The town, at the bottom, with its old palace, has nothing remarkable; but the sides are covered with delightful villas, one of which is notorious for the signature of the unhappy convention of Cintra. Mafra is a royal convent built by John V., in emulation of the Escurial; but though a stupendous pile, 700 feet square, and containing numberless suites of ill-furnished apartments, it ranks far below its model. Only five miles below Lisbon, of which it is considered a suburb, is Belem, the site of a palace and a very magnificent monastery, founded by Emanuel, and in which many of the royal family have been interred.

There are several other towns of some note in Portuguese Estremadura. St. Ubes or Setubal lies sixteen miles from Lisbon, on the coast south of the Tagus, on a long interior bay, the waters of which, evaporated by the heat of the sun, leave the excellent bay-salt, one of the national staples. The town is considerable, having been well rebuilt since the earthquake of 1755, when it was almost totally overthrown. The mountain of Ursabida, here extending into the sea, forms a bold and striking promontory, covered with trees and various vegetation. Ascending the Tagus, we come to Santarem, a considerable and ancient town, the Præsidium Julium of the Romans. It has an academy of history, established in 1747. Here the great French army, under Massena, remained long posted, unable to penetrate to Lisbon. Abrantes, higher up, is an important military position, situated on a height whence it commands the passage of the Tagus. Leiria, to the north, is an ancient town, in a most productive territory, and where a great annual fair is held for the supply of the peasantry of the neighbouring country round. At Batalha, is a church (*fig.* 328.), and monastery, which, united, form the finest structures in all Portugal. It is 541 feet by 416, and is considered by Mr. Murphy to be one of the noblest existing specimens of the Norman

328

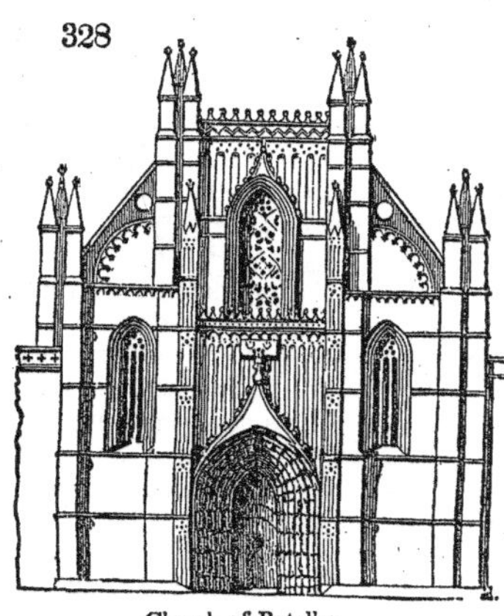

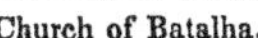

Church of Batalha.

329

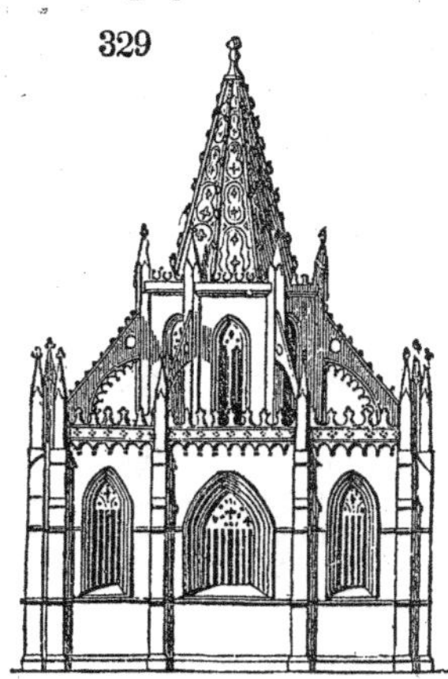

Mausoleum of King John.

Gothic. It is constructed entirely of marble, and the front appeared to him almost unrivalled in chaste and delicate ornament. Among the different parts, the mausoleum erected in honour of King John, is pre-eminently beautiful (*fig.* 329.). Vimiero is only a village, but celebrated for the signal victory gained by the British over the army of Junot. Three miles distant is Torres Vedras, a tolerable old town, but chiefly noted as the centre of the grand fortified lines formed by Wellington in 1810, which so completely baffled all the manœuvres by which the French had hoped to reconquer Portugal.

Alemtejo is an extensive province, comprising the greater part of Portugal south of the Tagus. The interior presents an extensive plain; but the frontier towards Spain is finely diversified with hills, wooded mountains, and deep valleys extremely well watered, and very fertile. It contains some large towns. Evora is situated on an eminence in a fine country, and is of great antiquity. Its origin has even been dated seven centuries before the Christian era. It is more clearly ascertained that the Romans made it a municipal town, and adorned it with some of their finest structures. There is a noble aqueduct, of which the piers are nine feet broad, and supported by buttresses; also a Temple of Diana built by Sertorius, in which great elegance is displayed. Elvas, on the Spanish frontier, immediately facing Badajos, is the strongest fortress in Portugal, and designed as the barrier of the kingdom. The works were constructed under the directions of the celebrated Count Schaumburg-Lippe; and the fort, bearing his name, is considered a masterpiece of the art. In this neighbourhood are also Villa Viçiosa, a pleasant town, and a favourite country residence of the Portuguese monarchs, who have here a handsome hunting-park; and Portalegre, a handsome little town in a delightful country, with a good cathedral. Southward, in the interior, is Beja, a Roman colony, and subsequently a strong Moorish fortress. After being nearly demolished, it was rebuilt by Alfonso III., and fortified by King Diniz, and is still a considerable town.

Algarve forms the extreme south of Portugal; and is a maritime province, bearing in an especial sense, the appellation of kingdom, since it long remained independent, and was a celebrated theatre of war between the Moors and the Christians. It is tolerably fertile in wine, fruits, and oil. Faro, the largest town, is also the principal seat of trade, and has a regular packet to Gibraltar. Lagos and Silves are also old little towns, the former on the sea-coast, with some shipping. Cape St. Vincent, the extreme point of Algarve, and the most south-westerly of the Peninsula, is celebrated for the signal victory gained by the British fleet over the Spanish, on the 14th of February, 1797.

Beira is a very extensive province or kingdom, filling nearly the whole centre of Portugal, between the Tagus and the Douro. Its surface presents considerable variety; the interior part has the usual mountainous character of Portugal, being traversed by the great chain called the Sierra d'Estrella. On the sea-coast, however, there are plains of considerable extent. The province produces plenty of wine, oil, and chestnuts, and has extensive pastures; but the grain is not sufficient for its consumption.

Coimbra (*fig.* 330.), the capital, is beautifully situated on the declivity of a hill, which rises above the Mondego; but the streets, as in other old Portuguese towns, are crowded, dirty, and very steep. In former times a residence of the kings of Portugal, it was strongly fortified, and has stood obstinate sieges; but the remains of its walls and towers are no longer sufficient to constitute it a fortress. It has been called the Athens of Portugal, from its extensive university, containing eighteen colleges, with forty professors, and about eight hundred students. Attached to it is a library of nearly 40,000 volumes, including numerous MSS.; but the actual value both of these and the printed works does not seem to have been fully investigated.

330

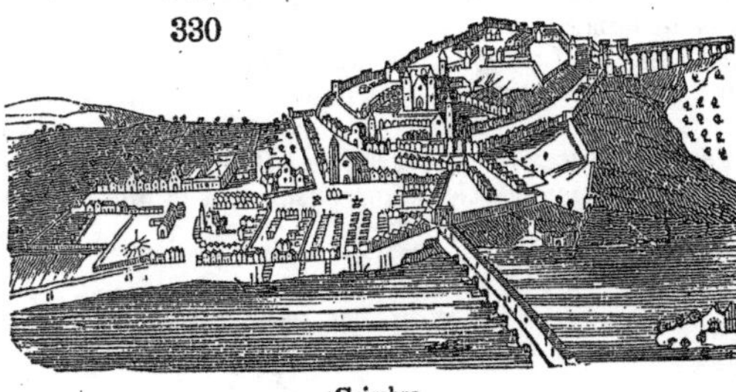

Coimbra.

Beira has other towns of some importance. Among these is Almeida, the northern barrier of the kingdom and a fortress of consequence, though not possessing the great strength of Elvas. It was twice taken in the last war, first by the French under Massena, and then by the British under Wellington. Castello Branco, on the southern frontier, notwithstanding its commanding situation, retains little importance. Lamego, near the southern bank of the Douro, is an ancient city, and the cradle of the Portuguese monarchy. Here, in 1143, the states-general for the first time met, recognised the fundamental laws, and acknowledged the sovereignty of Alfonso. Viseu, in the centre of the kingdom, is, like Lamego, an episcopal see, and has the greatest annual fair in Portugal.

Entre Douro e Minho forms the maritime part of Portugal, north of the Douro. Though the smallest, it is considered the most valuable, populous, and productive of all the provinces. Its peasantry have done much to redeem the reproach of torpor and sluggishness generally urged against their countrymen. This district is entirely covered with mountains, partly rugged and barren, but generally separated by fertile and well-watered valleys, cultivated to the utmost possible extent; and which, besides oil, fruit, and flax, are made to produce most copiously the wine called *port*, for which so ample a market exists in England.

Oporto, or Porto (*fig.* 331.), the ancient capital, and still the second city of the kingdom, is situated near the mouth of the Douro on the northern bank, though on the southern are two extensive suburbs, supposed to have constituted the ancient city. The modern town is well built, especially when compared with most others in the peninsula. The river affords a tolerably secure harbour, without any artificial aid, except an elevated and walled quay, to which the ships' cables may be fastened during the floods. These often come down with such force, that, without such a support, the vessels would be inevitably carried out into the

331

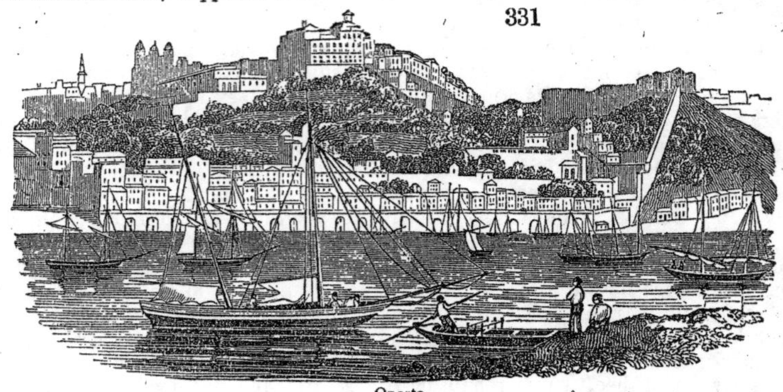

Oporto.

sea. The chief dependence of Oporto is its trade with England, which remains unimpaired amid the general diminution of that with America. There are about thirty English houses regularly settled here, besides a number of merchants who pay frequent visits to the place. The exportation of port wine, however, on which its trade rests, is generally cramped by the absurd policy of placing it entirely in the hands of an exclusive company,* who have adopted the pernicious practice of diluting the produce of the best vineyards with wine of those of an inferior quality, by which the character of the genuine port grievously suffers.

Braga, farther north, ranks as the capital of the province; and, though now far outstripped by Oporto, is of much more ancient fame. Under the Romans it was the metropolis of an extensive district, and its former greatness is still attested by numerous antiquities. It has made a distinguished figure in the ecclesiastical history of Portugal, and is the see of an archbishop, who is primate of the kingdom. Braga is a handsome town; well built, well paved, the streets spacious and clean. There is some industry, particularly a manufacture of small beaver hats, which supplies a great part of the kingdom. The adjacent country is hilly, but populous and pleasant. Valença is a small town, agreeably situated on the Minho, which separates it from Galicia.

Tras os Montes, or the province beyond the mountains, is of great extent, occupying the whole interior of Portugal north of the Douro. The Cantabrian chain, after traversing Asturias and Galicia, throws out branches which not only separate the territory from the rest of Portugal, but cover almost its whole surface. They leave only deep valleys, through which considerable rivers, too rapid however to be navigable, pour down into the Douro. It is much inferior to Entre Douro e Minho, both in populousness and cultivation; yet a considerable quantity of the port wine produced grows on the sides of its hills. The inhabitants are a race of active, hardy, and brave mountaineers. They rose in great force against the French, and have since somewhat less happily distinguished themselves by the ardour with which they fought in the cause of absolute power, and in resistance to every form of constitutional government.

The towns are small, and not regularly fortified; though, from the nature of the country, they form defensible military positions. Braganza is a city of ancient note, and gave the title of Duke to the first nobleman in the kingdom, even before he was raised to the throne, by the appellation of John IV. The kings of Portugal still retain the title of Dukes of Braganza. Chaves, the Aquæ Flaviæ of the Romans, still exhibits two baths and a magnificent bridge constructed by that people. Chaves gives the title of Marquis to a family, one of whom was the most active opponent of the French during their invasion; while another has lately been at the head of the anti-constitutional army, of which the head-quarters were always in Tras os Montes.

* [The Oporto wine company, which enjoyed this monopoly, was abolished in 1834.—Am. Ed.]

END OF THE FIRST VOLUME

www.ingramcontent.com/pod-product-compliance
Lightning Source LLC
LaVergne TN
LVHW021222110826
845150LV00002B/224

* 9 7 8 1 4 2 5 5 6 4 4 4 5 *